HISTORY
AND GENEALOGY
OF THE FAMILIES
OF
OLD FAIRFIELD

Compiled and Edited by

DONALD LINES JACOBUS

Volume I

Reprinted
With Additions and Corrections

CLEARFIELD

Originally Published
Fairfield, Connecticut
1930-1932

Reprinted
Two Volumes in Three

With
*Additions and Corrections
to History and Genealogy of
the Families of Old Fairfield*
(originally published as a
Supplement to The American
Genealogist, October 1943)

Genealogical Publishing Co., Inc.
Baltimore, 1976, 1991

Reprinted for
Clearfield Company by
Genealogical Publishing Co.
Baltimore, Maryland
2007

Library of Congress Catalogue Card Number 76-3279

Volume I ISBN-13: 978-0-8063-1297-2
Volume I ISBN-10: 0-8063-1297-1
Set ISBN-13: 978-0-8063-0719-0
Set ISBN-10: 0-8063-0719-6

Made in the United States of America

History and Genealogy

OF THE FAMILIES OF

OLD FAIRFIELD

VOLUME I.

Compiled and Edited by

DONALD LINES JACOBUS, M.A.

For

THE EUNICE DENNIE BURR CHAPTER

DAUGHTERS OF THE AMERICAN REVOLUTION

FAIRFIELD, CONNECTICUT

1930

GENEALOGICAL RESEARCH COMMITTEE

ANNIE BURR JENNINGS

LORETTA BRUNDIGE PERRY

HELEN TURNEY SHARPS, *Chairman*

THE TUTTLE, MOREHOUSE & TAYLOR COMPANY,
NEW HAVEN, CONN.

COMPILER'S PREFACE

On May 22, 1929, I was engaged to compile the history of the Fairfield families for the Eunice Dennie Burr Chapter, Daughters of the American Revolution, and on November 27, 1929, the date of present writing, the first volume is practically complete and the first section has been placed in the printer's hands. It can be asserted, without much fear of contradiction, that no genealogical work of equal magnitude has ever been compiled with such incredible rapidity.

Several factors have made this rapid progress possible. In the past, my work has taken me to Fairfield frequently, and in consequence I had a great deal of material on the early generations, which I contributed as a beginning for the work. My mother, Mrs. John I. Jacobus, has been a most capable assistant, when working in Fairfield, copying vital records and abstracting later probate records, while I was engaged on other parts of the work. Copies of material in printed sources and at the Fairfield Historical Society were typed for me by my secretary, Miss Pearl Beloff. Without this "staff" of clerical assistants, the work would have taken several months longer. I have also given my own time in no niggardly fashion, for many weeks working almost every evening on the task of compilation until one or two in the morning.

Our grateful thanks are due to the Fairfield Historical Society for their generosity in making available their valuable manuscript collections. The greatest single contribution is without question the carefully prepared genealogies of certain Fairfield families found in the manuscripts of the late Orrando Perry Dexter. This gentleman worked on the Fairfield records for seventeen years, and although he did not live to complete his work, the present volume owes so much to it that his name deserves a place as collaborator. I have never found an error in the finished section of his manuscripts, and on the other hand I have several times worked out difficult problems independently, only to find upon consulting his papers that he had preceded me in arriving at the same conclusions.

The copies of gravestone inscriptions and church records made by Mr. Winthrop H. Perry, Mr. Robert P. Wakeman, and others, and deposited at the Historical Society rooms, have also been extremely useful and have enabled the compiler to add many dates. Of particular service has been the excellent work of Mrs. Kate Perry in her *Old Burying Ground of Fairfield*.

The committee of the Daughters of the American Revolution, Miss Jennings, Miss Perry, and Mrs. Sharps, throughout the work have shown an attitude of understanding helpfulness whenever difficulties have arisen, and of broad vision in desiring to make this volume and the succeeding ones excellent in every respect. To Mrs. Sharps I am especially indebted for her generosity in lending a large quantity of collected material, which saved me considerable time and labor.

All references to the unpublished manuscripts of Gov. Winthrop were furnished by Col. Charles E. Banks of Boston, and are used by his gracious permission. The knowledge which we owe to this source, while not large in amount, is of the highest importance, since it is knowledge that could not be obtained from public record sources or in any other way.

I am indebted to Mr. Clarence A. Torrey, of Dorchester, Mass., for his helpful collaboration on the Burr family; to Mr. George C. Bryant, of Ansonia, Conn., for generosity in supplying data on several families with Milford connections; to Mr. Homer W. Brainard, of Hartford, Conn., for valuable information on a branch of the Gilbert family; to Mrs. Harry B. Houghton, of Bridgeport, Conn., for much data on the Westcott family; and to Miss Irene H. Mix, of Hartford, for her great kindness in looking up certain records at the State Library for use in the book.

Our account of the William Hill family, particularly of its important and interesting English connections, owes much to the generosity of Miss Grace A. Hill, of Richmond, Va., in permitting us to use the results of her researches.

A few years ago Mr. Francis B. Trowbridge, of New Haven, Conn., very kindly lent me some manuscript books compiled by his great-uncle, the historian E. Champion Bacon, to aid me in my work on New Haven families. By chance, one of these books contained brief abstracts of the first three volumes of Fairfield Probate Records, made in 1841. Although I felt it necessary to cover these records independently, so as to make more extended notes, Mr. Bacon's abstracts were useful for quick reference, as he had indexed them; and in two or three estates in the damaged first volume, his abstracts made so long ago contained a little more information than is now legible.

The willingness, even eagerness, of so many people to aid in a work of this nature, is extremely gratifying; and if through inadvertence I have omitted to make acknowledgment to some who have been helpful, I ask them to pardon the oversight and remind me of it, and the omission will be made good in the preface to the second volume.

For families with a Westchester County connection, the Miscellanea published for several years in the *New York Genealogical and Biographical Record* have been used extensively. Hall's' *Norwalk* and Huntington's *Stamford Registration* have been employed for vital records of those towns, corrected in a few instances from the original. It was not possible, however, to verify all these records, and it may be suspected that they contain a few slight errors. For Stratford and Woodbury vital records, I used my own verified copy made from the original. Milford records are either from my personal copy or Mr. Bryant's, and I am indebted to Mr. Bryant for several records from Newtown.

In a work of this size, it cannot be hoped that error will be entirely avoided. There is always the chance of overlooked typographical errors, as well as those politely termed "slips of the pen" which are usually mental lapses caused by fatigue. Finally, we have to admit the lack of verification or checking back. Frankly, I admire genealogical work performed with meticulous nicety, and try to employ it on smaller commissions. The present volume contains the early generations of the families of half a county, and one cannot paint a house with quite the same attention to detail that is devoted to painting a miniature. To employ the most meticulous methods on a work like this would require several years of time and a small fortune in money. Nevertheless, I believe that few mistakes will be found; and if any are noted, I shall be glad to have corrections sent to the committee for printing at the end of this volume or in the next volume.

ARRANGEMENT

The families are arranged in alphabetical order. Each family begins (wherever possible) with the first settler. His sons who are carried forward as heads of families are designated thus: +. Families are brought down in this volume at least to 1700, but the last generation included is given completely, so that on some lines the families are brought down to 1720 or considerably later. Individuals who will be carried to the second volume as heads of families are designated thus: X.

The public services of each individual are listed immediately after his name, before the genealogical statistics are given. Dates following military titles are those of appointment. The date of each session at which a Deputy served is stated.

Those who use the book are asked to remember that there are scarcely any vital records for the period before 1700, and that the extant church records do not begin until 1694. In consequence, the probate and land records constitute our chief sources of information. The earlier probate records are not in existence, and the first volume is so damaged as to be partly indecipherable. The earlier land records are mere entries of grants and sales, not copies of the deeds, and hence do not contain as much genealogical information as those of a slightly later date. In consequence of all this, the early generations of the Fairfield families are more difficult than are those of almost any other ancient town in the state. Much depends upon the trained judgment of the compiler and his ability to interpret correctly the significance of such records as are available. I have not hesitated to overwork the useful words, "perhaps," "possibly," and "probably," especially the last. Some relationships, while not susceptible of legal proof, I consider genealogically proved by strong circumstantial or collateral evidence, and have stated as facts, but where there has been the slightest doubt regarding the conclusions reached, I have felt that the only honest thing to do was to qualify with a "probably."

Brief abstracts of probate and land records are given, to show record evidence for most statements. The size of the work precluded giving specific references to volume and page. Personally, I cannot see that such references have much value. Often, when an old volume is provided with a modern index, it is entirely repaged, thus making a liar of anyone who has quoted the original page number; and the volumes themselves are sometimes renumbered. The old Fairfield books are for the most part well indexed; so that anyone who desires to inspect a certain record for himself should have little difficulty in finding it. As some of the earliest volumes of land records will probably be deposited with the State Library shortly, searchers are hereby warned to ascertain in advance whether the books they wish to consult are in Fairfield or Hartford.

Where the date of an inventory is stated, it is usually the date when it was taken, not the date when it was exhibited in Court; and it is often the closest approximation that can be obtained to the date of a man's death, which must be understood as falling between the making of his will and the inventorying of his estate. Finally, attention must be called to the large number of errors of date in "Family Book A" of the Fairfield Vital Records. Entire families of children were often entered in this book long after the births occurred, apparently depending on the faulty memory of the parents; and in consequence, it is not unusual to find two or three children in succession recorded as born *a year later* than their baptisms are entered in the church records. The latter were generally correct, as the entries were made at the time. A number of such discrepancies will be noted, which are not the fault of the compiler, but of the records themselves.

D. L. J.

ABBREVIATIONS

abt.	about	Exec'r	Executor
adm.	admitted	Exec'x	Executrix
adm'n	administration	g. s.	gravestone
Adm'r	Administrator	Inv.	Inventory
Adm'x	Administratrix	Leg.	Legislature
ae.	aged		[General Assembly]
b.	born	m.	married
bapt.	baptized	mo.	month
bur.	buried	prob.	probably
Cong.	Congregational	rec.	recorded,
d.	died		records
dau.	daughter	rem.	removed
dec'd	deceased	res.	residence
Epis.	Episcopal	s.	son
Est.	Estate	yr.	year

HISTORY AND GENEALOGY OF THE FAMILIES
OF OLD FAIRFIELD

Abbott, George.

Of Windsor 1640; rem. to Norwalk 1655, and d. in Feb. 1689/90.

Will 2 May 1689; eldest son John; three daus. Dorcas* Roots, Priscilla Clawson, Mary; son Jonathan; son Daniel, to live with John until 21; son George, under 21; codicil 4 Feb. 1689 [1689/90], mentions that Mary has married. Inv. Feb. 1689 [1689/90].

Inv. of Johanna Abbott, "last wife of George," presented 19 Mar. 1682. One son James Williams (under 21); two daus. Elizabeth and Sarah (under 18). Samuel Hayes and John Baldwin were appointed Adm'rs.

Children [by first wife]:

> John, d. at Norwalk in 1720; adm'n granted to widow Ruth, 28 June 1720; heirs, widow, one son, and two daus., Esther Jackson and Mary Scribner; he m. Ruth Ruscoe, dau. of John.
> Dorcas, d. at Woodbury, 15 May 1720; m. John Roots.
> Jonathan, received a grant from Norwalk, 1698, for service as a soldier; m. at Norwalk, 5 June 1696, Sarah Olmstead, dau. of Lt. John.
> Priscilla, m. [prob. Stephen] Clawson.
> Mary, m. ———.
> Daniel.
> George.

Abbott, Robert.

Of Watertown 1634, Wethersfield 1640, New Haven 1642, Branford 1649.

Died at Branford 31 Sept. 1658; Mary [his widow] m. (2) 4 Nov. 1659, John Robbins. Widow and two youngest children mentioned 1658; son Peter had a lunacy.

Estate of Robert who deceased 30 Sept. 1658. Distribution to children: Peter the eldest son; Matthew Roe; Deborah Abbott;

---

* Once called *Dorothy* in the recorded will, which we suppose a clerical error.

John; Joseph; Daniel; Abigail and Mary Abbott. The son John was apprenticed to William Lewis, Sr., 28 Dec. 1658, being then 9 yrs. 3 mos. 5 days old. John gave receipt to Robert Foote on account of John Robbins for his portion, 17 Mar. 1670/1. Joseph gave receipt to same for portion due from "my father-in-law" John Robbins, 2 Apr. 1677. Daniel gave receipt to same for portion left me by my father Robert Abbott which was due from my father-in-law, John Robbins, Nov. 1676. William Roberts gave receipt to Widow Sarah Foote for "my wives portion from her father Robert Abbot's estate", 5 Sept. 1684.

Children (last five recorded at Branford):

> Sarah, m. Matthew Rowe.
> +Peter.
> Deborah, m. (rec. New Haven) Oct. 1661, Nathan Andrews.
> John, b. 23 Sept. 1649 (by age at apprenticeship); bapt. at New Haven, 7 Oct. 1649.
> Abigail, b. 2 Oct. 1650, bapt. at New Haven, 1 June 1651.
> +Joseph, b 20 Apr. 1652.
> Benjamin, b. 10 Jan. 1653 [1653/4], d. young.
> +Daniel, b. 12 Feb. 1654 [1654/5].
> Mary, b. 13 Mar. 1657.

Abbott, Peter, s. of Robert.

He came to Branford 1658 to help his father weed corn and was taken with a lunacy; "no settled inhabitant there, but had lived sometimes in one plantation & sometimes in another."

Married Elizabeth Evarts, dau. of John of Guilford, murdered her at Fairfield, was tried, convicted, and executed 16 Oct. 1667.

Inv. taken 9 Aug. 1667. Adm'n granted to John Knowles and John Sturges. The child Hannah is left to care of Joshua Knowles. On 24 Nov. 1685, one of the Adm'rs being dec'd, John Sturges rendered account. He was ordered to deliver Est. to Hannah Abbott, dau. and heir.

Child:

> Hannah. Thomas Wilson on 25 Dec. 1686, being "Intristed upon yᵉ aconnt of Hannah abut her estat" entered a caveat against the home lot that was old John Cable's, now the lot of John Cable, Jr., in reference to an action of debt.

Abbott, Joseph, s. of Robert.

Born at Branford, 20 Apr. 1652.

Probably m. Anna Sanford, dau. of Thomas, b. 19 Feb. 1675.

Children, recorded at East Haven:

> Abigail, b. 15 Aug. 1700; m. 15 Mar. 1719/20 (rec. New Haven) Nathaniel Joslin.
>
> Mary, b. 14 Nov. 1707, d. 6 Apr. 1783 æ. over 70 (East Haven church).

Abbott, Daniel, s. of Robert.

Born at Branford 12 Feb. 1654 [1654/5].

Before the Court 1693 with Hannah Brooks, dau. of John, whom apparently he married.

Adm'n on estate granted 21 July 1729 to widow Hannah; children named, Joseph, Stephen, Deborah, Hannah, all of full age; res. Branford.

Children, recorded at New Haven:

> Deborah, b. 22 Apr. 1694; m. (Wallingford rec.) 16 Nov. 1724, Josiah Brockett.
>
> Joseph, b. 16 Jan. 1696 [1696/7]; m. (Branford rec.) 14 Apr. 1730, Hannah Marks.
>
> Hannah, b. 8 Jan. 1698 [1698/9]; m. (Branford rec.) 7 Dec. 1727, Benjamin Barnes.
>
> Daniel, b. 12 Sept. 1701.
>
> Stephen, b. (no record).

ADAMS FAMILY, FAIRFIELD

Adams, Edward.

He was of New Haven by 1640; Milford 1646; Fairfield 1650; and d. in 1671.

He m. Mary ———, who m. (2) Anthony Beers, and d. in 1687.

He had land granted to him in Milford, 19 Jan. 1645/6, "upon these conditions That he will both learn to dress Leather or Skins and alsoe follow His trade in the town." In 1653 and 1656 he entered for record several pieces of land in Fairfield.

Will dated 7 Aug. 1671; wife Mary; sons Samuel, Abraham; dau. Mary Murwin and her son Luke Guire; sons Nathaniel, John, Nathan. Inv. 11 Nov. 1671. Agreement 5 Feb. 1677 of Nathaniel (of age), respecting portion, and John and Nathan (under age), children of Edward; John chose John Banks for guardian; Anthony Beers and his wife chose Samuel Adams as guardian for Nathan. Adm'n on Est. of Mary Beers of Fairfield was granted, 2 Dec. 1687, to Sergt. Samuel Ward and Nathan Adams.

Edward gave land to dau. Mary, 26 Nov. 1668.

Abraham, Nathan, Daniel, Abraham, Jr., David, and John Adams, and Luke "Quire" of Fairfield agreed to divide that part of the long lots that were Edward Adams' and Joseph Patchen's, 21 Jan. 1713/4.

On 3 Jan. 1752, Stephen Adams, one of the representatives of Edward Adams, asked distribution of commons originally belonging to Edward. Distribution was made to the legal representatives: Capt. John Silliman, Stephen Adams, Samuel Bradley, Joseph Wakeman, John Jennings, 2d, heirs of Susannah Winton, David son of Nathan Jennings, Hannah wife of Jonathan Squire, Ellen wife of James Stewart, heirs of Luke Guire, Nathan Guire, Jonah Turney, heirs of Mary Marshall, heirs of John Adams. [Some of these were representatives by purchase, not descent.]

Children:
+Samuel.
    Mary, b. abt. 1647, d. abt. Apr. 1712; m. (1) 23 Feb. 1663, Luke Guire;
        (2) ——— Merwin; (3) Stephen Sherwood.
+Abraham, b. 9 Sept. 1650 (at Fairfield; Col. Rec.).
    Nathaniel, b. bef. 1656, d. bef. 1693, unm.
    John, b. after 1656, d. 1693. Will disapproved; Inv. 7 Nov. 1693.
        Brothers Samuel, Abraham, Nathan; sister Mary.
+Nathan, b. after 1656.

Adams, Samuel, s. of Edward.

He m. at Fairfield, 15 July 167—, Mary Meeker, dau. of Robert. She m. (2) Moses Lyon, and (3) John Thorpe.

Inv. 10 Feb. 1693/4. Widow Mary appointed Adm'x, with Daniel Meeker and Abraham Adams. Son Abram was bound out to Abraham Adams.

On 14 Mar. 1721, Daniel, David, and John Adams, Isaac Castle, Elijah Crane, and Elizabeth Adams, conveyed to Mr. John Denny the homelot of their father Samuel Adams dec'd; Mary Thorp confirmed the deed. The same grantors, 8 Mar. 1719/20, Elijah Crane in right of wife Abigail, and Isaac Castle of Woodbury in right of wife Sarah, agreed to divide lands of their bro. Abraham Adams, Jr.

Children, recorded at Fairfield:

Samuel, b. 1 Jan. 1677, d. 1698, s. p.

×Daniel, b. 17 May 1679; m. (1) Rebecca [prob. Cable]; m. (2) Sarah Turney, dau. of Benjamin, 2d.

Sarah, b. 3 Oct. 1680, d. at Woodbury, 24 Feb. 1707/8; m. Isaac Castle.

Abigail, b. 25 Mar. 1682; m. (1) Joseph Cable; (2) Elijah Crane.

Elizabeth, b. 3 Feb. 1684; res. Stratford, 1719.

Abraham, b. 1 Jan 1685, d. 1718; m. Sarah ———, who renewed Covenant at Fairfield Church, 16 Sept. 1716; only child, Sarah, bapt. 16 Sept. 1716, d. y. Adm'n granted, 12 Apr. 1718, to widow Sarah and bro. Daniel; child Sarah. Agreement, 21 Aug. 1719; Daniel and David Adams of Fairfield, John Adams of Greenwich, and Elizabeth Adams of Stratford, and Elijah Crane and Abigail of Fairfield, with Sarah, widow of Abraham Adams, Jr.

Jonathan, b. 31 Oct. 1686, d. y.

×David, b. 24 June 1689, bapt. 18 Jan. 1712/3, d. in 1723; will 5 Feb. 1722/3, proved 22 Apr. 1723; m. Abigail Silliman; she m (2) 22 Mar. 1737, John Hide.

Benjamin, b. 28 Dec. 1690, d. y.

×John, b. 6 Sept. 1692, bapt. 4 July 1714, d. at Greenwich in 1727; m. in 1717, Elizabeth Husted. Adm'n granted 5 Sept. 1727 to widow Elizabeth; she dead by 1730.

Adams, Abraham, s. of Edward.

Born at Fairfield, 9 Sept. 1650. Died 9 Aug. 1729 in 80th year; "a worthy founder and liberal benefactor to Trinity Church" (g. s.).

He was bapt. at Fairfield Church, 9 Dec. 1694; his daus. Deborah and Hannah were bapt. 20 Jan. 1694/5; Mary, Abigail, Susanna, and Elizabeth, 24 Feb. 1694/5.

He m. Martha ———, who m. (2) ——— Miller. It is not certain that she was mother of the children.*

Agreement made 10 Sept. 1729 between widow Martha, and children Deborah Bennet of Ridgefield, Daniel Morehouse and wife Hannah of Fairfield, Joseph Marshall and wife Mary of Horseneck, Fairfield County, John Whitlock and wife Abigail, John Winton and wife Susanna, and Benjamin Gilbert and wife Elizabeth, all of Fairfield, regarding Est. of their father Lt. Abraham Adams.

Children [by first wife]:

> Deborah, m. James Bennett of Ridgefield.
> Hannah, m. Daniel Morehouse.
> Mary, m. Joseph Marshall of Horseneck.†
> Abigail, m. John Whitlock.
> Susanna, b. abt. 1688, d. 7 Feb. 1749/50; m. abt. 1711, John Winton.
> Elizabeth, m. Benjamin Gilbert.

Adams, Nathan, s. of Edward.

Born after 1656; m. (1) about 1687, Mary James, dau. of Joseph.

Married (2) Anna ———.

Will 22 Aug. 1748, proved 6 Feb. 1748/9; son Stephen and Stephen's son Nathan; two grandchildren, sons of son Nathan dec'd; present wife Annah; daus. Ganda wife of Moses Knap, Sarah wife of Benjamin Sturgis, Ruth wife of Nathaniel Wilson, Mary wife of Luke Guire, and Avis wife of Daniel Crofut.

Children [by first wife], recorded (except Sarah) Fairfield Church:

> ✕Nathan, bapt. 23 Dec. 1694, d. in 1724; Inv. 6 Apr. 1724, presented 12 Feb. 1725/6 by widow Rebecca, now wife of Joshua Jennings; m. abt. 1714, Rebecca Clapham; she m. (2) at Christ Church, Stratford, 3 Feb. 1724/5, Joshua Jennings.
> Nathaniel, bapt. 23 Dec. 1694, d. y.

---

* Mr. Clarence A. Torrey, of Dorchester, Mass., rightly draws our attention to the fact that she must have been a second wife because in the agreement of heirs she was to receive two beds she "brought with her"; and suggests from circumstantial evidence that the mother of the Adams children *may* have been Sarah Lockwood.

† In 1752, Joseph Marshall, late of Greenwich, now of Northeast, Westchester County, N. Y., conveyed right in Fairfield from mother Mary Marshall of Greenwich, dec'd, which formerly belonged to my gr. father Abraham Adams of Fairfield, dec'd.

Ganda, bapt. 23 Dec. 1694; m. Moses Knapp.

Sarah, m. at Fairfield, 9 Feb. 1715, Benjamin Sturgis.

Ruth, bapt. 11 Oct. 1696, d. 13 June 1775 in 78 yr. (g. s., Fairfield);
m. Nathaniel Wilson.

Mary, bapt. 2 Oct. 1698; m. Luke Guire.

Johanna, bapt. 1 Sept. 1700, d. y.

Avis, bapt. 29 Nov. 1702; m. (recorded, date omitted) Daniel Crofut.

Nathaniel, bapt. 1 Oct. 1704, d. y.

✕Stephen, b. abt. 1708,* d. 5 Nov. 1794 ae. 86; will 23 Sept. 1793,
proved 25 Nov. 1794; m. (1) at Fairfield, 17 Oct. 1727, Sarah
Finch; m. (2) at Fairfield, 9 May 1764, Esther, widow of John
Hill, and dau. of Joseph Bulkley, bapt. 20 Dec. 1713, d. before 1793.

ADAMS FAMILY, MILFORD AND STRATFORD

Adams, ———.

Children:

+William.

+Freegrace.

Elizabeth, m. (rec. Milford) 1 June 1699, James Brisco.

(?) Sarah, m. (rec. Derby) 15 Apr. 1703, Moses Johnson.

Adams, William. Lt., Port Royal Expedition, Aug. 1710.

He was adm. to Milford-Church, 5 Nov. 1699; his first wife
was adm. 22 July 1711, and his second, June 1713. He d. after
26 Dec. 1742, when he conveyed land at Milford to William
Adams, Jr.

He m. (1) Abigail Oviatt, dau. of Thomas, b. at Milford,
17 Aug. 1674. On 23 Nov. 1708, Samuel Oviatt, soap boiler,
Thomas Oviatt, weaver, William Adams, weaver, in right of his
wife Abigail, and Josiah Whitmore, tailor, in right of his wife
Dorothy, all of Milford, sued for property they claimed by descent
from Thomas Oviatt dec'd.

He m. (2) Mary ———, who d. 2 Sept. 1713.

---

* Mr. Dexter's account of the Adams family identifies Stephen with the child bapt.
1 Oct. 1704, whose name in the baptismal record he supposes to be an error; but if
his age at death (in Trinity Church records) is correctly stated, this could not be.

Children [by first wife], recorded at Milford:

Abigail, bapt. 5 Nov. 1699; m. (rec. Stratford) 25 Feb. 1718/9, Isaac Stiles.

Mehitabel, bapt. 18 Feb. 1699/1700; m. abt. 1725, Ebenezer Blackman of Stratford, whose will 1753 made his bro.-in-law Samuel Adams an Exec'r.

Esther, bapt. 7 Dec. 1701.

Elizabeth, b. 3 Mar. 1704/5 [prob. 1703/4], bapt. 5 Mar. 1703/4.

Samuel, b. 3 May 1706, bapt. 28 Apr. 1706 [*sic*], d. at Litchfield, 12 Nov. 1788; Judge, Fairfield County Court; m. at Stratford, 7 Mar. 1728/9, Mary Fairchild; dau. of Samuel, 2d, b. at Stratford, 27 ——— 1708, d. at Litchfield, 29 Aug. 1803.

William, b. 3 June 1708, bapt. 7 June 1708, d. at Woodbridge, 19 May 1787; m. (1) Freelove Arnold; m. (2) at Woodbridge, 11 Sept. 1764, Rebecca, widow of John Thomas, and dau. of Daniel Alling, b. at New Haven, 5 Aug. 1716, d. at Woodbridge, 23 June 1802 ae. 88 (g. s.).

Adams, Freegrace.

Married (rec. Stratford) 8 Jan. 1700 [1700/1], Mary Galpin. On 7 May 1711, being then of Rye, he conveyed with wife Mary to Moses Galpin of Rye, land given me by my father and mother in law, John and Mary Galpin, reserving her dower right.

Died at Newtown in 1750.

Will dated 3 Aug. 1750, proved 27 Sept. 1750; wife Mary; four sons, John, Samuel, Ephraim, Abraham; daus. Abigail Kimberly, Experience Hard, Elizabeth Hull; gr. dau. Ann Prindle; daus. Sarah Stevens, Mehitabel and Abiah Adams; son John to pay £50 out of his part to bring up his dau. Sarah Curtis Adams; cousin Samuel Adams of Stratford, Exec'r.

Children (record incomplete):

John, m. (1) Sarah Curtis, dau. of Jonathan; m. (2) ———.

Samuel.

Abigail, m. at Newtown, last of Oct. 1725, Abraham Kimberly.

Ephraim.

Experience, bapt. 23 July 1704 (at Stratford, rec. Stratfield); m. Joseph Hard.

Elizabeth, m. abt. 1725, John Hull.

Sarah, m. ——— Stevens.

Abraham.

Mehitabel.

Abiah.

Allen, Samuel.

With Mary his wife, he sold a 2½ acre lot at Fairfield to Robert Meeker, 16 July 1663.

Allen, George.

Came in 1635 with wife Catharine, sons George, William and Matthew, and servant Edward Poole, and settled at Weymouth, Mass. In 1637 was a first settler in Sandwich; Constable there 1639. He served as Deputy to the Plymouth Gen. Court, 1640-1644. He was bur. 2 May 1648.

His will named sons Matthew, William, Samuel and Henry, and "my five least children" without naming them. Probably he had two sets of children; Catharine, his second wife, m. (2) John Collins, Sr., of Boston. Two of his sons, Henry and Gideon, settled in Milford, Conn.

Allen, Henry, s. of George.

Settled in Milford; rem. to Stratford soon after 1680. He conveyed land in Milford, 1686, calling himself formerly of Milford, now of Stratford.

He m. (1) Sarah ———, who was bapt. and adm. to Milford Church, 7 Oct. 1666, and d. in 1680; m. (2) Rebecca, widow of Robert Rose.

Inv. exhibited 8 Nov. 1690 by the widow. Samuel Sherman appointed Conservator of Estate. Two sons, Henry and John, and two daus.

Frances, wife of John Hall of Middletown, dau. of Henry Allen of Stratford dec'd, and sister of John Allen dec'd, conveyed 1704. [Stratford Deeds.]

Children [by first wife], recorded at Milford:

> Mary, b. 21 Oct. 1663, bapt. 7 Oct. 1666; adm. to Milford Church, Dec. 1687; d. Mar. 1693.
> Sarah, b. 5 Oct. 1666, bapt. 21 Oct. 1666, d. y.
> Miriam, b. 20 Apr. 1669, bapt. 25 Apr. 1669, d. y.
> Mercy, b. 8 Oct. 1671, bapt. 15 Oct. 1671, d. y.
> Henry, b. 2 May 1674, bapt. 3 May 1674; a tailor; m. Mercy Tibbals, dau. of Josiah and Mary (Sherwood), b. 2 May 1671. Their three children were bapt. together at Milford, 18 Oct. 1719. Children: Mary, b. 2 Aug. 1700, m. 5 Feb. 1724, Benoni Sage of Middletown;

Mercy, b. 4 July 1703, m. 25 Dec. 1723, Samuel Baldwin; Ruth, m. 10 Jan. 1725, Joseph Northrup.

Frances, bapt. 20 Aug. 1676; m. John Hall, of Middletown.

John, bapt. 19 Sept. 1680, d. at Stratford abt. 1704. Inv. 24 Mar. 1704; adm'n granted to bro. Henry of Milford. Distribution ordered between Henry Allen and his sister Frances Hall of Middletown equally.

Allen, Gideon, s. of George.

Came from Boston to Milford, where he m. Sarah Prudden, dau. of Rev. Peter. Lived in Boston a few years, then returned permanently to Milford, where he d. abt. 1693.

Adm'n granted, June 1693, to widow Sarah. Names and ages of children, Nov. 1694; eldest son Gideon; Sarah 18; George 18 (error for 14); Hannah 7; Abigail 4. His widow was living 1 Mar. 1699/1700, when she conveyed to her sons Gideon and George.

Children, first recorded at Boston, last five at Milford:

+Gideon, b. 9 Aug. 1671.

Sarah, b. (no record), abt. 1674, d. at Guilford, 8 Mar. 1712; m. John Leete of Guilford.

George, bapt. 31 Mar. 1678, d. at Milford, 7 Oct. 1734 (g. s.); m. (rec. Milford) 20 Nov. 1707, Frances Arnold. Will 8 July 1734, proved 13 Nov. 1734; wife Frances; bro. Gideon and his son George; sister Sarah Leete's five children, John, Gideon, Sarah, Patience, Mercy; brother Gideon; sister Hannah Whitman and her daus. Elizabeth and Frances; sister Abigail Foot and her sons John Shepherd and George Foot; son Edward, Exec'r.

Abigail, bapt. 5 Dec. 1680, d. y.

John, b. 19 Feb. 1682, d. y.

Hannah, b. 6 Oct. 1685, bapt. 29 Nov. 1685; m. in or after 1709, Zachariah Whitman, as his third wife.

Abigail, bapt. 9 Sept. 1688, d. at Newtown, 19 Dec. 1755; m. (1) 8 Oct. 1707, John Shepard; (2) Daniel Foote.

Allen, Gideon, s. of Gideon. Ens., east company, Fairfield, May 1712; Lt., first company, May 1721.

Born at Boston 9 Aug. 1671; called cordwainer in Milford records, which prove his removal to Fairfield. At baptism of children, called Sergt. 1710, Ens. 1713 to 1716, and Lt. 1721.

Conveyed 1729 to son and dau. Thomas and Sarah Couch; to son and dau. Thomas and Ann Hanford.

Will 22 Jan. 1750/1, proved 5 Feb. 1750/1; wife Jane; sons John, David, George; if George leaves no issue, the land to go equally to John and David; daus. Sarah Keeler, Abigail Wakeman, Mary Penfield, Hannah Gibbs; gr. dau. Sarah Hanford. Married (1) at Fairfield, 20 Jan. 1696, Anna Burr, dau. of Nathaniel. She d. there 14 Mar. 1747/8 ae. 72 (g. s.). He m. (2) 10 Aug. 1749, Jane, widow of Moses Dimon, and formerly of John Hill. "Widow Allen" d. at Reading, 22 July 1774 ae. (supposed) 98.

He d. at Fairfield, 25 Jan. 1750/1.

Children [by first wife], recorded at Fairfield:

Sarah, b. 1 Apr. 1697, bapt. 30 June 1700, d. at Ridgefield, 10 Mar. 1787 ae. 90; m. (1) 7 Dec. 1721, Thomas Couch; m. (2) 10 Nov. 1736, Timothy Keeler.

Anna, b. 6 June 1700, bapt. 30 June 1700, d. 27 Sept. 1747 in 47 yr. (g. s., Fairfield); m. (1) Thomas Hanford; (2) Gershom Burr.

Gideon, b. 1 Jan. 1702 [1702/3], bapt. 31 Jan. 1702/3, d. 28* May 1748. Adm'n granted 5 June 1748 to bros. Dr. John Allen and David Allen. Distribution: Sarah Keeler; Sarah Hanford, heir of Ann Burr dec'd; Abigail, wife of Joseph Wakeman; Mary wife of Peter Penfield; Hannah wife of Thomas Gibbs; John, David and George Allen. There was land in New Fairfield.

Abigail, b. June 1705, bapt. 24 June 1705, d. at Westport, 1 Jan. 1804 in 100 yr. (g. s.); m. 31 Oct. 1727, Joseph Wakeman.

Mary, b. 6 Aug. 1708, bapt. 8 Aug. 1708; m. 28 May 1730, Peter Penfield.

XJohn, b. 1 Dec. 1710, bapt. 3 Dec. 1710; grad. Yale 1729; Dr.; m. 17 Jan. 1750/1, Abigail Jessup, dau. of Edward, b. 9 May 1731.

David, bapt. 11 Jan. 1712/3, d. y.

Jonathan, bapt. 11 Jan. 1712/3, d. y.

XDavid, bapt. 4 July 1714, d. 8 Sept. 1777 in 64 yr. (g. s.); Lt.; m. 11 Oct. 1739, Sarah Gold, dau. of John; she d. Feb. 1778 in 60 yr. (g. s.).

Hannah, bapt. 18 Nov. 1716; m. 24 Mar. 1742/3, Thomas Gibbs of Milford.

George, bapt. 14 May 1721.

Allen, Gideon.

Perhaps a gr. son of George of Sandwich.

Married (1) abt. 1699, Mary Wright [New Haven County Ct. Rec.].

---

* 29 May 1748 in 46 yr. (g. s.).

Removed from Guilford to Fairfield, where he m. (2) Phebe, widow of John Bennett.

Children [by first wife], recorded at Guilford:

Gideon, b. 8 May 169[9], d. at Plymouth, 11 July 1778; m. (1) Rachel ———; (2) (Waterbury rec.) 6 Dec. 1751, Naomi (Luddington), widow of Josiah Tuttle; she m. (3) ——— Blakeslee.

XJoseph, b. 27 June 170[2],* d. (as did also his wife) between Mar. and Oct. 1776 (Westport Church); m. at Fairfield, 26 Mar. 1724, Rachel Bennett, dau. of John, b. Mar. 1702 [1702/3].

XEbenezer, b. 9 Oct. 170[4], d. 24 Mar. 1780 (Westport Church); m. (1) at Fairfield, 12 Nov. 1731, Deborah Bennett, dau. of John. She d. 15 Feb. 1757. He m. (2) 27 Apr. 1760, Tabitha Phillips.

Children [by second wife]:

XJohn, bapt. at Compo (Fairfield Church), 31 Oct. 1714, d. 30 Dec. 1791 (Westport Church); m. (1) at Fairfield, 23 Mar. 1739, Sarah Bennett, dau. of Deliverance. She was b. 8 Apr. 1716, d. 18 Apr. 1761 (g. s.). He m. (2) 12 Apr. 1768, Martha Lyon.

Mary, m. May 1739, Abraham Higgins.

Allyn, John, s. of Edward.

Edward Allyn, of Hartford, m. Rachel Steele, and had: John, b. 4 Mar. 1689 [1689/90?], d. at Fairfield in 1724/5; and Rachel, b. 20 Aug. 1694, m. 27 Apr. 1727, Timothy Seymour.

Called of "Fairfield East Parish", he m. at Stratford, 10 Jan. 1717/8, Rebecca Blackleach; dau. of Richard.

Inv. 23 Jan. 1724/5.

Rebecca m. (2) abt. 1726, Ens. Benjamin Rumsey, and (3) after 1734, John Curtis of Stratford. John Curtis and Rebecca his wife of Stratford conveyed, 1 Apr. 1737, to Timothy Seymour of Hartford and Rachel his wife, their right in a house at Greens Farms; and next year, Seymour sold land and house lately belonging to John Allen dec'd.

Ambler, Richard.

Born abt. 1611, was of Watertown, Mass., by 1637, and Boston 1643. He bought land in Stamford, 1650; gave age as 55 in 1666; freeman, 1669; living 1699.

---

* 25 June 1702, by Fairfield rec.

He m. (1) Sarah ———; and (2) Elizabeth ———, who d. 27 Mar. 1685.

Children [by first wife], recorded Watertown:

> Sarah, b. 4 Dec. 1639.
> Abraham, b. 27 Sept. 1641, d. y.
> +Abraham, b. 22 Sept. 1642.
> Others?

Ambler, Abraham, s. of Richard. Deputy (Stamford) to Conn. Leg., May 1674, May and Oct. 1677, May and Oct. 1678, May and Oct. 1679, May 1681, May 1682, Oct. 1690, May, July and Oct. 1691, Oct. 1692. Justice, 1699.

Born at Watertown, Mass., 22 Sept. 1642, d. at Stamford in 1699; m. (1) at Stamford, 25 Dec. 1662, Mary Bates; m. (2) Hannah ———.

Will 3 Aug. 1699, proved 24 Jan. 1699 [1699/1700]; wife Hannah, estate she brought at marriage; son John (Exec'r) to provide for his gr. father; dau. Mehitabel Ambler; gr. children Abraham, Abigail, and Sarah Brown. Inv. 8 Sept. 1699. On 7 Mar. 1715/6, the son John being dec'd, adm'n was granted to Martha Beach and Samuel Scofield.

Children [by first wife], recorded at Stamford:

> Mary, b. 15 Jan. 1663 [1663/4].
> Abraham, b. 5 Jan. 1665 [1665/6], d. before 1697; m. 12 Jan. 1692 [1692/3], Hannah Gold; she m. (2) 8 Sept. 1697, Jeremiah Andrews. Child: Abraham, b. 6 Sept. 1693; m. 4 Apr. 1717, Abigail Clawson. Adm'n on Est. of Abraham, Jr., was granted to Jonathan Gold, 5 Aug. 1713.
> John, b. 18 Feb. 1667 [1667/8], d. 4 Nov. 1711; will 3 Nov. 1711, proved 5 Feb. 1711/2; m. Martha [Wildman, dau. of Thomas of Bedford; she m. (2) ——— Beach]. They had three children: (1) John, b. 15 Feb. 1695 [1695/6], chose Samuel Blatchley of Stamford for guardian in 1713; m. Elizabeth Morehouse of Fairfield. (2) Stephen, b. 22 [———] 1698, chose John Stone of Stamford for guardian in 1713; m. 14 Dec. 1724, Deborah Hoyt. (3) Martha, b. 17 Mar. 1700 [1700/1].
> Joshua, b. 8 Sept. 1670.
> Sarah, b. 6 Oct. 1672.
> Mehitabel, d. 8 Feb. 1736/7; m. 3 Dec. 1702, James Slawson.

Andrews, Francis.

He settled in Hartford, 1639; removed to Fairfield.

Will 6 June 1662, proved 5 Mar. 1662/3; wife Anna; sons John, Thomas, Jeremiah, Abraham; daus. Elizabeth, Mary, Hester, Rebecca, Ruth; John Cramton and my dau. Hannah; gr. dau. Hannah Cramton.

His widow m. (2) before 1674, ———— Smith. Anna, late wife of Francis Andrews dec'd, sold to Simon Couch, 14 Mar. 1663 [1663/4]; and on 28 Feb. 1673 [1673/4] Couch had land entered which he had purchased of Ann Smith, Exec'x of the will of Francis Andrews.

Francis may have been bro. of William of Hartford and John of Farmington. It is at least worthy of note that John (son of Francis) and Thomas (son of William) m. sisters, daus. of John Kirby of Middletown; while Thomas (son of Francis) and Abraham (son of John) also m. sisters, daus. of Robert Porter of Farmington.

Children:

>Hannah, m. John Crampton of Norwalk.
>Elizabeth.
>+John, bapt. at Hartford, 27 Sept. 1646.
>+Thomas, bapt. at Hartford, 2 Jan. 1647 [1647/8].
>Mary, perhaps m. (1) Peter Norton of Fairfield, and (2) abt. 1670, Hugh Griffin.
>Esther.
>Rebecca, lived in Groves family, Stratford, prior to 1673; m. (rec. Norwalk) 7 July 1678, Samuel Benedict of Norwalk.
>+Jeremiah.
>+Abraham.
>Ruth.

Andrews, John, s. of Francis.

Bapt. at Hartford, 27 Sept. 1646; res. Fairfield.

Married Bethia Kirby, dau. of John and Elizabeth, b. at Middletown, 14 Feb. 1658 [1658/9]. On 21 Nov. 1700, Richard Osborn of Eastchester, N. Y., in right of wife Sarah Andrews, dau. of John Andrews of Fairfield dec'd, and John Andrews son of the above mentioned John, conveyed land in Middletown which had been conveyed to John Andrews dec'd by his mother-in-law Elizabeth Kirby.

Inv. 20 Dec. 1683. Left a boy and girl under age. Joseph Lockwood, Daniel Frost, Jr., and Samuel Benedict, Adm'rs.

Children, recorded at Fairfield:

+John, b. 24 Oct. 1679.
Sarah, b. 12 Jan. 1680 [1680/1]; m. Richard Osborn.

Andrews, Thomas, s. of Francis.

Bapt. at Hartford, 2 Jan. 1647/8; settled in Milford, where he was adm. to church, 19 Nov. 1670, and d. in 1718. He m. Elizabeth Porter, dau. of Robert, b. at Farmington, 11 Jan. 1653/4. She was adm. to Milford Church from Farmington, 3 Aug. 1679.

Adm'n granted, 24 Oct. 1718, to John Bronson of Waterbury, in right of wife Elizabeth, eldest dau. of the dec'd; John Andrews, only son, refused to act. In Feb. 1753, division of the unadministered estate of Thomas Andrews, Sr., was filed by Lawrence Clinton, Adm'r; shows that Thomas d. leaving heirs, John, Elizabeth, Mary, Sarah, Rebecca, Abigail, and Ruth; of whom Mary, Rebecca and Abigail d. without issue; distribution to the heirs of the other four.

Children, four recorded at Milford (all bapt. at Milford except the twins):

Elizabeth, b. 4 Nov. 1678, bapt. 10 Nov. 1678; m. (1) Eleazer Prindle; m. (2) abt. 1714/5 John Bronson of Waterbury.
Mercy, bapt. Aug. 1679, d. y.
Thomas, b. 10 Sept. 1681, bapt. 11 Sept. 1681, d. y.
Hannah, b. Jan. 1683 [1683/4], bapt. at Farmington, 31 May 1685.
Mary (twin), b. Jan. 1683 [1683/4], bapt. at Farmington, 31 May 1685; m. Samuel Allyn, of Middletown, b. 15 Mar. 1683/4, son of Obadiah and Elizabeth (Sanford) Allyn.
John, bapt. 7 Feb. 1685/6, d. at Milford abt. 1733; m. Sarah, widow of Jean Hiolle of Milford, and dau. of Stephen Valeau.*
Sarah, bapt. 30 Sept. 1688; m. 25 Feb. 1713/4, Samuel Northrup, bapt. 5 June 1687, son of Samuel and Sarah Northrup.
Ruth, bapt. 24 Aug. 1690, d. 27 Dec. 1730; m. Joel Northrup, son of Samuel.

---

* Etienne Valeau, a Huguenot of New York. We are indebted to George C. Bryant, Esq., of Ansonia, Conn., for the family of Thomas Andrews.

Rebecca, bapt. 21 May 1693, d. without issue.
Abigail, bapt. 23 June 1695, d. in 1723, unmarried; will 15 Jan. 1722/3,
proved 4 Mar. 1722/3.

Andrews, Jeremiah, s. of Francis. Deputy for Bedford, May 1697.

He m. at Stamford, 8 Sept. 1697, widow Hannah Ambler; dau. of John Gold.

Conveyed land at Stamford 1697, then called of Bedford.

Adm'n granted, 5 Aug. 1713, to Jonathan Gold and Daniel Weed, Jr.

Children, recorded at Stamford:

John, b. 31 Jan. 1700; m. Abigail ———.
Ann, b. 3 Aug. 1702, d. 10 May 1706.
Jeremiah, b. 5 Dec. 1705, d. 20 July 1713.
Jeremiah, d. 19 Dec. 1715.

Andrews, Abraham, s. of Francis. Deputy (Waterbury), May 1712.

He settled in Farmington; m. Rebecca ———, and d. in 1729. The *Andrews Memorial* calls her dau. of John Carrington, of which we have not seen evidence; but if true, she must have been sister of John of Waterbury, and presumably dau. of the John who was executed for witchcraft. Removed soon to Waterbury.

Children, recorded at Waterbury:

Rebecca, b. 16 Dec. 1672; m. William Hickock.
Mary, b. 10 Mar. 1674/5; m. Apr. 1693, Daniel Warner.
Hannah, b. 8 Sept. 1678; m. Zophar Northrup.
Abraham, b. 14 Oct. 1680; m. 5 Nov. 1702, Hannah Stevens, dau. of Thomas of Middletown.
Sarah, b. 16 Mar. 1683/4, d. 6 Mar. 1773; m. (1) 7 Apr. 1703, Joseph Lewis; m. (2) 14 May 1750, Isaac Bronson.
Rachel, b. 11 July 1686; m. Samuel Orvis.
John, b. 16 July 1688; m. Martha Warner, dau. of Thomas.
Thomas, b. 6 Mar. 1694; m. 2 Nov. 1725, Mary Turner, dau. of John.

Andrews, John, s. of John. Ens., west parish company, Fairfield, May 1715.

Born at Fairfield, 24 Oct. 1679, d. there in 1728.

Married (1) Eleanor Burr, dau. of Daniel, b. 26 Oct. 1680.

He m. (2) Abigail (Sturgis), widow of Simon Couch, who d. 14 Sept. 1730, ae. abt. 57 (g. s., Westport).

In 1708 he was called [Conn. Col. Rec.] brother-in-law of Deborah widow of Joseph Whelpley [she was born Deborah Burr].

Adm'n granted, 3 Dec. 1728, to Abigail and John Andrews. Dower in Est. of Ens. John was set to his widow Abigail, 6 Jan. 1729/30.

Children [by first wife], recorded at Fairfield:

XJohn, b. 6 Aug. 1707, bapt. 27 June 1708; Dea. John d. 28 Mar. 1771 ae. 63 yrs. 7 mos. 11 days (g. s., Westport); will 5 May 1769, proved 2 Apr. 1771; m. 28 Oct. 1730, Sarah Couch, dau. of Simon; b. 30 Mar. 1706, d. 9 Mar. 1783 in 77 yr. (g. s.).

Abigail, b. 17 June 1709, bapt. 14 Aug. 1709; m. (1) David Hill; m. (2) abt. 1739, Henry Rowland.

Eleanor, b. 9 Oct. 1711, bapt. 14 Nov. 1711; m. Elias Bixby of Ridgefield.

XDaniel, b. 20 Feb. 1714, bapt. 13 June 1714, d. 1800; Lt.; m. 8 Feb. 1741, Sarah Silliman. She was dau. of John, bapt. 23 Mar. 1717/8; d. 1795.

Abraham, b. 21 July 1717, d. y.

XEbenezer, b. 12 May 1720; m. Jan. 1746, Sarah Sturgis, dau. of Peter.

Applegate, John.

Prob. son of Thomas and Elizabeth of Weymouth, Mass.; was at Gravesend, L. I., 1650.

He bought land and house in Fairfield as early as 1663, from Mary Macock; and purchased from Samuel Forman 1667, and from Mr. John Pell 1671.

He m. Avis ———, who d. at Fairfield, 3 Feb. 1716/7 ae. near 80 (g. s.). He d. ae. 82 (g. s.).

Will 13 Nov. 1704; wife Avis, Exec'x; sons of bro. Thomas Applegate. Witnesses: John Meredith and Samuel Hubbell. Inv. 25 Dec. 1712. Mr. John Meredith of Newport, R. I., swore to will, 24 Jan. 1712/3.

Adm'n granted, 6 Feb. 1716/7, to Joseph Applegate, Avis being dec'd; and he gave bond with Abraham Higgins. The heirs are the children of Thomas Applegate of Middletown, Monmouth County, East Jersey, viz.: Thomas, John, Daniel, Joseph, Benjamin, and Richard. The Inv. of Est. of Avis, 5 Feb. 1716/7; Thomas Williams, Adm'r; nothing left after paying debts.

Avis conveyed 18 Jan. 1713/4 to loving kinsmen Benjamin and Joseph Applegate, now resident in Fairfield, sons of Thomas dec'd, who was one of the bros. of my dec'd husband John Applegate. She conveyed, 11 Oct. 1714, to Thomas, John, Daniel, and Richard, sons of Thomas Applegate of Middletown, N. J., dec'd, who was bro. to John Applegate of Fairfield dec'd.

John Williams and Theophilus Hull of Fairfield conveyed 18 Jan. 1703 [1703/4] to Mr. John Applegate one half of the long lot formerly belonging to Samuel Ward dec'd. On 20 Jan. 1715 [1715/6], John Williams conveyed land to Avis Applegate for £40, part of a debt of over £53 in silver money which he owed to John Applegate dec'd. She on 2 Feb. 1716/7, "for the love and respect which I bear unto John Williams of Fairfield and to his children", reconveyed the house and lot to him and his children, Elizabeth, Rebecca, Abiah, and Mary.

Bagley, John.

Married Mary, widow of Joseph Lyon, and dau. of Joseph Jackson.

Children, recorded at Fairfield Church:

Joseph, bapt. 2 June 1700.
Josiah, bapt. 12 July 1702; rem. to New York City; m. Anna Lockwood, dau. of John; on 23 Feb. 1753, Josiah Bagley of New York City was appointed Adm'r on Est. of Anna Bagley of said City.
James, bapt. 16 July 1704; m. Bethia Monroe, and had a dau. Lydia bapt. at Westport, 16 June 1742.
Mary, bapt. 13 Apr. 1707.
Sarah, bapt. 3 July 1709.
Ann, bapt. 20 Aug. 1711.

Baldwin, Nathaniel.

Second son of Richard of Cholesbury, co. Bucks, Eng.; a cooper, of Milford; his first wife Abigail d. there 22 Mar. 1648. She was prob. sister of William Camp, who was called uncle by his son John.

He settled in Fairfield, where he had a home lot recorded 13 Jan. 1653 [1653/4].

Inv. taken at Fairfield, 19 Oct. 1658. Widow Joan (previously married); three children by former wife living at Milford; also three children by present wife, under age. Eldest son John chose Mr. Pell guardian. Daniel receipted for portion 1663, and John 1665/6; Nathaniel of Milford receipted for himself and sister Abigail, 1668.

The will of Joanna Skidmore, wife of Thomas, in 1667, named children John, Daniel, Joanna and Abigail Westcott, and Sarah, Deborah and Samuel Baldwin.

His second wife was Joan, widow of Richard Westcott; she m. (3) Thomas Skidmore. She was sister of the wife of Robert Sanford of Hartford.

Thomas Skidmore and Cornelius Hull, Adm'rs of Est. of Nathaniel Baldwin, sold to Sarah and Deborah Baldwin land which they entered for record on 16 Apr. 1675. Four days later, Sarah Baldwin, joint proprietor with her sister Deborah Read, sold to her brother-in-law William Read all her interest. Samuel Baldwin had land by gift and also by purchase from his father-in-law Thomas Skidmore, recorded 26 Feb. 1677.

Children [by first wife], recorded at Milford:

> John, bapt. 2 June 1644; m. (rec. Fairfield and Milford) 19 Nov. 1663, Hannah Osborn, dau. of Richard; rem. to Newark, N. J. He had a dau. Hannah, who m. John Tichenor; and a son John (1675-1732) who m. Lydia Harrison (1683-1738).
> +Daniel, bapt. 2 June 1644.
> +Nathaniel, bapt. Jan. 1646.
> Abigail, b. abt. 1648.

Children [by second wife]:

> Sarah, b. abt. 1650.
> Deborah, b. abt. 1652; m. William Read.
> +Samuel, b. abt. 1655; bought from father-in-law Thomas Skidmore, 26 Feb. 1677 [1677/8]; and sold to Ezbon Wakeman land in the woods, being sometime Thomas Skidmore's building lot; recorded at Fairfield 6 Mar. 1679.

Baldwin, Daniel, s. of Nathaniel.

Married at Milford, 27 June 1665, Elizabeth Botsford, dau. of Henry.

Children, recorded at Milford:

> Daniel, b. 2 July 1666, d. 23 July 1666.
> Daniel, b. 3 Mar. 1667/8, d. in 1725; will 8 Mar. 1719, proved 2 May 1725; m. abt. 1689, Sarah Camp.

Elizabeth, b. 18 or 24 Apr. 1670.
Mary, b. 1 or 3 Aug. 1672, d. 1 Jan. 1672/3.
Samuel, b. 26 Dec. 1673, d. 26 Mar. 1674.
Nathaniel, b. 14 May 1676, d. 14 July 1676.
John, b. 26 Mar. 1679, bapt. 30 Mar. 1679.
Samuel, bapt. 6 Mar. 1684.

Baldwin, Nathaniel, s. of Nathaniel.

Called weaver, m. (1) at Milford, 12 Mar. 1670/1, Hannah Botsford, dau. of Henry.
Married (2) Martha Mitchell.

Children [by first wife] recorded at Milford:

Elizabeth, b. 9 June 1672; m. Stephen Parmelee, of Newtown.
Hannah, b. 11 July 1674, bapt. 12 July 1674; m. Samuel Sanford.
Esther, b. 14 Nov. 1676, bapt. 19 Nov. 1676, bur. 21 Nov. 1676.
Esther, b. 25 May 1683, bapt. 19 Dec. 1686; m. Samuel Sanford, of Newtown.
Samuel, b. 14 Jan. 1684 [1684/5], bapt. 19 Dec. 1686, d. y.

Child [by second wife]:

Daniel, bapt. 14 Oct. 1688, d. 6 Jan. 1711/2, unm.

Baldwin, Samuel, s. of Nathaniel.

Married Abigail Baldwin, dau. of John, b. at Milford, 15 Nov. 1658. She m. (2) John Wadham.
Distribution of Est. 21 Mar. 1710/1 to Mr. John Wadam "who hath married the widow"; eldest son Samuel Baldwin; Timothy Baldwin; Nathaniel Baldwin; Mr. Joseph and Abigail Starr; Ziba and Dorothy Tryon; and Samuel and Johanna Rose.

Children, recorded at Guilford:

Abigail, b. 14 Dec. 1678, d. 24 Aug. 1745; m. 24 June 1697, Joseph Starr.
Deborah, b. 8 Apr. 1681, d. 5 Dec. 1681.
Dorothy, b. 27 Dec. 1683; m. 1708, Ziba Tryon.
Joanna, b. 18 May 1686, d. at Branford, 1751; m. 18 Apr. 1705, Samuel Rose.
Samuel, b. 13 Jan. 1689.
Timothy, b. 14 Apr. 1691.
Nathaniel, b. 28 Nov. 1693.

Banks, John. Deputy (Fairfield) to Conn. Leg., Sept. 1651, May 1661, Oct. 1663, May and Oct. 1664, May and Oct. 1665, May and Oct. 1666, Oct. 1673, Oct. 1674, May and Oct. 1675, May and Oct. 1676, May and Oct. 1677, Oct. 1678, May and Oct. 1679, May and Oct. 1680, May and Oct. 1682, May and Oct. 1683. Deputy (Rye), May 1670, May 1671, May and Oct. 1672, Oct. 1677, May 1678, May 1680. Deputy (Greenwich), Oct. 1673, May and Oct. 1677, Oct. 1678. Commissioner for Fairfield, 1666. Member of War Council, Oct. 1675, May 1676; Committee on Indians, Oct. 1676; Committee on N. Y. boundary, Oct. 1674. Auditor of colony accounts, 1680, 1682. Received colonial grant of 100 acres, Oct. 1672.

Settled first in Windsor, where he was Clerk 1643 for weights and measures; came to Fairfield by 1649.

Presented Inv. of father Taintor's Est. at Fairfield, 1658. Married (1) ———, dau. of Charles Taintor.

Married (2) Mary, widow of Thomas Sherwood, 1st. She d. in 1694. [For her will, dated 6 Jan 1693 [1693/4], Inv. 13 Mar. 1693/4, see THOMAS SHERWOOD.]

Sergt. John Banks d. at Fairfield, 22 Jan. 1684 [1684/5]. His will, dated 12 Dec. 1684; codicil, 12 Jan. 1684 [1684/5]; wife Mary; sons John (land at Biram Neck and Horse Neck), Samuel (land at Rye), Obadiah, Benjamin; gr. child John, son of John Banks; dau. Susanna Sturgis and gr. child Jonathan Sturgis; gr. child Benjamin, son of Benjamin Banks; dau. Hannah Burr and gr. child Daniel Burr; son-in-law Daniel Burr; dau. Mary Taylor and her eldest dau.; mentioned land at Rye sold to George Kniffen. Inv. 27 Jan. 1684 [1684/5].

In 1678 and 1682, colonial records call him Lt., but no record of appointment found, and he was called Sergt. at death.

Children [by first wife]:

+John.
+Benjamin.
  Susanna, m. Jonathan Sturges.
  Joseph, d. abt. 12 Oct. 1682. Will 29 Oct. 1682 [date a mistake for Sept.]; bros. John, Obadiah, Samuel, Benjamin; sister Mary Taylor; to Mrs. Sarah Gold, Sr., £10; overseers, Maj. Nathan Gold and my father John Banks. Inv. 19 Oct. 1682. Samuel Morehouse and Daniel Burr, each ae. abt. 40, made oath; will made

abt. 14 days before Joseph's death; the date in the will was a
mistake.

+Samuel.

Hannah, m. Daniel Burr.

Mary, m. (called of Windsor) 27 Oct. 1670, Samuel Taylor [Col.
Rec.].

Obadiah, d. in Feb. 1691. Will 12 Feb. 1690 [1690/1]; cousin Joseph,
son of bro. John Banks; sister Mary Taylor; bro. Benjamin's two
eldest sons, Benjamin and Joseph; bro. Samuel; Rebecca dau. of
Sergt. John Wheeler of Fairfield dec'd; bro. Benjamin Banks, and
John Thompson, Exec'rs. Witnesses: Samuel Roberson, Josiah
Harvey. Inv. 27 Feb. 1690 [1690/1].

Banks, John, s. John.

Married at Stamford, 3 Apr. 1672, Abigail Lyon.

Settled at Greenwich; d. 14 July 1699.

Inv. of John of Greenwich who d. 14 July 1699 taken 10 Aug.
1699. Widow Abigail to administer. Dowry set, 4 May 1703, to
widow Abigail Banks. She was appointed guardian to youngest
son John, and Mercy chose her mother guardian. Joseph Banks
was appointed guardian to his bros. Daniel and Samuel.

Children:

Joseph, d. abt. 1712. Adm'n granted, 17 Apr. 1712, to widow Hannah.
Agreement at Greenwich, 17 Feb. 1729 [1729/30]; Hannah Lyon
widow of Joseph Banks, with her present husband John Lyon, Jr.;
only son Joseph Banks; George Gorham and wife Hannah (eldest
dau.); Abigail Banks (2d dau.); Mary Banks (3d dau.).

Mercy.

Daniel.

Samuel.

John, d. at Greenwich, abt. 1727. Inv. 12 Apr. 1727 presented by
Samuel Mills of Greenwich, Exec'r.

Banks, Samuel, s. of John.

On 14 July 1701, Samuel Banks, formerly living in Rye, now
in Westchester County, N. Y., being now disposed to go and
dwell in Tallbot County, Md., appointed his friend John Stoakham
of Westchester his attorney to dispose of Fairfield realty; witnessed (by mark) by Elizabeth Stoakham and Mary Stoakham, Jr.

He was living in 1708.

Banks, Benjamin, s. of John.

He had land by gift of father John, 3 Jan. 1679, in Sasqua field, sometime granted to Anthony Beers.

Called son of John, he m. at Fairfield, 29 June 1679, Elizabeth Lyon, dau. of Richard. She m. (2) abt. 1695, William Rowlandson. Benjamin receipted 1 Mar. 1680 to mother-in-law Margaret Lyon for £40 due wife Elizabeth under will of her father Richard Lyon.

Benjamin published warning, 25 July 1691, "not to traffic or barter with my wife Elizabeth." He purchased, 9 Feb. 1684 [1684/5], from his brothers John of Greenwich and Obadiah of Fairfield.

Will 21 Mar. 1691/2; wife Elizabeth; son Benjamin, land formerly my father John Banks's; son Joseph; daus. Elizabeth and Abigail Banks; bro. Daniel son of Mr. Jehu Burr sole Exec'r; codicil 2 May 1692; Inv. 5 July 1692.

Ages of children, 12 Mar. 1694 [1694/5]; Benjamin 13, Elizabeth 9, Abigail 5, Joseph 4. Daniel Burr and Elizabeth Rolison made oath; William Rolison had m. the widow. Adm'n granted to Daniel son of Jehu Burr, and Samuel Roberson. Distribution, 2 Aug. 1706; Benjamin, Joseph, and Abigail Banks, and Elizabeth Davis, eldest dau.

Children, first two recorded at Fairfield:

    ✕Benjamin, b. 30 Oct. 1682, d. 13 Jan. 1760 in 78 yr. (g. s. Greenfield); m. (1) Ruth Hyatt, who d. 20 May 1751 in 66 yr. (g. s.) or May 1750 æ. 67 (church rec.); m. (2) Elizabeth ———, who d. 27 Dec. 1758 in 63 yr. (rec. Greenfield church); m. (3) 23 July 1759 (rec. Greenfield) "Widow Whitney." She was Ann (Laborie), widow of Samuel Whitney of Stratford.

    Elizabeth, b. 26 Nov. 1685; m. Samuel Davis.

    Abigail, b. abt. 1688; m. 5 Mar. 1710, Daniel Knapp.

    ✕Joseph, b. [30 Dec. 1690 by age at death, making allowance for calendar change], d. 4 Jan. 1766 ae. 75 (g. s. Greenfield), ae. 75 yrs. wanting 5 days (church rec.); m. (rec. Greenfield church) 25 June 1712, Mary Sherwood [dau. of Benjamin], b. 8 Jan. 1693 (rec. Greenfield), d. 15 June 1770 ae. 77 (g. s.).

Barlow, John.

Settled in Fairfield, where he owned land at least as early as 1650.

Will 28 Mar. 1674; wife Ann; son John; daus. Elizabeth Frost, Martha Beers, Deborah Sturgis, Isabella Clapham, Ruth Bradley. Inv. 9 June 1674. The sons-in-law James Beers, John Sturgis, and Francis Bradley, made agreement with John Barlow, 20 Nov. 1674.

Inv. of his widow Ann's Est. 25 Feb. 1684 [1684/5].

Children:

> Ann, m. 13 Sept. 1650 (Col. Rec.) Samuel Drake; she called dau. of John.
> Elizabeth, d. 1686; m. Daniel Frost.
> +John.
> Martha, m. James Beers.
> Deborah, m. John Sturgis.
> Isabella, m. Peter Clapham.
> Ruth, m. Francis Bradley.

Barlow, Thomas.

He was prob. first at Windsor, being sued 1649 by Richard Samwis of that town. Settled in Fairfield, where he owned land at least as early as 1650. He bought a homelot from Thomas Sherwood, which Sherwood acknowledged 19 May 1684.

Married Rose (Sherwood) Rumble, dau. of Thomas Sherwood, 1st, and widow of Thomas Rumble of Stratford. She m. (3) Edward Nash.

Will 8 Sept. 1658; wife Rose; three daus. Phebe, Deborah, Mary, to receive portions at 16 yrs.; overseer, friend Mr. Thomas Pell; witnesses, Andrew Ward, John Banks. Inv. £465. In 1673 Phebe Barlow alias Olmstead receipted to Edward Nash and her mother; witnesses, Wm. Hamilton, Deborah and Mary Barlow. In 1679 Robert Steward of Norwalk and his wife Bethia, dau. of Thomas Rumble (who died before 4 Mar. 1653), whose widow Rose m. (2) Thomas Barlow and is now wife of Ed: Nash, etc.

James Olmstead of Norwalk and John Burritt of Stratford sold land in Fairfield, 9 Mar. 1691/2, to John Bulkley which was laid out to the children of Thomas Barlow; and the same grantors sold to Francis Bradley, 16 Mar. 1692/3. Joseph Burritt of Stratford, yeoman, with Mary his wife, 13 May 1714, released all right of reversion in a lot known as Barlow's lot, which father Mr. John Burritt sold to Rev. Joseph Webb of Fairfield.

Children, born at Fairfield:

Phebe, b. 27 Feb. 1650 [1650/1] (Col. Rec.); m. in 1673, James
Olmstead.

Deborah, m. (Stratford rec.) 1 May 1684, John Burritt.

Mary, d. 2 Sept. 1711; m. (Norwalk rec.) 1 May 1684, John Nash.

Barlow, John, s. of John.

He was husband of Abigail dau. of Robert and Susanna Lockwood in 1681.

Will 28 Jan. 1690 [1690/1]; wife Abigail; sons John, Joseph,
Samuel; daus. Abigail, Deborah, Elizabeth, Ruth. Inv. 6 Mar.
1690 [1690/1].

Children:

+John, b. abt. 1668.

Abigail, m. (1) Jonathan Rowland, d. 1691; m. (2) Samuel Denton,
of Hempstead, L. I.

+Joseph.

Deborah, b. abt. 1675, d. 4 Dec. 1726 in 52 yr. (g. s., Stratfield); m.
Col. John Burr.

Elizabeth, b. at Fairfield, 11 May 1677; m. Jeremiah Fowler of
Westchester, N. Y.

Ruth, m. John Morehouse.

+Samuel, b. abt. 1682.

Barlow, John, s. of John 2d. Lt., west company, Fairfield,
May 1705.

Born at Fairfield about 1668, d. there in 1715; renewed his
Covenant at Fairfield Church, 24 Feb. 1694/5.

Married about 1692, Ruth (Sherwood) Drake, dau. of Thomas
Sherwood, widow of Samuel Drake.

Will 31 July 1710, proved 6 Apr. 1715; wife Ruth; four sons,
John, Samuel, Joseph, Francis; four daus. Abigail, Ann, Sarah,
Deborah. Distribution made 22 Jan. 1717/8 to widow Ruth and
the four sons.

John Barlow, ae. 24, testified Sept. 1692 in the Disbrow witch
trial that the previous year he was in bed one night in the house
that "Ned" Jessup then lived in, etc.

Children, recorded at Stratford:

John, b. 6 Sept. 1693, bapt. 24 Feb. 1694/5.

✕Samuel, b. 14 Nov. 1695, bapt. 26 Apr. 1696, d. in 1734; adm'n granted, 8 Dec. 1734, to Sarah Barlow; m. Sarah (Sherman) Strong, widow of Benajah Strong; she m. (3) Samuel Rowland.

Abigail, b. 30 June 1697, bapt. 5 Sept. 1697, d. 16 Apr. 1743 ae. 47 (g. s., Greenfield) ; m. abt. 1716, William Hill.

Ann, b. 6 Oct. 1699, bapt. 19 Nov. 1699, d. at Westport, Nov. 1764; m. 1 Sept. 1720, Jeremiah Sturgis.

✕Joseph, b. 14 Apr. 1701, bapt. 18 May 1701; res. "Wostershear," N. Y., 1740; m. (1) Sarah Bradley, dau. of Joseph; m. (2) Experience Davis.

✕Francis, b. 11 July 1702, bapt. 16 Aug. 1702; res. Norwalk 1726, Stratford 1730, Newtown 1746; m. Elizabeth ———.

Sarah, b. 27 Feb. 1703 [1703/4], bapt. 5 Mar. 1703/4, d. 28 Nov. 1767 in 64 yr. (g. s., Greenfield); m. (1) Eliphalet Hull; m. (2) 1 Nov. 1738, Capt. David Banks.

Deborah, b. 10 Jan. 1705/6, bapt. 3 Mar. 1705/6, d. at Westport, 25 Jan. 1778; m. 13 Jan. 1725/6, Joseph Gorham.

Barlow, Joseph, s. of John 2d.

He d. between 6 July and 3 Oct. 1697; m. Sarah Read, dau. of William.

Inv. 3 Oct. 1697.

Agreement 3 Aug. 1698 between widow Sarah and Joseph's brothers John Burr, John Barlow (for himself and brothers Samuel Denton, Jeremiah Fowler and Samuel Barlow), and John Morehouse. Samuel Denton of "Homstead Village" [Hempstead], L. I., conveyed 1701 to John Barlow of Fairfield, right from brother-in-law Joseph Barlow dec'd.

Barlow, Samuel, s. of John. Ens., west end company, Fairfield, May 1715; Lt., second company, Oct. 1730.

Born about 1682, d. at Fairfield, 20 May 1745 in 63 yr. (g. s.).

Married Elizabeth Rumsey, b. abt. 1686, d. 10 Feb. 1752 in 66 yr. (g. s.).

Will 29 Apr. 1743, proved 19 June 1745; wife Elizabeth; sons Samuel, David; dau. Ann Barlow; daus. Elizabeth wife of Benjamin Sturgis, Abigail wife of Joseph Gold, Grace wife of Benjamin Lines; Eunice dau. of son Joseph dec'd. Adm'n was granted, 3 Feb. 1746/7, to son Samuel; and on 2 Feb. 1747/8 David Barlow, Exec'r, appealed from adm'n of Samuel Barlow.

Children, bapt. at Fairfield:

Gershom, bapt. 17 Feb. 1705/6, d. y.
XJoseph, bapt. 16 Mar. 1706/7, d. before 1743; m. ———.
Gershom, bapt. 19 Dec. 1708, d. y.
XSamuel, bapt. 22 Jan. 1709/10, d. at Redding, 20 Dec. 1773 ae. 63 (g. s.); will 20 Dec. 1773, proved 4 Jan. 1774; m. (1) 2 Aug. 1731, Eunice Bradley, dau. of Daniel; bapt. 30 May 1708; m. (2) 7 Aug. 1744, Esther Hull, dau. of Nathaniel; b. 11 June 1721, d. 28 Aug. 1775 ae. 54 (g. s.).
Daniel, bapt. 28 Oct. 1711, d. y.
Elizabeth, bapt. 20 June 1714; m. Benjamin Sturgis.
Abigail, bapt. 5 Aug. 1716; m. abt. 1738, Joseph Gold.
Mary, bapt. 2 Nov. 1718, d. y.
XDavid, bapt. 1 Mar. 1718/9; m. (1) 27 Dec. 1743, Susannah Hubbard, dau. of Zechariah, who d. 15 Oct. 1745 in 19 yr. (g. s.); m. (2) 29 Nov. 1750, Esther Sturgis, dau. of Jeremiah, b. 29 May 1722.
Ann, bapt. 8 Oct. 1721, d. at Stratfield, 26 July 1801 in 80 yr.; m. (1) 11 Mar. 1749/50, Joseph Sturgis of Stamford; m. (2) William Knowles of New Milford.
Grace, bapt. 24 May 1724; m. (1) at Greenfield, 30 May 1742, Benjamin Lines; m. (2) Jonathan Darrow.

Barley, George.

Although in the earliest generations the name of the *John Barlow* family was occasionally spelled *Barley* in the records, it was more usually *Barlow*. The connection of George with this family has not been ascertained. Although George's descendants seem to have adopted the form *Barlow,* it was almost always *Barley* in the first two generations.

He m. Mary Stilson, dau. of Vincent of Milford, whose will 1687 gave five shillings to his dau. Barly wife of George Barly, she having had portion.

He d. at Stratfield, by Nov. 1706.

Inv. of George of Stratford; adm'n granted, 27 Jan. 1706 [1706/7] to Widow Mary, with Samuel Hubbell. Five children. Samuel French appointed guardian to John, Elizabeth, and Nehemiah. Thomas Hawley appointed guardian for George and Mary. On 3 Feb. 1713/4, Samuel Hubbell being dec'd, adm'n was granted to the widow Mary Barley and son John Barley.

Children:

> John, b. [say 1688], d. at Stratford in 1755; will 1 Aug. 1748, proved
> 1 Sept. 1755; m. at Stratford, 10 Jan. 1716/7, Mary Sykes.
> Elizabeth, m. at Stratford, 27 Feb. 1717/8, Abraham Blackman.
> Nehemiah.
> ✕George, bapt. at Fairfield, 5 Jan. 1700/1; m. at Fairfield, 1 Apr. 1722,
> Mehitabel Staples [date 30 May 1723, by Stratford rec.].
> Mary, bapt. (with Ebenezer as children of Widow Barley) at Strat-
> field, 24 Nov. 1706; m. at Stratford, 11 Nov. 1723, Benjamin Lattin.
> Ebenezer, bapt. 24 Nov. 1706, d. y.

Barnum, Thomas.

He settled in Fairfield, and before 1678 sold his land there to
Alexander Bryan; rem. to Norwalk, and was a founder of
Danbury.

Est. of Thomas, Sr., of Danbury, who d. 26 Dec. 1695. Inv.
3 Jan. 1695/6, signed by Sarah Barnum. Son Thomas to administer with Thomas Pickett of Danbury. Five sons and five daus.
The widow had a prenuptial agreement.

Married (2) Sarah (Thompson), widow of John Hurd, Sr.
She returned to Stratford and d. there 24 Jan. 1717/8.

Children [by first wife], four recorded at Norwalk:

> +Thomas, b. 9 July 1663.
> (?) Sarah, m. (1) Thomas Pickett; m. (2) Samuel Hayes.
> +Richard.
> +Francis.
> John, b. 24 Feb. 1677 [1677/8].
> Hannah, b. 4 Oct. 1680.
> Ebenezer, b. 29 May 1682.
> Three other daus.

Barnum, Thomas, s. of Thomas.

Born at Norwalk, 9 July 1663, d. at Danbury in 1731.

Will of Thomas, Sr., of Danbury, 17 Dec. 1730, proved 27 Dec.
1731; sons, Thomas (eldest), Ephraim, Ebenezer, Joshua (4th
and youngest); wife Sarah; daus. Sarah Hoyt and Esther Judd;
grandson John Wilkes (his mother Susannah had portion in her
lifetime); youngest dau. Mary Barnum.

Children:

Thomas.
Sarah, m. [perhaps Joshua] Hoyt.
Ephraim, m. Mehitabel ——
Susanna, m. —— Wilkes.
Ebenezer, m. (by 1717) Abigail Skeels, dau. of John of Woodbury.
Esther, m. —— Judd.
Joshua.
Mary.

Barnum, Richard, s. of Thomas.

Married Mary Hurd, dau. of John of Stratford, b. 15 Aug. 1673. On 1 July 1720, they receipted to bro. Isaac Hurd for her right from father John, and "by Death of two of my sisters."

Will 14 Jan. 1739; five sons; gr. son Joseph, son of Joseph dec'd.

Children:

Benjamin, m. by 1722, Anna Forward.
John, will 1757; Capt.; m. Ruth ——.
Nathaniel, will 5 Feb. 1778; m. Thankful ——
Abner, m. at Stratfield, 9 Nov. 1732, Rachel Wakelee.
Bethuel, b. 17 Feb. 1705; m. Anna Goodsell.
Joseph, d. before 1739; m. 20 Oct. 1731, Mary Brackenburg.

Barnum, Francis, s. of Thomas.

Married (1) Deborah Hoyt, dau. of John of Danbury, and they joined on 28 Feb. 1712 [1712/3] in a mutual agreement of Hoyt heirs.

Married (2) Mary ——.

A conveyance was given by Francis to his six sons; and on 20 May 1741 his widow Mary conveyed to his son Abel her dower interest. [Private Deeds.]

Children [by first wife], daus. not known:

Isaac, m. Sarah Beardsley, dau. of Samuel, Jr., of Stratfield.
Samuel.
Thomas.
Nathan.
David.
Abel.

Bartram, John.

He petitioned the New Haven General Court, Oct. 1658, for divorce from a wife in Barbadoes, but the Court lacked knowledge of the circumstances and declined to act.

Inv. 8 Nov. 1675; "this is all that John Hurd Junr and his wife gave in"; John Hurd, Jr. made oath, 2 May 1676.

His widow Sarah doubtless m. Jacob Gray, for on 25 Feb. 1695 Ens. John Osborn recorded in Fairfield Deeds that he had purchased from John Bartram part of the long lot granted to Bartram's father-in-law Jacob Gray.

Children, one recorded at Stratford:
+John.
    Hannah, b. 28 June 1668.

Bartram, John, s. of John.

He bought from Albert Dennie, 26 Oct. 1692, the homelot that had been Joseph Cable's.

Sarah, wife of John, was bapt. at Fairfield Church, 23 Dec. 1694.

Adm'n granted, 27 Oct. 1740, to John Bartram.

Children, recorded at Fairfield:
    John, b. 23 Feb. 1690/1, d. y.
    Daughter, b. 10 May 1692, Sarah bapt. 23 Dec. 1694, d. y.
    XJohn, b. 9 Jan. 1693/4, bapt. 23 Dec. 1694, d. at Greenfield, 11 Dec. 1747; adm'n granted, 17 Dec. 1747, to Benjamin Sherwood and Joseph Rumsey; m. abt. 1718, Sarah, widow of Francis Bradley, and dau. of Joseph Jackson; she d. Mar. or Apr. 1753.
    Joseph, b. 8 Aug. 1696, bapt. 9 Aug. 1696.
    XEbenezer, b. 29 Apr. 1699, bapt. 30 Apr. 1699, d. 7 Dec. 1769 ae. 71 (g. s. Fairfield); m 15 May 1728, Elizabeth Williams, who d. 5 Dec. 1769 ae. 69 (g. s.).
    XDavid, bapt. 13 Dec. 1702, d. at Redding, 7 Feb. 1768; m. 14 Dec. 1730, Mabel Johnson [dau. of Moses].
    Sarah, bapt. 7 May 1704.

BASSETT FAMILY (FAIRFIELD)

Bassett, Thomas.

Came on the *Christian* 1635 aged 37. Served in Pequot War 1637. Settled in Windsor and made a freeman of Conn. Colony, Apr. 1640.

Received a homelot of 2½ acres in Fairfield, Aug. 1653, and was freed from training in Fairfield, 1659.

Before removing to Fairfield, he may have lived a short time in Stratford, and we must suppose it was his wife who was executed as a witch at Stratford in 1651.

He was one of four "poor men" whose debts were forgiven by the will of Dr. Pell, 1669. His Inv. taken 14 Jan. 1669/70; widow and children mentioned but not named. His administrators sold an acre in "Concord field", 4 May 1678, and Thomas Dickerson acknowledged next year that his father Dickerson gave the acre to Bassett.

He m. (2) after 1656, Johanna, widow of Thomas Beardsley of Fairfield, b. abt. 1634, by whom he had a family. On 25 Nov. 1661, he sold the house of Thomas Beardsley as his "successor." In May 1666 he testified, ae. 68, in the Benfield case, and his wife Johanna, ae. 32, also testified. This statement of his age identifies him with the Thomas who came on the *Christian*.

One child presumably was:
+Thomas.

Bassett, Thomas, [s. of Thomas?].

Married Sarah [Baldwin, dau. of Josiah?].
Died before 7 Feb. 1736/7.

Children, all bapt. at Milford 24 Oct. 1703:
> John, d. at Milford in 1759; m. Mary ———, who d. 23 Oct. 1752.
> Josiah, m. 25 Apr. 1717, Alice Canfield.
> Mercy, m. 27 Feb. 1719, Azariah Canfield.
> Abigail.
> Sarah, m. Nov. 1728, Walter Lewis.
> Thomas,* res. Derby; rem. to Newtown; m. 24 Aug. 1727, Sarah Pierson.
> Jerusha.

BASSETT FAMILY (STRATFORD)

Bassett, John.

Carpenter, took the oath at New Haven 1644. Mr. Evance hired him and his wife in England to be servants to Mr. Goodyear.

---

* Thomas of Stratford, will 10 Nov. 1752, proved 11 Mar. 1756; m. Ann ———; a different man, parentage not ascertained.

He bought Lieut. Seeley's house in 1646. Evidently went, or intended going, to England 1651, as the town, considering his usefulness and that he is "willing to come again", agreed to bear his charge in coming. Died between 17 and 20 Feb. 1652/3 at New Haven, but had bought land of Elias Bailey at Stamford the previous year.

His widow Margery and son Robert removed to Stamford. Goodwife Bassett made her will June 1653, proved May 1656; gave to her son Robert the house and lot at New Haven according to her husband's will; two daus. wives of John Emery and John Webb, and two, Sarah and Elizabeth, unmarried.

William Bassett of New Haven is sometimes included among the children of John, but we have found no evidence for so placing him.

Children:

+Robert.
    Daughter, m. John Emory.
    Daughter, m. John Webb.
    Sarah.
    Elizabeth, m. at Stamford, Oct. 1658, Isaac Finch.

Bassett, Robert, s. of John.   Chief Drummer, New Haven Col. Troop, June 1654.

Carpenter, took the oath at New Haven 1644.   Town drummer, 1645.   Removed to Stamford by 1651, and in 1653 was brought to New Haven for riotous support of Baxter and sedition in fiery speech aimed at tyranny of the colonial government; placed under bond of £100 to keep the peace.

Removed to Hempstead, L. I., where he died about 1670.

Children:

    Mary, b. 8 Mar. 1649/50, d. 17 Mar. 1649/50.
    Daughter, m. Daniel Pearsall of Hempstead.
    Sarah, m. (1) at Stratford, 8 Jan. 1673/4, Henry Hitt; m. (2) [prob. Simon] Lobdell [of Milford, as his second wife].
    John; will 24 May 1676; Inv. 3 Mar. 1684/5 included carpenter tools; will made at Stratford when called for service against the Indians; left to brother Robert "sword which was my father's." Probate mentions that Pearsall and Hitt consented to will of their bro.-in-law John Bassett, 6 Dec. 1685.
+Robert.

Bassett, Robert, s. of Robert.   Sergt., Stratford Trainband.

He m. Elizabeth Riggs, dau. of Samuel of Derby, b. June 1668, d. in 1746. Sergt. Robert d. at Stratford, 5 Aug. 1720. Inv. taken 30 Dec. 1720; adm'n granted to son Jonadab, 8 Dec. 1720. Distribution ordered to widow Elizabeth, sons Samuel, Jonadab, Robert, Ebenezer, and dau. Elizabeth. Will of Elizabeth, 21 Mar. 1744/5, proved 8 Apr. 1746; named same four sons and dau. Elizabeth wife of Francis "Witmore."

Children, recorded at Stratford:

> John, b. 23 June 1689, d. y.
>
> Samuel, b. 28 Nov. 1692, d. at Derby, 15 Sept. 1764; Capt.; m. 5 Jan. 1719, Deborah Bennett, dau. of Thomas, b. 15 Feb. 1695/6, d. July 1773.
>
> Jonadab, b. 20 July 1695, d. abt. 1779; will 29 May 1779; m. (1) at Stratfield, 28 May 1719, Mary Phippen; m. (2) 3 June 1756, Rebecca, widow of Robert Turney, and dau. of Daniel Burr, b. 29 Oct. 1710, d. at Trumbull, 7 Sept. 1794 in 84 yr. (g. s.); her will, 21 Mar. 1770, proved 3 Nov. 1794.
>
> Robert, b. 11 July 1699, d. in 1785; will 25 Oct. 1765, proved 4 Apr. 1785; m. (1) 21 Jan. 1730/1, Eunice Clark; m. (2) 25 Dec. 1763, Obedience (Mallory), widow of Edmund Curtis, Nathan Fairchild, and Benjamin Sherman.
>
> Elizabeth, b. 15 Dec. 1701; m. 19 Aug. 1725, Francis Whitmore.
>
> Ebenezer, b. 31 Jan. 1706/7, d. at Oxford, 17 July 1794 ae. 88; m. 2 Feb. 1742/3, Sarah Tomlinson. No issue. His will, 9 Apr. 1770, proved Nov. 1794; Sarah Whitmore of Derby, dau. of sister Elizabeth Whitmore of Killingly.

Bastard, Joseph.   Deputy (Fairfield), July 1691.

Born at Boston, Mass., 29 Sept. 1647, son of Joseph and Mary. Settled in Fairfield. Elizabeth, dau. of Joseph and Elizabeth, b. at Boston, 24 Dec. 1673, may have been his child by a first wife.

He m. abt. Sept. 1684, Hannah (Jordan) Wakeman, widow of Ezbon Wakeman, and dau. of John Jordan of Guilford. Hannah Bastard witnessed the will of Mrs. Sarah Burr, 8 June 1696, and was living when it was proved, 12 Aug. 1696, but d. before Nov. 1697.

Inv. 14 Nov. 1697; wife is deceased; two children. Adm'n granted, 10 Jan. 1697/8, to Nathan Gold and John Thompson.

On 5 Nov. 1685, Joseph Bastard recites that a marriage was consummated abt. 14 mos. before betwixt me and Hannah widow of Izbon Wakeman, "on which occasion (being a stranger) people have taken the freedom to discours very hardly of me, and when I have gone from whom on my ocation to Boston or els whear," and considering the "tenderness I bear her and issue I have now by her," give all estate in trust to Major Nathan Gold and Mr. John Burr.

Children:

> Ann, b. late in 1685 [assuming that she was the child referred to in her father's deed of trust]; m. Robert Rumsey.
> William, d. in 1707/8. Inv. 11 Feb. 1707 [1707/8]; Robert Rumsey, Adm'r.

Bateman, William.

He was of Concord, freeman 1641; rem. to Fairfield, presumably with the Jones party.

Will 24 Mar. 1656; one-half to son Thomas, now of Concord; one-half to son-in-law Henry Lyon; except £5 to gr. child Joseph Middlebrook, under 18. If Middlebrook dies, the £5 to be divided equally between Thomas and Henry. Witnesses: Andrew Ward, William Ward. Henry Lyon signed 27 Apr. 1657 a document now mostly illegible. Will exhibited 20 Oct. 1658.

Children:

> Thomas, of Concord, b. abt. 1615, d. 6 Feb. 1668/9 ae. 54; m. Martha ———.
> Daughter, m. Henry Lyon.
> Daughter, m. Joseph Middlebrook.

Bates, Robert.

He was of Wethersfield by 1640, soon rem. to Stamford.

He m. (2) (rec. Stamford) in 1657, Margaret Cross; widow of William of Fairfield.

He d. at Stamford, 11 June 1675.

Will 15 May 1675; gr. son John Bates; son John; dau. Mary Ambler and her children; son-in-law John Cross. Inv. June 1675.

Children [by first wife]:

Mary, m. 25 Dec. 1662, Abraham Ambler.
+John, b. abt. 1641.

Bates, John, s. of John. Ens., Stamford Trainband, Oct. 1685;
Deputy (Stamford) Aug. 1689, Oct. 1696.

Born abt. 1641; aged 25 in 1666.
He m. Sarah Cross, dau. of William.
Mrs. Sarah, "a usefull and skillful midwife", d. 18 Feb. 1711/2.
She gave her testimony as midwife, Oct. 1692, in the Clawson
witchcraft trial.

Children:

John, Lt., west company, Stamford, Oct. 1716; will 12 Feb. 1745/6,
proved 4 Aug. 1752; m. (1) 18 Jan. 1693/4, Elizabeth Lockwood,
dau. of Gershom of Greenwich; she d. 23 May 1702; m. (2) 28
Dec. 1702, Sarah Smith, who d. 20 Feb. 1726/7; m. (3) 15 Jan.
1727/8, Mrs. Hannah Mead.
Samuel, Lt., Stamford Trainband, May 1730; Inv. 27 Feb. 1754; m.
(1) 2 Mar. 1703/4, Sarah Scofield, who d. 17 Feb. 1717/8; m. (2)
21 Dec. 1727, Rachel Ferris.
Jonathan, Deputy for Stamford, Aug. 1710, May 1712, May 1714,
Oct. 1715, Oct. 1724, May and Oct. 1725, May and Oct. 1726,*
May and Sept. 1727, Oct. 1728, Oct. 1729, Oct. 1731, May 1732,
May and Oct. 1733, Oct. 1735, May 1743, Oct. 1745; m. 13 Dec.
1705, Joanna Selleck.

Baxter, Thomas.

Capt. Thomas "hath purchased" from Anthony Wilson land in
Fairfield; recorded 4 July 1657. The will of Thomas, going to
England, made 19 Dec. 1659; wife, Exec'x; children; overseers,
friends Nathan Gold, Michael Try and Andrew Ward.

Bridget divorced him for desertion, in May 1662, and m. (2)
John Palmer. Bridget Baxter sold to John Makew land which
he recorded 28 Mar. 1661. Bridget Palmer acknowledged, 16 Jan.
1667 [1667/8], that she sold land to Simon Couch before she m.
John Palmer.

---

* Called Joseph in Oct. 1726.

This was the Capt. Baxter who in 1653, armed with a commission from Rhode Island, during the war between England and Holland, made a nuisance of himself by seizing vessels along the coast of New England, English as well as Dutch. He carried things with such a high hand that New Haven Colony ordered his arrest and he was apprehended at Stamford, tried, fined £20, and compelled to give his bond for £100 to keep the peace. In the meanwhile, Rhode Island revoked his commission. The New Haven Colony records inform us that he had once lived among the Dutch, and after the trial "he had libertie to goe to Fairfeild to order his family occasions." Connecticut Colony also dealt severely with him, and his estate was attached by the Constable of Fairfield. It appears that the damage done was settled (though with heavy loss to the privateering captain), for in Oct. 1656 his bond was ordered returned by Conn. Colony.

In March 1661/2, Bridget Baxter petitioned for divorce, and a letter alleged to have been written by Baxter to his wife in England was put in evidence. Mr. Gould, Mr. Sherman, and Mr. William Hill were ordered to compare the letter with Baxter's other writings. In May, the divorce was granted; "and whereas the estate that her husband Baxter left with her is sold to pay debts, all excepting a bed and her wearing aparell," the Court prohibited the creditors from "seizing ye remainder, vntil ye Court see cause to ye contrary."

There was at least one child:

> Thomas, who eventually bought much of the Palmer property in Westchester, and in 1696 conveyed with his wife Rebecca to son Thomas.

Beach, John.

Came to New Haven with bros. Richard and Thomas, perhaps 1639 but first mentioned 1643 and took oath of fidelity the following year; rem. to Stratford 1652, and was an original proprietor of Wallingford 1670, but retained Stratford residence.

Died 16 June 1677, called Sr. of Stratford (probate rec.); Inv. of property at Stratford and Wallingford, amounting to about £344. Agreement 6 Nov. 1677 made by children who were of age, signed by John and Thomas Beach, Elizabeth Preston, and Mary Beach; they appointed Capt. Wm. Curtis, Mr. Israel Chauncey and Jehiel Preston, overseers of Est. and children in Stratford, and Mr. John Moss and Eliasaph Preston for those in Wallingford. Names and birth dates of the ten children given. Wife was called Mary at birth of child 1674.

Children, recorded at Stratford:

Elizabeth, b. 28 Mar. 1652 [20 Mar. by probate]; m. Eliasaph Preston.

+John, b. Apr. 1654.

Mary, b. Sept. 1656.

Thomas, b. May 1659, d. at Wallingford, 13 May 1741 ae. 82; m. (1) (rec. Wallingford) 12 May 1680, Ruth Peck, dau. of Paul and Martha (Hale) Peck, b. abt. 1660, d. 5 Dec. 1686; m. (2) Phebe Wilcoxson, dau. of Timothy, b. at Stratford, 2 Aug. 1669, d. 30 Apr. 1758.

+Nathaniel, b. Mar. 1662.

Hannah, b. Dec. 1665; m. (1) 3 Nov. 1681, Zechariah Fairchild; m. (2) 5 May 1708, Mr. John Burritt.

Sarah, b. Nov. 1667.

+Isaac, b. 27 June 1669.

+Joseph, b. 5 Feb. 1671 [1671/2] [1 Feb. by probate].

Benjamin, b. on or abt. 3 Mar. 1673/4; rem. to Wallingford, later to Hanover, N. J.; m. Mary Hitchcock, dau. of John, b. at Wallingford, 10 Dec. 1676.

Beach, John, s. of John.

Born Apr. 1654; res. Stratford; death entered, but date omitted, in Stratford, between entries dated Feb. and Apr. 1712.

Will 6 Nov. 1705, proved 2 Apr. 1712; wife Phebe, her former husband John Birdsey; son Ebenezer; eldest dau. Mary wife of Archibald Dunlap; daus. Mehitabel Beach, Hester Beach; codicil 14 Mar. 1711 mentions that dau. Mehitabel has married; bros. Nathaniel, Isaac, and Joseph Beach. Inv. 20 Mar. 1712. Receipt 14 Jan. 1723/4 given by Joseph Booth, Daniel Hubbell, and Mary Smith, to our uncles Nathaniel, Isaac and Lt. Joseph Beach.

Married (1) (Stratford rec.) 18 Dec. 1679, Hannah Staples of Fairfield. She was dau. of Thomas, b. [say 1659].

Married (2) Phebe, widow of John Birdsey, and dau. of William Wilcoxson, b. abt. 1651, d. 20 Sept. 1743 ae. 93.

Children [by first wife], recorded at Stratford (mother of last three called Hannah) :

> Mary, b. 14 July 1683, d. (Mary Smith, Widow) 4 Oct. 1725; m.
> (1) 15 June 1703, Mr. Archibald Dunlap; m. (2) as widow Mary
> Dunlap, 5 Jan. 1715/6, Mr. John Smith.
> Mehitabel, b. 30 Sept. 1690; m. by 1711, Joseph Booth.
> Ebenezer, b. 14 Sept. 1692, d. at Stratford in 1776; will 23 Jan. 1776,
> proved 8 Feb. 1776; m. (rec. Stratford) 28 Dec. 1715, Mehitabel
> Gibson of Milford.
> Hester, b. 3 May 1694; m. 17 May 1716, Daniel Hubbell.

Beach, Nathaniel, s. of John.

Born at Stratford, Mar. 1662, d. there 24 July 1747 ae. 84 yrs. 3 mos. (g. s.).

Married at Stratford, 29 Apr. 1686, Sarah Porter. She was dau. of Nathaniel, b. 3(?) Sept. 1667, d. 25 Mar. 1738 ae. 70 (g. s.).

Will 27 July 1744, proved 6 Nov. 1747; Andrew Beach of Branford, son of eldest son Ephraim dec'd; children of dec'd dau. Elizabeth wife of Nathan Wheeler; children of son David dec'd; son Josiah; children of son Nathaniel dec'd; dau. Sarah wife of Mr. John Beach of Redding; son Daniel; dau. Anna wife of Elnathan Beers; son Israel; residue to son James.

Children, recorded at Stratford (of Nathaniel and Sarah) :

> Ephraim, b. 25 May 1687, d. 15 Mar. 1716/7; m. 3 July 1712, Sarah
> Patterson, b. 17 Mar. 1694.
> Elizabeth, b. 11 or 12 Nov. 1689, d. at Stratford, 22 Jan. 1739/40
> in 51 yr. (g. s.) ; m. Nathan Wheeler.
> David, b. 15 May 1692, d. at Trumbull, 21 Apr. 1735 in 43 yr. (g. s.) ;
> m. 24 Jan. 1716/7, Hannah Sherman, who d. 19 Feb. 1772 in 77
> yr. (g. s.).
> Josiah, b. 18 Aug. 1694, d. at Trumbull, 17 Apr. 1759 in 65 yr. (g. s.) ;
> Lt.; m. (1) 25 Jan. 1721/2, Patience Nichols, who d. 25 Aug.
> 1749 ae. 48 (g. s.) ; m. (2) 3 June 1750, Abigail Wheeler.
> Nathaniel, b. 28 Dec. 1696, d. 20 Aug. 1734 in 38 yr. (g. s.) ; m. 3
> Nov. 1720, Sarah Burton; she m. (2) William Odell.
> Sarah, b. 12 Nov. 1691 [error in original for 1699], d. 1 Aug. 1756;
> m. Rev. John Beach.
> Daniel, b. 15 Jan. 1701/2, d. at Trumbull, 19 Feb. 1745/6 ae. 44 yrs.
> 1 mo. (g. s.) ; m. 3 Dec. 1724, Hester Curtis, bapt. 10 Feb. 1706.
> She m. (2) 17 June 1747, Ebenezer Hickock of Danbury.
> Anna, b. 10 Mar. 1704, bapt. 23 July 1704 (at Stratford, rec. Strat-
> field) ; m. 25 Jan. 1728, Elnathan Beers.

Israel, b. 3 May 1707, d. at Stratford in 1792; will 31 Oct. 1774, proved 27 Dec. 1792; m. 1 July 1731, Hannah Burritt.

James, b. 13 Aug. 1709, d. 16 Sept. 1752 in 44 yr.; will 23 June 1752, proved 8 Nov. 1752; m. 23 Dec. 1730, Sarah Curtis.

Beach, Isaac, s. of John.

Born at Stratford, 27 June 1669, d. there 30 Apr. 1741 ae. 71 yrs. 10 mos. (g. s.); m. 3 May 1693, Hannah Birdsey, b. 5 Feb. 1671/2, d. 15 Oct. 1750 in 79 yr. (g. s., Epis. Yard).

Will 12 Sept. 1740, proved 15 June 1741; wife Hannah; dau. Mary Wilcoks; dau. Hannah Prince; sons William, Elnathan, John.

Children by Hannah, recorded at Stratford:

William, b. 7 July 1694, d. 26 July 1751; m. (rec. Stratford) 30 Nov. 1725, Sarah Hull of Derby; she m. (2) Rev. Samuel Johnson.
Elnathan, b. 7 Jan. 1698, d. at Cheshire, 18 Aug. 1742 ae. 45 (g. s.); Capt.; m. (1) (rec. Wallingford) 9 May 1720, Abigail Ufford, b. May 1700, d. 2 Dec. 1738; m. (2) Hannah ———.
John, b. 6 Oct. 1700, d. at Newtown, 9 Mar. 1782; Rev.; m. (1) Sarah Beach, b. 12 Nov. 1699, d. 1 Aug 1756; m. (2) Abigail, widow of John Holbrook, and dau. of Abel Gunn of Derby.
Mary, b. 16 Dec. 1703; m. ——— Wilcox.
Hannah, b. 26 May 1709; m. ——— Prince.
Dinah, b. 14 Oct. 1713, d. 21 Dec. 1714.

Beach, Joseph, s. of John. Called Sergt. at birth of child 1713. Lt., north company, Stratford, May 1718.

Born at Stratford, 5 Feb. 1671 [1671/2]; Lt. Joseph d. there 17 Dec. 1737.

Married Abiah Booth, dau. of Ebenezer, b. 19 Oct. 1674.

Will 5 May 1736, proved 2 Jan. 1737/8; wife Abiah; daus. Sarah wife of Jonathan Nichols, Hannah wife of Zachariah Tomlinson, Abiah wife of Samuel Judson. Distribution 1739 to the three daus.

Adm'n on Est. of Abiah Beach, widow of Lt. Joseph, granted to Samuel Judson, 13 Mar. 1740/1.

Children by Abiah, recorded at Stratford:

Sarah, b. 13 July 1697; m. 22 Dec. 1713, Jonathan Nichols.
Agur, b. 8 Apr. 1699, d. 7 Mar. 1711/2.
Abraham, b. 29 Apr. 1701, d. 1 Mar. 1711/2.
Hannah, b. abt. 1704, d. at Stratford, 5 Oct. 1740 in 37 yr. (g. s.); m. 25 Mar. 1718/9, Zechariah Tomlinson.

Joseph, b. ——, d. 28 Feb. 1711/2.
Abiah, b. 12 Jan. 1712/3; m. 2 May 1734, Samuel Judson.

Beach, Benjamin, s. of Richard. Deputy (Stratford), May 1701, Oct. 1704, Aug. 1710.

Born at New Haven, Oct. 1644; d. at Stratford, 9 Apr. 1713. Inv. 13 Apr. 1713. Agreement for distribution made by Mrs. Mary Beach, the widow; Benjamin Beach, only son; Josiah Curtis; Edmund Lewis; and Mr. John Glover.

Married (1) Mary Peacock, dau. of John; who must have d. 1677.

Married (2) (rec. Stratford) 1 Feb. 1677/8, Sarah Welles. She was dau. of John of Hadley.

Married (3) 5 Dec. 1705, Mary Fairchild. She was widow of Samuel Fairchild, and dau. of Moses Wheeler; she m. (3) (rec. Wallingford) 31 July 1716, Thomas Yale.

Benjamin, Sr., conveyed 1707 to "onely son" Benjamin.

Children [by first wife], recorded at Stratford (mother of Bethia called Mary):

> Benjamin, b. 28 Oct. 1672, d. y.
> Bethia, b. 23 Apr. 1674; m. (1) William Bickley; m. (2) at Stratford, as Mist Bethyah Bickley, 14 July 1707, Mr. John Glover.*
> Mary, b. 19 Jan. 1676 [1676/7]; m. abt. 1698, Josiah Curtis.

Children [by second wife], recorded in Stratford (mother of Sarah called Sarah):

> Sarah, b. 24 May 1679, d. y.
> Hannah, b. Sept. 1681, d. at Stratford, 13 July 1756 in 75 yr. (g. s., Epis. Yard); m. 21 May 1702, Edmund Lewis.
> Benjamin, b. 1 Oct. 1683, "Sergt. Benjamin" d. 11 Nov. 1736 in 55 yr. (g. s., Unity); will Jan. 1735, proved 20 Dec. 1736; m. (1) 22 Dec. 1708, Martha Curtis; m. (2) at New Haven, 12 Mar. 1728/9, Jemima Talmadge, dau. of Thomas, b. 11 Feb. 1686.

Beach [UNPLACED.]

Ichabod Hubbard, son of SARAH BEACH of Stratford, chose Dea. Thomas Peat of Stratford for guardian, 27 Dec. 1739. He m. at Stratford, 30 Oct. 1751, Esther Wakelee.

---

* John Glover and Bethia Glover of Newtown conveyed 19 May 1714, excepting right of dower due to Mary widow of Mr. Benjamin Beach.

Beacham, Robert.

The surname is a corruption of Beauchamp, following the English pronunciation.

He was of Ipswich, Mass., 1648, of Norwalk by 1655, and removed to Fairfield by 1658. He acquired the right at Bankside or Maximus [Westport] which had belonged to Thomas Newton. He m. (1) Isabel ———, who joined him in a deed, 1659; m. (2) in 1668, Elizabeth, widow of Edward Jessup of Westchester.

Will of Robert of Maxemus Farms, 24 Nov. 1689; gr. children Robert and Susanna Lockwood; other two grandchildren John and Sarah Lockwood; land already given to Edward Jessup; wife Elizabeth; son-in-law Joseph Lockwood.

On 26 Jan. 1668 [1668/9], Robert Beacham and Elizabeth, formerly wife of Edward Jessup, acknowledged sale of land at Westchester to Thomas Hunt. On 29 Nov. 1684, Edward Jessup [Jr.] bought from Robert Beacham and also from Joseph Lockwood. Elizabeth Beacham, widow of Robert, conveyed all her estate to son Edward Jessup, 25 Dec. 1690.

The *Jessup Genealogy* suggests that Joseph Lockwood's wife may have been Hannah Jessup, stepdau. of Robert Beacham. Despite the fact that his will calls the Lockwood children his gr. children, that is possible; but in the want of definite proof, we follow the more generally accepted view.

Child [by first wife]:

    Daughter, m. Joseph Lockwood.

BEARDSLEY FAMILY (WILLIAM)

Beardsley, William. Deputy (Stratford) to Conn. Leg., Sept. 1645, Sept. 1649, May 1650, Sept. 1651, May 1652, Oct. 1653, Feb. 1657, May 1658.

A mason, of Stratford; came in *Planter,* 1635, aged 30, with wife Mary 26, dau. Mary 4, sons John 2 and Joseph ½.

Will 28 Sept. 1660; all my daus. that are now married, £10

apiece; sons Samuel and Joseph; wife; overseers, Mr. Blackman, Philip Groves, John Brinsmade, John Birdsey, Joseph Hawley; Daniel; son John; children; witnesses, Caleb Nichols, John
Welles. Inv. July 1661.

Children:

> Mary, b. abt. 1631; m. (rec. Wethersfield) May 1651, Thomas Welles
> [s. of Hugh]; settled in Hadley.
> +John, b. abt. 1633.
> +Joseph, b. abt. 1634.
> Ruth, m. Joseph Smith, of Jamaica, L. I.
> Rebecca, m. ——— Beebe.
> +Samuel.
> Hannah, m. Nathaniel Dickinson of Wethersfield; rem. to Hadley.
> +Daniel, b. abt. 1644.
> Sarah, m. (rec. Wethersfield) 8 Jan. 1668/9, Obadiah Dickinson, of
> Wethersfield and Hadley.

Beardsley, John, s. of William. Lt., Stratford Trainband,
May 1685; Lt., Stratfield Train Band, May 1697; Capt. of
same, May 1704.

Born abt. 1633; Capt. John d. at Stratford, 19 Nov. 1718.
Hannah wife of Capt. John d. at Stratford, Oct. 1718.

Will 21 Jan 1714/5 of John, Sr., of Stratfield; kinswoman
Deborah wife of Alexander Fairchild; wife Hannah (Exec'x);
John Beardsley son of brother Daniel; John Fairchild son of
Alexander. Inv. 3 Nov. 1718 of Capt. John.

[The death of his wife before him left a third of his estate
intestate, and from its distribution we learn much of the genealogy
of the early Beardsleys.]   Part of his estate was set to the children of Joseph Beardsley: John, Ephraim, Jonathan, Thomas, and
Josiah Beardsley, Elisabeth Pullford, and Joseph Beardsley.
Completing distribution, 3 Feb. 1720/1, the heirs of Mrs. Ruth
Smith, Mary Wells, Sarah Dickerson, and Hannah Dickerson, all
dec'd, had not received their portion; mention also of representatives of Samuel Beardsley dec'd; the heirs of Samuel had bought
the share of Mrs. Rebecca Beebe. [Fairfield Pro.] On 7 July
1721, Nathan Beardsley of Stratfield conveyed to John Hall of
the same, land formerly belonging to Capt. John Beardsley dec'd,

which was distributed to Mrs. Ruth Smith of Long Island as part of her right in his estate [Fairfield Deeds].

Beardsley, Joseph, s. of William.

Death recorded at Stratford, date omitted, between entries dated 19 Apr. and 4 May 1712.

Married at Stratford (not dated) Phebe Dayton of Brookhaven, L. I.

Children, recorded at Stratford:

> Joseph, b. 10 June 1666, d. in 1745; adm'n granted, 26 Aug. 1745, to Deborah Beardsley and Merriday Bostwick; m. (rec. Stratford) Nov. 1708, Deborah Stewart. She was dau. of Robert of Norwalk, b. May 1669; adm'n on her Est. was granted, 18 Apr. 1746, to John Clark of Stratford. Only recorded child: Joseph, b. 7 Nov. 1709.
> +John, b. 1 Nov. 1668.
> Hannah, b. 30 Apr. 1671.
> Thomas, d. in 1773; will 29 Mar. 1767, proved 9 Nov. 1773; m. 18 July 1707, Sarah Denman ["Dimin"].
> Ephraim, d. in 1734; will 23 Feb. 1733/4, proved 23 Mar. 1733/4; m. 30 Dec. 1708, Mehitabel Osborn.
> Jonathan.
> Josiah, m. 4 Dec. 1712, Mary Whittemore.
> Elizabeth, m. (1) 18 Nov. 1713, Edmund Pulford; m. (2) 8 Mar. 1722/3, Abraham Pullin.

Beardsley, Samuel, s. of William.

John Beardsley, Jr., and Jonathan Wakelee were appointed Adm'rs on Est. of Samuel of Stratfield, 10 Apr. 1707. Distribution ordered to Widow; five sons, William, Daniel, John, Benjamin, Nathan; two daus; eldest son is dec'd, had rec'd portion.

Married Abigail Clark, dau. of John of New Haven.*

Samuel, Sr., d. at Stratford, 24 Dec. 1706. His widow d. before 2 May 1727, when the third of his estate set to her was divided among the heirs: Hannah Parrack, Daniel Beardsley, Sarah Barnum, Jonathan Wakelee, John Beardsley, Nathan Beardsley.

---

* So stated by Winthrop; we are indebted to Mrs. Horatio Ford, of South Euclid, Ohio, for permission to use this information, obtained for her from unpublished Winthrop MSS. by Col. Charles E. Banks.

Children, recorded at Stratford:

> Abigail, b. 10 Aug. 1664, d. y.
> +Samuel, b. 1 Sept. 1666.
> +William, b. 22 Mar. 1668/9.
> +Daniel, b. 3 Apr. 1671.
> +John, b. 11 Oct. 1673.
> Ebenezer, b. 4 Feb. 1675 [1675/6].
> Benjamin, b. 25 Dec. 1677; Inv. 17 June 1712; Daniel and John Beardsley, Adm'rs. Distribution made 1727 to William, Daniel, John, and Nathan Beardsley, Jonathan Wakelee, John Parrocks, Sarah Barnum.
> Mary, b. 1 May 1680, d. after 1742; m. abt. 1704, Jonathan Wakelee.
> Hannah, b. 25 Oct. 1682; m. (1) John Parruck; m. (2) Edward Lacy.
> Nathan, b. 7 Oct. 1686; m. (1) at Stratfield, 13 June 1709, ———;
> m. (2) at Stratfield, 7 Jan. 1712 [1712/3], Elizabeth Hubbell.

Beardsley, Daniel, s. of William.

Born at Stratford, abt. 1644; d. there 7 Oct. 1730 in 86 yr. (g. s.).

Married Ruth Goodwin, dau. of Thomas of Milford, b. 2 Sept. 1662, d. 4 May 1732 in 71 yr. (g. s.). Her mother Ruth Rogers m. (2) Obadiah Wheeler and (3) Ephraim Stiles. A conveyance given by Daniel and Ruth Beardsley mentions that Ephraim Stiles married their mother Ruth Wheeler.

Children, recorded at Stratford:

> John, b. 18 Aug. 1681, d. 7 Nov. 1732 ae. 52 (g. s., Stratford); adm'n granted, 14 Nov. 1732, to Zechariah and Obadiah Beardsley. Est. distributed to bros. and sisters.
> Daniel, b. 17 Oct. 1684, d. at Stratford in 1766; will 3 Sept. 1765, proved 4 Aug. 1766; m. 6 Mar. 1717/8, Mary Bennett.
> Zechariah, b. 13 Nov. 1686, d. at Huntington, 17 Sept. 1748 in 62 yr. (g. s.); est. distributed 6 Dec. 1748; m. 4 June 1713, Elizabeth Curtis, who d. 1776 ae. 84.
> Ruth, b. 13 Oct. 1688, d. y.
> Nathan, d. at Stratford in 1760; will 2 Aug. 1746, proved 4 Feb. 1760; m. 26 June 1718, Dinah Curtis.
> Samuel, m. 25 Apr. 1723, Eunice Pulford.
> Rebecca, m. 30 May 1717, Ephraim Judson.
> Obadiah, d. in 1754; will dated 13 Apr. 1754, proved 18 June 1754; m. 21 Aug. 1729, Mary Porter.
> Sarah, bapt. (at Stratford, rec. Stratfield), 23 July 1704; m. 11 Aug. 1726, William Stannard of Saybrook.

Beardsley, John, s. of Joseph.

Born at Stratford, 1 Nov. 1668, d. there 29 Nov. 1735.
[Married Abigail Wakelee, dau. of Henry, b. abt. 1665, d. Aug. 1753 ae. 88.]*

Will 11 Nov. 1732, proved 9 Feb. 1735/6; blacksmith, of Stratford; wife Abigail (Exec'x); sons Caleb, John (Exec'r), Jehiel, Abraham, Andrew.

Children of John and Abigail, recorded at Stratford:

Caleb, b. 30 Nov. 1692; m. 21 Jan. 1722 [1722/3], Elizabeth Booth.
Jehiel, b. 16 Nov. 1693.
Abraham, b. 6 Mar. 1696 [1696/7], d. 9 July 1776 in 81 yr. (g. s., Huntington); will 29 May 1776, proved 5 Aug. 1776; m. 17 Apr. 1723, Esther Janes, who d. 11 Nov. 1772 in 74 yr. (g. s.).
Deborah, b. 6 Feb. 1699/1700.
John, b. 9 or 10 Mar. 1701/2; m. 29 Dec. 1725, Kezia Wheeler.
Andrew, b. 8 Mar. 1707/8, bapt. (at Stratford, rec. Stratfield), 3 Apr. 1709, d. in 1758; m. Sarah Porter, dau. of John, b. 26 Feb. 1712/3.

Beardsley, Samuel, s. of Samuel.

Born at Stratford, 1 Sept. 1666, d. there in 1690; m. but *not* Sarah Sherwood, as *Hist. of Stratford* falsely avers.

Inv. of Samuel, Jr., of Paquaneck, 2 Jan. 1690 [1690/1]. Widow made oath, 10 Mar. 1690/1; adm'n granted to widow and Nathaniel Sherman.

Only child:

Sarah, m. Isaac Barnum, of Danbury.

Beardsley, William, s. of Samuel.

Born at Stratford, 22 Mar. 1668/9.

Married (rec. Stratford) 5 July 1699, Elizabeth Brown. She was dau. of Ebenezer of New Haven, b. 13 May 1679; and was bapt. at Stratfield, 22 Apr. 1705.

Children, recorded at Stratford, bapt. at Stratfield:

William, b. 19 Apr. 1700, bapt. 16 June 1700; res. Stamford; m. Susanna ———.
Ebenezer, b. 2 Sept. 1701, bapt. 7 Sept. 1701.

---

* Proof of this statement, found in print, may exist but has not been located.

Samuel, bapt. 8 Aug. 1703, d. y.

Elizabeth, b. 25 Jan. 1705, bapt. 1 July 1705.

Samuel, b. 9 May 1707, bapt. 11 May 1707, d. at Stratford in 1761; will 25 Mar. 1760, proved 14 Jan. 1761; m. 17 May 1737, Eunice Brown of Waterbury.

Hannah, b. 9 Feb. 1708/9, bapt. 27 Mar. 1709, d. in 1762; will 9 Sept. 1762, proved 15 Dec. 1762; nephew Levi son of bro. William; niece Thankful Risden; niece Hannah Beardsley dau. of bro. Enos; two nieces Temperance and Elizabeth Beardsley, clothing and goods in bro. Jabez Beardsley's house; Elizabeth Risden dau. of cousin Risden.

Thankful, b. 1 Mar. 1710/1, bapt. 8 Apr. 1711.

Esther, bapt. 24 May 1713.

Lydia, bapt. 9 Feb. 1718.

Jabez, b. 28 Jan. 1720/1; rem. to Unadilla, N. Y.; m. (1) 20 Apr. 1741, Prudence Hubbell; m. (2) Eunice Summers.

Enos, b. 15 Oct. 1724, d. in 1757. Adm'n granted to Hezekiah Treadwell, 3 May 1757.

Beardsley, Daniel, s. of Samuel.

Born at Stratford, 3 Apr. 1671, d. in 1738.

Daniel Jr. m. (1) at Stratford, 3 Dec. 1695, Rebecca Jackson. She was dau. of Moses, b. 10 May 1674.

Daniel Jr. m. (2) at Stratford, 10 Aug. 1704, Ann Seeley.

Will proved 7 Feb. 1737/8; wife Ann; son Benjamin; dau. Abigail Fairchild; sons Robert, Daniel; dau. Ann; children of dau. Jemima dec'd; daus. Sarah, Rebecca, Jerusha, Esther, Tabitha.

Mary, Sarah, Ruth, Jerusha, Esther, Robert and Tabitha, children of Daniel Beardsley, chose him for guardian, 4 Feb. 1727 [1727/8], to take care of Est. that fell to them by the death of their brother David.

Will of Ann, 23 Apr. 1748, proved 2 Aug. 1748; sons Robert, Daniel; grandchild Eunice Wardam; daus. Ann Lake, Hester Beardsley, Tabitha Curtis; son-in-law Edward Lake, Exec'r.

Children [by first wife], two recorded at Stratford; bapt. at Stratfield:

David, b. 28 Aug. 1696, bapt. 27 Mar. 1698, d. in 1727; adm'n granted to Rebecca and Benjamin Beardsley, 24 Feb. 1726 [1726/7]; m. Rebecca ———. Distribution to Widow, Benjamin, Abigail, Ann, Rebecca, Jemima, Mary, Sarah, Ruth, Jerusha, Easter, Robert,

Tabitha. Another distribution, 21 Apr. 1753, was made to the Widow; Benjamin and Samuel Beardsley; Abigail wife of James Fairchild; Ann wife of Edward Lake; children of Jemima Worden; children of Rebecca Cole.

Benjamin, b. 24 Apr. 1698, bapt. 5 June 1698, d. in 1761; will 3 Nov. 1759, proved 7 Apr. 1761; m. Deborah Summers, bapt. 13 Mar. 1709.

Abigail, bapt. 31 Mar. 1700; m. 3 Apr. 1723, James Fairchild.

Samuel, bapt. 17 Jan. 1703.

Children [by second wife]:

Ann, bapt. 4 Nov. 1705; m. Edward Lake.

Rebecca, bapt. 7 Sept. 1707; m. ——— Cole.

Jemima, bapt. 19 June 1709; m. 18 Jan. 1727/8, Thomas Wordin.

Mary, bapt. 10 June 1711.

Sarah, bapt. 12 July 1713, d. in 1739. Will 13 Nov. 1738, proved 6 Mar. 1738/9; mother Ann Beardsley; four sisters, Ann Lake, Jerusha Beardsley, Hester Beardsley, Tabitha Beardsley.

Ruth, bapt. 1 Apr. 1716, d. in 1735. Will 11 Sept. 1735, proved 3 Nov. 1735; to brother Daniel Beardsley right in realty from Est. of brother David dec'd; to father.

Jerusha, bapt. 27 July 1718, d. in 1740. Will 10 May 1740, proved July 1740; eldest sister Abigail Fairchild; mother Ann Beardsley; sisters Ann Lake, Hester and Tabitha Beardsley.

Hester.

Robert, bapt. 26 May 1723, d. in 1766; will 30 Oct. 1765, proved 13 May 1766; m. Hannah ———.

Tabitha, m. Stephen Curtis.

Daniel, bapt. 25 July 1731, d. in 1756. Will 4 June 1756, proved 12 Dec. 1766; heirs of brother Robert Beardsley; Thomas Hawley, son of Ezra; Ezra Hawley, Jr.; heirs of Edward Lake, James Fairchild, Benjamin Beardsley, Thomas Worden, and Stephen Curtis; sister Hester. Distribution 25 Sept. 1769: children of Robert Beardsley (Sarah, Abijah, Daniel, Chauncey, Josiah, Hannah, Aaron, and Isaac); Thomas Hawley, son of Capt. Ezra; Ezra Hawley, Jr.; Hester Beardsley; children of Edward Lake dec'd; children of James Fairchild dec'd; children of Benjamin Beardsley dec'd; children of Thomas Worden dec'd; children of Stephen Curtis.

Beardsley, John, s. of Samuel.

Born at Stratford, 11 Oct. 1673, d. at Stratfield, late in 1753.

He m. (1) abt. 1701, Mary Wheeler, dau. of Sergt. John, b. abt. 1671.

He m. (2) at Stratfield, 27 Nov. 1711, Deborah Hull; dau. of Samuel of Fairfield.

Will 15 Apr. 1752, proved 6 Nov. 1753; wife Deborah; sons John, Obadiah, Samuel, Andrew, James; daus. Deborah wife of Josiah Treadwell, Abigail wife of Andrew Patterson, Experience wife of Richard Whitney, Martha wife of Abel Hubbell, and Hannah wife of Hezekiah Seeley; wife and bro. Samuel Hull, Exec'rs.

Children by first wife:

Mary, bapt. 27 June 1703.

John, bapt. 10 Sept. 1704; res. Stratfield and New Fairfield; m. Martha Odell, dau. of John, Jr., bapt. 21 Nov. 1708.

Obadiah, b. 2 June 1706; res. Stratfield and New Fairfield; m. 30 Nov. 1730, Mercy Jackson, dau. of Henry, bapt. 6 Dec. 1713.

Children by second wife:

Samuel, b. Oct. 1712, bapt. at Stratfield, 7 Dec. 1712.

Andrew, b. 19 Dec. 1713, bapt. at Stratfield, 20 Dec. 1713, d. 14 Mar. 1714.

Andrew, b. 24 Jan. 1715, bapt. at Fairfield, 7 Aug. 1715; m. at Fairfield, 1 Mar. 1743/4, Sarah Squire; dau. of Lt. Samuel; they joined 1774 in deed of Squire heirs.

James, b. 28 Jan. 1716/7, bapt. at Stratfield, 3 Feb. 1717; m. at Stratfield, 16 Sept. 1735, Rebecca Beardsley; dau. of Nathan, b. 6 Feb. 1715/6.

Deborah, b. 10 Sept. 1719; m. Josiah Treadwell.

Abigail, b. 20 Apr. 1721; m. Andrew Patterson.

Martha, b. 8 Jan. 1723, d. 9 Mar. 1726.

Experience, b. 26 Feb. 1726; m. at Stratfield, 4 Dec. 1750, Richard Whitney.

Martha, b. 22 Mar. 1728; m. Abel Hubbell.

Hannah, b. 30 Apr. 1730; m. at Stratfield, 27 Sept. 1750, Hezekiah Seeley.

BEARDSLEY FAMILY (THOMAS)

Beardsley, Thomas.

A Thomas "Beazley" m. at Milford, 20 Mar. 1649 [1649/50], Elizabeth Harvey [New Haven Col. Rec.]. Perhaps she was dau. of Josiah Harvey of Milford and Fairfield. Milford records are silent concerning this man, and we suppose that he was the Thomas Beardsley who was later in Stratford. There he bought land, 7 Feb. 1661 [1661/2]; the last entry, made 13 Feb. 1668

[1668/9], calls him dec'd; yet we find no probate action until 29 Mar. 1676, when his Inv. was taken by the Selectmen of Stratford.

Beardsley, Thomas.

Possibly son of the foregoing Thomas by a previous marriage. He settled in Fairfield; m. Johanna ———, b. abt. 1634, who m. (2) Thomas Bassett of Fairfield. Bassett sold Beardsley's house in 1661 as his "successor."

Inv. 5 July 1656, taken by Anthony Wilson, Humphrey Hide, and Alexander Knowles, sworn to by Johanna Beardsley.

Perhaps a child was:

> Abigail, m. 26 May 1684, Thomas Trowbridge. The marriage was rec. at New Haven, but being performed by Major Gold, must have taken place at Fairfield, which was therefore presumably the bride's home.

Beardsley [Unplaced.] Hannah, b. abt. 1693, d. 4 Jan. 1715/6 in 22 yr.; m. at Stratford, 14 Apr. 1715, Joseph Grimes.

Bedient, Mordecai.

Of Westchester, N. Y.

He m. Mary ———, who m. (2) Roger Townsend and (3) by 1677, Capt. Richard Osborn.

On 4 Dec. 1684, Richard Osborn of Westchester quitclaimed to Thomas Bedient of Woodbury all lands in Westchester formerly possessed by Mordecai Bedient dec'd and Mary his wife, afterwards called Mary Townsend, and Roger Townsend; Thomas to pay to his own dau. Abigail, £50, and two cows to Osborn's dau. Elizabeth.

Mordecai Bedient of Westchester conveyed, 22 Apr. 1685, to bro. Thomas Bedient, all right to Est. of Richard Osborn late dec'd or Mary his wife. John Bedient of Westchester conveyed, 26 July 1686, to Thomas Bedient, lands formerly possessed by Mordecai Bedient dec'd and by Mary his wife and Roger Townsend, lately in the tenure of Richard Osborn.

Children:

+Thomas.
    Mordecai, of Westchester.
    John, of Westchester.

Bedient, Thomas, s. of Mordecai.

He lived some years in Woodbury, but returned to Fairfield. Before 1680, he purchased land in Fairfield from his "father" Richard Osborn; and by 1688, called of Woodbury, bought from Thomas Shervington. The town of Fairfield granted him liberty, 27 Sept. 1697, to erect a grist mill or other mills on the Mill River.

Inv. at Fairfield, 12 Mar. 1698 [1698/9]. His widow Mary made return on his Est., 21 July 1699. Distribution ordered to the one son and six daus. (under age). Grace dau. of Mrs. Mary Bedient of Fairfield m. 15 Apr. 1713, Mr. John Segar [entered in Pro. Rec.].

He m. Mary Osborn, dau. of Richard, who in 1682 gave by deed to her three children.

Children:

(prob.) Dorothy, bapt. at Fairfield, 2 Nov. 1701.
    Abigail.
    Grace, m. 15 Apr. 1713, Mr. John Segar.
    Three other daus.
    ×John, m. 28 May 1723, Mary Morehouse.

Beebe, James, s. of John. Commissioner for Danbury, 1691-97*; Justice, 1701-11, 1716-21; Lt., Danbury Trainband, Oct. 1696; Capt., May 1710; Deputy (Danbury), Oct. 1707, Oct. 1708, May, June and Oct. 1709, May and Oct. 1710, Oct. 1711, May and Oct. 1713, Oct. 1714, Oct. 1715, Oct. 1718, Oct. 1719.

Born [perhaps at Broughton, co. Northampton, Eng.], abt. 1641, d. at Danbury, 22 Apr. 1728 ae. 87 (g. s.) He was of Hadley, where he m. (1) 24 Oct. 1667, Mary Boltwood, dau. of Robert; she d. 19 Aug. 1676. He rem. to Norwalk, where he m. (2) 19 Dec. 1679, Sarah Benedict, dau. of Thomas, Sr.

---

* Except 1694, when the name of Samuel Beebe appears instead; perhaps by **error** for James.

Children [by first wife], recorded at Hadley:

Mary, b. 18 Aug. 1668, d. young.
James, b. 9 Dec. 1669, d. young.
Rebecca, b. 8 Dec. 1670.
Samuel, b. 26 June 1672, d. at Litchfield, abt. 1731; m. Hannah ————,
   b. abt. 1672, d. at Canaan, 16 Nov. 1766.
Mary, b. in 1675.

Children [by second wife], first recorded at Norwalk:

Sarah, b. 13 Nov. 1680.
James, b. abt. 1682, d. at Danbury, in 1750; m. at Stratford, 22 Dec.
   1708, Abigail Sherman, dau. of Samuel, Jr., b. 4 Aug. 1688.

Beecher, Samuel, s. of Isaac.

Born at New Haven, 17 Oct. 1652, d. at Stratford, presumably;
m. at Stratford, 2 July 1691, Sarah Sherwood. She was widow
of John Sherwood, and dau. of John Hurd, b. 17 Feb. 1665/6.
Isaac Hurd paid to sister Sarah Beecher the portion given her by
will of her father, John Hurd [Stratford Deeds].

Samuel Beecher of Stratford bound his dau. Mary now near
four years old to be an apprentice to Thomas Minor of Woodbury, 14 Oct. 1697.

Children, recorded at Stratford:

Ruth, b. 1 Feb. 1691/2; m. 9 June 1719, Adam Blackman.
Mary, b. 16 Nov. 1693; m. 20 Dec. 1722, Jonathan Blackman.
Hester, b. 27 Nov. 1695; m. 11 June 1719, Nathaniel Code* of Preston.
Sarah, b. 24 Feb. 1702/3; m. 24 Mar. 1726, Jeremiah Burch.

BEERS FAMILY (ANTHONY)

Beers, Anthony.†

Res. Watertown, Mass., 1646, Roxbury, 1658; rem. to Fairfield, where he d. abt. 1679.

Samuel Wakeman before 1670 purchased from Richard Hubbell
a homelot that had once been Anthony Beers' lot.

---

* *Sic:* is Cady intended?

† Anthony and James Beers of Fairfield quite likely were brothers. Various statements of their paternity have appeared in print, such as that they were sons or nephews
of Capt. Richard Beers of Watertown, Mass., and a line of ancestry in England has
been assigned to the family, all without reference to wills or other documentary evidence. Although some of these statements may be true, they need corroboration, and
it is deemed wiser to begin the Fairfield families with Anthony and James.

Inv. 14 May 1679, taken by George Squire and Thomas Wilson; contained only personal property, at houses of Abraham Adams, Thomas Staples, Sr., and Daniel Silliman.

The Bible record of his gr. son Josiah begins: "Barnabas Beers the elder was son to ——— Beers who came to Fairfield with several children where he was soon drowned about the year 1676. His son Barnabas was settled at Stratford."

He m. (2) after 1671, Mary, widow of Edward Adams. Adm'n on her estate was granted to Sergt. Samuel Ward and Nathan Adams, 2 Dec. 1687.

Children, recorded at Watertown, Mass., youngest at Roxbury, Mass.:

> Samuel, b. 9 May 1647, d. y.
> +Ephraim, b. 5 July 1648.
> +John, b. 20 Jan. 1652.
> Esther, b. 16 Oct. 1654.
> Samuel, b. 2 May 1657, d. Sept. 1657.
> +Barnabas, b. 6 Sept. 1658, bapt. 17 Oct. 1658.

Beers, Ephraim, s. of Anthony.

Born at Watertown, Mass., 5 July 1648.

Children:

> John, m. ———.
> Anthony, m. ———.
> Esther, m. [Nathaniel?] Nichols.
> ✕Ephraim, b. (not found), d. 15 June 1759; res. Fairfield (Westport); adm'n granted 12 Dec. 1759; m. Susanna Meeker.
> Samuel, b. (not found), d. in 1772; res. Branford; will 1 Apr. 1771, proved 3 Nov. 1772; m. 8 Apr. 1713, Sarah Wheeler.
> Mary, b. (not found), d. in 1770; res. Norwalk; will 12 Mar. 1762, proved 6 Nov. 1770;* m. ——— Brush; no issue.

Beers, John, s. of Anthony.

Born at Watertown, Mass., 20 Jan. 1652.
Severely wounded 19 Dec. 1675 (K. Philip's War), had grant of relief 1677.

---

* Her will names all her nieces, the children of her bros. and sister, and is genealogically important to a study of this Beers family.

Will 9 Feb. 1682/3, proved 13 Mar. 1682/3; wife Mary; son Samuel; brother Barnabas Beers; sister Elizabeth Peck; sister Jonson of Salem.

Adm'n on Mary's Est. granted 12 June 1688.

Child by wife Mary, recorded at Stratford:

> Samuel, b. 9 Nov. 1679, d. at Newtown, 12 Mar. 1724/5; adm'n granted to widow Sarah, 26 Jan. 1727/8; m. 16 Jan. 1706/7, Sarah Sherman; dau. of Samuel, Jr., b. 16 Dec. 1681.

Beers, Barnabas, s. of Anthony.

Born at Roxbury, Mass., 6 Sept. 1658; d. at Stratford in 1714.
Married (1) at Stratford, 4 Apr. 1688, Elizabeth Wilcoxson.
She was dau. of John, b. July 1666, d. at Stratford, 11 Oct. 1694.
He m. (2) Mary ———.
Adm'n granted, Oct. 1714, to widow Mary and son Nathan.

Children [by first wife], recorded at Stratford:

> Mary, b. 27 Dec. 1689.
> Nathan, b. 1 Dec. 1691.
> Josiah, b. 8 Aug. 1693, d. at Stratford in 1763; will 25 Aug. 1762, proved 10 Feb. 1763; m. 10 May 1717, Elizabeth Ufford.

Probable children by second wife:

> Joseph, d. at Stratford in 1756; will 29 Jan. 1742/3, proved 6 Apr. 1756; m. 6 Mar. 1721/2, Sarah Clark.
> Abiel, m. 16 Jan. 1722/3, Elizabeth Commel.
> Elnathan, m. 25 Jan. 1728, Anna Beach; dau. of Nathaniel, b. 10 Mar. 1704.

BEERS FAMILY (JAMES)

Beers, James.

Prob. brother of Anthony.

He bought land in Fairfield from George Squire, 27 Apr. 1659.
He m. Martha Barlow, dau. of John, 1st, whose will 1674 named dau. Martha Beers.

On 26 Feb. 1682 [1682/3] and in other records he was called Sr., his son being then of mature age. He lived a short time at Woodbury, for he was called James Beers, Sr., of Woodbury on 6 Mar. 1684/5, when he purchased from John Osborn land on Sasco Hill.

Will 14 Nov. 1694, proved 28 Nov. 1694; wife Martha; son Joseph; daus. Martha wife of Joseph Bulkley, Deborah wife of Samuel Hull, and Elizabeth wife of John Darling; children of son James dec'd (only David named).

Will of Martha Beers, 22 Feb. 1697/8, proved 27 Mar. 1698; son John Darling; daus. Martha Bulkley, Deborah Hull, Elizabeth Darling.

Children:

+James.
Martha, m. Joseph Bulkley.
Deborah, m. Samuel Hull.
+Joseph.
Elizabeth, m. John Darling.

Beers, James, s. of James.

James Beers, Jr., had land by gift from father James, also by gift from Major Nathan Gold, recorded 2 May 1684.

Adm'n granted, 30 Apr. 1691, to Philip Lewis. Children: James (decrepit), David, Sarah, Mary; another son, Joseph, is dead, and the son James d. before the distribution 1697.

Nathan Gold was later Adm'r. John Marvin had land set to him in right of Mary his wife as part of her portion (no date).

Children, recorded at Fairfield:

James, b. 28 Jan.(?)* 1677; d. before 1697.
Sarah, b. 8 May 1678; m. (rec. Woodbury) 28 Sept. 1698, Sergt. John Judson, Jr.
Joseph, b. 11 July 1679, d. before 1697.
David, b. (no record).
Mary, b. abt. 1685, d. at Norwalk, 17 Apr. 1720 ae. 35 (g. s.); m. (rec. Norwalk) 22 Mar. 1704, John Marvin.

Beers, Joseph, s. of James.

Married Abigail Norton, dau. of Peter. "Abigail now wife of Joseph Beers of Fairfield" was named 1690 in will of Hugh Griffin as elder dau. of his wife. She m. (2) John Dunbar.

Inv. 6 Mar. 1695/6.

---

* Also read as Dec., but our reading compares more favorably with date of birth of next child.

James (son of Joseph) chose his cousin Francis Bradley guardian, 4 Apr. 1711. [Bradley was his father's first cousin on the Barlow side.]

John Dunbar as Adm'r of Est. of Joseph Beers, and his wife, paid legacies from the Est. of James Beers, father of said Joseph, of which said Joseph had been Exec'r.

Mutual distribution [in Land Records] made 6 Mar. 1718/9 by Joseph and James Beers of Fairfield and John Blackman of Newtown and Abigail his wife, of Est. of their father Joseph.

Children, recorded at Fairfield:

XJoseph, b. 18 Mar. 1688/9; conveyed 1712 land from father Joseph and gr. father James; m. 1 Mar. 1711, Hannah Whitlock, dau. of John.

Abigail, b. 24 Apr. 1692, bapt. 21 Oct. 1694, d. at Newtown, 27 Mar. 1762; m. John Blackman.

XJames, bapt. 21 Oct. 1694, d. 29 Apr. 1772 in 79 yr. (g. s.); Lt.; res. Fairfield; m. (1) 20 Jan. 1716, Hannah Rumsey, bapt. 30 Aug. 1696, d. 17 Mar. [1724?]; m. (2) 5 Aug. 1725, Olive Bulkley, bapt. 30 Aug. 1696, d. 5 Oct. 1774.

Belden, John, s. of William. Ens., Norwalk Trainband, May 1691; Lt., May 1705; Deputy for Norwalk, Oct. 1691, May 1705.

Born at Wethersfield, 9 Jan. 1649/50. He served in K. Philip's War, for which he received a grant of land at Norwalk, 12 Dec. 1676.

He m. Ruth [Hale?]; she m. (2) 4 Jan. 171[—], John Copp. He d. at Norwalk, 26 Nov. 171[3].

Inv. of Lt. John, 11 Mar. 1713/4; widow Ruth made oath. She had been granted adm'n, 15 Dec. 1713. One of his children, Ruth, was bapt. at Fairfield, 7 Oct. 1694.

Bell, Francis. Lt., Stamford Trainband, May 1655. Deputy (Stamford) to New Haven Leg., 1653-59, 1661-64; Magistrate, Stamford, 1652, 1654-56, 1658-1663. Confirmed Lt. by Conn. Colony, Oct. 1666.

Early at Wethersfield, rem. to Stamford 1641.

His wife Rebecca d. at Stamford, 17 May 1684; he d. 8 Jan. 1689 [1689/90].

Will 24 May 1689; son Jonathan, Sr., Exec'r; gr. son Jonathan Bell, Jr.; dau. Mary Hoyt; gr. child Hannah Bell now Betts; gr. child Rebecca Bell whom I brought up; dau. Tuttle's four sons, Jonathan, Simon, William, Nathaniel. Inv. 28 Jan. 1689 [1689/90]; the gr. child Rebecca is dec'd, and the Court ordered her legacy of £50 divided to Abraham Bell and the other five gr. children of Francis, *i.e.* Jonathan Bell's children.

Children:

+Jonathan, b. abt. 1641.
Rebecca, b. abt. 1643, d. at New Haven, 2 May 1676; m. Jonathan Tuttle.
Mary, b. abt. 1646 [testified 1692 ae. 46]; m. (1) Joshua Hoyt; m. (2) in 1691, Joseph Turney.

Bell, Jonathan, s. of Francis. Deputy (Stamford) to Conn. Leg., Oct. 1670, May 1674, Oct. 1675, May and Oct. 1676, May 1677, May 1680, Oct. 1681, Oct. 1682, May and Oct. 1683, May, July, and Oct. 1684, May and Oct. 1685, July and Oct. 1686, May 1687, June 1689, May and July 1691. Capt., Stamford Trainband, May 1698. Commissioner for Stamford and Greenwich, 1682-87, 1689, for Stamford, 1690-97; Justice, 1698.

Died at Stamford, 11 Mar. 1698 [1698/9]. He was consistently called Lt. in colonial records from 1674 until his promotion to Capt., but appointment not found. Perhaps the appointment of Francis as Lt. in 1666 is an error for Jonathan, since Francis was already Lt. by commission from New Haven Colony.

Married (1) at Stamford, 22 Oct. 1662, Mercy Crane; she d. 26 Oct. 1671.

Married (2) (rec. Stamford), 31 Oct. 1672, Susanna Pierson of Branford. She was dau. of Abraham, and d. 4 Jan. 1706/7.

Will 24 Nov. 1698; eldest son Jonathan; dau. Hannah Betts; sons Abraham, John; daus. Mercy, Susannah, Mary; wife Susannah. Inv. of Capt. Jonathan, 11 Mar. 1698/9. He owned a tanyard.

Children by first wife, recorded at Stamford:

Jonathan, b. 14 Feb. 1663 [1663/4], d. in Sept. 1745; will 6 Sept. 1745, proved 1 Oct. 1745; m. (1) 22 Mar. 1693, Grace Kitchell, who d.

Feb. 1693/4; m. (2) 14 Jan. 1701/2, Deborah Ferris, who d. 3 July 1724; m. (3) last day Feb. 1733/4, Mrs. Mary Brush.

Hannah, b. 29 Oct. 1665; m. John Betts, of Norwalk.

Rebecca, b. 6 Dec. 1667, d. 24 Sept. 1689.

Children by second wife, recorded at Stamford:

Abigail, b. 23 Feb. 1672/3, d. 5 June 1674.

Abraham, b. 22 June 1675, d. 6 July 1744; m. (1) 6 Apr. 1704, Hannah Hoyt, who d. 16 Nov. 1711; m. (2) 10 Mar. 1714, Mary Lewis.

Mercy, b. 5 Nov. 1678; m. (1) 15 Jan. 1701/2, John Holmes; m. (2) 13 July 1704, Samuel Hoyt; m. (3) 15 June 1716, Peter Ferris.

John, b. 16 Jan. 1681, d. at New Haven, 27 Oct. 1732; m. (1) 22 Feb. 1710/1, Sarah Slawson, who d. 11 Sept. 1713; m. (2) 19 Oct. 1714, Hannah Whiting of Southampton, who d. 16 Nov. 1732.

Daughter, b. and d. 3 Aug. 1683.

James, b. 11 Dec. 1684, d. y.

Susannah, b. 25 Dec. 1686.

Mary, b. 29 Sept. 1689.

Benedict, Thomas. Magistrate, Jamaica, 1663; Lt., Dec. 1663. Commissioner for Jamaica, 1664 (Conn. Col. appointment). Deputy to Hempstead Convention, 1665; Lt., Foot Company, Jamaica, Apr. 1665. Deputy (Norwalk) to Conn. Leg., May 1670, May 1675. Town Clerk, Norwalk; Selectman, 17 terms. One of committee to plant Danbury, 1684.

Son of William of co. Nottingham, he was born about 1617; came to New England abt. 1638, settled in Southold, L. I., lived in Huntington and Jamaica, L. I.; rem. 1665 to Norwalk, where he d. early in 1690. Deacon of church.

Married Mary Bridgum.

Will 28 Feb. 1689/90; wife Mary; sons Daniel and John Benedict; grandchild Thomas son of dau. Elizabeth Slawson; son James Benedict; gr. child Elizabeth Slawson; gr. child Thomas Benedict; gr. child Samuel Benedict; gr. child John, eldest son of son John; Joanna Benedict (mentions her grandmother); dau. Rebecca Wood; dau. Sarah; gr. child Mary Olmsted; gr. child Hannah Benedict; sons John and Samuel Benedict, overseers. Inv. 18 Mar. 1689/90.

Children:

+Thomas.

+John.

+Samuel.

+James, b. at Southold, 6 Feb. 1649 [1649/50] [New Haven Col. Rec.].
+Daniel.
Elizabeth, m. John Slawson, of Stamford.
Mary, m. at Norwalk, 17 July 1673, John Olmstead.
Sarah, m. at Norwalk, 19 Dec. 1679, James Beebe.
Rebecca, m. Dr. Samuel Wood, of Danbury.

Benedict, Thomas, s. of Thomas.

Married at Jamaica, L. I., Jan. 1664/5, Mary Messenger, dau. of Andrew.

She m. (2) before 1693, Dr. John Hull of Wallingford. When her son Thomas Benedict conveyed the homelot and house at Norwalk, 13 May 1693, Mary Hull also signed the deed. She d. by 1699.

Thomas, Jr., died 20 Nov. 1688; Inv. taken 22 Feb. 1688 [1688/9] by Thomas Benedict, Sr., Samuel Hayes, and Andrew Messenger. Mary Benedict made oath. Son and daus. under age. Thomas Benedict to administer with advice of Mr. Samuel Hayes and Andrew Messenger.

Children, recorded at Norwalk:

Mary, b. 4 Dec. 1666.
Thomas, b. 5 Dec. 1670, d. at Norwalk, 10 May 1743; Ens.; will 17 June 1738/9, proved 7 June 1744; m. (1) (rec. Norwalk), 13 May 169[—], Rachel Smith, dau. of Samuel, who d. 9 June 17[37]; m. (2) 14 Oct. 1740, Hannah Knapp of Danbury.
Hannah, b. 8 Jan. 1676 [1676/7], d. at Meriden, 12 Jan. 1767 ae. 91 (g. s.); m. (rec. Wallingford), 12 Dec. 1695, Samuel Royce.
Esther, b. 5 Oct. 1679, d. at Cheshire, 1 Jan. 1752 ae. 72 (g. s.); m. (rec. Wallingford), 11 May 1697, Joseph Ives.
Abigail, b. abt. 1682, d. abt. 1713; m. (rec. Wallingford), 14 Mar. 1709, Robert Royce.
Elizabeth.

Benedict, John, s. of Thomas.

Married at Norwalk, 11 Nov. 1670, Phebe Gregory, dau. of John.

Selectman, Norwalk, 1689, 1692-94, 1699; Deacon.

Children, three recorded at Norwalk:

Sarah.
Phebe, b. 21 Sept. 1673.

John, b. 3 Mar. 1675/6, d. at Norwalk, 16 Jan. 1766 in 90 yr. (g. s.);
Deacon; Sergt.; m. (1) before 1705, Anna St. John, dau. of Mark,
b. 8 Aug. 1674; m. (2) Mary ——, who d. 5 June 1749 ae. 72
(g. s.).

Jonathan, prob. d. y.

Benjamin, b. (no record), d. at Stamford, 3 July 1773; Deacon; res.
Ridgebury; m. Mary [perhaps Platt], who d. 30 Nov. 1771.

Joseph, of Ridgefield; m. (1) Anna ——, who d. at Ridgefield, 9
Dec. 1716; m. (2) 21 Mar. 1720/1, Mary (Groom), widow of
Samuel Pitman of Stratford.

James, b. 15 Jan. 1685 [1685/6], d. at Ridgefield, 25 Nov. 1762; Capt.;
m. 7 Apr. 1709, Sarah Hyatt, dau. of Thomas, b. Dec. 1686, d. 9
Feb. 1767 in 81 yr. (g. s.).

Mary.

Thomas, b. (no record), d. at Norwalk in 1763; Capt.; will 20 May
1763, proved 5 July 1763; m. in 1705, Millicent Hyatt, dau. of
Thomas, b. [1688?].

Benedict, Samuel, s. of Thomas.

Married (rec. Norwalk) 7 July 1678, Rebecca Andrews, dau. of
Francis, formerly of Fairfield.

He was an original founder of Danbury, 1685, and Deacon of
the Church.

Will 15 Apr. 1719, proved 1719; wife Rebecca; eldest son
Samuel; Samuel son of son Thomas dec'd; two youngest sons
Nathaniel and Abraham; daus. Rebecca, Esther; children of son
Thomas; Benoni to have half as much as a child's portion.

Children, four recorded at Norwalk:

Joanna, b. 22 Oct. 1673.

Samuel, b. 5 Mar. 1674/5, d. at Danbury in 1735; will 4 Mar. 1734/5,
proved 9 Apr. 1735; m. Abigail Pickett, dau. of Thomas, b. 30
July 1678.

Nathaniel, b. [say 1677], d. at Danbury in 1767; will 19 Jan. 1767,
proved 11 Dec. 1767; m. Sarah ——.

Thomas, b. 27 Mar. 1679, d. at Danbury in 1714; adm'n granted 6
Dec. 1714 to widow Elizabeth and Sergt. Francis Barnum; he m.
Elizabeth Hickock, dau. of Samuel of Waterbury, b. abt. 1682,
living at Danbury 1729; she m. (2) 21 June 1722, Samuel Smith
of Ridgefield.

Abraham, b. 21 June 1681, d. at Danbury in 1776; will 25 May 1774,
proved 28 Feb. 1776; m. Sarah ——.

Rebecca, m. 18 June 1712, Samuel Platt.

Esther.

Benedict, James, s. of Thomas. Deputy for Danbury, Oct. 1712.

Born at Southold, L. I., 6 Feb. 1649/50.

Married (1) at Norwalk, 10 May 1676, Sarah Gregory, dau. of John, Sr.

Married (2) Mar. 1707, Sarah, widow of Abraham Andrus of Farmington, and dau. of Robert Porter, b. 20 Dec. 1657.

He rem. to Danbury, and d. after 1717.

Children [by first wife], recorded at Norwalk:

> Sarah, b. 16 June 1677; m. Daniel Lockwood.
> Rebecca, b. abt. 1679, d. 20 Mar. 1709; m. (rec. Norwalk) 18 Jan. 1704/5, Samuel Keeler, Jr.
> Phebe, b. abt. 1682; m. Thomas Taylor.
> James, b. abt. 1685, d. at Danbury in 1761; Dea.; will 16 Sept. 1760, proved 23 June 1761; m. Mary Andrus, dau. of Abraham, bapt. at Farmington, 18 May 1689, d. after 1761.
> John, b. Oct. 1689, d. at Danbury, Feb. 1765; Capt.; will proved 25 Mar. 1771; m. Ruth ———.
> Thomas, b. 9 Nov. 1694, d. at Danbury, 4 July 1776; Dea.; m. Abigail Hoyt, dau. of John.
> Elizabeth, m. Daniel Taylor.

Benedict, Daniel, s. of Thomas.

He was a soldier in the Swamp Fight, K. Philip's War, 1675, a service for which he was granted 12 acres by the town of Norwalk.

Married Mary Marvin, dau. of Matthew 2d, b. abt. 1658.

Conveyed his Norwalk land, 25 Mar. 1690, and rem. to Danbury; d. after 1723.

Children:

> Mary.
> Daniel, d. at Danbury in 1776; will 26 Mar. 1762, proved 5 Aug. 1776; m. Rebecca Taylor, dau. of Thomas.
> Mercy.
> Hannah, m. Nathan Taylor.

Benfield, William.

Settled in Fairfield; was master of a boat which in 1655 made a trip from Milford to Stamford.

He was divorced from wife Elizabeth, 6 Dec. 1662; it having

been established by testimony of Mr. Thomas Mullenor of West-chester that in Apr. 1662 at the request of William Benfield, mariner, he sought out Benfield's wife in London, Eng., and found that she (Elizabeth Coulson) was living with a Dutchman and refused in no uncertain terms to return to her husband. The rarity of the surname leads us to guess that the Mary Benfield who figures prominently in the court records was the captain's second matrimonial venture; in which he fared no better than in the first.

In 1665, Mary Benfield of Fairfield, a married woman, but not living with her husband, had a child. Three men were suspected; Mary Benfield in her testimony refused to implicate anyone,—an instance of rare generosity. Many Fairfield people testified, and their affidavits contain valuable genealogical data.

BENNETT FAMILY (JAMES)

Bennett, James.

Freeman at Concord, Mass., 1639; rem. to Fairfield 1644, where he d. in 1659. Married Hannah Wheeler, dau. of Thomas. She m. (2) Joseph Middlebrook.

Inv. Aug. 1659. Widow Hannah; children, Thomas, James, John, Sarah, Hannah.

Will of Thomas Wheeler of Fairfield, 1654, mentioned son-in-law James Bennett, and Mary, James, Thomas, and John Bennett, children of dau. Hannah. Will of Ann Wheeler, 1659, named dau. Hannah and grandchildren Sarah and Hannah Bennett.

John Osborn having married Sarah dau. of James Bennett dec'd, gave receipt 9 Jan. 1673 to father Joseph Middlebrook; witnessed by Thomas Wilson and Hannah Bennett. Thomas, eldest son of James dec'd, receipted 15 May 1674 to father Joseph Middlebrook; witnessed by Wm. Hill and John Eggleston. James Bennett receipted to Joseph Middlebrook, 10 Dec. 1674. Hannah Bennett receipted to brother Thomas, 1677.

Children, first two recorded at Concord:

Hannah, b. 1 June 1640, d. at Fairfield, 29 Oct. 1650 [Col. Rec.].
+Thomas, b. 16 Oct. 1642.

+James, b. abt. 1645.
+John, b. abt. 1648.
  Mary, b. 20 Jan. 1651 [1651/2] [Col. Rec.], d. between 1654 and 1659.
  Sarah, b. abt 1654, d. early in 1726; m. abt. 1673, Capt. John Osborne.
  Hannah, b. abt. 1656; prob. m. (1) Lt. Nathaniel Seeley; m. (2)
  ————.

Bennett, Thomas, s. of James.

Born at Concord, Mass., 16 Oct. 1642, d. at Fairfield in 1704.
Freeman, Fairfield, 1664.   Married Elizabeth Thompson, dau. of
John, b. abt. 1644.   Thomas Bennett, Sr., conveyed 20 Sept. 1687
to his son Thomas, the home lot that was once John Thompson's.
  Thomas, ae. abt. 50, Thomas, Jr., aged 27 (mentioning his uncle
John Grumman, Sr.), and Elizabeth, ae. abt. 20, all testified in the
Disbrow witchcraft trial, June 1692.
  Inv. of Thomas, Sr., 17 June 1704.   Widow impowered to
receive and pay debts.   Agreement of heirs of Thomas 29 June
1704; widow Elizabeth, and children Thomas, John, and James
Bennett, Samuel Stewart, and Henry Hendricks, for themselves
and their minor brother Peter.
  Daniel Burchard of Cortland, Westchester County, N. Y., in
right of his wife Dorothy, dau. of Hannah Stewart late of Nor-
walk dec'd, who was dau. and one of the coheirs of Thomas
Bennett the first of Fairfield, moved for distribution, 18 July 1769.
Distribution was made, a double portion to the children and heirs
of Thomas, eldest son, and a single portion to children and heirs
of John, James, and Peter Bennett, Hannah late wife of Samuel
Stewart dec'd, and Elizabeth late wife of Henry Hendrix dec'd.
Samuel Hendrix appealed and gave bond with John Hendrix.

  Children, recorded at Fairfield:
    +Thomas, b. abt. 1665 (no record).
    +John, b. (by 1670; no record).
      Elizabeth, b. abt. 1672, d. at Westport, 4 Dec. 1755; m. Henry
      Hendrick.
    +James, b. 6 Aug. 1675.
      Hannah, b. 20 Aug. 1680; m. Samuel Stewart of Norwalk.
    +Peter, b. after 1684.

Bennett, James, s. of James.   Deputy for Fairfield, Oct. 1689,
May and Oct. 1695, May 1697, May 1699, May 1701, May 1702,

Oct. 1706, Oct. 1708, May and June 1709, Oct. 1710. Lt., Albany Expedition, Feb. 1692/3; Lt., Stratfield Trainband, May 1704. Justice, 1709-11, 1714-24. Admitted to Conn. Bar as attorney, Oct. 1708.

Born at Fairfield abt. 1645, d. there Oct. 1736. Married (1) abt. 1667, —— Joy, dau. of Walter. Their son Joseph was remembered in will of his uncle Joseph Joy; while their dau. Abigail named a son Joy Bishop. Married (2) after 1683, Mary, widow of Ephraim Booth, dau. of Jeremiah Osborn; b. at New Haven, 29 Mar. 1653; d. at Stratfield, 28 Nov. 1726 in 73 yr. (g. s.).

Married (3) Rebecca ——.

Will of James, Sr., 2 Oct. 1736, proved 6 Oct. 1736; wife Rebecca; daus. Mary Osborn, Abigail Bishop, Sarah Burritt; Sarah, Abiah, and Ann, children of dau. Anna Hawley dec'd; grandson James Bennett; sons Thomas, Jeremiah, Isaac; son Joseph dec'd. Capt. James Bennett appealed, 12 Mar. 1736/7. Distribution 7 Apr. 1738; Sarah Bryant(?); heirs of Anna Hawley; Abigail Bishop; Mary Osborn; Capt. Thomas Bennett; heirs of Joseph Bennett; Isaac Bennett; Jeremiah Bennett.

Lt. James was an original member of Stratfield Church, 1695, and his wife Mary joined by letter from Stratford, 1695. James Sr. and Mary Bennett witnessed will of Mrs. Abigail Hubbell, 11 Feb. 1705, and James Sr. (with Philip Lewis) witnessed the codicil 10 Dec. 1717; all three witnesses made oath, 5 Feb. 1717/8.

After death of his son James, Lt. James in 1714 confirmed gift of lands to the widow and children of his son.

Inv. of Est. of Mrs. Rebecca Bennett, 5 Dec. 1741; adm'n granted to John Mackintosh.

Children [by first wife], births not recorded:

+James, b. abt. 1668.
+Thomas, b. abt. 1669.
    Abigail, b. abt. 1671, d. at North Haven, 8 Nov. 1761 ae. over 90; m. (rec. New Haven) 11 Dec. 1695, James Bishop. Abigail Bishop of New Haven conveyed 1739 land at Stratfield inherited from father James Bennett, Esq.
    Mary, b. abt. 1673, d. at New Haven, in 1737; m. abt. 1691 Joseph

Osborn. Her three daus. with their husbands conveyed 1738 to Benjamin Bennett of Stratfield.

+Joseph.

Sarah, b. (no record) ;* m. at Stratford, 5 Dec. 1705, Peleg Burritt.

Children [by second wife] :

+Isaac, b. abt. 1685.

Anna, b. abt. 1691, d. at Stratfield, 14 Nov. 1727 in 36 yr. (g. s.) ; m. at Stratfield, 20 Feb. 1710/1, Gideon Hawley.

+Jeremiah, bapt. at Stratfield, 27 Dec. 1696.

Bennett, John, s. of James.

Born at Fairfield abt. 1648; m. Mary Thompson, dau. of John, b. abt. 1649. They had children Jeremiah, Ebenezer, Mary, and Samuel, bapt. at Fairfield Church, 6 Sept. 1696, the same day that the mother Mary renewed her Covenant. Shortly after, they removed to Cohansey, N. J.

The will of John Hurd, Sr., of Stratford, 1680, left ten shillings to John Bennett's wife Mary.

John Bennett of Fairfield in Cohansey alias Sasqua River, N. J., sold 7 May 1697 Fairfield land to Joseph Kirby. On 20 Oct. 1707, Jeremiah Bennett as attorney for his father John Bennett, both of "New Fairfield, West Jersey", conveyed land in Fairfield to Thomas Turney.

Bennett, Thomas, s. of Thomas.

Born at Fairfield abt. 1665. A weaver, of Compo (Westport), 1709.

Married Sarah Hubbard, dau. of William of Greenwich. She owned the Covenant at Fairfield Church, 31 Mar. 1695, and the first four children were bapt. same date.

Children, bapt. at Fairfield Church:

XDeliverance, b. 25 Dec. 1688 [O. S., by age at death], d. 18 Apr. 1761 ae. 72-3-13 (g. s., Westport) ; m. (rec. Fairfield) 5 Mar. 1708, Mary Bigg, b. abt. Oct. 1688, d. 14 Apr. 1761 ae. 72 yrs. and abt. 6 mos. (g. s.).

---

* Perhaps by second wife. Since we have no positive knowledge of the date of the first wife's death, the division of the children is made somewhat arbitrarily. It is possible that Isaac was the last child by the first wife, instead of the first by the second wife.

Sarah, b. abt. 1691.

XThomas, b. abt. 1693, d. 5 June 1781 in 88 yr. (g. s., Westport); m.
(1) 17 Mar. 1717, Mary Rowland, dau. of Israel. She d. 17 Apr.
1733, and he m. (2) 14 Oct. 1741, Mercy Scofield, who d. 8 June
1771 ae. 60 (g. s.).

Tabitha, b. abt. 1695; m. Daniel Sherwood, who d. in 1715.

Martha, bapt. 5 Nov 1699.

Mary, m. 3 Sept. 1728, Jonathan Cable.

Ruth, bapt. 17 Mar. 1705/6.

Ebenezer, bapt. 26 June 1709, settled in Wilton; m. Jemima ———.
He conveyed 1739 land at Compo Neck, bounded north on land
of Deborah dau. of John Bennett, now wife of Ebenezer Allen; his
wife Jemima conveyed her dower right; Thomas Bennett also
conveyed, as a reserve for life was made to him by Thomas Bennett,
father to Ebenezer.

Bennett, John, s. of Thomas.

Born at Fairfield by 1670. Called Jr. until his uncle John left
Fairfield. As John, Jr., he was one of the petitioners for church
at Stratfield 1691, but did not affiliate with it. His wife Phebe
renewed Covenant at Fairfield Church, 10 Mar. 1695.

Inv. of John of Compo (Westport), 24 May 1713. Adm'n
granted 2 Dec. 1713 to James Bennett.

Married Phebe ———. She m. (2) by end of 1713, Gideon
Allen.

Children, bapt. at Fairfield Church:

Deborah, bapt. 10 Mar. 1694/5, d. y.

XEdmund, bapt. 24 May 1696, d. at Westport, 15 July 1754; m.
Elizabeth, prob. dau. of Stephen Pierson of Derby; she m. (2) at
Westport, 22 Sept. 1755, Jonathan Mallory of Redding.

Abigail, bapt. 12 Jan. 1700/1.

Rachel, b. Mar. 1702 [1702/3], bapt. 2 May 1703, d. at Westport
between Mar. and Oct. 1776; m. at Fairfield, 26 Mar. 1724, Joseph
Allen.

Deborah, bapt. 4 Nov. 1705, d. 15 Feb. 1757; m. at Fairfield, 12 Nov.
1731, Ebenezer Allen.

Phebe, bapt. 4 May 1712, d. at Westport, 2 Dec. 1746. She was an
idiot, and in 1722 the Legislature gave power to Gideon Allen to
sell her realty; on 23 Jan. 1723/4, Joseph Patchen having kept her
nine months and agreed with the town to support her until she
reached 18 yrs. to save her mother and the town from charge, Allen
conveyed to Patchen all her right to lands from her father's estate.

Bennett, James, s. of Thomas.

Born at Fairfield, 6 Aug. 1675, d. at Ridgefield, 27 July 1725. He settled at "Bennetts Farms," on the Ridgefield-Danbury line. Married Deborah Adams, dau. of Abraham.

Adm'n granted, 10 Jan. 1726, to widow Deborah. Samuel Bennett of Danbury chose mother Deborah guardian, 2 Apr. 1726, and she was appointed guardian to Abraham and Deborah.

Deborah of Danbury conveyed, 23 Apr. 1731, to Nathan Adams land in Fairfield from father Abraham Adams, dec'd. In 1748 Deborah conveyed to Abiah wife of "my son Samuel" land at Bennetts Farms.

Children, bapt. at Fairfield:

> Gershom, bapt. 14 Sept. 1701; m. Sarah Gregory, dau. of Thomas, b. 4 Feb. 1709/10.
> Elizabeth, bapt. 9 May 1703; m. at Ridgefield, 29 Dec. 1726, Jonah Smith.
> Ephraim, bapt. 3 June 1705; m. Hannah ———.
> Hannah, bapt. 12 Mar. 1709/10; m. Israel Mead.
> Samuel, bapt. 13 July 1712; m. (1) Abiah Bennett, dau. of Joseph, bapt. at Stratfield, 22 Feb. 1707/8; m. (2) Mary ———.
> Abraham, bapt. 26 June 1715; Capt.; m. in 1737, Silence Hickox, dau. of Samuel, b. at Waterbury, 19 Sept. 1713.
> Deborah, m. at Ridgefield, 2 June 1737, Benjamin Wilson.

Bennett, Peter, s. of Thomas.

Born after 1684, living 1750 at New Fairfield; m. Elizabeth Rowland, dau. of Israel, Sr., bapt. 10 Mar. 1694/5.

Peter Bennett and Elizabeth his wife of New Fairfield conveyed 1750 to son John, land formerly Israel Rowland, Sr.'s; and a few days later John sold to Charles Duncomb the same land, specifying that it belonged to his gr. father Israel Rowland, dec'd.

Children (incomplete record):

> Henry, b. abt. 1712, d. at Sherman, 19 Sept. 1784 in 73 yr. (g. s.); Lt.; m. ———; adm'n granted 7 Oct. 1784, to Gideon Allen; distribution of Est. to his eight daus. or their heirs. Henry is placed hypothetically as son of Peter.
> Peter, bapt. at Fairfield, 31 Oct. 1714.
> John, m. at New Fairfield, 17 Jan. 1750, Abigail Hollister; dau. of Nathaniel, bapt. at New Milford, 12 Jan. 1734/5.

Bennett, James, s. of Lt. James.

Born at Fairfield, abt. 1668, d. at Stratfield abt. Dec. 1707.
Married Sarah Lewis, dau. of Philip. She m. (2) John Taylor of Norwalk.
Inv. 9 Mar. 1707/8 sworn to by widow Sarah. Heirs to Est. are eight children; sons aged 13, 5, 4 yrs., 10 wks.; daus. aged 16, 10, 7, 2.

Children, bapt. at Stratfield:

> Abigail, b. abt. 1691, bapt. 7 Nov. 1697; m. at Stratfield, 26 Jan. 1713/4, Zechariah Hubbell.
> ✕James, b. abt. 1694, bapt. 7 Nov. 1697, d. abt. 1750; mariner, of Stratfield; m. (1) Elizabeth Wakeman, dau. of Capt. John, b. 1 June 1695; m. (2) Tabitha Hubbell, dau. of Samuel, Sr., b. 24 Dec. 1700.
> Damaris, bapt. 12 Dec. 1697; m at Stratfield (rec. Newtown) 1 Dec. 1720, Enos Baldwin; he was son of Daniel and Sarah (Camp) Baldwin, bapt. at Milford, 30 Oct. 1698, d. at Newtown, abt. 1721; Damaris prob. m. (2) Samuel Bryan.*
> Philip, bapt. 25 June 1699, d. before 1707.
> Elizabeth, bapt. 8 Sept. 1700; m. at Norwalk (rec. Newtown, she called of Stratford) 12 July 1724, John Glover.
> Stephen, bapt. 21 June 1702; res. Stratfield, adm'n granted 6 Mar. 1738/9, to Gamaliel French; m. Abigail French, dau. of Sergt. Samuel, bapt. Jan. 1701/2.
> John, bapt. 9 Apr. 1704; mariner, of Stratfield, 1725; living 1730.
> Sarah, bapt. 12 May 1706; m. (before 24 Apr. 1729, as by deed at Fairfield) Noah Taylor of Norwalk.
> Ebenezer, bapt. (as son of James dec'd) 4 Jan. 1707/8; Inv. 4 Oct. 1733 of Ebenezer of Stamford, formerly of Fairfield.

Bennett, Thomas, s. of Lt. James.

Born at Fairfield, abt. 1669, d. at Newtown, 5 Apr. 1739.
Married at Stratford, 12 Apr. 1692, Mary Booth. She was dau. of Ephraim, b. 12 Nov. 1676, d. between 4 and 16 Sept. 1741.
Will of Capt. Thomas of Newtown, 20 Mar. 1738/9, proved 21 Apr. 1739; wife Mary; sons Abraham, Thomas, Ephraim; daus. Deborah Bassett, Eunice Booth, Rebecca Booth, Anna Bots-

---

* Samuel and Damaris Bryan of Stamford, 9 Apr. 1733, conveyed Newtown land formerly belonging to Enos Baldwin. The youngest Bryan child recorded at Stamford was named Lewis Enos.

ford, Damaris Botsford, Bethia; referred to will of his father, James Bennett, Esq.

Will of Mary of Newtown, 4 Sept. 1741, proved 16 Sept. 1741; son Abraham; daus. Mary Botsford, Deborah Bassett, Eunice Booth, Rebecca Booth; son Thomas; daus. Anna Botsford, Bethia Bennett; sons Joseph Botsford, Samuel Bassett, Daniel Booth, and Abiel Booth, exec'rs.

Children, five recorded at Stratford, two bapt. at Stratfield:

> Mary, b. 31 Aug. 1693; m. at Newtown, 9 Jan. 1718/9, Joseph Botsford.
>
> Deborah, b. 28 Feb. 1695/6, d. at Derby, July 1773; m. (rec. Derby) 5 Jan. 1719, Capt. Samuel Bassett.
>
> Ephraim, b. 23 Feb. 1698/9, d. y.
>
> Abraham, b. abt. 1701 (date not entered), d. at Newtown, in 1784; m. (1) at Newtown, 6 Apr. 1726, Christian Botsford, b. at Milford, 17 Aug. 1701, d. 7 Nov. 1769 (Newtown Church rec.); m. (2) Abigail (———) Judson, who d. in 1804.
>
> Eunice, b. abt. 1703 (date not entered), d. 16 May 1786 in 83 yr. (g. s., Newtown); m. Lt. Daniel Booth.
>
> Thomas, bapt. 25 Aug. 1706 (at Stratford, rec. Stratfield), d. at Southbury, 25 Aug. 1769 ae. 63; m. at Southbury, 18 Nov. 1736, Mercy Bronson.
>
> Rebecca, bapt. 3 Apr. 1709 (at Stratford, rec. Stratfield); m. Abiel Booth.
>
> Anna, b. abt. 1711, d. at Newtown, 3 June 1784; m. 2 May 1733, John Botsford.
>
> Damaris, b. 7 Sept. 1713 (Bible rec.); m. 1735 (Bible rec.) Amos Botsford.
>
> Bethia, b. abt. 1716, d. 26 Nov. 1754 ae. 38 (g. s., Newtown); m. 11 Nov. 1742 (Bible rec.) Gideon Botsford.
>
> Ephraim, b. abt. 1718, d. 7 Oct. 1779 in 62 yr. (g. s., Newtown); m. 19 June 1745, Ann Baldwin, dau. of Caleb, b. 18 Sept. 1727, d. 7 Nov. 1772 ae. 45 (g. s.).

Bennett, Joseph, s. of Lt. James.

He m. at Fairfield, 22 Jan. 1705/6, Elizabeth Whidden; dau. of Richard.

On 17 Jan. 1705/6, he had land entered on Fairfield records by gift from father James Bennett; also land in lieu of a legacy given him by his uncle Joseph Joy.

He renewed Covenant at Stratfield Church, 8 Feb. 1697; was a merchant there in 1706/7; d. before 1736.

Children, bapt. at Stratfield:

Richard, bapt. 13 Oct. 1706.
Abiah, bapt. 22 Feb. 1707/8; m. Samuel Bennett.
Sarah, bapt. 7 May 1710.
Joseph, bapt. 16 Dec. 1711; "distracted," 1739-48.
Widden, bapt. 6 Dec. 1713, d. in 1740/1; Inv. 24 Feb. 1740/1.
Mary, bapt. 16 Sept. 1716.

Bennett, Isaac, s. of Lt. James.

Born [say 1685], living (at home of son Gideon) 1762; m. (1) at Stratfield, Mar. 1708, Martha ———. She was bapt. at Stratfield, 9 Mar. 1712. He m. (2) Sarah ———, who was living 1762.

Of Stratfield, he conveyed 1739 to son Caleb, land that belonged to father James Bennett, Esq.; and Caleb, then of New Milford, sold the same property 1742. Of Stratford, he conveyed 1746 to sons William of Fairfield and Isaac of Stratford. Benjamin of Stratfield conveyed 1738, land bounded east on meadow of father Isaac Bennett, and west on land set to my aunt Abigail wife of James Bishop.

Children [by first wife], bapt. at Stratfield:

XWilliam, bapt. 26 Dec. 1708, d. at Easton, 16 Feb. 1788 in 80 yr. (g. s.); Lt.; Deacon; m. (1) 26 July 1731, Hannah Seeley, dau. of James, b. 23 May 1713, d. 28 Nov. 1743 in 31 yr. (g. s., Stratfield); m. (2) 3 Dec. 1744, Katharine Hawley, dau. of Thomas, b. 17 Feb. 1721/2, d. 22 July 1809 in 88 yr. (g. s., Easton).
XIsaac, bapt. 4 Mar. 1711, d. at Easton, 10 Dec. 1791 in 82 yr. (g. s.); Lt.; m. (1) abt. 1734, Mary, widow of Isaac Wheeler, 3d, and dau. of Jonathan Wakelee, b. 10 June 1708, d. 5 July 1768 (g. s.); m. (2) Eunice, widow of Sergt. James Hawley, and dau. of Henry Jackson, b. 7 Aug. 1715, d. 6 Sept. 1796 in 82 yr. (g. s., Stratfield).
Benjamin, bapt. 19 Apr. 1713, d. at Sherman, 10 Feb. 1792 in 79 yr. (g. s.); Deacon; m. (1) at New Milford, 4 Dec. 1740, Abiah Noble, dau. of John, b. at New Milford, 19 May 1721, d. there 22 Oct. 1758 ae. 37 (g. s.); m. (2) abt. 1759, Mary, widow of Dea. Daniel Noble, and dau. of Ens. William Gaylord, b. at New Milford, 22 Nov. 1725, d. at Sherman, 25 Jan. 1795 ae. 70 (g. s.).
Caleb, bapt. 9 Feb. 1716, d. at New Milford, 24 Mar. 1790 in 75 yr. (g. s.); m (1) at New Milford, 13 June 1746, Abigail Fowler, b. abt. 1727, d. 24 Nov. 1771 in 45 yr. (g. s.); m. (2) Sarah ———; possibly she m. before 1810 ——— Beebe.
Martha, bapt. 24 Nov. 1717.

Mercy, b. abt. 1721, d. at Stratfield, 5 Mar. 1819 ae. 98 (g. s.) ; m. 31 Aug. 1744, Dea. Abel Seeley.

Children [by second wife] :

Gideon, m. (1) before 1749, ———; m. (2) 30 Dec. 1762, Hannah Mallett, dau. of John, bapt. May 1739.

Nehemiah, m. July 1750, Ann Phippen, dau. of Benjamin, b. 15 Nov. 1727.

Beulah, bapt. at Stratfield, 19 Sept. 1731; m. at Stratfield, 10 Nov. 1749, John Barlow.

Bennett, Jeremiah, s. of Lt. James.

Bapt. at Stratfield, 27 Dec. 1696, d. there in 1773; m. ———, who d. in 1772.

Children, bapt. at Stratfield (record incomplete) :

Ann, bapt. 2 Sept. 1716.

Hezekiah, bapt. in 1719; m. at Trumbull, 14 June 1753, Hannah ———.

? Samuel, b. abt. 1726, d. 21 June 1731 ae. 7 (g. s., Trumbull).

BENNETT FAMILY (ISAAC)

Bennett, Isaac.

Not related, so far as records show, to the James Bennett family. Born abt. 1650, d. 23 May 1720 ae. abt. 70 (g. s., Shelton).

Married at Stratford, 2 June 1683, Elizabeth Rose. She was dau. of Robert, 2d, b. Feb. 1658/9.

Will 11 Jan. 1714/5, proved 1 July 1720; son Nathan; daus. Sarah Wheeler, Mercy Davis, Elizabeth Price; daus. Mary and Hannah, bed and furniture and £10 apiece; wife Elizabeth.

Children, recorded at Stratford :

Daniel, b. 9 Mar. 1683/4, d. s. p.; adm'n granted to Robert Wheeler, 14 Apr. 1714. Agreement of brother and sisters, 25 Nov. 1715; Nathan Bennit, Sarah wife of Robert Wheeler, Marcy wife of Samuel Davis, Elizabeth wife of Ephraim Price of Newark, Mary and Hannah Bennit.

Sarah, d. abt. 1773; m. June 1708, Robert Wheeler.

Mercy, m. June 1708, Samuel Davis.

Elizabeth, m. 13 Nov. 1712, Ephraim Price of Newark, N. J.

Mary, m. 6 Mar. 1717/8, Daniel Beardsley.

Hannah.
Nathan, b. 6 Aug. 1697,* d. 19 Sept. 1748 ae. 51 (g. s., Shelton);
Capt.; m. 25 Feb. 1723/4, Deborah Curtis, b. 28 Sept. 1699, d. 16
Sept. 1785 in 87 yr. (g. s.).

BENNETT FAMILY ("SHIPWRIGHT")

Bennett, James.

Prob. son of an earlier James, of New London.

Shipwright, settled in Stratfield, and m. (2) Mary (Couch),
widow of Thomas Grumman. He went to Va. or Md. as a shipwright, leaving his wife and children, 1699, and she divorced him
Oct. 1703, after six years of marriage. She m. (3) by contract
dated 24 Oct. 1727, Samuel Jennings.

Mary, wife of James, "Shipwright", owned Covenant 10 May
1696, at Stratfield Church. He was bapt. there 9 Aug. 1696.

Children, bapt. at Stratfield:†

Elizabeth, bapt 10 May 1696.
Mary, bapt. 10 May 1696.
Benjamin, bapt. 4 Apr. 1697; m. at Stratford, 28 Jan. 1724/5, Hannah
Curtis.

Bickley, William.

Of Stratford, will 24 Feb. 1706/7, proved 24 Apr. 1707; all
estate to wife Bethia; friends Joseph Curtis and Jonathan Pitman,
overseers. Mrs. Bethia Glover declined further adm'n, 26 Jan.
1707/8, and it was granted to John Glover of Stratford.

He m. Bethia Beach, b. 23 Apr. 1674; she m. (2) 14 July 1707,
John Glover.

Bingham, Abel, s. of Thomas. Deputy (Windham), May
1721, May 1723, May and Oct. 1724.

Son of Dea. Thomas and Mary (Rudd) Bingham, b. at
Norwich, 25 June 1669, d. at Windham, 25 Mar. 1745. He settled

---

* I read birth date 1687; so also Cothren; Orcutt gives 1697, which agrees with age
at death. If 1697 is correct, how could he sign agreement in 1715, when a minor?
† The two daus. were by a former wife unless James married Mary earlier than the
record of divorce indicates.

in youth at Stratfield; rem. abt. 1707 to Windham, where he was chosen deacon 1729, and served as Selectman.

Married (rec. Fairfield) 16 May 1694, Elizabeth Odell.

The births of his children were entered in Windham after he settled there.   See *Bingham Genealogy* for further particulars.

Children, first six bapt. at Stratfield:

> Abigail b. and bapt. 7 June 1696; m. Francis Griswold.
> Mary, b. 17 Dec. 1697, bapt. 19 Dec. 1697; m. 7 Nov. 1717, John Abbe.
> John, b. 9 Feb. 1700, bapt. 11 Feb. 1700; m. Mary Moulton.
> Elizabeth, b. 27 Mar. 1702, bapt. 29 Mar. 1702; m. 7 Feb. 1727, Samuel Coggeswell.
> Abel, b. 17 June 1704, bapt. 18 June 1704.
> Ann, b. 13 Sept. 1706, bapt. 15 Sept. 1706; m. (1) Thomas Baldwin of Norwich; m. (2) ——— Hough.
> Jemima, b. 24 Oct. 1708; m. Ebenezer Jennings.
> Jonathan, b. 17 Aug. 1712.
> David, b. 12 Sept. 1714.

Birdsey, John.

Married (1) Philippa ———, with whom he was admitted to Milford Church, 23 Aug. 1640; they were dismissed to Stratford, 19 Mar. 1649.

Married (2) in 1688 Alice, widow of Henry Tomlinson; marriage agreement dated 8 Oct. 1688.

"Deacon" John d. at Stratford, 4 Apr. 1690.   His widow Alice d. 25 Jan. 1697/8.

Will 22 Aug. 1689; calls himself aged; son John; son-in-law and dau. Timothy and Joanna Wilcoxson; wife Alice, referring to marriage agreement.   Inv. sworn 12 June 1690.

Children, recorded at Stratford:

> +John, b. 28 Mar. 1641.
> Johanna, b. 18 Nov. 1642; m. 28 Dec. 1664, Timothy Wilcoxson.

Birdsey, John, s. of John.

Called son of John, he m. (Stratford rec.) 11 Dec. 1669, Phebe Wilcoxson, dau. of William.   He d. 9 Jan. 1697/8.   His widow m. (2) John Beach.

Will 20 May 1693; wife Phebe, Exec'x; sons Abel, Joseph;

daus. Hannah Beach, Dinah Birdsey. Inv. 9 Feb. 1697/8. Ages of children: Hannah 26, Abel 19, Joseph 16, Dinah 9.

Children, recorded at Stratford:

Hannah, b. 5 Feb. 1671; m. 3 May 1693, Isaac Beach.

Mary, b. 2[—] Nov. 1675, d. 17 June 1691.

Sarah, b. 9 May 1678, d. 21 Jan. 1678 [1678/9].

Abel, b. 30 Nov. 1679, d. at Stratford, 14 May 1747 in 68 yr. (g. s.); Lt.; will 12 May 1747, proved 2 June 1747; m. (1) 8 June 1704, Comfort Welles, who d. 29 June 1717; m. (2) 25 Feb. 1717/8, Mrs. Mercy Denton of Hempstead, L. I., who d. 6 Feb. 1763; her will 12 Sept. 1757, proved 2 Mar. 1763.

Joseph, b. 22 Feb. 1681/2, d. at Stratford, 25 June 1757 ae. 75; will 3 Dec. 1756, proved 4 July 1757; m. (1) 10 June 1708, Sarah Thompson, who d. 3 May 1726 in 41 yr.; m. (2) 11 Oct. 1726, Mrs. Tabitha Walker. She was widow of John Walker, and dau. of Edward Wooster.

Elizabeth, b 21 Oct. 1685, d. 13 Nov. 1692.

Dinah, b. abt. 1688.

Bishop, (Rev.) John.

The first minister at Stamford.

He m. (1) Rebecca ———; m. (2) Joanna, widow of Capt. Thomas Willett and previously of Rev. Peter Prudden of Milford, and dau. of Rev. John Boyse of Halifax, co. York, Eng.

Will 16 Nov. 1694, proved 12 Mar. 1694/5; to be buried between his two wives Rebecca and Joanna who [he says with comfortable assurance] are fallen asleep in Jesus and gone to Heaven before me; I feel that the gospel is going from New England for the neglect and contempt it hath found here; sons Stephen, Joseph, Ebenezer, Benjamin; dau. Whiting.

Joseph Bishop, Exec'r of father's will, set out land, 18 Oct. 1695, to Mr. Joseph Whiting of Southampton, in consideration of legacy due him from will of my father Bishop.

Children [by first wife]:

+Stephen.

Daughter, m. Mr. Joseph Whiting, of Southampton, L. I. He was b. at Lynn, 6 Apr. 1641; grad. Harvard 1661; minister at Southampton from 1682 until his death, 7 Apr. 1723.

+Joseph.

Mary, d. 25 July 1658.

+Ebenezer, b. abt. 1666.

+Benjamin.

Bishop, Stephen, s. of John.   Deputy for Stamford, Oct. 1700, Oct. and Dec. 1707, Oct. 1708, May, June and Oct. 1709.

He d. at Stamford, 3 Dec. 1722 [1723?].

Married Mercy ———.

Inv. of Mr. Stephen Bishop who d. 3 Dec. 1723; adm'n granted to son John.   Five children: John, Stephen, Isaac, Rebecca wife of Elisha Holly, Abigail wife of John Seeley.

Children, recorded at Stamford:

John, b. abt. 1682, d. abt. 1757; will 16 Apr. 1752, proved 12 Jan. 1758; m. (1) 10 May 1704, Mary Talmadge, b. at New Haven, 3 Feb. 1682/3, d. 23 Sept. 1725; m. (2) 24 Jan. 1725/6, widow Sarah Lewis of Fairfield; she was widow of Nathan Lewis, and dau. of Capt. John Osborn, b. abt. 1689, d. 30 Apr. 1729; m. (3) Abigail ———.

Abraham, b. 28 Oct. 1684, d. 29 Oct. [1712] ae. 28.

Stephen, b. 28 Oct. 1684, d. in 1731; will 21 July 1731, proved 3 Aug. 1731; m. 4 June 1713, Waitstill Waterbury, who d. 5 July 1730.

Theophilus, b. 1 Feb. 1687, d. 13 Sept. 1710 ae. 24.

Isaac, b. 30 Oct. 1689, d. in 1759; Dea.; adm'n granted 3 July 1759; m. 22 May 1718, Susanna Finch.

Rebecca, b. 9 Apr. 1692, m. 24 Jan. 1715/6, Elisha Holly.

Abigail, b. 15 July 1696, d. 1 Sept. 1757; m. by 1720, John Seeley.

Bishop, Joseph, s. of John.   Justice, 1704, 1711, 1714-33; Lt., Stamford Trainband, Oct. 1709; Capt., Oct. 1710.

The Worshipful Joseph, Esq., d. at Stamford, 14 Sept. 1733.

He m. (rec. Stamford) 3 Nov. 1691, Elizabeth Knowles.   She was dau. of John of Fairfield, b. abt. 1669, d. at Stamford, 29 Apr. 1754 ae. 85.

Will of Joseph, Sr., 8 June 1727, proved 21 Nov. 1733; wife Elizabeth, Exec'x; children, Joseph (Exec'r), Charles, Andrew, Alexander, Hannah, Sarah Davenport, Rebecca, Elizabeth, Mary, Martha.

Children, recorded at Stamford:

Joseph, b. 16 Oct. 1692; m. 1 Feb. 1722, Hannah Holly.

Alexander, b. 15 Apr. 1694, d. 21 Oct. 1706.

Charles, b. 5 May 1695.

Andrew, b. 3 Oct. 1696, d. 10 Sept. 1753; adm'n granted 19 Feb. 1760; m. (1) 7 Mar. 1734, Mary Crissy, who d. 14 Aug. 1743; m. (2)

1 Dec. 1748, Hannah Thorp [prob. widow of Charles Thorp, and dau. of Nathan Ferris, b. 20 June 1704].

Hannah, b. 8 July 1698; prob. m. 11 June 1728, John Ketchum, of Stamford, from Huntington, L. I.

Nathan, b. 29 Oct. 1699, d. y.

Elizabeth, b. 3 June 1700, d. 12 Jan. 1705/6.

Sarah, b. 27 Dec. 1701; m. 6 Sept. 1721, John Davenport.

Rebecca, b. 17 Aug. 1703.

Helena, b. 1 Apr. 1705, d. 6 June 1721.

Elizabeth, b. 6 Sept. 1706; perhaps m. 10 Feb. 1737/8 (as his second wife), John Penoyer.

Mary, b. 21 July 1708, d. 19 Aug. 1766.

Martha, b. 31 Oct. 1709; perhaps m. 3 Dec. 1748 (as his second wife), Nathaniel Crissey.

Alexander, b. 5 Jan 1710/1; m. Susanna ———.

Bishop, Ebenezer, s. of John.

Born abt. 1666, d. at Stamford, 12 Mar. 1710 ae. 44; m. 2 Oct. 1700, Sarah Slawson; dau. of John, b. 20 Jan. 1667/8, d. 11 Jan. 1743/4.

He testified Aug. 1692, ae. 26, in the Clawson witchcraft trial.

Children, recorded at Stamford:

Sarah, b. 14 July 1701, d. 27 Nov. 1743; m. 14 Dec. 1721, John Jeffrey.

Ann, b. 19 Sept. 1702; m. 20 Jan. 1723/4, John Dean.

Samuel, b. 18 Oct. 1704; m. 25 Mar. 1736, Rebecca Slawson.

Ebenezer, b. 19 Mar. 1705/6, d. 4 Oct. 1743; Dr.; will 28 Sept. 1743, proved 10 Oct. 1743, named mother, bros. Samuel and Thomas, cousin Stephen Bishop (Exec'r), landlord David Dibble, and sisters Sarah and Ann.

Thomas, b. 6 Mar. 1709/10, d. 12 Nov. 1743; adm'n granted, 6 Dec. 1743, to Samuel Bishop; distribution ordered to Samuel Bishop, heirs of Sarah Jeffery, and Ann wife of John Dean.

Bishop, Benjamin, s. of John.

He d. at Stamford, 25 Jan. 1727/8; m. 24 Aug. 1696, Susannah Pierson. She was dau. of Rev. Abraham, and d. 2 Nov. 1748.

Inv. presented 6 Aug. 1733 by Benjamin Bishop, Adm'r.

Children, recorded at Stamford:

Abigail, b. 3 Oct. 1697.

Susannah, b. 2 July 1699.

Benjamin, b. 28 Nov. 1701; m. (1) 25 Apr. 1728, Mary Guernsey, who d. 18 June 1736; m. (2) 11 Nov. 1736, Rachel Bates.

James, b. 3 Apr. 1704; m. abt. 1735, Abigail ———.
Ruth, b. 13 June 1706.
David, b. 26 June 1708.
Nathan, b. 13 Sept. 1711; m. 9 Nov. 1742, Sarah Ferris of Greenwich.
Hannah, b. 6 May 1714; prob. m. 4 Aug. 1736, Charles Hoyt.

Bispham, Robert. [Surname often spelled Bisbom.]

Married before 1685, Susanna Hendrick, dau. of Henry; she m. (2) by 1694, Philip Price, and renewed her Covenant at Fairfield Church, 17 Feb. 1694/5, having a Bispham and a Price child bapt. that date, and her two other Bispham children a few weeks later.

John Middlebrook purchased, 16 May 1707, from Rebecca and Margery Bispham their share in the homelot of their father Robert Bispham dec'd, now in the occupancy of said Middlebrook.

Children:

Elizabeth, bapt. 17 Feb. 1694/5; m. by 1702, John Middlebrook.
Margery, bapt. 7 Apr. 1695.
Rebecca, bapt. 7 Apr. 1695.

Blackleach, Richard. Deputy for Stratford, Apr. 1690, Oct. 1695, May 1696, May 1698, May 1699; Commissioner for Stratford, 1695-98; Justice, 1698-1701; Commissary for Army at Albany, May 1690.

Testified 1687 aged 33; d. at Stratford, 4 Sept. 1731.

Mr. Richard m. (1) (rec. Stratford) 8 Dec. 1680, Miss Abigail Hudson of New Haven. She was dau. of John, b. 25 Mar. 1654; d. 10 Mar. 1712/3 ae. 60 (g. s., Stratford).

He m. (2) at Stratford, 27 Aug. 1717, Elizabeth de la Porte alias Poisson [widow of Edward]. She was born Harris, and widow successively of Samuel Wheeler and Hugh Nesbitt, Blackleach being her fourth husband.

The will of John Hudson, Sr., 1690, named Richard Blackleach husband of dau. Abigail. The will of John Hudson, 3d, 1721, named his cousins, children of Richard Blackleach of Stratford; Samuel and Joseph Blackleach appealed from probate. The will of Mrs. Sarah Chauncey (née Hudson, sister of Abigail), 1711, named Isaac Chauncey of Hadley, son of husband Israel of Stratford dec'd; dau. Sarah wife of son Isaac Chauncey; brother Richard Blackleach; sister Abigail wife of Richard Blackleach, money in hands of John Hudson; nephews Richard, Samuel, and Joseph Blackleach; nieces Rebecca and Abigail Blackleach.

Children [by first wife], not recorded:

+Richard, b. abt. 1681.

Sarah, b. abt. 1682, d. at Hadley, 29 June 1720 ae. 38 (g. s.) ; m. Rev. Isaac Chauncey.

Samuel, b. (no record), living 1721.

Rebecca, m. (1) at Stratford, 10 Jan. 1717/8, John Allen of "Fairfield, East Parish"; m. (2) abt. 1726, Benjamin Rumsey; m. (3) after 1734, John Curtis.

Joseph, b. abt. 1694, d. 20 June 1756 in 62 yr. (g. s., Huntington) ; m. at Stratford, 5 Dec. 1723, Ann Hawley, dau. of Samuel, Jr., b. 14 Jan. 1704/5, d. 20 Mar. 1771 in 66 yr. (g. s.).

Abigail, m at Stratford, 29 Aug. 1716, Dr. James Laboree.

Blackleach, Richard, s. of Richard.

Born at Stratford, abt. 1681, d. there in 1750.

Married (1) Sarah Wheeler, dau. of Moses.

Married (2) at Stratford, 2 Feb. 1715/6, Mehitabel Laboree of Guilford.

Will 27 Feb. 1747/8, proved 2 Oct. 1750; Mehitabel and Blackleach, dau. and son of Peleg Burritt, Jr., of Stratford; dau. Sarah wife of Edward Jessup of Fairfield.

Child [by first wife] :

Sarah, b. abt. 1700, d. 18 Nov. 1783 in 84 yr. (g. s., Westport) ; m. at Stratford (rec. also Fairfield) 7 Dec. 1724, Capt. Edward Jessup.

Children by Mehitabel, recorded at Stratford:

Mehitabel, b. 26 Jan. 1716/7; m. Peleg Burritt, Jr.

Mary, b. 20 Nov. 1719, d. y.

Blackman, (Rev.) Adam.

The surname was more generally Blakeman in the early generations.

From co. Stafford, matriculated at Christ's College, Oxford, 28 May 1617 in 19 yr.; preached in cos. Leicester and Derby;

came over abt. 1638, and was a short time at Guilford. First
minister at Stratford, 1640, where he d. 7 Sept. 1665.

Will 16 Mar. 1664/5; sons John, James and Samuel have had
portions; wife; son Benjamin; son Atwater's son Joshua; dau.
Mary Atwater; son John's children; wives of sons James and
Samuel; son Deliverance provided he returns; Joseph Blackman; to dau. Blackman if she marry not John Thomas; overseers, Brother Groves, bro. Booth, bro. Hawley.

Inv. 22 Sept. 1665.

Will of Jane Blackman 20 Sept. 1671; son Deliverance, £30;
sons James and Benjamin; son James's wife; son Benjamin and
gr. son Adam Blackman, land to be divided when latter reaches 21,
and if Adam dies, Benjamin to have all; three daus. of son
James; son Samuel's son Adam and eldest dau.; servant Sarah
Nichols; James's dau. Mary; gr. child Joseph Blackman, the
homelot; Mr. Israel Chauncey, £5; servant Nathaniel, £5 at
end of his time; overseers, Mr. Chauncey, Elder Groves, Joseph
Hawley. Inv. 23 Jan. 1673 [1673/4].

Children:

+John.
+James.
  Mary, b. abt. 1636, d. at Salem, Mass., 9 Mar. 1708/9 ae. 72 (g. s.);
     m. (1) (rec. New Haven) 6 May 1651, Joshua Atwater, of Boston,
     Mass.; m. (2) in 1676, Rev. John Higginson, of Salem.
+Samuel.
  Benjamin, grad. Harvard 1663; ordained at Malden 1674; of Saco
     1678; rem. to Boston; m. 1 Apr. 1675, Rebecca Scottow, who d.
     21 Mar. 1715. In 1715, Thomas Goodwill of Boston and Rebecca
     his wife, only surviving child and heir of Mr. Benjamin Blackman
     of Stratford dec'd, conveyed land.
+Deliverance.

Blackman, John, s. of Adam.

Married Dorothy Smith, dau. of Rev. Henry of Wethersfield.
Dorothy, widow of John, m. (2) at Stratford, last of Oct. 1665,
Francis Hall. She m. (3) early in 1692, Mark St. John of Nor-
walk; and (4) Dea. Isaac Moore of Farmington.

Will 19 Jan. 1661/2, proved 26 Nov. 1662; wife; children
Joseph and others; overseers, my father, my brother Birdsey,
my uncle Wheeler, and brother James Blackman; witnesses,

Adam and James Blackman. Inv. of James, deceased in Apr. 1662, presented 26 Nov. 1662.

Dorothy More of Farmington conveyed 1699 to grandchild Joseph Blackman, land in Stratford.

Will of Dorothy Moore of Farmington, late wife of Dea. Isaac, 21 May 1700, proved 17 Apr. 1706; gr. child Joseph Blackman, my dwelling house, reserving a room for Mary Hall, dau. of my husband Francis Hall; Joseph's bros. John and Samuel; my sons John and Ebenezer Blackman; land at Hatfield; Abigail and Rebecca, daus. of son Joseph; Dorothy and Elizabeth, daus. of son Ebenezer; overseers, Mr. Joseph Curtis and Mr. Israel Chauncey.

Children:
+John.
+Ebenezer.
+Joseph.

Blackman, James, s. of Adam.

Will at "Orinoge" 18 July 1689, proved 7 Nov. 1689; wife Miriam; sons; eldest son Zechariah; two unm. daus. Elizabeth and Martha; five daus. "disposed of", Sarah Cunny, Mary Searles, Hannah Gilbert, Miriam Northrop, Jane Russell; overseers, brothers Samuel Wheeler, Moses Wheeler, Ephraim Stiles, and son-in-law Joseph Northrop.

Married (1) ——— Stiles, dau. of Francis.

Married (2) Miriam Wheeler, dau. of Moses, b. 28 Mar. 1647. She m. (2) Edward Groom, by whom she had a dau. Mary.

Will of Miriam Groom of "Oronoge" dated at Milford, 4 Oct. 1693; eldest son Zachariah Blackman; sons Adam and James Blackman; Miriam wife of Joseph Northrop; Mary Groom; Martha Blackman; dau. Jane; witnessed by George Clark and Jobamah Gunn. Inv. at Stratford and Milford, 6 Nov. 1693.

Children [by first wife], recorded at Stratford:
Sarah, b. 25 Apr. 1658, d. at Boston, 17 Apr. 1694; m. abt. 1677, John Coney, Jr.
Mary, b. 25 Apr. 1661; m. George Searles.
Hannah, b. 21 Jan. 1664 [1664/5], d. before 1695; m. abt. 1687, John Gilbert.

Children [by second wife], recorded at Stratford:

Jane, b. 26 Oct. 1668; m. (1) at New Haven, 12 June 1687, Joseph Russell;* m. (2) Thomas Griffin; m. (3) at Stratford, 24 May 1698, James Clark, Jr.

Miriam, b. 8 Feb. 1670 [1670/1]; m. (1) Joseph Northrop; m. (2) John Smith of Milford, and with second husband conveyed 1727 to brother Zechariah Blackman land inherited from grandfather Moses Wheeler.

Elizabeth, b. [say 1673], d. in 1691; Inv. 17 Sept. 1691; George Searles appointed Adm'r.

Martha, b. abt. 1676, d. at West Springfield, 18 Aug. 1746 in 70 yr.; m. (1) Francis Ball; m. (2) (rec. Springfield) 8 May 1701, Benjamin Stebbins.

Zechariah, b. 26 May 1678, d. at Stratford in 1765; will 10 Mar. 1752, proved 5 Mar. 1765; m. (1) 27 Dec. 1704, Elizabeth Denman of Derby, who d. 23 Mar. 1731/2; m. (2) at New Haven, 19 June 1733, Mrs. Dinah Sherman; widow of John Sherman, and dau. of Daniel Thomas, b. 26 Dec. 1678, d. in 1769.

Adam, b. 1 Jan. 1683 [1683/4]; m. 6 Apr. 1708, Bathsheba Pierson.†

James, b. 4 Dec. 1686, d. at Stratfield, 29 Oct. 1709 in 23 yr. (g. s.). Nuncupative will; two bros. to have lands; John Love and Samuel Henries of Stratfield testified 14 Mar. 1709/10. Adm'n granted to bros. Zechariah and Adam, 13 Dec. 1709; Agur Tomlinson gave bond. The Adm'rs exhibited receipts from Jane Clark, Miriam Smith, and Martha Stebbins, sisters of the dec'd, that they are satisfied.

Blackman, Samuel, s. of Adam.

Married latter end of Nov. 1660, Elizabeth Wheeler, dau. of Moses. She m. (2) 6 Dec. 1670, Mr. Jacob Walker.

He d. at Stratford, 27 Nov. 1668.

Inv. exhibited 12 Mar. 1668/9. Widow; children and ages, Adam 3, daughters 5 and 1.

In 1712 Zechariah Blackman and Johanna Watkins of Stratford, and Thomas Ingersoll and Abigail his wife of Springfield, conveyed land laid out to Rev. Adam Blackman [deed signed also by David Watkins].

Children, recorded at Stratford:

Son, b. Jan. 1661 [1661/2], d. abt. 11 Mar. following.

Abigail, b. 11 Dec. 1663; m. (1) 4 Dec. 1679, Hezekiah Dickinson; m. (2) Thomas Ingersoll of Springfield, Mass.

---

* He was of East Haven, but his Inv. taken 17 Nov. 1688 is recorded at Fairfield; widow Jane and child; adm'n granted to James Blackman of Stratford.

† An Adam m. at Stratford, 9 June 1719, Ruth Beecher.

Adam, b. 14 Sept. 1665, d. y.
Johanna, b. 4 Dec. 1667; m. (1) 4 Dec. 1688, Joseph Watkins; m.
(2) Jesse Lambert; m. (3) as Johanah Lambert of Stratford, 24
Nov. 1725(?),* Mr. Samuel Camp, of Newark, N. J.

Blackman, Deliverance, s. of Adam.

Inclined to wildness in his youth, he was accused of the paternity
of Mary Benfield's child in 1665.
He settled in Stonington, and m. Hannah ———.

Children:

Adam, bapt. May 1687.
Hannah, bapt. Mar. 1693/4.

Blackman, John, s. of John.

Married Mary Kimberly, dau. of Abraham, b. 4 May 1668.
Will 30 Sept. 1706, proved 18 Nov. 1706; only son Abraham;
brother Ebenezer's son John. Abraham Blackman chose his uncle
Abraham Kimberly for guardian, 8 Nov. 1711.

Child, recorded at Stratford:

Abraham, b. 25 Oct. 1694; m. 27 Feb. 1717/8, Elizabeth Barley.

Blackman, Ebenezer, s. of John.

Married (1) at Stratford, 24 Oct. 1681, Patience Wilcoxson.
She was dau. of John, b. 1 Feb. 1663 [1663/4].
Married (2) at Stratford, 3 Nov. 1692, Abigail Curtis. She
was dau. of Jonathan, b. 17 Oct. 1671.

Children [by first wife], recorded at Stratford:

Dorothy, b. 18 Mar. 1682/3, d. at Newtown, 28 Jan. 1721/2; m. at
Stratford, 2 Jan. 1704/5, Daniel Foote.
John, b. 4 Apr. 1685, d. at Newtown, 25 Jan. 1764; m. Abigail Beers,
b. at Fairfield, 24 Apr. 1692, d. at Newtown, 27 Mar. 1762.
Elizabeth, b. 10 Feb. 1688 [1688/9]; m. at Stratford, 25 Jan. 1710/1,
Edward Fairchild.

Children [by second wife], recorded at Stratford (mother 1696
to 1702 was Abigail):

Ebenezer, b. 9 Aug. 1693, d. at Stratford in 1753; will 28 May 1753,
proved 24 Aug. 1753; m. abt. 1725, Mehitabel Adams.

---

* Orcutt read date as 1723, Cothren as 1720.

Jonathan, b. 24 Apr. 1696; m. 20 Dec. 1722, Mary Beecher.
David, b. 6 Jan. 1697/8, d. Mar. 1702/3.
Abigail, b. 20 Nov. 1700, d. Mar. 1702/3.
Nathan, b. 29 Sept. 1702; m. Sarah Welles.
Sarah, b. 3 Apr. 1705; prob. m. 2 Nov. 1737, Joseph Booth; and if so,
    d. Apr. 1784 in 76 yr. (g. s., Stratfield).
David.

Blackman, Joseph, s. of John.

Married (Stratford rec.) 14 July 1674, Hannah Hall.   She was
dau. of Francis.

Children, recorded at Stratford:

Joseph, b. 12 Apr. 1675; m. (1) 14 Sept. 1697, Elizabeth Seeley; m.
    (2) 29 Jan. 1704/5, Hester Wheeler.
+John, b. abt. 1677.
Abigail, b. 12 Aug. 1680; m. 6 Nov. 1701, William Smith.
Samuel, living 1700, prob. not living 1714.
Benjamin, m. 26 Mar. 1706, Rebecca Smith.
Rebecca,* m. 1 Dec. 1708, William Curtis.
(?) Josiah, d. at Stamford, 17 June 1747; m. at Stamford, 5 Aug. 1714,
    Sarah Brown.

Blackman, John, s. of Joseph.

Born abt. 1677, d. at Fairfield abt. 1732; m. (rec. Stratford)
29 Apr. 1701, Jemima Hurlbut.   She was dau. of Thomas, bapt.
at Woodbury, Aug. 1680; she m. (2) Nathaniel Whitehead, and
d. at Westport, 4 Feb. 1757.

Adm'n granted, 4 Apr. 1732, to Gideon Hurlbut and John
Blackman.

His widow Jemima was appointed guardian to the daus. Jemima
and Abigail, 2 Jan. 1732/3; Mary chose Ephraim Jackson for
guardian, and he was appointed for Sarah.

Adam, son of John, chose Capt. Samuel Couch for guardian,
4 Apr. 1732; Couch desired to be discharged, 24 Jan. 1736, and
he chose John Blackman. On 20 Aug. 1737, Adam refused to
appear, and the Court appointed Ephraim Jackson guardian.

Peter Blackman, a minor of Fairfield, ae. abt. 20, refusing to
choose a guardian, the Court appointed Nathaniel Whitehead,
5 Mar. 1744/5.

---

* Hannah, dau. of Rebecca Blackman, bapt. at Milford, 2 Feb. 1706/7.

Children, four bapt. at Fairfield:

Dorothy, m. William Williams, of Cortlandt, Westchester County, N. Y., with whom she conveyed 1744 to Ephraim Jackson land in Fairfield (west parish) from father John Blackman dec'd.

×John, b. [say 1705], bapt. 10 Aug. 1707, d. abt. 1737; adm'n granted to Ann, 2 Aug. 1737; m. Ann Jackson, dau. of Joseph, bapt. 2 July 1710, d. at Oxford, 17 July 1777 ae. 68; she m. (2) Samuel Chatfield of Redding and Oxford.

Martha, b. Oct. 1708 [error for 1707], bapt. 9 Nov. 1707; m. June 1730, Ephraim Jackson.

Gershom, bapt. 1 Jan. 1709/10.

Rebecca, bapt. 11 May 1712; m. 25 Jan. 1735, William Jacocks.

Mary.

Adam.

Sarah.

Jemima, possibly m. Nathaniel Whitehead, Jr.

Abigail; an Abigail Blackman d. at Westport, 26 Aug. 1772.

×Peter, b. abt. 1725, d. before 4 Apr. 1780, when Est. was distributed; m. 18 Oct. 1746, Abigail Beers, who d. in 1792; will 3 Nov. 1792, proved 22 Dec. 1792.

Blackman (UNPLACED).   SARAH m. at Stratford, 6 Sept. 1720, Jeremiah Greenman.

Bloomer, Robert.

He witnessed receipt given at Fairfield by John Westcott, 1666. Philip Galpin of Rye conveyed, 20 Feb. 1672, to Robert Bloomer of Rye, and the latter on 3 Mar. 1672/3 to Simon Roberts of Boston.

He sold, 14 Apr. 1682, to Mr. Jehu Burr, land laid out to Stephen Sherwood. On 12 Jan. 1684 [1684/5], John Banks conveyed to his son Obadiah land brought from Robert Blumer.

Booth, Richard.

The Booth chart compiled by George Munson Booth of Chicago, Ill., states that Richard was bapt. at Great Budworth, co. Cheshire, Eng., Aug. 1608, a son of Edward (d. 1628), who was a son of William of Twemlow, co. Cheshire (by his wife Ellen, dau. of John Davenport of Davenport), who was a son of Edward of Twenlow, who was a son of Sir William Booth of Dunham Massie, co. Cheshire (d. 1519). The earlier generations of this pedigree are authentic, but I know not the authority for the connection of this line with Richard of Stratford.

He was one of the founders of Stratford, and in Mar. 1687/8 gave his age in an affidavit as abt. 81. From the terms of the will of his son Ephraim, it is likely that his wife Elizabeth was sister of Mr. Joseph Hawley.

No probate found.

Children, recorded at Stratford:

> Elizabeth, b. 10 Sept. 1641, d. at Woodbury, 24 Oct. 1732; m. 19 Oct. 1658, John Minor.
> Anna, b. 14 Feb. 1643 [1643/4].
> +Ephraim, b. 1 Aug. 1648.
> +Ebenezer, b. 18 or 19 Nov. 1651.
> +John, b. 5 Nov. 1653.
> +Joseph, b. 8 Mar. 1656.
> Bethia, b. 18 Aug. 1658; m. 9 Nov. 1676, Joseph Curtis.
> Johanna, b. 21 Mar. 1661.

Booth, Ephraim, s. of Richard.

Born at Stratford, 1 Aug. 1648, d. there in 1683.

Will 26 Feb. 1682 [1682/3]; daus. Mary, Johanna, Bethia, under 18; son Richard; wife Mary; uncle Mr. Joseph Hawley, brothers Ebenezer Booth, John Booth, and Joseph Curtis, and cousin Samuel Hawley, overseers. Inv. 9 Mar. 1682/3.

Married at New Haven, 9 June 1675, Mary Osborn. She was dau. of Jeremiah, b. 29 Mar. 1653 (First Church, New Haven); m. (2) Lt. James Bennett, and d. 28 Nov. 1726 in 73 yr. (g. s., Stratfield).

Children, recorded at Stratford:

> Mary, b. 12 Nov. 1676, d. at Newtown, Sept. 1741; m. 12 Apr. 1692, Thomas Bennett.
> Johanna, b. Sept. 1678, d. at Stratfield, 28 Jan. 1761 in 84 yr. (g. s.); m. (1) John Sherwood; m. (2) Oct. 1721 [error for 1701], Thomas Hawley. In 1698 Johannah Sherwood, widow of John of Fairfield, conveyed to brother Thomas Bennett of Stratford, land from father Ephraim Booth, dec'd. In 1712 Thomas and Johannah Hawley conveyed one-third of land from father Ephraim Booth, excepting dower of widow Mary Benit, widow of Ephraim Booth.
> Bethia, b. (by age at death) 1680, d. 7 Sept. 1780; m. 14 May 1702, Samuel Hawley, Jr. Shortly before her marriage, 1702, she conveyed to Thomas Bennett right from her father Ephraim Booth.
> Richard.

Booth, Ebenezer, s. of Richard.

Born at Stratford, 18 or 19 Nov. 1651; d. there in 1732.
Will of Ebenezer of Stratford, husbandman, 2 Nov. 1732; daus.
Deborah, Elizabeth, Abigail; son Ebenezer dec'd, mentioning his
eldest son Nathaniel; sons Benjamin, Edward.
Married (1) Hannah ———.
Married (2) Elizabeth Jones, dau. of Richard of Haddam.
She d. June 1709 [Conn. Archives]. After her father's death, her
mother (née Elizabeth Carpenter) with her second husband John
Chappel conveyed land that had belonged to Richard Jones. That
was in 1674, and in 1747 the Jones heirs brought suit, questioning
the legality of the sale. All the heirs were specified, and much
Booth data are found in these papers [Private Controversies, Conn.
Archives].

Children [by first wife], recorded at Stratford (Abiah's mother
called Hannah):

> Abiah, b. 19 Oct. 1674, d. in 1741; m. Lt. Joseph Beach.
> Richard, b. 9 May 1679.

Children [by second wife]:

> ✕Ebenezer, d. 11 Feb. 1726 [1726/7] [Conn. Archives]; Inv. 29 June
> 1727; adm'n on Est. of Ebenezer of Newtown granted, 3 Oct. 1727,
> to widow Mary; m. 8 Sept. 1709, Mary Clark; dau. of James, b.
> 10 Jan. 1686/7.
> Deborah, m. (1) 31 May 1709, John Prindle, of Derby; m. after
> 1712, Walter Harris, of Lebanon.
> Martha, d. in 1727 [Conn. Archives]; m. 26 Jan. 1715/6, James Booth.
> Edward, d. at Stratford, in 1761; Inv. 29 Oct. 1761.
> Elizabeth, m. 21 Jan. 1722 [1722/3], Caleb Beardsley.
> Abigail, m. 21 Jan. 1724/5, David Lake.
> Benjamin.

Booth, John, s. of Richard. Sergt., Stratford Train Band;
Deputy for Stratford, Oct. 1696.

Born at Stratford, 5 Nov. 1653.
Married (1) (Stratford rec.) 14 June 1678, Dorothy Hawley,
who d. 29 May 1710.
Sergt. John m. (2) 31 Jan. 1714/5, widow Hannah Clark. She

was widow of James Clark, previously of Patrick Falconer, and dau. of Gov. William Jones.   Mrs. Hannah Booth, wife of Sergt. John, d. 29 May 1717.

Children [by first wife], first recorded at Stratford:

> Thomas, b. 13 Mar. 1679 [1679/80], d. at Stratford in 1740; Inv. exhibited 7 Oct. 1740; m. (1) 22 Jan. 1700 [1700/1], Elizabeth Judson, who d. 29 July 1702; m. (2) 11 Apr. 1705, Elizabeth Coney.
>
> Jonathan, rem. to Newtown; m. (rec. Stratford) 11 Aug. 1703 (by Mr. Purdy, J. P. at Rye) Hester Galpin.
>
> Ann, b. abt. 1688, d. at Stratford, 23 Sept. 1774 in 86 yr. (g. s.); m. 22 May 1707, Ambrose Thompson.
>
> Ephraim, d. at Stratford, 27 Nov. 1733; Sergt.; adm'n granted to Sarah and Andrew Booth, 1 Jan. 1733/4; m. (1) 24 Jan. 1710/1, Rachel Nichols; m. (2) by 1728, Sarah ———.
>
> ? Mary, b. abt. 1692, d. at Stratford, 2 Nov. 1740 in 49 yr. (g. s.); m. (1) 20 Sept. 1710, Agur Fairchild; m. (2) 12 Mar. 1712/3, Benjamin Brooks.
>
> John, m. (rec. Stratford) 9 Jan. 1717/8, Elizabeth Mallory of New Haven.
>
> ? Sarah, m. Izrahiah Wetmore.

Booth, Joseph, s. of Richard.

Born at Stratford, 8 Mar. 1656, d. there 31 Aug. 1703.

He m. (1) Hannah Wilcoxson, dau. of John, b. 14 Feb. 1664/5, d. 10 July 1701 ae. 38 (g. s.); m. (2) Elizabeth ———.

Will 14 Aug. 1703, proved 3 Jan. 1703/4; deeds of gift to sons mentioned; wife Elizabeth; dau. Hannah (under 18); sons James, Joseph, Robert, David, Nathan; balance to six sons and daus.; friend Sergt. John Hawley, Exec'r.

Children:

> James, b. abt. 1687, d. at Stratford, 20 Aug. 1765 ae. 78 (g. s.); will 11 Aug. 1765, proved 28 Aug 1765; m. (1) 26 Jan. 1715/6, Martha Booth; dau. of Ebenezer, d. in 1727 [Conn. Archives]; m. (2) Martha, widow of Samuel Peck, and dau. of Ens. George Clark; bapt. 26 May 1695, d. 3 Dec. 1747 in 52 yr. (g. s.); m. (3) Sarah ———.
>
> Joseph, b. abt. 1689, d. 2 May 1763 in 75 yr. (g. s., Stratfield); Deacon; Inv. 11 June 1763; m. (1) by 1711, Mehitabel Beach, b. 30 Sept. 1690; m. (2) Rebecca Morehouse, b. 26 Apr. 1693; m. (3) 2 Nov. 1737, Sarah Blackman, who d. Apr. 1784 in 76 yr. (g. s., Stratfield).

Robert, m. 27 Nov. 1712, Ann Hollister.

Hannah, b. (no record), d. in 1767; m. (rec. Fairfield) 2 May 1723, Nathaniel Silliman.

David, b. abt. 1700, d. at Trumbull, 21 June 1773 in 74 yr. (g. s.) ; will 10 Nov. 1747, proved 7 Sept. 1773; m. 7 June 1727, Ann Mills of Windsor, who d. 19 Nov. 1793 in 91 yr. (g. s.).

Nathan, d. at Stratford, 17 Aug. 1714; adm'n granted, 6 Sept. 1714, to James and Joseph Booth.

Zechariah, d. at Stratford in 1762; will 17 Apr. 1760, codicil 15 Mar. 1762, proved Sept. 1762; m. (1) 12 June 1718, Anna Curtis; m. (2) abt. 1734, Sarah ———. He received deeds from bro. David of Stratford and bro. Joseph of Stratfield in 1721/2.

Bostwick, Arthur.

Settled in Stratford before 1650.

He m. (2) Ellen, quite likely the childless widow of a bro. of Henry Tomlinson, and she appears to have come over with her first husband bringing a young relative Elizabeth Bourn, who m. (1) Mr. John Welles and (2) John Wilcoxson.

Agreement with wife. Ellen, 9 Feb. 1674 [1674/5] ; signed also by John Bostwick, and mention made of "sd Arthurs other children"; witnessed by Henry Tomlinson and John Minor. Ellen's estate was appraised 28 Jan. 1674 [1674/5] by William Curtis, Henry Tomlinson, and John Minor; included "yᵉ halfe of yᵉ girle" £6, and "yᵉ other halfe of yᵉ girle by agreement between Arthur Bostick and Ellene," £6; recorded at Stratford, 21 May 1677.

She d. in 1677/8 before Arthur, and claim to part of her estate was made (and allowed) by Mrs. Elizabeth Wilcockson, sometime Elizabeth Bourne, next of kin with her children to the dec'd, Elizabeth having been brought by the dec'd and "Mr. Tomlin" from her natural friends. The residue was ordered divided between: children of Hannah Porter for care of her; her husband "After Bostock"; John Bostwick and his wife and the wife of her son Johnson of New Jersey; and Temperance and Sarah Welles, daus. of said Elizabeth by her first husband.

John Bostwick on 4 Feb. 1677/8 recorded land he had by gift from his father Arthur Bostwick and by exchange with his mother Ellen Bostwick, also by purchase from Mr. John Welles.

In New Haven records, Apr. 1663, Thomas Johnson claimed a debt on behalf of "his father in law Bausticke of Stratford."

Children [by first wife]:

> Ellen, m. by 1651, Thomas Johnson of New Haven, who rem. 1666 to Newark, N. J., where he d. 5 Nov. 1695 ae. 64.
> +John.
> Perhaps other daus. not known.

Bostwick, John, s. of Arthur.

Married Mary Brinsmade, dau. of John, b. 24 July 1640. She m. (2) William Read of Fairfield, and d. at Stratford in 1704.

Inv. of John of Stratford, 5 Nov. 1689. Widow Mary, and children.

Inv. of Est. of Mary Reed of Stratford, 28 Dec. 1704; adm'n granted to her son Zachariah Bostwick.

Children, recorded at Stratford:

> +John, b. 4 May 1667.
> +Zachariah, b. 24 July 1669.
> +Joseph, b. 11 May 1672.
> Mary, b. 14 Feb. 1674 [1674/5].
> Elizabeth, b. 1 Oct. 1677.
> Jane, b. 13 Apr. 1680; m. (rec. Woodbury) 13 Nov. 1705, John Nichols.
> Benjamin, b. abt. 1684, d. 15 May 1739 ae. abt. 55 (g. s., New Milford); m. (rec. New Milford) 2 May 1711, Zerviah Johnson of Woodbury.

Bostwick, John, s. of John.

Born at Stratford, 4 May 1667.

Married Abigail Walker, b. 18 Feb. 1671/2, dau. of Joseph.

Stratford Deeds call him of Derby, 1705. In 1708 he settled in New Milford.

Children by Abigail, first recorded at Stratford, last at New Milford:

> John, b. 12 Oct. 1688; Deacon John d. at New Milford, 12 June 1741; Major John d. 15 June 1741 in 53 yr. (g. s.); m. (rec. New Milford) 30 Jan. 1711/2, Mercy Bushnell of Danbury; she m. (2) 14 Oct. 1742, William Gaylord, and (3) Capt. James Lockwood. Mrs. Mercy Lockwood, formerly wife of Major John Bostwick, d. at New Milford, 5 Sept. 1767.
> Robert, m. (rec. New Milford) 9 Jan. 1720/1, Rachel Holmes of Bedford.
> Ebenezer, m. 11 Apr. 1717, Rebecca Bunnell.

Joseph, d. 27 Sept. 1796; Capt.; m. (rec. New Milford) 23 July 1724, Rebecca Wheeler of Stratfield.

Nathaniel; Capt.; m. (1) 7 Oct. 1727, Esther Hitchcock, who d. 13 Dec. 1747; m. (2) Jerusha (Beecher) Baldwin, widow of Capt. Theophilus Baldwin.

Lemuel, b. abt. 1704, d. at New Milford, 8 Apr. 1791 in 87 yr.; m. (rec. New Milford) 5 Nov. 1729, Anna Jackson of Stratfield.

Sarah, m. 5 Nov. 1724, William Warriner.

Daniel, b. abt. 1708, d. 23 Dec. 1782 ae. 74; m. 14 Dec. 1736, Hannah Hitchcock.

Hannah, m. 18 Jan. 1731/2, Benjamin Benedict of Ridgefield.

Mary, b. 8 Feb. 1714/5; m. 26 July 1733, Zerubbabel Canfield.

Bostwick, Joseph, s. of John.

Born at Stratford, 11 May 1672; d. at New Milford, in 1726. Married (rec. Stratford) 14 June 1698, Ann Buss.

Abraham Bostwick of New Milford informed, 8 Apr. 1726, that his father Joseph Bostwick of New Milford is dec'd; adm'n granted to his [Abraham's] mother Ann with Abraham her eldest son. On 6 Mar. 1726/7, the heirs are named as Widow Ann; Abraham Bostwick, only surviving son; Hannah; Rebecca wife of Benjamin Fippeny; Elisabeth; Eunice; Abigail wife of Jonathan Hurd (she had rec'd full portion).

Children, first three born at Stratford:

Abigail, b. 24 Sept. 1700; m. (rec. Stratford) 28 Jan. 1719/20, Jonathan Hurd.

Abraham, b. 5 Sept. 1702; m. (1) at New Milford, 14 Sept. 1732, Hannah Collins, dau. of Daniel of Milford; she d. 18 Dec. 1742, and he m. (2) Hannah (Tid) Lum.

Hannah, b. 3 Jan. 1704/5.

Rebecca, bapt. at Stratfield, 21 Aug. 1709; m. (rec. Stratford, she called of New Milford) 30 Jan. 1726/7, Benjamin Phippen.

Elizabeth, m. (rec. Stratford) 22 Mar. 1731, Samuel Benjamin.

Eunice, m. at Trumbull, 1 Jan. 1735/6, John Middlebrook.

Bostwick, Zechariah, s. of John.

Born at Stratford, 24 July 1669, d. there Aug. 1734. Married (1) Elizabeth ———.

Married (2) Kezia Talmadge, dau. of Thomas, b. at New Haven, 27 Apr. 1688; living 1737.

Will 6 Aug. 1734, proved 21 Aug. 1734; wife "Coziah"; sons David, Jonathan, Zachariah, Ephraim, Mariday; have given portions to all my daus. Mary, Martha, Parnal, Susanna, and Elizabeth.

Children [by first wife]:

> Mary, b. 19 Feb. 1691/2; m. ———— Fadden.
> ✕David, b. 26 Oct. 1693, d. in 1758; will 8 Oct. 1752, proved 8 July 1758; m. (1) 26 Feb. 1719/20, Sarah Nichols; m. (2) 3 Sept. 1726, Elizabeth MacKenzie of Fairfield.
> Martha, b. 28 Nov. 1695; m. (1) 12 Jan. 1715/6, Ebenezer Sherman; m. (2) Sept. 1728, Isaac Clark.
> Jonathan, b. 1 Apr. 1697, d. in 1738, unm. Will 17 June 1738, proved 17 Aug. 1738; two brethren, Zachariah and Ephraim; bro. Meredith; sisters Susanna Hurd, Parnel Brown; Abigail Sherman, dau. of sister Martha Clark; bro. Meredith to pay £5 to Zachariah Fadden, son of our sister Mary dec'd.
> Susanna, b. 22 Nov. 1700; m. David Hurd.
> Parnell, b. 15 Apr. 1702; m. 22 July 1727, Joseph Brown.
> Elizabeth, b. 12 May 1704, bapt. 23 July 1704 (at Stratford, rec. Stratfield); m. 8 Sept. 1726, Isaac Curtis.
> Zachariah.
> Ephraim.
> Meredith, m. Hannah Hanford, dau. of Capt. Elnathan of Norwalk; she m. (2) at Greenwich, 15 Feb. 1764, John Perott or Parrott, s. of James of St. Martin's in the Fields, London, Eng.

Bouton, John.

Married Alice ————, b. abt. 1610; she m. (2) abt. 1647, Matthew Marvin, and d. abt. Dec. 1680.

Children:

> +John.
> +Richard.
> Bridget, m. at Norwalk, in 1655, Daniel Kellogg.

Bouton, John, s. of John. Deputy (Norwalk) to Conn. Leg., Oct. 1669, Oct. 1671, Oct. 1673, May 1674, May 1675, Oct. 1676, May and Oct. 1677, May 1678, Oct. 1679, May 1680, May 1681, May and Oct. 1682, May 1683, May and Oct. 1685. Sergt., Norwalk Trainband.

Married (1) at Norwalk, 1 Jan. 1656 [1656/7], Abigail Marvin, dau. of Matthew.

Married (2) after 1689, Mary, widow of Jonathan Stevenson, and previously of Thomas Allen.

Will of John, Sr., 25 Dec. 1706, proved 27 Jan. 1706 [1706/7];
wife Mary; grandchild John Bowton of Danbury; sons Mathew
and Joseph Bowton; dau. Rachel Sension; son Thomas Bowton;
dau. Elizabeth Warrin; son Richard Bowton; dau. Mary Bowton;
three sons Joseph, Thomas and Richard. Matthew Sension,
"Edman Waren", and James Betts, sons-in-law to the dec'd,
appealed.

On 16 July 1720, Mary Bouton of Norwalk distributed property
to son Thomas Bouton, dau. Mary Morehouse, to "Thomas and
Richard", geese to Thomas Bouton, he to give one gander and two
geese to John Betts' wife; my three gr. children Thomas Bouton,
Richard Bouton and Mary Morehouse land at "Compow in Fairfield"; my gr. children Mary Hayes, Ruth Bouton, and Gabriel
Morehouse.

Children [by first wife], recorded at Norwalk:

+John, b. 30 Sept. 1659.
Matthew, b. 24 Dec. 1661.
Hannah, m. James Betts.
+Joseph.
Rachel, b. 15 Dec. 1667; m. abt. 1690, Matthew St. John.
Abigail, b. 1 Apr. 1670, d. y.
Mary, b. 26 May 1671, d. y.
Elizabeth, m. 6 Oct. 1698, Edmund Waring.

Children [by second wife]:

Thomas, d. s. p.
Richard, m. Mercy Platt, dau. of John, 2d.
Mary, m. Lemuel Morehouse.

Bouton, Richard, s. of John.

Settled in Fairfield, where he d. in 1665.

Married Ruth Turney, dau. of Benjamin, b. at Concord, 28 Jan.
1643/4, d. at Fairfield in 1666.

Inv. 21 June 1665, presented by Widow. Joseph Middlebrook
and wife testified that Richard the day he died gave his Est. to
Ruth his wife, excepting tools. Court decrees if Ruth be with
child, the child to have its share; if no issue, then John son of
John Bouton to have the tools.

Inv. of Ruth Bouton, 7 Nov. 1666. Matthew Marvin, Sr.,
Robert Turney, and John Bouton, relations to Ruth the dau. of
Richard and Ruth Bouton, consent that the child be placed with

Marvin until 18; if he dies, then with John Bouton, the child's uncle; and if he dies, then with Robert Turney; if the child dies, then the land to go to Benjamin Turney of Fairfield, and £7-14-6 to Thomas Morehouse of Fairfield, and the rest divided among the nearest relations.

Child:

> Ruth, b. late in 1665; m. (rec. Stratford) Dec. 1698, Moses Wheeler. Ruth Bouton had land in Fairfield recorded 14 Feb. 1692 (in right of her mother), possessed by her and her parents for thirty years last past.

Bouton, John, s. of John, 2d.

Born at Norwalk, 30 Sept. 1659.

Prob. m. Mary Hayes, dau. of Nathaniel.

On 8 Mar. 1699, John Bouton, Jr., of Danbury, receipted to father-in-law Nathaniel Hayes of Norwalk for part of that pasture lot "where I Builded a House in Norwalk." In a deed recorded 7 Apr. 1704, John, Jr., and Matthew Bouton, now of Danbury, conveyed to Richard Holmes a right in Norwalk deeded to them by father Bouton.

Inv. "2d day 1704/5" at Danbury of Est. of John Bouton who died "the Next day after the date above writed." Children: John, married; Sarah Bouton, of age; Abigail 16; Mary 12; Nathaniel 10; Eleazer, abt. 3½. The son John made oath to Inv. 14 Mar. 1704/5, and gave bond as adm'r with Matthew Bouton of Danbury. The son Nathaniel was placed as ward with Matthias St. John of Norwalk, Nov. 1706, and Mary Bouton chose James Hayes as her guardian.

Children:

> John, b. [say 1684]; res. Stamford; m. by 1704 [perhaps Mercy Hickock, b. abt. 1688].
> Sarah, b. [say 1686].
> Abigail, b. abt. 1688.
> Mary, b. abt. 1692.
> Nathaniel, b. abt. 1694; res. Stamford; m. abt. 1720, Hannah Betts, dau. of John of Norwalk.
> Eleazer, b. 1701; res. Stamford; m. (1) abt. 1722, Elizabeth Seymour, dau. of Capt. Matthew; m. (2) Mary (Pettit) Bouton.*

---

* According to the Seymour Genealogy in *New Eng. Hist. and Gen. Register,* 1918; which calls her widow of Eleazer's bro. John. Further research is needed here; John Bouton did not m. Mary Pettit until 18 Feb. 1731/2.

Bouton, Joseph, s. of John.

Born [say 1665], d. at Norwalk in 1747.

Married Mary Gregory, dau. of Jachin.

Will of Joseph, Sr., 20 Dec. 1746, proved 23 Feb. 1746/7; wife Mary; daus. Sarah Hanford and Dinah Benedict; son-in-law Dea. John Benedict, "in consideration of his taking ye whole cair & charge of my beloved brother Thomas Boutten boath in sickness & in health to ye end of my s^d brother's day"; gr. son Joseph Bouton; sons Jachin and John.

Bradley, Francis.

He was apprenticed to Gov. Theophilus Eaton, of New Haven, his time expiring before 1650; rem. to Branford, where he was living in 1657; and by 1660 had settled in Fairfield. He bought from Stephen Sherwood, 1674/5.

He had a bro. John Bradley who lived in Red Lyon Street near the Cross Keys in Holborn, London, Eng. A letter from this brother, dated 24 Jan. 1695 [1695/6] and stating that he was then in his 74th year, was sent to Francis through Mr. Wilson of New York, and a copy made on Fairfield records. The suggestion that they derived from the Coventry Bradleys seems not unlikely.

Married Ruth Barlow, dau. of John, Sr.

Will 22 Jan. 1688 [1688/9]; wife Ruth; sons John, Francis, Daniel, Joseph; daus. Ruth wife of Thomas Williams, and Abigail Bradley. Inv. 22 Oct. 1689.

Children:

+John.
+Francis.
  Ruth, m. Thomas Williams.
+Daniel.
+Joseph.
  Abigail.
  Mary, b. at Fairfield, 5 Dec. 1677.

Bradley, John, s. of Francis.

Married Hannah Sherwood, dau. of Thomas; she m. (2) Cornelius Jones.

Inv. 14 Apr. 1703. Widow Hannah Bradley and Francis

Bradley, Adm'rs. 4 Apr. 1707, two sons and four daughters. Abigail chose mother Hannah Jones guardian; father-in-law Cornelius Jones appointed guardian for John, Elizabeth, Ruth, and Joseph. Receipts 7 Mar. 1716/7 from Elizabeth and John, and 24 Apr. 1717 from Abigail, to father-in-law Cornelius Jones of Stamford, for their portions, also from Samuel Bradley in behalf of Abigail and Ruth. Joseph and Hannah chose their brother John guardian, 24 Apr. 1717, and Ruth chose Samuel Bradley.

John renewed his Covenant at Fairfield Church, 21 Sept. 1701, and the four elder children were bapt. the same day.

Children, bapt. at Fairfield:

John, b. abt. 1693, d. at Greenfield, 5 Dec. 1773 ae. over 80; m. Martha Darling, dau. of John. At Greenfield Church he was entered among the members (as bapt. 21 Sept. 1701), with Martha his wife, and no children.

Abigail, b. abt. 1695, d. at Kent, 22 Apr. 1772; m. at Stratfield Church, 17 Oct. 1717, Ephraim Hubbell.

Elizabeth, b. abt. 1697; m. (rec. Stamford) 16 Jan. 1717/8, Charles Holly.

Ruth, b. abt. 1699.

XJoseph, bapt. 14 June 1702, d. at Fairfield in 1770; will 7 Feb. 1770, proved 5 Mar. 1770; m. (rec. Fairfield) 20 June 1724, Olive Hubbell, dau. of Samuel, bapt. 15 Feb. 1707/8.

Hannah, bapt. 19 Sept. 1703.

Bradley, Francis, s. of Francis.

Married Sarah Jackson, dau. of Joseph; she m. (2) John Bartram.

Sarah wife of Francis renewed her Covenant of Fairfield Church, 3 Dec. 1699.

Inv. 4 Dec. 1716; widow Sarah, six sons, one dau. Francis chose John Sturgis guardian; Samuel chose Mr. Gershom Bulkley. On 13 Dec. 1717, Ephraim chose Nathan Adams, Jr., for guardian, and the Court appointed Thomas Turney for Gershom and Peter, Nathan Adams for Hellinah, and Luke Guire for John.

The will of Sarah Bartram, 9 Mar. 1753, proved 16 Apr. 1753; dau. Sarah Rumsey; dau. Ellen Sherwood; heirs of son Ephraim dec'd; sons Francis, Samuel, John, Peter, Gershom. [The dau. Sarah Rumsey was by her second husband.]

Children, bapt. at Fairfield:

×Francis, b. 29 May 1699 (rec. Greenfield), bapt. 3 Dec. 1699, d. at Greenfield in 1786; will 23 Feb. 1786, proved 3 Apr. 1786; m. at Fairfield, 29 Apr. 1719, Mary Sturgis, dau. of John, b. 8 Aug. 1699.

×Samuel, b. 29 Sept. 1701 (rec. Greenfield), bapt. 26 Oct. 1701, d. 12 Oct. 1772 ae. 71 (g. s., Greenfield); m. at Fairfield, Nov. 1724, Sarah Whelpley, b. 17 Jan. 1707, d. 12 Sept. 1777 (g. s., Greenfield).

×Ephraim, bapt. 19 Sept. 1703, d. at Westport, 5 Oct. 1748; ae. 45 (g. s.); m. Sarah Scribner, who m. (2) Mar. 1749, Daniel Bradley.

×John, b. Nov. 1705, bapt. 30 Dec. 1705, d. Oct. 1776; Lt.; m. (1) 13 Jan. 1725/6, Sarah Gilbert, b. 12 Feb. 1705/6 (rec. Greenfield), d. 14 Apr. 1766 ae. 61; m. (2) 11 Oct. 1768, Widow Mary Silliman [widow of Robert Silliman and formerly of Abijah Morehouse; prob. dau. of Henry Summers, Jr.], b. abt. 1718, d. 18 May 1776 in 58 yr.

Eleanor, bapt. 22 Feb. 1707/8, d. at Greenfield, 29 Mar. 1793 ae. 85 (g. s.); m. at Fairfield, 9 Feb. 1723, Benjamin Sherwood.

×Peter, bapt. 17 Dec. 1710, d. at Greenfield, 2 Aug. 1768; will 4 June 1760, proved 1 Nov. 1768; m. (1) (rec. Greenfield) 5 Nov. 1735, Damaris Dimon, b. Sept. 1714, m. (2) Oct. 1756, Sarah Price, widow of Lemuel Price, and dau. of Joseph Middlebrook, bapt. 8 Feb. 1712/3.

×Gershom, bapt. 7 Dec. 1712, d. 15 Jan. 1795 in 83 yr. (g. s., Easton); will proved 5 Feb. 1795; m. (1) Sarah Sherwood, dau. of Benjamin, bapt. 12 Aug. 1711; m. (2) Elizabeth Osborn, bapt. 28 June 1719; m. (3) Jane Dimon, dau. of Moses, bapt. 17 Oct. 1722, d. 3 Feb. 1755 ae. 32 yrs. 5 mos. 12 days (g. s., Greenfield); m. (4) Deborah Burr, dau. of Ebenezer, bapt. 27 Apr. 1735, d. 3 Sept. 1832 in 99 yr. (g. s., Easton).

Bradley, Daniel, s. of Francis.

Married Abigail Jackson, dau. of Joseph. She renewed her Covenant at Fairfield Church, 16 Jan. 1698/9.

Inv. 1 July 1713; widow Abigail, two sons, four daus. Sergt. John Odell and Francis Bradley, Adm'rs 1 Dec. 1714; Odell later released, and Daniel Burr, Sr., appointed. On 3 Mar. 1713/4, Francis Bradley appointed guardian to Daniel, Mary, and Eunice; Joseph Jackson, guardian to Abigail, Martha, and James. Martha chose Sergt. John Odell guardian, 5 Jan. 1714 [1714/5]. Abigail chose uncle Francis Bradley guardian, 6 Apr. 1715. On 22 Nov. 1716, Francis Bradley being deceased, Samuel Bradley was appointed guardian to James, and Sergt. John Odell to Abigail, Eunice and Mary.

Children, bapt. at Fairfield:

Daniel, bapt. 15 Jan. 1698/9, d. y.

Mary, bapt. 9 Mar. 1700/1, d. y.

Martha, bapt. 4 Oct. 1702; m. Ebenezer Hull.

XDaniel, bapt. 11 June 1704, d. at Ridgefield, 23 Apr. 1765; Capt.; m. (1) (rec. Fairfield) June 1724, Esther Burr, bapt. 31 Jan. 1702/3, d. 29 Dec. 1741; m. (2) (rec. Fairfield) Mar. 1743, Mary Fitch, who d. 21 Dec. 1746; m. (3) Mar. 1749, Sarah Bradley, widow of Ephraim, and dau. of Thomas Scribner.

Abigail, bapt. 19 May 1706; m. at Fairfield, 3 Mar. 1725, Solomon Sturgis.

Eunice, bapt. 30 May 1708; m. at Fairfield, 2 Aug. 1731, Samuel Barlow.

Mary, bapt. 14 May 1710; m. (by 1729) Daniel Dean of Danbury.

XJames, bapt. 11 May 1712, d. at Ridgefield, in 1784; m. at Redding, 4 Dec. 1735, Abigail Sanford.

Bradley, Joseph, s. of Francis.

He renewed his Covenant at Fairfield Church, 3 Feb. 1705/6.

Inv. 1 Nov. 1714; widow Ellen, three sons, two daus. Samuel Bradley appointed guardian for Sarah, Mary, and David; and the widow for Joseph and Nathan.

Children, bapt. at Fairfield:

Sarah, bapt. 3 Feb. 1705/6; m. Joseph Barlow.

Deborah, bapt. 3 Feb. 1705/6, d. y.

Mary, bapt. 12 May 1706; m. James Redfield.

XDavid, bapt. 2 May 1708; m. at Fairfield, 25 Apr. 1731, Damaris Davis, bapt. 5 Sept. 1714.

XJoseph, bapt. 8 Apr. 1711, d. 26 June 1776 in 76(?) yr. (g. s., Greenfield); m. (1) at Fairfield, 9 Nov. 1732, Jerusha Turney, dau. of Robert, who d. 16 Jan. 1746/7; in 34 yr. (g. s.); m. (2) 11 Apr. 1747, Mary Squire, dau. of Lt. Samuel, who d. 24 May 1776 in 61 yr. (g. s., Greenfield).

Nathan, bapt. 18 Oct. 1713.

Bradley, Samuel.

Settled in Fairfield, and m. Phebe Sherwood, dau. of Thomas. He and his wife were bapt. at Fairfield Church, 25 May 1712, and had children bapt. there: Deborah and Ann, 25 May 1712; Samuel, 15 Nov. 1713; Benjamin, 11 Mar. 1715/6; Phebe, 16 Mar. 1717/8.

Brewster, Francis.

A merchant, came to New Haven by 1641, when his household consisted of nine persons. He was prob. a large owner of the ill-fated "Great Ship" (under Capt. Lamberton) in which he was lost in 1646. He was a man of large estate, and dignified with the prefix of respect ("Mr."). His wife Lucy, tried and fined in 1646 for offensive remarks, referred to her Pastor in England and a neighbor Mrs. Bennett cast out of the church there; she had evidently lived in Mass. Bay before coming to New Haven. Edward Parker said Mrs. Brewster "had a notable pate." Bamfield Bell was called a kinsman of Mr. Brewster.

Late in 1647 Mrs. Brewster m. (2) Dr. Thomas Pell, and by 1650 they rem. with the younger Brewster children to Fairfield. A son, Joseph, was mentioned in New Haven in 1645, then a youth in his late 'teens. In 1654, Mrs. Pell and her daus. Elizabeth and Mary were witnesses in that *cause célèbre,* the Staples suit against Mr. Ludlow, the girls being then apparently not much if at all over twenty.

The ancestry of Mr. Brewster in England has been located, but we are not at liberty to print it. Presumably Joseph, Elizabeth, and Mary, were the youngest surviving children. From the will of Dr. Pell, their stepfather, we deduce that one daughter m. a French and had a son Nathaniel, and that another m. a White and had children Elizabeth, Mary, and Nathaniel. This Nathaniel White was prob. he who lived 1684 in Eastchester, N. Y., and d. there Oct. 1690, leaving children William and Sarah. It is not certain that all the older children came to this country or remained here; and the Sir Francis Brewster, merchant of Dublin, who had a ship wrecked near New London about 1671, may have been a connection.

We have no hesitancy in affirming that Rev. Nathaniel Brewster of Brookhaven was an older son of Francis. (1) Students of the Elder William Brewster family have found no evidence for placing him there. (2) Francis was a man of means and social standing, who could have educated a son at college. (3) In 1649, Nathaniel appears in Walderswich, co. Suffolk, Eng., as attorney for Thomas Pell. (4) In 1665, when the church at New London voted to give Mr. Brewster "a call", Mr. Pell was asked to use his influence. (5) Nathaniel's dau. Abigail and her husband Daniel Burr of Fairfield received valuable legacies in the will of Dr. Pell. (6) Nathaniel had a grandson named Francis. (7) Apparently two daus. of Francis named a son Nathaniel, after their brother. Against this array of strong circumstantial evidence, we can set merely the laudable desire of many descendants to claim a Mayflower line; a claim which is not (and should not be) admitted by the Mayflower Society.

NATHANIEL BREWSTER, b. in or before 1618, was graduated from Harvard College 1642, went to England, where from 1643 to 1663 he labored in the ministry, beginning at Neatishead and Irsted; m. (1) abt. 1644, Abigail Reynes, dau. of John of Norfolk; in 1649 was in Walderswich, as mentioned above; was settled at Alby, co. Norfolk, 1651; sent to Ireland by Cromwell, 1655, and is said to have received degree of B.D. from University of Dublin, 1656; was back in Alby by 1662, and the following year returned to America. After preaching for short periods in Boston, and Eastchester, he was settled as pastor in Setauket, Brookhaven, L. I., from 1664 until his death. His will was proved May 1695.*

Doubtless it was in Ireland abt. 1656 that he m. (2) Sarah Ludlow, dau. of Roger.

Children of Rev. Nathaniel [by first wife]:

> John, b. abt. 1645.
> Abigail, b. abt. 1647, d. between 1672 and 1678; m. at Stamford, Feb. 166[8?], Daniel Burr, of Fairfield.

Children of Rev. Nathaniel [by second wife]:

> Sarah, b. abt. 1656; m. Jonathan Smith.
> Timothy, b. abt. 1658; m. Mary Hawkins.
> Daniel, bapt. at Alby, 31 Oct. 1662; m. abt. 1693, Anna Jayne, dau. of William.
> Hannah, b. abt. 1669; m. (1) John Muncey; m. (2) Samuel Thompson.

Brinsmade, John. Deputy (Stratford) to Conn. Leg., Oct. 1671, May and Oct. 1672.

He settled in Charlestown, Mass., by 1636, and was made freeman, 2 May 1638; m. Mary Carter, dau. of Thomas. He rem. to Stratford.

---

* Details of his career are largely from the unpublished genealogy compiled by Mrs. May Lillian Sullivan.

Agreement of heirs of John, Sr., of Stratford, 3 Nov. 1673; widow Mary; sons John, Daniel, Paul, Samuel; daus. Mary Bostwick (had part of portion at marriage) and Elizabeth Brinsmade; signed also by John Bostwick [Mary did not sign]. Inv. £519, shows he was a blacksmith; about 60 books; land at Stratford and Derby.

Children, recorded at Charlestown:

> Mary, b. 24 July 1640, d. at Stratford in 1704; m. (1) John Bostwick; m. (2) after 1689, William Read, of Fairfield.
> John, b. 2 Mar. 1642/3.
> +Daniel.
> +Paul.
> Samuel.
> Elizabeth.

Brinsmade, Daniel, s. of John.

Married Sarah Kellogg, dau. of Daniel of Norwalk, b. Feb. 1659/60; she m. (2) John Betts of Norwalk.

Inv. 7 Oct. 1702. Widow Sarah; children and ages: Mary 18, Daniel 15, Abigail 11, Samuel 8, Ruth 2. The son Daniel on 18 Mar. 1708 chose his uncle Abraham Nichols of Stratford for guardian, and Samuel chose his father-in-law John Betts of Norwalk. [Nichols m. sister of Sarah Kellogg.]

Children:

> Mary, b. abt. 1684, d. at Stratford, 26 July 1712; m. at Stratford, 3 May 1708, Samuel Wheeler.
> Daniel, b. abt. 1687, d. at Trumbull, 27 Mar. 1757 in 70 yr. (g. s.); will 8 Mar. 1757, proved 5 Apr. 1757; m. (1) abt. 1715, Mercy ———, who d. 15 Apr. 1731 in 35 yr. (g. s.); m. (2) abt. 1732, Hannah Mix, dau. of Nathaniel of New Haven; she d. without issue, abt. 1763.
> Abigail, b. abt. 1691, d. at Norwalk, 16 Nov. 1766 in 75 yr.; m. (rec. Norwalk) 23 Feb. 1709/10, Moses Comstock.
> Samuel, b. abt. 1694.
> Ruth, b. abt. 1700; m. Stephen Betts, of Norwalk, with whom she conveyed 1731 right from her father.

Brinsmade, Paul, s. of John.

Inv. taken 15 Mar. 1696, included clothes of a deceased child, realty in Stratford and Farmington [the latter came by his wife].

His brother Daniel made oath to Inv. 26 Mar. 1696, two days after adm'n was granted to Ens. James Judson and Benjamin Curtis. Names and ages of children: John 13½, Zachariah 10, Elizabeth 11, Esther 6, Deborah 3½.

Married (rec. Stratford) 30 Oct. 1678, Elizabeth Howkins. She was dau. of Anthony of Farmington, and d. before Paul.

Children, first recorded at Stratford:

Amy, b. 16 Oct. 1679, d. before Mar. 1696.

John, b. 1682, d. at Milford, 19 Jan. 1753 in 71 yr. (g. s.); m. (rec. Derby) 28 July 1703, Abigail Wheeler; dau. of Ephraim, b. 8 Feb. 1683/4.

Elizabeth, b. abt. 1684, d. at Stratford, 6 Jan. 1763 in 79 yr. (g. s.); m. 6 Mar. 1706/7, Daniel Hawley.

Zechariah, b. abt. 1685, d. at Stratford, 22 Nov. 1741; in 56 yr. (g. s.); m. (rec. Stratford) 26 Oct. 1700 [error for 1710],* Sarah Cobbett of Fairfield, who d. 2 June 1737; or 9 June 1736 ae. 48 yrs. 6 mos. (if g. s. reading is correct).

Esther, b. abt. 1689, d. abt. 1785; m. 11 Dec. 1712, William Wilcoxson.

Deborah, b. abt. 1692, d. abt 1758; m. 13 Jan. 1714/5, John Wilcoxson, Jr.

Brooks, John.

Married at Stratford, 25 Mar. 1685, widow Sarah Peat. She was widow of John Peat, Jr., and dau. of Richard Osborn of Fairfield.

Will 11 Mar. 1694 [1694/5]; only son Benjamin; brother-in-law John Osborn of Fairfield, Exec'r; overseers, Dea. Thomas Welles and John Beach of Stratford. Inv. 19 Mar. 1694/5.

Child, recorded at Stratford:

Benjamin, b. 17 Oct. 1685, d. 30 Dec. 1745 in 61 yr. (g. s.); will 17 Dec. 1745, proved 7 Jan. 1746; m. 12 Mar. 1712/3, widow Mary Fairchild, who d. 2 Nov. 1740 in 49 yr. (g. s.). She was widow of Agur Fairchild, née Booth.

Brown, Peter.

A baker, was at New Haven 1639, rem. abt. 1647 to Stamford. Married (1) Elizabeth ———, who d. at Stamford, 21 Sept. 1657; m. (2) 25 July 1658, Unica [widow of Clement] Buxton.

---

* This entry is duplicated, and given correctly.

He d. 22 Aug. 1658. Unica m. (3) 9 Mar. 1658/9, Nicholas Knapp.

Will of Peter of Stamford presented at New Haven Colony Court, dated 19 Aug. 1658, and the Inv. taken 29 Nov. 1658, attested by widow Brown and Thomas Brown.

Thomas Brown conveyed 1683 to bro. Deliverance Brown, both of Rye.

Children [by first wife], two bapt. at New Haven:

> Thomas, b. abt. 1638, aged 22 in 1660 when he testified in behalf of Francis Brown of Stamford; settled in Rye by 1665, and d. abt. 1694.
>
> Hachaliah, b. perhaps 1640, settled in Rye and was propounded for freeman of Conn. Colony, May 1670; d. abt. 1720; m. Mary, prob. dau. of John Hoyt.
>
> Mercy, bapt. 6 Apr. 1645.
>
> Elizabeth, bapt. 1 Aug. 1647; m. John Purdy of Fairfield; she called Thomas and Hackaliah Brown her brothers.
>
> Deliverance, of Rye; Deputy for Rye to Conn. Leg., May 1697; Justice, 1698; m. by 1678, Mary Purdy, dau. of Francis.
>
> Ebenezer, d. at Stamford, 21 Aug. 1658.

Brown, Francis [prob. bro. of Peter]. Deputy (Stamford) to the Conn. Leg., May 1665, May 1667, Oct. 1668, May 1669.

Sometimes confused with the Francis Brown of New Haven who m. Mary Edwards and had a different family.

He was apprentice of Henry Wolcott of Windsor, bought his freedom 1649; m. (1) prob. a relative of Nathaniel Ruscoe; bought and sold at Farmington, 1656. He settled in Stamford, and m. there (2) 17 Dec. 1657, Martha Chapman. She was widow of John Chapman of Stamford, and previously widow of Thomas Lawrence of Milford. He m. (3) Judith, widow of John Ogden of Stamford, and dau. of Lt. John Budd, and rem. with her to Rye, N. Y.

He conveyed 15 Dec. 1684 to son Joseph, who was to make a payment to "my daughter Mary Hallebort." [Stamford Deeds.]

The will of Francis, being ill, 5 Feb. 1685 [1685/6], recorded 6 Nov. 1686; wife Judith, mentioning her former husband, John Ogden; to son Joseph, house and land in Stamford; to child Mercy Brown; sons "Benninonie" Galpin, Thomas "Hollibird", and Jonathan Scudder. [Rye Records.]

Despite the recording of the will, he recovered and signified his intention of renewing its terms from year to year. He gave conveyances as late as 1707.

Child [by first wife] :

> Mary, b. abt. 1655; mentioned by Winthrop as ae. 12 in 1667, dau. of Francis Brown of Stamford, but then living with Nathaniel Ruscoe of Hartford as his adopted dau. Ruscoe called her his kinswoman in his will 1673. She m. Thomas Hurlbut, of Fairfield.

Children [by second wife] :

> +Joseph, b. abt. 1658.
> Rebecca, b. [say 1662], d. at Woodbury, 8 Feb. 1743; m. by 1682, Benjamin Galpin.
> Sarah, m. Jonathan Scudder, of Huntington, L. I. His will, 9 Dec. 1690, proved 22 Oct. 1691, named son Jonathan, two younger daus. Abigail and Rebecca, wife Sarah, dau. Sarah (non compos mentis) ; overseers, Capt. Epenetus Platt and my bro. Eliphalet Jones.
> Mercy.

Brown, Joseph, s. of Francis.

He m. Mary ———, and d. in 1738; Mary, "ancient widow", d. 3 July 1744.

Will of Joseph, Sr., 21 Sept. 1736, proved 28 Apr. 1738; wife; sons Nathaniel, Nathan, Jonathan; gr. children, sons of son Joseph dec'd (Joseph, David, Peter) ; gr. dau. Eunice Brown; son Francis; two daus. Sarah Blackman, Mary Skelding; sons Francis and Nathaniel, Exec'rs.

Children, recorded at Stamford:

> Francis, prob. the son b. 24 Dec. 1686; m. 18 June 1713, Mercy Webb.
> Joseph, prob. the son b. 11 Mar. 1689; d. 3 May 1730; m. (1) 21 Apr. 1720, Elizabeth Buxton, b. 7 June 1696, d. 27 Mar. 1725; m. (2) 2 Jan. 1725/6, Mary Hoyt, who d. 2 Aug. 1728; widow of Benjamin Hoyt; m. (3) 16 Jan. 1728/9, Ruth Scofield. She m. (2) Benjamin Close.
> Hannah, b. 21 Sept. 1692, d. y., unless the name is a misreading of Sarah.
> Sarah,* m. 5 Aug. 1714, Josiah Blackman.
> Nathaniel b. 16 June 1696; m. 20 Apr. 1725, Anna Brush.
> Nathan, b. 29 Oct. 1697; m. Ruth Brush.
> Jonathan, b. 14 May 1701, d. 17 Apr. 1747; will 16 Apr. 1747, proved 7 July 1747; m. 19 Nov. 1730, Mary Slawson.

---

* Sarah, child of Sarah Brown, b. 17 June 1712.

David, b. 22 Mar. 1703/4, d. 31 Aug. 1711.
Mary, b. 5 Oct. 1705; m. 5 Sept. 1726, Thomas Skelding.

Brown, James.

Of Branford 1679, rem. to Norwalk.
He m. Rebecca Ruscoe, dau. of John of Norwalk; prob. widow of Peter Clapham, whose widow Rebecca is known to have m. a Brown; and since Clapham d. in 1698, this would make her Brown's second wife and mother of only his youngest child. As Rebecca Browne she joined 1702 in agreement of heirs of John Ruscoe.
Inv. 2 Mar. 1701/2. Ages of five children stated. Widow Rebecca appointed Adm'x with Mr. Andrew Messenger and Mr. Samuel Betts, all of Norwalk. On following 19 Mar., there being some difficulties, Messenger refused, and Mr. Joseph Platt was appointed to act with Betts and the widow. Betts asked for discharge, 7 Mar. 1709/10, and the son James Brown replaced him. As late as 4 Apr. 1711, Capt. Joseph Platt and the widow Rebecca Brown appeared as Adm'rs, and James Brown had some time since entered on the work of adm'n with his mother.

Children [by first wife], births from Pro. Rec.:
> James, b. Nov. 1682; m. (rec. Norwalk) 20 Dec. 1714, Joanna Whitehead, dau. of Samuel of Elizabeth, N. J.
> Sarah, b. 23 Oct. 1686.
> Elisha, b. 15 Nov. 1688.
> Isaac, b. 25 Feb. 1690/1 [1 Mar. 1690 by Norwalk rec.]; m. Sarah Lockwood, dau. of John of Fairfield.

Child [by second wife]:
> John, b. 6 Oct. 1700; m. (rec. Norwalk) 6 May 1729, Mary Raymond, dau. of Samuel.

Brundish, John. [The name is also spelled Brundage.]

A tanner, came to Watertown, Mass., thence to Wethersfield with first settlers. The name later was spelled Brundage.
Inv. 27 Oct. 1639. Widow Rachel and five children; two older girls, a boy, and two younger girls, all under 16 yrs.
An original unrecorded deed, dated 20 May 1639, witnessed by Andrew Ward, Edmund Wood, and Robert Rose (the last by mark), not signed by the grantor John Brundish; the second part,

dated 23 Nov. 1639, is a confirmation given by the widow as Adm'x, and states: "but Providence so disposing of the aforesayd John Brundishe that before the tym that the mony was due & yᵉ writing (?) confermed He put an end unto his lyf." Hence he d. between 20 May and 27 Oct. 1639, which disposes of suggestions that he was killed by Indians in 1637.*

The widow Rachel m. Anthony Wilson of Fairfield, about 5 Aug. 1642, as the badly defaced probate record in Fairfield mentions agreement of that date. At Rachel's death (1648?), Anthony Wilson was to have the homelot in Fairfield that was Rachel Brundish's, and to pay legacies to the children, John Brundish, Mary wife of Francis Purdy, Bethia Brundish and Posthume. The tanner's tools had been sold, and John was to have the money.

John Brundish of Rye, on 24 May 1667, having formerly sold to his father-in-law Anthony Wilson, land in Fairfield, exempts such lands as the heirs of Francis Purdy possess, except that Joseph Taylor now possesses the remainder of my lands not above exempted.

Children:

Mary, b. [1629 or earlier]; m. by 1645, Francis Purdy.
Daughter, d. between 1639 and 1648.
+John, b. abt. 1635 [Winthrop called him ae. 30 in 1666].
Bethia, b. abt. 1637; of Fairfield, ae. 16, in 1654 [New Haven Col. Rec.]; possibly m. Joseph Taylor, of Westchester.
Posthume, b. in 1639 (so her name signifies); m. (we suppose) John Winter, of Westchester, whose wife in several deeds 1692-94 rejoiced in the unusual name of "Posthumy."

Brundish, John, s. of John. Deputy (Rye) to Conn. Leg., May 1681.

Born about 1635; rem. from Fairfield to Rye, where he was the first Town Clerk, and Deputy 1677; d. in 1697.

Inv. 2 Oct. 1697, taken by Samuel Kniften, Hachaliah Brown, and John Lyon. Widow Hannah; children John, Daniel, Joshua, Ruth Scofield, Mary Brundage, Hannah Brundage. Deliverance Brown and George Lane of Rye appointed to make distribution. [Fairfield Pro. Rec.]

---

* For this deed we are indebted to Col. Charles E. Banks.

The four sons, John, Joseph, Daniel, and Joshua, made agreement at Rye, 5 Dec. 1698, making allowance for their mother's dower.

Children:

John.
Joseph.
Daniel.
Ruth, m. (rec. Stamford) 14 Sept. 1689, Richard Scofield.
Joshua.
Mary.
Hannah.

Bulkeley, (Rev.) Peter.

Born at Odell, co. Bedford, Eng., 31 Jan. 1582/3, scion of an ancient family of co. Cheshire, and son of Rev. Edward and Olive (Ilsby) Bulkeley of Odell; m. at Goldington, co. Bedford, 12 Apr. 1613, Jane Allen, of that parish, who d. at Odell and was buried 8 Dec. 1626; m. (2) in 1634, Grace Chetwood, b. abt. 1602, d. at New London, Conn., 21 Apr. 1669 (see Bradstreet's Journal). She was dau. of Sir Richard Chetwood, by his second wife Dorothy Needham; who was sister of Sir Robert Needham, of Shenton, co. Shropshire (created Viscount Kilmorey in 1625), dau. of Robert and Frances (Aston) Needham, and granddau. of Thomas Needham by his wife Anne Talbot; who was dau. of Sir John Talbot, of Grafton, co. Worcester, by his first wife Margaret Troutbeck, Sir John being a grandson of John Talbot (1413-1460), second Earl of Shrewsbury.*

Educated (B.D.) at St. John's College, Cambridge, he succeeded his father in the parish of Odell, but leaning towards Puritanism, was at length silenced for non-conformity. In May 1635 the shipping lists show the names of Peter Bulkley, aged 50, embarked in the *Susan & Ellin,* and Grace Bulkley, aged 33, in the *Elizabeth & Ann.* On the former, the names Ben: Buckley and Daniell Bulkley, aged 11 and 9 respectively, appear in the list. Some of the children presumably came under fictitious names.

He lived in Cambridge, Mass., a while, then founded Concord,

---

* This interesting ancestry, first suggested by the present writer in the *New England Hist. and Gen. Register,* vol. 76, p. 311, has since been accepted by the Heralds' College and the editor of Burke's *Peerage,* insofar as the one disputed point, the parentage of Anne Talbot, is concerned.

where he "buried a great estate" in the wilderness. A scholar, composer of Latin verses, author of the *Gospel Covenant;* served Concord as preacher until shortly before his death on 9 Mar. 1658/9.

Children [by first wife] :

> Edward, bapt. 12 June 1614, d. at Chelmsford, Mass., 2 Jan. 1696, and buried at Concord.
> Mary, bapt. 24 Aug. 1615, buried 13 Jan. 1615/6.
> +Thomas, bapt. 13 Apr. 1617.
> Nathaniel, bapt. 29 Nov. 1618, buried 11 Feb. 1628/9.
> John, bapt. 6 Feb. 1619/20.
> Mary, bapt. 1 Nov. 1621.
> Joseph, bapt. 4 May 1623.
> +Daniel, bapt. 28 Aug. 1625.
> Jabez, bapt. 24 Dec. 1626, buried 2 Dec. 1629.

Children [by second wife] :

> Gershom, b. Dec. 1635, d. at Glastonbury, 2 Dec. 1713 ae. 77 yrs. 11 mos.; minister at New London and Wethersfield; Chirurgeon, K. Philip's War, 1676; Deputy for Wethersfield, May 1679; licensed as physician in Conn., Oct. 1686; Justice under Gov. Andros, 1687; m. (rec. Concord), 6 Oct. 1659, Sarah Chauncey.
> Eleazer, b. 1638.
> Dorothy, b. at Concord, 2 Aug. 1640.
> +Peter, b. at Concord, 12 Aug. 1643.

Bulkley, Thomas, s. of (Rev.) Peter.

Bapt. at Odell, co. Bedford, Eng., 13 Apr. 1617, d. at Fairfield in 1658.,

Married Sarah Jones, dau. of Rev. John, b. abt. 1620, d. in 1683; she m. (2) Anthony Wilson of Fairfield.

Inv. 4 June 1658. Widow; two sons; and daus.; children under age. Overseers, Mr. Hill and Mr. Hull.

The will of Sarah Wilson, "sometimes Sarah Bulkley", dated 26 Apr. 1677, codicil 15 Feb. 1680, proved 2 Jan. 1683 [1683/4] ; dau. Sarah wife of Eleazer Browne of New Haven; dau. Rebecca wife of Joseph Whelplie of Fairfield; dau. Hannah; sister-in-law, Mr. Eliphalet Jones' wife; sister Elizabeth Hill; two sons John and Joseph Bulkley; brother-in-law Mr. Gershom Bulkeley of Wethersfield, and Samuel Wakeman, overseers. Witnesses: Gershom Bulkley and Israel Chauncey.

John and Joseph Bulkley made agreement to divide lands, 10 Mar. 1683/4. On 15 Feb. 1672, Joseph Bulkley entered for record lands received from mother Sarah Wilson, of which the first parcel was the homelot given to Mr. Thomas Bulkley dec'd by will of his bro. Daniel Bulkley dec'd.

Children:

    Sarah, b. at Concord, Mass., 12 Aug. 1640, d. at New Haven in 1723; m. Eleazer Brown.
    +John.
    +Joseph, b. abt. 1648 (testified in Disbrow trial 1692, ae. 44).
    Rebecca, d. in 1690; m. Joseph Whelpley.
    Hannah.

Bulkley, Daniel, s. of (Rev.) Peter.

Bapt. at Odell, co. Bedford, Eng., 28 Aug. 1625, he came with his father and lived in Concord; joined his brother Thomas in Fairfield, where he was granted six acres. Died probably by 1648, and willed his land to Thomas Bulkley, who sold it to Robert Woolly, and the latter resold to Thomas Dunn, all before 5 Mar. 1649 [1649/50], when Dunn had the land recorded to himself.

Bulkley, (Dr.) Peter, s. of (Rev.) Peter.

Born at Concord, Mass., 12 Aug. 1643, d. at Fairfield, in 1691. Married Margaret ———, who d. before him.

On 29 June 1688, Peter Bulkley of Fairfield, apothecary, with Margaret his wife, mortgaged his dwelling house and land for £90 to Francis Foxcroft of Boston, merchant. Foxcroft was bringing suit to foreclose at the time of Peter's death.

Will dated 25 Mar. 1691; two eldest daus. Grace and Margaret; "that fflock bed yt is at Hanna Shermans there let it remaine: or if young James Bennit have it it shall be only upon Courtisey"; Peter to be apprenticed to James to learn weaving; a mare now at Daniel Silliman's; brother Gershom, sole Exec'r. The Exec'r refusing, adm'n was granted to John and Joseph Bulkley and Samuel Robinson, any two of them. Inv. 17 July 1691; included medicine and books in English and Latin.

Peter's five children were named in the will of his brother, Rev. Gershom of Wethersfield.

Children:

> Grace, b. [say 1672]; m. (rec. Wethersfield) 20 Sept. 1692, Corp. Ebenezer Kilbourn.
>
> Margaret, b. [say 1674].*
>
> +Gershom, b. [say 1676].
>
> +Peter, b. at Fairfield, 25 Dec. 1683.
>
> Dorothy, b. [say 1687], d. at Fairfield in 1734; m. Sergt. David Osborn.

Bulkley, John, s. of Thomas.

Inv. 22 Apr. 1707. Adm'n granted to his dau. Sarah Bulkley and to Joseph Whelpley. Distribution made to the five daus., Sarah, Esther, Hannah, Elizabeth, and Olive. Elizabeth chose Joseph Whelpley guardian in 1707; and in 1708, her guardian being deceased, the "Worshipfull Mr. Peter" [Burr] was appointed her guardian. Sarah Bulkley was appointed guardian to Olive in 1707; and in Apr. 1710 Olive chose her brother Joseph Perry guardian.

In 1694, John's wife was called Esther (in the church rec.). Quite likely she was Esther Burr, dau. of the second Jehu, who in her father's will 1690 was stated to have received her portion, signifying that she was then married.

He purchased 1694 from his uncle Eliphalet Jones of Huntington, one-sixth of an orchard in Fairfield left to latter by his father Mr. John Jones; he had bought another share of the orchard from the widow of John Jones, Jr., 1679/80; and in 1692 another sixth from Peregrine Stanborough [husband of the eldest dau. of Ruth (Jones) James].

Children, two youngest bapt. at Fairfield:

> Sarah, d. abt. 1710; m. Joseph Perry; no issue.
>
> Esther, b. 30 Jan. 1683/4 (by age at death), d. at Fairfield, 18 Mar. 1725/6 ae. 42 yrs. 1 mo. 19 days (g. s.); m. Joseph Bulkley (her first cousin).
>
> Hannah, d. between 1722 and 1725; m. Peter Bulkley, s. of Dr. Peter.
>
> Elizabeth, bapt. 26 Aug. 1694; m. abt. 1711, Nathaniel Whitehead.
>
> Olive, bapt. 30 Aug. 1696, d. at Fairfield, 5 Oct. 1774; m. at Fairfield, 5 Aug. 1725, Lt. James Beers.

---

* In his work on the Bulkeley Genealogy for Mrs. Benjamin Patterson Bole of Cleveland, Ohio, the editor of the present work made every effort to learn the marriage of Margaret, without success. See footnote under JOHN THORP. If Margaret's birth can be placed a little earlier, she might be the Margaret ———— who m. in 1688 Benjamin Gardner of Wethersfield and named a son Peter.

Bulkley, Joseph, s. of Thomas.

Born abt. 1648, d. prob. late in 1719; m. Martha Beers, dau. of James. She was named as his wife in wills of her father 1694 and mother 1698.

Adm'n granted, 6 Jan. 1719/20, to son Joseph. Distribution made to widow Martha; five sons, Joseph, Peter, Daniel, Thomas, John; dau. Sarah Bulkley. John chose his mother Martha guardian. A mutual distribution was made 4 Jan. 1719/20 between the five sons and Joshua Jennings in right of wife Sarah (sister to the said Bulkleys) to divide the Est. of their father Joseph.

Children, recorded at Fairfield:

XJoseph, b. 9 May 1682, d. 6 May 1750 ae. 68 (g. s., Fairfield); m. (1) Esther Bulkley, b. 30 Jan. 1683/4, d. 18 Mar. 1725/6 ae. 42 yrs. 1 mo. 19 days; m. (2) Ruth Jennings, bapt. 11 Apr. 1708, d. abt. 1787; she m. (2) 14 Mar. 1754, Capt. Seth Samuel Burr.

XPeter, b. 21 May 1684, d. at Fairfield, 15 Oct. 1752 in 69 yr. (g. s.); called weaver and Jr.; m. [at Stratfield, 25 Oct. 1709]* Hannah Ward, who d. abt. 1772.

XDaniel, b. abt. 1689; m. (1) Hannah ———, who d. 1724 to 1727; m. (2) (rec. Fairfield Church) 21 May 1728, Hannah Johnson; dau. of Moses.

XThomas, b. abt. 1691, d. at Westport, 25 May 1756; m. Abigail ———, who d. at Westport, 15 Apr. 1765.

Sarah, bapt. 23 Sept. 1694, d. 17 Sept. 1724 ae. 31 (g. s., Fairfield); m. Joshua Jennings; no issue.

Gershom, bapt. 13 Sept. 1696, d. y.

XJohn, bapt. 22 Mar. 1701/2, d. at Fairfield between 2 Oct. and 5 Nov. 1751; m. Martha [perhaps Morehouse, bapt. 7 Sept. 1712], who d. in 1759, having m. (2) 1 Nov. 1752, Gershom Whitehead.

Bulkley, Gershom, s. of (Dr.) Peter. Quarter-Master, Fairfield County Troop of Horse, Oct. 1718; Cornet, Oct. 1722; Capt., May 1726.

Born presumably at Fairfield, abt. 1676, d. there 9 Apr. 1753; m. (1) abt. 1700, Eunice Hanford, dau. of Rev. Thomas of Norwalk, b. Mar. 1676, d. by 1706; m. (2) by 1706, Rachel Talcott, b. 23 Feb. 1681/2, d. before 1753. She was dau. of Lt.-Col. John Talcott of Hartford, and half-sister of Gov. Joseph Talcott.

Will 5 Apr. 1753, proved 30 Apr. 1753; daus. Eunice, Rachel,

---

* The wife's name is not given, and the date may belong to the other Peter.

and Grace, £100 apiece; sons Gershom, Hezekiah, Peter, and Talcott.

Child [by first wife], bapt. at Fairfield:
Eunice, bapt. 4 Jan. 1701/2; m. abt. 1723, Eleazer Smith.

Children [by second wife], bapt. at Fairfield:
Rachel, bapt. 16 Mar. 1706/7.
✕Gershom, bapt. 27 Mar. 1709, d. at Greenfield, 27 Sept. 1802 in 96 yr. (g. s.); m. 17 May 1736, Sarah Banks, b. 1 Feb. 1715/6, d. 7 May 1791 in 76 yr. (g. s.).
Grace, bapt. 27 May 1711, d. y.
✕Hezekiah, bapt. 29 Nov. 1713, d. at Fairfield in 1788; will 9 Sept. 1788, proved 22 Dec. 1788; m. (1) 4 Jan. 1739, Catherine Hill, bapt. 2 June 1717; m. (2) at Redding, 20 Sept. 1768, Sarah Rumsey; widow of Joseph Rumsey, and dau. of John Bartram, b. 14 May 1719.
✕Peter, bapt. 5 Feb. 1715/6, d. at Westport, 12 May 1804 in 89 yr. (g. s.); m. 9 Apr. 1740, Ann Hill, bapt. 28 Feb. 1719/20, d. 11 Apr. 1795 ae. 76 (g. s.).
Jonathan, bapt. 18 May 1718, d. y.
Grace, bapt. 12 Feb. 1720/1, d. at Westport, 21 Feb. 1772 in 52 yr. (g. s.); m. 9 Nov. 1741, John Burr.
✕Talcott, b. 21 Aug. 1724, bapt. 23 Aug. 1724, d. at Westport, 26 Apr. 1810 ae. 86; Lt.; m. 19 June 1753, Esther Bradley, b. 30 Mar. 1733.

Bulkley, Peter, s. of (Dr.) Peter.

Born at Fairfield, 25 Dec. 1683, d. there 18 July 1753 in 70 yr. (g. s.); m. (1) Hannah Bulkley, dau. of John, who d. between 1722 and 1725; m. (2) Abigail ———, b. abt. 1702, d. 12 Jan. 1795 ae. 92 (g. s.).*

He was a cooper, and often called Sr. to distinguish him from his cousin Peter (son of Joseph). On 9 May 1722, Peter Bulkley, cooper, and Hannah his wife, conveyed to him in trust certain buildings which descended to Hannah from her father John Bulkley, the deed reciting that Hannah's "weakness and sickness hath been very great", and referring to Peter's "tender care and great kindness." She did not long survive, and there were no children, as her relatives conveyed their interest to Peter after her death.

---

* This Peter and his family have usually been confused with Peter (son of Joseph, see above) and his family. For proof of the correction made herein, see *N. Y. Gen. and Biog. Record*, vol. 60, pp. 234 *et seq.*

Will 17 July 1753, proved 27 Aug. 1753; wife Abigail; dau. Hannah; son Jonathan.

Will of Abigail, 15 Nov. 1794, proved 17 Jan. 1795; dau. Hannah Burr; dau.-in-law Hannah, widow of son Jonathan; Jonathan's children, Peter, Jonathan, Abigail, Thomas, Hannah, Harry, and James.

Children [by second wife], bapt. at Fairfield:

Hannah, bapt. 16 Oct. 1726, d. at Fairfield, 23 July 1818 ae. 91 (g. s.) ; m. (1) James Morehouse; m. (2) 9 Jan. 1766, Ebenezer Burr.

Abigail, bapt. 13 Apr. 1729, d. y.

XJonathan, b. 3 Oct. 1732, bapt. in 1732, d. at Fairfield, 13 Apr. 1789 in 57 yr. (g. s.); m. 21 Jan. 1762, Hannah Hoyt, dau. of James, b. abt. 1741, d. 4 Mar. 1817 ae. 76 (g. s.).

Bunkham, Cornelius.

Married after 1702, Hannah, widow of John Green of Fairfield, and dau. of John Hobby of Greenwich.

Hannah Buncom and her two Green children were bapt. at Fairfield, 16 Sept. 1705.

He d. at Westport, 12 Jan. 1745/6; Widow Hannah d. 15 Oct. 1749.

Will 26 Dec. 1745, proved 15 Jan. 1746; wife Hannah; gr. child Thomasin Green, dau. of John, £50;` other six children of John Green, £5 each; Richard Elwood of Fairfield, my Great Bible; Daniel Buckingham of Fairfield, £10; Joseph Gorham of Fairfield, £60; Deborah wife of Benjamin Gregory, £5; residue to wife, Daniel Buckingham, and Joseph Gorham, equally.

Child, bapt. at Fairfield:

Thomasin, bapt. 2 July 1710, d. y.

Burch, Jeremiah.

Married (rec. Stratford) June 1696, Elizabeth Wheeler.

Children, recorded at Stratford:

Elizabeth, b. 15 Dec. 1697; m. 12 Sept. 1717, William Lamson.

Jeremiah, b. 10 June 1699; m. 24 Mar. 1726, Sarah Beecher.

Mary, b. 10 June 1701.

Burgess, Richard

Of Sandwich, Mass., 1643; of Fairfield by 1650, where he had a grant from the town, 8 Sept. 1676.

Married (1) ———; m. (2) in 1677, Phebe Peacock, dau. of John, by marriage agreement dated 20 Oct. 1677.

Inv. 4 May 1685; widow Phebe; dau. Jane; overseers, James Clark and Benjamin Beach. Phebe gave a power of attorney to John Applegate to manage her estate, which she revoked 11 Mar. 1685 [1685/6], and gave one to Mr. Samuel Sherman, Jr., and Mr. Josiah Nichols.

Child [by first wife]:

Jane, m. (rec. Fairfield) 24 Jan. 1689, Isaac Hall.

Burr, Jehu.   Deputy for Springfield to Conn. Leg., Apr. 1638, Sept. 1641; for Fairfield, Sept. 1645, Apr. 1646.

He came in the Winthrop Fleet, 1630, settled in Roxbury, Mass., and was made freeman, 18 May 1631. In 1633 he served on a committee with William Pynchon, the Colony Treasurer; and in 1636 went with Pynchon to Springfield, of which he was appointed Collector by Conn. Colony. He rem. to Fairfield soon after 1641. He may have married more than once. The mother of Jehu, Jr., was quite likely sister of John Cable, Sr. There was prob. some relationship between the Burrs and the family of Nathaniel Perry.

He d. by 1654,* and perhaps even earlier. On 17 Feb. 1670 [1670/1], the younger Jehu had recorded a homelot adjoining his own homelot, of which he "hath had quiet possession above this sixteen years." Immediately beneath, under date 12 Jan. 1673 [1673/4], is entered a description of the same lot, autographed by his bro. John, from whom he had purchased it, apparently a ratification of the purchase. The next entry, same date, is the younger Jehu's own homelot which he "hath by his father's will Jehu dec'd", bounded by the lot bought from his bro. John.

Children:

+Jehu, b. [say 1625].
+John, b. abt. 1633.

---

* Unless, indeed, he returned to England, as did Pynchon; turning over his lands to his children. But the compiler does not favor that solution. There are references to his will, which must have been probated at an early date not to be found on record.

+Nathaniel.
   Elizabeth, m. (1) Nehemiah Olmstead; m. (2) Obadiah Gilbert; m.
   (3) 1674, Capt. Nathaniel Seeley.
+Daniel, b. abt. 1642.

Burr, Jehu, s. of Jehu.   Deputy (Fairfield) to Conn. Leg., Oct.
1659, Oct. 1660, May 1661, May and Oct. 1663, May and Oct.
1668, May 1669, May and Oct. 1670, May 1672, May and Oct.
1673, May 1674, May and Oct. 1675, May 1676, May 1678, Oct.
1679, May and Oct. 1680, May 1682, May 1683 to May 1685
inclusive, May 1686, May 1691; Commissioner for Fairfield,
1664, 1668 to 1687 inclusive, 1689-92.   Lt., Fairfield County
Troop, Aug. 1673; member of War Council, Oct. 1675, May
1676; Commissioner for Indians, May 1680.   Colonial grant
of 200 acres, May 1673.

   Born prob. by 1625, d. at Fairfield in 1692; m. (1) after 1655,
Esther, widow of Joseph Boosey of Westchester, and perhaps dau.
of Andrew Ward; m. (2) by 1666, Elizabeth Prudden, dau. of
Rev. Peter, bapt. at Milford, 11 Mar. 1642/3.

   Will 11 Jan. 1689 [1689/90], proved 31 Oct. 1692; wife (name
not stated); sons Daniel, Peter, Samuel (the last a minor); dau.
Esther had received portion; daus. Elizabeth, Sarah, Joanna,
Abigail, all under 18; gr. child Mary, only child of dec'd dau.
Mary by son-in-law Samuel Wakeman; bros. John and Nathaniel,
overseers.*

---

* Col. Charles E. Banks sends us the following autograph letters of Jehu Burr from
the unpublished Winthrop Mss. XI. 98:
   Right Worshipfull
   I Presume your Worshipe is not Ignorant That Captain Winthrope when he went
for New Yorke bought a horse of me for which he was to give me fiveteen pond out
of the Country rate: these are to request your Worship that order may be given to
the treasurer to pay me the said fiveteen pound and the bill shall be returrned to you
upon the recete of the debte having not else to troble your Worship I take leve to
remain
                                        Your humble servant
Fairfield   JEHU BUR
26: Jany. '64

   Right worshipful
   After my respects psented thes are to requste you to pay 8*li* for me to this
barer Joshua Holkem: He desires to have it paid to Mr Richerts if hee excepte it there
Pray take a receite of him for my accounte: not else but remaine youeres
                                        to comand
                                              JEHU BUR

The problem of Jehu's wives is so difficult as to require special consideration. We have been assisted by a discussion of the problem with Mr. Clarence A. Torrey, of Dorchester, Mass., who however must not be understood to endorse the conclusions herein stated in their entirety. The *Ward Gen.* and *Burr Gen.* follow the *Hist. of Fairfield* in supposing that Jehu m. (1) Mary Ward, dau. of Andrew, and (2) widow Esther Boosey. This can be positively disproved. Joseph Boosey, of the Wethersfield family, settled in Westchester and d. in 1655, leaving his entire estate to his wife Esther. She m. Jehu Burr, and with him conveyed her interest in Boosey property 27 Feb. 1661 [1661/2], for £64, the deed at Wethersfield stating that James Boosey gave the land to his son Joseph Boosey first husband "unto the said Easter and now the wife of the said Jehu Burr." In consequence, she must have been mother of the elder Burr children, Daniel, whose birth must certainly be placed as early as 1660, and Esther, named after herself.

The Prudden letters, discovered and published* by Mr. George C. Bryant, prove just as positively that Jehu m. Elizabeth dau. of Rev. Peter and Joanna (Boyse) Prudden of Milford. Her mother Joanna had an income from English estates, which she left by will to her children. Letters written by Rev. John Prudden, brother of Elizabeth, and accounts kept by him, prove that her share was paid for a time to Peter Burr. In 1707 he wrote: "I have not sent any share to Peter Burr: being fully persuaded that he understands the Letter of his Grand-mothers Will better then to think that his mother had any Right in this Revenue to convey to another after her decease."

Elizabeth Prudden was therefore mother of Peter Burr, b. 1668, and as every one of the five younger Burr children had Prudden names, we have little hesitancy in assigning them to Elizabeth. The only child whose maternity is in doubt is Mary Burr who m. Samuel Wakeman and d. abt. 1688 leaving an only child, Mary Wakemán. She was prob. older than Peter, hence b. abt. 1666.

Mary Burr's dau. Mary Wakeman lived in girlhood in Milford, and her deed conveying Fairfield property was witnessed by Sylvanus Baldwin (who m. Mildred Prudden, sister of Elizabeth). Left a double orphan, we can only conclude that she had gone to

---

* *New England Hist. and Gen. Register,* Jan. 1930.

live with relatives of her grandmother in Milford. This deed is convincing evidence that her mother Mary Burr (b. abt. 1666) was dau. of Jehu by his Prudden wife. Elizabeth witnessed a deed with Jehu, 24 May 1667, but the above considerations make it necessary to set the date of their marriage in 1665, or 1666 at the latest. This is three or at most four years after the last date on which Jehu's first wife Esther is known to have been living.

The will of Hester Ward (widow of Andrew) in 1665 named her living children, including dau. Mary Burr, and several sets of grandchildren in such terms as might imply that they were all the grandchildren she had. At the end, almost as an afterthought, she gave ten shillings apiece to Daniel and Hester Burr, without specifying relationship to herself, or even their parentage.

Unquestionably, the Daniel and Hester Burr referred to were the eldest children of Jehu, then young children of perhaps five and three years of age. It was natural to assume, as previous writers did, that Mary Ward m. Jehu Burr and was mother of these children. But we have shown that Esther was the first wife, and mother of Daniel and Esther, hence this theory, formerly widely accepted, is untenable.

Mary Ward was married by 1659, for she was among the daus. not given legacies in Andrew Ward's will because they had received portions at marriage; and her mother's will proves that she was wife of a Burr in Dec. 1665. It is very improbable that she was wife of Jehu, since his marriage to Elizabeth Prudden must be placed as early as 1665-66. The only Fairfield Burr available as her husband was Jehu's brother John, whose marriage to Sarah Fitch did not occur much before 1673, when he was nearing forty. A prior marriage for him was not only possible, but probable. The will in 1684 of Moses Dimon (who m. Abigail Ward) called John Burr and Samuel Ward his brethren, and it is difficult to explain why this term was applied to John Burr unless he had been the husband of Mary Ward, sister of Dimon's wife.

The only problem remaining is why Mrs. Hester Ward gave small legacies to [Jehu's children] Daniel and Hester Burr. The compiler's personal belief is that their mother, the widow Esther Boosey, was a dau. of Andrew and Hester Ward.* Her name,

---

* Mr. O. P. Dexter's valuable notes state that Mary Ward "m. a Burr, probably Jehu." He says of Mrs. Hester Ward that "she gives also to Daniel and Esther

like that of other married daus., would not appear in Andrew's will, and she died before Mrs. Ward. The only objections to this theory are: (1) Mrs. Ward's will did not specifically call the Burr children her grandchildren. However, she did refer to them so casually, that we infer it would be clear to her contemporaries how they were related to her and why it was natural for her to remember them. (2) She gave legacies of £9 to several groups of her grandchildren, in such terms as might lead to the supposition that she had no other grandchildren. This objection seems to us entirely negative, for wills of that period were often not drawn with the meticulous phrasing of a modern will drawn by an attorney. The failure of Mrs. Ward to give the Burr children an equal amount with other groups of her grandchildren is susceptible of explanation. The Boosey estate which Esther inherited was worth upward of £64, and the Burr children were the eventual heirs; this was more than seven times the legacies which Mrs. Ward gave to the other groups of grandchildren, so she could have considered them already well provided for.

However, the evidence is insufficient to *prove* that Esther was dau. of the Wards; and the theory is equally tenable that she was a niece or other relative of Mrs. Ward; and named after her.

Children [by Esther]:

+Daniel, b. abt. 1660.
    Esther (or Hester), b. [say 1663]; perhaps m. John Bulkley.

Children [by Elizabeth]:

    Mary, b. [say 1666], d. abt. 1688; m. Samuel Wakeman.
+Peter, b. abt. Mar. 1668.
    Elizabeth, m. Samuel Hubbell.
    Sarah, perhaps m. Nathan Gold, 2d.
    Samuel, living apparently 1696, when an agreement between his guardian Mr. Daniel Burr and his bro. Peter Burr was recorded.
    Joanna, d. 1 Sept. 1749; m. Ens. John Curtis, of Woodbury.
    Abigail.

Burr, children of Jehu Burr by Esther, widow of Joseph Boosey; I strongly suspect this Esther was another dau. of Andrew and Esther Ward: which immediately raises the question whether the Puritans permitted a man to marry his dec'd wife's sister." The undeniable abhorrence with which such marriages were regarded makes it impossible to suppose that Jehu m. both Esther and Mary, if they were sisters.

Burr, John, s. of Jehu. Deputy for Fairfield, May 1666, Oct. 1667, Oct. 1668, May 1670 to Oct. 1671 inclusive, May 1674, Oct. 1685, May, July and Oct. 1686, Jan., Mar. and Oct. 1687, May, June and Oct. 1689, Apr. 1690. Assistant, 1690 to 1694 inclusive. Commissioner for Fairfield, 1679-87, 1689. Capt., Fairfield Trainband, Apr. 1690; Commissary, Fairfield County, Feb. 1693; Sergeant-Major, Fairfield County, Oct. 1694.

Born abt. 1633; testified 1681 ae. 48.

Married Sarah Fitch, dau. of Thomas of Norwalk, who was mother of his children. As he was nearly forty when the first of his ten children was born, and possessed a homelot and lands, a prior marriage is likely, and he may have m. (1) before 1659, Mary Ward, who d. after 1665 without issue [see discussion under his bro. Jehu]. He bought lands of Charles and Michael Taintor, prior to 14 June 1656.

Will of John, Sr., 19 Mar. 1693/4; wife Sarah; son John (Exec'r), homelot I dwell upon, formerly Strickland's and Pinkney's; son Samuel, farm in the woods, and four years in College; son Jonathan, land in the new field, formerly Westcott's and Joseph Bishop's; son David, homelot I bought of John Cable; dau. Mary, £100 at 18 or marriage; dau. Deborah, the same; dau. Sarah already portioned; bro. Nathaniel Burr and cousin Peter Burr, overseers; I have not rec'd from my father Fitch my wife's portion. Witnesses: John Edwards, Eliphalet Hill. Inv. 5 Nov. 1694.

Children, recorded at Fairfield:

+John, b. 2 May 1673.
    Sarah, b. 25 July 1675, d. "15 of 1697/8"; m. 29 June 1692, Rev. Charles Chauncey.
    Seth, b. 21 June 1677, d. y.
    Samuel, b. 2 Apr. 1679, d. 7 Aug. 1719 ae. 40 yrs. 4 mos. 5 days (g. s., Fairfield). Res. Cambridge 1702 when he receipted to brother John, Executor of will of father John. Will of Samuel of Charlestown, Mass., 2 May 1717; wife Elizabeth; daus. Sarah and Rebecca; sons John and Samuel; mentioned gr. gr. father Stedman. Graduated Harvard 1697; master of Grammar School, Charlestown. He m. (1) 16 Dec. 1700, Dorothy, widow of Samuel Shove of Boston, and dau. of Henry and Elizabeth (Stedman) (Upham) Thompson; b. at Boston, 26 Oct. 1671, d. 20 Feb. 1701/2 ae. 30 (g. s., Cambridge). He m. (2) 19 June 1707, Elizabeth dau. of Thomas and Rebecca (Trerice) Jenner, b. 11 Feb. 1670/1. By

1st wife he had: Sarah, b. 17 Oct. 1701, m. 20 Nov. 1723, Thomas
Edwards, goldsmith, of Boston. By 2d wife he had: John, b. 14
Apr. 1708; Samuel, b. 28 May 1709; and Rebecca, b. 14 Mar. 1710/1,
m. 25 Oct. 1733, John Leppington.
Ebenezer, b. 7 Feb. 1681, d. y.
Mary, b. 19 Aug. 1683, d. prob. abt. 1717; m. abt. 1702, John Osborn.
Ebenezer, b. 9 Feb. 1684 [1684/5], d. y.
Deborah, m. at Stratfield, 24 Mar. 1713/4, Timothy Treadwell.
Jonathan, d. s. p. abt. 1710; Inv. 4 Jan. 1710 [1710/1], presented by
bro. Mr. Samuel Burr 25 Apr. 1712. Distribution 28 Feb. 1726/7
to bros. and sisters; heirs of Mr. John Burr; heirs of Mr. Samuel
Burr; heirs of Mrs. Sarah Chauncey; heirs of Mrs. Mary Osborn;
Deborah Treadwell, only sister now living. The distribution had
been requested by Israel Chauncey of Fairfield, son of Rev. Mr.
Charles Chauncey of Stratfield who had m. one of Jonathan's
sisters, and by Thomas Hill in right of his wife Mary, and Andrew
Burr, dau. and son of Jonathan's bro. John.
David, d. y.

Burr, Nathaniel, s. of Jehu. Deputy for Fairfield, Oct. 1692,
Mar. and Oct. 1693, Feb. 1694, Oct. 1695, Jan. 1697, May and
Oct. 1698, May 1700.

Married (1) after June 1659, Sarah Ward, dau. of Andrew.
The will of Hester Ward, 1665, gave legacies to her grandchildren
Sarah and Nathaniel, children of her dau. Sarah Burr.

Married (2) Hannah, widow of Samuel Wakeman, dau. of
Dep.-Gov. Stephen Goodyear.

Died at Fairfield 26 Feb. 1712.

Will 22 Nov. 1711; wife Ann; sons John and Daniel; four
children of dec'd son Nathaniel; daus. Abigail wife of John
Wheeler, Esther wife of John Sloss, Ann wife of Gideon Allen,
Rebecca wife of Capt. Samuel Sherwood, and Mary wife of Dr.
James Laborie.

Children [by first wife]:

Sarah, b. abt. 1662, d. y.
+Nathaniel, b. abt. 1664.
Abigail, b. abt. 1668, d. 7 Feb. 1711/2; m. 22 Mar. 1692, John Wheeler.
+John, b. abt. 1672.
Anna, b. abt. 1675, d. 14 Mar. 1747/8 ae. 72 (g. s., Fairfield); m. 20
Jan. 1696, Gideon Allen.
+Daniel, b. [say 1677].

Esther, d. 1722; m. (1) John Sloss; m. (2) by marriage contract dated 3 May 1722, Rev. Samuel Cooke.

Rebecca, b. abt. 1681, d. 16 May 1721 ae. 40 (g. s., Stratfield); m. 30 Nov. 1704, Capt. Samuel Sherwood.

Mary, m. Dr. James Laborie.

Burr, Daniel, s. of Jehu. Commissary, Fairfield County, May 1690.

Born abt. 1642; testified 1682 ae. 40; d. in 1695. He bought a house and homelot from Andrew Ward, 24 Dec. 1668; deed witnessed by William Ward and John Burr. He bought land from Mr. John Pell, 25 July 1672.

Married (1) (rec. Stamford) Feb. 166[9?], Abigail Brewster. She was dau. of Rev. Nathaniel of Brookhaven, L. I., whose will 16 Mar. 1684/5 named his gr. children Daniel and Abigail Burr. The will of Dr. Thomas Pell of Fairfield 1669 gave legacies to Daniel Burr and Abigail his wife. Pell was stepfather of Rev. Nathaniel Brewster.

He m. (2) at New Haven, 11 Dec. 1678, Abigail Glover. She was dau. of Henry and Helena, b. 31 July 1652, d. abt. 1720/1.

Inv. of Est. of Daniel, Sr., 5 Nov. 1695.

Inv. of Est. of Abigail, 25 Jan. 1721. Probate names her heirs as: one son Samuel; children of dec'd dau. Helena wife of John Andrews (viz.: John, Abigail, Helena, Daniel, Ebenezer); children of dec'd dau. Deborah wife of Joseph Perry (viz.: Sarah, Abigail, Joseph, Daniel, Nathaniel); and Mehitabel's one dau. Mehitabel Strong.

Distribution of land that belonged to Daniel Burr 1st, 2 Aug. 1751, to the heirs of Daniel Burr dec'd, to Samuel Burr, to the heirs of Ellen dec'd, to the heirs of Deborah dec'd, and to Abigail. Another distribution ordered 8 May 1769 to the following: heirs of Daniel Burr, dec'd, eldest son of the dec'd; heirs of Ellen Andrews, dec'd; heirs of Abigail Sherman, dec'd; heirs of Deborah Perry, dec'd; and Seth Samuel Burr.

Children [by Abigail Brewster], recorded at Fairfield:
+Daniel, b. 30 July 1670.
    Abigail, b. 14 Mar. 1671 [1671/2], d. at Stratford, 2 Mar. 1730/1; m. (1) Daniel Lockwood; m. (2) at Fairfield, 26 June 1700, Elnathan Hanford; m. (3) (rec. Stratford) 26 Nov. 1707, Nathaniel Sherman; had issue by all three.

Children [by Abigail Glover], recorded at Fairfield:

Ellen [also called Helena], b. 26 Oct. 1680; m. Ens. John Andrews.

Deborah, d. abt. 1718; m. (1) Joseph Whelpley; m. (2) Joseph Perry; had issue by both.

Mehitabel, d. before 1713; m. Benajah Strong.

+Seth Samuel [often called Samuel], b. 20 June 1694, bapt. 19 Aug. 1694.

Burr, Daniel, s. of Jehu 2d.

Born about 1660. He was called Mr. and "of Upper Meadow" to distinguish him from his cousin.

Married (1) Hannah Banks, dau. of John, whose will in 1684 calls her wife of Daniel Burr.

Married (2) Mary Sherwood, dau. of Stephen.

Married (3) Elizabeth Pinkney, dau. of Philip.

Greenfield Church Records in listing his family gives him by first wife a dau. Hannah, by second wife Jehu and Mary. Mary Burr was called second wife of David Meeker.

Distribution of Daniel's Est., 1 Aug. 1727; widow; eldest son Jehu; Stephen; Peter; Moses; Aaron; Hannah Burr; Mary Meeker; Elizabeth Hull; Jane Sherwood; Esther Bradley.

Elizabeth Burr was appointed guardian, 5 Sept. 1727, to her son David Burr (non compos mentis); Stephen Burr was appointed guardian to Moses son of Daniel; Peter Burr was appointed guardian to his brother Moses.

Child [by first wife], recorded at Fairfield:

Hannah, b. 16 June 1681.

Children [by second wife]:

×Jehu, b. [say 1687], d. at Fairfield in 1757; by 1710 was of Newtown with first wife Hannah; will 28 Sept. 1757, proved 1 Nov. 1757, named wife Sarah, brother Stephen Burr, sons Jehu and Daniel, nine daus., and others.

Mary, b. [say 1689], bapt. 30 May 1708, d. at Greenfield, 30 Aug. 1763 in 74 yr.; m. by 1720, David Meeker.

Children by Elizabeth, bapt. at Fairfield:

Elizabeth, b. (rec. Greenfield) 12 Apr. 1696, bapt. 20 Sept. 1696, d. 11 Nov. 1760 ae. 64 (Redding Church); m. 29 Nov. 1716, Nathaniel Hull.

×Stephen, bapt. 3 Oct. 1697, d. at Redding in 1778; Deacon; will 20 Aug. 1776, proved 1 Oct. 1778; m. (1) 8 June 1721, Elizabeth Hull, dau. of Cornelius, bapt. 15 Oct. 1699, d. at Redding, 26 Nov. 1760 ae. 62; m. (2) at Redding, 12 Apr. 1761, Abigail Hall.

✕Peter, bapt. 23 July 1699, d. at Redding, abt. 1779; m.˄(1) Abigail ———, who d. at Redding, 19 Mar. 1736; m. (2) at Redding, 7 May 1736, Rebecca Ward.

Jane, bapt. 27 Apr. 1701, d. 10 Mar. 1779 ae. 78 (g. s., Westport) ; m. 8 Mar. 1722, Samuel Sherwood.

Esther, bapt. 31 Jan. 1702/3, d. 29 Dec. 1741; m. June 1724, Daniel Bradley.

Philip, bapt. 28 Jan. 1704/5, d. y.

David, bapt. 14 Mar. 1707/8, d. y.

David, bapt. 1 Jan. 1709/10, *non compos mentis* 1727, d. at Redding, 10 Apr. 1766 ae. 56; adm'n granted, 17 June 1766, to Stephen Burr.

Moses, bapt. 28 Mar. 1714, d. in 1740; grad. Yale 1734; M.A.; licensed to preach, 1738.

Aaron, b. 4 Jan. 1715/6, bapt. 4 Mar. 1715/6, d. at Princeton, N. J., 24 Sept. 1757; grad. Yale 1735; M.A.; Rev.; m. at Newark, 29 June 1752, Esther Edwards, dau. of Rev. Jonathan; parents of Aaron Burr, Vice-President, U. S. A.

Burr, Peter s. of Jehu 2d. Graduated Harvard, 1690. Deputy for Fairfield, Oct. 1700, May and Oct. 1701 (speaker), Oct. 1702; Assistant, 1703-24. Major of Militia, Fairfield County, Oct. 1708; Committee of War, Fairfield County, May 1704, Oct. 1709; Commissioner on N. Y. boundary, Oct. 1713. Justice, 1701, 1702; Judge, Fairfield County Court, 1708-24; Judge, Superior Court, 1711-16, and Chief Judge, 1723, 1724; Judge, Fairfield Probate Court, Oct. 1723, May 1724.

Born about Mar. 1668; Hon. Peter d. 25 Dec. 1724 ae. 56 yrs. 9 mos. (g. s., Fairfield) ; m. (1) Abigail ———, who in 1706 witnessed with him a deed given by [his cousin] Zachariah Walker. He m. (2) Sarah (Osborn), widow of Jonathan Sturges, who m. (3) (recorded Milford) 1 June 1726, Gov. Jonathan Law; she d. at Milford, 17 June 1727.

Inv. 18 Feb. 1724/5; adm'n granted to widow Sarah and eldest son Thaddeus. On 28 Feb. 1725/6, Hon. Jonathan Law of Milford, now husband of Mrs. Sarah Law, and Thaddeus Burr, rendered account of adm'n; two sons, Thaddeus and Gershom; two daus., Abigail and Eunice. Eunice Burr receipted 21 June 1727 to bro.-in-law Ephraim Burr, late her guardian. In distribution, Ephraim Burr (for his wife) is named in lieu of Abigail.

Children [by first wife], bapt. at Fairfield:

XThaddeus, bapt. 8 Sept. 1700, d. 28 Mar. 1755 in 55 yr. (g. s., Fairfield); m. 26 Nov. 1725, Abigail Sturges, dau. of Jonathan; b. 8 Sept. 1704, d. 26 June 1753 in 49 yr. (g. s.).

Abigail, bapt. 25 Oct. 1702, d. 8 July 1780 ae. 78 (g. s., Fairfield), m. 7 Jan. 1724/5, Ephraim Burr.

Gershom, b. 30 Apr. 1705 (by age at death), bapt. 6 May 1705, d. 2 Sept. 1747 ae. 42 yrs. 4 mos. 2 days (g. s., Fairfield); m. Ann (dau. of Gideon Allen), widow of Thomas Hanford, b. 6 June 1700, d. 27 Sept. 1747 in 47 yr. (g. s.), or 29 Sept. (town rec.). Sarah Hanford, only child to Ann Burr, late widow of Gershom, requested distribution; one-half of moveables were set to the heirs of the widow Ann; the rest of Est. was divided equally between Thaddeus Burr, Abigail wife of Ephraim Burr, and Eunice wife of Benjamin Wynkoop.

Sarah, bapt. 14 Dec. 1707, d. 2 Dec. 1723 ae. 16 (g. s., Fairfield).

Eunice, bapt. 2 July 1710; m. 22 Nov. 1730, Benjamin Wynkoop.

Burr, John, s. of John. Commissary, Fairfield County, Mar. 1704.

Born at Fairfield, 2 May 1673, d. in 1705; m. Elizabeth Hanford, dau. of Rev. Thomas of Norwalk, who d. before 1708. Elizabeth renewed her Covenant at Fairfield Church, 31 Mar. 1695.

Inv. Nov. 1705. Widow, Mrs. Elizabeth Burr, to administer, with Mr. John Edwards and Moses Dimon. On 29 Apr. 1708, Edwards and Dimon rendered accounts; paid out for Mary and Deborah Burr's legacies, £124 [they were sisters of John]. Remains for distribution, £1146. Son Andrew; daus. Mary, Ann, Elizabeth. John Edwards appointed guardian to Elizabeth, and Mary chose him for guardian. Sergt. Moses Dimon appointed guardian for Andrew and Ann. Andrew had housing by will of his grandfather Maj. John Burr. Distribution to the four children was made 3 Aug. 1711.

Children, bapt. at Fairfield:

Mary, b. 13 Oct. 1694 (by age at death, computed to Old Style), bapt. 31 Mar. 1695, d. 19 Dec. 1763 ae. 69 yrs. 1 mo. 26 days (g. s., Fairfield); m. (rec. Fairfield) 9 Dec. 1715, Capt. Thomas Hill.

XAndrew, b. 27 Sept. 1696, bapt. 1 Nov. 1696, d. at Fairfield, 9 Nov. 1763 ae. 67; Col.; will 24 Nov. 1760, proved 20 Feb. 1764; m. (1) 30 Apr. 1719, Sarah Sturges, dau. of Jonathan; b. 22 Dec. 1701,

d. 9 Dec. 1745 ae. 45 yrs. wanting 13 days (g. s., Fairfield) ; m. (2) 6 Aug. 1747, Sarah Stanley of Hartford, who d. 29 Aug. 1769 ae. 61 (g. s.).

Ann, b. 25 Mar. 1699, bapt. 30 Apr. 1699, d. at Norwalk, 25 Feb. 1733/4; m. 17 Feb. 1724, Josiah Thatcher of Norwalk, and they conveyed 1726, to Thomas Hill and Andrew Burr, their interest in Est. of Jonathan Burr.

Elizabeth, bapt. 2 Feb. 1701/2, d. 3 Aug. 1769 in 69 yr. (g. s., Woodbridge) ; m. (1) John Wheeler; m. (2) at Stratfield, 3 Apr. 1733, Ezra Dibble; m. (3) Capt. Ebenezer Beecher of Woodbridge. On 16 Apr. 1726, Elizabeth widow of John Wheeler conveyed to her brethren Thomas Hill and Andrew Burr, her interest in Est. of Jonathan Burr.

Ebenezer, bapt. 25 June 1704, d. y.

Burr, Nathaniel, s. of Nathaniel. Deputy for Fairfield, Oct. 1697.

Born about 1664, d. at Fairfield in 1700/1.

Married Susannah Lockwood, dau. of Sergt. Joseph, whose will in 1715 named his dau. Susanna's children Nathaniel, Ephraim, Sarah, and Ann Burr. The four children were also referred to in the will of their grandfather Burr. Susannah Burr conveyed 1709 to her sons Nathaniel and Ephraim.

Susannah wife of Nathaniel, Jr., renewed her Covenant at Fairfield Church, 23 Dec. 1694, and the first two children were bapt. the same date.

Inv. 27 Jan. 1700/1 ; widow Susannah made oath. Sergt. Joseph Lockwood gave bond with his dau., the widow Susannah. Distribution ordered, 26 Nov. 1702, to four children, Nathaniel, Ephraim, Sarah, and Annah; Susannah was appointed guardian to her youngest child Ephraim. Nathaniel Burr was released, 7 Apr. 1703, as guardian for Nathaniel, Sarah and Annah Burr, children of his dec'd son Nathaniel, and Sergt. Robert Lockwood was appointed. Later, Lockwood was released, and Ens. Benjamin Rumsey, father-in-law of the three children, was appointed their guardian. Nathaniel, son of Nathaniel, Jr., chose his bro. John Silliman for guardian, 2 Mar. 1714/5.

Children, bapt. at Fairfield :

Joseph, b. (say 1691), d. y.
Nathaniel, b. (say 1693), d. y.

Sarah, bapt. 20 Jan. 1694/5, d. in 1716. Inv. 10 Dec. 1716; sister Ann
wife of John Silliman, and two brothers Nathaniel and Ephraim.
Anna, bapt. 5 Apr. 1696, d. 1 Oct. 1740 in 45 yr. (g. s., Fairfield) ; m.
abt. 1716, Capt. John Silliman.
XNathaniel, bapt 15 May 1698, d. in 1761; will 25 May 1761, proved 21
Aug. 1761; m. 10 Nov. 1726, Martha Silliman, bapt. 24 Aug. 1701,
d. 18 Mar. 1753.
XEphraim, b. 5 Apr. 1700 (by age at death), bapt. 14 Apr. 1700, d. 29
Apr. 1776 ae. 76 yrs. 13 days (g. s., Fairfield) ; will 18 Aug 1769,
codicil 6 Apr. 1776, proved 1776; m. 7 Jan. 1724/5, Abigail Burr,
dau. of Maj. Peter, bapt. 25 Oct. 1702, d. 8 July 1780 ae. 78 (g. s.).

Burr, John, s. of Nathaniel. Deputy for Fairfield, May 1704,
Oct. 1705, May 1708, May and Aug. 1710, May and June 1711,
May 1712, Oct. 1713, May and Oct. 1714, May 1717, Oct. 1718,
May and Oct. 1719, May 1720, May 1721, May 1723, Oct. 1723
(speaker), May 1724 (speaker), Oct. 1724, May and Oct. 1725,
May 1726, Oct. 1727, Oct. 1728, May 1729; Assistant, 1729-39.
Major, Expedition to Port Royal, Aug. 1710; Capt., Fairfield
County Troop, May 1714; War Council, July 1711; Major,
Fairfield County, May 1725; Colonel, 4th Regt., Oct. 1739.
Justice, 1711, 1714-29; Judge, Fairfield County Court, 1726-44;
Judge, Fairfield Probate Court, Dec. 1726 to 1744.

Born about 1672; Col. John d. 13 June 1750 in 79 yr. (g. s.,
Stratfield).

Married (1) Deborah Barlow, dau. of John, b. abt. 1675, d.
4 Dec. 1726 in 52 yr. (g. s., Stratfield).

Married (2) in 1727, Elizabeth (Hawley), widow of Joseph
Wakeman. She was b. 6 May 1679, d. 18 Aug. 1753 in 74 yr.
(g. s.).

Will 26 Apr. 1750, proved 18 June 1750; wife Elizabeth
(referring to marriage covenant dated 29 Mar. 1727) and her
dau. Mary; dau. Abigail Hubbell; dau. Mary Smedley; gr. son
Ebenezer Dimon, son of said dau. Mary; gr. sons William and
David Dimon; sons John and William Burr.

Children [by first wife], bapt. at Stratfield:

XJohn, bapt. 28 Aug. 1698, d. 13 Sept. [O. S.] 1752 in 55 yr. (g. s.,
Stratfield) ; Capt.; m. (rec. Fairfield) 18 Oct. 1722, Katharine
Wakeman, who d. 25 Sept. 1753 in 53 yr. The will of Capt. John,

20 July 1752, proved 3 Oct. 1752, named his wife, seven daus. and four sons, .referred to father Col. John dec'd, maintenance of brother Joseph Burr; brother William, Exec'r.

Abigail, bapt. 16 Mar. 1701, d. 6 Apr. 1780; m. 25 May 1727, Eleazer Hubbell.

Deborah, bapt. 22 Apr. 1705, d. 28 Nov. 1726 in 22 yr. (g. s.).

Mary, bapt. 4 July 1708, d. 12 Sept. 1766 in 58 yr.; m. (1) Ebenezer Dimon; m. (2) at Fairfield, 4 Jan. 1747/8, Col. James Smedley.

✕William, b. 9 Dec. 1711, bapt. 10 Feb. 1712, d. 5 May 1769 in 58 yr. (g. s., Stratfield); m. (1) (rec. Fairfield) 4 Aug. 1736, Mary Wakeman, dau. of Capt. Joseph, who d. 19 Mar. 1742/3 in 33 yr. (g. s.); m. (2) (rec. Fairfield) 16 May 1744, Charity, widow of Joseph Strong, and dau. of John Welles, Jr., of Stratford. Charity d. 2 Oct. 1769 in 48 yr. (g. s.); will of Charity, 2 Aug. 1769, proved 16 Oct. 1769.

Joseph, b. 22, bapt. 27 June 1714; incompetent, living 1752.

Burr, Daniel, s. of Nathaniel.

Born at Fairfield [say 1677], d. there in 1722; prob. m. (1) 7 Nov. 1705, Abigail Stratton;* m. (2) Mary Jennings, dau. of Joshua, b. abt. 1690, d. 11 Oct. 1748 in 59 yr. (g. s., Westport).

He was called Jr. and "Town" to distinguish him from his cousins. Daniel, Jr., renewed his Covenant at Fairfield Church, 1 June 1707; Mary wife of Mr. Daniel "Town" was bapt. 16 Sept. 1716.

Will 9 Apr. 1722, proved 25 June 1722; calls himself son of Nathaniel; wife Mary; four sons, Nathaniel, James, John, David; two daughters, Rebecca and Mary Burr; brother John Burr, Exec'r. Robert Turney and Rebecca his wife of Stratford, and Nathan Adams and Mary his wife of Norwalk, receipted for their portions to mother Mary Burr, 3 Jan. 1742/3.

Will of Mary Burr, widow of Daniel, 9 Mar. 1742/3, proved 6 Dec. 1748; eldest son John; son David; daus. Rebecca wife of Robert Turney and Mary wife of Nathan Adams.

Children [by first wife], bapt. at Fairfield:

✕Nathaniel, bapt. 1 June 1707, d. 8 Nov. 1784; Capt.; m. 23 Nov. 1732, Mary Turney, dau. of Robert, bapt. 26 Oct. 1712.

✕James, bapt. 23 Jan. 1708/9, d. in 1782; res. Monroe; m. Deborah Turney, dau. of Robert, bapt. June 1711.

---

* See *Book of the Strattons,* vol. 1, p. 104. We are indebted to Mr. Clarence A. Torrey for this marriage.

Children [by second wife], bapt. at Fairfield:

Rebecca, bapt. 29 Oct. 1710, d. at Trumbull, 7 Sept. 1794 in 84 yr.
(g. s.); m. (1) Robert Turney; m. (2) 3 June 1756, Jonadab
Bassett.

✕John, bapt. 1 Feb. 1712/3, d. at Westport, 9 Apr. 1783 ae. 70 yrs. 3
mos. (g. s.); m. (1) 14 Oct. 1735, Elizabeth Nash, dau. of Thomas,
who d. 29 Mar. 1740; m. (2) 9 Nov. 1741, Grace Bulkley, dau.
of Gershom, bapt. 12 Feb. 1720/1, d. 21 Feb. 1772 in 52 yr. (g. s.).

✕David, b. 13 Apr. 1719 [if g. s. is correctly read], bapt. 8 Mar. 1718/9,
d. at Westport, 29 Aug. 1792 ae. 73 yrs. 4 mos. 5 days (g. s.);
will 23 Apr. 1781, proved 6 Sept. 1792; m. 8 Apr. 1741, Abigail
Silliman, dau. of John.

Mary, bapt. 31 July 1721, d. at Westport, 15 Mar. 1806 ae. 84; m.
Nathan Adams.

Burr, Daniel, s. of Daniel.

Born at Fairfield, 30 July 1670. "Deacon Burr" d. at Greenfield, 4 Nov. 1748, ae. abt. 78.

Married (1) Esther Perry, dau. of Nathaniel.

Married (2) Abigail ———.

His family, entered in Greenfield Church records with great
incompleteness, included his wife Abigail, his children Joseph,
Timothy, Abigail, James, and Jabez, bapt. as adults, and Daniel
himself was called "Jr." In 1726 his wife was admitted under
the name Hannah, an error unless he had three wives.

Children [by first wife]:

✕Joseph, bapt. 20 Feb. 1725/6 as an adult; m. (rec. Fairfield) 3 Mar.
1725, Hannah Hide, bapt. 14 Mar. 1707/8.

✕Timothy, b. abt. 1702, bapt. 26 June 1726, d. 27 July 1772 in 69 yr.
(g. s., Greenfield); will 21 July 1772, proved 15 Sept. 1772; m.
(rec. Greenfield) 6 Mar. 1728, Sarah Rowland, who d. 27 Sept.
1788 in 83 yr.

Children [by second wife]:

Abigail.

✕James, m. (1) (rec. Fairfield) 12 Dec. 1731, Hannah Osborn, Widow
[prob. Hannah Hubbell, widow of Joseph Osborn], who d. 11 Aug.
1743; m. (2) Jan. 1746, Mary Barlow.

✕Jabez, bapt. 4 Nov. 1739 as an adult, d. at Redding, 29 Apr. 1770;
will 17 Apr. 1770, proved 1 May 1770; m. Elizabeth ———, who
d. at Redding, 16 Nov. 1760 ae. 42.

Burr, (Seth) Samuel, s. of Daniel. Deputy for Fairfield, May 1728 to Oct. 1731 inclusive, Oct. 1733, May 1734, May 1735, Oct. 1739, May 1741 to Oct. 1743 inclusive, Oct. 1744, May 1745, May and Oct. 1746, May 1747, Oct. 1748, Oct. 1751 to May 1754 inclusive. Lt., Fairfield First Company, May 1729; Capt., Oct. 1738. Justice, 1739-41.

Born at Fairfield, 20 June 1694, d. there 21 Mar. 1773 in 79 yr. (g. s.); m. (1) June 1722, Elizabeth Wakeman, dau. of Joseph, bapt. 19 Apr. 1702, d. 16 June 1753 in 51 yr. (g. s.); m. (2) 14 Mar. 1754, Ruth, widow of Joseph Bulkley, and dau. of Matthew Jennings, bapt. 11 Oct. 1708, d. abt. 1787.

Elizabeth wife of Sergt S. Samuel renewed her Covenant at Fairfield Church, 15 Sept. 1723, and he was called Sergt. at bapt. of children 1723 and 1726; beginning with 1732, the church records call him simply Samuel.

Children [by first wife], recorded at Fairfield:

Mehitabel, b. 28 May 1723, bapt. 1 Sept. 1723, d. in 1761; m. abt. 1744, Joseph Squire.

Seth, b. Jan. 1725/6, bapt. 6 Feb. 1725/6, d. at Fairfield, 22 Dec. 1764 ae. 39 (g. s.).

✕Samuel, b. Nov. 1728,* bapt. 24 Sept. 1727, d. 20 Mar. 1791; m. 31 May 1753, Eunice Sturgis, dau. of Solomon.

✕Daniel, b. 2 July 1730, bapt. 12 July 1730; m. 22 Jan. 1756, Ann Silliman.

✕Ebenezer, b. Oct. 1732, bapt. in 1732, d. 1767 ae. 35 (g. s.); adm'n granted 13 Apr. 1767; m. 26 Feb. 1759, Amelia Silliman, dau. of Ebenezer, b. 30 Oct. 1736, d. 1794 ae. 58 (g. s.); she m. (2) Abel Gold.

✕Nehemiah, b. 18 Apr. 1734, bapt. 5 May 1734, d. in 1815; Ens.; m. 21 Apr. 1762, Sarah Osborn, b. 27 May 1741.

Ellen, b. Nov. 1736, bapt. 18 Jan. 1735/6, d. 18 June 1777; m. 19 Dec. 1754, Abel Gold.

Elizabeth, b. Sept. 1738, bapt. 16 Oct. 1737; m. 21 Jan. 1756, Samuel Silliman.

Abigail, bapt. 18 Mar. 1738/9, d. y.

Charles, b. Aug. 1741, bapt. 3 Sept. 1741, d. 15 Mar. 1800 ae 58; m. Elizabeth ———, who d. 10 July 1813 ae. 69.

Burritt, William.

An early settler of Stratford. Inv. 28 May, 1651; £140.

Will of Elizabeth of Stratford, 2 Sept. 1681; son Steven Burrit;

---

* Birth date apparently in error.

dau. Mary Smith; five shillings to each of six grandchildren; to
Mr. Chauncey, 20 shillings; to David Mitchell, 20 shillings; to
John Minor, 10 shillings; residue to son John Burrit, in confirma-
tion of my deed of 5 Apr. 1675. Witnesses: Daniel Mitchell,
Abraham Mitchell. Inv. 23 Oct. 1683, £55.

Children:
+Stephen, b. abt. 1641.
Mary, m. ——— Smith.
+John.

Burritt, Stephen, s. of William. Ens., Stratford Trainband,
June 1672; Ens., Fairfield County Dragoons, Sept. 1675; Com-
missary of Army, Nov. 1675; Lt., Fairfield County Troop,
Jan. 1675; Deputy for Stratford, May 1681, May 1691; Capt.,
Trainband, May 1692.

Capt. Stephen d. 24 Jan. 1697/8 in 57 yr. (g. s.).
Inv. of Capt. Steven, 4 Mar. 1697/8. Widow Sarah made oath.
Six children and ages: Elizabeth 22, Peleg 19, Josiah 17, Israel
11, Charles 8, Ephraim 5.
Married 8 or 28 Jan. 1673 [1673/4] (duplicate entries, Strat-
ford), Sarah Nichols, dau. of Isaac.

Children, recorded at Stratford:
Elizabeth, b. 7 July 1675.
William, b. 29 Mar. 1677, d. y.
Peleg, b. 5 Oct. 1679; m. 5 Dec. 1705, Sarah Bennett.
Josiah, b. abt. 1681; m. 10 Mar. 1702/3, Mary Peat.
Israel, b. abt. 1687, d. at Durham, in 1750; Deacon; m. (1) 4 Mar.
   1718/9, Sarah Coe; m. (2) Sarah Chauncey, dau. of Rev. Nathaniel.
Charles, b. abt. 1689, d. in 1761; will 23 Jan. 1761, proved 26 Feb.
   1761; m. 18 Apr. 1717, Mary Lockwood.
Ephraim, b. abt. 1692; m. (1) 14 Feb. 1721/2, Mary Fairchild, who d.
   18 Aug. 1726; m. (2) 15 Jan. 1728, Mrs. Sarah Lewis.

Burritt, John, s. of William. Deputy for Stratford, Oct. 1693,
Oct. 1698, May 1704.

Adm'n granted, 17 Feb. 1726/7, to Joseph Burritt of Stratford,
John being called father of Joseph, who was the only "heir in
law." Inv. showed good estate.

Married (1) at Stratford, 1 May 1684, Deborah "Barley". She was dau. of Thomas Barlow.

He m. (2) at Stratford, 5 May 1708, Mis^t Hannah Fairchild. She was widow of Zechariah Fairchild, and dau. of John Beach.

He m. (3) 9 May 1726, Mercy Wheeler; prob. widow of Moses Wheeler, and previously of Thomas Lattin.

Mr. John Burit d. at Stratford, 1 Feb. 1726/7.

Child by Deborah, recorded at Stratford:

> Joseph, b. 12 Mar. 1685, d. in 1752; will 10 Mar. 1750, proved 5 Mar. 1752; m. 25 Nov. 1708, Mary Wakelee.

Burroughs, John.

Married at Stratford, 10 Jan. 1694/5, Patience Hinman.

Inv. 11 Mar. 1712 [1712/3]. Steven and Edward, sons of John, chose uncles Edward Hinman and Ens. Richard Hubbell guardians. On 14 Apr. 1713, Ens. Richard Hubbell and Edward Hinman were granted adm'n on Est. of John; Patience, widow of John, being dec'd. Distribution ordered 1722 at request of Joseph; Steven has improved his part. John chose Ens. Edmund Lewis guardian, 9 Oct. 1722, and Eden chose John Thompson.

Children of John and Patience, recorded at Stratford:

> Stephen, b. 25 Feb. 1694 [1694/5]; m. 3 Mar. 1719/20, Ruth Nichols.
> Edward, b. 14 Mar. 1696.
> Hannah, b. 23 Nov. 1697; m. 7 Dec. 1720, Eliphalet Curtis.
> Eunice, b. 1 Sept. 1699; m. 11 Sept. 1727, Jonah Curtis.
> Joseph, b. 23 Nov. 1701, d. 6 Jan. 1765 ae. 63 (g. s., New Haven); m. at New Haven, 13 Jan. 1725/6, Lydia Munson, b. 22 Nov. 1707, d. 12 Sept. 1769 ae. 62 (g. s.).
> Bathsheba, b. 26 Sept. 1703; m. 5 Apr. 1726, Sevignion Lewis.
> John, b. 31 Aug. 1705, bapt. (Stratfield rec.) 10 Feb. 1706, d. at Newtown abt. 1726/7. Adm'n granted, 20 Feb. 1726/7, to Stephen Burrows and Eliphalet Curtis. Distribution made to brothers and sisters: Stephen, Edward, Joseph, Eden, Hannah, Eunice, Bashua, Patience.
> Eden, b. 10 July 1707, bapt. (Stratfield) 7 Sept. 1707, d. 9 Mar. 1771 ae. 64 (g. s., New Haven); m. (rec. Wallingford) 27 Dec. 1733, Lydia Austin, b. abt. 1713, d. 1775; no issue.
> Ephraim, b. in 1708, bapt. (Stratfield) 24 Apr. 1709, d. y.
> Patience, b. 2 Jan. 1709/10, bapt. (Stratfield) 11 Mar. 1711; m. at Stratfield, 29 Jan. 1736, David Sanford.

Burrough, Mr. Edward.

He was a sea captain; d. at Stratford, 29 Apr. 1732; m. (1) at Stratford, 20 Apr. 1710, Mrs. Abigail Gaskell; widow of Samuel Gaskell and previously of Dr. Nathaniel Hudson, and dau. of Rev. Nathaniel Chauncey, b. 14 Oct. 1677, d. in 1720; m. (2) 11 Sept. 1722, Ann Judson; dau. of Samuel, b. 15 Oct. 1695.

Will 18 Apr. 1732, proved 8 May 1732; all realty to only beloved son, Zechariah Burroughs; daus. Abigail, Sarah, and Elizabeth Burroughs, £30 each.

Children [by first wife]:

> Zechariah, b. 19 Feb. 1712/3, d. in Antigua in 1737.
> Abigail, b. 31 May 1715; m. (rec. Wallingford) 28 Feb. 1736, Jotham Ives.
> Sarah.

Child [by second wife]:

> Elizabeth, bapt. 30 Dec. 1722,* d. 14 Jan. 1745/6; m. 2 Feb. 1743/4, James Curtis.

Burton, Solomon.

Married at Stratford, 1 Aug. 1687, Mercy Judson.

Children, recorded at Stratford:

> Benjamin, b. 3 Aug. 1692, d. in 1765; will 13 Feb. 1764, proved 22 June 1765; m. 7 Dec. 1714, Bethia Curtis.
> Joseph, b. [say 1695], d. 30 Dec. 1721; adm'n granted to bros. Benjamin and Judson, 8 Jan. 1721/2; widow Anna made oath to Inv.; m. 30 Nov. 1720, Anna Ufford, dau. of Lt. Samuel, b. 8 Aug. 1702. She m. (2) 22 Aug. 1723, William Patterson.
> Judson, b. [say 1698], d. in 1774; will 24 June 1771, proved 7 Mar. 1774; m. 9 Jan. 1721/2, Eunice Lewis.
> Sarah, b. [say 1700]; m. (1) 3 Nov. 1720, Nathaniel Beach; m. (2) William Odell.

Bushnell, Francis, s. of Richard.

He m. at Norwalk, 12 Oct. 1675, Hannah Seymour, dau. of Thomas; and settled in Danbury.

Inv. Oct. 1697; Samuel Knapp of Danbury made oath.   Adm'n

---

* By *Hist. of Stratford,* but the record is not found in Stratford Cong. Church register, and may be from that of the Epis. Church. Possibly the date is inaccurate.

granted to Samuel Pickett and Samuel Knapp. The seven children named, under 18; Abigail chose Ens. Thomas Taylor for guardian.

Children, first two recorded at Norwalk:

>   Hannah, b. 22 Aug. 1676; m. Samuel Knapp.
>   Mary, b. 21 Dec. 1679; m. John Taylor.
>   Abigail, m. Rev. Seth Shove, of Danbury. They had a dau. Mary bapt. at Fairfield, 8 Nov. 1696.
>   Lydia, m. John Fitch.
>   Mercy, d. at New Milford, 5 Sept. 1767; m. (1) (rec. New Milford), 30 Jan. 1711/2, John Bostwick; m. (2) at New Milford, 14 Oct. 1742, William Gaylord; m. (3) Capt. James Lockwood of Norwalk.
>   Rebecca, [m. Theophilus Taylor?].
>   Judith.

Butler, Richard.

Inv. 18 May 1676. Agreement made by Thomas Hicks, Mary Hicks, Benjamin Peat, Phebe Peat.

Benjamin and Samuel Peat, Jr., of Stratford, conveyed 1713 land from grandfather Richard Butler dec'd. John Washbourne of Flushing, L. I., Gent., conveyed 1712 to Daniel Beardsley, right in Stratford land. John Hicks of Flushing, L. I., eldest son of Thomas Hicks by his wife Mary, dau. of Richard Butler of Stratford, with Samuel Simmons and his wife Phebe, John Isman and his wife Elizabeth, and Sarah Rushmore, all of Flushing, three daus. of Thomas and Mary, appointed 1712 their brother Jacob Hicks to act as their attorney.

Distribution 1713 of Est. of Mrs. Mary Hicks of Cornberry Neck, L. I.; grandson John Washbourne; heirs of Mary Hicks, a dau., and of Thomas Hicks: John Hicks; Jacob Hicks; Phebe Hicks; Sarah Hicks; Elizabeth Hicks.

Children:

>   Mary, m. (1) 17 June 1655, John Washburn; m. (2) Thomas Hicks.
>   Phebe, m. Benjamin Peat.

Butler, (Dr.) John.

On 9 Mar. 1686/7, John Butler, merchant, now resident in Stratford, conveyed 70 acres to David "Rennals", merchant, resident in Fairfield.

Inv. of Mr. John of Stratford, 26 June 1696; Mrs. Mary made oath. He had a ship, and a farm at Saugatuck.

Cable, John.

Settled in Springfield, 1636; removed to Fairfield 1644.

Will 4 Apr. 1682; wife Ann; gr. child John Cable; gr. child John Knowles; dau. Rebecca; kinsman Jehu Burr and John Burr, overseers. Witnesses: Ezbon Wakeman, John Banks. Inv. 21 Sept. 1682. John Cable gave acquittance, 13 Mar. 1694/5, to Jehu and John Burr, Adm'rs of his grandfather's Est.

Sarah Cable, mentioned 1654 in the Staples slander trial, was prob. his first wife, unless she was an otherwise unknown dau. He m. (2) Ann, widow of Roger Betts of Branford.

Children [by first wife]:
+John, b. at Springfield, 12 Jan. 1640 [1640/1].
Rebecca, m. John Knowles.

Cable, John, s. of John.

Born at Springfield, 12 Jan. 1640 [1640/1].
Inv. 7 Nov. 1673.
Widow Elizabeth m. before 19 Dec. 1683, Thomas Sherwood. In 1685, since the eldest son John had his gr. father's lands, distribution was ordered to Joseph, Elizabeth, Sarah, and Rebecca (all minors).

Children:
+John.
Elizabeth.
Sarah, m. abt. 1690, Robert Churchill.
Rebecca, prob. m. Daniel Adams.
+Joseph.

Cable, John, s. of John 2d.

Married Abigail Sherwood. Isaac Sherwood, Sr., conveyed 1708 to son-in-law John Cable. Abigail m. (2) 1 Dec. 1727, Thomas Pike, and d. between 27 Oct. and 18 Dec. 1735.

He conveyed, 1 Mar. 1708, to bro.-in-law Daniel Sherwood the house which stands upon the acre I had of my father-in-law Isaac Sherwood.

Will 12 June 1724; wife Abigail; sons George, Jonathan, John, Andrew, Daniel, Isaac; daus. Margery Patchen and Abigail Cable. Inv. 8 Aug. 1724.

Distribution 28 Mar. 1727; widow; children George, Jonathan, John, Andrew, Daniel, Isaac, and Margery Cable, and Abigail wife of Jacob Patchen.*

Daniel and Isaac chose George Cable for guardian, 27 Nov. 1735.

Real Est. of John Cable which was set to his widow for life, was distributed 18 Dec. 1735 to the six sons.

A deed was given 9 Jan. 1727/8 by Thomas Sherwood to Abigail former wife of John Cable, she being then already wife of Thomas Pike, so another deed was given, and the Pikes conveyed the property, 27 Oct. 1735, to their son John Cable, and to John's dau. Emitt.

Children:

> Margery, b. [say 1701], d. at Wilton, 1 Apr. 1788; m. [say 1723], Joseph Patchen.
>
> ✕George, b. abt. 1703, d. at Westport, 17 Sept. 1763 in 60 yr. (g. s.); will 30 Aug. 1763, proved 26 Sept. 1763; m. (rec. Fairfield) 17 Feb. 1729, Sarah Shaw, who d. 29 Jan. 1787 (Westport Church).
>
> ✕Jonathan, b. [say 1705]; m. (rec. Fairfield) 3 Sept. 1728, Mary Bennett, dau. of Thomas.
>
> Abigail, b. [say 1707], d. at Wilton, 15 Feb. 1795/6; m. [say 1725], Jacob Patchen.
>
> ✕John, b. [say 1709], d. 24 Mar. 1760; will 7 Mar., proved 22 Apr. 1760; Ens.; m. 26 Sept. 1733, Ann Davis, who d. in 1773.
>
> ✕Andrew, b. [say 1712], d. before 4 Aug. 1761, when adm'n was granted to widow; m. Rebecca Wheeler, who d. 23 Feb. 1799 ae. 80 yrs. 9 days (g. s., Stratfield).
>
> ✕Daniel, b. [say 1714], d. in 1760; Inv. 5 May 1761; m. (rec. Fairfield) 7 June 1739, Sarah Crane.
>
> Isaac, b. [say 1716].

---

* There is a difficulty regarding the marriages of the daus. The will 1724 calls them Margery Patchen and Abigail Cable. The distribution 1727 states that Margery *Cabel* had over £20 in her father's lifetime, and over £21 from the Executrix "as she saieth" while Abigail had received her portion (over £42) from the Executrix, as appeared by a receipt from her husband Jacob Patching. We can only suppose that *Cabel* is an error in the distribution, for Margery would hardly have received half of her portion from her father unless married, as his will shows.

Cable, Joseph, s. of John 2d.

Married Abigail Adams, dau. of Samuel, b. 25 Mar. 1682; she m. (2) Elijah Crane.

He "listed him self to go a Volentere to war", *therefore* Mrs. Sidenham in behalf of her husband Mr. William Sidenham entered caveat against the house and land of Joseph Cable, 16 Apr. 1690; thus was patriotism rewarded.

Conveyed 1702 land from John Cable, Jr., dec'd.

Joseph, son of Joseph, chose Thomas Sanford guardian, 1 Feb. 1715; there being three more sons, the Court appointed Daniel Adams guardian for Samuel, and Elijah Crane for William and Benjamin.

Benjamin, son of Joseph, chose his uncle [———][11] Adams guardian, 7 Feb. 1726/7.

Children:

> Joseph, b. abt. 1700/1; prob. lived in Salem, Westchester County, N. Y.; m. and had a family, untraced.
> ╳Samuel, b. [say 1705], d. in 1740; will 2 Jan. 1739/40, proved 23 May 1740; m. (rec. Stratfield) 27 July 1731, Ann Wheeler. She was dau. of Timothy.
> William, b. [say 1708], d. at New Haven abt. 1761; m. (1) Sarah
> ———, b. abt. 1711, d. 15 Aug. 1751 ae. 40 (g. s.); m. (2) Mary (Hall), widow of Nathaniel Brown, b. 20 Aug. 1723, d. 29 Feb. 1784 ae. 62 (g. s.).
> ╳Benjamin, b. abt. 1712, d. at Norwalk in 1795; will 28 Jan. 1783, proved 10 Sept. 1795; m. Martha ———.

Castle, Henry.

He had a grant at Fairfield, 25 Dec. 1678.

His wife received a legacy 1667 in will of Daniel Finch, and doubtless she was his stepdau., and dau. of Thomas Dickerson. The first six children of Henry and Abigail were bapt. together at Woodbury, Sept. 1686, and we assume that the mother was Abigail Dickerson. Mary dau. of Roger and Elizabeth (Dickerson) Knapp in her will 1711, referred to her "aunt Casle".

Henry, Sr., d. at Woodbury, 2 Feb. 1697/8, after a year's illness; "The Widow" Castle d. there, Dec. 1725.

Widow Abigail made oath to Inv. of Henry, Sr., of Woodbury, who d. 2 Feb. 1697/8. Adm'n granted to son Henry. Ages of children: Henry 31, Samuel 29, Isaac 25, William 10, Abigail 22, Mary 20, Mercy 13.

Children, bapt. at Woodbury:
+Henry, b. abt. 1666.
+Samuel, b. abt. 1668.
Isaac, b. abt. 1672, d. 25 July 1727; m. (1) Sarah Adams, dau. of Samuel of Fairfield, b. 3 Oct. 1680, d. at Woodbury, 24 Feb. 1707/8; m. (2) abt. 1716, Joanna ———.
Abigail, b. abt. 1675.
Mary, b. abt. 1677; m. 17 May 1698, Joseph Hurlbut, Jr.
Mercy, b. abt. 1684.
William, bapt. July 1688; m. at Stratfield, 1 Feb. 1710/1, Rebecca; she was dau. of John Seeley; the "wife of William" d. Dec. 1725.

Castle, Henry, s. of Henry.

Married (1) (rec. Woodbury) 12 Apr. 1699, Hannah Squire; dau. of Thomas. She d. 7 May 1714, and he m. (2) abt. 1715, Ruth ———.
Agreement of heirs, 13 Feb. 1745; Henry Castle, Luke Castle, Roger Brownson, Jr., Samuel Benedict, Hannah Castle.

Children by Hannah, recorded at Woodbury:
Henry, b. 12 Feb. 1699/1700.
Hannah, b. 22 May 1702.
Ruth, b. 6 Aug. 1705, d. at New Milford, 4 Mar. 1788 in 83 yr. (g. s.) ; m. (rec. New Milford) 11 Jan. 1732/3, Roger Bronson, Jr.
Jemima, b. 3 Mar. 1708/9; m. Samuel Benedict.
Luke, b. 21 Mar. 1710/1.

Child by Ruth, recorded at Woodbury:
Nathaniel, b. 7 Nov. 1716, d. 11 Sept. 1720.

Castle, Samuel, s. of Henry.

Born abt. 1668, d. 2 Apr. 1707 in 29(?) yr. (g. s., Stratford).
Married Susanna, widow of Samuel Nichols, previously widow of Thomas Fairchild, 2d.

Child, bapt. at Woodbury:
Susannah, bapt. Sept. 1693.

Chapman, John.

An original settler at New Haven, 1638, sold 1647 and rem. to Fairfield; and soon after to Stamford. On 13 Jan. 1653 [1653/4], Richard Osborn entered land at Fairfield purchased from George Hull as agent for John Chapman.

Married Martha, widow of Thomas Lawrence of Milford; she m. (3) at Stamford, 17 Dec. 1657, Francis Brown.

Inv. June 1665 attested by the wife of Francis Brown. Widow; daus. Mary and Elizabeth, under 18, only heirs.

Eleazer Slawson, husband of Mary Chapman, and Elizabeth Chapman, conveyed 7 Mar. 1673/4 to father-in-law Francis Brown. Eleazer Slawson, 12 Dec. 1672, acknowledged receiving from Francis Brown, Adm'r on Est. of John Chapman, portion due my wife Mary. John Judson of Stratford, with consent of wife, sold 1674 to father-in-law Francis Brown, ¼ of house Brown now lives in; witnessed by Eliphalet Jones and Eleazer Slawson. Thomas Lawrence conveyed 23 Oct. 1677 to bro.-in-law John Judson. [Stamford Deeds.]

Children:

> Mary, m. Eleazer Slawson.
> Elizabeth, m. at Stratford, 12 Mar. 1673/4, John Judson.

Chauncey, (Rev.) Israel. Chaplain, K. Philip's War, and member of Council of War, Oct. 1675. Granted 200 acres, Oct. 1681.

Son of Rev. Charles and Catharine (Eyre) Chauncey; grad. Harvard Coll. 1661; minister at Stratford over 38 yrs.

Married (1) at Stratford, 8 Jan. 1667 [1667/8], Mary Nichols, dau. of Isaac.

Married (2) at New Haven, 11 Nov. 1684, Sarah Hudson. She was dau. of John, b. 5 Apr. 1657, d. in 1711.

Rev. Mr. Israel, pastor of the Church in Stratford, d. 14 Mar. 1702/3; in 59 yr. (g. s.).

Children [by first wife], recorded at Stratford:

> +Charles, b. 3 Sept. 1668.
> Isaac, b. 5 Oct. 1670, d. 2 May 1745 ae. 74 (g. s., Hadley); grad. Harvard Coll. 1693; minister at Hadley, Mass.; m. (1) Sarah

Blackleach, dau. of Richard b. abt. 1682, d. 29 June 1720 ae. 38 (g. s.); m. (2) Abiel, widow of Rev. Joseph Metcalf, and dau. of Rev. William and Alice (Bradford) Adams of Dedham.
Robert, b. 25 Oct. 1677; settled in Bristol, Eng.

Chauncey, (Rev.) Charles, s. of Israel. Granted remuneration as Chaplain to Army, Oct. 1690, and as Chaplain and physician, Oct. 1691. Preached Election Sermon, 1702.

Born at Stratford, 3 Sept. 1668; grad. Harvard Coll. 1686; minister at Stratfield, where he d. Dec. 1714 ae. 48 (g. s.).

Married (1) (rec. Fairfield) 29 June 1692, Sarah Burr. She was dau. of John, b. 25 July 1675, d. "15 of 1697/8." He, of Stratfield, m. (2) 16 Mar. 1698/9, Sarah Wolcott, dau. of Mr. Henry of Windsor. She d. 5 Jan. 1703/4. He m. (3) 4 Mar. 1710, Elizabeth, widow of Matthew Sherwood, and dau. of Samuel Morehouse. She m. (3) at Stratfield, 10 Apr. 1716, Lt. Richard Miles of New Haven.

Will of Charles Chauncey of Fairfield, Clerk, 24 Dec. 1714, proved 6 July 1715; wife Elizabeth, mentioning income from Est. at Lambeth near Bristol in Great Britain which descended from father Mr. Israel Chauncey of Stratford dec'd; son Israel, farm given unto my gr. father Mr. Charles Chauncey near Merrimack River, Mass. Bay; son John, lands in Stratford from my father and by purchase from my bro. Robert of Bristol, Gt. Britain; sons Robert and Ichabod Wolcott, estate in Stratfield; dau. Abiah Chauncey; overseers, Rev. Joseph Webb of Fairfield, and Rev. Timothy Cutler of Stratford. Abiah chose Rev. Samuel Cook of Stratfield for guardian, 6 June 1716; and Ichabod Wolcott chose the same guardian, 1 Dec. 1718. Lt. Richard Hubbell was appointed to administer, but failing to distribute, on 29 Apr. 1719 Lt. Richard Miles, in right of wife Elizabeth who was the widow, applied for distribution.

Children by first wife, recorded at Fairfield:

XIsrael, b. 29 June 1693, d. in 1737; adm'n granted, 1 Feb. 1736/7; m. 2 Feb. 1720/1, Martha Wakeman; dau. of John, b. 24 Sept. 1700.
John, b. 7 Nov. 1695, bapt. at Stratfield 10 Nov. 1695; m. (rec. Stratford) 1 Jan. 1721/2, Mist Eunice Brewster of Brookhaven.

Children by second wife, recorded at Fairfield, bapt. at Stratfield:

Abiah, b. 22 Jan. 1699/1700, bapt. 28 Jan. 1700; m. (rec. Wallingford) 20 Feb. 1727, Col. Benjamin Hall.

✕Robert, b. 30 Oct. 1701, bapt. 2 Nov. 1701, d. in 1753; adm'n granted, 25 Aug. 1753; m. Hannah Wheeler, dau. of Samuel, bapt. at Stratfield, 31 Jan. 1703.

Ichabod Wolcott, b. 5 Jan. 1703/4, bapt. 9 Jan. 1704; grad. Yale Coll. 1723; went to England 1726 and d. there before 1742.

Church, Joseph.

Of Fairfield, Inv. 4 Jan. 1723 [1723/4]; Jonathan Sturgis, Adm'r.

Churchill, Robert.

He was usually called Churcher.

Sarah, wife of Robert, was bapt. at Fairfield Church, 10 Feb. 1694/5. She was dau. of John Cable, Jr. Robert receipted, 24 Jan. 1694/5, to father-in-law Thomas Sherwood, Adm'r by virtue of marriage with my wife's mother, for portion of wife Sarah in Est. of her father John Cable.

He m. (2) ———, dau. of John Thomas of Woodbury, who was his wife in 1709. Prob. she was Rebecca, b. at New Haven, 20 Sept. 1680.

Will 3 Nov. 1733, proved 8 Jan. 1734; eldest son Nehemiah; daus. Eleanor Sherwood, Sarah Churcher, Patience Oysterbank; son Robert, Exec'r with Capt. Gershom Bulkley.

On 22 Dec. 1722, Robert Churcher, Jr., attested respecting a twelfth part of the Est. of John Thomas, Jr., of Woodbury, dec'd, which David Leavenworth bought of my sister Patience, that she hath power now to dispose of the same.

Children, bapt. at Fairfield Church, first two as of Robert and Sarah, the next two as of Robert:

Abigail, bapt. 17 Feb. 1694/5, d. y.
Sarah, bapt. 17 Feb. 1694/5.
Ellen, bapt. 20 Oct. 1695, d. at Westport, 1 Oct. 1754; m. Thomas Sherwood.
Nehemiah, bapt. 27 Mar. 1698.

Children [by second wife]:

Robert, d. at Westport, 31 Mar. 1776.
Patience, d. at Westport, 29 Nov. 1760; m. Jacob Oysterbank.

Clapham, Peter.

He was called cousin [*i. e.*, nephew] in the will of Anthony Wilson of Fairfield. By 1660, he had land in Fairfield, purchased from William Ward.

He m. (1) Isabella Barlow, dau. of John, whose will 1674 called her Isabella Clapham. He m. (2) abt. 1694, Rebecca [Ruscoe, dau. of John]; she m. (2) [James] Brown, and d. at Fairfield, 3 June 1730 in 75* yr. (g. s.). On 29 Jan. 1716/7, Nathan Adams, Jr., of Fairfield, yeoman, as attorney for Rebecca Brown of Fairfield, formerly wife of Peter Clapham of Norwalk, dec'd, quit-claimed her right of dowry in Hoyt's Island to Thomas Merwin.

Inv. taken 1 Mar. 1698 showed Est. in Norwalk and Fairfield; he d. 18 Feb. 1697/8. Children's ages: Rebecca, abt. 3, Elizabeth, abt. 2, and Peter, b. 15 May 1698. A writing called his will exhibited 26 Apr. 1698; not proved. Thomas Murwane of Fairfield and John Platt of Norwalk appointed to administer; Widow and children, Peter, Abigail Murwane, Rebecca, and Elizabeth.

Jonathan Reynolds and Joshua Knapp of Greenwich were appointed guardians of the three children, 22 Jan. 1702 [1702/3]. John Platt and Rebecca Clapham of Norwalk, as Adm'rs, conveyed 7 Dec. 1698 to Thomas Merwin, as portion of his wife Abigail, land at Hoyt's Island and a negro Jack.

Nehemiah Smith of Norwalk and wife Elizabeth, dau. of Peter Clapham of Norwalk dec'd, conveyed 4 Feb. 1714/5 to Nathan Adams, Jr. On 10 Sept. 1714, Nathan Adams, Jr., of Fairfield, and Rebecca Adams alias Clapham his wife, conveyed land at Clapham Spring to Gideon Allen. Nehemiah Smith and Elizabeth his wife conveyed land 1718, reserving life use to Rebecca Brown of Fairfield.

Child [by first wife]:

>   Abigail, m. Mar. 1678 [1678/9], Thomas Merwin.

Children [by second wife]:

>   Rebecca, b. abt. 1695; m. (1) abt. 1714, Nathan Adams; m. (2) at Christ Church, Stratford, 3 Feb. 1724/5, Joshua Jennings.
>   Elizabeth, bapt. at Fairfield, 19 Sept. 1697; m. by 1715, Nehemiah Smith, of Norwalk. They conveyed land at Compo, 24 Feb. 1725/6,

* We suspect that either the date or age has been misread, and that she was about a decade younger than would appear from the date and age stated.

Joshua Jennings and Rebecca his wife joining in the deed, and mentioning father Peter Clapham.

Peter, b. 15 May 1698, d. in 1716. He chose bro.-in-law Nathan Adams of Fairfield for guardian, 7 Apr. 1714. Thomas Merwin of Fairfield informed the Court, 1 Jan. 1716 [1716/7], that his bro -in-law Peter Clapham is dead, and was granted adm'n.

CLARK FAMILY (JAMES)

Clark, James, s. of James.

From New Haven, settled in Stratford.

Married (1) Deborah Peacock, dau. of John, bapt. at Milford, Feb. 1644/5, d. at Stratford, 14 Dec. 1705 in 61 yr. (g. s.).

Married (2) Hannah, widow of Patrick Falconer, and dau. of Gov. William Jones. She m. (3) 31 Jan. 1714/5, Sergt. John Booth, and d. 29 May 1717.

Will 1 July 1709, proved 3 Feb. 1713/4; marriage agreement with Mrs. Hannah Falconer; sons James, John, Isaac, Ephraim; daus. Sarah Janes, Deborah Jones, dau. Fullford, dau. Mary Clark; wife's dau. Hannah Falconer and wife's son Patrick Falconer. Mr. William Janes, Mr. Isaac Jones, and Abraham Fulford appealed.

Children [by first wife], recorded at Stratford:

+James, b. 12* Feb. [1664/5].
  Sarah, b. 11 Jan. 1666 [1666/7], d. 16 Oct. 1739 in 72 yr. (g. s., Epis. yard, Stratford) ; m. 26 Nov. 1685, William Janes.
+John, b. 17 Mar. 1668/9.
  Deborah, b. 10 Oct. 1672, d. at New Haven, 28 May 1735 ae. 63 (g. s.) ; m. (rec. New Haven) 21 Nov. 1692, Isaac Jones.
  Phebe, b. 15 July 1675; m. Abraham Fulford, with whom she conveyed 1710 to brother Isaac Clark.
  Isaac, b. 17 Jan. 1677 [1677/8].
+Isaac, b. 25 Sept. 1679.
+Ephraim, b. (no record).
  Mary, b. 10 Jan. 1686 [1686/7] ; m. 8 Sept. 1709, Ebenezer Booth.

Clark James, s. of James 2d.

Born at Stratford, 12 Feb. 1664/5. James, Jr., d. at Stratford, 29 Feb. 1712.

---

* 24 written over 12.

James, Jr., m. at Stratford, 24 May 1698, widow Jane Griffin. She was dau. of James Blackman, b. 26 Oct. 1668, and had m. (1) Joseph Russell and (2) Thomas Griffin.

Zechariah, son of James, chose Zechariah Blackman of Stratford guardian, 5 Mar. 1718/9.

Children, recorded at Stratford:

> Nathan, b. 6 Nov. 1696, d. 31 Dec. 1701.
> Deborah, b. 4 Jan. 1700/1.
> Zechariah, b. 8 June 1702, d. 4 Oct. 1785 in 84 yr. (g. s., Monroe); m. 21 Nov. 1727, Eunice Staples of Fairfield.
> Adam, b. 21 Jan. 1704/5; res. Redding; m. and had issue.
> Martha, b. 1 July 170[7].

Clark, John, s. of James 2d. Lt., Port Royal Expedition, Aug. 1710.

Born at Stratford, 17 Mar. 1668/9.

Married at Stratford, 11 Aug. 1692, Sarah Titherton. She was dau. of Daniel, b. 12 Oct. 1673.

John Clark, Sr., and Sarah Clark, conveyed 1714 to son Daniel land originally belonging to Daniel Titherton.

Children by Sarah, recorded at Stratford:

> Daniel, b. 25 Oct. 1693, d. abt. 1720. Adm'n on Est. granted, 15 Dec. 1720, to Isaac Clark and John Porter. Distribution to brothers and sisters (children of John): Ichabod, Sarah, Elizabeth, Mary, Ann, Eunice.
> John, b. 3 May 1696, d. y.
> Sarah, b. [say 1698]; m. 6 Mar. 1721/2, Joseph Beers.
> John, b. 30 Sept. 1700, d. y.
> Elizabeth, b. 1 Dec. 1702; m. (1) 24 Apr. 1723, Joseph Wakelee; m. (2) at Woodbury, 23 Sept. 1729, John Squire.
> Mary, bapt. 14 Oct. 1705 (at Stratford, rec. Stratfield).
> Ichabod, b. [say 1707]; m. 4 Oct. 1733, ———.
> Ann, b. (31 Aug. 1709 by age at death), d. 14 Mar. 1729 ae. 19 yrs. 6 mos. 14 days (g. s.); m. 20 Dec. 1728, Samuel Judson.
> Eunice, b. [say 1711]; m. 21 Jan. 1730/1, Robert Bassett.

Clark, Isaac, s. of James 2d.

Born at Stratford, 25 Sept. 1679.

Married (1) 4 Nov. 1702, Elizabeth Sherman; dau. of Samuel, Jr., b. 20 Jan. 1678/9. She divorced him.

He m. (2) Sept. 1728, Martha Sherman. She was widow of Ebenezer Sherman, and dau. of Zechariah Bostwick.

Inv. 5 Nov. 1748, exhibited by Ephraim Clark, Adm'r. James, son of Isaac, chose Joseph Brown guardian, July 1744. Joseph, a minor, chose Ebenezer Sherman of Stratford guardian. Distribution 27 Mar. 1750: James, eldest son; Joseph, youngest son.

Children by second wife:

> James, bapt. Nov. 1729; m. 5 Jan. 1750, Phebe Blackman.
> Dinah, bapt. Nov. 1729, d. y.
> Joseph, bapt. Oct. 1731; m. Isabella Elizabeth ———.
> Isaac, bapt. June 1739, d. y.

Clark, Ephraim, s. of James 2d.

Married (rec. Stratford) 28 July 1703, Hester Belding.

Will 14 June 1756, proved 22 Feb. 1764; wife Hester; daus. Deborah, Elizabeth, Ruth; heirs of dec'd daus., Abigail and Hester; sons Ephraim, Nathan, David (Exec'r); grandchild Hester wife of Nehemiah Hide, dau. of dec'd son Samuel Clark.

David Clark, agreement with mother Hester 1764.

Children by Hester, recorded at Stratford:

> Abigail, b. 2 May 1704, bapt. 23 July 1704 (at Stratford, rec. Stratfield); m. ———.
> Deborah, b. 22 Aug. 1705, bapt. 10 Feb. 1706 (at Stratford, rec. Stratfield).
> Samuel, b. 16 Nov. 1707, d. in 1733; Inv. 16 Mar. 1733; m. 26 Oct. 1731, Elizabeth Loring; who as Widow Elizabeth m. (2) 2 June 1736, Samuel French, Jr.
> Hester, b. 22 Aug. 1709, d. 6 July 1744; m. Nov. 1728, Peter Curtis.
> Elizabeth, b. 4 May 1711.
> Ephraim, b. 6 Nov. 1712, d. 5 Mar. 1789 ae. 77; m. 8 July 1736, Mehitabel Beardsley.
> Ruth, b. 1 July 1716.
> David, b. 5 May 1718, d. in 1772; will 6 May 1772, proved 9 June 1772; m. (1) 5 May 1741, Sarah Hickox of Norwalk, who d. 12 Mar. 1743 ae. 18 yrs. 12 days (g. s.); m. (2) Oct. 1743, Abigail Peck of Milford.
> Nathan, b. 6 Jan. 1720, m. 1740, Mary Blagge.

CLARK FAMILY (ROBERT)

Clark, Robert.

Died at Stratford, 16 Nov. 1694.

Married (1) Sarah, widow of Francis Stiles; she d. in 1682/3 [for her will, see STILES]. He m. (2) ———.

Samuel Sherman, Ephraim Stiles, and Daniel Beardsley, appointed Exec'rs 23 Nov. 1694. Children: John 10, Hannah 7.

Children [by second wife]:

> John, b. abt. 1684, d. in 1765; will 8 Mar. 1763, proved 2 Apr. 1765; m. (1) Jane Clark, dau. of Ens. George of Milford, bapt. 8 Sept. 1689; m. (2) Rebecca ———.
> Hannah, b. abt. 1687; m. (rec. Stamford) 22 Aug. 1711, Ephraim Stevens.

CLARK FAMILY (MILFORD)

Clark, George, s. of George. Ens., Milford trainband, May 1693; Deputy for Milford, Oct. 1708, May and Oct. 1719, May and Oct. 1720, Oct. 1721, May and Oct. 1722, May and Oct. 1723, May and Oct. 1724, May and Oct. 1725.

Son of Dea. George, bapt. at Milford, 30 Apr. 1648, d. there 19 July 1734 in 87 yr. (g. s.); m. (1) Deborah Gold, dau. of Nathan; adm. to Milford Church Sept. 1686, and d. 2 June 1697; m. (2) Rebecca, widow first of Samuel Baldwin and next of Job Prince, and dau. of Gamaliel and Sarah (Purchase) Phippen, bapt. at Boston 1 Mar. 1656/7, d. at Milford, 17 Oct. 1712 ae. abt. 54 (g. s.); m. (3) Phebe, widow of Isaac Knell, and dau. of Caleb Nichols, bapt. 12 Nov. 1671.

We are indebted to the manuscript genealogy compiled by George C. Bryant, of Ansonia, Conn., for much of the data on this family.

Children [by first wife], rec. Milford:*

---

* The following conveyances by Clark heirs of their interest in the Gold farm may be of interest. On 5 Feb. 1725, John Talcott of Hartford and Joseph Talcott of Bolton appointed their uncle George Clark of Milford their attorney, and on 25 Feb. 1724/5, Nathan Talcott of Milford gave power of attorney to his uncle George Clark to sell land in Fairfield. On 22 Feb. 1724/5, Samuel Beard and Sarah his wife, Thomas Baldwin and Jerusha his wife, Samuel Peck and Martha his wife,

Sarah, b. 21 June 1678, bapt. 26 Sept. 1686; m. 8 July 1696, Samuel
Beard, son of John and Anna (Hawley) Beard, b. 4 Feb. 1669/70,
d. in 1754.

Abigail, b. 1 Apr. 1680, bapt. 26 Sept. 1686, d. at Hartford, 24 Mar.
1704/5; m. Gov. Joseph Talcott.

George, b. 3 Apr. 1682, bapt. 26 Sept. 1686, d. at Woodbridge, 21 Aug.
1762 ae. 82 (g. s.); m. Mary Coley, dau. of Samuel, b. 14 Jan.
1684/5.

Deborah, bapt. 26 Sept. 1686; m. (1) Job Prince, b. 10 Nov. 1680,
d. in 1704; m. (2) 14 Jan. 1704/5, Samuel Prince, b. 20 Sept. 1675,
d. abt. 1722; m. (3) Joshua Judson, b. at Stratford, 23 Jan. 1677/8,
d. 27 Nov. 1735 in 58 yr. (g. s.); m. (4) Thomas Tibbals, b. 22
Aug. 1679, d. 1 Sept. 1750 ae. 71.

Nathan, bapt. 27 Mar. 1687, d. at Milford, 3 Sept. 1729 in 43 yr.
(g. s.); m. 29 June 1710, Elizabeth Fowler, dau. of William and
Anna (Beard), bapt. 20 Sept. 1691; she m. (2) 19 June 1744, Enos
Camp.

Jane, bapt. 8 Sept. 1689, d. by 1734; m. John Clark, of Stratford.

Jerusha, bapt. 5 June 1692, d. Apr. 1728; m. 17 Jan. 1711/2, Thomas
Baldwin, bapt. 1 Jan. 1698/9, d. abt. 1773.

Martha, bapt. 26 May 1695, d. 3 Dec. 1747 ae. 52 (g. s., Stratford);
m. (1) 5 May 1714, Samuel Peck, son of Joseph and Mary (Camp),
bapt. 13 July 1690, d. abt. 1728; m. (2) James Booth.

Silence, bapt. 6 June 1697; m. (1) 20 May 1714, Samuel Buckingham, son of Samuel and Sarah, bapt. 21 Nov. 1694, d. 29 Dec. 1749
in 56 yr. (g. s.); m. (2) Ebenezer Smith, son of Benjamin and
Sarah (Phippen), bapt. 31 Jan. 1691/2, d. in 1763.

Child [by third wife]:

Abigail, b. [4 Jan. 1713/4], d. 29 Nov. 1746 ae. 32 yrs. 10 mos. 25
days (g. s.); m. 25 Nov. 1730, Ebenezer Curtis.

Clawson, Stephen.

The name is spelled Clason, Cloyson, etc.

He m. at Stamford, 11 Jan. 1654/5, Elizabeth Periment, b. abt.
1631. She, as aged widow, d. 10 May 1714.

On 28 May 1692, complaint was made by Sergt. Daniel West-

Samuel Buckingham and Silence his wife, and Nathan Clark, all of Milford, and
Joshua Judson and Deborah his wife, and John Clark and Jane his wife, all of Stratford, conveyed to bro. George Clark of Milford, right from mother Deborah Clark.
Samuel Beard, Jr, of Ripton and Nathan Beard of Waterbury conveyed, 27 Feb.
1733/4, to bro. James Beard of Ripton, land in Reading which our uncle Lt. George
Clark conveyed to us [Clark's deed to them, dated one day before, is also on record].
On 15 Jan. 1735 [1735/6], George Clark of Milford conveyed to nephew John Talcott
of Bolton and Joseph Talcott of Hartford and Nathan Talcott of New Milford, all
right in Reading in Farm called ye Golds Farm.

cott that she had bewitched his servant girl, and a bill was found against her by the Grand Jury. The water test was applied, and it was found that she swam like a cork when put in water bound hand and foot. A lot of stupid and ridiculous testimony was taken, but there was also testimony in her favor given by some of her neighbors, and the Petit Jury returned a verdict of not guilty. When the son Jonathan died, 1685, his mother Elizabeth, ae. 54, and bro. Stephen, Jr., ae. 28. testified concerning his will.

Children, rec. Stamford:

Jonathan, b. 11 Feb. 1655/6, d. 10 June 1685; m. 16 Dec. 1680, Sarah Roberts, b. 4 Sept. 1661, d. 30 Aug. 1684. They had: Stephen, b. 2 Dec. 1681; and Sarah. Jonathan's Inv. 18 July 1685, presented by his father Stephen; Stephen Clawson, Sr., and David Clawson appointed adm'rs.

Stephen, b. 17 Feb. 1657/8; perhaps m. Priscilla Abbott, dau. of George of Norwalk.

Rebecca, b. 1 Mar. 1659/60.

Son, b. 18 May 1662; prob. David, who d. 29 Mar. 1721; and he prob. m. 1 Dec. 1692, Mary Holmes.

Samuel, d. 6 May 1723; m. 7 Dec. 1693, Hannah Dunham, who d. 8 Mar. 1720/1.

Others?

Close, ———.

Goodman Close was mentioned in the will of William Frost, 1645, and was an early settler in Fairfield, where he d. by 1653. His widow Elizabeth m. George Stuckey and d. at Stamford, 4 Sept. 1656.

Children:

Hannah, m. 9 June 1657, Joshua Knapp.

Joseph, d. before 1660.

+Thomas.

Mary, m. 25 June 1668, Samuel Holly.

Close, Thomas, s. of ———.

He d. at Greenwich in 1709.

Will 30 Dec. 1708, proved 12 Feb. 1708/9; dau. Sarah; dau. Hannah; three children of son Thomas; son Joseph; son Benjamin; dau. Elizabeth; dau. Ruth; son John; dau. Lydia; five shillings to each of foregoing; to wife, residue of moveables for life, and those outdoors not expended to be divided between daus. Hannah, Elizabeth and Ruth, and those within doors to dau. Lydia after her mother's decease; son Joseph with his mother, Exec'rs.

Children :*

> Sarah, b. 10 Dec. 1670.
> Hannah, b. 12 Mar. 1672; m. Johannes Luqueer, of Newtown, L. I.
> Thomas, b. 16 Dec. 1674, d. at Greenwich in 1707; m. Feb. 1703, Hannah Knapp. Births of children entered in Fairfield Pro. Rec.: Sarah, b. 9 Nov. 1703; Hannah, b. 29 Mar. 1705; Thomas, b. 28 Nov. 1706. Adm'n on Est. of Thomas of Horseneck granted, 28 Oct. 1707, to his father Thomas Close, with Joseph Close and Caleb Knapp.
> Joseph, b. 20 Nov. 1676, d. 4 Oct. 1760; m. in 1701, Rebecca Tompkins, b. in 1679, d. 13 Nov. 1761.
> Benjamin, b. 18 May 1679, d. Mar. 1759; m. (1) ——; m. (2) Ruth (Scofield) widow of Joseph Brown, Jr.
> Mary, b. in 1682; m. Moses Hunt.
> Elizabeth, b. 5 Aug. 1684.
> Ruth, b. 1 Nov. 1687.
> John, b. 8 Apr. 1689.
> Lydia.

Clugston, Michael.

He m. by 1694, Mary Wakeman, dau. of Rev. Samuel; she m. (2) abt. 1706, Thomas Staples.

Inv. 4 Jan. 1697 [1697/8]. Distribution 14 Aug. 1706; Widow Mary Clugston; children John, Samuel, Mary. Lt. Joseph Wakeman guardian of the sons, Mary Clugston of the dau.

Mary Clugston of Fairfield conveyed 22 Aug. 1706 to her three children, her right in Est. of her brother Jabez Wakeman dec'd.

John Cluckstone of Fairfield gave a release, 23 May 1717, to father-in-law Thomas Staples, "by virtue of marriage with my Mother Mary Staples Administratrix on the Estate of my father Micaell Cluckstone late of Fairfield deceased."

Children, bapt. at Fairfield Church:

> XJohn, bapt. 23 June 1695, d. 23 Mar. 1758 ae. 64 (Redding Church rec.); Inv. of Est. 18 Apr. 1758; m. (1) at Stratfield, 11 June 1718, Elizabeth Welles [dau. of Samuel], who d. 1 Sept. 1745; m. (2)

---

* Births from *Ye Historie of Greenwich.*

(rec. Fairfield Church) 24 Mar. 1747/8, Elizabeth Rowlinson [23 Mar. 1749 by town rec.], who d. 17 May 1759 ae. 55 (Redding Church).

Samuel, bapt. 17 Nov. 1696, d. at Norwalk in 1751; m. Deborah Ketchum. No issue. Will 8 Apr. 1751, proved 27 Nov. 1751; Church of England in Norwalk; brother John Cluckstone; sister Mary Perry; residue to cousins Jonathan Ketchum and Esther Perry alias Cannon, wife of John Cannon, Jr.

Mary, bapt. 18 Sept. 1698; Mary, wife of Capt. Thomas Edwards of Stratford formerly the wife of Joseph Perry of Fairfield and dau. of Michael Clugston of Fairfield, d. 8 Nov. 1773 (Fairfield rec.).

Cobbitt, Samuel.

Deacon, of Fairfield. Whence he came we have not learned, but suspect a connection with that Samuel (son of Rev. Thomas Cobbett of Lynn) who was grad. from Harvard Coll. 1663, but whose later history was unknown to Savage [*Gen. Dict.*] except that in the Harvard catalogue of 1698 he was marked as living.

Inv. of Mr. Samuel of Fairfield, 3 Mar. 1712/3. Adm'n granted, 6 May 1713, to widow Sarah Cobbitt and Zechariah Brinsmade.

Zechariah and Sarah Brinsmade, and Sarah Cobbitt, all of Stratford, conveyed 20 July 1714 to Mr. Joseph Perry, land bounded north on David Ogden, on all other sides by the mill pond.

Child:

Sarah, b. abt. 1688, d. at Stratford, 2 June 1737; or (if g. s. is correctly read) 9 June 1736 ae. 48 yrs. 6 mos.; m. (rec. Stratford), 26 Oct. 1700 [error for 1710],* Zechariah Brinsmade.

Coe, Robert, s. of Robert.

Bapt. at Boxford, co. Suffolk, Eng., 19 Sept. 1626; came with father, 1634, and followed his migrations, Watertown, Mass., Wethersfield 1635, Stamford 1641; but remained in Connecticut when the rest of the family rem. to Hempstead, L. I., 1644, or else soon returned; settled in Stratford, and d. in 1659.

Inv. 20 Oct. 1659. Children: Susanna 6½; Sarah 3½; John 1½.

---

* A later duplicate entry gives the year correctly.

Married Hannah Mitchell, dau. of Matthew of Stamford, bapt. at South Ouram, co. York, Eng., 26 June 1631, d. at New Haven, 2 Apr. 1702.

She m. (2) by 1667, Nicholas Elsey, of New Haven.

Children, recorded at Stratford:

    Hannah, b. 17 Dec. 1651, d. y.
    Susanna, b. abt. 1653, d. 3 Apr. 1746 ae. 93 (g. s., New Haven); m. (rec. New Haven) 11 Jan. 1671 [1671/2], John Alling.
    Sarah, b. abt. 1656; m. (1) abt. 1680, Timothy Gibbard; m. (2) abt. 1687, Jeremiah Osborn; both of New Haven.
    +John, b. abt. 1658.

Coe, John, s. of Robert 2d. Ens., Stratford Trainband, May 1698; Lt., May 1706; Capt., Oct. 1709. Deputy (Stratford), Oct. 1701, Oct. 1715.

Born about 1658; Capt. John d. at Stratford, 19 Apr. 1741 in 83 yr. (g. s.).

Married 20 Dec. 1682,* Mary Hawley, dau. of Joseph, b. 16 July 1663; d. 9 Sept. 1731 in 69 yr. (g. s.).

Will 29 Jan. 1739/40, proved 5 May 1741; five sons, Robert, Joseph, John, Ephraim, Ebenezer; by deeds of gift gave Robert and Joseph lands in Durham, John lands in Haddam, Ephraim lands in Middletown; to son Ebenezer lands in Stratford; children Hannah wife of James Curtis of Durham, Katharine wife of David Calhoun of Stratford, Mary wife of Samuel Pickett of Durham, and Abigail wife of John Guthrie of Durham; grandchild Mary Burritt, dau. of late dau. Sarah wife of Israel Burritt of Durham; Lt. Samuel Ufford, Lt. Abiel Birdsey of Stratford, and son Ebenezer, Exec'rs.

Children, recorded at Stratford :†

    Job, b. 1 May 1683, d. y.
    Robert, b. 21 Sept. 1684, d. at Middlefield, 2 Feb. 1762 ae. 77; Ens., Durham, Oct. 1718; m. 21 Dec. 1708, Barbara Parmelee, dau. of John, b. at Guilford, 23 June 1689, d. at Bristol, 26 Sept. 1774 ae. 85.

---

* The date not found in Stratford rec., is presumably from Coe Fam. Bible. The excellent Coe history has supplied this and some other dates.

† The last six children were entered as of John and Mary; John was called Ens. at birth of children 1693 and 1698, and Lt. 1704; showing that the entries were not made soon after the event.

Joseph, b. 3 Feb. 1686, d. at Durham, 15 July 1754 ae. 68; Ens., May 1722, Lt., May 1725, Capt., May 1729; m. at Durham, 21 Nov. 1708, Abigail Robinson, dau. of David, b. at Guilford, 3 Apr. 1690, d. at Durham, 6 July 1775 ae. 85.

Hannah, b. 14 Apr. 1689, d. at Durham, Mar. 1758; m. abt. 1708, James Curtis.

Mary, b. 11 Aug. 1691, d. at Durham, 19 Feb. 1763; m. 27 Nov. 1712, Samuel Pickett.

John, b. 5 Dec. 1693, d. at Durham, 24 Sept. 1751 in 58 yr.; m. 22 Dec. 1715, Hannah Parsons, dau. of Samuel, b. abt. 1698, d. at Durham, 14 Oct. 1760 ae. 62.

Sarah, b. 26 Mar. 1696, d. at Durham, 6 Feb. 1731/2; m. 4 Mar. 1718/9, Israel Burritt.

Ephraim, b. 18 Dec. 1698, d. at Durham, 10 Nov. 1765 in 67 yr.; m. at Middletown, 28 Nov. 1723, Hannah Comfort Miller, dau. of Benjamin, who d. at West Granville, Mass., Feb. 1793 ae. 88.

Katharine, b. 23 Sept. 1700; m. (1) 11 Nov. 1725, Joseph Fairchild; m. (2) 24 Aug. 1728, David Calhoun.

Abigail, b. 11 Nov. 1702, d. at Southbury, Mar. 1747; m. 1 June 1727, John Guthrie.

Ebenezer, b. 18 Aug. 1704, d. at Stratford, 26 Mar. 1766 ae. 62 (g. s.); Ens., May 1740, Lt., Oct. 1744, Capt., May 1750; m. 18 Dec. 1728, Mary Blackman, dau. of Zechariah, b. 2 Sept. 1705; d. 23 May 1773 in 68 yr. (g. s.).

Coley, Samuel.

He was adm. to the church in Milford, 25 Oct. 1640, and d. there in 1684.

Married Ann Prudden, dau. of James. She was adm. to Milford Church, 14 Feb. 1640/1, and d. 3 Oct. 1689.

Will 22 Mar. 1677/8; wife Anne; son Peter Coley; dau. Sarah Baldwin; son Samuel Coley; daus. Abilene Chapin, Mary Simpson, Hannah Garnsey; son Thomas Coley. Inv. 26 Sept. 1684.

Will of Anne Coley, widow of Samuel, Sr., 13 Feb. 1688/9; children Peter, Samuel, and Thomas Coley, Abilene Chaping, Sarah Baldwin, Mary Stream, Hannah Gernsey; son-in-law Joseph Gernsey, Exec'r. Inv. 11 Nov. 1689.

Children, recorded at Milford:

+Peter, bapt. 25 Apr. 1641.

Abilena, bapt. 12 Mar. 1643; m. Japhet Chapin, of Springfield, Mass.

Samuel, bapt. Feb. 1646, res. Milford, but death not found; m. 25

Oct. 1669, Mary "Curtes" [Curtis]. Only known child: Mary, b. 14 Jan. 1684/5, m. Lt. George Clark.

Sarah, bapt. 24 Sept. 1648; m. Joseph Baldwin, of Hadley, Mass.

Mary bapt. 23 Nov. 1651, d. in 1705, without issue; m. (1) Peter Simpson; m. (2) John Stream, Jr., of Milford; m. (3) after 1689, [Joseph] Lockwood, of Fairfield.

Hannah, b. 10 Oct. 1654, bapt. 15 Oct. 1654; m. 10 Apr. 1673, Joseph Guernsey.

Thomas, b. 20 Apr. 1657; m. Martha Stream, dau. of John.

Coley, Peter, s. of Samuel.

Bapt. at Milford, 25 Apr. 1641; settled in Fairfield and d. in 1690.

Married Sarah Hide, dau. of Humphrey. His wife Sarah and children Samuel, Sarah, Peter, and Mary, were named 1679 in her father's will. She m. (2) Thomas Sherwood, 2d, as his fourth wife.

Inv. 31 Mar. 1690; left widow Sarah; son Samuel had an estate from his grandfather; Peter the second son; three daus. Sarah Coley, Mary wife of Nicholas Johnson, and Ann Coley. Children's ages 5 Apr. 1690: Sarah 22, Ann 18 last Jan., Mary 13, Elizabeth 8, Hannah 6, one son Peter. Agreement of heirs 15 Mar. 1694/5; Samuel Coley, Nicholas Johnson in right of wife, Sarah Coley, Sarah Coley Widow, and Peter Coley.

On 19 June 1705, Elizabeth, wife of Samuel Westcott of Cohansey, N. J., yeoman, and dau. of Peter Coley of Fairfield, receipted to bro. Peter; witnesses, Sarah Jennings, John Meredith. William Rowlinson of Fairfield, yeoman, receipted 20 Mar. 1704 to Peter Coley for wife Sarah's portion; witnesses, John and Elizabeth Meredith. Samuel Coley gave discharge to Est. of his father Peter, 6 Feb. 1691/2; and Nicholas Johnson of Fairfield receipted, 25 Oct. 1696, to bro. Peter Coley and my wife's mother as Exec'rs.

Children, recorded at Fairfield:

+Samuel, b. [say 1664].
Sarah, b. abt. 1668; m. William Rowlandson.
+Peter, b. 12 June 1671.
Ann, b. 13 Jan. 1673.
Mary, b. 23 Apr. 1677; m. Nicholas Johnson.
Elizabeth, b. 1 Dec. 1680; m. Samuel Westcott, of Cohansey, N. J.
Hannah, b. abt. 1683.

Coley, Samuel, s. of Peter.

Married (1) abt. 1685, Esther Frost, dau. of Daniel.

Married (2) Mary ———.

Adm'n granted, 6 May 1713, to bro. Peter and son Daniel.

Distribution 10 June 1714; Daniel Coley, Samuel Coley, Jemima King, John Coley, Mary Coley, Esther Coley, Ann Coley.

He renewed his Covenant at Fairfield Church, 2 June 1695, and three children by Esther were bapt. same day. His wife Mary was bapt. 28 Nov. 1703. He conveyed to William Sprague, 25 June 1696, the homelot which his gr. father Humphrey Hide gave him.

Richard King of Fairfield and his wife Jemima King alias Coley conveyed 18 Nov. 1715; and Ephraim Raymond of Norwalk and Mary his wife conveyed, 28 July 1724, right from her father Samuel Coley dec'd.

Children [by first wife], bapt. at Fairfield:

> Daniel.
> Jemima; m. (1) Richard King; m. (2) by 1730, Buckland Williams.
> Abigail, d. abt. 1715; m. (rec. Fairfield) 23 Dec. 1714, William Gray.
> Esther, bapt. 15 Aug. 1703; m. William Fountain of Norwalk.

Children [by second wife], bapt. at Fairfield:

> Samuel, bapt. 5 Dec. 1703.
> Mary, bapt. 5 Dec. 1703; m. Ephraim Raymond.
> XJohn, bapt. 17 Mar. 1705/6, d. at Westport, 6 June 1775; will 14 Feb. 1774, proved 4 July 1775; m. 22 July 1728, Mercy Gregory, dau. of Benjamin; she was bapt. at Stratfield, 31 Oct. 1708, d. 29 Jan. 1773 in 65 yr. (g. s., Westport).
> Ann, bapt. 1 Aug. 1709; m. (rec. Norwalk) 1 Jan. 1729/30, John Kellogg. They conveyed 1730 right from her father Samuel Cooley, dec'd.

Coley, Peter, s. of Peter.   Sergt., Fairfield Trainband.

Born at Fairfield, 12 June 1671.

Married Hannah Couch, dau. of Simon, and gave receipt for her portion 1703.   She m. (2) Joshua Hoyt.

He renewed his Covenant at Fairfield Church, 4 Aug. 1700.   He was called Sergt. at bapt. of children 1710 to 1721.

Children, bapt. at Fairfield:

> Hannah, bapt. 4 Aug. 1700; m. Jonathan Beebe.
> XPeter, bapt. 30 Aug. 1702, d. at Ridgefield, in 1743; will 17 Nov. 1742, proved 5 July 1743; m. Ruth Treadwell, dau. of Ephraim, bapt. 23 May 1708; she m. (2) James Tongue.
> Simon, bapt. 30 Jan. 1703/4.
> Elizabeth, bapt. 24 Mar. 1706; m. 15 Dec. 1726, Jeremiah Jennings.
> XAndrew, bapt. 25 July 1708; rem. to Woodbury and conveyed 1735 land from father Peter dec'd; m. ———.
> Ebenezer, bapt. 8 Oct. 1710, d. y.
> Ebenezer, bapt. 4 May 1712, d. in 1735; Inv. Mar. 1734/5; Jonathan Beebe, Adm'r; Est. distributed 2 Jan. 1735/6 between brothers and sisters; agreement signed by Peter Coley, Jonathan Beebe and wife Hannah, Simon, Andrew and David Coley, Joshua Hait and wife Hannah, Jeremiah Jennings and wife Elizabeth.
> XDavid, b. 29 Jan. 1715, bapt. 13 Mar. 1714/5; m. 16 Dec. 1740, Mary Hide.
> XJonathan, bapt. 30 June 1717; m. 6 Dec. 1739, Lucy Sturgis, dau. of John.
> Mary, bapt. 18 June 1721.

Commell, John.

He m. Jane Peat, dau. of John, b. 17 Oct. 1677; she m. (2) 6 Mar. 1706/7, Bezaleel Sherman.

Child:

> Elizabeth, chose her uncle Samuel Peat for guardian, 23 Dec. 1719; m. at Stratford, 16 Jan. 1722/3, Abiel Beers.
> ?Sarah, m. 6 Nov. 1727, David Baldwin.

Comstock, Christopher. Deputy (Norwalk) to Conn. Leg., Oct. 1686, May and June 1689, May 1690.

Prob. son of William of New London. He settled in Fairfield; rem. to Norwalk, and was nominated for a freeman of Conn. Colony, Oct. 1667.

He m. (rec. Norwalk) 6 Oct. 1663, Hannah Platt, dau. of Richard of Milford; and d. 28 Dec. 1702.

In 1654 he testified to visiting the convicted witch, Goodwife Knapp, in company with Thomas Shervington and Goodwife Baldwin. In 1692 he served on the Grand Jury which indicted Mercy Disbrow and others for witchcraft.

Will 22 Dec. 1701, proved 4 Jan. 1702/3; wife Hannah; sons Moses, Samuel; daus. Hannah Comstock and Mercy Comstock; every grandchild to have a Bible; wife, Exec'x, and friends Rev. Stephen Buckingham and James Olmstead, overseers.

Children, recorded at Norwalk:

+Daniel, b. 21 July 1664.
Hannah, b. 15 July 1666.
Abigail, b. 27 Jan. 1669 [1669/70], d. 9 Feb. 1689 [1689/90].
Mary, b. 19 Feb. 1671 [1671/2], d. 17 Oct. 1749; m. 18 Dec. 1693, James St. John.
Elizabeth, b. 7 Oct. 1674; m. Ebenezer St. John.
Mercy, b. 12 Nov. 1676; m. (1) abt. 1706, Nathan Olmstead; m. (2) John Williams.
+Samuel, b. 6 Feb. 1679 [1679/80].
+Moses, b. 4 May 1685.

Comstock, Daniel, s. of Christopher.

Born at Norwalk, 21 July 1664, d. in 1694.

He m. (rec. Norwalk) 13 June 1692, Elizabeth Wheeler, dau. of John of Fairfield "at the Black Rock." She renewed her Covenant at Stratfield Church, 26 Aug. 1694; and m. (2) Sergt. Samuel Welles.

Inv. 6 Nov. 1694, calls him of Norwalk; widow Elizabeth and only son.

Child:

Daniel, bapt. at Stratfield, 26 Aug. 1694; rem. from Stratfield to Kent, 1741; m. (1) at Stratfield, 10 Nov. 1713, Sarah Odell; dau. of John, b. 10 Aug. 1694; m. (2) between 1727 and 1735, Mary, widow of Samuel Morehouse.

Comstock, Samuel, s. of Christopher. Deputy (Norwalk) to Conn. Leg., Oct. and Nov. 1711, Oct. 1714, May 1720, Oct. 1723, Oct. 1725, Oct. 1726, Oct. 1727, Oct. 1728, Oct. 1729, Oct. 1730, Oct. 1738. Ens., south company, Norwalk, May 1710; Lt., Oct. 1724; Capt., May 1730.

Born at Norwalk, 6 Feb. 1679/80, d. there 26 Oct. 1752; m. 27 Dec. 1705, Sarah Hanford, dau. of Rev. Thomas.

Will 26 Aug. 1743, proved 6 Feb. 1753; wife; sons Nathan,

Daniel, David, Exec'rs; daus. Lydia, Sarah Betts, Mary Trow-bridge; legacy to Nehemiah Mead. On 10 Jan. 1754, Daniel Betts, Jr. (and wife Sarah) of Norwalk, and John Trowbridge (and wife Mary) of Danbury, and Lydia Comstock of Norwalk, receipted to Nathan, Daniel, and David Comstock, Exec'rs of will of father Capt. Samuel.

Children, recorded at Norwalk:

Sarah, b. 25 Mar. 1707; m. Daniel Betts, Jr.
Samuel, b. 12 Nov. 1708, d. y.
Mary, b. 5 Aug. 1710; m. John Trowbridge, of Danbury.
Nathan, b. abt. 1713, d. at Wilton, 12 Oct. 1794; m. 7 Mar. 1738/9, Bethia Strong, dau. of Benajah of Stratfield.
Daniel, d. in 1757; res. Norwalk and Danbury; m. Abigail Dickinson, dau. of Rev. Moses.
David, b. abt. 1720, d. at Norwalk, 19 Nov. 1783; m. Rebecca Grumman, dau. of Samuel, b. 24 Sept. 1727, d. at Danbury, 3 Jan. 1812.
Lydia.

Comstock Moses, s. of Christopher.

Born at Norwalk, 4 May 1685, d. there 18 Jan. 1766 in 82 yr.; m. (rec. Norwalk) 23 Feb. 1709/10, Abigail Brinsmade, dau. of Mr. Daniel of Stratford; b. abt. 1691, d. 16 Nov. 1766 in 75 yr.

Will 24 Jan. 1754, proved 11 Feb. 1766; wife Abigail; daus. Sarah, Phebe; sons Abijah, Moses; three daus. Abigail, Hannah, Martha; two gr. children Ruth and Isabel Hanford, daus. of late dau. Dinah Hanford; gr. sons Moses son of Samuel Hanford, and Moses Comstock Eells; son Abijah and son-in-law Samuel Hanford, Exec'rs; negro man and woman to remain with my wife, and at her death to choose which of my children they will live with. Distribution ordered 3 Sept. 1766 to eldest son Abijah, Moses, Abigail wife of John Eells, Hannah wife of Phineas Hanford, heirs of Dinah wife of Samuel Hanford, Sarah Comstock and Phebe Comstock.

Children:

Abigail, m. Rev. John Eells, of New Canaan.
Hannah, m. Phineas Hanford.
Abijah, b. 19 Nov. 1721, d. at Norwalk, June 1797; m. 30 May 1745, Deborah Benedict, b. 8 Jan. 1728.

Martha, b. abt. 1723, d. 4 Aug. 1814 ae. 91; m. 1 July 1742, Ambrose
Olmstead.
Moses, d. in 1789; m. 30 June 1748, Elizabeth St. John.
Sarah, b. abt. 1727, d. 1796 ae. 70, unm.
Dinah, m. Samuel Hanford.
Phebe, b. abt. 1731, d. 1817 ae. 86, unm.

Coney, John.

A cooper, of Boston, d. there 24 Dec. 1670; m. 20 June 1654,
Elizabeth Nash, dau. of Robert of Boston.

Children, recorded at Boston:

John, b. 5 Jan. 1655 [1655/6], d. 29 Aug. 1722; m. (1) Sarah Black-
man, dau. of James of Stratford, b. 25 Apr. 1658, d. 17 Apr. 1694;
m. (2) 8 Nov. 1694, Mary, widow of John Clark, and dau. of
Joshua and Mary (Blackman) Atwater, b. 15 Jan. 1659/60, d. 12
Apr. 1726. His two wives were first cousins, and he had children
by both.
Sarah, b. 22 May 1660.
Joseph, b. 27 Apr. 1662.
Elizabeth, b. 2 Apr. 1664, d. 16 June 1664.
William, b. 5 July 1665.
Thomas, b. 26 Sept. 1667.
Mary, b. 10 Mar. 1668 [1668/9].
Rebecca, b. 18 June 1670; m. 7 Dec. 1692, Jolief Price.
Elizabeth, b. 24 Feb. 1671 [1671/2], prob. d. y.
Benjamin, b. 16 Oct. 1673, d. at Stratford, 27 Feb. 1720/1; m. (1) at
Stratford, 18 Nov. 1702, Anna Fairchild, who d. 23 July 1703; m.
(2) at New Haven, 18 Dec. 1705, Mehitabel Glover, dau. of John,
b. 1 May 1679; she m. (2) at Stratford, 21 Sept. 1721, Rev. Joseph
Webb of Fairfield. The will of Benjamin, 25 Dec. 1716, proved 11
Apr. 1721; wife Mehitabel; bros. John and Nathaniel Coney;
sister Elizabeth Booth.
Nathaniel, of Boston, m. (1) before 1700, Elizabeth ———; m. (2)
6 Sept. 1711, Abigail Ager.
Elizabeth, b. abt. 1679, if the statement is correct that she d. at Newtown in 1776 ae. 97; m. at Stratford, 11 Apr. 1705, Thomas Booth.

Cook, John.

Came to Stratford as servant to Richard Butler, and had land
by gift from Butler as well as from the town by 1668.

Inv. 23 July 1689, presented by Moses Wheeler, Sr. Adm'n
granted to Joseph Curtis.

Cosier, Richard.

Of Branford 1680, servant then of Jonathan Rose; ran away, and "in his flight rid through Branford with his sword drawn & pistol cockt threatening mischief to any that should seize him." Prob. he m. (1) Abigail Stewart, dau. of Robert, b. at Norwalk, middle of Aug. 1664, who in 1688 was called Abigail Cosier. Certainly he m. (2) or (3) Abigail Brown, gr. dau. of Abraham Ambler. On 18 Nov. 1709, Richard and Abigail Cosier receipted to John Ambler, Exec'r of will of our gr. father Abraham Ambler, for the £5 legacy given to Abigail Brown, now wife of Richard Cosier.

Inv. of Richard of Norwalk, 26 Nov. 1712. Widow Abigail; children's ages: John, about 19; Thomas, about [left blank]; Hezekiah, 4 on 3 July last; Josiah, 2 on 1 Mar. last. Thomas chose his uncle Mr. John Reed of Norwalk for guardian, 23 Jan. 1719/20.

Child [by first wife] :*
    John, b. abt. 1693.

Child [perhaps by a sister of John Reed] :
    Thomas, b. [say 1704].

Children [by Abigail Brown] :
    Hezekiah, b. 3 July 1708.
    Josiah, b. 1 Mar. 1709/10.

Couch, Simon.

Born about 1633; testified 1681 ae. 48; m. Mary ———.† He bought land in Fairfield from Anna widow of Francis Andrews, 14 Mar. 1663/4, from William Hayden, 24 May 1664, and from Robert Beacham, 25 May 1665.

Four of the name came to Connecticut, but not early. WILLIAM d. at Guilford, 12 Sept. 1689; no family known. SAMUEL settled

---

* A widow Abigail Cosier [prob. widow of one of the elder sons of Richard] m. at Fairfield Church, 24 Dec. 1729, Andrew Sinclair. Abigail Cosier [possibly dau. of the widow] had a child Margaret bapt. at Fairfield, 21 Sept. 1735.

† Mrs. Schenck with happy certainty calls her dau. of Francis Andrews, which is not impossible; yet the records she quotes do not specify the relationship as her quotations seem to imply.

at Milford; m. Pity,* childless widow of Charles Deal, by whose gift he had Charles Island; m. (2) in 1691 Mary, widow of Vincent Stilson. His will, June 1693, referred to marriage agreement with wife Mary; his homelot in Milford, Charles Island, etc., to dau. Elizabeth Couch living in St. Mary Ottery, co. Devon, Eng.; but if she come not over in seven yrs., then all to Nathaniel, son of Capt. Samuel Eells of Hingham, Mass. THOMAS bought land from John Stiles in Wethersfield, 1665, and m. (1) 22 Nov. 1666, Rebecca ———, who d. 1 Mar. 1671/2; m. (2) Hannah ———. Inv. of Thomas, 24 Mar. 1687; widow Hannah; ages of children: Susannah 20, Simon 18, Rebecca 15, Hannah 13, Thomas 12, Mary 11, Sarah 8, Abigail 6, Martha 3. Legacy to children from their uncle Simon Couch mentioned. Simon was certainly brother of Thomas of Wethersfield, and prob. also of Samuel of Milford.

Will 22 Dec. 1687, proved 15 Mar. 1687/8; wife Mary; eldest son Thomas; 2d son Simon; 3d son Samuel; brother's son Thomas Couch that lives with me; brother's dau. living at John Grumman's; cousin Susannah Couch living at Milford; eldest daus., Mary and Martha; daus. Sarah and Hannah.

Inv. of Mary Couch, 22 May 1691, exhibited 27 Dec. 1691. Adm'n granted to Simon and Samuel Couch. Order to distribute to the children: Thomas ("if he never come into this Country again"); Simon; Samuel; widow Mary Grumman; Martha, Hannah and Sarah Couch.

Mary Couch conveyed 1689 to brother Thomas. Samuel Couch receipted 1694 to brother Simon for legacy from mother Mary dec'd. Abraham Finch receipted 1697 for legacy from father-in-law Couch. Peter Coley receipted 1703 for legacy of Hannah Couch, his present wife.

Children:

> Thomas, d. in 1691. Will 8 Apr. 1689, proved 2 Dec. 1691; "voyaging to England"; mother Mary Couch; brother Simon's eldest son; brother Samuel's eldest son.
>
> +Simon.
>
> Mary, m. (1) Thomas Grumman; m. (2) after 1691, James Bennett,

---

* She m. Deal on 3 July 1672, her surname being omitted; and it is said that she was an Indian.

"Shipwright"; divorced him 1703 and m. (3) by contract dated
24 Oct. 1727, Samuel Jennings.

+Samuel.

Martha, m. Abraham Finch.

Sarah.

Hannah, m. (1) abt. 1699, Peter Coley; m. (2) Joshua Hoyt.

Couch, Simon, s. of Simon.

He m. Abigail Sturgis, dau. of John, whose father's will 1698
called her his wife. She m. (2) Ens. John Andrews, and d. 14
Sept. 1730 ae. abt. 57 (g. s., Westport). Abigail wife of Simon
renewed her Covenant at Fairfield Church, 3 May 1696.

Will 2 Mar. 1712/3, proved 7 Apr. 1713; wife Abigail and
brother-in-law Jonathan Sturgis; son Thomas, who had land left
him by my brother Thomas; son Simon; slaves; five daus.
Abigail, Hannah, Sarah, Isabel, Deborah. The births of the children (see below) are given in the probate records. Distribution
made 20 Feb. 1718/9 to those named in will, the only married dau.
being Abigail Edwards.

Will of Abigail Andrews, 7 Feb. 1729/30, proved 22 Sept. 1730;
daus. Abigail Edwards, Hannah Osborn, Sarah Couch, Isabel
Rumsey, Deborah Couch; sons Thomas and Simon Couch.

Anthony Batterson of Norwalk, 23 Feb. 1724/5 quitclaimed to
Thomas and Simon Couch any pretense of right to land or any
other estate which did belong to Mr. Simon Couch dec'd, being
father of the said Thomas and Simon. [His interest does not
appear.]

Children, bapt. at Fairfield Church:

Abigail, b. 31 Jan. 1693/4, bapt. 3 May 1696; m. (recorded Norwalk)
4 May 1713, William Edwards.

✕Thomas, b. 9 June 1695, bapt. 3 May 1696, d. 1 Apr. 1736 ae. 40 yrs.
9 mos. 22 days (g. s., Westport); will 6 Dec. 1735, codicil 2 Feb.
1735/6, proved 20 Apr. 1736; m. 7 Dec. 1721, Sarah Allen, b.
1 Apr. 1697. She was dau. of Lt. Gideon; m. (2) 10 Nov. 1736,
Timothy Keeler, and d. 10 Mar. 1787 ae. 90.

Simon, b. 6 July 1697, bapt. 15 Aug. 1697, d. 10 Apr. 1770 ae. 72 yrs.
9 mos. 13 days (g. s., Westport), prob. misreading for 19 Apr., as
given by Church record; Ens., west parish, Fairfield, Oct. 1733;
Capt., May 1735; m. 18 May 1721, Abigail Jennings, dau. of Joshua,
b. 16 Feb. 1700 (by age at death), d. 14 July 1765 ae. 65 yrs. 4 mos.
15 days (g. s.). His will, 17 Mar. 1770, proved 21 Apr. 1770, freed

two slaves, and gave residue to his nephew and adopted son Simon Couch of Redding.

Hannah, bapt. 27 Aug. 1699; m. 4 Nov. 1724, Samuel Osborn.
John, bapt. 9 May 1702, d. y.
Solomon, bapt. 27 Aug. 1704, d. y.
Sarah, b. 30 Mar. 1706, bapt. 12 May 1706, d. 9 Mar. 1783 in 77 yr. (g. s., Westport); m. 28 Oct. 1730, John Andrews.
Isabel, b. 17 Sept. 1708, bapt. 17 Oct. 1708, d. 7 Nov. 1754; m. in 1729, Benjamin Rumsey.
Deborah, b. 30 Mar. 1710, bapt. 14 May 1710; m. Jacob Jones, of Ridgefield.

Couch, Samuel, s. of Simon. Ens., west company, Fairfield, June 1709; Lt., Oct. 1709; Capt., Oct. 1710; Deputy (Fairfield), Oct. 1710, Oct. 1712, May and Oct. 1720, May 1733, Oct. 1734; Justice, 1723-39.

Married Edrea Hurlbut, dau. of Thomas, 2d, and with her and her brothers and sisters conveyed rights in Woodbury inherited from her father. Doubtless she was the young widow of Benjamin Gilbert when she m. Couch. Born about 1674, she d. 24 Nov. 1737 ae. 63 (g. s., Westport). Edra, wife of Samuel, renewed Covenant at Fairfield Church, 3 May 1696. At bapt. of children 1711 to 1715, Samuel was called Capt.

Will 12 May 1739, proved 3 Dec. 1739; advanced in years; legacies to sons Samuel, Benjamin, John (at College, to have out of his estate education for four years), and Ebenezer; daus. Eunice wife of Reuben Taylor and Abigail Couch; gr. son Joseph Jackson; residue equally to children, Samuel, Benjamin, Ebenezer, and Solomon Couch, Mary Couch, Edry Frost, Eunice Taylor, Elizabeth Todd, and Abigail Couch.

Samuel, Benjamin, Ebenezer, and Solomon Couch, Joseph Crane and wife Mary, Joseph Frost and wife Adra, Nathaniel Hibbard and wife Abigail, all of Fairfield, Reuben Taylor and wife Eunice of Norwalk, and Rev. Jonathan Todd and wife Elizabeth of Guilford, conveyed 15 June 1741 to brother John Couch of Fairfield, land in Redding.

Children, bapt. at Fairfield:

Mary, bapt. 3 May 1696, d. 9 Jan. 1766 ae. 70 (Bible rec.); m. Joseph Crane; res. Fairfield 1741, Dukesfield, Dutchess Co., N. Y., 1744.

Adrea, bapt. 7 Aug. 1698, d. 23 July 1753; m. 27 Aug. 1724, Joseph Frost.

✕Samuel, bapt. 22 Sept. 1700, d. at Westport, 18 May 1775; will 2 Nov. 1774, proved 20 June 1775; m. 13 Sept. 1726, Elizabeth Sturges, dau. of John; bapt. 29 Aug. 1708, d. 20 July 1787.

✕Benjamin, bapt. 27 Dec. 1702, d. 27 Sept. 1748 in 47 yr. (g. s., Westport); m. Mary ———, who m. (2) (rec. Westport) 19 Dec. 1749, Moses St. John, of Norwalk.

Martha, bapt. 18 Feb. 1704/5, d. abt. 1728; m. Nov. 1727, Ephraim Jackson.

Eunice, bapt. 2 Mar. 1706/7; m. Reuben Taylor, of Norwalk.

✕Ebenezer, bapt. Apr. 1709, d. 23 Mar. 1797 ae. 88 (g. s., Redding); will 6 June 1796; m (1) 18 May 1731, Ann Crane, dau. of Jonathan; m. (2) Eunice ———.

Elizabeth, bapt. 22 July 1711, d. at East Guilford, 18 Dec. 1783 in 73 yr.; m. 9 Jan. 1735, Rev. Jonathan Todd.

✕Solomon, bapt. 24 May 1713, d. 26 Sept. 1748 in 36 yr. (g. s., Westport); adm'n on Est. granted to Deborah and John Couch, 1 Nov. 1748; m. Deborah Silliman, dau. of Daniel, who m. (2) at Westport, 11 May 1760, David Bulkley, and d. in 1766. The dower set to widow Deborah Couch, late Deborah Bulkley, dec'd, was ordered distributed to her children, 23 Sept. 1766.

Abigail, bapt. 4 Sept. 1715, d. at Westport, 15 Nov. 1776; m. 24 Apr. 1740, Nathaniel Hibbard.

✕John, res. Redding; m. Sarah ———.

Coventry, Jonathan.

Of Marshfield, Mass., 1651. With Ephraim Wheeler, he witnessed a deed given at Fairfield, 12 Apr. 1654, by Thomas Wheeler to Francis and Elizabeth Hall. If he lived in Fairfield, he was there but a short time.

Crane, Elijah, s. of Benjamin.

Born at Wethersfield abt. 1665, son of Benjamin and Mary (Backus) Crane.

He renewed Covenant at Stratfield Church, 8 Feb. 1697; Mary [his wife] was received to full communion, 22 Oct. 1699.

Married (1) Mary Sherman, dau. of Theophilus of Wethersfield, mentioned as his wife 1711 in her father's will.

Married (2) (by 1715) Abigail, widow of Joseph Cable, and was appointed guardian of two of her Cable sons, 1 Feb. 1715 [1715/6]. She was dau. of Samuel Adams, b. 25 Mar. 1682, and was called wife of Crane in settlement of Est. of her brother Abraham Adams, 1718.

Daniel Adams of Fairfield was appointed guardian to Abigail, Sarah, Elizabeth, Israel, and Benjamin, children of Elijah Crane of Fairfield, dec'd, 7 Feb. 1726/7; and on 26 Apr. 1727, Capt. Samuel Couch was appointed guardian to Benjamin.

Children [by first wife], bapt. at Stratfield:

Abigail, bapt. 29 May 1698, d. y.
Deborah, bapt. 2 Apr. 1699.
Mary, bapt. 15 Sept. 1700.
Israel, bapt. 28 Mar. 1703, d. y.
Comfort, bapt. 16 June 1706, d. at Huntington, 20 Sept. 1792 ae. 88; m. (rec. Stratford) 3 Dec. 1730, Joseph Goodwin.
Elijah, bapt. 7 Nov. 1708, d. at Stratford, 3 Oct. 1740; adm'n granted, 13 Feb. 1743/4, to Benajah Mallory; m. at Stratford, 3 Aug. 1732, Elizabeth Wakelee; she m. (2) 20 Jan. 1742/3, Benajah Mallory.
Jabez, bapt. 9 May 1714, d. at Norwalk in 1748; will 2 July 1748, proved 26 Sept. 1748; named wife Ann, dau. Mary Sherman Crane, son William, and dau. Lucretia. He m. (1) Elizabeth Fitch, dau. of Nathaniel; m. (2) Ann ———.

Children [by second wife]:

Abigail, bapt. 24 June 1716;* m. 14 Sept. 1744, Andrew Trubee.
Sarah, m. 7 June 1739, Daniel Cable.
Elizabeth.
Israel.
Benjamin.

Crofut, Daniel, s. of Joseph.

Doubtless son of Joseph and Mary (Hillier) Crofut of Springfield, b. 23 Jan. 1669/70. His father was of Springfield by 1658, and was under Capt. William Turner at the Falls Fight, K. Philip's War, 1676.

He settled in Fairfield and m. Phebe, widow of William Lyon; she m. (3) Samuel Jackson, and (4) Zechariah Lawrence.

Will 23 Jan. 1706/7, proved 28 May 1707; wife Pheby, Exec'x; three sons; son-in-law Nathaniel Lyon.

Zachariah Lawrence of Fairfield conveyed, 3 June 1736, to Daniel Crowfoot, David Crowfoot, and Gabriel Jackson, children

---

* Eunice, dau. of Abigail Crane, bapt. 30 Nov. 1740.

of wife Phebe Lawrence, late of Fairfield, dec'd, all her moveable Est. [Fairfield Probate.]

Children, bapt. at Fairfield:

XDaniel, bapt. 9 Aug. 1702, d. at Redding, in 1772; adm'n granted, 25 Aug. 1772; m. (rec. Fairfield, date omitted) Avis Adams. She was dau. of Nathan, bapt. 29 Nov. 1702, d. after 1772.

XJoseph, bapt. 10 Dec. 1704; m. abt. 1725, Lydia Canfield, dau. of Ebenezer.

XDavid, bapt. 8 Sept. 1706, d. at Redding, in 1767; will 23 June 1767, proved 7 July 1767; m. (1) Mary ———; m. (2) Naomi ———.

Crofut, James, s. of Joseph.

Born at Springfield, Mass., 23 Jan. 1666/7, son of Joseph and Mary (Hillier) Crofut; settled in Norwalk, rem. to Danbury, and d. in 1724. We may guess that he m. a dau. [Percy?] of Judah Gregory.

Inv. 2 Nov. 1724 taken by Israel Curtis and John Hoyt. Inv. at Norwalk taken by Mr. Benjamin Lines and Matthew Gregory, 7 Oct. 1724. Joseph Gregory one of the Adm'rs. Widow and eight children, named as below.

Children:

James, d. at Danbury in 1767; will 5 May 1761; agreement of heirs, 7 July 1767; m. at New Haven, 4 Dec. 1723, Lydia Bristol, dau. of Eliphalet, b. 1 Nov. 1701.

Josiah, d. at Danbury in 1763; will 31 Oct. 1763, proved 29 Nov. 1763; m. Sarah ———.

Matthew, d. at Danbury in 1782; Inv. 12 May 1782; m. ———.

Hannah.

Mary.

Elizabeth.

Sarah.

Lydia.

Crooker, William.

He was of Stratford as early as 1647, and in 1649 was husband of a dau. of Henry Gregory.

His name appears in the list of freeholders of Oyster Bay, L. I., 1685.

Cross, William.

Served in the Pequot War, 1637; settled early in Windsor, removed by 1644 to Wethersfield, and finally to Fairfield, where he d. in 1655.

Inv. 7 Sept. 1655, taken by George Hull and Alexander Knowles; the widow and orphans mentioned. Mr. Ward, Mr. Hill, and John Banks, to care for the estate.

Margaret Cross [his widow] m. (rec. Stamford) in 1657, Robert Bates.

Children:
+Nathaniel.
+Samuel.
+John.
Sarah, d. at Stamford, 18 Feb. 1711/2; m. John Bates.
Hannah, d. at Stamford between 1675 and 1682; m. John Jagger.
Mary, d. at Stratford, 7 Oct. 1687; m. (rec. Stratford) 19 Jan. 1672/3, John Pickett, Jr.

Cross, Nathaniel, s. of William.

He m. (1) Abigail ———.
He m. (2) at Stamford, 6 Nov. 1696, Hannah Knapp. She m. (2) 31 Mar. 1715, Samuel Palmer.
He d. at Stamford, 28 Oct. 1714.
Adm'n granted, 2 Feb. 1714/5, to widow Hannah. Deborah Cross, dau. of Nathaniel, chose father-in-law Samuel Palmer guardian, and he was appointed for John, Sarah and Mary Cross.
Distribution of his lands made by mutual agreement of his heirs, 11 Jan. 1730/1; Deborah Cross wife of John Knapp; Sarah Cross wife of Israel Holly; Hannah Cross wife of Sergt. John Waterbury; Mary Cross; and John Cross. [Stamford Deeds.]

Children [by first wife], recorded at Stamford:
Hannah, b. 23 Feb. 1687 [1687/8]; m. 30 Nov. 1710, John Waterbury.
Abigail, b. 8 Apr. 1694, d. 5 Sept. 1710.

Children [by second wife]:
Deborah, b 17 Feb. 1701 [1701/2], d. 4 Dec. 1735; m. 23 May 1723, John Knapp.

Nathaniel, b. 13 Apr. 1703, d. 28 Oct. 1714.*
Sarah, b. [say 1705]; m. 25 Feb. 1724/5, Israel Holly.
John, b. 16 Jan. 1707 [1707/8].
Mary, b. 15 Apr. 171—.

Cross, Samuel, s. of William. Lt., north company, Windsor, Oct. 1698; Capt., Oct. 1705.

Settled in Windsor, and m. 12 July 1677, Elizabeth (Fox), widow of Edward Chapman. He d. 5 Nov. 1707.

On 15 Feb. 1671 [1671/2], William Hill entered land for record at Fairfield, purchased from Samuel Cross.

Will 31 July 1707, proved 5 Jan. 1707/8; wife Elizabeth; son-in-law Simon Chapman; bro. John Cross; the dau. which bro. Nathaniel Cross had by his first wife; cousins John Bates, Samuel Bates, Jonathan Bates, Sarah Ketchum, Jonathan Jagger, Hannah Webb, James Pickett, Mary Hoyt, and Ephraim Phelps.

Children, recorded at Windsor:

Hannah, b. 11 June 1678, d. 7 July 1680.
Samuel, b. and d. 10 Dec. 1679.

Cross, John, s. of William.

He m. (1) at Windsor, 3 Nov. 1686, Mary (Hull), widow of John Grant, bapt. at Windsor, 8 Oct. 1648, d. there 29 June 1720; m. (2) Mary ———. He d. 23 July 1721.

In 1718 he was appointed to accompany the Conn. Commissioners on the N. Y. Boundary, as he had been present at the running of the line, indicating that he had lived in Stamford in his youth. His first wife was dau. of Josias Hull, and granddau. of George Hull of Fairfield.

Adm'n granted, 1 Aug. 1721, to Simon Chapman of Windsor, and Joshua Hoyt of Stamford was added, 5 Dec. 1721. Distribution ordered to the widow Mary; and to the heirs of his brother and sisters, viz.: of Nathaniel Cross dec'd, of Sarah Bates dec'd, of Mary Pickett dec'd and of Hannah Jagger dec'd.

Child:

Hannah, b. 10 Apr. 1694, d. Dec. 1696.

---

* *Stamford Registration,* perhaps by error, gives same date of death for father and son.

Crow, John, Jr.

Son of John and Elizabeth (Goodwin) Crow, of Hartford and Hadley. Settled in Fairfield, and died at sea, unmarried. Inv. 1 June 1667. The next February an agreement was made by [his father] John Crow, Sr., on behalf of the younger children, and [his elder sisters and their husbands] Giles and Esther Hamlin, and William and Elizabeth Warren.

Giles Hamlin (of Middletown) was a witness to the Wethersfield deed given 1661/2 by Jehu and Esther Burr.

Curtis, John.

Married at Nazing, co. Essex, Eng., 19 Apr. 1610, Elizabeth Hutchins.

He may be the John who was at Roxbury 1638, and Wethersfield 1639; in any case, he d. soon. The widow Elizabeth Curtis was in Stratford as early as 1650, and d. in 1658.

Will of Elizabeth Curtiss of Stratford, proved 4 June 1658; grandchildren John and Jonathan Curtiss, sons of John and William; to grandchildren John, Israel, Jonathan, and Sarah, children of said John and William, my house and lot when they come to age of 20; grandchild Mary Curtiss daughter of Thomas Curtiss; residue to sons John and William; my Bible to grandchild John (son of John), and a Bible for Jonathan Curtiss (son of my son William).

Children, bapt. at Nazing:

+John, bapt. 26 Feb. 1614/5.
+William, bapt. 21 June 1618.
+Thomas, bapt. 12 Mar. 1619/20.

Curtis, John, s. of John. Sergt., Stratford Train Band.

Bapt. at Nazing, co. Essex, Eng., 26 Feb. 1614/5. Came aged 21 on the *Safety* in 1635, was at Roxbury, Mass., for a time, resided 1639 in Wethersfield, and settled 1640 in Stratford.

Elizabeth wife of John, Sr., d. at Stratford, 9 Mar. 1681/2. John, Sr., d. there 2 Dec. 1707 ae. abt. 96. Statements to the effect that Elizabeth was a Welles are based on a misinterpretation of a deed at Stratford; he was called uncle by John Welles [son of Hugh] who m. his niece Sarah Curtis.

Children, recorded at Stratford:

John, b. 14 Oct. 1642, d. at Newark, N. J., 17 Sept. 1704; m. Hannah, widow of Abraham Kimberly.

+Israel, b. 3 Apr. 1644.

Elizabeth, b. 2 May 1647.

Thomas, b. 14 Jan. 1648 [1648/9], d. at Wallingford in 1736; Deputy for Wallingford, Sept. and Oct. 1689, May and Oct. 1717, May 1718; Ens., Wallingford Trainband, Oct. 1704; m. at Wallingford, 9 June 1674, Mary Merriman, dau. of Capt. Nathaniel, b. at New Haven, 12 July 1757; had 12 children.

+Joseph, b. 12 Nov. 1650.

+Benjamin, b. 30 Sept. 1652.

Hannah, b. 2 Feb. 1654 [1654/5], d. 21 Oct. 1728 in 74 yr.; m. Benjamin Lewis.

Curtis, William, s. of John. Deputy for Stratford, Oct. 1667, May and Oct. 1668, May and Oct. 1669, May and Oct. 1670, May 1671 (called Lt. Joseph by error), May and Oct. 1672, May and Oct. 1673, May and Oct. 1674, May and Oct. 1675, Oct. 1676, May and Oct. 1677, May and Oct. 1678, May and Oct. 1679, May 1680, Oct. 1681, May and Oct. 1682, May, July and Oct. 1684, May 1685, Oct. 1686, Jan. and Mar. 1687, May and June 1692. Commissioner for Stratford, 1671-75, for Stratford and Woodbury, 1676-79, for Stratford, 1680-87, 1689-97. Called Lt., Oct. 1667; Capt., Stratford Trainband, June 1672; Second Military Officer, Fairfield County, June 1672; Capt., Fairfield County Troop, Nov. 1673, Oct. 1675; Militia Committee, June 1672; War Committee, Aug. 1673.

Bapt. at Nazing, co. Essex, Eng., 21 June 1618; Capt. William d. at Stratford, 21 Dec. 1702.

Will 15 Dec. 1702, proved 31 Dec. 1702; sons Daniel, Ebenezer, Zechariah, Josiah; daus. Sarah Wells, Elizabeth Rose; son Joshua Curtis; Jonathan the son of Jonathan Curtis.

He m. (2) Sarah, widow of Ens. William Goodrich of Wethersfield, and dau. of Matthew Marvin of Norwalk, bapt. at Great Bentley, co. Essex, Eng., 27 Dec. 1631, d. abt. 1702.

Children [by first wife], recorded at Stratford:

Sarah, b. 10 Oct. 1642; m. abt. 1658, John Welles.

+Jonathan, b. 14 Feb. 1644 [1644/5].

+Joshua, b. 6 Oct. 1646.

Abigail, b. 26 Apr. 1650, d. y.
+Daniel, b. 16 Nov. 1652.
Elizabeth, b. 16 Feb. 1654 [1654/5]; m. (1) Mercy Moss of New Haven; m. (2) John Rose of Branford.
+Ebenezer, b. 26 July 1657.
+Zachary, b. 14 Nov. 1659.
+Josiah, b. 30 Aug. 1662.

Curtis, Thomas, s. of John.

Baptized at Nazing, co. Essex, Eng., 12 Mar. 1619/20; m. ———.

Had a child mentioned in his mother's will:

Mary, prob. the "Mary Curtes" who m. (rec. Milford) 25 Oct. 1669, Samuel Coley. Mary Coley, Milford, 2 Oct. 1692, is in the list of those who renewed Covenant and had children bapt. at Stratford Church.

Curtis, Israel, son of John. Deputy (Woodbury), May and June 1689, May and Oct. 1691, May, June and Oct. 1692, May, Sept. and Oct. 1693, Oct. 1695, May* and Oct. 1696, May 1699, May 1703, Oct. 1704; Commissioner for Woodbury, 1691-97; Lt., Woodbury Trainband, Oct. 1690.

Born at Stratford, 3 Apr. 1644; Lt. Israel d. at Woodbury, 28 Oct. 1704 in 61 yr. An original proprietor of Woodbury, 1672.

Agreement 10 Nov. 1704 to divide Est. of Lt. Israel Curtis; widow Rebecca Curtis; daus. Hannah wife of Thomas Minor and Rebecca wife of Ephraim Minor; three sons, Israel, John, Stephen.

Children, recorded at Stratford:

Israel, b. 18 Mar. 1666/7, d. y.
+Israel, b. 12 May 1668.
+John, b. first week of Oct. 1670.
Stephen, b. 24 Aug. 1673, d. at Woodbury, after long sickness, 11 June 1723 ae. 50; Deputy (Woodbury) May 1718; m. 2 Nov. 1699, Sarah Minor.
Hannah, b. abt. 1675; m. at Woodbury, abt. 1692, Thomas Minor.
Rebecca, bapt. at Woodbury, Nov. 1678, d. 13 Mar. 1763 ae. 96; m. at Woodbury, 21 Aug. 1701, Ephraim Minor.
Ruth, bapt. Apr. 1681, d. y.
Josiah, bapt. Nov. 1683, d. y.
Ruth, bapt. Sept. 1687, d. y.

---

* Called Lt., John by error.

Curtis, Joseph, s. of John.   Deputy (Stratford), May and July 1686, May and Oct. 1689, May 1690, May 1691, May and June 1692, May and Sept. 1693, May 1694; Assistant, 1698-1721; Ens., company raised for war, Mar. 1692/3; Commissioner for Stratford, 1692-97; Associate Judge, Fairfield County Court, 1698; Judge of County Court, 1711, 1725; Committee of War, Fairfield County, Oct. 1709; Justice, 1722-28.

Born at Stratford, 12 Nov. 1650; d. at Stratford in 1742.

Married at Stratford, 9 Nov. 1676, Bethia Booth.   She was dau. of Richard, b. 18 Aug. 1658.   Wife was called Bethia at birth of children 1687 and 1699.

Children, recorded at Stratford:

Elizabeth, b. 17 Jan. 1677 [1677/8]; m. 5 Dec. 1694, Samuel Ufford.
Anna, b. 1 Sept. 1679.
Mary, b. abt. 1682, d. 16 Apr. 1767 in 83 yr. (g. s., Trumbull); m. (1) 26 Dec. 1704, Joseph Nichols; m. (2) Henry Hawley.
Ephraim, b. 31 Dec. 1684, d. at Stratford, 9 May 1775 in 92 yr. (g. s.); will 22 Dec. 1766, proved 4 Jan. 1776; m. 26 June 1707, Elizabeth Stiles; dau. of Ephraim, b. 18 Feb. 1687/8, d. 5 Oct. [1778] in 91 yr. (g. s.).
Joseph, b. 6 Nov. 1687, d. at Stratford, July 1738; will 1 July 1738, proved 2 Aug. 1738; m. 5 July 1711, Elizabeth Welles.
Nathan, b. 21 Feb. 1689/90; m. 23 June 1715, Eunice Judson.
Josiah, b. 31 Mar. 1692, d. 26 Apr. 1708.
Bethia, b. 10 Mar. 1695/6; m. 7 Dec. 1714, Benjamin Burton.
Eleazer, b. 30 July 1699, d. 21 Oct. 1699.
Ebenezer, b. 1 Aug. 1699, d. May 1700.
Eliphalet, b. 1 Aug. 1699; m. 7 Dec. 1720, Hannah Burroughs.

Curtis, Benjamin, s. of John.   Deputy (Stratford), Oct. 1697, Jan. 1698, Oct. 1700, Oct. 1703, May 1705, May 1706, May, Oct. and Dec. 1707, Oct. and Nov. 1711, Oct. 1712, Oct. 1714, May and Oct. 1721, Oct. 1722; Naval Officer, Port of Stratford, May 1714.

Born at Stratford, 30 Sept. 1652; d. there in 1733.

Adm'n was granted, 19 June 1733, to John Curtis and Zachariah Booth.

Married (1) at Stratford, 23 Mar. 1680/1, Esther Judson. She was dau. of Joseph, b. 20 Aug. 1660.   Mrs. Hester, wife of Benjamin, d. 27 Aug. 1713.

Mr. Benjamin m. (2) at Stratford, 1 Dec. 1714, Mis[t] Bathsheba Stiles. She was widow of Ephraim Stiles, and dau. of Henry Tomlinson, b. 3 Jan. 1661/2. A prenuptial agreement with her, dated 27 Nov. 1714, appointed Samuel Walker trustee, and gave her power to dispose at her own will of personal estate and negroes. She d. 9 Feb. 1735 ae. 74 (g. s.).

Children [by first wife], recorded at Stratford:*

John, b. 18 Feb. 1681/2, d. in 1745; will 3 Sept. 1745, proved 19 Sept. 1745; m. (1) 19 Feb. 1706/7, Margaret Pickett, b. 14 Aug. 1686, d. 8 Oct. 1714; m. (2) 3 Nov. 1715, Hannah Johnson, dau. of Col. Ebenezer of Derby, b. 6 Dec. 1680; m. (3) after 1734, Rebecca, widow of Ens. Benjamin Rumsey, and previously of John Allyn, and dau. of Richard Blackleach.

Ruth, b. 11 Jan. 1683 [1683/4], d. 23 Apr. 1721; m. 15 Nov. 1705, John Thompson.

James, b. 4 May 1686, d. at Durham, 1 Nov. 1765; m. abt. 1708, Hannah Coe, dau. of John, b. 14 Apr. 1689.

David, b. [say 1694], d. in 1760; will 30 Mar. 1754, proved 26 Dec. 1760; m. (1) 26 Nov. 1719, Dinah Wakelee, who d. June 1725; m. (2) 10 Nov. 1725, Hester Hurd; her will June 1773, proved 14 June 1775.

Anna, b. abt. 1697, d. at Stratford, 18 May 1733 in 37 yr. (g. s.); m. 12 June 1718, Zechariah Booth.

Esther, d. 26 Aug. 1701.

Esther, bapt. at Stratford (rec. Stratfield) 10 Feb. 1706, d. at Bethel, 25 Aug. 1775 in 70 yr. (g. s.); m. (1) at Stratford, 3 Dec. 1724, Daniel Beach; m. (2) 17 June 1747, Capt. Ebenezer Hickok.

Curtis, Jonathan, s. of William.

Born at Stratford, 14 Feb. 1644/5; d. there in 1681.

In Stratford Deeds, he had land by gift from his father Lt. William Curtis and by gift from his father-in-law John Thompson.

Inv. 10 Oct. 1681; widow Abigail, two sons and two daus.

Wife was called Abigail at birth of child 1679. She was dau. of John Thompson, b. 1 May 1646, and she m. (2) Nicholas Hughes, and (3) 1 Aug. 1695, Mr. Samuel Sherman, and d. 2 Mar. 1731. Abigail Sherman conveyed 1708 to son Jonathan Curtis land from former husband Nicholas Huse. In 1692 Abigail

---

* His children were not all recorded, and he prob. had more daus. than appear. As candidates for missing daus., we incline to the opinion that Martha who m. 22 Dec. 1708, Benjamin Beach, and Phebe who m. 5 Oct. 1711, Ephraim Hawley, belong in this family, born between James and David. Possibly Dinah who m. 26 June 1718, Nathan Beardsley, belongs here also, though more doubtful.

and Sarah Curtis receipted to their mother for right from brother William Curtis and uncle John Thompson, referring to father Jonathan Curtis dec'd. In 1709 Abigail Sherman conveyed to son Jonathan Curtis, who obliged himself to satisfy her son-in-law Francis Griffin with portion due from Est. of her dec'd husband Jonathan Curtis and her son William Curtis.

Children, recorded at Stratford:

> Abigail, b. 17 Oct. 1671; m. 3 Nov. 1692, Ebenezer Blackman.
> Sarah, b. 12 Sept. 1673, d. July 1707; m. 25 Nov. 1697, Francis Griffin.
> William, b. in 1675, d. y.
> +Jonathan, b. 28 June 1679.

Curtis, Joshua, s. of William.

Born at Stratford, 6 Oct. 1646; d. at Cohansey, N. J., in 1705. An original proprietor of Woodbury, 1672.

Inv. of Joshua who d. at Cohansey, est. in Stratford, taken 22 Jan. 1705/6 by Joseph, Zechariah, and Josiah Curtis.

Distribution made 7 Feb. 1708/9 to his son and three daus. (rec. Stratford); William Curtiss; Mary wife of John Marcy; Anna Rowell; Bethyah Daighton.

Children, three bapt. at Woodbury:

> William, m. 1 Dec. 1708, Rebecca Blackman.
> Anna, bapt. Dec. 1681; m. Thomas Rowell of Salem, N. J.
> Bethia, bapt. Feb. 1685/6; m. ——— Dayton.
> Mary, bapt. Sept. 1688; m. John Marcy of Salem, N. J.

Curtis, Daniel, s. of William.

Born at Stratford, 16 Nov. 1652, d. there 6 Feb. 1718/9 in 67 yr.

Possibly his wife was Mary Jennings.

Adm'n granted to widow Mary, 19 Feb. 1718/9. Son Abel and dau. Esther chose mother for guardian. Three sons, Daniel (rec'd portion), Abel, Hezekiah; four daus. Elizabeth, Esther, Abigail, Rebecca.

Children:

> Daniel, d. at Stratford, Oct. 1763; m. 11 May 1736, Mary Curtis, dau. of Joseph, who d. Oct. 1782 ae. 68.

Hezekiah, b. abt. 1708, d. at Stratford, 9 Oct. 1771 in 64 yr. (g. s.) ;
m. Mehitabel Hubbell, dau. of Richard, who d. in 1790 ae. 77.
Elizabeth, m. 16 Dec. 1723, Elisha Blagge.
Abel, d. in 1730. Adm'n granted to Hezekiah Curtis, 23 Oct. 1730.
Esther.
Abigail.
Rebecca.

Curtis, Ebenezer, s. of William. Ens., Stratford Trainband,
May 1706; Lt., north (or second) company, Oct. 1709.
Deputy (Stratford), May 1724.

Born at Stratford, 26 July 1657, d. there 10 Dec. 1751. He m.
Ruth Porter, dau. of Nathaniel, b. 22 Nov. 1669, d. 28 May 1739
in 70 yr. (g. s.).

Will 6 Feb. 1749/50, proved in 1751; children of son Ebenezer
dec'd; children of dau. Ruth Sherman dec'd; children of dau.
Deborah Bennett; dau. Sarah Nichols; son-in-law Theophilus
Nichols, Exec's. Inv. of Lt. Ebenezer, 14 July 1752, sworn to by
Capt. Theophilus Nichols, Exec'r.

Children of Sergt. Ebenezer and Ruth, recorded at Stratford:
Hannah, b. 30 Apr. 1691, d. s. p.
Samuel, b. 27 Sept. 1693, d. 18 Mar. 1715/6.
Ruth, b. 7 Jan. 1695/6, d. 9 Nov. 1726; m. 22 [Nov.] 1720, Nathaniel
Sherman.
Deborah, b. 28 Sept. 1699, d. 16 Sept. 1785 in 87 yr. (g. s., Shelton) ;
m. 25 Feb. 1723/4, Nathan Bennett.
Sarah, b. 7 Apr. 1702, d. 26 Sept. 1769 in 68 yr. (g. s., Epis. Yard,
Stratford) ; m. 2 Jan. 1723/4, Theophilus Nichols.
Ebenezer, b. (no record), d. in 1749; will 23 Oct. 1749, proved 5 Dec.
1749; m. (1) 25 Nov. 1730, Abigail Clark, who d. 29 Nov. 1746
ae. 32 yrs. 10 mos. 25 days (g. s.) ; she was dau. of Ens. George
of Milford; m. (2) Mary ———.

Curtis, Zachariah, s. of William.

Born at Stratford, 14 Nov. 1659; d. there 12 June 1748 ae. 89.
He m. Hannah Porter, dau. of Nathaniel, b. 10 Apr. 1665, d.
14 Feb. 1738 ae. 73.
Distribution of Est. of Hannah Curtis (by order of Court, Apr.
1749) : Nathaniel Curtis (double portion) ; heirs of Zachariah

Curtis dec'd; Elizabeth Beardsley; heirs of Isaac Curtis dec'd; Jeremiah Curtis, "Clerk."

Children:

Nathaniel, b. [say 1690], d. in 1760; will 29 Nov. 1760, proved 23 Dec. 1760; m. 27 Nov. 1712, Hannah Welles; dau. of John of Hartford.

Elizabeth, b. abt. 1692, d. at Huntington, 22 May 1776 ae. 84 (g. s.); m. 4 June 1713, Zechariah Beardsley.

Zachariah, b. abt. 1697, d. at Trumbull, 18 Feb. 1746 in 49 yr. (g. s.); will 18 Feb. 1745/6, proved 28 Feb. 1745/6; m. 9 Jan. 1721/2, Mary Mitchell; dau. of Daniel, b. 27 Feb. 1701, d. 3 Jan. 1745 ae. 43 (g. s.).

Isaac, b. [say 1700], d. in 1741; adm'n granted, 3 Mar. 1740/1, to Daniel Porter and Nathaniel Curtis; m. 8 Sept. 1726, Elizabeth Bostwick.

Jeremiah, bapt. 26 May 1706, d. at Southington, 31 Mar. 1795 ae. 89; grad. Yale Coll. 1725; Rev. (pastor at Southington 1728-54); m. (1) 7 Jan. 1730, Hannah Burnham, dau. of Rev. William, who d. 10 Apr. 1772; m. (2) 4 May 1774, Rachel (Merchant), widow of Joseph Guernsey, who d. 21 Oct. 1794 ae. 88.

Curtis, Josiah, s. of William. Ens., south (or first) company, Stratford, Oct. 1709; Capt., May 1714. Deputy (Stratford), May 1716.

Born at Stratford, 30 Aug. 1662; d. there in 1745.

He m. (1) at Stratford, July 1692, Abigail Judson; dau. of Joseph, b. 15 Sept. 1669.

He m. (2) abt. 1698, Mary Beach, dau. of Benjamin, b. 19 Jan. 1676/7.

Adm'n cum testamento annexo granted, 20 Nov. 1745, to Abraham Curtis. Will 15 June 1745, proved 9 Nov. 1745; son William; dau. Abigail wife of Capt. Hezekiah Hooker of Woodbury; dau. Eunice wife of Lt. Robert Welles of Stratford; sons Abraham, Josiah, Benjamin, Peter; dau. Mary wife of Mr. John Patterson of Stratford; son Matthew; dau. Mehitabel Curtis; son Charles; wife Mary, Exec'x.

Will of Mary, 13 Apr. 1757, proved 20 Apr. 1759; sons Josiah, Benjamin, Peter, Matthew, Charles; daus. Eunice Welles, Mary Patterson, Mehitabel Curtis.

Children by Abigail, recorded at Stratford:

William, b. 22 Sept. 1693, d. at Stratford in 1767; will 12 June 1767, proved 7 July 1767; m. 24 Mar. 1725/6, Prudence Judson.

Sarah, who m. 19 Mar. 1712/3, John Wilcoxson, and d. soon after without issue, was prob. dau. of Josiah.

Abigail, m. 18 Dec. 1716, Hezekiah Hooker.

Children by Mary, recorded at Stratford:

Eunice, b. 1 Aug. 1699; m. 24 Oct. 1720, Robert Welles.

Abraham, b. 10 May 1701, d. at Stratford, 7 Sept. 1779 ae. 79 (g. s.); m. 25 Feb. 1724/5, Elizabeth Welles, who d. 31 Aug. 1770 in 68 yr. (g. s.).

Josiah, b. 6 Jan. 1702/3, d. 26 May 1773 in 71 yr. (g. s.); m. 28 Nov. 1727, Mary Judson of Woodbury.

Benjamin, b. 25 Dec. 1704, d. 28 July 1782 in 78 yr. (g. s., Newtown); m. 17 Aug. 1727, Elizabeth Birdsey, b. 17 Dec. 1706, d. 23 Feb. 1773 in 67 yr. (g. s., Newtown).

Peter, b. 1 Apr. 1707, d. in 1766; will 10 Oct. 1758, proved 5 Aug. 1766; m. (1) 4 Nov. 1728, Hester Clark, who d. 6 July 1744; m. (2) Mary Hawley.

Matthew, b. 16 Dec. 1708, bapt. 3 Apr. 1709 (at Stratford, rec. Stratfield), d. y.

Mary, b. 25 July 1711; m. 4 June 1730, John Patterson.

Matthew, b. 1 Dec. 1712, d. at Newtown, 29 Nov. 1796; m. (1) 2 June 1737, Phebe Judson; m. (2) Abigail Thompson of Fairfield.

Charles, b. 1 Jan. 1715/6; m. abt. 1736, Desire ———.

Mehitabel, b. 1 Jan 1715/6.

Curtis, Israel, son of Israel. Deputy for Danbury, May 1719, May 1720.

Born at Stratford, 12 May 1668; res. Woodbury and Danbury. He m. abt. 1693, Mary Morehouse, dau. of Samuel of Fairfield.

Children, recorded at Woodbury:

Samuel, bapt. Jan. 1694/5.

Josiah, bapt. Apr. 1697, d. at Danbury, in 1741; adm'n granted, 4 Jan. 1741/2, to David Hoyt; m. Hannah ———.

Stephen, b. 22 Apr. 1699, bapt. Apr. 1699, d. at Danbury, in 1741; will 23 Jan. 1740/1, proved 2 Mar. 1740/1; m. Abigail ———. His will called Francis Knapp brother.

Rebecca, b. 22 July 1701.

Son, stillborn 22 July 1701.

Curtis, John, s. of Israel. Ens., Woodbury Trainband, May 1714. Deputy for Woodbury, May 1715, Oct. 1717, Oct. 1718, Oct. 1721.

Born first week of Oct. 1670, d. at Woodbury, 14 Apr. 1754; m. abt. 1696, Joanna Burr, dau. of Jehu, 2d; she d. 1 Sept. 1749. The evidence of her identity is entirely circumstantial. She named her eldest dau. Elizabeth (after her mother), and a son Peter (after her bro. Hon. Peter Burr). Her son Peter named a son Peter Burr Curtis; and her dau. Eunice named a son Burr Stoddard.

Children, recorded at Woodbury:

> Elizabeth, bapt. Sept. 1697; m. 17 Jan. 1716/7, John Mitchell.
> Hannah, b. 1 Nov. 1699 at night, bapt. Nov. 1699, d. y.
> Elnathan, b. 2 Feb. 1701 [1701/2], but bapt. as Nathan, May 1702; Nathan d. at Woodbury, 19 Oct. 1761; m. May 1732, Martha Preston; dau. of William, b. 23 Apr. 1709, d. 23 June 1764 ae. 53.
> Abigail, b. 29 Feb. 1703/4, bapt. Mar. 1703/4; m. 6 Jan. 1723/4, David Hurd.
> Esther, b. 5 Apr. 1706, bapt. Apr. 1706; m. at Stratford, 20 Dec. 1734, Joseph Judson.
> Joanna, b. 5 Sept. 1708, bapt. Sept. 1708; m. 4 Dec. 1729, Eliakim Stoddard.
> John, b. 3 Feb. 1710/1, bapt. Feb. 1710/1, killed by lightning 1743; m. Abiah ———.
> Olive, b. 6 May 1713, bapt. May 1713, d. 26 Sept. 1749; m. 14 Jan. 1733, Gideon Stoddard.
> Peter, b. 1 Jan. 1715/6, d. at Lanesboro, Mass., 12 Mar. 1775; m. 27 Nov. 1747, Mrs. Mary Chittenden, who d. 4 July 1810.
> David, b. 21 Jan. 1717/8, d. at Woodbury, 15 Sept. 1782 ae. 65; m. Eunice Stiles, b. 18 Aug. 1717, d. 5 Mar. 1783 ae. 65.
> Eunice, b. 20 Mar. 1720; m. 1 Aug. 1739, Abijah Stoddard.

Curtis, Jonathan, s. of Jonathan.

Born at Stratford, 28 June 1679, d. there in 1770.

He m. (1) Hannah ———.

He m. (2) at Stratford, 24 Dec. 1718, Mary Summers.

Adm'n granted, 6 Nov. 1770, to Timothy Curtis. Distribution made, 15 Aug. 1771; sons Jonah, Jonathan, Israel, and Stephen had rec'd portions in father's lifetime; son Timothy; dau. Mary wife of John Haynes; Hannah Washburn, dau. of Edmund Curtis dec'd, eldest son of the dec'd; Sarah wife of Asa Chambers, dau.

of Sarah Adams dec'd, dau. of the dec'd; Thaddeus Bennett, Benjamin Bennett, Mary wife of David Beardsley, Sarah wife of Solomon Plant, and Ann Bennett, children of Hannah Bennett dec'd, dau. of the dec'd.

Children by Hannah, recorded at Stratford:

> Edmund, b. 26 June 1702, d. 20 Oct. 1726; adm'n granted to Obedience Curtis, 4 July 1727; m. 12 Dec. 1723, Obedience Mallory; dau. of John, b. at New Haven, 11 Apr. 1704, d. after 1785; she m. (2) 14 Feb. 1728, Nathan Fairchild; m. (3) 20 Nov. 1740, Benjamin Sherman; m. (4) 25 Dec. 1763, Robert Bassett.
>
> Jonah, b. 26 Oct. 1703, d. by 1792; will proved 27 May 1792; m. 11 Sept. 1727, Eunice Burroughs.
>
> Hannah, b. 24 Aug. 1705, bapt. 10 Feb. 1706 (at Stratford, rec. Stratfield); m. 28 Jan. 1724/5, Benjamin Bennett.
>
> Sarah, m. John Adams.
>
> Jonathan, b. abt. 1710, d. at Monroe, 8 Sept. 1787 in 77 yr. (g. s.); m. Eunice Summers, who d. in 1796 in 77 yr. (g. s.).

Children [maternity uncertain]:

> Israel.
> Stephen.
> Mary, m. at Stratford, 6 Sept. 1739, John Haynes.
> Timothy.

Darling, John.

Married Elizabeth Beers, dau. of James, and was called his wife in her father's will 1694 and her mother's will 1698.

Adm'n granted to his son John, 11 Feb. 1718/9; there are four sons, John, James, Joseph, Benjamin, and two daus., Hannah and Martha. Joseph and Benjamin Darling chose bro.-in-law John Bradley guardian.

Children, bapt. at Fairfield:

> Hannah, b. [say 1689], d. at Fairfield, 20 Oct. 1774; m. (rec. Norwalk) 17 Apr. 1709, Richard Whitney.
>
> Martha, m. John Bradley.
>
> ✕John, bapt. 24 Mar. 1694/5; m. Abilene Jessup, dau. of Edward, bapt. 13 Sept. 1696.
>
> James, bapt. 17 Apr. 1698.
>
> ✕Joseph, bapt. 29 June 1701.
>
> ✕Benjamin, bapt. 28 Feb. 1702/3; m. 6 Jan. 1725/6, Mary Hide.

Davis, John.

His grant from the town of Fairfield was recorded 21 Oct. 1679. He was adm. an inhabitant to a ten-acre lot in Woodbury, 2 June 1687. He conveyed for love to son John, 30 June 1704.

Marriage intended, 26 Dec. 1672, between John Davis and Lydia Waller, Adm'x of her dec'd husband Joseph Waller's Est. [Fairfield Pro. Rec.].

Lydia Davis bapt. 17 Nov. 1695 (Fairfield Church). Mary and Samuel, children of John, Jr.(?), bapt. 19 Jan. 1695/6.

John Davis of Fairfield, 27 Aug. 1707, conveyed to his sons John and Samuel, land in Woodbury, which John, Jr., and Samuel of Fairfield sold 26 Nov. 1708. John had other lands laid out on the Shepaug River, Woodbury.

Inv. 25 Feb. 1712/3. Samuel Davis, Adm'r.

Children (record incomplete) :

+John, b. [say 1674].
(prob.) Mary, b. abt. 1678, d. at Greenfield, 27 Jan. 1758 ae. 80 (g. s.) ; m. (rec. Greenfield) 15 May 1699, John Thorp.
+Samuel, b. [say 1680].
Rebecca, who testified July 1703 that Jonathan Squire's wife [Mary] "came to father John Davises", etc. [Conn. Archives.]*

Davis, John, s. of John.

Inv. of John, Jr., Est., 31 Oct. 1709. John Davis Adm'r of his son's Est.

Children (record incomplete) :

Mary, m. (rec. Fairfield, called dau. of John), 8 May 1718, Samuel Lyon.

Davis, Samuel, s. of John.

Blacksmith of Fairfield, conveyed land 1708, signing with his mark. He conveyed 1706, land formerly belonging to father-in-law Benjamin Banks.

He m. (1) Elizabeth Banks, dau. of Benjamin, b. 26 Nov. 1685. She was bapt. at Fairfield Church, Aug. 1714.

---

* This does not mean, as we interpret the passage, that Mary Squire was dau. of John Davis, but refers to Rebecca's father.

He m. (2) Hannah, widow of Joseph Smith.

The death of Samuel, and under it the death of Lydia Davis, are entered without date in Greenfield records.

Will 22 Mar. 1739/40, proved 6 May 1740; of parish of Greenfield; wife Hannah; daus. Rachel, Olive Smith; son Jabez; daus. Sarah, Elizabeth; gr. child Sarah Barlow; daus. Ann Cable, Damaris Bradley.

Elizabeth chose Capt. Thomas Hill for guardian, 1740; Rachel chose John Bradley, Jr., 1741.

Children, bapt. at Fairfield Church, first four on 5 Sept. 1714:

    XJabez, b. [say 1705], d. at Fairfield in 1791; adm'n granted, 6 June 1791; m. 3 Aug. 1726, Rebecca Rowland.
    Experience, m. Joseph Barlow.
    Ann, m. 26 Sept. 1733, John Cable.
    Damaris, m. 25 Apr. 1731, David Bradley.
    Lydia, bapt. 12 Feb. 1715/6, d. y.*
    Olive, bapt. 1 June 1718; m. Samuel Smith.
    Sarah, bapt. 14 May 1721, d. at Westport, 26 Oct. 1802 ae. 82 (g. s.); m. 19 Nov. 1740, Caleb Disbrow.
    Elizabeth, bapt. 2 June 1723.
    Rachel, bapt. 2 Aug. 1724, d. at Westport, 15 Feb. 1789; m. 20 Feb. 1742, Richard Elwood.

Denman, Philip.

The Constable of Stratford, 29 Sept. 1679, forewarned Philip Denman and "his mate Collens" out of town; and warned him and Daniel Collins, 12 Nov. 1679, from "Stratford side yᵉ river", Pagesutt [Derby].

He d. at Derby, 20 Aug. 1698; m. Apr. 1677, Hasadiah, who (though the Derby entry of marriage omits her surname) was almost certainly dau. of William and Elizabeth (Prudden) Slough, bapt. at Milford, 26 Nov. 1648 [see JAMES PRUDDEN]. Philip and his wife conveyed rights in Milford, and as no other female blessed with this rare name appears in early Milford records, no doubt of the identification can be entertained.

Will 20 Aug. 1698; wife; son Micah; daus. Mary, Elizabeth, Sarah, Hannah. Inv. 22 Aug. 1698.

---

* Adm'n on Est. of Lydia Davis of Fairfield granted, 2 Dec. 1740, to Jabez Davis. There is nothing to show whether she was his sister or grandmother.

Children, recorded at Derby:

> Mary, b. Apr. 1678.
>
> Elizabeth, b. July 1680, d. at Stratford, 23 Mar. 1731/2; m. (rec. Stratford) 27 Dec. 1704, Zechariah Blackman.
>
> Sarah, b. 15 Sept. 1682; m. (rec. Stratford) 18 Dec. 1707, Thomas Beardsley.*
>
> Micah, b. 22 [———] 1684, d. at Derby in 1769. His will, 5 Feb. 1763, proved May 1769, made his nephew John Coe of Derby his heir. [Coe was gr. son of Micah's sister Elizabeth.]
>
> Hannah, b. 10 May 1686.

Dennie, Albert.

He first appears in Fairfield records as having land from Thomas Shervington as security for a note dated 13 Nov. 1686; so did not come to Fairfield without means, and received the prefix "Mr." indicative of social standing.

Arrested 1689 on suspicion of murdering an Indian woman, he was represented by Mr. John Burr; and as no more is heard of the matter, and he afterwards married the minister's dau., the suspicion seems to have been ill founded.

Married Elizabeth Wakeman, dau. of Rev. Samuel.

Inv. 7 June 1708; adm'n granted to Capt. John and Lt. Joseph Wakeman; three children. John and Grizzel chose uncle Lt. Joseph Wakeman for guardian; and he was appointed guardian of James.

Adm'n on his estate was granted 13 May 1708 in New York.

Children, bapt. at Fairfield:

> ╳John, bapt. 7 Oct. 1694; m. (1) Mary Edwards, dau. of John, bapt. 7 July 1695; m. (2) Sarah Webb, dau. of Rev. Joseph, bapt. 30 Jan. 1702/3.
>
> Grizzel, bapt. 28 Feb. 1696/7, d. at Westport, 10 June 1754; m. Rev. Daniel Chapman.
>
> Margaret, bapt. 30 Apr. 1699, d. y.
>
> Annabel, bapt. 30 Nov. 1701, d. y.
>
> ╳James, bapt. 14 Feb. 1702/3, d. in 1759; adm'n granted 23 Feb. 1759; m. (1) 13 Apr. 1731, Mrs. Eunice Sturges; dau. of Jonathan, b. 4 Jan. 1708/9, d. 16 Oct. 1740; m. (2) Sarah Thompson, dau. of David, bapt. 24 May 1724; she m. (2) Dr. Francis Forgue, and d. 24 Jan. 1796 ae. 72 (g. s., Fairfield).

---

* We suppose that this Sarah was Beardsley's wife, though in the marriage record her name looks like "Dimin".

Dickerson, Thomas.

The name was usually spelled Dickerson, but occasionally Dickinson, of which it was a variant.

He had a grant of a homelot in Fairfield, 16 Feb. 1656, which he sold to John Foster.

Inv. of Thomas of Fairfield, 11 Sept. 1658. Widow Mary; a son, and daus., under 18. His widow m. (2) by 1660 Daniel Finch, as his third wife, and by him had a son Nathaniel. She m. (3) a Pinion, whom we identify as Nicholas Pinion, who came from Lynn, Mass., to the Iron Works at East Haven, where he d. Apr. 1676. The convenient death of Nicholas' wife Elizabeth in 1667, the same year that Mary lost her Finch husband, left him an eligible widower for this alliance.

On 20 Feb. 1677 [1677/8], Thomas Dickerson [Jr.], reciting that my bro. Joseph James hired of my mother Mary Pinion the land she had in Fairfield pertaining to the estate of my father Dickerson dec'd, receipted to James for the full rent for the whole number of years James had had the farm.

Children:

    Elizabeth, b. [say 1637], d. in 1691; will mentioned brother Thomas Dickerson; m. (1) [say 1655], Roger Knapp; m. (2) —— Wake.

    Mary, b. [say 1640]; m. Joseph James.

    Abigail, b. [say 1645], d. at Woodbury, Dec. 1725; m. Henry Castle.

    +Thomas, b. [say 1652].

    Sybil, b. [say 1655]; m. (1) Josiah Knapp; m. (2) James Nicholson, whose will named his bro.-in-law Nathaniel Finch.

Dickerson, Thomas, s. of Thomas.

He m. (1) Hannah Hendrick, dau. of Henry, who was his wife in 1685 and 1691; m. (2) Lydia ——. She m. (2) Thomas Sharp, of Stratfield and Newtown.

Inv. 14 Feb. 1699/1700. Children that date: Thomas, 11 next July; Daniel, 5 this 20 Feb.; Nathaniel, 3 next July; Elizabeth, 7 next June; Sibell, 4 mos. old. Widow Lydia Adm'x with Benjamin Sherman. In 1706, the widow "or she who was the Widow" to have dower, indicating remarriage. The dau. Sybil chose Richard Whitney for guardian, 6 Jan. 1713/4, as did also Daniel a month later.

Lydia Dickinson of Stratford, widow of Thomas, gave a conveyance 17 Jan. 1705/6, and signed as "Dickinson alias Sharp." [Stratford Deeds.]

Children, recorded at Stratford:

> Mary, b. 16 May 1679, or 26 May by Fairfield rec.; m. John Cully of Stonington, and on 4 Sept. 1710 conveyed to Nathaniel Knapp land in Stratfield which had belonged to her dec'd father Thomas Dickerson.
>
> Elizabeth, b. (rec. Fairfield) 12 Jan. 1681 [1681/2], d. y.
>
> Hannah, b. 7 Feb. 1686/7.
>
> Thomas, b. 16 July 1689; in May 1709, described as "a poor decrepid person", ae. abt. 20, he was granted liberty by the Conn. Leg. to sell land in Stratford to pay doctors.

Children [by Lydia]:

> Elizabeth, b. 9 June 1693.
>
> Daniel, b. 20 Feb. 1694/5.
>
> Nathaniel, b. [July 1697]; m. Susanna Lockwood, dau. of Robert of Fairfield.
>
> Sybil, b. [Oct. 1699].

Dimon, Thomas.

He settled early in Fairfield; was a mariner and ship-owner.

Inv. 19 Oct. 1658, included a bark of twelve tons. Sons Moses and John over 14.

Son Thomas apprenticed by Court to William Ward for five years [hence was prob. 16 in 1658]; John was apprenticed to Maj. Nathan Gold until 21 yrs. old.

Children:

> +Moses, b. [say 1638].
>
> +John, b. [say 1640].
>
> +Thomas, b. abt. 1642.

Dimon, Moses, s. of Thomas.

He purchased land from John Purdy, 19 Dec. 1670; and witnessed deed from John Burr to Jehu Burr, 1672/3.

He m. [2 May 1670 by *Ward Gen.*] Abigail Ward, dau. of Andrew. She m. (2) (by marriage contract, 2 June 1685), Edward Howard.

Will 21 Mar. 1683 [1683/4]; wife Abigail; son Moses; daus. Abigail, Hester, Grace; brethren John Burr and Samuel Ward, overseers. Inv. 15 Apr. 1684.

The overseers by the will complained 9 Feb. 1685 [1685/6] against Edward Howard, Exec'r by marriage. Howard thereupon engaged to pay the portions to the children. On 16 Mar. 1687/8, Abigail Howard complained that she wanted comforts and provisions for herself and child; the Court ordered her to live with one of the overseers of Moses Dimon's estate at the charge of her husband Howard until he provides.

Children, recorded at Fairfield:

+Moses, b. 7 Oct. 1672.
   Abigail, b. 20 Aug. 1676; m. 1700, Samuel Smedley.
   Thomas, b. 15 Sept. 1678, d. y.
   Hester, b. (no record); is prob. the Esther, b. [between Sept. 1681 and Sept. 1682], d. 11 Sept. 1744 in 63 yr. (g. s., Fairfield), who m. abt. 1707, Capt. Samuel Rowland.
   Grace, b. (no record, say 1683/4).

Dimon, John, s. of Thomas.

Born [say 1640]; settled in New London, and m. Rebecca, widow of Tobias Minter, and dau. of James Bemis; she m. (3) 2 Aug. 1682, Benedict Satterlee.

Children:

   John, b. abt. 1675.
   Sarah, b. abt. 1676.
   Jonathan, b. abt. 1678.

Dimon, Thomas, s. of Thomas.

Born abt. 1642, d. at New London in 1687; m. at New London, 22 Sept. 1670, Elizabeth Bradley, dau. of Peter and Elizabeth (Brewster).

He was a mariner.

Children, recorded at New London:

   Elizabeth, b. 14 Aug. 1672; m. Robert Lattimore.
   Thomas, b. 22 July 1675.
   Moses, b. 14 May 1677.
   Ruth, b. 22 Sept. 1680; m. Benjamin Shapleigh.
   John, b. 25 July 1686, d. in 1687.

Dimon, Moses, s. of Moses.   Lt., east company, Fairfield, May 1709; Deputy (Fairfield), Oct. 1722; Justice, 1723-36.

Born at Fairfield, 7 Oct. 1672.   Capt. Moses d. 7 Aug. 1748 ae. 77 (g. s., Fairfield).

Married (1) Jane Pinkney, dau. of Philip.

He m. (2) Jane (Dirck), widow of Moses Gilbert.

He m. (3) (by marriage agreement, 7 Mar. 1737/8), Jane, widow of John Hill.   She m. (3) (Fairfield Church) 10 Aug. 1749, Lt. Gideon Allen, and d. at Redding, 22 July 1774 ae. (supposed) 98.

Will 4 Nov. 1745, proved 26 Aug. 1748; wife Jane, mentioning marriage jointure; eldest son Moses, land from my father Moses dec'd; sons John, Ebenezer; daus. Abigail wife of Joseph Hill and Damaris wife of Peter Bradley.

Adm'n granted, 6 Sept. 1748, to Mr. James Smedley and Mr. David Rowland.   Distribution, 28 Apr. 1749, to Moses and John Dimon; heirs of Ebenezer Dimon dec'd; Abigail wife of Joseph Hill; Damaris wife of Peter Bradley.

He was called Lt. at bapt. of child 1709, and Capt. 1712, 1714; and Capt. in probate 1748.

Children [by first wife], bapt. at Fairfield:

×Moses, b. 4 Apr. 1698 (rec. Greenfield), bapt. 17 Apr. 1698, d. at Greenfield, 28 Nov. 1766 in 69 yr.; Capt. and Deacon; will 5 Mar. 1765, proved 23 Dec. 1766; m. (rec. Greenfield) 27 Apr. 1721, Hannah Gilbert, b. 29 Dec. 1700, d. 24 July 1767 in 67 yr. She was dau. of Moses.

×John, bapt. 17 Nov. 1700, d. 4 May 1764 in 64 yr. (g. s., Fairfield); Capt.; will 25 Feb. 1761, proved 28 June 1764; m. 10 May 1727, Elizabeth Wheeler, b. 2 Apr. 1704, d. 8 Feb. 1786 in 84 yr. (g. s.).

Thomas, bapt. 29 Aug. 1703, d. y.

×Ebenezer, bapt. 18 Mar. 1704/5, d. 28 May 1746 in 42 yr. (g. s., Fairfield); grad. Yale 1728; Sheriff; will 1 May 1746, proved 1 July 1746; m. (abt. 1729/30), Mary Burr, dau. of Col. John, bapt. at Stratfield, 4 July 1708. She m. (2) 4 Jan. 1747/8, Col. James Smedley, and d. 12 Sept. 1766.

Abigail, bapt. 17 Aug. 1707, d. 25 Apr. 1774 in 67 yr. (g. s., Greenfield); m. 30 Mar. 1731, Joseph Hill.

David, bapt. 20 Nov. 1709, d. y.

Damaris, bapt. 24 Aug. 1712, d. y.

Damaris, b. Sept. 1714 (rec. Greenfield), bapt. 31 Oct. 1714, d. between 1750 and 1756; m. (rec. Greenfield) 5 Nov. 1735, Peter Bradley.

Disbrow, Thomas.

Lived at Compo (Westport) in Fairfield.

He m. Mercy, perhaps Hollingsworth, b. [say 1640], certainly dau. of Susanna the second wife of Rev. John Jones of Fairfield. Mercy had children by previous husband Nichols when she m. Disbrow. She was convicted of witchcraft 1692, but reprieved.

Inv. recorded 28 Mar. 1709. Widow Mercy to have dower, and only son (Thomas) the balance, 6 Feb. 1711/2.

Samuel Coley, 13 Feb. 1688 [1688/9] hath purchased of Thomas Disbrow with consent of Disbrow's mother-in-law "shusanah Jons" and wife Marcy Disbrow.

John Nichols received a deed 1699 from his father-in-law [stepfather] Thomas Disbrow. He also had dealings with the younger Thomas, as in 1712 when Thomas Disbrow conveyed to brother John Nichols, mentioning Est. of father Thomas Disbrow dec'd and Est. of grandmother Jones.

Thomas Disbrow [Jr.] of Fairfield, yeoman, considering what is due from estate of father Thomas Disbrow to my bro. John Nichols of Fairfield on account of what my said father received of estate of grandmother Jones dec'd that did belong unto my said bro. Nichols, conveyed to him.

Child:

    XThomas, b. [say 1680-85], d. at Westport, 30 Sept. 1757; adm'n granted, 4 Oct. 1757; m. (rec. Fairfield) Oct. 1708, Abigail "Goding," who d. 19 Apr. 1756. She was dau. of Samuel Godwin of Eastchester.

Downs, John, s. of John.

Born at New Haven, 25 Nov. 1672; settled in Fairfield, where he purchased from John Seeley a house and land on 1 Aug. 1699.

Married (1) Mary Perry, dau. of Nathaniel.

He m. (2) at Stratfield, 25 May 1713, Deborah Odell, dau. of John, b. 28 Aug. 1682. She d. (as wife of John) 23 May 1745 ae. abt. 63 (Greenfield Church).

John renewed Covenant at Fairfield Church, 27 Mar. 1697 [1698]. He d. in 1753 in old age (Greenfield Church).

Children [by first wife], bapt. at Fairfield:

John, bapt. 27 Mar. 1698.
Nathaniel, bapt. 25 Feb. 1699/1700, d. y.
Joseph, bapt. 28 Dec. 1701, d. y.
XJoseph, bapt. 21 Mar. 1702/3, d. at Greenfield, 19 Feb. 1783 in 80 yr.;
    m. (1) Rebecca ———; m. (2) Hannah ———, b. abt. 1709, d. at
    Greenfield, 18 Nov. 1783 in 75 yr.
XDavid, bapt. 3 Mar. 1705/6, d. 13 Feb. 1759 ae. 53 (g. s., Greenfield);
    will 4 Feb. 1759, proved 1 May 1759; m. 3 Jan. 1733/4, Elizabeth
    Rowland, who d. 12 June 1769 ae. abt. 56 (Greenfield Church).
Mary, bapt. 12 Mar. 1709/10.

Child [by second wife], bapt. at Fairfield:

XNathaniel, bapt. 12 Sept. 1714, d. at Greenfield, 21 Oct. 1779; m.
    Sarah Chauncey, dau. of Israel, b. abt. 1722, d. at Greenfield, 6 Aug.
    1775 in 54 yr.

Drake, Samuel.   Deputy for Fairfield, Oct. 1662.

Of Fairfield by 1650, when he was granted a homelot; rem.
1665 to Eastchester, N. Y., where according to Inv. he d. 10 May
1686.

Married at Fairfield, 13 Sept. 1650, Ann Barlow, dau. of John.
[Col. Rec.]

Samuel of Eastchester conveyed Fairfield land, 8 Feb. 1677
[1677/8] to son Samuel.

Will 10 May 1686, proved 2 June 1686; aged and weak; wife
Ann; son Samuel Drake of Fairfield; dau. Mary Drake, £25;
son Joseph; sons-in-law Joseph Jones, Leffelane Slater, Richard
Headley; gr. children Samuel Headley and Robert, under 21;
Joseph, Samuel, Mary, and Hannah Jones; Martha and Elizabeth
Slater; son Joseph Drake, sole Exec'r; sons Samuel and John
Drake, overseers.

Children:

John.
Joseph, b. abt. 1663; ae. 47 in 1710 Census of Eastchester; m. at
    Eastchester, 31 Dec. 1685, Mary Shute. Joseph, Sr., of Eastches-
    ter, conveyed 1709/10 Fairfield land my bro. Samuel gave by will
    to my son Joseph and sold by latter to me.
Rebecca, m. (1) by 1677, Joseph Jones, of Stamford; gave receipt
    1682 to father-in-law Samuel Drake for wife Rebecca's portion; m.
    (2) by 1691, ——— Rogers, of Eastchester.

Daughter, [perhaps Ruth], m. Leffelane Slater.*
+Samuel.
Hannah, m. Richard Headley† of Eastchester and Mamaroneck, b. abt. 1642 (aged 38 in 1680). He was a carpenter, and acknowledged receipt of wife Hannah's portion in 1681.
Mary.

Drake, Samuel, s. of Samuel.

Lived at Fairfield, d. in 1690/1; m. Ruth Sherwood, dau. of Thomas; she m. (2) John Barlow, 3d, cousin of her first husband. Will 12 Dec. 1691; mother Ann Drake; sister Rebecca Rogers living in Eastchester; cousin Joseph, son of bro. Joseph Drake of Eastchester; to Daniel Lockwood, gun and sword; dear wife Ruth. Inv. 17 Feb. 1691 [1691/2].

A child recorded at Eastchester, Samuel, b. 12 Jan. 1687/8, must have d. young.

Dunbar, John.

Son of Robert and Rose, b. at Hingham, Mass., 1 Dec. 1657; m. (1) 4 July 1679, Mattithiah Aldridge. She was prob. mother of his dau. Sarah, b. abt. 1691, d. at New Haven, 25 Apr. 1764 ae. 73, who m. 16 Feb. 1720/1, William Diodati; and of his son John, bapt. at Fairfield, 21 Oct. 1694, d. at Wallingford, 13 May 1746, who m. at Wallingford, 14 June 1716, Elizabeth Fenn; and possibly of older children who d. y.

He m. (2) abt. 1696/7, Abigail, widow of Joseph Beers, of Fairfield, and dau. of Peter Norton. She did not long survive, and after an unsuccessful attempt to m. Rebecca Thomas, dau. of John of Woodbury, which was frustrated by the maiden's objecting father, he did m. (3) at New Haven, 24 July 1700, Elizabeth Beecher, dau. of John, b. abt. 1675, d. in 1758. By her he had seven children, all of whom d. y. or unm. except Elizabeth (m. Shubael Painter) and Lydia (m. Ebenezer Hull). He d. at New Haven in 1733.

---

* His name is so given in *N. Y. Gen. and Biog. Record;* yet at births of children his name is impossibly printed "Ruth" Slater in Scharff's *Hist. of Westchester County.* The children were: Martha, b. 31 Mar. 1683; Elizabeth, b. 4 Feb. 1685/6; John, b. 29 May 1687; Michael, b. 18 Nov. 1689; and Ruth, b. 13 Mar. 1694.
† This name is often misread Hoadley.

Dunn, Thomas.

Born abt. 1610, came over 1635 ae. 25 on the *Defence* with the Rev. John Jones family, his name appearing on the ship list directly under theirs; d. at Fairfield, 1660, unmarried. He was granted a homelot at Fairfield, 5 Mar. 1649 [1649/50], and prior to that date had purchased from Robert Wooly six acres originally laid out to Daniel Bulkley. Before 3 Dec. 1653 he purchased also from Thomas Wheeler, Jr.

Will 3 May [no year stated], proved 5 Dec. 1660; entire Est. to Mr. John Jones. Witnesses, Thomas James, Charles Taintor.

A man of this name was at Weymouth, freeman of Mass., 1647; rem. to Rehoboth; and the name is seen at New Haven, Mar. 1647/8, in the list of those who swore fidelity. But we cannot assert that this was the Fairfield man.

Dunning, Benjamin, s. of Theophilus.

Res. Jamaica, L. I.
The two sons settled and married in Stratfield.

Children:

> Benjamin, b. [say 1675], d. at Newtown, 21 Mar. 1739; testified in Disbrow trial, June 1692, ae. above 16 yrs.; will 23 Mar. 1737, proved 3 Apr. 1739; m. (1) abt. 1700, Mary Seeley, dau. of John; m. (2) 1710, Elizabeth Minor.
>
> John, b. [say 1685], d. at Wilton, in 1734; will 22 Dec. 1733, proved 11 Feb. 1733/4; m. abt. 1712, Sarah Lambert.
>
> Hannah, m. (rec. Stratford) 11 Mar. 1708/9, Isaac Hurd.

Edwards, Thomas.

He was a master mariner, of Boston, later of Stratford, where he d. in 1708.

Adm'n on Est. of Mr. Andrew How of Milford was granted to his widow Mary, June 1697; but on 16 Nov. 1697, having presented the Inv., she resigned, and William Wheeler of Milford succeeded her as Adm'r.

Edwards bought land in Stratford, 1694, then called mariner, late of Boston, now resident in Stratford. Mr. Thomas Edwards of Stratford m. 25 Nov. 1679, Mist. Mary How of Milford; the figures are transposed in the original record at Stratford, and the date should be 1697.

On 5 July 1706, John Edwards of Fairfield, attorney for Mr. John Mico* of Boston, who is attorney for Mrs. Elizabeth Harper of Yarmouth, co. Norfolk, Eng., Exec'x to the will of Mr. John Harper of Yarmouth dec'd, quitclaimed to Mr. Thomas Edwards late of Boston, mariner, now inhabitant of Stratford; witnesses, Benjamin and Sarah Fairweather.

Inv. of Capt. Thomas of Stratford, 6 May 1708. Mrs. Mary made oath and was granted adm'n. Mr. John Edwards, attorney to Mr. John Micko of Boston, and Mrs. Mary Edwards of Stratford, creditors of the estate, which was insolvent.

There was another Thomas Edwards, who m. at Dorchester, Mass., 10 Mar. 1670/1, Mary Birch, and settled in Stonington, Conn., where his marriage and births of nine children are recorded; and still another, early at Wethersfield.

Children of Thomas and Sarah, recorded at Boston:
>Thomas, b. 6 Feb. 1663 [1663/4].
>John, b. 8 Oct. 1666; mariner, of Boston, petitioned Conn. Leg. June 1709 to rescind order for sale of lands of his father, Capt. Thomas of Stratford.
>Daniel, b. 16 Mar. 1669 [1669/70].

Edwards, John. Deputy (Fairfield), Oct. 1702, May 1706, Oct. 1711, Oct. 1712, May 1718; Naval Officer, Port of Fairfield, May 1714; Justice, 1714-21.

Clothier, of Fairfield, where he purchased realty from Joseph Rowland, 12 Nov. 1691; adm. to Stratfield Church before 1731. Prob. he was related to Capt. Thomas of Stratford.

Married (1) Mary Hanford, dau. of Rev. Thomas of Norwalk, b. 30 Nov. 1663. She was living 1705, dead 1723.

Married (2) Mary ———, who d. 6 Mar. 1749 in 82 yr. (g. s., Stratfield).

Mr. John Edwards d. in Aug. 1744 ae. 82 (g. s., Stratfield).

Will of John, Sr., of Stratfield, 3 Dec. 1735, codicil 4 July 1737, proved 23 Sept. 1744; wife Mary; dau. Abigail Wheeler; children of late dau. Mary Dennie; eldest son William; sons Thomas,

---

* John Mico m. at Boston, 20 Aug. 1689, Mary Brattle.

John, Joseph; land at Sackett's Farm, N. Y., Stratford, and Fairfield; gave £30 to Church of Christ in Stratfield for a silver
vessell; had slaves and a large estate. Witnesses: John Odell,
Samuel Odell, and (Rev.) Samuel Cooke. Codicil witnessed by
Obadiah and Mercy Beardsley and Samuel Cooke. The son William appealed.

Will of Mary Edwards, widow of John of Stratford, 15 Feb.
1745/6, proved 4 Apr. 1749; Mary and Sarah, daus. of Thomas
Edwards, and his wife Sarah; Prudence, Rhoda, Eunice, Joseph,
and William, children of Joseph Edwards; son-in-law Joseph
Edwards, youngest son of husband Mr. John Edwards dec'd.
Witnesses: James Beardsley, Ebenezer Wakelee, Theophilus
Nichols.

Children* [by first wife], bapt. at Fairfield:

×William, b. [no record, say 1691], d. before 1754; res. Norwalk and
   Stratford; m. (rec. Norwalk) 4 May 1713, Abigail Couch. She
   was dau. of Simon, b. 31 Jan. 1693/4.
×Thomas, b. [say 1693], bapt. 7 July 1695; Capt.; res. Stratford; m.
   (1) Sarah ———; m. (2) Mary, widow of Joseph Perry, and dau.
   of Michael Clugston, bapt. 18 Sept. 1698.
Mary, bapt. 7 July 1695; m. John Dennie.
×John, bapt. 14 Aug. 1698, d. by 1784; will 3 Sept. 1766, proved 2 Feb.
   1784; m. (1) Rebecca Porter; m. (2) Hannah ———.
Samuel, bapt. 8 Dec. 1700, d. y.
Abigail, bapt. 25 Apr. 1703; m. Ebenezer Wheeler.
×Joseph, bapt. 17 June 1705; m. (rec. Stratford) 18 Dec. 1731,
   Prudence Wakelee.

Eggleden, John.

The name is a variant of Iggleden, and John may have been a
stepson of Joseph Patchen, as the two men first appear in Fairfield at about the same time.

He had grant of land from town of Fairfield, 9 Feb. 1652.

Inv. 20 Oct. 1659; widow and child; Nathaniel Seeley,
overseer.

His widow Peaceable m. (by contract July 1661) Daniel Silli-

---

* The death of Elizabeth Edwards, prob. a member of John's family [an older
dau.?], 22 Feb. 1709/10, was recorded at Fairfield.

man. There was some complaint about treatment of her son, and the child was apprenticed to Joseph Middlebrook, Mar. 1663/4.

Child:

> John, d. y. Joseph Middlebrook, Sr., [formerly his guardian] conveyed 12 June 1679 to Daniel Silliman, Adm'r of Est. of John Egleton, Jr., for use of the legatees the sons of Peaceable Sillevant the natural mother of the dec'd.

Everts, John.

Of Concord, Mass.; freeman, Mar. 1638; rem. to Guilford 1650, and d. 10 May 1669.

He m. (2) at New Haven, 27 May 1663, Elizabeth, widow of John Parmelee, formerly widow of —— Bradley; she d. Jan. 1683.

Records of his estate named the four sons, and the child of their sister Elizabeth Abbott.

Children, two youngest recorded at Concord:

> +James.
> Daniel, d. at Guilford, 5 Dec. 1692; m. (1) Mary ——, who d. 31 Mar. 1663; m. (2) 1 Mar. 1663/4, Rebecca Dowd, dau. of Henry, who d. 10 Oct. 1703.
> Elizabeth, d. at Fairfield, 1667; m. Peter Abbott.
> John, b. 29 Feb. 1639/40, d. at Guilford, 28 Dec. 1692; m. (1) 14 Sept. 1665, Mary French, dau. of Thomas; m. (2) 5 Dec. 1676, Mary Bow, who d. 25 Apr. 1700.
> Judah, b. 27 Oct. 1642, d. at Guilford, in 1696; m. 3 Aug. 1670, Mary Hayden, dau. of William.

Everts, James, s. of John.

He m. Lydia Goodrich, dau. of Richard. She was insane in old age.

He received a grant of a homelot at Fairfield, entered 29 Jan. 1655 [1655/6]; purchased part of Joseph Patchen's lot by 22 Apr. 1658; and sold to Thomas Oliver. He sold to Richard Hubbell, 1 Sept. 1665, shortly before removing to Eastchester, N. Y.; and he later returned to Guilford, where he d. Apr. 1684.

Inv. June 1684.

Children, three recorded at Eastchester 1667-1671:

Mary, b. at Guilford, 17 Mar. 1662, d. June 1734; m. 3 June 1684, John Munger.

John, b. [say 1664]; m. 23 Oct. 1688, Sarah Crampton, b. 17 Dec. 1669.

Jonathan, b. 12 Nov. 1667, d. at Guilford in 1696. His heirs were bros. and sisters: John and James Evarts, Mary Munger, Lydia Bishop, Judah Evarts, ae. 23, Hannah Evarts, ae. 19, Joseph, ae. 17, and Dorothy, ae. 13.

James, b. 15 Feb. 1669 [1669/70], d. 3 Jan. 1739; m. 7 Mar. 1694, Mary Carter, b. abt. 1674, d. 30 Mar. 1751.

Judah, b. 16 Mar. 1671 [1671/2], d. 28 Oct. 1748; m. 5 Sept. 1706, Mary Eggleston.

Lydia, b. perhaps 1675, d. 27 Dec. 1750; m. 19 Aug. 1692, Caleb Bishop.

Hannah, b. at Guilford, 22 Sept. 1677, d. 18 Jan. 1757; m. 26 Aug. 1701, John Crampton.

Joseph, b. 24 Feb. 1679/80, d. 21 Dec. 1767; m. 21 Apr. 1713, Hannah Scranton, who d. 26 Mar. 1789.

Dorothy, b. abt. 1683; m. 6 Apr. 1710, Samuel Munger.

Fairchild, Thomas. Deputy (Stratford) to Conn. Leg., Apr. 1646, Sept. 1654, May 1655, Oct. 1655, Oct. 1658, May 1659, Oct. 1659, May 1660, May 1664, Oct. 1664, Oct. 1665, May and Oct. 1666, May 1667; Commissioner for Stratford, 1664, 1666-70; war committee for Stratford, Oct. 1654.

Mr. Thomas "ffayrechilde" d. at Stratford, 14 Dec. 1670. He was a merchant, an original and prominent settler of Stratford.

Will 7 Dec. 1670; wife Katharine; son Samuel (his ferry land); son Zechariah; dau. Dinah; dau. Thomas; dau. Emm. Inv. 10 Jan. 1670 [1670/1].

Married (1) ——— Seabrook, dau. of Robert. Stratford Deeds, 1670, mention land that Thomas and Samuel Fairchild had by gift of grandfather Robert Seabrook.

Married (2) Katharine Craig, by contract 22 Dec. 1662, she being sister of widow Elizabeth Whiting of London, Eng.; his will made no provision for children by Katharine [Col. Rec.]. His widow m. (2) at Stratford, 8 Nov. 1675, Sergt. Jeremiah Judson.

Zechariah Fairchild had land by gift from brethren Samuel and Thomas Fairchild and Jehiel Preston, and mother Mrs. Katharine Judson [Stratford Deeds].

Children [by first wife], recorded at Stratford:
+Samuel, b. 31 Aug. 1640.
Sarah, b. 19 Feb. 1641 [1641/2]; m. Jehiel Preston.
John, b. 1 May 1644.
+Thomas, b. 26 Feb. 1645 [1645/6].
Dinah, b. 14 July 1648.
+Zechariah, b. 14 Dec. 1651.
Emm, b. 23 Oct. 1653; m. 20 Apr. 1676, Hachaliah Preston.

By Katharine, recorded at Stratford:
+Joseph, b. 18 Apr. 1664.
John, b. 8 June 1666.
Priscilla, b. 20 Apr. 1669; m. abt. 1688, Benjamin Peat.

Fairchild, Samuel, s. of Thomas.

Born at Stratford, 31 Aug. 1640; d. there in 1705.

He testified, May 1701, ae. abt. 60, that in younger days he was often at Knell's Island.

He m. Mary Wheeler, dau. of Moses, b. 13 Sept. 1655. She m. (2) 5 Apr. 1705, Benjamin Beach, and (3) 31 July 1716, Thomas Yale.

Inv. 7 Mar. 1704/5. Distribution of Est. ordered to Widow Mary; double portion to eldest son; two other sons to share alike.

Children:
Robert, d. before 1716.
XSamuel, b. abt. 1682, d. at Redding, 28 Feb. 1761 in 79 yr. (g. s.);
Lt.; m. (1) 3 Jan. 1705/6, Ruth Beach, dau. of Thomas, b. at Wallingford, 24 Oct. 1683, d. 30 Jan. 1721/2; m. (2) (rec. Stratford) 24 Jan. 1722/3, Dinah Burwell of West Haven; dau. of Samuel, b. 28 Oct. 1694; d. at Redding, 8 May 1769 in 76 yr. (g. s.).
Anna, d. 23 July 1703; m. 18 Nov. 1702, Benjamin Coney.
Edward, m. 25 Jan. 1710/1, Elizabeth Blackman.

Fairchild, Thomas, s. of Thomas.

Born at Stratford, 26 Feb. 1645/6; d. at Woodbury, 27 Mar. 1686 [Pro. Rec.].

Inv. of Thomas of Woodbury, 16 Apr. 1686. Widow Susanna.

Ages of children: Emm, over 14; Samuel, 10 next Jan.; Ruth, 8 next 15 Jan.; Alexander, 6 next Feb.; Katharine, 1½.

The widow Susanna was wife of Samuel Nichols 1691, and of Samuel Castle 1708 [Fairfield Probate].

Children, bapt. at Woodbury, eldest born at Stratford:

Emm, b. 30 Aug. 1672, bapt. 11 Apr. 1676.
Sarah, b. abt. 1675, bapt. 11 Apr. 1676, d. y.
Samuel, b. Jan. 1676/7, bapt. Apr. 1678; m. at Stratford, 22 Nov. 1699, Mary Lewis.
Ruth, b. 15 Jan. 1678/9, bapt. Jan. 1678/9, d. at Woodbury, 28 May 1727; m. at Woodbury, 3 Nov. 1697, Joseph Hickox.
✗Alexander, b. Feb. 1680/1, bapt. Apr. 1681, d. 1727; adm'n granted, 6 June 1727; m. Deborah Jackson.
Sarah, bapt. Feb. 1682/3, d. y.
Katharine, bapt. May 1685.

Fairchild, Zechariah, s. of Thomas.

Born at Stratford, 14 Dec. 1651, d. there 23 June 1703.

Married at Stratford, 3 Nov. 1681, Hannah Beach. She was dau. of John, b. Dec. 1665, and m. (2) 5 May 1708, John Burritt.

Died intestate; adm'n granted, 6 Sept. 1703, to widow Hannah and John Beach. Six sons and two daus. (minors). Guardians appointed for children: Capt. Matthew Sherwood for Caleb and Agur; John Beach for James; Joseph Beach for Mary; Isaac Beach for Zechariah; Widow Hannah Fairchild for Abiel. David chose his uncle Nathaniel Beach for guardian. Matthew Sherwood having died, Agur chose Lt. Agur Tomlinson, 14 Mar. 1709/10.

Children, recorded at Stratford (mother 1691 to 1704 called Hannah):

Mehitabel, b. 29 Mar. 1683, d. 27 Sept. 1684.
Hannah, b. 1 Aug. 1685; m. 12 Dec. 1706, Daniel Searles.
David, b. 16 May 1688, d. at Newtown 1743; adm'n granted, 1 Feb. 1742/3; m. 20 Apr. 1711, Deborah Hawley, b. 21 Apr. 1692.
Agur, b. 1 Oct. 1691, d. at Stratford, 4 May 1712; m. 20 Sept. 1710, Mary Booth. She m. (2) 12 Mar. 1712/3, Benjamin Brooks, and d. 2 Nov. 1740 in 49 yr. (g. s.).
Caleb, b. 10 Sept. 1693, living 1723 at Stratfield, where he had children bapt.: Hezekiah, 10 Feb. 1717, and Sarah, May 1719.
James, b. 12 Feb. 1695/6, d. at Stratford in 1761; will 23 May 1759,

codicil 12 Feb. 1761, proved 9 Apr. 1761; m. 3 Apr. 1723, Abigail
Beardsley, dau. of Daniel of Stratfield.
Mary, b. 7 May 1698, bapt. (Stratfield) 5 June 1698, d. 18 Aug.
1728; m. 14 Feb. 1721/2, Ephraim Burritt.
Zechariah, b. 21 Nov. 1701, bapt. (Stratfield) 30 Nov. 1701.
Abiel, b. 15 Jan. 1703/4; m. 8 Aug. 1728, Lois Riggs.

Fairchild, Joseph, s. of Thomas.

Born at Stratford, 18 Apr. 1664, d. there 25 July 1713.
Married Joanna Wilcoxson, dau. of Timothy, b. 8 July 1667.
Mrs. Johanah d. at Stratford 15 Aug. 1713.
Inv. 2 Mar. 1713/4; dates of birth of children (except
Jeremiah) stated in Pro. Rec. Adm'n granted to Timothy and
Joseph. Various heirs gave receipts; Katharine and Joanna
Fairchild, 14 Apr. 1724; John and Sarah Wildman, 26 Mar. 1724;
Phebe Fairchild, and John as guardian to bro. Thomas, 4 Dec.
1727; Nathan and John, 12 Dec. 1727.

Children, recorded at Stratford:

Timothy, b. 9 Dec. 1687, d. 28 Nov. 1726; will 19 Nov. 1726, proved
20 Jan. 1726/7; m. 15 Nov. 1715, Sarah Thompson of New Haven.
Joseph, b. 28 Dec. 1689, d. 20 Apr. 1727 in 37 yr. (g. s.); adm'n
granted, 2 May 1727, to widow and Capt. John Coe; m. 11 Nov.
1725, Katharine Coe; she m. (2) 24 Aug. 1728, Mr. David Calhoun.
Joseph's Est. was distributed, 4 June 1732, to widow Katharine Calhoun and only child Joanna.
Jeremiah, b. 27 Dec. 1691, d. y.
Nathan, b. 29 Jan. 1692/3, d. 9 Jan. 1730/1 ae. 38 (g. s.); will 7 Jan.
1730/1, proved 2 Feb. 1730/1; m. (1) (rec. Stratford) 22 Apr. 1724,
Phebe St. John of Norwalk, who d. 26 Sept. 1726; m. (2) 14 Feb.
1727/8, Obedience Curtis, widow of Edmund Curtis, and dau. of
John Mallory, b. at New Haven, 11 Apr. 1704; she m. (3) 20 Nov.
1740, Benjamin Sherman, and (4) 25 Dec. 1763, Robert Bassett.
Sarah, b. 26 Nov. 1694; m. (1) 19 Apr. 1716, John Wildman; m.
(2) (as "Mrs. Sarah Fairchild") 12 July 1727, William Peat.
Johanna, b. 2 Feb. 1696/7; m. (rec. Fairfield) 3 Feb. 1727, Samuel
Hull.
Katharine, b. 11 Apr. 1699; m. (rec. Fairfield) 11 Feb. 1724/5, Joseph
Sanford.
John, b. 19 June 1701; m. 26 Dec. 1723, Johanna Phippen.
Phebe, b. Dec. 1704, d. 20 Oct. 1728. Will 7 Oct. 1728, proved 19
Nov. 1728; cousin Daniel Fairchild; cousin Sarah Fairchild (all
that was given me by my grandmother Wilcoxson); cousin Johanna

Fairchild; sister Sarah Peat; three sisters, Sarah, Johanna and
Katharine; bro. William Peat, Exec'r.
XThomas, b. 4 May 1712, d. at Redding, in 1748; will 20 Dec. 1747,
proved 29 Mar. 1748; m. at Fairfield, 22 Sept. 1737, Mary Hall;
dau. of Jonathan; she d. in 1748 (adm'n granted, 6 Dec. 1748).

Fairweather, Benjamin, s. of John. Cornet of Troop, Fairfield County, May 1717.

Although his birth is not found in Boston records, he was
undoubtedly son of John Fairweather of Boston, prob. by his
first wife Sarah Turner (dau. of Robert), and grandson of
Thomas Fairweather. The name was often spelled Fayerweather.

His son Joseph in his will 1732 called Capt. John Fairweather
of Boston his uncle.

Married Sarah, widow of Ephraim Wheeler, dau. of Capt.
Matthew Sherwood. She was b. abt. 1676, m. (3) Anthony
Nouquier, and d. 25 May 1743 in 67 yr. (g. s., Stratfield).

He d. 6 [———] 1725 in [———] yr. (g. s., Stratfield).

Will 20 Aug. 1725, proved 2 Nov. 1725; wife Sarah, Exec'x;
sons John, Joseph, Thomas, Benjamin; daus. Penelope, Sarah,
Mary.

Agreement of John Fairweather of Stratfield (for himself and
bro. Joseph dec'd, whose right he purchased) with bros. Thomas
of Norwalk and Benjamin, with regard to 1,300 acres at Merryall
given by will of Mr. Benjamin Fairweather to his four sons;
Sarah Fairweather signed with him; 23 Aug. 1737.

Will of Sarah Nouquier, widow of Anthony, 13 May 1743,
proved 31 May 1743; son Andrew Wheeler; son Benjamin
Fayerweather; children of dau. Catherine late wife of Peter
Hubbell of Newtown; dau. Mary wife of John Holberton; dau.
Abiah wife of John Cornwell; dau. Penelope wife of Richard
Hubbell; dau. Sarah wife of Daniel Morris; children John and
Thomas; friend David Sherman, Jr., of Stratfield, Exec'r.

Children, bapt. at Stratfield:

XJohn, b. 28 Dec. 1703, bapt. 2 Jan. 1704, d. at Stratfield, in 1749;
adm'n granted, 8 May 1749; m. Ann ———, b. 27 Apr. 1712 (g. s.),
d. 24 Sept. 1773 (g. s., Stratfield).
Penelope, b. 18 Feb. 1705/6, bapt. 24 Feb. 1706, d. 29 Aug. 1791 in
87 yr. (g. s., Stratfield); m. (rec. Fairfield) 9 Dec. 1735, Richard
Hubbell.

XJoseph, b. 4 Nov. 1707, bapt. 16 Nov. 1707, d. at Stratfield, 3 Sept.
    1732; will 23 Aug. 1732, proved 5 Dec. 1732; m. Abigail ———.
Thomas, b. 17 Oct. 1709, bapt. 23 Oct. 1709; res. Norwalk; m. Mary
    Hanford, dau. of Thomas, Jr.
Walter, b. 17 Dec. 1711, bapt. 24 Feb. 1712, d. 26 Dec. 1717 ae. 6
    (g. s., Stratfield).
Sarah, b. 22 Sept. 1713, bapt. 27 Sept. 1713, d. 16 Apr. 1761 in 48 yr.
    (g. s., Stratfield); m. (1) (rec. Stratfield) 22 Mar. 1733, Matthew
    MacHard; m. (2) (rec. Fairfield) 9 July 1741, Daniel Morris.
Mary, b. 13 Jan. 1715/6, bapt. 4 Mar. 1716; m. John Holburton.
XBenjamin, b. 1 Oct. 1717, bapt. 6 Oct. 1717, d. 20 June 1791 in 74 yr.
    (g. s., Stratfield); Lt.; m. (Fairfield Church) 7 Jan. 1741/2,
    Elizabeth Beach.
Twin brother, b. 1 Oct. 1717, d. in half an hour.
James, b. 24 Aug. 1721, d. 29 Aug. 1721.

Fanton, Jonathan.

He m. (1) after 1688, Mehitabel Staples, dau. of Thomas, b.
abt. 1651, d. before 1693.

He m. (2) Sarah Hide, dau. of John, b. 25 Sept. 1670. She m.
(2) William Hill, and d. at Greenfield, 29 Sept. 1760 in 90 yr.

Adm'n granted, 6 Jan. 1713 [1713/4], to widow Sarah, with
her bro. John Hide. Inv. 1 Feb. 1713/4.

Child [by first wife]:
    Mehitabel.

Children [by second wife], bapt. at Fairfield:
    Sarah, bapt. 18 Nov. 1694.
    Ellen, bapt. 17 May 1696; m. 9 Jan. 1717, Ebenezer Lyon.
    Ann, bapt. 14 Aug. 1698, d. at Waterbury, 17 Dec. 1765; m. (rec.
        Waterbury) 3 Nov. 1724, Richard Welton.
    XJonathan, bapt. 22 Sept. 1700, d. in 1738; Inv. Dec. 1738; m. Sarah
        Hide, dau. of John, 2d.
    Mary, bapt. 2 May 1703; m. (Fairfield Church) 18* Nov. 1728,
        Gershom Scott of Waterbury.
    John, bapt. 5 Jan. 1706/7, d. y.
    XJohn, bapt. 10 Oct. 1708; b. 22 Aug. 1709, by Greenfield rec., obviously
        in error for 1708; d. 18 Nov. 1795 ae. 90 (g. s., Easton); m. (1)
        Nov. 1731 (Fairfield rec.) or 28 Oct. 1732 (Greenfield rec.), Mary
        Rowland, b. Aug. 1711 (Greenfield rec.); m. (2) 12 Feb. 1755,
        Widow Eunice Lyon. She was widow of Ephraim.

---
* 17, by Waterbury record.

Ferguson, John.

Name spelled "ffagason" in Stratford records.
Prob. rem. to Westchester, N. Y.

Children, recorded at Stratford:

Mary, b. Aug. 1660.
Sarah, b. Aug. 1662.
Abigail, b. 1 May 1664.

Ferris, Zechariah. Served in K. Philip's War, 1676.

Married at Charlestown, Mass., 17 Nov. 1673, Sarah Blouds.
Admitted to Stratfield Church by letter from Charlestown, 19
Sept. 1705.
Will of Zechariah, Sr., 14 Aug. 1710, proved 16 Apr. 1711;
wife; sons Zechariah and Samuel; dau. Sarah; friend Capt.
David Sherman and Benjamin Fairweather, Exec'rs and overseers.
Widow Sarah swore to Inv.

Children, recorded at Charlestown:

Zechariah, b. 24 Sept. 1674, bapt. 6 Feb. 1675/6; m. abt. 1699, Sarah
———. Admitted to full communion, Stratfield, 23 May 1708, dis-
missed to New Milford, 18 Nov. 1716.
Sarah, bapt. 12 Nov. 1676; m. Joseph Halsted of Hempstead, L. I.,
with whom he sold in 1712 to Samuel Ferris of Newtown, right to
property once in occupation of David Jenkins, which descended to
Sarah Ferris now Halsted by her father's will.
Richard, b. 30 Mar. 1679, bapt. at Boston, 6 Apr. 1679, d. 23 July 1679.
Hannah, bapt. 18 July 1680, d. y.
Samuel, b. (no record), d. at Newtown, abt. 1764; will 7 Sept. 1764;
m. abt. 1710, Martha ———. Martha renewed Covenant, Strat-
field, 21 Oct. 1711; living 1764.

Finch, Daniel.

Constable for Wethersfield, 26 Apr. 1636. Removed to Stam-
ford by 1641, and to Fairfield by 1649. Entered for record at
Fairfield, 4 Jan. 1653 [1653/4], land purchased from Richard
Lattin.

Estate left at Fairfield committed to the management of his
grandson Abraham Finch, for the use of Daniel or to satisfy other
just demands, May 1657.

Agreement of marriage, 25 Dec. 1657, with Elizabeth Thompson [widow of John].

Married (3) by 4 Apr. 1660, Mary, with whom he conveyed on that date. She was widow of Thomas Dickerson, and mother of several of the legatees named in Finch's will. She m. (3) Nicholas Pinion of East Haven.

Will 5 Mar. 1666/7; son Nathaniel "my books", he under 18; 40 shillings to grandson Abraham Finch; 20 shillings to Roger Knap's wife, 10 shillings to Joseph James' wife and £7 to Henry Castel's wife; 10 shillings to John Sturgis; 20 shillings apiece "unto the Two Children that be with ther Mother" [his second wife's children?]; of Nathaniel, he said, "his mother shall give him" [showing that Nathaniel was by third wife]. Witnesses: John Sturgis, Henry Castle. Inv. 11 Mar. 1666/7.

Child [by first wife]:

+Abraham.

Child [by third wife]:

+Nathaniel, b. [say 1662].

Finch, John.

Perhaps bro. of Daniel; bought house and lot of Henry Akerly at Stamford, 1652.

Called Sr. in testifying, 1653.

Died at Stamford, 5 Sept. 1657. Martha [his widow] m. Sept. 1658, John Green.

Prob. children:

+John.
+Isaac.
+Samuel.
  Joseph, m. at Stamford, 23 Nov. 1670, Elizabeth Austin.

Finch, Abraham, s. of Daniel.

Killed by Nepaupuck at Wethersfield, for which Nepaupuck was beheaded 30 Oct. 1639; Abraham was murdered 30 Oct. 1637.

Inv. taken 3 Sept. 1640 by Samuel Smith and Nathaniel Foote; £137. Adm'n granted to his widow, who was to maintain the child or commit him to his grandfather Abraham* Finch; the latter offered to educate him.

His widow Dorothy m. (2) John Edwards, and (3) Richard Tousley of Saybrook.

Child:

+Abraham.

Finch, Nathaniel, s. of Daniel.

Born at Fairfield abt. 1662, d. at Norwalk, abt. 1719.

Adm'n granted 27 Jan. 1720/1 to son Samuel. Distribution ordered 10 Mar. 1720/1 to Widow; eldest son Samuel; the other two children, Nathaniel and Lydia; John, one of the sons, is also deceased. He was of Norwalk at death.

He came to East Haven [doubtless with his mother when she m. Pinion], where by 1691 he m. Mary Hemingway, b. 5 July 1668, d. about 1692, dau. of Samuel. He next m. her sister Elizabeth, but the marriage was denounced by all parties concerned and invalidated by the Court, and Elizabeth m. thereafter Zachariah How and Samuel Brockett.†

He next removed to Branford, where he m. (3) Mary dau. of William Hoadley, widow of Jonathan Frisbie and Robert Darby.

Nathaniel of Branford in 1697 leased land he owned in Fairfield; on 5 Feb. 1693/4, when he was of New Haven, he sold Fairfield property to Albert Dennie.

Child [by first wife], recorded at New Haven:

Samuel, b. 17 Feb. 1691/2; on 28 Dec. 1719, being of Norwalk, conveyed to Lt. John Taylor of Norwalk, land my father Nathaniel dec'd bought of Daniel Sherwood in Fairfield, adjoining land distributed to mother-in-law Mary Finch.

Child [by second wife], recorded at New Haven:

Daniel, b. 19 May 1694, d. 1766; had family in East Haven and North Haven.

Children by third wife, recorded at Branford:

John, b. 20 Dec 1699, d. s. p. 1720/1.

Nathaniel, b. 25 Oct. 1701; res. Norwalk; m. 24 Nov. 1725, Hannah Raymond.

Lydia, b. 19 Apr. 1705; m. at Branford, 2 Jan. 1729, Joseph Elwell.

---

* It is believed that this record is in error, and that Daniel was intended. See Appendix for a full consideration of this problem.

† The New England Congregationalists long shared the prejudice of their English brethren against marriage to a deceased wife's sister, considering the relation as incestuous in nature.

Finch, John [son of John?].

Married Hannah, sister of Jonathan and Samuel Marsh, and widow of Launcelot Fuller of New Haven, shortly after 8 Nov. 1652; in Dec. 1656 she had returned to New Haven (as wife of John Finch of Westchester) to obtain medical treatment for her lame [Fuller] child, and was then pregnant. In June 1657 she was helped out of Mr. Westerhouse's estate, apparently in settlement of a debt; and was still in New Haven, Feb. 1664/5.

John Finch of New York, shopkeeper, perhaps the son of above John and Hannah, was named as "cousin" in will of John Marsh of New York, millwright, 1713; Finch had wife Elizabeth and daus. Ann and Sarah.

Finch, Isaac, s. of John.

He m. (1) (rec. Stamford) Oct. 1658, Elizabeth Bassett; dau. of John. He m. (2) Ann ———.

Inv. 16 Nov. 1702; widow Ann to administer with her two sons, John and Isaac.

Children [by first wife], recorded at Stamford:

> John, b. 20 Sept. 1659; perhaps m. Sarah Pettit, b. 27 Aug. 1666.
> [Isaac], b. 12 Apr. 1662.
> -Abraham, b. 5 July 1665 (before day).
> Elizabeth, b. 14 Nov. 1669.
> Martha, b. 19 June 1672.

Children [prob. by second wife, but perhaps they belong to Isaac, Jr.]:

> Rebecca, b. 17 Mar. 1682/3.
> Sarah, b. 23 Jan. 1686/7.
> Jacob, b. 9 Oct. 1691, d. 15 Apr. 1702.
> Benjamin, b. 29 June 1695.

Finch, Samuel, s. of John.

Of Stamford, made freeman Oct. 1669; m. Sarah Hoyt, dau. of Simon.

Samuel, Sr., d. at Stamford, 23 Apr. 1698; his widow Sarah d. 19 Mar. 1712/3.

Will 28 Sept. 1697; wife Sarah; sons Samuel, Joseph; daus.

Sarah Holly, Martha Mead, Susannah Seeley, Rachel Finch. Inv. 20 May 1698.

Adm'n on Est. of Widow Sarah granted to Joseph Finch, 1 July 1713.

Children:

> Sarah, m. 2 Dec. 1686, Jonathan Holly.
> Samuel, m. Sarah ———; they had children recorded at Stamford: Mary, b. 2 Mar. 1692/3; Susannah, b. 3 Mar. 1693/4, m. 22 May 1718, Isaac Bishop; Sarah, b. 25 Sept. 1695, d. 23 Jan. 1715; Abigail, b. 15 July 1697, d. 23 Jan. 1715; Hannah, b. 23 Mar. 1700/1; Martha, b. 23 July 1703.
> Martha, m. ——— Mead.
> Susannah, m. in 1692, Obadiah Seeley.
> Rachel.
> Joseph, d. at Stamford, 18 Dec. 1752; m. 7 Aug. 1703, Abigail Seeley.

Finch, Abraham, s. of Abraham.

He was made freeman of Conn., May 1658. On 20 Oct. 1664, he sold Fairfield property to Robert Turney, and we hear of him no more. He witnessed deed of Jehu and Esther Burr (recorded at Wethersfield), 1661/2. He lived chiefly at Saybrook, and d. there unmarried.

Finch, Abraham, s. of Isaac.

Born at Stamford, 5 July 1665; m. Martha Couch, dau. of Simon of Fairfield. Gave receipt, 1697, for legacy from his father-in-law Couch.

He testified Sept. 1692 in the Clawson witch trial as Abraham Finch, Jr., ae. abt. 26.*

He purchased land in Fairfield from James Newton, 7 Apr. 1696.

Martha Finch renewed her Covenant at Fairfield Church, 6 Sept. 1696, and Abraham had children bapt. there:

> Isaac, bapt. 13 Sept. 1696.
> Elizabeth, bapt. 15 May 1698.

Fitch, Thomas. Clerk, Norwalk Train Band, Feb. 1657; Ens., May 1665; Capt., Fairfield County Troop, Aug. 1673, and Feb.

---

* Abraham Finch of Stamford was freed from training because of constant lameness, Mar. 1684/5.

1676 (K. Philip's War); Commissioner for Norwalk, 1669-87, 1689-94, and for Danbury, 1686-87, 1689-90; Deputy (Norwalk), May 1673.

Eldest son of Thomas and Anna (Reeve) Fitch of Bocking, co. Essex, Eng., b. abt. 1612, d. at Norwalk in 1704; m. at Bocking, 1 Nov. 1632, Anna Stacey. He was instrumental in bringing other members of his family to New England; among his bros. were Rev. James of Norwich, Samuel the Hartford school master, and Capt. Joseph. The latter was with him in Norwalk, but finally settled in Windsor.

Will 6 Oct. 1696; gr. son Thomas Fitch; two gr. sons John and Nathaniel Fitch; dau. Ann now wife of John Thompson of Farmington; dau. Mary now wife of Capt. Matthew Sherwood; son John and John's wife; son Capt. Matthew Sherwood and cousin Sergt. John Platt, overseers; mentioned his great expense in the civil wars in England, and the transportation of himself and family. Inv. 14 Apr. 1704. John Fitch as Exec'r engaged to give to the children of his dec'd sister Burr the same amount which his other sisters had by will.

Richard Lyon of Fairfield gave by will 1678 £7 to his "cousin" Mary Fitch. She is usually supposed to be the dau. of Thomas; but since that Mary must have m. several years before that date, we cannot agree. Thomas Fitch, Jr., had a dau. Mary, b. abt. 1668, but it is not clear how she could have been related to Lyon. The John Platt called "cousin" by Thomas Fitch was husband of a sister of the wife of Thomas Fitch, Jr.

Children:

+Thomas.
-:-John.
   Mary, b. abt. 1644, d. at Stratfield, 25 Dec. 1730 ae. abt. 87 (g. s.); m. Matthew Sherwood.
   Ann, m. (1) Stephen Hart, Jr., of Farmington; m. (2) John Thompson.
   Sarah, m. [say 1672] Maj. John Burr, of Fairfield.

Fitch, Thomas, s. of Thomas. Sergt., Norwalk Trainband.

Died at Norwalk in 1684; m. Ruth Clark, dau. of George, "Jr." or "Farmer" of Milford, bapt. 20 Feb. 1641/2; she m. (2) Robert

Plumb of Milford, and (3) 3 July 1706, John Wheeler of Woodbury.

Inv. May 1684. Widow Ruth; ages of children: Sarah, 21; Thomas, 19, Mary 16; Samuel, 2½.

Children:

> Sarah, b. abt. 1663; m. John Ford, of Milford.
> Thomas, b. abt. 1665, d. in 1731; is said to have m. three times; will 29 Apr. 1731, proved 5 May 1731, named wife Rachel, sons Samuel, Thomas, and James, and dau. Elizabeth Raymond. The son Thomas had a distinguished career, and was Gov. of Conn. 1754-65.
> Mary, b. abt. 1668, d. between 1705 and 1712; m. Daniel Terrell, of Milford.
> Samuel, b. in 1681, prob. d. young.

Fitch, John, s. of Thomas.

He m. at Norwalk, 3 Dec. 1674, Rebecca Lindall, dau. of Dea. Henry and Rosamond, b. at New Haven, 20 Oct. 1653.

Children, recorded at Norwalk:

> John, b. 29 Sept. 1677, d. in 1748; will 26 Jan. 1747/8, proved 5 Apr. 1748; m. Lydia Bushnell, dau. of Francis.
> Rebecca, b. 15 Jan. 1679/80.
> Nathaniel, b. 6 Nov. 1682, d. in 1743; will 5 Apr. 1742, proved 20 June 1743; m. (1) ———; m. (2) by 1729, Sarah, widow of Daniel Frost, and dau. of Benjamin Seeley, b. [say 1690]; m. (3) Anna, widow of William Mallory.

Foote, Daniel.

Son of Nathaniel and Elizabeth (Smith) Foote, b. prob. at Hadley abt. 1652.

His wife Sarah d. at Stratford, 26 Mar. 1704 in 46 yr. (g. s.).

Children, recorded at Stratford:

> John, b. 17 June 1680; res. Newtown; m. 13 July 1715, Sarah Prindle.
> Daniel, b. 10 Jan. 1681 [1681/2]; res. Newtown; m. (1) 2 Jan. 1704/5, Dorothy Blackman, who d. at Newtown, 28 Jan. 1721/2; m. (2) Abigail, widow of John Shepard, and dau. of Gideon Allen.
> Hannah, b. 13 Feb. 1683 [1683/4]; m. 7 Dec. 1704, Richard Beach; res. Durham and Hebron.

Jehiel, b. 17 Mar. 1685/6, d. at Stratford 2 Sept. 1740 in 55 yr. (g. s.) ;
   m. Susannah ———.
✕Solomon,* of Fairfield, m. [say 1715] Elizabeth Osborn.
Mary,* m. (rec. Stratford) 10 Dec. 1713, Caleb Dayton.
Peter, b. abt. 1698, d. at Stratford, 8 Dec. 1753 in 56 yr. (g. s.) ; will
   4 Dec. 1753, proved 15 Jan. 1754; to Daniel Foot, my house; to Mrs.
   Sarah wife of Mr. James Beach of Stratford, £50; residue to sons
   of late bro. Jehiel Foot, viz.: Joseph, Daniel, George, Jehiel;
   cousin Daniel Foot, Exec'r.

Ford, Timothy.

He was an original signer of the New Haven Covenant, 1639,
and took the oath of allegiance 1644. He removed to Fairfield,
where he was a land owner before 1650. He returned to New
Haven, where he was fined in 1652 for defect in his arms, and
being a new comer, he said that the requirements were different
"where he came from."

He d. at New Haven, 28 Aug. 1684, his wife having d. 25 July
1681. He had five children, who remained in New Haven.

Forman, Samuel.

He had land recorded in Fairfield, 16 Jan. 1667 [1667/8],
formerly purchased of Simon Couch.

He m. (1) ———. Winthrop wrote in 1660: Sam Firman his
wife at Fairfield sister to Thos Hous wife he hath had 6 or 7 children & all dead but one which is about 1½ years.

He m. (2) 25 Mar. 1662, Miriam Hoyt, dau. of Simon.

He settled in Oyster Bay, L. I.

Forward, Joseph, s. of Samuel.

Born at Windsor, 10 Nov. 1674, son of Samuel and Ann; d. at
Danbury in 1704.

Married Lydia Gregory, dau. of Judah, b. at Norwalk, 9 Jan.
1676/7. She m. (2) Thomas Wildman.

Inv. of Joseph of Danbury, 3 Oct. 1704. Widow Forward
made oath; ages of the four children stated. On 3 Nov. 1707,
"Lydia Forward that was, and now Wildman", widow of Joseph
Forward, appeared in Court. Thomas Wildman who m. the

---

* Hypothetically placed as child of Daniel.

widow appointed guardian to Lydia and Mercy. Joseph Gregory to be guardian for Ann. Hannah's "unckle" took her. Daniel Benedict, Sr., and Thomas Taylor, Jr., appointed distributors.

Children (ages in Fairfield Probate Rec.) :

> Lydia, b. 2 Apr. 1698, d. in 1721; m. (rec. New Milford) 15 June 1720, David Noble.
>
> Ann, b. 15 Mar. 1699/1700; m. Benjamin Barnum, with whom she conveyed in 1722 to father-in-law Thomas Wildman, calling herself second dau. of Joseph Forward.*
>
> Hannah, b. 18 Jan. 1701/2; m. (rec. Norwalk) 27 Mar. 1723, William Jarvis.
>
> Mercy, b. 16 Feb. 1703/4.

Fossecar, John.

He was at New London, 1648; rem. to Fairfield, where he bought land from Edward Adams, recorded 29 May 1656, and sold to Giles Smith before 6 Nov. 1658.

Married Elizabeth, widow of Peter Johnson.

Foster, John.

On 17 Feb. 1671 [1671/2], land was entered for Daniel Lockwood on west side of "Sascoe" Hill, which was sold by Henry Gray to Robert Lockwood, and originally had been John Foster's.

He bought land from Thomas Dickerson.

Fountain, Aaron.

Married (1) by 1681, Mary Beebe, dau. of Samuel of New London. Samuel Beebe conveyed, Dec. 1681, to his son-in-law Aaron Fountain, land at New London.

Married (2) prob. by 1690, Hannah ――――, mother of John Winton, who was bapt. as her child 29 May 1698. We suppose her to have been widow of Andrew Winton.

On 20 Aug. 1717, Aaron Fountain surrendered to his son-in-law John Mills, his interest in Samuel Beebe's estate of New London. [Stamford Deeds.]

---

* *Hist. of Danbury* (1896), p. 52.

Child [by first wife]:

> Mary, m. (rec. Stamford) at Fairfield, 2 Oct. 1702, John Mills, she being called dau. of Aaron Fountain by his wife Mary dau. of Mr. Samuel Beebe of New London.

Children [by second wife]:

> ✗Aaron, bapt. at Fairfield, 5 June 1698, d. at Westport, 15 Apr. 1760; m. Elizabeth ———.
>
> Moses, bapt. 5 June 1698; rem. abt. 1740 from Norwalk to Bedford, N. Y.; m. at Norwalk, 13 Aug. 1719, widow Elizabeth Gregory. She was widow of Thomas Gregory and dau. of Joseph Ketchum.
>
> Hannah, bapt. 5 June 1698.
>
> Samuel, bapt. 29 May 1698.
>
> William, bapt. 26 May 1700; m. Esther Coley, dau. of Samuel, bapt. 15 Aug. 1703.
>
> John, bapt. 9 May 1702; res. 1725 Stamford; in 1730, being "late of Fairfield now of Ridgefield", he conveyed Fairfield land to William Truesdell of Ridgefield.

Fountain, James.

Inv. of James of Greenwich, 8 Jan. 1710. Children, Judith and Magdeline. Anthony Nouguier and Alexander Resseguie appointed guardians to the children.

He m. Maudlin (Daniel), widow of "goodman" Samuel Street of Wallingford. She m. (3) Luke Hayes of Farmington, and (4) in 1716, Dennis Higgins.

"Modlin", a girl of about 6 years that formerly belonged to a Frenchman, was apprenticed June 1662 by the townsmen of Stratford, with her father's consent, to John Minor. Perhaps she was the Maudlin Daniel whose marriage to Samuel Street in 1684 was recorded at Wallingford; but if so, she had a child by Fountain born when she was nearly 50 yrs. old. Her three children by Street all d. young.

Children, recorded at Wallingford:

> Judith, b. 5 Apr. 1704; m. (rec. Norwalk) 11 Mar. 1724, Robert Smith.
>
> Maudlin, b. 26 May 1706; m. John Smith.

French, Samuel, s. of Thomas. Sergt., Stratfield Trainband.

Born at Guilford, 21 Aug. 1667; d. at Stratfield, 20 Dec. 1732 ae. 65 (g. s.). He received land by deed from his uncle Mr. Jonathan Pitman, and was chief heir in his uncle's will 1728.

Married Abigail Hubbell, dau. of Richard, as shown by will of her father 1699. Abigail French of Stratfield conveyed 12 Feb. 1740/1, land from father Richard Hubbell of Fairfield dec'd. Samuel renewed Covenant at Fairfield Church, 2 Dec. 1694. Abigail renewed Covenant at Stratfield Church, 8 Feb. 1697, and Samuel was admitted to full communion, 8 Mar. 1697. Will 22 Dec. 1732, proved 15 Jan. 1733; wife Abigail; sons Samuel and Gamaliel; daus. Deborah Weed, Abigail Bennett, Elizabeth Slater, Thankful Taylor, Martha French, Sarah Mallett; son Ebenezer.

Children, first bapt. at Fairfield, the others at Stratfield:

XSamuel, bapt. 2 Dec. 1694; m. Mary Sherman, dau. of Benjamin, b. 24 Feb. 1696/7.

Deborah, bapt. 2 Aug. 1696 [the parents are not stated], d. y.

XEbenezer, bapt. 5 Nov. 1699, d. after 1764; m. Eleanor Smith, dau. of Samuel of Fairfield, bapt. 8 Apr. 1711.

Abigail, bapt. 11 Jan. 1701/2; m. 8 Oct. 1724, Stephen Bennett.

Elizabeth, bapt. 11 June 1704; m. ——— Slater.

XGamaliel, bapt. 30 June 1706, d. 1783; will 12 June 1780, proved 5 Nov. 1783; m. (1) Hannah ———, who d. 10 Oct. 1745 ae. 33 (g. s., Stratfield) ; m. (2) (Fairfield Church) 7 Aug. 1749, Sarah Redfield, dau. of James, bapt. 27 Mar. 1726, d. 27 May 1758 in 32 yr. (g. s.).

Thankful, bapt. 23 Jan. 1707/8; m. (rec. Norwalk) 2 Aug. 1729, Josiah Taylor.

Martha, bapt. 27 May 1711.

Deborah, bapt. 16 Aug 1713; m. ——— Weed.

Sarah, b. abt. 1717, d. 5 Dec. 1742 in 26 yr. (g. s., Stratfield) ; m. by 1733, John Mallett.

French, Samuel, joiner, of Stratford, was an immigrant from England; member of Christ Church (Epis.), Stratford; buried 3 Sept. 1763 (Huntington Epis. Church); will 3 Dec. 1762, proved 26 Sept. 1763; wife Mary; sons Samuel, Jeremiah, John, Jonathan, Thomas, Joseph; daus. Mary Booth, Susanna Demmon, Ann Beardsley, Elizabeth Beardsley, Hannah Leavenworth.

Frenchard, Francis.

He had land in Fairfield, which was sold to Joseph James.

Frost, William.

From Nottingham, Eng. [Lechford].

Will 6 Jan. 1644/5, proved in 1645; eldest son Daniel; Rebecca and Sarah Frost; son Abraham; dau. Elizabeth and John Gray; Luke Watson; Susanna and Johanna Watson, daus. of Elizabeth Gray; John Gray's own two children; Henry and Lydia Gray and Jacob their son; Mary dau. of Henry Gray; to Mary Rylie and her children, all my goods and lands in Old England; to town of Uncowah [Fairfield] £10 towards meeting house; Henry Gray of Uncowah, Exec'r; Ephraim Wheeler and Daniel Frost, overseers; Goodman Close had some of his cattle "to winter"; son Abraham to have housing and lands bought from John Strickland. Witnesses: Ephraim Wheeler, Francis and Mary Purdy.

Children:
+Daniel.
    Elizabeth m. (1) —— Watson; m. (2) John Gray.
    Lydia, m. Henry Gray.
    Mary, m. —— Riley.
    Abraham.

Frost, Daniel, s. of William.

He m. (1) ——; m. (2) Elizabeth Barlow, dau. of John, whose will 1674 called her Elizabeth Frost.

Will 23 Feb. 1682; wife Elizabeth; sons Daniel, Joseph, Isaac; daus. Rebecca Booth, Sarah Smith, Rachel Rumsey, Hannah Thorp, Hester Frost.

Inv. 15 Dec. 1684. Controversy 10 Mar. 1684/5 between Daniel Frost [Jr.] and Robert Rumsey, John Thorp and Samuel Smith, in right of their wives.

Inv. of Est. of Elizabeth Frost, 13 Aug. 1686; Robert Rumsey made oath. Agreement of heirs; two sons, Daniel and Joseph Frost; four sons-in-law Samuel Smith, Robert Rumsey, John Thorp, and Samuel Coley, who married four of her daus.

In 1663, Sarah Frost signed release to father Daniel for legacy from her gr. father William Frost; acknowledged 1682 as Sarah Smith. Simon Booth and Rebecca his wife of York County, Mass., released father Daniel Frost from paying a legacy from gr. father William Frost, received through Mr. James Hill of Boston.

Child [by first wife]:

Rebecca, m. [5 Jan. 1663/4], Simon Booth, of York County, Me., and Enfield, Conn.

Children [by second wife]:

Sarah, m. in 1665, Samuel Smith.
+Daniel.
+Joseph.
Rachel, m. Robert Rumsey.
Hannah, m. John Thorp.
Isaac, d. in 1684, unm. Will 23 Dec. 1684, proved 10 Mar. 1684/5; three sisters, Sarah Smith, Rachel Rumsey, Hannah Thorp; bro. Daniel and sister Esther Frost; cousin John, son of bro.-in-law Samuel Smith, my sword; cousin Elizabeth Smith, dau. of same; residue to bro. Joseph. Inv. 26 Feb. 1684 [1684/5].
Esther, m. abt. 1685, Samuel Coley.

Frost, Daniel, s. of Daniel.   Sergt., Fairfield Trainband.

Married Mary Rowland, dau. of Henry; she m. (2) Moses Jackson.

Will 15 Dec. 1707, proved 4 Feb. 1707/8; wife Mary and son Daniel, Exec'rs; son Isaac; son William; daus. Abigail, Mary, Elizabeth, Rebecca Frost. Witnesses: Nathan Gold, Joseph Webb. Inv. 27 Jan. 1707/8 called him Sergt. Daniel; widow Mary made oath.

William, son of Daniel, chose his father-in-law Moses Jackson for guardian, 6 Mar. 1717/8.

Children, bapt. at Fairfield:

XDaniel, d. before 1729; m. Sarah Seeley, dau. of Benjamin, b. [say 1690]; she m. (2) by 1729, Nathaniel Fitch, of Norwalk.
Abigail, m. John Sherwood.
Mary, perhaps d. at Westport, 17 Oct. 1751.
XIsaac, bapt. 26 Aug. 1694, d. at Westport, 28 Mar. 1761; adm'n granted, 7 Apr. 1761; m. Abigail ———, who d. 22 Mar. 1761.
Rebecca, bapt. 4 July 1697.
William, bapt. 16 June 1700, d. in 1733, unm. Inv. 3 Sept. 1733, sworn by Isaac Frost, Adm'r. Agreement of his heirs, 27 Nov. 1735; Isaac and Daniel Frost, John Sherwood and Abigail his wife, Mary and Rebecca Frost, all of Fairfield, Nathaniel and Elizabeth Green of Stamford.
Elizabeth, m. (rec. Stamford) 16 Feb. 1721/2, Nathaniel Green.

Frost, Joseph, s. of Daniel.

Married Elizabeth Hubbell, dau. of Richard.

She m. (2) Samuel Hull, as his second wife.

Inv. exhibited 11 Mar. 1698 [1698/9]. Widow Elizabeth; two sons and two daus. Distribution made in 1707 to Widow, eldest son Joseph, Abner, Ellin, and Sarah Frost. Sergt. Daniel Frost was appointed guardian to Joseph's son Joseph.

Distribution ordered, 6 Aug. 1712, of the dower set to Elizabeth Hull dec'd, widow of Joseph Frost.

On 8 Nov. 1718, Abner Frost, and Henry and Sarah Wakelee, of Stratfield, and Jacob and Hellenah Weed of Danbury, children and heirs of Elizabeth, late wife of Samuel Hull, and formerly wife of Joseph Frost of Fairfield and dau. of Sergt. Richard Hubbell of Stratfield, conveyed to Joseph Frost.

Children:

   XJoseph, m. at Fairfield, 27 Aug. 1724, Adrea Couch, dau. of Samuel.
   Ellen, m. at Stratfield, 29 Oct. 1718, Jacob Weed.
   XAbner, bapt. at Fairfield, 16 Feb. 1695/6; res. Stratfield, 1723, and Elizabeth, N. J., 1731; m. at Stratfield, 24 Sept. 1723, Rebecca Hall. She was dau. of Francis, b. 23 Nov. 1703.
   Sarah m. (rec. Stratford) 26 Jan. 1710/1, Henry Wakelee.

Galpin, Philip.

Married (1) at New Haven, shortly after June 1646, Elizabeth Smith, who had been servant of Mrs. Leech.

Married (2) Hannah Jackson, dau. of Henry of Fairfield, whose will 1682 called her Hannah Galpin; she m. (2) Stephen Sherwood.

He removed to Fairfield 1657, and to Rye by 1665. Will 27 Mar. 1684, proved 19 Nov. 1684; wife; son John and his eldest son John; sons Samuel, Benjamin, Joseph, Jeremiah, Moses; daus. Sarah, Hannah; the rest of my daus., five shillings apiece; overseers, Thomas Lyon, Sr., and Gershom Lockwood.

Benjamin Galpin receipted to the widow Galpin at Rye, 29 Oct. 1685. Richard Walter, Jr., and Robert Traves receipted, 22 May 1686 to Mother Galpin for portions willed to wives by their father. John Galpin gave receipt, 13 Feb. 1685, to mother-in-law Hannah Galpin for the legacy of Samuel Galpin from his father's estate.

Stephen Sherwood and wife Hannah, Adm'rs of Philip Galpin's Est., receipted 9 Nov. 1688. Division of homestead of Philip between Joseph and his younger brother Moses, agreement 15 Feb. 1688, with Stephen Sherwood, husband of Hannah the widow of Philip Galpin. [Rye Deeds.]

Children [by first wife], two recorded at New Haven:

+John.
+Samuel, b. 17 July 1650.
   Joseph, b. 17 June 1652; res. Rye, N. Y.
+Benjamin.
   Daughter, m. Richard Walter, Jr.
   Daughter, m. Robert Travis.

Children [prob. by second wife]:

   Moses, of Rye, bachelor in 1711 when he sold land inherited from father Philip. He was a weaver.
   Jeremiah.
   Sarah.
   Hannah.

Galpin, John, s. of Philip.

Lived in Rye, and m. Mary Morgan, dau. of John. On 9 Aug. 1704, he gave to wife Mary land formerly purchased by John Morgan, "my wife's father", with remainder to daus. Mary and Ruth. On 6 Jan. 1703/4, he conveyed, as John, Sr., with wife Mary to dau. Susanna wife of James Murray. He d. abt. 1706. The deeds prove that the wives of Freegrace Adams and Jonathan Booth were also his daus.

Children:

   John, named in grandfather's will 1684.
   Susanna, m. (1) James Murray; m. (2) John Hawkins.
   Mary, m. (rec. Stratford) 8 Jan. 1700 [1700/1], Freegrace Adams.
   Ruth, prob. m. Nathaniel Bailey.
   Hester, m. at Rye (rec. Stratford), 11 Aug. 1703, Jonathan Booth.

Galpin, Samuel, s. of Philip.

Born at New Haven, 17 July 1650.
Married (1) at Stratford, 22 Mar. 1676/7, Esther Thompson. She was dau. of John, b. Jan. 1649/50, d. 27 Aug. 1678.

Married (2) Elizabeth St. John, dau. of Mark, b. at Norwalk, 6 Dec. 1656. The will of Mark St. John, 1693, mentioned son-in-law Samuel Galpin. She m. (2) Edward Camp, of Milford. Inv. 22 Mar. 1697/8; widow Elizabeth made oath. Five children: Elizabeth 13, Samuel 9, Caleb 6, Abigail 2, Mary ½. Adm'n granted 26 Apr. 1698 to widow and Mr. John Hawley.

On 7 Mar. 1710/1, Caleb son of Samuel chose Francis Griffin for guardian; Abigail and Mary chose their mother Elizabeth Galpin.

Elnathan Peat and wife Mary conveyed 1716 to brother Caleb Galpin.

Will of Elizabeth Camp of Kensington, 24 July 1728, proved 28 Nov. 1732; three daus. Elizabeth, Abigail, Mary; two sons, Samuel and Caleb.

Child [by first wife], recorded at Stratford:
Esther, b. 19 Aug. 1678, d. y.

Children [by second wife]:
Elizabeth, b. abt. 1684.
Samuel, b. abt. 1688.
Caleb, b. abt. 1691; m. (rec. Stratford) 24 Feb. 1713/4, Elizabeth Baldwin of Milford.
Abigail, b. abt. 1695.
Mary, b. abt. 1697; m. 4 Nov. 1714, Elnathan Peat.

Galpin, Benjamin, s. of Philip. Sergt., Woodbury Trainband.

Sometimes called Benoni; was apprentice of Michael Try in Fairfield, 1676. Sergt. Benjamin d. at Woodbury, 6 Jan. 1730/1.

He m. Rebecca Brown, dau. of Francis of Rye, N. Y.; she d. 8 Feb. 1743.

Will 5 Jan. 1729/30, proved 2 Feb. 1730/1; wife Rebecca; sons Joseph, Samuel; daus. Elizabeth, Martha, Rebecca, Sarah, Rachel, Thankful. Receipts of portions dated 4 Feb. 1730/1, given by John Camp, Ebenezer Warner, Joseph Andres for his mother, and Thankful Terrill.

Children, recorded at Woodbury:
Elizabeth, bapt. Mar. 1682/3; m. 19 Dec. 1704, Benjamin Andrus, of Farmington.

Martha, bapt. Apr. 1685, d. 17 Apr. 1745; m. 19 Dec. 1704, Dr. Ebenezer Warner.

Benjamin, bapt. May 1687, d. 13 Feb. 1704/5.

Rebecca, bapt. Nov. 1689; m. John Camp.

Joseph, bapt. Apr. 1693, d. 13 Sept. 1749; m. abt. 1739, Joanna ———.

Sarah, bapt. Feb. 1696/7; m. 30 Oct. 1718, David Mitchell.

Rachel, b. 31 Aug. 1699.

Samuel, b. 6 Apr. 1703, d. 31 Dec. 1789 ae. 85; Sergt.; m. (1) abt. 1728, Ruth Curtis, b. 14 Jan. 1707/8, d. 13 Nov. 1745; m. (2) at Fairfield, 4 Feb. 1745/6, Ann Sherwood.

Thankful, b. 18 Oct. 1706; m. (1) Timothy Terrill; m. (2) Lt. John Hunt.

Gaskell, Samuel.

Called Samuel, Jr., of Boston, he m. at Stratford, 12 Jan. 1703/4, Abigail, widow of Dr. Nathaniel Hudson of Stratford, and dau. of Rev. Nathaniel Chauncey. She was b. 14 Oct. 1677, and m. (3) 20 Apr. 1710, Edward Burrough.

Of Stratford, will 31 Jan. 1706/7; wife Abigail; sister Mary Gaskell; friend Mr. Benjamin Coney, Exec'r, with wife [he refused]. Inv. 2 May 1707.

Gibbs, Thomas.

Of "Corelinoe" [Carolina], merchant, made separation agreement with wife Elizabeth Gibbs, resident at New York, 17 Sept. 1681; the dau. Rebecca besides the dau. now in Barbadoes to be under care of Thomas; the dau. Martha to be under care of Elizabeth, and the negro woman Hagar to remain with her until Martha is 21 or married. [Fairfield Pro. Rec.]

Gilbert, Thomas.

Born in England about 1582; was in Braintree, Mass., by 1640, when his family consisted of seven heads.

He bought house and lot in Windsor from Francis Stiles, 24 Jan. 1644, which he later sold to John Drake and his son Jacob Drake. He afterwards bought part of the homelot of Thomas Gunn, but by 1658 had sold this to Thomas Bissell and removed to Wethersfield, where he d. 5 Sept. 1659. Doubtless he was the ——— Gilbert, aged 77, treated by Dr. Winthrop in 1659.

On 24 Mar. 1653/4, Lydia Gilbert was indicted for witchcraft, for causing the death of Henry Stiles (who boarded with the Gilberts in Windsor) in Oct. 1651 by the accidental discharge of a gun in the hands of Thomas Allyn. She was convicted and, we must believe, executed. It must also be believed that Lydia was wife of Thomas Gilbert. This has been disputed because the probate records mention that the funeral expenses of Thomas' wife were to be paid out of his estate, which might imply that she d. not long before him in 1659. But he could have m. again between 1654 and 1659.

The estate of Thomas was ordered distributed to those who are below assigned to him as children. It is certain that these heirs were six brothers and a sister; and there is no reasonable doubt that Thomas was their father.

Children, prob. all b. in England:

+Jonathan, b. abt. 1618.
  Ezekiel.
  Sarah, b. abt. 1624; m. Joel Judkins, of Braintree, Mass.
+Josiah, b. abt. 1628.
+John, b. abt. 1630.
+Thomas.
+Obadiah.

Gilbert, Jonathan, s. of Thomas. Indian Interpreter and Marshal, Conn. Colony, Apr. 1646, and for greater part of period 1646-1682; a trooper under Maj. Mason, Mar. 1658, and commissioned Cornet of Troop of Horse, Oct. 1668; Collector of Customs, Hartford, Mar. 1659; Deputy (Hartford) to Conn. Leg., May 1677, Oct. 1677, May 1678, May 1681.

Born about 1618, d. at Hartford, 10 Dec. 1682 in 64 yr. (g. s.).

Married (1) (rec. Hartford) 29 Jan. 1645/6, Mary White; dau. of John. The will of Elder John White, 1683, named grandson Jonathan Gilbert, "son of my daughter Mary."

He m. (2) abt. 1650, Mary Welles, b. abt. 1626, d. 3 July 1700 in 74 yr. (g. s.). She was dau. of Hugh.

In Aug. 1661 he received a colonial grant of 350 acres, for services to the colony. He was several times Townsman of Hartford. In 1654 he received permission to set up a warehouse at the general landing place. The General Court in 1662 granted him liberty to keep an ordinary at his house at Cold Spring. Will 10 Sept. 1674, proved 1 Mar. 1683; wife Mary (sole Exec'x); sons Samuel (under 21), Ebenezer, Jonathan, Thomas, Nathaniel; daus. Lydia Richison, Sarah Belcher, Mary Holton, Hester and Rachel Gilbert; Ebenezer to have 300 acres in Farmington; Hannah Kelly (evidently an indentured servant); grandchildren John Rossiter, Andrew Belcher, Jonathan Richeson; desired Capt. John Allyn, "my brother John Gilbert", and Sergt. Caleb Stanley, to be helpful to wife. Inv. £2484.

Will of Mary, 23 May 1700; described herself as "widow and innholder"; sons Thomas, Samuel, and Ebenezer; grandson Thomas Dickinson; daus. Lydia Chapman and Rachel Marshfield; children of late dau. Sarah Belcher; children of dau. Lydia which she had by husband Richardson dec'd; two sons of late grandson Jonathan Richardson; son-in-law Charles Dickinson. Inv. £562.

Children [by first wife], recorded at Hartford:

> Jonathan, b. 11 May 1648, d. at Middletown, 1 Feb. 1697/8; m. Dorothy Stow, dau. of Rev. Samuel, who d. 4 July 1698.
>
> Mary, b. 15, bapt. 17, Dec. 1649; d. without surviving issue; m. (1) abt. 1668, John Rossiter, of Killingworth; m. (2) Samuel Holton, of Northampton, Mass.

Children [by second wife], first two recorded at Hartford:

> Sarah, b. 25 July 1651, d. at Charlestown, Mass., 26 Jan. 1688/9; m. at Hartford, 1 July 1670, Mr. Andrew Belcher. He was a noted merchant, of Boston. Their son, Jonathan, was Royal Governor of Massachusetts and afterwards of New Jersey, and founder of Princeton College.
>
> Lydia, b. 3 Oct. 1654; m. (1) Jonathan Richardson; m. (2) ———— Chapman.
>
> Thomas, b. abt. 1656, d. at Boston; m. (1) Lydia Ballett; m. (2) at Boston, 24 Sept. 1708, Mary (Lilly) Trowbridge.
>
> Nathaniel, b. (no record), d. before 1700, unm.
>
> Samuel, b. abt. 1663, d. at Salem, 5 Aug. 1733 ae. 70 (g. s.); Capt.; m. 2 Oct. 1684, Mary Rogers, dau. of Samuel of New London; she d. 30 Sept. 1756 in 91 yr. (g. s.).
>
> Ebenezer, d. at Kensington, 11 Aug. 1736; m. Esther Allyn, b. 29 Jan. 1676/7, d. 4 Oct. 1750.
>
> Esther, m. Charles Dickinson.
>
> Rachel, m. 22 Sept. 1686, Josiah Marshfield.

Gilbert, Josiah, s. of Thomas.

Born abt. 1628, d. at Wethersfield, abt. Sept. 1688. He testified, Oct. 1684, ae. 56, and stated that he became in 1651 tenant farmer for Lt. Hollister, holding the farm twelve years. He m. (1) abt. 1651, Elizabeth Belcher, b. abt. 1632, d. at Wethersfield, 17 Oct. 1682 ae. 50; m. (2) Jan. 1687/8, Mary, widow of John Ward and dau. of William Harris. The antenuptial agreement with Mary was dated 18 Oct. 1687 [always read as 1681, which is impossible, as her first husband was then living, and it is stated in probate records that the marriage took place Jan. 1687/8].

On 2 Mar. 1695/6, Jonathan Deming, Sr., John Riley, Jacob Williams, and Simon Willard, in right of their wives, who were all daus. of Josiah Gilbert, complained that no action had been taken on his estate, and appointed their uncle Francis Whitmore of Middletown to represent them. The Inv. appraised the personal estate as of value on 29 Sept. 1688, which was prob. the date of Josiah's death; taken 17 Mar. 1695/6. Children named, each sex in order of birth: Benjamin, Josiah, Eleazer, Moses, Caleb, John; Elizabeth Deming, Lydia Riley, Sarah Williams, Mary Willard, Amy Gilbert. A charge was allowed for bringing up John, son of Josiah, from last week of Mar. 1689 to Apr. 1697 (seven years).

It was mentioned on 1 Sept. 1721 that Josiah's widow was lately dec'd.

Children [by first wife,] recorded at Wethersfield:

Benjamin, b. 22 Sept. 1652, d. at Wethersfield, 9 Dec. 1711 ae. abt. 59; Sergt.; m. 25 Nov. 1680, Mary Riley.

Elizabeth, b. 28 Mar. 1654, d. at Wethersfield, 3 Sept. 1714; m. 5 Dec. 1673, Jonathan Deming, Sr.

Lydia, b. Dec. 1656; m. John Riley, of Newington.

Josiah, b. 12 Sept. 1659, d. at Wethersfield, 2 Feb. 1704/5. Will 24 Jan. 1704/5; bro. Benjamin; bro. Moses; sister Mary wife of Simon Willard; bro. Caleb; sister Elizabeth Deming; cousins Josiah and Mary Willard, children of bro. Willard; sister Amy Gilbert.

Sarah, b. 1 Dec. 1661; m. 10 Dec. 1685, Capt. Jacob Williams.

Eleazer, b. 20 Sept. 1663.

+Moses, b. 12 Apr. 1666.

Caleb, b. 10 June 1668.

Mary, b. 18 Nov. 1670; m. Simon Willard.

Amy, b. 12 Apr. 1672, d. at Wethersfield, in 1739, unm. Adm'n granted to Jacob Williams, 1 Jan. 1739/40.

Child [by second wife]:
    John, perhaps b. Mar. 1688/9, living 1697.

Gilbert, John, s. of Thomas. Corpl., Hartford Train Band.

Born about 1630; d. at Hartford, 29 Dec. 1690 (probate rec.). Married at Hartford, 6 May 1647, Amy Lord. She was dau. of Thomas, bapt. at Towcester, co. Northampton, Eng., 30 Nov. 1626; d. 8 Jan. 1691.

Will 1 Aug. 1690; to wife, land given us by our Mother Lord; sons Thomas, Joseph, James; dau. Dorothy Palmer.

Children, recorded at Hartford:
    John, b. 16 Jan. 1647 [1647/8], d. y.
    Dorothy, b. abt. 1651; m. abt. 1672, Moses Palmer of Stonington.
    John, b. 19 Feb. 1652 [1652/3], d. y.
    Elizabeth, b. 12 Feb. 1655 [1655/6], living 1669, d. bef. 1690.
    Thomas, b. 4 Sept. 1658, d. abt. 1706; glazier, Hartford; Inv. 16 Mar. 1705/6, £33; adm'n granted to bro. Joseph; m. in 1681, Deborah Beaumont.
    James, b. (no record), d. abt. 1697. Adm'n granted, 4 Mar. 1696/7, to Thomas and Joseph Gilbert.
    Amy, b. 3 Apr. 1663, d. y.
    Joseph, b. 3 Apr. 1666.

Gilbert, Thomas, s. of Thomas.

Of Windsor, rem. 1655 to Springfield, Mass., where he d. 5 June 1662; m. 31 July 1655, Catherine, widow of Nathaniel Bliss, and dau. of Samuel Chapin. She m. (3) 28 Dec. 1664, Samuel Marshfield.

Children, recorded at Springfield:
    Sarah, b. 19 Feb. 1655 [1655/6]; m. 9 Aug. 1676, Samuel Field of Hatfield.
    +John, b. 18 Oct. 1657.
    +Thomas, b. 15 Mar. 1659 [1659/60].
    Henry, b. 1 Mar. 1661 [1661/2].

Gilbert, Obadiah, s. of Thomas.

On 11 Jan. 1670 [1670/1] he entered his homelot at Fairfield of which he had had quiet possession above eight years.

Will of Obadiah of Fairfield, 23 Aug. 1674; wife Elizabeth; dau. Sarah Olmsted; sons Obadiah, Benjamin, Joseph; brothers Jonathan and Josiah Gilbert, overseers. Inv. 16 Sept. 1674.

Married Elizabeth, widow of Nehemiah Olmstead, dau. of Jehu Burr. She m. (3) Capt. Nathaniel Seeley.

Elizabeth Seeley conveyed to her sons Obadiah and Benjamin Gilbert as Exec'x of her husband Gilbert's will; recorded 21 June 1688.

Children:

+Obadiah.
+Benjamin.
+Joseph.

Gilbert, Moses, s. of Josiah.

Born at Wethersfield, 12 Apr. 1666, d. at Fairfield in 1713.

Married at New York City, 4 Apr. 1694, Jannetje Dirck; she m. (2) Capt. Moses Dimon. Called Jane in Fairfield records, she was dau. of Dirck Evertszen and Elizabeth Lubberts (also called Elizabeth Fluyt), and was bapt. at New York, 3 Oct. 1674.

Inv. 15 Feb. 1714/5. Widow Jane appointed Adm'x, 7 Oct. 1713 [perhaps should be 1714]; one son Josiah, who chose mother Jane for guardian; four daus. Elizabeth, Hannah, Sarah, and Cattern; of the last three, Jane was appointed guardian.

Josiah Gilbert chose Zechariah Blackman for guardian, 19 Nov. 1714.

Sarah Gilbert receipted 4 Jan. 1725/6 to father-in-law Moses Dimon; Catherine Gilbert did likewise, 22 Nov. 1729.

Children, bapt. at Fairfield:

×Josiah, b. (no record), d. at Fairfield, 4 Dec. 1760; will 4 Dec. 1760,
    proved 29 Dec. 1760; m. 14 June 1722, Sarah Lord.
Elizabeth.
Hannah, b. at Fairfield, 29 Dec. 1700, d. at Greenfield, 24 July 1767
    in 67 yr.; m. (rec. Greenfield) 27 Apr. 1721, Moses Dimon, Jr.

Sarah, bapt. 16 Feb. 1706/7, d. at Greenfield, 14 Apr. 1766 ae. 61;
m. (rec. Greenfield) 13 Jan. 1725/6, John Bradley, Jr.
Catherine, bapt. 3 July 1709, d. at Greenfield, 9 Apr. 1777 ae. 68; had
son Benoni [Dimon], b. 12 Sept. 1725; m. (rec. Greenfield) 8 Apr.
1730, John Wakeman.
Margaret, bapt. 20 Aug. 1711, d. y.

Gilbert, John, s. of Thomas.

Born at Springfield, 18 Oct. 1657, d. at Stratford, in 1709. He
m. (1) Hannah Blackman, dau. of James, b. 21 Jan. 1664/5. He
m. (2) at Stratford, 2 July 1695, Hannah Canfield; dau. of
Thomas, b. at Milford, 20 Nov. 1667. She m. (2) 20 Feb. 1710/1,
John Osborn, Sr.
Inv. Sept. 1709. Widow Hannah made oath; adm'n granted
to her with Zechariah Blackman. Ages of children: Thomas, 13
last Apr.; Josiah, 10 last Mar.; John, 8 last Mar.; Sarah, 3 on
last 10 Nov. On 22 Nov. 1710, Josiah chose Mr. Ephraim Sti
for guardian; the Court appointed Jonathan Gilbert for John; the
mother Hannah was chosen by Thomas and appointed for Sarah.
Ephraim Stiles being dead, Josiah chose Zechariah Blackman,
19 Nov. 1714. On 23 June 1719, Jonathan Gilbert, guardian to
John, having absented himself, John chose Jonathan Stiles; who
reported, 16 Nov. 1720, that John, Jr., had died, and distribution
was ordered to his bros. Thomas and Josiah, and sister Sarah.
Agreement, 13 Mar. 1723/4 to divide Est. of father John Gilbert; Thomas Gilbert, Josiah Gilbert, Jabez Harger and Ann his
wife, Sarah Gilbert; mention dower of mother, and bro. John
dec'd.

Child [by first wife], recorded at Stratford:
Anna, b. June 1688; m. 24 Jan. 1704/5, Jabez Harger.

Children [by second wife], recorded at Stratford:
Thomas, b. 16 Apr. 1696, d. in 1760; will 26 Mar. 1752, proved
4 Aug. 1760; m. (1) (rec. Stratford) 19 Dec. 1717, Jemima Silli-
man of Fairfield, who d. 17 Sept. 1718; m. (2) 18 Dec. 1718,
Elizabeth How, dau. of Daniel, b. at Wallingford, 28 Jan.
1699/1700.
Josiah, b. 24 Mar. 1699, d. in 1777; Inv. exhibited 3 Nov. 1777; m.
Sarah ———.

John, b. 13 Mar. 1701/2, d. in 1720.
Sarah, b. 10 Nov. 1705; m. 24 Aug. 1724, John Marchant.

Gilbert, Thomas, s. of Thomas.

Born at Springfield, 15 Mar. 1659/60, d. there 14 May 1698; m.
(1) 4 Aug. 1680, Abilene Marshfield, who d. 26 Nov. 1689; m.
(2) 9 Apr. 1690, Anna Bancroft. She m. (2) James Sexton, of
Westfield.

Children [by first wife] :
　Thomas, b. 3 Nov. 1681.
　Samuel, b. 4 Sept. 1683.
　Sarah, b. 11 Sept. 1685, d. 14 Oct. 1685.
　Jonathan, b. 4 Nov. 1686; m. at Stratford, 5 Aug. 1707, Margery
　　Searles, and had children recorded there :* Abilene, b. 11 Jan. 1708;
　　Phebe, b. 1 Jan. 1709/10; Katherine, b. 8 Mar. 1712.
　John, b. 28 Feb. 1687 [1687/8], d. y.
　Ebenezer, d. 4 Jan. 1691 [1691/2].

Children [by second wife] :
　John, b. 16 Mar. 1691; m. at Stratford, 25 Nov. 1714, Patience Lattin.
　Margaret, b. 27 Mar. 1693.
　Sarah, b. 18 Jan. 1694 [1694/5].
　Anna, b. 16 Feb. 1696 [1696/7], m. Joseph Segar.

Gilbert, Obadiah, s. of Obadiah.

Married Abigail ———.
He was bapt. at Fairfield Church, 19 May 1695.
Widow Abigail (guardian of Sarah and Margret, children of
Obadiah dec'd) gave receipt 4 Dec. 1728 to Benjamin and John
Gilbert, Adm'rs. Elizabeth and Marah Gilbert gave receipt,
4 Dec. 1728, to mother Abigail and brothers Benjamin and John.

Children, bapt. at Fairfield:
　×Benjamin, bapt. 19 May 1695; m. Elizabeth Adams, dau. of Abraham,
　　bapt. 24 Feb. 1694/5.
　×John, bapt. 23 May 1697; m. 29 June 1721, Jemima Williams.
　Elizabeth, bapt. 8 Sept. 1700.

---

* Omitted in Orcutt's *History of Stratford.*

Abigail, bapt. 11 Apr. 1703, d. y.

Mary, b. 3 Mar. 1705, bapt. 29 Apr. 1705, d. at Greenfield, Nov. 1750 ae. abt. 42; m. (rec. Greenfield) 20 Jan. 1728/9, Edmund Ogden.

Joseph, bapt. 25 Aug. 1706.

Abigail, bapt. 15 May 1709.

Sarah, b. 20 Dec. 1711, bapt. 9 Mar. 1711/2; m. (rec. Greenfield) 15 July 1733, James Grey.

Margaret, bapt. 21 Apr. 1717; m. Gershom Thorp, with whom she conveyed 14 Mar. 1738/9 to John Gilbert land from her father Obadiah Gilbert.

Gilbert, Benjamin, s. of Obadiah.

Married Adrea Hurlbut, dau. of Thomas, 2d; she m. (2) Capt. Samuel Couch.

Inv. 1 July 1693, taken by Philip Lewis and Thomas Jones; widow "Adry" made oath.

Prob. no children.

Gilbert, Joseph, s. of Obadiah.

He was bapt. at Fairfield Church, 19 May 1695.

Will 28 Dec. 1699; wife Mary; only son Joseph (a minor); brother Obadiah Gilbert.

Inv. 14 Feb. 1699 [1699/1700].

Child:

Joseph.

Gilbert, William.

Of Stratford; adm'n granted, 5 Sept. 1727, to Frances Gilbert.

Frances, doubtless his widow, m. at Stratford, Dec. 1728, John Keyes, and d. 14 Dec. 1768.

Glover.

HENRY, soap boiler, of New Haven, d. there 2 Sept. 1689; Springfield records call him bro. of Thomas Cooper of that place; m. Helena, most likely sister of William Davis of New Haven; she d. 1 Mar. 1697/8. They had several daus., of whom Abigail, b. 31 July 1652, m. 11 Dec. 1678, Daniel Burr of Fairfield; and an only son:

JOHN, bapt. at New Haven, 8 Oct. 1648, d. there 29 Jan. 1679 [1679/80] ; m. 7 Dec. 1671, Joanna, dau. of Stephen Daniel by his wife Anna, dau. of Mr. Thomas Gregson. Joanna, b. 1 Sept. 1652, m. (2) 28 Dec. 1682, Mr. William Thompson of New Haven, and by him had seven children, of whom the following daus. m. Stratford men; Jane, b. 29 Oct. 1683, d. at Stratford, 28 Sept. 1743, m. 22 Dec. 1707, John Moss; Abigail, b. 18 Oct. 1685, m. 11 Dec. 1707, Richard Hubbell; and Sarah, bapt. 19 Jan. 1691/2, m. (1) 15 Nov. 1715, Timothy Fairchild, and (2) 12 July 1729, William Peet.

John and Joanna (Daniel) Glover had three daus., of whom Mehitabel, b. 1 May 1679, m. (1) 18 Dec. 1705, Benjamin Coney of Stratford, and (2) 21 Sept. 1721, Rev. Joseph Webb of Fairfield, and (3) 7 July 1741, John Thompson of Stratford; and an only son:

JOHN, b. at New Haven, 20 Nov. 1674, d. at Newtown, 30 June 1752; m. (1) (rec. New Haven) 27 Nov. 1700, Mrs. Margery Hubbard, says the record, which we take to be a mistake for Hubbell [see JOHN HUBBELL]. They rem. to Stratford, where she d. 14 Mar. 1703/4. He m. (2) at Stratford, 14 July 1707, Mrs. Bethia Bickley; widow of William Bickley, and dau. of Benjamin Beach, b. 23 Apr. 1674. He settled early in Newtown; but lived for a time in Rye, returning to Newtown by 1745; and m. (3) Susannah ———. His will 1749, proved July 1752, named wife Susannah, eldest sons John and Henry, son Benjamin, dau. Susannah, and youngest sons Isaac and Arnold.

Children by first wife:

> John, b. at New Haven, 30 Dec. 1701; m. (rec. Newtown) 12 July 1724, Elizabeth Bennett; dau. of James, bapt. at Stratfield, 8 Sept. 1700.
>
> Henry, b. at Stratford, 8 Oct. 1703, d. at Newtown, 12 Feb. 1784 ae. 81 (g. s.); Capt.; m. (rec. Newtown) 10 Apr. 1735, Prudence Stoddard, who d. 20 Aug. 1782 ae. 73 (g. s.).

Child by second wife:

> Benjamin, b. May 1708; m. (rec. Newtown) 10 Oct. 1733, Mary Burwell; dau. of Ens. Samuel of New Haven.

Children by third wife:

> Susannah.
>
> Isaac, d. in 1756, unm.; will 1755, proved Apr. 1756, named father

John dec'd; mother Susannah; bro. Arnold; sister Susannah Glover. Arnold.

Godfrey, Christopher.

He bought land at Compo (Westport), 29 Dec. 1686. Perhaps he was related to Robert Godfrey who received a grant of land at Oyster Bay, 1679.

Anne Godfrey renewed Covenant at Fairfield Church, 17 July 1698. She, aged 27, testified 1692 in Disbrow witch trial.

He d. 26 Nov. 1715 ae. 58 (g. s., Stratford; the day of month perhaps misread).

Inv. 17 Nov. 1715. Adm'n granted to widow Ann, 4 Jan. 1715/6.

On 7 Jan. 1723/4, Patrick Bulmore of Norwalk, with wife Mary, dau. to Christopher Godfrey dec'd and sister to Isaac Godfrey dec'd, conveyed to Christopher Godfrey. Another deed, 1725, recites that Christopher, Samuel, and John Godfrey, Isaac Godfrey dec'd, Elizabeth wife of John Elwood, and Mary wife of Patrick Bulmore, were children of Christopher Godfrey.

John Elwood and Elizabeth his wife, dau. of Christopher Godfrey dec'd, and sister of Isaac Godfrey dec'd, conveyed 25 May 1734 to Christopher Godfrey.

Children, bapt. at Fairfield, the first five on 17 July 1698:

XChristopher, b. abt. 1685/6, d. 20 Aug. 1758 in 73 yr. (g. s., Westport), m. 11 Feb. 1711, Margery Sturges [also called Margaret], who d. 4 Nov. 1759 in 71 yr. (g. s.).

Samuel, res. Hempstead, L. I. In 1725, John Ellison of Hempstead entered caveat against lands of Samuel Godfrey, formerly of Fairfield, lately resident in Hempstead.

Elizabeth, d. at Westport, 24 Feb. 1764; m. John Elwood.

Mary, m. Patrick Bulmore.

Abigail, d. young.

XJohn, bapt. 23 Apr. 1699.

Isaac, bapt. 14 Feb. 1702/3, d. before 1724, unm.

Godwin, George.

Married at Fairfield, 21 Feb. 1651 [1651/2], Ellen Smith [Col. Rec.]. She was dau. of Giles.

He entered, 5 Jan. 1653 [1653/4], lands purchased from Nathan Gold.

Will (no date); wife Ellen; sons Samuel and John (under 18); dau. Mary (under 7); Thomas Sherwood and Samuel Forman overseers; will and Inv. proved 20 Oct. 1658.

Children:

> Mary, m. (1) Joseph Jackson; m. (2) Joseph Seeley, and rem. to Cohansey, N. J.
> +Samuel.
> John, d. in K. Philip's War; will 1 Dec. 1675, proved 10 Feb. 1675/6; says he is "prest a soldier"; sister Mary Jackson; uncle John Smith; brother Samuel Godwin.

Godwin, Samuel, s. of George.

Born about 1655; settled in Eastchester, N. Y.; d. before 1697. Of Eastchester, 1682, he sold to John Sturgis, Sr., the homelot in Fairfield which his father George Godwin gave him.

Married ———, dau. of the first Henry Gray of Fairfield; q. v. for deed in which Godwin's daus. joined.

He is said to have m. [secondly?] Sarah Fowler, dau. of Henry and Rebecca (Newell) Fowler. Samuel Goding of Eastchester conveyed 1682 to bro.-in-law Henry Fowler [Eastchester Deeds]. She m. (2) Edward Hancock of Eastchester.*

John, Mary, and Abigail "Godin" are listed in the Eastchester Census of 1698 under Edward, Sarah, Elias, and Susannah Hancock.

Children [by first wife]:

> John, b. [say 1677]; m. and had children rec. at Eastchester: Samuel, b. 26 Jan. 1699 [1699/1700]; John, b. 1 May 1702; Solomon, b. 3 Oct. 1704.
> Sarah, m. John Jackson.
> Mary, gave rec't to John Godwin and his father-in-law Edward Hancock and his mother Sarah Hancock, for her portion; she m. abt. 1701, Christopher Sturges of Fairfield, rem. to Stamford, and d. there 17 Feb. 1746.
> Abigail, d. 30 Sept. 1757; m. (rec. Fairfield) Oct. 1708, Thomas Disbrow.

---

* *N. Y. Gen. and Biog. Record*, 58: 262. Hancock had a son Elias b. 15 Dec. 1693.

GOLD FAMILY (FAIRFIELD)

Gold, Nathan. Ens., Fairfield Trainband, before 1656; Lt., May 1657; Chief Military Officer, Fairfield County, June 1672; Major, Fairfield County, Aug. 1673; member of Conn. War Council, Nov. 1673, July 1675, May 1676. Patentee, Royal Charter, 1662. Assistant, Conn. Col., 1657, 1659-87, 1689-94. Commissioner, N. Y. Boundary, 1683, 1684. Judge of Pleas for Fairfield County under Andros, 1687. Colonial grant of 300 acres, 1667, and of 800 acres [in Danbury], 1687.

Son of John Gould, of Kings Langley, yeoman (will 30 June 1633, proved 18 July 1633), by wife Judith (will 6 May 1650, proved 3 Sept. 1650). Judith m. (2) by license 20 Sept. 1639, Simon Gould, of Bovingdon, co. Herts, a distant cousin of her first husband. She was buried at Watford, co. Herts, 15 May 1650. She left money to be sent to New England "for my son Nathan and my daughter Sarah their own children"; other children, Hannah, Mary, Abel, Lydia, Elizabeth; another son, Zaccheus, died before her, "ultra marinis coelebs", unmarried.*

Nathan is first seen at Milford, whence he soon removed to Fairfield; m. (1) between 1648 and 1655, Martha, widow of Edmund Harvey. In 1657, Winthrop wrote of Gold's wife at Fairfield as suffering from "hypocondraiaca." Perhaps she did not long survive; Martha's name has not been found in Fairfield records following her marriage to Gold, though he was later recorded as responsible for the portions of her children.

When Mrs. Mary Benfield was examined in 1665 at the house of the magistrate, Nathan Gold, she was questioned privately by Mrs. Sarah Gold and Mrs. Beatrice Risden. In 1682, Joseph Banks gave £10 by will to Mrs. Sarah Gold, Sr., making Maj. Gold one of the overseers. In Sept. 1692, "Sary" Gold testified with Ann Wakeman [widow of Rev. Samuel Wakeman] in the

---

* From researches of Col. Charles E. Banks on behalf of Mrs. Finley J. Shepard, of New York City. Nathan Gould of Salisbury, Mass., testified 1682 aged 68 that "he came into this Country and Town" Sept. 1652; if this means (as we should ordinarily understand the words) that he did not come to New England until 1652, then he could not have been Judith's son who was here in 1650, and we must identify Nathan of Fairfield as the son of John and Judith. The Salisbury man has usually been considered the son of Judith; and it is at least a curious coincidence that he had a gr. dau. named Judith. Nathan of Fairfield, however, was a man of wealth, as we should expect Judith's son to be, while Nathan of Salisbury was a yeoman.

witchcraft trials. No further reference to her is found, and when Nathan Gold made his will in 1694, he had no wife living.

The term "Mrs." implied respect, not necessarily the married state, and intrinsically there is no reason why Mrs. Sarah Gold cannot be identified with the sister of Maj. Gold who came to this country. Yet we do not favor that interpretation. It was very unusual for a man to bring a young sister from England, and maintain her unmarried in his household for more than forty years. Again, Nathan's sister had a considerable inheritance, yet there is no record of Sarah's owning any land in her own right, nor is any will or conveyance found by which she disposed of property. Martha is known to have been ill in 1657, and if she died then, all the children could have been by a second wife, and we believe that she was the Sarah whose name appears from 1665 to 1692.

It is interesting in this connection to study the names of the children and grandchildren. Nathan named his second dau. Sarah, his fourth, Martha. It was a common practice to name a dau. after a deceased first wife. Among the grandchildren, the names are found distributed thus:

Deborah named her 1st dau. Sarah, her 6th dau. Martha.
Sarah named her 2nd dau. Sarah.
Nathan named his 2nd dau. Sarah, his 4th dau. Martha.
Abigail named her 1st dau. Sarah.
Martha named her 3rd dau. Sarah, her 2nd dau. Martha.

It will be seen that all five children named a child Sarah, while but three named a child Martha; and of the latter, only Martha (in naming a dau. for herself) gave that name the preference over Sarah. Although such evidence is not conclusive, it accords well with the belief that Sarah was mother of the children.

In 1663, Capt. Robert Seeley accused Nathan Gold of speaking against the King, and he indignantly protested his innocence.

Will 1 Mar. 1693/4, proved 29 Mar. 1693/4; only son Nathan; four daus., the wife of John Thompson, Deborah wife of George Clarke, Abigail wife of Jonathan Selleck, and Martha Selleck.

Children :*

    Deborah, b. [say 1659], d. at Milford, 2 June 1697; m. abt. 1677, Ens. George Clark.

*Of course Nathan had no dau. who m. Josiah Harvey, his "son-in-law" [stepson].

Sarah, b. abt. 1661, d. at Fairfield, 4 June 1747 in 87 yr. (g. s.) ; m. 25 Apr. 1684, John Thompson.

+Nathan, b. abt. 1663.

Abigail, b. [say 1665], d. at Stamford, 20 Dec. 1711; m. 5 Jan. 1685, Jonathan Selleck, Jr.

Martha, b. [say 1668], d. at Stamford, 1 Dec. 1712; m. (1) John Selleck; m. (2) 18 Apr. 1695, Rev. John Davenport.

Gold, Nathan, s. of Nathan. Ens., Fairfield Train Band, Apr. 1690; Capt., Oct. 1695. Deputy for Fairfield to Conn. Leg., May 1692, Oct. 1694. Commissioner [Judge] for Fairfield, 1693, 1694. Assistant, Conn. Col., 1695 to 1708; Dep.-Gov., 1708 until death 1723. Judge, Fairfield Probate Court, Oct. 1698, May 1701 to 1723; Judge, Fairfield County Court, May 1701 to May 1708; Judge, Court of Assistants at New Haven, 1703, and in New Haven and Fairfield Counties, 1704; Judge, Superior Court of Conn., from May 1711, and Chief Judge from May 1717 to 1723. Committee of War for Fairfield County, Oct. 1709.

Married (1) Hannah Talcott, who d. 28 Mar. 1696 [by Talcott Fam. Rec.].

Mrs. Sarah d. at Fairfield, 17 Oct. 1711; was his second wife, and perhaps dau. of Jehu Burr, 2d. Nathan and Sarah Gold witnessed a deed, Oct. 1707.

Hon. Nathan, Lt.-Gov. of Conn., d. 3 Oct. 1723 ae. 60 (g. s.). Will 13 Sept. 1723, proved 27 Nov. 1723; eldest son John; son Nathan; sons Samuel and Hezekiah; son-in-law Rev. Thomas Hawley of Ridgefield who m. dau. Abigail; dau. Martha Gold; sons Onesimus, David, Joseph; to Sarah Clark, £5. John Gold appealed.

Inv. 14 Nov. 1723. A distribution was made to eldest son John, 2d son Nathan, 3d son Samuel, Onesimus, David, and Joseph. Receipts were given by Hezekiah Gold, Thomas Hawley, Onesimus Gold, David Gold.

Children [by first wife], recorded at Fairfield:

Abigail, b. 14 Feb. 1687; m. Rev. Thomas Hawley, of Ridgefield.

×John, b. 25 Apr. 1688, d. 23 Sept. 1766 in 79 yr. (g. s., Fairfield) ; adm'n on Est. granted 13 Oct. 1766; m. Jemima Sherwood, dau. of John, bapt. 14 Jan. 1696/7.

✕Nathan, b. 6 Apr. 1690, d. before 28 Sept. 1761 (distribution of Est.) ;
m. ———.

✕Samuel, b. 27 Dec. 1692, bapt. 26 Aug. 1694, d. 11 Oct. 1769 in 77 yr.
(g. s., Fairfield) ; m. (rec. Fairfield) 7 Dec. 1716, Esther Bradley.

✕Hezekiah, bapt. 17 Feb. 1694/5, d. 22 Apr. 1761 in 67 yr. (g. s.,
Stratford) ; grad. Harvard, 1719; Rev.; m. (rec. Stratford) 23
May 1723, Mary Ruggles of Guilford, who d. 2 July 1750 in 48 yr.
(g. s.).

Sarah, bapt. 23 July 1696, d. y.

Children [by second wife], bapt. at Fairfield:

Sarah, bapt. 3 Mar. 1699/1700, d. y.

✕Onesimus, bapt. 19 Oct. 1701, d. at Greenfield, 6 Mar. 1773 ae. over
70; m. Eunice [prob. Hubbell, dau. of Samuel, Jr., bapt. 21 Mar.
1703].

David, bapt. 3 Dec. 1704.

Martha, bapt. 8 Feb. 1707/8; m. (rec. New Haven) 4 Apr. 1728,
Mr. Samuel Sherman.

✕Joseph, bapt. 21 Oct. 1711, m. abt. 1738, Abigail Barlow, dau. of
Samuel.

GOLD FAMILY (STAMFORD)

Gold, John.

He was noted in New Haven records as a youth in 1661, and
appears to have resided there for several years thereafter; rem.
to Stamford.

Married Hannah Slawson, dau. of George; who m. (2) at
Stamford, 20 Sept. 1714, Dea. Samuel Hoyt as his third wife.

John, Sr., d. at Stamford, 14 July 1712.

Jonathan Gold, having rec'd a homelot and dwelling house from
his father John Gold, released all claim to his Est., 12 July 1712.
[Stamford Deeds.]

Children :*

Sarah, m. at Stamford, 1 Dec. 1692, Israel? Finch.

Hannah, m. (1) at Stamford, 12 Jan. 1692 [1692/3], Abraham
Ambler; m. (2) at Stamford, 8 Sept. 1697, Jeremiah Andrews.

Mary, m. at Stamford, 11 Oct. 1699, Eliphalet Lockwood.

+John.

Ann, m. at Stamford, 16 Jan. 1706/7, John Pettit.

Jonathan; Inv. of Est. of Sergt. Jonathan, 8 Oct. 1730.

---

* Some of the children are placed hypothetically or by circumstantial evidence.

Gold, John, s. of John.

Married at Stamford, 3 Apr. 1707, Hannah Higginbothom. She was dau. of Richard and Elizabeth (Munson) (Cooper) Higginbothom, and m. (2) John Seymour.

John, Jr., d. at Stamford, 27 Mar. 1720.

Inv. 4 Feb. 1722/3; adm'n granted to Hannah and Sergt. Jonathan Gold. Widow; four children, John, Munson, Sarah, Hannah.

Children, recorded at Stamford:

John, b. 17 Nov. 1707.
Munson.
Child, d. 8 Sept. 1712.
Hannah, d. 12 Dec. 1715.
Sarah.
Hannah, b. abt. 1716; m. by 1733, James Hoyt, of Norwalk; gave receipt for wife's portion to her mother and guardian, Hannah Seymour.

Gray, Henry. Deputy for Fairfield, Apr. 1643, Oct. 1656, Feb. 1657.

Of Fairfield by 1643.

Married Lydia Frost, dau. of William, whose will 1645 named her, her husband, and children Jacob and Mary.

Inv. Oct. 1658. Son Jacob chose John Cable for guardian, 1658.

On 9 Dec. 1734, Isaac, David and Samuel Gray, Thomas Disbrow and Abigail his wife, John Nott and Martha his wife, and Sarah Jackson "Widow Woman", all of Fairfield, and Christopher Sturges and wife Mary of Stamford, conveyed to Jacob Gray and Will Gray, Jr., of Fairfield, interest in land in West Parish laid out to said Jacob Gray, eldest son of Jacob Gray late of Fairfield, who was eldest son of Henry Gray one of the five Farmers of Maxamus.

Children:

+Jacob.
Mary.
+Henry, b. abt. 1645.
Daughter, m. Samuel Godwin of Eastchester.

Gray, John.

Prob. bro. of Henry; m. abt. 1640, Elizabeth, widow of ——— Watson, and dau. of William Frost. They had two children in 1645 when Frost made his will.

He removed, perhaps to Newtown, L. I.

Gray, Jacob, s. of Henry.

Having a legacy from gr. father William Frost, he bound himself 17 Nov. 1662 not to sell without consent of uncle Daniel Frost and Cornelius Hull.

Married (1) Joanna Smith, bapt. at Hartford, 25 Mar. 1649; dau. of Giles, whose will 1669 called her Johanna Gray.

Married (2) Sarah, widow of John Bartram of Stratford.

He d. at Fairfield, 6 Mar. 1712.

Inv. 12 Mar. 1712. Widow Sarah and son Jacob, Adm'rs. Isaac Jennings of Fairfield assigned to bro.-in-law Joseph Gray of Newtown, right in Est. of father-in-law Jacob Gray, Sr., 29 Mar. 1712. Samuel Umberfield of New Haven assigned to bro.-in-law Jacob Gray right in Est. of father-in-law Jacob Gray.

Inv. of Sarah Gray, who d. in Stratford, 16 Dec. 1716, taken 2 Feb. 1716/7. Adm'n on estate of Sarah widow of Jacob Gray, Sr., was granted to her son-in-law Charles Lane.

Jacob conveyed 11 acres to dau. Rebecca Gray for her portion, 6 May 1690. Jacob, Sr., in case son Jacob marry with Hannah Seeley the dau. of Lt. Nathaniel and leave her a widow, she shall have north-east end of my house during widowhood. He conveyed land to son Joseph, 20 Feb. 1707/8; also to son Jacob, with reservation for himself and wife Sarah. He conveyed to son Joseph, 24 Dec. 1709, reserving life use to himself and wife Sarah, and Joseph with his bro. Jacob obligated themselves to pay father and mother £5 a year and to pay portions to daus. of Jacob, Sr.

Child [by first wife], recorded at Fairfield:
    Rebecca, b. 1 Jan. 1670 [1670/1].

Children [by second wife], recorded at Fairfield:
    Sarah, b. 9 Oct. 1677, prob. m. Samuel Humphreville [Umberfield] of West Haven.
    Mary, b. 7 July 1679; m. Isaac Jennings.

✕Jacob, b. 10 Dec. 16 [81], d. at Greenfield, 26 Dec. 1742 ae. abt. 61; will 21 Oct. 1742, proved 13 Jan. 1742/3; m. Hannah Seeley, dau. of Lt. Nathaniel.
✕Joseph, b. [say 1683]; m. Sarah ———.
Joanna, m. Charles Lane.

Gray, Henry, s. of Henry.

Born about 1653; d. at Westport, 21 Nov. 1731 in 87 [77?] yr. (g. s.).
He testified 1692, ae. abt. 39, at Disbrow witch trial, and called Jacob Gray his brother.
Married (1) ———.
Married (2) about 1700, Hannah, widow of Samuel Gunn, and dau. of Andrew Sanford.
Married (3) Margaret ———, who d. at Westport, 29 Aug. 1754.
Will 19 Nov. 1731, proved 21 Dec. 1731; wife Margret; sons Samuel, Isaac, William, David; gr. son Benjamin Gray; gr. dau. Elizabeth Gray; daus. Deborah Dickason, Mary Crane, Martha Gray.

Children [by first wife], all bapt. at Fairfield, 30 Apr. 1699:

✕Isaac, d. at Westport, 7 Nov. 1745; m. ———.
✕Henry, d. at Westport, 29 May 1713 [Pro. Rec.]; m. (1) Sarah ———; m. (2) Elizabeth ———.
✕William, d. at Westport, 27 Aug. 1761; m. (1) 23 Dec. 1714, Abigail Coley, dau. of Samuel, who d. abt. 1715; m. (2) 31 Oct. 1716, Elizabeth Meeker, bapt. 29 Mar. 1696, d. at Westport, 6 July 1772.
David.
Deborah, m. ——— Dickerson.
Mary, m. ——— Crane.

Child [by second wife]:

✕Samuel, bapt. 25 June 1704; m. (1) 24 Oct. 1734, Eleanor Sturgis, dau. of Christopher, b. 19 Oct. 1704, d. 4 Feb. 1762 in 58 yr. (g. s.); m. (2) at Westport, 19 June 1763, Joanna Stone of Providence, who d. 15 Jan. 1770.

Child [by third wife]:

Martha, bapt. 6 Mar. 1714/5; m. (1) in 1731, John Nott; m. (2) at Westport, 15 July 1759, Joseph Patchen.

Green, John.

Records of this man are meagre and confusing. Born abt. 1614, he testified 28 Nov. 1672, then ae. abt. 58, regarding the settlement of Fairfield, hence was an original settler. Records of the Hartford Particular Court locate him at Fairfield in 1649 and 1654. With Ann Greene (presumably his wife) he witnessed a Fairfield deed, 1659. He entered his lands for record, 26 Mar. 1669, and other purchases in 1681 and 1683.

A John Green had a son John b. at New Haven, 26 Dec. 1651, but otherwise does not appear in New Haven records. He may be the same whose wife Mary d. at Stamford, 14 Nov. 1657; and who m. there (2) Sept. 1658, Martha Finch, presumably widow of John. He was Deputy for Stamford, Oct. 1668, May and Oct. 1669, May 1670, May and Oct. 1671, May and Oct. 1673, and Oct. 1674. We suppose him father of Joseph, Benjamin, and perhaps John, of Stamford in the next generation. Of these, Benjamin had a dau. Sarah bapt. at Fairfield, 10 May 1696.

No record of the family of John of Fairfield appears, unless he was father of the two children (given below) who were born in the 1690's. No distinction is made between a John, Sr. and Jr., yet we would not readily assume that the original John m. a young woman and became a father at 75 years of age or upwards. Attempts to identify him with the Stamford John do not solve this difficulty, and they seem to have been distinct individuals. However that may be, we shall assume that the original John of Fairfield was father of a younger John, to whom all the *following* records and statements pertain.

He m. Hannah Hobby, dau. of John of Greenwich; she m. (2) Cornelius Bunkham, and d. at Westport, 15 Oct. 1749. She was called Hannah Bunkham in her father's will, 1707.

He gave his negro Harry, 24 June 1699, freedom from slavery after his own decease, only Harry to work five years for any master for £20 which he shall add to my estate for use of my sons, and to pay my father Hobby for boarding him. [Fairfield Deeds.]

He disposed of his Est. to wife Hannah, son John, and dau. Hannah Green, 1702 [Fairfield Deeds]. Cornelius and Hannah Bunkham of Fairfield conveyed 1712 to our son John Green right in Est. of his father John Green dec'd.

Hannah Buncom was bapt. at Fairfield, 16 Sept. 1705; the two Green children were bapt. same date.

Children, bapt. at Fairfield 16 Sept. 1705:

XJohn, b. [say 1690], d. at Norwalk in 1752; will 10 Mar. 1752, proved 8 May 1752; m. Rebecca Gregory, dau. of Thomas.
Hannah.

Gregory, Henry.

William Gregory of Nottingham, Eng., Gent., in his will 18 June 1650, proved 5 Feb. 1651, gave a legacy to his bro. Henry Gregory, and £5 to each of Henry's children, except £10 to "my Cousin Perrie, my said brother Henry's daughter", they being now in New England (but apparently the last statement does not apply to Cousin Perrie).

He was of Springfield by 1643. A shoemaker, of Stratford, his workmanship was complained of 1647; he was spoken of as an old man, and his sons John and Judah and dau. the wife of William Crooker testified. Died at Stratford in 1655.

Inv. 19 June 1655, taken by John Welles and Thomas Fairchild. Eldest son John, and other children (not named).

Children (record incomplete):

Daughter, m. ——— Perry; quite likely remained in England.
+John.
Daughter, m. William Crooker.
+Judah.
Elizabeth, d. at Norwalk, 24 Jan. 1680 [1680/1]; m. Richard Webb.

Gregory, John, s. of Henry. Deputy for Norwalk, Oct. 1659, Oct. 1662, May 1663, May 1665, Oct. 1667, May 1668, May and Oct. 1669, Oct. 1670, Oct. 1671, May 1672, May 1674, Oct. 1675, Oct. 1677, May 1679, Oct. 1680, May 1681.

Admitted member of New Haven Court, 24 Feb. 1644/5; shoemaker, early rem. from New Haven to Norwalk, where he d. in 1689; m. Sarah ———, who d. in Oct. 1689.

Will 15 Aug. 1689; wife Sarah; children; two daus. to receive equally, and son-in-law James Benedict to have as much as' John Benedict had.

Will of Sarah Gregory, widow, of Norwalk, 9 Oct. 1689; friends, Mr. Thomas Hanford and Sergt. John Platt, overseers; witnesses, John Fitch and James Betts. Inv. 28 Oct. 1689. Agreement 1 Nov. 1689; sons-in-law John Benedict, James Benedict; sons John, Jakin, Judah, Joseph, Thomas Gregory.

Children:

+John, b. [say 1636].
+Jachin, b. [say 1640].
+Judah, b. [say 1642].
Joseph, bapt. at New Haven, 26 July 1646.*
+Thomas, bapt. at New Haven, 19 Mar. 1648.
Phebe, b. [say 1650]; m. at Norwalk, 11 Nov. 1670, John Benedict.
Sarah, b. [say 1654]; m. at Norwalk, 10 May 1676, James Benedict.

Gregory, Judah, s. of Henry.

Settled in Springfield, Mass., and there m. 20 June 1643, Sarah Burt; she m. (2) 4 Sept. 1649, Henry Wakelee of Stratford. Samuel Gregory was called uncle of Samuel Summers.

Children:

+Samuel, b. [say 1645].
Sarah, b. [say 1647]; m. by 1668, Henry Summers.

Gregory, John, s. of John. Deputy for Norwalk, Oct. 1695.

Married at New Haven, 18 Oct. 1663, Elizabeth Moulthrop.

Children, recorded at Norwalk:

Elizabeth, b. Jan. 1665.
Sarah, b. Dec. 1667.
Jonathan, b. June 1671.
Abigail, b. June 1672.
Mary, b. Dec. 1674.
John, b. abt. 1676 (no record), d. 18 Jan. 1751 in 75 yr.; m. (1) abt. 1704 ———; m. (2) abt. 1717, Mary Smith, dau. of Ebenezer and Clement (Denton) of Long Island.

---

* A Joseph Gregory m. Hannah Russell, dau. of John of New Haven, b. 17 Feb. 1689; and conveyed inherited Russell land with her in 1730.

Gregory, Jachin, s. of John.   Deputy for Norwalk, May 1695.
Inv. 22 Feb. 1697 [1697/8].   Ages of children: Thomas 25,
Samuel 23, Matthew 19, Jachin 15, Mary 28, Sarah 20.   Adm'n
granted to Mary Gregory and her two eldest sons.

Children, recorded at Norwalk:

> Mary, b. 5 Dec. 1669; m. Joseph Bouton.
> John, b. 25 Jan. 1670 [1670/1], d. y.
> +Thomas, b. 17 Jan. 1672 [1672/3].
> Samuel, b. 10 Mar. 1675/6.
> Sarah, b. 15 Sept. 1678; m. John Seymour.
> Matthew, b. 17 Dec. 1680, d. May 1777; Deacon; Lt.; m. Hannah
> ———, who d. 29 June 1767 ae. 80.
> Jachin, b. 10 May 1682, d. in 1747; m. Wait Taylor, dau. of John, b.
> abt. 1693.

Gregory, Judah, s. of John.

Married at Norwalk, Hannah Hoyt, dau. of Walter.
Removed to Danbury, and d. in 1733.

Children, recorded at Norwalk:

> Hannah, b. 24 Sept. 1665.
> John, b. 17 Mar. 1668.
> Percy, b. 11 Feb. 1671; [m. James Crofut?].
> Joseph, b. 16 July 1674; m. (recorded Woodbury, without date, he
> called of Danbury) abt. 1701, Hannah Preston.
> Lydia, b. 9 Jan. 1676 [1676/7]; m. (1) abt. 1697, Joseph Forward;
> m. (2) Thomas Wildman.
> Josiah, b. 13 July 1679.
> Benjamin, b. 26 Mar. 1682.

Gregory, Thomas, s. of John.

Bapt. at New Haven, 19 Mar. 1648; d. at Norwalk in 1693.
He received a grant from Norwalk, for service as a soldier in
K. Philip's War.
Married (rec. Norwalk) 25 Dec. 1679, Elizabeth Pardee, dau.
of George of New Haven.   She m. (2) Lt. John Olmstead.
Inv. Nov. 1693; £356.   Son and daus.
Rebecca chose Ebenezer Gregory for guardian (apparently
1705).   The Adm'rs have paid to the children Ebenezer, Phebe,

and Rebecca, 1707. John Benedict and Elizabeth Olmstead, Adm'rs of Est. of Thomas Gregory, gave receipt to the Adm'rs of Est. of Lt. John Olmstead.

Children, recorded at Norwalk:

Martha, b. 31(?) Apr. 1680.
Ebenezer, b. abt. 1683, d. 30 May 1760 ae. 77; m. at Norwalk, 13 Dec. 1711, Mary Fitch, dau. of John.
Phebe, m. Thomas Hurlbut.
Rebecca, b. abt. 1691; m. John Green.

Gregory, Samuel, s. of Judah.

Came to Stratford with his mother when she m. Henry Wakelee. He m. Rebecca Wheeler, dau. of Ephraim, and on 21 Apr. 1682 had land recorded at Fairfield in right of his wife Rebecca, being her legacy from her father Ephraim Wheeler, dec'd.
Inv. of Sergt. Samuel of Stratfield, June 1702; adm'n granted, 18 June 1702, to widow Rebecca and sons Samuel and Benjamin. Three sons, five daus. (not named).
Children [named in Fairfield Deeds]: Samuel, Benjamin, Ebenezer Gregory; Abigail wife of Edward Lacy; Sarah wife of James Seeley; Martha wife of George Hull; Rebecca wife of Ezekiel Sanford; Johanna wife of Jonathan Rudd.

Children:

Rebecca, b. abt. 1673, d. at Redding, Nov. 1765 ae. 92 (g. s.); m. Ezekiel Sanford.
Abigail, b. [say 1676]; m. (rec. Fairfield) 23 July 1702, Edward Lacy.
+Samuel, b. abt. 1678.
+Benjamin, b. [say 1680].
Sarah, b. [say 1682]; m. at Stratfield, 21 Jan. 1702/3, James Seeley.
Martha, b. [say 1690]; m. abt. 1711, George Hull.
Johanna, b. [say 1693]; m. (rec. Norwich) 27 Oct. 1720, Jonathan Rudd.
+Ebenezer, bapt. at Stratfield, 6 Dec. 1696.

Gregory, Thomas, s. of Jachin.

Born at Norwalk, 17 Jan. 1672/3; d. there in 1712.
Married Elizabeth Ketchum, dau. of Joseph. She m. (2) 13 Aug. 1719, Moses Fountain.

Widow Elizabeth appointed Adm'x, 6 Apr. 1712. Inv. £536. Ages of the four children stated.

Benjamin Gregory of Goshen, Samuel Gregory of New Fairfield, and Gershom Bennett and wife Sarah of Ridgefield, conveyed 1751 to David Whelpley of Norwalk, land from father Thomas Gregory dec'd [Norwalk Deeds].

Children, births recorded in Probate Records:

> Benjamin, b. 17 Dec. 1702.
> Samuel, b. 22 Mar. 1704/5.
> Elizabeth, b. 22 Sept. 1707; m. David Whelpley.
> Sarah, b. 4 Feb. 1709/10; m. (1) Ebenezer Nash; m. (2) Gershom Bennett, of Ridgefield.

Gregory, Samuel, s. of Samuel. Ens., Stratfield company, Oct. 1727.

Born about 1678; Ens. Samuel d. at Stratfield, 11 Dec. 1743 in 66 yr. (g. s.).

Married at Fairfield, 28 Dec. 1699, Mary "Sillaven."

Will 8 Feb. 1742/3, proved 4 Feb. 1743/4; wife Mary; daus. Beulah Treadwell, Miriam Hartshorn; eldest son Thaddeus; son Enoch; bro. Ebenezer Gregory, £30; gr. son Gilead Treadwell; gr. son Selah Gregory; gr. son Gilead Gregory; residue to sons Thaddeus and Enoch, Exec'rs.

Children, bapt. at Stratfield:

> ×Thaddeus, bapt. 13 July 1701, d. 30 Dec. 1777 in 77 yr. (g. s., Stratfield); m. Rebecca Smith, dau. of Samuel, b. 20 Mar. 1704.
> Beulah, bapt. 8 Aug. 1703; m. ——— Treadwell.
> ×Enoch, bapt. 28 Dec. 1707, d. abt. 1776; will 23 Jan. 1764, proved 12 Jan. 1777; m. Esther Smith, dau. of Samuel, bapt. 22 May 1709, d. 16 July 1790 in 83 yr. (g. s., Stratfield).
> Gilead, bapt. 25 May 1712.
> Miriam, bapt. 3 Jan. 1714; m. (rec. Stratfield and Norwich) 2 Nov. 1732, Ebenezer Hartshorn.
> Jemima, bapt. 1 Oct. 1717 (at home, because of sickness, Mr. Bennet and James Seeley, present), d. y.

Gregory, Benjamin, s. of Samuel.

He d. at Stratfield in 1738; m. Abigail Sturges, dau. of John. Will 25 Aug. 1733, proved 9 Feb. 1737/8; wife Abigail; chil-

dren Ithamar Gregory, Abiah Meeker, Mercy Coley; children
Ebenezer and Zaccheus Gregory; if either of latter die under 21
without issue, my bro. Ebenezer Gregory to have his portion,
bro. Samuel Gregory.

Children, two bapt. at Stratfield:

Abigail, m. 1 Aug. 1722, Samuel Meeker.
Mercy, bapt. 31 Oct. 1708; m. 22 July 1728, John Coley.
XIthamar, bapt. 8 Oct. 1710.
Ebenezer.
Zaccheus.

Gregory, Ebenezer, s. of Samuel.

Bapt. at Stratfield, 6 Dec. 1696, d. there in 1750; m. Mary
Odell, dau. of Samuel.

Adm'n granted, 3 Apr. 1750, to Mary Gregory.

Moses Johnson and Naomi his wife of Hanover, Morris County,
N. J., conveyed 1755 to Jedediah Gregory of Stratford, land set
to Naomi out of Est. of Ebenezer Gregory. [Stratford Deeds.]

Griffin, Hugh.

An earlier man of this name lived at Sudbury, Mass., to whom
the Stratford settler may have been related.

He m. (Stratford rec.) 20 July 1652, Dorothy Skidmore, dau.
of Thomas.

His wife Dorothy d. at Stratford, and was buried about the last
of Apr. 1670. He m. (2) Mary, widow of Peter Norton.*

He sold land at Fairfield to Alexander Bryan by 1678.

He d. at Stratford, 10 Sept. 1691.

Will of Hugh Grifen of Orinage, 9 Sept. 1690; half of lands
in commons of Stratford to my sons John, Thomas, and Samuel;
my wife's dau. Mary Norton; her elder dau. Abigail now wife of
Joseph Bears of Fairfield has received portion; my daus. Mary
and Dorithy; youngest dau. Hannah (under 18); son Francis one
half of land in Stratford commons and residue; my wife. Inv.
17 Sept. 1691. Children, Francis ae. 19 and Hannah ae. 16.
Widow Mary.

---

* Swan's notes state that she was dau. of Francis Andrews of Fairfield, but we have
not found the proof.

Children [by first wife], recorded at Stratford:

╫John, b. 25 Sept. 1654.
╫Samuel, b. 22 Feb. 1656 [1656/7].
Mary, b. 26 Apr. 1659.
╫Thomas, b. 7 May 1662.
Son, b. 14 Nov. 1664.
Sarah, b. 2 June 1667; [name apparently changed to Dorothy after death of her mother Dorothy two yrs. later].
Hannah, b. 12 Jan. 1669 [1669/70], bur. last of Apr. 1670.

Children [by second wife]:

╫Francis, b. abt. 1672.
Hannah, b. abt. 1675; m. 26 Feb. 1701/2, James Wakelee.

Griffin, John, s. of Hugh.

Born at Stratford, 25 Sept. 1654.
He m. Sarah ———.

Children:*

Samuel, b. 14 Aug. 1698; settled in Newtown.
Hugh.
✕John; perhaps the John of Redding who m. Sarah Nash.

Griffin, Samuel, s. of Hugh.

Born at Stratford, 22 Feb. 1656/7, d. at Derby in 1691; m. Elizabeth ———.

Apprentice of [his gr. father] Thomas Skidmore, and apparently served in King Philip's War [see *Conn. Col. Rec.* vol. 3, p. 39].

Inv. Derby, 14 July 1691. Widow Elizabeth; children's ages, Phebe 6, Elizabeth 4.

Children:

Phebe, b. abt. 1685; m. Obadiah Rogers, of Huntington, L. I.
Elizabeth, b. abt. 1687; m. Jonathan Wicks, of Huntington, L. I.

---

* The first rec. at Stratford; the other two are given on authority of *Hist. of Stratford*. Was another son Jonathan, who m. at New Haven, 16 May 1717, Mehitabel Mallory? Her sister Elizabeth m. John Booth of Stratford, who on 22 Apr. 1721 "to incourige my Brother in law Jonathan Griffin of Newhaven to settle with me on my farm in Ripton" gave him four acres for a homelot. Jonathan became the pioneer of Quaker Farms, Oxford.

Griffin, Thomas, s. of Hugh.

Born at Stratford, 7 May 1662; d. Feb. or Mar. 1703.

Married Jane, dau. of James Blackman, b. 26 Oct. 1668, who had previously been wife of Joseph Russell. She m. (3) 24 May 1698, James Clark, Jr. In Stratford Deeds 1709, mention of Jane Clark (widow of Thomas Griffin) and her dau. Miriam Griffin. At Court 8 Apr. 1703, the will and Inv. of Thomas Griffin were approved. The witnesses, Edward Hinman and Francis Griffin, made oath 25 Feb. 1702/3 to the will which was apparently nuncupative; wife Jane; dau. Miriam; Mr. Samuel Fairchild, John Griffin, Edward Hinman, and Francis Griffin, overseers.

Child:

Miriam.

Griffin, Francis, s. of Hugh.

Born at Stratford about 1672; d. 24 Sept. 1759 ae. 89 (g. s., Woodbridge).

Married (1) 25 Nov. 1697, Sarah Curtis. She was dau. of Jonathan, b. 12 Sept. 1673, d. July 1707. He m. (2) (rec. Stratford) 30 May 1708, Jemima Darling of Jamaica; she d. 12 Dec. 1775 ae. 85 (g. s., Woodbridge). No issue.

Will 19 Apr. 1747, proved Dec. 1759; wife Jemima. In Feb. 1761, Griffin Bradley of New Haven in behalf of Samuel Griffin of Newtown, nephew of Mr. Francis Griffin, appealed.

Will of Jemima, 3 July 1760, proved 19 May 1778; two daus. of my sister Hannah Winter of New York; residue to Thomas Darling, Esq., of New Haven.

Grimes, ———.

The surname is a variant of Graeme or Graham. Henry Grimes of Hartford had several children, of whom the three sons were Benjamin (b. abt. 1662, of Hartford), John (b. abt. 1665), and Joseph (b. abt. 1667, of Wethersfield). The history of John has not been learned, and he may have been the unknown Grimes who m. Mary Harvey, dau. of Josiah of Fairfield, b. 25 May 1669. Mary renewed Covenant at Fairfield Church, 5 Apr. 1696.

Child, bapt. at Fairfield:

> Joseph, b. abt. 1691, bapt. 5 Apr. 1696, d. at Stratford, 4 Mar.
> 1716/7; in 25 yr. (g. s.). Inv. 21 Apr. 1717. Estate distributed
> 25 Mar. 1718 to uncle Thomas Harvey, aunt Martha Harvey, and
> Samuel Peat Jr. and wife Abigail (sister of Thomas Harvey). He
> m. at Stratford, 14 Apr. 1715, Hannah Beardsley, who d. 4 Jan.
> 1715/6; in 22 yr. (g. s.). Only child: Joseph, b. 27 Dec. 1715, d.
> 30 Jan. 1715/6.

Grimes, William.

Of Greenwich, will 18 July 1671; estate to be disposed by
Joseph Mead, John Reynolds, and Eliphalet Jones for good of
the town. Inv. 1671.

Groom, Edward.

Married, doubtless early in 1690, Miriam, widow of James
Blackman, dau. of Moses Wheeler. She was b. 28 Mar. 1647.

Child of Edward and Miriam, recorded at Stratford:

> Mary, b. 19 Nov. 1690; m. (1) 23 Nov. 1716, Samuel Pitman; m.
> (2) [21 Mar. 1720/1], Joseph Benedict, of Ridgefield. She was
> the "daughter Benedict" mentioned in will of her father-in-law
> Jonathan Pitman. In 1727 Joseph Benedict and Mary his wife
> of Ridgefield conveyed to brother Zechariah Blackman of Strat-
> ford, land that descended from Moses Wheeler, Sr.

Groves, Philip. Deputy (Stratford) to Conn. Leg., Apr.
1642, May 1648, May 1651, May 1653, May 1654, May 1655,
Oct. 1655, Feb. 1657, May 1660, Oct. 1660, May 1661, Oct.
1661, Oct. 1662, May 1663, Oct. 1663, May 1665; Judge (Stratford), May 1654, May 1655, May 1656; war committee for
Stratford, May 1653, Oct. 1654.

Goodman Grove, of Milford, shoemaker, testified 1647; leather
sealer for Stratford, Oct. 1656; Grand Juror for Stratford, May
1660.

Mr. Philip d. at Stratford, 10 Feb. 1675 [1675/6].

Will of Philip Grove, "Ruling Elder", 30 Jan. 1672/3; wife
Ann; four motherless grandchildren Nathaniel, Hannah, Sarah,
and Ruth Porter; son-in-law Nathaniel Porter; sister Susanna

Grant, Widow, at Hanwell near Banbury; brother John Groves in parish of Leget Grove three miles from Bristol; Rebecca Andrews that formerly lived with me; Nathaniel Humiston my servant; overseers, Mr. Israel Chauncey, Capt. William Curtis, and Mr. Joseph Hawley. Codicil 25 Jan. 1676; dau. Elizabeth Porter* and her child John Porter; friend John Pickett, Sr., to be an overseer. Inv. 14 Feb. 1675/6.

Child:

> Hannah, m. Nathaniel Porter.

Grover Samuel.

Came in *Truelove*, 1635, ae. 16. He had a lot in Fairfield, which was sold to Alexander Bryan, and by him to Roger Knapp before Oct. 1654.

Grumman, John.

Settled in Fairfield and d. in 1685; m. Sarah Try, dau. of Michael, who d. in 1691. In 1653/4 he entered land and dwelling house purchased from Richard Lattin which was sometime Timothy Ford's.

Will 2 June 1685, proved 3 Nov. 1685; sons John, Samuel, Thomas, Michael; dau. Sarah; wife Sarah; legacy to Thomas Oliver; friends Jehu Burr and Simon Couch, overseers.

Inv., widow Sarah Groman, 8 Apr. 1691; John Gruman, Samuel Jennings, and Samuel Roberson appointed adm'rs. Distribution made to John Gruman, Sarah wife of Samuel Jennings, and Mary Gruman dau. of Samuel dec'd.

Children:

> +John.
> +Samuel.
> +Thomas.
> Michael, d. in 1691, unm. Inv. made 8 Apr. 1691; est. distributed to Mary dau. of Samuel Gruman, to John Gruman, and Sarah Jennings.
> Elizabeth, d. between 1677 and 1685, unm.
> Sarah, m. abt. 1691, Samuel Jennings.

---

* She of course was the second wife of his son-in-law.

Grumman, John, s. of John.

Married (1) Esther Thompson, dau. of John, b. about 1654.
Married (2) Esther, widow of Nathaniel Perry, and dau. of
Richard Lyon. When common lands were set out to the heirs
of Richard Lyon, Sr., 10 Mar. 1723/4, Esther's portion was set
to her three Perry children and to Samuel Grumman "a repre-
sentative of his mother Esther." This proves that Samuel was the
only surviving child by Esther Lyon; as there is proof that the
eldest son John was by the first wife, she must have been mother
of the other children unless there was an intervening unknown
wife between Esther Thompson and Esther Lyon.

"Hester Groment", aged 34, testified 1692 in the Disbrow witch
trial; this was the second wife.

Inv. 20 May 1695; left a widow, four sons and a dau. On
13 Feb. 1701, John Gruman represented to the Court that his
uncle Sergt. John Thompson together with Ezekiel Sanford were
adm'rs of the Est. of his father John. Joseph, son of John,
was of age to receive his portion, 30 Nov. 1709. On 23 May 1710,
John Gruman (who had succeeded Thompson and Sanford as
adm'r), made a division with the consent of Joseph Gruman,
Ezekiel Sanford in behalf of Thomas Gruman, David Sherman in
behalf of Samuel Gruman, "my sister Abigail having received her
portion."

Children [by first wife] :
+John, b. abt. 1680.
  Abigail, b. 1 Aug. 1685; m. 20 Jan. 1709, Joseph Jennings.
  Joseph, b. abt. 1688; sold 13 Apr. 1716, calling himself yeoman, all
    right in Try's long lot, his own share and that of his brother
    Thomas; soon after removed to Newark, N. J., where he was
    living 1730; m. and had children, including Nehemiah (1718-1797)
    of Wilton and Ichabod (1723-1789) of Newark.
  Thomas, b. abt. 1690, d. at Newark, N. J., 1714; yeoman, will
    26 Mar. 1714, named brother Joseph (Exec'r) and brother Samuel
    (under age).

Child [by second wife] :
  Samuel, b. abt. 1694, d. at Norwalk, 21 Aug. 1747 ae. 53 (g. s.) ; m.
    (called "late of Fairfield") at Norwalk, 10 Jan. 1721/2, Rebecca
    Betts, dau. of Daniel. She d. 24 May 1790 in 94 yr. (g. s.).

Grumman, Samuel, s. of John.

Died at Fairfield, 12 Mar. 1690/1.

Married Mary Hubbard, dau. of William; she m. (2) Jacob
Patchen. Mary Grumman, dau. of Mary, wife of Jacob Patchen,
was bapt. at Fairfield, 24 Mar. 1694/5.

Inv. 25 Mar. 1690/1; left widow.

Child:

> Mary, b. abt. 1690, d. in 1780; m. Gideon Morehouse. She and her
> husband joined other Grumman heirs in a law suit 1714, for
> possession of land claimed under will of Michael Try.

Grumman, Thomas, s. of John.

Died at Fairfield, 10 Mar. 1690/1.

Married Mary Couch, dau. of Simon. She m. (2) James
Bennett, shipwright, of Stratfield; and (3) by prenuptial contract
dated 24 Oct. 1727, Samuel Jennings, Sr. [widower of Sarah
Grumman].

Inv. 8 Apr. 1691 presented by widow Mary. The widow was
to have what remained after payment of debts, except the entailed
part of the Est.

On 11 Aug. 1697, James Bennett, shipwright, of Stratford, sold
land which was granted by the town to John Grumman. On 19
Sept. 1704, Mary Bennett, formerly the wife of Thomas Grumant,
approved a bill of sale made by Samuel Couch. [Fairfield Deeds.]

Child:

> Sarah, b. 6 Mar. 1690/1, d. 30 Mar. 1690/1.

Grumman, John, s. of John 2d.

Born at Fairfield about 1680.

Married Ruth ———, with whom he conveyed 1710, land
bounded on land of sister Abigail.

John Grumman of Fairfield conveyed 1737 to son John of
Norwalk, land inherited from his uncle Thomas Grumman dec'd.

Children, recorded at Fairfield (first four bapt. 5 July 1713):

> Esther, b. 1 Jan. 1704 [1704/5].
> Silence, b. 15 Apr. 1708.
> John, b. 3 July 1710; settled in Wilton; m. Damaris ———, by whom
> he had two children bapt. at Fairfield: David, 21 Apr. 1734; and
> Jedediah, 12 Jan. 1735/6.

Thankful, b. 5 Jan. 1712/3; m. (rec. Norwalk) 30 Oct. 1734, Ephraim Lockwood.

Elizabeth, b. 3 July 1717, bapt. 4 Aug. 1717.

Ebenezer, b. 7 July 1720, bapt. 21 Aug. 1720, d. at South Salem, Westchester Co., N. Y., 29 Aug. 1793; m. at Ridgefield, 12 Nov. 1742, Deborah ———. He had two children recorded at Ridgefield, and others bapt. at South Salem.

Guire, Luke.

The surname is also spelled Guyer and Wire.

His mother was Mary Adams, dau. of Edward; she m. (2) ——— Merwin and (3) Stephen Sherwood. The will of Mary Sherwood, 22 Mar. 1711/2, proved 7 May 1712; gr. son Luke Guire; gr. daus. Hellinah, Mary, Hannah Guire; gr. son Ebenezer Guire.

He m. Rebecca Odell, dau. of John; she m. (2) Robert Turney. Rebecca Guire renewed Covenant at Fairfield Church, 14 June 1696.

Inv. 11 Apr. 1699. Ages of children: Luke 10, Ebenezer 6, Elinah 7½, Mary 4, Hannah 2, John 9 months. Widow Rebecca to administer with her brother John Odell, Jr.

Samuel Hall, Jr., of Chestnut Ridge [Redding] conveyed 3 Feb. 1715/6 to Luke Guire of Fairfield, land from wife's father Luke Guire, referring to wife's brother Ebenezer Guire.

Children, bapt. at Fairfield:

XLuke, b. abt. 1689, bapt. 14 June 1696, d. at Westport, 10 May 1751; m. abt. 1711, Mary Adams, dau. of Nathan.

Helena, b. abt. 1691, bapt. 18 Apr. 1697, d. after 1752; called also Ellen and Eleanor; m. James Stewart, of Norwalk and Kent.

Ebenezer, b. abt. 1693, bapt. 18 Apr. 1697.

Mary, b. abt. 1695, bapt. 14 June 1696; m. Jonah Turney, with whom she conveyed, 25 Jan. 1722/3, land from father.

Hannah, b. abt. 1697, bapt. 18 Apr. 1697, living 1752; m. (1) Samuel Hall; m. (2) after 1730, Jonathan Squire.

John, b. abt. July 1698, bapt. 21 Aug. 1698, d. before 1712.

Hale, Thomas. Granted 50 acres for Pequot War service, Oct. 1671.

Settled first in Roxbury, Mass.; freeman, May 1634. Went to Hartford with first settlers, and served in Pequot War, 1637, receiving a lot in Soldier's Field, Hartford. Returned to Roxbury to m. Feb. 1639/40, Jane Lord, a servant, member of Roxbury church; rem. from Hartford to Norwalk by 1651, with bro. Samuel. In Charlestown, Mass., he m. (2) 14 Dec. 1659, Mary Nash, dau. of William, and was made freeman there 1671; the church in Charlestown admitted him 14 Aug. 1670 by letter from Norwalk. In Norwalk, in 1674, Thomas Hale "that was formerly an inhabitant accepted on his returning."

Winthrop, under date 23 Mar. 1666, states of Martha Peck, ae. 45, wife of [Dea.] Paul Peck of Hartford: "She is sister of Sam: Hale of Wethersfield & hath a brother Tho: Hale at Charltown."*
Inv. 19 Feb. 1678 [1678/9]; estate at Charlestown and Norwalk. [Fairfield Pro.]

His widow was relieved in Charlestown, 1679, was adm. to the church in 1687, and was living 1696. A dau. by the second wife, Mary, m. at Charlestown, 24 Mar. 1697/8, Elias Brigden.

His bro. Samuel served also in the Pequot War; was Deputy for Norwalk, Oct. 1656, Feb. and Oct. 1657, May and Oct. 1660, and for Wethersfield, May 1665; removing permanently to the latter place. He too received a colonial grant, for 60 acres, for the Pequot War service, May 1671. The grant for 110 acres to the two brothers was not laid out until 1703, when Thomas Dickinson of Glastonbury, who had purchased the rights of the heirs of Thomas and Samuel, had the land surveyed to him.

The town of Norwalk, 12 Dec. 1676, granted to John Belden the remainder of the swamp that shall be left, "when his Father Hales is laid out."†

A child by his first wife was Thomas, bapt. at Hartford, 19 Jan. 1650 [1650/1].

Hall, Francis. Deputy for Stratford, May 1661, May 1676, Oct. 1677, Oct. 1678, May and Oct. 1679, May and Oct. 1680, May 1685.

An original signer of New Haven Covenant, 4 June 1639. Had three in family 1641. Brought John and Thomas Whitehead from England, nephews of Thomas Alcott in "the Bay" [Mass.] and of

---

* For this valuable excerpt, which discloses the maiden name of the mother of the Hartford Pecks, we are under special obligation to Col. Charles E. Banks.

† From Hall's *Norwalk;* Selleck appears to have read "Hales" as "Haies", and may be right.

Mr. Alcott of Roxbury. Bought land from Thomas Fugill which he sold to John Meigs, 1649, and rem. to Stratford. He purchased land in Fairfield in 1654, and in 1659 in Stratford. On 12 Apr. 1654, being then of Stratford, he purchased with his wife Elizabeth, land in Fairfield from Thomas Wheeler, yeoman. Married (1) Elizabeth ———, who d. at Fairfield, 6 July 1665. She inherited a house and land in England, which he sold about 1664, and in 1687 their son Isaac entered a caveat to prevent his father from selling Fairfield lands, which he claimed for the children of Elizabeth. Married (2) at Stratford, last of Oct. 1665, Dorothy, widow of John Blackman. She was dau. of Rev. Henry Smith of Wethersfield, and m. (3) early in 1692, Mark St. John of Norwalk, and (4) Dea. Isaac Moore of Farmington. He d. (rec. Fairfield) 5 Mar. 1689/90. Will of Francis "of Stratford." 6 May 1686, proved 14 Mar. 1689 [1689/90]; wife, referring to her last husband John Blackman; sons Isaac, Samuel; daus. Mary, Elizabeth, Rebecca, Hannah.

Children [by first wife]:

+Isaac.

Mary, b. abt. 1635 [Winthrop called her ae. 24 in 1659], d. at Stratford in 1716; will 1 Dec. 1714, proved 28 Nov. 1716; Samuel Hall, son of brother Samuel; cousin Joseph Blackman and his dau. Sarah; cousin Benjamin Blackman and his wife; Josiah Blackman; cousin Adam Blackman; cousin Rebeckah Curtiss; brother Ebenezer Blackman's three sons, Ebenezer, Jonathan and Nathan; cousins William and Abigail Smith.

Elizabeth, d. at Stratford in 1694; Inv. 30 Apr. 1694; adm'n granted to bro. Samuel Hall; on 6 Nov. 1694, Samuel being dec'd, his widow Susannah was appointed to complete the adm'n.

Rebecca, d. (rec. Fairfield) 2 Mar. 1690.

Hannah, m. at Stratford, 14 July 1674, Joseph Blackman.

+Samuel.

Hall, Isaac, s. of Francis. Granted £30, Oct. 1690, for service as Chirurgeon to the Army. Granted 150 acres, May 1697, having served as surgeon and lost one son in service.

Physician, of Stratfield, where he d. in May 1714.

Married (rec. Fairfield) 16 Jan. 1666 [1666/7], Lydia Knapp, dau. of Nicholas; she d. in Dec. 1716.

Isaac, Francis, John, Mary, and Abigail, children of Isaac Hall, Sr., bapt. at Stratfield, 28 Apr. 1700.

Nuncupative will of Dr. Hall, 13 May 1714; wife Lydia; dau. Sarah; gr. dau. Lydia Lane; Inv. 25 May 1714. James Bennett, Sr., and Johannah Odell, testified to will 12 Oct. 1714. Adm'n to widow with her sons Francis and John. Will of Lydia, widow of Dr. Isaac, 1 Dec. 1716, proved 19 Dec. 1716; son John Hall; dau. Abigail Jacox and her children.

Agreement 23 Oct. 1714, between Sarah Hall by power from my husband Joseph Hall, and William Stites by marriage with Mary, and Thomas Jecox by marriage with Abigail, and Ezekiel Baldwin by marriage with Hannah, which are the daus. of the dec'd Dr. Isaac Hall, all resident in Queens County, N. Y.,— appoint our brethren Francis and John Hall of Stratfield our attorneys to adjust controversy with our cousin Samuel Hall, heir to our dec'd uncle Samuel Hall.

Isaac, Francis, John, and Jonathan Hall, all of Stratfield, for themselves and with authority from our Brethren that married our sisters Sarah, Elizabeth, Mary, Abigail, and Hannah, who with us are heirs to Est. of our father Mr. Isaac Hall, late of Stratfield; make agreement, 20 Jan. 1714/5, with Samuel Hall, only surviving son and heir of our dec'd uncle Mr. Samuel Hall also of Stratfield, with respect to the Est. of our grandfather Mr. Francis Hall also of Stratfield dec'd.

Children, recorded at Fairfield:

+Isaac, b. 8 Nov. 1667.
    Sarah, b. 3 Mar. 1668 [1668/9]; m. Joseph Hall, of Hempstead, L. I. They conveyed, 21 May 1717, to Francis and John Hall.
    Lydia, b. 21 Sept. 1670, d. y.
    Elizabeth, b. 11 Nov. 1672; m. Samuel Lane, of Rye, N. Y. They conveyed, 9 May 1717, to Francis and John Hall, right from father Isaac.
    Samuel, b. 14 Sept. 1674, d. y.; prob. the son who d. in war 1690.
+Francis, b. 26 Sept. 1676.
    John, b. 8 Feb. 1677 [1677/8], d. after a few hours.
+John, b. 3 Jan. 1679 [1679/80].
    Mary, b. 7 Aug. 1681; m. William Stites, of Queens Co., L. I.
    Abigail, b. 1 Apr. 1683; m. Thomas Jacocks, of Queens Co., L. I., 1714, of Stratfield 1717 when they conveyed to Francis and John Hall right from father Isaac.

+Jonathan, b. 2 Dec. 1684.
Hannah, m. Ezekiel Baldwin, of Hempstead, L. I. They conveyed,
22 May 1717, to Francis and John Hall, right from father Isaac.

Hall, Samuel, s. of Francis.

Served as soldier under Capt. Seeley, King Philip's War, and
in the Narragansett Fort Fight, Dec. 1675, fell with two bullets
in each thigh, but crawled away, cutlass in hand, and after great
suffering from exposure and loss of clothing, survived to receive
50 shillings in compensation from a grateful General Assembly
in 1678.

Called son of Francis, m. (1) (rec. Fairfield), 20 Mar. 1682/3,
Mary ———. She d. 1 Feb. 1685 [1685/6], and he m. (2) 16
Mar. 1686/7, Hannah ———, who d. 17 Nov. 1687.

He m. (3) [say 1688/9] Susannah ———; she m. (2) Dea.
Isaac Wheeler. Susannah Hall was adm. to full communion,
Stratfield Church, 5 Jan. 1695/6.

Inv. 8 Nov. 1694; Widow Susannah to administer with Lt.
James Bennett and Mr. Nathaniel Sherman. Names of children:
Samuel, David. On 18 Sept. 1699, Ens. Isaac Wheeler was
appointed to care for the estate, and to have the improvement of
it until the children reach 14 yrs.

The two surviving sons were mentioned in the will of their stepfather. The son Samuel sold land 22 Feb. 1715/6, his mother
Susannah Wheeler consenting.

Children by first wife:
  Francis, b. 27 Feb. 1683 [1683/4], d. y.
  Edward, b. 8 Jan. 1685 [1685/6], d. 12 Mar. 1686/7.

Child by second wife:
  James, d. 17 Dec. 1690.

Children by third wife:
  +Samuel, b. [say 1692]; renewed Covenant at Stratfield, 2 Nov. 1712;
    was only surviving son and heir 1714 when he made agreement with
    his cousins.
  David, b. [say 1694], d. unm. between 1712 and 1714; renewed
    Covenant at Stratfield, 26 Oct. 1712.

Hall, Isaac, s. of Isaac.

Born at Fairfield, 8 Nov. 1667; d. at Redding, 4 July 1741.

Married (rec. Fairfield) 24 Jan. 1689, Jane Burgis. Jane Hall and her child Isaac, belonging to Isaac Hall, Jr., bapt. at Stratfield, 11 Aug. 1695.

Will of Isaac of Redding, 17 Apr. 1736, proved 1 Aug. 1741; wife Jean; son Asa Hall; dau. Jean Squire; son Burgis Hall; daus. Lydia Judd, Anna Corns; gr. son David Hall, residue of land; son Joshua Hall, my smith's shop and cast irons. Witnesses: Moses Knapp, John Mallory, John Read. Asa, the Exec'r, was to have "my Doctor Books, Chirurgeons Implements & Carpenter Tools."

Children, recorded at Fairfield (bapt. at Stratfield except youngest):

David, b. 2 Jan. 1689/90.
Rebecca, b. 13 Jan. 1691, d. 3 Feb. 1691.
Isaac, b. 14 Oct. 1692, bapt. 11 Aug. 1695; m. and had son David, who chose Asa Hall for guardian, 27 Dec. 1739.
✕Samuel, b. 2 Oct. 1695, bapt. 17 Nov. 1695; of Chestnut Ridge, Redding; Est. distributed, 18 Mar. 1730; m. Hannah Guire, dau. of Luke, bapt. 18 Apr. 1697; she m. (2) Jonathan Squire.
Lydia, b. 25 Sept. 1698, bapt. 25 Sept. 1698; m. —— Judd.
Burgis, b. 8 Nov. 1701, bapt. 16 Nov. 1701; m. Abigail ——.
[Did she m. (2) at Redding, 12 Apr. 1761, Dea. Stephen Burr?]
Jesse, b. 14 Dec. 1703, bapt. 19 Dec. 1703.
✕Asa, b. 9 Feb. 1706, bapt. 17 Feb. 1706, d. at Danbury in 1771; adm'n on Est. granted 22 Apr. 1771; m. Rachel Meeker, dau. of Daniel.
✕Joshua, b. 4 Nov. 1708, bapt. 21 Nov. 1708, d. at Redding in 1789; adm'n on Est. granted 25 Sept. 1789; Capt.; m. —— Williams, dau. of Thomas.
Anna, b. 26 Dec. 1710, bapt. 1 July 1711, m. at Redding, 12 Nov. 1734, George Corns.
Jane, b. 15 Nov. 1712, bapt. 14 Dec. 1712, d. 24 July 1714.
Jane, b. 9 Oct. 1714, bapt. at Fairfield, 9 Jan. 1714/5; m. Zechariah Squire.

Hall, Francis, s. of Isaac. Sergeant, Stratfield Trainband.

Born at Fairfield, 26 Sept. 1676.

Married at Stratfield, 8 Dec. 1702, Margaret Stites; presumably dau. of Richard of Hempstead.

Will 16 June 1758, proved 6 Jan. 1761; son Richard, Exec'r;

gr. sons James and Eleazer Hall; gr. daus. Molly and Margaret Hall; daus. Rebecca Frost, Margaret Jackson; gr. daus. Hannah and Lois Hall.

Children, recorded at Stratfield:

> Rebecca, b. 23 Nov. 1703, bapt. 19 Dec. 1703; m. 24 Sept. 1723, Abner Frost.
>
> ✕Francis, b. 24 Aug. 1705, bapt. 26 Aug. 1705, d. 26 Feb. 1734/5 in 30 yr. (g. s., Stratfield); m. Ann Seeley, dau. of James. She m. (2) 7 Oct 1736, Zechariah Sanford.
>
> Margaret, b. 5 Oct. 1707, bapt. 12 Oct. 1707; m. (rec. Fairfield) 24 May 1727, Gabriel Jackson.
>
> Sarah, b. 18 Feb. 1710, bapt. 19 Mar. 1710, d. 25 Oct. 1717.
>
> Richard, b. 20 Apr. 1712, d. 28 May 1712.
>
> ✕Richard, b. 9 Apr. 1713, bapt. 12 Apr. 1713; will 27 May 1768, proved 14 June 1768; m. 30 June 1731, Hannah Booth, who d. in 1768.
>
> Benjamin, b. 13 Feb. 1716/7, bapt. 17 Feb. 1717, d. 25 Aug. 1738 in 21 yr. (g. s., Stratfield).

Hall, John, s. of Isaac.

Born at Fairfield, 3 Jan. 1679/80; d. at Stratfield, 17 Apr. 1749 in 71 yr. (g. s., Stratfield).

Married Abigail Summers, dau. of Henry.

He conveyed land to son Elnathan, 7 June 1743.

Will of John of Stratford, 26 Mar. 1749, proved 1 May 1749; wife Abigail; dau. Abigail wife of Ezra Hawley; son Zachariah Hall; three sons, Elnathan, John, Jabez. The widow and children made agreement for distribution, 13 Mar. 1750.

Children, recorded at Stratfield:

> Zachariah, bapt. 27 Apr. 1701.
>
> Abiah, bapt. 4 Nov. 1705, d. y.
>
> ✕Elnathan, bapt. 19 Aug. 1711, d. at New Fairfield in 1774; Capt.; m. (1) 28 Dec. 1732, Hannah Hawley, who d. 9 Apr. 1741 in 26 yr. (g. s., Stratfield); m. (2) Hannah ———.
>
> David, bapt. 28 Feb. 1714, d. y.
>
> Abigail, b. [late in 1715], d. 18 Apr. 1786 in 71 yr. (g. s., Stratfield); m. 30 Jan. 1734/5, Capt. Ezra Hawley.
>
> ✕John, bapt. 19 May 1717; m. (1) Sarah ———, who d. 6 Apr. 1739 ae. 26 (g. s., Stratfield); m. (2) Martha Hall, dau. of Samuel, b. 9 Apr. 1717.
>
> Jabez.
>
> Gershom, b. abt. 1721, d. 16 Nov. 1746 in 26 yr. (g. s., Stratfield).

Hall Jonathan, s. of Isaac.

Born at Fairfield, 2 Dec. 1684; d. at Stratfield in 1718/9; m. Mary, perhaps dau. of Edward Lacy.

His wife Mary was bapt. at Stratfield, 3 Mar. 1717; their five children, 16 June 1717.

Inv. 28 Jan. 1718/9. Adm'n granted to bros. Francis and John Hall. Ichabod, youngest son, being in infancy, Edward Lacy was appointed his guardian, 29 Feb. 1718/9; and their uncle Francis Hall was soon after appointed guardian to the other four children. Distribution of Est. 8 Jan. 1723/4; eldest son Wm.; second son Ichabod; Kezia, Charity, and Mary Hall. William's gr. father Isaac Hall and uncle John Hall mentioned. Ichabod chose his uncle John Hall for guardian, 22 Jan. 1732/3.

Children:

> William.
>
> Kezia, m. Joseph Hubbell, with whom she conveyed 4 Jan. 1725/6 to uncle John Hall, mentioning gr. father Isaac Hall and uncle Francis Hall.
>
> Charity, m. Nathaniel Risden, of Stratfield, with whom she conveyed land to uncle John Hall, 20 Apr. 1730, bounded north on uncle Francis Hall's land, being a third of a lot with sister Kezia's part on east, and Mary's part on west.
>
> Mary, d. in 1748; m. (rec. Fairfield) 22 Sept. 1737, Thomas Fairchild, with whom she conveyed land to Elnathan Hall, 29 Mar. 1740.
> ✕Ichabod.

Hall, Samuel, s. of Samuel.

Married at Stratfield, 29 July 1714, Sarah Silliman. She was dau. of Robert, bapt. 16 Sept. 1694.

Will of Samuel of Fairfield, 4 Apr. 1764, proved 13 Jan. 1768; wife Sarah; son Samuel (farm on Chestnut Hill); gr. son Daniel, son of late son Nathaniel Hall dec'd; sons Ebenezer, David, Abel (Exec'r), Joseph; daus. Martha wife of John Hall, Sarah wife of Joseph Booth, Mary wife of Sylvanus Morehouse; gr. daus. Sarah, Mabel, Rebecca, children of son Nathaniel dec'd.

Children, recorded at Stratfield:

> David, b. 12 July 1715, d. 15 Feb. 1725/6 ae. 10 yrs. 7 mos. (g. s., Stratfield).

Martha, b. 9 Apr. 1717, bapt. 14 Apr. 1717; m. John Hall.
Samuel, b. 16 Dec. 1718, bapt. 21 Dec. 1718; m. Catherine ———.
XNathaniel, b. 3 Nov. 1720, d. in 1761; adm'n granted 15 June 1761;
    m. Rebecca ———, who d. by 1774.
Ebenezer, b. 12 Mar. 1723.
Sarah, b. 20 Feb. 1724/5; m. Joseph Booth.
Mary, b. 18 Sept. 1726; m. 3 Nov. 1747, Sylvanus Morehouse.
David, b. 20 June 1728.
Abel, b. 12 July 1730, d. at Trumbull, 7 Mar. 1809 in 79 yr. (g. s.);
    m. 6 Sept. 1751, Rebecca Hall; dau. of Richard, b. abt. 1735, d.
    11 Jan. 1810 ae. 74 (g. s.).
Seth, bapt. 20 Aug. 1732, d. y.

Hanford, (Rev.) Thomas. Colonial grant of 200 acres, Oct.
1674.

His mother, Eglin, was sister of Timothy Hatherly, the founder
of Scituate, and came over in 1634, ae. 46, with her daus. Lettice
(who m. 8 Apr. 1635, Edward Foster) and Margaret (who m.
1636, Isaac Robinson). Thomas appears to have come later, perhaps after completing his education, and was in Scituate by 1643;
taught school in Roxbury, Mass.; freeman of Mass., 1650, and
soon after settled in Norwalk.

Married (1) Hannah Newberry, dau. of Mr. Thomas of
Dorchester, Mass.

Married (2) (rec. Norwalk) 22 Oct. 1661, widow Mary Ince.
She was dau. of Richard Miles of New Haven, and widow of
Jonathan Ince.

Inv. 4 Jan. 1693 [1693/4]. Heirs named: Theophilus, "whether
living or dead uncertain"; Elizar; Elnathan; Samuel; Mary;
Hannah; Elizabeth; Eunice, 18 next Mar.; Sarah, 16 next May.
Widow Mary and her son Eliezar, and son-in-law Mr. John
Edwards, appointed Adm'rs. They made a return, 13 Mar.
1693/4. Another Inv. of Rev. Thomas presented, 2 Apr. 1711;
distribution ordered to heirs; one son and three daus. are dec'd
leaving children, and three sons and two daus. living.

Inv. of Theophilus Hanford of Norwalk, 29 June 1705; adm'n
granted to John Edwards, John Burr, and Joseph Platt. A later
record shows that John Burr was dead by 12 Dec. 1705. Distribution made to surviving brothers and sisters, Thomas, Eliazar,
and Samuel Hanford, Mary Edwards, Hannah Platt, Elizabeth

Burr Widow, and Sarah Hanford, and to heirs of dec'd Elnathan
Hanford and Unice wife of Gershom Bulkley.

On 22 Jan. 1722/3, Gershom Bulkley of Fairfield and Eunice
Bulkley his dau. by his former wife Eunice who was one of the
daus. of Rev. Thomas Hanford, conveyed to Joseph Platt of
Norwalk, right that belongs to us in revertion after the death of
the widow. On 26 Jan. 1722/3, Thomas, Eleazer, and Samuel
Hanford, Joseph Platt in right of his wife Hannah, and by
purchase from Gershom Bulkley and his dau. Eunice, Samuel
Comstock and Sarah his wife, all of Norwalk, and John Edwards
in behalf of his children (the heirs of his wife Mrs. Mary Edwards
dec'd), Thomas Hanford, and Thomas Hall in behalf of the heirs
of Mrs. Elizabeth Burr dec'd, all of Fairfield, conveyed to Thomas
Hanford their right in the dower set to Mrs. Mary Hanford, the
widow, in the Est. of Rev. Thomas Hanford. [Norwalk Deeds.]

Children [by second wife], first seven recorded at Norwalk·
>Theophilus, b. 29 July 1662, d. by 1705, unm. [See above.]
>Mary, b. 30 Nov. 1663; m. John Edwards, of Stratfield.
>Hannah, b. 28 June 1665; m. Joseph Platt.
>Elizabeth, b. 9 Jan. 1666 [1666/7], d. before 1708; m. John Burr, of
>   Fairfie'd.
+Thomas, b. 18 July 1668.
+Eleazer, b. 15 Sept. 1670.
+Elnathan, b. 11 Oct. 1672.
+Samuel, b. 5 Apr. 1674.
>Eunice, b. Mar. 1675/6 (by probate rec.), d. by 1706; m. abt. 1700,
>   Gershom Bulkley.
>Sarah, b. May 1678 (by probate rec.); m. at Norwalk, 27 Dec. 1705,
>   Samuel Comstock.

Hanford, Thomas, s. of Thomas.

Born at Norwalk, 18 July 1668; d. there 7 June 1743 in 75 yr.
(g. s.).

Married Hannah (Lockwood), widow of John Burwell, and dau.
of Gershom Lockwood. She d. at Norwalk, 28 Dec. 1745 ae. 78
yrs. 5 days.

Will 9 May 1733, proved 22 Aug. 1743; wife Hannah; sons
Theophilus, Thomas, Elnathan; my brother Gershom Lockwood;
daus. Elizabeth Waren, Catherine Raymond, Mary Fayerweather.

Will of Hannah, 21 Feb. 1744/5, proved 14 Jan. 1745/6; three sons Theophilus, Thomas, Elnathan; dau. Elizabeth wife of Edmund Waren, Jr.

Children:

> Catherine, d. at Norwalk, 2 Oct. 1741; m. 24 Dec. 1719, John Raymond, Jr.
> Mary, m. Thomas Fairweather.
> Elizabeth, m. Edmund Waring, Jr.
> Theophilus.
> Thomas, b. ———, d. 1748; will 4 Sept. 1747, proved 2 Feb. 1747/8; m. Mary Seymour, dau. of John.
> Elnathan, b. abt. 1707, d. 24 Aug. 1764 in 58 yr. (g. s., Norwalk); Capt.; m. (1) Sarah St. John, b. abt. 1706, d. in 1751; m. (2) Hannah ———.

Hanford, Eleazer, s. of Thomas.

Born at Norwalk, 15 Sept. 1670; d. there before 1728.

Married Hannah Frisbie, dau. of Jonathan, b. at Branford, 14 Aug. 1693, d. in 1759. She m. (2) John Reed of Norwalk.

Eunice and Phinehas chose Capt. Samuel Hanford for guardian, 2 Apr. 1728; and John Reed was appointed guardian to Mary and Eleazer. Distribution, not made until 4 May 1759: Widow; eldest son Phineas; Eleazer; Mary wife of Elisha Alvord; heirs of Eunice Whitney; heirs of Sarah Darrow.

John Reed (for his wife Hannah, and as guardian to his son-in-law Eleazer and dau.-in-law Mary Hanford), Phineas Hanford, and John Darrow and wife Sarah of Norwalk, conveyed 19 May 1737 to Josiah Whitney and Eunice his wife of Norwalk, right in Est. of Mr. Eleazer Hanford dec'd. [Norwalk Deeds.]

Children:

> Eunice, b. abt. 1712; m. 30 Oct. 1729, Josiah Whitney.
> Phinehas, b. abt. 1714, d. at Norwalk in 1788; Capt.; Est. distributed 5 July 1788; m. (1) Ruth Scribner, dau. of Thomas; m. (2) Hannah Comstock, dau. of Moses.
> Sarah, b. abt. 1716, d. at Norwalk, 11 Dec. 1749 in 34 yr. (g. s.); m. 30 Oct. 1735, John Darrow, late of New London.
> Mary, b. abt. 1718, d. abt. 1811; m. (1) in 1758, Elisha Alvord, of Fairfield; m. (2) at Greenfield, 23 Nov. 1778, Thomas Sherwood.
> ✕Eleazer, b. abt. 1720; m. 1745, Ann Taylor, dau. of Noah, who d. 1802.

Hanford, Elnathan, s. of Thomas.

Born at Norwalk, 11 Oct. 1672; settled in Fairfield.

Married (1) abt. 1695, Sarah Wilson, dau. of Thomas.

Married (2) at Fairfield, 26 June 1700, Widow Abigail Lockwood. She was widow of Daniel Lockwood, and dau. of Daniel Burr, b. 14 Mar. 1671/2. She m. (3) (rec. Stratford) 26 Nov. 1707, Nathaniel Sherman, and d. 2 Mar. 1730/1.

Will 28 Dec. 1701, proved 23 Jan. 1701/2; wife Abigail, mentioning right in Est. of her former husband Daniel Lockwood; wife pregnant, the child to have lands in Norwalk from Est. of father Thomas dec'd; two children Thomas and Hannah; uncle Samuel Wilson, Exec'r. [Wilson was uncle of his first wife.]

Ellen Hanford, dau. of Elnathan of Fairfield, being dec'd, distribution of lands at Norwalk willed her by her father was ordered, 3 Jan. 1710 [1710/1] to his son Thomas and dau. Hannah. Mr. John Edwards and Lieut. Moses Dimon, distributors.

Children [by first wife], bapt. at Fairfield:

Hannah, bapt. 8 Mar. 1695 [1695/6].

Thomas, bapt. 20 May 1699, d. at Fairfield, 14 May 1731 in 32 yr. (g. s.,); Sheriff, Fairfield County, 1727; will, proved 6 July 1731, named only dau. Sarah and wife Ann; m. Ann Allen, dau. of Gideon, b. 6 June 1700, d. 27 Sept. 1747, having m. (2) Gershom Burr. Ann, wife of Thomas, renewed Covenant at Fairfield Church, 17 Dec. 1721. Children: (1) Sarah, bapt. 21 Jan. 1721/2, d. y. (2) Sarah, b. 11 Feb. 1728/9, bapt. 16 Feb. 1728/9; m. 10 May 1752, Mr. Ebenezer Wakeman. Thomas Hanford conveyed, 23 Apr. 1723, land laid out to gr. father Thomas Wilson.

Samuel, bapt. 20 May 1699, d. y.

Child [by second wife]:

Eleanor [or Ellen], bapt. 22 Mar. 1701/2, d. by 1710.

Hanford, Samuel, s. of Thomas. Deputy for Norwalk, Oct. 1705, May and Dec. 1707, May 1708, May 1711, May 1714, Oct. 1717, Oct. 1719, May 1720, Oct. 1722, Oct. 1733, May and Oct. 1735, May and Oct. 1736, May and Oct. 1737. Lt., north company, Norwalk, May 1710; Capt., Oct. 1719. Justice, 1711, 1723, 1724, 1735-51.

Born at Norwalk 5 Apr. 1674; d. there 2 Feb. 1751 in 77 yr. (g. s.).

Married Isabel Haynes, dau. of William.

Will 19 Dec. 1750, proved 17 Feb. 1750/1; wife Isabel; sons Samuel and Thaddeus (land in Canaan), Haynes, Hezekiah, William; three gr. daus. Hannah, Betty, and Sarah, daus. of dec'd dau. Isabel Hall.

Children:

> Isabel, m. Jonathan Hall.
> Samuel, b. abt. 1710, d. 28 Mar. 1795; Capt.; m. (1) Dinah Comstock, dau. of Moses; m. (2) 22 Mar. 1757, Mary (Lockwood), widow of Martin Kellogg.
> Thaddeus.
> Haynes.
> Hezekiah, b. abt. 1722, d. 2 May 1812; m. 7 Oct. 1743, Deborah Hoyt, b. 1726, d. 15 Sept. 1803 in 78 yr. (g. s.).
> William.

Hard, James.

Of Derby and Newtown; m. Elizabeth Tomlinson, dau. of William.

James Hard and Elizabeth his wife conveyed, 4 Apr. 1712, to brothers John and Isaac Tomlinson right from father William Tomlinson dec'd. [Derby Deeds.]

Children, recorded at Newtown:

> James, b. at Derby, 7 Jan. 1695/6 [8 Jan. 1694/5 by Derby rec.]; will 14 Dec. 1764, proved 13 June 1766; m. Hannah Kimberly, dau. of Abraham, b. 19 Jan. 1698.
> Ruth, b. at Derby, 10 Feb. 1705/6 [1704/5 by Derby rec.].
> Joseph, b. 1 Sept. 1707; m. Experience Adams, dau. of Freegrace.

Harger, Jabez.

Of Stratford, rem. to Derby, where he d. in 1678.

Married 5 Nov. 1662 (Stratford rec.) Margaret Tomlinson, dau. of Henry. Wife was called Margaret at birth of child 1674. She m. (2) John Tibbals, and d. at Derby, 17 Mar. 1697/8.

Children, first seven recorded at Stratford:

> Samuel, b. 29 Sept. 1663, d. at Derby, 18 Feb. 1697; m. (rec. Derby) 9 May 1693, Hannah, widow of Isaac Stiles, and dau. of Robert Rose; she m. (3) 28 Mar. 1700, John Tibbals.

Sarah, b. 5 Feb. 1665 [1665/6].

Anna, b. 23 Feb. 1667 [1667/8]; m. at Derby, 5 Feb. 1684 [1684/5], John Chatfield.

Mary, b. 17 Feb. 1669 [1669/70], d. abt. 17 Mar. 1672/3.

Abigail, b. 2 Mar. 1671/2; m. by 1692, John Davis of Derby.

Ebenezer, b. 25 Dec. 1674, d. 31 Mar. 1736 ae. 61 (g. s., Derby); m. at Derby, 15 Sept. 1698, Abigail Tibbals, b. abt. 1677, d. 25 Dec. 17[33] ae. 56 (g. s.).

Abraham, b. 1 Apr. 1677, d. at Huntington, in 1721; Lt.; Inv. 28 Feb. 1721; m. at Derby, 19 May 1703, Hannah Riggs, dau. of Samuel, b. 24 Feb. 1683.

Jabez, b. abt. 1679, d. at Derby before 1738; m. at Stratford, 24 Jan. 1704/5, Ann Gilbert.

Harvey, Edmund. Deputy for Fairfield, May 1647.

Admitted to Milford Church, 13 Sept. 1640, where his death at Fairfield on 22 May 1648 is entered next his name.

Inv. 21 June 1648; wife; a dau. in England ae. 22; two daus. in New England ae. 18 and 14; a son of 7 and dau. of 2.

Nathan Gold m. the relict; the two children Josyas and Hannah mentioned.

He prob. m. (1) ———, mother of the older children. He m. (2) Martha ———, who m. (2) Nathan Gold. Martha was adm. to Milford Church, 20 June 1641.

The land records state that Maj. Nathan Gold, having m. the widow of Edmund Harvey, agreed at a Court held 18 June 1655 to assume the debts and pay legacies to Josiah and Hannah Harvey (entered 4 Mar. 1679).

Children [by first wife]:

Daughter, b. abt. 1626; was in England 1648.

Daughter, b. abt. 1630; prob. Elizabeth who m. 20 Mar. 1649 [1649/50], Thomas Beardsley [New Haven Col. Rec.].

Daughter, b. abt. 1634.*

Children [by second wife]:

+Josiah, bapt. at Milford, 27 Dec. 1640.

Hannah, b. abt. 1646; living 13 Feb. 1669 [1669/70], when with Josiah Harvey she witnessed a deed of Nathan Gold's.

---

* I do not consider it likely that the Ann Harvey who m. at New Haven, 24 May 1661, Thomas Wheadon, was a dau. of Edmund. There was an Ann Small, an apprentice girl, mentioned earlier as about to m. Francis Harvey, a Frenchman, and it may have been the same who m. Wheadon.

Harvey, Josiah, s. of Edmund. Chirurgeon to Army, Oct. 1675.

Physician, of Fairfield. Bapt. at Milford, 27 Dec. 1640; d. early in 1698. Married Mary Staples, dau. of Thomas. Josiah and Mary Harvey witnessed a deed given by Benjamin Turney, Apr. 1671.

Inv. 27 Mar. 1698; Mary Harvey, Adm'x. Agreement of widow with Thomas and Martha Harvey. The other children, Mary Grimes and Abigail Peat, have rec'd portions. On 24 May 1704, Samuel Peat, Jr., of Stratford, in right of wife Abigail dau. of Josiah Harvey, assigned to Thomas Harvey of Fairfield, yeoman. Mary Grimes of Fairfield gave rec't, 31 July 1707, for full portion in Est. of father Josiah Harvey dec'd.

Josiah's wife Mary and dau. Hannah were accused of witchcraft 1692 (together with Hannah's grandmother Staples and others), but no indictment was found against them.

Children, recorded at Fairfield:

Mary, b. 25 May, 1669; m. ——— Grimes.
Abigail, b. 8 Jan. 1671 [1671/2]; m. Samuel Peat, Jr.
Hannah, b. 7 June 1675, d. between 1692 and 1698, unm.
Martha, b. 12 Oct. 1677, d. at Greenfield, 17 Feb. 1770 in 93 yr. She conveyed, 13 Oct. 1762, with John Goodsell, presumably her conservator.
Thomas, b. 23 Jan. 1680 [1680/1], d. at Greenfield, 12 Aug. 1747 ae. abt. 67; will 24 July 1747, proved 17 Aug. 1747; referred to sister Mary; sister Martha, "who always lived with me"; sister Abigail Peat and her dau. Abigail wife of Samuel Deforest. He m. Elizabeth, widow of Edward Wooster, dau. of Joseph Watkins, b. 10 Aug. 1702, d. 2 Mar. 1737/8. Only child: Elizabeth, b. Feb. 1737/8, d. ae. 10 days.

Harvey, Richard. Called Sergt. 1670.

Tailor, came in the *Planter,* 1635, ae. 22, with Ann Harvey, ae. 22, presumably his wife, but it is not certain that he was Richard of Stratford.*

He m. (1) Margaret ———, who d. at Concord, Mass., 2 Dec. 1639.

He m. (2) ———.

---

* Winthrop in 1668 wrote "Richard Harvie of Southold his wife is Deacon Howes(?) daughter." A different Richard?

Mary wife of Thomas Jeffrey had land at Stratford by gift of her father Richard Harvey, 1676. In 1686, calling himself of Stratford, now resident in Fairfield, he conveyed to son-in-law John Hide of Fairfield; deed witnessed by Josiah Harvey and John Burr.

Inv. 4 Nov. 1689.

John Hide represented at Court 25 Dec. 1705 that considerable was due from Harvey's Est. to his dec'd father John Hide, and was granted adm'n.

Children [by first wife], recorded at Concord:

Twin daus., b. 25 and 26 Nov. 1639, both buried 28 Nov. 1639.

Children [by second wife], recorded at Stratford:

Elizabeth, b. 25 July 1644, d. in 1701; m. John Hide.
Mary, b. 15 Sept. 1647; m. 1 May 1674, Thomas Jeffrey.
Sarah, b. 13 Feb. 1649.

Hawkins, Robert.

Came in the *Elizabeth and Ann*, 1635, ae. 25; with Mary, ae. 24, his wife; settled in Charlestown; freeman, 25 May 1636.

Quite early he owned land in Fairfield, which came into possession of Thomas Wheeler, Jr., who conveyed it in 1650.

Prior to 1649 a Mr. Hawkins had a lot in New Haven, being an absentee owner, and the Hawkins lot was referred to as late as 1660; apparently he never resided in New Haven, or but for a short time; and whether he was Robert or another, cannot be determined.

Children, recorded at Charlestown:

Eleazer, bapt. 25 Dec. 1636.
Zechariah, bapt. 25 Oct. 1639; accepted to be made a freeman of Connecticut, May 1664, with other inhabitants of Setauket, L. I.; unless this was another, perhaps an uncle, of identical name.*
Joseph, bapt. 3 Apr. 1642, d. at Derby in Oct. 1682; will 12 Oct. 1682, Inv. 1 Nov. 1682; m. 8 Apr. 1668, Abigail Holbrook, dau. of Richard of Milford.

---

* "Zachary Hawkings" of Brookhaven d. in 1698; will 17 Nov. 1698 named wife Mary, eldest son Zachary, sons Joseph, Eleazer; gr. children Nathaniel Brewster, Zachary Smith; daus. Martha and Hannah (under age).

Hawley, Joseph. Deputy for Stratford, May 1658, Oct. 1665, Oct. 1667, May and Oct. 1668, May and Oct. 1669, May and Oct. 1670, May and Oct. 1671, Oct. 1673, May and Oct. 1674, Oct. 1675, May 1677, May 1678, Oct. 1680, May and Oct. 1681, May and Oct. 1682, May 1683, May and Oct. 1684, Oct. 1685, May and June 1687. Commissioner for Stratford, 1682-87, 1689-91.

He was named as uncle in will of Ephraim Booth, 1683; perhaps he m. a sister of Richard Booth, or vice versa. His sister Hannah m. (1) John Ufford of Milford, whom she divorced, and (2) Capt. John Beard. A bro. was prob. Thomas of Roxbury, whose dau. Dorothy, bapt. 20 June 1658, m. John Booth of Stratford.

"J. H." d. at Stratford 20 May 1690 (g. s.).

Will 17 Sept. 1689, of Joseph Hawley, yeoman, sometime Justice of the Peace; wife Katharine; sons Samuel, Ephraim, John; Samuel's son Joseph; gr. children John and Joseph Chapman at Saybrook; daus. Hannah Nichols and Mary Coe; land at Woodbury; Capt. John Beard to put a final issue to any difference; Mr. Israel Chauncey, £5. Inv. 4 June 1690.

Children, recorded at Stratford:

+Samuel, b. abt. 1648.
Joseph, b. 9 Jan. 1649 [1649/50], d. y.
Elizabeth, b. 26 Jan. 1651 [1651/2], d. at Saybrook, 10 May 1676; m. (rec. at Saybrook) 7 June 1670, Capt. John Chapman.
+Ebenezer, b. 17 Sept. 1654.
Hannah, b. 26 May 1657; m. (1) 13 Dec. 1678, Josiah Nichols; m. (2) 22 June 1692, John Wolcott, of Windsor; m. (3) after 1713, —— Porter; living 1726.
+Ephraim, b. 7 Aug. 1659.
+John, b. 14 June 1661.
Mary, b. 16 July 1663, d. 9 Sept. 1731; m. [20 Dec. 1682], John Coe.

Hawley, Samuel, s. of Joseph. Deputy for Stratford, Oct. 1690, Oct. 1695, Oct. 1697, Jan. 1698, Oct. 1700, May and Oct. 1708, May and June 1711.

Born abt. 1648, d. at Stratford, 24 Aug. 1734 in 87 yr. (g. s.).

Married (1) (rec. Stratford) 20 May 1673, Mary Thompson of Farmington.

Married (2) Patience, widow of John Hubbell, dau. of Isaac Nichols, b. 2 Feb. 1659/60.

Will 15 Apr. 1734, proved 24 Sept. 1734; having lived to see my children disposed of in marriage, and given them portions, all remaining estate to wife Patience.

Children [by first wife], recorded at Stratford (mother of first three called Mary):

> Samuel, b. 14 May 1674, d. in 1754; m. 14 May 1702, Bethia Booth, b. in 1680, d. 7 Sept. 1780.
>
> Joseph, b. 6 Jan 1675 [1675/6], d. at Farmington, 20 Nov. 1752 in 77 yr. (g. s.); Capt.; m. 7 June 1697, Elizabeth Wilcoxson, dau. of Timothy, b. 6 Nov. 1673, d. 10 Sept. 1762 in 89 yr. (g. s.).
>
> Thomas, b. 30 July 1678, d. at Stratfield, 6 May 1722 ae. 44 (g. s.); Deacon; m. Oct. 1721 [error for 1701], Johanah Sherwood, widow. She was dau. of Ephraim Booth, b. Sept. 1678, and widow of John Sherwood. She d. 28 Jan. 1761 in 84 yr. (g. s.).
>
> Matthew, b. 7 Nov. 1680; "M. Hawley" d. 1693 (g. s.).
>
> Ebenezer, b 25. Feb. 1682 [1682/3].
>
> Jehiel, b. 5 Apr. 1685, d. at Durham, 19 July 1727; adm'n granted, 5 Sept. 1727, to widow Hope; m. 13 Dec. 1708, Hope Stow, dau. of Ichabod, b. 31 Oct. 1690, d. 23 Jan. 1763.
>
> Elizabeth, b. 30 Mar. 1687, d. at Windsor, 3 Nov. 1765; m. 19 Dec. 1706, Lt. Charles Wolcott.

Children [by second wife]:

> Ephraim, b. abt. 1691, d. in 1771; res. New Milford; m. 5 Oct. 1711, Phebe Curtis.
>
> Katharine, b. abt. 1695, d. 2 Feb. 1696 [1696/7] in 2 yr. (g. s.).
>
> Stephen, d. in 1790; m. 21 July 1720, Mary DeForest.
>
> Benjamin, d. at Hawleyville, 8 May 1765; m. (1) 18 Feb. 1724/5, Mary Nichols; m. (2) Experience Dibble.
>
> Nathaniel, b. abt. 1702, d. 7 Jan. 1754 in 52 yr. (g. s.); m. 12 Dec. 1723, Mary Ufford, dau. of Samuel, b. 16 Apr. 1704.

Hawley, Ebenezer, s. of Joseph.

Born at Stratford, 17 Sept. 1654; d. at Fairfield, 3 Oct. 1681 [Pro. Rec.].

Married Hester Ward, dau. of William. Marriage agreement, 19 Apr. 1678, between Ebenezer, son of Mr. Joseph Hawley of Stratford, and Hester Ward, daughter of Mrs. Deborah Topping of Southampton. She m. (2) at Fairfield, 17 Oct. 1682, Ephraim

Nichols of Stratford; m. (3) Nov. 1691, Eliphalet Hill, and (4) Robert Lord.

Inv. 27 Dec. 1681. Widow Hester; lands in reversion due from Mr. Hawley at Stratford; children, William and Elizabeth.

Children, recorded at Fairfield:

> Elizabeth, b. 6 May 1679, d. at Fairfield, 18 Aug. 1753 in 74 yr. (g. s.); m. (1) by 1698, Capt. Joseph Wakeman; m. (2) in 1727, Col. John Burr.
> William, b. abt. 1681, d. y.

Hawley, Ephraim, s. of Joseph.

Born at Stratford, 7 Aug. 1659, d. there 18 Apr. 1690.

Married (rec. Stratford) 4 Dec. 1683, Sarah Welles of Wethersfield. She m. (2) 19 Oct. 1692, Lt. Agur Tomlinson, and d. 29 June 1694.

Order of distribution 14 Dec. 1706; double portion to eldest son, and single to two other children; they had also Est. from their gr. father Mr. Joseph Hawley.

Children, recorded at Stratford:

> Daniel, b. 20 Sept. 1684, d. 28 July 1750 in 66 yr. (g. s.); m. 6 Mar. 1706/7, Elizabeth Brinsmade, b. abt. 1684, d. 6 Jan. 1763 in 79 yr. (g. s.).
> Gideon, b. 30 Jan. 1687/8, d. at Stratfield, 16 Feb. 1730/1 in 43 yr. (g. s.); m. at Stratfield 20 Feb. 1710/1, Anna Bennett, b. abt. 1691, d. 14 Nov. 1727 in 36 yr. (g. s.).
> Abiah, b. 18 Sept. 1690, d. at East Windsor, 16 June 1716; m. 5 Nov. 1707, William Wolcott.

Hawley, John, s. of Joseph. Lt., Fairfield Troop raised for war, May 1704; Lt., Stratford Trainband, May 1709; Capt., north company, Stratford, Oct. 1709. Deputy for Stratford, Oct. 1702, Oct. 1705, May, Oct. and Dec. 1707, Oct. 1709, Oct. 1710, May 1712, May 1713, May 1714, May and Oct. 1716, Oct. 1719, May and Oct. 1720, May and Oct. 1721, May 1722, Oct. 1723, May 1724. Justice, 1720-28.

Born at Stratford, 14 June 1661, d. there 27 July 1729 ae. 68 yrs. 1 mo. (g. s.).

Married (rec. Stratford) 23 Apr. 1686, Deborah Pierson, who d. 3 Dec. 1739 in 73 yr. (g. s.).

Will 16 Mar. 1727/8, proved 23 Dec. 1729; daus. Hannah and Mary; wife; lands in Durham, Haddam and Stratford to four sons Henry (eldest), John, Nathan, and Joseph; children of dau. Deborah dec'd, all lands in Newtown; gr. child John Porter, son of dau. Sarah dec'd, £10, which I have delivered to his gr. father John Porter.

He was called Sergt. at birth of children 1700 and 1702, and Lieut. 1706.

Children, recorded at Stratford:

> Henry, b. 26 Jan. 1686/7, d. at Stratford, 18 Feb. 1752; m. (1) 18 June 1713, Mary Pickett; dau. of Daniel, b. 15 Jan. 1692/3; m. (2) Mary (Curtis), widow of Joseph Nichols.
>
> Hannah, b. 13 Oct. 1689; m. 14 Mar. 1708/9, Joseph Judson.
>
> Deborah, b. 21 Apr. 1692; m. 20 Apr. 1711, David Fairchild.
>
> John, b. 4 Jan. 1693 [1693/4], d. in 1742; estate distributed 6 Sept. 1742; m. 20 Dec. 1716, Sarah Walker; dau. of Robert, b. 23 July 1697.
>
> Mary, b. 6 July 1697, d. at Fairfield (Redding), 14 Feb. 1748; m. (rec. Fairfield) 20 Sept. 1723, John Read.
>
> Nathan, b. 15 Mar. 1699/1700, d. 24 Feb. 1747; m. 6 Aug. 1719, Silence Mallory.
>
> Katharine, b. 6 Mar. 1701/2.
>
> Sarah, bapt. at Stratford, 10 Feb. 1705/6 (rec. Stratfield); m. 25 Mar. 1725, Daniel Porter.
>
> ×Joseph, bapt. at Stratford, 27 Apr. 1707 (rec. Stratfield), d. at Redding, 12 Dec. 1771 ae. 66; m. 25 Jan. 1727/8, Hannah Walker; dau. of John, b. abt. 1710, d. 16 July 1769 ae. 59.

Hayden, William. Deputy for Killingworth, Oct. 1667. His heirs granted 50 acres, Oct. 1671, for Pequot War service.

Perhaps from Hinton Blewitt, co. Somerset, Eng., came to Dorchester 1630, and was made freeman 1634; came early to Hartford and served in the Pequot War, 1637, receiving a lot in Soldiers' Field, Hartford; sold his Hartford property 1643, but had settled in Windsor prob. by 1640. He was a farmer, had also a stone quarry at Windsor.

His wife d. at Windsor in 1664; she was sister of Sarah, wife first of Francis Stiles and second of Robert Clark of Stratford.

He m. (2) Margaret, widow of William Wilcoxson of Stratford, and in 1665 went with the first settlers to Killingworth, where he d. 27 Sept. 1669.

Children [by first wife], recorded at Windsor:

Daniel, b. 2 Sept. 1640, d. at Windsor, 22 Mar. 1712/3; Lt.; m. 17 Mar. 1664, Hannah Wilcoxson; dau. of William; she d. 19 Apr. 1722.

Nathaniel, b. 2 Feb. 1642/3, d. at Killingworth, 20 Apr. 1706 ae. 63; m. 17 Jan. 1677, Sarah Parmelee; dau. of John of Guilford; she d. 19 May 1717.

Mary, b. 6 June 1648; m. Judah Evarts of Guilford.

Hayden, William.

Came to Fairfield, where he m. before 1661 the widow of John Tompkins [q. v.], and resided for a time, then rem. to Eastchester, N. Y., where he was living in 1687. His estate in Fairfield, by virtue of an execution, was acquired by the children of John Thompson of that place, by 1672; he having been an overseer of Thompson's estate in 1658. He witnessed a deed given 4 June 1659 by Grace Perry to her son Isaac Nichols.

Hayes, Nathaniel.

He and his bro. Samuel were most likely children of the first wife of Nathaniel Richards of Norwalk, for Samuel called Richards "father" and received a legacy in his will.

Named in Norwalk, 1655 list; had seven children, 1672. He and Samuel were among the Norwalk freemen, 1669, and among the petitioners for establishment of Danbury, 1672. From an entry made by Winthrop, it appears that he was a kinsman of Nicholas Olmstead of Hartford.

Married Mary Kimberly, dau. of Thomas, whose will 1672 named his gr. children Nathaniel, Mary and Elizabeth Hayes.

Will of Nathaniel, Sr., of Norwalk, 27 Apr. 1705; son Nathaniel, £30; son Samuel, £15; dau. Rachel Messenger, land; son James, residue. Witnesses, Peter Burr, William Haines.

Inv. £398, taken 12 Mar. 1706/7 by William Haines, Andrew Messenger, Samuel Hayes.

Will of Rachel Messenger, 17 Apr. 1738, proved 1 Sept. 1740; her cousin Thomas Hayes; half of residue to brother Samuel Hayes, a quarter to brother James, and a quarter to John, Nathaniel and Eleazer "Boughtens"; brother James and friend Mr. Samuel Fitch, Exec'rs.

John Bouton, Jr., of Danbury, receipted 8 Mar. 1699 to father-in-law Nathaniel Hayes of Norwalk for land where he built his house in Norwalk.

Children:

> Nathaniel, d. in 1748. Adm'n granted, 4 Oct. 1748, to Sarah Hayes and Elnathan Hanford. Inv. £1,887. Distribution to widow Sarah and only child Mary Hayes. The dau. Mary m. Abner Holmes.
>
> Mary, prob. m. John Bouton, 3d.
>
> Elizabeth.
>
> Samuel, settled in Danbury; m. (1) a dau. of James Pickett, and (2) after 1712, Sarah (Barnum?), widow of Thomas Pickett.
>
> Rachel, d. in 1740; m. Andrew Messenger.
>
> James, b. ——, d. in 1747; will Apr. 1747, proved 5 Dec. 1747; m. 1 Apr. 1703, Mary Allen; dau. of Thomas and Mary Allen, and stepdau. of John Bouton, 2d.

Hayes, Samuel. Deputy for Norwalk, May and July 1686, May, June and Oct. 1687, Oct. 1689, May and June 1692, May, Sept. and Oct. 1693, May 1694, May 1695, May 1696, May and Oct. 1697, Jan., May and Oct. 1698, Oct. 1699, May 1700, May 1701, Oct. 1702, Oct. 1703.

Born about 1641, d. at Norwalk, 7 Dec. 1712 ae. 72 (g. s.).

Married about 1665, —— Moore, dau. of Isaac of Farmington. He had one child in the 1672 list. His widow Elizabeth d. at Norwalk, 3 Nov. 1729. Perhaps she was a second wife and widow of James Pickett of Danbury [*q. v.*]; unless indeed the widow Elizabeth Pickett m. his bro. Nathaniel; but since Nathaniel did not name a wife in his will 1705, and this woman was living 1711, that supposition is less likely, unless indeed Nathaniel had a pre-nuptial contract with her and in consequence omitted to mention her in his will.

Children, recorded at Norwalk:

> Child, b. abt. 1666, d. y.
>
> Sarah, b. 19 Sept. 1673; m. Capt. Matthew Seymour.
>
> Isaac, b. 27 Aug. 1682, d. 5 Jan. 1711/2; Inv. £700 taken 5 Jan. 1711/2, mentioned "Est. in reversion to return to the heirs of the dec'd Isaac Haies at the decease of his father and mother Mr. Samuel and Mrs. Elizabeth Hayes. He m. 10 July 1701, Elizabeth Sherwood, dau. of Isaac of Fairfield; she m. (2) abt. 1713 Andrew Sanford of Milford.

Hedges, Stephen.

Owned land in Fairfield by 1653.

Will of Mr. Stephen, aged, sick and weak, 10 June 1682; to Hannah wife of Lt. Ezbon Wakeman, £20; to Lt. Cornelius Hull, £5, and to Cornelius Hull, Jr., £14; the foregoing as recompense for care in his sickness; residue to brother Thomas Hedges son of my father Roger Hedges of Westbury under Salisbury Plain, and in his default to brother William, and in his default to brother Joseph, and in his default to brother John, and if all my brothers are dead, then to the eldest son of brother Thomas, the heir to come personally and make claim within three years; signed with mark. Inv. 25 Dec. 1683.

Anthony Hedges came over in 1684, fortified with a document from inhabitants of Westbury under Salbury Plain, co. Wiltshire, Eng., stating that Thomas, Andrew and William, sons of Roger, died without male issue, and that Joseph died leaving the son Anthony; Thomas left an only child, Hannah, wife of Christopher Stantiall; signed by John Watts, Mayor, Samuel Gibbs, Michael Whatly, Henry Belton, John Barter(?), Nicholas Clift, Benjamin Norway, Edmund Bayley, Philip Withers, John Leigh, James Dean.

Anthony disposed of his uncle's property and vanished; prob. returned to England. Rebecca Hull of Fairfield had by gift from Anthony Hedges, land in Fairfield, 21 Aug. 1685.

There was also a Stephen Hedges who m. before 1684 a dau. of John Stratton of Easthampton, L. I.; oddly enough, she was sister of Cornelius Stratton who m. Martha dau. of Cornelius Hull of Fairfield.

Hendrick, Henry.

A Dutchman, also called Hendrick Hendrickson; entered land at Fairfield, 31 Jan. 1655 [1655/6], previously purchased of William Hill. His wife Hannica, also called Hannah, m. (2) Daniel Silliman.

Will 11 Mar. 1683 [1683/4], proved 18 June 1684; wife Hannica, alias Hannah, house for life, Exec'x; daus. Susanna (already rec'd part of portion), Hannah, Elizabeth, Mary; son Henrick, the homelot, etc. Inv. 31 May 1684.

Robert Bisbum receipted 27 Oct. 1685 to mother-in-law Hannah Henerickson now Silliman, for portion of wife Susanna from her father Henry Hendrickson; and Thomas Dickerson for wife Hannah, and Nathaniel Wilson for wife Elizabeth, receipted in similar terms.

Inv. of Est. of Mary Hendrick, 6 June 1691. Adm'n granted to Jonathan Morehouse. Agreement, 6 Dec. 1691, between widow Silliman and her sons-in-law Thomas Dickerson, Nathaniel Wilson, and Philip John Prise, and her own son Henry Hendrickson, concerning Est. of her dau. Mary.

Children:

> Susanna, m. (1) Robert Bispham; m. (2) Philip John Price.
> Hannah, m. Thomas Dickerson.
> Elizabeth, m. Nathaniel Wilson.
> Mary, d. abt. 1691, unm. [See above.]
> +Henry.

Hendrick, Henry, s. of Henry.

He was bapt. at Fairfield Church, 17 Mar. 1694/5; his wife Elizabeth renewed Covenant, 31 Mar. 1695.

Married Elizabeth Bennett, dau. of Thomas, b. abt. 1672; Widow Elizabeth d. at Westport, 4 Dec. 1755.

Will 12 June 1740, proved 27 Oct. 1741; wife Elizabeth, Exec'x; son John; children of dau. Elizabeth Smith dec'd,— Jabez, Abigail, and Sarah Smith (mentioning "my wife their grandmother"); daus. Hannah Jennings, Sarah Stewart; children of son Henry dec'd; sons James and David Hendrick.

Children, bapt. at Fairfield:

> ✕John, bapt. 31 Mar. 1695; m. in 1728, Phebe Coe, who d. 21 Apr. 1752 ae. 50 (g. s., Westport).
> Elizabeth, bapt. 11 Apr. 1697; m. ———— Smith.
> ✕Henry, bapt. 15 Oct. 1699, d. in 1734; John Hendrick appointed Adm'r; Inv. 15 June 1734; m. Elizabeth Luff, dau. of John of Stratfield.
> Hannah, bapt. 26 Apr. 1702; m. Daniel Jennings.
> Peter, bapt. 18 Feb. 1704/5, d. in 1735, unm. Adm'n granted to James Hendrick.
> Sarah, bapt. 15 June 1707; m. John Stewart, 3d, of Norwalk. They conveyed, 1739, to John Hendrick, right inherited from brother Peter.

James, bapt. 2 July 1710, d. by 1766. Inv. 2 Sept. 1766, presented by Samuel Hendrick. Adm'n granted, 3 May 1768, to John Hendrick, Jr. Distribution to bros. and sisters: John Hendrick; heirs of Henry Hendrick, Jr.; heirs of David Hendrick; Hannah wife of Daniel Jennings; heirs of Elizabeth Smith; heirs of Sarah late wife of John Stewart.

×David, bapt. 20 Jan. 1716/7, d. 5 Nov. 1756 on way home from army (rec. Westport); m. at Westport, 22 Nov. 1743, Mary Fountain, who d. at Westport, 9 Nov. 1780.

Herdman, John.

His name appears at Lynn, 1647. We suppose him to be the man who was at Braintree with wife Sarah, 1652 to 1654; before 1659 he had come to Fairfield, where he d. in 1665.

In the company of Cable, Post, and "Lockwood's son," in 1659 he dined too well one night in Milford, created a disturbance, and kicked the marshal, and when fined by the Milford magistrate spoke rashly of those in authority, for which offense the New Haven Court fined him heavily. Sigismund Richalls of Branford gave bond of £50 for Herdman's good behavior, and it appears also paid his fine, though Richalls like Herdman was a man of small estate and left but £14 when he d. in 1683.

Inv. presented 1 Nov. 1665. Tools, etc., in house of William Gibbons in New Haven. Thomas Lyon and John Grumman to administer. Est. to be divided equally to all the children.

Children, recorded at Braintree:
> Mary, b. 7 Nov. 1652.
> John, b. 10 Nov. 1654.
> Prob. others.

Hickock, ———.

Surname spelled Hickok, Hickox, etc.

An unknown of this name m. Elizabeth ———, who m. (2) William Adams of Farmington. When the Inv. of Adams' Est. was taken 6 Sept. 1655, the two Adams children were listed, together with Samuel Heacock, aged 12, and Joseph Heacock, aged 10.

This man was not the Mr. William Hickock who had a lot in

the original New Haven division of land, but who apparently never came over and was living in London at a considerably later date.

Children:

+Samuel, b. abt. 1643.
+Joseph, b. abt. 1645.

Hickock, Samuel, s. of ———. Sergt., Waterbury Trainband.

Born about 1643, d. at Waterbury early in 1695. Married Hannah Upson, dau. of Thomas of Farmington. Inv. 28 Feb. 1694/5, taken by Timothy Stanley, John Hopkins, and Thomas Judd. Children's ages: Samuel 26, William 22, Thomas 20, Joseph 17, Stephen 11, Benjamin 9, Ebenezer 2, Hannah 24, Mary 14, Elizabeth 12, Mercy 6.

Children:

+Samuel, b. abt. 1668.
Hannah, b. abt. 1670, d. at Watertown, 17 July 1750; m. at Waterbury, 16 Apr. 1696, John Judd.
William, b. abt. 1672, d. at Waterbury, 4 Nov. 1737, m. abt. 1699, Rebecca Andrews, dau. of Abraham, Sr.
Thomas, b. abt. 1674, d. at Waterbury, 28 June 1728; Deacon; m. at Waterbury, 27 Mar. 1700, Mary Bronson, dau. of Sergt. Isaac; she m. (2) 23 Nov. 1748, Dea. Samuel Bull, and d. 4 July 1756.
Joseph, b. abt. 1677, d. at Durham, in 1725; adm'n granted 6 July 1725 to brother Stephen and son Joseph; m. (rec. Waterbury) 8 Feb. 1699/1700, Elizabeth Gaylord, dau. of Joseph.
Mary, b. abt. 1680, d. at Waterbury, 21 Mar. 1713; m. 9 Nov. 1697, John Bronson.
Elizabeth, b. abt. 1682, living at Danbury 1729; m. (1) Thomas Benedict, of Danbury; m. (2) 21 June 1722, Samuel Smith, of Ridgefield.
Stephen, b. abt. 1684, d. at Durham, in 1726; adm'n granted 19 Apr. 1726 to widow Ruth; m. abt. 1711, Ruth Gaylord, dau. of Joseph. She m. (2) David Johnson.
Benjamin, b. abt. 1686, d. at Norwalk, in 1745; res. Stamford and Norwalk; will 17 June 1745, proved 27 Nov. 1745; m. (1) ———; m. (2) 3 Feb. 1713/4, Sarah (Lockwood) Selleck, widow of Nathaniel Selleck and dau. of Gershom Lockwood. She m. (3) 9 Mar. 1755, Samuel Kellogg.
Mercy, b. abt. 1688; [perhaps m. John Bouton, and if so, lived in Stamford 1729].
Ebenezer, b. abt. 1692, d. at Bethel, 8 July 1774 in 83 yr. (g. s.) ; Capt.,

Danbury; m. (1) [perhaps Rebecca Keeler, dau. of Ralph, 2d];
m. (2) at North Stratford, 17 June 1747, Esther (Curtis), widow
of Daniel Beach, and dau. of Benjamin Curtis; bapt. 10 Feb. 1706,
d. 25 Aug. 1775 in 70 yr. (g. s.).

Hickock, Joseph, s. of ———.

Born about 1645, d. at Woodbury in 1687. Married Mary
Carpenter, dau. of David of Farmington, b. Aug. 1650. She m.
(2) Samuel Hinman.
Inv. 12 Aug. 1687, included land at Waterbury. Children's
ages: Joseph, 14; Benjamin, 12, 5 Jan. next; Samuel, 14 weeks;
Mary, 9, 15 May last; Elizabeth, 6, next June. Widow Mary
made oath at Woodbury, 31 Oct. 1687. The Court appointed
Samuel Hickock of Waterbury, Capt. Minor, Mr. John Sherman,
and Jonathan Hough, overseers.

Children:

> Joseph, b. abt. 1673, d. at Woodbury "of a cancer", 20 Oct. 1717;
> Inv. 20 Oct. 1717; m. at Woodbury, 3 Nov. 1697, Ruth Fairchild,
> who d. 28 May 1727.
> Benjamin, b. 5 Jan. 1675/6, d. 15 Jan. 1745 ae. 69 (g. s., Southbury);
> Dea.; m. at Woodbury, 3 Nov. 1697, Hannah Skeels, who d. 17
> Jan. 1746 ae. 68 (g. s.).
> Mary, b. 15 May 1678; m. (rec. Waterbury) 8 Feb. 1699/1700, Joseph
> Gaylord.
> Elizabeth, b. June 1682, m. at Woodbury, 20 Nov. 1701, John
> Gaylord.
> Samuel, b. July 1687, bapt. at Woodbury, Sept. 1687, d. there 5 June
> 1727; m. Ellen ———. She prob. m. (2) Ebenezer Squire.

Hickock, Samuel, s. of Samuel.

Born about 1668, d. at Waterbury, 3 June 1713. Married 16
Apr. 1690, Elizabeth Plumb, dau. of John of Milford. She d.
at Waterbury, 17 Oct. 1749.

Children, recorded at Waterbury:

> Daughter, b. and d. May 1691.
> Ebenezer, b. 6 Oct. 1692; res. Waterbury 1736, Milford 1739, Nor-
> walk 1746; m. (1) Dec. 1714, Esther Hine, dau. of Thomas; m.
> (2) 28 Aug. 1729, Abigail Stevens, dau. of Samuel of West Haven.
> Samuel, b. 3 Nov. 1694, d. 7 July 1713.

John, b. 18 Nov. 1696, bapt. at Milford, 20 Dec. 1696; m. 18 Nov. 1719, Mary Gaylord, dau. of Joseph.

Hannah, b. 21 Apr. 1699, bapt. at Milford.

Elizabeth, b. 6 Apr. 1702, bapt. at Milford, 14 June 1702.

Son, b. and d. 3 Mar. 1704.

Gideon, b. 6 Sept. 1705; m. 15 Aug. 1734, Sarah Upson, dau. of Stephen.

Sarah, b. 6 Dec. 1707; m. John Platt of Norwalk.

Silence, b. 19 Sept. 1713; m. 1737, Abraham Bennett.

Hide, Humphrey.

Bought land at Windsor, 1645, which he sold 1653 and rem. to Fairfield, where a grant of two acres was entered 11 Mar. 1649 [1649/50]. On 12 Feb. 1671 [1671/2], he conveyed to son John; contingent heirs, daus. Sarah and Hannah.

Will 12 Nov. 1679; wife Ann all lands for life, and residue; she to be sole Exec'x; son John, provided for at marriage, to have gun and sword; dau. Sarah and her children Samuel, Sarah, Peter, and Mary Coley; dau. Hannah; children of son John,—John, Elizabeth, Sarah, and Mary; loving friends John Gregory of Norwalk and Robert Clarke of Stratford, overseers.

Inv. 27 Aug. 1684.

Children:

+John.

Sarah, m. (1) Peter Coley; m. (2) Thomas Sherwood, 2d.

Hannah, m. William Sprague.

Hide, John, s. of Humphrey.

Married Elizabeth Harvey, dau. of Richard of Stratford [*q. v.*].

Inv. 1 Nov. 1689, sworn to by Elizabeth Hide. Mutual agreement, 18 Mar. 1692/3, by Elizabeth Hide, and Sarah, Mary, John and Elizabeth Hide.

Benjamin Rumsey, Jonathan Fanton, and Edward Jesup, children and heirs of Est. of John Hide, Sr., receipted 6 Jan. 1696 to brother John Hide, with consent of our mother.

Elizabeth Hide sold a negro boy, seven years old, for £30 to John Hide, 16 Nov. 1698.

Will of Elizabeth, 9 June 1701, proved 18 Nov. 1701; daus.

Elizabeth Jessup, Sarah Fanton, Mary Rumsey; son John Hide (Exec'r) and his eldest son. The Exec'r declined; adm'n granted to John Hide and Benjamin Rumsey.

On 9 Feb. 1721/2, Jonathan Fanton conveyed to John Hide [Jr.] right in land of gr. father John Hide dec'd set to me from father Jonathan Fanton's estate, undivided with the rest of the long lot belonging to my uncle John Hide and Benjamin Rumsey.

Children, all but John recorded at Fairfield:

+John, b. 1 May 1668 (by both Stratford and Greenfield records, with
    which age at death agrees; but date conflicts with birth of the
    next child as rec. at Fairfield).
Elizabeth, b. 23 Aug. 1668 [1669?]; m. Edward Jessup.
Sarah, b. 25 Sept. 1670, d. at Greenfield, 29 Sept. 1760 in 90 yr.;
    m. (1) Jonathan Fanton; m. (2) (by prenuptial agreement, 29 Feb.
    1715/6), William Hill.
Mary, b. 26 July 1672; m. Benjamin Rumsey. He conveyed 9 Feb.
    1721/2 to John Hide, right in land he had from father-in-law John
    Hide with his wife Mary.

Hide, John, s. of John.

Born at Stratford, 1 May 1668; Dea. John d. 5 Nov. 1744 ae. 76½ (rec. Greenfield). He renewed Covenant at Fairfield Church, 3 Mar. 1695, and his wife Rachel was bapt. 2 Apr. 1710.

Married Rachel Rumsey, b. 6 Oct. 1671 (rec. Greenfield), d. at Greenfield, 14 June 1738 ae. 67 (g. s.). She was called Rachel Hide in will of her father Robert Rumsey, 1710.

Will 25 Oct. 1744, proved 15 Nov. 1744; sons John, Daniel; daus. Damaris Whitlock, Sarah widow of Jonathan Fanton, Elizabeth wife of John Bell, Hannah wife of Joseph Burr, Mary, Rachael, Abigail wife of Jonathan Malery.

Children, recorded at Greenfield, bapt. at Fairfield Church:

×John, b. 6 Oct. 1692, bapt. 3 Mar. 1694/5, d. at Westport, 15 Jan.
    1761 (g. s., which gives birth-date); Deacon; m. (1) (rec. Fair-
    field) 22 Apr. 1718, Rachel Holmes, who d. 30 Sept. 1736 in 37 yr.
    (g. s., Westport); m. (2) 22 Mar. 1737, Abigail (Silliman),
    widow of David Adams.
Elizabeth, b. 9 Aug. 1694, bapt. 3 Mar. 1694/5; m. (rec. Fairfield)
    10 June 1736, John Bell.
Damaris, b. 2 Sept. 1696, bapt. 11 Oct. 1696; m. (rec. Fairfield) 24
    Jan. 1716, Thomas Whitlock.

Daniel, b. 31 Mar. 1700, bapt. 5 Apr. 1700, d. [———] 1771 in 71 yr.
(g. s., Huntington); Capt.; m. (1) Deborah Perry, who d. 17
Feb. 1754 ae. 56 (g. s.); m. (2) Mary ———.
Abigail, b. 20 May 1702, bapt. 21 June 1702; m. Jonathan Mallory.
Sarah, b. 25 Dec. 1703, bapt. 16 Apr. 1704, living 1757; m. Jonathan
Fanton.
Mary, b. 8 Oct. 1705, bapt. 11 Nov. 1705; m. (rec. Fairfield) 6 Jan.
1725/6, Benjamin Darling.
Hannah, b. 28 Sept. 1707, bapt. 14 Mar. 1707/8; m. (rec. Fairfield)
3 Mar. 1725, Joseph Burr.
Joseph, bapt. 2 Apr. 1710, d. y.
Rachel, b. 6 Feb. 1713, bapt. 2 May 1714; m. (1) Robert Lord; m.
(2) as "Lord alias Hide", 23 June 1746, Richard Livesey.

Higbee, Edward.*

Early of Stratford (1640?); New London by 1648; perhaps
Stratford again; Middletown 1674; Jamaica, L. I., 1677;
Huntington, L. I., 1683; d. in 1699. He had a grant of 300 acres
from Conn. Colony in 1665.

He m. (1) Jedidah Skidmore, dau. of Thomas, whose will 1684
named his grandchild John Higby.

He m. (2) [Lydia] Smith, sister of Joseph Smith of Jamaica,
who in 1668 was called (by Winthrop) brother of Goody Higbee.
In 1669 Winthrop stated ages of three children of Edward Higby:
Patience 6 (or 8), Sarah 4, Nathaniel 1.

In 1688 he was called bro.-in-law by Jeremy Adams of Huntington (son of John, son of Jeremy of Hartford). He prob. m. (3)
by 1684, Abigail (Adams) Betts.

Child [by first wife]:

John, b. abt. 1649; in 1669 Winthrop mentions him, ae. 20, in Windsor at Nathaniel Bissell's. He m. 1 May 1679, Rebecca Treadwell,
dau. of Edward, and sister of Samuel of Fairfield. He settled in
Middletown and d. in 1688 (Inv. 28 Dec. 1688); his widow d. by
Mar. 1708. His son Edward chose his uncle Samuel Treadwell for
guardian, 11 Sept. 1700; m. 29 Nov. 1706, Rebecca Wheeler, dau.
of Joseph of Stratfield, and returned to Middletown, dying 21 Nov.
1775.

---

* Our account of this family is fragmentary, and the printed sources utilized may
not be entirely dependable. We have not had the opportunity to consult the *Higbee
Genealogy*.

Children [by second wife], record incomplete:
Patience, b. abt. 1662.
Sarah, b. abt. 1664.
Nathaniel, b. abt. 1667.

Higgins, Abraham.

Born about 1665, d. at Westport, 20 Mar. 1757, in 92 yr. (or 21 Mar. by g. s.).

Married Sarah Middlebrook, dau. of Joseph, b. 12 Nov. 1675; renewed Covenant at Fairfield, 24 Mar. 1695, and d. at Westport, 24 Mar. 1756.

Will 14 Jan. 1744/5, proved 19 Apr. 1757; wife Sarah; daus. Sarah and Mary; son Samuel; dau. Martha; son Abraham.

Children, bapt. at Fairfield:
Abigail, bapt. 24 Mar. 1694/5.
Sarah, bapt. 26 Nov. 1699; m. at Fairfield, 20 Jan. 1723, Nathaniel Squire.
Mary,* b. [say 1701].
Phebe, who m. (rec. Greenfield) 3 June 1727, Noah Sherwood, should perhaps be placed in this family, as Abraham Higgins, Jr., was appointed guardian of her son Noah. Her age at death would place her birth about 1703; d. at Greenfield, 22 Apr. 1774 ae. 71.
Abraham, bapt. 23 Sept. 1705, d. y.
XSamuel, bapt. 20 Sept. 1708, d. in 1789; will 24 Mar. 1788, proved 7 Dec. 1789; m. Miriam Belden, dau. of William of Norwalk, b. 11 Nov. 1714.
Martha, bapt. 9 Apr. 1710.
XAbraham, bapt. 24 July 1715; m. at Fairfield, May 1739, Mary Allen.

HILL FAMILY (WILLIAM)

Hill, William. Deputy (Windsor) to Conn. Leg., Aug. and Sept. 1639, Jan. 1640, Feb., Sept. and Nov. 1641, Apr. and Aug. 1642, Mar. and Sept. 1643, Apr. and Sept. 1644.

Son of James Hill of Lyme Regis, co. Dorset, Eng., who was Mayor of Lyme Regis, 1603. The will of James, 10 May 1620, proved 5 May 1621, named son William and dau. Mary Hill, with

---

* A Mary Higgins d. at Westport, 11 Aug. 1757.

others. The will of Mary Godwyn of Lyme Regis, last of Mar.
1665, proved 6 June 1665, named her three cousins, William,
James, and Ynatius, sons of my brother William Hill in New
England, £150 between them.

He m. at St. Mary Archer, Exeter, co. Devon, 28 Oct. 1619,
Sarah Jourdain, dau. of Ignatius and Elizabeth* of Exeter, co.
Devon; she was bapt. at St. Mary Archer, 4 Mar. 1598/9, and m.
(2) after 1663, Edmund Greenleaf† of Boston. The will of
Ignatius,‡ 1 Mar. 1635, proved 16 Oct. 1640, named wife Elizabeth, children of son William Hill, and others, specifying Lyme as
his birthplace. The will of Elizabeth, widow of Ignatius, 20 June
1645, proved 9 Mar. 1649, gave £20 to grandchild Joseph Hill.

He came to Dorchester, Mass., by 1633, probably on *Mary and
John* 1630; removed before 1639 to Windsor, and not long before
his death to Fairfield, where he d. in Sept. 1649. On 11 May 1654,
lands were entered in Fairfield records, formerly given by the town
to William Hill, Sr.

Will 9 Sept. 1649, proved 15 May 1650; wife Sarah; children
Sarah (has had portion), William, Joseph, Ignatius, James, Elizabeth. Inv. at Windsor, 24 Sept. 1649; at Fairfield, 16 Nov. 1649.

Will of Edmund Greenleaf of Boston, 22 Dec. 1668, named his
wife's three sons, William, Ignatius, and James Hill, to whom
their aunt gave £50 apiece; he sent something to Ignatius in
Barbadoes.

---

* Elizabeth, wife of Ignatius Jourdain, was sister of Sir Simon Baskerville, and
dau. of Thomas Baskerville of Exeter, co. Devon, Bailiff in 1590, by his wife, dau. of
Richard Perry, Bailiff in 1585. Her brother Simon, of London, was physician to
James I and Charles I; the latter knighted him.

† Capt. Edmund Greenleaf, bapt. at St. Mary's La Tour, Ipswich, co. Suffolk, 2 Jan.
1573/4, son of John and Margaret; d. at Boston, 24 Mar. 1671; m. (1) Sarah Dole,
who d. 18 Jan. 1662/3.

‡ Ignatius, son of William Jourdain of Lyme Regis, bapt. there 17 Aug. 1561;
began his business life among his kinsmen in Exeter; in 1576 was sent by his employer
to Guernsey, where he was converted; m. (1) at St. Mary Archer, Exeter, 24 June
1589, Katherine Bodlie, dau. of John, who was buried 4 May 1593; m. (2) 5 Aug.
1593, Elizabeth Baskerville. In 1599 he was appointed a Bailiff of Exeter; member
of the Chamber, 1608; Receiver of the City, 1610; Sheriff of Exeter, 1611; Mayor,
1617; Deputy Mayor, 1624, for three months during the plague, all the magistrates having fled; Member of Parliament from Exeter, 1625, also 1625-6 and 1627-8. He was
a Puritan, and in 1639 when the proclamation touching the rebellious practices in
Scotland was read in Exeter Cathedral, Alderman Jourdain was one of three who put
on their hats in silent protest. For this he was commanded either to apologize or to
appear before the Council in London. He did neither; but did not long survive; buried
18 June 1640. His widow Elizabeth was buried 18 Oct. 1649.

On 1 Feb. 1673 [1673/4], the younger William Hill entered for record at Fairfield lands of which half were his portion, and the rest granted him by his father-in-law Greenleaf and his mother.

Children:

Sarah, d. 23 Aug. 1653; m. at Windsor, 17 Sept. 1646, Joseph Loomis.
+William.
Joseph, prob. d. s. p.
Ignatius, of Barbadoes and Boston; will 12 Jan. 1675/6, named brother Sergt. James and referred to legacy of £50 from aunt Mary Goodwin sent over from England.
James, Sergt., of Boston; m. 10 Apr. 1662, Hannah Henchman; had children rec. at Boston: Hannah, b. 21 Mar. 1664/5; James, b. 21 Feb. 1666/7; Ignatius, b. 6 Nov. 1668; and Elizabeth, b. 15 June 1670.
Elizabeth, m. [say by 1650], Anthony Wilson; whose will 1662 referred to mother Hill and brothers William, Ignatius, and James Hill.

Hill, William, s. of William. Deputy (Fairfield) to Conn. Leg., Sept. 1651, May and Oct. 1652, May 1653, May and Sept. 1654, May and Oct. 1655, Oct. 1658, Oct. 1659, Oct. 1661, Oct. 1665, Oct. 1666, May and Oct. 1667, May and Oct. 1668, May 1669, May 1671. War committee, Fairfield, May 1653. Commissioner for Fairfield, 1666 to 1678 inclusive, and was Clerk of the Fairfield County Court, May 1666. Colonial grant of 150 acres, Oct. 1672. Town Recorder.

Married Elizabeth Jones, b. in England early in 1635, dau. of Rev. John. She was named as Elizabeth Hill in her father's will 1665, and as sister in will 1677 of Sarah (Jones) (Bulkley) Wilson.

He d. at Fairfield, 19 Dec. 1684. Deacon, Fairfield Church.

Inv. 25 Dec. 1684. Adm'n granted to widow Elizabeth; the dau. Sarah and four sons. On 24 Feb. 1728/9 his undivided commonage was partitioned by agreement of his heirs, Dea. William Hill (son of William dec'd), William Hill, Jr., and Eliphalet Hill (sons of Eliphalet), and John Hill (son of John).

Elizabeth Hill conveyed 1694 to her four sons, referring to dec'd husband William Hill, and dec'd father Jones.

Children:

Sarah, d. 28 Mar. 1697; m. 15 Apr. 1686, Richard Whidden.
+William, b. abt. 1661.
+Eliphalet.
+John.
Joseph, d. in 1696, unm. Adm'n granted, 17 Sept. 1696, to William
  and John Hill. Distribution 4 Apr. 1711 to two brothers John and
  William; heirs of Eliphalet Hill,—two sons, William and
  Eliphalet; heirs of Richard Widden,—two daus. Elizabeth and
  Sarah.

Hill, William, s. of William, 2d.

Born about 1661, d. at Fairfield, 19 Apr. 1739 in 78 yr. (g. s.).
Deacon, Fairfield Church.

Married (1) (rec. Fairfield) 7 Oct. 1691, Abigail Osborn, dau.
of David of Eastchester, dec'd. She was prob. the "A. H." who
d. 27 Apr. 1712 (g. s.). He m. (2) Sarah ———, who d. at
Fairfield, 28 Mar. 1715. He m. (3) (by prenuptial agreement,
29 Feb. 1715/6) Sarah Fanton. She was widow of Jonathan Fanton, and dau. of John Hide, b. 25 Sept. 1670, d. at Greenfield,
29 Sept. 1760 in 90 yr.

Will 21 Jan. 1728/9, proved 24 Apr. 1739; wife Sarah; three
sons, Joseph, William, David; two grandchildren, Joseph and
Abigail Squire. On 3 Nov. 1766, Samuel Rowland in right of
his wife Abigail (granddau. of Wm. Hill dec'd) asked for adm'n
on the part of Est. bequeathed in his will to David Hill; Joseph
and William Hill, only surviving children, appealed.

Children [by first wife], recorded at Fairfield:

Abigail, b. 8 Jan. 1694 [1694/5], bapt. 24 Mar. 1694/5, d. before 1719;
  m. 1715, Joseph Squire.
XJoseph, b. 1 Apr. 1699, bapt. 14 May 1699, d. 6 Mar. 1797 in 98 yr.
  (g. s., Greenfield); Deacon; m. 30 Mar. 1731, Abigail Dimon, dau.
  of Moses, bapt. 17 Aug. 1707; d. 25 Apr. 1774 in 67 yr. (g. s.).
XWilliam, b. 16 May 1702, bapt. 12 July 1702, d. ———; Cornet of
  Horse, 1744; res. Redding; m. (1) 28 Apr. 1725, Hannah Morehouse. She was dau. of Daniel, bapt. 24 Sept. 1704; d. 10 Aug.
  1729. He m. (2) 28 Feb. 1730, Rebecca Sanford; dau. of Ezekiel,
  b. 21 Nov. 1710, d. abt. Nov. 1730. He m. (3) 6 May 1731, Mary
  Ogden.
David, b. 3 Apr. 1710 [prob. error for 1706], bapt. 7 Apr. 1706, d. in
  1736/7; m. Abigail Andrews, who m. (2) Henry Rowland. She

was dau. of John, b. 17 June 1709. Their only child Abigail, b. 8 July 1732, d. y. David's will, 7 Feb. 1736/7, proved 30 Mar. 1737; gave £10 out of charity to poor widow Rowlandson; bros. Joseph and William Hill; wife Abigail, Exec'x.

Hill, Eliphalet, s. of William, 2d.   Deputy (Fairfield) to Conn. Leg., Oct. 1691, May 1694.

Married at Fairfield, Nov. 1691, Esther Nichols, dau. of William Ward. She was widow of Ebenezer Hawley, and after of Ephraim Nichols; and m. (4) Robert Lord.

Inv. 30 Jan. 1695 [1695/6]; his wife's dowry in her husband Nichols' estate mentioned. Adm'n granted to bros. William and John Hill, 23 Apr. 1696. They refused, and Lt. James Bennett and Abraham Adams were appointed. Bennett refused, so Adams administered. Mr. Nathaniel Burr and Mr. John Edwards were appointed to act with Adams, 10 Feb. 1696 [1696/7], because of difficulties. Part of Inv. could not be "gained from Robert Lord and Esther"; they explained losses.

Children, recorded at Fairfield:

 XWilliam, b. 17 Nov. 1692, d. 25 Apr. 1775 ae. over 80 (Greenfield Church); will 25 Feb. 1775, proved 16 May 1775; m. (1) abt. 1716, Abigail Barlow, dau. of John, b. 30 June 1697; d. 16 Apr. 1743 ae. 47 (g. s., Greenfield); m. (2) Esther (Sturgis) Lines, widow of Benjamin Lines, bapt. 2 Mar. 1700/1.
 Eliphalet, b. 11 Jan. 1694/5, bapt. 3 Mar. 1694/5; res. Huntington, L. I., 1725.

Hill, John, s. of William, 2d.

Married Jane ———; she m. (2) 1738, Moses Dimon, and (3) 10 Aug. 1749, Lt. Gideon Allen; Widow Allen d. at Redding, 22 July 1774 ae. (supposed) 98.

Adm'n granted to widow Jane, 5 Sept. 1727. Distribution to widow, John Hill, and Gershom Morehouse [not dated, apparently 1728].

Will of Jane Allen of Reading, 9 Feb. 1762, proved 16 Aug. 1774; dau. Sarah wife of Gershom Morehouse; gr. children Nathan, Esther, Sarah, Isaac, Joseph, Gershom, Elizabeth, and Ruth, a bond against Nathan Hill to be equally divided; gr. son Gershom Morehouse, Exec'r.

Children:

Sarah, bapt. 25 May 1701; m. 22 Apr. 1725, Gershom Morehouse.

XJohn, bapt. 29 June 1707, d. at Fairfield, 17 Dec. 1759; will 7 Dec.
1759, proved 15 Jan. 1760; m. 27 Jan. 1729, Esther Bulkley. She
was dau. of Joseph, bapt. 20 Dec. 1713; and m. (2) 9 May 1764,
Stephen Adams.

HILL FAMILY (THOMAS)

Hill, (Capt.) Thomas.

Married abt. 1685/6, Abigail Wakeman, dau. of Ezbon.

On 9 Nov. 1685, at Flushing, L. I., Thomas Hill, mariner, gave
a bond to Mr. Elias Doughty of Flushing and Mr. Jacob Walker
of Stratford, feofees in trust for Abigail Wakeman of Fairfield,
dau. of Mr. Izbon Wakeman dec'd, a minor with whom Hill
intended marriage.

Nathaniel Fryer of Portsmouth, N. H., mariner, owner of half
the ketch *The Two Brothers* (32 tons), conveyed 21 Sept. 1686
to Thomas Hill, late of London, mariner, now of Fairfield.

Joseph Bastard bought land, 5 Feb. 1686 [1686/7], from
Thomas Hill and Abigail his wife.

Thomas Hill, mariner, now of Fairfield, 20 July 1688, referring
to marriage covenant, made Joseph Lockwood and Jacob Walker
feofees in trust.

He died before 1711.   Thomas Hill, son of Thomas of Fairfield,
dec'd, chose his uncle Robert Rumsey for guardian, 6 Mar. 1710/1.

Children:

XThomas, b. [say 1692], d. in 1770; Capt.·; will 27 Dec. 1769, proved
10 Aug. 1770; m. (1) at Fairfield, 9 Dec. 1715, Mary Burr. She
was dau. of John, b. 13 Oct. 1694 (by age at death), d. 19 Dec.
1763 ae. 69 yrs. 1 mo. 26 days (g. s., Fairfield). He m. (2) (by
marriage Covenant, 13 Apr. 1764), Hannah ———.

Benjamin, bapt. 3 Nov. 1695; m. by 1717, Ann Wakeman, dau. of
John, b. 24 Mar. 1698. On 4 Jan. 1716/7, he sold to his bro.
Thomas a full third interest in lands which his father Thomas Hill
(with wife Abigail, only child of Ezbon Wakeman) died seized of,
to which Thomas and Benjamin Hill were the only heirs. On 9
Dec. 1717, with wife Ann dau. of John Wakeman, he sold land
set to her in the distribution of her father's Est. He had one child,
Abigail, bapt. at Fairfield, 26 Apr. 1719.

Hinman, Edward.

Of Stratford by 1652, and received a homelot in Woodbury by 1681.

Married Hannah Stiles, dau. of Francis.

The will of Sarah wife of Robert Clark of Stratford (formerly Stiles) in 1677 mentioned children of her dau. Hannah Hinman dec'd.

Will of Sergt. Edward of Woodbury, 17 Nov. 1681; he died 26 Nov. 1681; sons Titus, Samuel, Benjamin; daus. Hannah, Mary, Patience, under 18; dau. Sarah Roberts and her two children; son Edward to have land in Stratford, and to be apprenticed to "some honest & religious tender man", preferably to Jehiel Preston of Stratford; brother Ephraim Stiles to be overseer at Stratford; Samuel Stiles, overseer at Woodbury.

Children, recorded at Stratford:

Sarah, b. Sept. 1653; m. William Roberts.
+Titus, b. Jan. 1655 [1655/6].
+Samuel, b. last of June 1658.
+Benjamin, b. Sept. 1662.
Hannah, b. 15 July 1666.
Mary,* m. —— Clark.
Patience, m. 10 Jan. 1694/5, John Burroughs.
+Edward.

Hinman, Titus, s. of Edward.

Lt., Woodbury Trainband, May 1710; Capt., May 1714. Deputy for Woodbury, May 1699, Oct. 1712, Oct. 1713, May and Oct. 1714, Oct. 1715, Oct. 1716, May 1719, Oct. 1720.

Born at Stratford, Jan. 1655/6; d. at Woodbury, 5 Apr. 1736 ae. 80 (g. s.); m. (1) Hannah Coe, dau. of John of Rye, who d. 4 Jan. 1702/3; m. (2) 14 June 1703, Mary Hawkins, dau. of Robert, b. at Derby, 11 June 1677, d. at Southbury, June 1756 ae. 80.

Children [by first wife], bapt. at Woodbury:

Ephraim, bapt. 26 July 1685.
Joseph, bapt. June 1687; m. 16 Nov. 1714, Esther Downs.

---

* Abraham, son of Mary Hinman, bapt. at Woodbury, July 1697.

Andrew, bapt. Apr. 1690; Lt., south company, Woodbury, Oct. 1727; Capt., May 1733; m. (rec. Woodbury), 29 Aug. 1711, Mary Noble; dau. of John, b. 16 Oct. 1692.

Titus, bapt. June 1695, d. at Southbury, 5 Apr. 1736; m. at New Milford, abt. 8 June 1721, Sarah Noble; dau. of John, b. 22 Mar. 1699.

Ebenezer, b., bapt., and d. 4 Jan. 1702/3.

Children [by second wife], recorded at Woodbury:

Hannah, b. 21 Mar. 1703/4, bapt. Mar. 1703/4, d. y.

Eleazer, b. 17 Apr. 1705, bapt. Apr. 1705; Lt. of the Troop in 13th Regt., Oct. 1744; m. Hannah Scovill, dau. of John, b. at Waterbury, 19 Mar. 1706/7.

Timothy, b. 4 Mar. 1708 [1708/9], bapt. Mar. 1708/9, d. at Southbury, 11 Dec. 1769; Capt., Southbury company, May 1754; m. Emm Preston, who d. 20 Sept. 1794 ae. 78.

Mary, b. 6 Feb. 1713 [1713/4]; m. 30 July 1739, Rev. David Bostwick, of New Milford, Jamaica, L. I., and New York City.

Hannah, b. 12 Mar. 1720/1; m. (1) 13 Dec. 1739, Samuel Twitchell; m. (2) 13 Apr. 1749, John Pierce of Southbury.

Hinman, Samuel, s. of Edward.

Born at Stratford, last of June 1658; lived in Woodbury, and d. 7 Nov. 1713. He m. after 1687, Mary, widow of Joseph Hickock, and dau. of David Carpenter, b. Aug. 1650. No issue.

Will 7 June 1710, proved 2 Dec. 1713; wife Mary; kinsman Ephraim Hinman, eldest son of brother Titus; kinsman Benjamin Hinman, son of brother Ben; kinsman Abraham Wooster, son of sister Mary Clerk; lands to be divided between these three after death of wife, Wooster not to alienate his share until forty years old; my girl Sarah Taylor; witnesses, Anne Knowles and Anne Huthwitt. Ann Knowles now Ann Hinman, and Ann Huthwitt, gave oath to will, 2 Dec. 1713.

Hinman, Benjamin, s. of Edward. Deputy for Woodbury, May and June 1711.

Born at Stratford, Sept. 1662; Sergt. Benjamin d. at Woodbury, 26 May 1727.

He m. (rec. Woodbury) 12 July 1684, Elizabeth Lum, who was

bapt. at Woodbury, May 1683. Justice Richbell performed the marriage ceremony.

Inv. of Benjamin, Sr., who d. 26 May 1727, made 26 Oct. 1727. Agreement of heirs (mentioning the heir of Rachel) was signed by Noah Hinman, John and Elizabeth Hurd, Benjamin, Jr., and Hannah Hurd, Nathan and Eunice Hurd, Samuel and Annis Martin, Wait Hinman, Ephraim Baldwin, and Mercy Hinman.

Children, recorded at Woodbury:

Annis, bapt. Apr. 1685, d. y.

Hannah, bapt. Oct. 1686, d. at Roxbury, 29 Feb. 1756; m. Benjamin Hurd.

Adam, bapt. Jan. 1687/8, d. 23 Dec. 1717.

Noah, bapt. July 1689, d. at Southbury, 14 Nov. 1766 ae. 76; Dea. and Judge of County Court; m. (1) 28 Feb. 1710/1, Anna Knowles, who d. 10 Feb. 1719/20; m. (2) Sarah Scovill, who d. 23 Apr. 1741; m. (3) Mrs. Wildman.

Benjamin, bapt. Apr. 1692, d. in 1727; Inv. 22 June 1727; m. 18 Dec. 1718, Sarah Sherman, who d. 19 May 1727 ae. 37.

Elizabeth, bapt. Feb. 1692/3; m. John Hurd.

Eunice, bapt. May 1696, d. 23 Mar. 1792 ae. 96; m. 7 Nov. 1718, Nathan Hurd.

Annis, bapt. Sept. 1697; m. 15 Jan. 1715/6, Samuel Martin, and had 17 children.

Rachel, b. 12 Sept. 1700, d. 26 May 1727; m. Ephraim Baldwin; he conveyed with other Hinman heirs 1727, on behalf of his son Jonas.

Edward, b. 25 Oct. 1702, d. in 1726.

Samuel, b. 1 Dec. 1704, d. 21 May 1727.

Wait, b. 16 Oct. 1706, d. at Southbury, 29 Apr. 1775 ae. 69; Ens., Woodbury south company, Oct. 1740; Capt., Oct. 1743; m. 11 June 1729, Ann Hurd, who d. 27 Dec. 1785 ae. 83.

Mercy, b. 23 Dec. 1709; m. David Barnum.

Hinman, Edward, s. of Edward.

His widow Hannah d. at North Stratford, 25 July 1777 on her 99th birthday [Old Style], which would place her birth 14 July 1678. Hinman in *Conn. Puritans* calls her Hannah Jennings, but no place for her has been found in the Jennings family of Fairfield. The name may be due to confusion with the wife of her son Ebenezer.

Children, recorded at Stratford:

Jonah, b. 5 Nov. 1700; rem. to Newark, N. J., where he d. 9 Sept. 1758 ae. 58 (g. s.); m. Elizabeth ———, who d. 21 Apr. 1772 ae. 64 yrs. 2 mos. 7 days (g. s.).

Hannah, b. 3 Mar. 1702 [1702/3], m. 16 Jan. 1722/3, Mr. Thomas Allen, of Newark, N. J.

Zechariah, b. 27 Jan. 1704/5.

Samuel, b. 6 Jan. 1705/6; res. Litchfield and Goshen, being one of the first settlers of the latter place; Ens., Goshen east company, Oct. 1751; Lt., Oct. 1752; Capt., Oct. 1756.

Justus, b. 28 Dec. 1707; m. Hannah Judson, dau. of Joshua.

Ebenezer, b. 5 Oct. 1709, d. at Southbury, 18 Nov. 1795 ae. 86; m. 4 June 1739, Obedience Jennings, who d. 15 Dec. 1812 ae. 92.

Sarah, b. Oct. 1711.

John, b. 4 Nov. 1713; res. Trumbull; m. (1) Eunice Curtis; m. (2) 15 Aug. 1754, Anna Nichols.

Rachel, b. 4 Dec. 1715.

Eunice, b. 16 Aug. 1717.

Amos, b. 18 Oct. 1720; m. Abigail ———.

Charity, b. 6 June 1723.

Hitt, Henry.

Married at Stratford, 8 Jan. 1673 [1673/4], Sarah Bassett. She was dau. of Robert; and m. (2) [Simon] Lobdell.

Inv. of Henry of Woodbury, 20 Mar. 1689/90; included property in Stratford. Widow; children's ages: Sarah 14, Margerit about 10, Henry 7, John and Mie (twins) 4, James about 2.

Samuel Sherman of Stratford, adm'r of Est. of Henry Hitt of Woodbury, with consent of the adm'x Sarah Lobdell, sold 4 Mar. 1698/9 to Benjamin Hinman. [Woodbury Deeds.]

Children, first recorded at Stratford, the rest bapt. at Woodbury:

Sarah, b. 23 Feb. 1675 [1675/6].

Margaret, bapt. Apr. 1679.

Henry, bapt. Feb. 1682; lived in Westchester County.

John, bapt. Apr. 1686; m. Hannah ———; had children recorded in Branford.

Amy, bapt. Apr. 1686.

James, bapt. Feb. 1688, d. at Branford early in 1712. The Inv. was sworn to 17 Mar. 1711 [1711/2] by the adm'rs John and Henry Hitt, who exhibited receipts from the heirs, 14 Feb. 1712/3.

Hobby, John. Deputy for Greenwich, Oct. 1682, May 1696, May 1697, May 1701.

He was a member of the petit jury which tried the witchcraft cases, 1692.

Will of John of Greenwich, 24 Apr. 1707; sons Thomas, Benjamin, Jonathan; daus. Hannah Bunkham, Martha Morehouse; daus. of dec'd dau. Rebecca Hardy,—Rebecca and Hannah Hardy; daus. Mary Holmes, Rachel James; gr. children, John Hobby, Mary Holmes; son Jonathan and son-in-law Stephen Holmes, Exec'rs. Inv. 26 May 1707.

Hollingsworth, Richard.

Came from London in the *Blessing* 1635, aged 40, with wife Susan or Susanna, ae. 30, and children William 7, Richard 4, Elizabeth 3, and Susan 2. He settled as a shipwright in Salem, Mass., and d. in 1654.

His widow Susanna perhaps m. (2) Rev. John Jones of Fairfield. Winthrop in 1666 treated Mary "Holsworth", ae. 26, whom he called dau. of the wife of Mr. Jones, Pastor of Fairfield.

Susannah Hollingworth of Salem, widow, conveyed to Humphrey Woodbury of Salem, 2 Dec. 1667. This militates against the conclusion that she had married Jones; yet he was then dead, and it is not unknown for a woman doubly a widow to use the first husband's name when conveying right in his estate. "Old Goodwife Hollingworth" was admitted by Humphrey Woodbury, Sr., into his cottage and he agreed to support her; but if he dies, she was to be admitted an inhabitant; this entry, from Salem town records, 12 Dec. 1675, indicates that she had been living elsewhere and had returned to Salem.

Children:*

    William, b. abt. 1628, d. in 1667; m. Eleanor ——, who d. 22 Nov. 1689 ae. 59 (g. s.). Children: William, b. abt. 1655, d. 7 Nov. 1688 ae. 33 (g. s.); Mary, m. 1 Sept. 1675, Philip English, and was accused of witchcraft during the great Salem delusion; Susanna, b. 4 Mar. 1658/9.

    +Richard, b. abt. 1630.

    Elizabeth, b. abt. 1632.

    Susan, b. abt. 1634; m. 24 Nov. 1650, Robert Starr.

---

* Job Hilliard of Salem by first wife Sarah had a dau. Sarah who m. by 1674 —— Hollingsworth.

Hypothetical children :*
  Mary, b. abt. 1637.
  Mercy, b. [say 1640]; m. (1) —— Nichols; m. (2) Thomas
    Disbrow, of Fairfield.

Hollingsworth, Richard, s. of Richard.

Born in England about 1630, d. at Milford in 1683; m. at
Boston, 23 Aug. 1659, Elizabeth Powell, dau. of "Elder" Michael,
b. at Boston, 16 June 1641, d. at Milford, 10 Jan. 1706 ae. 68(?)
(g. s.). She m. (2) Richard Bryan of Milford, and (3) 24 Oct.
1705, Gov. Robert Treat.

He was a mariner, of Salem, Mass., and Milford, Conn.

Inv. 7 Sept. 1683; small estate, but included Latin and English
books.

Adm'n on Est. of Mrs. Elizabeth Treat late Hollingsworth of
Milford was granted, 2 Mar. 1705/6, to dau. Mrs. Abigail Beard
and her husband Mr. John Beard, the son Richard declining.
Distribution was ordered to the three children. On the Est. of
Mrs. Elizabeth Treat sometime Hollingsworth of Milford, a
quietus est was granted, Nov. 1711, to Mrs. Abigail Beard. Caleb
and Richard Hollingsworth of Milford gave receipt, 3 Apr. 1711,
to sister Mrs. Abigail Beard for share from mother's Est.

Children, recorded at Salem, Mass.:
  Richard, b. 9 Aug. 1661, d. Aug. 1662.
  Benjamin, b. 28 June 1663, d. y.
  John, b. 12 May 1665, d. y.
  Abigail, b. 1 Mar. 1667/8; m. 15 Mar. 1704/5, John Beard, of Milford.
  Joseph, b. 4 May 1670, d. at Milford in Apr. 1698, unm.; Inv. 26
    Apr. 1698, exhibited by his mother Mrs. Elizabeth Bryan. His
    sister Abigail Hollingworth, ae. abt. 29, testified to Joseph's nun-
    cupative will, dated 9 Apr. 1698, mentioning his mother and bro.
    Richard.
  Caleb, b. 22 Dec. 1673, d. abt. 1731, unm. Adm'n granted, 28 Apr.
    1731, to Richard Hollingsworth.
  +Richard, bapt. at Milford, 19 Sept. 1680.

---

* It must be understood that the theory suggested is merely a theory. The second
wife of Rev. John Jones may have been a Holdsworth; see further discussion under
JONES. In 1673 the second Richard Hollingsworth stated that his father came to this
country about 40 yrs. before and brought a family of *twelve* with him. Perhaps some
of the children were born here, if the testimony was inexact.

Hollingsworth, Richard, 3d, s. of Richard, 2d.

Bapt. 19 Sept. 1680; m. Ruth Lewis, dau. of Philip of Fairfield; in old age she m. (2) Stephen Munson (1679-1768) of New Haven.

Lived in Fairfield several years; in 1733 was of Milford and conveyed to Richard, Jr., right from Est. of bro. Caleb of Milford dec'd.

Children, first three bapt. at Stratfield, 15 Apr. 1711, two at Fairfield:

> Richard, m. at Milford, 16 June 1735, Ann Baldwin.
> Mary, m. at Milford, 7 Jan. 1730/1, Thomas Hine, Jr.
> Elizabeth, m. at Milford, 20 Apr. 1727, William Hine, of Milford and Derby.*
> ✕Joseph, bapt. 14 Jan. 1712/3, d. at Fairfield in 1776; m. (1) at Fairfield, 4 Nov. 1734, Ann Jennings; m. (2) Ruth ———.
> Abigail, bapt. 2 June 1723, d. at New Haven, 23 Feb. 1793 ae. 70 (g. s.) ; m. (rec. New Haven, called of Milford) 21 May 1741, Samuel Munson.

Holly, John. Magistrate for Stamford, May 1654, May 1655; Deputy (Stamford) to New Haven Leg., May 1663; Deputy (Stamford) to Conn. Leg., Oct. 1670, and for Greenwich, May 1673. Commissioner for Stamford and Greenwich, 1667-81, and most of that period for Rye also.

Mr. John d. at Stamford, 25 May 1681.

Will 14 Apr. 1681; wife Mary; sons Samuel, John, Increase, Elisha, Jonathan; daus. Elizabeth Turney, Bethia Weed, Hannah Hoyt; dau. Abigail.

Children:

> Samuel, b. abt. 1641, d. at Stamford, 13 May 1709 in 68 yr. (g. s.) ; m. 25 June 1668, Mary Close. Samuel Holly, Sr., ae. abt. 50, testified Aug. 1692 in the Clawson witchcraft trial.
> Elizabeth, m. Robert Turney.
> Bethia, d. at Stamford, 24 Dec. 1713; m. 16 Nov. 167—, Jonas Weed.

---

* Her name is stated as Abigail in the marriage record. No Abigail Hollingsworth can be found suitable for this marriage; a son by Elizabeth was given the Hollingsworth name *Richard;* and we conclude that the original entry erred in the name Abigail. William Hine's wife *Elizabeth* was adm. to Milford Church, 20 July 1729, and the two eldest children were bapt. as *Elizabeth's* children. The second child was Abigail (bapt. 1730) who in William Hine's will 1781 received "all my moveables that belonged to my *first* Wife her Mother". This proves that his first wife was *Elizabeth.*

John, d. 22 Sept. 1716; m. 2 Apr. 1679, Hannah Newman, who d. 24 Jan. 1712.

Increase, d. 1 Mar. 1726/7; Ens., Stamford Trainband, Oct. 1699; Lt., May 1707; m. 2 Apr. 1679, Elizabeth Newman.

Hannah, d. 7 Dec. 1710; m. 16 Nov. 167—, Dea. Samuel Hoyt.

Abigail.

Elisha, b. 6 Mar. 1658/9, d. 28 Oct. 1719; Deputy for Stamford, May 1700, May and Oct. 1701, May and Oct. 1704, May and Oct. 1707, May and Oct. 1708, Oct. 1709, Oct. 1710, May 1711, May 1713; Justice, 1711; m. 2 Dec. 1686, Martha Holmes, who d. 4 Aug. 1721.

Jonathan, b. 1 Mar. 1662/3, d. 12 Oct. 1712; m. 2 Dec. 1686, Sarah Finch; dau. of Samuel, who d. 16 Jan. 1750/1 ae. 88.

Holmes, Francis.

He was of Stamford by 1658, when he and Richard witnessed a deed. The surname was first spelled Homes.

Will 6 Sept. 1671; wife; sons John, Stephen; dau. Ann Dean; son Richard; servant Cornelius; son John's eldest son. Inv. 14 Feb. 1675/6.

Agreement of heirs, 3 Mar. 1675/6; widow Ann; children, John, Richard, and Stephen Holmes, and Samuel and Ann Dean.

In the Clawson witchcraft trial, Oct. 1692, Richard Holmes, ae. abt. 55, testified that his mother had been midwife in Stamford.

Children:

+John.
+Stephen.
  Ann, m. Samuel Dean.
+Richard, b. abt. 1637.

Holmes, John, s. of Francis.

He m. at Stamford, 12 May 1659, Rachel Waterbury.

Removed from Stamford to Bedford.

Children, recorded at Stamford:*

  John, b. 8 Oct. 1660, d. y.
  Mary, b. 25 Sept. 1662; m. 1 Dec. 1692, [prob. David] Clawson.
  Stephen, b. 14 Jan. 1664, d. at Greenwich in 1710; Inv. 13 Dec. 1710; m. 18 Nov. 1686, Mary Hubby.

---

* The younger children are added on the authority of Mead's *Hist. of Greenwich.*

Sarah, m. 25 Feb. 1691, Jonathan Miller.
Rachel, b. 7 Dec. 1669.
John, b. 18 Oct. 1670.
?David.
?Richard.
?Joseph.
?Jonathan.
Rose, m. 9 Apr. 1702, John Westcott.

Holmes, Stephen, s. of Francis.

He d. at Stamford, 15 May 1710.

Widow Martha d. 13 Mar. 1727/8.

Will 6 Sept. 1707; son Samuel; son John's son John; son Stephen; five daus. Mary Slawson, Martha Holly, Rebecca Jaggers, Abigail Hait, Sarah Waterbury; wife Martha. Inv. 14 Nov. 1710.

Children:

> Martha, d. 4 Aug. 1721; m. 2 Dec. 1686, Elisha Holly.
> John, d. 6 July 1703; m. 15 Jan. 1701/2, Mercy Bell.
> Stephen, m. 7 Sept. 1704, Margaret Gibbs; dau. of John of New Haven. They had two surviving children: Hannah, m. Joseph Bishop; and Martha, m. Jonas Weed.
> Rebecca, d. 1 Apr. 1749; m. 22 Aug. 1700, Jonathan Jagger.
> Abigail, m. 30 Apr. 1702, John Hoyt.
> Mary, m. abt. 1704, John Slawson.
> Sarah, m. 16 Jan. 1706/7, John Waterbury.
> Samuel, d. 16 June 1734; perhaps m. 4 Sept. 1725, Anne Orry of Stratford (rec. also at Stratford, 4 Nov. 1725).

Holmes, Richard, s. of Francis.

Born abt. 1637, d. in 1704.

Will of Richard of Norwalk, 31 Oct. 1704, proved 6 Dec. 1704; wife Sarah all est. for life; to her near kinswoman Mehitabel Warner now with me, my now dwelling house, lands, etc.; smith tools; to Jonathan son of Jonathan Stevenson dec'd, former servant whom I brought up from a child, £10; to Samuel Hayes, Sr., of Norwalk, 40 shillings; to Thomas and Richard the two youngest sons now of John Bouton, Sr., of Norwalk, 20 shillings apiece; residue to the now daus. of well beloved brothers, John

Holmes, Sr., of Bedford, and Stephen Holmes, Sr., of Stamford. Inv. 23 Nov. 1704; widow made oath.

Sarah Holmes, widow of Richard and Exec'x of his will, reported dec'd at Court 4 Dec. 1706. Adm'n granted to Mr. Samuel Hayes and John Bouton. Sundry children of Robert Warner of Middletown dec'd are next of kin. On 27 Jan. 1706/7, John Bouton being dec'd, John Benedict appointed in his place.

Howard, Edward.

Perhaps he was the man of this name who m. at Boston, 7 June 1661, Hannah Hawkins, dau. of Thomas, the Boston baker.

He m. (by marriage contract, 2 June 1685) Abigail, widow of Moses Dimon. She was dau. of Andrew Ward.

He was sworn as Clerk for the County of Fairfield, 13 Apr. 1688; on 29 Nov. 1689, Mr. Edward Howard, formerly Clerk, was ordered to deliver to Nathan Gold, present Clerk, all documents, etc.

Hoyt, Simon. [Surname also spelled Hoit, Hait, Haight, etc.]

Son of John and Ruth, born at Upway in Dorchester, co. Dorset, Eng., 20 Jan. 1590.

Of Charlestown 1628, Dorchester 1630, Scituate 1635; came to Windsor abt. 1639, where he sold his holdings in 1646. The Old Goody Hoyt who d. 1644 at Windsor may have been his mother.

He received a grant of land at Fairfield, 6 Mar. 1649, having previously purchased land there from John Green. Not long before his death, he rem. to Stamford, where he d. 1 Sept. 1657.

Married (1) at Upway, Dec. 1612, Deborah Stowers, dau. of Walter, b. at Dorchester 1 May, bapt. 5 June, 1593; and her brother Nicholas Stowers, as well as the Spragues, all from Upway, accompanied the Hoyts with Gov. Endicott to New England on the *Abigail*.

Married (2) Susanna Smith, with whom he joined the church at Scituate, Apr. 1635. She m. (2) Robert Bates of Stamford and d. early in 1674.

Agreement, 1 Feb. 1673/4, of Moses, Joshua, Samuel, and Benjamin Hoyt, Thomas Lyon, Samuel Finch, and Samuel Firman, to distribute Est. of dec'd mother, Susanna Bates.

Children by first wife, recorded at Upway:*

+John, b. 12 Mar. 1614.
+Walter, b. 9 June 1616.
Thomas, b. 20 Sept. 1618.
Deborah, b. 9 Aug. 1620, d. 3 June 1628.
+Nicholas, b. 10 Nov. 1622.
Ruth, b. 2 Jan. 1625, d. 9 May 1627.

Children by second wife:

+Moses.
Daughter, m. Thomas Lyon.
Sarah, d. at Stamford, 19 Mar. 1712/3; m. Samuel Finch.
+Joshua.
Miriam, m. 25 Mar. 1662, Samuel Forman.
+Samuel.
+Benjamin, b. at Windsor, 2 Feb. 1644 [1644/5].

Hoyt, John, s. of Simon.

Born (bapt.?) at Upway, co. Dorset, 12 Mar. 1614, d. at Rye, N. Y., in 1684.

He lived at Fairfield, 1650 to 1665; sold homelot there to Peter Clapham and rem. to Eastchester, 1665, and to Rye, 1676. Patentee of Eastchester, 1666.

Married (2) at Fairfield abt. 1659, Mary, widow of Francis Purdy, and dau. of John Brundish.

Will 29 Aug. 1684; wife Mary; two youngest sons, John and Simon; two daus., Mary Brown and Rachel Norton; overseers, Joshua and Samuel Hoyt, and John Brundish.

Children:

Samuel.
Mary, m. [Hachaliah?] Brown.
Rachel, m. ——— Norton.
John.
Simon.

---

* Given on authority of the *Constant Journal*, p. 417. As it was most unusual for the parish registers to specify dates of birth and death, perhaps the dates given should refer to baptism and burial.

Hoyt, Walter, s. of Simon. Deputy for Norwalk, Oct. 1658, Oct. 1659, Oct. 1661, May and Oct. 1667, Oct. 1668, May 1670, May 1671, Oct. 1673, Oct. 1674, May 1676, May 1678, Oct. 1681. Sergt., Norwalk Trainband, May 1659.

Born (bapt.?) at Upway, co. Dorset, 9 June 1616, he was granted land in Windsor, 1640; one of the first settlers at Norwalk, where he d. late in 1698 or the first days of 1699. In 1684, making oath as witness to the will of John Hoyt of Rye, he stated his age as abt. 65; in his will 1696, he stated it as abt. 78. Married (1) ———; m. (2) Rhoda, widow of John Taylor. Will 11 Feb. 1695/6, proved 11 Apr. 1699; two sons, John of Danbury and "Zaraball." Inv. 10 Jan. 1698 [1698/9].

Children [by first wife] :*

> Elizabeth, m. at Norwalk, Sept. 1663, Samuel St. John.
> +John, b. at Windsor, 13 July 1644.
> Hannah, m. at Norwalk, 20 Oct. 1664, Judah Gregory.
> Child of "Hoyt", d. at Windsor 1647.

Child [by second wife] :

> +Zerubbabel, b. [say 1652].

Hoyt, Nicholas, s. of Simon.

Born (bapt.?) at Upway, co. Dorset, 10 Nov. 1622, d. at Windsor, 7 July 1655; m. at Windsor, 12 June 1646, Susanna Joyse, a widow with one dau. She d. 4 July 1655.

Inv. 30 July 1655. Abigail Joyse, 10½, his wife's dau.; his children, Samuel 8 yrs. 14 wks., Jonathan 6 yrs. 1 mo., David 4 yrs. 11 wks.

Children, recorded at Windsor:

> Samuel, b. 1 May 1647, d. Sept. 1712; rem. by 1672 to Eastchester, by 1683 to Flushing; m. Sarah ———.
> Jonathan, b. 7 June 1649, d. at Guilford, 21 Mar. 1696/7; m. (1) 6 Mar. 1671/2, Sarah Pond, who d. 16 Oct. 1676; m. (2) Mary ———.
> David, b. 22 Apr. 1651, d. in captivity to the Indians, May or June 1704; Deacon and Lt.; rem. by 1682 to Deerfield; m. (1) 3 Apr.

---

* There may have been more daus., as Walter evidently portioned them at marriage, and did not mention them in his will. The two given above were called daus. of Walter in the marriage entries.

1673, Sarah Welles, dau. of Thomas, who d. in 1676; m. (2) Mary Wilson; m. (3) Abigail, widow of Joshua Pomeroy, and dau. of Nathaniel Cook; she m. (3) 25 Aug. 1708, Dea. Nathaniel Royce. Daniel, b. 10 Apr. 1653, d. 15 July 1655.

Hoyt, Moses, s. of Simon.

He bought land in Fairfield from Mr. George Hull before 21 May 1658; also from Richard Vowles and William Heyden. He sold land with a house in 1661; and in 1665 removed to East-chester, where he was an original settler.

There he was prominent; kept the ordinary in 1679 and 1682; deputy constable, 1683; town commissioner, 1686; townsman, 1700. With wife Elizabeth he gave conveyances to his children and others, 1701-03, and d. in or after 1712.

Children:

> Abigail, b. [say 1659]; m. by 1679, Henry Fowler, who received deed from his father-in-law, 1703.
> Moses, b. before 1662, d. in 1711/2; received deed from father, 1702; will 5 Jan. 1711, proved 14 Mar. 1711/2, named wife Elizabeth, and eight children, all minors.
> Mary, b. [say 1670]; m. abt. 1693, Edmund Ward, and received deed from her father, 1702.

Hoyt, Joshua, s. of Simon. Deputy for Stamford, Oct. 1681, Oct. 1682, Oct. and Nov. 1683, May and Oct. 1684, Oct. 1685, Oct. 1686, Jan. 1687.

Born before 1641, d. at Stamford in 1690; m. Mary Bell, dau. of Francis. She m. (2) in 1691, Joseph Turney.

He was drummer at Stamford, 1667.

Inv. 4 Nov. 1690; widow Mary made oath.

Children, recorded at Stamford:

> Mary, b. 22 Dec. 1664. Prob. she (or sister Rebecca) m. Joseph Ferris [called son-in-law 1717 in deed from Mrs. Mary Turney], who had children born 1688-1706 [including Nathan, b. 1694, called gr. son-in-law 1713 in deed from Joseph Turney].
> Rebecca, b. 21 Sept. 1667.
> Joshua, b. 4 Oct. 1670, d. at Stamford, 1 Jan. 1744/5; planter; bought land in Fairfield, 1736; m. (1) (rec. Stamford) 16 Mar. 1698,

Mary Pickett, dau. of John, b. 30 Mar. 1677, d. 10 Nov. 1732; m.
(2) Hannah, widow of Peter Coley, and dau. of Simon Couch.

Sarah, b. 17 Apr. 1674, d. 10 Dec. 1715; m. 11 Apr. 1706, Peter
Ferris, Jr.

Samuel, b. 3 July 1678, d. at Stamford, 10 Aug. 1738; blacksmith; m.
(1) 24 Oct. 1700, Susannah Slawson, who d. 26 Mar. 1706/7; m.
(2) 31 Dec. 1707, Mary Weed; widow of Jonas Weed and dau.
of Daniel Scofield.

Hannah, b. 1 Sept. 1681; perhaps m. 6 Apr. 1704, Abraham Bell, and
if so, she d. 16 Nov. 1711.*

Moses, b. 7 Oct. 1683, d. at Stamford, 2 Nov. 1731, unm.; incapable.

Abigail, b. 20 Aug. 1685; m. 1 Jan. 1707/8, John Holly.

Hoyt, Samuel, s. of Simon. Deputy for Stamford, Apr. and
May 1690, May 1692, May 1693, May and Oct. 1697, Jan. 1698,
May and Oct. 1699, Oct. 1703, May and Oct. 1704, Oct. 1716.
Ens., Stamford Trainband, May 1698. Justice, 1699-1702,
1707-11.

Deacon; d. at Stamford, 7 Apr. 1720. He m. (1) 16 Nov.
1671, Hannah Holly, dau. of John, who d. 7 Dec. 1710; m. (2)
Rebecca ———, who d. 8 Dec. 1713; m. (3) 20 Sept. 1714, Mrs.
Hannah Gold, Sr.; widow of John Gold, and dau. of George
Slawson. Prob. she was "ye aintiant Widow Hait" who d. 27
Jan. 1729/30.

Children [by first wife], recorded at Stamford:

Samuel, b. 27 July 1673, d. at Stamford, 9 Dec. 1711; m. 13 July
1704, Mercy Holmes; widow of John Holmes, and dau. of Capt.
Jonathan Bell; she m. (3) 15 June 1716, Peter Ferris.

John, b. 9 Jan. 1675, d. at Stamford, 10 Dec. 1732; Deacon, Deputy;
m. 30 Apr. 1702, Abigail Holmes.

Hannah, b. 23 Mar. 1679/80, d. without issue, and prob. young.

Jonathan, b. 11 June 1683, d. at Stamford in 1769; Deacon, Col.,
Deputy, Judge of Probate; m. 1 Apr. 1710, Melicent Penoyer.

Joseph, b. 12 June 1686, d. 19 or 20 May 1730; m. 6 June 1728,
Hannah Finch; she next m. Thomas Waterbury.

Ebenezer, b. 29 Nov. 1689, d. y.

Nathan, b. 24 Mar. 1691, d. at Stamford in 1772; adm'n granted, 12
Apr. 1772; m. 3 June 1714, Mary Finch.

Nathaniel, b. 1 Apr. 1694, d. 27 July 171[1].

---

* See Hannah, dau. of Benjamin Hoyt.

Hoyt, Benjamin, s. of Simon.

Born at Windsor, 2 Feb. 1644/5, d. at Stamford, 26 Jan. 1735/6 in 91 yr.; m. (1) 5 Jan. 1670, Hannah Weed; dau. of Jonas; she d. 9 Nov. 1711, and he m. (2) Abigail ———, who d. 4 Mar. 1729/30.

Children [by first wife], recorded at Stamford:

> Benjamin, b. 9 Dec. 1671, d. at Stamford in 1747; will 28 Sept. 1744, proved Aug. 1747; m. 10 June 1697, Elizabeth Jagger; dau. of Jeremy, Jr., b. abt. 1679.
>
> Mary, b. 20 Sept. 1673, d. 24 Feb. 1749/50 ae. 77; m. 23 Feb. 1698 [1698/9], Joseph Webb.
>
> Hannah, b. 3 June 1676; perhaps m. 17 Apr. 1701, Daniel Scofield.*
>
> Simon, b. 14 Mar. 1677 [1677/8], prob. d. y.
>
> Samuel, b. [say 1680], d. at Stamford abt. 1767; Capt., Deacon; will 9 June 1761, proved 23 Feb. 1767; m. (1) 29 Mar. 1705, Mary Jagger; dau. of Jeremy, Jr., b. abt. 1683; m. (2) after 1746, Elizabeth, widow of Jonathan Clason, née James of Long Island; her will, 26 Dec. 1760, proved 5 May 1767.
>
> Jonas, b. [say 1682], d. at Stamford, 3 Dec. 1711; m. 15 Dec. 1705, Sarah Smith; she m. (2) 17 Feb. 1714, Thomas June.

Hoyt, John, s. of Walter.

Born at Windsor, 13 July 1644, d. at Danbury about 1711; m. (1) at Norwalk, 14 Sept. 1666, Mary Lindall, dau. of Dea. Henry of New Haven.

Married (2) Hannah ———.

He settled in youth in Fairfield, and sold land there 12 Apr. 1666 to Peter Coley; rem. to Norwalk.

On 28 Feb. 1712, agreement was made for distribution between Hannah Hoit, widow of John of Danbury; Mary Hoit, widow of Nathaniel of Danbury; John, Samuel, Thomas, Joshua, and Benjamin, sons of said John Hoit and brethren of said Nathaniel; and Francis Barnum and wife Deborah, dau. of said John.

Children [by first wife], recorded at Norwalk:

> John, b. 21 June 1669, d. at Danbury, abt. 1746; will 23 Dec. 1745, proved 22 Apr. 1746; m. Hannah Drake, dau. of John of Simsbury.
>
> Samuel, b. 17 Oct. 1670, d. s. p. in 1751; will 27 Oct. 1749, proved 3 June 1751; children of dec'd brothers John, Thomas, Joshua,

---

* See Hannah dau. of Joshua Hoyt.

Benjamin; homestead to cousin David Hoit; cousins Lt. David and Thomas Hoit, exec'rs.

Thomas, b. 5 Jan. 1674 [1674/5], d. before 1749; m. ———.

Mary, b. 1 Sept. 1677, d. y.

Deborah, b. 28 Dec. 1679; m. Francis Barnum.

Joshua, b. [say 1681], d. in 1726/7; adm'n granted 7 Feb. 1726/7 to widow Sarah and brother John; m. Sarah [perhaps dau. of Thomas Barnum].

Benjamin, b. [say 1683], d. abt. 1722; adm'n granted 11 Feb. 1722 to widow Mary and brother John; m. Mary ———; she m. (2) (rec. Stamford) 12 Jan. 1725/6, Joseph Brown and d. 2 Aug. 1728.

Nathaniel, b. [say 1686], d. in 1712/3; Inv. 4 Mar. 1712/3 presented by brothers Benjamin and John; m. Mary, prob. dau. of Theophilus Hull of Fairfield.

Hoyt, Zerubbabel, s. of Walter.

Born [say 1652], d. at Norwalk between 1727 and 1738; Deacon; m. (1) ———; m. (2) before 1725, Mehitabel, widow of John Keeler, and dau. of John Rockwell.

Children, recorded at Norwalk:

Abigail, b. 2 Feb. 1675 [1675/6].

Joseph, b. abt. 1678, d. at Norwalk in 1730/1; will 28 Dec. 1730, proved 22 Jan. 1730/1; m. Sarah, [prob. dau. of James Pickett].

Daniel, b. 1 Jan. 1681, d. at Norwalk by 1764; Deacon; m. (1) [perhaps Elizabeth Keeler, dau. of John, b. 19 Mar. 1678]; m. (2) (by marriage covenant, 21 Apr. 1748) Sarah, widow of John Starr of Danbury.

Caleb, b. [say 1683], d. at Norwalk, 11 Apr. 1755; m. 25 Feb. 1707/8, Mehitabel Blatchley, widow of Joseph, and dau. of John Keeler; she d. 21 Mar. 1755.

Hannah, b. [say 1685]; m. 6 July 1704, Joseph Whitney.

Rhoda, m. 19 Apr. 1710, John Keeler, Jr.

Hubbard, William, s. of George.

Son of George and Mary* Hubbard of Guilford.

He bought land in Greenwich, 1658, and in 1663 owned also in Stamford. In 1683 he bought land of his son John Austin in Greenwich. In 1684, called "Sr.", he conveyed to sons George and William. Perhaps he m. Catherine, widow of that first John Austin who d. at Stamford 24 Aug. 1657.

---

* Not Bishop, as usually stated.

Will of William, Sr., of Fairfield, 10 Oct. 1702; son-in-law Jacob Patchen, Exec'r; son-in-law Thomas Bennett; son William, meadow at Greenwich; residue equally to daus. Mary Patchen and Sarah Bennett. Witnesses: Thomas Jones, John Thompson, John Meredith. Inv. 7 Nov. 1702.

Children:

+George, b. [say 1663].
    Mary, b. [say 1666], d. at Wilton, 25 Mar. 1754; m. (1) by 1689, Samuel Grumman, of Fairfield; m. (2) by 1692, Jacob Patchen.
    Sarah, b. [say 1668]; m. by 1688, Thomas Bennett, of Fairfield.
    William, b. [say 1670], d. in 1723; m. Hannah Mead.

Hubbard, George, s. of William.

Of Greenwich, Inv. 12 Dec. 1688, taken by Samuel Hayes and James Bennett. Widow Abigail and son.

Hubbell, Richard. Sergt., Fairfield Trainband. Deputy (Fairfield) to Conn. Leg., May 1678, May 1679, May 1681.

Was he not a son of that Richard Hubbell who m. at Bewdley, co. Worcester, Eng., 30 Apr. 1621, Sarah Wakeman, sister of John and Samuel Wakeman, the New Haven colonists?

Born [in England] about 1627, d. at Stratfield, 23 Oct. 1699 in 72 yr. Took oath of fidelity, New Haven, 7 Mar. 1647/8; admitted planter, Guilford, 25 Feb. 1653/4. Tried for sedition 1662, as one of a party which supported Dr. Bray Rossiter against the authorities of New Haven Colony. Accepted as freeman, resident at Fairfield, 13 Oct. 1664.

He acquired a good estate, and was an original member of Stratfield Church, 1695.

Married (1) [prob. in New Haven] abt. 1651, Elizabeth Meigs, dau. of John of Guilford.

He m. (2) about 1669, Elizabeth Gaylord, dau. of Samuel, b. at Windsor, 4 Oct. 1647. She is probably buried at Stratfield, grave marked "E. H. 1688." The will 1690 of her brother Samuel Gaylord named Samuel Hubbell the son of Richard Hubbell "which he hath by my sister Elizabeth Gaylord", the distinction being necessary because Richard had two living sons named Samuel, one by his former wife.

He m. (3) (by marriage contract 16 Apr. 1688), Abigail Walker, widow of Joseph. She was dau. of Rev. Peter Prudden. Will of Richard of Pequonnock, 5 Apr. 1699, proved 20 Nov. 1699; heirs of dec'd son John, and to John's son Richard; son Samuel, Sr.; Ebenezer, son of son Ebenezer; son Richard; daus. Elizabeth Frost, Mary Newton, Martha Wakeman; son Samuel, Jr.; daus. Abigail French, Sarah Hubbell; sons James, Joseph, John; residue to wife Abigail for life, she and Samuel, Sr., to be Exec'rs. Witnesses: Isaac Knapp, Jonathan Pitman. Inv. 3 Sept. 1699 taken by Matthew Sherwood and James Bennett. Will of Abigail of Stratfield 11 Feb. 1705, codicil 10 Dec. 1717, proved 5 Feb. 1717/8; two daus. Abigail Bostwick, Johannah Odell; living son John Hubbell; son Robert Walker.

Children [by first wife], three recorded at Guilford:

+John, b. abt. 1652, called eldest son in deed from father.
+Richard, b. abt. 1654.
James, buried 12 Dec. 1656.
+Samuel, b. 6 Nov. 1657.
Elizabeth, b. 16 Nov. 1659; m. (1) Joseph Frost; m. (2) Samuel Hull.
Mary, b. abt. 1661; m. James Newton.
Martha, d. 5 June 1710; m. 24 Apr. 1687, Capt. John Wakeman.
+Ebenezer.

Children [by second wife]:

+Samuel, b. abt. 1670.
Abigail, b. abt. 1672, d. after 1741; m. abt. 1693, Samuel French of Stratfield.
+James, b. abt. 1674.
Sarah, d. 17 Dec. 1726; m. 25 June 1699, Josiah Stevens, of Killingworth.

Children [by third wife]:

Joseph, b. abt. 1689, d. by 1700. Inv. 25 Mar. 1700. Distribution to brothers and sisters, Richard, James, Samuel, Sr., Samuel, Jr., and John Hubbell, Jr.; Elizabeth wife of Samuel Hull, Mary, wife of James Newton, Martha wife of John Wakeman, Abigail wife of Samuel French, and Sarah wife of Josiah Stevens.
+John, b. abt. 1691.

Hubbell, John, s. of Richard. Lt. for expedition to Albany, Apr. 1690.

Born about 1652, d. in 1690.

Married Patience, called his wife at birth of child 1685, who m. (2) Samuel Hawley. Without much question she was dau. of Isaac Nichols, b. at Stratford, 2 Feb. 1659/60, and sister of Temperance (Nichols) Preston who m. her husband's brother Samuel Hubbell, Sr. She named her dau. Margery after her mother, and son Josiah after her eldest brother.

In 1683, the town of Derby granted him the lot formerly granted to Josiah Nichols and afterwards to Jonathan Nichols, provided he lived there seven years. He did for a time reside in Derby, but returned to Stratford.

He served in King Philip's War, 1675/6, for in 1678 he received a colonial grant of 100 acres, as compensation for loss of a finger. Commissioned Lt. for the Albany expedition 1690, he there lost his life. His eldest son Richard had a colonial grant of 100 acres, Oct. 1706.

Inv. 13 Oct. 1690; widow Patience; ages of children; Margery 9, Richard 6, Josiah 2. Josiah Nichols and Samuel Hubbell, Sr., appointed to administer the estate, with the widow, who by 23 Sept. 1691 had m. Samuel Hawley.

Children, the second recorded at Stratford:

> Margery, b. abt. 1681, d. 14 Mar. 1703/4; renewed Covenant at Stratford, 11 Jan. 1697/8; m. (by Israel Chauncey, rec. New Haven) 27 Nov. 1700, Mr. John Glover. Though called Mrs. Margery Hubbard, the "Mrs." was a title of respect often conferred on maidens of good family, and Hubbard an error of the New Haven clerk for Hubbell. Marriage by the Stratford minister (Chauncey, who was husband of Margery's aunt Mary Nichols) implies Stratford as the home of the bride. The Glovers removed from New Haven to Stratford, and Margery's brother Richard m. her husband's half-sister Abigail Thompson.
>
> ×Richard, b. 20 Jan. 1684 [1684/5], d. 27 Nov. 1758 ae. 74; Capt.; will 3 Dec. 1751, proved 2 Jan. 1759; m. (rec. Stratford) 11 Dec. 1707, Abigail Thompson of New Haven.
>
> ×Josiah, b. abt. 1688, d. at Stratfield in 1752; will 12 July 1752, proved 1 Sept. 1752; m. 18 June 1713, Martha Ufford, dau. of Samuel, b. 28 Sept. 1695.

Hubbell, Richard, s. of Richard. Ens., Stratfield company, Oct. 1709; Lt., May 1714. Deputy (Fairfield), May 1713, May and Oct. 1715, May and Oct. 1716, Oct. 1717.

Born about 1654, d. at Stratfield in 1738.

Married (1) at Fairfield, 5 Nov. 1685, Rebecca Morehouse, who d. 2 Apr. 1692. She was dau. of Samuel.

Married (2) (rec. Fairfield) 12 Oct. 1692, Hannah Swillaway, of Malden, Mass.; dau. of Henry and Margaret.

Hannah dau. of Henry Swillaway was b. at Malden, Feb. 1665/6. Margaret Swillaway of Malden m. there 15 Aug. 1687, Robert Smith of Charlestown. Adm'n on the Est. of Mrs. Margaret Smith of Stratfield, formerly of Boston, was granted, 7 Jan. 1712/3, to Ens. Richard Hubbell. Mary Swillaway was bapt. at Stratfield, 8 Nov. 1696. Hannah was bapt. as wife of Lt. Richard, at Stratfield, 12 Jan. 1717/8.

Will 12 Nov. 1734, proved 8 Aug. 1738; wife; eldest son Peter of Newtown; son Ebenezer, shoemaker and tanner; son Jonathan, land at Newtown; son Zachariah and his son Phineas; sons Richard, Eleazer; son Nathaniel brought up at College and in ministry in Jersey; daus. Elizabeth, Margery, and Abigail, money in addition to what they had rec'd. Ebenezer Hubbell asked disapproval of will, and Court rejected it. Zachariah Hubbell appealed. Inv. £2,845.

Children by first wife, recorded at Fairfield:

XPeter, b. 10 Aug. 1686, d. at Newtown in 1780; will 1 May 1770, proved 22 Feb. 1780; m. (1) at Stratfield, 19 Jan. 1709/10, Katharine Wheeler, who d. 16 Mar. 1742 in 49 yr.; m. (2) Sarah ———.

XEbenezer, b. 19 or 20 Sept. 1687, d. 6 Mar. 1761 in 74 yr. (g. s., Easton); m. Sarah Titherton, b. 31 Jan. 1696/7, d. 20 May 1788 in 93 yr. (g. s.).

Elizabeth, b. 23 Oct. 1689; m. at Stratfield, 7 Jan. 1712/3, Nathan Beardsley.

XJonathan, b. 25 Mar. 1692, d. 6 Sept. 1766 ae. 73 (Newtown Church); m. at Stratfield, 18 Nov. 1713, Peaceable Silliman, dau. of Daniel, 2d.

Children by second wife, recorded at Fairfield, bapt. at Stratfield:

XZachariah, b. 26 Aug. 1694, bapt. 23 June 1695; m. at Stratfield, 26 Jan. 1713/4, Abigail Bennett.

✕Richard, b. 20 Oct. 1696, bapt. 18 Oct. 1696, d. 27 June 1787 in 93 yr.
    (g. s., Stratfield); Dea.; m. (rec. Fairfield) 9 Dec. 1725, Penelope
    Fairweather, bapt. 24 Feb. 1706, d. 29 Aug. 1791 in 87 yr. (g. s.).
Hannah, b. 7 July 1698, bapt. 10 July 1698, d. y.
✕Eleazer, b. 15 Aug. 1700, bapt. 18 Aug. 1700, d. at New Fairfield,
    3 Sept. 1770; Capt.; res. Willington, New Fairfield; m. 25 May
    1727, Abigail Burr, bapt. 16 Mar. 1701, d. 6 Apr. 1780.
Nathaniel, b. 11 Aug. 1702, bapt. 16 Aug. 1702, d. at Lebanon, N. J.,
    in 1761; Yale Coll. 1723; Rev.; will dated 11 July 1760, proved
    28 May 1761; m. (1) at New Haven, 5 Mar. 1721/2, Esther Mix;
    m. (2) Elizabeth (———) Marsh, who d. in 1779.
Margery, b. 19 Jan. 1705, bapt. 21 Jan. 1705; m. ———.
Abigail, b. 19 Sept. 1709, bapt. 23 Sept. 1709; m. ———.

Hubbell, Samuel, Sr., s. of Richard. Ens., Stratfield company,
Oct. 1708; Lt., Oct. 1709. Deputy (Fairfield), Oct. 1703, Oct.
1711.

Born at Guilford, 6 Nov. 1657, d. at Stratfield, 18 Sept. 1713
ae. 57. Married (1) 4 Apr. 1687, Elizabeth Wilson, who d.
4 Jan. 1687/8.

Married (2) 17 Apr. 1688, Temperance Preston. Certainly she
was the widow of Jehiel Preston, after whom she named her eldest
son by Hubbell; and almost as certainly was she dau. of Isaac
Nichols, b. at Stratford, 17 May 1662.

Inv. of Lt. Samuel, 10 June 1714, presented by Mrs. Temperance
Hubbell. Children's ages stated (births given below), Daniel,
Ephraim, Stephen, David, Tabitha, Joseph. Adm'n granted to
the widow Temperance and her son Daniel.

Child by first wife, recorded at Stratfield:

Benoni, b. 29 Dec. 1687, d. 20 Jan. 1687/8.

Children by second wife, recorded at Stratfield:

Elizabeth, b. 29 Dec. 1689, d. 4 Jan. 1689 [1689/90].
Jehiel, b. 27 Jan. 1689/90, d. 3 May 1693 ae. 4.
✕Daniel, b. 8 Aug. 1691, d. 11 Dec. 1735 in 45 yr. (g. s., Stratfield);
    Capt.; m. 17 May 1716, Esther Beach, b. 3 May 1694.
Katharine, b. 11 Mar. 1693, d. 19 Dec. 1697.
✕Ephraim, b. 11 Oct. 1694, d. at Kent, 4 Nov. 1780; Capt.; m. 17 Oct.
    1717, Abigail Bradley, b. abt. 1695, d. 22 Apr. 1772.
✕Stephen, b. 16 Feb. 1695 [1695/6], bapt. 17 Feb. 1695/6, d. 29 Apr.
    1792 in 98 yr. (g. s., Stratfield); m. 10 Jan. 1720, Abigail Squire,
    bapt. 11 Nov. 1694, d. 1 Aug. 1777 in 84 yr. (g. s.).

✕David, b. 1 July 1698, bapt. 3 July 1698, d. in 1753; m. Eunice Sanford, bapt. 26 Aug. 1705.

Abiel, b. 15 Jan. 1699 [1699/1700], bapt. 21 Jan. 1699/1700, d. 3 Mar.
1699 ae. 2 mos.

Tabitha, b. 24 Dec. 1700, bapt. 29 Dec. 1700; m. James Bennett.

✕Joseph, b. 29 Oct. 1702, bapt. 1 Nov. 1702; m. Kezia Hall, dau. of
Jonathan.

Hubbell, Ebenezer, s. of Richard.

Settled in New London, and d. in 1698. Married Mary Harris,
dau. of Gabriel. She m. (2) Ebenezer Griffin.

Children, recorded at New London:

Elizabeth, b. 1693, bapt. 14 Jan. 1693/4; m. (published 20 Sept. 1713),
Joshua Appleton. On 18 Mar. 1737/8, Joshua Appleton, Jr., of
New London conveyed to father Joshua Appleton land in Fairfield
inherited from uncle Ebenezer Hubbell.

Ebenezer, bapt. 22 Dec. 1695, d. in 1720, unm.

Hubbell, Samuel, Jr., s. of Richard.

Married Elizabeth, with whom he renewed Covenant at Fairfield Church, 19 May 1695. She was quite likely dau. of the
second Jehu Burr, and sister of Hon. Peter and aunt of Thaddeus
Burr, an identification suggested by the recurrence of the names
Peter and Thaddeus among her grandchildren. Furthermore, he
acted in a fiduciary capacity for Mary, the orphan dau. of Samuel
and Mary (Burr) Wakeman, whose mother was sister of Elizabeth
Burr.

Children, bapt. at Fairfield:

Hannah, bapt. 19 May 1695, d. 11 Aug. 1743; m. (1) Joseph Osborn;
m. (2) 12 Dec. 1731, James Burr.

✕Nathan, b. (rec. Greenfield) 1 Dec. 1699, bapt. 3 Dec. 1699, d. at
Wilton, 6 Feb. 1761; m. (rec. Greenfield) 5 Dec. 1723, Martha
Finch, b. (rec. Greenfield) 7 Jan. 1702, d. at Wilton, 1 Dec. 1755
ae. 53.

Eunice, bapt. 21 Mar. 1703; m. Onesimus Gold.

Abigail, bapt. 15 July 1705.

Olive, bapt. 15 Feb. 1707/8; m. 20 June 1724, Joseph Bradley.

✕David, bapt. 2 Sept. 1711; m. Martha Middlebrook, dau. of Jonathan.

✕Samuel, bapt. 30 May 1714, d. 4 Sept. 1757; m. Abigail ———, bapt.
as his wife 4 Oct. 1741, d. in 1782.

Hubbell, James, s. of Richard.   Sergt.

Born about 1674; d. Oct. 1777 ae. 104 (Bible record, quoted by *Hubbell Gen.*).

Married Patience Summers, who d. 29 Sept. 1753 in 71 yr. (g. s., Trumbull).

Children, recorded at Stratford, bapt. at Stratfield:

> XAndrew, b. 22 June 1707 [error for 1706], bapt. 23 June 1706, d. at Stratford in 1777; will 3 July 1777; m. (1) abt. 1726, Sarah Parruck, dau. of John, bapt. 19 June 1709, d. 20 July 1736; m. (2) 2 Dec. 1736, Mary Welles.
> Abiah, b. 10 Aug. 1709 [error for 1708], bapt. 19 Sept. 1708.
> Sarah, b. 12 Sept. 1712 [error for 1711], bapt. 6 Apr. 1712.
> XElnathan, b. 22 Sept. 1718 [error for 1717], bapt. 6 Oct. 1717, d. 21 July 1788 ae. 71 (g. s., Bennington, Vt.); m. Mehitabel Sherwood, b. abt. 1720.
> Patience, b. 8 Apr. 1722.

Hubbell, John, s. of Richard.

Born about 1691, after death of his half-brother John; d. at Stratfield, 8 Apr. 1774 in 85 yr. (g. s.).

He was sometimes called "Jr." to distinguish him from his older nephew, son of his half-brother John.   Receipted for his portion of father's estate, 17 Mar. 1712.

Married at Stratfield, 6 Nov. 1711, Ann Welles.

Children, bapt. at Stratfield:

> Jerusha, bapt. 14 June 1713.
> XBenjamin, bapt. 6 Oct. 1717, d. 24 Feb. 1793 in 76 yr. (g. s., Stratfield); m. Mary Porter, b. abt. July 1721, d. 29 Aug. 1813 ae. 92 yrs. 1 mo. (g. s.).
> John, accidentally shot and killed by brother Benjamin [*Hubbell Gen.*].

Hughes, Nicholas.

Served in King Philip's War, 1675, and was granted land in New Haven for his service.   Removed to Stratford, where he d. in 1692.

Married Abigail Thompson, dau. of John, b. at Stratford, 1 May 1646, d. there 2 Mar. 1731.   She was widow of Jonathan Curtis, and m. (3) 1 Aug. 1695, Mr. Samuel Sherman.

Will 18 Apr. 1690; shop and tools; son-in-law William Curtis, and his brother Jonathan and sister Sarah Curtis; wife Abigail (Exec'x); Capt. William Curtis and Ambrose Thompson, overseers. Inv. Nov. 1692. Samuel Hughes, brother of Nicholas, not mentioned in will, signed off his right, 1 Nov. 1692.

Hull, George. At Dorchester, Mass., 1630; freeman 1633, Deputy to Mass. Leg., May 1634; removed to Windsor with first settlers, which he served as Deputy to Conn. Leg., May and Nov. 1637, Mar. and Apr. 1638, Aug. and Sept. 1639, Jan. and Apr. 1640, Feb., Apr., Sept. and Nov. 1641, Apr. and Aug. 1642, Mar., Apr. and Sept. 1643, Apr. and Sept. 1644, Sept. and Dec. 1645, and Apr. 1646; removed to Fairfield about 1647, and was Deputy May 1649, May 1650, May 1651, Oct. 1655, May 1656. Magistrate for Fairfield, May 1654.

Married (1) at Crewe Kerne, co. Somerset, Eng., 27 Aug. 1614, Thomasin Mitchell of Stockland.

Married (2) Sarah, widow of David Phippen, who d. in Aug. 1659.

He entered at Fairfield in 1653 land purchased from Charles Taintor.

Will (date not seen); wife Sarah; sons Josias and Cornelius; cousin Jane Pinkney; four daus. Mary, Martha, Elizabeth, Naomi. Inv. 25 Aug. 1659.

Will of Sarah, widow of George, Aug. 1659; house at Boston; son Gamaliel; son George Phippen; daus. Rebecca Vickers, Sarah Yeo; cousins Jane and Philip Pinkney; four sons Benjamin, Joseph, Gamaliel, and George Phippen. Inv. 25 Aug. 1659.

Children [by first wife], three bapt. at Crewe Kerne:

> Mary, bapt. 27 July 1618, d. at Windsor, 18 Aug. 1685; m. Humphrey Pinney, of Dorchester.
> Josias, bapt. 5 Nov. 1620, d. at Killingworth, 16 Nov. 1675; m. at Windsor, 20 May 1641, Elizabeth Loomis, dau. of Joseph. Deputy (Windsor) to Conn. Leg., May and Oct. 1659, May 1660, Oct. 1662; Lt., Killingworth Trainband, Oct. 1666; Deputy (Killingworth) May 1667, May and Oct. 1668, May and Oct. 1669, Oct. 1671, May and Oct. 1672, May and Oct. 1673, May 1674; Commissioner for Killingworth, 1671.
> Martha.

Elizabeth, bapt. 16 Oct. 1625, d. at Windsor, 2 May 1680; m. at Windsor, 4 Dec. 1646, Samuel Gaylord.

+Cornelius, b. abt. 1627.

Naomi.

Hull, Cornelius, s. of George. Deputy (Fairfield) to Conn. Leg., Feb. 1657, May 1658, May 1659, May and Oct. 1660, Oct. 1662, May 1663, Oct. 1664, May 1667, Oct. 1676, Oct. 1677. Lt., Major Treat's Life Guard, Feb. 1676; Lt., Fairfield County Troop, May 1676 (K. Philip's War). Received colonial grant of 100 acres, Oct. 1677.

Born in England about 1627; d. at Fairfield, prob. in latter half of Sept., 1695.

Married Rebecca Jones, dau. of Rev. John, b. in England abt. 1633; who prob. m. (2) Mr. Joseph Theale, of Bedford, N. Y.

Will 16 Sept. 1695; sons Samuel, Theophilus, and Cornelius; daus. Rebecca Hull, Sarah wife of Robert Silliman, and Mártha wife of Cornelius Stratton; grandchild George, son of Cornelius. Inv. 7 Oct. 1695.

Children:

+Samuel.

+Theophilus.

+Cornelius, b. abt. 1655.

Rebecca, m. between 1695 and 1713, John Lyon, Sr., of Byram Neck. On 8 Aug. 1715, John Lyon of Greenwich, with wife Rebecca, formerly Rebecca Hull, conveyed interest in homelot of Cornelius Hull dec'd.

Sarah, prob. m. (1) John Knapp; m. (2) by 1691, Robert Silliman.

Martha, m. (1) ——— Smith; m. (2) by 1695, Cornelius Stratton, of Easthampton, L. I.

Hull, Samuel, s. of Cornelius.

Married (1) Deborah Beers, named as his wife in will 1694 of her father James Beers.

Married (2) Elizabeth, widow of Joseph Frost, and dau. of Sergt. Richard Hubbell.

Married (3) Jane ———.

Will 15 Nov. 1718, proved 18 Aug. 1720; wife Jane, referring to Est. she had; son Cornelius; son Josiah (under 21), referring to "my former wife who was daughter of Richard Hubbell";

two daus. Rebecca Morehouse and Deborah Beardsley; dau. Martha; dau. Sarah (under 18) ; residue to son Samuel, Exec'r.

Children [by first wife], two bapt. at Fairfield:

Rebecca, m. at Stratfield, 8 Aug. 1706, Jonathan Morehouse.
Deborah, m. at Stratfield, 27 Nov. 1711, John Beardsley.
Martha, bapt. 9 Sept. 1694.
XSamuel, bapt. 26 Apr. 1696, d. at Fairfield, abt. 1787; will 13 Mar. 1765, proved 8 Mar. 1787; m. (rec. Fairfield) 3 Feb. 1727, Joanna Fairchild, dau. of Joseph, b. 2 Feb. 1696/7.

Children [by second wife], bapt. at Fairfield:

Cornelius, bapt. 23 June 1700; res. Norwalk.
XJosiah, bapt. 12 Apr. 1702, d. at Stamford, will dated 5 Dec. 1740, proved 8 Jan. 1740/1; m. (rec. Norwalk) 27 July 1727, Hannah Prindle, dau. of Eleazer of Milford.

Child [by third wife], bapt. at Fairfield:

Sarah, bapt. 28 Mar. 1714; m. 5 Nov. 1735, John Lane.

Hull, Theophilus, s. of Cornelius. Ens., west end company, Fairfield, May 1705; Lt., June 1709; Capt., Oct. 1709; Committee of War, Fairfield County, Oct. 1709; Deputy (Fairfield) May 1708, Oct. 1709.

Married Mary Sanford, dau. of Ezekiel, b. 3 Apr. 1670, d. in 1712. He and his wife renewed Covenant at Fairfield Church, 26 Aug. 1694.

Capt. Theophilus d. at Fairfield, 5 June 1710.

Will 4 June 1710, proved 2 Aug. 1710; wife Mary; two daus. Mary and Ann, £50 apiece; four sons, Theophilus, Eliphalet, John, Jabesh; all children under age; cousin Sarah Seeley that lived with me, £18. [Sarah Seeley was prob. step-dau. of his wife's sister Rebecca (Sanford) Seeley.]

Nuncupative will of Mary, widow of Theophilus, made abt. two days before her death, witnessed by Sarah Silliman and Elizabeth Jackson, who made oath 14 Apr. 1712; she gave to Sarah Seeley 40 shillings; to daus. Mary and Ann, £16 apiece, and her clothing equally; residue to all her children. Adm'n granted to Sergt. Ezekiel and Thomas Sanford. Theophilus, son of Capt. Theophilus, chose Nathaniel Hoyt of Danbury for guardian; and Anna chose Cornelius Hull.

Children, bapt. at Fairfield:

Mary, bapt. 26 Aug. 1694; m. prob. Nathaniel Hoyt, of Danbury.

Ann, bapt. 26 Aug. 1694.

XTheophilus, bapt. 23 May 1697, d. at Redding, will 7 June 1748, proved 31 Oct. 1748; m. abt. 1719, Sarah Sherwood, dau. of Samuel, bapt. 29 Mar. 1696.

XEliphalet, b. 5 Feb. 1700/1 [age at death], bapt. 20 Mar. 1701, d. 14 Mar. 1737 ae. 36 yrs. 1 mo. 9 days (g. s., Greenfield); will 9 Mar. 1736/7, proved 22 Mar. 1736/7; m. Sarah Barlow, b. 27 Feb. 1703/4, d. 28 Nov. 1767; she m. (2) at Greenfield, 1 Nov. 1738, David Banks.

XJohn, bapt. 2 Apr. 1704, d. at Newtown, 28 May 1761; adm'n granted 22 June 1761; m. Elizabeth Adams, dau. of Freegrace.

XJabez, bapt. 10 Feb. 1705/6; m. Mary Thorp, b. 17 Feb. 1705/6.

Hull, Cornelius, s. of Cornelius.

Born about 1655; d. at Greenfield, 7 May 1740 ae. 85 (g. s.). Married Sarah Sanford, dau. of Ezekiel, b. 25 Mar. 1666, d. in 1753.

Will 18 Apr. 1734, signed 21 Jan. 1734/5, proved 12 Aug. 1740; wife Sarah; daus. Rebecca Meeker, Elizabeth Burr, Martha Sherwood, Eleanor Pherrey; gr. dau. Sarah Sanford; sons George, Nathaniel, Ebenezer, John, Cornelius.

Will of Widow Sarah, 16 Jan. 1743/4, proved 25 June 1753; sons George, Nathaniel, Cornelius, Ebenezer; gr. dau. Sarah Sanford; dau. Martha; children of son John; daus. Rebecca, Elizabeth, Martha, Eleanor; Capt. Moses Dimon, Jr., and my son Daniel Sherwood, Exec'rs.

Children, bapt. at Fairfield:

XGeorge, b. abt. 1686, d. 9 Feb. 1769 ae. 83 (Redding Church); adm'n granted, 18 Feb. 1769; m. abt. 1711, Martha Gregory.

Sarah, b. abt. 1690, bapt. 26 Aug. 1694, d. by 1720; m. David Meeker. Her dau. Sarah (Meeker) who m. 11 Jan. 1732/3, Samuel Sanford, was named in wills of both grandparents.

Rebecca, b. abt. 1693, bapt. 26 Aug. 1694; m. Joseph Meeker.

XNathaniel, b. (rec. Greenfield) Mar. 1695, bapt. 7 Apr. 1695, d. 16 July 1749 ae. 54 (g. s., Greenfield); will 13 July 1749, proved 8 Aug. 1749; m. (rec. Greenfield) 29 Nov. 1716, Elizabeth Burr, b. 12 Apr. 1696, d. 11 Nov. 1760 ae. 64 (Redding Church); adm'n on her Est. granted 3 Dec. 1760.

XEbenezer, bapt. 20 June 1697; m. Martha Bradley, dau. of Daniel, bapt. 4 Oct. 1702.

Elizabeth, bapt. 15 Oct. 1699, d. at Redding, 26 Nov. 1760 ae. 62; m. 8 June 1721, Stephen Burr.

Martha, b. (rec. Greenfield) 15 June 1701, bapt. 13 July 1701, d. at Greenfield, 19 Sept. 1782 in 83 yr. (g. s.); m. abt. 1727, Daniel Sherwood.

✕John, b. abt. 1703, d. in Cuba in 1741; will 16 Sept. 1740, proved 15 Sept. 1741; [?m. (2) at New Milford, 1 Nov. 1737, Abigail (Prindle) Gillet].

Eleanor, bapt. 15 Sept. 1706, d. at Redding in 1762; adm'n granted 2 Mar. 1762; m. Ebenezer Ferry.

✕Cornelius, bapt. 14 May 1710, d. 26 Dec. 1787 ae. 78 (g. s., Greenfield); m. 24 Aug. 1731, Abigail Rumsey, bapt. 4 Mar. 1710/1, d. 7 June 1776 ae. 66 (g. s.).

Hull, John, s. of Richard. Surgeon, K. Philip's War, 1675-76; Deputy for Derby, May 1689.

Bapt. at New Haven, 24 May 1640, d. at Wallingford, 6 Dec. 1711 ae. 80 (g. s.); rem. to Stratford in 1662, and to Derby abt. 1673, and finally settled in Wallingford; noted as a physician.

Married (1) Mary, quite prob. dau. of Richard Beach of New Haven and sister of Benjamin Beach of Stratford; if so, b. at New Haven, June 1642.

Married (2) abt. 1690, Tabitha, widow of Edward Wooster, and dau. of Henry Tomlinson. She d. abt. 1691; he m. (3) by 1693, Mary (Messenger), widow of Thomas Benedict of Norwalk; and he m. (4) (by Capt. Gold, rec. at Wallingford) 21 Sept. 1699, Rebecca Turney. She was widow of Benjamin Turney, and dau. of Ralph Keeler.

Children [by first wife], five recorded at Stratford, four at Derby:

John, b. 14 Mar. 1661/2, d. at Derby, 9 Nov. 1714; m. Mary Merwin, dau. of Miles and Sarah (Platt) Merwin, b. at Milford, 23 Jan. 1665/6.

Samuel, b. 4 Feb. 1663 [1663/4], d. y.

Mary, b. 31 Oct. 1666, d. at Derby, 5 Sept. 1696; m. at Derby, 23 Dec. 1685, John Prindle.

Joseph, b. 16 Feb. 1668 [1668/9], d. at Derby, 5 Oct. 1744 ae. 76; Capt.; m. (1) (rec. Derby) 20 Jan. 1691 [1691/2], Mary Nichols, dau. of Caleb, b. abt. 1665/6, d. 6 Apr. 1733 in 68 yr. (g. s.,); m. (2) at Derby, Nov. 1735, Hannah (Botsford), widow of John Prindle.

Benjamin, b. 10 Apr. 1672, d. at Wallingford, 30 Mar. 1741; Dr.; m.
(1) at Wallingford, 14 Sept. 1693, Elizabeth Andrews, dau. of
Samuel, b. 17 July 1674, d. 27 Apr. 1732; m. (2) 22 Jan. 1733,
widow Hannah Parmelee.
Richard, b. 16 Oct. 1674, d. y.
Ebenezer, b. 16 Mar. 1678/9, d. at Wallingford, 9 Nov. 1709; m.
7 Mar. 1706, Lydia Mix, dau. of Daniel, b. end of July 1682, d.
in 1710. They had three children, of whom Rebecca, b. abt. 1708,
m. Thomas Nash of Fairfield [proved by Wallingford Deeds].
Jeremiah, b. 28 Sept. 1679 [1681/2?], d. at Wallingford, 11 May 1736;
Dr.; m. 24 Mar. 1711, Hannah Cook, dau. of Samuel, b. 28 May
1693, d. 22 Nov. 1735.
Andrew, b. 15 July 1685, d. y.

Hunnewell, William.

Of Stratford, lived in John Sherwood's house and d. there.
Inv. 13 Aug. 1688. Adm'n granted to John Beardsley, Jr.

Hurd, Adam.

Brother of John, Sr., is said to have had wife Hannah.

Children:

+John, called Jr.
Perhaps daus.

Hurd, John. Deputy (Stratford) to Conn. Leg., May 1649,
May and Oct. 1656, Oct. 1657.

Of Windsor before 1640, rem. early to Stratford. Some suppose
that the original John, who had the above service as Deputy, was
father of the John (called Sr. to distinguish him from the other
John, the son of Adam) who m. Sarah Thompson. Our research
has not been extensive enough to decide this question with
certainty, but no evidence has been seen for this conclusion.

John, Sr., m. (Stratford rec.) 1 Dec. 1662, Sarah Thompson,
dau. of John, b. in 1642. Winthrop referred to her in 1663 as
aged 21.

John, Sr., d. at Stratford, 4 Feb. 1681/2; by a second record
14 Feb. "or there abouts." His widow m. (2) Thomas Barnum
of Danbury. The widow Sarah Barnum, "formerly the wife of
John Hurd senʳ" d. at Stratford, 24 Jan. 1717/8.

Will 18 Feb. 1679 [1679/80]; dear wife Sarah; sons John, Isaac; daus. (under 18); to Samuel Galpin, 20 shillings; to Mary wife of John Bennet of Fairfield, ten shillings if she demand it within a year after my decease; to Abigail wife of Samuel Bissell of Windsor, five shillings if she demand etc.; to Philip Travers if he demand etc.; eldest son under 21; friends Mr. Zackery Walker of Woodbury and Robert Clarke of Stratford, with my brethren John and Ambrose Thompson, overseers. Proved 14 Mar. 1681 [1681/2] and Inv. exhibited.

Children, recorded at Stratford, two bapt. at Woodbury:

+John, b. 16 Dec. 1664.
Sarah, b. 17 Feb. 1665 [1665/6]; m. (1) 23 Apr. 1685, John Sherwood; m. (2) 2 July 1691, Samuel Beecher.
Hannah, b. 27 Sept. 1667; m. 14 July 1693, Samuel Titherton.
+Isaac, b. 2 June 1669.
Jacob, b. 16 Nov. 1671, d. y.
Mary, b. 15 Aug. 1673, bapt. Aug. 1673; m. Richard Barnum, of Danbury.
Esther, b. 20 Aug. 1676, bapt. May 1678 (unless a second Esther), d. y.
Abigail, b. 12 Feb. 1679 [1679/80], d. in 1683.

Hurd, John, s. of Adam.

Called Jr. at births of all children. In Stratford Deeds, John, Jr., bought land from his "uncle", John Hurd, Sr. He m. 10 Dec. 1662, Ann, widow of Joshua Judson.

He and his wife settled estate of John Bartram, 1675.

Joseph Hurd and Benjamin Hurd, Sr., of Woodbury, and Ebenezer Hurd of Killingworth, agreed to divide land of father John Hurd, 27 Nov. 1716. [Woodbury Deeds.]

Children, recorded at Stratford:

Sarah, b. 10 Dec. 1664.
Joseph, b. 4 Feb. 1665 [1665/6], d. at Woodbury, 18 Jan. 1751; distribution made 8 Feb. 1750/1; m. Jane Munn, dau. of Samuel, who d. 27 Jan. 1760.
Benjamin, b. 16 Feb. 1666 [1666/7], d. at Woodbury, 21 May 1754; Sergt.; will 21 Mar. 1747/8, proved 18 June 1754; m. Sarah Kimberly, dau. of Abraham, b. 1 Aug. 1672, d. 20 Sept. 1749.

Ebenezer, b. 9 Nov. 1668, "sun an houre high in ye morning"; m. Sarah Lane, dau. of Robert, b. 24 Feb. 1666/7.
Ruth, b. 12 Feb. 1670 [1670/1].
John, b. 17 Aug. 1673.

Hurd, John, s. of John.

Born at Stratford, 16 Dec. 1664, d. there 7 Mar. 1731/2. His stone states d. in 68 yr., without date.

Married (1) 5 Jan. 1692 [1692/3], Abigail Wallis; dau. of Richard of Norwich, b. abt. 1670; step-dau. of Henry Wakelee; she d. 28 Aug. 1728.

Married (2) Abigail –

Will 4 Mar. 1731/2, proved 16 Mar. 1731/2; wife Abigail, mentioning marriage covenant; sons Jonathan (my Great Bible), David, John, Ebenezer, Nathan, Jabez, Enos, Ephraim; daus. Esther wife of David Curtis and Abigail Hurd.

Children [by first wife], recorded at Stratford:

Jonathan, b. 27 Apr. 1694, d. at Stratford in 1757; adm'n granted, 23 Aug. 1757; m. 28 Jan. 1719/20, Abigail Bostwick.

Hester, b. 9 May 1696; m. 10 Nov. 1725, David Curtis.

David, b. 24 Mar. 1699, d. at Huntington, 19 Sept. 1758 in 61 yr. (g. s.); will 2 July 1758, proved 5 Dec. 1758; m. Susanna Bostwick, dau. of Zechariah, who d. in 1776; her dower distributed, 7 Oct. 1776.

John, b. 14 Feb. 1700/1 (8 Feb. 1701 by duplicate entry), d. in 1754; adm'n granted, 2 July 1754, to widow Sarah; m. Sarah ———.

Ebenezer, b. 7 Apr. 1703, bapt. 30 May 1703 (at Stratford, rec. Stratfield), d. at Huntington, 7 May 1788 ae. 87 (g. s.); m. (1) 26 Jan. 1731/2, Abigail Hubbell, who d. 1 July 1756 in 45 yr. (g. s.); m. (2) Rebecca ———, who d. 16 Apr. 1783 ae. [—] (g. s.).

Nathan, b. 11 Oct. 1705, bapt. 17 Feb. 1706 (at Stratford, rec. Stratfield), d. at Stratfield in 1761; will 21 Feb. 1761, proved 12 Mar. 1761; m. ———.

Jabez, b. 12 Mar. 1707/8; m. (1) 9 Sept. 1727, Phebe Burritt; m. (2) 19 Apr. 1764, Sarah Caldwell.

Abigail, b. 8 Feb. 1710/1.

Enos, b. 12 Mar. 1712/3; m. Elizabeth ———.

Ephraim, b. 20 Sept. 1715; m. Ann ———.

Hurd, Isaac, s. of John.

Born at Stratford, 2 June 1669, d. there 28 Nov. 1732; m. (rec. Stratford) 11 Mar. 1708/9, Hannah Dunning.

Marriage intended, 20 Feb. 1708/9, between Isaac Hurd of Stratford and Hannah Dunning, dau. of Benjamin of Jamaica, L. I. [Stratford Deeds.]

Will 19 Apr. 1732, proved 1 May 1732; wife Hannah, Exec'x, with Lt. Abel Birdsey.

Hurlbut, Thomas. Colonial grant, Oct. 1671, for service in Pequot War, 1637. Clerk, Wethersfield Trainband, June 1649.

Born [in England] prob. not much before 1615; d. at Wethersfield, Sept. 1689.

The surname is often spelled Hollabut, Holabird, and various other ways. The *Hurlbut Gen.* gives an impossible account of the succession of three Thomas Hurlbuts, where there were but two.

He came prob. with Lion Gardiner to Saybrook 1635, and his part in the Pequot War is narrated by Capt. Gardiner in his *Relation.* He settled in Wethersfield, where he was blacksmith. In 1662, the town granted him land on which to set a shop and little house.

In 1670 he was listed in the town of Wethersfield with seven persons in his household, whom we take to be himself, his wife, and five sons; the only other Hurlbut listed separately was (his son) Samuel, with three persons. [The Wyllys Papers.]

Died Sept. 1689; Inv. £58, includes blacksmith tools; taken 6 Mar. 1689/90 by Robert Welles and Samuel Butler. Widow Elizabeth; ages of children: Timothy 9, Nathaniel 7, Ebenezer 4. Adm'n granted to Stephen Hurlbut; Est. insolvent.

The names of the six elder sons were not stated in the probate records, as they were not minors; and they had received their portions apparently by deeds of gift from their father before his last marriage.

Children [by first wife]:

    John, b. at Wethersfield, 8 Mar. 1642 [1642/3], d. 30 Aug. 1690 [Pro. Rec.]; Sergt., of Middletown; m. at Wethersfield, 15 Dec. 1670, Mary Deming. He was a blacksmith.

    Samuel, b. [say 1645], d. at Wethersfield, 6 Dec. 1710; m. Mary ———. Farmer; bought house 1668; drew land 1670 and 1694; had deed from father 1677.

    +Thomas, b. in 1650/1.

Joseph, b. [say 1652], d. at Woodbury, called "the aged", 13 July 1732; m. Rebecca ———. Sold to his father 1678, and rem. to Woodbury.

Stephen, b. [say 1655]; m. at Wethersfield, 12 Dec. 1678, Phebe ———. He had deed of house from his father 1681; had a shop; drew land 1692.

Cornelius, b. [say 1658]; m. Rebecca Butler, dau. of Thomas.

Children [by last wife Elizabeth] :

Timothy, b. abt. 1680.

Nathaniel, b. abt. 1682, d. at Simsbury, 12 May 1756; m. (1) at Woodbury, 19 Oct. 1708, Sarah Jenners; m. (2) Jan. 1727/8, Mary ———.

Ebenezer, b. abt. 1685, d. at Simsbury, 3 May 1756; res. Guilford 1705, Windsor 1707, Simsbury 1716; m. at Windsor, 11 May 1710, Hannah Winchell.

Hurlbut, Thomas, s. of Thomas 1st.

Born at Wethersfield in 1650/1, d. at Fairfield in 1697. Blacksmith; received land for shop from father, 1671; bought from Thomas Williams 1673, and from William Hills, Jr., and wife, 1676.

With his brother Joseph he removed to Woodbury, about 1678, and not long before his death settled in Fairfield, where he bought from Josiah Harvey, 27 Mar. 1690. The will of Francis Brown of Rye, dated 5 Feb. 1685 [1685/6], recorded 6 Nov. 1686, mentioned his son Thomas Hollibird. His wife was Mary Brown, b. abt. 1655.

Thomas "Halliberth", the jailkeeper at Fairfield, ae. 41, testified June 1692 in Disbrow trial.

Inv. taken by John Bulkley and John Edwards exhibited 2 Nov. 1697. Samuel Couch to take estate into his hands and secure it. Mr. John Edwards appointed, 5 Dec. 1698, to reckon with the debtors. Elijah, son of Thomas, chose brother Gideon guardian, 1 Dec. 1714.

On 9 Feb. 1725/6, Thomas, Gideon, and Elijah Hurlbut, Samuel Couch and Edrei his wife, and John Blackman and Jemima his wife, all of Fairfield, and Ebenezer Mead and Kezia his wife of Bedford, Westchester County, N. Y., conveyed land, in Woodbury, calling themselves sons and daus. of Thomas Hurlbut of Woodbury dec'd.

Children:*

Adrea, b. abt. 1674, d. 24 Nov. 1737 ae. 63 (g. s., Westport); m. (1) Benjamin Gilbert; m. (2) Capt. Samuel Couch.

Jemima, bapt. at Woodbury, Aug. 1680, d. at Westport, 4 Feb. 1757; m. (1) (rec. Stratford) 29 Apr. 1701, John Blackman; m. (2) Nathaniel Whitehead.

Jerusha, bapt. at Woodbury, Apr. 1682, d. y.

XThomas, bapt. at Woodbury, Dec. 1684, d. at Norwalk; adm'n granted 24 Jan. 1754; m. Phebe Gregory, dau. of Thomas.

XGideon, bapt. at Woodbury, Aug. 1688, d. at Westport, 9 Mar. 1757 in 70 yr. (g. s.); m. Margaret ———, who d. 28 Feb. 1754 in 54 yr. (g. s.).

Kezia, m. Ebenezer Mead.

Elijah, bapt. at Fairfield, 3 Nov. 1696; res. Fairfield 1726, Windham 1743.

Husted, Robert.

Of Boston 1640, and joined the Braintree settlers that year, rem. soon after to Stamford, where he d. in 1652, and his widow Elizabeth d. in 1654.

Will 8 July 1652; wife Elizabeth; children, Robert, Angel, Ann.

Children:

Robert, freeman Oct. 1663; rem. 1664 to Westchester.

+Angel.

Ann, m. abt. 1653, Richard Hardy.

Husted, Angel, s. of Robert.

Will of Angel, Sr., of Greenwich, 5 Apr. 1706; wife; sons Jonathan, Joseph and Angel Husted, and dau. Elizabeth "Bawldin", to each one shilling, "having formerly given them"; to son Moses, five shillings; residue to sons John and Samuel. Inv. 19 Apr. 1706 attested by the widow Rebecca.

Husted, Jonathan, s. of Angel. Sergeant, Greenwich Trainband.

---

* All apparently by Mary Brown, with possible exception of Adrea, who could have been by a possible former wife.

He m. by 1681, Mary Lockwood, dau. of Robert; she m. (2) Joseph Knapp of Greenwich.

Will 29 July 1705, proved 23 May 1706; to wife Mary, all Est. until my cousin Jonathan Jessup now dwelling with me be 21 yrs.; one-half of realty forever to wife, and one-half to said cousin; carpenter tools. Inv. 13 May 1706 attested by Mary Huested.

On 4 Oct. 1711, Mary wife of Joseph Knapp of Greenwich, by consent of husband and in right of former husband Jonathan Husted, conveyed to "my loving cousin Jonathan Jesup now living with me", lands in Greenwich and Stamford.

Hyatt, Thomas.

In 1633, the will of John Russell of Dorchester, Mass., named his brothers Henry Russell and Thomas Hyatt.

He had a grant of a house lot at Stamford, 7 Dec. 1641, and d. there 9 Sept. 1656. He m. Elizabeth ———, who m. (2) 6 Oct. 1657, Cornelius Jones.

Inv. not presented until 16 June 1662; left widow and six children.

Children:

> Caleb, gave receipt for portion to father-in-law Jones, 23 Dec. 1661; settled in Rye by 1678.
> Ruth, m. John Westcott.
> Deborah, received her portion of her father's estate, 30 Nov. 1669; m. (rec. Fairfield) 24 Oct. 1672, Moses Jackson.
> John, of Stamford, sold land 1668, rem. to Rye between 1680 and 1683, and to Yonkers before 1689, when he gave a final discharge to his father-in-law Jones; prob. m. his stepsister Mary Jones, dau. of Cornelius.
> Rebecca, received her portion 13 Oct. 1674; m. at Milford (but called of Stamford) 13 Nov. 1678, Thomas Hine, Jr.; she d. by 1684, when he m. again.
> +Thomas, received his portion 21 Oct. 1674.

Hyatt, Thomas, s. of Thomas.

He was of Norwalk by 1671, and received land from the town, 1677, for service as a soldier in K. Philip's War.

Married at Norwalk, 10 Nov. 1677, Mary St. John, dau. of Matthias.

Inv. of Thomas of Norwalk taken 28 Mar. 1698; £182. Children: Rebecca abt. 19, Thomas 18, Mara 16 next May, Ruth 14 next May, Sarah 12 next Dec., Millison abt. 12, John 7 next Jan., Elizabeth 4, Ebenezer 1. Widow Mary made oath. Adm'n granted to her and Ebenezer St. John.

Children, first recorded at Norwalk:

Rebecca, b. beginning of Oct. 1678.

Thomas, b. abt. 1680, d. at Ridgefield in 1760; will 10 June 1759, proved 5 Feb. 1760; m. Experience ———.

Mary, b. May 1682.

Ruth, b. May 1684, d. 20 May 1755 in 66 yr. (g. s., Greenfield) ; m. Benjamin Banks.

Sarah, b. Dec. 1686, d. at Ridgefield, 9 Feb. 1767 in 81 yr. (g. s.) ; m. 7 Apr. 1709, James Benedict.

Millicent, b. [say 1688?] ; m. in 1705, Thomas Benedict.

John, b. Jan. 1691/2.

Elizabeth, b. abt. 1694.

Ebenezer, b. abt. 1697, d. at Norwalk, in 1767; will 22 July 1766, proved Apr. 1767; m. Elizabeth ———.

Jackson, Henry.

Came from London aged 29 on *Elizabeth and Ann*, 1635; settled first in Watertown, Mass., where he was a lessee of fishing rights. Rem. to Fairfield, where he made an agreement with the town about the tide mill, 2 Feb. 1648 [1648/9] ; and sold the mill to Thomas Morehouse, 1653.

He bought land in Fairfield, 16 June 1650, from Thomas Wheeler, Jr.

Will 11 Nov. 1682, proved 22 Sept. 1686; son Moses, house at "Poquanocke"; son Samuel already had land; gr. child Moses Jackson, land at Compo; son John; gr. child Samuel Jackson; wife; the old negro woman; sons John, Moses, and Samuel, and dau. Hannah; Maj. Nathan Gold and Mr. Josiah Harvey, overseers; portion due to Est. of my son Joseph per her father Godwin's will; five children of son Joseph. Inv. 21 June 1686.

Adm'n was granted, 13 Jan. 1718/9, to the gr. sons John and Robert Jackson, on undivided lands belonging to the Est. of Henry Jackson; distribution ordered to the legal representatives of the sons, John (eldest), Moses, Samuel, and Joseph. Distribution, dated Stratfield, 3 Jan. 1720; heirs of John Jackson, viz.

Moses and John Jackson, and Susanna Lyon; heirs of Moses Jackson, viz. Robert Jackson and Deborah Smith; heirs of Samuel Jackson, viz. Daniel, Jonathan, Ebenezer, and Gabriel Jackson, Hannah Jennings, Deborah Fairchild, Rachel Lyon, and Abigail; and Sarah wife of John Bartram.

Children:

+John, b. abt. 1640.
Hannah, m. (1) Philip Galpin; m. (2) Stephen Sherwood.
+Moses.
+Samuel.
+Joseph.

Jackson, John, s. of Henry.

Born abt. 1640, he testified on 4 Aug. 1680 ae. 40.

Married Elizabeth Smith, dau. of Giles, whose will 1669 called her Elizabeth Jackson.

He settled in Eastchester, where he lived several years, but returned to Fairfield.

Inv. 11 Nov. 1689. Widow Elizabeth made oath. Adm'n granted to Joseph Seeley and Moses Jackson, Jr.

Children, the three youngest recorded at Eastchester:

Elizabeth, perhaps the nameless dau. b. at Stamford, 21 July 1662; m. Isaac Sherwood, who gave receipt to Moses Jackson, 10 May 1692, for portion of wife in Est. of father-in-law John Jackson.
+Moses.
Susanna, b. 10 Sept. 1670; m. Samuel Lyon.
+John, b. 27 Oct. 1674; gave receipt to bro. Moses, 26 Dec. 1699, for portion in Est. of father John Jackson.
Margery, b. 14 July 1677, d. y.

Jackson, Moses, s. of Henry.

Married (1) (rec. Fairfield) 24 Oct. 1672, Deborah Hyatt; dau. of Thomas of Stamford.

Married (2) widow Esther Seeley, prob. widow of Obadiah. Esther Jackson, with her sons Nathaniel Seeley and Robert Jackson (son of Moses), were bapt. at Stratfield, 22 Nov. 1696.

Moses Jackson, Sr., with Abigail Seeley his wife's dau., and Deborah his own dau., were bapt. 6 Feb. 1698.

"M. J." d. 13 Nov. 1712 (g. s., Stratfield).

Will 7 Mar. 1710 [1710/1], proved 4 Dec. 1712; dau. Rebecca Beardsley's children, David, Benjamin, Abigail; dau. Deborah Smith's children, Deborah, Rebecca, Sarah, Hester; sons-in-law Daniel Beardsley, Samuel Smith; son Robert. Receipt of Deborah Smith to brother Robert Jackson dated Stratfield, 17 June 1713.

Children [by first wife], recorded at Fairfield:

> Rebecca, b. 10 May 1674; m. (rec. Stratford), 3 Dec. 1695, Daniel Beardsley, Jr.
>
> Deborah, b. 8 Feb. 1678; m. (1) at Fairfield, 27 Oct. 1699, as his second wife, Samuel Smith; m. (2) by 1716, Thomas Bailey.

Child [by second wife]:

+Robert.

Jackson, Samuel, s. of Henry.

Married (1) ———. We may suspect that her name was Jedidah, for both her son Henry and dau. Abigail conferred this uncommon name on their respective eldest daus. Thomas Skidmore had a dau. named Jedidah, who m. Edward Higbee, and was of proper age to be mother or aunt of Samuel Jackson's wife.

Married (2) Phebe, widow of William Lyon and Daniel Crofut; she m. (4) Zachariah Lawrence.

Will 30 Aug. 1712; wife, Exec'x; to daus. Hannah, Deborah, Rachel, and Abigail, moveable Est.; lands already disposed to sons by deed.

Inv. 12 Feb. 1714/5; Widow Phebe. She appeared under the name Phebe Lawrence, 2 Mar. 1715.

Children [by first wife], three recorded at Fairfield, younger ones bapt. at Stratfield:

> Samuel, b. 19 June [167—], d. y.
>
> Nathaniel, b. 6 Mar. [167—], d. y.
>
> Hannah, b. 17 Mar. 167[—], bapt. 6 Apr. 1701; m. (1) at Stratfield, 15 Apr. 1709, Nathaniel Lyon; m. (2) Matthew Jennings.
>
> Joshua, d. in 1698; Inv. 10 Jan. 1698 [1698/9]; m. Elizabeth Sanford, dau. of Ezekiel, b. 6 Sept. 1679; she m. (2) Joseph Jackson, and (3) Thomas Chambers. Only child: Joshua, bapt. at Stratfield, 16 Oct. 1698, d. y. Adm'n on Joshua's Est. granted to widow Elizabeth and her father-in-law Samuel Jackson, who promised to add £10 for the use of widow and child of his son, and gave to

his gr. son Joshua his right in the pasture and lot of [his own] father Henry Jackson.

+Henry, b. abt. 1679, bapt. 6 Apr. 1701.

Deborah, b. ——, bapt. 6 Apr. 1701; m. [in 1701], Alexander Fairchild.

+Daniel.

Rachel, m. Moses Lyon, of Newtown.

+Jonathan, bapt. 21 July 1695; chose Sergt. John Odell for guardian, 5 Jan. 1714/5. He, of Stratfield, blacksmith, conveyed 1717 part of gr. father Jackson's long lot held in common with bro. Ebenezer. Of Newtown, he conveyed 1728.

Abigail, b. [say 1696], d. at Woodbury, 2 Nov. 1772; m. (rec. Woodbury) 6 Nov. 1717, Cornelius Bronson, Jr. They conveyed to James Dennie, 16 June 1743, one-thirtieth of land that originally belonged to Henry Jackson.

+Ebenezer, bapt. 16 Oct. 1698; chose Henry Jackson for guardian, 5 Jan. 1714/5; resided Wilton. He, of Norwalk, conveyed 1721 land given by father Samuel to bro. Jonathan and myself, also one-eighth of gr. father Jackson's long lot.

Bethia, bapt. 11 May 1701, d. y.

Child [by second wife], bapt. at Stratfield:

+Gabriel, bapt. 9 Jan. 1709.

Jackson, Joseph, s. of Henry.

Married Mary Godwin, dau. of George. She m. (2) Joseph Seeley, and rem. to Cohansey, N. J.

Inv. 31 Oct. 1681. Widow Mary; one son and four daus. Father Henry living. Matthew Sherwood and Samuel Morehouse appointed overseers. On 12 Apr. 1687, Joseph Seeley, now husband of the widow, was to receive the portions for the five children. On 17 Mar. 1687, Hannah Galpin, dau. of Henry Jackson, testified that portion given by George Godwin to his dau. Mary, sometime wife of Joseph Jackson, had been paid.

Francis Bradley receipted 1704 to Joseph Seeley for his wife's portion in Est. of her father Joseph Jackson, Sr. Capt. Matthew Sherwood and Lt. James Bennett, Sr., overseers of Est. of Joseph Jackson, receipted 1698/9 to Joseph Seeley late of Fairfield, for portion of Abigail Jackson, now wife of Daniel Bradley.

Children:

Mary, m. (1) Joseph Lyon; m. (2) abt. 1699, John Bagley.

Sarah, b. ——, d. in 1753; m. (1) abt. 1698, Francis Bradley; m. (2) John Bartram.

Abigail, m. abt. 1697, Daniel Bradley.
Eleanor.
+Joseph.

Jackson, Moses, s. of John.

Married (1) Hannah Trowbridge, dau. of William, b. at New Haven, 6 July 1668.

Married (2) after 1707, Mary, widow of Daniel Frost, and dau. of Henry Rowland. Moses Jackson's wife d. at Stratfield, 3 Jan. 1733/4.

Will 1 Feb. 1745/6, proved 14 Apr. 1746; equal shares to dau. Margery, dau. Thankful, and children of dau. Elizabeth Jennings; son-in-law Nathan Meeker, Exec'r.

Children [by first wife]:

Gershom, b. at Fairfield, 23 Nov. 1689, d. y.
Margery, m. Nathan Meeker.
Thankful.
Elizabeth, m. in 1717, Michael Jennings.

Jackson, John, s. of John.

Born at Eastchester, N. Y., 27 Oct. 1674, d. at Stratfield in 1727. Married Sarah, dau. of Samuel Godwin.

His children John, David, Rebecca, Sarah, and Helen, were bapt. at Stratfield, 17 Oct. 1714, and Abram two weeks later.

Adm'n granted, 14 Mar. 1726/7, to widow Sarah. The same year, Sarah was appointed guardian to her sons Joseph and Stephen, and was chosen by dau. Helen. Distribution: Widow, David, Joseph, Stephen, Rebecca, Helen.

Children:

✕John, d. at North Fairfield in 1784; Inv. 21 June 1784; m. (1) Abigail Summers, bapt. 21 Oct. 1705; m. (2) 19 July 1753, Abigail Nichols of Greenfield.
David, b. before 1707, since at Stratfield he was called "Sr." to distinguish him from cousin of like name born that year; called of Fairfield at first purchase in Newtown, 19 Mar. 1744/5; called of Newtown 1754 when he conveyed right in Fairfield laid out to heirs of Henry Jackson, dec'd; conveyed to sons 1779 and d. before 28 May 1784 when his widow Rachel conveyed to the sons; lived in Newbury [Brookfield], est. distributed 22 Dec. 1792; m.

(1) ——; m. (2) at Second Church, New Haven, 1 Feb. 1759,
Rachel (Sanford) (Warner) Sperry, b. at New Haven, 1 May
1710, widow of Benjamin Warner and Enos Sperry.

Rebecca, m. John Jones, of Stratfield, with whom she conveyed 1728
to bro. John Jackson, part of homelot that was father John
Jackson's.

Sarah, d. s. p.

Helen, m. Thomas Nichols.

Abraham, d. unm. in 1741. Will 4 Aug. 1740, proved 5 May 1741;
all estate to nephew John Jones; friend John Wilson, Exec'r.

XJoseph, m. Deborah Lyon, dau. of Nathaniel; she m. (2) in 1754,
Joseph Beach of Stratford.

Stephen, m. ("of Fairfield") at Darien, 3 Oct. 1745, Mary Waterbury, dau. of David of Stamford.

Jackson, Robert, s. of Moses.

Married (rec. Stratfield) 18 Apr. 1706, Sarah Huttin.

Rem. from Stratfield to Norwalk. In 1755, David Benedict
and wife Tabitha, John Nash, Jr., and wife Sarah, Robert Watson and wife Esther, Fountain Smith and wife Hannah, Jonathan
Darrow and wife Abigail, and Philadelphia Jackson, all of Norwalk, conveyed as heirs to land laid out to Henry Jackson, dec'd.

Children, recorded at Stratfield:

Abiah, b. 16 July 1707, bapt. 20 July 1707.

Rebecca, bapt. 12 Nov. 1710; "R. J." d. 14 May 1712 (g. s.,
Stratfield).

Tabitha, b. 9 [Sept.] 1713, bapt. 27 Sept. 1713; m. David Benedict.

Sarah, b. 16 Oct. 1715, bapt. 4 Mar. 1716; m. (rec. Norwalk) in
1736, John Nash.

Esther, b. 9 Aug. [1718], bapt. 10 Aug. 1718; m. Robert Watson.

Abigail, b. 22 Oct. 1720, d. 20 July 1756 ae. 35 yrs. 9 mos. (Bible
record); m. 27 Sept. 1743, Jonathan Darrow.

Hannah, m. Fountain Smith.

Philadelphia.

Jackson, Henry, s. of Samuel.

Born about 1679, d. at Stratfield, 15 Sept. 1717 ae. 38 (g. s.).

Married 16 Jan. 1703/4, Mary Wheeler, dau. of Isaac; b. abt.
1683, d. at Stratfield, 18 Sept. 1743 in 61 yr. (g. s.); she m. (2)
Capt. Samuel Sherwood.

Distribution, 28 Nov. 1723; widow; David, Isaac, Jedidah, Anna, Deborah, Mary, and Eunice Jackson.

The son Isaac chose his mother Mary Sherwood for guardian, 4 June 1728; Dr. John Wheeler was surety.

Children, recorded at Stratfield:

Jedidah, b. 17 Apr. 1705, bapt. 22 Apr. 1705; m. Ebenezer Lacy.
David, b. 14 Mar. 1707, bapt. 16 Mar. 1707, d. at New Milford, 26 Dec. 1754 ae. 47 (g. s.); m. Hannah ———, b. abt. 1714, d. 11 June 1784 ae. 70 (g. s.)
Anna, b. 12 Jan. 1708/9, bapt. 27 Feb. 1709; m. (rec. New Milford) 5 Nov. 1729, Lemuel Bostwick.
Deborah, b. 13 Jan. 1710/1, bapt. 22 Jan. 1711; m. 14 Dec. 1732, Joseph Lake, of Trumbull.
✕Isaac, b. 11 May 1712, bapt. 18 May 1712, d. in Sept. 1777; will 1 Sept. 1777, proved 20 Sept. 1777; m. at Trumbull, 14 Nov. 1734, Rachel Nichols; dau. of Daniel.
Mercy, b. 30 Nov. 1713, bapt. 6 Dec. 1713; m. 30 Nov. 1730, Obadiah Beardsley; rem. to New Fairfield.
Eunice, b. 7 Aug. 1715, d. at Stratfield, 6 Sept. 1796 in 82 yr. (g. s.); m. (1) 19 July 1733, James Hawley; m. (2) Isaac Bennett.
Sarah, b. 19 Aug. 1717, bapt. 1 Sept. 1717, d. before 1723.

Jackson, Daniel, s. of Samuel.

He rem. to Newtown, and by 1734 to Dover, N. Y.

He m. Mary Preston, dau. of Jehiel, who d. at Stratfield, 7 Aug. 1734 (at Capt. Hubbell's).

Child:

✕Samuel, bapt. at Stratfield, 20 Aug. 1710.
Others?

Jackson, Jonathan, s. of Samuel.

Bapt. 21 July 1695; blacksmith, of Stratfield 1717; of Newtown 1728; settled in Wilton, where his children were recorded.

Children:

Moses, b. 10 July 1719.
Samuel, b. 7 Jan. 1720/1, m. 10 Dec. 1741, Hannah Bedient?
Deborah, b. 16 Oct. 1722, d. Dec. 1731.
Abigail, b. 10 Feb. 1724/5.
Eunice, b. 9 Nov. 1727.
Sarah, b. 14 Aug. 1729.

Jackson, Ebenezer, s. of Samuel.

Bapt. 16 Oct. 1698; settled in Wilton, where his children were recorded.

He m. Esther Abbott, dau. of John.

Children:
> Mary, b. 3 May 1717.
> Ebenezer, b. 2 May 1719.
> Joshua, b. 12 Jan. 1720/1.
> John, b. 5 Apr. 1723.
> Abraham, b. 16 Jan. 1725/6.
> Daniel, b. 13 Apr. 1728.

Jackson, Gabriel, s. of Samuel.

Bapt. at Stratfield, 9 Jan. 1709.
Married at Fairfield, 24 May 1727, Margaret Hall, dau. of Francis.

Children, recorded at Fairfield:
> Samuel, b. 19 Mar. 1728.
> Mehitabel, b. 27 Mar. 1730, d. Jan. 1738.
> Patience, b. 25 Sept. 1733; m. 11 Sept. 1752, Nehemiah Jennings.
> Francis, b. 11 Mar. 1736, d. Jan. 1738.
> Francis, b. 3 June 1740.
> Benjamin, b. 30 July 1743.
> Mehitabel, b. 30 Sept. 1745.

Jackson, Joseph, s. of Joseph.

He d. at Stratfield, 29 Sept. 1714; m. 23 Nov. 1699, Elizabeth (Sanford), widow of his cousin Joshua Jackson. She was dau. of Ezekiel, b. 6 Sept. 1679; she m. (3) Thomas Chambers, of Stratfield.

Adm'n granted to widow Elizabeth, 8 Nov. 1714. Inv. 7 Feb. 1714/5. Distribution 10 Aug. 1721 to Widow, and Ephraim, Elizabeth, Sarah, and Ann Jackson.

On 14 Mar. 1719/20, Thomas Chambers receipted for payment made to Joseph Jackson dec'd, late husband to Elizabeth, my now wife, who was Adm'x.

On 1 Mar. 1728/9, Ephraim Jackson, Nathaniel and Elizabeth

Seeley, and Ann Jackson, conveyed to Thomas Morehouse and Sarah his wife, all right in one-third of our father Joseph Jackson's house, now held by "our mother Chambers."

Children, bapt. at Stratfield:

Joseph, b. 19 Sept. 1700, bapt. 20 Oct. 1700, d. 15 Aug. 1707.

Elizabeth, b. and bapt. 15 Nov. 1702, d. at Stratfield, 9 Dec. 1781 in 79 yr. (g. s., Stratfield); m. Nathaniel Seeley.

XEphraim, b. 13 Oct. 1704, bapt. 22 Oct. 1704, d. at Redding, 5 May 1768 ae. 65 or 66; m. (1) Nov. 1727, Martha Couch; dau. of Samuel, bapt. 18 Feb. 1704/5, d. abt. 1728; m. (2) June 1730, Martha Blackman, b. Oct. 1708.

Sarah, b. 26 Nov. 1706, bapt. 1 Dec. 1706, d. 14 Mar. 1706/7.

Sarah, b. 29 Oct. 1708, bapt. 12 Dec. 1708; m. Thomas Morehouse, Jr.

Ann, b. 1 July 1710, bapt. 2 July 1710, d. at Oxford, 17 July 1777 ae. 68; m. (1) John Blackman; m. (2) Samuel Chatfield.

Mary, b. 11 Oct. 1712, bapt. 12 Oct. 1712, d. 1 Apr. 1714.

James, (Rev.) Thomas, s. of Rev. Thomas.

In 1653 was mentioned the house in Fairfield which was once his. He witnessed the will of Thomas Dunn (probated 1660) by which Dunn gave his property to Rev. John Jones. Is it not likely then that he was the husband of Ruth James named in the will 1665 of her father Rev. John Jones? Ruth was b. abt. 1628, and her husband may have lived in Fairfield a year or so subsequent to their marriage.

What Thomas James was this? Thomas, son of Rev. Thomas of Charlestown, came with his father to New Haven in 1639, and remained here some years after his father left. He was ordained in Easthampton, L. I., in 1651, and remained there as minister, dying 14 June 1696. Made freeman in 1645, we may suppose him b. abt. 1624, hence of fitting age to marry Ruth Jones, b. abt. 1628, dau. of another minister. The elder chroniclers report the likely tradition that his education in England was not completed, hence he studied under New England clergymen before his ordination.

This man had left New Haven by Jan. 1648/9, when he was one of the absentee lot owners to whom the Secretary was ordered to write with regard to keeping up fences. He sold land in Oct. 1649, and the last mention of him in New Haven was in

1655 when Thomas Johnson entered for record land which he had bought from Thomas James through his agent Mr. Wakeman.

Between 1648, by which year doubtless he had rem. from New Haven, and 1651, when he began to preach in Easthampton, we have three years to account for. Since a Thomas James (as mentioned above) lived in Fairfield and left there before 1653, what more likely than that he was the same man, who settled in Fairfield to study under Rev. John Jones, having married his preceptor's dau.? For that he had a wife by 1647 is proved by the "seating" of New Haven meeting-house early that year. His appearance in Easthampton coincides with his disappearance from Fairfield.

It is here necessary to dissipate the claim that James had a group of children bapt. at New Haven. Savage, followed by others, has attributed to him four children, Elisha, Nathaniel, Abel, and Abigail, bapt. 19 Mar. 1647/8, and a dau. Ruth bapt. 24 Mar. 1649/50. Not one of these belonged to Thomas James. In the first place, he had left New Haven before the youngest was bapt. Secondly, it is inherently improbable that a minister's son, himself a candidate for the ministry, would have allowed four children to accumulate before having them baptized. Finally, these five children belonged to William Janes the school-teacher, for he had three known sons with the names of those three allegedly bapt. to Thomas James; while the birth of Ruth dau. of William Janes is recorded as occurring a month prior to the bapt. of Ruth "James". The always careful Mr. Henry White, whose edited copy of the New Haven First Church baptisms pub. in Vol. 9 of the *New Eng. Hist. and Gen. Register* has been followed by Savage and others, is responsible for this group of pseudo-Jameses; nor should he be blamed by any who have experienced the delight of discriminating between such names as "Mr. James" and "Mr. Janes" in the cramped faded handwriting of 1650.*

We conclude that Rev. Thomas James m. (1) Ruth Jones; he m. (2) 2 Sept. 1669, Katharine Blux.†

Will of Thomas James, Preacher, of Easthampton, 5 June

---

* Since writing the above, we find that the compiler of the *Janes Family* (1868) had reached the same conclusion (see p. 78).

† Marriage on authority of Pelletreau in *Early Long Island Wills.* Katharine may have been mother of Mary and Elizabeth, the stepdaus. named by James in his will.

1696; eldest dau. Sarah wife of Peregrine Stanborough; second dau. Mary wife of John Stratton; third dau. Hannah wife of James Dyment; son-in-law Thomas Harris in behalf of his wife, my fourth dau. Ruth; gr. children Mary Stanborough and Mary Stratton; dau.-in-law Anne wife of Mr. Abraham Howell, £20 provided she bring in no after reckoning upon account of her first husband, my son Nathaniel, dec'd; eldest gr. son John Stanborough; two daus.-in-law Mary wife of Mr. John Mulford and Elizabeth wife of Mr. Joseph Osborn; sons-in-law Stanborough, Stratton, Dyment, and Harris, Exec'rs; two sons-in-law Mulford and Osborn, overseers. He died 14 June 1696.

Children [prob. all by first wife]:

Sarah, b. [say 1648]; m. (rec. Southampton, L. I.) 15 Dec. 1664, Mr. Peregrine Stanborough.*

On 4 June 1692, John Bulkley of Fairfield entered his purchase from Peregrine Stanborough of Southampton, L. I., of the sixth part of the orchard or lot where said Bulkley's house standeth now. Bulkley was gr. son of Rev. John Jones, and this deed confirms the surmise that Mrs. Peregrine Stanborough was gr. dau. of the same through her mother Mrs. Ruth James.

Nathaniel, m. Ann Wakeman, dau. of Rev. Samuel of Fairfield; she m. (2) 2 Oct. 1690, Capt. Abraham Howell, of Southampton.

Mary, b. abt. 1654, d. 14 Feb. 1718 ae. 64; m. John Stratton, Jr., of Easthampton, bro. of Cornelius Stratton who m. Martha Hull of Fairfield, gr. dau. of Rev. John Jones through her mother Rebecca.

Hannah, m. James Dyment.

Ruth, m. Thomas Harris.

James, Joseph.

Apparently not related to Rev. Thomas James. He rented a farm in Fairfield for several years prior to 1678 from his wife's mother; and had a grant from the town, Jan. 1680 [1680/1]; d. in 1687. In Oct. 1679, the Conn. Assembly granted him 50 shillings per annum because of disablement; "a wounded soldier in the late warrs."

He m. Mary Dickerson, dau. of Thomas. She received a legacy in the will of [her stepfather] Daniel Finch.

He conveyed, 5 Dec. 1687, to Nathan Adams, who hath m. my dau. Mary with my consent.

* He d. in Jan. 1701/2; for his will, see *Early Long Island Wills*, p. 233.

Adm'n granted 6 Jan. 1687 [1687/8] to widow Mary and to Abram Adams.

Child:

> Mary, b. [say 1665]; m. abt. 1687, Nathan Adams.

Janes, William.

Born about 1648; d. at Stratford, 17 Nov. 1726 in 79 yr. (g. s., Epis. yard).

He is usually attributed as a son to the earlier William of New Haven and Northampton; if so, we should guess his age at death overstated or misread, and that he was born perhaps a decade later than above stated.

Married at Stratford, 26 Nov. 1685, Sarah Clark. She was dau. of James, b. 11 Jan. 1666/7, d. 16 Oct. 1739 in 72 yr. (g. s.).

Distribution 16 June 1727 of Est. of William Jeans: Widow Sarah; Mary wife of Nathan Smith; Sarah wife of Thomas Salmon; Elizabeth wife of John Outman; Esther wife of Abraham Beardsley; Deborah wife of Samuel Watkins; Michael Jeans.

Will of Sarah Jeans, 3 Oct. 1738, proved 6 Nov. 1738; children Michael Jeans, Mary Smith, Sarah Salmon, Elizabeth Oatman; Deborah Loring, Esther Beardsley; sons-in-law Nathan Smith and Thomas Salmon, Exec'rs.

Land at Stratford laid out, 19 Feb. 1727/8, to Thomas Salmon, Nehemiah Loring, and John Outman in right of their wives, daus. of William Janes dec'd.

Children, recorded at Stratford:

> Michael, b. 29 Sept. 1686; settled in Charleston, S. C., but returned to the north.
> Hester, b. 21 Mar. 1688, d. y.
> Mary, b. "26 of 1692/3"; m. at Stratford, 22 July 1714, Nathan Smith of Milford.
> Sarah, b. 20 Mar. 1693/4, d. 15 Mar. 1750 ae. 55 (g. s., Epis. Yard, Stratford); m. Thomas Salmon.
> Elizabeth, b. 5 Nov. 1695; m. John Outman.
> Deborah, b. 9 Sept. 1697; m. (1) 17 Jan. 1716/7, Samuel Watkins; (2) 29 Oct. 1727, Nehemiah Loring.
> Esther, b. abt. 1699, d. 11 Nov. 1772 in 74 yr. (g. s., Huntington); m. 17 Apr. 1723, Abraham Beardsley.

Jeffrey, Thomas.

Married at Stratford, 1 May 1674, Mary Harvey, dau. of Richard, b. 15 Sept. 1647.

Inv. of Est. taken 8 Apr. 1690 by Samuel Sherman and Samuel Galpin. Widow Mary made oath; adm'n granted to her, with advice of Samuel Galpin and Josiah Nichols.

Jenkins, David.

An original settler of Woodbury, 1673.
He m. after 1683, Grace, widow of Thomas Leavenworth.
He d. at Newtown, 19 Dec. 1736.

Children, bapt. at Woodbury:
> Grace, bapt. Mar. 1687/8.
> Alice, bapt. Mar. 1689/90, d. 9 Jan. 1708/9 in 20 yr. (g. s., Stratford).

Jenners, John.

Settled in Stratford; rem. to Brookhaven, L. I.; m. Alice Pigg, dau. of Robert and Margaret.

The will of Robert Pigg of New Haven, dated 28 Mar. 1660, named his dau. Alice and her son Thomas and her other children.

Children, recorded at Stratford:
> Mary, b. 14 Oct. 1648.
> Thomas, b. 20 Apr. 1651.
> Others.

Jennings, Joshua.

An early settler of Hartford; fined for a trivial offense, he left Hartford in 1650 and settled in Fairfield.

Married at Hartford, 22 Dec. 1647, Mary Williams. She m. (2) at Fairfield, 16 Dec. 1680, George Slawson, of Stamford; with whom she made a marriage covenant dated 18 Nov. 1680.

Will 25 Feb. 1674 [1674/5]; to son Joshua, my carpenter, joiner, wheelwright and turning tools; to rest of my sons, Joseph, Michael, John, Samuel, Matthew, and Isaac, and to my daus. Mary and Elizabeth, 20 shillings apiece; to wife Mary, residue, housing, lands, chattels, etc.; friends Major Gold and Mr. Wakeman to be helpful to my wife; witnesses, Josiah Harvey, Mary Staples. Inv. 27 Nov. 1675.

Goodwife Slawson demanded goods which had been in possession of her son-in-law John Smith, John and his wife being deceased; she made oath 9 Dec. 1690 that the goods were hers and "she would never give them to her daughter said Smith's wife if she would proceed in the match with said Smith."

Will of Mary Slawson, 27 Mar. 1697; sons Matthew, Isaac, and Samuel Jennings; dau. Mary Curtis, all her wearing apparel and £30 out of Est. at Stamford; dau.-in-law Hannah Jennings; son Joseph Jennings; grandchild John Smith, £5; five sons, Joshua, Joseph, Samuel, Matthew, Isaac. Inv. 10 Jan. 1697 [1697/8].

Children:

+Joshua.
+Joseph.
    Mary, m. [Daniel?] Curtis.
+Samuel.
+Matthew.
    John, d. unm. before 1697.
+Isaac, b. abt. 1673.
    Elizabeth, m. John Smith.

Jennings, Joshua, s. of Joshua.

Married Hannah Lyon, dau. of Richard, b. about 1681, d. Nov. 1743 in 83 yr. (g. s., Westport). He receipted to "mother Lyon" for his wife's portion, 17 Aug. 1688.

Joshua, Sr., was bapt. at Fairfield Cong. Church, 1 June 1712.

Adm'n on his estate was granted, 31 July 1716, to widow Hannah and son Joshua. Distribution 13 Feb. 1718 to Joshua and Moses Jennings, daus. Mary Burr and Hannah Sturges, Abigail Jennings, and widow Mary Jennings [the last obviously by mistake for Hannah]. Abigail chose her brother Joshua guardian; he refused, and she chose her brother-in-law Peter Sturges. Moses chose his brother Joshua guardian.

On 21 Jan. 1730/1, there being land of Joshua not inventoried, viz. the whole right of Isaac Sherwood in commons, a third of the right of Thomas Lyon in commons, and a fifth of commons which belonged to Mary Slosson sometime resident in Stamford ("mother of our father"): agreement for distribution was made by Joshua Jennings, Mary Burr, Peter Sturges and Hannah his wife, and Simon Couch and Abigail his wife, who referred to their brother Moses Jennings dec'd.

Will of Hannah, 25 Jan. 1742/3, proved 30 Nov. 1743; three daus. Mary, Hannah, Abigail; gr. son Joshua Jennings, Jr.; son Joshua.; son-in-law Simon Couch and gr. son Samuel Sturges, Exec'rs.

Children:

XJoshua, b. abt. 1686, d. at Westport, 2 Jan. 1746; m. (1) abt. 1719, Sarah Bulkley, dau. of Joseph, bapt. 23 Sept. 1694, d. 17 Sept. 1724 ae. 31 (g. s., Fairfield); m. (2) at Christ Church, Stratford, 3 Feb. 1724/5, Rebecca (Clapham), widow of Nathan Adams, Jr., b. abt. 1690, d. 1748.

Mary, b. abt. 1690, d. at Westport, 11 Oct. 1748 in 59 yr. (g. s.); m. Daniel Burr.

Hannah, b. abt. 1692, d. 6 Aug. 1771 in 80 yr. (g. s., Fairfield); m. Peter Sturges.·

Abigail, b. 16 Feb. 1699/1700 (by age at death, with allowance for calendar change), d. 14 July 1765 ae. 65 yrs. 4 mos. 15 days (g. s., Westport); m. 18 May 1721, Capt. Simon Couch.

Moses, bapt. with Abigail 26 Dec. 1714, d. in 1727. Adm'n granted, 19 May 1727, to Joshua Jennings and Simon Couch. His Est. was distributed, 17 Aug. 1727, to Joshua Jennings, Mary Burr, Hannah wife of Peter Sturges, and Abigail wife of Simon Couch. He had received 1720 a conveyance from Joshua Jennings, Daniel Burr and wife Abigail, Peter Sturgis and wife Hannah, and Abigail Jennings, of their right in house of father Joshua dec'd.

Jennings, Joseph, s. of Joshua.

Married Abigail Turney, dau. of Robert, b. 25 Feb. 1661.

He was bapt. at Fairfield Church, 14 May 1699. He conveyed, 9 Nov. 1721, to son Joseph, two acres that "was his grandfather Turnies", reserving life use to my wife Abigail, and referring to bro. Matthew Jennings.

Adm'n on his estate was granted, 1 Aug. 1727, to Abigail and Ebenezer Jennings.

Children, bapt. at Fairfield:

XJoseph, b. (no record), d. in 1768; will 9 May 1768, proved 2 Aug. 1768; m. 20 Jan. 1709, Abigail Grumman, b. 1 Aug. 1685.

XJohn, b. (no record), d. in 1762; adm'n granted, 13 June 1762; m. Sarah ———, who d. in 1776; her dower distributed, 8 July 1776.

Ebenezer, b. abt. 1692, bapt. 28 Oct. 1694, d. 9 Apr. 1768 in 76 yr. (g. s., Fairfield); m. Rebecca Silliman, who d. 2 Jan. 1790 in 85 yr. (g. s.); no issue. Will 8 June 1763, proved 3 May 1768; wife Rebecca, life use, with provision for my sister Martha for life, and liberty to sell real estate, if necessary, with approval of Rev. Noah Hobart; residue to my relations; kinsman Andrew Jennings, Exec'r.

Abigail, bapt. 28 Oct. 1694.

Sarah, bapt. 22 Aug. 1697; m. (Fairfield Church) 19 Nov. [1718 or 1719], Joseph Squire.

Martha, bapt. 11 Aug. 1700.

Ann, bapt. 12 Mar. 1703/4; m. 4 Nov. 1734, Joseph Hollingworth.

Jennings, Samuel, s. of Joshua.

Married (1) Sarah Grumman, prob. in 1691, when he gave a receipt to John Grumman for wife's legacy from her grandfather Michael Try. She renewed her Covenant at Fairfield Church, 9 Sept. 1694.

Married (2) by prenuptial contract dated 24 Oct. 1727, Mary widow of "James Bennitt Carpenter." She was dau. of Simon Couch, and widow first of Thomas Grumman.

On 23 Dec. 1692, he divided with bro.-in-law John Grumman, interest in estate of Michael Grumman dec'd which he had by marriage with "Sarah Grumman my now wife."

Will 23 Jan. 1728/9, proved 7 Dec. 1732; wife Mary; children of late son Michael dec'd; sons Samuel, Nathan; son-in-law Daniel Lyon; daus. Sarah Lyon, Eunice Jennings; nephew Joseph Jennings; codicil, 20 Nov. 1732, dau. Eunice Jennings now Lyon. Distribution 1734; heirs of Michael; Samuel Jennings; Nathan Jennings; Daniel Lyon; Elnathan Lyon.

Children [by first wife], recorded at Fairfield:

XMichael, b. 3 Dec. 1693, bapt. 9 Sept. 1694, d. in 1727; adm'n granted to Samuel Jennings, 6 June 1727; m. in 1717, Elizabeth Jackson, dau. of Moses.

Elizabeth, bapt. 7 Mar. 1696/7, d. y.

Patience, bapt. 25 Sept. 1698, d. y.

Sarah, b. 9 Feb. 1699 [1699/1700], bapt. 11 Feb. 1699/1700; m. 7 Aug. 1718, Daniel Lyon.

XSamuel, b. 16 Mar. 1702/3, bapt. 22 Mar. 1701/2 [the church record must be presumed correct], d. in 1741; will 12 June 1740, proved 7 Oct. 1741; m. (Fairfield Church) 2 Oct. 1728, Johanna Risden.

Eunice, b. 13 Dec. 1704, bapt. 2 Jan. 1704/5; m. Elnathan Lyon.

Dorothy, bapt. 14 Sept. 1707, d. y.
Dorothy, b. 11 Nov. 1709, bapt. 13 Nov. 1709, d. y.
XNathan, b. 13 Mar. 1710/1, bapt. 18 Mar. 1710/1, d. 12 May 1757 in 47 yr. (g. s., Fairfield); adm'n granted, 30 June 1757; m. (1) Ann Adams, dau. of David, bapt. 12 Feb. 1715/6, d. before 1743; m. (2) Abigail ———.
Benjamin, bapt. 20 Sept. 1713, d. y.

Jennings, Matthew, s. of Joshua.

Married (1) Mary ———, who renewed Covenant at Fairfield Church, 5 Sept. 1697.
Married (2) Hannah, widow of Nathaniel Lyon, and dau. of Samuel Jackson.
Will 20 Dec. 1737, proved 8 May 1738; wife Hannah; dau. Hannah; sons Daniel, Jeremiah; Ruth Bulkley, Mary Ogden, Rebecca Middlebrook, Hannah Jennings.

Children [by first wife], bapt. at Fairfield:

Matthew, b. in 1695, bapt. 5 Sept. 1697, d. y.
Elizabeth, b. in 1697, bapt. 31 Oct. 1697, d. y.
XDaniel, b. in 1700, bapt. 7 Apr. 1700, d. abt. 1778; m. Hannah Hendrick.
XJeremiah, b. in 1703, bapt. 11 Apr. 1703, d. by 1780; Inv. 19 June 1780; m. 15 Dec. 1726, Elizabeth Coley.
Mary, b. in 1705, bapt. 2 Sept. 1705, d. y.
Ruth, bapt. 11 Oct. 1708, d. abt. 1787; m. (1) Joseph Bulkley; m. (2) 14 Mar. 1754, Seth Samuel Burr.
Mary, b. abt. 1710, d. at Greenfield, 31 May 1768 ae. abt. 60; m. 1 Jan. 1730, John Ogden.
Sarah, d. y.
Rebecca, m. 2 June 1734, Jonathan Middlebrook.

Child [by second wife]:

Hannah, bapt. 10 July 1720, d. 28 Jan. 1796 in 76 yr. (g. s., Stratfield); m. 29 June 1738, John Knapp.

Jennings, Isaac, s. of Joshua.

Born about 1673, d. 10 July 1746 in 73 yr. (g. s., Fairfield).
Married (1) Mary Gray, dau. of Jacob, b. 7 July 1679.
Married (2) Abigail Morehouse, dau. of Samuel, bapt. at Stratfield, 21 Mar. 1708.
Adm'n granted, 21 Aug. 1746, to son Isaac. Will 10 June 1746, proved 21 Aug. 1746; sons Josiah, Isaac, John; daus.

Abigail, Sarah, and Mary Smith. Distribution Jan. 1747/8; Isaac, John, Josiah; Mary wife of John Smith; Abigail and Sarah Jennings.

Children [by first wife], recorded at Fairfield:

XIsaac, b. 11 July 1692 [should be 1702], bapt. 11 Oct. 1702, d. at Fairfield, 16 Mar. 1760 ae. 58 (g. s.); will 20 Jan. 1758, proved 27 Mar. 1760; m. 1 June 1731, Phebe Staples, dau. of John, bapt. 16 Mar. 1706/7, d. in 1768; her will, 20 June 1768, proved 19 July 1768.

Mary, b. 4 July 1695 [should be 1705], bapt. 19 Aug. 1705; m. John Smith.

XJohn, b. 24 Mar. 1706 [should be 1707], bapt. 11 May 1707, d. 12 May 1799 in 93 yr. (g. s., Greenfield); m. 20 Jan. 1731, Sarah Winton, dau. of John, b. 16 Feb. 1711/2, d. 13 Dec. 1791 ae. 79 (g. s.).

Josiah, b. 1 Apr.(?) 1711, bapt. 27 May 1711.

David, b. 6 Sept. 1714, bapt. 31 Oct. 1714, d. y.

Children [by second wife], bapt. at Fairfield:

Abigail, bapt. 14 Sept. 1729.

Sarah, bapt. 14 May 1732; m. Mar. 1756, Samuel Bostwick.

Jessup, John.

Came to Mass. by 1637, removed to Wethersfield with first settlers, and apparently was dead by Feb. 1637/8, when the Conn. General Court ordered creditors to present claims. His widow married John Whitmore, who was of Wethersfield by 1639, and the Whitmores removed in 1641 to Stamford, doubtless with the Jessup children. Here Whitmore was murdered by the Indians, Oct. 1648. In 1652, the widow Joanna Whitmore sold land in Stamford.

In a court case 1657, it was testified that "Edward Jessup and his mother widow Whitmore went from Stamford to live elswhere". [New Haven Col. Rec.]

Probable children:

John, removed from Wethersfield to Stamford 1641, and to Southampton, L. I., by 1653.

+Edward.

A daughter, presumably, who m. John Burroughs. He was at Salem, Mass., by 1637; of Newtown, L. I., 1657, and d. Aug. 1678 ae. 61, having m. (2) widow Elizabeth Reed. Burroughs was called brother-in-law in will of Edward Jessup; who also gave a legacy to his cousin [niece] Johanna Burroughs. Note that the child Johanna was named after her grandmother.

Jessup, Edward, s. of John. Magistrate at Newtown, 1659, 1660, 1661, 1662. Magistrate for Westchester, appointed by Conn. Leg., Oct. 1663, May 1664. Patentee, Westchester, 1666.

In testimony taken 1672, he was referred to as an original lot-owner at Fairfield (1639). After his stepfather's death, he appears in Stamford records, 1649. The Fairfield land, he sold to Thomas Barlow before 1653. He was a pioneer of Newtown, L. I., 1652, and in 1661 bought land in Jamaica which was sold in 1691 by his son Edward of Fairfield. In 1663 he removed to Westchester, N. Y., where he d. in 1666.

Will 6 Aug. 1666, proved 14 Nov. 1666; dau. Elizabeth Hunt; dau. Hannah Jessup (under 18); son Edward (under age); gr. child Mary Hunt; cousin Johanna Burroughs; to Derrick Gasson, a cow; to wife Elizabeth, Exec'x, most of Est.; overseers, Mr. Richard Cornhill, J. P., Mrs. Sarah Bridges, bro.-in-law John Burroughs, and Ralph Hunt.

His widow Elizabeth m. in 1668, Robert Beacham of Fairfield, and took her two younger children there with her. She was living 25 Dec. 1690, when she conveyed to son Edward all her property.

Edward Jessup of Fairfield conveyed right in cattle belonging to his father Jessup, to Thomas Hunt, Jr., 23 July 1682. A letter from Elizabeth Beacham to her son-in-law Thomas Hunt, Jr., 27 Mar. 1682, gave her son Edward power to dispose of any estate that belongs to him. "I give Edward power to dispose of any of my daughter Hannah's jades, for I have order from my son Joseph and his wife both." [Westchester Deeds.]

Children:

>   Elizabeth,* m. Thomas Hunt, Jr., of Westchester.
>   Hannah, m. Joseph ———.†
> +Edward, b. abt. 1663.

---

* Perhaps dau. of Edward by an earlier marriage. The other two children were certainly by Elizabeth, and apparently were some years younger than their sister.

† The *Jessup Genealogy* suggests that Hannah may have been wife of Joseph Lockwood, which would make her stepdau. instead of actual dau. of Robert Beacham (see his will). This is a plausible theory, but evidence is insufficient to substantiate it.

Jessup, Edward, s. of Edward.

Born about 1663, d. at Stamford, 28 Dec. 1732 in 70 yr. (g. s.).
Aged 29, he testified 1692 in Disbrow witchcraft trial.
He m. (2) Elizabeth Hide, dau. of John, b. 23 Aug. 1668.   She
renewed her Covenant at Fairfield Church, 13 Sept. 1696; d. at
Stamford, 2 Oct. 1747 in 79 yr. (g. s.).
Will 17 Aug. 1731, proved 5 Jan. 1732/3; wife Elizabeth; sons
Joseph (Exec'r), Jonathan; daus. Hannah, Elizabeth; son
Ebenezer; daus. Abilene, Deborah, Sarah.   The son Jonathan,
and John Reynolds who m. a dau., appealed 5 Feb. 1733; but on
20 Feb. joined with John Smith and Elizabeth his wife in quit-
claiming all right in Est. to the Exec'r.   Abilene receipted 1734
for her bequest.
Elizabeth Jessup of Stamford, will 15 Sept. 1747, proved 6 Oct.
1747; sons Edward and Joseph; daus. Abilene, Deborah, Sarah,
who (called "my three daughters") were to have residue; gr. dau.
Elizabeth Darling.

Children [by first wife] :

> Jonathan, d. at Greenwich in 1757; adm'n granted to Sarah, 2 Aug.
> 1757; m. Sarah ———, who m. (2) Timothy Knapp. The will
> of Jonathan Husted of Greenwich, 1705, gave to cousin Jonathan
> Jessup, "now dwelling with me", half his estate; and in 1711
> Husted's widow conveyed to cousin Jonathan Jessup, "now living
> with me", lands in Greenwich and Stamford. The will of Jabez
> Sherwood of Greenwich, 1704, gave lands to Jonathan Husted
> and his wife; and to Jonathan Jessup, son of Edward of Fair-
> field, his carpenter's tools, and his hat.*
> Hannah, b. [say 1692]; m. John Reynolds, of Greenwich.
> Elizabeth, b. (rec. Greenfield) 11 Feb. 1693 [1693/4]; m. Aug. 1710,
> John Smith.

Children [by second wife], bapt. at Fairfield Church:

> Abilene, bapt. 13 Sept. 1696; m. John Darling.
> XEdward, bapt. 7 Mar. 1696/7, d. at Westport, 30 Sept. 1750 in 54
> yr. (g. s.) ; m. (rec. Fairfield) 7 Dec. 1724, Sarah Blackleach.
> She was dau. of Richard, 2d, b. abt. 1700, d. 18 Nov. 1783 in 84
> yr. (g. s.). Edward received by deed his father's homestead at
> Maximus [Westport].

---

* It is clear from these wills that Jonathan Jessep cannot be identified with the son
bapt. 1707, and the excellent *Jessup Genealogy* errs in this particular. We know that
Jonathan was under 21 in 1705 and should guess, from the terms of the wills, that
he was born not later than 1690. His mother may have been a dau. of Angel
Husted, and he was adopted by his childless uncle Jonathan Husted, for whom he
was prob. named.

Joseph, bapt. 4 June 1699, d. at Montreal, Canada, in 1778 ae. 79; m. at Stamford, 14 Aug. 1734, Abigail James; she was dau. of Henry, and d. 6 May 1743 in [——] yr. (g. s., Stamford). He rem. to Nine Partners, N. Y., abt. 1744; loyalist.

Deborah, bapt. 12 July 1702, d. at Stamford, 1 Mar. 1769; m. at Stamford, 23 Feb. 1740/1, Obadiah Stevens.

John, bapt. 3 Aug. 1707, d. y.

Sarah, bapt. 15 Mar. 1712/3, d. at Stamford, 11 Dec. 1792 in 82 yr. (g. s.); m. (rec. Stamford) 11 Nov. 1736, Jonathan Dibble.

Ebenezer, bapt. 21 Mar. 1713/4, d. at Stamford in 1741, unm. Inv. 28 Apr. 1741; mariner.

Johnson, Peter.

Called a Dutchman, was at Boston before 1638, when Richard Rawlings was permitted to buy the house that had been his.

Of Fairfield, d. before 1650, when his widow Elizabeth was in prison, where a child was born to her. This child was apprenticed to Nathaniel Ruscoe, son of the jail-keeper in Hartford, who was to have £5 from Newton's property; and Ruscoe's will gave a legacy to Benoni Newton, his former apprentice. It appears that the child was son of widow Elizabeth Johnson by Thomas Newton, who was seized, charged with a capital crime, but broke jail and escaped, never returning to Fairfield.

The estate of Peter Johnson was ordered distributed to "the Mother and Children", 1 Mar. 1654/5.

The widow Elizabeth m. John Fossecar. The Inv. of John Johnson was taken 12 Aug. 1659. His mother swore to it, and distribution was ordered to his two brothers when they reached the age of 21; John Fossecar gave bond for the small legacies due to Moses and Ebenezer Johnson, and land of their brother John dec'd was mentioned.

Children:

John, d. unm. in 1659.

+Moses, b. abt. 1641.

+Ebenezer, b. abt. 1645.

Johnson, Moses, s. of Peter. Sergt., Woodbury Trainband.

Born about 1641; Sergt. Moses d. at Woodbury, 30 Oct. 1713 in 72 yr. Cothren's statement that he was son of Moses of Stratford does not merit consideration, for there was no earlier Moses. He himself was of Stratford before settling in Woodbury, and prob. lived with Moses Wheeler the ferryman. In 1659, when he was 17 or 18, he witnessed a deed obtained by Wheeler from the Indians to land which was later in the bounds of Woodbury, the other witness being Wheeler's son Samuel, a youth of 14. Perhaps because of the early age of the witnesses, a confirmatory affidavit was later obtained from the Indian who acted as interpreter and placed on record at Woodbury. Some have erroneously assumed, from the above circumstances, that there was an earlier Moses, of whom this Moses was son.

He drew land at Voluntown for service in K. Philip's War.

He m. Mary Rose, dau. of Robert, b. 20 Apr. 1655.

Will of Moses, Sr., of Woodbury, "under the infirmity of age", 10 Mar. 1713, proved 26 Nov. 1713; wife Mary; sons Moses and Solomon; daus. Zerujah Bostwick, Mary Stiles, Elizabeth Wells [error in recording for Weller] ; land granted by town to son John dec'd, to be divided equally among all my children. Witnesses: John Sherman, Sr., John Skeels, Sr.

Est. of John Johnson of Woodbury; Inv. presented 1 Jan. 1713/4 by Francis Stiles, Adm'r; no wife or children surviving; distribution to two brothers and three sisters (named as in will of Moses, except that Elizabeth was correctly called Weller).

Children, bapt. at Woodbury:

Zeruiah, bapt. Apr. 1682; m. (rec. New Milford) 2 May 1711, Benjamin Bostwick.

Rebecca, bapt. July 1684, d. 21 Jan. 1709/10, unm.

John, bapt. Apr. 1686, d. at Stratfield, 9 Nov. 1709 on return from Wood Creek Expedition (rec. at Woodbury).

Sarah, bapt. Aug. 1688, d. 22 Jan. 1709/10, unm.

Mary, bapt. Apr. 1690; m. at Woodbury, 21 Sept. 1709, Francis Stiles.

Elizabeth, bapt. Oct. 1691, d. 18 Sept. 1770 ae. 79 (g. s., Roxbury) ; m. abt. 1712, Thomas Weller.

Moses, bapt. May 1693, d. 23 Apr. 1760 ae. 67 (g. s., Southbury) ; m. (rec. Woodbury) 6 Oct. 1715, Prudence Jenner.

Solomon, bapt. Jan. 1694/5, d. 30 July 1778 ae. 84 (g. s., Southbury) ; m. (1) Mary Hickock, dau. of Benjamin, b. 15 Sept. 1703, d. 13 June 1735 "as was thought when his house was burnt"; m. (2) 30 June 1736, Hannah Noble, dau. of John, b. (rec. New Milford), 2 Nov. 1697.

Johnson, Ebenezer, s. of Peter. Lt., Derby Trainband, May 1685; granted £4, May 1686, for services in late Indian War;

Capt. of volunteers, New Haven and Fairfield Counties, Sept. 1689; Capt. for Albany Expedition, Apr. 1690; Capt., Troops to march to New York, June 1697; Sergt.-Major, New Haven County, May 1704, and retired May 1709 because of age and long service; Lt.-Col., Expedition against Port Royal, Aug. 1710; granted 200 acres, Oct. 1698; granted £6, Feb. 1706/7, for travel of himself and son to Albany on public service. Deputy (Derby) Oct. 1685, May, July and Oct. 1686, Jan., Mar., May, June and Oct. 1687, May 1689, Apr. and Oct. 1690, May and Oct. 1691, May 1693, May and Oct. 1695, May and Oct. 1698, Oct. 1699, May and Oct. 1700, May and Oct. 1701, May and Oct. 1702, May and Oct. 1703, May and Oct. 1704, May 1705, Oct. 1706, Apr., May, Oct. and Dec. 1707, May and June 1711, May and Oct. 1715, May 1716, May and Oct. 1717, May and Oct. 1718, May and Oct. 1719, May and Oct. 1721, May and Oct. 1722, May 1723; Committee on R. I. Boundary, Oct. 1702; guardian of Paugasset Indians, Mar. 1704. Commissioner for Derby, 1690, 1692-97; Justice, 1698-1705, 1707, 1710, 1711, 1714-24.

Born about 1645, d. at Derby, 18 Sept. 1726 ae. 81 (g. s., Derby); m. (1) (rec. Stratford) 16 Nov. 1671, Elizabeth Wooster. She was dau. of Edward. He m. (2) (rec. Derby, bride's name omitted) 23 Nov. 1676, Hannah Holbrook, dau. of Richard of Milford.

He drew land at Voluntown for service in K. Philip's War.

Child [by first wife], recorded at Stratford:

Elizabeth, b. 20 Dec. 1672, d. in 1757; m. 1692, Jeremiah Johnson.

Children [by second wife], recorded at Derby, except youngest at Wallingford:

Eunice, b. 22 Aug. 1678; m. abt. 1700, Adino Strong of Southbury.
Hannah, b. 6 Dec. 1680; m. (rec. Stratford) 3 Nov. 1715, John Curtis.
Peter, b. 9 Oct. 1684, d. at Derby in 1765; m. (1) abt. 1708, Martha ———, who d. 7 May 1720; m. (2) abt. 1722, Mary Baldwin, dau. of Obadiah.
Ebenezer, b. 22 Feb. 1686 [1686/7], d. 10 Sept. 1751 ae. 65 (g. s., Derby); Lt.; m. 19 Feb. 1718/9, Elizabeth Hine, dau. of John, bapt. at Milford, 1 Mar. 1691, d. 18 Jan. 1760 ae. 67 (g. s.).
Israel, b. 13 Apr. 1689, bapt. at Milford, 27 Apr. 1690, d. 31 Jan. 1712/3; Lt.; unm.

Alexander, bapt. at Milford, 10 Apr. 1692, d. 29 Apr. 1727 in 36 yr. (g. s., Derby).

Timothy, b. 23 Dec. 1693, bapt. 10 June 1694, d. after 1773; m. (rec. Derby) 21 Feb. 1724/5, Abigail Brewster, who d. 15 Dec. 1773.

Charles, b. 29 Dec. 1696/7, d. 30 Oct. 1738 in 42 yr. (g. s., Derby); Sergt.; m. 16 Aug. 1726, Sarah Wooster. She was dau. of Abraham, and m. (2) Rev. Jacob Hemingway of East Haven. No issue.

Johnson, George.

He m. (rec. Stratford) 4 Jan. 1694/5, Hannah Dorman. She was dau. of Edmund, b. at New Haven, 1 Mar. 1676/7. He d. at Stratford, 2 Jan. 1714 [1714/5]; she d. in 1724.

Adm'n granted, 2 Feb. 1714/5, to Thomas Leavenworth and Hannah Johnson; three sons and five daus. Hannah was appointed guardian, 4 May 1715, to Robert, Margaret, Joseph and Thankful. Thomas Leavenworth was chosen guardian by John, 2 Feb. 1714/5, and appointed for Hannah and Elizabeth.

His son John's estate was distributed in 1767 to: bro. Joseph; sister Margaret Bunnell; sister Thankful Baldwin; sister Elizabeth Upson; children of dec'd sister Mary Stratton; Sarah Chatfield, only surviving child of sister Hannah Wooster; Joseph, Jr., and Ephraim, legal representatives of bro. Robert, whose share they had purchased.

Children, recorded at Stratford (wife called Hannah in 1706 and 1709):

Mary, b. 10 Oct. 1695; m. 5 Sept. 1717, Thomas Stratton.

John, b. 15 Apr. 1697, d. at Stratford in 1766, unm. Adm'n granted, 16 Sept. 1766, to Joseph Johnson.

Hannah, b. 5 Apr. 1699; m. (rec. Derby) 22 May 1725, Samuel Wooster.

Elizabeth, b. 28 Aug. 1701, d. in 1797; m. (1) (rec. Waterbury) 25 Dec. 1721, James Prichard, of Milford and Waterbury; m. (2) at Waterbury, 28 Nov. 1750, Stephen Upson.

Robert, b. 29 Jan. 1703/4; m. at Stratford, 21 Mar. 1727/8, Sarah Chapman.

Margaret, b. 22 Sept. 1706; m. at Stratford, 1 Jan. 1728/9, Gershom Bunnell.

Joseph, b. 22 Jan. 1708/9, bapt. (at Stratford, rec. Stratfield) 3 Apr. 1709; m. Rachel ———.

Thankful, m. (rec. Milford), 27 Mar. 1733, Noah Baldwin.

Johnson, Nicholas.

Married Mary Coley, dau. of Peter, b. at Fairfield, 23 Apr. 1677.

Johnson, Herman.

Complained of, June 1685, for theft from Joseph Lockwood's barn.

JONES FAMILY (FAIRFIELD)

Jones, (Rev.) John.

Born abt. 1593, co. Northampton; matriculated sizar from Queens College, Cambridge, Michaelmas 1608, as John "Johnes"; B.A., 1612/3; M.A., 1616; ordained deacon at Peterboro, 19 Dec. 1613; prob. Rector of Abbot's Ripton, co. Huntington, 1619-1630, when he was deprived.*

Sailed 1635 on *Defence* with [wife] Sarah ae. 34, and [children] Sarah 15, John 11, Ruth 7, Theophilus 3, Rebecca 2, Elizabeth 6 mos. Mather tells of a dangerous crossing, the ship springing a leak in the first storm.

He settled at Concord, Mass., with Rev. Peter Bulkeley, after being entertained upon arrival by Gov. Winthrop in his Boston house. Ordained pastor at Concord, 6 Apr. 1637; removed with other Concord settlers to Fairfield, 1644.

Married (1) Sarah ———, b. about 1601.

Married (2) after 1654, Susanna ———, b. about 1605, perhaps widow of Richard Hollingsworth† of Salem. Winthrop in 1663 notes Mary "Holsworth", ae. 26 yrs., dau. of the wife of Mr. Jones, Pastor of Fairfield. Susanna's dau. Mercy m. (1) a Nichols and (2) Thomas Disbrow, and was tried for witchcraft in 1692.

---

* For this identification we are indebted to Col. Charles E. Banks and the late J. Gardner Bartlett.

† Holdsworth is nearer to Winthrop's spelling of the name than is Hollingsworth, but we have been able to find scarce any records of the former name. Joseph and Joshua Holdsworth were living in Boston around 1670; the former died and left property by nuncupative will to bro. Joshua. While Susanna may have been the widowed mother of these Holdsworths, nothing has been found to prove it. The suggested Hollingsworth theory fits the known facts well. Winthrop is usually exact, but that is not to say that he was infallible, in the writing of names.

Will 17 Jan. 1664 [1664/5]; wife Susanna, Exec'x, £50 he promised her; he owed the heirs of Capt. Cullick £7; children John Jones, Eliphalet Jones, Sarah Wilson, Widow, Ruth James, Rebecca Hull, Elizabeth Hill; Mr. Gold and Mr. Pell, overseers. Inv. 9 Feb. 1664 [1664/5].

Children [by first wife]:

Sarah, b. abt. 1620, d. in 1683; m. (1) abt. 1638, Thomas Bulkley; m. (2) abt. 1659, Anthony Wilson.

John, b. abt. 1624; grad. Harvard Coll. 1643; freeman, 1645; preacher, Nevis, Bermuda; d. early; m. Mary ———, and had a son John. She m. (2) John Osborn, of Easthampton, L. I. On 24 Feb. 1679 [1679/80], Mary Osborn, as attorney for her husband John Osborn and son John Jones, sold to John Bulkley all right of her husband and son in Mr. Jones's orchard.

Ruth, b. abt. 1628; m. abt. 1646, Rev. Thomas James; rem. to Easthampton, L. I.

Theophilus, b. abt 1631, d. y.

Rebecca, b. abt. 1633; m. (1) Cornelius Hull; prob. m. (2) after 1695, Joseph Theale.

Elizabeth, b. abt. 1635; m. William Hill.

Eliphalet, b. at Concord, 9 Jan. 1640/1; d. at Huntington, L. I., abt. 1732; entered Harvard Coll. 1662, but did not graduate; freeman, Greenwich, 1669; assistant pastor at Stamford, 1672; also preached at Rye; rem. to Huntington, L. I., 1675, was pastor there until after 1719; m. Martha Lawrence, dau. of Thomas, bapt. at Milford, 9 Aug. 1646. No issue.

Jones, Thomas.

A homelot was granted to him in Fairfield, 12 Jan. 1649 [1649/50]. He, of Huntington, conveyed 21 Mar. 1667/8 to son Thomas, all rights in Fairfield.

Will of Thomas of Huntington, 16 Feb. 1669, proved by wife Katharine 2 Mar. 1669; eldest son Thomas, my best cloak; three youngest sons; son John; wife.

Jones, Thomas, s. of Thomas. Deputy (Fairfield), May 1685, Oct. 1704.

Married at Fairfield, 5 Mar. 1670/1, Abigail Rowland, dau. of Henry.

He acknowledged, 2 May 1673, that his father had sold his homelot to John Bulkley. Unable to find a deed for land which his father bought from Nathan Gold "many years since", Gold gave him a new deed, 17 Mar. 1684/5.

Will 16 Feb. 1714/5, proved 20 Feb. 1723/4; "greatly advanced in years"; wife Abiall [*sic*]; dau. Abigail Wells of Stratfield; son John Jones; dau. Martha Jones.

Children:

    ✗John, m. Rebecca Jackson, dau. of John of Stratfield.
      Abigail, m. (rec. Stratfield) 6 Nov. 1711, Sergt. [Samuel] Welles.
      Martha, b. at Fairfield, 25 Oct. 1683.

JONES FAMILY (STAMFORD)

Jones, Cornelius.

Married (2) at Stamford, 6 Oct. 1657, Elizabeth Hyat. She was widow of Thomas.

Will 2 June 1690, proved 10 Mar. 1690/1; sons Joseph, Ebenezer; gr. child Ruth Hyat (under 18); dau. Mary Hyat (had considerable portion); Lt. Jonathan Bell and Abraham Ambler, Exec'rs. Inv. 31 Oct. 1690. Joseph was dead by 1691, leaving a widow, three sons and two daus.

Children [by first wife], recorded at Stamford:

    Ebenezer, b. 20 Aug. 1646.
    [Ma]ry, b. Feb. 1647/8; m. [John?] Hyatt.
    Cornelius, b. Nov. 1649, d. at Fairfield in 1676; Inv. 9 Nov. 1676.
    +————, b. May 1652. } Doubtless one of these was Joseph, the
    ————, b. Jan. 1653/4. } other d. y.

Jones, Joseph, s. of Cornelius.

He m. by 1677, Rebecca Drake, dau. of Samuel of Eastchester; she m. (2) abt. 1691, ———— Rogers, of Eastchester.

Inv. of Est. of Joseph, dec'd in year 1690; widow Rebecca made oath, 10 Mar. 1690/1. Children's ages: Mary 13, Hannah 11, Joseph 9, Samuel 6, Cornelius 3. Abraham Ambler and Daniel Scofield of Stamford appointed Adm'rs, 3 Nov. 1691. A late distribution (1703/4) of the estates of Joseph and Cornelius Jones was made to Joseph, Samuel, and Cornelius Jones, Cornelius

Seeley in right of his wife, and David Miller in right of his wife Hannah.

Children, recorded at Stamford:

> Mary, b. 4 Jan. 1677 [1677/8]; m. Cornelius Seeley, of Bedford.
> Hannah, b. 16 Mar. 1679/80; m. David Miller.
> Joseph, b. 20 Dec. 1682.*
> Samuel, b. 1 Mar. 1684/5; estate distributed 18 Oct. 1707.
> Cornelius, b. 1 Mar. 1687/8; m. Hannah (Sherwood), widow of John Bradley.

Jordan, John.

Perhaps he was bro. of Mr. Thomas Jordan, who was Deputy for Guilford to the New Haven Colony Leg., May 1653, and May 1654; and Commissioner to Mass. Colony, June 1653, and June 1654; who returned to England, leaving here a dau. Elizabeth, who was m. 1 June 1669 to Andrew Leete, by his father, Dep.-Gov. William Leete.

Mr. John was early at Guilford, where his will was presented 1 Sept. 1650, but we fail to find its terms recorded. His widow Anne m. (2) by 1654, Mr. Thomas Clark, who was bur. at Guilford, 10 Oct. 1668. Mrs. Anne Clark d. at Saybrook, 1 Jan. 1671/2, and adm'n on her estate was granted to Abraham Post.

On 2 Dec. 1658, John Jordan, ae. above 12, testified concerning a dispute between his father [Thomas Clark] and John Hill. Anne, wife of Thomas Clark, and his dau.-in-law [stepdau.] Mary Jordan, also testified.

In 1658 Winthrop mentioned Mary Jordan (ae. 17), dau. of Thomas Clark's wife of Guilford, but living at Jeremy Steele's for the present; and in 1659 he mentioned Mary Jordan (ae. 20) and Elizabeth Jordan (ae. 17) at Guilford.

Children:

> Mary, b. abt. 1640; servant of Rev. John Davenport in 1661; m. Abraham Post of Saybrook, and d. 23 Mar. 1684.
> Elizabeth, b. abt. 1642; m. 17 Nov. 1664, Daniel Hubbard.
> John, b. by 1646; in 1677 gave a deed at Guilford with his wife Deborah,† who d. that year. In 1680, John of Middletown sued

---

* Was he perchance the Joseph Jones who m. at Stratford, 10 Sept. 1705, Hannah Lewis, and had a family there?

† See footnote under WALTER JOY for her possible identity.

Jonathan Hoyt of Guilford, and in 1684 John of Saybrook sued Mrs. Joanna Chittenden of Guilford (as Adm'x of her husband's estate), for land that had belonged to his father Mr. John Jordan dec'd.

Hannah, b. [say 1648]; m. (1) at Stratford (but called of Guilford), 28 June 1666, Ezbon Wakeman; m. (2) abt. Sept. 1684, Mr. Joseph Bastard; and left by each husband a surviving dau., whence descended branches of the Hill and Rumsey families of Fairfield.

Joy, Walter.

Walter Joy's wife at Milford was treated by Winthrop, 1657. We are unable to connect him with the Hingham family, and no relationship is known to Peter Joy of Salem. He left little record of himself or family, but for reasons which will presently appear we believe that his wife was Deborah and that she m. (2) Thomas French of Guilford, as his second wife.

The first link in the chain of evidence is the too brief record of the estate of Isaac Joy, whose Inv. presented 9 June 1675 showed a small property at Milford and Guilford; he left a mother who lived at Guilford; three brothers and one sister related by the father and mother; and there were two children related by the mother only.

A study of Guilford families reveals that Thomas French, between 1660 and 1667, acquired a second wife Deborah, by whom he had two children,—Samuel 1667, and Abigail 1669. This answers the requirements of the case perfectly. Furthermore, Thomas French and Deborah his wife, of Guilford, conveyed on 10 Mar. 1678 and also on 21 July 1679, to Joseph Joy of Guilford.

Joseph Joy was of Fairfield when he died, and his will, 28 Apr. 1690, states that he was leaving with the expedition against the French in Canada; gave legacies to his cousins Joseph Bennett, Deborah Joy, and Mary Joy; and gave the residue of his estate to Walter Joy, son of his brother Jacob; brother Jacob and Samuel Hubbell, Sr., Exec'rs. Inv. 24 Sept. 1690. Jacob reported deceased, 15 Feb. 1691 [1691/2]; Walter Joy was also dec'd, his share ordered to his sisters Deborah wife of Andrew Ward and Mary Joy.

Abraham Joy of Fairfield, making a voyage to Boston, left his estate to his brother Joseph, who presented the Inv. 16 Aug. 1687; Isaac Wheeler appointed Adm'r.

Jacob Joy received a grant from the town of Guilford, 23 Feb. 1669/70, and soon after removed to Killingworth.

The three own brothers mentioned in the record of Isaac's estate are therefore placed as Jacob, Joseph, and Abraham. Of these, Jacob and Joseph are known to have resided in youth in Guilford, and Joseph and Abraham resided in Fairfield at death. Lt. James Bennett was father of the Joseph named as cousin [nephew] in Joseph Joy's will, and Bennett's dau. Abigail m. and named a son Joy Bishop. We can therefore place the own sister as wife of James Bennett.

With regard to the half-brother, Samuel French, Talcott's manuscript history of Guilford families states that he d. young, but nothing to substantiate this has been found except that no record of him after his birth appears in Guilford records. The age at death of Sergt. Samuel French of Stratfield agrees with the birth of the Guilford Samuel, and patient search has failed to disclose any other Samuel with whom the Stratfield man can be identified. The eldest dau. of Sergt. Samuel French was named Deborah, as was also the eldest dau. of Jacob Joy; and this is what we should expect if Deborah was their mother.

We therefore conclude that Walter Joy m. Deborah ———, who m. (2) Thomas French.*

Children:

> Jacob, a blacksmith, of Killingworth, d. in 1690; m. 23 May 1671, Elizabeth (Spencer) Wellman, and had four children: Deborah (1673-1752), m. Andrew Ward (1669-1756), ancestress of Henry Ward Beecher; Jacob (1675-d. y.); Walter 1677-d. y.); and Mary (1680-   ), m. Peter Ward (1676-1763). His Inv. taken Fairfield, 29 Jan. 1690 [1690/1]; house in Killingworth mentioned; widow Elizabeth made oath; she to administer with Capt. Matthew Sherwood and James Bennett, Jr.
>
> Daughter, m. Lt. James Bennett.
>
> Isaac, d. in 1675, unm.
>
> Joseph, of Fairfield, d. in war, 1690, unm.
>
> Abraham, of Fairfield, d. in 1687, unm.

---

* Deborah (———) (Joy) French perhaps m. (3) John Jordan and d. in 1677. John Jordan and Deborah his wife of Guilford conveyed to John French [stepson of Mrs. Deborah French], 12 Apr. 1677; Jonathan Pitman witnessed the deed, which states that Deborah died before the ensealing and delivery. [Guilford Deeds.]

Judson, William.

Early at Concord, Mass.; was at Hartford, Conn., in 1639; removed to Stratford by 1644. Later he became interested in the iron works at East Haven village, and settled in New Haven, where he took oath of fidelity 1647, having bought that year the house and orchard of Henry Browning.

Married (1) Grace ———, who d. at New Haven, 29 Sept. 1659. He m. (2) Elizabeth, widow of Benjamin Wilmot, Jr., and previously of ——— Heaton.

In 1660 he gave his Stratford lands to his three sons. Will 20 Nov. 1661, mentions his old age; eldest son Joseph; sons Joseph and Jeremiah to have his interest in the iron works near Stony River; his wife's daus. Hannah, Mercy, and Elizabeth Wilmot; servant Peter Simpson. Inv. 15 Dec. 1662. His widow d. in 1685, leaving a will.

Children [by first wife]:
+Joseph, b. abt. 1619.
+Jeremiah, b. abt. 1621.
+Joshua.

Judson, Joseph, s. of William. Deputy (Stratford) to Conn. Leg., Oct. 1658, May 1659, Oct. 1659, Oct. 1661, May 1662, Oct. 1662, May 1663, Oct. 1663, May 1664, May 1665, May 1666, Oct. 1666, May 1667. Called Ensign, Oct. 1663; Lt., Stratford Trainband, June 1672; Capt., Fairfield County Troop, May 1676 (K. Philip's War) "if Capt. Selleck be disenabled." Committee of defence, July 1665. One of the six Stratford men who were granted permission, Oct. 1667, to purchase "Potatuke", and was one of the four patentees of Pomperaug (Woodbury), May 1672. Lt., Woodbury Trainband, May 1684. Deputy (Woodbury) to Conn. Leg., May and Oct. 1684, May and Oct. 1685, May and Oct. 1686. Commissioner for Woodbury, 1684, 1685, 1686, 1687, 1689.

Born in England about 1619, d. 8 Oct. 1690 ae. 71 (g. s., Stratford).

Married at Windsor, 24 Oct. 1644, Sarah Porter, dau. of John, bapt. at Felsted, co. Essex, Eng., 15 Mar. 1624/5, d. 16 Mar. 1696/7 ae. 70 (g. s.).

Will 27 Feb. 1679 [1679/80]; "now of Woodbery"; wife Sarah; eldest son John, £300; son James, £300; daus. Sarah Howell and Grace "Priden", £10 each; daus. Hannah, Easter, Ruth, and Abigail, £50 apiece; son John, Exec'r; overseers, friends Mr. Zachary Walker, brother Jeremiah Judson, Mr. Joseph Hawley, and Samuel Sherman, Jr. Inv. at Woodbury, 28 Oct. 1690; at Stratford, 6 Jan. 1690 [1690/1].

In 1691 John Judson of Woodbury conveyed to Benjamin Curtis and Hester his wife, her portion by will of Joseph Judson.

Children, born at Stratford:

> Sarah, b. 2 Mar. 1645 [1645/6]; m. 11 Nov. 1664, Edmund Howell of Southampton.
> +John, b. 10 Dec. 1647.
> +James, b. 24 Apr. 1650.
> Grace, b. 19 Feb. 1651 [1651/2]; m. (1) 30 Dec. 1669, Samuel Prudden, of Milford; m. (2) Thomas Clark, of Milford.
> Joseph, b. 10 Mar. 1654, d. 1 Feb. 1677/8.
> Hannah, b. 31 Dec. 1657; m. 12 June 1689, Samuel Wadsworth, of Farmington.
> Esther, b. 20 Aug. 1660, d. 27 Aug. 1713; m. 23 Mar. 1680/1, Benjamin Curtis.
> Joshua, b. 27 Oct. 1664, d. y.
> Ruth, b. 27 Oct. 1664; m. Samuel Welles of Hartford. They conveyed 1720 to their kinsman David Judson, land laid out to their father Lt. Joseph Judson.
> Phebe, b. 29 Oct. 1666.*
> Abigail, b. 15 Sept. 1669; m. July 1692, Josiah Curtis.

Judson, Jeremiah, s. of William. Sergt., Stratford Train Band. Deputy (Stratford), Aug. 1689; Commissioner for Stratford, 1689-94.†

Mr. Jeremiah Judson d. at Stratford, 15 May 1700; ae. 79 (g. s.).

He m. (1) Sarah Foote.

Married (2) at Stratford, 8 Nov. 1675, Katharine Fairchild [née Craig, widow of Thomas]. She d. at Stratford, in May 1706.

---

* Apparently d. y. The *Hist. of Stratford* says, d. 1 Nov. 1676; Cothren does not give death record, and the present writer did not find it in Stratford.

† In 1692 he was erroneously called "Mr. Jeri: Curtice," the other two Commissioners that year both being named Curtis.

Will 21 Feb. 1697/8, proved 10 Dec. 1700; wife Katharine, mentioning marriage covenant; two gr. children Mary and Elizabeth, daus. of son Isaac; gr. child Elizabeth Tomlinson; dau. Sarah Sturges; gr. child Mary Watkins; dau. Mercy Burton; residue to son Jeremiah. Inv. 11 June 1700. Solomon Burton and Jeremiah Judson made agreement with regard to their mother-in-law Mrs. Katharine Judson. Lt. Agur Tomlinson appealed.

On 7 Mar. 1738, Samuel Welles and Mary his wife, Benjamin Burton, Judson Burton, and Nathan Curtis and Eunice his wife, all of Stratford, and Nathan, David, and Jeremiah Sturges of Fairfield, and William Odell and Sarah his wife of Fairfield, and Benoni Sherman and Sarah his wife of Newtown, conveyed land. On 28 Mar. 1751, Solomon Sturges of Fairfield conveyed to Solomon Burton of Stratford, right from gr. father Jeremiah Judson and mother Sarah Sturges. [Stratford Deeds.]

Children [by first wife], recorded at Stratford:

+Isaac, b. 13 Mar. 1653 [1653/4].
Mary, b. 31 Dec. 1655, d. y.
Elizabeth, b. 24 Feb. 1658 [1658/9]; m. 13 Dec. 1681, Agur Tomlinson.
Sarah, b. 7 Apr. 1662; m. (1) David Watkins; m. (2) Joseph Sturges, of Fairfield.
Mercy, b. 15 June 1665; m. 1 Aug. 1687, Solomon Burton.
+Jeremiah, b. 1 Mar. 1670/1.

Judson, Joshua, s. of William.

He m. Ann ——— who m. (2) 10 Dec. 1662, John Hurd, Jr.

The record of his estate, in part obliterated, mentions eldest son Joshua, second son Samuel, the dau., and if the widow be with child. Joseph and Jeremiah Judson, with Mr. Sherman and Mr. Tuttle(?), overseers. The date is gone, but most likely 1661.

Children, recorded at Stratford:

Ann, m. Arthur Perry.
Joshua, b. 3 Dec. 1658.
+Samuel, b. 27 Aug. 1660.

Judson, John, s. of Joseph.

Born at Stratford, 10 Dec. 1647; d. at Woodbury, 12 Jan. 1709/10 in 63 yr. Freed from training, June 1685.

Inv. 14 Jan. 1709/10; estate in Woodbury, Stratford, and Stamford. Adm'n granted to sons John and Joseph. Distribution 18 Apr. 1710; Widow, Mrs. Mary Judson, half of house in Woodbury; Isaac, Daniel, Jonathan, Eliphalet Judson; Martha Preston, Mary Judson; Ephraim Judson (lands in Stratford); Jeremiah Judson (lands in Stratford or Stratfield). [The three eldest sons had received lands by gift.]

Married (1) (Stratford rec.) 12 Mar. 1673/4, Elizabeth Chapman. She was dau. of John. Wife called Elizabeth at birth of child 1678, and in all the baptismal records.

Married (2) Hannah, widow of Samuel Ward and previously of Jonathan Nichols, and dau. of Mr. Anthony Howkins. She was b. at Farmington abt. 1661, and d. at Woodbury, 23 July 1698.

Married (3) 5 July 1699, Mary Orton of Farmington. The marriage covenant mentions her father Tudor and her two sons, John and Samuel Orton (under 16), and Judson's two houses, at Stratford and Woodbury.

Children by first wife, three recorded at Stratford; bapt. at Woodbury:

> John, b. 12 Mar. 1675/6, d. at Woodbury, 6 Apr. 1722; Sergt.; m. 28 Sept. 1698, Sarah Beers of Fairfield.
>
> Joshua, b. 23 Jan. 1677/8, bapt. Jan. 1678/9(?), d. 27 Nov. 1735 in 58 yr. (g. s., Stratford); will 25 Nov. 1735, proved 8 Dec. 1735; m. (1) at Stratford, 24 Apr. 1712, Mary Nichols; m. (2) Deborah, dau. of Ens. George Clark, and widow of Job Prince and Samuel Prince; she m. (4) Thomas Tibbals.
>
> Joseph, b. 24 Oct. 1679, bapt. Aug. 1680, d. at Woodbury, 22 Mar. 1758; Lt.; m. 13 Feb. 1706/7, Mary Walker.
>
> Chapman, bapt. Dec. 1681, d. 8 May 1700.
>
> Jonathan, bapt. Dec. 1682; m. 22 Aug. 1711, Mary Mitchell.
>
> Ephraim, bapt. Dec. 1685, d. y.
>
> Martha, bapt. Dec. 1686; m. June 1705, William Preston.
>
> Eliphalet, bapt. Feb. 1688/9.
>
> Ephraim, bapt. Sept. 1694, d. at Huntington, 14 Nov. 1782 in 88 yr. (g. s.); Deacon; m. (1) at Stratford, 30 May 1717, Rebecca Beardsley, who d. 16 Dec. 1754 in 59 yr. (g. s.); m. (2) Abigail ———, who d. 9 Feb. 1774 in 66 yr. (g. s.).

Children [by third wife], recorded at Stratford:

> Isaac, b. 3 June 1700 (late in the night), d. at Woodbury, 14 May 1789 ae. 90; m. (1) 29 Nov. 1727, Elizabeth Hawley, who d. 12

July 1731 ae. 25; m. (2) 22 Nov. 1731, Rebecca, widow of Gideon Hollister, and dau. of Benjamin Sherman.

Daniel, b. 6 or 7 Feb. 1701/2 (very early in the morning), d. at Woodbury, 29 Dec. 1766; m. Abigail ———.

Mary, b. 11 Apr. 1703, m. (rec. Stratford) 28 Nov. 1727, Josiah Curtis, Jr.

Jeremiah, b. 31 Oct. 1705.

Judson, James, s. of Joseph. Deputy (Stratford) to Conn. Leg., Oct. 1689, Apr. 1690, Oct. 1691, Oct. 1692, Oct. 1694, Oct. 1696, Oct. 1698, May 1699, May 1700, May and Oct. 1701, May and Oct. 1703, Oct. 1705, May and Oct. 1706, Apr. 1707, May and Oct. 1708, May and June 1709, Oct. 1711, Oct. 1712, May and Oct. 1713, May and Oct. 1714, Oct. 1715, May 1718, and Oct. 1719. Lt., Fairfield County Dragoons, Apr. 1690; Lt., Stratford Trainband, May 1697; Lt. of Co. to march to N. Y., June 1697; Capt., Trainband, May 1698. Committee of Safety, Fairfield County, May 1704. Justice, 1701-11, 1714-21.

Born at Stratford, 24 Apr. 1650; Capt. James d. 25 Feb. 1721 ae. 71 (g. s., Stratford).

Married (1) (rec. Stratford), 18 Aug. 1680, Rebecca Welles. She d. 5 Nov. 1717 ae. 62 (g. s.).

He m. (2) (rec. Stratford) 22 Oct. 1718, Mrs. Anne Steele of Wethersfield. She was widow of James Steele, and dau. of Samuel Welles.

Will of Capt. James, 17 June 1713, proved 5 Apr. 1721; wife Rebecca; to son Joseph, his present dwelling house; to son James, his present dwelling house; to son David, my dwelling house; three daus., Hannah, Sarah, and Phebe, £150 apiece; codicil 2 May 1718, mentions death of wife Rebecca, and gives to daus. Hannah Lewis, Sarah Chauncey, and Phebe Lewis. Inv. 7 Mar. 1721. Mrs. Ann Judson, his widow, agreed with heirs what she should receive.

Children [by first wife], recorded at Stratford:

Hannah, b. 30 May 1681, d. 2 July 1756 ae. 75 (g. s.); m. 11 Nov. 1702, James Lewis.

Sarah, b. 16 Feb. 1682 [1682/3]; m. 12 Oct. 1708, Rev. Nathaniel Chauncey, of Durham.

Rebecca, b. 25 Feb. 1684 [1684/5], d. y.

Joseph, b. 10 Jan. 1686 [1686/7], d. at Stratford in 1755; will 15
Sept. 1749, proved 18 Aug. 1755; Capt.; m. (1) 14 Mar. 1708/9,
Hannah Hawley; m. (2) 20 Dec. 1734, Esther Curtis.
James, b. 1 Apr. 1689, d. at Stratford in 1744; Inv. 4 Sept. 1744;
m. 18 Dec. 1712, Martha Lewis.
Phebe, b. 2 Oct. 1691, d. 11 Sept. 1753 ae. 62 (g. s.); m. 29 June
1714, Joseph Lewis.
David, b. 7 Aug. 1693, d. 5 May 1761 ae. 67 yrs. 9 mos. (g. s., Stratford); Capt.; will 8 Mar. 1758, proved 8 May 1761; m. 29 Oct.
1713, Phebe Stiles, dau. of Ephraim, b. 25 Mar. 1696, d. 20 May
1765 ae. 69 yrs. 2 mos. (g. s.); adm'n on her est. granted 10 June
1765.

Judson, Isaac, s. of Jeremiah.

Born at Stratford, 13 Mar. 1653 [1653/4]; d. there in 1687.
Married (Stratford rec.) 5 Dec. 1678, Mary Hicks.
Inv. 15 June 1687; widow Mary granted adm'n. One son,
three daus. Overseers: Sergt. Jeremiah Judson, Mr. Thomas
Hicks, Benjamin Peat, James Judson, Samuel Hawks. On 7
Nov. 1693 it was reported that but two of the children were
surviving.

Children, recorded at Stratford:
Mary, b. 10 Oct. 1679; m. 15 Dec. 1698, John Welles.
Elizabeth, b. 10 Oct. 1681, d. 29 July 1702 in 21 yr. (g. s.); m. 22
Jan. 1700, Thomas Booth.
Phebe, b. 11 Sept. 1683, d. y.
William, b. 4 Jan. 1685 [1685/6], d. y.

Judson, Jeremiah, s. of Jeremiah. Lt., south company, Strat-
ford, Oct. 1709; Capt., May 1720. Deputy for Stratford,
May 1715, May 1719.

Born 1 Mar. 1670/1; d. 9 Feb. 1734 ae. 63 (g. s., Stratford).
He m. at Stratford, 24 Apr. 1695, Mary Welles.
Will of Capt. Jeremiah, 18 Jan. 1733/4, proved 19 Feb. 1733/4;
wife Mary; to dau. Eunice, wife of Nathan Curtis of Stratford,
100 acres in Woodbury; gr. son Jeremiah Judson Curtis, son of
Nathan; if he die under 21, then gr. son Judson Curtis to inherit;
wife and son-in-law Nathan Curtis and gr. son Jeremiah Judson
Curtis (when he comes of age), Exec'rs.
Will of Mary, widow of Jeremiah, 17 July 1751, proved 5 Nov.
1751; dau. Eunice wife of Nathan Curtis, giving her my Little

Negro Girl called Hester, and after her decease my gr. dau. Eunice Curtis shall have her; female children of dau. Eunice, my gr. children Eunice Curtis, Mary wife of Nathaniel Curtis, Jr., Anna wife of Joseph Gorham, Phebe, Charity, and Mary Curtis; my brethren, Thomas and Robert Welles, Exec'rs.

Child, recorded at Stratford:

> Eunice, b. in 1695; m. 23 June 1715, Nathan Curtis.

Judson, Samuel, s. of Joshua.

Born at Stratford, 27 Aug. 1660, d. there Jan. 1725/6.
He m. Mary ———.
Will (date gone), proved 1 Mar. 1725/6; wife Mary; eldest son Joshua; dau. Ann Burroughs; three daus. Prudence, Mary, Martha.

Children, recorded at Stratford:

> Ann, b. 15 Oct. 1695; m. 11 Sept. 1722, Mr. Edward Burroughs.
> Joshua, b. 31 Mar. 1698, d. at Stratford in 1752; will 28 Feb. 1752, proved 7 July 1752; m. (1) 8 Nov. 1721, Abigail Prindle, who d. 18 Feb. 1721 [1721/2]; m. (2) 5 Mar. 1727/8, Mary Welles.
> Prudence, b. 19 Sept. 1700; m. 24 Mar. 1725/6, William Curtis.
> Samuel, b. 21 Sept. 1704; m. (1) 20 Dec. 1728, Ann Clark, b. [31 Aug. 1709], d. 14 Mar. 1729 ae. 19 yrs. 6 mos. 14 days (g. s.); m. (2) 2 May 1734, Abiah Beach, b. 12 Jan. 1712/3.
> Mary.
> Martha.

Judson [UNPLACED]. PHEBE m. 30 Dec. 1725, Thomas Ufford.

No place for Phebe is found, and the record is believed to be in error. Probably Phebe Welles, whose mother was a Judson, was intended.

Keeler, Ralph.

He settled in Hartford by 1640; went with first settlers to Norwalk. He m. (2) about 1663, Sarah, widow of Henry Whelpley, and formerly widow of Edward Treadwell. She m. (4) Thomas Skidmore of Fairfield, and d. late in 1684.

Will 20 Aug. 1672; aged 59; wife Sarah; eldest son Ralph; sons John, Samuel; youngest son Jonah; daus. Rebecca, Elizabeth; friends Daniel Kellogg and John Bouton, Sr., overseers.

Inv. Sept. 1672. Thomas Morehouse m. eldest dau., not mentioned in will; Court ordered share paid to her.

Children [by first wife]:

+John.
+Ralph.
    Daughter, m. Thomas Morehouse, of Fairfield.
+Samuel.
    Jonah, d. in 1674. His brothers John, Ralph, and Samuel, divided Est., 11 Mar. 1673/4.
    Rebecca, bapt. at Hartford, 9 Feb. 1650 [1650/1]; m. (1) (rec. Fairfield) 16 Nov. 1671, Benjamin Turney, of Fairfield; m. (2) (rec. Wallingford) 21 Sept. 1699, Dr. John Hull.
    Elizabeth, m. (1) (rec. Norwalk) 17 July 1673,* James Pickett; m. (2) ——— Hayes.

Keeler, John, s. of Ralph.   Deputy (Norwalk), Oct. 1698.

Son of Ralph, m. (rec. Norwalk) 18 June 1679, Mehitabel Rockwell, dau. of John of Stamford. She m. (2) before 1725, Dea. Zerubbabel Hoyt.

Will 27 Feb. 1718/9, proved 3 May 1720; sons John and David; daus. Elizabeth Hait, Mehitabel Hait, Hannah Gregory, Sarah Hait; daus. Jemima and Ruth Keeler; wife Mehitabel.

Children, recorded at Norwalk:

    Elizabeth, b. 19 Mar. 1678; m. [perhaps Daniel] Hoyt.
    John, b. 26 Dec. 1682; m. 19 Apr. 1710, Rhoda Hoyt.
    Mehitabel, d. at Norwalk, 21 Mar. 1755; m. (1) 14 Oct. 1703, Joseph Blatchley; m. (2) 25 Feb. 1707/8, Caleb Hoyt.
    Hannah, m. ——— Gregory.
    Sarah m. [Joshua?] Hoyt.
    David.
    Jemima.
    Ruth.

Keeler, Ralph, s. of Ralph.

Married Grace Lindall, dau. of Henry, b. 31 Mar. 1656.

He was called son-in-law in will of Nathaniel Richards, 1681; Grace Keeler was called dau. in will of Rosamond Richards, 1683.

Will 23 Mar. 1716, proved 30 June 1721; two sons Ralph and

---

* The record says *Rebecca* instead of Elizabeth; but Pickett's wife is called Elizabeth in later records, while on the other hand Rebecca's marriage to Turney is recorded at Fairfield, and she appears as Rebecca in later records.

Ebenezer; grandson Nathan Olmstead; wife Grace; dau. Rebecca "Hitchcock." Inv. 2 Mar. 1720/1.

Children:

> Ralph.
> Sarah, m. 7 Dec. 1702, Nathan Olmstead.
> Ebenezer.
> Rebecca, m. [Ebenezer?] Hickock.

Keeler, Samuel, s. of Ralph. Deputy (Norwalk), Oct. 1701, Oct. 1703, May 1704, May 1706, May, June and Oct. 1709.

Born abt. 1655, d. at Ridgefield, 19 May 1713 ae. 58; m. (rec. Norwalk) 10 Mar. 1681/2, Sarah St. John, dau. of Mark, b. 18 Jan. 1659/60, d. at Ridgefield, 15 Apr. 1714.

He received a grant of 12 acres in Norwalk, for service in the Great Swamp Fight, K. Philip's War.

Inv. of Samuel of Ridgefield, 17 June 1713; no widow; only five sons surviving, viz. Samuel, Joseph, Jonah, [name omitted], Timothy.

Children:

> Samuel, b. abt. 1683, d. 8 Aug. 1763; Lt., Expedition against Port Royal, Aug. 1710; m. (1) 18 Jan. 1704/5, Rebecca Benedict, dau. of James of Danbury; she d. 20 Mar. 1709, and he m. (2) 11 Dec. 1712, Sarah Betts, dau. of Thomas, who d. 12 Jan. 1777.
> Joseph, b. abt. 1684, d. 29 Nov. 1757 ae. 74; m. Elizabeth Whitney.
> Jonah, d. 24 May 1767; m. (rec. Ridgefield), 5 Nov. 1713, Ruth Smith, dau. of Samuel of Norwalk.
> Benjamin, d. 1719; m. Hannah ———.
> Timothy, m. (1) at Ridgefield, 19 May 1720, Abigail Osborn, dau. of Richard, who d. 24 Nov. 1735; m. (2) 10 Nov. 1736, Sarah Couch, widow of Thomas; she was dau. of Lt. Gideon Allen, b. 1 Apr. 1697, d. 10 Mar. 1787 ae. 90.

Kellogg, Daniel. Deputy (Norwalk), Oct. 1679, May 1680, Oct. 1683.

Son of Martin and Prudence (Bird), bapt. at Great Leighs, co. Essex, Eng., 6 Feb. 1630; d. at Norwalk in 1688.

Winthrop in 1661 mentioned Daniel Kelluck and his wife of Norwalk, and their children John, aged 3, and Sarah, 1½.

Married at Norwalk, in 1655, Bridget Bouton, dau. of John.

Inv. 5 Dec. 1688. Children: Sarah, Mary, Rachel, "married away"; Elizabeth, above 20; Daniel, 18 next May; Samuel, 15; Lydia, 13 next Apr.; Benjamin and Joseph, twins, 11. Widow Bridget made oath, 5 Mar. 1688 [1688/9]. Inv. of Benjamin, 2 Nov. 1702. Adm'n granted to brother Daniel. Agreement by the sons and sons-in-law of Daniel Kellogg for distribution of Est. of their brother Benjamin, signed by Daniel, Samuel, and Joseph Kellogg, Abraham Nichols, John Clark, and Sarah Brinsmade. One of the sisters, Mary Platt, Widow, hath not signed but sent her consent.

Children, recorded at Norwalk:

John, b. abt. 1657, d. y.
Sarah, b. Feb. 1659 [1659/60]; m. (1) by 1683, Daniel Brinsmade, of Stratford; m. (2) John Betts, of Norwalk.
Mary, b. Feb. 1661 [1661/2]; m. (rec. Milford) 5 May 1680, Joseph Platt.
Rachel, b. Feb. 1663 [1663/4]; m. (rec. Stratford) 3 Dec. 1684, Abraham Nichols.
Elizabeth, b. Aug. 1668, d. in 1690, unm.; Inv. 3 Nov. 1690.
+Daniel, b. 7 May 1671.
Samuel, b. latter end of Feb. 1673 [1673/4], d. at Wilton, 13 Oct. 1757; m. (1) 6 Sept. 1704, Sarah Platt, dau. of Dea. John, who d. 10 Nov. 1750 ae. 72; m. (2) 9 Mar. 1755, Sarah (Lockwood), widow first of Nathaniel Selleck and second of Benjamin Hickock.
Lydia, b. [Apr. 1676]; m. (1) John Clark of Milford; m. (2) (rec. Milford) 7 June 1705, Thomas Oviatt.
Benjamin, b. abt. 1678, d. in 1702, unm.
Joseph (twin), b. abt. 1678; m. (1) (rec. Norwalk) 25 Nov. 1702, Sarah Plumb, dau. of John of Milford, who d. 17 Aug. 1712; m. (2) 10 Oct. 1712, widow Mary Lyon. She was widow of Andrew of Norwalk.

Kellogg, Daniel, s. of Daniel.

Born at Norwalk, 7 May 1671, d. there in 1709; m. Elizabeth Preston, dau. of Eliasaph, b. at Wallingford, 29 Jan. 1677.

Inv. 28 July 1709. Children's ages: Daniel 10, John 8, Benjamin 5, Joanna 3, Eliasaph abt. 1 week.

Children:

Daniel, b. 7 May 1698; m. Eunice Jarvis.
John, b. abt. 1701; m. (rec. Norwalk) 1 Jan. 1729/30, Ann Coley, dau. of Samuel of Fairfield.

Benjamin, b. abt. 1704, d. at Cheshire, Dec. 1748; m. abt. 1728, Elizabeth Curtis, dau. of Samuel, b. at Wallingford, 11 Jan. 1707/8; she m. (2) 20 Mar. 1749, Thomas Andrews.

Joanna, b. abt. 1706, d. before Mar. 1720.

Eliasaph, b. abt. 21 July 1709; m. at Norwalk, 13 June 1734, Rachel Benedict, dau. of Ens. Thomas.

Ketchum, Edward.

Of Ipswich 1635, freeman 9 Mar. 1636/7.

Married Sarah ————, who m. (2) Henry Whitney of Huntington, L. I., later of Norwalk.

Of Stratford, will presumably 1655; wife Sarah; son John; daus. Mary, Hannah, Hester; not much of will now decipherable, and other children may have been mentioned. Inv. 9 June 1655.

In 1660 Henry Whitney complained at Huntington, L. I., against Joseph Whitman for stealing his dau.'s affections contrary to her mother's mind. Edward Frencham deposed that "good Cechom coming to us when I was in Milford" gave his consent for Whitman to marry her. Samuel Blackman also testified. The Court desired "Sara Cechum" to appear.

Children [in part hypothetical]:

Sarah, m. abt. 1660, Joseph Whitman, of Huntington, L. I.

Samuel, of Newtown, Brookhaven, and Huntington, L. I.

John, of Brookhaven and Newtown, L. I., d. in 1697.

Rebecca, m. (rec. Norwalk, called dau. of Edward of Stratford) 14 Feb. 1677 [1667/8?], Thomas Taylor.

Mary.

Hannah.

Hester.

Edward, of Huntington, L. I.

+Joseph.

Ketchum, Joseph, s. of Edward.

Married at Norwalk, 3 Apr. 1679, Mercy Lindall, dau. of Henry of New Haven.

Will 4 May 1730, proved 3 July 1730; wife Sarah; eldest son Nathaniel and son Joseph, Exec'rs; sons John, Samuel; daus. Elizabeth wife of Moses Fountain, Deborah wife of Samuel Clugston, and Hannah wife of Daniel Olmsted of Ridgefield.

Children, recorded at Norwalk:

> Nathaniel, b. 23 Jan. 1679 [1679/80], d. at Wilton in 1738; Lt.,
> Wilton Trainband, Oct. 1727; Capt., Oct. 1730; will 9 Sept. 1738,
> proved 21 Dec. 1738; m. (rec. Norwalk) 12 June 1710, Sarah
> Wakelee, dau. of Deliverance.
> Sarah, b. 19 Feb. 1681 [1681/2].
> Hannah, m. (rec. Ridgefield) 9 May 1711, Daniel Olmsted.
> Elizabeth, m. (1) Thomas Gregory; m. (2) 13 Aug. 1719, Moses
> Fountain.
> Joseph, Lt., south company, Norwalk, May 1730; Capt., first com-
> pany, May 1739.
> John.
> Samuel.
> Deborah, m. Samuel Clugston.

Kimberly, Thomas. Corp., New Haven Trainband, Aug.
1642. Marshal, New Haven Colony, 1643-61.

He m. (1) Alice ———, who d. at New Haven, 10 Oct. 1659;
m. (2) Mary, widow of William Preston of New Haven, and
presumably dau. of Robert Seabrook of Stratford.

Will 11 Jan. 1672 [1672/3]; wife Mary; dau. Abiah Boardman and her three children; Hachaliah and Joseph Preston; gr.
children Nathaniel, Elizabeth, and Mary Hayes; sons Nathaniel,
Thomas; son Abraham, his wife Hannah and dau. Mary.

Children [by first wife]:

> Thomas, d. at New Haven, Feb. 1705; m. Hannah Russell, dau. of
> James, who d. 28 Nov. 1714; no issue.
> +Abraham.
> Mary, m. Nathaniel Hayes of Norwalk.
> +Nathaniel.
> Eleazer, bapt. at New Haven, 17 Nov. 1639, d. at Glastonbury, 3 Feb.
> 1709 ae. 70 (g. s.); m. (1) abt. 1662, Mary Robbins, b. at
> Wethersfield, 20 Jan. 1641/2; m. (2) by 1680, Ruth Curtis, dau.
> of Thomas, who d. at Wethersfield, 29 Dec. 1683.
> Abiah, bapt. 19 Dec. 1641, d. at Wethersfield, 6 Jan. 1722/3; m. abt.
> 1665, Isaac Boardman.

Kimberly, Abraham, s. of Thomas.

Married Hannah ———, who m. (2) John Curtis.
John Blackman, Sr., of Stratford, and Benjamin Hurd, of
Woodbury, legatees of our late mother Hannah Curtis dec'd,

by virtue of marriage with our present wives, the daus. of said Hannah, conveyed 21 Oct. 1701 to brother Abraham Kimberly of Stratford all right in dwelling house which belonged to our mother.

Children, recorded at New Haven:

>Hannah, b. 11 Jan. 1655 [1655/6].
>Mary, bapt. 25 July 1659, d. y.

Born Albemarle County, Carolina, recorded Stratford:

>Mary, b. 4 May 1668; m. John Blackman.
>Sarah, b. 1 Aug. 1672, d. 20 Sept. 1749; m. Benjamin Hurd, of Woodbury.
>+Abraham, b. 4 Mar. 1674/5.

Kimberly, Nathaniel, s. of Thomas.

He lived in West Haven and d. in 1705; in 1668 Winthrop mentioned his wife Miriam.

Will 26 Oct. 1705, proved Nov. 1705; called himself a tailor; dau. Elizabeth Mallory; dau. Sarah Blakeslee; gr. child Deborah Kerby; gr. son Abiel Kerby; dau. Mary Chittenden; only s. Nathaniel; wife. Appended note states that Abiel was a mistake for Abiah.

Children:

>Sarah, m. 20 Nov. 1684, Samuel Blakeslee.
>Elizabeth, m. (1) 30 Dec. 1686, John Mallory; m. (2) Benjamin Barnes of Waterbury.
>+Nathaniel.
>Abiah, d. 28 Apr. 1704; m. Joseph Kirby.
>Mary, m. Joseph Chittenden of Guilford.

Kimberly, Abraham, s. of Abraham.

Born in Albemarle County, "Carolina", 4 Mar. 1674/5, d. at Newtown, in 1727.

Married at Stratford, 11 May 1696, Abigail Fitch. She was dau. of Thomas Fitch of Wethersfield, and only surviving child by his *first* [not second] wife, Abigail Goodrich, dau. of Ens. William and Sarah (Marvin) Goodrich. Her grandmother, Sarah (Marvin) Goodrich, m. (2) Capt. William Curtis of Stratford, and may have brought Abigail Fitch, whom she remembered in

her will, to Stratford to live with her.   Thomas Fitch was son of
Samuel [bro. of Thomas of Norwalk and Rev. James of Nor-
wich] by wife Susanna, widow of William Whiting of Hartford.
In 1701 he bought the interest of his sisters in his mother's
homestead, and in 1706 bought right in Stratford land from
Eleazer Kimberly of Glastonbury [his uncle]; and in 1706 sold
the property bought from Eleazer, as well as land laid out to
Thomas Kimberly.   In 1724, being of Newtown, he sold.   [Strat-
ford Deeds.]

Adm'n granted, 26 July 1727, to son Abraham.

Agreed division of Est. of father Abraham Kimberly, 17 May
1742, made by Abraham Kimberly, John Lake and Abigail his
wife, James Heard and Hannah his wife, Joseph Prindle and
Sarah his wife, Thomas Leavenworth and Mary his wife, all of
Newtown, Gideon Kimberly of Wilton, Thomas Kimberly of
Woodbury, Josiah Smith and Prudence his wife of Stratford, and
John Curtiss and Abiah his wife of Woodbury.

Children, first three recorded at Stratford:

> Hannah, b. 19 Jan. 1698; m. James Hard, of Newtown.
> Abigail, b. 25 Apr. 1699; m. at Newtown, 4 Jan. 1715/6, John Lake.
> Abraham, b. 29 Apr. 1702; m. last of Oct. 1725, Abigail Adams.
> Sarah, bapt. at Stratford (rec. Stratfield), 23 July 1704; m. Joseph
> Prindle.
> Gideon, res. Newtown and Wilton; m. 9 Oct. 1735, Mary Osborn.
> Jedediah, bapt. at Stratfield, 4 July 1708, d. y.
> Mary, m. 10 Jan. 1731/2, Thomas Leavenworth.
> Abiah, m. John Curtis, of Woodbury.
> Prudence, m. at Stratfield, 8 Oct. 1735, Josiah Smith of Stratford.
> Thomas, m. at Woodbury, 28 Jan. 1742, Lois Tuttle.

Kimberly, Nathaniel, s. of Nathaniel.

He lived in West Haven, and d. in 1720; m. 22 Sept. 1692,
Hannah Downs, dau. of John, b. 19 Jan. 1670 [1670/1].   He
was called Lt.; record of appointment not found.

Adm'n was granted, 5 Dec. 1720, to his widow Hannah; all
seven children were named.

On 29 Aug. 1721, John Lyon and Hannah his wife of "Colony
of Conn." conveyed land which our father Nathaniel Kimberly of
New Haven bought of John Mallory.   On 3 June 1747, Zuriel
Kimberly of New Haven, Abraham Kimberly, Joseph Parmelee

and Abigail his wife, all of Guilford, Thomas Pike and Hannah his wife, and Benjamin Treadwell and Mary his wife, all of Fairfield, conveyed to bro. Nathaniel Kimberly of New Haven right from father Nathaniel Kimberly dec'd.

Children, recorded at New Haven:

> Hannah, b. 13 Apr. 1694; m. (1) John Lyon and (2) Thomas Pike, both of Fairfield.
> Abigail, b. 28 July 1696, d. at Guilford, 28 Nov. 1763; m. (rec. Guilford) 19 Sept. 1716, Joseph Parmelee.
> Mary, b. 24 July 1698; m. Benjamin Treadwell, of Fairfield.
> Nathaniel, b. 11 Mar. 1700, d. at West Haven, 15 Aug. 1780 ae. 80 (g. s.); m. 22 Apr. 1724, Hannah Candee, b. in 1703, d. 13 Jan. 1781 ae. 77 (g. s.).
> Bathshua, b. 28 Feb. 1703; m. Samuel Wilson.
> Zuriel, b. 25 Nov. 1706; m. (1) 26 Nov. 1730, Hannah Hill, b. Dec. 1702, d. 8 June 1766 ae. 64; m. (2) 17 Dec. 1766, Martha Hitchcock, widow of John.
> Abraham, b. 22 Mar. 1709, d. at Guilford, 19 Feb. 1797; m. (1) (rec. Guilford) 7 Mar. 1732, Mary Sherman; m. (2) ———.

Kirby, Joseph, s. of John.

Born at Middletown, 17 July 1656, d. there 2 Dec. 1711 in 56 yr. On 7 May 1697, John Bennett of Cohansey, N. J., sold to Joseph "Curby" of Middletown, land in Fairfield. He lived there a couple of years, then removed to West Haven, and finally returned to Middletown.

His sister Bethia, b. 14 Feb. 1658/9, m. John Andrews of Fairfield.

He m. (1) at Wethersfield, 10 Nov. 1681, Sarah Markham; m. (2) Abiah Kimberly, dau. of Nathaniel, who d. at New Haven, 28 Apr. 1704; m. (3) (rec. New Haven), 17 Oct. 1704, Mary Plumb, dau. of John, b. at Milford, 15 May 1673.

The will of Nathaniel Kimberly, 26 Oct. 1705, named grandchildren Deborah and Abiah Kirby. The latter name was written Abiel in the will, but an appended note explains that it was an error of dictator or scribe for Abiah.

Children [by first wife], first five recorded at Middletown as children of Joseph and Sarah:

> Elizabeth, b. 20 Feb. 1682/3; m. at New Haven, 31 Oct. 1704, James Brown.

Sarah, b. 10 Aug. 1685; m. at Milford, 9 Apr. 1712, Samuel Baldwin.

Deborah, b. 27 Mar. 1688, d. y.

John, b. 16 Feb. 1691, d. at Middletown, 25 Feb. 1760; m. 3 Mar. 1718, Hannah Stow.

Mary, b. 10 June 1693, d. at New Milford, 17 Feb. 1771; m. (rec. New Milford), 10 Dec. 1717, Benoni Stebbins; she called of Milford at marriage.

Joseph, bapt. at Middletown, 9 June 1695, d. y.

Bethia, bapt. at Fairfield, 10 July 1698; m. Nathaniel Sanford.

Children [by second wife] :

Deborah, bapt. at New Haven, 29 Sept. 1700; m. John Pierson.

Abiah, b. [say 1702], named in grandfather's will.

Roger, b. at New Haven, 14 Apr. 1705, an impossible date, prob. an error for 1704, as the entry occurs in a group of 1704 births; d. 12 June 1793 ae. 95, an impossible age (g. s., Milton); m. Martha ———.

Children [by third wife] :

Joseph, b. at New Haven, 14 May 1705, d. Dec. 1725.

Susanna, bapt. at Middletown, 29 Dec. 1706, d. at Milford in 1733, unm. Will 27 Mar. 1733, proved 7 May 1733; friend Daniel Smith; sister Margaret Kirby, all right in Est. of gr. father John Plumb; sisters Sarah wife of Samuel Baldwin, Jr., Mary wife of Benoni Stebbins, and Bethia wife of Nathaniel Sanford; residue to all her brothers and sisters.

Margaret, b. at Middletown, 2 Sept. 1709, d. in 1780; m. Nathaniel Wooster of Oxford.

Knapp, Roger.

Very early settled at New Haven, as he relinquished his right, signing by his mark, to any of the land purchased by the New Haven colonists from the Indians 11 Dec. 1638. Took oath of fidelity, New Haven, July 1644; had been in Delaware Bay before 1644, and was a poor man. His wife and children were mentioned 1647. He removed to Fairfield, and was one of four "poor men" to whom the will of Dr. Pell, 1669, gave their debts to him.

Married (1) ———, executed for witchcraft 1653.

Married (2) Elizabeth Dickerson, dau. of Thomas. The will of [her stepfather] Daniel Finch, 1667, gave a legacy to the wife of Roger Knapp. The will of her dau. Mary named her "aunt Casle", the wife of Henry Castle being also a legatee in the will of Daniel Finch [stepfather of Elizabeth Dickerson and of Abigail wife of Henry Castle].

The pitiful story of the trial and execution of "Goody Knapp" of Fairfield, as disclosed by testimony in the famous Staples slander suit, may be found in New Haven Colony Records. As Roger was the only Knapp appearing in Fairfield records at that period, we hesitate not to make him husband of "Knapp's wife" as she was also called.

Will 21 Mar. 1672/3, proved 20 Sept. 1675; wife Elizabeth; sons Jonathan, Josiah; dau. Lydia; sons Roger, John, Nathaniel; daus. Elizabeth, Mary.

Will of Elizabeth Wake, 7 July 1691, exhibited 9 Nov. 1691, not approved; son Nathaniel Knap; will of son Roger, lately dec'd; two daus. Mary and Sarah Knap; dau. Phebe; son-in-law Charles Lane and my dau. Elizabeth; brother Thomas Dickerson, and Jonathan Morehouse, Exec'rs. Inv. of widow Wake of Fairfield, and her son Roger, 23 Sept. 1691. Court ordered distribution, ⅓ to three grandchildren (children of Charles Lane her son-in-law), ⅓ to dau. Mary and ⅓ to dau. Phebe.

Children [by first wife]:

> Jonathan, d. abt. 1676, unm. Inv. 1 Feb. 1675 [1675/6]. Lydia Mills released Josiah Knapp, Adm'r of brother Jonathan's Est., of legacy due her, 1678.
> +Josiah.
> Lydia, m. ———— Mills.

Children [by second wife]:

> Roger, d. in 1691. Will 31 Mar. 1691, proved 23 Sept. 1691; mother; brother Nathaniel; sister's children. Court ordered distribution to Susanna, Charles and Alexander Lane, children of Charles who m. Elizabeth Knapp, sister to Roger; and remainder to his sister Mary Knapp.
> John, d. between 1675 and 1691. Inv. (he some years dec'd) taken 13 Dec. 1705. Distribution ordered between Nathaniel Knapp, Mary Knapp, and Charles Lane in right of his wife. He prob. m. Sarah Hull, who m. (2) Robert Silliman.
> Nathaniel, d. in 1713. Inv. 1 May 1713 showed Est. at Stratfield and Norwalk; included a tinker's anvil; m. at Stratfield, 28 May 1712, ———— ————. No issue. He sold for two pair of men's shoes and 1½ bushels of wheat, to Robert Silliman, 21 Feb. 1706/7, his right in the long lot of his father Roger Knapp, dec'd.
> Elizabeth, m. Charles Lane. He sold, 17 Feb. 1707/8, to Robert Silliman, my right in my bro.-in-law John Knapp's part of his

father Roger Knapp's long lot, set to me in right of dec'd wife
Elizabeth; also my share in commonage of my mother-in-law,
widow of Roger.

Mary, d. 23 Nov. 1711, unm. Will 19 Nov. 1711, proved 3 Jan.
1711/2; sister Phebe wife of Samuel Henrik; "I acknowledge
Nath[ll] son of said Sam[ll] and Phebe to be my the said Mary's
child"; brother Nathaniel Knap; "my boy Nath[ll]"; Susannah
Thomas; Alexander Lane; my aunt Casle. We take the passages
relating to her sister Phebe's son to mean that she adopted him as
her son and chief heir; for Nathaniel was bapt. at Stratfield as
child of Samuel Henries, and his birth-record entered later at
Newtown calls him son of the same. In 1713, Benjamin Fairweather was appointed Adm'r (succeeding her dec'd brother
Nathaniel), and reported all legacies paid except what is due to
Samuel Henrick's son.

Sarah, b. perhaps after father's will was made 1673, but called dau.
Sarah Knap in her mother's will 1691.

Child of Widow Elizabeth Knapp (presumably by her later
Wake husband) :

Phebe, m. abt. 1704, Samuel Henricks or Henry, of Stratfield and
Newtown.

Knapp, Josiah, s. of Roger.

He m. Sybil Dickerson, dau. of Thomas; she m. (2) James
Nicholson.

He entered caveat 3 Feb. 1686 against lands of Joseph James
for portion due his wife. [James was husband of Sybil's sister
and perhaps had been her guardian.]

Inv. 13 Mar. 1689/90; two sons and widow.

Moses Knapp conveyed to Daniel Knapp, 9 Apr. 1712, a right
from gr. father Roger Knapp. Moses and Daniel Knapp as
heirs to Josiah dec'd conveyed, 10 Mar. 1708/9, to Robert Silliman, right in the long lot that was formerly Roger Knapp's.

Children, first two recorded at Fairfield, fourth bapt. there as
son of Sybilla Niccolson:

Mary, b. 7 Nov. 1677, d. y.

Jonathan, b. 21 Apr. 1680, d. y.

✗Moses, d. in 1755; adm'n granted to Ganda Knapp, 17 Nov. 1755;
m. Ganda Adams, dau. of Nathan.

✗Daniel, bapt. 21 June 1696, d. abt. 1771; will 14 Mar. 1768, proved
28 Jan. 1771; m. at Fairfield, 5 Mar. 1710 [1710/1], Abigail
Banks.

Knapp, Christopher.

Died at Fairfield, 17 Jan. 1709/10. His nuncupative will, 5 Jan. 1709, proved 21 Feb. 1709 [1709/10], gave his estate to the poor.

Knell, Nicholas.

Colonial grant of 50 acres, May 1668, and 50 acres more, May 1669. Quite likely he was a veteran of the Pequot War (1637).

He was an early settler in Fairfield, but sold his property there to George Stukey, who in turn conveyed it to Giles Smith, who entered it for record 17 Dec. 1651. Just when he left Fairfield cannot be determined, but he settled permanently in Stratford before 1650.

Married Elizabeth, widow of Thomas Knowles of New Haven. Will 24 Mar. 1670/1, proved 14 Mar. 1675/6; wife Elizabeth; two sons, Isaac and John; overseers, Richard Booth, Mr. Isaac Nichols, and Mr. Joseph Hawley.

Described as "y^t aged benefacto^r in ye Countrey", he d. 2 Apr. 1675.

Children, recorded at Stratford:

> John, b. 24 Oct. 1651, bur. 16 Jan. 1651 [1651/2].
> Elizabeth, b. 3 May 1653, d. at Woodbury, 19 Jan. 1729/30; m. abt. 1678, John Mitchell, of Woodbury.
> Isaac, b. Feb. 1655, d. 2 Nov. 1708 in 57 yr. (g. s., Stratford); m. at Woodbury, 28 Dec. 1697, Phebe Nichols, bapt. 12 Nov. 1671; she m. (2) Ens. George Clark, of Milford.
> John, b. 17 Nov. 1657.

Kniffen, George.

Of Stratford, bought house in Rye 1666 from John Budd, Sr.; d. in 1694.

He m. a sister of Nathan Whelpley, whose will 1686 called Samuel Kniffen his sister's son; and she may have been mother of all the children.

He conveyed land in Rye, 1684, to son-in-law John Stoakham. His will was proved 7 Dec. 1694.

Children:

> Joseph.
> Ebenezer, of Rye, will 17 Oct. 1722, proved 16 Aug. 1723; wife

Anna; son Ebenezer; daus. Anna and Sarah; wife and bros. George and Joseph Kniffen, Exec'rs.

Jonathan.

George.

Nathan, living at Rye 1732, when he and his sons Nathan, Andrew, Caleb, and Amos, received legacies under will of William Proboy.

Samuel, of Rye; adm'n granted to widow Mary, 26 Feb. 1707/8.

Knight, William.

Inv. of William of Fairfield, ship carpenter, not dated; prob. 1684.

KNOWLES FAMILY (FAIRFIELD)

Knowles, Alexander. Magistrate for Fairfield, May 1654, May 1661; Assistant, Conn. Col., 1658; war committee for Fairfield, Oct. 1654.

Freeman, Mass., 7 Dec. 1636.

Will (date gone); sons Joshua, John; gr. children John, Thomas, Elizabeth, Mary, and Lydia Ford; gr. child John Knowles; "our dau. at Milford"—also called dau. Elizabeth; wife. Mr. Gold and John Burr, overseers. Witnessed by Philip Pinkney. Inv. 8 Dec. 1663.

Children:

Elizabeth, m. (1) Thomas Ford, (2) Eleazer Rogers, both of Milford. By her first husband she had: Elizabeth; John (1654); Thomas (1656); Mary (1658), m. John Rogers; Lydia (1660), m. John Newton; and by her second husband: Hannah (1663), m. Joseph Camp; Sarah (1665), m. Abraham Nichols; Samuel (1668); and Joseph (1671).

Joshua, d. at Fairfield, 26 Jan. 1711 [1711/2], without issue. He had land recorded 23 Mar. 1690 by gift from his father-in-law Sergt. John Wheeler. He m. Judanne Wheeler, b. abt. 1661. Adm'n granted, 5 Mar. 1711/2 to Capt. Joseph Bishop of Stamford, Mr. Dugall MacKenzie of Fairfield, and Mr. Joseph Rogers of Milford. Agreement 28 May 1713 of heirs of Est. of uncle Mr. Joshua Knowles, joined by: Dugall Makenzy and wife Sarah, Joseph Bishop of Stamford and wife Elizabeth, and John Cressy of Stamford and wife Rebecca,—they being daus. of John Knowles; Joseph Rogers of Milford, son of Elizabeth formerly

Knowles; John Rogers of Milford and wife Mary, Lydia Newton of Milford, Joseph Camp of Milford and wife Hannah, and Abraham Nichols of Stratford and wife Sarah,—all daus. of said Elizabeth.
+John.

Knowles, John, s. of Alexander.

Married Rebecca Cable, dau. of John, whose will 1682 named his grandchild John Knowles.

Will 1 Nov. 1673; eldest son John, all housing and lands; son Joshua; brother Joshua Knowles has taken my son Joshua as his own child; three daus. Sarah, Elizabeth, Rebecca; sister Elizabeth Rogers; to John Loom (who hath been very helpful to me in my sickness); bro. Joshua and friends Mr. Jehu Burr and Mr. John Burr, overseers. Witnessed by John Lume. Inv. 8 Dec. 1673.

Jehu and John Burr gave an account of their adm'n, 10 Mar. 1684/5; mention made of legacy left by John Cable, Sr., to his gr. child John Knowles (son of John) who has died, and the legacy is to be divided between the three daus. Sarah Knowles, same date, chose Mr. John Burr for guardian.

Receipt 26 Nov. 1687 of Sarah and Elizabeth, daus. of John Knowles, to uncle Joshua Knowles and the overseers. Receipt 24 June 1690 of Jonathan Morehouse and Rebecca Knowles [apparently on eve of marriage]. Heirs of John Knowles, 23 Jan. 1693 [1693/4], his son being deceased, are his three daus., Sarah (Exec'x to her dec'd husband Samuel Wakeman, Jr.), Elizabeth (wife of Joseph Bishop of Stamford), and Rebecca (wife of Jonathan Morehouse).

Children:

John, d. after 1682, unm.
Joshua, d. y. after 1673.
Sarah, m. (1) abt. 1689, Samuel Wakeman; m. (2) 18 Nov. 1696, Dugall MacKenzie.
Elizabeth, b. abt. 1669, d. at Stamford, 29 Apr. 1754 ae. 85; m. (rec. Stamford) 3 Nov. 1691, Joseph Bishop.
Rebecca, b. [say 1671]; m. (1) 16 Apr. 1690, Jonathan Morehouse; m. (2) John Cressy, of Stamford.

KNOWLES FAMILY (STRATFORD)

Knowles, Thomas.

Took the oath of fidelity, New Haven, July 1644. He and "Goody" Knowles had seats in the meeting-house, Mar. 1646/7. He died between Feb. and May 1648, his widow being referred to the latter month as in need.

Married Elizabeth, *not* dau. of Gov. Francis Newman. She was still a widow, Nov. 1649, but married (2) by 1650 Mr. Nicholas Knell, of Stratford.

Eleazer and Thomas Knowles had land in Stratford by gift from father Nicholas Knell.

Children:

+Eleazer.

>Thomas, b. abt. 1648, d. at Stratford, 17 Nov. 1705; in 57 yr. (g. s.); Ens., Stratford Trainband, May 1697; Lt., May 1698; Deputy for Stratford, Oct. and Nov. 1691, May 1702, and May 1703; m. Mary ———. No issue. His will proved 14 Dec. 1705: cousin Isaac, son of brother Eleazer Knowles of Woodbury; wife Mary; the eldest son of Benjamin Nichols.

Knowles, Eleazer, s. of Thomas.

Settled in Woodbury, where he d. 31 Jan. 1730/1.

He m. Mary ———, who d. ("Aged Widow") 24 Oct. 1732.

Will 1 May 1724, proved 8 Mar. 1731; sons Thomas, Isaac, Samuel; daus. Mary wife of Samuel Sherman, and Elizabeth; to Adam and Elizabeth, children of Noah Hinman.

Children, recorded at Woodbury:*

>Thomas, b. 26 Dec. 1683, bapt. Dec. 1683.
>Mary, b. 22 Mar. 1687/8, bapt. Mar. 1686/7; m. 22 Dec. 1709, Samuel Sherman.
>Anna, b. 15 Jan. 1689 at night, bapt. Jan. 1688/9; m. 28 Feb. 1710/1, Noah Hinman.
>Samuel, b. 30 Apr. 1691, bapt. May 1691, d. at Southbury, 8 Mar. 1772 ae. 81; Lt.; m. (1) Huldah ———, who d. 1 Feb. 1726/7; m. (2) Elizabeth ———; m. (3) at Southbury, 28 Oct. 1744, Mary, widow of Moses Wooster, and dau. of Joseph Hawkins, 2d, b. at Derby, 1 Apr. 1700.
>Isaac, b. 29 July 1696, bapt. July 1696.
>Elizabeth, b. 30 Mar. 1698, bapt. Mar. 1698.

---

* Some of the baptismal dates, from Cothren, may be erroneous.

Laborie, (Dr.) James. Chirurgeon, Port Royal Expedition, Aug. 1710, and Chaplain on the transport brigantine *Mary;* Lt., Fairfield County Troop, May 1714.

Completed study of theology in Academy of Geneva, 1688, and was ordained at Zürich; went to England and officiated in French churches of London; came to America in 1698, and after ministering to French colony in New Oxford, Mass., had charge of French church in New York, 1704 to 1706. He then engaged in the practice of medicine, and rem. to Stratford.

Married (1) Jeanne Resseguie, (2) Mary Burr, dau. of Nathaniel.*

On 12 Apr. 1711, expecting to be called to serve in the war, he appointed his brother Anthony Laborie of Guilford, "Gentleman and Chyrurgeon", trustee for his wife Mary, with whom he had received a considerable estate in marriage. [Stratford Deeds.]

Will of James of Fairfield, "Phisition", 17 Mar. 1730/1, proved 4 May 1731; to son James, all my Instruments of chirurgery and all my French writings; son John, "if he Comes again"; daus. Ann, Jeanne, Mary; grandson John Laborie; wife Mary, sole Exec'x.

Children [by first wife]:

> James, b. abt. 1692, d. 26 Dec. 1739 in 48 yr (g. s., Epis. Yard, Stratford); Dr.; m. at Stratford, 29 Aug. 1716, Abigail Blackleach.
> John.
> Ann, m. (1) at Stratford, 18 Jan. 1721/2, Samuel Whitney; m. (2) at Greenfield, 23 July 1759, Benjamin Banks.
> Jeanne, bapt. at French Church, N. Y., 10 Mar. 1705/6.
> Mary [perhaps her mother was Mary Burr].

Lacy, Edward.

The six children of Edward and Sarah were bapt. at Fairfield Church, 20 Jan. 1694/5.

Children:

> ✕Edward, rem. to New Fairfield; m. (1) (rec. Fairfield) 23 July 1702, Abigail Gregory; m. (2) Hannah (Beardsley), widow of John Parruck; m. (3) (rec. Greenfield) 18 May 1748, Rebecca Grey.
> ✕John, d. at Stratfield, in 1761; will 31 May 1754, proved 3 Mar.

---

* Coll. of the Huguenot Society of America, vol 1, p. 110. For the reference, and bapt. of the dau. Jeanne, acknowledgment is made to Mr. Clarence A. Torrey.

1761; m. Ruth (Wakelee), b. 27 Aug. 1681, widow of Ephraim
Treadwell, and dau. of Jacob Wakelee.

Sarah, m. (1) Samuel Trowbridge; m. (2) (Fairfield Church), 26
May 1743, Edward Treadwell.

Henry, rem. to Newark, N. J.; m. (Stratfield Church), 11 Dec.
1716, Hannah Morehouse. They had a son, Joseph, bapt. at Stratfield, 8 Sept. 1717.

Mary, perhaps m. Jonathan Hall.

Elizabeth.

Lake, Thomas.

Married Sarah Peat, dau. of John, b. 3 Oct. 1665.

Will 9 Mar. 1726, proved 5 Feb. 1728; wife Sarah; dau. Sarah
Lake; sons John, David, Joseph, Thomas, James, Edward.

Children of Thomas and Sarah, recorded at Stratford:

John, b. 22 Nov. 1688, d. at Newtown in 1768; will 13 Aug. 1768,
proved 27 Sept. 1768; m. (rec. Newtown) 4 Jan. 1715/6, Abigail
Kimberly.

Charity, b. 16 Mar. 1691, or by duplicate entry, 16 Mar. 1690/1; m.
at Stratford, 20 June 1717, William Peat.

David, b. 10 Mar. 1693, or by duplicate entry, 20 Mar. 1692/3; m.
at Stratford, 21 Jan. 1724/5, Abigail Booth.

Joseph, b. 15 Apr. 1696, d. Dec. 1786 in 91 yr. (g. s., Trumbull);
m. (Trumbull Church), 14 Dec. 1732, Deborah Jackson. She was
dau. of Henry.

Sarah, b. 15 Jan. 1697/8.

Thomas, b. 23 Feb. 1700/1; m. at Stratford, 15 Feb. 1727/8, Elizabeth Walker.

James, b. 28 Jan. 1702/3; settled in New Milford; m. Mary Rogers,
dau. of John and Mary (Ford) Rogers of Milford.

Edward, b. 15 Dec. 1705, bapt. (rec. Stratfield) 19 May 1706; m.
Ann Beardsley, dau. of Daniel.

Lancaster, Walter.

He received from the town of Fairfield a grant of a homelot,
4 Jan. 1653; purchased 1656/7 a house and lot from Richard
Perry. He sold a homelot before 29 Sept. 1657 to Alexander
Knowles. He sold 26 Nov. 1672 to Henry Jackson, and some
of his holdings were sold to Giles Smith and Peter Clapham.

Lane, Robert. Deputy (Stratford), May and July 1686;
Deputy (Killingworth) May 1699, Oct. 1700, Oct. 1701, Oct.

1703, May 1705, Oct. 1706, May 1707, Oct. 1709, Oct. 1711, May and Oct. 1712, May and Oct. 1713, May and Oct. 1714, May 1715.

Married at Stratford, 19 Dec. 1665, Sarah Pickett. She was dau. of John. Robert d. at Killingworth, 12 Apr. 1718, and his widow Sarah, 11 Mar. 1725.

Children, recorded at Stratford:

> Sarah, b. 24 Feb. 1666 [1666/7]; m. Ebenezer Hurd.
> Hannah, b. 28 Dec. 1668; m. at Killingworth, 21 Nov. 1695, Nathaniel Wilcoxson.
> Daniel, b. 27 July 1671, d. 17 Mar. 1673/4.
> John, b. 12 July 1674, d. at Killingworth, 2 Oct. 1759; Dr.; m. (1) at Killingworth, 31 Dec. 1700, Lydia Kelsey, who d. 2 Apr. 1710; m. (2) 16 Jan. 1711, Hannah Parks.
> Elizabeth, b. 31 Jan. 1676 [1676/7].
> Margaret, b. 18 or 25 Aug. 1679; m. at Killingworth, 5 Dec. 1699, Theophilus Crane.
> Rebecca, b. 7 Mar. 1682 [1682/3].
> Jonathan, b. 16 Oct. 1685, m. Mercy ———, who d. at Killingworth, 13 Nov. 1727 in 36 yr.
> Mary, b. 23 Sept. 1688.

Lane, Charles.

Married Elizabeth Knapp, dau. of Roger of Fairfield, who d. before 1708.

Children:

> Susanna, b. ———, d. at Roxbury, 18 May 1767; m. Jeremiah Thomas.
> ✕Charles, b. ———, d. at Stratford in 1762; will 27 June 1755, proved 1 Jan. 1763; m. (1) by 1710, Joanna Gray, dau. of Jacob of Fairfield; m. (2) at Stratford, 2 Feb. 1720/1, Achsah Mallory. She was dau. of Peter. He was a warden of Christ Church, Stratford, for Ripton [Huntington], 1724.
> ✕Alexander, m. by 1717, Sarah ———.

Lattin, Richard.

Was first at Concord, by 1640.

Name spelled Lettin; bought from Thomas Jones a lot in Fairfield by 1649, which he sold to John Grumman 11 Jan. 1653.

He bought 8 acres from Charles Taintor, by 1653. Thomas Beardsley of Fairfield acknowledged a debt to him in 1652; and in 1654 he brought action for debt against Thomas Dunn and Roger Knapp.

Christian Lattin in 1661 sued "Henderickson" for slander; case referred by the Court at Hartford to that at Fairfield.

Richard went over about 1654 to Hempstead, L. I., to Oyster Bay in 1660, and to Huntington in 1661. About 1664 he returned to Oyster Bay, where he bought a large tract from the Indians. His first wife appears to have remained at Fairfield and d. there. In 1668 he m. Jean, widow of Thomas Ireland of Hempstead, whither he removed again, and d. 1672/3.

Children [by first wife], two recorded at Concord:

> Josiah, b. 20 Feb. 1640/1, d. at Oyster Bay in 1720; m. ———.
> Son, b. 12 Sept. 1643.
> Daughter, m. William Hudson.
> Daughter, m. John Robbins, of Oyster Bay.
> Hannah, m. John Davis, of Brookhaven.
> +Thomas, supposed son of Richard.

Lattin, Thomas, [s. of Richard].

The will of Michael Griswold of Wethersfield, 10 Sept. 1678, named dau. Abigail Lattin and her dau. Ann. Abigail Griswold was b. 8 June 1655, and was perhaps first wife of Thomas Lattin.

He m. Mercy, prob. dau. of Henry Wakelee. She m. (2) 31 Aug. 1721, Mr. Moses Wheeler, and presumably (3) 9 May 1726, Mr. John Burritt.

He d. at Stratford, 24 Feb. 1712/3.

Land laid out at Stratford, 25 July 1721, to Thomas, David and Benjamin Lattin, sons of Thomas.

If the Woodbury Church records as printed by Cothren may be depended on (they contain many palpable errors), Thomas had a dau. Phebe bapt. there in 1681.

Children, recorded at Stratford:

> Patience, b. 31 Dec. 1688; m. 25 Nov. 1714, John Gilbert.
> Thomas, b. 18 Nov. 1693, d. at Huntington, 22 Oct. 1776 ae. 83 (g. s.); Lt., Capt. Josiah Starr's Co., Cape Breton Expedition, July, 1745; m. 19 Apr. 1722, Mary Skidmore, b. abt. 1697, d. 18 June 1773 ae. 76 (g. s.).
> David (twin), b. 18 Nov. 1693, d. at Stratford in 1750; will 9 Oct.

1750, proved 19 Nov. 1750; m. 8 Nov. 1721, Comfort Titherton; no issue. Will mentions wife Comfort; land which when under distraction he conveyed to Abigail Titherton and she to my wife; two bros. Thomas and Benjamin Lattin. Comfort m. 30 Oct. 1754, Nathan Summers.

Jacob, b. 9 Nov. 1696, d. y.

Benjamin, b. 13 Apr. 1702; m. 11 Nov. 1723, Mary Barley.

Law, Richard. Deputy (Stamford) to New Haven Leg., May 1653, May 1654, May 1655, May 1656, May 1657, May 1658, May 1659, May 1661, May 1662, May and Oct. 1663, Jan. and May 1664; Magistrate for Stamford, 1653-63; Assistant (provisional appointment, Conn. Col.), Oct. 1664; Deputy (Stamford) to Conn. Leg., Oct. 1665, Oct. 1666, Oct. 1669, May 1672; Commissioner for Stamford, Greenwich and Rye, 1665-80, for Stamford and Greenwich, 1681-86, and for Stamford, 1687.

Of Wethersfield by 1638; rem. to Stamford.

He m. Margaret Kilbourne, dau. of Thomas.

Children:

+Jonathan, b. abt. 1636.

Abigail, m. at Stamford, 11 May 1663, Jonathan Selleck.

Sarah, m. at Stamford, 28 Oct. 1669, John Selleck.

Law, Jonathan, s. of Richard.

Born abt. 1636, d. at Milford, 9 Jan. 1711/2 in 75 or 76 yr.; m. at Milford, 1 June 1664, Sarah Clark; dau. of George, Sr., bapt. 7 Apr. 1644, d. at Milford, 15 Feb. 1705/6(?); 1704 (g. s.).

Child, recorded at Milford:

Jonathan, b. 6 Aug. 1674 [1672 by g. s.], d. 6 Nov. 1750 (g. s., Milford); Gov. (1742-50); m. (1) 20 Dec. 1698, Ann Eliot, who d. 16 Nov. 1703; m. (2) 14 Feb. 1704/5, Abigail Arnold, who d. 14 Dec. 1705; m. (3) 1 Aug. 1706, Abigail Andrew; dau. of Rev. Samuel, bapt. 29 Jan. 1686, d. 25 Sept. 1724; m. (4) 1 June 1726, Sarah Burr; widow of Peter Burr and previously of Jonathan Sturges, dau. of David Osborn, b. [say 1673], d. 17 June 1727; m. (5) 11 Jan. 1730, Eunice Andrew; widow of Samuel Andrew, Jr., and dau. of John Hall, b. at Wallingford, 7 Mar.

1700, d. at New Haven, 2 June 1774 ae. 74; she m. (3) in 1751, Joseph Pitkin of Hartford. [See *Treat Genealogy* for good account of Gov. Jonathan's children.]

Lawrence, Thomas.

Adm. to church at Milford, 4 Dec. 1642, and d. in 1648. His wife Martha was adm. 11 Feb. 1644/5, and was dismissed to Stamford. She m. (2) John Chapman of Stamford, and (3) 17 Dec. 1657, Francis Brown.

Children, bapt. at Milford:

> Martha, bapt. 9 Aug. 1646; m. Rev. Eliphalet Jones, of Huntington, L. I.
> +Thomas, bapt. 3 Dec. 1648, posthumous.

Lawrence, Thomas, s. of Thomas.

Bapt. at Milford, 3 Dec. 1648; d. at Stamford, 16 Aug. 1691.

He m. after 1674, Hannah, widow of Caleb Knapp, and dau. of Henry Smith, both of Stamford.

Of Stamford, will 26 July 1691; sister Rebecca "Gampin" [Galpin], 50 shillings; dau.-in-law Hanna, 40 shillings; son-in-law Samuel Knap; kinswoman Martha Slauson, 40 shillings and land; nephew Eleazer Slauson, Jr., son of sister Mary, land; sister Sarah Scudder; nephew Jonathan Scudder; my brother-in-law Eliphalet Jones and sister Martha Jones; nephew Joseph Brown, Jr.; brother-in-law Joseph Brown, Sr.; friends Abraham Ambler and Daniel Weed, Exec'rs. Inv. 16 Aug. 1691; estate carried in his lifetime to Long Island mentioned. Son-in-law John Knap made oath to Inv. 6 Nov. 1691.

Some of those named in the will were children of his mother by her subsequent marriages to Chapman and Brown [*q. v.*].

Leavenworth, John.

Of Woodbury, brother of Thomas, Sr.

Inv. 12 Oct. 1702. Adm'n granted to his cousin [nephew] Thomas Leavenworth; distribution ordered between said Thomas and his brother John.

Leavenworth, Thomas.

Inv. of Thomas of Woodbury, 20 Nov. 1683. Widow; two sons; one dau.

Testimony 6 Nov. 1702 of David Jenkins, husband to Grace Jenkins which was formerly the wife of Thomas Levinsworth, that John and Thomas Levinsworth both of Woodbury did acknowledge themselves to be own brothers, and we testify that Thomas and John Levinsworth now resident in Stratford are the abovesaid Thomas Levinsworth's children. [Woodbury Deeds.]

Testimony 29 Oct. 1702 of Joseph Hurd and William Marks of Woodbury that Mr. John Levensworth "if he did not come againe" gave his whole accommodations or lands to his two kinsmen Thomas and John Levinsworth equally. [Woodbury Deeds.]

Children:

+Thomas, b. abt. 1673.
+John.
Daughter, prob. d. y.

Leavenworth, Thomas, s. of Thomas.

Born about 1673; Doct. Thomas d. 4 Aug. 1754 in 81 yr. (g. s., Huntington); m. Mary Dorman. She was dau. of Edmund, b. at New Haven, 12 May 1680; d. June 1768 in 89 yr. (g. s.).

Will 6 July 1748, codicil 25 July 1749, proved 15 July 1754; wife Mary; son James; two grandsons Nathan and Ebenezer (sons of son David dec'd); sons John, Zebulon, Thomas, Mark; daus. Mary wife of Joseph Perry, Hannah wife of Nichols Moss, and Sarah wife of Abner Perry; son Edmund.

Children, some recorded at Stratford:

James, b. 1 Sept. 1699, d. at Stratford, Aug. 1759; m. 23 Aug. 1720, Hester Trowbridge.
David, b. 12 Oct. 1701, d. at Woodbury, 10 Apr. 1735; m. 3 June 1730, Sarah Hurd.
Ebenezer, b. 7 Apr. 1706, bapt. (rec. Stratfield) 30 June 1706, d. in 1734. Will 25 May 1734, proved 6 Aug. 1734; of Ripton; father Thomas; brother Edmund; brothers and sisters.
John, b. 3 Nov. 1708, bapt. (rec. Stratfield) 26 Dec. 1708, d. 20 Jan. 1785 in 77 yr. (g. s., Roxbury); m. (1) abt. 1735, Deborah Moss, dau. of William, b. at Derby, 10 Feb. 1714/5, d. at Wood-

bury, 1 Jan. 1746; m. (2) 29 Jan. 1747, Mary Bronson, who d. 24 Dec. 1803 ae. 85 (g. s., Roxbury).

Zebulon, d. at Roxbury, 2 May 1778; m. abt. 1743, Esther ——, who d. 24 June 1793.

Mark, b. abt. 1712, d. 20 Aug. 1797 in 86 yr. (g. s., Waterbury); grad. Yale Coll. 1737; Rev. at Waterbury 57 yrs.; m. (1) 6 Feb. 1739/40, Ruth Peck, dau. of Jeremiah, who d. 8 Aug. 1750 in 32 yr. (g. s.); m. (2) 4 Dec. 1750, Sarah Hull, dau. of Capt. Joseph, who d. 7 May 1808 ae. 82 (g. s.).

Thomas, b. ——, d. at Woodbury in 1781; adm'n granted 16 Nov. 1781; m. (1) abt. 1743, Elizabeth Davis, dau. of Samuel of Stratford, who d. 24 Apr. 1758; m. (2) at Woodbury, 10 Oct. 1758, Rhoda Olds, who d. 1 May 1794.

Mary, b. abt. 1716, d. at Shelton, 4 Nov. 1809 ae. 93 (g. s.); m. Joshua Perry [name Joseph in her father's will is an error].

Hannah, b. abt. 1719, d. 15 Oct. 1789 ae. 70 (g. s., Mt. Carmel); m. (1) (rec. Derby) 25 Mar. 1740, Nichols Moss; m. (2) abt. 1761, Lt. Jonathan Dickerman.

Sarah, b. 6 Oct. 1722; m. Rev. Abner Perry.

Edmund, b. abt. 1725, d. 28 July 1785 in 61 yr. (g. s., Huntington); Capt.; m. Abigail Beardsley, who d. 18 Mar. 1804 ae. 82 (g. s.).

Leavenworth, John, s. of Thomas.

Blacksmith, of Stratford; rem. to Newtown, where he d. in 1762.

Married Phebe Wooster, dau. of Thomas.

Will 26 Jan. 1762, proved 22 Feb. 1762; wife Phebe; three daus. Alice Camp, Sarah Botsford, Abigail Turner; son Thomas Leavenworth; three gr. children John Camp, Jabez Botsford, Jeremiah Turner, Jr.; son Lemuel Camp.

Children:

Thomas, m. at Newtown, 10 Jan. 1731/2, Mary Kimberly. She was dau. of Abraham, b. abt. 1710, d. 21 Mar. 1773 ae. 63 (g. s., Southbury).

Alice, m. at Newtown, 19 Mar. 1730, Lemuel Camp.

Sarah, b. abt. 1713, d. at Newtown, 1 Mar. 1789; m. Moses Botsford.

Abigail, m. Jeremiah Turner.

Levins, John.

Settled in Stratford; m. at New Haven, 23 Nov. 1674, Elizabeth Preston, dau. of Edward, b. 29 Sept. 1655. They rem. to Woodstock; she m. (2) 24 Mar. 1699, Peter Aspinwall.

Children, recorded at Stratford (mother of first two called Elizabeth):

> James, b. 9 Dec. 1675, d. 23 Apr. 1678.
> Peter, b. 9 Nov 1677.
> James, b. 24 Oct. 1679.

Lewis, Benjamin.

He was among the first settlers of Wallingford, 1670; rem. to Stratford by 1679.

Married Hannah Curtis, dau. of John, b. 2 Feb. 1654/5, d. 21 Oct. 1728 in 74 yr.

Despite prominence of family, births of children were not recorded in Stratford, we find no death record of Benjamin, and no probate. Several of the children are placed circumstantially.

Children, first two recorded at Wallingford:

> John, b. 30 Sept. 1672.
> Mary, b. 9 Nov. 1674; m. 22 Nov. 1699, Samuel Fairchild.
> James, b. abt. 1677, d. at Stratford, 29 Jan. 1766 ae. 89 (g. s., Epis. Yard); Capt.; m. at Stratford, 11 Nov. 1702, Hannah Judson, b. 30 May 1681, d. 2 July 1756 ae. 75 (g. s., Epis. Yard).
> Edmund, b. abt. 1679, d. 14 May 1757 in 78 yr. (g. s., Epis. Yard, Stratford); Col.; m. 21 May 1702, Hannah Beach, b. Sept. 1681, d. 13 July 1756 in 75 yr. (g. s.).
> Joseph, b. abt. 1682, d. 3 July 1756 ae. 74 (g. s., Epis. Yard, Stratford); m. 29 June 1714, Phebe Judson, b. 2 Oct. 1691, d. 11 Sept. 1753 ae. 62 (g. s.).
> Hannah, b. [say 1684]; m. 10 Sept. 1705, Joseph Jones.
> Martha, b. [say 1691]; m. 18 Dec. 1712, James Judson.
> Abigail, b. [say 1694]; m. 1 Dec. 1715, Samuel Prindle.
> Benjamin, b. abt. 1696, d. at Stratford, 7 July 1759 in 63 yr. (g. s.); m. 24 Dec. 1719, Sarah DeForest; dau. of David, b. 9 Nov. 1698, d. 8 June 1765 in 66 yr. (g. s.).
> Eunice, m. 9 Jan. 1721/2, Judson Burton.

Lewis, Philip, s. of William, 2d. Deputy (Fairfield), May 1698.

Son of William and Mary (Hopkins), and gr. son of William and Felix (Whiting?) Lewis.

Bapt. at Hartford, 13 Dec. 1646; lived with his father's family in Farmington; settled in Hartford; removed to Fairfield, 1692.

On 8 Aug. 1692, being of Hartford, he bought from John "Butteler" of Hartford, merchant, as attorney to Francis Foxcroft of Boston, merchant, land in Fairfield.

Married Sarah Ashley, dau. of Robert of Springfield, Mass., b. 23 Aug. 1648.

In 1709 Philip Lewis and Elizabeth Lewis the younger witnessed a deed.

Inv. 4 Dec. 1723 presented by his dau. Sarah Taylor.

Jonathan Sturges of Fairfield, attorney for Philip Lewis of Boston, and Richard Hollingsworth of Fairfield in right of wife Ruth one of the daus. of Philip Lewis late of Fairfield dec'd, dissatisfied with action of Probate Court, 13 Oct. 1725. [Superior Court Rec.]

Philip Lewis of Boston, Mass., mariner, conveyed 13 Feb. 1727 [1727/8] to John Thompson of Fairfield, tailor, house in Fairfield; a witness was Thomas Lewis.

> Children, two bapt. at Hartford:
>
>> Sarah, m. (1) abt. 1690, James Bennett of Stratfield; m. (2) John Taylor of Norwalk.
>> Philip, mariner, of Boston, Mass.; m. at Boston, 15 Apr. 1703, Martha Hender.
>> ✕Nathan, m. abt. 1710, Sarah Osborn, dau. of Capt. John, b. [say 1689], d. 30 Apr. 1729. She m. (2) 24 Jan. 1725/6, John Bishop, of Stamford.
>> Ruth, m. (1) Richard Hollingsworth; m. (2) Stephen Munson, of New Haven.
>> Thomas, bapt. 29 Nov. 1685.
>> Abigail, bapt. 8 Apr. 1692.

Lockwood, Robert.   Sergt., Fairfield Trainband, May 1657.

Came to America about 1630, brother of Edmund; settled in Watertown, Mass.; freeman of Mass. Bay, Mar. 1636/7. Removed to Fairfield about 1646; freeman of Conn., May 1652.

Married Susannah, prob. dau. of Richard Norman of Salem, Mass. She m. (2) Jeffrey Ferris.

Inv. 11 Sept. 1658. Widow Susanna to administer; nine children: eldest son Jonathan, Joseph, Daniel, Ephraim, Gershom, John, Abigail, Sarah, Mary; Deborah, being married, hath rec'd portion.

Jeffrey Ferris agreed to pay portions to the children, and mention was made of what he shall pay William Ward and Joseph and Daniel Lockwood on account of the children.

Children, first six recorded at Watertown:

+Jonathan, b. 10 Sept. 1634.
Deborah, b. 12 Oct. 1636; m. (1) before 20 Oct. 1658, Ens. William Ward; m. (2) John Topping, of Southampton, L. I.
+Joseph, b. 6 Aug. 1638.
+Daniel, b. 21 Mar. 1640.
+Ephraim, b. 1 Dec. 1641.
+Gershom, b. 6 Sept. 1643.
John, d. in 1677, unm. Inv. abt. 1677, presented by Ephraim Lockwood.
Abigail, m. John Barlow, Jr. He receipted, 28 Dec. 1681, for the portion of his wife Abigail in Est. of father-in-law Robert Lockwood and mother-in-law Susannah Ferris.
Sarah, d. 1 Mar. 1650 [1650/1] (Col. Rec.).
Sarah, b. 27 Feb. 1651 [1651/2] (Col. Rec.); possibly she was the first wife of Lt. Abraham Adams.
Mary, m. (1) Jonathan Husted, of Greenwich, who receipted for her portion, 1 Dec. 1681; m. (2) Joseph Knapp, of Greenwich.

Lockwood, Edmund, s. of Edmund.

Son of Edmund of Cambridge, Mass., and nephew of Robert of Fairfield. He settled in Stamford by 1651, and d. there, 31 Jan. 1692 [1692/3]; m. (rec. Stamford) 7 Jan. 1655 [1655/6], Hannah Scott, who d. 12 Apr. 1706. She was dau. of Thomas and Elizabeth Scott of Ipswich, Mass.

He was propounded for freeman of Conn. Colony, 12 May 1670. Freed from training, June 1685.

Inv. 28 Feb. 1692/3. Widow; sons Joseph, Daniel, Edmund; daus. Mary, Abigail, and another not named. Adm'n was granted to the son Joseph, with Jonas Weed; the latter declined to act, and Abraham Ambler, Sr., was appointed in his place.

Another Inv. 30 Jan. 1706/7 [after death of the widow]; distribution ordered to the three sons and three daus.

Children:

Mary, m. 2 Mar. 1692/3, Joseph Garnsey.
Abigail, m. ——— Cook.

Joseph, m. (1) 19 May 1698, Elizabeth Ayres, who d. 16 Dec. 1715;
m. (2) 10 Aug. 1715 (*sic*), Margery Webb, who d. 2 Jan. 1736/7.
Daniel, m. 5 Nov. 1702, Charity Clemence.
Edmund, d. at Stamford, 8 Feb. 1739/40. Will 8 Jan. 1739/40,
proved 4 Mar. 1739/40; bros. Daniel and Joseph Lockwood of
Stamford; three sisters, Mary Garnsey, Abigail Cook, Sarah
Lounsbury; cousin Edmund, son of bro. Daniel; cousin Deborah
wife of Nathaniel Webb, dau. of bro. Daniel.
Sarah, m. 19 June 1707, Michael Lounsbury.

Lockwood, Jonathan, s. of Robert. Deputy for Greenwich,
May and Oct. 1671, May 1673, Oct. 1674, Oct. 1676, May 1683.
Commissioner on N. Y. boundary, Oct. 1674. Called Sergt.
1673, and Lt. 1674.

Born at Watertown, Mass., 10 Sept. 1634, d. at Greenwich, 12
May 1688; m. Mary Ferris, dau. of Jeffrey. She m. (2) in 1696,
Thomas Merritt of Rye, and d. at Greenwich 1707/8.

Inv. 31 Jan. 1707/8 of Marah Merrit of Greenwich. Her prenuptial agreement with Merritt was made 3 June 1696. Her
children and heirs: Robert, Gershom, and Joseph Lockwood,
Abigail Baxter, and Still John Lockwood.

Children:

Robert, d. at Greenwich in 1732/3; will 7 May 1731, proved 23 Jan.
1732/3; wife Mary; sons Jonathan, Samuel, David; daus. Phebe
Austin, Mary Wiatt, Susannah [?Jsestiles], and Deborah.
Jonathan, d. at Greenwich, 9 Nov. 1689. His bro. Robert made oath
to Inv.; adm'n granted to Gershom and Robert Lockwood, both
of Greenwich.
Gershom.
Joseph.
Abigail, m. ——— Baxter.
Still John, d. at Greenwich abt. 1757; Inv. exhibited 3 May 1757;
no widow; distribution ordered to children John, Gilbert, William,
Abigail, Elizabeth, Mary, Susannah, Ann, Deborah.

Lockwood, Joseph, s. of Robert. Sergt., Fairfield Trainband.
Deputy (Fairfield), Oct. 1681, May 1696.

Born at Watertown, Mass., 6 Aug. 1638, d. at Fairfield, in
1717.

Married (1) ——— Beacham, dau. of Robert, who apparently
d. before her father made his will (1689).

As he was the only Fairfield Lockwood of suitable age for the marriage, we dare assert that he m. (2) after 1689, Mary (Coley), widow first of Peter Simpson and later of John Stream, Jr., all of Milford, where she was bapt. 23 Nov. 1651. She d. in 1705, and was Mary Lockwood of Fairfield when her estate was administered. [New Haven County Court Rec.]

Will 17 June 1715, sealed 29 Apr. 1717, proved 10 June 1717; gr. son Robert, son of Robert dec'd; gr. son Daniel Lockwood; dau. Susanna's children,—Nathaniel, Ephraim, Sarah and Ann Burr; residue to son John (Exec'r). Called Sergt.; Inv. 27 Jan. 1717/8.

Children [by first wife, all mentioned in will of her father]:

+Robert.

Susanna, m. (1) Nathaniel Burr, Jr.; m. (2) Ens. Benjamin Rumsey.

+John.

Sarah, d. s. p.

Lockwood, Daniel, s. of Robert.

Born at Watertown, Mass., 21 Mar. 1640, d. at Fairfield in 1691; m. Abigail Sherwood, dau. of Thomas.

Inv. 30 May 1691. Ages of children: Daniel 22, Abigail 17, Mary 10 (she very sickly and weak). The widow Abigail affirmed the inventory, refusing to swear.

Will of Abigail Lockwood of Fairfield, 29 Jan. 1691/2; son Daniel (Exec'r); dau. Abigail wife of Samuel Roberson; dau. Mary; brothers Joseph Lockwood and Matthew Sherwood, overseers.

On 26 June 1700, the widow and son Daniel who were to distribute the Est. of Daniel, Sr., being dec'd, and the youngest dau. Mary not having rec'd her portion, the widow of the younger Daniel was to distribute. Portion paid, 4 Mar. 1700/1, to Mary dau. of Daniel, Sr., now wife of Nathan Morehouse.

Children:

+Daniel, b. abt. 1669.

Abigail, b. abt. 1674; m. 20 Aug. 1691, Samuel Robinson.

Mary, b. abt. 1681; m. abt. 1701, Nathan Morehouse.

Lockwood, Ephraim, s. of Robert.

Born at Watertown, Mass., 1 Dec. 1641; d. at Norwalk in 1685; m. at Norwalk, 8 June 1665, Mercy St. John, dau. of Matthew, Sr.

Aged about 43, will 13 Jan. 1685; wife; second son Daniel; lot lying between Robert Steward and Samuel Sention [St. John] my brother; son Ephraim; eldest son John (Exec'r with his mother); son Eliphalet; son Joseph; son James (had Est. by will of uncle); Sarah (to have at 18); Mark Sention and John Fitch, overseers. Witnesses: Samuel Hayes, Sr., and Samuel Belden.

Inv. 20 July 1685; Mercy Lockwood made oath, 2 Nov. 1685. The birth dates of the children are entered in the Probate records.

Inv. of Mercy Lockwood of Norwalk, 1 Feb. 1694 [1694/5]. The son Ephraim died a minor after death of his father Ephraim, Sr.; Inv. of John of Norwalk also dec'd; surviving heirs, 12 Mar. 1694/5, Daniel, Eliphalet, Joseph, James, and Sarah Lockwood.

Children, all but James recorded at Norwalk:

> John, b. 19 Mar. 1665/6, d. by 1690, unm. Inv. 2 Mar. 1690 [1690/1]; house purchased by him and his mother; land given him by his father. Adm'n granted to Mercy Lockwood and her son Daniel.
>
> Daniel, b. 13 Aug. 1668, d. at Norwalk in 1712; m. Sarah Benedict, dau. of James, b. 16 June 1677.
>
> Sarah, b. 3 Nov. 1670; m. in 1695, John Platt, Jr.
>
> Ephraim, b. 1 May 1673, d. y.
>
> Eliphalet, b. 27 Feb. 1675 [1675/6]; m. 11 Oct. 1699, Mary Gold, dau. of John of Stamford.
>
> Joseph, b. 1 Apr. 1680, d. at Norwalk in 1760; will 16 Apr. 1758, proved 2 Dec. 1760; m. (1) 14 Aug. 1707, Mary Wood, dau. of John of Stamford; m. (2) Hannah ———.
>
> James, b. 21 Apr. 1683; Capt.; m. (1) 23 Oct. 1707, Lydia Smith, dau. of Samuel; m. (2) Mercy (Bushnell), widow of William Gaylord, and previously of Maj. John Bostwick.

Lockwood, Gershom, s. of Robert.

Born at Watertown, Mass., 6 Sept. 1643, d. at Greenwich, 12 Mar. 1718/9 ae. 77 (g. s.); m. (1) Ann [?Millington] of Windsor.

He m. (2) abt. Oct. 1716, Elizabeth, widow of Gideon Wright, and dau. of John and Elizabeth (Montgomery) Townsend.

Adm'n granted, 1 Apr. 1719, to widow Elizabeth and son Gershom. The Inv. mentions "about thirty acres of Land at Windsor which came to him by his first wife."

Agreement 28 Mar. 1719: Widow Elizabeth; Gershom and Joseph Lockwood of Greenwich, sons of Gershom; Hannah wife of Thomas Hanford of Norwalk and Sarah wife of Benjamin Hecox of Stamford, daus. of Gershom; and John, Nathaniel, Elizabeth, and David Bates, children of Elizabeth Bates of Stamford dec'd, one of the daus. of Gershom. The prenuptial contract of the widow with Gershom was dated 2 Oct. 1716.

Children [by first wife]:

> Gershom, Deputy for Greenwich, May and Aug. 1710, Oct. 1715, May and Oct. 1719, Oct. 1720, Oct. 1721, May 1723, May and Oct. 1724, May and Oct. 1726, Sept. 1727, May and July 1728; Justice; m. Mary [perhaps dau. of John Weed, b. at Stamford, 21 Apr. 1684].
>
> Hannah, m. (1) abt. 1686, John Burwell;* m. (2) Thomas Hanford.
>
> Elizabeth, d. at Stamford, 23 May 1702; m. (rec. Stamford), 18 Jan. 1693/4, John Bates.
>
> Joseph, d. at Greenwich in 1748; will 16 Dec. 1748, proved 2 Jan. 1749; m. [perhaps Sarah Green, b. at Stamford, 19 Apr. 1684, dau. of Benjamin Green whose will 1725 named dau. Sarah Lockwood].
>
> Sarah, b. abt. 1679, d. at Wilton, 27(?) Feb. 1765 ae. 86 (g. s.); will 10 Jan. 1765, proved 23 Feb. 1765; m. (1) (rec. Stamford) 25 Jan. 1699/1700, Nathaniel Selleck; m. (2) 3 Feb. 1713/4, Benjamin Hickock; m. (3) 9 Mar. 1755, Samuel Kellogg of Norwalk.

Lockwood, Robert, s. of Joseph.

Married Mary ———.

Adm'n granted, 3 Aug. 1715, to Sergt. Joseph Lockwood and to Mary Lockwood, widow of the dec'd. Inv. taken 14 June 1715. On 9 Nov. 1715, action was taken on minor children, Daniel, Abigail, Joseph, Gershom, Jehiel; Mary Lockwood appointed guardian to last two: John Silliman to Abigail and Joseph; and John Lockwood to Daniel.

Distribution ordered 11 Dec. 1735, and made 2 Apr. 1736, of

---

* Will of John Burwell, last day of Apr. 1690; wife, Exec'x; child; if wife should be with child; father Gershom Lockwood, and cousin John Browne of Newark, N. J., overseers.

the part of Est. of Robert Lockwood of Fairfield which was set to his widow as dower. Heirs: eldest son Robert; Daniel; Joseph; Jehiel; Gershom; Mary Dunkins; Susanna Dickinson. Adm'n on Est. of Mary Lockwood of Fairfield granted, 22 Nov. 1736, to Gershom Lockwood.

Children:

×Robert.

    Joseph, living in 1761; was prob. the Joseph of Sharon who conveyed Fairfield land in 1768.

    Mary, d. ("Widow Mary Dunkins") at Westport, 15 Aug. 1749; m. John Dunkins.

    Sarah, d. in 1716. Inv. 23 Aug. 1716. Distribution ordered to five brothers, Robert, Daniel, Joseph, Jehiel, Gershom, and three sisters, Mary, Susanna, Abigail.

×Gershom, d. at Westport in 1748. Adm'n granted, 5 Apr. 1748, to Abraham Higgins, Jr.; m. Jane Frost, who d. at Westport, 7 Jan. 1774.

×Daniel, d. in 1733. adm'n granted, 28 Jan. 1733/4.

    Susanna, m. Nathaniel Dickinson, of Stratford, with whom she conveyed 1736 land from father Robert Lockwood "which originally belonged to Robert Beacham granfather to s^d Susanah."

    Abigail, d. in 1723. Adm'n granted, 29 Nov. 1723, to John Silliman of Fairfield. Distribution ordered to surviving brothers and sisters,—Robert, Joseph, Gershom, Daniel, Jehiel, Mary, and Susanna Lockwood.

    Jehiel, d. in 1761; adm'n granted, 20 Mar. 1761, to Daniel Dunkins. Distribution ordered to brothers and sisters or their heirs, viz.: (1) Daniel and Abigail, children of Robert Lockwood dec'd; (2) Joseph Lockwood; (3) Wait Lockwood; (4) Zadoc, Benajah, Nathan, Nathaniel, Robert, Abigail wife of John Kinny, Sarah wife of Samuel Eastern, and Naomi, children of Susannah Dickinson dec'd; (5) William, John, Mary wife of Ebenezer Munroe, and Daniel, children of Mary Dunkins dec'd; (6) Gershom, Stephen, Frost and Mabel, children of Gershom Lockwood dec'd.

Lockwood, John, s. of Joseph. Deputy for Fairfield, Oct. 1726.

Will 5 Apr. 1735, proved 30 Nov. 1736; wife Elizabeth; three sons, Joseph, John and Ephraim (Exec'rs); daus. Sarah wife of Isaac Brown of Norwalk, Anna Bagley, Grace Williams, Elizabeth Matthews, Susanna Lockwood.

Ephraim, son of John, chose Capt. John Silliman for guardian, 30 Dec. 1736; and Susanna chose Josiah Bagley, 4 July 1737.

Children:

Sarah, m. Isaac Brown of Norwalk.
Anna, m. Josiah Bagley.
XJoseph, m. 1 Nov. 1737, Agnes Money of Ireland.
XJohn, d. at Westport, abt. 1784; will 13 Feb. 1784, proved 17 Jan.
1785; m. 8 Feb. 1731, Abigail Morehouse, dau. of Gideon.
Grace, m. William Williams of "west parish", Fairfield.
Elizabeth, m. Robert Matthews.
Susanna, d. at Westport, 6 June 1747; m. David Adams.
Ephraim, res. 1 Jan. 1744/5 at Crosswicks, Burlington County, N. J.,
and on that date called himself formerly of Fairfield when convey-
ing right to land from his father John Lockwood.

Lockwood, Daniel, s. of Daniel.

Born at Fairfield about 1669, d. there about 1698; m. Abigail
Burr, dau. of Daniel, b. 14 Mar. 1671/2. He and his wife
renewed their Covenant at Fairfield Church, 23 Sept. 1694. She
m. (2) 26 June 1700, Elnathan Hanford; and (3) 26 Nov. 1707,
Nathaniel Sherman of Stratford, where she d. 2 Mar. 1730/1.

Inv. 11 Mar. 1698 [1698/9?]. Widow Abigail and her
brother Daniel Burr to administer. On 26 June 1700, the widow
of Daniel, Jr., was to marry Elnathan Hanford; two daus., aged
6 and 4. On 19 Nov. 1707, Nathaniel Sherman of Stratford was
appointed guardian to Abigail and Mary.

The part of the Est. which was set as dower to the widow
Abigail was distributed, 20 Jan. 1735/6, to the heirs: the legal
representatives of Abigail Gorham, dec'd; and Mary wife of
Charles Burritt.

Children, recorded at Fairfield:

Abigail, b. 28 May 1694, bapt. 23 Sept. 1694, d. at Fairfield, 23 Jan.
1724/5 ae. 31 (g. s.); m. 11 May 1715, Joseph Gorham [date 7
Apr. 1715 by Stratford rec.].
Mary, b. 14 Jan. 1695 [1695/6], bapt. 29 Mar. 1696; m. (rec. Stratford) 18 Apr. 1717, Charles Burritt.

Lord, Robert, s. of William.

Born at Saybrook, Aug. 1651, d. at Fairfield in 1739; son of
William Lord, and gr. son of Thomas and Dorothy (Bird) Lord
who came from Towcester, co. Northampton, Eng., 1635.

Married Esther, dau. of Ens. William Ward, who had been
wife, first of Ebenezer Hawley, second of Ephraim Nichols, and

third of Eliphalet Hill. Born abt. 1664, she d. [date gone, 1732]
ae. 67 (g. s., Fairfield).

Will of Esther wife of Robert Lord, 8 Jan. 1730, proved 8 Feb.
1731/2; sons Robert and Ebenezer Lord; Church of England in
Fairfield; other three sons have had portions by deed; daus.
Elisabeth, Deborah, Esther, Sarah, Abigail.

Distribution of Est. of Hester Lord, 4 Oct. 1751; Elizabeth
late wife of Col. John Burr; Ignatius Nickolls (by deed of gift
from his mother Hester Lord); heirs of Deborah late wife of
Joseph Wheeler; heirs of Hester wife of David Wheeler; William
Hill and Eliphalet Hill (by deeds of gift from their mother);
heirs of Robert Lord dec'd; heirs of Ebenezer Lord dec'd; Sarah
wife of Josiah Gilbert; Abigail wife of Ebenezer Stevens.

Children, bapt. at Fairfield:
> Mary, bapt. 21 Aug. 1698, d. y.
> Abigail, bapt. 5 Apr. 1700; m. Ebenezer Stevens.
> Sarah, bapt. 29 Mar. 1702; m. 14 June 1722, Josiah Gilbert.
> ✕Robert, m. abt. 1730, Rachel Hide, b. 6 Feb. 1713. Rachel "Lord
> alias Hide" m. at Greenfield, 23 June 1746, Richard Livesey.
> ✕Ebenezer, d. in 1750; Inv. 10 Nov. 1750; m. Abigail ———.

Ludlow, Roger. Assistant, Mass. Bay Col., Feb. 1630, and
Dep. Governor, 1634. Commissioner appointed by Mass. to
govern Conn., Mar. 1636; Assistant, Conn. Col., Apr. 1636,
Sept. 1636, Mar. 1637, May 1637, Nov. 1637, Feb. 1638, Mar.
1638, Apr. 1638, Apr. 1640, Apr. 1641, Apr. 1643, Apr. 1644,
Apr. 1645, Apr. 1646, May 1647, May 1649, May 1650, May
1651, May 1652, May 1653; Dep. Governor, Conn. Col., Apr.
1639, Apr. 1642, May 1648; Commissioner to Saybrook,
Pequot War, June 1637; Commissioner to United Colonies,
May 1648, May 1651, May 1652, May 1653.

As chief founder of Fairfield, the career of Roger Ludlow
would merit lengthy consideration, were it not that Mrs. Schenck
wrote a long and excellent account, to which we can refer the
reader for fuller detail, published in her *Hist. of Fairfield*, Vol. 1,
pp. 303-323. We therefore confine our comments for the most
part to genealogical considerations.

We are indebted to the investigations of the late Col. Joseph L.
Chester for most of our knowledge of the antecedents of Roger

Ludlow in England. He came from a younger branch of the Ludlows of Hill Deverill, co. Wilts, a family whose pedigree is traced to William Ludlow and Margaret Rymer his wife; through their son John Ludlow and Lora Ringwood his wife; through their son William Ludlow and Joan More his wife; through their son George Ludlow and Edith Windsor his wife; all happily without one definite date to serve as a guide. With the last marriage, however, we enter a field in which dates of a sort are readily obtainable; for Edith Windsor was third dau. of Andrews*, first Baron Windsor (descended from an elder branch of the family to which the famous FitzGeralds belonged), by his wife Elizabeth, dau. of William Blount, Baron Montjoy. Sir Andrews Windsor was born before 1479, when he was mentioned in his father's will, and himself died in 1543. It is well to bear these dates in mind, for as Edith was married before her father made his will, her birth can be placed pretty definitely as between 1510 and 1520.

George Ludlow, Esq., by his said wife Edith, had two sons, Edmund and Thomas. The elder continued the Hill Deverill line, and was grandfather of Edmund Ludlow, one of the regicides who condemned King Charles I. The younger son, Thomas, is supposed to be the ancestor of the Ludlows of Warminster, co. Wilts, who also had estates at Maiden Bradley, co. Wilts, and at Butleigh, co. Somerset. The undoubted father and mother of Roger Ludlow were Thomas Ludlow and Jane Pyle, who were of Dinton, co. Wilts, when Thomas died in 1608. Col. Chester assumed, and Mrs. Schenck followed him, that Roger's father Thomas was identical with Thomas, second son of George and Edith. An analysis of the chronology shows that this was possible. If we suppose Edith, as above, born around 1515, and her second son Thomas as late as 1555,† he could have been husband of Jane Pyle, who must have been very old when she died in 1650; if a decade younger than her husband, she would have been 85 at death.

Thomas Ludlow of Dinton, will 19 Nov. 1607, proved 8 June 1608, named dau. Ann (under 21 and unmarried), wife Jane, and

---

* Not Andrew, as usually printed. He was given the name of his mother, Elizabeth Andrews.

† Either Col. Chester made a slip, or Mrs. Schenck misunderstood his statement, for it was Edith's father who d. 1543, and if she died that year, as stated, the chronology is too long to admit of her being grandmother of Roger.

son Gabriel; lands at Butleigh and goods at Warminster; brother, Sir Gabriel Pyle, overseer.

Jane Pyle was dau. of Thomas of Babton, co. Wilts, sister of Sir Gabriel (d. 1627); and her eldest nephew Francis Pyle was born 1589. In her will, 10 Dec. 1646, proved 6 July 1650, she called herself widow, of Baycliffe, co. Wilts; gave to the poor of Maiden Bradley and of Warminster; to son Roger Ludlow and to son George Ludlow, her two wedding rings; her dau.-in-law Phillis Ludlow and Thomas, Francis, John, Ann, Elizabeth, and Sarah, children of her son Gabriel, received the bulk of her estate.

Gabriel, the eldest son of Thomas, was preparing in 1638 to emigrate to New England, but the outbreak of the Civil War may have caused him to change his plans, and we suppose he was the Capt. Gabriel Ludlow who fell at Newbery, 24 Sept. 1644. His widow Phillis and children remained in England.

The youngest son, George, came to Dorchester, Mass., removed to York, Va., and left a will dated 8 Sept. 1655, in which he made Thomas, eldest son of his dec'd bro. Gabriel Ludlow, his heir; and his nephew Jonathan, "eldest son of my brother Roger Ludlow, who lives at Dublin in Ireland", his contingent heir; with bequests to the children of Gabriel and Roger. Adm'n was granted at Canterbury, 1 Aug. 1656, to Roger Ludlow, father of Jonathan, Joseph, Roger, Anne, Mary, and Sarah Ludlow, nephews and nieces of the testator.

It may be suggested that Roger Ludlow named Windsor after his grandmother, Edith Windsor, through whom he was connected with the higher aristocracy, his not distant cousin, the sixth Baron Windsor (with whom the male line ended in 1642), having been Rear-Admiral of a British fleet in 1623.*

Mr. Ludlow came over in the *Mary and John* in 1630, being one of the first Assistants chosen for the governing of the Mass. Bay Colony. He was a founder of Dorchester, and gave good service to the Colony as Assistant, Deputy-Governor, and Justice. His ambition to be elected Governor was thwarted by his own aristo-

* Col. Charles E. Banks has a different theory of the choice of the name Windsor for the Conn. town, which we leave for him to make public in due season. It should always be remembered that the choice of a name cannot always be attributed to a single factor. When a name was proposed, it may have appealed for utterly diverse reasons to several of the prominent settlers; and the reasons stated above should have made the choice of the name Windsor agreeable to Ludlow, even if he did not select it.

cratic temper which was not in sympathy with the republican form of government. In 1635 he joined others in establishing a settlement on the Connecticut River, and despite disputes and discouragements, led a large company from Dorchester to Windsor in Apr. 1636. The founders of Conn. Colony at first operated under a commission granted by the General Court of Mass., under which Ludlow's name was foremost of the commissioners appointed to govern the settlement. Ludlow was the *de facto* Governor of the Conn. plantations until they became a separate colony, and Haynes, under the newly adopted Constitution, was in Apr. 1639 elected the first Governor, with Ludlow as Deputy-Governor. As chief of the governing Commissioners, the responsibility of the hard years from 1637 to 1639, including the Pequot War, fell largely on his shoulders, and the election of Haynes as Governor must have seemed to him a usurpation of an honor which he had rightfully earned.

Ludlow had been educated in law, having been admitted to the Inner Temple, Nov. 1612. This training made him useful to the Colony, both in the formulation of the Conn. Constitution of 1639, the first written constitution in history, and in the codification of the laws.

In 1639 the Conn. General Court granted him the privilege of making a settlement at Pequonnock, but instead he settled at Uncoway, thus becoming the principal founder of Fairfield. Here he resided until he left New England, being elected Magistrate [Assistant] of the Colony each year. In Fairfield he was the leading citizen, in charge both of judicial and military matters.

In 1653, the England of Cromwell being at war with Holland, much uneasiness was felt by the New Englanders because of the proximity of the Dutch in New Amsterdam. Fairfield being so close to the Dutch settlement, Ludlow was one of the foremost of those who wished to take immediate warlike action. Suspicions of his motives were aroused, and in disgust he decided to remove. In a semi-confidential conversation with Rev. Mr. Davenport of New Haven, Ludlow repeated some of the gossip started by others about Mrs. Staples, charging her with witchcraft, and Mr. Davenport had the poor judgment to disclose what was said, which led to the suit brought against Mr. Ludlow by the incensed husband, and a fine of £10 for slander. He sold his Fairfield holdings to Mr. Alexander Bryan of Milford, and Nathan Gold eventually acquired the Ludlow homestead.

Mr. Ludlow, probably after a farewell visit to his bro. George in Virginia, returned abroad, and in 1655 was living at Dublin, Ireland. Here, about 1656, his dau. Sarah m. Rev. Nathaniel Brewster, later of Brookhaven, L. I., and through her he left a branch of American descendants.

An able and useful man, Mr. Ludlow possessed great qualities which were somewhat marred by defects of temperament. His natural temper was proud and inclined to arrogance, and he lacked the suavity and tact to win popularity. The question of ambition is one impossible to solve, for we cannot delve into his inner motives; so far as can be judged from his actions, he may not have been more ambitious than others his equal in birth, education, and ability. His energy and capacity for leadership are shown in his being a chief founder of three towns, as well as of Conn. Colony. The thing that gives him more than local importance, and an enduring place in history, is his work in the field of jurisprudence, which was able, sound, and as liberal as could be expected for the era. His real monument is the first Constitution of Connecticut.

Luff, John.

Daniel Tharp of Norwalk and Hephzibah his wife conveyed 4 Feb. 1730/1, one-fifth of land in Stratfield which was father John Luff's. Henry Hendrick of Fairfield and Elizabeth his wife conveyed same, 25 Apr. 1729, mentioning right from brother William Luff dec'd. John Luff of Stratfield conveyed same, 2 Mar. 1730/1.

Children:

> Hephzibah, d. at Westport, 16 Mar 1752; m. by 1731, Daniel Thorp.
> Elizabeth, m. Henry Hendrick.
> John.
> Sarah, bapt. at Stratfield 11 Jan. 1712/3; m. (1) (rec. New Haven) 12 May 1725, John Elcock; m. (2) (Superior Court rec.) 9 June 1735, Peter Brown, who soon deserted her, and she divorced him 1739.
> William, d. s. p.

Lyon, Henry.

Admitted to Milford Church, 25 Feb. 1648/9; dismissed to Fairfield; where he was granted a homelot, 1652. He m. a dau. of William Bateman.

He entered for record at Fairfield, 9 Feb. 1655 [1655/6], land purchased of Richard Lyon, a house purchased of William Bateman, and land given him by the latter.

He rem. to Newark, N. J.

Lyon, Richard.

Married Margaret ———, who d. in 1705. Her Inv. taken 23 Mar. 1705, exhibited by Richard Lyon, Apr. 1705.

Will 12 Apr. 1678; son Moses, who was to pay "to my Cosen Mary fitch" £7; sons Richard, William, Samuel, Joseph; dau. Hester Perry; son-in-law Nathaniel Perry; wife Margaret (Exec'x); daus. Betty, Hannah and Abigail (all under 19). Witnesses, Nathan Gold, Mary Murwin. Inv. 17 Oct. 1678.

He conveyed to sons Richard and Moses, 1677/8; and Moses purchased from his mother Margaret, 1681.

Richard and Samuel Lyon agreed 1699 on distribution of Moses Lyon's property; the owners of the other four parts are Joshua Jennings, Samuel Smith, William Rowleson, and Esther Grumman. Samuel Lyon bought of Esther Grumman, his brother Joseph Lyon, and also from Samuel Jennings right in land which latter bought from Joshua Jennings, Samuel Smith and William Rowleson which befell by the death of their brother. [Fairfield Deeds.]

Distribution 10 Mar. 1723/4 of commonage to heirs of Richard Lyon, who left five sons, Moses (eldest, dec'd without heirs), Richard, Samuel, William dec'd, Joseph dec'd, and four daus., Hannah, Esther dec'd, Elizabeth dec'd, Abigail dec'd. The children of William are Nathaniel (dec'd, left children), William and Benjamin. Joseph had two sons, Joseph, and David (dec'd left children). Children of Esther: Joseph Perry, Esther (dec'd, wife of Daniel Burr, left children), Mary (dec'd, wife of John Downs, left children), and Samuel Grumman. Children of Elizabeth: Benjamin and Joseph Banks, also Elizabeth (dec'd, wife of Samuel Davis, left children). Abigail left dau., wife of William Odell.

Children:

+Moses.
+Richard, b. abt. 1653.
Elizabeth, m. (1) at Fairfield, 29 June 1679, Benjamin Banks; m. (2) abt. 1695, William Rowlandson.
Esther, b. abt. 1658; m. (1) Nathaniel Perry; m. (2) John Grumman.
Hannah, b. abt. 1661, d. Nov. 1743 in 83 yr. (g. s., Westport); m. Joshua Jennings, who receipted 17 Aug. 1688 to mother Lyon for his wife's portion.
+William.
+Samuel.
+Joseph.
Abigail, b. [say 1673], d. 6 Mar. 1698; m. at Fairfield, 9 Jan. 1696 [1695/6], Samuel Smith.

Lyon, Thomas.

Born abt. 1621, d. at Greenwich in 1690; m. (1) Martha Winthrop, dau. of Henry and Elizabeth (Fones) Winthrop, and granddau. of the first Gov. Winthrop. She was bapt. at Groton, co. Suffolk, Eng. 9 May 1630, and was stepdau. of Robert Feke who founded Greenwich in 1640. He m. (2) Mary Hoyt, dau. of Simon.

He purchased land in Fairfield from Thomas Shervington before 11 May 1654, and from Simon Hoyt before 12 Jan. 1658 [1658/9], and sold to Daniel Frost before 1 Nov. 1675. Settled in Greenwich.

Will of Thomas, Sr., 6 Dec. 1689; wife Mary; son John, the mill at Rye; son Thomas, homelot lying up Byram River; son Samuel; son Joseph, dwelling house; rights in Greenwich; five daus. Mary, Abigail, Elizabeth, Sarah, Deborah. Inv. at Greenwich, 7 Sept. 1690.

In May 1703, John and Mary Wilson of Rye petitioned the Conn. Leg. for the return of 300 acres in Greenwich; Samuel and Joseph Lyon, sons of Thomas dec'd, ordered to pay £50 or return land.

On 30 Oct. 1707, John Lyon of Rye, and Thomas and Samuel Lyon of Byram, sold to Joshua Jennings, the long lot, building lot, and first and second dividends of lands at Compo, laid out to our father Thomas Lyon, sometime of Fairfield. [Fairfield Deeds.]

Children [by first wife] :

Infant, d. y.

Mary, b. Aug. 1649; [either she or her mother m. before 1691, John Wilson, of Bedford and Rye].

Children [by second wife] :

Abigail, m. at Stamford, 3 Apr. 1672, John Banks.

John, of Byram Neck; m. Rebecca Hull, dau. of Cornelius of Fairfield.

+Thomas.

Elizabeth, m. John Marshall.

Deborah, m. —— Cove.

Sarah, m. —— Merritt.

Samuel, d. at Greenwich in 1713; Inv. 28 Nov. 1713; adm'n granted to Thomas Lyon. Left no issue, but eight bros. and sisters, two of the latter being also dec'd; distribution ordered to Thomas Lyon (who had also bought shares of his sisters Abigail and Mary); John Lyon; Joseph Lyon; Sarah Merritt; Deborah Cove; and children of Elizabeth Marshall dec'd.

Joseph.

Lyon, Moses, s. of Richard.

Married after Feb. 1693/4, Mary, widow of Samuel Adams, and dau. of Robert Meeker. She m. (3) John Thorp.

Inv. 2 Mar. 1697/8; the widow's dowry in Adams' estate mentioned. Samuel Lyon was to "preserve the creatures", i.e. the livestock; John Edwards to administer. Distribution; widow Mary; brothers; Joshua Jennings, William Roleson, Samuel Smith, in right of their wives, and Esther Grumman, who were sisters of the dec'd.

Lyon, Richard, s. of Richard.

Born about 1653, d. Jan. 1740 ae. 87 (Redding Church).

Mary wife of Richard, bapt. at Fairfield, 9 Feb. 1695/6.

Children, recorded at Fairfield:

XSamuel, b. 27 Dec. 1688, bapt. 5 Apr. 1696, d. in 1767; Inv. 18 Aug. 1767; m. Hannah [?Dickerson].

Sarah, b. 14 Feb. 1691, bapt. 5 Apr. 1696.

XEbenezer, b. 15 Aug. 1694, bapt. 5 Apr. 1696, d. in 1773; will 28 Jan. 1741/2, proved 6 Apr. 1773; m. 9 Jan. 1717, Ellen Fanton.

×Daniel, b. 3 Oct. 1697, bapt. 3 Oct. 1697; m. 7 Aug. 1718, Sarah
Jennings.

Hannah, b. 14 May 1701, bapt. 15 June 1701.

×Nathan, b. 28 Nov. 1703, bapt. 13 Feb. 1703/4, d. at Redding, 21 Nov.
1757 in 54 yr. (g. s.); will 25 Aug. 1757, proved Dec. 1757; m.
Abigail, widow of Robert Meeker.

Jonathan, bapt. 1 June 1708.

Lyon, William, s. of Richard.

Married Phebe ————. She m. (2) by 1701, Daniel Crofut;
(3) Samuel Jackson; (4) Zachariah Lawrence.

Will 4 Nov. 1699; wife Phebe; sons Nathaniel, William,
Moses; "if my wife should have another child by me." Inv. 23
Dec. 1700.

Samuel Jackson and Phebe Jackson, alias Phebe Lyon, formerly
wife of William Lyon dec'd, sold land 6 May 1714, given her by
former husband.

Moses Lyon of Newtown, husbandman, sold 2 Nov. 1720, to
mother Phebe Lawrence of Stratfield.

Children, bapt. at Fairfield:

×Nathaniel, bapt. 9 Sept. 1694, d. at Fairfield in 1718; Inv. 10 Sept.
1718; m. at Fairfield, 15 Apr. 1709, Hannah Jackson; she m. (2)
Matthew Jennings.

×William, bapt. 16 Feb. 1695 [1695/6], d. at Newtown in 1745; will
10 May 1745, proved 29 Aug. 1745; m. abt. 1715, Elizabeth Dickerson, dau. of Thomas, b. at Stratford, 9 June 1693.

×Moses, bapt. 8 May 1698, d. at Newtown, 20 Apr. 1745; will 12
Feb. 1744/5, proved 29 Aug. 1745; m. abt. 1720, Rachel Jackson.

×Benjamin, bapt. 8 Sept. 1700, d. at Newtown in 1746; will 2 July
1745, proved 29 May 1746; m. abt. 1725, Elizabeth Platt, dau. of
John, Jr., b. at Norwalk, 11 June 1699.

Lyon, Samuel, s. of Richard.   Sergt.

He was bapt. at Fairfield Church, 18 Mar. 1704/5, with the
four eldest children.

Married Susanna Jackson, dau. of John, b. 10 Sept. 1670.
Susanna, wife of Sergt. Samuel, bapt. at Fairfield Church, 19
Oct. 1718.

Will 17 July 1732, proved 21 Sept. 1733; wife Susan; youngest son Ephraim; four sons, John, Samuel, James, Ephraim; four daus. Margery, Abigail, Ann, Jemima.

Children, recorded at Fairfield:

×John, d. in 1735; will 13 Dec. 1734, proved 4 Feb. 1734/5; m. Hannah Kimberly, dau. of Nathaniel, b. at New Haven, 13 Apr. 1694. She m. (2) Thomas Pike.

×Samuel, d. in 1767; will 19 Feb. 1767, proved 11 Nov. 1767; Inv. 4 Dec. 1767; called "2d" and Ens.; m. at Stratfield, 8 May 1718, Mary Davis [dau. of John, by Greenfield rec.].

Margery, m. 9 Aug. 1727, John Meeker.

×James, b. 21 Mar. 1704; m. 14 Dec. 1732, Abigail Rowland, who d. 26 Mar. 1752.

Abigail, bapt. 12 May 1706, d. Sept. 1757; m. 2 Jan. 1724, Daniel Morehouse.

×Ephraim, bapt. 27 Sept. 1708, d. in 1751; will 14 May 1751, proved 2 June 1751; m. Eunice Thorp, dau. of John, b. 18 Mar. 1710. She m. (2) 12 Feb. 1755, John Fanton, and d. 2 Oct. 1762.

Ann, bapt. 6 Aug. 1710.

Jemima, bapt. 1 Apr. 1713.

Lyon, Joseph, s. of Richard.

Married Mary Jackson, dau. of Joseph. She m. (2) John Bagley.

He was bapt. at Fairfield Church, 28 July 1695, and his wife Mary renewed Covenant same date.

Inv. 11 Mar. 1697/8. Samuel Lyon gave bond to pay portions to the two sons. John Bagley, father-in-law of the children Joseph and David, to have charge of their portions in place of Samuel Lyon, 13 Nov. 1700.

David, son of Joseph, chose father-in-law John Bagley for guardian, 2 Apr. 1712. Joseph and David gave a receipt to their uncle Samuel Lyon, 2 Aug. 1718.

Children, bapt. at Fairfield:

Joseph, bapt. 28 July 1695, d. at Cohansey, N. J., by 1729; adm'n granted to Thomas Jones of Cohansey, 12 May 1729. On 10 Nov. 1718, being still of Fairfield, he made his bro. David attorney to recover lands descended from our father Joseph dec'd, or from our mother Mary dec'd, who was one of the daus. of Joseph Jackson dec'd.

×David, bapt. 27 June 1697, d. abt. 1723; will 4 June 1722, proved
7 Feb. 1723; m. Elizabeth ———, prob. niece of the wife of
Thomas Nash.

Lyon, Thomas, s. of Thomas.

Will of Thomas of Greenwich, 2 Apr. 1739; proved 1 May
1739; wife Abigail; daus. Abigail, Elizabeth, Jemima, Mary,
Deborah; sons Thomas (land in Rye), Samuel of Rye, Jonathan,
David (land in Greenwich), Joseph, Gilbert; each son to pay
their mother Abigail Lyon £2 during her life; gr. son Thomas
Lyon.

MacKenzie, Dougal.

Married at Fairfield, 18 Nov. 1696, Sarah, widow of Samuel
Wakeman. She was dau. of John Knowles.

Will 4 Jan. 1728/9, proved 10 Feb. 1728/9; £100 to Trinity
Church (Epis.); wife Sarah; daus. Abigail Thompson, Ann
Caner, Elizabeth Bostwick, Mary Mackenzy; sons-in-law Mr.
Henry Caner and David Thompson, Exec'rs.

Agreement, 19 Jan. 1732/3, of the four daus. with their husbands (including Jonathan and Mary Cutler) to divide real estate
given them by will of father and by deed of Mrs. Sarah Mackenzy
to her children.

Children, recorded at Fairfield:

Abigail, b. and bapt. 4 Aug. 1700; m. David Thompson.
John, b. 18, bapt. 19 Oct. 1701, d. 10 Oct. 1707 (g. s.).
Daniel, b. 30 Apr., bapt. 2 May 1703, d. 10 Oct. 1707 (g. s.).
Ann, b. 17, bapt. 18 Feb. 1704/5; m. (Christ Church, Stratford) 25
Aug. 1728, Rev. Henry Caner.
Elizabeth, bapt. 29 Sept. 1706; m. (Christ Church, Stratford) 3
Sept. 1726, David Bostwick.
Mary, bapt. 10 Oct. 1708, d. at New Haven, 1 Jan. 1792 ae. 83; m.
Jonathan Cutler, of Fairfield and New Haven.
Samuel, bapt. 8 Oct. 1710, d. y.

Macock, Peter. [Surname also spelled Meacock.]

He had land at Greenwich 1650, and a house in Fairfield 1653.
Mary Macock sold Fairfield property to John Applegate by

1662/3. We suppose that she was widow of Peter; and by 1664 she was the "pretended wife" of Thomas Case. There was evidently some illegality about her remarriage to Case, who was of Newtown, L. I.; and the Magistrates at Newtown were required by Gov. Nicolls, acting upon information received from the Council of Conn. Colony, to obtain security from Case to protect Mary and her children in property held under the will of her former husband. On 21 Apr. 1665, Gov. Nicolls declared Thomas Case and Mary Meacock free from the tie of wedlock.*

The surname was not common in New England, but occurs early in Southampton, L. I. Peter may have been bro. of Capt. Thomas Macock, who had a grant of land in Milford 1660 and rem. 1662 to Guilford, where he d. in 1707; m. Lettice [prob. Atred], step-dau. of Humphrey Spinning, who d. at Guilford, 5 Sept. 1715. The will of Thomas, 1 Nov. 1701, codicil 2 Feb. 1704, proved 28 May 1707; wife Lettice; kinsman Samuel Smithson of "Brafield near to Northampton in old England." No issue; Smithson came over and settled in Guilford.

Mallet, John.

Lewis Liron of Milford on 20 Mar. 1710 conveyed to Mr. John Mallet of Stratfield, land purchased of "Mr. Johanne Koartland" of New York. John conveyed, 7 Jan. 1739/40, to dau. Joanna wife of Zachariah Angevine of Stratfield, in consideration of £100 bequeathed to her by the will of her uncle Mr. Lewis Liron of Milford, etc.

Died at Stratfield, 28 Sept. 1745 in 72 yr. (g. s.); his widow Joanna d. 16 Sept. 1764 in 101 yr. (g. s.).

Will of John of Fairfield, 3 Dec. 1744, proved 8 Oct. 1745; eldest son David; son John; son Peter; dau. Joanna Anjevine, already rec'd above £300; wife Joanna.

Children, recorded at Fairfield, bapt. at Stratfield:

> David, b. 10 Jan. 1704 [1704/5], bapt. 29 Apr. 1705, d. 22 Aug. 1777 ae. 77(?) (g. s., Trumbull); m. Esther ———, who d. 16 Jan. 1787 in 76 yr. (g. s.). His will, 15 Mar. 1775, named wife Esther, sons Joseph, John, David, and dau. Esther wife of John Wheeler.
> Lewis, b. 14 Aug. 1708, bapt. 21 Nov. 1708.

---

* Library Bulletin, History No. 2, University of the State of New York, pp. 153, 166.

Joanna, b. 10 Mar 1710, bapt. 29 Oct. 1710; m. Zachariah Angevine.
Peter, b. 31 Mar. 1711; m. Mary Booth, dau. of Ebenezer, b. 22 Feb. 1716.
John, b. 16 Oct. 1712; m. Sarah French, dau. of Sergt. Samuel.*

Mallory, Peter.

He took the oath of allegiance at New Haven, 5 Aug. 1644. He and his wife, recently married, were before the Court, 6 Feb. 1648/9, and the record mentions that he was "subject to distraction, haueing sometime bine distempered that way." He bought a house, orchard and land from Nathaniel Seeley, 5 Aug. 1651. He d. in 1698 or 1699; his wife Mary d. Dec. 1690.

He prob. m. Mary Preston, dau. of William, bapt. at Chesham, co. Bucks, Eng., 13 Dec. 1629.† She was about 19 yrs. old when Peter married, and no other marriage has been found for her. Peter named his youngest son William, and some of the Mallorys followed the migrations of the Prestons to Stratford and Woodbury. John Hunter signed the oath of allegiance immediately under Peter; his will 15 May 1648 gave his small estate to Sarah wife of William Meeker [she was dau. of William Preston], to Peter Mallory, and to Mary widow of William Preston. Hunter and Mallory perhaps lived with the Preston family until the death of Hunter and marriage of Mallory.

There were eleven children,‡ of whom the second and eleventh were:

+Peter, b. 27 July 1653.
+William, b. 2 Sept. 1675.

Mallory, Peter, s. of Peter.

Born at New Haven, 27 July 1653, d. at Stratford in 1720; m. (1) 28 May 1678, Elizabeth Trowbridge, dau. of William and

---

* Will of John of Stratford, 26 June 1767, proved 2 July 1776; wife Martha; dau. Prudence Daugh; son Matthew; daus. Sarah Sears, Mehitabel Beardsley, Eunice Beardsley, Hannah Bennett, Mercy, Ruth, and Olive Mallet; sons John, Edmund, Henry.

† The present writer suggested this theory years ago to Prof. Franklin B. Dexter, who stated it as fact in his *First Church, New Haven.* Although likely, it is still unproved.

‡ For whom, see *Families of Ancient New Haven,* vol. 5, p. 1122.

Elizabeth (Lamberton), b. 5 Jan. 1661 [1661/2]; m. (2) Abigail ———.

Children [by first wife], recorded at New Haven:

Peter, b. 22 Apr. 1679, d. y.
Caleb, b. 3 Nov. 1681, d. at New Milford, 20 Aug. 1716; m. at New Haven, 13 Feb. 1706/7, Miriam Blakeslee, b. 2 May 1688, d. 23 June 1776; she m. (2) 13 Dec. 1716, Thomas Pickett.
Peter, b. 2 Aug. 1684, d. y.
Elizabeth, b. 27 Apr. 1687; m. at Stratford, 10 Dec. 1712, George Welton.
Judith, b. 2 Sept. 1689; m. (rec. Milford) 24 Jan. 1711, Jeremiah Canfield.
Benjamin, b. 3 Apr. 1692; m. (rec. Stratford) 22 Dec. 1715, Eunice Butler of Wethersfield.
Stephen, b. 12 Oct. 1694; m. Mary ———.
Ebenezer, b. 29 Nov. 1696.
Zaccheus, b. 22 May 1699; m. (rec. Stratford) 17 Apr. 1722, Sarah Rice.
Abigail, b. 5 Aug. 1701.
Achsah, b. [say 1703]; m. at Stratford, 2 Feb. 1720/1, Charles Lane.
Zipporah, b. 15 Dec. 1705; m. at Trumbull, 18 Mar. 1731, Jeremiah Johnson.
Peter, b. 1 Mar. 1708; m. Mary Beardsley, dau. of Thomas.

Mallory, William, s. of Peter.

Born at New Haven, 2 Sept. 1675; d. at Fairfield in 1738.

His wife Anna renewed Covenant at Fairfield Church, 17 Dec. 1699. She m. (2) Nathaniel Fitch, with whom she conveyed 1741 to son Ebenezer Mallory.

Will 6 June 1738, proved 5 Dec. 1738; wife Anna; children Jonathan, Mary, Rebecca, Sarah, John, Ann, William, Peter, Ebenezer.

Children, bapt. at Fairfield, except youngest at Greenfield:

✕Jonathan, bapt. 17 Dec. 1699, settled in Redding; m. (1) Abigail Hide, dau. of John, b. 20 May 1702, living 1747; m. (2) at Westport, 22 Sept. 1755, Elizabeth Bennett. She was widow of Edmund Bennett, and dau. of Stephen Pierson, b. at Derby, 12 Jan. 1699.
Mary, bapt. 22 Aug. 1703; m. at Stratfield, 24 Feb. 1727, Alexander Fairchild.
Rebecca, bapt. 24 Feb. 1705/6; m. Benjamin Williams.
Sarah, bapt. 11 July 1708.

XJohn, bapt. 3 Dec. 1710, d. at Redding in 1785; will 8 Mar. 1779, proved 29 Apr. 1785; m. 15 Apr. 1735, Elizabeth Adams.

Anna, bapt. 17 May 1713.

XWilliam, bapt. 22 Apr. 1716, d. at Danbury in 1770; adm'n granted 27 Nov. 1770; m. Eunice Gray, dau. of Jacob.

XPeter, bapt. 30 Nov. 1718, m. at Redding, 28 Feb. 1737, Joanna Hall.

XEbenezer, bapt. 14 May 1721, d. at Fairfield in 1762; m. at Redding, 6 Apr. 1744, Hannah or Johanna Knapp, dau. of Moses.

Lydia, bapt. 20 Oct. 1723, d. y.

Deborah, bapt. 22 May 1726, d. y.

Martin, William.

He m. Abigail Nichols, dau. of Caleb, b. 6 Feb. 1663/4.

Of Woodbury, d. 4 July 1715; adm'n granted to widow Abigail, who was appointed guardian to his dau. Phebe.

Children, recorded at Woodbury:

Joseph, bapt. Nov. 1691, d. 12 Apr. 1740; m. 18 Aug. 1718, Sarah Harris.

Samuel, bapt. Mar. 1693; m. 15 Jan. 1715/6, Annis Hinman, bapt. Sept. 1697, d. 13 Mar. 1750.

Caleb, b. 26 Mar. 1698, bapt. Mar. 1697/8, d. 14 Sept. 1776 ae. 79; m. (1) 26 June 1729, Elizabeth Walker; m. (2) Sarah ———.

Phebe, b. 13 Jan. 1703/4, bapt. Jan. 1703/4; m. 3 June 1730, Daniel Curtis.

Marvin, Matthew. Deputy (Norwalk) to Conn. Leg., May 1654.

Son of Edward and Margaret, bapt. at Great Bentley, co. Essex, Eng., 26 Mar. 1600. Came on the *Increase,* 1635, with wife and five children; an original settler in Hartford same year, and of Norwalk, 1651.

Married (1) by 1622, Elizabeth ———, b. abt. 1604, d. abt. 1642; m. (2) abt. 1647, Alice, widow of John Bouton.

Will 20 Dec. 1678; ae. 80 or thereabouts; wife Alice; son Matthew of Norwalk; gr. child Matthew, son of Matthew Marvin; son Samuel Smith; son John Bowton and my dau. Abigail his wife; gr. child Richard Bushnell; Francis Bushnell; four daus. Mary Adgate of Norwich, Hannah Semer, Abigail Bouton, and Rebecca Clarke of Farmington. Inv. 13 July 1680.

Will of Alice, ae. 70 or thereabouts, 1 Dec. 1680; son John Bouton; dau. Bridget Kellogg; dau. Rachel Smith; gr. child Sarah Brinsmade; gr. child Ruth Bouton; gr. child Rachel Bouton. Inv. 9 Jan. 1680/1.

Children [by first wife], first four bapt. at Great Bentley:

> Elizabeth, bapt. 15 Sept. 1622, d. at Norwich in 1708; m. before 1650, John Olmstead of Hartford and Norwich; no issue. Her will, 15 Oct. 1689, besides relatives of her husband named her kinsman "Sergt. Richard Baskett (written now Richard Bushnell)", brother Adgate's three children, Sarah, Rebecca, and Thomas, brother's eldest dau. Abigail; kinsman Samuel Lothrop, Exec'r.
> +Matthew, bapt. 8 Nov. 1626.
> Mary, bapt. 15 Dec. 1628, d. at Norwich, 29 Mar. 1713; m. (1) at Hartford, 11 Oct. 1648, Richard Bushnell; m. (2) 1659, Dea. Thomas Adgate.
> Sarah, bapt. 27 Dec. 1631, d. at Stratford abt. 1702; m. (1) at Hartford, 4 Oct. 1648, Ens. William Goodrich; m. (2) Capt. William Curtis of Stratford.
> Hannah, b. abt. Oct. 1634, d. after 1680; m. at Norwalk, 5 Jan. 1653 [1653/4], Thomas Seymour.
> Abigail, b. abt. 1637, d. abt. 1681; m. at Norwalk, 1 Jan. 1656 [1656/7], John Bouton.
> Rebecca, b. abt. 1639; m. John Clark, of Farmington.

Children [by second wife], bapt. at Hartford:

> Samuel, bapt. 6 Feb. 1647 [1647/8], d. y.
> Rachel, bapt. 30 Dec. 1649; m. Samuel Smith, of Norwalk.

Marvin, Matthew, s. of Matthew. Deputy for Norwalk, May 1694, May and Oct. 1697.

Bapt. at Great Bentley, co. Essex, 8 Nov. 1626, d. at Norwalk about 1712; m. abt. 1650, Mary ———.
Freed from training, 9 Mar. 1685/6.

Children:

> Matthew, b. abt. 1656, d. at Norwalk, 7 Oct. 1691; m. abt. 1688, Rhoda St. John, dau. of Mark, b. 12 Aug. 1666. Inv. exhibited 3 Nov. 1691 by Rhoda; one child Mary, ae. 2. Agreement 6 Nov. 1691 by Matthew Marvin, Sr., and Rhoda widow of Matthew, and her father Mark Sention.

Mary, b. abt. 1658; m. Daniel Benedict.

Mercy, b. abt. 1660, d. at Norwalk, 22 July 1711 ae. 51 (g. s.) ; m. abt. 1698, William Haynes.

Sarah, b. abt. 1662; m. 13 Jan. 1680, Thomas Betts.

Samuel, b. abt. 1664, d. soon after 1754; Lt.; m. abt. 1701/2, Hannah Platt, dau. of John, b. 15 Dec. 1674.

Elizabeth, b. 2 Dec. 1671, d. 9 Apr. 1703; m. 6 Nov. 1700, Joseph Platt.

Hannah, b. abt. 1675, d. at Huntington, L. I., abt. 1703; m. Epenetus Platt.

John, b. 2 Sept. 1678, d. at Sharon, 9 Feb. 1774; Sergt.; m. (1) 22 Mar. 1704, Mary Beers, dau. of James of Fairfield, b. abt. 1685, d. at Norwalk, 17 Apr. 1720 ae. 35 (g. s.) ; m. (2) 27 Apr. 1721, Rachel St. John, dau. of Matthias.

Mayo alias Cohoe.

John "Makew" purchased land in Fairfield from Bridget Baxter, entered for record 28 Mar. 1661.

John Mayo alias Cohoe was granted a homelot of 1½ acres by the town, 24 Nov. 1673. He sold to Nathan Gold before 19 Aug. 1675, Gold not to have possession until Mayo's death.

John Mahue alias Cohue d. 19 Jan. 1685 [1685/6].

Inv. of Est. of John Mayhew taken 21 Jan. 1685 [1685/6] by Robert Turney, Jacob Joy and Samuel Morehouse. Adm'n granted to Samuel Morehouse, Sr.

Meeker, Robert.

Prob. bro. of William Meeker of New Haven, 1646, who m. Sarah Preston, dau. of William, and had children recorded at New Haven: Benjamin, b. 17 Mar. 1649 [1649/50] ; Sarah, b. 7 Feb. 1653 [1653/4] ; Mary, b. 6 Oct. 1656; Child, b. Dec. 1663, d. 1663; John, b. 7 Sept. 1666. This family removed to Newark, N. J.

Robert m. at New Haven, 16 Sept. 1651, Susan Turberfield. She was from Barbadoes, and had been servant of Mrs. Van Goodenhousen (formerly Mrs. Nathaniel Turner) of New Haven.

Will 12 Nov. 1683, proved 10 Mar. 1684/5; sons, John, Daniel; dau. Mary and son-in-law Samuel Adams; wife Susanna.

Children:

+John.

+Daniel.

Mary, m. (1) at Fairfield, 15 July 167[—], Samuel Adams; m. (2) after Feb. 1693/4, Moses Lyon; m. (3) after Mar. 1698, John Thorp.

Meeker, John, s. of Robert.

Married Elizabeth ————, who was bapt. at Fairfield Church, 1 Mar. 1695 [1695/6].

Will 26 Jan. 1721/2, proved 6 June 1727; wife Elizabeth; daus. Sarah Sherwood, Susanna Beers, Elizabeth Gray; sons John, Robert, Nathan, Ebenezer; daus. Deborah, Abigail.

Children, bapt. at Fairfield:

Sarah, bapt. 29 Mar. 1696, d. at Westport, 17 Jan. 1749; m. 16 Mar. 1709, David Sherwood.

Susanna, bapt. 29 Mar. 1696; m. Ephraim Beers.

Elizabeth, bapt. 29 Mar. 1696, d. at Westport, 6 July 1772; m. 31 Oct. 1716, William Gray, as his second wife.

XJohn, bapt. 18 Apr. 1697; m. 9 Aug. 1727, Margery Lyon.

XRobert, bapt. 11 Sept. 1699, d. in 1727; adm'n granted to Samuel Squire and Abigail Meeker, 11 June 1727; m. Abigail ————; she m. (2) Nathan Lyon. On 3 Jan. 1727/8, Abigail Lyon, wife of Nathan, was appointed guardian to her two sons, Ephraim and Robert Meeker.

Deborah, bapt. 24 May 1702; [?m. Samuel Adams].

XNathan, bapt. 28 May 1704, d. in 1751; adm'n granted to widow Margery, 2 July 1751; m. Margery Jackson, dau. of Moses.

XEbenezer, bapt. 25 May 1707.

Abigail, bapt. 14 May 1710; m. 27 Oct. 1731, Joseph Disbrow.

Meeker, Daniel, s. of Robert.

Married Elizabeth Ogden, dau. of Richard; she d. after 1735.

He was bapt. at Fairfield Church, 17 Feb. 1694/5, and his wife Elizabeth, 7 July 1695. He d. between 23 and 26 Dec. 1716.

Adm'n on Est. of Daniel, Sr., granted 26 Dec. 1716 to widow Elizabeth and son Joseph. Samuel chose his brother Daniel for guardian, 21 Mar. 1716/7. Nuncupative will 23 Dec. 1716; wife Elizabeth; two sons Joseph and Benjamin; son Samuel; youngest sons Jonathan and Isaac; dau. Rachel Meeker; as for sons Daniel and David and dau. Hannah Meeker, he had done pretty well for them. Thomas Lyon of Newark, N. J., in right of wife Hannah, appeared Mar. 1720/1 and appealed from probate of will; Mr. John Stone of Stamford was his attorney.

Children, first five bapt. at Fairfield, July 1695:

Daniel.

✕David, b. abt. 1687, d. at Greenfield, 14 Apr. 1754 ae. 67 (g. s.); Dea.; m. (1) Sarah Hull, dau. of Cornelius, b. abt. 1690, d. by 1720; m. (2) Mary Burr, dau. of Daniel, b. abt. 1689, d. at Greenfield, 30 Aug. 1763 in 74 yr.

✕Joseph, b. ———, d. at Fairfield in 1752; will 27 Apr. 1752, proved 11 July 1752; m. Rebecca Hull, dau. of Cornelius.

Hannah, m. Thomas Lyon, of Newark, N. J.

Elizabeth, bapt. with four preceding, July 1695; no further record.

Benjamin, bapt. 9 Oct. 1698, d. in 1728, unm. Will 10 Oct. 1721, proved 5 Mar. 1727/8; mother Elizabeth Meeker; sister Rachel Meeker; brothers Joseph and Samuel, Exec'rs; brothers Jonathan and Isaac.

✕Samuel, bapt. 25 Aug. 1700, d. at Greenfield, 25 Feb. 1770; will 25 Jan. 1770, proved 27 Mar. 1770; m. (1) 1 Aug. 1722, Abigail Gregory; m. (2) Abial ———, who d. 1 May 1776.

Esther, bapt. 18 July 1703, d. y.

✕Jonathan, b. 25 May 1707, bapt. 25 May 1707, d. at Redding 1765; will 14 Mar. 1765, proved 5 May 1765; m. 18 Jan. 1731, Abigail Parruck, b. 18 Sept. 1712.

Isaac, bapt. 20 Aug. 1710, d. in Apr. 1735, s. p. Will 2 Apr. 1735, proved 10 Apr. 1735; wife; mother Elizabeth Meeker; brother Jonathan (Exec'r); brothers Joseph and Samuel; sister Rachel Hall; brothers Daniel and David and sister Hannah; Church of Christ in Fairfield west Parish. He m. Anna ———, who m. (2) 24 Oct. 1736, David Knapp. On 21 Apr. 1735, Ann Meeker, widow of Isaac, conveyed all right in his estate to Jonathan Meeker, Samuel Meeker, and Asa Hall.

Rachel, m. Asa Hall.

Merwin, Miles.

He was nephew of Mrs. Abigail (d. at Windsor, 18 May 1684), widow first of John Branke (d. 27 May 1662), and afterwards of Rev. John Warham (d. 1 Apr. 1670). Her Est. ordered distributed to Elizabeth, John, Abigail, Thomas, Samuel and Miles, children of her cousin Miles Merwin.

Tanner, of Milford, where he d. 23 Apr. 1697.

Married (1) Elizabeth ———, who was mentioned by Winthrop in 1657, with dau. Abigail ae. 5, and son Thomas. The wife of Miles joined Milford Church, June 1661, and d. 10 July 1664. Married (2) Sarah, widow of Thomas Beach, and dau. of Dea. Richard Platt; she d. 15 May 1670. Married (3) at Stamford, 30 Nov. 1670, Sarah, widow of Daniel Scofield. She d. 5 Mar. 1697/8.

Children [by first wife] :

> Elizabeth, b. abt. 1648, admitted to Milford Church, 18 Apr. 1669; m. abt. 1669, Samuel Canfield, of Norwalk.
>
> John, b. abt. 1650, d. at Milford, 15 Jan. 1727/8; m. (1) 12 Apr. 1683, Mary (Welch), widow of Israel Holbrook; m. (2) 6 Jan. 1704/5, Elizabeth (Canfield), widow of Theophilus Baldwin.
>
> Abigail, b. abt. 1652; m. Daniel Scofield, 2d, of Stamford.
>
> +Thomas, b. abt. 1654.
>
> Samuel, b. 21 Aug. 1656, d. at Milford, 12 Jan. 1705/6; m. (1) at New Haven, 13 Dec. 1682, Sarah Wooding, b. 13 Sept. 1654, d. 9 Mar. 1690/1; m. (2) Hannah ———, who m. (2) abt. 1707, Isaac Beecher, and d. in 1741.
>
> Miles, b. 14 Dec. 1658, d. at Milford, 18 Sept. 1724; m. at New Haven, 20 Sept. 1681, Hannah (Wilmot), widow of Samuel Miles, bapt. 21 May 1648.
>
> Daniel, b. 28 June 1661, bapt 30 June 1661, d. y.

Children [by second wife] :

> Martha, b. 23 Jan. 1665 [1665/6], bapt. 28 Jan. 1665/6; m. 20 Sept. 1685, James Prime.
>
> Mary, b. 23 Jan. 1665 [1665/6], bapt. 28 Jan. 1665/6; m. abt. 1690, John Hull of Derby.
>
> Hannah, b. 15 Nov. 1667, bapt. 17 Nov. 1667; m. 20 Dec. 1683, Abel Holbrook.
>
> Deborah, b. 24 Apr. 1670, bapt. 24 Apr. 1670, d. 10 Oct. 1706; m. Samuel Burwell.

Merwin, Thomas, s. of Miles.

Born at Milford about 1654, and called of Milford when he first bought land in Fairfield, 18 Dec. 1678. He was of Norwalk, 25 July 1690, when he bought land from David Reynolds of Fairfield, and was of Fairfield again, 23 Mar. 1691 [prob. 1691/2], when he bought from Robert Churcher.

Married Abigail Clapham, dau. of Peter. A marriage record

at top of a page, only partly legible, in Fairfield, contains the name Abigail Clapham and date Mar. 1678 [1678/9]. Thomas and Abigail Merwin witnessed a deed of sale of a negro boy by Elizabeth Hide, Nov. 1698.

Samuel and Thomas Marwin of Fairfield agreed, 4 Mar. 1733/4, to divide land "that formerly belonged to our grandfather Peter Clapham" late of Fairfield, dec'd.

He renewed his Covenant (as Thomas Murruin of Fairfield) at Stratford, 15 July 1694, and prob. his eldest son Samuel was then and there bapt.

This branch adopted the spelling Murwin in the early generations, though in the old records the spelling Marwin is often found.

Children, bapt at Fairfield :*

⨯Samuel, b. (no record), d. in 1777; will 23 Dec. 1767, proved 19 May 1777; m. 5 July 1722, Abigail Wheeler.

⨯Thomas, bapt. 29 Mar. 1696, d. at Greenfield, 27 Nov. 1769 in 73 yr. (g. s.) ; will 16 Oct. 1769, proved 22 Dec. 1769; m. (1) Aug. 1717, Ruth Morehouse; she was dau. of John, b. 21 Apr. 1699; m. (2) July 1742, Mary Smith, Widow.

Abigail, bapt. 27 May 1699.

Messenger, Andrew, s. of Andrew. Deputy (Norwalk), May 1691,† Oct. 1696, Oct. 1700, Oct. 1701, May 1702.

Settled in Norwalk, where he m. (1) in 1685, Rebecca (Pickett), widow of James St. John; m. (2) Rachel Hayes, dau. of Nathaniel. No issue.

Will 19 Aug. 1727, proved 9 Nov. 1730; wife Rachel; cousin Zachariah Mills, Sr., of Bedford; cousins Samuel son of Mr. John Messenger of Jamaica, L. I., and Nehemiah, second son of Mr. Daniel Messenger of Hartford; to Abigail Messenger, younger sister of said Samuel, £20; John Bartlett and Thomas Fitch, Jr., Exec'rs.

Will of Rachel, 17 Apr. 1738, proved 1 Sept. 1740; cousin Thomas Hayes; half of residue to bro. Samuel Hayes, a quarter to bro. James, and a quarter to John, Nathaniel, and Eleazer Bouton; bro. James and friend Mr. Samuel Fitch, Exec'rs.

---

* There may have been older daus.

† Erroneously called Edward.

On 1 Jan. 1717/8, Jabez Crowell of Fairfield, formerly of Boston, mariner, being dec'd, adm'n was granted to Mr. Thomas Messenger of Boston, who gave bond with Andrew Messenger of Norwalk. Jabez Crowell had m. at Boston, 5 May 1713, Sarah Messenger, by whom he had Elizabeth, b. 17 Jan. 1713/4, and Thomas, b. 18 Jan. 1714/5. This Sarah Messenger, b. 17 Apr. 1688, was dau. of Thomas, who was son of Henry of Boston. The Crowell record is important, for Andrew was prob. cousin of Thomas whose bondsman he was, and the first Andrew was therefore bro. of Henry of Boston.

Middlebrook, Joseph.

Of Concord, rem. to Fairfield with the Jones party in 1644. Grant from the town entered 28 Jan. 1649 [1649/50].

Married (1) ——— Bateman, dau. of William, whose will 1656 named his grandson Joseph Middlebrook [Jr.].

Married (2) Mary, widow of Benjamin Turney, and in 1661 paid legacies to the Turney heirs.

Married (3) Hannah, widow of James Bennett, and dau. of Thomas Wheeler. In 1673 and 1674 the children of James Bennett gave receipts to their father-in-law Joseph Middlebrook.

His dau. Phebe intending marriage, 12 June 1679, with Samuel Wilson, Joseph gave her land.

Inv. 22 Nov. 1686. Agreement 24 Mar. 1686 [1686/7] states that Joseph, Sr., left only two children, a son Joseph, and dau. Phebe wife of Samuel Wilson.

Child [by first wife]:
+Joseph.

Child [by second wife]:
Phebe, m. in 1679, Samuel Wilson.

Middlebrook, Joseph, s. of Joseph.

Born by 1650, living 1710.

Married (1) Sarah ———, with whom he conveyed, 20 Apr. 1688, to Samuel Wilson.

Married (2) Bethia ———, living 1710. She must be the wife of Joseph Middlebrook whose death "in an advanced age" is entered in Greenfield records without date, but apparently in 1746.

He granted land to his son-in-law Abraham Higgins, which he confirmed 24 Feb. 1706/7. He also conveyed lands to his sons John and Joseph.

Jonathan Middlebrook, having received from his father Joseph his whole estate, bound himself 5 Jan. 1709 [1709/10] to maintain his father and mother-in-law "whilst she Continue with him"; and to pay £5 apiece after his father's death to his brothers John and Joseph, sister Hannah Middlebrook, and mother-in-law Bethia Middlebrook.

No probate.

Children [by first wife], recorded at Fairfield:

> Sarah, b. 12 Nov. 1675, d. at Westport, 24 Mar. 1756; m. by 1694, Abraham Higgins.
>
> Hannah, b. 25 June 1677, living unm. 1710.
>
> ×John, b. 25 Oct. 1678, d. 10 Oct. 1769 in 91 yr. (g. s., Trumbull); will 27 Mar. 1755, proved 6 Mar. 1770; m. (1) by 1702, Elizabeth Bispham, dau. of Robert; m. (2) (rec. Stratford) 4 Aug. 1727, Widow Mary Porter; widow of Nathaniel Porter and dau. of John Odell, b. abt. 1693, d. 13 Aug. 1771 in 79 yr. (g. s.).
>
> ×Joseph, b. 15 Apr. 1680, d. at Greenfield, 3 Jan. 1763 ae. almost 83; m. abt. 1703, Deborah ———, b. abt. 1681, d. Oct. 1780 in 100 yr.
>
> ×Jonathan, b. (no record), d. at Fairfield in 1754; will 29 Mar. 1754, proved 4 June 1754; m. (rec. Fairfield) 31 Jan. 1712, Martha Squire, dau. of Sergt. Thomas of Woodbury.

Miller, John.

One of the first settlers in Wethersfield, and a founder of Stamford, where he d. in 1642; m. Mary ———, who m. (2) Obadiah Seeley.

Inv. of John Miller "deceased anno 1642" taken 24 Feb. 1665/6 by Richard Newman and Robert Usher. Widow and three children, John (eldest son), Jonathan and Joseph. Seeley had built a house on Miller's land, which is to be enjoyed by the widow for life, and then to belong to the children of Miller, they paying its value to the children of Seeley.

The sons settled in Bedford, N. Y.

Mills, Mr. Richard.

A very early settler in Stratford, removed abt. 1650. His meadow at Stratford was long known as Mills' Lordship, or the Lordship farm, for what reason does not appear, unless originally it was applied in a jocular sense. He prob. m. (1) a dau. of Francis Nichols. In 1654 and 1660 he was living at Stamford, where a son of his died 25 Dec. 1660. He m. (2) the widow of Vincent Simkins of Stamford, and is mentioned in New Haven Colony records as teaching school around Stamford.

SAMUEL, prob. son of Richard, bought land in Stratford from uncle Caleb Nichols, 1668; rem. to Southampton, L. I.; m. Mary ————. On 9 Mar. 1684/5, a copy of his will was presented; he lately deceased upon Long Island. Samuel Sherman, Jr., was appointed Adm'r, 3 Nov. 1685; in 1706 he was ordered to deliver the Stratford property to Richard, son and only heir of Samuel.

RICHARD, prob. another son of Richard, m. Lydia Knapp, dau. of Roger,* and lived in Greenwich.

Mills, John [s. of Richard?].

Of Milford, purchased not long before 29 July 1692 from John Grumman, house in Fairfield that had once been Robert Seeley's. The identity of this Milford man is not known, but he could not have remained there long. It was probably the same John who bought land in Stratford; on 29 Sept. 1718, John Mills of Cohansey, West Jersey, weaver, conveyed to Joseph Seeley land in Stratford which his father John Mills of Cohansey, dec'd, bought in 1693 from Isaac Bennett.

The town of Stamford granted four acres to Mr. Mills, ship carpenter, 21 June 1687. John Mills, shipwright, sold his pink, the *Blossom*, of 70 tons, built in Stamford. In 1693/4, Jonathan and John Selleck entered caveat against all the lands of John Mills, Sr. John, Mary, and John Mills sold, 18 Jan. 1695. Another deed names his sons as John, William, and Robert. "Ye antient widow mary mills" who d. 19 Nov. 1732 was prob. widow of John, Sr. This Stamford John was probably a son of Richard.

---

* Not dau. of Nicholas Knapp, as Mead's *Hist. of Greenwich* asserts; Lydia the dau. of Nicholas m. 16 Jan. 1666, Dr. Isaac Hall.

The son William d. by 1710 leaving a widow and perhaps children.

The family of the son, John, Jr., will appear in Volume II.

Minor, John, s. of Thomas. Deputy (Stratford) to Conn. Leg., Oct. 1676; Deputy (Woodbury), Nov. 1683, May and Oct. 1684, May and Oct. 1685, May and Oct. 1686, May and June 1687, May 1689, May 1692, Oct. 1695, May 1696, May 1697, Oct. 1698, May 1703, Oct. 1705, May and Dec. 1707, May and Oct. 1708, May and June 1709, May 1710. Capt., Woodbury Trainband, May 1684. Commissioner for Woodbury, 1679-87, 1689-97; Justice, 1698-1719.

Son of Thomas and Grace (Palmer) Miner, bapt. at Charlestown, Mass., 30 Aug. 1635, d. at Woodbury, 17 Sept. 1719, in 85 yr.; married at Stratford, 19 Oct. 1658, Elizabeth Booth, dau. of Richard, b. at Stratford, 10 Sept. 1641, d. at Woodbury, 24 Oct. 1732.

Will 17 Aug. 1719, proved 14 Nov. 1719; wife Elizabeth; sons John, Thomas, Joseph, Ephraim; son William Gaylord "in complement of my daughter"; daus. Elizabeth Walker, Grace Grant, Sarah Curtis, Abigail Treadwell, Johanna Gaylord. Inv. of Capt. John who *died* 16 Sept. 1719.

Children, recorded at Stratford, bapt. at Woodbury:

+John, b. 9 Sept. 1659.
+Thomas, b. 29 May 1662.
  Hannah, b. 2 Aug. 1664, d. before May 1683.
  Elizabeth, b. 16 Jan. 1667, d. at Woodbury, 19 Dec. 1749; m. Dea. Zechariah Walker.
  Grace, b. 20 Sept. 1670, bapt. 28 Sept. 1670, d. at Windsor, 16 Apr. 1753; m. 11 Apr. 1688, Samuel Grant; ancestors of Pres. Grant.
+Joseph, b. 4 Mar. 1672/3.
+Ephraim, b. 24 Oct. 1675, bapt. Oct. 1675.
  Sarah, b. 19 June 1678, bapt. June 1678; m. 2 Nov. 1699, Stephen Curtis.
  Abigail, bapt. Feb. 1680/1; m. (1) at Woodbury, 8 Feb. 1699/1700, John Treadwell of "Fairfield-Village" [Stratfield]; m. (2) (rec. New Haven) 22 Nov. 1721, Lt. Richard Miles.
  Joanna, bapt. at Woodbury, July 1683, d. at New Milford, 24 May 1741; m. 12 Feb. 1706/7, Ens. William Gaylord.

Minor, John, s. of John.

Born at Stratford, 9 Sept. 1659, d. at Woodbury, 14 Mar. 1731; m. Sarah Rose, dau. of Robert, b. Aug. 1664.

Children, recorded at Woodbury:

> Samuel, bapt. 14 Nov. 1686, d. 22 Dec. 1734.
> Elizabeth, bapt. 6 July 1690; m. 1710, Benjamin Dunning, of Newtown.
> Hannah, bapt. 29 Jan. 1692/3; m. 10 Aug. 1720, Thomas Mallory.
> John, b. 19 Dec. 1697, bapt. 27 Feb. 1697/8, d. 2 May 1761; m. 18 Nov. 1731, Mary Judson.
> Sarah, b. 7 Apr. 1709; had son Daniel, b. 13 Mar. 1730; m. 3 Mar. 1730 [1730/1], Moses Matthews.

Minor, Thomas, s. of John. Deputy (Woodbury) to Conn. Leg., May 1698.

Born at Stratford, 29 May 1662, d. at Woodbury, 15 June 1722. Married Hannah Curtis, dau. of Israel, b. abt. 1675.

Children, recorded at Woodbury:

> Josiah, bapt. 8 July 1693, d. in 1766; m. (1) 6 July 1715, Mary Hurlbut, who d. 9 Dec. 1733; m. (2) 9 Oct. 1734, Mary (Shove), widow of —— Barnum, who d. 30 Mar. 1768.
> Samuel, bapt. 11 May 1697, d. 2 Mar. 1767 ae. 71; Deacon; m. (1) Hannah ——, who d. 16 Apr. 1727; m. (2) Rachel ——, who d. 12 Sept. 1777.
> Peter, b. and bapt. 10 Dec. 1700, d. 10 June 1703.
> Thomas, bapt. 28 Feb. 1702/3, d. 6 June 1796 ae. 93; m. (1) Feda Murray, who d. 3 Oct. 1749; m. (2) at Fairfield, 4 Sept. 1751, Tabitha Treadwell, bapt. 24 Apr. 1715, d. 29 Feb. 1792 ae. 77.
> Peter, b. 1 Dec. 1705, d. 29 Aug. 1796 ae. 91; m. (1) 9 Oct. 1734, Judith Squire, b. 19 Apr. 1716, d. 11 May 1768; m. (2) ——.
> Clement, b. 22 Mar. 1710, d. 26 Sept. 1718.
> Hannah, b. 19 June 1712, d. 27 June 1712.
> Peace, b. 19 July 1713, d. 24 June 1714.
> Clement, b. 11 Dec. 1719, d. 25 Dec. 1719.
> Clement, b. abt. 1723, d. 11 Mar. 1798 ae. 75; Deacon; m. (1) June 1744, Mary Barnum, who d. 30 Aug. 1749; m. (2) ——, who d. 17 Aug. 1785; m. (3) ——, who d. 21 May 1798 ae. 70.

Minor, Joseph, s. of John. Ens., Woodbury Trainband, May 1710; Lt., May 1714; Capt. of north Woodbury Co., Oct. 1722; Col. of 13th Regt., Oct. 1739. Deputy (Woodbury) to

Conn. Leg., Nov. 1711, May 1712, May and Oct. 1713, Oct. 1714, May and Oct. 1715, Oct. 1716, May and Oct. 1717, May 1718, May 1719, May and Oct. 1720, Oct. 1721, May 1722, May 1723, Oct. 1724, Oct. 1725, May and Oct. 1726, May and Sept. 1727, May and Oct. 1728, May 1729, May and Oct. 1730, May and Oct. 1732, Feb. and May 1733, May and Oct. 1736, Oct. 1738, and May, July and Aug. 1745. Auditor of colony accounts, 1722, 1723. Judge of Probate, Woodbury District, 1728-56. Justice, 1720-56.

Born (presumably at Woodbury) 4 Mar. 1672/3, d. there 30 Oct. 1774 in 102 yr.; m. 12 July 1710, Susanna Root, b. at Fairfield, 13 May 1678, d. 26 Apr. 1738.

Children, recorded at Woodbury:

> Joseph, b. 12 Apr. 1711, d. 19 Aug. 1749; m. 22 Dec. 1741, Jane Nichols, who d. 28 Oct. 1743.
> Sarah, b. 3 Apr. 1713; m. 23 Nov. 1737, John Judson.
> Susanna,* b. 21 Nov. 1718; m. 6 Aug. 1755, Ebenezer Warner, as his second wife.
> David, b. 26 May 1721; m. (1) 6 Feb. 1746, Prudence Martin; m. (2) Elizabeth ———, who d. 17 Jan. 1788 ae. 63.

Minor, Ephraim, s. of John. Deputy (Woodbury) to Conn. Leg., May 1724, May and Oct. 1734, May 1735. Sergt., Trainband.

Born at Woodbury, 24 Oct. 1675, d. there 16 Sept. 1762 ae. 87; m. 21 Aug. 1701, Rebecca Curtis, dau. of Israel, b. abt. 1681, d. 13 Mar. 1763 ae. 96.

Children, recorded at Woodbury:

> Timothy, b. 10 Dec. 1702; m. 11 June 1729, Elizabeth Judson.
> Jehu, b. 30 June 1705, d. 15 Feb. 1790 ae. 85; Deacon; m. 18 Nov. 1731, Mary Judson, who d. 28 Sept. 1762.
> Matthew, b. 2 Sept. 1708, d. 21 Nov. 1778 ae. 70; Capt.; m. (1) 9 Oct. 1734, Sarah Preston, who d. 12 Jan. 1760; m. (2) Mary ———.
> Rebecca, b. 30 Jan. 1712; m. 30 June 1736, Elnathan Judson.
> Ephraim, b. 15 July 1715, d. 24 May 1783 ae. 68; m. 20 Nov. 1739, Mary Martin.

---

* Patience dau. of Susanna Minor, b. 15 Feb. 1742.

Mitchell, Matthew. Committee (i.e. Deputy, for Wethersfield) to Conn. Leg., May 1637; Assistant, Feb. to Apr. 1638; Magistrate for Stamford, 1643.

Born 1590 in South Ouram parish, Halifax, co. York, Eng.; m. 16 Apr. 1616, Susan Butterfield, of Ovenden. Came to Boston in the *James,* landing 17 Aug. 1635; in 1636 removed to Concord, Mass., and soon after to Springfield. He was one of the first settlers in Saybrook, where he suffered heavy property loss, from the Indians, besides having employees and a brother-in-law (Samuel Butterfield) killed. Removing to Wethersfield, he was a member of the General Court which declared war on the Pequots.

In Wethersfield, he was a large land owner and was chosen Recorder, in 1640, but the Court rejected the choice, and he withdrew with Denton and his flock to Stamford, where he d. in 1645. Was much the wealthiest settler there, his tax being about three times that of Thurstan Raynor, the next largest tax-payer. He was one of the four persons chosen at Wethersfield to regulate the Stamford settlement, and the first Selectman chosen there, Nov. 1641.

Will presented 16 June 1646; son Jonathan, £100; daus. Susanna and Hannah, £80 each; son David, £40; "my wife may by all right claim the rest." Inv. £1,700.

Children, six bapt. at South Ouram, one at Ovenden, one at North Ouram:

> Abigail, bapt. 26 Apr. 1618; d. y.?
> +David, bapt. 14 Nov. 1619.
> Sarah, bapt. 14 Oct. 1621; m. Samuel Sherman.
> Martha, bapt. 26 Oct. 1623, d. 22 Nov. 1623.
> Jonathan, bapt. 19 Dec. 1624; Harvard 1647; noted preacher, of Cambridge, Mass.; d. 9 July 1668; m. 19 Nov. 1650, Margaret (Boradel), widow of Rev. Thomas Shepard; grandfather of Chief Justice Sewall of Mass.
> Susanna, bapt. 14 Oct. 1627; m. Rev. Abraham Pierson, of Southampton, L. I., 1640, Branford 1644, and Newark, N. J., 1667. He was b. abt. 1612, d. 9 Aug. 1678.
> Matthew, bapt. 5 July 1629, d. 4 Oct. 1629.
> Hannah, bapt. 26 June 1631, d. at New Haven, 2 Apr. 1702; m. (1) Robert Coe, of Stratford; m. (2) by 1667, Nicholas Elsey, of New Haven.

Mitchell, David, s. of Matthew.

Bapt. at South Ouram, co. York, Eng., 14 Nov. 1619; d. at Stratford in Mar. 1686.

Will 11 Mar. 1685/6; wife Elizabeth (sole Exec'x); sons Matthew, John, Abraham, Daniel; daus. Martha (rec'd part of portion), Elizabeth, Susanna, Grace. Sons Matthew and John and my kinsman John Sherman and Mr. Israel Chauncey, overseers. Inv. 29 Mar. 1686.

Children:

  +Matthew.
  +John.
    Martha, m. abt. 1685, Nathaniel Baldwin, of Milford, as his second wife.
    Elizabeth.
  +Abraham.
    Susanna.
  +Daniel.
    Grace, m. at Stratford, 26 Nov. 1701, William Pixlee.

Mitchell, Matthew, s. of David.

Married Mary Thompson, dau. of John of Stratford, b. 20 July 1655, d. at Woodbury, 18 Jan. 1710/1 in 56 yr.

Settled in Woodbury; "Deacon Matthew Mitchell ye Aged" d. 11 Sept. 1736.

Children:

    Mary, bapt. Feb. 1678/9, d. y.
    Jonathan, bapt. July 1683, d. at Woodbury, 5 May 1744; agreement of heirs, 29 May 1744; m. (1) at New Haven (rec. Woodbury) 25 Jan. 1705/6, Hannah Jenners, who d. 7 Nov. 1732; m. (2) 24 Apr. 1735, Elizabeth, widow of Samuel Squire, and dau. of John Mitchell, bapt. May 1693, d. in 1761.
    Mary, bapt. July 1687; m. 22 Aug. 1711, Jonathan Judson.
    David, bapt. Oct. 1692, d. at Woodbury in 1757; will 29 June 1756, proved 3 Dec. 1757; m. 30 Oct. 1718, Sarah Galpin, dau. of Benjamin, bapt. Feb. 1697.

Mitchell, John, s. of David. Ens., Woodbury Trainband, May 1705. Deputy (Woodbury), Oct. 1709.

Married Elizabeth Knell, dau. of Nicholas of Stratford, b. 3 May 1653, d. at Woodbury, 19 Jan. 1729/30.

Settled in Woodbury; Ens. John d. 3 June 1732.

Will 1 Feb. 1723/4, proved 3 July 1732; wife Elizabeth; sons John and Knell; daus. Elizabeth Squire and Martha Hurd.

Children, bapt. at Woodbury:

David, bapt. Nov. 1679, d. y.
David, bapt. Apr. 1680/1, d. y.
Elizabeth, bapt. Nov. 1683, d. y.
Elnathan, bapt. Oct. 1686, d. y.
John, bapt. Feb. 1688/9, d. 22 Apr. 1748; Lt.; will 14 Mar. 1744/5, last codicil 8 Mar. 1747/8, proved 31 May 1748; m. (1) 17 Jan. 1716/7, Elizabeth Curtis, d. 14 May 1738; m. (2) Mary ———, who d. 4 Jan. 1745; m. (3) by Jan. 1745/6, Sarah (Harris), widow of Joseph Martin, who d. 3 Sept. 1749.
Knell, bapt. Apr. 1690/1, d. at Woodbury in 1746; will 10 July 1746, proved 8 Dec. 1746; m. Martha Terrill, b. 19 Nov. 1697, d. 1 Oct. 1730.
Elizabeth, bapt. May 1693, d. at Woodbury in 1761; will 21 Feb. 1760, proved 7 July 1761; m. (1) abt. 1714, Samuel Squire; m. (2) 24 Apr. 1735, Jonathan Mitchell.
Martha, bapt. Mar. 1696/7; m. 11 Feb. 1719/20, Abraham Hurd.

Mitchell, Abraham, s. of David.

Married Sarah Wheeler, b. 24 Feb. 1663/4, dau. of John of Woodbury, whose will 1712 named his gr. children Nathan, Hannah, and Sarah Mitchell.

Children, first bapt. at Woodbury:

Hannah, bapt. Aug. 1688.
Nathan, of Stratford 1718, when he sold land bequeathed to his "mother Sarah Wheeler by her grandfather Thomas Wheeler."
Sarah*, d. at Roxbury, 28 Mar. 1760; m. (rec. Woodbury) 11 Oct. 1721, Ebenezer Thomas.

Mitchell, Daniel, s. of David.

Married Susannah Sherman, dau. of Samuel, Jr., b. 22 July 1670.

Adm'n on Est. of Daniel of Stratford was granted to Peter Pixlee, 14 Apr. 1746.

* Benjamin, son of Sarah Mitchell, b. at Woodbury, 4 Nov. 1718.

Children, recorded at Stratford:

> Mary, b. 27 Feb. 1701, d. at Trumbull, 3 Jan. 1745 ae. 43 (g. s.); m.
> 9 Jan. 1721/2, Zechariah Curtis.
> Elizabeth, b. 9 Sept. 1703, bapt. at Stratfield, 5 Nov. 1704.

Monroe, David.

He settled in Norwalk as early as 1690. The family early
spread into the present Westport and Greenfield. The name was
most generally spelled Munrow in the early generations, and sometimes was abbreviated to Row in the records.

Of Norwalk, will 1 Mar. 1731/2, proved 20 Sept. 1733; wife
Rebecca; son Amos Monrow; dau. Elizabeth Wood and her son
David Wood; gr. son David Monrow, "son to my son Law Joseph
Monrow"; dau. Levina Morehouse; dau. Experience Norris; dau.
Martha Beers (her mother-in-law my wife); dau. Bethiah Bagley; dau. Christian Sanders; gr. dau. Mary Miller, land adjoining my son Solomon Monrow's land; gr. son David, son of my
son Solomon Monrow; sons Solomon and Amos; Joseph Platt
and Solomon Monrow, Exec'rs.

Children, recorded at Norwalk:*

> Mary, b. Feb. 1690 [1690/1]; prob. m. —— Miller.
> Elizabeth, b. Aug. 1693; m. at Ridgefield, 28 May 1715, Jonathan
> Wood, son of Jonathan and Mary.
> Martha, b. May 1696; m. John Beers, of Norwalk.
> Christian, b. Apr. 1699; m. George Saunders.
> Susanna, b. 12 Feb. 1700; prob. m. Joseph Munrow.
> Experience, b. 9 Feb. 1702; m. John Norris.
> ✕Amos, b. 9 May 1704, d. abt. 1757; m. Sarah ——.
> Solomon, b. 31 Jan. 1705 [1705/6]; purchased land at Norwalk from
> Joseph Munrow, 1727; m. Thankful Morehouse, bapt. 23 July 1710;
> and had issue, including a son David.
> Lavinia, b. 31 Jan. 1707 [1707/8]; m. 10 Mar. 1727, Jehu Morehouse.
> Bethia, b. 5 Aug. 1711; m. James Bagley.

Morehouse, Thomas. Deputy (Fairfield) to Conn. Leg., Sept. 1653.

---

* For the record of the children, and of some of the descendants to appear in
Volume II, we are largely indebted to Mr. Frederick Wood, of Springfield, Delaware
County, Pa.

He settled early in Wethersfield, where his holdings adjoined those of Thomas Sherwood, with whom he removed to Stamford in 1640/1, selling his Wethersfield property to George Wyllys. He last settled in Fairfield, where in 1653 he purchased Henry Jackson's tide mill.

Will 4 Aug. 1658; wife Isabel; "if wife is with child"; eldest dau. Hannah (rec'd portion); son Samuel (Exec'r), double portion; three other sons, Thomas, John, Jonathan; dau. Mary; "my mill and mill lot." Inv. Oct. 1658.

Children:

    Hannah, m. ———.
    +Samuel, b. abt. 1642.
    +Thomas.
    Mary, possibly m. Joseph Patchen, Sr., as his second wife.
    John, resided in 1684 in Southampton, L. I.; Ens., Fairfield County
        Troop, May 1676.
    +Jonathan.

Morehouse, Samuel, s. of Thomas.

Born about 1642, d. at Fairfield in 1687.

Married Rebecca Odell, dau. of William, whose will 1676 named his dau. Rebecca Morehouse and gr. children Samuel, Thomas, and John Morehouse. She was b. at Concord, 17 July 1642.

Will 9 Dec. 1687, proved 13 Mar. 1687/8; wife; sons Samuel, Thomas (Exec'r), John, Daniel (land in Concord field), James; daus. Rebecca, Elizabeth, Hannah, Mary, Ann, last three under 18; Lt. Sherwood and John Seeley, overseers.

Receipt of Benjamin Rumsey, 26 Apr. 1698, to Thomas Morehouse, Jr., Exec'r of will of Samuel Morehouse, for dec'd wife Hannah's portion. Receipt of Matthew Sherwood, 21 Dec. 1696, to brother-in-law Thomas Morehouse, for wife's portion in Est. of father-in-law Samuel Morehouse. Receipt of Richard Hubbell, 1 Mar. 1691/2, the same. Receipt of Ann Morehouse, 7 June 1700, to sister Mary Morehouse* for legacy from will of father Samuel. Rebecca, widow of Samuel, receipted to son Thomas. Israel Curtis receipted, 24 June 1696, to bro.-in-law Thomas Morehouse, for portion by will of father-in-law Samuel Morehouse.

---

* She was widow of the Executor, Thomas Morehouse.

Samuel Morehouse, Sr., receipted for portion from Est. of father Samuel.

Children:

+Samuel.
Rebecca, d. 2 Apr. 1692; m. 5 Nov. 1685, Richard Hubbell.
+Thomas.
Elizabeth, m. (1) Matthew Sherwood, Jr.; m. (2) 4 Mar. 1710, Rev. Charles Chauncey; m. (3) at Stratfield, 10 Apr. 1716, Lt. Richard Miles, of New Haven.
+John.
Hannah, m. Benjamin Rumsey.
Mary, m. abt. 1693, Israel Curtis.
+Daniel, b. abt. 1679.
James, d. s. p.
Ann, unm. 1700.

Morehouse, Thomas, s. of Thomas.

Married (1) ———, eldest dau. of Ralph Keeler of Norwalk, who was his wife in 1672.

Married (2) Martha Hobby, dau. of John, whose will 1707 called her Martha Morehouse. She was bapt. at Fairfield Church, 1 Nov. 1696.

Will 16 Aug. 1716, proved 7 Dec. 1725; wife Martha, mentioning Est. from her father John Hobby of Greenwich dec'd; son Lemuel; all my children by my former wife, they have rec'd their share.

Children [by first wife] :*

+Thomas.
+Nathan.
Mary, m. (1) (rec. Stratford) 12 May 1696, John Peat; m. (2) at Stratfield, 4 Dec. 1712, John Corbet; m. (3) (rec. Stratford) 5 Sept. 1723, Benjamin Peat.
+Gideon, b. abt. 1682.

Child [by second wife]:

+Lemuel, bapt. 1 Nov. 1696.

---

* Probably there were more daus. Mary is placed hypothetically as dau. of Thomas.

Morehouse, Jonathan, s. of Thomas.

Married (1) Mary Wilson, dau. of Edward, who was his wife 1684.

Married (2) at Fairfield, 16 Apr. 1690, Rebecca Knowles. She m. (2) by 1707, John Cressey of Stamford, and d. 21 Aug. 1727. Before 4 Oct. 1672, he purchased from Joseph Patchen, Sr., his house on Wolf Pit Plain "which sometimes pertayned" to Thomas Morehouse; by 23 Mar. 1676, purchased from his bro. Samuel Morehouse; and by 22 Mar. 1681, purchased from Joseph Patchen, Sr., all his interest within the bounds of Fairfield. On 9 Nov. 1684, he bought from his bro. John Morehouse of Southampton. He was Adm'r of the Est. of Joseph Patchen, Jr., 1689.

On 20 Sept. 1716, David Morehouse of Elizabeth, N. J., for himself and as attorney for brethren Jonathan and John and sisters Mary and Tryal Morehouse, all children of Jonathan Morehouse dec'd who m. Rebecca dau. of John Knowles (mentioning her present husband John Cressey of Stamford); also Joshua Morehouse, David Webster in right of wife Mercy, Jonathan Sturdivant of Norwalk in right of wife Deborah, and Hannah Morehouse of Stratfield, daus. of said Jonathan dec'd; conveyed to Mrs. Abigail Couch.

Children [by first wife], two recorded at Fairfield:

+Jonathan, b. 1 Jan. 1677 [1677/8].
Martha, b. 2 Nov. 1679; d. s. p.?
David, settled in Elizabeth, N. J.
Deborah, m. John Sturdivant.
Mercy, m. (rec. Stamford) 1 Dec. 1709, David Webster; and in 1711 they, of Stamford, conveyed to Simon Couch one-fifteenth of the John Knowles lot.*

Children [by second wife], four bapt. at Fairfield:

John, bapt. 7 Oct. 1694.
Hannah, bapt. 7 Oct. 1694; m. at Stratfield, 11 Dec. 1716, Henry Lacy. They, of Newark, N. J., conveyed 1730 land deeded to her by her mother and father-in-law John Cressey and Rebecca his wife, one of the children of John Knowles.
Joshua, bapt. 8 Mar. 1695 [1695/6]; res. Elizabeth, N. J., 1720, settled soon after in Stamford; m. Ann ———.
Mary.
Elizabeth, bapt. 9 May 1702; m. by 1722, John Ambler, of Stamford.
Tryal.

---

* Perhaps she was by the second wife.

Morehouse, Samuel, s. of Samuel.

He settled in Stratfield, and d. late in 1732.

Adm'n granted to Noah Morehouse, 5 Dec. 1732. Inv. 1 Jan. 1732/3.

John Man and Hannah his wife of Stratfield agreed with three brothers Noah Morehouse, Isaac Jennings, and Daniel Morehouse, to quitclaim right to Est. of father Samuel Morehouse of Fairfield dec'd [Fairfield Deeds].

Children, younger ones bapt. at Stratfield:

XNoah, b. [say 1688], d. Feb. 1750; will 7 Feb. 1749/50, proved 28 Feb. 1749/50; m. at Stratfield, 6 Oct. 1708, Martha [Summers, dau. of Henry].

XSamuel, b. [say 1690], d. at Stratfield in 1727; will 3 Nov. 1725, proved 5 Dec. 1727; m. Mary ———; she m. (2) Daniel Comstock, Sr.

Mary, bapt. 14 Mar. 1697, d. y.

Elizabeth, bapt. 1 Feb. 1702, d. y.

Hannah (twin), bapt. 1 Feb. 1702, d. at Stratfield, 20 Sept. 1777; m. (rec. Stratford) 28 Apr. 1726, John Man.

XDaniel, b. by 1705, d. in 1759. Adm'n granted to son Daniel, 1 Mar. 1759; m. at Fairfield, 2 Jan. 1724, Abigail Lyon, bapt. 12 May 1706, d. Sept. 1757.

Abigail, bapt. 21 Mar. 1708; m. abt. 1728, Isaac Jennings.

Morehouse, Thomas, s. of Samuel.

Married at Boston, Mass., 3 Apr. 1690, Mary Hill, dau. of Eliphalet and Ann, b. at Boston, 1 Apr. 1670; she m. (2) in 1700, Joseph Sturges, and d. 9 July 1746 in 77 yr. (g. s., Fairfield).

Inv. 12 Mar. 1706. Mary Sturges, who was his widow, to have dower, 1 Mar. 1708; distribution to children ordered. John Morehouse appointed guardian 1708 for Thomas and Mary; Sergt. Matthew Sherwood for John and Rebecca. Distribution 14 Feb. 1719/20; sons Thomas and John; receipts from the daus.

Thomas Morehouse, eldest son, John Morehouse, and Joseph Booth in right of wife Rebecca, children of Thomas Morehouse, acknowledged receipt, 7 Feb. 1722/3, of the dower of their mother Mrs. Mary Sturgis. The next day, Joseph Sturges and Mary his wife conveyed to Joseph Booth of Stratfield land formerly belonging to the Est. of Thomas Morehouse, former husband of Mary.

Children, births recorded 1704 at Fairfield, all but first bapt. at Fairfield:

> Catherine, b. 22 June 1691, bapt. at Boston, 7 Aug. 1698; m. Samuel Allen; res. Westerly, R. I., 1717; Lebanon, 1735. They, of Westerly, conveyed 15 July 1717 to bro. Thomas Morehouse of Westerly.
>
> Rebecca, b. 26 Apr. 1693, bapt. 5 June 1698; m. Joseph Booth of Stratfield.
>
> Thomas, b. 18 Nov. 1695, bapt. 5 June 1698; res. Westerly, R. I., 1717; Stonington, 1724; Saybrook, 1725. He, of Westerly, conveyed 8 Nov. 1718 to John Morehouse of Fairfield.
>
> Mary, b. 30 June 1696, bapt. 5 June 1698; m. David Tillison, of Lyme. They, of Lyme, conveyed 6 Sept. 1717 to bro. Thomas Morehouse of Westerly.
>
> John, b. 20 Sept. 1698, bapt. 25 Sept. 1698, d. at Stratfield in 1724; Inv. 10 Nov. 1724; m. Eunice ———; no issue. She m. (2) Samuel St. John of Norwalk, with whom she conveyed land in Fairfield, 1729, making reservation of the life interest of Mary widow of Joseph Sturges. His will, 8 Jan. 1723/4, proved 3 Mar. 1723/4, named his bro. and three sisters, but was not accepted by Court [Pro. Files].

Morehouse, John, s. of Samuel.

Married Ruth Barlow, dau. of John, 2d.

Will 28 Mar. 1727, proved 31 May 1727; wife Ruth; son Stephen of Chestnut Ridge; sons Gershom, Abijah, John, Ephraim, James; daus. Ruth Marwin, Ann Morehouse. Thomas Marwin, Jr., receipted 7 Dec. 1727 to Stephen and Gershom Morehouse, the Exec'rs, for legacy of wife Ruth and for that of Ann Morehouse the youngest dau., and for part of the portion of James, one of the sons. Receipt 7 Dec. 1727 of Ruth Morehouse for dower, and portion of son John.

John renewed his Covenant at Fairfield Church, 21 May 1704, the eldest three children being bapt. the same date.

Children, recorded at Fairfield:

> Ruth, b. 21 Apr. 1699; m. Aug. 1717, Thomas Merwin.
>
> ×Stephen, b. 12 July 1701, d. at Redding, 22 May 1767 in 66 yr. (g. s.); will 7 Mar. 1767, proved 10 June 1767; m. (1) 1 Mar. 1722, Abigail Treadwell, bapt. 11 Oct. 1702, d. 6 Sept. 1759 in 56 yr. (g. s.); m. (2) Ann, widow of George Halloway of Cornwall, and dau. of John and Mary (Wolcott) Eliot of Windsor, b. 12 Feb. 1710; she m. (3) at Redding, 29 Nov. 1767, Dea. Joseph Banks.

✕Gershom, b. 18 Nov. 1703, d. at Redding, 11 June 1768 ae. 64; m. 22 Apr. 1725, Sarah Hill, dau. of John, bapt. 25 May 1701.

Elizabeth, b. 24 Mar. 1706, bapt. 31 Mar. 1706, d. y.

Elizabeth, bapt. 16 May 1708, d. y.

James, b. 21 Mar. 1710, bapt. 19(?) Mar. 1709/10, d. y.

✕Abijah, bapt. 27 Apr. 1712, d. in 1753; will 30 Aug. 1753, proved 2 Oct. 1753; m. abt. 1737, Mary [prob. dau. of Henry Summers, Jr.], b. abt. 1718, d. at Greenfield, 18 May 1776 in 58 yr. She m. (2) 14 Dec. 1756, Robert Silliman, and (3) 11 Oct. 1768, Lt. John Bradley.

✕John, bapt. 19 Sept. 1714, d. 1785; will 25 Dec. 1780, proved 1 Aug. 1785; m. Mary Stewart, dau. of James of Norwalk.

✕Ephraim, bapt. 28 Aug. 1716, d. in 1760; will 21 Sept. 1759, proved 20 Feb. 1760; m. Eunice Wheeler, dau. of David, b. 24 Dec. 1717, d. 9 Apr. 1785; she m. (2) John Nichols.

Ann, b. 14 Sept. 1718, bapt. 2 Nov. 1718, d. 5 Nov. 1755; m. 7 Apr. 1736, James Morgan.

✕James, bapt. 11 Nov. 1722, d. after 1753; m. Hannah Bulkley, dau. of Peter, bapt. 16 Oct. 1726, d. 23 July 1818 ae. 91 (g. s., Fairfield); she m. (2) 9 Jan. 1766, Ebenezer Burr.

Morehouse, Daniel, s. of Samuel. Ens., first company, Fairfield, May 1721.

Born about 1679, d. at Fairfield, 24 May 1739 in 61 yr. (g. s.); m. Hannah Adams, dau. of Lt. Abraham.

Aged 19, he testified Mar. 1698 to the nuncupative will of Sarah Merwin of Milford.

He was called Sergt. at baptism of children, 1712 and 1714.

Will of Ens. Daniel, 8 May 1738, proved 23 Jan. 1738/9; wife Hannah; daus. Katherine Tayler, Rebecca Wakeman; son-in-law Stephen Wakeman; gr. dau. Hannah Hill, my silver tankard; gr. son Daniel Hill; residue to son Abraham.

Children, bapt. at Fairfield:

✕Abraham, bapt. 22 Dec. 1700, d. 3 May 1761 in 61 yr. (g. s., Fairfield); m. 12 Apr. 1722, Elizabeth Patterson, b. at Stratford, 28 Jan. 1700 [1700/1].

Sarah, bapt. 10 Jan. 1702/3, d. y.

Hannah, bapt. 24 Sept. 1704, d. 10 Aug. 1729; m. 28 Apr. 1725, William Hill of Redding.

Daniel, bapt. 29 Dec. 1706, d. y.

Samuel, bapt. 29 May 1709, d. y.

Rebecca, bapt. 24 Feb. 1711/2, d. in 1761; m. 28 Apr. 1727, Stephen Wakeman.

Catherine, bapt. 29 Aug. 1714; m. Thomas Taylor.

Morehouse, Thomas, s. of Thomas, 2d.

Died at Westport, 6 Sept. 1748. Widow Mary d. at Westport, 20 Dec. 1758.

In 1721 he bought property east of the Saugatuck River, in Green's Farms parish (Westport), and in 1732 purchased fifty acres in Wilton parish, Norwalk, where he settled. Will of Thomas of Norwalk, 13 Feb. 1747/8, proved 4 Oct. 1748; wife Mary; sons Jehu, Thomas; daus. Mary Bedient, Sarah Mills; Thankful Monrow, Hannah Sherwood, Elizabeth Raymond; son Elisha. Will of Mary of Norwalk, 18 May 1756, proved 11 Feb. 1761; daus. Bedient, Mills, and Raymond; grand daus., daus. of John Sherwood dec'd, daus. of Solomon Monroe, and daus. of son Thomas; children of son Elisha; gr. dau. Molly.

In 1734 Thomas conveyed to his son Stephen the easterly half of his farm in Wilton, reserving life use for himself and wife.

Children, bapt. at Fairfield:

×Jehu, bapt. 5 Jan. 1700/1, d. at Westport, May 1778; m. 10 Mar. 1727, Lavinia Munroe; dau. of David of Norwalk, b. 31 Jan. 1707/8.

Mary, bapt. 16 May 1702; m. 28 May 1723, John Bedient.

Sarah, bapt. 6 Feb. 1703/4; m. —— Mills.

Jethro, bapt. 3 Feb. 1705/6, d. s. p.

Thomas, bapt. 16 May 1708.

Thankful, bapt. 23 July 1710; m. Solomon Munroe.

×Stephen, bapt. 10 Aug. 1712, d. at Wilton, 21 Sept. 1738; m. at Wilton, Nov. 1733, Sarah St: John; she m. (2) 13 May 1740, Ebenezer Hurlbut.

Hannah, bapt. 4 Sept. 1715; m. John Sherwood.

Elisha, m. ——.

Elizabeth, m. —— Raymond.

Morehouse, Nathan, s. of Thomas, 2d. Ens., company at Greens Farms, Oct. 1727.

Married abt. 1701, Mary Lockwood, dau. of Daniel.

Ens. Nathan d. at Westport, 31 Oct. 1753. Mary Morehouse, widow, of Norwalk, d. at Westport, 23 Jan. 1761.

Will 9 Oct. 1753, proved 29 Nov. 1753; wife Mary; three sons, Nathan, Jabez, Thaddeus; heirs of son David dec'd; dau. Mary

Whitlock; dau. Sarah Hayes; gr. dau. Mary Hilton; dau.
Abigail Dixon; son Jabez and Nathaniel Hubbard, Exec'rs.

Children:

    ✕David, d. in 1733; adm'n granted to Nathan Morehouse, 10 Aug.
        1733; m. ———.

    Mary, m. (1) ——— Hilton; m. (2) 4 May 1746, Daniel Whitlock.

    Sarah, b. abt. 1707, bur. 5 Aug. 1793 ae. 86 (Trinity Church rec.);
        m. (1) ——— Hayes; m. (2) 3 Oct. 1755, James Davis.

    ✕Nathan, d. in 1784; will 25 Feb. 1784, proved 3 May 1784; m. 4
        Mar. 1740, Elizabeth Ogden, dau. of Joseph.

    ✕Jabez, m. 18 Sept. 1738, Sarah Ogden, dau. of Joseph.

    ✕Thaddeus, d. at Wilton in 1785; will 22 Feb. 1783, proved 20 June
        1785; m. (1) 2 Apr. 1746, Martha Williams; m. (2) 24 Oct.
        1773, Abigail (Hickock), widow of William Bennett, who d. 30
        Dec. 1800 in 83 yr. (g. s., Westport).

    Abigail, m. ——— Dixon.

Morehouse, Gideon, s. of Thomas, 2d.

Born about 1682, d. at Westport, 12 May 1753 ae. abt. 71
(g. s.); m. Mary Grumman, dau. of Samuel, b. abt. 1690, d. at
Redding, 13 Sept. 1780 ae. 90 (g. s.).

Will 23 Mar. 1753, proved 7 Aug. 1753; wife Mary; sons
Samuel, Gideon, Zaccheus, John; dau. Abigail wife of John
Lockwood. Distribution made 1754 (not recorded until 20 Feb.
1760) made to same except heirs of the son John dec'd.

Children:

    ✕Samuel, b. 10 Oct. 1710, d. 17 Jan. 1776 ae. 65 yrs. 3 mos. 14 days
        (g. s., Westport); Lt.; m. 20 Aug. 1743, Abigail Frost, dau. of
        Isaac.

    Abigail, m. 8 Feb. 1731, John Lockwood.

    ✕Gideon, b. abt. 1718, d. at Westport, 29 Jan. 1771 (g. s.); Deacon;
        m. (1) 3 Feb. 1742, Sarah Godfrey, dau. of Christopher, who d.
        12 June 1756 ae. 38 yrs. 3 mos. (g. s., Westport); m. (2) 13 Sept.
        1756, Eunice Sturges, dau. of Eleazer, b. 16 Aug. 1731, d. 6 Mar.
        1819 ae. 89.

    ✕Zaccheus, b. abt. 1722, d. at Redding, 4 Oct. 1780 in 59 yr. (g. s.);
        m. 24 Dec. 1744, Abigail Sturges, dau. of John.

    ✕John, b. abt. 1727, d. 13 June 1753; adm'n granted to widow Mary,
        9 Aug. 1753; m. 16 May 1745, Mary Jessup, dau. of Edward, b.

28 Sept. 1729, d. 29 Mar. 1815 ae. 85 (g. s.); she m. (2) 30 July 1754, Gershom Sturges; and (3) 7 Feb. 1765, Samuel Taylor of Norwalk.

Morehouse, Lemuel, s. of Thomas, 2d.

Bapt. at Fairfield, 1 Nov. 1696; m. Mary Bouton, dau. of John. Settled in Ridgefield, where he d. in 1768. Will 7 Apr. 1768, proved 3 May 1768; three sons, Lemuel, James, John; two daus. Rebecca, Hannah. Distribution agreement, 7 June 1768; eldest son Lemuel; son James; youngest son John; dau. Rebecca wife of Comfort Stevens of Danbury; youngest dau. Hannah wife of Aaron Osborn of Ridgefield.

Children, recorded at Ridgefield:

> Gabriel, b. 14 Sept. 1718, d. in 1748; adm'n granted, 5 Dec. 1748, to widow Rebecca. She was appointed guardian to the children, Adonijah, Daniel, Joshua, and Martha, with Caleb Lobdell as surety on her bond. Daniel chose David Lobdell for guardian, 6 Mar. 1758, and Joshua chose Benjamin Bennett. The widow Rebecca was wife of Timothy Wood in 1762.
> Nathan, b. 12 Jan. 1720.
> Mary, b. 4 Sept. 1722.
> Rachel, b. 11 Feb. 1727; m. 9 Mar. 1747/8, Thomas Northrup.
> Lemuel, b. 20 Dec. 1728; Ens., Ridgefield 2d. Co., May 1767; Lt., Oct. 1769; Capt., May 1771; Deputy for Ridgefield, May and July 1775; m. 6 June 1750, Rachel Osborn.
> Thomas, b. 12 Nov. 1730.
> Rebecca, b. 9 July 1732; m. Comfort Stevens, of Danbury.
> James, b. 30 Sept. 1734.
> Hannah, b. 20 Mar. 1737; m. Aaron Osborn, of Ridgefield.
> John, b. 10 June 1739; m. 14 Mar. 17—, Deborah Brush.

Morehouse, Jonathan, s. of Jonathan.

Born at Fairfield, 1 Jan. 1677/8.
Married at Stratfield, 8 Aug. 1706, Rebecca Hull, dau. of Samuel.

Children, recorded and bapt. at Stratfield:

> ×Jonathan, b. 9 Mar. 1708, bapt. 14 Mar. 1708, m. by 1730.
> Rebecca, b. 2 Feb. 1710, bapt. 5 Feb. 1710.
> Martha, b. 26 Jan. 1712, bapt. 7 Sept. 1712, perhaps m. (1) John Bulkley and (2) 1 Nov. 1752, Gershom Whitehead.

Jabez, b. June [1714], bapt. 6 June 1714; res. Redding 1739, Ridge-
field 1743; m. at Ridgefield, 9 Nov. 1738, Mary ———.*
David, b. 16 Dec. 1716.
Joshua, b. 5 Apr. 1719, bapt. abt. Apr. 1719.

Morehouse, Mary.

Of Fairfield, had child recorded at Stratford:

Benoni, b. 9 Jan. 1709/10, and bapt. by Rev. Mr. Cutler. The will
of Dea. Edmund Lewis of Stratford, 1757, gave to Benoni Morehouse the interest of £16 for support in his old age, and the
principal if needed, provided that "he will live with one of my sons
and be governed by him."

Munn, Daniel.

Of Milford, nuncupative will sworn to 13 June 1666 by Robert
Denison and Mrs. Sarah Whitman. He gave all Est. to Mary
Riggs, only she to carry it kindly to "any of my brethren" if they
come as strangers [from England]. Adm'n granted to Mary
Riggs.

Munn, Samuel.

Prob. younger bro. of Daniel, and came over after his death.

He m. Mary ———; she m. (2) John Bartlett, and d. at
Woodbury, 10 Feb. 1713/4.

Inv. of Samuel of Woodbury, 30 Oct. 1690; widow and
children.

On 14 July 1713, his children, all having arrived at lawful age,
made agreement; Mary Bartlett, the widow; the two sons, Daniel
and Samuel; the three daus., Jane wife of Joseph Hurd, Mary
wife of Ebenezer Bronson, and Amy wife of Joseph Allis.
[Woodbury Deeds.]

---

* His will, 13 Sept. 1753, proved 1 Dec. 1753; wife Mary; eldest son Jabez;
eldest dau. Mary; dau. Rebecca; wife pregnant; two youngest sons, Josiah, Jonathan; children all under age; wife, Stephen Smith and Jacob Smith of Ridgefield,
Exec'rs. Widow Mary of Ridgefield was appointed guardian, 17 Dec. 1754, to Jabez,
Josiah, Mary, Jonathan, Rebecca, and Benjamin, and gave bond with Nathan Wilson.

Children, bapt. at Woodbury:

> Jane, bapt. Oct. 1680, d. 27 Jan. 1760; m. Joseph Hurd.
> Amy, bapt. Oct. 1680; m. Joseph Allis.
> Mary, bapt. Nov. 1681; m. 13 Aug. 1702, Ebenezer Bronson.
> Daniel, bapt. Feb. 1684, d. 11 June 1761; Dr.; will 27 Feb. 1761, proved 6 July 1761; m. (1) Anna Wheeler, dau. of Thomas of Milford; m. (2) Elizabeth ———.
> Samuel, bapt. Apr. 1687; m. abt. 1708, Abigail Stiles, bapt. Apr. 1689.

NASH FAMILY (STRATFORD-NORWALK)

Nash, Edward.

Of Stratford, rem. to Norwalk by 1654.

Married (2) after 1658 Rose (Sherwood) (Rumble) Barlow, dau. of Thomas Sherwood, 1st, of Fairfield, widow of Thomas Rumble and Thomas Barlow.

Freed from training, 9 Mar. 1685/6. In 1668 Winthrop mentioned the wife (ae. 40) of Nash the tanner at Norwalk.

Inv. of Edward of Norwalk, 2 Aug. 1699. John Nash made oath to it, 7 Nov. 1699. Deliverance Wakelee appeared and agreed to accept £30 (in addition to what he hath had from his father-in-law Edward Nash) as in full of his wife's portion; the rest distributed to the son John.

Children [by first wife], recorded at Stratford:

> Anna, b. 18 Jan. 1651 [1651/2]; "Hannah" m. at Stratford, 3 Dec. 1678, Deliverance Wakelee.
> +John, b. (no record).

Nash, John, s. of Edward.

Married (rec. Norwalk) 1 May 1684, Mary Barley [Barlow], dau. of Thomas of Fairfield. She d. 2 Sept. 1711.

John of Norwalk, renewed Covenant at Fairfield Church, 23 June 1695, and his two sons were bapt. same date.

Inv. 14 Mar. 1712/3; sons John and Nathan made oath.

Children, recorded at Norwalk:

> John, b. 25 Dec. 1688; m. (rec. Norwalk) 19 May 1709, Abigail Blakeslee, dau. of Ebenezer of New Haven.
> Nathan, b. 26 Jan. 1692/3, d. at Norwalk in 1753; m. Mary ———.

Will 9 Jan. 1753, proved 6 Mar. 1753; wife Mary; cousin Mary Reed, dau. of my bro. John Nash, £300; heirs of Samuel Nash dec'd, £50 equally; cousin Abigail Nash, £50; Minister of Church of England, £200; sons of my bro. John Nash,—Edward, John, Nathan, Abraham, Micajah, and Ebenezer,—residue equally.

NASH FAMILY (BRANFORD-FAIRFIELD)

Nash, John.

Blacksmith, of Branford; his parentage is a problem. Thomas Nash, blacksmith, of New Haven, had three sons, John, Joseph, and Timothy. Of these, the families of Maj. John of New Haven and of Timothy of Hadley are well established by records. Corp. Joseph, by first wife Mary, had a son John, b. at New Haven, 12 July 1650; he rem. to Hartford, m. (2) Margaret, widow of Arthur Smith, by whom he had an only dau., and his will, 1678, gives his estate to his wife and dau., specifying that if his dau. die without issue, his eldest bro. Capt. John of New Haven should inherit his lands. These are singular provisions for a man to make if he had a son living; yet the excellent *Nash Genealogy* advances strong reasons for accepting John of Branford as the son of Joseph born in 1650, supposing him to have received his full portion during his father's lifetime. A son usually received his portion in realty, and no records have been found to show that John ever received anything from Joseph. In view of the terms of Joseph's will, we prefer to leave John's connection unsolved until stronger evidence is adduced.

He m. at Branford, 22 Aug. 1677, Elizabeth (Hitchcock), widow of Anthony Howd; and d. in 1683.

Children, recorded Branford:
> Joseph, b. 1 Aug. 1678, d. at Fairfield in 1702, unm. Inv. 2 Apr. 1702; adm'n granted to Thomas Nash.
> +Thomas, b. 28 Jan. 1679 [1679/80].
> Elizabeth, b. 15 Aug. 1681; m. Stephen Foote.

Nash, Thomas, s. of John. Lt., company in west parish, Fairfield, May 1715; Capt., Greens Farms Co., Oct. 1727.

Born at Branford, 28 Jan. 1679/80; Capt. Thomas d. at Westport, 8 June 1748 in 69 yr. (g. s.). Sarah, widow of Capt.

Thomas, d. 20 Feb. 1760 in 83 yr. (g. s.). He was called deacon in Green's Farms records.

Blacksmith; received a grant from town of Fairfield, 18 Nov. 1701.

He relinquished to the town of Fairfield, 15 Mar. 1710/1, land laid out to Thomas Lyon, also part of building lot laid out to "Sarah Wils" dec'd.

The will 1722 of David[3] Lyon (b. 1697, son of Joseph[2], Richard[1]), named Thomas Nash as his uncle. How this relationship came about, we can hazard no guess unless Nash's wife Sarah was aunt of Lyon's wife Elizabeth. The possibility has suggested itself that Nash's wife was Sarah Whelpley, b. 30 June 1676, dau. of Joseph and Rebecca (Bulkley) Whelpley, and gr. dau. of the Sarah (Jones) (Bulkley) Wilson part of whose building lot came into possession of Nash, as her age was right and her history unknown after 1698; but evidence is inconclusive, and the suggestion is not made with undue confidence.

On 3 Nov. 1732, he conveyed to son-in-law John Griffin, as part of portion of my dau. Sarah, his wife, land in Redding.

Thomas and Jonathan Nash, 11 Dec. 1749, divided right in commonage from father Thomas Nash dec'd. Will 16 June 1741; wife Sarah; dau. Sarah Griffin; two gr. children Daniel and John Burr; sons Thomas and Jonathan; negro servants Prince and Ham. Distribution of Est. of Capt. Thomas, 3 Mar. 1760; only surviving son Thomas; heirs of Jonathan Nash; Sarah wife of John Griffin, the lot at Redding; gr. child Daniel Burr.

Children, bapt. at Fairfield, births from Bible records:

Joseph, bapt. with next two children, 4 Jan. 1712/3, d. young.

XThomas, b. 3 Aug. 1708, d. at Westport, 2 Aug. 1769 ae. 61 yrs. less 12 days (g. s., correct allowing for calendar change); Capt. and Deacon; m. (rec. Fairfield) 28 Sept. 1731, Rebecca Hull; not called "of Fairfield" as Mrs. Schenck too hastily asserts; but was dau. of Ebenezer Hull of Wallingford; she d. 22 Apr. 1791 in 84 yr. (g. s.).

Sarah, b. 20 Mar. 1712; m. abt. 1732, John Griffin of Redding.

XJonathan, b. 17 Oct. 1714, bapt. 4 Sept. 1715, d. at Westport, 9 Oct. 1757; adm'n granted, 8 Nov. 1757; m. 14 Mar. 1754, Sarah Andrews; dau. of John, b. 6 Aug. 1731. She m. (2) 24 Jan. 1764, Nathan Godfrey.

Elizabeth, b. 3 Mar. 1717, d. 29 Mar. 1740; m. 14 Oct. 1735, John Burr.

Nettleton, Samuel.

From Wethersfield to Branford, 1644, with the original settlers; also bought land at Fairfield. His wife Mary* d. at Branford, 29 Oct. 1658.

Died at Branford and not long after his wife died; Inv. recorded at Branford, £77; the land at Fairfield appraised by Henry Jackson, Francis Hall, Henry Whelpley; house and land at Branford. John Ufford received Est., and gave bond to pay the children on demand. Schedule of amounts due to the heirs, John Nettleton (double share), John Ufford, Mary, Esbell, Sarah and Betty Nettleton, and Samuel Nettleton. Mary Nettleton receipted 13 May 1659 to brother Ufford; Thomas Smith receipted for wife's portion, 8 Dec. 1659, to brother John Ufford. On 26 Oct. 1658, Thomas Smith of Milford on behalf of John Nettleton son of Samuel of Branford, leased the Fairfield land to Richard Williams. Action on this estate is found both at Branford and at Fairfield.

Children:

Hannah, m. at Branford, 10 July 1656, Thomas Smith.
Martha, m. at Milford, abt. July 1657, John Ufford.
Mary.
Isabel, m. (rec. Guilford) 19 Mar. 1659, George Chatfield.
John, d. at Killingworth, 18 Mar. 1690/1; m. at Killingworth, 29 May 1670, Martha Hull.
Sarah, m. (rec. Middletown) 6 June 1666, Thomas Miller.
Betty [name erroneously rendered Lettice in previous accounts].
Samuel, m. at Milford, 8 Feb. 1681 [1681/2], Martha Baldwin.

Newton, Thomas. Deputy (Fairfield) to Conn. Leg., Apr. 1645.

Married (1) Dorothy ———.
Married (2) at Flushing, L. I., 31 Mar. 1648, Joan Smith, dau. of Richard, Sr., who d. in 1664.

An original settler in Fairfield, he was one of the five farmers at Green's Farms [Westport], 1648. A man of substance and influence, he was charged in 1652 with being the father of the Widow Elizabeth Johnson's child, which as he was a married man

---

* It has always been a matter of wonder to the compiler why, when the name Mary happened to be spelled "Marie" in early records, some family historians should insist on retaining the spelling Marie or even convert it into Maria.

was then a capital offense under the laws of Conn. Colony. Through the connivance of friends, he was delivered from jail while awaiting trial and sought refuge under the Dutch government. He settled in Newtown, L. I., where also he was prominent, and d. before May 1683.

His farm at Maximus, Green's Farms, or Bankside, as variously known, came into possession of Robert Beacham, from whom it descended to the progeny of Joseph Lockwood.

Children [by second wife] :

> Thomas.
>
> Abigail, b. abt. 1654, d. in 1745; m. Lodowick Updike, of Loyd's Neck, L. I.
>
> +James.
>
> Israel, d. at Kingston, R. I., in 1720; will proved 9 June 1720; brother James; nephew Richard Updike.

Newton, James, s. of Thomas. Capt., first company, Colchester, May 1716; Deputy (Colchester), May 1713, May and Oct. 1714, May 1715, May and Oct. 1716, May and Oct. 1717, May and Oct. 1718, May and Oct. 1719, May 1720, May and Oct. 1721, May and Oct. 1722, Oct. 1723.

Married Mary Hubbell, dau. of Sergt. Richard.

He settled in Fairfield, where he was bapt. 30 Dec. 1694; removed to Kingston, R. I., where he resided 1703, 1713; removed to Colchester.

James of Kingston, R. I., conveyed 5 Jan. 1703 [1703/4] to Richard Hubbell all right in Est. of Joseph Hubbell of Killingworth dec'd.

Children (second to fifth recorded at Colchester, but not born there) :

> Dorothy, b. at Fairfield, 22 Mar. 1681 [1681/2]; m. Quintin Crawford, of Stratfield.
>
> Alice, b. 28 Feb. 1686; m. by 1709, Robert Ransom of Colchester.
>
> James, b. 3 Apr. 1690, d. 4 Aug. 1756; m. at Colchester, 31 May 1716, Susanna Wyatt.
>
> Ann, b. 13 Apr. 1692, bapt. at Fairfield, 16 Dec. 1694, d. 14 Aug. 1769; m. at Colchester, 3 Jan. 1710/1, Jonathan Kellogg.
>
> Israel, b. 5 Mar. 1694, bapt. at Fairfield, 16 Dec. 1694, d. at Cape Breton, 24 May 1745; Major; m. by 1716, Hannah Butler.

Mary, bapt. at Fairfield, 23 Apr. 1699, d. 10 Jan. 1754; m. at Colchester, 11 July 1717, Jonathan Welles.

Abigail, b. at North Kingston, R. I., Mar. 1703/4, d. 15 June 1778; m. at Colchester, 25 Dec. 1723, Lt. Azariah Loomis.

NICHOLS FAMILY (FRANCIS)

Nichols, Francis. Sergt., Stratford Trainband, Oct. 1639.

It should hardly be necessary to refute the foolish assertion that he was brother* of Gov. Richard Nicolls of New York, though he may have been related to that family. He was one of the founders of Stratford in 1639, where the Conn. General Court placed him in charge of military affairs. He d. abt. 1650; Inv. in Stratford, 1655.

Married (1) ———; m. (2) Anne Wines, dau. of Barnabas of Southold, L. I.; she m. (2) John Elton of Southold, (3) Capt. John Tooker, and (4) abt. 1691, Christopher Youngs, 2d.

Children [by first wife] :

+John.
+Isaac.
?Daughter, m. Richard Mills.
+Caleb.

Child [by second wife] :

Anne, m. abt. 1675, Christopher Youngs, 3d, of Southold.

Nichols, John, s. of Francis.

Settled in Fairfield, where he d. in 1655; m. (1) ———; m. (2) Grace ———, who m. (2) Richard Perry.

Inv. June 1655; widow Grace. Children: Hester, Elizabeth, Hannah, Isaac, Sarah, John. Overseer, Isaac Nichols.

Grace Perie now of fairfield widow, conveyed 4 June 1659 to son Jsacke now apprentist with Jzacke Nichols of Stratford and my three other children Samuell Nichols John Nichols and Sarah.

Children [by first wife] :

Esther.
Elizabeth.
Hannah.

---

* Capt. Francis Nicolls, brother of Richard, belonged to a strongly Royalist family; followed the King into exile, 1649, and died on the Continent.

Children [by second wife] :

+Isaac.

Sarah.

John, d. in K. Philip's War, 1676. Inv. 2 May 1676 presented by brother Isaac Nichols. Had interest in cattle in New London; also his wages due from the Country.*

+Samuel, b. abt. 1655.

Nichols, Isaac, s. of Francis. Deputy (Stratford) to Conn. Leg., May 1662, Oct. 1664.

Will 28 Sept. 1694, proved 5 Nov. 1695; wife Margery; son Benjamin; children of dau. Mary Chauncey; dau. Sarah Burritt; children of son Isaac dec'd; children of son Jonathan dec'd; children of son Ephraim; daus. Patience, Temperance, Elizabeth Webb, Margery.

Children, recorded at Stratford:

Mary, b. 2 Feb. 1647 [1647/8]; m. 8 Jan. 1667 [1667/8], Rev. Israel Chauncey, of Stratford.

Sarah, b. 6 Nov. 1649; m. 8 Jan. 1673/4, Stephen Burritt.

+Josiah, b. 29 Jan. 1651 [1651/2].

+Isaac, b. 12 Mar. 1654.

+Jonathan, b. 20 Dec. 1655.

+Ephraim, b. 16 Dec. 1657.

Patience, b. 2 Feb. 1659 [1659/60]; m. (1) abt. 1680, Lt. John Hubbell; (2) in 1691, Samuel Hawley.

Temperance, b. 17 May 1662; m. (1) Jehiel Preston; (2) at Stratfield, 17 Apr. 1688, Samuel Hubbell, Sr.

Margery, b. 30 Nov. 1663.

+Benjamin, b. 2 Feb. 1665 [1665/6].

Elizabeth, b. 2 Apr. 1668, d. at Fairfield, 15 Feb. 1718 aged 50 yrs. 10 mos. 15 days (g. s.); m. (rec. Fairfield and Derby) 8 July 1691, Rev. Joseph Webb.

Nichols, Caleb, s. of Francis.

Married Anne Ward, dau. of Andrew; she was called Ann Nichols in will of her mother Hester Ward, 1665. Mrs. Anne Nickols "departed this Life on ye 23d of July 1718 in ye 98th yeare of her age as is supposed on good grounds."

---

* Possible ancestor of the Nichols family of Westport, *q.v.* below.

Will of Caleb, Sr., of Woodbury, 14 Aug. 1690, proved 8 Nov. 1690; wife Ann; oldest son Samuel and his child Josiah; sons John, Caleb, Abraham; three daus. Mary, Anna, Phebe; friends Mr. Zachariah Walker, Capt. John Minor, and John Sherman, overseers. Widow was called Hannah when she swore to Inv. [Caleb's will did not name married daus.]

Abraham, Caleb and John Nichols, Joseph Hull in behalf of Mary his wife, Phebe wife of Isaac Knell, and Anna Nichols the widow, agree to a distribution, Est. of Caleb Nichols, 28 May 1702. [Woodbury Deeds.]

Children, recorded at Stratford:

> Sarah, b. 1 Dec. 1650; m. 20 Oct. 1674, Moses Wheeler, Jr.
> Anne, b. 5 Mar. 1651 [1651/2], d. y.
> Esther, b. 18 Feb. 1652 [1652/3], m. John Prentice, of New London.
> Joseph, b. 25 Dec. 1656, d. y.
> +Samuel, b. 29 Mar. 1658.
> Andrew, b. 28 Nov. 1659, d. y.
> +Abraham, b. 19 Jan. 1661 [1661/2].
> Abigail, b. 6 Feb. 1663 [1663/4]; m. William Martin, of Woodbury.
> Mary, b. abt. 1665/6, d. 6 Apr. 1733 in 68 yr. (g. s., Derby); m. (rec. Derby) 20 Jan 1691 [1691/2], Capt. Joseph Hull.
> Hannah, b. Aug. 1667, living unm. 1706.
> +Caleb, b. Feb. 1668 [1668/9].
> Phebe, bapt. at Woodbury, 12 Nov. 1671; m. (1) at Woodbury, 28 Dec. 1697, Isaac Knell of Stratford; m. (2) Ens. George Clark of Milford.
> +John, bapt. Mar. 1675/6.

Nichols, Isaac, s. of John.

Called "son of John sometimes of Fairfield", he m. (Stratford rec.) 15 Aug. 1672, Esther Clark. She was dau. of John of New Haven, bapt. 1 Mar. 1645. He was also called "Cousin" Isaac in Stratford records to distinguish him from his uncle. He settled in Derby, where he was Deacon. He d. at Derby, 20 Dec. 1713. Esther d. 14 Jan. 1716/7.

Adm'n granted to brother Samuel and widow Esther, 4 Jan. 1714. Distribution to widow and only dau.

Children, four recorded at Stratford:

Grace, b. 6 June 1673, d. at Derby, 2 Mar. 1701/2.

Alice, b. 25 Nov. 1674, d. y.

John, b. 10 Oct. 1676, d. y.

Samuel, b. 26 Dec. 1678, d. y.

Esther, d. at Derby, 23 Nov. 1712; m. 9 June 1708, Richard Holbrook; no issue.

Abigail, m. (1) 5 Jan. 1708, Edward Riggs; m. (2) 18 Mar. 1714, William Moss.

Nichols, Samuel, s. of John. Ens., Derby Trainband, Oct. 1709.

Born at Fairfield about 1655, d. at Derby in 1736/7; m. in May 1682, Mary Bowers, dau. of Rev. John and Bridget (Thompson) Bowers of Derby. No issue. She d. at Derby, 9 Dec. 1736.

Will 3 Sept. 1736, proved 7 Feb. 1736/7; cousin John Bowers of Derby, son of Nathaniel Bowers of Newark; cousin Nichols Moss, son of William; cousin Mary wife of Jonah Tomlinson of Derby.

Nichols, Josiah, s. of Isaac. Deputy (Stratford), May and June 1689, May 1690.

Born at Stratford, 29 Jan. 1651 [1651/2], d. there 25 June 1692 [error for 1691], ae. 39 (g. s., Stratford).

Married at Stratford, 13 Dec. 1678, Hannah Hawley. She was dau. of Joseph, b. 26 May 1657, and she m. (2) 22 June 1692, Mr. John Wolcott, of Windsor, and (3) ———— Porter.

Deed of gift 16 Mar. 1690/1, proved 3 Nov. 1696; brother Benjamin; cousin Jonathan, second son of brother Jonathan; wife Hannah.

Nichols, Isaac, s. of Isaac.

Born at Stratford 12 Mar. 1654, d. there in 1690.

Inv. 13 May 1690; widow Mary to administer with Josiah Nichols; "the children."

Married Mary Baldwin, dau. of Ens. Richard of Milford, b. in Nov. 1653. This is proved by deed from her mother to Isaac Nichols, in original Milford land records now (1929) in private hands.* After Isaac's death, Mary returned temporarily to Milford, where her twin children were bapt. as sons of widow Mary Nichols of Stratford Church, born after father's death. She m. (2) Daniel Comstock of Lyme, with whom she conveyed 22 Nov. 1711 to "our brother Barnabas Baldwin" land in Milford.

Children, three recorded at Stratford, two bapt. at Milford:

Francis, b. 3 June 1676.

Richard, b. 26 Nov. 1678, d. 20 Sept. 1756† in 78 yr. (g. s., Stratford) ; will 25 Sept. 1755, proved 8 Oct. 1755; m. (1) 3 June 1702, Comfort Sherman; dau. of Theophilus; she d. 11 Feb. 1726/7 ; m. (2) Elizabeth (Sherman) Clark, who was divorced from her former husband Isaac Clark.

Joseph, b. 1 Nov. 1680, d. y.

Joseph, b. abt. 1686, d. 10 Mar. 1733 in 47 yr. (g. s., Waterbury) ; lived first at Newtown, L. I., bought land in Derby 20 May 1715, and abt. 1728 rem. to Waterbury; m. Elizabeth Wood.

Isaac, bapt. 20 July 1690, prob. the Isaac, b. abt. 1684, d. at Derby, 12 Apr. 1733 in 49 yr. (g. s.) ; who m. 14 Nov. 1723, Agnes, widow of Abel Gunn, and dau. of Joseph and Abigail (Holbrook) Hawkins. She was b. 6 Nov. 1681, and d. in 1757, having m. (3) Samuel Camp.

Jonathan, bapt. 20 July 1690.‡

Nichols, Jonathan, s. of Isaac.

Born at Stratford, 20 Dec. 1655, d. there in 1689.

Married (rec. Stratford) 21 Dec. 1681, Hannah Howkins. She was dau. of Mr. Anthony Howkins and granddau. of Gov. Welles, and was b. at Farmington abt. 1661. She m. (2) Sergt. Samuel Ward; and (3) John Judson of Woodbury, where she d. 23 July 1698.

Inv. 28 Oct. 1689. Ages of children: Josiah 7, Jonathan 2, Mary 4. Adm'n granted to widow, with advice of Mr. Israel Chauncey, Mr. Samuel Hawley, and Josiah Nichols. Widow returned account, 23 Sept. 1691; the two sons were to be placed out to learn trades at 16.

---

* Also, Isaac Nichols, Jr., of Stratford conveyed land in Derby, 22 Mar. 1674/5, and called Elizabeth Fowler of Milford his mother-in-law. She was Mary Baldwin's mother, Elizabeth (Alsop) (Baldwin) Fowler.

† Obviously a misreading; prob. 29 Sept. 1755.

‡ A Jonathan Nichols of Saybrook, will 14 Oct. 1772, proved 21 Dec. 1772, named three gr. daus. Rebecca, Sarah, and Lydia, the children of son Jonathan Nichols of Saybrook dec'd; dau. Mary wife of Aaron Cone, and Sarah wife of Samuel Parmelee, both of Saybrook.

Will of Hannah wife of John Judson of Woodbury, 22 July 1698; two sons Josiah and Jonathan Nichols; dau. Mary Nichols; dau. Hannah Ward.

Children, recorded at Stratford:

> Josiah, b. 21 Oct. 1682, d. 18 Nov. 1734, unm.
> Mary, b. 16 Jan. 1684 [1684/5]; m. 24 Apr. 1712, Joshua Judson.
> Jonathan, b. 12 Sept. 1687, d. 6 Nov. 1760 in 73 yr. (g. s., Stratford);
> m. 22 Dec. 1713, Sarah Beach, dau. of Sergt. Joseph.

Nichols, Ephraim, s. of Isaac. Ens., Fairfield Trainband (appointment not found).

Born at Stratford, 16 Dec. 1657, d. at Fairfield, in 1690/1.

Called of Stratford, he m. at Fairfield, 17 Oct. 1682, Esther Hawley. She was widow of Ebenezer Hawley and dau. of William Ward. As Esther Nicolls, dau. of William Ward, she m. (3) Nov. 1691, Eliphalet Hill; and she m. (4) Robert Lord.

Inv. of Ens. Ephraim, 9 Mar. 1690/1. Widow Easter appointed with Sergt. Joseph Lockwood to administer the estate and to take care of the children. Joseph Lockwood and Eliphalet and Easther Hill receipted as Adm'rs, 31 May 1693, to Isaac Nichols of Stratford.

Children, recorded at Fairfield:

> ✕Ignatius, b. 17 Dec. 1683, d. 17 Dec. 1758 in 75 yr. (g. s., Green-field); m. Abigail Staples, b. abt. 1689, d. 12 Dec. 1745 ae. 57 (g. s.).
> Deborah, b. 1 Jan. 1685 [1685/6], d. at Greenfield, 14 Sept. 1748; m. 7 Dec. 1705, Joseph Wheeler.
> Esther, b. 18 Dec. 1689; m. 20 Mar. 1716/7, David Wheeler.

Nichols, Benjamin, s. of Isaac.

Born at Stratford, 2 Feb. 1665/6, d. at Stratford in 1715.

Married (1) Abigail ———.

Married (2) 1711, Rebecca, widow of John Seeley, and dau. of Ezekiel Sanford, b. 13 Dec. 1672. She m. (3) at Stratfield, 24 May 1716, John Mann, and d. (rec. Stratford) Mar. 1725/6.

Adm'n granted, 2 Feb. 1714/5, to Jonas Wooster of Stratford. Inv. 9 Apr. 1717 presented 8 Oct. 1718.

Children [by first wife] :

Jane, m. Jonas Wooster.

Patience, b. abt. 1701, d. at Trumbull, 25 Aug. 1749 ae. 48 (g. s.) ; m. at Stratford, 25 Jan. 1721/2, Josiah Beach.

Ephraim, b. abt. 1706, d. (rec. Woodbury, as son of Benj.) 23 Feb. 1725/6 in 20 yr.

Child [by second wife], bapt. at Stratfield:

×John, bapt. 28 Sept. 1712, d. at Stratfield, 5 July 1785; m. (1) 11 Dec. 1737, Rebecca Sherwood, who d. 12 Sept. 1749 in 36 yr. (g. s., Stratfield) ; m. (2) 25 Dec. 1751, Huldah, widow of Elijah Nichols, and dau. of Ambrose Thompson, b. 31 Mar. 1709/10, d. 16 Apr. 1759 in 49 yr. (g. s.) ; m. (3) Eunice, widow of Ephraim Morehouse, and dau. of David Wheeler, b. 24 Dec. 1717, d. 9 Apr. 1785.

Nichols, Samuel, s. of Caleb.

Born at Stratford, 29 Mar. 1658, d. at Woodbury in 1691; m. Susanna, widow of Thomas Fairchild. She m. (3) Samuel Castle.

Inv. 11 Aug. 1691. Widow Susanna; child Josiah aged 4 yrs., 25 July last. Overseers of the Est. of Thomas Fairchild, former husband to the above named widow, mentioned. Distribution to widow and son ordered. On 14 Mar. 1708, Samuel Castle was Adm'r of Est. of Samuel Nichols; portions of Thomas Fairchild's children; allowance for bringing up the child of Nichols; Susanna Castle, relict of said Nichols.

Children, bapt. at Woodbury:

Josiah, b. 25 July 1687, bapt. Sept. 1687, d. at Danbury in 1743; adm'n granted to widow Mehitabel, 26 Oct. 1743, and she was chosen as guardian by sons Daniel and Samuel, 22 Jan. 1744/5; m. after 1719, Mabel, widow of John Griswold of New Milford, sister of Rev. Daniel Boardman. She was dau. of Daniel, b. at Wethersfield, 30 May 1689.

Andrew, bapt. Mar. 1688/9, d. y.

Nichols, Abraham, s. of Caleb.

Born at Stratford, 19 Jan. 1661 [1661/2].

Married (1) (rec. Stratford) 3 Dec. 1684, Rachel Kellogg; she was dau. of Daniel of Norwalk, b. Feb. 1663.

Married (2) after 1708, Sarah Rogers, dau. of Eleazer of Milford, b. 5 Oct. 1665. She was widow of Samuel Buckingham of

Milford (b. 1 Nov. 1668, d. 29 Oct. 1708). On 24 June 1735, Abraham Nichols and Sarah his wife of Stratford conveyed to their son Samuel Buckingham of Milford, land that was "Joshua Knowleses late of Fairfield." [See KNOWLES.]

Children of Abraham and Rachel, recorded at Stratford:

Joseph, b. 21 Sept. 1685, d. 17 Sept. 1743 in 59 yr. (g. s., Trumbull); Capt.*; will 14 Sept. 1743, proved 5 Oct. 1743; m. 26 Dec. 1704, Mary Curtis. She was dau. of Joseph, b. abt. 1682; she m. (2) Henry Hawley, and d. 16 Apr. 1767 in 83 yr. (g. s.).

Daniel, b. Apr. 1687, d. at Stratford, May 1740; will 4 May 1740, proved 18 May 1740; m. Hannah Peat, dau. of Samuel, b. 12 Aug. 1694.

Hester, b. 31 Oct. 1689; m. 21 Feb. 1711/2, Nathan Peat.

Rachel, b. 9 Nov. 1691; m. 24 Jan. 1710/1, Ephraim Booth.

Abraham, b. 15 Sept. 1696; m. 25 Dec. 1718, Abigail Walker.

Eunice, b. 7 Dec. 1698; m. (1) 29 Jan. 1718/9, Charles Patterson; m. (2) 2 May 1728, Nathaniel Sherman.

Ruth, b. Mar. 1701; m. 3 Mar. 1719/20, Stephen Burroughs.

Phebe, b. 22 July 1703, bapt. at Stratfield, 7 Nov. 1703; m. 7 Jan. 1724/5, Thomas Peat.

Nichols, Caleb, s. of Caleb.

Born at Stratford, Feb. 1668/9; Caleb, Jr., of Woodbury d. in Stratford of a cancer (rec. Woodbury), 14 Apr. 1706.

Will of Caleb of Woodbury, 6 Mar. 1706; sister Hannah Nichols for her care of him in his sickness; eldest bro. Abraham Nichols, and bro. John, and sisters Abigail Martin, Mary Hull, Annah Nichols, Phebe Knell. Inv. 14 Apr. 1706.

Nichols, John, s. of Caleb. Sergt.

Bapt. at Woodbury, Mar. 1675/6. Sergt. John d. there, 24 Apr. 1727.

Married (rec. Woodbury) 13 Nov. 1705, Jane Bostwick of Stratford.

---

* In 1710 the Conn. Leg. ordered payment to widow Sarah Parret for nursing Joseph Nichols and two other soldiers, proving that he served against the French, 1709/10.

Children, recorded at Woodbury:

Sarah, bapt. Mar. 1706/7.*

Caleb, b. and bapt. Dec. 1708, d. 17 June 1710.

John, b. 28 Apr. 1711, bapt. Apr. 1711, d. 4 Apr. 1791 ae. 78; Lt.; m. (1) 2 Feb. 1731/2, Elizabeth Preston, who d. 1 Feb. 1732/3; m. (2) 6 Nov. 1735, Abigail Judson, who d. May 1749; m. (3) 14 Jan. 1756, Mary Tuttle, who d. 9 May 1768.

Caleb, b. 18 Mar. 1713, bapt. Mar. 1712/3, d. 1 Apr. 1727.

Andrew, b. 6 Oct. 1715, bapt. Oct. 1715.

Joseph, b. 28 Jan. 1718, bapt. 2 Feb. 1718, d. in 1760; grad. Yale College 1734; m. Sept. 1739, Phebe Smith.

Mary, b. 7 July 1720, bapt. 10 July 1720.

Samuel, bapt. 10 Mar. 1723; m. ———.

NICHOLS FAMILY (WESTPORT)

Nichols, ———.

He m. Mercy, dau. of Mrs. Susanna Jones by her former husband (Holdsworth or Hollingsworth). She m. (2) Thomas Disbrow, and was tried for witchcraft, 1692.

The only member of the Francis Nichols family who could possibly have been her husband was John[3] (*John[2], Francis[1]*), who d. in K. Philip's War, 1676, but the probate records do not indicate that this man left widow and children. If Mercy's husband was not this John, he was of some other Nichols family.

A Mercy Niccolson was divorced from John Niccolson, Oct. 1677, he having deserted her for over five years. Knowing that the name Wilcoxson became shortened in some branches to Wilcox, it is tempting to surmise that in John Nicholson we have the first husband of the witch Mercy, and that James Nicholson may have been his son, and a brother or half-brother of John and Nathaniel Nichols. But we hardly dare do more than suggest the possibility.

Children:

+John.

+Nathaniel.

Nichols, John, s. of ———.

Thomas Disbrow of Fairfield conveyed 1712, "what is due from Est. of my father Thomas Disbrow dec'd to my brother John

---

* A Sarah Nichols m. at Stratford, 26 Feb. 1719/20, David Bostwick.

Nicoles of Fairfield" on account of what my said father rec'd of grandmother Jones' estate. On 4 June 1718, John Nickols and Thomas Disbrow, sons of Mercy Disbrow late of Fairfield dec'd, mention "our brother Nathaniel Nicoles of Fairfield" and land given to said Nathaniel by our said mother Mercy Disbrow.

John Nichols of Fairfield conveyed for love to son Samuel of Norwalk, 7 Apr. 1736. Samuel and Thomas Nichols of Fairfield conveyed, 1 Aug. 1726, to Ephraim Nichols, land bounded on that of our father John Nichols.

Abigail wife of John d. at Westport, 2 Feb. 1749.

John was bapt. at Fairfield Church, 31 Mar. 1694/5, and had children bapt. there:

> Ebenezer, bapt. 16 June 1695.
> Samuel, bapt. 21 Mar. 1696/7, living 1736 in Norwalk.
> ✕Solomon, bapt. 23 Apr. 1699, d. before 1734; m. Mary ———; she m. (2) ——— Stone.
> Thomas, bapt. 28 July 1700.
> Joseph, bapt. 10 Sept. 1704.
> ✕Benjamin, bapt. 12 Aug. 1711; m. 13 Oct. 1730, Elizabeth Trowbridge.
> Margery, bapt. 12 Aug. 1711.

Nichols, Nathaniel, s. of ———.

Prob. he m. (1) Esther Beers, dau. of Ephraim. The will of her sister Mary (Beers) Brush (1771) named Esther's daus. Esther, Mary, Elizabeth and Rebecca Nichols.

Died at Westport, 6 Mar. 1762; Hannah, wife of Nathaniel, d. 29 Nov. 1749.

Adm'n granted to Phineas Chapman, 8 Apr. 1762.

He conveyed, 30 July 1730 to son David Nichols, his deed mentioning another son Ephraim, and his own bro. John Nichols. John Finch of Fairfield conveyed to John Allen, Jr., right in land that Allen purchased of my gr. father Nathaniel Nichols.

Children (record incomplete):

> ✕Ephraim, m. Sarah ———.
> ✕David, m. Mary ———.
> ?Esther.
> ?Mary.
> ?Elizabeth.
> ?Rebecca, perhaps the Rebecca of Norwalk on whose estate Nehemiah Mead was Adm'r in 1773.

Nicholson, James.

Res. Fairfield.

Married Sybil, widow of Josiah Knapp, and dau. of Thomas Dickerson. No issue.

On 6 Jan. 1685 [1685/6], he mortgaged to Peter Bulkley for £10, housing, lands and tan "fates"; released 13 Apr. 1689.

Will 2 Aug. 1709, proved 10 Nov. 1709; makes son-in-law [step-son] Daniel Knapp his heir; bro.-in-law Nathaniel Finch, sole Exec'r. [Finch was his wife's half-brother.]

Norton, Peter.

Married Mary [dau. of Francis Andrews?].

Inv. 1 Sept. 1670.

Hugh Griffen of Orinoake in Stratford had married widow of Peter Norton, who died in Fairfield leaving two daus. Abigail and Mary, and agreed to pay £5 to each within two years, 5 July 1687.

Children:

> Abigail, m. abt. 1688, Joseph Beers.
> Mary [? b. abt. 1665, d. at Stratford, 28 Nov. 1748 ae. 83; m. John Skidmore. When Mary's half-brother Francis Griffin died, John Skidmore's grandson Griffin Bradley contested Griffin's will, and his interest does not clearly appear unless this Mary was his grandmother. Hence this marriage is tentatively suggested for her.]

Nouguier, Anthony.

In 1705 he entered on Fairfield records his naturalization papers, showing that he became a British subject, 22 June 1694, certified at London the following 11 July.

Merchant and money lender of Fairfield; d. at Fairfield, 23 Oct. 1740 in 86 yr. (g. s.).

He m. (1) Jane ————, who d. 24 Oct. 1739 in 87 yr. (g. s.).

He m. (2) Sarah, widow successively of Ephraim Wheeler and Benjamin Fairweather, and dau. of Capt. Matthew Sherwood; b. abt. 1676, d. at Stratfield, 25 May 1743 in 67 yr. (g. s.).

Will 7 Oct. 1740, proved 6 Nov. 1740; to wife, Sarah, all estate for life, and service of negro servant Elizabeth, also absolutely £3,000 of debts due me by bonds; to Yale College, £150; to

Fairfield Church, £200, Rev. Noah Hobart to have use of it; to Public School in First Society, £150; to friend, Capt. Thomas Hill, my homestead after my wife's death; to French Church in Boston, £100; to the poor of Fairfield, £150; negro servant Elizabeth to be free after wife's death; servant girl Ann to be free at 18, and to have £100; to cousin, Mr. Daniel Aurault of Newport, R. I., the residue.

Daniel Ayrault was son of a Huguenot refugee, Dr. Pierre Ayrault, and cousin of Dr. Nicholas Ayrault of Wethersfield.* The wife of Pierre was prob. Nouguier's sister.

Odell, William.

He came from Newport, co. Buckingham, Eng.† Statements that he was a member of the Wodhull family of Thenford, co. Northampton, are absurdly irrelevant.

Of Concord by 1639; rem. to Southampton, L. I., 1642; and later to Fairfield, where a grant of land was recorded 8 Apr. 1660.

Will 6 June 1676; son William; gr. child Samuel Morehouse, son of dau. Rebecca, and his brothers Thomas and John Morehouse; gr. child John Odell, son of John; to Goody Knap, four yards of new red cloth; dau.-in-law Mary Odell; son John Odell and dau. Rebecca Morehouse; son-in-law Samuel Morehouse and son John Odell, Exec'rs. Inv. 12 June 1676.

Children:

+John.
James, b. at Concord, 2 Jan. 1639/40, buried there 4 Apr. 1641.
Rebecca, b. at Concord, 17 July 1642; m. Samuel Morehouse.
William, b. abt. 1644; founder of the Westchester County Odells.

Odell, John, s. of William.

Died at Stratfield in 1707; m. Mary ———, who d. in 1711/2.

Inv. Stratfield, 16 May 1707; widow Mary made oath. Will 22 Apr. 1707, proved 6 May 1707, gave dau. Mary £15 and each other dau. £1; wife Mary, Exec'x.

Inv. of widow Mary Odell of Stratfield, 22 Jan. 1711/2. The son Samuel made oath; his sister Deborah mentioned.

---

* See *Ancestry of William Francis Joseph Boardman* (1906), pp. 109-113.
† *N. Y. Gen. and Biog. Record*, vol. 44, p. 118.

Children, recorded at Fairfield:

+John, b. abt. 1666.

Elizabeth, m. 16 May 1694, Abel Bingham.

Rebecca, m. (1) Luke Guire; m. (2) Robert Turney.

+Samuel, b. 10 Mar. 1677.

Hannah, b. 20 Oct. 1679, d. 14 June 1756 in 77 yr. (g. s., Stratfield);
m. (1) abt. 1700, Nathaniel Seeley; m. (2) Jacob Sterling.

Deborah, b. 28 Aug. 1682, d. at Greenfield, 23 May 1745 ae. abt. 63;
m. (rec. Stratfield) 25 May 1713, John Downs.

Mary, b. abt. 1693, d. at Trumbull, 13 Aug. 1771 in 79 yr. (g. s.); m.
(1) abt. 1713, Nathaniel Porter; m. (2) at Stratford, 4 Aug. 1727,
John Middlebrook.

Odell John, s. of John.

Born about 1666, d. at Stratfield, 1 June 1743 ae. 77 (g. s.).
Married Sarah Wheeler, dau. of Isaac, b. about 1665, d. 25 Oct.
1743 in 79 yr. (g. s.).

With wife Sarah he conveyed, 22 Feb. 1725/6, to son Hezekiah,
her reversion in estate now in possession of our mother-in-law
[stepmother] Susanna Wheeler, widow of our father Dea. Isaac
Wheeler.

Will 22 Nov. 1742, proved 6 June 1743; wife Sarah; sons
William, Hezekiah; gr. sons Gershom and Azariah; daus. Ann,
Martha; children of dau. Bethia dec'd; children of dau. Sarah
dec'd.

Will of Sarah, 19 Oct. 1743, proved 29 Oct. 1743; son William;
son Hezekiah, right inherited from father Deacon Wheeler of
Stratfield dec'd; gr. dau. Abigail Odell; dau. Martha; the dau.
of my dau. Bethia dec'd; daus. of my dau. Sarah dec'd; friend
David Sherman, Jr., of Stratford, Exec'r.

Ann Gill of Middletown, dau. of John Odell of Stratfield, conveyed 7 Nov. 1743 to bro-in-law John Beardsley, Jr., of Stratfield, land which John Odell willed to my sister Martha wife of
John Beardsley, heirs of my dec'd sister Sarah Comstock, and
heirs of my dec'd sister Bethia Squire, equally with me. On 30
Mar. 1744, Daniel Comstock, Jr., of Kent, eldest son of Sarah
Comstock, dau. of John Odell, conveyed to uncle John Beardsley.

Children, first four recorded at Fairfield, last seven at Stratfield:

Ann, b. 6 Mar. 1688/9; m. (1) at Stratfield, 10 Nov. 1713, Beraiah
Bacon, of Middletown; m. (2) ——— Gill, of Middletown.

John, b. 5 Nov. 1690, d. y.

Bethia, b. 27 Feb. 1692/3; m. at Stratfield, 1 Feb. 1710/1, Jonathan Squire.

Sarah, b. 10 Aug. 1694, bapt., at Fairfield, 11 Nov. 1694; m. at Stratfield, 10 Nov. 1713, Daniel Comstock, of Norwalk.

XWilliam, b. 17 July 1697, bapt. 18 July 1697, d. at Stratfield in 1772; will 23 Sept. 1772, proved 9 Nov. 1772; m. (1) at Stratfield, 2 Oct. 1718, Abigail Smith, b. 23 Sept. 1696, d. Jan. 1736 in 40 yr. (g. s.) ; m. (2) Sarah (Burton), widow of Nathaniel Beach, Jr.

Tabitha, b. 20 Apr. 1699, bapt. 23 Apr. 1699.

XHezekiah, b. 22 Sept. 1700, bapt. 13 Oct. 1700; m. Deborah Smith, b. 28 Mar. 1702, d. 27 June 1756 in 55 yr. (g. s.).

Gershom, b. 28 Sept. 1702, bapt. 18 Oct. 1702.

Mary, b. 26 Mar. 1704, bapt. 26 Mar. 1704, d. y.

John, bapt. 17 Feb. 1706.

Martha, b. 9 Nov. 1708, bapt. 21 Nov. 1708; m. John Beardsley, Jr., of Stratford.

Odell, Samuel, s. of John. Ens., Stratfield Trainband, May 1722.

Born at Fairfield, 10 Mar. 1677, d. in 1727.

Married Joanna Walker, dau. of Joseph, b. at Boston, 5 May 1677.

Johanna and Samuel Odell appointed Adm'rs of Samuel's Est., 6 June 1727. John son of Samuel of Stratfield chose Jacob Sterling for guardian, 5 Dec. 1727. Hannah Odell chose mother Johanna for guardian, 7 May 1728.

Children, bapt. at Stratfield:

Eunice, bapt. 12 Mar. 1704.

XSamuel, bapt. 16 Dec. 1705, d. at Stratfield, 7 June 1775 in 69 yr. (g. s.) ; m. (1) at Stratfield, 25 Jan. 1733, Judith-Ann Wheeler; dau. of John, b. 16 Jan. 1705/6; m. (2) at Greenfield, 19 Sept. 1751, Sarah, widow of Thomas Banks, and dau. of Samuel Osborn, bapt. 29 Nov. 1713.

Mary, bapt. 21 Mar. 1708; m. Ebenezer Gregory.

John, bapt. 20 Aug. 1710.

Hannah, bapt. 3 Jan. 1714.

Ogden, Richard.

Was at Stamford by 1641 with brother John; stone-masons. Richard settled in Fairfield, where he was the miller. He bought six acres on old Mill River from Giles Smith, and no deed having been given, Eluzar and John Smith (sons and Executors of Giles) gave a deed 9 Feb. 1669 [1669/70].

Inv. of Richard, Sr., of Fairfield, 8 Apr. 1687; widow Mary made oath. Three sons, Richard, David, John; three daughters "of the deceased aliue ye wife of Sarj^t Samuel Ward the wife of Daniel Meker ye wife of Daniel Silleman Juni^r"; and John Pine had a child in marriage with a dec'd dau. of Richard. Samuel Ward and John Osborn, Adm'rs.

Statements that the dau. who m. Ward was named Alice are based on a clumsy reading of the word "alive" in the above record.

On 27 Oct. 1690, John Ogden chose Sergt. Samuel Ward for guardian. The widow of Richard was then also dec'd, and Samuel Ward and Joseph Bastard were ordered to finish the adm'n.

Richard, Sr., entered for record 2 Apr. 1679, land purchased from John Sturgis. He entered into a covenant with the town, 20 Dec. 1680, with regard to "ye mell now standing by ye old mell rever"; and after his death the matter was taken up, Oct. 1690, with his sons Richard, David, and John (the last by his guardian Samuel Ward) and the daus.

Children:

+Richard, b. [say 1655].
Daughter, m. John Pine.
Daughter, m. Samuel Ward.
Elizabeth, m. Daniel Meeker.
Abigail, m. Daniel Silliman, Jr.
+David, b. [say 1668].
John, b. [say 1672]; on 5 July 1705, was of New Fairfield, Cohansey, N. J.; when he conveyed to Jonathan Sturges land from dec'd father Richard Ogden, by agreement of brethren Richard and David, and Samuel Ward "which was my Guardian."

Ogden, John. Deputy (Rye) to Conn. Leg., Oct. 1674.

Married Judith Budd, dau. of Lt. John. On 19 July 1683, John Budd of Rye conveyed to "Judete Browne", dau. of his dec'd father, and to the heirs of her son Joseph Ogden, a lot in accordance with his father's will.

In May 1682, called John of Rye, he was granted 20 acres by the Conn. General Court.

Inv. of John of Stamford, 7 Aug. 1682, sworn to by "Jude" Ogden. Adm'n granted to Judith.

She m. (2) by 1683, Francis Brown of Rye, who in 1687 through the medium of Joseph Horton, Sr., of Rye, conveyed to his wife Jude all his estate in Rye; she to provide for her husband a comfortable maintenance for life, and to pay the legacies of the children of John Ogden, dec'd, as they come of age.

Francis and Jude Brown, adm'rs of Est. of John Ogden, gave lands 12 Dec. 1690 to Joseph Ogden son of John for his legacy.

Francis Brown of Rye conveyed, 5 June 1700, to son-in-law David Ogden; to son-in-law Richard Ogden, 11 June 1700; and with wife Judith to son Richard Ogden, 19 Feb. 1706/7, land "which was our son Richard Ogden's own father's, John Ogdens."

Children:

>Joseph, of Rye, d. abt. 1715; m. Mary ———.
>Hannah; conveyed to Hackaliah Brown, 11 Nov. 1684, land confirmed to her as part of her portion by Francis Brown, she being his dau.-in-law.
>Richard.
>David, of White Plains.

Ogden, Richard, s. of Richard.

Married Sarah ———, who m. (2) prob. late in 1700, Thomas Staples, 2d.

Inv. 25 Jan. 1697 [1697/8]; widow Sarah to administer. Distribution ordered 31 Dec. 1700 to widow, three sons and two daus.; Joseph was 21, and desired his portion, 22 Oct. 1701; and Richard chose Mr. Samuel Cobbit for guardian, while Sarah chose Mr. Peter Burr; Thomas Staples their father-in-law being appointed guardian for Jonathan and Mary.

Distribution 17 Aug. 1705; Widow, Richard, Jonathan, Sarah; and Thomas Staples for his ward Mary. "There has been great devastations the Barn Blown down, the house much decayed, and the Mill Burnt."

Children, first four bapt. at Fairfield as of Richard and Sarah, 27 Jan. 1694/5:

>×Joseph, b. abt. 1680.
>Richard, b. [say 1683].
>Sarah, b. [say 1686].

Jonathan, b. [say 1689].

Mary, bapt. 19 Apr. 1696; m. Robert Travis, of Rye, N. Y., with whom she conveyed, 9 Aug. 1723, to David Ogden land set to her from Est. of father Richard Ogden, bounded on land set to her brother Jonathan and sister Sarah Ogden.

Ogden, David, s. of Richard.

Died at Fairfield by 1715. On 18 Feb. 1725/6, Mary Ogden, dau. of David Ogden who died above ten years ago, and no Inv. taken, agreed with eldest brother David Ogden of Fairfield to accept £120 as full portion.

He m. Abigail Sherwood, dau. of Thomas, 2d; she d. at Greenfield, 1 May 1744 in 74 yr. (g. s.).

Children:

X David, b. abt. 1695, d. at Fairfield, 13 Mar. 1768 in 74 yr. (g. s.); will 31 Oct. 1765, proved 5 Apr. 1768; m. at Fairfield, 14 Dec. 1724, Abigail Osborn, bapt. 5 Mar. 1703/4, d. 14 Sept. 1783 in 81 yr. (g. s.).

X John, b. by 1697, d. at Greenfield, 7 June 1777 ae. upwards of 80; will 24 Mar. 1772, proved 7 July 1777; m. at Fairfield, 1 Jan. 1730 [24 Jan. 1728/9 by Greenfield rec.], Mary Jennings, b. abt. 1710, d. at Greenfield, 31 May 1768 ae. abt. 60.

Mary.

Oliver, Thomas.

He acquired the Anthony Beers land in Fairfield, and sold it to Thomas Sherwood, 9 Feb. 1670 [1669/70], purchasing from Sherwood the same date.

Thomas Oliver assigned all his property to John Wheeler, 2 Mar. 1685/6, Wheeler agreeing to maintain him for life. He was freed from training, 9 Mar. 1685/6.

Olmstead, James.

Son of James and Jane (Bristow), bapt. at Great Leighs, co. Essex, Eng., 4 Dec. 1580, d. at Hartford in 1640; m. at Great Leighs, 26 Oct. 1605, Joyce Cornish, who was buried at Fairsted, co. Essex, 21 Apr. 1621.

He came on the *Lion* to Boston in 1632, with his two sons, and three children of his brother Richard, and settled in Cambridge, Mass. In 1636 removed to Hartford.

Will: two sons Nicholas and Nehemiah; promise of brother
Loomis regarding my son Nicholas' wife's portion; cousin Rebecca
Olmstead that now dwelleth with me; servant Will Corby. Inv.
28 Sept. 1640. Agreement of Nicholas and Nehemiah Olmstead
for his kinsmen Richard and John Olmstead to have £5 each.

Children, two bapt. at Great Leighs, five at Fairsted, co. Essex:

Faith, bapt. 7 Jan. 1606/7, buried at Fairsted, 3 Mar. 1627.
Frances, bapt. 14 Feb. 1608/9, buried 14 Feb. 1608/9.
Mabel, bapt. 30 Sept. 1610, buried 18 Feb. 1621.
Nicholas, bapt. 15 Feb. 1611/2, d. at Hartford, 31 Aug. 1684; m.
    Sarah Loomis. Served in Pequot War, 1637; Corp., Conn. Col.
    Troop, Mar. 1658; Lt., Hartford County Troop, Aug. 1673; Lt.,
    Hartford Trainband, Oct. 1673 (declined). Served as Lt. in K.
    Philip's War, July 1675, and Aug. 1675 as Capt. of Hartford
    County Dragoons. Deputy (Hartford) to Conn. Leg., Oct. 1672,
    May 1673. The Hayes family of Norwalk was related to him or
    his wife.
James, bapt. 22 Jan. 1614/5, d. y.
+Nehemiah, bapt. 10 Nov. 1618.
Mary, bapt. 18 Apr. 1621, buried 24 Apr. 1621.

Olmstead, Richard.

Son of James and Jane (Bristow), bapt. at Great Leighs, co.
Essex, Eng., 22 Mar. 1579, buried at Fairsted, co. Essex, 16 Nov.
1641. He m. Frances Slany, buried 10 Sept. 1630, sister of
Thomas Slany of London, haberdasher, whose will, proved 28 July
1638, gave legacies to Joseph, his sister Holmested's youngest son,
to his niece Sarah Holmestead, and to his nephew Richard
Holmestead. Thomas Slany also gave legacies to the three children of his sister Bazie, one of whom was doubtless John Bazie
of Hartford, who was called cousin in the will of Capt. Richard
Olmstead of Norwalk.

Children:

+Richard, bapt. 20 Feb. 1612.
Mary, bapt. 6 July 1615.
+John, bapt. 16 Feb. 1617.
Sarah, bapt. 2 Nov. 1620.
Rebecca, brought to America by her uncle James, m. Thomas Newell,
    and d. at Farmington, 24 Feb. 1698.
Joseph, bapt. 2 Dec. 1627.

Olmstead, Nehemiah, s. of James. Sergt., Fairfield Trainband, May 1657.

Bapt. at Fairsted, co. Essex, Eng., 10 Nov. 1618, d. at Fairfield in 1657; m. Elizabeth Burr, dau. of Jehu. She m. (2) Obadiah Gilbert, and (3) Capt. Nathaniel Seeley.

Inv. 6 Oct. 1657. Widow and minor dau.

On 27 Jan. 1671 [1671/2], land was recorded which Nehemiah Olmstead "did purchase of his bro.-in-law Jehu Burr." On 15 Mar. 1675 [1675/6], Nehemiah having died and left a widow and one child, Sarah, and she is now of age and married to Robert Seeley, he demanded her portion, and an agreement was made with Elizabeth Seeley, the Adm'x.

Child:

Sarah, m. abt. 1675, Robert Seeley.

Olmstead, Richard, s. of Richard. Served in the Pequot War, 1637, for which he received lot in Soldier's Field, Hartford, and in 1669 a colonial grant of 60 acres. Sergt., Norwalk Trainband, May 1653; Sergt., Conn. Col. Troop, same date; Lt., Norwalk Trainband, May 1659; Capt. of same, Oct. 1680; Muster Master, Fairfield County, Nov. 1673. Deputy (Norwalk) to Conn. Leg., May 1653, Sept. 1654, May 1658, Oct. 1660, May 1661, May 1662, May and Oct. 1663, May and Oct. 1664, Oct. 1665, May and Oct. 1666, May 1667, May and Oct. 1668, May 1669, May 1671, and May 1679; Commissioner for Norwalk, 1678-85.

Bapt. at Fairsted, co. Essex, Eng., 20 Feb. 1612, d. at Norwalk, early in 1687.

Brought to America by his uncle James, in 1632, he settled in Cambridge, Mass., and in 1636 removed to Hartford. In 1646 he was Constable, and fence-viewer in 1649. About 1650 he removed to Norwalk.

He m. (1) ———; (2) ———, prob. wid. of Thomas Smith.

Will 30 Sept. 1684; aged 76 yrs. or thereabout; son John, dwelling-house; eldest son James; the clothes of my first wife and dau. dec'd, to my sons and their wives; cousin Nicholas Olmstead of Hartford, £1; cousin Baizie's two daus., Elizabeth

Peck and Lydia Baker, £1 apiece; to Samuel Smith the bed that was my last wife's etc.; friend Sergt. John Platt, overseer. Inv. of Capt. Richard, 23 Feb. 1686 [1686/7].

Children [by first wife]:

+James.
+John, bapt. at Hartford, 30 Dec. 1649.
Daughter, d. unm.

Olmstead, John, s. of Richard. Surgeon, K. Philip's War, 1675.

Bapt. at Fairsted, co. Essex, Eng., 16 Feb. 1617, d. at Norwich, 2 Aug. 1686; m. before 1650, Elizabeth Marvin, dau. of Matthew, bapt. at Great Bentley, co. Essex, 15 Sept. 1622. No issue.

Will, not dated; aged about 60; wife Elizabeth sole Exec'x; servants to have liberty at death of wife; exhibited 22 Sept. 1686.

Elizabeth's will, 15 Oct. 1689; two sons of husband's brother, Richard Olmstead of Norwalk,—Lt. James and Ens. John; nine children of brother and sister Newell of Farmington; and several of her own relatives.

Olmstead, James, s. of Richard. Lt., Norwalk Trainband, Oct. 1680; Capt., May 1691. Deputy (Norwalk) to Conn. Leg., Oct. 1691, Oct. 1692, Oct. 1693, May 1699. Committee of Safety, Fairfield County, May 1704. Commissioner for Norwalk, 1690-98, and Justice, 1698-1724. Selectman, 1671, 1682-85; Town Clerk, 1678-1707, 1721.

Born prob. at Hartford; d. at Norwalk in 1731; m. in 1673, Phebe Barlow, dau. of Thomas of Fairfield.

Will 28 Apr. 1731, proved 12 June 1731; sons Joseph, John; son Nathan dec'd had had portion.

Children, recorded at Norwalk:

James, b. 17 Apr. 1675, d. y.
Joseph, b. 10 Mar. 1676/7, d. at Norwalk in 1748; will 27 Jan. 1747/8, proved 14 Nov. 1748; m. Mehitabel Warner, dau. of Robert of Middletown, b. abt. 1673.

Nathan, b. 27 Apr. 1678, d. in 1716.   Inv. 12 Feb. 1716 [1716/7] ;   m. (1) 7 Dec. 1702, Sarah Keeler;   m. (2) abt. 1706, Mercy Comstock, b. 12 Nov. 1676.

Samuel, b. 13 May 1683, d. y.

John, b. 14 Aug. 1692, d. in 1748;   adm'n granted, 1 Nov. 1748;   m. 29 Feb. 1717/8, Mary Small, dau. of Robert, once of Norwalk.

Olmstead, John, s. of Richard.   Ens., Norwalk Trainband, May 1674;   Lt., May 1691.   Selectman, 1699, 1703.

Bapt. at Hartford, 30 Dec. 1649, d. at Norwalk in 1704.

Married (1) at Norwalk, 17 July 1673, Mary Benedict, dau. of Thomas.

Married (2) Elizabeth, widow of Thomas Gregory, and dau. of George Pardee, b. at New Haven, 10 June 1660.

Inv. 22 Dec. 1704/5 (*sic*).   Children: Daniel abt. 19 (Thomas Read guardian) ;   Richard 17 (Samuel Sension guardian) ;   John 4 (Samuel Betts guardian) ;   Mary 18 [error for 28] ;   Jane;   Sarah;   Rebecca;   Elizabeth;   Eunice abt. 15 (Samuel Marvin guardian) ;   Deborah 10 or 11;   Abigail abt. 8 (Joseph Platt guardian) ;   Anna abt. 6 (Samuel Keeler guardian).   Thomas Read, Samuel Sension, and Benjamin Wilson, sons-in-law to Lt. John Olmstead, Adm'rs. John Benedict and Elizabeth Olmstead, as Adm'rs of Est. of Thomas Gregory, gave receipt to Est. of Lt. John Olmstead.

Distribution 17 Apr. 1705: Widow;   eldest son Daniel;   Thomas Reed, Benjamin Wilson, Annah Olmsted, Jonathan Abut, Samuel St. John;   Richard, John, Elizabeth, Eunice, Deborah, and Abigail Olmsted.

Children [by first wife] :

Mary, b. abt. 1675;   m. at Norwalk, 9 May 1694, Thomas Read.

Jane, b. abt. 1677;   m. abt. 1700, Benjamin Wilson.

Sarah, b. abt. 1679;   m. at Norwalk, 5 June 1696, Jonathan Abbott.

Rebecca, b. abt. 1681;   m. Samuel St. John.

Elizabeth, b. abt. 1683;   m. at Norwalk, 14 June 1710, Henry Whitney.

Daniel, b. abt. 1685;   m. (rec. Ridgefield) 9 May 1711, Hannah Ketchum.

Richard, b. abt. 1687;   m. (rec. Ridgefield) 22 Apr. 1714, Mary Betts, dau. of Samuel and Judith of Norwalk.

Eunice, b. abt. 1689.

Deborah, b. abt. 1693.

Children [by second wife] :

Abigail, b. abt. 1696.

Anna, b. abt. 1698, m. in 1720, Robert Andrus.

XJohn, b. abt. 1700; m. (1) abt. 1726, Mindwell Sherwood, dau. of Benjamin, b. 8 Sept. 1696; m. (2) ————.

Osborn, Richard. Colonial grant of 80 acres, May 1671, for service in Pequot War.

Came to Hingham, Mass., 1635; rem. to Windsor with first settlers, and served in Pequot War 1637. He came to New Haven, 1639, and moved to Fairfield by 1652. He settled in Westchester, N. Y., by 1682, and d. there abt. 1685.

At New Haven, he signed the Fundamental Agreement, June 1639, and took the oath of allegiance, 1644; had three in his family, 1641; sold his property there in Apr. and May 1652.

On 26 May 1674 he gave land in Fairfield to his dau. Priscilla wife of Cornelius Seeley; and it was recorded, 25 Nov. 1678, that Thomas Bedient had land by gift from his father-in-law, Capt. Richard Osborn.

On 27 Oct. 1682, being of Westchester, he gave his Fairfield lands to his son John, who was to pay £1 apiece to the eldest dau.'s five children, £2 apiece to dau. Priscilla's two sons and £1 apiece to her two daus., £1 apiece to dau. Sarah's seven children, £1 apiece to dau. Mary's three children, and to dau. Elizabeth, £50. [Fairfield Deeds.]

His first wife, mother of his children, is not known. On 12 June 1677, he appears in Westchester records as husband of Mary, widow of Roger Townsend. She had previously been widow of Mordecai Bedient.

Will of Capt. Richard of Westchester, 19 Dec. 1684; gr. child Richard, son of David of Eastchester; children; property in Fairfield County; legacies to Bridget wife of neighbor Justice John Palmer and her dau. Bridget Palmer; Capt. John Pell of Westchester County and son John Osborn, of Fairfield, Exec'rs; Thomas Bedient a witness.

Children [by first wife] :

Hannah, m. at Fairfield, 19 Nov. 1663, John Baldwin, of Milford; rem. to Newark, N. J.

Sarah, m. (1) by 1662, John Peat, and (2) 28 Mar. 1685, John
Brooks, both of Stratford.
+David.
Mary, m. Thomas Bedient.
Priscilla, b. abt. 1650, d. after 1710; m. by 1674, Cornelius Seeley, of
Bedford, N. Y.
Elizabeth, b. 3 Mar. 1650, d. 3 Mar. 1651 [Col. Rec.].
+John.
Elizabeth.

Osborn, David, s. of Richard.

Settled in Eastchester, where he d. in 1679; m. Abigail Pinkney,
dau. of Philip.

Inv. 22 Apr. 1679. The widow Osborn's children are men-
tioned, Nov. 1679, "before her second marriage"; one son, Richard.
The widow Abigail asked adm'n, 11 June 1679, for her father Mr.
Philip Pinkney and Nathaniel Tompkins.

Caveat of Thomas Bedient of Fairfield, 9 Dec. 1697, as attorney
to the orphans of David Osborn, Sarah and Abigail, now the wives
of Jonathan Sturges and William Hill.

Richard son of David of Eastchester chose his uncle, John
Pinkney of same, for guardian, 30 Jan. 1689/90, but his uncle,
John Osborn of Fairfield, 14 Mar. 1690.

Children:

Abigail, b. [say 1671], d. at Fairfield, prob. 27 Apr. 1712; m. (rec.
Fairfield) 7 Oct. 1691, William Hill, of Fairfield.
Sarah, b. [say 1673], d. at Milford, 17 June 1727; m. (1) (rec. Fair-
field) last day of July 1692, Jonathan Sturges; m. (2) after 1711,
Hon. Peter Burr; m. (3) (rec. Milford) 1 June 1726, Gov. Jona-
than Law.
+Richard, b. abt. 1676.

Osborn, John, s. of Richard. Ens., Fairfield Trainband, Oct.
1695; Capt., Fairfield County Troop, May 1704; Capt., west
company in Fairfield, May 1705. Deputy for Fairfield, Oct.
1699, May 1704, May and June 1709.

Remained in Fairfield; Capt. John d. 15 July 1709. Married
(by receipt 1673) Sarah Bennett, dau. of James, b. about 1653, d.
early in 1726.

Widow Sarah and Sergt. Samuel Osborn granted adm'n. Six children, and the heirs of Hannah Rumsey dec'd. Joseph and Elizabeth chose mother guardian, 28 Apr. 1710. Distribution: widow; Samuel, John, David, Joseph, Sarah, Elizabeth Osborn.

On 21 Apr. 1714, Solomon Foote conveyed to uncle James Bennett as trustee, realty distributed to me through marriage with wife Elizabeth from her father Capt. John Osborn's Estate.

Joseph Osborn, Solomon Foote and Elizabeth his wife, and Nathan Lewis and Sarah his wife, conveyed 1719 to David Osborn, right in dowry of mother Sarah Osborn.

Will of Sarah, 27 Sept. 1723, proved 2 Feb. 1725/6; sons Samuel, John, David, Joseph; gr. dau. Sarah Squire; daus. Sarah Lewis and Elizabeth Foote.

Children:

> Hannah, b. 26 July 1677; m. Isaac Rumsey.
> +Samuel, b. abt. 1680.
> +John, b. abt. 1683.
> +David, b. [say 1686].
> Sarah, b. [say 1689], d. at Stamford, 30 Apr. 1729; m. (1) Nathan Lewis, of Fairfield; m. (2) (rec. Stamford), 24 Jan. 1725/6, John Bishop.
> +Joseph, b. [say 1692].
> Elizabeth, bapt. 24 May 1696; m. Solomon Foote.

Osborn, Richard, s. of David. Justice, 1717-34.

Aged 34 in 1710 Census of Eastchester, N. Y.

Removed from Eastchester to Ridgefield, 1713. Married (1) by 1699, Sarah Andrews, dau. of John, b. at Fairfield, 12 Jan. 1680/1, d. at Ridgefield, 6 Nov. 1719; m. (2) by 1724, Sarah ———.

Samuel Osborn of Bedford, John and Joseph Osborn living on the Oblong, all in Westchester County, N. Y., Jonathan and Jeremiah Osborn of Ridgefield, and Daniel Osborn of Norwalk, conveyed 15 Nov. 1749 to John Andrews of Fairfield, right from mother Sarah Osborn who was dau. to John Andrews formerly of said Fairfield.

Children, recorded at Ridgefield:

David, b. Nov. 1700; m. Rachel Keeler, dau. of Joseph, b. 4 Oct. 1706.
Abigail, b. July 1702; m. 19 May 1720, Timothy Keeler.
John, b. May 1704; m. 28 Sept. 1726, Patience Ketchum.
Joseph, b. Sept. 1706; m. 18 Apr. 1728, Mary Hyatt.
Samuel, b. Nov. 1708; m. 1 Jan. 1732/3, Sarah Simkins.
Jonathan, b. Nov. 1710; m. 3 Jan. 1732, Rebecca ———.
Sarah, b. Dec. 1712.
Hezekiah, b. 30 Apr. 1715, d. at Ridgefield in 1738/9; Inv. 26 Feb.
1738/9.
Jeremiah, b. 17 Dec. 1717; m. 11 Jan. 1738/9, Rebecca ———.
Daniel, b. 14 Oct. 1719, d. in 1763; m. at Greenfield, 15 Nov. 1744,
Sarah Osborn, bapt. 5 May 1726, d. at Lenox, Mass., 13 Mar. 1819
ae. 93.

Osborn, Samuel, s. of John.   Sergt., Fairfield Trainband.

Born about 1680, d. at Fairfield, 2 Apr. 1752 ae. 72 (g. s.) ; m.
(1) abt. 1700, Abigail Rumsey, dau. of Robert, b. abt. 1680, d.
5 Aug. 1724 ae. abt. 44 (g. s.) ; m. (2) at Fairfield, 4 Nov. 1724,
Hannah Couch, dau. of Simon, bapt. 27 Aug. 1699, d. 30 Aug.
1774 in 76 yr. (g. s.).

His wife Abigail was bapt. at Fairfield Church, 26 Dec. 1703.
He was called Sergt. at bapt. of children, 1711, 1713 and 1727.
As Samuel, Sr., he renewed his Covenant, 24 Oct. 1725.

Will 2 Aug. 1751, proved 7 Apr. 1752; wife Hannah; children
Samuel, Daniel, Thaddeus, Joseph, Jeremiah, Hannah, Abigail wife
of Eleazer Sturgis, Ann, Sarah, Eunice, Abigail, Isabel, Mary,
Ellen, Martha. Distribution 20 Sept. 1774; heirs of Samuel,
Jr.; Daniel; Thaddeus; Joseph; heirs of Jeremiah; Hannah
widow of David Sturges; Abigail wife of Eleazer Sturges; Ann
wife of Jacob Cadwell; Sarah wife of Samuel Odell, Esq.;
Eunice widow of David Burr; Abigail widow of Cornelius Wine-
koop; Isabel wife of Archabel Cambel; Mary wife of Liman
Hall; Ellin wife of Woolcut Hawley; Martha Osborn.

Children [by first wife], bapt. at Fairfield:

XSamuel, b. abt. 1701, bapt. 2 Jan. 1703/4, d. at Fairfield, 7 June 1754
in 54 yr. (g. s.) ; m. abt. 1723, Abigail Sturges, dau. of Joseph.
Hannah, bapt. 2 Jan. 1703/4; m. David Sturges.
Abigail, bapt. 27 Apr. 1707; m. 23 Apr. 1724, Eleazer Sturges.
Ann, bapt. 15 July 1711, m. Jacob Cadwell.
Sarah, bapt. 29 Nov. 1713; m. (1) Thomas Banks; m. (2) 19 Sept.
1751, Samuel Odell, of Stratfield.

Children [by second wife], recorded at Fairfield:

XDaniel, b. 10 Oct. 1725, bapt. 31 Oct. 1725, d. 27 Apr. 1804 ae. 79 (g. s.); Deacon; m. 19 Jan. 1757, Elizabeth Burr, dau. of Andrew, b. 22 June 1726, d. 5 Oct. 1815 in 90 yr. (g. s.).

Thaddeus, b. 1 Dec. 1726, bapt. 8 Jan. 1726/7, d. in 1797. Adm'n granted, 3 Oct. 1797, to Daniel Osborn, with Hezekiah Nichols as surety.

Eunice, b. 16 Feb. 1727/8, bapt. 24 Mar. 1727/8, d. 1 Dec. 1789; m. 11 Dec. 1751, Col. David Burr.

Abigail, b. 1 Sept. 1729, bapt. 5 Oct. 1729; m. 12 Mar. 1758, Cornelius Wyncoop, Jr., of New York, N. Y.

Isabel, b. 1 Feb. 1730/1, bapt. 14 Mar. 1730/1; m. Archibald Campbell, with whom she conveyed 1766, land from father's Est.

Joseph, b. 22 Feb. 1733, bapt. 15 Apr. 1733, d. 4(?) Oct. 1776 in 44 yr. (g. s.); m. at Westport, 23 Jan. 1765, Mary Couch; no issue; she m. (2) at Fairfield Church, 10 Dec. 1778, Jedediah Hull of Greenfield. Joseph's will, 1 Oct. 1776, proved 4 Nov. 1776; wife Mary, Exec'x; two bros. Daniel and Thaddeus; two nephews Daniel and Jeremiah, sons of bro. Daniel; six sisters, Eunice Burr, Abigail Wyncoop, Isabel Cammel, Ellen Hawley, Mary Hall, Martha Osborn.

Jeremiah, b. 30 Sept. 1734, bapt. 19 Nov. 1734, d. 8 Oct. 1757, unm.

Mary, b. 8 Aug. 1736, bapt. 17 Oct. 1736; will 10 Oct. 1793, Burke County, Ga; m. Lyman Hall; they, of Charleston, S. C., conveyed 22 Mar. 1762, land from her father's Est. He was Signer of Declaration of Independence, and Gov. of Georgia.

Ellen, b. 8 Feb. 1738, bapt. 23 Apr. 1738; m. 29 Nov. 1764, Wolcott Hawley.

Martha, b. 17 May 1739, bapt. 12 Aug. 1739, d. 7 Mar. 1788, unm. Will 12 Feb. 1788, proved 17 Mar. 1788; sister Ellen wife of Wolcott Hawley; niece Elizabeth Campbell; sister Abigail Wyncoop, Exec'x; nephew James Wyncoop to have my great Bible, also my geese and all right in my brother Joseph's Est.

Osborn, John, s. of John. Ens., west end company, Fairfield, Oct. 1709; Lieut., Oct. 1710; Capt., May 1715. Deputy for Fairfield, Oct. 1726, May and Sept. 1727.

Born about 1683; Capt. John d. at Fairfield, 13 Oct. 1760 in 78 yr. (g. s.). Married (1) abt. 1702, Mary Burr, dau. of John, b. 19 Aug. 1683, d. prob. abt. 1717.

Married (2) Thankful Silliman, widow of Daniel, and dau. of Joseph Howes, b. Apr. 1692.

He renewed his Covenant at Fairfield Church, 7 Mar. 1703. Mary and Deborah Silliman were bapt. there, 2 Nov. 1729, as daus. of Capt. Osborn's present wife.

Will 4 July 1760, proved 4 Nov. 1760; wife Thankful; three sons, Jonathan, John, Howes; gr. dau. Mary dau. of John; daus. Abigail, Mary, Thankful, Elizabeth, Sarah, Martha, Lydia; gr. son Jonathan son of Jonathan; gr. son John son of Howes; residue to son Stephen.

John Osborn of Fairfield, yeoman, and wife Mary, on 1 Sept. 1715, having rec'd from Samuel Burr of Charlestown, Mass., Exec'r of will of Jonathan Burr of Fairfield dec'd, land which was bequeathed by latter to their son Jonathan, released all right in Jonathan Burr's Est.

Children [by first wife] :

Abigail, bapt. 5 Mar. 1703/4, d. 14 Sept. 1783 in 81 yr. (g. s., Fairfield) ; m. 14 Dec. 1724, David Ogden.

John, bapt. 7 Oct. 1705, d. y.

XJonathan, bapt. 21 Dec. 1707; m. Sept. 1733, Catherine Wheeler, dau. of Joseph, b. 16 Nov. 1712.

Mary, bapt. 11 Feb. 1711/2, d. y.

XJohn, bapt. 6 Feb. 1714/5, d. at Westport, 23 Apr. 1775; m. 15 Apr. 1741, Abigail Bulkley, dau. of Thomas, who d. at Westport, 7 May 1796.

Mary, bapt. 17 Feb. 1716/7, d. y.

Children [by second wife] :

Mary, bapt. 20 Aug. 1721, d. 29 Dec. 1787; m. 5 Nov. 1740, Nathaniel Perry.

XHowes, bapt. 3 Feb. 1722/3, d. at Fairfield, 29 Aug. 1807 ae. 85 (g. s.) ; m. 6 Feb. 1755, Mary Bulkley, dau. of Peter, bapt. 17 Oct. 1731, d. 25 Nov. 1812 ae. 81 (g. s.).

Thankful, bapt. 2 May 1725, d. 13 Apr. 1812 ae. 87 (g. s.) ; m. 10 Nov. 1743, Samuel Beers.

Elizabeth, bapt. 28 May 1727; m. (1) 5 Nov. 1747, Jabez Bulkley; m. (2) 9 Dec. 1761, Jonathan Darrow, Sr.

Sarah, bapt. 8 Dec. 1728, d. at Fairfield, 8 Apr. 1776 in 48 yr (g. s.) ; m. 10 Jan. 1754, Jonathan Lewis.

Martha, bapt. 13 Sept. 1730, d. 30 Jan. 1810 ae. 80; m. 14 June 1770, Jabez Thorp.

Lydia, m. 23 Jan. 1771, David Edwards of North Stratford.

XStephen, b. 4 Feb. 1739 (Bible rec.), bapt. 18 Mar. 1738/9, d. at Fairfield, 28 Oct. 1822 ae. 84 (g. s.) ; m. 17 Dec. 1778, Grizzel Osborn; dau. of Eleazer, b. 14 Mar. 1751, d. 14 Jan. 1840 (Bible record).

Osborn, David, s. of John. Sergt., Fairfield Trainband.

Born about 1686, died late in 1727; married Dorothy Bulkley, dau. of Dr. Peter, who d. in 1734. Her parentage is based on cumulative circumstantial evidence in public records; also, her name as "Buckley" appears to have been handed down in old family records.

Inv. 6 Feb. 1727/8 presented by Capt. John Osborn and Dorothy Osborn, who were appointed Adm'rs, 19 Dec. 1727. William Osborn released, 19 Mar. 1732/3, to bros. and sisters, Eleazer and David Osborn, Dorothy, Hannah and Grace Osborn, and Sarah wife of Joseph Sherwood, right in Est. of father David. On 1 May 1733, Dorothy chose her mother Dorothy for guardian, and she was appointed guardian to Hannah, Grace, and David; Eleazer chose Peter Bulkley, Sr., for guardian.

On 7 May 1734, William Osborn was appointed guardian to Grace and David, children of Dorothy Osborn dec'd. Grace chose Joseph Sherwood, 5 Sept. 1738; and David chose Peter Bulkley, 2 Mar. 1741/2.

Eleazer Osborn, Joseph Sherwood and Sarah his wife, and Nathan Thorp and Dorothy his wife, conveyed 29 Mar. 1739 to John Ogden, land originally from Richard Osborn and father David dec'd, also one-half of what was set to Hannah Osborn now dec'd in distribution of said David's Est.

Children, bapt. at Fairfield:
David, bapt. 8 Feb. 1707/8, d. y.
XWilliam, b. 16 Apr. 1708 [error for 1709, family record], d. at Weston, 16 Feb. 1795 in 86 yr. (g. s.) ; m. (1) 16 Feb. 1741 [error for 1731, family record], Elizabeth Turney, b. abt. 1715, d. 16 Feb. 1741 in 26 yr. (Bible) ; m. (2) Mary Lyon, b. 15 Oct. 1714, d. 6 Jan. 1796 in 82 yr. (g. s.).
Sarah, bapt. June 1711 ; m. 17 Feb. 1731, Joseph Sherwood.
John, bapt. 8 Nov. 1713, d. y.
XEleazer, b. 26, bapt. 29 Jan. 1715/6, d. 20 May 1788 in 73 yr. (g. s., Fairfield) ; Lieut.; m. 29 June 1738, Hannah Bulkley, dau. of Peter, b. 29 Aug. 1719, d. 19 Nov. 1812 ae. 93 (g. s.).
Dorothy, bapt. 3 Nov. 1717, d. at Weston, 14 Sept. 1794 ae. 77 (g. s.) ; m. 3 May 1738, Nathan Thorp.

Hannah, bapt. 5 Feb. 1720/1, d. before 1739.
Grace, b. 7 Jan. 1725 (Bible record), bapt. 10 Jan. 1724/5, d. abt.
1807; m. at Greenfield, Jan. 1749/50, John Stratton.
✕David, bapt. 6 Aug. 1727, d. 15 Jan. 1772 in 45 yr. (g. s., Greenfield);
m. Mindwell Sherwood.

Osborn, Joseph, s. of John.

Born perhaps abt. 1692, d. at Fairfield late in 1731; m. Hannah
Hubbell, dau. of Samuel, bapt. 19 May 1695. Widow Hannah
Osborn m. 12 Dec. 1731, James Burr, and d. 11 Aug. 1743.

Joseph and Hannah renewed their Covenant at Fairfield Church,
7 June 1719.

Adm'n granted, 21 Dec. 1731, to John and Hannah Osborn.
Widow Hannah Osborn was appointed guardian to son Nathan,
5 Dec. 1732. Nathan Osborn was appointed guardian to Peter,
son of Joseph, 6 Dec. 1743; Sarah, Abigail, and Olive chose
Nathan Hubbell guardian. Olive Osborn gave a receipt, 3 Dec.
1747, to uncle Nathan Hubbell of Wilton.

Agreement of heirs of John Osborn, 23 Apr. 1751, relating to
lands distributed to heirs of Joseph and David: Samuel, John,
William, Daniel, Eleazer, and Sarah Osborn; Gershom Bradley
as guardian to Peter Osborn; Gershom and Hannah Thorp; David
Osborn; Zephaniah and Olive Clark; Daniel and Abigail Squire.
[Fairfield Deeds.]

Daniel Osborn and Sarah his wife of Norwalk conveyed 1747
land that was their father's Joseph Osborn dec'd.

Children, three bapt. at Fairfield, four at Greenfield:

Elizabeth, bapt. 28 June 1719, d. abt. 1739; m. Gershom Bradley.
✕Nathan, bapt. 5 Feb. 1720/1, d. at New Fairfield in 1760; adm'n
granted, 4 Dec. 1760; m. (1) Sarah Hurlbut, dau. of Gideon; m.
(2) 22 Dec. 1748, Grizzel Lyon.
Hannah, bapt. 21 June 1724; m. Jan. 1745/6, Gershom Thorp.
Sarah, bapt. 5 May 1726; m. 15 Nov. 1744, Daniel Osborn.
Abigail, bapt. (no date, doubtless 1727), d. 12 Sept. 1815 ae. 90
(g. s.); m. (1) Sept. 1746, Daniel Squire; m. (2) 22 July 1756,
Nathan Beers.
Olive, bapt. 7 Sept. 1729; m. 31 Oct. 1749, Zephaniah Clark.
✕Peter, bapt. 23 May 1731; res. Easton to 1783; rem. to Fredericks-
burg, Dutchess Co., N. Y.; res. 1789, Stephentown, Westchester
Co., N. Y.; res. 1803, Stamford, Delaware Co., N. Y.; m. (1)
1752, Lois ———, who d. 29 June 1758 ae. abt. 24; m. (2) 14 Mar.
1759, Elizabeth Banks, dau. of John, b. 11 Feb. 1741, d. 23 Apr.
1760 ae. 18 yrs. 2 mos.; m. (3) 1762, Sarah ———.

OSBORN FAMILY (STRATFORD)

Osborn, John.

He m. (1) ———.

He m. (2) at Stratford, 20 Feb. 1710/1, Hannah Gilbert, widow [of John]; she was dau. of Thomas Canfield, b. at Milford, 20 Nov. 1667.

Receipts were given in 1728 to bro. Samuel Osborn for legacies in the Est. of their father John of Stratford, by James and Sarah Peat, John Osborn, Mary Osborn, Ephraim Beardsley for wife's legacy; also by the widow Hannah Osborn.

Children [by first wife]:

> John, m. at Stratford, 14 July 1709, Prudence Blagge.
> Mehitabel, m. at Stratford, 30 Dec. 1708, Ephraim Beardsley.
> Samuel, d. at Stratford in 1737; m. at Stratford, 1 Nov. 1727, Mary Jones.
> Sarah, m. at Stratford, 14 Nov. 1716, James Peat.
> Mary.

Palmer, John, s. of William.

Born abt. 1633, testified 1 May 1666, ae. 33, in the Benfield case; d. in or shortly before 1692.

Married Bridget Baxter, who had divorced her former husband, Capt. Thomas Baxter, May 1662. She was Palmer's wife by May 1666.

John Palmer purchased land in Fairfield, from Robert Rumsey and John Barlow which was recorded 14 Feb. 1669; Palmer to maintain fence in accordance with town order of 15 Mar. 1668.

He removed to Westchester, where he was a neighbor of Capt. Richard Osborn, whose will 1684 gave legacies to Palmer's wife Bridget and dau. Bridget. With his wife Bridget he conveyed 1689 to Thomas Baxter [his stepson] land which he owned in partnership with his bro. Joseph Palmer. On 30 Nov. 1692, his widow Bridget and three daus., with their husbands, as named below, conveyed to Thomas Baxter.

Children:

> Mary, m. Francis Doughty, of Flushing.
> Abigail, m. Thomas Farrington, of Flushing.
> Bridget, unm. in 1692.

Parruck, John.

In 1710 the Conn. Leg. paid the widow Sarah "Parret" for nursing Joseph Nichols and two other soldiers. Was she mother of John?

Married Hannah Beardsley, dau. of Samuel, b. at Stratford, 25 Oct. 1682. She m. (2) Edward Lacy.

Will 26 Dec. 1726, proved 16 Jan. 1726/7; son Elnathan; daus. Hannah, Abigail, Abiah; dau. Sarah had portion; wife Hannah and friend Thomas Sherwood of Stratford, Exec'rs.

Children, bapt. at Stratfield:

> John, bapt. 8 Dec. 1706, d. y.
> Sarah, bapt. 19 June 1709; m. Andrew Hubbell.
> Hannah, bapt. 17 Dec. 1710, d. 20 July 1736; m. (rec. Newtown) 6 Apr. 1727, John Sherwood.
> Abigail, b. (rec. Fairfield) 18 Sept. 1712, bapt. 2 Nov. 1712; m. (rec. Fairfield) 18 Jan. 1731, Jonathan Meeker.
> John, bapt. 26 Aug. 1716, d. y.
> Abiah, m. (rec. Fairfield) 24 Aug. 1738, Caleb Lyon.
> ✕Elnathan, b. (rec. Fairfield) 18 Feb. 1724; m. at Stratfield, 22 Nov. 1750, Mary Hill, dau. of William.

Patchen, Joseph.

Born abt. 1610; testified as Joseph, Sr., ae. 56, in the Benfield case, 1 May 1666. He settled first in Roxbury, Mass., where he m. (1) 18 Apr. 1642, Elizabeth, widow of Stephen Iggleden, Jr. She came from Biddenden, co. Kent, on the *Castle*, in 1638, with husband and children, of whom the former d. on the passage. Another passenger d. at sea and left money to Elizabeth for her care of him.

"Goodwife Patchin, a poor old woman," who joined Roxbury Church in 1649, may have been mother of Joseph. Yet his wife Elizabeth must have been considerably, perhaps a decade, older than himself, and in the view of that period a woman of 50 years was sometimes qualified for the term "old."

He rem. to Fairfield by 1652, was granted a homelot 1655/6, and was one of four "poor men" whose debts were forgiven by Dr. Pell in his will 1669. He was living 1689, when his son was still "Jr."

He m. (2) Mary ———,* who also testified in the Benfield
case, 1666. Much of his property in Fairfield came into possession of the Edward Adams family, prob. not by inheritance. Quite
likely there was relationship, but just what we cannot say; Patchen
realty may have been turned over to the Adamses in return for
maintenance.

Joseph may have been stepfather of John Eggleden of Fairfield; if we may suppose that Elizabeth named a child John by
both husbands, a duplication sometimes found.

Children [by first wife], recorded at Roxbury:

> Joseph, b. 14 Apr. 1643, bapt. 24 Mar. 1650, d. at Fairfield in 1689,
> apparently unm. He was appointed 1680 to sweep the meeting-
> house. Inv. 10 Dec. 1689; Est. insolvent; no land; clothing and
> tobacco at house of Nathan Adams. Adm'n granted to Jonathan
> Morehouse.
>
> John, b. 20 Dec. 1644, bapt. 24 Mar. 1650; was living, a poor old man,
> at Stratfield in 1712, when he was provided for in the will of Dea.
> Isaac Wheeler, whose servant he had been for thirty years.

Prob. child [by second wife]:

+Jacob, b. abt. 1663.

Patchen, Jacob, [s. of Joseph].

Born about 1663; d. at Wilton, 15 Feb. 1749 aged 87 or 88.

Freeman, Fairfield, 18 Mar. 1689/90.

Married Mary, widow of Samuel Grumman, by 1692 when
Patchen was administrator in right of his wife on Grumman's
estate. She was dau. of William Hubbard of Greenwich, whose
will named her as wife of Patchen, 1702. Mary d. at Wilton,
25 Mar. 1754. Samuel Adams purchased from Jacob Patchen
with consent of Patchen's wife, 1692/3, part of the long lot laid
out to John Grumman dec'd.

Jacob was bapt. at Fairfield church, 17 Mar. 1694/5, and Mary
renewed her Covenant, 24 Mar. 1694/5, three children being bapt.
on latter date: Joseph, of Jacob and Mary Patchen; Abigail, of
Jacob; and Mary Grumman, of Mary. Jacob of Norwalk conveyed 13 Nov. 1746 to son Jacob, land in Fairfield.

---

* Possibly dau. of Thomas Morehouse. See JONATHAN MOREHOUSE.

Children, bapt. at Fairfield:

>Abigail, bapt. 24 Mar. 1694/5; m. in 1714, William Stirling.
XJoseph, bapt. 24 Mar. 1694/5; rem. to Wilton; m. [say 1723], Margery or Margaret Cable, dau. of John, 3d, who d. 1 Apr. 1788.
Sarah, bapt. 22 May 1698.
XJacob, bapt. 2 Nov. 1701, d. at Wilton, 4 Apr. 1764; will 29 Mar. 1764, proved 1 May 1764; m. [say 1725], Abigail Cable, dau. of John, 3d, who d. 15 Feb. 1795/6.
Martha, bapt. 12 Sept. 1703.*
XSamuel, bapt. 30 June 1706; m. Margaret Morehouse, dau. of Noah.

Patterson, Andrew.

Came from Scotland as a political refugee, 1685 to Perth Amboy, N. J., and thence the next year to Stratford.

Married at Stratford, 19 Feb. 1690 [1690/1], Elizabeth Peat. She was dau. of John, b. 19 Feb. 1669/70.

He d. at Stratford, 2 Dec. 1746 ae. 87 (g. s.).

Will 8 May 1742, proved 15 Dec. 1746; wife Elizabeth; gr. sons Abraham, James, and Elnathan Patterson; two sons, William and John.

Children, recorded at Stratford:

>Sarah, b. 17 Mar. 1694; m. 3 July 1712, Ephraim Beach.
Charles, b. 4 Apr. 1696, d. abt. 1726; m. 29 Jan. 1718/9, Eunice Nichols; she m. (2) 2 May 1728, Nathaniel Sherman.
William, b. 2 July 1698, d. 31 Dec. 1758 ae. 60; m. 22 Aug. 1723, widow Anna Burton; widow of Joseph Burton, and dau. of Lt. Samuel Ufford, b. 8 Aug. 1702, d. 22 Apr. 1778 ae. 75.
Elizabeth, b. 28 Jan. 1700 [1700/1]; m. (rec. Fairfield) 12 Apr. 1722, Abraham Morehouse.
Hannah, b. 18 Apr. 1703, bapt. at Stratfield, 30 May 1703, d. 13 Mar. 1760; m. (rec. Newtown) 16 Apr. 1724, Joseph Murray.
Mary, b. 27 Mar. 1706, bapt. at Stratfield, 2 June 1706; m. John Adams, of Newtown.
John, b. 24 June 1711, d. at Piermont, N. H., 20 Jan. 1806 in 95 yr.; grad. Yale Coll. 1728; m. at Stratford, 4 June 1730, Mary Curtis; dau. of Josiah; she d. 18 July 1789 in 78 yr.

Peacock, John.

Of New Haven 1639, Milford 1641, and Stratford 1651; d. in 1670.

---

* Abraham, son of Martha Patchen, bapt. 26 Nov. 1727.

Married Joyce ———, who was adm. to Milford Church, 19 Dec. 1641, and dismissed to Stratford, 7 Dec. 1651.

Will 4 Mar. 1670; son-in-law James Clark; wife Joyce; daus. Phebe and Mary. Inv. 30 Oct. 1670.

Marriage agreement between Richard Burgess and Phebe Peacock, 20 Oct. 1677.   Phebe wife of Richard Burgess and dau. of John Peacock dec'd conveyed 1678 to her bro.-in-law Benjamin Beach; also to James Clark and his children by his wife Deborah, dau. of the dec'd. [Stratford Deeds.]

Children, three bapt. at Milford:

> John, bapt 16 Jan. 1641/2, d. y.
> John, bapt. 19 Nov. 1643, d. y.
> Deborah, bapt. Feb. 1644 [1644/5], d. at Stratford, 14 Dec. 1705; m. James Clark.
> Phebe, b. [say 1647]; m. in 1677, Richard Burgess.
> Mary, b. [say 1650], d. abt. 1677; m. abt. 1670, Benjamin Beach.

Peat, John.

Jo: Peat, a husbandman, ae. 38, from Duffield, co. Derby, came in the *Hopewell,* Apr. 1635.   The name in Stratford, where he early settled, was often spelled Peake, then Peat, and at last more generally Peet.

John, Sr., d. at Stratford, 1 Sept. 1684.   No probate found.

Perhaps his last wife was Ann "Peacke", whose Inv. was taken 29 Apr. 1687 by John Green and Joseph Lockwood.

When the estate of John Charles of Branford was distributed in 1673, a share went to John Peat for the children he had by his deceased wife, a dau. of Charles. It is uncertain what John Peat this was. It is well established that John, Jr., m. Sarah Osborn, and almost equally certain that she was mother of his seven children. The children of John Charles (except the dau. who m. Peat) were all born in the 1630's and 1640's. It is a question whether he could have had a dau. old enough to be wife of John Peat, Sr., and mother of the two sons, neither of whom could have been born much later than 1640. These sons were adults with families of their own in 1673, and ought to have been mentioned as receiving the Charles legacy in their own right if they were the gr. children, instead of their father receiving it for them.

Granting that it was possible for Charles to have had a dau. born by abt. 1620, she would have been over 20 yrs. younger than John Peat, Sr., and just old enough to be mother of his sons. The fact that John Charles, Jr., lived a few years in Stratford agrees with the assumption that his sister m. a Stratford Peat. Perhaps the Charles girl was a second wife of John Peat, Sr., and had daus. by him. But the evidence at hand is insufficient for a positive conclusion.

Children :*
+John.
+Benjamin.

Peat, John, s. of John.

John, Jr., son of John, Sr., d. at Stratford, 28 Jan. 1677/8.

Will 17 Jan. 1677/8; wife Sarah; son Samuel (mentions a mare his grandfather gave him) ; sons John, Joseph; daus. Sarah, Hannah, Elizabeth, Jane; friends Capt. William Curtis, Israel Chauncey, my bro. Benjamin Peat, my bro. John Osborn, and William Roberts, overseers. Inv. 20 Feb. 1677/8.

Married Sarah Osborn, dau. of Richard; she m. (2) 25 Mar. 1685, John Brooks. The "deed of gift" given by Richard Osborn 1682, provided £1 apiece for the seven children of his dau. Sarah.

Samuel and John Peat, Sarah Lake, Hannah Wakelee, and Elizabeth Patterson, children of John Peat of Stratford dec'd, conveyed 1694 to mother Sarah Brooks and father-in-law John Brooks.

Children, recorded at Stratford:
+Samuel, b. 26 Dec. 1663.
 Sarah, b. 3 Oct. 1665; m. Thomas Lake.
 Hannah, b. 6 Dec. 1667; m. [Jacob?] Wakelee.
 Elizabeth, b. 19 Feb. 1669 [1669/70]; m. 19 Feb. 1690 [1690/1],
   Andrew Patterson.
+John, b. 28 Nov. 1672.
 Joseph, b. 10 Mar. 1674/5, d. in 1694. Inv. 6 Nov. 1694; distribution
   to brothers and sisters, Samuel and John Peat, Sarah Lake, Hannah
   Wakelee, Elizabeth Patterson, Jane Peat.
 Jane, b. 17 Oct. 1677; m. (1) John Commell; m. (2) 6 Mar. 1706/7,
   Bezaleel Sherman.

* Prob. daus. also, not known.

Peat, Benjamin, s. of John.

Will 14 Apr. 1704, proved 12 July 1704; eldest son Benjamin; son Samuel; dau. Mary Burrit had portion at marriage; residue to wife Phebe, Exec'x. Inv. June 1704.

Married Phebe Butler, dau. of Richard. Wife was called Phebe at birth of child 1677.

He d. at Stratford, 1 May 1704. His widow was living 1725. Phebe Peat of Stratford conveyed 24 Feb. 1724/5 to son Samuel "for his inCourigment towards My Maintenance & support in my old age" all right from the estate of my father Richard Butler and from the estate of my Dear Husband Benjamin Peat dec'd. Benjamin Peat and Samuel Peat, Jr., conveyed 1713, land from grandfather Richard Butler dec'd.

Children, recorded at Stratford:

    Samuel, b. 19 Sept. 1663, d. y.
   +Benjamin, b. 31 Aug. 1665.
   +Samuel, b. 15 Mar. 1670/1, or 14 Mar. 1670 (second entry).
    Thomas, b. 29 Mar. 1674, d. y.
    Alice, b. 10 Oct. 1677, d. y.
    Mary, b. 10 Oct. 1683; m. 10 Mar. 1702/3, Josiah Burritt.

Peat, Samuel, s. of John, 2d. Lt.

Born at Stratford, 26 Dec. 1663; Lt. Samuel d. 14 Sept. 1747 in 84 yr. (g. s., Stratford).

Married (1) abt. 1688, Mary ———.
Married (2) 1 June 1698, Elizabeth Smith.

Children of Samuel Sr. and Mary, recorded at Stratford:

    Nathan, b. 28 Nov. 1689; m. 21 Feb. 1711/2, Hester Nichols.
    Elnathan, b. 4 Aug. 1692; m. 4 Nov. 1714, Mary Galpin.
    Hannah, b. 12 Aug. 1694; m. Daniel Nichols.

Peat, John, s. of John, 2d.

Born at Stratford, 28 Nov. 1672; Sergt. John d. 1 Feb. 1709/10.

Married (rec. Stratford) 12 May 1696, Mary Morehouse. She m. (2) at Stratfield, 4 Dec. 1712, John Corbett, and (3) 5 Sept. 1723, Benjamin Peat.

Inv. 13 Mar. 1709/10; widow Mary to administer. Dates of birth of children are appended. Mary wife of John Corbett of

Stratford, formerly widow of John Peat, 9 Mar. 1718/9; distribution ordered to four sons and three daus. On 25 Feb. 1712/3, Joseph and David chose mother Mary Corbett for guardian, and she was appointed for the five younger children.

Mary Corbit wife of John of Stratford, formerly widow of John Peat, Adm'x, 9 Mar. 1718/9; distribution ordered; four sons and three daus., Joseph, David, Daniel, John, Sarah, Mary and Hanna Peat.

Children of John and Mary, recorded at Stratford, four bapt. at Stratfield:

> Joseph, b. 4 Jan. 1696 [1696/7]; m. Eleanor ———.
> David, b. 30 June 1698; m. 1 Oct. 1719, Mary Titherton.
> Sarah, b. 4 Aug. 1700 [4 June by probate].
> Mary, b. 3 Dec. 1702 [2 Dec. by probate], bapt. 30 May 1703; m. Daniel Bronson, of Danbury.
> Hannah, b. 22 Dec. 1704, bapt. 26 Aug. 1705; m. Joseph Seeley.
> John, b. 23 Apr. 1707, bapt. 3 Aug. 1707.
> Dinah, b. 30 Mar. 1709, bapt. 29 May 1709; m. John Luff, Jr.
> Daniel, b. (no record).

Peat, Benjamin, s. of Benjamin.

Born at Stratford, 31 Aug. 1665, d.

Married (1) Priscilla Fairchild, dau. of Thomas, b. 20 Apr. 1669.

Married (2) 5 Sept. 1723, Mary Corbett; agreed by marriage covenant "to take her body without her estate." She was Mary Morehouse, and had been wife first of John Peat and second of John Corbett.

Children of Benjamin and Priscilla, recorded at Stratford:

> Butler, b. 1 Sept. 1689.
> James, b. 27 Mar. 1691; m. 14 Nov. 1716, Sarah Osborn.
> William, b. 1 May 1694; m. (1) 20 June 1717, Charity Lake; m. (2) 12 July 1727, Mrs. Sarah Fairchild.
> Richard, b. 30 Aug. 1696; m. at Woodbury, 11 Mar. 1724/5, Sarah Curtis.
> Thomas, b. 15 July 1698; Deacon Thomas "of North Stratford & the King's Post-rider for 32 years" d. 12 Oct. 1760 in 63 yr. (g. s., Trumbull); m. 7 Jan. 1724/5, Phebe Nichols.
> Josiah, b. 1 Apr. 1700.
> Katharine, b. 18 July 1701.
> Anna, b. 30 Jan. 1703/4, bapt. at Stratford (rec. Stratfield) 23 July 1704.

Peat, Samuel, s. of Benjamin.

> Born at Stratford, 15 Mar. 1670/1; called Jr. to distinguish him from his cousin.
>
> Married by 1698 Abigail Harvey, dau. of Josiah.
>
> Child of Samuel Jr. and Abigail, recorded at Stratford:
>> Abigail, b. 30 Mar. 1707, bapt. at Stratford (rec. Stratfield) 27 Apr. 1707; m. 30 Dec. 1725, Samuel Deforest.

Pell, Thomas. Served in Pequot War, 1637. Magistrate at Fairfield, May 1661. Deputy for Fairfield, May 1664, May 1665.

> He came in the *Hopewell,* 1635, ae. 22; apparently came down to Saybrook and served under Capt. Mason, 1637. He came to New Haven by 1642; in 1646 was sued by Mr. Caffinch for slander; and in 1647 he attached £200 of Mr. Selleck's goods. About Oct. 1647 he m. Lucy, widow of Mr. Francis Brewster. Although not a Puritan, and very independent in character, he was useful as a surgeon, and his social standing permitted him liberties denied to lesser men. He refused to take the Oath of Fidelity at New Haven, saying he had taken the oath to the King in England, and should not take it here. The Court tried to compel him to pay a fine which had been imposed on his wife before he m. her, and though summoned several times, he refused to pay, or absented himself, leading to a charge of contempt; but the fine was apparently still unpaid in 1650 when he rem. to Fairfield. There he was prominent; and he bought a large tract from the Indians in Westchester County.
>
> Will 21 Sept. 1669, proved 30 Sept. 1669; denied natural issue of his body; God has taken to himself my beloved wife Lucy; nephew John Pell in old England, only son of my only brother John Pell, Doctor of Divinity, which he had by his first wife; bro. John Pell's daus.; if my bro. hath a son or sons by his last wife; to Abigail wife of Daniel Burr, the best bed, silver spoons, etc.; to Daniel Burr, all my horses or colts in New England and New York (excepting mares); my son French; Nathaniel French; Elizabeth White; Mary White; Nathaniel White; set his servant Barbery at liberty, gave her a bed, etc.; "my antient mayd", Katherine Roystin; Daniel Burr and John Banks, Exec'rs; I give

these poor men their debts,—Joseph Patchen, James Everts, Thomas Bassett, Roger Knapp.

His nephew John Pell came over 1670, sold the Fairfield property inherited under his uncle's will, and settled on the Westchester County property; whence the Pells of Pelham Manor.

Perry, Richard. Clerk, New Haven Trainband, July 1644.

One of the original and considerable signers and settlers of New Haven; made free, 29 Oct. 1640; took oath of allegiance, 1644; Secretary, May 1646, and Oct. 1646; but the following Apr. was going on a voyage for the comfort of his family, and resigned the office. He bought land, however, Sept. 1647; and the next month had leave to go on the *Phœnix*. In Sept. 1649 he sold house and lot to Thomas Kimberly.

This Richard was a young man, married to a dau. of Mr. Richard Malbon, who was an original settler of New Haven, and Capt. of the artillery company. Malbon had an unmarried dau. Martha, and prob. a son Nathaniel. Malbon returned to England abt. 1648, and in 1655 lived in London; d. before 1661.

In Feb. 1650/1 it was stated that Mr. and Mrs. Perry "are goeing away"; the next month, Mr. Perry desired to carry some things to England which his father [Mr. Malbon] had written for. He appears no more in New Haven records.

Unless his plans were suddenly changed, it must be supposed that he returned to England in 1651. He had five children, Mary, Micajah, Samuel, John, and Grace, bapt. 1640-49. Savage suggests, and is followed by others, that Richard of New Haven rem. to Fairfield. This does not appear probable, for the Fairfield man was certainly there before 1650, and not one of the five children recorded at New Haven appears in Fairfield records.

PERRY FAMILY (FAIRFIELD)

Perry, Richard.

He was a land owner in Fairfield prior to 1650 (grant recorded 18 Mar. 1649), and prob. was related to the Burrs or m. a dau. of Jehu Burr, Sr. Not only were Burrs guardians of his children, but his son Nathaniel made them his contingent heirs should his own children die.

Inv. 10 Sept. 1658, small estate, £106; widow had dower in house at Fairfield before she married him; children, not named. Adm'n granted to Jehu Burr and William Hayden. Jehu and John Burr appointed guardians to children.

He m. (2) abt. 1656, Grace, widow of John Nichols.

Children [by first wife]:

+Nathaniel.
Apparently one or more others, who prob. d. y.; see will of Nathaniel.

Perry, Nathaniel, s. of Richard.

Married Esther Lyon, dau. of Richard, b. abt. 1658; she m. (2) John Grumman.

He had land recorded in Fairfield as heir to estate of his dec'd father; and purchased Peter Norton's lot from Hugh Griffin.

Will 1 Jan. 1681 [1681/2]; wife Hester; son Joseph; daus. Hester and Mary. If all children die, residuary heirs to be Daniel son of Jehu Burr and John son of John Burr. Inv. 23 Jan. 1681 [1681/2].

Children:

+Joseph, b. abt. 1676.
Esther, b. [say 1678]; m. Daniel Burr.
Mary, b. [say 1680]; m. by 1697, John Downs.

Perry, Joseph, s. of Nathaniel.

Born about 1676, d. at Fairfield, 9 Aug. 1753 ae. 77 (g. s.).

Married (1) abt. 1708, Sarah Bulkley, dau. of John, who d. abt. 1710 without issue.

Married (2) abt. 1710, Deborah, widow of Joseph Whelpley, and dau. of Daniel Burr, who d. abt. 1718.

Married (3) abt. 1718, Mary Clugston, dau. of Michael, bapt. 18 Sept. 1698; she m. (2) Capt. Thomas Edwards of Stratford and d. 8 Nov. 1773.

Will 15 Mar. 1753, proved 7 Sept. 1753; wife Mary; dau. Abigail wife of Joseph Wheeler, £100; dau. Sarah, £700; dau. Esther wife of John Cannon, £5; dau. Mary wife of Gershom Banks, £700; sons Joseph, Nathaniel, Daniel, Samuel, Michael, Ebenezer; to the six sons, "all my Land which I had by my first wife Sarah Bulkley."

He conveyed 1708 to Nathaniel Nichols, land to Compo laid out to father John Bulkley dec'd. On 8 May 1710 he conveyed to Joseph Bulkley, Sr., land which descended to him by virtue of marriage with Sarah Bulkley my late dec'd wife.

Children [by second wife], bapt. at Fairfield:

Abigail, bapt. 8 Feb. 1710/1; m. 10 Sept. 1729, Joseph Wheeler.

Esther, bapt. 15 June 1712, d. y.

XJoseph, bapt. 20 Sept. 1713, d. at Fairfield, 20 Aug. 1753 in 40 yr. (g. s.); adm'n granted 2 Oct. 1753; m. 11 Nov. 1736, Sarah Bulkley, dau. of Peter, bapt. 29 Nov. 1713; she m. (2) at Greenfield, 17 Apr. 1760, Thomas Wheeler, and d. 22 Apr. 1789 in 76 yr. (g. s., Greenfield).

XDaniel, bapt. 29 Jan. 1715/6; m. (1) 8 Oct. 1740, Mary Sturges, dau. of Peter, b. [say 1721], d. 31 Oct. 1742; m. (2) 1 Jan. 1744/5, Sarah Wilson.

XNathaniel, bapt. 16 Mar. 1718/9; d. 2 July 1798; m. 5 Nov. 1740, Mary Osborn, dau. of Capt. John, bapt. 20 Aug. 1721, d. 29 Dec. 1787.

Children [by third wife], bapt. at Fairfield:

XSamuel, b. (rec. Greenfield) 13 May 1719, bapt. [May or June] 1719, d. 1 June 1796; m. (1) 28 Apr. 1742, Sarah Whitlock, b. 27 Apr. 1720, d. at Greenfield, 18 Nov. 1759 in 40 yr.; m. (2) 15 Apr. 1760, Widow Mary Smith.

XMichael, bapt. 29 Oct. 1721, d. 10 Sept. 1797; m. 8 Dec. 1742, Grace Sturges, who d. 18 Sept. 1788.

Mary, bapt. 28 Mar. 1725; m. 14 Feb. 1752, Gershom Banks.

Sarah, bapt. 10 Mar. 1727/8, d. at Fairfield, 27 Dec. 1798 ae. 72 (g. s.); m. 15 Apr. 1756, Nathan Bulkley.

Esther, bapt. 12 Mar. 1731/2; m. (rec. Norwalk) 1 Dec. 1750, John Cannon.

XEbenezer, bapt. 9 Apr. 1738, d. at Fairfield, 26 Apr. 1804 in 67 yr. (g. s.); m. 24 Dec. 1760, Martha Sherwood, dau. of Daniel, b. 9 Mar. 1739/40, d. 10 Jan. 1814 in 75 yr. (g. s.).

PERRY FAMILY (STRATFORD)

Perry, Arthur.

Son of Arthur and Elizabeth (Crowell) Perry, b. abt. 1651; d. at Stratford in 1709; m. Anna Judson, dau. of Joshua.

Inv. 14 Apr. 1709; widow Annah; children William, Samuel, Annah, and Elizabeth had rec'd part of portion; Josiah chose mother Anna guardian; Daniel chose Sergt. Abraham Wooster guardian.

Children, recorded at Stratford, of Arthur and Anna:

William, b. 29 June 1677, d. in 1738; will 14 Mar. 1718, proved at Derby, 18 Dec. 1738; wife Sarah, Exec'x; brother Josiah; Inv. calls him cordwinder, of Stratford; adm'n granted to Yelverton Perry, 12 Dec. 1738; m. Sarah Stiles.

Anna, b. 22 Jan. 1678 [1678/9].

Samuel, b. 4 Feb. 1681/2; m. Elizabeth Wheeler, dau. of Moses, b. 8 Aug. 1687.

Sarah, b. 16 Jan. 1682/3.

Elizabeth, b. 25 Sept. 1684.

Yelverton, b. 20 Aug. 1686; served in Port Royal Expedition, 1710.

Seth, b. 24 Jan. 1687/8, d. in Feb. 1745/6; will 5, proved 15 Feb. 1745/6, named cousin Abner Perry of Stratford; Samuel Adams of Stratford, Exec'r.

Ruth, b. 5 May 1690, d. at Oxford, 27 Jan. 1767 in 77 yr.; m. Isaac Trowbridge of Stratford, with whom she conveyed 1721 to bro. Yelverton Perry land from Est. of her father.

Daniel, b. 14 Apr. 1692.

Joshua, b. 22 Dec. 1694, d. Oct. 1777 ae. 84 (g. s., Shelton); m. Mary Leavenworth, who d. 4 Nov. 1809 ae. 93 (g. s.)

Caleb, b. Aug. 1696, d. at Oxford abt. 1750; m. (rec. Stratford) 29 Jan. 1721/2, Hannah Bennett; dau. of Isaac of Stratford.

Deborah, b. 29 Mar. 1697, d. 17 Feb. 1754 ae. 56 (g. s., Huntington); m. Daniel Hide; conveyed 1727 land in Stratford to bro. Yelverton Perry from Est. of her father.

Josiah, b. 31 Aug. 1699, d. at Oxford in 1790 ae. 90½; m. Anna ———, who d. 9 Apr. 1768 ae. 62 (Oxford Church rec.).

Pettit, John.

Married at Stamford, 13 July 1665, Sarah Scofield. She was dau. of Daniel, and d. abt. 1684.

Inv. 5 June 1676. Widow Sarah; eldest son and two others; daus. Sarah and Bethia. The widow's share in her bro. Joseph's estate mentioned. On 8 Dec. 1684, Sarah chose Abraham Ambler for guardian, and John chose Daniel Scofield; the three other children referred to, "their mother being dec'd."

Children, recorded at Stamford:

Sarah, b. 27 Aug. 1666.

John, b. 26 Oct. 1668, d. at Stamford, 17 Dec. 1715; Inv. 23 July 1716; m. (1) Mary ———, who d. 23 Oct. 1702; m. (2) 16 Jan. 1706/7, Ann Gold, who d. 26 Jan. 1719/20 [Ann called Hannah in Probate Rec.].

Solomon, b. 20 Aug. 1672.

Mercy, b. 9 Nov. 1674; m. (rec. Milford) 26 May 1697, Jeremiah Beard.

Bethia, b. abt. 1676; unm. when named 1698 in will of grandmother Sarah (———) (Scofield) Merwin of Milford; perhaps m. (1) abt. 1699, Theophilus Miles, and (2) 24 Oct. 1705, Josiah Tibbals, Jr., and d. at Milford, 21 Mar. 1714/5.

Phippen, David.

Son of Robert, from Weymouth, or Melcombe Regis, co. Dorset, Eng.; came to Hingham, Mass., 1635; freeman, 3 Mar. 1636; rem. to Boston 1641, and d. in 1650.

Will proved 31 Oct. 1650; wife Sarah, house I dwell in, and shop; lots for Benjamin, Gamaliel, and George; my son-in-law Thomas Yeo; son George Vicars, a cow; son Joseph Phippen, exec'r with my wife; land in Hingham.

His widow Sarah m. George Hull of Fairfield, and d. Aug. 1659, naming her children in her will.

Children:

Joseph, of Hingham, rem. 1644 to Boston, was at Falmouth, and rem. 1665 to Salem, where he d. in 1687; m. Dorcas Wood.

Rebecca, m. George Vicars.

+Benjamin.

+Gamaliel.

Sarah, m. abt. 1650, Thomas Yeo.

George.

John, b. and d. July 1637.

John, b. and d. July 1640.

Phippen, Benjamin, s. of David.

Of Boston, blockmaker, d. abt. 1678.

Married (1) Wilmot ———.

Married (2) Eleanor ———.

Children [by first wife]:

David, b. 6 Nov. 1651.

Benjamin, b. 6 Apr. 1653, bapt. 10 Apr. 1653, d. 28 May 1654.

Benjamin, b. 19 Jan. 1654 [1654/5], bapt. 28 Jan. 1654 [1654/5], d. 20 Sept. 1655.

Benjamin, b. 15 July 1656.

Sarah, b. 13 Apr. 1658.

Mary, m. (rec. Stratford) 13 June 1680 (or 30 June 1681 by duplicate entry), Nathaniel Sherman.

+James, b. 30 Jan. 1663 [1663/4].

Rebecca, b. 10 Aug. 1666; m. (rec. Stratford) 6 June 1683, Benjamin Sherman.

Children [by second wife] :

Thomas, b. 1 Dec. 1671.

John, b. 1 June 1673.

+Joseph, b. 30 Nov. 1676.

Phippen, Gamaliel, s. of David.

Married Sarah Purchase.

Children, recorded at Boston:

Sarah, bapt. 30 Dec. 1649 ae. abt. 6 days; m. (1) Robert Haughton; m. (2) at Milford, 9 Feb. 1682, Benjamin Smith.

Gamaliel, b. 12 Mar. 1651 [1651/2], bapt. 14 Mar. 1652, d. 8 Sept. 1652.

Hannah, b. 25 July 1653, bapt. (as Anna) 31 July 1653; m. William Gibson.

Rebecca, b. 12 Feb. 1656 [1656/7], bapt. 1 Mar. 1657, d. at Milford, 17 Oct. 1712 ae. abt. 54 (g. s.) ; m. (1) Samuel Baldwin; m. (2) Job Prince; m (3) Ens. George Clark.

Elizabeth, b. 10 Aug. 1659, bapt. 15 Aug. 1659; said to m. ———— Spencer.

Gamaliel, b. 16 Feb. 1663.

Ann, b. 28 Apr. 1666; m. at Boston, 16 May 1686, William Wheeler.

Mehitabel, b. 27 Apr. 1668, d. at Milford, 15 Dec. 1721 in 54 yr. (g. s.) ; m. (1) Thomas Ford, Jr., of Milford; m. (2) Samuel Clark, of Milford.

Phippen, James, s. of Benjamin.

Born at Boston, 30 Jan. 1663/4, d. at Stratford, 12 Aug. 1717; m. Joanna ————, who m. (2) 8 Mar. 1722, Lemuel Sherwood; she d. at Stratfield, 9 May 1727.

Widow Joanna made oath to his Inv. 3 June 1718. Four sons and three daus. On 13 Feb. 1729/30, Jonadab Bassett was relieved from guardianship of James Phippen, and John Fairchild was appointed.

Children, recorded at Stratford:

> Joanna, b. 17 Jan. 1695/6; m. 26 Dec. 1723, John Fairchild.
>
> Mary, b. 27 Sept. 1697; m. at Stratfield, 28 May 1719, Jonadab Bassett.
>
> Benjamin, b. 14 Jan. 1701/2; m. 30 Jan. 1726/7, Rebecca Bostwick of New Milford.
>
> Sarah, b. 30 Mar. 1705, bapt. at Stratfield, 20 May 1705, d. at New Milford, 27 Jan. 1743/4; m. (at Trumbull, rec. New Milford) 6 Jan. 1740/1, Samuel Prindle.
>
> James, b. 10 Aug. 1710; m. at Trumbull, 14 July 1734, Hannah Smith.
>
> Son.
>
> Daughter.

Phippen, Joseph, s. of Benjamin.

Born 30 Nov. 1676.

He settled in Fairfield, and d. in 1733.

Will 3 Feb. 1732/3, proved 6 Feb. 1732/3; wife Elizabeth; sister Mary English; Ebenezer Silliman and Samuel Burr of Fairfield, Exec'rs.

Child:

> Joseph, d. at Fairfield, 10 July 1712 ae. abt. 26(?) (g. s.). Adm'n granted, 7 Aug. 1712, to father Joseph Phippen.

Pickett, John.   Deputy for Stratford, May 1673, May 1675.

He settled at Salem, Mass., by 1648; rem. to Stratford 1660; Constable, 1667, Selectman, 1669.

John, Sr., d. 11 Apr. 1684; his wife "Margett" d. 6 Oct. 1683 (Stratford rec.). John "Pigott's" wife of Stratford was mentioned by Winthrop as aged 41 yrs. in 1663.

Will 26 Feb. 1683/4; "stricken in years"; son Daniel, my dwelling house and home lot; sons John, Daniel, James, Thomas; dau. Sarah; Abigail wife of Thomas Pickett; dau. Rebecca Sention; son John's little boy John; James' little boy John; John Lane; Thomas' little boy; my dau. Lane; sons John and Daniel, Exec'rs; friends Israel Chauncey, Deacon Timothy Wilcoxson, and Sergt. Jehiel Preston, overseers. Witnesses: David Mitchell, Isaac Knell. Inv. 15 Apr. 1684.

Children, bapt. at Salem:

+John, bapt. 19 Nov. 1648.
+James, bapt. 19 Nov. 1648.
    Sarah, bapt. 19 Nov. 1648, d. at Killingworth, 11 Mar. 1725; m. at Stratford, 19 Dec. 1665, Robert Lane.
+Thomas, bapt. 19 Nov. 1648.
    Rebecca, bapt. 30 June 1650; m. (1) (rec. Norwalk) 31 Dec. 1673, James St. John; m. (2) abt. 1685, Andrew Messenger.
+Daniel, bapt. 25 Jan. 1651/2.
    Jacob, bapt. 3 Sept. 1654, d. y.

Pickett, John, s. of John.

Bapt. at Salem, Mass., 19 Nov. 1648, d. at Stratford between 14 and 26 Dec. 1690.

Will 14 Dec. 1690; son James; daus. Rebecca and Mary; bro. Daniel Pickett, sole Exec'r; friends Thomas Welles and Samuel Sherman, overseers.

Married 19 Jan. 1672/3, Mary "Crose." She was dau. of William Cross, and d. 7 Oct. 1687.

Children, recorded at Stratford:

    Rebecca, b. last of Dec. 1673, d. in 1693. Inv. 13 Mar. 1693; Daniel Pickett made oath. Distribution to brother James and sister Mary Pickett.
    Mary, b. 30 Mar. 1677, d. at Stamford, 10 Nov. 1732; m. (rec. Stamford) 16 Mar. 1698, Joshua Hoyt.
    John, b. 5 Jan. 1678 [1678/9], d. y.
    Sarah, b. 8 Mar. 1681 [1681/2], d. y.
    James, b. 5 Jan. 1686 [1686/7], d. in 1707/8. Inv. 26 Jan. 1707/8; included money due from Robert Lane of Killingworth; Joshua Hait of Stamford made oath. Distribution ordered to only sister, Mary wife of Joshua Hoyt.

Pickett, James, s. of John.

Bapt. at Salem, Mass., 19 Nov. 1648, d. at Danbury in 1701/2.
Married at Norwalk, 17 July 1673, Elizabeth* Keeler, dau. of Ralph; she m. (2) ——— Hayes.
Inv. 13 Feb. 1701 [1701/2]; widow and son John to administer.
On 26 Oct. 1711, Elizabeth Hayes of Norwalk, John Pickett and Samuel Hayes of Danbury, and Joseph Hoyt of Norwalk, con-

---

* Called *Rebecca* in marriage record; see footnote under RALPH KEELER.

veyed land which was my husband's and our father's Mr. James Pickett late of Danbury dec'd. [Norwalk Deeds.]

Children [by first wife], recorded at Norwalk:

> James, b. 7 May 1674, d. young.
> John, b. 16 Sept. 1675, d. at Danbury, 23 May 1712 [Pro. Rec.]; m. Catherine ———. Adm'n granted to widow and Francis Barnum. Births of children in Pro. Rec.: James,* b. 8 Jan. 1702/3; Elizabeth, b. 5 Oct. 1704; John, b. 29 Apr. 1707; Rebecca, b. 10 Mar. 1709; David, b. 11 Mar. 1710/1.
> Sarah, b. 17 Apr. 1678; m. Joseph Hoyt.
> Elizabeth, b. 2 Nov. 1680; m. Samuel Hayes, of Danbury.
> Samuel, b. 30 Mar. 1683, d. y.

Pickett, Thomas, s. of John.

Bapt. at Salem, Mass., 19 Nov. 1648, d. at Danbury, early in 1712.

Called son of John, Sr., he m. (1) (rec. Stratford) 16 Nov. 1676, Abigail Seymour, dau. of Thomas of Norwalk, b. Jan. 1655/6.

He m. (2) Sarah, prob. dau. of Thomas Barnum. She m. (2) Samuel Hayes, and quit her dower right.

Inv. exhibited 6 Feb. 1711/2. The births of children are appended. Adm'n granted to widow Sarah and son Ephraim. On 5 Mar. 1712, the Court appointed Richard Barnum of Danbury guardian to Joseph; Samuel Benedict of Danbury guardian to Benjamin; and the mother Sarah guardian to Ebenezer.

Children, first three recorded at Stratford, all except Jacob in Pro. Rec.:

> Abigail, b. 30 July 1678; m. Samuel Benedict.
> Hannah, b. 20 May 1680, d. at New Milford, 1 Mar. 1716 [1715/6]; m. John Noble.
> Jacob, b. 16 Feb. 1680 [*sic;* 1681/2?], d. y.

[Perhaps the rest of the children were by the second wife:]

> Ephraim, b. 1 Mar. 1686.
> Thomas, b. 22 Nov. 1689, d. at New Milford, 17 June 1774 in 86 yr.; Dr.; m. at New Milford, 13 Dec. 1716, Miriam Mallory; she was

---

* This James settled in Norwalk and m. 14 Apr. 1726, Deborah Stewart, dau. of Lt. James. He d. in 1750; distribution mentioned widow and six children.

widow of Caleb Mallery, and dau. of Samuel Blakeslee, b. at New Haven, 2 May 1688, d. 23 June 1776.

Sarah, b. 21 Sept. 1694; m. ———— Videto.

James, b. 2 June 1697; adm'n granted to James Pickett, 24 Nov. 1741.

Joseph, b. 28 Mar. 1700, d. at Danbury by 1766; distribution 13 Oct. 1766; m. Abigail Seeley, dau. of John, b. 9 Mar. 1698/9.

Benjamin, b. 15 Apr. 1703, d. at Danbury in 1724. Inv. 3 Apr. 1724; distribution to five brethren, Ephraim, Thomas, James, Joseph, Ebenezer, and two sisters, Sarah Videto of Danbury, Abigail wife of Samuel Benedict, and Thomas Noble of New Milford, only son of Hannah.

Ebenezer, b. 12 Oct. 1706; m. Elizabeth Knapp, dau. of Timothy and Elizabeth (Seymour) of Greenwich, b. 22 Aug. 1710.

Pickett, Daniel, s. of John.   Deputy (Stratford), Oct. 1709; Sergt., Stratford Trainband.

Bapt. at Salem, Mass., 25 Jan. 1651/2.

Married (rec. Stratford), 13 Sept. 1683, Mary Ufford.   Wife called Mary, and he Sergt., at birth of child 1701.

Sergt. Daniel d. (date omitted), entered at Stratford between deaths dated 29 Feb. and 19 Apr. 1712.

Will 16 Mar. 1712, proved 4 June 1712; wife Mary; sons Samuel, Daniel; dau. Margaret Curtis; daus. Mary, Comfort, Rebecca, Prudence, Phebe; wife Exec'x. Witnesses: Joseph Curtis, Daniel Uffoot.

Will of Mary, 5 Mar. 1729, proved 9 Feb. 1732/3; two sons and four daus, disposed of in marriage (their father Daniel Pickett dec'd) ; two younger daus. Prudence and Phebe; sons Samuel, Daniel; son-in-law John Curtice; three surviving daus.; sons-in-law Henry Hawley and Ebenezer Thompson, Exec'rs. Witnesses: John Thompson, Nathan Peet, Martha Thompson.   Inv. 27 Nov. 1732.

Children, recorded at Stratford:

Samuel, b. 23 Nov. 1684, d. 30 June 1689.

Margaret, b. 14 Aug. 1686; m. 19 Feb. 1706/7, John Curtis.

Daniel, b. 27 Feb. 1687/8, d. y.

Samuel, b. 31 Oct. 1689; m. 27 Nov. 1712, Mary Coe.

Daniel, b. 1 Oct. 1691.

Mary, b. 15 Jan. 1692 [1692/3], d. in 1753; m. 18 June 1713, Henry Hawley.

Comfort, b. 6 Sept. 1694, d. at Huntington, 7 Nov. 1773 ae. 78; m. 7 Aug. 1712, Ebenezer Thompson.

Rebecca, b. 5 Mar. 1700/1; m. 12 Oct. 1727, John McEwen.

Prudence.

Phebe, bapt. at Stratford (rec. Stratfield) 27 Apr. 1707.

Pike, Thomas.

Married (1) at Fairfield, 1 Dec. 1727, Abigail, widow of John Cable, and dau. of Isaac Sherwood. She d. between 27 Oct. and 18 Dec. 1735.

He m. (2) prob. not long after 1735, Hannah, widow of John Lyon of Fairfield, and dau. of Nathaniel Kimberly, b. at New Haven, 13 Apr. 1694; and they were both living in 1747, when they joined other Kimberly heirs in a deed.

His last conveyance in Fairfield was dated 29 July 1758.

Adm'n on Est. of Thomas Pike of New Fairfield was granted, 13 Mar. 1760 to Nathan Stuart. [Danbury Pro.]

Perhaps he had a former wife, before the two noted above, and the Hannah Pike who d. at Woodbury, 31 Oct. 1732, may have been a dau.

Pinkney, Philip.

Of Fairfield by 1650; had a grant of land from the town, 14 Feb. 1666 [1666/7]. Sold to Nathan Gold, 13 Feb. 1669 [1669/70]; sold also to James Beers. He and his wife Jane were perhaps drawn to Fairfield by the marriage of their aunt, Mrs. Sarah Phippen, to George Hull. They rem. to Eastchester, N. Y.

Will 9 Jan. 1688/9, proved 28 Feb. 1688/9; son Thomas, Exec'r; sons John, William, Thomas, lands in Eastchester; unmarried daus., Elizabeth, Jean, Ann, Deborah, £10 each; daus. already married, 12 pence each.

Of the older married daus., one was Abigail who m. (1) (say 1670) David Osborn (d. 1679), and (2) ———; another was Hannah who m. Thomas Pickering of Eastchester. The dau. Elizabeth m. by 1695, Daniel Burr, of Fairfield; and the dau. Jane m. by 1697 Moses Dimon, of Fairfield.

Pitman, Jonathan.

This surname was found early at Salem, Mass., where it was also spelled Pitnam and Pickman.

Mr. Jonathan m. at Stratford, 29 Nov. 1681, Miss Temperance Welles. She was dau. of Mr. John, b. abt. 1654, d. after 1728.

He d. at Stratford, 1 Dec. 1731 ae. 91 (g. s., Episcopal Yard). Will 13 Mar. 1727/8, proved 6 Dec. 1731; "antient and under ye decays of Nature"; wife Temperance, life use of moveable estate; to my dau. Benedict £5 and my cupboard in ye celler; residue to cousin Samuel French of Stratford; cousin Samuel French and cousin John Thompson, Exec'rs; overseers, Capt. John Welles, Joseph Welles, Nathaniel Curtis.

Children, recorded at Stratford:

> Jonathan, b. 4 Nov. 1682, d. y.
> Jonathan, b. 25 May 1685, d. y.
> Robert, b. 16 Oct. 1687, d. y.
> Samuel, b. 5 Feb. 1691/2, d. at Stratford, 18 May 1717; ae. 25 yrs. 3 mos. 13 days (g. s., Congregational Yard); m. 23 Nov. 1716, Mary Groom; dau. of Edward, b. 19 Nov. 1690. Only child: Samuel, b. 28 Sept. 1717, d. 29 Mar. 1721. He was school-teacher at Stratford; his widow m. (2) (rec. Ridgefield) 21 Mar. 1720/1, Joseph Benedict.

Plasted, Roger.   [York County, Me.]

Of "Quamphegon, Ottrie township, on Pusscataway Reuar in Yorksheer", he bought 6 July 1659 from Robert Beacham of Bankside, Fairfield. John Plasted of "Pascataway Rever" sold 3 Aug. 1683 to Joseph Lockwood [Beacham's son-in-law].

Platt, Richard.

Probably son of Joseph, bapt. at Bovingdon, co. Hertford, Eng., 28 Sept. 1603.

Among the early settlers of New Haven, he was listed in 1641 with a family of four persons and a good estate. Removed to Milford in 1639 with the founders of that town; chosen a deacon of Milford Church, 1669.

Married Mary ———, who was buried at Milford, 24 Jan. 1675/6.

Will 4 Aug. 1683; son John and four Bibles for his children; son Isaac and three Bibles for his children; son Epenetus and three Bibles for his children; son-in-law Christopher Comstock and his wife, and three Bibles for their children; Samuel Beach, referring to what he had already given him; Hannah and Deborah Merwin, two Bibles; aid for education of Elder Buckingham's son, and for education of the son of Epenetus; son Josiah and five Bibles for his children; two Bibles for Josiah Whitmore and his sister; son Joseph and two Bibles for his children. Inv. 13 Feb. 1684 [1684/5].

Children, four younger recorded at Milford:

Mary, b. [say 1633], d. at Middletown, 11 June 1669; m. (1) (rec. New Haven) 1 May 1651, Luke Atkinson; m. (2) 3 Jan. 1667, Thomas Wetmore [Whitmore].

Sarah, b. [say 1634], d. at Milford, 15 May 1670; m. (1) Thomas Beach; m. (2) abt. 1665, Miles Merwin.

+John, b. [say 1636].

+Isaac, b. [say 1638].

Epenetus, bapt. 2 July 1640, d. at Huntington, L. I., in 1693; will 1 Sept., proved 13 Nov. 1693; m. in 1667, Phebe Wood, dau. of Jonas; her will 12 Jan. 1696/7, proved 24 July 1697.

Hannah, bapt. 1 Oct. 1643; m. (rec. Norwalk) 6 Oct. 1663, Christopher Comstock.

Josiah, bapt. in Nov. 1645, d. at Milford, 1 Jan. 1724/5; will 20 Aug. 1717, proved 1 Feb. 1724/5; m. at Milford, 2 Dec. 1669, Sarah Canfield, dau. of Thomas.

Joseph, bapt. 1 Apr. 1649, d. at Milford abt. 1705; m. (rec. Milford) 5 May 1680, Mary Kellogg; dau. of Daniel, b. Feb. 1662.

Platt, John, s. of Richard. Deputy for Norwalk, Oct. 1678, Oct. 1680, Oct. 1681, May and Oct. 1682, May, Oct. and Nov. 1683, May and Oct. 1684, May and Oct. 1685, May, July and Oct. 1686, Jan. 1687, May and July 1691, Oct. 1692, Mar. 1693, Oct. 1694; Sergt., Norwalk Trainband.

Born [say 1636], d. at Norwalk late in 1705; m. at Milford, 6 June 1660, Hannah Clark, dau. of George, "farmer."

Made freeman, Oct. 1667; deacon of Norwalk Church.

Will of John of Norwalk, husbandman, 6 Nov. 1705, proved 15 Dec. 1705; wife Hannah; three daus. Hannah Marvin, Sarah Kellogg, Mary Benedict; sons John, Samuel, Joseph.

Children, recorded at Norwalk:

+John, b. June 1664.
Josiah, b. 28 Dec. 1667, d. y.
+Samuel, b. 26 Jan. 1670 [1670/1].
+Joseph, b. 17 Feb. 1672/3.
Hannah, b. 15 Dec. 1674; m. abt. 1701/2, Samuel Marvin.
Sarah, b. 21 May 1678, d. at Wilton, 10 Nov. 1750 ae. 72; m. 6 Sept. 1704, Samuel Kellogg.
Mary, m. [perhaps Benjamin] Benedict.

Platt, Isaac, s. of Richard.   Recorder at Huntington, 1687; Capt. of Militia.

Born [say 1638]; d. at Huntington, L. I., 31 July 1691; m. Elizabeth Wood, daughter of Jonas "of Oram."

He did not, as so often stated, m. (1) at Milford, 12 Mar. 1640, Phebe Smith.   No marriages were entered in either town or church records there of so early a date; and the statement is obviously due to carelessness in confusing him with another Isaac Platt of Milford who did m. Phebe Smith, but on 12 Mar. 1740, just a century later.

Children, rec. Huntington, L. I.:

Elizabeth, b. 15 Sept. 1665; m. John Wood, of Huntington.
XJonas, b. 16 Aug. 1667; m. Sarah Scudder, and had a family; of whom the sons Obadiah and Timothy rem. to Fairfield and will appear in the second volume of the present work. Other sons mentioned in printed sources were Jesse and Isaac. Sarah Platt who m. at Fairfield, 17 Jan. 1734, Elias Bates, was possibly a dau. of Jonas.
John, b. 29 June 1669.
Mary, b. 26 Oct. 1674.
Joseph, b. 8 Sept. 1677.
Jacob, b. 29 Sept. 1682.

Platt, John, s. of John.

Born at Norwalk, June 1664, d. there in 1736; m. in May 1695, Sarah Lockwood, dau. of Ephraim of Norwalk, b. 3 Nov. 1670.

He was prob. the Mr. John Platt of Norwalk who m. [second] at New Haven, 20 Nov. 1722, Mrs. Mary Smith; perhaps widow of Ebenezer Smith who had d. in 1714.

Will 13 Mar. 1735/6, proved 17 Apr. 1736; sons John, Josiah; four daus. Mercy wife of Richard Bouton, Sarah wife of Nathan Whitney, Elizabeth wife of Benjamin Lyon, and Abigail wife of Samuel Waring.

Children:

> Mercy,* m. Richard Bouton.
> Sarah, b. 30 May 1697; m. Nathan Whitney.
> Elizabeth, b. 11 June 1699; m. Benjamin Lyon.
> John, b. 2 Apr. 1702; m. Sarah Hickock, dau. of Samuel, Jr., b. at Waterbury, 6 Dec. 1707.
> Abigail, b. 12 Feb. 1707/8; m. Samuel Waring.
> Josiah.

Platt, Samuel, s. of John.

Born at Norwalk, 26 Jan. 1670/1, d. there 4 Dec. 1713; m. (rec. Norwalk) 18 June 1712, Rebecca Benedict, dau. of Samuel of Danbury.

Will 3 Dec. 1713, proved 15 Dec. 1713; wife Rebecca; minor dau.; John and Josiah, sons of bro. John; Joseph, son of bro. Joseph.

Child, recorded at Norwalk:

> Rebecca, b. 9 Apr. 1713, d. in 1790; m. Jabez Raymond.

Platt, Joseph, s. of John.   Deputy (Norwalk), May 1705, Oct. 1706, Apr. and Oct. 1707, Oct. 1708, Oct. 1709, May and Aug. 1710, Oct. and Nov. 1711, Oct. 1712, Oct. 1713, Oct. 1714, Oct. 1716, Oct. 1718, May and Oct. 1719, Oct. 1720, May 1721, Oct. 1722, Oct. 1724, Oct. 1725, Oct. 1726, Oct. 1727, May, July and Oct. 1728, Oct. 1729, Oct. 1730, May 1731, May and Oct. 1732, Feb., May and Oct. 1733, Oct. 1734, Oct. 1737, Oct. 1738, May 1739; Capt., north company, Norwalk, May 1710; Justice, Oct. 1713 to May 1743; Commissioner, N. Y. Boundary, Apr. 1720.

---

* Her birth is not given in Hall's *Norwalk;* Mr. Frederick Wood gives it from Norwalk records as 6 Jan. 1690. If correct, this would mean that her father had a first wife before his marriage to Sarah Lockwood, which is possible. However, Sarah Lockwood's mother was named Mercy; Mercy Platt, if born 1690, would have been older than her husband; and I suspect that the date of her birth may have been 6 Jan. 1695 [1695/6], which would make her the eldest child by Sarah Lockwood.

Born at Norwalk, 17 Feb. 1672/3, d. there 12 June 1748, in 76 yr. (g. s.); m. (1) at Norwalk, 6 Nov. 1700, Elizabeth Marvin, dau. of Matthew. She d. 9 Apr. 1703; he m. (2) 26 Jan. 1703/4, Hannah Hanford, dau. of Rev. Thomas.

He received a grant, 1698, from the town of Norwalk, for service as a soldier in war.

Will 18 Oct. 1744, proved 26 July 1748; wife Hannah; gr. son Joseph Platt Cook; son Joseph; gr. daus.; cousin Rebecca wife of Jabez Raymond.

Child by first wife:

> Elizabeth, b. 2 Dec. 1701, d. at Stratfield, 16 May 1732; m. Rev. Samuel Cooke.

Children by second wife:

> Hannah, b. 29 Oct. 1704, d. y.
> Joseph, b. 9 Sept. 1710, d. at Norwalk, Mar. 1777; grad. Yale Coll. 1733; m. Hannah Whitman, dau. of Zechariah.

Porter, John. Deputy (Windsor) to Conn. Leg., Aug. 1639, Oct. 1646, May 1647.

Of Felsted, co. Essex, Eng., m. at Messing, co. Essex, 18 Oct. 1620, Anna White, bapt. at Messing, 13 July 1600, dau. of Robert and Bridget (Allgar) White. Came to New England with family 1638, prob. in *Susan and Ellen,* and settled in Windsor.

His wife died in 1647 (Windsor Church rec.); he d. at Windsor, 21 Apr. 1648. His will, dated 20 Apr. 1648, mentioned his "sonne Joseph Judgson."

For children, see *Porter Genealogy,* or *The Ancestry of William F. J. Boardman,* p. 307; two of the eleven children were:

> Sarah, bapt. at Felsted, 15 Mar. 1624/5, d. 16 Mar. 1696/7 ae. 70 (g. s., Stratford); m. 24 Oct. 1644, Joseph Judson, of Stratford.
> +Nathaniel, b. 19 July 1640.

Porter, Nathaniel, s. of John. Sergt., Stratford Train Band.

Born at Windsor, 19 July 1640, d. at Stratford, Jan. 1679/80.

Will 10 Jan. 1679 [1679/80]; Inv. 30 Jan. 1679 [1679/80]; son John one-half of house and homelot at 21, the other half at death of my wife Elizabeth, who was to have use of all housing and lands until John should come to age, and thereafter one-half; dau. Mary Porter, £40; residue to six children, Nathaniel, Hannah, Sarah, Ruth, John, and Mary Porter; friends, cousin Nicholas Camp, Samuel Eells, Jehiel Preston, and John Birdsey, overseers.

Inv. of Elizabeth, 21 Feb. 1683 [1683/4], presented by Jehiel Preston, who was appointed to administer with Camp, Eells, and Birdsey.

Receipts given 16 Dec. 1692 by Robert Royce and Mary Royce formerly Porter dau. of Nathaniel of Stratford; by Ebenezer and Ruth Curtis, John Porter, Sarah Porter, and Nathaniel Porter, the last-named of Fairfield. Receipts exhibited 10 July 1696.

Married (1) Hannah Groves, dau. of Philip. The children of Hannah Porter shared in the estate of Ellen Bostwick, 1677, in recompense for care given her.

Married (2) Elizabeth Baldwin, dau. of John, bapt. 19 Aug. 1649.

Sergt. Nathaniel d. at Stratford 14 Jan. 1679 [1679/80]; Elizabeth d. 6 Feb. 1683 [1683/4].

Children [by first wife], recorded at Stratford:

> Hannah, b. 10 Apr. 1665, d. 14 Feb. 1737/8 ae. 73 (g. s.); m. Zachariah Curtis.
>
> Sarah, b. 3(?) Sept. 1667, d. 25 Mar. 1738 ae. 70 (g. s.); m. 29 Apr. 1686, Nathaniel Beach.
>
> Ruth, b. 22 Nov. 1669, d. 28 May 1739 in 70 yr. (g. s.); m. Ebenezer Curtis.
>
> +Nathaniel, b. 27 Aug. 1672.

Children [by second wife], recorded at Stratford (mother of John & Mary called Elizabeth):

> +John, b. 28 Mar. 1674.
>
> Samuel, b. 17 July 1675, d. same month.
>
> Mary, b. 28 Feb. 1676/7, d. at Meriden, 11 Mar. 1759; m. (rec. Wallingford) 2 June 1692, Dea. Robert Royce.

Porter, Nathaniel, s. of Nathaniel.

Born at Stratford, 27 Aug. 1672, d. at Stratfield, 1727.

Married (1) abt. 1699, Rebecca, widow of Isaac Wheeler, Jr., and dau. of Sergt. John Wheeler, b. abt. 1672.

Married (2) abt. 1713, Mary Odell, dau. of John, b. abt. 1693; she m. (2) 4 Aug. 1727, John Middlebrook, and d. at Trumbull, 13 Aug. 1771 in 79 yr. (g. s.).

Lands recorded to him in Stratford 3 Feb. 1690 [1690/1], given him by his grandfather Mr. Philip Groves.

Will 24 Jan. 1726/7, proved 17 Feb. 1726/7; wife Mary; daus. Rebecca, Hannah, Abigail, Mary, Sarah; sons John, Samuel, Nathaniel; wife and bro.-in-law Sergt. John Odell, Exec'rs.

Distribution, 1 Jan. 1727/8; Widow; John, Rebecca, Hannah, Abigail, Samuel, Nathaniel, Mary, Sarah. Theophilus Hull was appointed guardian of Samuel, 6 June 1727, and of Nathaniel, 5 Sept. 1727.

Children [by first wife], bapt. at Stratfield:

> John, bapt. 17 Nov. 1700, d. at Trumbull, 6 May 1781 in 83 yr. (g. s.); Ens.; m. Hannah Sanford, dau. of Thomas, b. abt. 1703, d. at Stratfield, 28 Oct. 1763 in 61 yr. (g. s.).
> Rebecca, bapt. 25 Oct. 1702; m. John Edwards.
> Hannah, bapt. 8 July 1705, d. at Trumbull, 1 June 1790 in 85 yr. (g. s.); m. 23 May 1734, John Turney.
> Abigail, bapt. 6 June 1708.

Children [by second wife]:

> Nathaniel, bapt. 21 Nov. 1714, d. y.
> Samuel, bapt. 17 Nov. 1717, d. at Stratfield, 13 Sept. 1795 in 78 yr. (g. s.); m. Abiah ———, who d. 9 July 1801 in 76 yr. (g. s.).
> Nathaniel, b. abt. 1719.
> Mary, b. [July 1721 by age at death], d. 29 Aug. 1813 ae. 92 yrs. 1 mo.; m. Benjamin Hubbell.
> Sarah.

Porter, John, s. of Nathaniel. Ens., south company, Stratford, May 1720; Deputy (Stratford), Oct. 1717, Oct. 1718.

Born at Stratford, 28 Mar. 1674, d. there in 1758.

Married at Stratford, 8 Oct. 1696, Mary Titharton.

Will 11 Nov. 1747, proved 23 Feb. 1758; wife Mary; gr. child Comfort dau. of Abel Thompson of Wallingford; dau. Elizabeth wife of Benjamin Atwater of Wallingford; dau. Mary wife of Obadiah Beardsley of Ripton; two gr. children Anna and Comfort Beardsley, daus. of Andrew Beardsley by his dec'd wife Sarah of Stratford; son Daniel of Stratford, Exec'r.

Children, recorded at Stratford; three bapt. there (but rec. at Stratfield):

>Daniel, b. 16 July 1697; m. (1) 25 Mar. 1725, Sarah Hawley; m. (2) 5 Feb. 1729/30, Mary Judson.
>
>Nathaniel, b. 16 Aug. 1699, d. y.
>
>Stephen, b. 3 Mar. 1701/2, d. y.
>
>Mary, b. 14 June 1704, bapt. 23 July 1704; m. 21 Aug. 1729, Obadiah Beardsley.
>
>Elizabeth, b. 1 Dec. 1706, bapt. 27 Apr. 1707, d. 13 Jan. 1774 ae. 66 (g. s., Wallingford); m. (rec. Wallingford) 28 Nov. 1732 Benjamin Atwater.
>
>Sarah, bapt. 3 Apr. 1709, d. y.
>
>Comfort, b. 4 May 1710, d. at Wallingford, 29 Aug. 1738; m. (rec. Wallingford) 20 Apr. 1737, Abel Thompson.
>
>Sarah, b. 26 Feb. 1712/3; m. Andrew Beardsley.

Porter, Jonathan.

Of Huntington, L. I.; gave all estate to wife during life; Giles Smith of Fairfield m. Eunice widow of said Porter, and Smith is now dec'd; Porter had three daus.; Eunice has rec'd her estate from Smith's Exec'rs, and the legatees gave release 21 June 1670, affirming that "our mother" has rec'd etc. Signed by Eunice Porter, James Chichester, Edward Hornett, Stephen Jarvis.

Preston, William.

His ancestry as stated in Cothren's *Hist. of Ancient Woodbury* (vol. 1, p. 663) is absurdly impossible.

His will mentions land at Giggleswick, co. York, inherited by elder bro. and himself from his father. The late James Shepard, of New Britain, Conn., obtained a record to the effect that William, son of Adam and Isabel (Braithwhet) Preston, was bapt. at Giggleswick, 23 Jan. 1590/1, but we do not know how authentic the record is.

He settled in Chesham, co. Bucks, where he m. (1) 11 Oct. 1613, Elizabeth Sale, bapt. 8 June 1590, bur. 22 Feb. 1633/4. Shortly before coming to New England, he m. (2) Mary, perhaps dau. of Robert Seabrook, and in his will refers to the monetary assistance of his wife in bringing himself and his children to this country. She was born abt. 1601, and d. after 1680, having m. (2) Thomas Kimberly, with whom she rem. from New Haven to Stratford.

His son Edward, ae. 13, came in Mar. 1634/5 in the *Christian*, with the Stiles family, Thomas Bassett [of Fairfield], and others. William, ae. 44, Mary [his wife], ae. 34, and Elizabeth, 11, Sarah, 8, Mary, 6, and John, 3, came in the *Truelove*, Sept. 1635. The family settled in New Haven, where William d. in 1647. In 1657, Winthrop wrote of Goody Kimberly, G. Preston's daughter. This was two years before Thomas Kimberly's first wife died, and Goodwife Preston became his second wife. Winthrop's note seems to imply that she had a daughter already married to a son of Kimberly's. The only Kimberly to whom this could apply was Abraham, son of Thomas, who had a child born in New Haven in 1656. This Abraham was survived by a widow Hannah, but whether she was the same wife whom he had in 1657 cannot be asserted. William and Mary Preston were m. by 1635, and their eldest child could have been a daughter who m. Abraham Kimberly.

Children [by first wife], rec. Chesham:

> William, bapt. 5 Oct. 1614, bur. 4 June 1633.
> John, b. [say 1617], bur. 18 Nov. 1623.
> Edward, bapt. 14 Nov. 1619, d. iu 1699; m. Margaret Hurst, of Boston, who (unless he m. again) was the wife who d. 28 Dec. 1690.
> Daniel, bapt. 3 Mar. 1621, d. at Dorchester, Mass., 10 Nov. 1707; m. Mary ———.
> Elizabeth, bapt. 18 Jan. 1623, d. 29 Aug. 1693 ae. 68 (g. s., New Haven); m. Joseph Alsop.
> Sarah, bapt. 18 July 1626; m. William Meeker.
> Mary, bapt. 13 Dec. 1629; prob. m. Peter Mallory.
> John, bapt. 4 Mar. 1632; lived in Massachusetts.

Children [by second wife], rec. New Haven:

> +Jehiel, bapt. 14 June 1640.
> +Hachaliah, bapt. 9 Apr. 1643.
> +Eliasaph, bapt. 9 Apr. 1643.
> Joseph, bapt. 24 Jan. 1645/6, d. at New Haven in 1733; Sergt.; m. Joanna, widow of Henry Stevens, and dau. of Philip Leek, b. 22 Jan. 1657; no issue.

Preston, Jehiel, s. of William. Sergt., Stratford Trainband. Deputy for Stratford, May 1676, Oct. and Nov. 1683.

Bapt. at New Haven, 14 June 1640; d. at Stratford in 1684.

Married (1) Sarah Fairchild, dau. of Thomas, b. 19 Feb. 1641/2.

Married (2) [say 1682], Temperance, whom we hesitate not to identify as the dau. of Isaac Nichols, b. 17 May 1662; she m. (2) at Stratfield, 17 Apr. 1688, Samuel Hubbell, Sr.

Inv. 24 Sept. 1684 of Sergt. Jehiel of Stratford. Widow Temperance. Samuel Preston, Adm'r. The child Mary Preston, and the son.

Children [by first wife], recorded at Stratford:

> Samuel, b. 1 July 1663, d. in 1707, unm. Adm'n granted, 15 Apr. 1707, to bro.-in-law Daniel Jackson.
>
> Joseph, b. 10 July 1665, d. y.

Child [by second wife]:

> Mary, b. [say 1683]; m. Daniel Jackson. Mary Preston of Stratfield conveyed 1704; in 1707 Daniel Jackson of Stratfield and Mary his wife conveyed right from brother Samuel Preston of Stratford dec'd.

Preston, Hachaliah, s. of William.

Bapt. at New Haven, 9 Apr. 1643, d. at Woodbury, 20 Nov. 1692.

Married at Stratford, 20 Apr. 1676, Emm Fairchild. She was dau. of Thomas, b. 23 Oct. 1653, d. at Woodbury, 25 Feb. 1732/3.

Children, first recorded at Stratford, all bapt. at Woodbury:

> William, b. 21 Mar. 1676 [1676/7], bapt. Aug. 1680, d. at Woodbury, 5 Sept. 1754 ae. 78; Deputy for Woodbury, many years; Lt.-Col., 13th Regt., Oct. 1739;; m. June 1705, Martha Judson.
>
> Hannah, bapt. Aug. 1680; m. (no date, but placed among 1701 marriages) Joseph Gregory, of Danbury.
>
> Lydia, bapt. Nov. 1682.
>
> Sarah, bapt. Nov. 1683; m. (rec. Stratford) 3 Feb. 1714/5, Joseph Welles.
>
> Jehiel, bapt. Oct. 1686, d. at Woodbury, 22 May 1727; m. 27 Dec. 1714, Mary Huthwitt.
>
> Emm, bapt. 3 Mar. 1688/9, d. at Woodbury in 1729; m. 22 July 1714, John Sherman.
>
> Remember, bapt. Oct. 1691, d. 15 Feb. 1698 [1698/9].

Preston, Eliasaph, s. of William.

Bapt. at New Haven, 9 Apr. 1643; d. at Wallingford, in 1707, where he was deacon of the church. He followed his mother and bro. Jehiel to Stratford, but rem. abt. 1676 to Wallingford.

He m. (1) Mary ———; m. (2) Elizabeth Beach, b. 28 Mar. 1652, dau. of John of Stratford, she being called his wife in probate, 1677; m. (3) abt. 1694, Martha, widow of Samuel Munson, and dau. of William Bradley, bapt. at New Haven, Oct. 1648. She m. (3) Capt. Daniel Sherman* of New Haven, and was living 1722.

Child by Mary, recorded at Stratford :†

Mary, b. 12 Apr. 1674, d. at Wallingford, 28 Nov. 1755; m. (1) 9 July 1690, Caleb Merriman; m. (2) 18 Mar. 1708, Samuel Munson.

Children [by second wife], recorded at Wallingford:

Elizabeth, b. 29 Jan. 1676 [1676/7]; either she or her sister Hannah d. y., and the other (prob. Elizabeth) m. Daniel Kellogg, of Norwalk.

Hannah, b. 12 July 1678, prob. d. y.

Eliasaph, b. 26 Jan. 1679 [1679/80], d. at Wallingford, 4 Jan. 1763; m. (1) 31 Jan. 1704, Rebecca, widow of Benjamin Royce, and dau. of Timothy Wilcoxson, b. at Stratford, 13 July 1680, d. 2 Sept. 1716; m. (2) 2 Jan. 1717 [1717/8], Deborah Merwin, dau. of Samuel, bapt. at Milford, 15 Mar. 1691.

Joseph, b. 10 Mar. 1681/2, d. after 1762; m. 7 July 1708, Jane Cook, dau. of Henry.

Esther, b. 28 Jan. 1683 [1683/4], d. 4 July 1764; m. 9 Dec. 1702, James Benham.

Lydia, b. 5 May 1686; m. James Dorchester, of Springfield, Mass.

Jehiel, b. 25 Aug. 1688, d. 24 Nov. 1689.

---

* The usually accurate *Munson Record* states that she m. (3) Matthew Sherman, caused by misreading her name in a deed as "Mrs. Matthew" instead of "Mrs. Martha."

† The statement that Eliasaph had a first wife Mary and that she was mother of the eldest child is based solely on the Stratford record of birth of Mary daughter of Eliasaph and *Mary* Preston. There is no record of the marriage nor of Mary's death, in Stratford or Wallingford. The compiler personally believes that the name Mary for the mother of the first child was an error of Stratford recorder. If the mother was Elizabeth Beach, this child was the first grandchild born to John and Mary Beach. The Beaches were old residents in Stratford, Preston a new-comer. In the birth entry, between "Mary" and Preston," is what looks like a "B" crossed out. The recorder may have had in mind the child's grandmother Mary Beach, started to write "Beach" instead of Preston, crossed it out, but failed to correct the name Mary. While plausible, this theory is not proved, and we have followed the record. In some printed works, a date of death has been assigned the wife Mary, which is fictitious and not found in the records.

Price, Philip.

Also known as Philip John Price, prob. was Dutch.

Married Susanna, widow of Robert Bispham, and dau. of Henry Hendrick. She renewed her Covenant at Fairfield Church, 17 Feb. 1694/5.

Children, bapt. at Fairfield:

    ✕Lemuel, bapt. 17 Feb. 1694/5, d. at Greenfield, 24 Dec. 1748; will 16 Dec. 1748, proved 3 Jan. 1748/9; m. (1) Mary ———; m. (2) Sarah Middlebrook, dau. of Joseph, bapt. 8 Feb. 1712/3; she m. (2) Oct. 1756, Peter Bradley.

    Mary, b. Feb. 1696/7, bapt. 18 Apr. 1697, d. at Greenfield, [abt. Jan.] 1776 in 80 yr.; m. at Stratford, 1 Nov. 1722, William Williams. Her name is given as Middlebrook in the marriage record, but no Mary Middlebrook of proper age appears. The baptismal date of Williams' wife as stated in Greenfield records accords with baptism of Mary Price. John Middlebrook married Elizabeth Bispham, elder half-sister of Mary Price, and she may have been living in his family when married, which would explain the error of the Stratford recorder.

Prudden, Rev. Peter.

Born prob. in vicinity of Kingswalden, co. Hertford, Eng.

First minister and a founder of Milford, where he d. July 1656.

He m. Joanna Boyse, dau. of Rev. John of Halifax, co. York, Eng. She m. (2) at Milford, 19 Sept. 1671, Capt. Thomas Willett; m. (3) Rev. John Bishop, of Stamford, and d. early in 1683.

Will of Mrs. Joanna Bishop, 8 Nov. 1681; eldest son Samuel; second son John; five daus. Joanna, Elizabeth, Abigail, Sarah, Mildred; two children of late dau. Mary Walker; husband Mr. John Bishop. Inv. 22 Mar. 1682/3.

Children, bapt. at Milford:

    Joanna, bapt. 30 Aug. 1640; m. Thomas Chittenden, of Guilford.

    Mary, bapt. 4 Dec. 1641; m. Rev. Zechariah Walker, of Stratford.

    Elizabeth, bapt. 11 Mar. 1642/3; m. Jehu Burr, of Fairfield.

    Samuel, bapt. 18 Feb. 1643/4, d. at Milford in 1685; m. at Stratford, 30 Dec. 1669, Grace Judson, dau. of Ens. Joseph; she m. (2) Thomas Clark of Milford.

    John, bapt. Nov. 1645, d. at Newark, N. J., 11 Dec. 1725; grad. from Harvard College, 1668; Rev.; m. Grace ———.

Abigail, bapt. 13 Feb. 1647/8, d. abt. Jan. 1717/8; m. (1) at Milford, 14 Nov. 1667, Joseph Walker, of Stratford; m. (2) (by marriage contract, 16 Apr, 1688) Sergt. Richard Hubbell, of Stratfield.

Sarah, b. 9 May 1650 [New Haven Col. Rec.], bapt. 12 May 1650, living 1700; m. Gideon Allen.

Peter, bapt. 30 May 1652, d. 10 June 1652.

Mildred, bapt. 14 May 1653, d. at Milford, 6 Jan. 1711/2; m. at Milford, 20 Sept. 1671, Sylvanus Baldwin.

Prudden, James.

Most likely brother of Rev. Peter, and perhaps the same James whose wife "Eiz" [Elizabeth?] was buried at Kingswalden, co. Hertford, Eng., 27 May 1618.

He was admitted to the church in Milford, 13 Oct. 1639, and d. there Aug. 1648.

Children:

Ann, d. at Milford, 3 Oct. 1689; m. abt. 1640, Samuel Coley.

Elizabeth, m. (1) by 1647, William Slough, of Milford, who was excommunicated from the church and executed at New Haven for "horrible depravity"; m. (2) at Milford, 18 Dec. 1653, Roger Pritchard. She had children by her first husband (*Slough*): I. Hasadiah, bapt. 26 Nov. 1648; m. by 1677, Philip Denman of Derby. II. James, b. 28 Jan. 1649 [1649/50], d. 10 Feb. 1649 [1649/50] [New Haven Col. Rec.].

Purdy, Francis.

An early settler in Fairfield.

Married by 1645, Mary Brundish, dau. of John; she m. (2) abt. 1659, John Hoyt, and removed with him from Fairfield to Rye, taking her children with her.

Inv. 14 Oct. 1658; Widow made oath. Five children, John, Francis, [Joseph], Daniel and Mary, all minors. John to have double portion; John Hoyt shall take care of the mare.

On 2 May 1678, Moses Dimon purchased land in Fairfield from Deliverance Browne, John Purdy, Francis Purdy, and Joseph Purdy, all of Rye.

In Rye Deeds, we find that Joseph sold land 1679 bounded by land laid out to the children of his brother John; that widow Elizabeth Purdy with John Brundish as adm'rs of John Purdy's Est., sold 1679 land in which John's bro. Francis had an equal share.

Children:

> John, d. in 1678; m. Elizabeth Brown, bapt. 1 Aug. 1647. Inv. at
> Fairfield, 26 Dec. 1678; widow Elizabeth made oath. She desired
> that "my father John Hoit and my brother Thomas Browne might
> stand overseers, or my brother Hacaliah Browne."
> Francis, b. abt. 1650, living at Rye 1722; m. ———.
> Joseph, will 5 Oct. 1709; Justice, Representative; m. Elizabeth,
> [dau. of John Ogden?].
> Mary, m. Deliverance Brown, of Rye.
> Daniel, d. y.

Quinby, William.

He settled in Stratford before 1652, and did not long survive.
His lands were sold to Joshua Atwater, and resold, 1 Apr. 1657,
to Henry Tomlinson; and his widow Ann m. (2) 28 Nov. 1657,
George Stuckey of Stamford. After Stuckey's death in 1660, the
family rem. to Westchester, N. Y.

Children (record incomplete):

+John.

Quinby, John, s. of William.

Agreement of Ann Stuckey of Westchester, 24 Feb. 1661, with
her son John Quinby of the same, gave him land in Stratford, and
mentioned his children Sarah and Deborah. [Westchester Deeds.]

He remained in Westchester, and was progenitor of a family
there. On 4 Mar. 1698/9, John Quinby, Sr., of Westchester, conveyed with Deborah his wife to their son-in-law Erasmus Alton
and Elizabeth his wife.

Children, second recorded at Stratford:

> Sarah.
> Deborah, b. 28 [or 20] Apr. 1654.
> John, m. Anne ———.
> Charles.
> Elizabeth, m. Erasmus Alton.
> Josiah, m. 17 June 1689, Mary Mullinex.
> Mary.

Ratliffe, William. Deputy (Greenwich) to Conn. Leg., May 1670.

He m. at Stamford, 29 Oct. 1659, Elizabeth Theale, dau. of Nicholas, b. at Watertown, Mass., 24 Oct. 1640.

By 1667 he had rem. to Greenwich, and d. abt. 1676.

Inv. 3 May 1676 of Est. of William Ratclift of Greenwich lately dec'd. Two children's names and ages are appended: Mary abt. 13½, and Mary abt. 10. The second Mary we take to be a clerical blunder for Elizabeth.

Children, first recorded at Stamford:

> Mary, b. 27 Oct. 1662, perhaps d. y. after 1676.
> Elizabeth, b. abt. 1666; m. (1) Ezekiel Sanford, of Milford; m. (2) Zechariah Baldwin, of Milford; with the latter she sold the inherited Ratliffe property at Greenwich in 1689.

Rawlinson, William.

Stratford, with its usual facility for duplicating Fairfield names,* comes close in William Rawlinson, sometimes called Rawlins, to duplicating William Rowlandson of Fairfield. Yet they appear to have separate histories. The Stratford man d. there 22 Feb. 1712, and his wife, who d. before him, is said to have been named Jane.

Will of William of Stratford, 13 Feb. 1712, proved 15 Mar. 1711/2; to Elizabeth Beardsley, for her care of him; adopted son, Caleb Dayton, sole heir; overseers, Hon. Nathan Gold and Mr. Joseph Curtis.

Reed, William.

He settled at Stratford before 1650; rem. to Norwalk by 1656.

Inv. of William of Norwalk presented 20 Oct. 1659. Adm'n granted to Isaac Moore and Walter Hoyt.

Was he perhaps father of John of Norwalk, and of William of Fairfield, whose families follow?

---

* Each town had its own Thomas Sherwood, John Thompson, and Wheeler, Bennett, Rowland, Perry, Bassett, and Beardsley families.

Reed, John.

He was from Rye, N. Y., when he settled in Norwalk, where he d. at a great age in 1730.

John Reed, Sr., conveyed to son-in-law David Tuttle, 17 Oct. 1699. On 19 Dec. 1720, John Reed "Jr. the 1st", Thomas Reed, and David Tuttle, all of Norwalk, partitioned land laid out to their father, Mr. John Reed, Sr.

Children:

+John.
+Thomas.
    Mary, m. 24 Nov. 1698, David Tuttle.

Read, William.

Settled in Fairfield before 1673, and d. between 7 May and 23 June 1697.

He purchased land in Fairfield from Cornelius Hull prior to 1673; bought from his sister-in-law Sarah Baldwin in 1675, and from Daniel Westcott in 1681. In 1675 he had land by gift from Thomas Skidmore.

Married (1) Deborah Baldwin, dau. of Nathaniel; she was stepdau. of Thomas Skidmore.

Married (2) after 1689, Mary, widow of John Bostwick, and dau. of John Brinsmade; she d. in 1704.

He conveyed the Hedges lot to his children, Sarah and Abigail Read, and the rest of his lands to son John Read, 2 Sept. 1693, and gave them another conveyance, 7 May 1697, the dau. Sarah then being called Barlow.

Inv. 25 June 1697. Before his death he made legal conveyance to his son John and two daus. Sarah Barlow and Abigail Reed of his whole estate, and the widow by agreement received satisfaction in lieu of the dower she could claim; adm'n granted to son John, and son-in-law Joseph Barlow, and dau. Abigail. The widow Mary acquitted the estate, 23 June 1697.

Children [by first wife], two recorded at Fairfield:

    Sarah, m. Joseph Barlow.
    Abigail, b. 1 Mar. 1677/8.
+John, b. 29 Jan. 1679 [1679/80].

Reed, John, s. of John.

He m. 28 Mar. 1687, Elizabeth Tuttle, dau. of John, b. at New Haven, 19 Nov. 1666.

Inv. 26 Oct. 1724. Adm'n granted to sons John and Daniel. Widow; four sons living,—John, Daniel, Samuel, William; legal representatives of Eleazer Reed dec'd; three daus. Elizabeth Green, Experience St. John, Mehitabel Reed.

Children, recorded at Norwalk:

Ann, b. 23 Dec. 1687, d. y.
John, b. 24 Feb. 1689 [1689/90], d. at Norwalk in 1775; will 18 Feb. 1774, proved 23 Dec. 1775;* m. (1) ———; m. (2) by 1728, Hannah, widow of Eleazer Hanford, and dau. of Jonathan Frisbie, b. at Branford, 14 Aug. 1693, d. in 1759; m. (3) Mary ———.
Elizabeth, b. 14 Sept. 1692; m. at Norwalk, 12 Nov. 1719, Jacob Green.
Eleazer, b. 6 June 1695.
Daniel, b. 13 June 1697, d. at Norwalk in 1775; m. abt. 1720, Elizabeth Kellogg, dau. of Joseph and Sarah (Plumb).
Experience, b. 13 Mar. 1700; m. Jacob St. John.
Samuel, b. 24 Oct. 1702, d. at New Canaan in 1760; m. Sarah Kellogg, dau. of Joseph and Sarah (Plumb).
Mehitabel.
William, b. 16 Nov. 1708, d. at New Canaan, 2 Aug. 1793; m. at Norwalk, 28 Nov. 1729, Rachel Kellogg, dau. of Joseph.

Reed, Thomas, s. of John.

He m. at Norwalk, 9 May 1694, Mary Olmstead, dau. of Lt. John.

Will 4 Jan. 1752, proved 13 Mar. 1758; sons Thomas (Exec'r), John of Stamford, Elias of Stamford, Nathan of Norwalk; four daus. Mary Weed of Stamford, Eunice Bell of Stamford, Elizabeth Reed of Norwalk, Temperance Warren of Norwalk. Jonathan Bell of Stamford was appointed Adm'r of the intestate part of the estate, 21 June 1758. Receipts given by Jonathan and Eunice Bell, Solomon and Temperance Waring, Thomas Reed, Mary Weed, John Reed, Elias Reed, Nathan Reed.

---

* Will named wife Mary, with whom he had a marriage agreement; dau. Martha; three children of dau. Esther; children of dau. Ann dec'd, viz. Eliakim, Ann, Abigail, Moses, and Hannah; son Thaddeus; two sons of son John dec''d, viz. John and Moses. The dau. Ann m. 7 Dec. 1738, Eliakim Waring.

Children, recorded at Norwalk:

Mary, b. 2 May 1695; m. [Nathaniel?] Weed.

Eunice, b. 26 Feb. 1696/7; m. (at Norwalk, rec. Stamford), 24 Jan. 1716, Jonathan Bell, of Stamford.

Thomas, b. 7 May 1699; m. 2 Oct. 172[8], Sarah Benham, dau. of John of West Haven, b. 11 July 1700.

John, b. 7 Aug. 1701.

Elizabeth, b. 7 Oct. 1703.

Ann, b. 6 July 1706, d. 9 Feb. 1709/10.

Temperance, b. 16 Oct. 1708; m. Solomon Waring.

Elias, b. 10 Mar. 1711; m. (rec. Stamford), 13 Mar. 1740, Mary Todd.

Nathan, b. 13 Aug. 1713; m. 22 Dec. 1737, Mary Peck, dau. of Samuel, Jr., of Greenwich, b. 12 May 1716.

Read, John, s. of William. Member of Committee to revise laws of Conn. Colony, May 1709. Attorney-General of Mass., 1723, 1725, 1726, 1727.

Born at Fairfield, 29 Jan. 1679/80; grad. from Harvard College, 1697; d. at Boston, Mass., 7 Feb. 1748/9 ae. 69.

Married Ruth Talcott, dau. of John of Hartford, and half-sister of Gov. Joseph Talcott. She was b. 12 Sept. 1677, d. at Boston, 20 July 1759 ae. 81.

He renewed his Covenant, Fairfield Church, 14 May 1699. He studied for the ministry and preached for a time at Waterbury, Hartford and Stratford; but preferring the law, was adm. to the bar in 1708, and was appointed Queen's Attorney.

In 1714 he bought a large tract at Lonetown (Redding), and there established a "manor" which his son John enjoyed after him. In 1722 he removed to Boston, where he gained a great reputation as an attorney.

Adm'n on Est. of Hon. John Read of Boston was granted, 25 Mar. 1749, to John Read of Fairfield.

Agreement 7 Oct. 1756: John Read of Fairfield, Ruth Hunn, widow, of Fairfield, Charles Morris and Mary his wife of Halifax, Nova Scotia, Abigail Miller, widow, of Milton, Mass., William Read of Boston, Gent., and Henry Paget and Deborah his wife of Smithfield, R. I., children and heirs of John Read of Boston dec'd; mention their mother Ruth Read, widow.

The estate of Ruth Hunn of Redding was distributed, 1 May 1770, to bros. and sisters: John Read of Redding, William Read of Boston, heirs of Abigail wife of Joseph Miller, Mary wife of Charles Morris of Halifax, and Deborah wife of Henry Paget of Providence.

Children:

> John, bapt. at Fairfield, 14 May 1699, d. y.
>
> Ruth, b. abt. 1699, d. at Redding, 8 Aug. 1766 ae. 67; m. 14 Sept. 1737, Rev. Nathaniel Hunn, minister at Redding 1733-49; no issue.
>
> ✕John, b. abt. 1701, d. at Redding, 30 Oct. 1786 ae. 85 (g. s.); Justice, Deputy, Colonel, leading citizen of Redding parish, for whom the town was named. He m. (1) 20 Sept. 1723, Mary Hawley of Stratford, who d. 14 Feb. 1748; m. (2) 19 Dec. 1750, Sarah Bradley, dau. of Samuel, b. 27 Nov. 1726, d. 8 May 1774 ae. 47 (g. s.).
>
> Rachel, b. at Stratford, 14 Feb. 1703/4, d. y.
>
> Abigail, m. at Boston, 3 Mar. 1728 [1728/9], Joseph Miller of Milton, Mass.
>
> William, bapt. at Stratford (rec. Stratfield) 10 Feb. 1706, said to have d. at Boston, Sept. 1780 ae. 70, unm.; lawyer; Judge of the Admiralty Court, 1766, of the Superior Court, 1770.
>
> Mary, b. 14 Apr. 1716 [so given in *Hist. of Redding*]; m. Capt. Charles Morris, b. at Boston, 8 June 1711; lived 15 yrs. at Hopkinton; rem. to Halifax, Nova Scotia, where he became Chief Justice.
>
> Deborah, b. abt. 1717/8, d. Apr. 1793 in 76 yr.; m. (1) at Boston, 24 July 1739, Henry Welsted; m. (2) at Boston, 31 Jan. 1749 [1749/50], Henry Paget, of Smithfield, R. I.

Redfield, James.

Born abt. 1646, son of William Redfin of Cambridge and New London; settled in New Haven, 1669, Tisbury, Martha's Vineyard, 1671, and Saybrook, 1676. By 1693 he rem. to Fairfield. In 1713 he conveyed his Saybrook property to his son Theophilus; and in 1719 with wife Deborah conveyed Fairfield property to their son James.

He m. (1) at New Haven, May 1669, Elizabeth How.

He m. (2) Deborah, widow of Benjamin Seeley, and dau. of John Sturges.

James may have had other children besides those listed below, especially daus.; but the Sarah given him by the *Redfield Genealogy* was his stepdau. Sarah Seeley; and Margaret did not m. his "son-in-law" [stepson] John Seeley.

Children [by first wife], eldest recorded at New Haven:

Elizabeth, b. 31 May 1670.

Theophilus, b. abt. 1682, d. at Killingworth, 14 Feb. 1759 in 77 yr. (g. s.); Sergt.; m. 24 Dec. 1706, Priscilla Grinnell, dau. of Daniel; she d. 12 Jan. 1770 in 81 yr. (g. s.).

Children [by second wife]:

Margaret, bapt. 7 Oct. 1694.

✗James, bapt. 25 Oct. 1696, d. at Fairfield in 1743; adm'n granted, 4 Oct. 1743; m. (1) Sarah Smith, dau. of Samuel, b. 2 Jan. 1706/7; m. (2) Mary Bradley, dau. of Joseph, bapt. 12 May 1706; m. (3) by 1742, Sarah Thorp, dau. of John, b. 27 Jan. 1711/2, d. in 1758.

Reynolds, David.

A merchant, settled in Fairfield before 1687, when he bought 70 acres from Dr. John Butler. On 9 Mar. 1687/8, Mr. David "Renald" recorded land with buildings which he had purchased from Isaac Hall with consent of his dau. Sarah Hall.

Richards, Nathaniel. Deputy (Norwalk) to Conn. Leg., Oct. 1658.

Came to Boston in the *Lion,* 1632; settled at Cambridge, freeman 6 Nov. 1632; rem. to Hartford 1636, and to Norwalk 1652, where he was prominent, and d. in 1681/2.

Perhaps he m. (1) the mother of Nathaniel and Samuel Hayes. He m. (2) 15 Mar. 1663/4, Rosamund, widow of Dea. Henry Lindall of New Haven. Rosamond's will, 1683, named her daus. Mary Hoyt, Rebecca Fitch, Grace Keeler, and Mercy Ketcham.

Will 7 Oct. 1681; aged 77 yrs.; wife "Rozimon", Exec'x; son Joseph Ketcham, house and homestead; sons John Hoyt, John Fitch, and Ralph Keeler, lands; also refers to preceding as his four sons-in-law; to Samuel Hayes, my pasture lot; to Rev. Mr. Thomas Hanford; to Rebecca "Garuet" (now Rebecca Waller), one cow and one yearling heifer. Inv. 9 Feb. 1681 [1681/2]. Agreement of heirs made 14 Mar. 1681/2 by widow, the four sons-in-law and Samuel Hayes, refers to land sold to Samuel Baldwin.

His stepchildren, children of Henry Lindall, were:

Mary, bapt. 19 July 1646; m. at Norwalk, 14 Sept. 1666, John Hoyt.

Sarah, bapt. 29 Oct. 1648, d. y.

Hannah, b. 7 Jan. 1650 [1650/1], bapt. 12 Jan. 1650 [1650/1], d. y.

Rebecca, b. 20 Oct. 1653, bapt. 20 Oct. 1653; m. at Norwalk, 3 Dec. 1674, John Fitch.

Grace, b. 31 Mar. 1656, bapt. 5 Apr. 1656; m. Ralph Keeler.

Mercy, b. 18 Dec. 1658, bapt. 30 Jan. 1658 [1658/9]; m. at Norwalk, 3 Apr. 1679, Joseph Ketcham.

Risden, Robert.

A mariner, of Boston 1654; came abt. 1663 to Fairfield, where he d. abt. 1666.

He m. Beatrice ———, who d. abt. 1667. In 1665 she testified in the Benfield case.

Mr. Risden complained to New York authorities that Ann Furse, his covenant maid servant, had fled to Long Island, 1665 [N. Y. Col. Records].

Inv. of Mr. Robert, 21 Jan. 1666 [1666/7]. It was reported on 20 June 1667 that his wife was also dec'd; five children; a considerable Est. both "in these parts" and in the Island of Nevis.

Children,* three recorded at Boston:

Elisha, b. 25 Jan. 1654/5. On 8 May 1678, as eldest son, ae. 22, he confirmed what had been done in his father's Est. Land was set out to him in Fairfield, 1681.

Mary, b. 15 June 1659.

Sarah, b. 29 May 1662.

Robert, joined Stratford Church, 25 July 1689, and d. there 12 Dec. 1727.

One other.

Roberts, William.

Married Sarah Hinman, dau. of Edward, b. Sept. 1653.

Will of William of Woodbury, undated, proved 7 Feb. 1690 [1690/1].

---

* The estate of John Scott of Wallingford, 8 Dec. 1713, was ordered distributed in eight equal shares, to Edmund, Samuel, George, David, Jonathan, and Robert Scott, Sarah wife of Roger Terrill, and Robert Risden. There is here something of mystery. The six Scotts were brothers, sons of the first Edmund Scott of Farmington (prob. by his second wife Elizabeth (Fuller) Upson). They had a seventh brother, Joseph, who d. at Farmington in 1708, and was prob. father of the John whose estate was distributed. They had also two sisters (prob. half-sisters) on the paternal side, as well as Upson half-brothers and sisters on the maternal side, who are not mentioned in the distribution, showing that only John's uncles and aunts of the "whole blood" participated. It would appear likely that Mrs. Terrill and Robert Risden, who participated, were connected on the side of John Scott's mother. As a tentative hypothesis, Robert Risden's sister Sarah m. Roger Terrill of Woodbury; Mary Risden or another sister m. Joseph Scott and was mother of John. While possible, this theory is far from proved.

Widow Sarah. Ages of children: Zechariah, 11 next July; Sarah, 7 next Aug.; Hannah, 4 last Jan.; Amos, 2 next July.

Children, first two recorded at Stratford (mother of first called Sarah):

> Hannah, b. 18 Oct. 1677, d. y.
> Zechariah, b. 3 July 1680.
> Sarah, b. Aug. 1684.
> Hannah, b. Jan. 1686/7.
> Amos, b. July 1689. On 1 Mar. 1712 he, of Flushing, L. I., conveyed right in Woodbury that came from father William Roberts, dec'd.

Robinson, Samuel.

He purchased 1¼ acres in Fairfield, from Edward Adams, 6 Mar. 1670 [1670/1].

He m. Constance ——, who d. by 1680; he d. in 1674.

Inv. 9 Aug. 1674; his widow made oath, 19 Feb. 1674 [1674/5].

Samuel Robinson (being the sole heir of his father Samuel and mother Constance Robinson, both dec'd), had land recorded, 25 Dec. 1680. [Fairfield Deeds.]

Child:

+Samuel.

Robinson, Samuel, s. of Samuel.

He m. at Fairfield, 20 Aug. 1691, Abigail Lockwood, dau. of Daniel.

Will 2 Apr. 1698, proved 26 Apr. 1698; wife Abigail, Exec'x; dau. Damaris; overseers, John Edwards, Elnathan Hanford.

Child, recorded at Fairfield:

> Damaris, b. 13 Apr. 1696.

Root, Richard.

The surname was spelled Roots until after 1700.

Of Lynn, was of Salem church, 1636; freeman, 9 Mar. 1636/7; rem. to Fairfield.

Married Margery ——, who m. (2) before 1653, Michael Try.

On 31 Dec. 1653, lands formerly granted to Richard Root dec'd, now in possession of Michael Try by virtue of marriage with Margery Root whose these lands were after her husband's decease, were entered as "now Try's for ever."

Clearly he had no children; but was uncle of John Root, who by an extension of the term called Michael Try his uncle, Try being husband of his uncle's widow.

Root, John.

Born about 1645, d. at Woodbury, 25 May 1723 in 78 yr. He was nephew of Richard Root of Salem and Fairfield, and without much doubt was son of Josiah of Salem, who came in the *Hercules* 1635; Josiah had son Josiah, and daus. Bethia and Susanna, names that were repeated among John's children.

On 16 Jan. 1673 [1673/4] he had land at Fairfield by gift from his uncle Michael Try.

He m. abt. 1677, Dorcas Abbott, dau. of George of Norwalk, whose will 1689 named his dau. Dorcas Roots. Mrs. Dorcas Root d. at Woodbury, 15 May 1720.

Children, first two recorded at Fairfield, all bapt. at Woodbury:

> Susanna, b. 13 May 1678, bapt. Apr. 1685, d. 26 Apr. 1738; m. at Woodbury, 12 July 1710, Ens. Joseph Minor.
> Mary, b. 19 Jan. 1679 [1679/80], bapt. Apr. 1685; m. Robert Warner.
> Sarah, bapt. Apr. 1685.
> John, bapt. Apr. 1685, d. y.
> Josiah, bapt. Mar. 1688, d. at Woodbury in 1727; m. at Woodbury, 3 July 1717, Elizabeth Huthwitt.
> Bethia, bapt. Dec. 1690, d. 23 July 1700.
> John, bapt. May 1693, d. at Woodbury, 3 Aug. 1757; m. (1) at Woodbury, 4 Sept. 1717, Ruth Hickock, b. 31 July 1700, d. 23 Apr. 1741; m. (2) Elizabeth Treadwell.
> Joseph, b. 9 June 1698, bapt. June 1698, d. in 1761; m. Susanna ———.
> Thomas, d. at Woodbury, 3 June 1727; m. Sarah Hickock, dau. of Benjamin; she m. (2) 8 Jan. 1728, Joseph Prime.
> Bethia, b. 7 Feb. 1702/3.

Rose, Robert, s. of Robert. Colonial grant of 50 acres, May 1668, for service in Pequot War (1637).

Born about 1619, came with his parents on the *Frances* in 1634 aged 15. Settled in Wethersfield, rem. to Branford, and soon after 1655 to Stratford, where he d. early in 1683.

Married Rebecca ————. She m. (2) in 1685, Henry Allen.

On 1 Nov. 1679, Robert Rose of Stratford conveyed to son-in-law Moses Johnson of Woodbury, land in Woodbury, "granted to me as gratification for servis don by me in ye pequad war."

Inv. 9 Mar. 1682/3. Widow Rebecca; children Mary Johnson, Rebecca Stevens, and Elizabeth, Sarah, Hannah, and Mercy Rose. Agreement 10 June 1685 between Rebecca Rose, widow; Moses Johnson; Isaac Bennett for himself and his brother-in-law Obadiah Stephens; and John Minor, Jr.; making allowance for their two sisters-in-law Hannah and Mercy Rose.

In 1685 Moses Johnson of Woodbury conveyed to father-in-law Henry Allyn of Stratford all right in Est. of Robert Rose lying undivided between the children of said Rose. A mutual distribution was made 1686 by the heirs to Est. of Robert Rose, viz.: Henry Allyn in behalf of Moses Johnson; Obadiah Stephens of Stamford; Isaac Bennet and wife Elizabeth, for himself and in behalf of John Minor, Jr., and Hannah Rose.   [Stratford Deeds.]

Children, recorded at Stratford:

> Mary, b. 20 Apr. 1655; birth rec. at Branford, 15 Apr. 1655; m. Moses Johnson, of Woodbury.
> Rebecca, b. 14 July 1657; m. Obadiah Stevens, of Stamford.
> Elizabeth, b. Feb. 1658 [1658/9]; m. 2 June 1683, Isaac Bennett.
> Dorcas, b. Apr. 1661, d. y.
> Sarah, b. Aug. 1664; m. John Minor, Jr.
> Hannah, b. [say 1668]; m. (1) Isaac Stiles, Jr.; m. (2) (rec. Derby) 9 May 1693, Samuel Harger; she m. (3) 28 Mar. 1700, John Tibbals.
> Mercy, b. 3 Mar. 1672/3, d. at Stratford abt. 1733. Adm'n granted, 25 Jan. 1733 [1733/4], to Nathan Bennett of Stratford.

Rowland, Henry.

Of Fairfield, where he purchased land before 1650.

Will 30 Dec. 1690, proved 4 Jan. 1691 [1691/2]; wife Rebecca; son Joseph (and his dau. and three other children); sons Jonathan, Israel, Henry; daus. Elizabeth Wheeler, Abigail wife of Thomas Jones, Rebecca wife of Eluzer Smith, and Mary wife of Daniel Frost, and their children; gr. child Jonathan Smith; friends, Capt. John Burr and Sergt. John Thompson, overseers. Inv. 29 Dec. 1691.

Will of Rebecca, 12 Dec. 1691; "old"; son Joseph; daus. Eliza-

beth Wheeler, Abigail Jones, Rebecca Smith, Mary Frost; son
Israel.   Inv. 6 Nov. 1694.

Henry, Sr., conveyed to son Jonathan the house where he lived,
28 Oct. 1689, he to pay to my wife Rebecca £2-10 per annum.

Children:

> +Joseph, b. abt. 1647.
> +Jonathan.
> Elizabeth, m. by 1673, Sergt. John Wheeler.
> Abigail, m. at Fairfield, 5 Mar. 1670/1, Thomas Jones.
> Rebecca, m. Eluzai Smith.
> Mary, m. Daniel Frost.
> +Israel.
> Henry, d. unm. in 1691. Inv. 5 Jan. 1691 [1691/2]; adm'n granted
> to Thomas Jones, who conveyed 16 Dec. 1693 to the heirs,—Joseph
> and Israel Rowland, Elizabeth Wheeler, Daniel Frost, Eluzer Smith
> and Thomas Jones in right of their wives, and Jonathan Rowland's
> children.

Rowland, Samuel.

An early settler of Stratford, possibly brother of Henry of Fairfield; d. early leaving a will, of which the only mention is found
in Stratford Deeds.

Child:

> Elizabeth, d. abt. 1709; m. James Rogers, of Milford and New Lon-
> don, who sold Rowland land to Francis Hall; conveyance confirmed
> in 1662 by Samuel Rogers of New London, who mentioned his
> grandfather Rowland's will.

Rowland, Joseph, s. of Henry.

Born about 1647; m. Sarah Wilson, dau. of Anthony.   No death
or probate record found.

His "now wife Sarah" was mentioned 26 Dec. 1681; on 25 Mar.
1686/7, the Exec'rs of the Est. of Anthony Wilson dec'd made
agreement with Joseph Rowland who m. the dau. and only heir.

On 15 Feb. 1705 [1705/6], Joseph Rowland, Sr., conveyed for
love to son Joseph.   On 21 Sept. 1709, Thomas Clark gave receipt
to Joseph Rowland, Jr., for payment of a mortgage from my
father Joseph Rowland; witnessed by Philip Lewis and Elizabeth
Lewis the younger.   Joseph conveyed, 21 Dec. 1716, to Samuel

Lyon of Fairfield, land I had by my wife Sarah, only dau. of Anthony Wilson, having already given to sons Joseph, Samuel, and James Rowland.

Children:

> Elizabeth, prob. m. Thomas Clark.
> ✕Joseph, d. at Fairfield in July 1728; will 4 July 1728, proved 6 Aug. 1728; m. Abigail Whitlock, dau. of David.
> ✕Samuel, b. abt. 1679, d. at Fairfield, 4 Nov. 1748 in 62 [69?] yr.; Capt.; m. (1) Esther, prob. dau. of Moses Dimon; b. abt. 1682, d. 11 Sept. 1744 in 63 yr. (g. s.); m. (2) Sarah, widow of Samuel Barlow and previously of Benajah Strong, and dau. of Capt. David Sherman.
> ✕James, b. ———, d. at Fairfield in 1750; adm'n granted 20 Aug. 1750; m. Mary ———.
> ✕Henry, b. abt. 1691, bapt. at Stratfield (on own account), 16 Nov. 1712, d. at Stratfield, 29 June 1775 ae. abt. 84 (g. s. erected 1879); m. (1) at Stratfield, 25 Sept. 1718, Tamar Sherman, bapt. 2 Mar. 1696, d. 21 Apr. 1737 in 42 yr. (g. s.); m. (2) Abigail, widow of David Hill, and dau. of John Andrews, b. 17 June 1709; m. (3) Mary ———.

Rowland, Jonathan, s. of Henry.

He m. Abigail Barlow, dau. of John, 2d; she m. (2) before Nov. 1697, Samuel Denton of Hempstead, L. I.

Inv. 17 Nov. 1691.

Child :*

> Jonathan, of Hempstead, L. I., who conveyed Fairfield land in 1713: m. Martha Seaman, dau. of Benjamin.

Rowland, Israel, s. of Henry.

Married Elizabeth, most likely Turney, dau. of Robert, b. 15 July 1668.

Elizabeth renewed her Covenant at Fairfield Church, 24 Feb. 1694/5. Israel conveyed to two daus., Mary and Elizabeth.

Will 6 Nov. 1719, proved 24 Feb. 1719/20; children Israel, John, Mary Bennett, Elizabeth Bennett, Bethia Gray, Rebecca, Deborah and Judith Rowland.

The widow Elizabeth Rowland m. (2) (by contract 10 June 1724) John Staples.

---

* No record of other children found.

Children, all but first bapt. at Fairfield:

Mary, bapt. 10 Mar. 1694/5, d. 17 Apr. 1733; m. at Fairfield, 17 Mar. 1717, Thomas Bennett.

Elizabeth, bapt. 10 Mar. 1694/5; m. Peter Bennett.

Bethia, bapt. 13 June 1697; m. ———— Gray.

✗Israel, m. ———— Williams, dau. of Thomas. Israel conveyed, 22 May 1729, to Benjamin Franklin of Chestnut Ridge [Redding], land I bought of my father Thomas Williams.

Rebecca, bapt. 5 Apr. 1702; m. 3 Aug. 1726, Jabez Davis.

Deborah, bapt. 3 Oct. 1703, d. at Greenfield, 12 Aug. 1774 ae. 68; m. 24 May 1723, Thomas Staples, "Sr."

Judeanne [called Judith in will], bapt. 2 June 1706.

✗John, bapt. 1 Oct. 1710; m. 13 Dec. 1738, Sarah Lyon, dau. of Samuel.

Rowlandson, William.

He m. (1) abt. 1695, Elizabeth, widow of Benjamin Banks, and dau. of Richard Lyon. The name in print has usually been converted into Robinson, but in Banks probate records is spelled Rolison, and in Col. Rec. he is called Rowlandson of Fairfield.

He m. (2) by 1704, Sarah Coley, dau. of Peter, b. abt. 1668.

Mary and Elizabeth Rowlandson were bapt. at Fairfield, evidently as infants or children, 15 July 1722; Elizabeth m. 24 Mar. 1747/8, John Clugston. In 1737 the poor widow Rowlandson received £10 "out of charity" by the will of David Banks. Presumably she was mother of Mary and Elizabeth.

Roystin, Katharine. [Surname may be Royston.]

This woman deserves special mention as the earliest female doctor's assistant found in New England. She lived some years in New Haven; in 1658 was a member of the household of Sergt. Thomas Jeffreys, and in 1661 gave testimony concerning his estate. Dr. Nicholas Augur of New Haven mentioned her in his will 1669; and the same year, she received a legacy in the will of Dr. Thomas Pell, then of Fairfield, who called her his "antient mayd." Whether single or widowed does not appear, but we may believe that she did domestic work in the homes of others, and that physicians welcomed her services.

A Thomas Royston came on the *Elizabeth*, 1635, ae. 25; a

Katharine Jones, ae. 28, came on the same ship; both, we judge unmarried. The ship was bound for Virginia, but as the surname is not found in Savage, a clue may be found here.

Rumble, Thomas.

Born abt. 1613, he came to Boston in the *Truelove,* Sept. 1635 ae. 22. He came to Saybrook and was in the Pequot War, 1637, under Lion Gardiner. Settled in Stratford and d. abt. 1649.

He m. Rose Sherwood, dau. of Thomas, b. abt. 1622, and she m. (2) Thomas Barlow and (3) Edward Nash.

The probate records show that he d. before 4 Mar. 1653, but he must have d. by 1650, as his widow had a child by her second husband, b. 1651.

Child:

Bethia, m. (rec. Norwalk) 12 June 1661, Robert Stewart.

Rumsey, Robert.

He m. Rachel Frost, dau. of Daniel.

He recorded a homelot, by grant from the town of Fairfield, 9 Feb. 1669 [1669/70].

He conveyed land, 28 Nov. 1710, to his son Robert, and in default of heirs, to his son Benjamin.

Will 28 Nov. 1710, proved 20 Nov. 1712; wife Rachel; sons Benjamin, Isaac, Daniel, Robert; three daus. Rachel Hide, Abigail Osborn, Elizabeth Barlow; gr. dau. Hannah Rumsey; gr. s. Isaac Rumsey.

Adm'n on undivided estate granted, 5 Apr. 1756, to John Andrews. On 19 Apr. 1756, a part of Robert's estate which was intestate was ordered divided among the seven heirs (or their representatives), Benjamin, Isaac, Daniel, Robert, Rachel, Abigail, Elizabeth.

Children:

+Benjamin, b. abt. 1667.
Rachel, b. 6 Oct. 1671 (rec. Greenfield), d. 14 June 1738 ae. 67 (g. s., Greenfield); m. abt. 1691, John Hide.
+Isaac.
Daniel.

Abigail, b. abt. 1680, d. at Fairfield, 5 Aug. 1724 ae. abt. 44 (g. s.); m. abt. 1700, Samuel Osborn.

+Robert.

Elizabeth, b. abt. 1686, bapt. at Fairfield, 4 Oct. 1702, d. 10 Feb. 1752 in 66 yr. (g. s., Fairfield); m. abt. 1705, Samuel Barlow.

Rumsey, Benjamin, s. of Robert. Ens., west company, Fairfield, Oct. 1710.

Born about 1667, d. at Westport, 3 Nov. 1732 ae. 65 (g. s.); was called Sergt. at bapt. of child 1709.

He m. (1) Hannah Morehouse, dau. of Samuel, who was called dec'd in 1698 when he receipted for her portion.

He m. (2) by 1696, Mary Hide, dau. of John, b. 26 July 1672.

He m. (3) Susannah, widow of Nathaniel Burr, Jr., and dau. of Sergt Joseph Lockwood.

He m. (4) abt. 1726, Rebecca, widow of John Allyn, and dau. of Richard Blackleach; she m. (3) John Curtis, of Stratford.

Adm'n granted, 5 Dec. 1732, to Rebecca and Benjamin Rumsey.

Benjamin Rumsey, James Dickson and Hannah his wife, John Davice and Ann his wife, Lewis Macdonald and Sarah his wife, Salathiel Denmore and Ruth his wife, and Rebecca Rumsey (guardian to Abigail Rumsey), all of Fairfield, and all (except Rebecca) children of Benjamin Rumsey dec'd, made agreement 30 Dec. 1734. James Dickson, formerly of Fairfield, now living in Courtlandt, Westchester County, N. Y., conveyed with wife Hannah, 1740; and on 3 Oct. 1747 James Dickerson and wife Hannah of "Sciners Farm," Westchester County, conveyed to Ralph Isaacs of Norwalk, right to land from sister Abigail Rumsey of Stratford.

Child [by first wife]:

Hannah, b. [say 1693]; m. (rec. Norwalk) 8 Dec. 1709, James Dickson.

Children [by second wife], bapt. at Fairfield:

Joseph, bapt. 2 Nov. 1701, d. in 1726; adm'n granted, 7 Feb. 1725/6, to father Benjamin. Distribution, 22 Nov. 1726, to James Dixon in right of wife Hannah, John Davis in right of wife Ann, Sarah Rumsey, Ralph Isaacs in right of wife Mary, Benjamin Rumsey and Ruth Rumsey.

Ann, bapt. 2 Nov. 1701, d. at Westport, 28 Feb. 1746; m. John Davis.

Sarah, bapt. 2 Nov. 1701; m. Lewis MacDonald, of Fairfield.

Mary, bapt. 30 Oct. 1703; m. (rec. Norwalk) 7 Mar. 1725/6, Ralph Isaacs.

XBenjamin, b. abt. 25 May 1707, d. at Westport, 12 Nov. 1781; Lt.; m. in 1729, Isabel Couch, dau. of Simon, b. 17 Sept. 1708, d. 7 Nov. 1754.

Ruth, bapt. 1 Aug. 1709; m. Salathiel Denmore.

Child [by fourth wife]:

Abigail, b. prob. after 1726, d. at Stratford by 1747.

Rumsey, Isaac, s. of Robert.

He m. by 1694, Hannah Osborn, dau. of John, b. 26 July 1677. She renewed her Covenant at Fairfield Church, 30 Aug. 1696.

Isaac Rumsey, John Squire and Sarah his wife, and James Beers, conveyed 21 Dec. 1725, part of land that was our grandfather's, Capt. John Osborn, set to us as representatives of our mother Hannah Rumsey dec'd.

Children, bapt. at Fairfield:

Sarah, bapt. 30 Aug. 1696; m. abt. 1717, John Squire.

Hannah, bapt. 30 Aug. 1696, d. 17 Mar. [1724?]; m. 20 Jan. 1716, James Beers.

Isaac, bapt. 12 June 1698.

Rumsey, Robert, s. of Robert.

He m. Ann Bastard, dau. of Joseph. She renewed her Covenant with Fairfield Church, 27 Feb. 1708/9.

Robert Rumsey in right of wife Ann made agreement, 3 Nov. 1714, with Thomas Hill son of Capt. Thomas Hill dec'd concerning division of all lands that formerly belonged to Lt. Ezbon Wakeman dec'd, and Mr. Joseph Bastard and Capt. Thomas Hill died possessed of. With wife Ann "only daughter of Joseph Bastard", he conveyed 6 Feb. 1716/7 to Capt. Joseph Wakeman. [Fairfield Deeds.]

Children, bapt. at Fairfield:

William, bapt. 27 Feb. 1708/9, d. at Westport, 3 Jan. 1748 [1748/9] in 41 yr. (g. s.). Adm'n granted, 12 Jan. 1748/9, to Joseph Rumsey and Cornelius Hull. Distribution 1764 to heirs of Joseph Rumsey dec'd, Nathan Rumsey, Abigail wife of Cornelius Hull, Elizabeth wife of Joseph Jennings, Jr., Ann wife of Benjamin Jennings, Rachel wife of Charles Lewis, Hannah wife of Seth Hull, heirs of Daniel Rumsey dec'd, and John Rumsey.

Abigail, bapt. 4 Mar. 1710/1, d. at Greenfield, 7 June 1776 ae. 66 (g. s.); m. 24 Aug. 1731, Cornelius Hull.

Elizabeth, bapt. 13 Sept. 1713, d. at Sharon, 19 Dec. 1785 in 73 yr. (g. s.); m. (1) Zechariah Bostwick, Jr.; m. (2) 30 Aug. 1744, Joseph Jennings, Jr.

Rachel, bapt. 15 Apr. 1716, living 1765; m. Charles Lewis.

✗Joseph, bapt. 28 Sept. 1718, d. at Redding, 26 Nov. 1760 ae. 40; will 27 Dec. 1754, proved 3 Dec. 1760; m. 16 Aug. 1738, Sarah Bartram, dau. of John, b. 14 May 1719; she m. (2) at Redding, 20 Sept. 1768, Hezekiah Bulkley.

Ann, bapt. 8 Oct. 1721; m. Benjamin Jennings.

Daniel, bapt. 22 Dec. 1723, d. at Redding, 7 Feb. 1761 ae. 37. Inv. presented 20 Apr. 1761.

✗John, m. 19 Mar. 1752 [probably error for 1750], Esther Jones.

Hannah, bapt. 31 Mar. 1728; m. 24 Dec. 1747, Seth Hull.

Nathan, bapt. 19 Apr. 1730.

St. John, Matthias. [Surname spelled Sention usually before 1700.]

Came to Dorchester, Mass., about 1632; freeman, 3 Sept. 1634. Removed to Windsor about 1640, and in 1654 to Norwalk, where he d. abt. Jan. 1669/70.

Will 19 Oct. 1669; youngest son James; my wife, his mother; sons Samuel Sention and Ephraim Lockwood; residue, double portion to son Matthias, one part to son Mark, and the other two parts to sons Samuel Sention and Ephraim. Inv. Jan. 1669 [1669/70].

Children:

+Matthias, b. abt. 1630.
+Mark, b. abt. 1634.
+Samuel, b. abt. 1639.
  Mercy, d. in 1694; m. 8 June 1665, Ephraim Lockwood.
+James, b. abt. 1649.

St. John, Matthias, s. of Matthias.

Born abt. 1630, d. at Norwalk in Dec. 1728; m. Elizabeth ———.
Adm'n granted to widow Elizabeth, 5 Sept. 1732.

Children:

Mary, m. 10 Nov. 1677, Thomas Hyatt.

Ebenezer, b. abt. 1660; m. Elizabeth Comstock, b. 7 Oct. 1674.

Matthias, b. abt. 1667, d. at Wilton, 17 Aug. 1748; m. abt. 1690, Rachel Bouton, b. 16 Dec. 1667.

James, b. abt. 1674, d. at Norwalk in 1754; will 27 Oct. 1750, proved 28 June 1754; m. 18 Dec. 1693, Mary Comstock, b. 19 Feb. 1671/2, d. 17 Oct. 1749.

St. John, Mark, s. of Matthias. Deputy for Norwalk, Oct. 1672, Oct. 1676, Oct. 1678, May and Oct. 1684.

Born abt. 1634, d. at Norwalk, 12 Aug. 1693.

Married (1) abt. 1655, Elizabeth Stanley, dau. of Timothy of Hartford, b. abt. 1635.

Married (2) (marriage covenant, 21 Jan. 1691/2), Dorothy, widow of Francis Hall and previously of John Blackman, and dau. of Rev. Henry Smith of Wethersfield. She m. (4) Dea. Isaac Moore of Farmington.

Will not dated; aged abt. 59; son Joseph; daus. Lois and Rachel Sention, Annah, Elizabeth, Sarah, Rhoda; Joseph Lockwood, my sister's son; three sons, Joseph Sention, Samuel Galpin, and Samuel Keeler, Exec'rs. Inv. 2 Oct. 1693. Marriage Covenant with Dorothy Hall of Stratford recorded.

Children [by first wife], recorded at Norwalk:

Elizabeth, b. 6 Dec. 1656, d. at Kensington in 1732; m. (1) Samuel Galpin; m. (2) Edward Camp, of Milford.

Sarah, b. 18 Jan. 1659 [1659/60], d. at Ridgefield, 15 Apr. 1714; m. 10 Mar. 1681/2, Samuel Keeler.

Joseph, b. 1664, d. 26 Sept. 1731; m. 5 Mar. 1695/6, Sarah Betts, dau. of Thomas, b. abt. 1665, d. 26 Aug. 1755.

Rhoda, b. 12 Aug. 1666, living 1702; m. abt. 1688, Matthew Marvin.

Lois, b. 1669, d. 12 Jan. 1752 ae. 82; m. 3 Jan. 1705/6, Samuel Carter.

Rachel, b. 1671; m. John Judd, of Farmington.

Anna, b. 8 Aug. 1674; m. John Benedict.

St. John, Samuel, s. of Matthias.

Born abt. 1639, d. at Norwalk, 14 Jan. 1684 [1684/5], error for 1685/6.

Married at Norwalk, Sept. 1663, Elizabeth Hoyt, dau. of Walter.

Will 11 Jan. 1685 [1685/6]; wife Elizabeth; dau. Elizabeth (under 18); son Thomas (under 22); sister Lockwood; wife and Sergt. John Platt, Exec'rs; brother Mark Sention, overseer. Inv. exhibited Nov. 1686; wife was then dead, and only heir was the dau. Elizabeth; John Bouton was joined with Platt in the adm'n. Elizabeth dau. of Samuel ae. between 13 and 14.

Children, recorded at Norwalk:

> Sarah, b. Jan. 1664 [1664/5], d. 5 Jan. 1685 [1685/6].
> Thomas, b. Oct. 1666, d. young.
> Elizabeth, b. Apr. 1673; m. at Norwalk, 7 Mar. 1690 [1690/1], John Raymond, Jr.

St. John, James, s. of Matthias.

Born abt. 1649, d. at Norwalk, 9 May 1684; m. (recorded Norwalk) last day of Dec. 1673, Rebecca Pickett, dau. of John of Stratford. No issue; she m. (2) in 1685, Sergt. Andrew Messenger.

Will 9 May 1684; aged abt. 35; wife Rebecca; Joseph son of Mark Sention; Thomas son of Samuel Sention; James son of Matthias Sention; James son of Ephraim Lockwood. Inv. 30 May 1684. Agreement 9 Mar. 1684 [1684/5] between the widow Rebecca, and Matthias, Mark and Samuel Sention and Ephraim Lockwood.

Samfield, Austin.

Purchased two acres at Fairfield from George Hull, prior to May 1658.

Inv. 12 Dec. 1661; left widow and no children; small estate.

Sanford, Thomas.

Born about 1608, son of Ezekiel (bapt. at Much Hadham, co. Herts, 20 Feb. 1585/6) and ———— (Warner) Sanford, and nephew of Andrew Warner the emigrant. The family lived in Hatfield Broad Oak and Stanstead Mountfitchet, co. Essex, Eng.

Of Dorchester, 1634-40; rem. to Milford, where he was adm. to the church, 9 Jan. 1641/2.

His wife Sarah was adm. to Milford church, 15 Dec. 1642, and d. 14 May 1681, he dying the following Autumn.

Will 23 Sept. 1681; eldest son Ezekiel; sons Thomas, Ephraim, Samuel; ⸱daus. Sarah wife of Richard Shute of Eastchester, and Elizabeth wife of Obadiah Allyn of Middletown; gr. children Sarah Shute and Thomas Allyn; Sarah Whitlock that was his maid. Inv. 21 Oct. 1681.

Children, all except first two bapt. at Milford:

+Ezekiel, b. abt. 1637.

Sarah, b. abt. 1639; m. Richard Shute, of Eastchester, N. Y.

Mary, bapt. 16 Jan. 1641/2, d. y.

Samuel, bapt. 30 Apr. 1643, d. at Milford, 27 Nov. 1691; Inv. 8 Dec. 1691; m. (rec. Milford) 16 Aug. 1674, Hannah Bronson, dau. of Richard of Farmington.

Thomas, bapt. Dec. 1644, d. at New Haven, after 1721; m. at New Haven, 11 Oct. 1666, Elizabeth Payne.

Ephraim, bapt. 17 May 1646, d. at Milford in 1687; Inv. 12 June 1687; m. at New Haven, 18 Nov. 1669, Mary Powell; dau. of Thomas, bapt. 20 July 1645; she m. (2) Nathaniel Baldwin.

Elizabeth, bapt. 27 Aug. 1648; m. at Milford, 26 Oct. 1669, Obadiah Allyn.

Sanford, Andrew.

Brother of Thomas, he was bapt. at Stanstead Mountfitchet, co. Essex, 1 Nov. 1617, and d. at Milford in 1684. He settled in Hartford, where his uncle Andrew Warner lived; freeman, May 1657. His first wife, Mary, was indicted with him for witchcraft; she was convicted, 13 June 1662, and presumably executed.

He rem. to Milford 1667, and had a second wife, of whom not even her given name has been learned, with whom he joined the church in 1671. The younger children belonged to the second wife, and five were bapt. together at Milford in 1671.

Much light on this family is shed by the (as yet) unpublished Winthrop documents. As a physician, in 1661, he treated the Sanford children and specified their ages as follows: Andrew, above 16 yrs., Mary 14½, Elizabeth 13, and Ezekiel 6. Later in the same year, he noted the youngest dau. (ae. 14) of Andrew Sanford, pumpmaker, which is important in indicating that Andrew's daus. Hannah, Martha, etc., were born after 1661, and hence were by the second wife. Again, in 1663, Winthrop noted Andrew (ae. 20), son of Andrew of Hartford.

Will 6 Sept. 1684, proved 12 Nov. 1684; children,—only Ezekiel, Mary and Hannah named. Inv. 16 Oct. 1684.

Children [by first wife]:

+Andrew, b. abt. 1643.

Mary, b. abt. 1646, d. in 1689, unm. Inv. 12 Apr. 1689. The Court ordered £1 to the sister that is weakly, and £1 to the youngest sister; one-third of residue to Andrew Sanford, only natural brother, and two-thirds to four sisters.

Elizabeth, b. abt. 1648, d. y., quite likely in 1661.

Ezekiel, b. abt. 1656, bapt. at Milford, 4 June 1671, d. in 1685, without issue. Inv. 11 Jan. 1685 [1685/6]; tools left at Mr. Wm. Maltby's of Branford; estate at Greenwich and Bedford belonging to his widow out of her father's estate. Adm'n granted to his widow Elizabeth, 9 June 1686. He m. Elizabeth Ratleff, dau. of William of Greenwich; she m. (2) Zechariah Baldwin. On 31 Mar. 1704, receipt was given by Henry Grey of Fairfield and his wife Hannah, who was sister to Ezekiel Sanford, to their brother Andrew Sanford, Sr.; by Joseph Tuttle and Elizabeth Tuttle alias Sanford of New Haven, to Zechariah Baldwin and Elizabeth his wife, formerly widow of Ezekiel Sanford; and by Joseph Beard for his late wife Sarah Beard alias Sanford of Milford, to the same. On 4 Apr. 1704, receipt was given by Pelatiah Holbrook and Martha his wife of Milford, who was sister to Ezekiel Sanford, to their brother Andrew Sanford, Sr., and Zechariah Baldwin.

Thomas, b. abt. 1658, perhaps was son of Andrew, and if so, d. y.; mentioned by Winthrop 1667 ae. 9, as at Mr. Richards' in Hartford; perhaps left with Mr. Richards by Andrew temporarily upon his removal to Milford.

Children [by second wife], first four bapt. at Milford, 4 June 1671:

Hannah, m. (1) Samuel Gunn, of Milford; m. (2) in 1700, Henry Gray, of Fairfield. On 12 Nov. 1700, Mr. Andrew Sanford, Adm'r of the Est. of Samuel Gunn, informed the Court that the widow was about to marry out of the Colony [by which County must have been meant], and Mrs. Hannah Grey alias Gunn is mentioned 19 Mar. 1700/1.

Martha, m. (1) Pelatiah Holbrook; m. (2) after 1707, —— Arnold.

Elizabeth, m. (rec. New Haven) 20 Nov. 1691, Joseph Tuttle.

Abigail, bapt. with the others, d. y.

Son, b. 30 Mar. 1673, called Nathaniel in baptismal record, d. y.

Samuel, b. 27 Jan. 1674 [1674/5], d. y.

Sarah, b. 7 Apr. 1677, d. between 1701 and 1704; m. at Milford, 1 Apr. 1701, Joseph Beard.

Sanford, Ezekiel, s. of Thomas.

Born about 1637, d. at Fairfield in 1683; m. (rec. Fairfield), 25 Apr. 1665, Rebecca "Wiekle." She was possibly dau. of James or Henry Wakelee.

He received a grant of land from the town of Fairfield, 16 Jan. 1673 [1673/4].

Inv. 1683; widow, eldest son Ezekiel, other son Thomas; daus. Sarah, Mary, Rebecca, Martha, Elizabeth. Agreement of children, 2 Nov. 1697, signed by Ezekiel and Thomas Sanford, Cornelius Hull for wife Sarah, Theophilus Hull for wife Mary, John Seeley for wife Rebecca, Martha and Elizabeth Sanford.

Children, recorded at Fairfield:

Sarah, b. 25 Mar. 1666, d. in 1753; m. abt. 1685, Cornelius Hull.
+Ezekiel, b. 6 Mar. 1668.
Mary, b. 3 Apr. 1670, d. after 1710; m. abt. 1690, Theophilus Hull.
Rebecca, b. 13 Dec. 1672, d. at Stratfield, Mar. 1725/6; m. (1) abt. 1690, John Seeley; m. (2) in 1711, Benjamin Nichols; m. (3) at Stratfield, 24 May 1716, John Mann.
+Thomas, b. 2 May 1675.
Martha, b. 29 June 1677; m. Nathaniel Hoyt.
Elizabeth, b. 6 Sept. 1679; m. (1) Joshua Jackson; m. (2) 23 Nov. 1699, Joseph Jackson; m. (3) Thomas Chambers.

Sanford, Andrew, s. of Andrew.

Born (prob. at Hartford) abt. 1643, d. at Milford in 1705; m. (1) at Milford, 8 Jan. 1667 [1667/8], Mary Botsford, dau. of Henry.

He m. (2) abt. 1688, Sarah Gibbard, dau. of Mr. William of New Haven, bapt. 20 Oct. 1648. In 1701, he appeared in right of his wife, an heir to Est. of Mrs. Anne Andrews and Timothy Gibbard; Timothy was her brother, and Mrs. Andrews her mother.

He was released from training, Nov. 1696, because of a sore eye. Andrew conveyed, 30 June 1705, to his dau. Hannah widow of Daniel Tuttle, and to Tuttle's two sons, Daniel and Andrew.

Adm'n on Mr. Andrew's estate was granted, Sept. 1705, to his son Andrew. Inv. 10 Dec. 1705. Inv. was also made at Milford, 8 Nov. 1705, of the Est. of Elizabeth Harwood late of Milford dec'd "wch was in ye hands of Andrew Sanford." This woman was in 1686 late of Boston and now of Milford, and was widow of Henry Harwood of Boston. How she was connected with the Sanfords has not been ascertained.

Jonathan Osborn and Samuel Chatterton of New Haven conveyed, 29 Mar. 1752, land laid out in Milford in name of "our mother" Sarah Sanford of Milford dec'd. These were representatives of the second wife of Andrew, Osborn being son-in-law and Chatterton grandson. New Haven Deeds and the will of the dau. Abigail also give evidence bearing on the second marriage and family of Andrew.

Children, by first wife, recorded at Milford:

> Mary, b. 16 Nov. 1668; m. (1) (rec. New Haven) 10 Nov. 1691, Thomas Tuttle; m. (2) at New Haven, 23 Dec. 1707, Daniel Johnson.
>
> Hannah, b. 19 Feb. 1669 [1669/70]; m. Daniel Tuttle, of Milford.
>
> Samuel, b. 17 Mar. 1671/2, d. 16 Mar. 1697/8, unm.
>
> Andrew, b. 13 July 1673, d. at Milford, 23 Apr. 1747 in 73 yr. (g. s.); Capt.; pump maker; m. (1) Hannah Raymond, dau. of John, b. at Norwalk, Dec. 1679; m. (2) abt. 1713, Elizabeth, widow of Isaac Hayes of Norwalk, dau. of Isaac Sherwood. His wife Hannah was adm. to Milford Church from Norwalk, 11 Dec. 1699. The *Sanford Genealogy,* by a mistaken interpretation of a deed in Milford, erroneously makes Hannah dau. of John Platt.
>
> Elizabeth, b. 5 Mar. 1674/5, d. in 1675.
>
> Esther, b. 6 May 1677.
>
> Mercy, b. 1 July 1679; m. Joshua Palmer, of Branford. Mercy Palmer of Branford conveyed, 29 Aug. 1735, to her "only brother" Capt. Andrew Sanford of Milford.
>
> Ezekiel, b. 11 July 1683, d. y.

Children [by second wife], recorded at Milford:

> Abigail, bapt. 9 June 1689, d. at New Haven, Sept. 1757; m. (1) abt. 1728, Samuel Chatterton; m. (2) at New Haven, 1 Oct. 1735, Isaac Jones.
>
> Ann, bapt. 26 Apr. 1691, d. at New Haven, 27 July 1734; m. (rec. New Haven) 9 Sept. 1723, Jonathan Osborn.

Sanford, Ezekiel, s. of Ezekiel. Sergt., Fairfield Trainband.

Born at Fairfield, 6 Mar. 1668, d. at Fairfield, 2 Mar. 1728/9 ae. 62 (g. s.); m. by 1697, Rebecca Gregory, dau. of Samuel, b. abt. 1673, d. at Redding, Nov. 1765 ae. 92 (g. s.).

He was called Sergt. at bapt. of children, 1710 to 1719. He renewed his Covenant at Fairfield Church, 27 May 1705.

Will 29 Jan. 1728/9, proved 25 Mar. 1729; wife Rebecca; daus. Rebecca, Abigail; eldest son Joseph; sons Samuel, Lemuel, Zechariah, Ezekiel, Ephraim.

Children, recorded at Fairfield:

✗Joseph, b. 27 Mar. 1698, bapt. 27 May 1705, d. at Redding abt. 1780; Lt.; will 2 Nov. 1779, proved 11 Jan. 1781; m. 11 Feb. 1724/5, Catherine Fairchild.

✗Lemuel, b. 16 Dec. 1699, bapt. 27 May 1705, d. 21 Apr. 1780 in 81 yr. (g. s., Redding); Deacon; m. 12 May 1730, Rebecca Squire, bapt. 17 June 1705, d. 26 Mar. 1779 in 75 yr. (g. s.).

✗Zechariah, b. 24 Nov. 1701, bapt. 27 May 1705, d. in 1787; will 23 Jan. 1783, proved 19 Feb. 1787; m. (1) at Stratfield, 7 Oct. 1736, Ann Hall; she was widow of Francis Hall, and dau. of James Seeley, b. 20 Jan. 1707, d. 21 Sept. 1779; m. (2) Sarah ———.

✗Ezekiel, b. 27 July 1704, bapt. 27 May 1705, d. at Stratfield, 19 July 1774; will 17 Feb. 1774, proved 2 Aug. 1774; m. 13 June 1733, Sarah Treadwell, bapt. 2 June 1706, d. after 1774.

✗Samuel, b. 20 Feb. 1706/7, bapt. 23 Feb. 1706/7, d. 6 Nov. 1768 ae. 61 yrs. 8 mos. 16 days (g. s., Redding); Capt.; m. 11 Jan. 1732/3, Sarah Meeker, b. abt. Nov. 1715, d. 31 Oct. 1803 ae. 87 yrs. 11 mos.

✗Ephraim, b. 12 Feb. 1708/9, bapt. 27 Mar. 1709; b. 12 Feb. 1708, d. 2 Feb. 1761 ae. 52 yrs. 11 mos. 21 days (g. s., Redding); Capt.; m. 7 Oct. 1730, Elizabeth Mix, b. at New Haven, 9 Nov. 1713, d. 21 Jan. 1777 ae. 62 yrs. 6 mos. 18 days (g. s., Redding).

Rebecca, b. 21 Nov. 1710, bapt. 26 Nov. 1710, d. abt. Nov. 1730; m. 28 Feb. 1730, William Hill.

Abigail, bapt. 29 Aug. 1714; m. at Redding, 4 Dec. 1735, James Bradley.

Elnathan, bapt. 1 Sept. 1716, d. 26 Apr. 1727 ae. 9 (g. s.).

Ruth, bapt. 28 June 1719.

Sanford, Thomas, s. of Ezekiel.

Born at Fairfield, 2 May 1675, d. at Stratfield, 20 May 1757 in 83 yr. (g. s.); m. abt. 1700, Hannah Stevens, dau. of James of Killingworth, where she was b. 8 Apr. 1679. She d. at Stratfield, 18 May 1755 in 75 yr. (g. s.).

Thomas renewed his Covenant at Fairfield Church, 26 Aug. 1705. He removed to Meriden by 1739, and by 1750 returned to Stratfield. In 1742 he, then "of Wallingford", bought land in Killingworth, which he conveyed same year to his son David.

Will (undated), proved 6 Dec. 1757; son Ebenezer; wife Hannah, Exec'x; dau. Sarah Andrews ("if she remain a

Widow") ; gr. son Joseph Andrews (under 21) ; residue to children, Thomas, Ebenezer, and David Sanford, Elizabeth wife of Thomas Lee, Hannah wife of John Porter, Eunice wife of David Hubbell, Mary wife of Thomas Wheeler, Sarah Andrews, Tabitha wife of Benjamin Andrews, and Tamar wife of Ebenezer Hubbell.

Children, bapt. at Fairfield:

Elizabeth, b. abt. 1701, bapt. 26 Aug. 1705; m. 15 Nov. 1721, Thomas Lee, of Guilford.

Hannah, b. abt. 1703, bapt. 26 Aug. 1705, d. at Stratfield, 28 Oct. 1763 in 61 yr. (g. s.) ; m. John Porter.

Eunice, bapt. 26 Aug. 1705; m. David Hubbell.

Thomas, bapt. 4 Oct. 1707, d. at Trumbull, 19 Apr. 1767 in 60 yr. (g. s.) ; will 12 Apr. 1767, proved 11 May 1767; to wife Abiah; the Church of Christ in North Stratford; surviving brothers [sic] Ebenezer Sanford, David Sanford, Eunice Hubbell, Tabitha Andrews, Tamar Hubbell; heirs of dec'd sisters. His widow Abiah m. (2) 2 Apr. 1777, John Middlebrook, and d. at Trumbull, 26 Nov. 1781 in 60 yr. (g. s.).

✗Ebenezer, bapt. 6 Nov. 1709, d. at Easton, 16 Apr. 1786 in 78 yr. (g. s.) ; m. 14 Feb. 1739/40, Sarah Chapman, dau. of Robert of East Haddam, who d. 20 Mar. 1809 in 92 yr. (g. s.).

✗David, bapt. 24 Feb. 1711/2, d. at Warwick, N. Y., in 1767; res. Meriden and North Killingworth; m. at Stratfield, 29 Jan. 1736, Patience Burroughs, b. 2 Jan. 1709/10.

Mary, bapt. 2 May 1714, d. 24 Feb. 1753 in 39 yr. (g. s., Greenfield) ; m. Thomas Wheeler.

Sarah, bapt. 11 Nov. 1716; m. —— Andrews.

Tabitha, bapt. 25 Jan. 1718/9; m. Benjamin Andrews, of Middletown.

Tamar, bapt. 16 Aug. 1724; m. Ebenezer Hubbell.

Scofield, Daniel.

Will 4 Sept. 1669; wife ——; dau. Sarah and her two children; sons Daniel, John, Joseph; dau. Mercy.

Inv. of Daniel of Stamford, 10 Feb. 1669/70.

Sarah [his widow] m. at Stamford, 30 Nov. 1670, Miles Merwin, and d. at Milford, 5 Mar. 1697/8. Her nuncupative will was presented by Theophilus Miles, ae. 21, Daniel Morehouse, ae. 19, and Sarah Deane, ae. 35; she said, 3 Mar. 1698, that she gave the £10 rec'd from will of her dec'd husband Miles Merwin, equally to her gr. son John Finch for his children, her son Samuel Camp, and Mercy Beard and Bethia Pettit, the last three of Milford; and £5 due her at Bedford to gr. son Finch; her sons at Stamford had had enough.

Children:

Sarah, m. 13 July 1665, John Pettit.
Daniel, "Sr." d. at Stamford, 10 Oct. 1714; Inv. 22 Nov. 1714; m. Abigail Merwin, dau. of Miles, who survived him. Agreement of heirs, 29 Nov. 1714; widow Abigail; Daniel, Joseph, and Samuel Scofield; Samuel Hoyt (smith) and Mary his wife; Samuel Weed and Abigail his wife; Samuel Bates and Sarah his wife; Daniel Weed, Jr., and Elizabeth his wife.
John, d. 27 Mar. 1699; m. 12 July 1677, Hannah Mead.
Joseph, d. in K. Philip's War; Inv. Mar. 1675/6, "to his wages in the service against the common enemy". Heirs: brothers Daniel, John; sisters, Sarah Pettit, Mercy Scofield.
Mercy, b. latter end of Nov. 1657; m. (rec. Milford) 6 Jan. 1681 [1681/2], Samuel Camp.

Scribner, Benjamin. [Surname originally Scrivener.]

He m. at Norwalk, 5 Mar. 1679/80, Hannah Crampton, dau. of John.

Inv. 15 Oct. 1704. Widow Hannah. Ages of children: Thomas, 24 next Mar.; Benjamin, 22 next May; Ruth, 15 next Mar.; Lydia, 7 this Dec.; Elizabeth, 5 next July; Abigail, 3 next Jan.

Children, first recorded at Norwalk:

Thomas, b. 31 Mar. 1681, d. at Norwalk in 1747; will 12 Apr. 1743, proved 21 Apr. 1747; wife; sons Benjamin, Thomas, Philip, Zaccheus, Uriah; daus. Sarah wife of Gershom* Bradley, Ruth wife of Phineas Hanford, Wait wife of Nathan Disbrow, and Hannah Scribner; friends Capt. Samuel Clugston and Mr. Samuel Fitch, Exec'rs. Prob. m. Mary Abbott, dau. of John.
Benjamin, b. May 1683, d. at Norwalk in 1752; will 1 Jan. 1750/1, proved 2 Jan. 1753; wife Abigail; son Matthew of Fairfield in Reading Parish, two lots in Norwalk, on condition that he pay £10 each to my daus. Hannah Gray and Rachel Fairchild of Reading; son Abraham of Norwalk, residue, on condition that he provide for my wife for life, and pay legacies to five of my daus., £10 to Lydia, £10 to Abigail, £25 to Elizabeth, £25 to "Esibel", and £50 to Ruth.

---

* Error for Ephraim Bradley.

Ruth, b. Mar. 1690.
Lydia, b. Dec. 1697.
Elizabeth, b. July 1700.
Abigail, b. Jan. 1701/2.

Seabrook, Robert.

An elderly man, one of the early settlers in Stratford, he did not long survive. His will is not found, and our only knowledge of it comes from mention made of it in Stratford Deeds, where land was entered to the following persons which they had by gift from their grandfather Robert Seabrook:—Samuel Fairchild, Thomas Fairchild, Jehiel Preston, John Wheeler's wife, Samuel Stiles's wife, and perhaps others not noted. From this we deduce that he had daus. who m. Thomas Fairchild, William Preston,* and Thomas Sherwood; the wives of Wheeler and Stiles were daus. of Sherwood.

Preston was from Chesham, co. Buckingham, and the name Seabrook is common in that county, where at Wingrave a Robert Seabrook m. 12 Sept. 1596, Alice Goodspeed, bapt. 19 Aug. 1576, dau. of Nicholas, Jr., and Margaret Goodspeed. She was a cousin of Roger Goodspeed, the Barnstable settler. If this was the emigrant Robert, he may have married more than once; but unless research in England be made, we have only vague surmise on which to build.

Children (perhaps others):

?Mary, b. abt. 1601, living in 1680; m. (1) abt. 1635, William Preston, and came with him to New England in 1635 ae. 34; m. (2) Thomas Kimberly, of New Haven and Stratford.

Daughter, b. by 1620; m. by 1639, Thomas Fairchild, of Stratford.

Sarah, b. abt. 1623; m. by 1642, Thomas Sherwood, of Stratford.

Searles, George.

He d. at Stratford, 2 Aug. 1706; m. Mary Blackman, dau. of James, b. 25 Apr. 1661.

---

* Jehiel Preston had land entered in Stratford, 8 Oct. 1670, "by gift from his Grandfather Mr. Robt Seabrook." As he was then the husband of Sarah Fairchild, a gr. dau. of Seabrook, there is a possibility that the land was in right of his wife; but the land of other husbands of Seabrook gr. daus. was entered as being given by Seabrook to their *wives*. The evidence is insufficient for certainty.

Children:

Daniel, d. at Stratford, 16 Nov. 1719; Inv. 19 Jan. 1719 [1719/20];
adm'n granted, 8 Apr. 1720, to widow Hannah and Isaac Beach;
m. 12 Dec. 1706, Hannah Fairchild, dau. of Zechariah, b. 1 Aug.
1685.

Margery, m. 5 Aug. 1707, Jonathan Gilbert.

Sarah, m. Nathaniel Cogswell, and was of Elizabethtown, N. J., 1746,
when she conveyed Stratford land inherited from father George
Searles.

Sedenham, William.   Sheriff, Fairfield County, under Andros,
1687.

With Nathan Gold, Jr., William Sydenham witnessed a deed
given by Nathan Gold, Sr., 17 Mar. 1684/5.   William "Sedenam"
entered land at Fairfield, 7 Mar. 1689/90, previously purchased
from Joseph Rowland.   On 29 June 1688, Dr. Peter Bulkley
mortgaged his Fairfield property to Francis Foxcraft of Boston,
the deed being witnessed by Thomas Hill and "frances" Sedenham; and on 31 Mar. 1691, Mistress Sedenham of Fairfield as
attorney for Mr. Foxcraft entered caveat against house and land
of Mr. Peter Bulkley, foreclosure proceedings being contemplated.

We suppose that the wife of William was Frances; but as Mr.
Foxcraft's name was also spelled "frances" in the same document,
hesitate to affirm it positively.

Seeley, Robert.   Lt. (second in command under Mason),
Pequot War, May 1637; Marshal (New Haven), Oct. 1639,
to Nov. 1642; Lt., New Haven Train Band, Aug. 1642; Lt.,
Artillery Co., Mar. 1645; Capt., Artillery Co., May 1648; Capt.,
New Haven Col. Troop, June 1654; in command of New
Haven Col. Troops against Ninigret, Oct. 1654; Lt. (chief
military officer), Huntington Train Band, May 1663 (and
referred to as Capt.); Judge (Huntington town), May 1663,
May 1664; Deputy (Huntington) to Conn. Leg., May 1664.

Resided at Watertown, Mass., 1631-34; at Wethersfield, 1635;
New Haven, 1639; Huntington, L. I., 1662.   He m. (1) ———;
m. (2) (N. Y. Mar. Licenses) 22 Dec. 1666, Mary Walker [née
Manning, widow Walker].

Adm'n granted, 19 Oct. 1668, to widow Mary.   She referred to
Capt. John Manning as her brother.

Children (list incomplete; no positive proof that Obadiah belongs here) :

+Obadiah.
+Nathaniel.

Seeley, Obadiah [s. of Robert?].

Married Mary ———, widow of John Miller.
He d. at Stamford, 25 Aug. 1657.
Inv. of Obadiah Seeley (deceased Anno 1657) taken 24 Feb. 1664/5 by William Newman and Robert Usher. Widow Mary made oath, 7 Nov. 1666; three children, Obadiah, Cornelius and Jonas.

Children:

+Obadiah.
+Cornelius, b. abt. 1650.
+Jonas.
Habakuk, d. at Stamford, 13 Aug. 1658.

Seeley, Nathaniel, s. of Robert. Called Sergt., May 1674; Lt., second in command of army, K. Philip's War, Nov. 1675; Capt., Fairfield County Dragoons, Nov. 1675.

He settled in Fairfield as early as 1657; m. (1) abt. Oct. 1649, Mary Turney, dau. of Benjamin. She testified 7 June 1650 that she was then married 8 mos. [New Haven Rec.]. He m. (2) in 1674, Elizabeth, widow of Obadiah Gilbert, previously widow of Nehemiah Olmstead, and dau. of Jehu Burr.

He was killed in the Great Swamp Fight, K. Philip's War.

Inv. 5 Feb. 1675 [1675/6]. Widow Elizabeth; mention made of her former husband, Obadiah Gilbert, and dau. Sarah. Children: Nathaniel, Robert, Benjamin, Joseph, John, Mary, Sarah, Phebe, Rebecca. Capt. Nathaniel having m. Elizabeth widow of Obadiah Gilbert, she made a mutual agreement, 14 Mar. 1675/6, with Nathaniel and Robert Seeley on behalf of Seeley's children.

Children [by first wife] :

+Nathaniel, b. abt. 1650.
+Robert, b. abt. 1653.
+Benjamin, b. abt. 1657.

+Joseph, b. abt. 1659.
+John, b. by 1661.
Mary, perhaps m. Jonathan Squire.
Sarah, m. Samuel Squire, who was appointed his attorney by bro. Joseph Seeley, 1696.
Phebe.
Rebecca.

Seeley, Obadiah, s. of Obadiah.

Probably m. Esther ———, who m. (2) Moses Jackson of Stratfield.
Inv. 25 July 1680, presented by Jonas Seeley.

Children [the younger two bapt. at Stratfield as children of Moses Jackson's wife] :

Obadiah, d. at Stamford, 4 Sept. 1745; m. at Stamford, 5 Dec. 1692, Susanna Finch.
Benjamin, b. abt. 1673, d. 5 Sept. 1696, unm. Inv. of Benjamin of Stamford, 31 Oct. 1696; brother Obadiah appointed Adm'r.
?Nathaniel.
?Abigail, m. at Stamford, 7 Aug. 1703, Joseph Finch.

Seeley, Cornelius, s. of Obadiah.

Born about 1650, d. after 1710, when he was living in Bedford, N. Y., ae. 60, with wife of same age; m. Priscilla Osborn, dau. of Capt. Richard, b. abt. 1650.

Children [record incomplete] :

Elizabeth, m. Joseph Hunt.
Cornelius, b. abt. 1673; m. Mary Jones, dau. of Joseph, b. at Stamford, 4 Jan. 1677/8.
Sarah, b. abt. 1676.
Joseph, b. abt. 1685; m. Martha ———.

Seeley, Jonas, s. of Obadiah.

Lived in Stamford, where he d. in 1703; m. (1) ———.
He m. (2) abt. 1689, Mary, widow of John Waterbury; she d. 31 Dec. 1738.
Will 20 Mar. 1702/3, disapproved. Inv. 5 Mar. 1704/5; widow Mary; eight children. On 13 Feb. 1721/2, it was represented that Jonas, Martha and Susanna had died after distribution was

granted; surviving children, Ebenezer, Nathaniel, Eliphalet, eldest son Samuel, and dau. Sarah.

Children [by first wife], first recorded at Stamford:

> Sarah, b. Feb. 1684/5, d. 27 Feb. 1727; m. 29 July 1707, Jonathan Holmes, of Greenwich and Bedford.
>
> Samuel, b. abt. 1687, d. after 1721/2; m. at Stamford, 13 May 1709, Charlotte Popino.

Children [by second wife], recorded at Stamford:

> Martha, b. 20 Sept. 1690, d. 25 May 1710.
>
> Jonas, b. 22 July 1692, d. in 1710.
>
> Susanna, b. 12 June 1694, d. 1 July 1710.
>
> Ebenezer, b. 18 Jan. 1696/7, d. at Goshen, N. Y., in 1767; Lt., New Canaan Co., Oct. 1737; will proved 7 Mar. 1767; m. (1) at Stamford, 22 Jan. 1718/9, Mercy Dean; m. (2) Eunice, widow of ———— Davenport.
>
> Nathaniel, b. 23 Aug. 1699.
>
> Eliphalet, b. 20 Aug. 1701, d. 3 May 1784; Ens., New Canaan Co., May 1743; Lt., Oct. 1747; m. 4 Dec. 1724, Sarah Holly.

Seeley, Nathaniel, s. of Nathaniel. Lt., Fairfield Trainband, May 1685.

Born about 1650, d. at Fairfield, 28 Mar. 1687 [prob. should be 1688]; m. abt. 1677, Hannah, prob. dau. of James Bennett, b. abt. 1656. She was about to marry again in 1692, but the name of her second Romeo appears not.

Inv. 12 Dec. 1688; adm'n granted to widow Hannah with James Bennett.

The widow being about to remarry, James Bennett was continued as Adm'r, with Samuel Squire "to help him."

Children, recorded at Fairfield, last three bapt. at Stratfield:

> +Nathaniel, b. 24 May 1678.
>
> +James, b. 19 Apr. 1681, bapt. 5 July 1696.
>
> Hannah, b. 10 July 1683, bapt. 5 July 1696; m. Jacob Gray.
>
> +Ebenezer, bapt. 5 July 1696.

Seeley, Robert, s. of Nathaniel.

Born about 1653, d. at Fairfield in 1690; m. by 1676, Sarah Olmsted, dau. of Nehemiah. Sarah Seeley was bapt. at Stratfield, 28 Oct. 1694, and four children of Widow Sarah were bapt. there in 1696. Robert receipted 16 Mar. 1675, in right of wife Sarah dau. of Nehemiah Olmstead dec'd, to Elizabeth Seeley, Adm'x [she was Elizabeth (Burr) (Olmstead) (Gilbert) Seeley].

Inv. 30 June 1690.

Sarah Seeley widow of Robert gave receipt for her dowry, 27 Oct. 1692, to Mr. John Edwards of Fairfield. Joseph and John Seeley, and Sarah Seeley the relict, Adm'rs, conveyed 7 Feb. 1692/3, to John Edwards the house of Robert Seeley dec'd.

Children (the first placed here hypothetically) :

> Elizabeth, m. (rec. Stratford) 14 Sept. 1697, Joseph Blackman.
> +Robert, bapt. 23 Aug. 1696.
> Nathaniel, bapt. 23 Aug. 1696; lived in Hempstead, L. I., 1711.
> Sarah, bapt. 23 Aug. 1696.
> +Nehemiah, bapt. 12 July 1696.

Seeley, Benjamin, s. of Nathaniel.

Born about 1657, lived in Fairfield and Easthampton, L. I.

He m. Deborah Sturges, dau. of John; she m. (2) James Redfield.

John Sturges, Sr., purchased 4 Oct. 1681, from his son-in-law Benjamin Seeley, formerly of Fairfield, now of Easthampton, the west part of the house formerly belonging to the latter's father Nathaniel dec'd.

Children:

> +John, b. [say 1683].
> Sarah, b. [say 1690]; m. (1) Daniel Frost; with whom she conveyed, 10 Jan. 1720/1, to brother James Redfield, Jr.; m. (2) by 1729, Nathaniel Fitch, of Norwalk.

Seeley, Joseph, s. of Nathaniel.

Born about 1659; aged 36 in 1696; lived in Fairfield, rem. to Cohansey, N. J.

He m. Mary, widow of Joseph Jackson, and dau. of George Godwin.

On 12 Apr. 1695, Joseph Lyon, having m. Mary dau. of Joseph Jackson dec'd, gave receipt to father-in-law Joseph Seeley, who had m. the Adm'x.

On 9 Nov. 1706, Joseph Seeley, of Cohansey, N. J., sold to

John Edwards of Fairfield land which formerly belonged to my father dec'd.

Children (incomplete record), two recorded at Fairfield:

> Ephraim, b. 9 Sept. 1684, d. at Cohansey, N. J., in 1723; will 9 Mar. 1722/3, proved 10 Apr. 1723; m. Mary ————.
> Samuel, b. 12 Apr. 1686.
> Benjamin (prob. s. of Joseph), d. at Cohansey, N. J., in 1722; Est. settled 20 Mar. 1721/2.

Seeley, John, s. of Nathaniel.

Born by 1661, d. at Stratfield in 1710; m. (1) Sarah Squire, dau. of George, whose will 1690 named John Seeley as his son-in-law. She d. abt. 1690, and he m. (2) abt. 1690, Rebecca Sanford, dau. of Ezekiel, b. 13 Dec. 1672, d. at Stratfield, Mar. 1725/6. She m. (2) in 1711, Benjamin Nichols, and (3) at Stratfield, 24 May 1716, John Mann.

Will 4 Feb. 1709/10, proved 18 Apr. 1710; sons, John, Joseph, David; daus. Mary "dunin", Ann Beardsley; daus. Sarah, Hannah, Abigail, Ruth, Elizabeth, and Martha, under 18; wife Exec'x, with advice of Lt. James Bennett and bro. Ezekiel Sanford.

Ruth Seeley of Stratfield receipted 11 Aug. 1720 to father-in-law John Man for legacy from father John Seeley's will. Joseph Seeley, for himself and as guardian to his brethren David Seeley and John Nichols, receipted 12 Nov. 1726 to father-in-law John Mann, mentioning mother Rebecca Man and uncle Ezekiel Sanford. Elizabeth Seeley receipted, 15 Sept. 1726, to John Man. Matthew Sherman and Hannah his wife receipted, 21 Nov. 1726, to father-in-law John Man, mentioning uncle Ezekiel Sanford. Samuel Castle of Woodbury receipted, 2 Oct. 1726, for himself and wife Martha, to father-in-law John Man. Joseph Pickett of Danbury and Abigail his wife receipted to John Man. William Castle of Woodbury receipted, 2 Oct. 1726, to John Man for amount due him "upon ye acco^tt of marying one of ye daughters of Rebecca Man dec'd." [Stratford Deeds.]

Children [by first wife]:

> Mary, m. abt. 1700, Benjamin Dunning.
> Ann, m. (rec. Stratford) 10 Aug. 1704, Daniel Beardsley, Jr.
> Sarah, b. abt. 1690, bapt. at Stratfield, 28 Oct. 1694; prob. m. at Stratfield, 28 May 1713, Job Sherman.

Children [by second wife], births recorded in Probate Rec., bapt. at Stratfield, the first six bapt. together, 28 Mar. 1703:

> Rebecca, b. 26 Nov. 1691, d. at Woodbury, Dec. 1725; m. at Stratfield, 1 Feb. 1710/1, William Castle.
>
> Hannah, b. 9 Mar. 1692/3; m. Matthew Sherman.
>
> John, b. Feb. 1694/5, d. before 8 May 1722.
>
> +Joseph, b. 10 Mar. 1696/7.
>
> Abigail, b. 9 Mar. 1698 [1698/9]; m. Joseph Pickett, of Danbury.
>
> Ruth, b. June 1702; m. (rec. Stratford) 11 Aug. 1720, Thomas Thompson.
>
> Elizabeth, b. 28 Nov. 1703, bapt. 23 Apr. 1704; m. at Newtown, 16 Oct. 1728, Nathaniel Sanford.
>
> Martha, b. 30 June 1706, bapt. 7 July 1706; m. Samuel Castle, of Woodbury.
>
> David, b. 31 July 1707, bapt. 31 Aug. 1707; res. 1730, Newark, N. J.

Seeley, Nathaniel, s. of Nathaniel, 2d.

Born at Fairfield, 24 May 1678, d. in Apr. 1703; m. abt. 1700, Hannah Odell, dau. of John, b. 20 Oct. 1679; she m. (2) Jacob Sterling, and d. 14 June 1756 in 77 yr. (g. s., Stratfield).

Will 5 Apr. 1703, proved 13 Apr. 1703; wife Hannah; son Nathaniel; brother John Odell, Exec'r. Inv. 20 Apr. 1703.

Child:

> ✕Nathaniel, bapt. at Fairfield, 22 June 1701, d. at Stratfield, 27 Mar. 1786 in 85 yr. (g. s.); m. Elizabeth Jackson, dau. of Joseph, bapt. 15 Nov. 1702, d. 9 Dec. 1781 in 79 yr. (g. s.). They conveyed land in Stratfield, 6 Feb. 1723/4, near the mansion house of our kinsman Henry Jackson dec'd.

Seeley, James, s. of Nathaniel, 2d. Lt., Stratfield Trainband, May 1723.

Born at Fairfield, 19 Apr. 1681, d. at Stratfield in Mar. 1729; Deacon of Stratfield Church.

Married at Stratfield, 21 Jan. 1702/3, Sarah Gregory, dau. of Samuel.

Will 5 Aug. 1727, codicil 12 Mar. 1728/9, proved 1 Apr. 1729; wife Sarah; sons Nathan, James, Abel; dau. Sarah Trowbridge; daus. Ann, Hannah; friend Daniel Hubbell of Stratfield, Exec'r. Sarah Seeley was appointed guardian to Abel and James, and chosen by Nathan, 7 Oct. 1729; Hannah chose Lt. Daniel Hubbell guardian.

Children, recorded at Stratfield:

> Sarah, b. 29 Jan. 1703/4, bapt. 2 Apr. 1704, d. at New Fairfield, 15 Mar. 1752; m. at Stratfield, 30 Aug. 1722, Samuel Trowbridge.
>
> James, b. 1 Apr. 1706, d. 7 June 1706.
>
> Ann, b. 20 Jan. 1707, bapt. 6 July 1707, d. 21 Sept. 1779; m. (1) Francis Hall; m. (2) 7 Oct. 1736, Zechariah Sanford.
>
> Seth, b. 15 May 1710, bapt. 21 May 1710, d. 29 July 1727 in 18 yr. (g. s., Stratfield).
>
> Hannah, b. 23 May 1713, bapt. 24 May 1713, d. at Stratfield, 28 Nov. 1743 in 31 yr. (g. s.); m. at Fairfield, 26 July 1731, William Bennett.
>
> ✕Nathan, b. 22 Mar. 1714 [1714/5], bapt. 24 Aug. 1715, d. 30 Apr. 1766 in 52 yr. (g. s., Stratfield); Ens.; will 22 Mar. 1766, proved 20 May 1766; m. Eunice Wakelee, who d. 6 June 1745 in 28 yr. (g. s.).
>
> Rebecca, bapt. 5 May 1717, d. y.
>
> Eunice, bapt. 13 June 1719, d. y.
>
> Stephen, b. 16 May 1721, d. 4 July 1721.
>
> James, b. 22 July 1722, d. at Bethel, 5 Dec. 1809; will 30 Sept. 1807; m. (1) Hannah ———, who d. 12 Nov. 1802 in 87 yr. (g.s.); m. (2) 6 July 1803, Mabel, widow of Seth Trowbridge of New Fairfield, previously widow of Joseph Barnum of Danbury.*
>
> ✕Abel, b. 7 Sept. 1725, d. 9 May 1810 in 85 yr. (g. s., Stratfield); Deacon; m. 31 Aug. 1744, Mercy Bennett, b. abt. 1721, d. 5 Mar. 1819 ae. 98 (g. s.).

Seeley, Ebenezer, s. of Nathaniel, 2d.

Bapt. at Stratfield, 5 July 1696, d. there 24 July 1717; m. abt. 1713, Jerusha Sherman, dau. of Capt. David, b. abt. 1693. She m. (2) (rec. New Milford), 1 Nov. 1720, Rev. Daniel Boardman of New Milford, and d. there 30 Aug. 1777 in 85 yr. (g. s.).

Will 30 Mar. 1717, codicil 2 July, proved 26 Aug. 1717; wife Jerusha; mentioned gr. father Nathaniel Seeley dec'd; brother James Seeley; sister Hannah Gray; father-in-law Capt. David Sherman.

Children, bapt. at Stratfield:

> Eunice, bapt. 2 May 1714, d. y.
>
> Ebenezer, b. 6 Nov. 1717, bapt. 10 Nov. 1717 (posthumous), d. at Kent, in 1790; will proved 26 Apr. 1790; m. Elizabeth Comstock.

---

* We are indebted to Mr. Henry M. Bradley, Jr., of Derby, Conn., for the children by first wife: Sarah (1743-1780), m. 1767 Samuel Crofut; Hannah (1746-1787), m. Benajah Benedict; Anne (1750-1806), m. Timothy Taylor; Eunice (1757-1847), m. Joshua Taylor.

Seeley, Robert, s. of Robert.

Bapt. at Fairfield (adult), 23 Aug. 1696; on 14 Mar. 1710/1, being then of Hempstead, L. I., he conveyed, for himself and brother Nathaniel of the same place, one-sixth of Capt. Nathaniel Seeley's commonage inherited from father Robert dec'd. He returned to Conn., settled in Newtown and later in Redding.

Will 12 Mar. 1753, proved 12 Apr. 1753; wife Ann; sons Nehemiah, Robert; daus. Sarah Benedict, Mary Beers, Amy Foot; gr. son Nehemiah Seeley; son-in-law John Beers, Exec'r.

Distribution to children, Redding Parish, 3 Dec. 1766: Nehemiah Seeley, Jr.; Amy wife of Joseph Davis; Mary wife of John Beers; Robert Seeley; Sarah widow of John Benedict.

Children, bapt. at Newtown, 4 June 1723, Episcopal records:
>Nehemiah.
>Robert, d. at Newtown in 1774; adm'n granted, 1 Feb. 1774; m. in 1734, Mary Fairchild.
>Sarah, m. John Benedict.
>Amy, m. (1) abt. 1731, John Foote, of Newtown; m. (2) Joseph Davis.
>Mary, m. by 1735, John Beers, of Newtown.

Seeley, Nehemiah, s. of Robert.

Bapt. 12 July 1696; settled in Newtown; m. Miriam Botsford, dau. of Henry.

Children, three rec. Newtown:
>Anna, b. 30 Jan. 1719/20.
>×Abel, b. 11 Feb. 1733/4, d. at Redding, 2 Mar. 1819 ae. 85; m. Rebecca Guire, who d. 19 Nov. 1808.
>×Nehemiah, b. 27 Feb. 1735/6, d. at Redding in 1780; m. (1) 12 Apr. 1755, Abigail Guire; m. (2) at Redding, 26 Sept. 1769, Sarah Dibble of Ridgefield.

Seeley, John, s. of Benjamin.   Sergt., Fairfield Trainband.

Born [say 1683], d. at New Milford, 20 May 1740. Called Sergt. at bapt. of child, Dec. 1712. He rem. to Newtown, thence to New Milford; m. Martha ———, who was his wife in 1712, 1729 and 1735, hence mother of all the children.

On 10 May 1704, he sold to Joseph Jennings, his right in his gr. father Capt. Nathaniel Seeley's homelot.

On 4 Mar. 1718/9, he, of Newtown, conveyed to bro. [half-bro.] James Redfield, Jr., land in Fairfield.

Will 2 May 1740, named wife Martha, all his children, and Ruth's dau. Abigail Hamblin.

Children, last three recorded at New Milford:

> John, prob. rem. to Pownal, Vt.
> Mary, m. at New Milford, 12 Nov. 1728, Obadiah Weller.
> Benjamin, bapt. at Fairfield, Dec. 1712, killed at Ridgefield 28 Apr. 1777; Ens., north company, New Fairfield, May 1745; Lt., Oct. 1750; 2d Lt., 9th Co., 4th Regt., Army, Aug. 1755; 1st Lt., 7th Co., 3d Regt., Mar. 1756; adm'n granted 4 Nov. 1777; m. at New Milford, 11 Apr. 1735, Deborah Hitchcock, dau. of Samuel.
> Joseph, b. [say 1714], living 1785; m. 28 July 1735, Thankful (Bart-lett), widow of Jonathan Weller.
> Ephraim, b. [say 1716]; res. 1746 Woodbury, 1768 Pownal, Vt.; m. Kezia ———.
> Ruth, b. [say 1719].*
> Nathaniel, b. [say 1721], d. in 1757; adm'n granted 1 Dec. 1757; m. at New Milford, 9 May 1745, Abigail Howard.
> Justus, b. [say 1724], d. at Litchfield in 1795; will 25 Oct., proved 14 Dec. 1795; m. (1) 10 Mar. 1746/7, Elizabeth Gibbs; m. (2) Phebe ———.
> Nehemiah, b. [say 1726].
> Ebenezer, b. 25 Sept. 1729, bapt. 2 Nov. 1729.
> David, b. 4 Sept. 1731, bapt. 10 Oct. 1731; res. Kent; m. Sybil ———.
> Sarah, bapt. 31 Mar. 1734; m. June 1750, Benjamin Ruggles.

Seeley, Joseph, s. of John.

Born 10 Mar. 1696/7; d. at Stratford in 1766; m. Hannah Peat, dau. of John, b. 22 Dec. 1704.

Will 16 Mar. 1762, proved 25 Apr. 1766; wife Hannah; eldest son John; sons Benjamin, Joseph, David, Seth, Micah, Gideon, Elnathan, Justus, Israel; daus. Rebecca, Hannah Lake, Ruth, Dinah; wife and friend Joseph Nichols, Exec'rs.

Children, rec. Stratford:

> John, b. 18 Sept. 1724; m. 25 Jan. 1744, Charity Hinman.
> Benjamin, b. 6 July 1726; m. Deborah Loring, b. Nov. 1728.
> Joseph, b. 5 Apr. 1728, d. at Stratford in 1778; m. Jerusha Hubbell, dau. of Andrew, b. 19 May 1729. Will 6 Oct. 1777, proved 24 Feb. 1778; wife Jerusha; seven sons, Michael, Ephraim, Gideon, Ezra, Agur, Lyman, John; five daus. Sarah, Jerusha, Hannah, Naomia, Beulah.
> Rebecca, b. 21 Jan. 1730.

---

* Abigail Hamlin dau. of Ruth Seeley, single woman, b. at New Milford, 25 May 1739, bapt. 19 Aug. 1739.

David, b. 4, bapt. 6 Feb. 1732; m. 17 Dec. 1755, Susannah Curtis; perhaps m. (2) Beulah Gregory, b. 16 Mar. 1736.

Seth, b. 16, bapt. 23 Dec. 1733, bur. 21 Jan. 1812 ae. 78 (Trinity Church rec.).

Gideon, b. 13, bapt. 21 Dec. 1735; m. Betty Wheeler, dau. of David.

Michael, b. 25 Jan. 1737.

Hannah, b. 17 Sept. 1738.

Elnathan, b. 4 Mar. 1741.

Justus, b. 1 May 1743.

Israel, b. 9 Sept. 1744, d. at Stratford in 1776; m. Betty ———. Adm'n granted, 8 Oct. 1776. Distribution 3 June 1777: widow Betee; only son Lewis.

Ruth, b. 7 Nov. 1746.

Dinah, b. 23 Jan. 1748.

Selleck, Jonathan, s. of David. Deputy for Stamford, May 1670, May 1671, May 1672, May 1673, May 1675, May 1676, May 1683, May 1685, May 1687; Assistant, 1695 to 1700 inclusive; Peace messenger to New York, May 1674; Commissioner, N. Y. Boundary, Oct. 1674; called Lt. as early as 1670 in Col. Records (appointment not found); Capt., Stamford Trainband, July 1675; Capt., Fairfield County Troop, K. Philip's War, Jan. 1676; Commissioner for Stamford and Greenwich, 1689, and for Stamford, 1690-94; Sergt.-Major, Fairfield County, May 1696; Judge, Fairfield County Court, 1698 (relieved 1700).

Born at Boston, 20 May 1641; Maj. Jonathan d. at Stamford, 10 Jan. 1712/3.

He m. at Stamford, 11 May 1663, Abigail Law; dau. of Richard.

Will 21 Dec. 1712, proved 3 Feb. 1712/3; gr. son Jonathan Selleck; gr. son Gold John Selleck; gr. dau. Theophila Selleck; gr. dau. Abigail Selleck; gr. son Jacob Moon, son of Dr. Jacob Moon of New York; Rev. John Davenport, pastor in Stamford, all my Latin, Greek and Hebrew books; gr. son Nathan Selleck, residue.

Children, two recorded at Stamford:

+Jonathan, b. 11 July 1664.

David, b. 27 Jan. 1665 [1665/6], d. y.

John, m. Martha Gold, dau. of Maj. Nathan; she m. (2) 18 Apr. 1695, Rev. John Davenport.

Selleck, John, s. of David.   Deputy (Stamford), July 1686.

Born at Boston, 21 Apr. 1643; merchant with his bro. Jonathan, and Capt. of a vessel.   His ship was captured by the French, 1689, and he never returned.

He m. 28 Oct. 1669, Sarah Law; dau. of Richard.

Inv. 5 Mar. 1699/1700; widow Sarah made oath.   Distribution: Nathaniel Selleck, John Selleck, Mr. John Potter in right of his wife, Joannah Selleck, Susannah Selleck.

Children, recorded at Stamford:

> Sarah, b. 22 Aug. 1670; m. 30 Aug. 1698, John Potter.
> David, b. 27 Dec. 1672, d. in 1707. Inv. 17 Sept. 1707. John Holly and Jonathan Bates, Adm'rs. They appealed against the settlement (15 May 1708) of the Est. of their father-in-law Mr. John Selleck.
> Nathaniel, b. 7 Apr. 1678, d. at Stamford, 14 Aug. 1712; m. 25 Jan. 1699/1700, Sarah Lockwood; dau. of Gershom of Greenwich; she m. (2) 3 Feb. 1713/4, Benjamin Hickock, and (3) 9 Mar. 1755, Samuel Kellogg.
> John, b. 7 June 1681, d. 12 Nov. 1706. Will 11 Nov. 1706, proved 10 Mar. 1706/7; bro. Nathaniel Selleck; mother; sisters Susannah and Johanna the wives of John Holly and Jonathan Bates.
> Susannah, b. 2 Feb. 1683 [1683/4], d. 20 Sept. 1745; m. 6 Jan. 1703/4, John Holly.
> Johanna, b. 31 May 1686; m. 13 Dec. 1705, Jonathan Bates.

Selleck, Jonathan, s. of Jonathan.   Deputy (Stamford), May 1705, May and Oct. 1706, Apr. and May 1707, May 1708; Justice, 1699-1703, 1705-10; Surveyor for Fairfield County, 1700.

Born at Stamford, 11 July 1664; Capt. Jonathan d. 11 June 1710.

He m. (rec. Stamford) 5 Jan. 1685, Abigail Gold; dau. of Maj. Nathan; she d. 20 Dec. 1711.

Will 19 Jan. 1708/9, codicil 15 Apr. 1709, proved 5 Feb. 1710/1; son Nathan, my gun that is called Whenham's gun; gr. son Jacob Moon (his mother, my dau. Abigail Moon dec'd); dau. Theophila Selleck, two silver spoons, of which one hath her gr. father and gr. mother Gold's name on it; son Jonathan; dau. Abigail Selleck; son Gold John Selleck; mentioned will of my father-in-law Nathan Gold, Esq.   Inv. of Capt. Jonathan, 5 Feb. 1710 [1710/1].

Children, recorded at Stamford:

Nathan, b. 12 Sept. 1686; m. (1) 12 Aug. 1708, Susannah Hooker, who d. 5 Oct. 1709; m. (2) (at Jamaica, L. I.), Dec. 1710, Mrs. Mary Sands, who d. 15 July 1712; m. (3) (at Hempstead, L. I.), 1 Jan. 171[3], Mrs. Sarah Sands.

Abigail, b. 3 Apr. 1688, d. 19 Nov. 1706; m. 11 Jan. 1704/5, Dr. Jacob Moene, of New York, who after his wife's death returned there from Stamford and m. again.

Theophila, b. 11 Feb. 1694/5; m. 25 Feb. 1720, Samuel Penoyer, of Stamford, with whom she conveyed 1740 to Ebenezer Silliman one-sixteenth part of Maj. Nathan Gold's right in Fairfield commons, inherited from mother Abigail Selleck dec'd.

Jonathan.

Abigail, b. [6 Feb. 1706/7], d. at Fairfield, 16 Mar. 1772 ae. 65 yrs. 1 mo. wanting 1 day (g. s.); m. (rec. Fairfield) 8 Oct. 1728, Ebenezer Silliman.

Gold John.

Seymour, Richard.

Son of Robert and Elizabeth (Waller), bapt. at Sawbridge-worth, co. Hertford, Eng., 27 Jan. 1604/5, d. at Norwalk in 1655; m. at Sawbridgeworth, 18 Apr. 1631, Mercy Ruscoe, dau. of Roger and Sarah, b. abt. 1610. She m. (2) 25 Nov. 1655, John Steele of Farmington.

Came to Hartford in 1639; signed agreement for the planting of Norwalk, 19 June 1650, and became one of the first settlers there; Selectman, 1655.

Will 29 July 1655, proved 25 Oct. 1655; wife Mercy; eldest son Thomas; other three sons, John, Zachary, Richard.

Children, three bapt. at Sawbridgeworth:

+Thomas, bapt. 15 July 1632.

Mary, bapt. 9 Jan. 1634/5, buried 3 Apr. 1635.

Mercy, bapt. 8 July 1636, d. y.

John, b. [say 1639], d. at Hartford in 1713; will 10 Dec. 1712, proved 3 Aug. 1713; m. Mary Watson, dau. of John.

Zachariah, b. abt. 1642, d. at Wethersfield, Aug. 1702 ae. abt. 60; will 14 Apr. 1702, proved 11 Nov. 1702; m. at Wethersfield, 9 Feb. 1687/8, Mary Gritt; she m. (2) Joseph Hollister.

Richard, b. [say 1645], d. at Farmington, in 1710; Inv. 29 Nov. 1710; Capt.; m. Hannah Woodruff, dau. of Matthew, b. abt. 1648 [ae. 21 in 1669].

Seymour, Thomas, s. of Richard. Deputy (Norwalk), Apr. 1690.

Bapt. at Sawbridgeworth, co. Hertford, 15 July 1632, d. at Norwalk in 1712; m. (1) at Norwalk, Jan. 1653 [1653/4], Hannah Marvin, dau. of Matthew.

He m. (2) between 1690 and 1697, Elizabeth, widow of Thomas Wildman of Bedford.

Will 22 Sept. 1712, proved 7 Nov. 1712; wife Elizabeth; son John; gr. son Thomas Seamer; sons Matthew and John; surviving daus.; dau. Elizabeth Knapp. Inv. 15 Oct. 1712.

Children [by first wife], recorded at Norwalk:

> Hannah, b. 12 Dec. 1654; m. 12 Oct. 1675, Francis Bushnell.
> Abigail, b. Jan. 1655 [1655/6]; m. (rec. Stratford) 16 Nov. 1676, Thomas Pickett.
> Mary, b. Sept. 1658; m. (rec. Saybrook) May 1682, Joshua Bushnell.
> Sarah, b. Sept. 1658.
> Thomas, b. Sept. 1660, d. y.
> Mercy, b. Nov. 1666.
> +Matthew, b. May 1669.
> Elizabeth, b. Dec. 1673, d. at Greenwich, 17 June 1713; m. (rec. Greenwich) 16 Mar. 1699, Timothy Knapp.
> Rebecca, b. Jan. 1675 [1675/6]; m. 13 Apr. 1704, Jonathan Reynolds.
> +John, b. [say 1678].

Seymour, Matthew, s. of Thomas. Deputy (Norwalk), Oct. 1712, Oct. 1713; Lt., north company, Norwalk, May 1710; Capt., Oct. 1729.

Born at Norwalk, May 1669, d. there late in 1735; m. (1) Sarah Hayes, dau. of Samuel, b. at Norwalk, 19 Sept. 1673, living 1712; m. (2) Catherine ———.

Will 4 Jan. 1734/5, proved 6 Jan. 1735/6; wife Catherine; sons Matthew, Samuel, Thomas, Jehiel; youngest son Daniel (under age, Catherine is called his mother); daus. Hannah St. John, Elizabeth Bouton, Ruth Smith, Sarah Bouton, Catherine, Susanna; wife and brother John Seymour, exec'rs.

Children [by first wife]:

> Matthew, b. abt. 1691, bapt. at Fairfield, 7 Oct. 1694, d. at Ridgefield, 30 Apr. 1768 in 77 yr.; will 26 June 1766, proved 7 June 1768; m. (rec. Ridgefield) 14 June 1722, Hannah Smith, dau. of Thomas, bapt. at Milford, 24 Oct. 1703, living 1766.

Samuel, bapt. at Fairfield, 17 Nov. 1695, d. at New Canaan, abt. 1754; will 22 Nov. 1753, proved 5 Feb. 1754; m. Mary Lyon, dau. of Andrew of Norwalk.

Hannah, b. [say 1697], d. at Ridgefield, 22 Aug. 1768; m. (rec. Ridgefield) 7 June 1721, Nathan St. John.

Elizabeth, b. [say 1700]; m. abt. 1722, Eleazer Bouton.

Thomas, b. abt. 1702, d. at New Canaan, 11 Apr. 1796 ae. 94; Capt.; m. (1) by 1727, Elizabeth Betts, dau. of Thomas, b. 23 Oct. 1699; m. (2) abt. 1747, Elizabeth ———, who d. 23 Aug. 1794 ae. 70.

Jehiel, b. [say 1704], d. at Huntington, L. I., in 1753; adm'n granted 11 Dec. 1753; m. (1) Mary Jarvis, dau. of William; m. (2) at Huntington, 11 Aug. 1751, Rachel Wright.

Ruth, b. [say 1707]; m. at Ridgefield, 12 June 1729, Jabez Smith.

Sarah, b. [say 1710]; m. by 1734, John Bouton.

Children [by second wife]:

Catherine, d. in 1735, unm.

Susanna, m. by 1743, Josiah Rusco.

Daniel, d. at Norwalk abt. 1759; m. Ann Betts, dau. of Matthew, b. 29 Mar. 1729, living 1789.

Seymour, John, s. of Thomas.

Born [say 1678], d. at Norwalk in 1746; m. (1) Sarah Gregory, dau. of Jachin, b. 15 Sept. 1678; m. (2) abt. 1723/4, Hannah, widow of John Gold, Jr., and dau. of Richard and Elizabeth (Munson) (Cooper) Higginbothom.

Will 28 Apr. 1746, codicils 5 and 26 May, proved 5 Aug. 1746; wife Hannah and son John, Exec'rs; dau. Mary wife of Thomas Hanford; daus. Sarah Trowbridge, Abigail Selleck, Rebecca Bouton, Martha Jarvis; gr. sons John Seymour, and Munson Jarvis, son of Samuel and Martha Jarvis.

Children [by first wife]:

Mary, m. Thomas Hanford.

Sarah, m. in 1725, Daniel Trowbridge.

Abigail, m. 5 Nov. 1729, John Selleck.

John, b. abt. 1710, d. at Norwalk, 8 Sept. 1796 ae. 85; m. (1) Ruth Belden, dau. of William, b. 18 Jan. 1712/3, d. 29 May 1782; m. (2) at New Canaan, 4 Feb. 1784, Elizabeth Wood of Huntington, L. I.

Rebecca, d. in 1775; m. (1) at Norwalk, 6 July 1734, Elijah Whitney; m. (2) by 1744, John Bouton; m. (3) by 1758, Capt. Joseph Starr, of Danbury.

Child [by second wife]:

Martha, b. abt. 1726, d. 1 Dec. 1803; m. 18 Dec. 1741, Samuel Jarvis, of Stamford.

Sharp, Thomas.

He settled in Stratfield, and m. Lydia, widow of Thomas Dickerson.

They rem. to Newtown abt. 1711.

Inv. of Thomas of Newtown, 5 Aug. 1712. Ages of children: Thomas, 11 next Mar.; Marcy, 8 on 10 Oct.; William, 6 on 14 July; John, 4 on 1 next Feb.; Elizabeth, 6 mos. Lydia Sharp appeared 8 Oct. 1712 and presented Inv. The Court appointed Joseph Curtis guardian of William and Mary, 3 June 1713. The Court appointed Richard Nichols guardian of John and Thomas, 1 July 1713, and made him Adm'r. Thomas, eldest son, desired distribution, 25 Nov. 1729.

Thomas Sharp was appointed Adm'r of the Est. of his bro.-in-law Jonathan Mills of Stratford, 12 Dec. 1709; which may be the clue to the identity of Sharp's wife.

Children, all recorded at Newtown, first four born at Stratfield:

Thomas, b. 18 Mar. 1702, d. at Newtown, 17 Apr. 1765 in 64 yr.; will 23 Mar., proved 3 June 1765; m. (1) Feb. 1745, Sarah ———, who d. 14 Jan. 1754; m. (2) 1755, ——— ———.

Mary, b. 10 Oct. 1703 [1704 by Pro. Rec.]; m. Noah Parmelee, of Newtown.

William, b. 19 Aug. 1705 [1706 by Pro. Rec.].

John, b. 1 Feb. 1708/9.

Elizabeth, b. 18 Apr. 1712.

Shaw, Nathaniel.

He m. at Boston, Mass., 12 July 1698, Margaret Jackson.

Inv. 6 Jan. 1712/3; widow Margaret made oath. She had been appointed Adm'x, 2 Oct. 1712, and guardian to Nathaniel, Sarah, and Thomas, 6 May 1713. On 5 Aug. 1713, the dau. Margaret asked that Edward Sturgis, mariner, formerly chosen as her guardian, be freed, and her mother Mrs. Margaret Shaw appointed.

Children, last four bapt. at Fairfield:

Margaret, b. at Boston, 12 May 1699.

Thomas, b. at Boston, 19 Nov. 1700, d. y.

Nathaniel, bapt. 26 Sept. 1703.*

---

* Nathaniel Shaw d. at Westport, 21 May 1758, or by gravestone 22 May 1758 æ. (30?); if age be correctly read, cannot be the same Nathaniel, but I suspect the reading. His will, 14 Apr. 1758, proved 5 July 1758; loving cousin, Thomas Freeman of Boston; Samuel Gray of Fairfield, Exec'r. John Shaw had a dau. Mary b. at Boston 26 Mar. 1714, and Mary Shaw m. at Boston, 10 May 1737, Thomas Freeman.

John, bapt. 11 Nov. 1705, no further record.
Sarah, bapt. 11 Apr. 1708; d. at Westport, 29 Jan. 1787; m. at Fair-
field, 17 Feb. 1729, George Cable.
Thomas, bapt. 21 Oct. 1711.

Shaw, Christopher.

Children, four bapt. together at Fairfield, 20 Aug. 1710:

Mary.
Eleanor.
Sarah.
Abigail.

Sherman, Edmund.

Born at Dedham, co. Essex, Eng., abt. 1572, d. at New Haven
in 1641. He may have m. Joan Makin, dau. of Tobias of
Fingringhoe, but the evidence seen does not seem conclusive.

He came with some of his children to New England, was at
Wethersfield 1635, and rem. shortly before his death to New
Haven.

Children, bapt. at Dedham:

Edmund, bapt. 23 June or Oct. 1599, came to Watertown, Mass.,
where he was freeman and selectman 1636; returned to Dedham.
Ann, bapt. 15 Sept. 1601.
Joan, bapt. 13 Dec. 1603.
Hester, bapt. 1 Apr. 1606, d. at Fairfield in 1665; m. Andrew Ward.
Richard, bapt. 16 Oct. 1608, buried at Dedham, 27 Oct. 1647; m.
Mary ———.
Bezaleel, bapt. 17 Sept. 1611.
John, b. 26 Dec. 1613, bapt. 4 Jan. 1613/4; B.A. (Trinity Coll., Cam-
bridge) 1629, A.M. 1633; of Watertown, Mass., Wethersfield, and
Milford, returned 1647 to Watertown, where he was third minister,
and d. 8 Aug. 1685 ae. 72; m. (1) Mary, prob. sister of John Gibbs
of New Haven; she d. at Milford 8 Sept. 1644; m. (2) Mary
Launce, who d. at Watertown, 9 Mar. 1710.
Child, bapt. 18 June 1616; prob. Grace, who m. John Livermore and
d. at Chelmsford, Mass., 14 Jan. 1690 ae. 75.
+Samuel, bapt. 12 July 1618.
Another dau.

Sherman, Samuel, s. of Edmund. Served in the Pequot War.
Deputy (Stratford) to Conn. Leg., Oct. 1660; Assistant, Conn.
Col., Oct. 1662, 1663-67. Commissioner for Stratford, 1671-75,

for Stratford and Woodbury, 1676-79, for Stratford, 1680-84, for Fairfield, 1685-88.

Bapt. at Dedham, co. Essex, Eng., 12 July 1618, d. at Stratfield, 5 Apr. 1700 ae. 80 (g. s.). He came with his father to Wethersfield, and (prob. there) m. abt. 1640, Sarah Mitchell, dau. of Matthew, bapt. 14 Oct. 1621. With the Mitchells and others, he joined the migration to Stamford.

He remained in Stamford until 1650, rem. to Stratford, and finally in 1685 to Fairfield, where he located in the Stratfield section.

Children, recorded at Stratford:
+Samuel, b. 19 June 1641.
+Theophilus, b. 28 Oct. 1643.
+Matthew, b. 21 Oct. 1645.
+Edmund, b. 4 Dec. 1647.
+John, b. 8 Feb. 1650 [1650/1].
    Sarah, b. 8 Feb. 1653, d. at Guilford, 1713; m. Josiah Rossiter.
+Nathaniel, b. 21 Mar. 1656.
+Benjamin, b. 29 Mar. 1662.
+David, b. 15 Apr. 1665.

Sherman, Samuel, s. of Samuel. Deputy (Stratford), Oct. and Nov. 1683, Oct. 1685, May and Oct. 1687, May 1693, Oct. 1699.

Born 19 June 1641, d. at Stratford 20 Feb. 1718/9.

Called son of Mr. Samuel, he m. (1) (Stratford rec.) 19 June 1665, Mary Titherton, dau. of Daniel.

He m. (2) 1 Aug. 1695, Abigail Huse. She was widow of Nicholas Huse, formerly of Jonathan Curtis, and was dau. of John Thompson, b. 1 May 1646, d. 2 Mar. 1731.

Adm'n granted to son Daniel and to John Leavenworth, 24 Feb. 1718/9. Agreement of heirs of Samuel Sherman, 8 Oct. 1719; Daniel Sention of Norwalk, James Beebe of Danbury, Samuel Beers of Newtown, Daniel Sherman, Daniel Mitchell, and Isaac Clark.

Children [by first wife], recorded at Stratford, baptisms at Woodbury:
    Mary, b. 9 May 1666, bapt. 8 May 1670, d. y.
+Daniel, b. 23 Mar. 1668/9, bapt. 8 May 1670.
    Susanna, b. 22 July 1670, bapt. 24 July 1670; m. Daniel Mitchell.
    Sarah, b. 26 Mar. 1673, bapt. 4 May 1673, d. y.

Grace, b. 8 July 1676, bapt. in 1676; m. Daniel St. John, of Norwalk.
Elizabeth, b. 20 Jan. 1678/9; m. (1) 4 Nov. 1702, Isaac Clark;
  divorced him and m. (2) Sept. 1728, Richard Nichols.
Sarah, b. 16 Dec. 1681; m. 16 Jan. 1706/7, Samuel Beers.
Abigail, b. 4 Aug. 1688; m. 22 Dec. 1708, James Beebe, of Danbury.

Sherman, Theophilus, s. of Samuel.

Born 28 Oct. 1643, d. at Wethersfield, in 1711/2; m. (1) Comfort Robbins, dau. of John and Mary (Welles) Robbins, b. at Wethersfield, 12 Oct. 1646. Her mother was niece of Gov. Thomas Welles.

He m. (2) by 1697, Mary, widow of John Coltman of Wethersfield. She was m. to Coltman in 1667, and lost her first husband abt. 1688. In 1691 belated probate action on the Coltman estate was taken, and it may be surmised that the widow was on the point of remarriage at that time. On 14 Apr. 1697, in asking for distribution, the widow was called Mary Sherman.

Will 13 Apr. 1711; son Theophilus, all land in Wethersfield, he to be Exec'r; daus. Mary wife of Elijah Crane and Comfort wife of Richard Nichols, land near the bounds of Stratford or Stratfield; wife Mary. Inv. 27 Feb. 1711/2.

Children [by first wife]:

Mary, m. Elijah Crane.
Comfort, d. at Stratford, 11 Feb. 1726/7; m. (rec. Stratford) 3 June
  1702, Richard Nichols.
Theophilus, d. at Wethersfield, abt. 1746; adm'n granted, 7 June
  1746, to Theophilus Nichols of Stratford, with John Robbins, Jr.,
  of Wethersfield as surety.

Sherman, Matthew, s. of Samuel.

Born 21 Oct. 1645, d. at Stratfield in 1698; m. Hannah ———, who d. in 1713.

A modern monument erected by Rowland B. Lacey in the Stratfield Cemetery in 1885, states the name of Matthew Sherman's wife as Hannah Bulkley.

Inv. Apr. 1698; widow Hannah granted adm'n.

Inv. of Hannah, widow of Matthew, undated. Adm'n on Est. of Widow Hannah of Stratfield was granted, 6 Jan. 1713 [1713/4] to son David.

Children, first recorded at Stratford:

> David, b. 11 Oct. 1692, d. at Stratfield, 8 July 1752 in 60 yr. (g. s.);
> Lt., Stratfield Co., May 1741; will 7 Sept. 1750, proved 4 Aug.
> 1752; m. (1) 11 June 1718, Dinah Royce of Wallingford; dau. of
> Dea. Robert, b. 24 Feb. 1696; she d. at Stratford, 13 Apr. 1732
> in 37 yr. (g. s.); m. (2) 25 Feb. 1735/6, Sarah Thompson.
>
> Hannah, bapt. at Fairfield, 7 Apr. 1695, d. at Trumbull, 19 Feb. 1772
> in 77 yr. (g. s.); m. 24 Jan. 1716/7, David Beach.
>
> Jabez, bapt. at Stratfield, 26 Sept. 1697; settled in Woodbridge;
> m. ———.

Sherman, Edmund, s. of Samuel.

Born at Stamford, 4 Dec. 1647, d. at Stratford in 1683; m.
Susannah Hardy, dau. of Richard of Stamford. She m. (2)
——— Raynor.

Inv. 5 Nov. 1683; widow Susanna made oath. Three sons and
one dau. (all minors).

On 9 Jan. 1694 [1694/5] it was recorded that Charles Douglas
hath by purchase from Susannah Rayner eight acres in the woods,
confirmed to Douglas by the *said Susannah Sherman.* [Stratford
Deeds.]

Children, recorded at Stratford:

> +Bezaleel, b. 1 Jan. 1674 [1674/5], bapt. at Woodbury, 11 Apr. 1676.
> Samuel, b. 8 Jan. 1678 [1678/9].
> Edmund, b. 20 Mar. 1680 [1680/1].
> Matthew, b. 8 Jan. 1683 [1683/4].

Sherman, John, s. of Samuel. Deputy (Woodbury) to Conn.
Leg., Oct. 1699, May 1700, Oct. 1701, May and Oct. 1704, Oct.
1705, Oct. 1706, May, Oct. and Dec. 1707, May and Oct. 1708,
May and June 1709, May, Aug., and Oct. 1710, Deputy and
Speaker of the House, May, June, and Oct. 1711, May and
Oct. 1712. Assistant of Conn. Colony, 1713-22. Justice,
1702-11, 1723-25, 1727-28. Commissioner to deal with Indians,
Feb. 1707. Capt., Woodbury company, May 1711. Judge of
Probate, Woodbury District, Oct. 1719 to May 1728. Deacon
and Town Clerk.

Born at Stratford, 8 Feb. 1650/1, d. at Woodbury, 13 Dec.
1730; m. Elizabeth ———, who d. at Woodbury, 1 Oct. 1744.

Children, recorded at Woodbury:

> Hannah, bapt. 18 July 1680, d. 30 July 1744; m. 8 Jan. 1706/7, Josiah Crittenden of Guilford.
>
> Samuel, bapt. 13 Aug. 1682, d. at Woodbury, 25 Feb. 1757; Deacon; m. 22 Dec. 1709, Mary Knowles.
>
> Elizabeth, bapt. 12 Oct. 1684, d. at Woodbury, 15 Apr. 1747; m. 23 July 1713, Roger Terrill.
>
> John, bapt. 17 June 1687, d. at Woodbury, 20 May 1727 ae. 40 (g. s.); m. 22 July 1714, Emm Preston, dau. of Hachaliah, bapt. 3 Mar. 1688/9, d. in 1729.
>
> Sarah, bapt. 19 Jan. 1689/90; m. 18 Dec. 1718, Benjamin Hinman, Jr.
>
> Mary, bapt. 20 Mar. 1691/2; m. 3 Jan. 1715/6, Rev. Anthony Stoddard.
>
> Susanna, bapt. 25 Nov. 1694, d. at New Milford, 9 Apr. 1750 in 61(?) yr. (g. s.); m. 4 June 1722, David Noble.
>
> Ichabod, b. 27 Apr. 1700, d. at Woodbury, 20 Jan. 1760, unm.

Sherman, Nathaniel, s. of Samuel. Deputy (Stratford), Oct. 1694, May 1695, May 1700, May 1702.

Born at Stratford, 21 Mar. 1656, d. there 19 Apr. 1712.

Married (1) (duplicate records, Stratford) 13 June 1680 or 30 June 1681, Mary Phippen.

Married (2) (rec. Stratford) 26 Nov. 1707, Abigail Hanford of Fairfield. She was widow of Elnathan Hanford, previously widow of Daniel Lockwood, and dau. of Daniel Burr. She d. at Stratford, 2 Mar. 1730/1.

Inv. sworn to by widow Abigail, 2 July 1712. Distribution Feb. 1728/9 to Widow, Sarah, Peninah, and Naomi.

John Lewis and Sarah his wife, Peninah Sherman, and James Lewis and Naomi his wife, all of Stratford, conveyed right in Fairfield lands, 6 July 1750.

Children by Abigail, recorded at Stratford:

> Sarah, b. 3 Sept. 1708, bapt. at Fairfield, 17 Oct. 1708; m. 7 Dec. 1727, John Lewis.
>
> Peninah, b. 5 Apr. 1710; prob. m. abt. 1752, Joseph Nichols.
>
> Naomi, b. 5 May 1712, d. 27 Jan. 1797 in 85 yr. (g. s., Stratford); m. (1) 2 Dec. 1731, James Lewis, Jr.; m. (2) 22 Mar. 1767, Timothy Sherman.

Sherman, Benjamin, s. of Samuel. Deputy (Stratford), May 1711.

Born at Stratford, 29 Mar. 1662.

Married (rec. Stratford) 6 June 1683, Rebecca Phippen.

Children, recorded at Stratford :*

Abigail, b. 10 Apr. 1684.

John, b. 30 Nov. 1685, d. y.

Wilmet, b. 21 Jan. 1688; m. (rec. at Newtown) 15 Sept. 1714, Jeremiah Turner.

Job, b. 7 Apr. 1690, d. at Newtown, in 1750; m. at Stratfield, 28 May 1713, Sarah Seeley.

Nathaniel, b. 1 Dec. 1692, d. at Stratford in 1767; will 28 Aug. 1766, proved 13 Oct. 1767; m. (1) 22 [Nov.] 1720, Ruth Curtis, who d. 9 Nov. 1726; m. (2) 2 May 1728, widow Eunice Patterson. She was dau. of Abraham Nichols, b. 7 Dec. 1698.

Martha, b. 20 Dec. 1695.

Mary, b. 24 Feb. 1696/7.

Enos, b. 15 Apr. 1699; m. 28 Jan. 1724/5, Abigail Walker.

Rebecca, b. 18 Jan. 1700 [1700/1]; m. (1) at Stratford, 28 Mar. 1723, dau. of John, b. [? at Windham, 15 June 1726], d. at Stratford, 23 Sept. 1783; she m. (2) 27 Oct. 1765, Abraham Judson.

Benjamin, b. 23 Jan. 1702 [1702/3], bapt. at Stratfield, 11 Apr. 1703; m. at Trumbull, 20 Nov. 1740, widow Obedience Fairchild. She was widow of Nathan Fairchild and previously of Edmund Curtis, and dau. of John Mallory, b. at New Haven, 11 Apr. 1704. She m. (4) 25 Dec. 1763, Robert Bassett, and was living 1785.

Samuel, b. 10 Feb. 1705, bapt. 29 Apr. 1705, d. at Stratford, in 1764; will 19 Oct. 1759, proved 21 Mar. 1764; m. abt. 1748, Sarah Hurd, dau. of John, b. [? at Windham, 15 June 1726], d. at Stratford, 23 Sept. 1783; she m. (2) 27 Oct. 1765, Abraham Judson.

James, b. 15 Dec. 1706, bapt. 2 Mar. 1707, d. at New Haven, 19 Jan. 1786 ae. 79; m. at Stratfield, 17 Jan. 1733/4, Sarah Cooke, dau. of Rev. Samuel, b. at New Haven, 8 June 1713, d. at New Haven, 18 Feb. 1802 ae. 89.

Timothy, b. 4 Jan. 1709, d. at Stratford, in 1788; will 24 Sept. 1787, proved 5 Jan. 1789; m. (1) Elizabeth ———, who d. 10 Dec. 1766 in 52 yr. (g. s.); m. (2) 22 Mar. 1767, Naomi, widow of James Lewis, and dau. of Nathaniel Sherman, b. 5 May 1712, d. 27 Jan. 1797 in 85 yr. (g. s.).

Sherman, David, s. of Samuel. Ens., Stratfield Trainband, Oct. 1703; Lt., Oct. 1708; Capt., Oct. 1709. Deputy (Fairfield), Oct. 1709.

Born at Stratford, 15 Apr. 1665; Capt. David d. at Stratfield, 1 Jan. 1753 in 88 yr. (g. s.). He m. Mercy Wheeler, dau. of Isaac, b. abt. 1670, d. 19 Aug. 1745 in 75 yr. (g. s.).

Adm'n granted, 24 Jan. 1753, to Theophilus Nichols.

In 1753, Jerusha Boardman of New Milford, Samuel and

---

* The Mindwell bapt. at Fairfield, 4 Oct. 1696, often attributed to him, undoubtedly was Mindwell Sherwood, dau. of Benjamin, b. 8 Sept. 1696.

Eunice St. John of Norwalk, Nathaniel and Mercy Sherwood, John and Dorothy Wheeler, Benajah Barlow, and Edmund Rowland, all of Stratfield, conveyed to Jabez Hubbell of Stratfield.

David at bapt. of children was called Ens. 1704, Lt. 1709, Capt. 1711.

Children, all but first two bapt. at Stratfield:

Sarah, b. [say 1691]; m. (1) at Stratfield, 8 Oct. 1713, Benajah Strong; m. (2) Samuel Barlow; m. (3) Samuel Rowland.

Jerusha, b. abt. 1693, d. at New Milford, 30 Aug. 1777 in 85 yr. (g. s.); m. (1) abt. 1713, Ebenezer Seeley; m. (2) (rec. New Milford) 1 Nov. 1720, Rev. Daniel Boardman.

Tamar, bapt. 2 Mar. 1696, d. at Stratfield, 21 Apr. 1737 in 42 yr. (g. s.); m. at Stratfield, 25 Sept. 1718, Henry Rowland.

Abiah, bapt. 21 Oct. 1697, d. 28 May 1717 ae. 19 (g. s., Stratfield).

Eunice, bapt. 21 Jan. 1700; m. Samuel St. John, of Norwalk.

Esther, bapt. 6 Apr. 1702.

Mercy, bapt. 21 May 1704, d. at Stratfield, 26 July 1779 in 76 yr. (g. s.); m. Nathaniel Sherwood.

Prudence, bapt. 13 Oct. 1706; m. at Stratfield, 4 Apr. 1733, Col. Robert Dennison.

Elnathan, bapt. 29 May 1709, d. 15 Apr. 1717 ae. abt. 8 (g. s., Stratfield).

Mehitabel, bapt. 6 May 1711.

Dorothy, bapt. 29 Aug. 1714, d. at Stratfield, 9 Oct. 1800 in 87 yr. (g. s.); m. John Wheeler.

Sherman, Daniel, s. of Samuel, 2d.

Born at Stratford, 23 Mar. 1668/9, d. at Newtown, 15 Feb. 1740/1.

Married at Stratford, 19 Dec. 1694, Rebecca Wheeler; dau. of Dea. Isaac, b. abt. 1672, d. at Newtown, 2 Sept. 1751.

Will 21 Oct. 1729, proved 18 May 1741; wife Rebecca; gr. sons Ebenezer and Daniel, sons of Ebenezer Sherman formerly of Stratford dec'd; sons Samuel, Benoni; dau. Ann Burrill of New Haven.

Children, recorded at Stratford:

Ebenezer, b. 20 Oct. 1695, d. at Stratford in 1727; m. 12 Jan. 1715/6, Martha Bostwick, b. 28 Nov. 1695. Daniel Sherman was appointed guardian of Ebenezer's three children, 2 May 1727. Martha m. (2) Sept. 1728, Isaac Clark.

Ann, b. 3 Dec. 1697; m. at Stratford, 26 Dec. 1723, Stephen Burwell, of New Haven.

Benoni, b. 11 Feb. 1699/1700, d. at Newtown in 1765; will 5 Apr. 1765, proved 3 June 1765; m. (rec. Stratford, without date), Sarah Sturges of Fairfield.

Samuel, b. 6 Dec. 1707, d. at Newtown, 10 Jan. 1747/8; m. (1) Elizabeth ———, who d. 10 Dec. 1736; m. (2) Mary ———.

Sherman, Bezaleel, s. of Edmund.

Born at Stratford, 1 Jan. 1674/5, d. there in 1717; m. (rec. Stratford), 6 Mar. 1706/7, widow Jane Commell. "Here note y[t] bezeliel sherman cloathed y[e] wid Jane connel before he was married to her at his cost & charge as is testifyed by Mis[t] Adams & her daughter." She was dau. of John Peat, b. 17 Oct. 1677; and widow of John Commell of Stratford.

Inv. 16 Nov. 1717; widow Jane made oath, 20 Dec. 1717. Children's ages: Edmund, 6 yrs. 5 mos.; Ebenezer, 4 yrs. 3 mos.; Bezaleel, 6 wks.; Susannah, 9 yrs. 9 mos. Distribution made in 1721 to Widow, Edmund, Ebenezer, Susannah.

Children, last recorded at Stratford:

> Susannah, b. abt. Mar. 1707/8, bapt. at Stratfield, 20 June 1708; m. abt. 1726, Thomas Brown, of Greenwich.
> ✕Edmund, b. abt. July 1711; m. at Redding, 2 July 1740, Rebecca Lee.
> Ebenezer, b. abt. Sept. 1713; gave receipt, Sept. 1734, to former guardian, uncle Andrew Patterson; m. Abiah Booth, dau. of James.
> Bezaleel, b. Oct. 1717, d. y.

Shervington, Thomas.

Born prob. not later than 1625, d. at Fairfield in 1702; as his younger dau. was a minor when he died, it may be inferred that he m. more than once, and that his later wife was considerably his junior in years. The surname was often written Sherrington, which likely approximates the pronunciation.

He had a grant of land in Fairfield prior to 14 June 1650, and added to it by purchase from Henry Whelpley and Richard Perry. Freed from training, 9 Mar. 1685/6. With consent of his wife, whose name does not appear, he sold land 22 Oct. 1689 to Jonathan Sturges. Mary Shervington was complained of 1685, for selling rum to Indians.

Inv. 29 May 1702; adm'n granted to son-in-law Jeremiah Wood and Thomas Staples. Distribution ordered to two daus., Mary

wife of Jeremiah Wood and Sarah Shervington.   Sarah chose her
bro.-in-law Jeremiah Wood for guardian.

Children:

> Mary, m. Jeremiah Wood. He, of Hempstead, L. I., conveyed 22
> Dec. 1702 to Gideon Allen land from Est. of Thomas Shervington.
> Sarah.

SHERWOOD FAMILY (FAIRFIELD)

Sherwood, Thomas.

On some branches of this family we have been greatly assisted
by Mrs. G. E. Fellows, of Salt Lake City, Utah; but the editor
assumes responsibility for the conclusions stated.

Thomas came to Boston in the *Frances,* Apr. 1634, ae. 48, with
wife Alice, ae. 47, and children Anna (14), Rose (11), Thomas
(10), and Rebecca (9). He came to Wethersfield with the first
settlers, 1635, was a carpenter, and sold his lands to George
Wyllys, 25 Mar. 1640. He removed to Stamford, where he lived
until 1648, when he sold to John Holly, and settled in Fairfield.
He may have been related to Thomas Morehouse, whose holdings
adjoined his in Wethersfield, and who accompanied him in his
subsequent migrations.

If the age of the son Thomas was misstated in the ship's list,
he could have been the Thomas son of Thomas and Alice bapt. at
St. Michael's, London, Eng., 23 Jan. 1630.

Will 21 July 1655, proved 25 Oct. 1655; children by former
wife, Thomas, Jane, Tamsen, Margaret, Sarah, Hannah, Rose,
Rebecca; wife Mary, and children by her, Stephen, Matthew,
Mary, Ruth, Abigail, Isaac.

Fairfield Deeds mention 18 Jan. 1658 [1658/9] that "John
Banks hath married Mary Sherwood the relict."

His widow Mary m. (2) John Banks and d. in 1694.*

Will of Mary Banks, 6 Jan. 1693 [1693/4]; son Stephen Sherwood's dau. Ruth; son Matthew Sherwood's dau. Mary; Hannah
"Lumis"; dau. Ruth; sons Stephen, Isaac; residue to son

---

* Statements that this Mary was a Fitch seem to confuse her with her son Matthew's
wife, who was Mary Fitch.

Matthew; Ens. Wheeler and James Bennett, Sr., overseers. **Inv.** 13 Mar. 1693/4.

Children [by first wife]:
> Jane.
> Thomasin.
> Margaret.
> Sarah.
> Hannah, b. abt. 1620.
> Rose, b. abt. 1622; m. (1) Thomas Rumble; m. (2) Thomas Barlow; m. (3) Edward Nash.
> +Thomas, b. abt. 1624.
> Rebecca, b. abt. 1625.

Children [by second wife]:
> +Stephen; conveyed 1680/1 to "my father Banks."
> +Matthew, b. abt. 1644.
> Mary.
> Ruth, m. at Windsor, 4 June 1663, Joshua Holcomb.
> Abigail, d. in 1692; m. abt. 1668, Daniel Lockwood.
> +Isaac.

Sherwood, Thomas, s. of Thomas.

He m. (1) Sarah Wheeler, dau. of Thomas, Sr. She and her son Thomas were named in the will of her father 1654. She was dead by 1659, when the will of her mother Ann Wheeler named grandchild Sarah Sherwood and Annis Sherwood, wife of her son-in-law.

He m. (2) by 1659, Ann Turney, dau. of Benjamin, b. abt. 1637.

He m. (3) between 1673 and 1683, Elizabeth, widow of John Cable.

He m. (4) Sarah, widow of Peter Coley, and dau. of Humphrey Hide. Marriage agreement dated 24 June 1695.

His son Thomas had received his "portion" and given a discharge for it, but on 9 Nov. 1681 Thomas, Sr., discharged him from his discharge.

Inv. 12 Mar. 1698 [1698/9]. Adm'n granted to Benjamin and Samuel Sherwood.

Agreement 14 Mar. 1700 between Benjamin, Samuel, and Isaac Sherwood, sons of Thomas dec'd; Benjamin was to pay certain amounts to his sister Phebe Sherwood and to John Bradley towards his wife Hannah's portion. On 11 Mar. 1728/9, Isaac Sherwood of Norwalk, Abigail Ogden, John Bradley, Sr., Joseph Banks, and Benjamin Sherwood, Jr., of Fairfield, quitclaimed to Benjamin Sherwood, Sr., Samuel Sherwood, and Daniel Sherwood, their interest in the Est. of Thomas Sherwood.

Children [by first wife] :

+Thomas.
Sarah, m. John Whitlock.

Children [by second wife, except possibly the last two] :

Mary, m. David Whitlock.
+Benjamin, b. abt. 1669.
+Samuel.
Ruth, m. (1) Samuel Drake; m. (2) John Barlow.
Hannah, m. (1) John Bradley; m. (2) Cornelius Jones, of Stamford.
Abigail, b. abt. 1671, d. at Greenfield, 1 May 1744 in 74 yr. (g. s.) ;
    m. David Ogden. In 1732 Abigail Ogden sold right in long lot of
    father Thomas Sherwood dec'd.
+Isaac, b. [say 1675].
Phebe, m. Samuel Bradley.

Sherwood, Stephen, s. of Thomas.

He m. (1) by 1661, Rebecca Turney, dau. of Benjamin, b. at Concord, Mass., 16 Feb. 1639/40.

He m. (2) Hannah, widow of Philip Galpin, and dau. of Henry Jackson.

He m. (3) Mary, widow of —— Merwin, and previously of —— Guire, and dau. of Edward Adams, b. abt. 1647, d. abt. Apr. 1712. Her will, 22 Mar. 1711/2, proved 7 May 1712, named her Guire grandchildren.

On 25 May 1727, Nathaniel, Jonathan, Samuel and John Sherwood of Rye conveyed to Benjamin Baker "our hassocky meadow."

Children :

+Stephen.
+Joseph.
Daniel, d. at Fairfield in 1715; m. Tabitha Bennett; no issue. **Inv.**
    3 May 1715; widow Tabitha to administer, and gave bond with
    Thomas Bennett. On 6 Apr. 1716, Nathaniel Sherwood of Rye,
    and Jehu and Mary Burr, children of Mary Burr alias Sherwood

dec'd, who was one of the sisters of Daniel Sherwood dec'd, conveyed their interest to John and Thomas Sherwood of Fairfield.

Mary, m. Daniel Burr.

+Nathaniel.

Jabez, d. at Greenwich in 1704. Will 7 Oct. 1704, proved 6 Nov. 1704; to Jonathan Husted and his wife, all my land in Greenwich; to Jonathan Jessup, son of Edward of Fairfield, my carpenter's tools; sister-in-law Elizabeth Sherwood of Rye; bro. Nathaniel; to bro. Stephen, property in Rye; to cousin Stephen Sherwood of Rye, my gun; sister Ruth Merritt, wearing apparel, except my hat to Jonathan Jessup and two shirts to Mary wife of Jonathan Husted. Adm'n granted to Stephen Sherwood, Jonathan Husted, and John Pettit.

Jonathan.

Samuel.

Andrew.

John.

Ruth, m. —— Merritt.

Sherwood, Matthew, s. of Thomas. Ens., Fairfield County Troop, Aug. 1673; Ens., Fairfield Trainband, Oct. 1685; Lt., Apr. 1690; Capt., Fairfield County Troop raised for war service, Apr. 1690; Capt. of Troop raised June 1697. Deputy for Fairfield, May and June 1692; Commissioner for Fairfield, 1694-96, for "Fairfield Village," 1697; Justice, 1698-1708.

Born abt. 1644, d. at Stratfield, 26 Oct. 1715 in 72 yr. (g. s.).

He m. (1) Sarah Turney, dau. of Benjamin, b. at Concord, 11 Dec. 1641.

He m. (2) Mary Fitch, dau. of Thomas of Norwalk, b. abt. 1644, d. 25 Dec. 1730 ae. abt. 87 (g. s.)

Will 14 Apr. 1713, proved 21 Dec. 1715; sons Samuel, Lemuel; Ruth Treadwell, gr. dau. of son Matthew dec'd; gr. dau. Jemima Sherwood, dau. of son John dec'd; two eldest daus. Mary Fitch and Sarah Fayerweather; dau. Ann Trowbridge; wife Mary.

Will of Mary Sherwood of Stratfield, 9 July 1726, proved 2 Feb. 1730/1; my daus.; dau. Mary Bradford, mentioning legacy given her by her gr. mother Sherwood alias Banks; sons Samuel and Lemuel; Church of Christ in Stratfield; daus. Mary Bradford, Sarah Fayerweather, Ann Fairchild; gr. dau. Jemima Gold.

Child [by first wife]:

+Matthew.

Children [by second wife] :

+John.

Mary, m. (1) Capt. Daniel Fitch, of Norwich; m. (2) Joseph Bradford.

Sarah, b. abt. 1676, d. at Stratfield, 25 May 1743 in 67 yr. (g. s.) ; m. (1) Ephraim Wheeler; m. (2) Benjamin Fairweather; m. (3) Anthony Nouguier.

+Lemuel.

+Samuel, b. abt. 1681.

Ann, m. (1) abt. 1708, Joseph Trowbridge; m. (2) Caleb Fairchild, and rem. to Hanover, N. J.

Sherwood, Isaac, s. of Thomas.

He m. Elizabeth Jackson, dau. of John, perhaps b. 21 July 1662.
Received a grant of land from town of Eastchester, 1676, and was of Rye in 1678. In 1687 he bought land at Compo (Westport), where he was living in 1733.

He conveyed to son Isaac, Jr., 21 Aug. 1727, mentioning other sons David and John, and reserving life use for himself and wife Elizabeth.

Children:

Elizabeth, b. [say 1681]; m. (1) (rec. Norwalk) 10 July 1701, Isaac Hayes, of Norwalk; m. (2) abt. 1713, Andrew Sanford, of Milford.

+Daniel, b. abt. 1686.

+Isaac.

+John.

+David.

Abigail, b. [say 1679], d. late in 1735; m. (1) [say 1700], John Cable, 3d; m. (2) 1 Dec. 1727, Thomas Pike.

+Thomas.

Sherwood, Thomas, s. of Thomas, 2d.

Married Sarah ———, and d. in 1699; she m. (2) ——— Waterbrook, of New Rochelle, N. Y.

Thomas Sherwood and Sarah his wife, of "Mile Square, in Manor of Phillips", conveyed 24 Aug. 1697 to dau. Evis Sherwood. [Westchester Deeds.]

On 24 Nov. 1709, "we the children of" Thomas Sherwood dec'd conveyed to bro. William Sherwood the proper heir of Thomas

Sherwood deceased 1699; signed by Rebecca and Mary Sherwood, Ruth Waterbrook, and Margery Sherwood. Signed also by Nathaniel Taylor, Samuel Baylor, and John Quinby, prob. as witnesses. Sarah Waterbrook of New Rochelle conveyed to son William Sherwood; Thomas the son of Thomas was under 21, and was expected to sign later. [Fairfield Deeds.] William later conveyed the Fairfield property to Samuel Sherwood.

Children:

>William, rem. to Cape May, N. J.
>Rebecca.
>Mary.
>Ruth, m. —— Waterbrook.
>Margery.
>Thomas, b. after 1688. On 5 Nov. 1714, he conveyed to Samuel Sherwood, one of the sons of his gr. father Thomas, part of the latter's long lot, to which he claimed he was rightful heir by gift from his father Thomas, although his elder bro. William, sometime inhabitant of Cape May, had already given a conveyance, as pretended heir, to the same grantee. Prob. he was of Oyster Bay, L. I., 1723.
>Evis.

Sherwood, Benjamin, s. of Thomas, 2d.

He m. Sarah ——, and d. at Greenfield, ae. abt. 67 or 68, date not stated.

Children, recorded at Greenfield (also at Fairfield except the youngest), bapt. at Fairfield:

>Mary, b. 8 Jan. 1692/3, d. at Greenfield, 15 June 1770 ae. 77 (g. s.); m. 25 June 1712, Joseph Banks.
>Mindwell, b. 8 Sept. 1696, bapt. 4 Oct. 1696; m. John Olmstead.
>XBenjamin, b. 1 Mar. 1700/1, bapt. 30 Mar. 1701, d. at Greenfield, 19 Jan. 1763 in 63 yr. (g. s.); will 5 Aug. 1760, proved 14 Feb. 1763; m. 9 Feb. 1723/4, Eleanor Bradley, b. 22 Feb. 1707/8, d. 29 Mar. 1793 ae. 85 (g. s.).
>XJoseph, b. 21 Nov. 1702 (Fairfield rec.) or 1 Dec. 1702 (Greenfield rec.), bapt. 31 Jan. 1702/3, living 1753; m. at Fairfield, 17 Feb. 1731, Sarah Osborn, bapt. at Fairfield, June 1711, d. after 1793.
>XNoah, b. 8 May 1707, bapt. 29 June 1707, d. at Greenfield, 4 Apr. 1734 ae. almost 27; m. 3 June 1727, Phebe Higgins, b. abt. 1703, d. at Greenfield, 22 Apr. 1774 ae. 71; she m. (2) 2 Oct. 1739, Robert Rogers.
>Sarah, bapt. 12 Aug. 1711, d. by 1738; m. Gershom Bradley.

Sherwood, Samuel, s. of Thomas, 2d.

Will 15 Mar. 1724/5, proved 22 June 1725; daus. Ann, Sarah, Abigail; Lydia dau. of my dau. Sarah Hull; sons Daniel, Samuel. He renewed Covenant at Fairfield Church, 29 Mar. 1696.

Children, bapt. at Fairfield:

Sarah, bapt. 29 Mar. 1696; m. abt. 1719, Theophilus Hull.

✕Samuel, bapt. 18 Feb. 1699/1700, d. at Westport, 2 June 1768 in 69 yr. (g. s.); Capt.; will 29 Nov. 1759, proved 21 June 1768; m. at Fairfield, 8 Mar. 1722, Jane Burr, dau. of Daniel, bapt. 27 Apr. 1701, d. 10 Mar. 1779 ae. 78 (g. s.); her Inv. 25 Mar. 1779.

Abigail, bapt. 18 Oct. 1702.

Ann, bapt. 13 May 1705; perhaps m. at Fairfield Church, 4 Feb. 1745/6, Samuel Galpin, of Woodbury, as his second wife.

✕Daniel, b. (rec. Greenfield) 5 Apr. 1708, bapt. 27 June 1708, d. at Greenfield, 20 Feb. 1784 ae. 77 (g. s.); m. abt. 1727, Martha Hull, b. 15 June 1701, d. 19 Sept. 1782 in 83 yr. (g. s.).

Sherwood, Isaac, s. of Thomas, 2d.

He settled in Norwalk; m. Mary ———; and d. in 1748. Isaac of Norwalk conveyed to bro. Samuel, 1706.

Adm'n granted, 4 Oct. 1748, to son Isaac of Norwalk. Distribution 26 Jan. 1748/9; Widow; Isaac Sherwood; Rebecca wife of Robert Cleyland; Elizabeth wife of Benjamin Keeler; children of John Sherwood dec'd.

Children:

Isaac, Ens., 1st Co., Norwalk, May 1746.

Rebecca, m. Robert Cleyland.

Elizabeth, m. Benjamin Keeler.

✕John, m. Hannah Morehouse, dau. of Thomas, 3d, bapt. 4 Sept. 1715.

Sherwood, Matthew, s. of Matthew.

He d. at Stratfield in 1709 ae. 22 (g. s.) [the age is wrongly read, and may be 42].

He m. Elizabeth Morehouse, dau. of Samuel. She m. (2) 4 Mar. 1710, Rev. Charles Chauncey of Stratfield; and (3) 10 Apr. 1716, Lt. Richard Miles of New Haven.

Will 12 July 1709, codicil 13 Sept. 1709, proved 21 Nov. 1709; wife Elizabeth; dau. Sarah Treadwell and son Timothy Treadwell; if dau. should leave no issue, then to bro. Samuel Sherwood's son Nathaniel and bro. Thomas Morehouse's son John.

Child:

> Sarah, d. by 1715; m. abt. 1705, Timothy Treadwell.

Sherwood, John, s. of Matthew.

He m. Johanna Booth, dau. of Ephraim, b. at Stratford, Sept. 1678. She m. (2) Oct. 1701, Thomas Hawley, and d. at Stratfield 28 Jan. 1761 in 84 yr. (g. s.).

Inv. of John of Stratford, 7 Oct. 1696. Matthew Sherwood, Jr., and the widow to administer. Widow Johanna and dau. Jemima. Capt. Matthew, father of John, engaged 26 June 1697 to give his gr. child Jemima £100.

Child, recorded at Stratford:

> Jemima, b. 17 Jan. 1696/7, bapt. at Stratfield, 14(?) Jan. 1696/7; m. John Gold, of Fairfield.

Sherwood, Lemuel, s. of Matthew.

Deacon of Stratfield Church, and Town Clerk of Fairfield. He d. 2 Sept. 1732.

He m. (1) after 1706, Ann Wheeler, dau. of Sergt John, b. abt. 1684.*

He m. (2) at Stratfield, 17 May 1711, Experience Wheeler, dau. of Isaac; she d. 27 Aug. 1721 ae. 35.

He m. (3) 8 Mar. 1722, Joanna Phippen, widow of James; she d. 9 May 1727.

He m. (4) 27 June 1728, Ann Silliman, dau. of Robert, bapt. 12 Mar. 1698/9.

Will of Dea. Lemuel, 4 Aug. 1732, proved 1 Oct. 1732; wife Ann; daus. Ann, Abiah, Mehitabel; son Matthew is to confirm Sergt. John Odell and his son William and Lt. John Burr in lands Lemuel had sold them which accrued from Est. of father Wheeler in right of Lemuel's late wife Experience, mother of said son Matthew; lands to sons Matthew and Samuel; wife and eldest

---

* The manuscript Sherwood Genealogy suggests that Nathan of Stamford was son of Lemuel by his first wife. Proof of this has not been found. Nathan had no deeds at Fairfield. His first purchase at Stamford, 28 July 1727, calls him of Fairfield. He m. by 1730, Ann Pettit, dau. of John, b. 27 Apr. 1708. They had eleven children recorded at Stamford, two of whom were named Matthew and Lemuel, names that occur in this branch of the family.

son Matthew, Exec'rs; to sons Andrew and Samuel their mother's dower in my real estate.

Distribution, 14 Feb. 1732/3, to widow Ann; 29 Sept. 1733, to Ann, Abiah and Mehitabel Sherwood, daus. of Dea. Lemuel; 4 Dec. 1734, to Matthew and Samuel, sons of Dea. Lemuel.

He conveyed 1712 to Jonathan Wheeler, land he had with wife Ann Wheeler, now dec'd.

David Middlebrook and Abiah his wife, and Elnathan Hubbell and Mehitabel his wife, all of Stratford, conveyed 18 Mar. 1749 to bro. John Brooks of Stratford, right from our mother Experience Wheeler dec'd.

Children [by second wife], recorded and bapt. at Stratfield:

Matthew, b. 12 Apr. 1712, bapt. 6 July 1712.
Hannah, b. 11 Dec. 1713, bapt. 13 Dec. 1713, d. y.
Andrew, bapt. 24 Apr. 1715.
Ann, b. 22 Aug. 1716, bapt. 26 Aug. 1716; m. John Brooks, of Stratford.
Abiah, b. 26(?) Mar. 1718, bapt. 20 Mar. 1718; m. David Middlebrook.
Mehitabel, b. 21 Feb. 1719/20; m. Elnathan Hubbell.

Children [by fourth wife], recorded and bapt at Stratfield:

Experience, b. 12 Apr. 1729, d. 11 Aug. 1730/1.
Samuel, b. 9 July [1731]; is said to have d. at Bennington, Vt., 9 Feb. 1788 in 58 yr.; ?m. at Greenfield, Feb. 1754, "Ev: Sherwood." His wife was Ruth, dau. of John Sherwood.
Hannah, bapt. 21 Feb. 1733 (posthumous), d. 26 Feb. 1732/3.

Sherwood, Samuel, s. of Matthew.   Ens., Stratfield Trainband, May 1714; Capt., May 1722.

Born abt. 1681; Capt. Samuel d. at Stratfield, 10 Nov. 1732 in 52 yr. (g. s.).

He m. (1) 30 Nov. 1704, Rebecca Burr, dau. of Nathaniel, b. abt. 1681, d. at Stratfield, 16 May 1721/2 ae. 40 (g. s.). [The date as read is impossible, and usually given 16 May 1721; perhaps should be 16 Mar. 1721/2.]

He m. (2) Mary, widow of Henry Jackson, and dau. of Isaac Wheeler, b. abt. 1683, d. 18 Sept. 1743 in 61 yr. (g. s.).

Will 7 Nov. 1732, proved 11 Dec. 1732 [called Capt. in Inv.]; wife Mary; five eldest daus., Sarah, Mary, Abigail, Rebecca, and Esther, to have the linen that was their own mother's; dau.

Prudence; ~sons John and Nathaniel, Exec'rs; Capt. Daniel Hubbell to be guardian to my son Thomas; Sergt. David Sherman to be guardian to my son Andrew.

Children [by first wife], recorded and bapt. at Stratfield:

XJohn, b. 22 Sept. 1705, bapt. 4 Nov. 1705, d. at Stratfield, 17 Sept. 1779 in 74 yr. (g. s.); Capt.; will 26 Nov. 1772, proved 4 Oct. 1779; pastor of Baptist Church at Stratfield; m. at Stratfield, 14 June 1733, Mary Walker, who d. 12 June 1767 in 58 yr. (g. s.).

XNathaniel, b. 15 Sept. 1707, bapt. 21 Sept. 1707, d. at Stratfield, 2 Oct. 1784 in 78 yr. (g. s.); m. Mercy Sherman, bapt. 21 May 1704, d. 26 July 1779 in 76 yr. (g. s.).

Sarah, b. 23 Oct. 1709, bapt. 18 Dec. 1709; m. at Stratfield, 16 Nov. 1732, Daniel Fitch.

Mary, b. 1 Mar. 1710/1, bapt. 8 Apr. 1711; m. 9 June 1742, George Dolbeare.

Abigail, b. Oct. 1713(?), bapt. 23 Nov. 1712; prob. m. Ebenezer Lord.

Rebecca, b. 12 Oct. 1715(?), bapt. 21 Nov. 1714; m. (rec. Fairfield) 1 Dec. 1737, John Nichols.

Esther, b. 23 Nov. 1717(?), bapt. 25 Nov. 1716; m. 15 Dec. 1736, John Bradford, of Montville.

XThomas, b. 11 Mar. 1719, bapt. 15 Mar. 1719, d. at Easton, 15 Sept. 1798; m. (1) Ann Burr, b. 7 Sept. 1726, d. 3 Dec. 1777 in 52 yr. (g. s.); m. (2) at Greenfield, 23 Nov. 1778, Mary (Hanford) Alvord, b. abt. 1718.

XAndrew, b. 21 Mar. 1721, d. at Stratfield, 23 Nov. 1767 in 47 yr. (g. s.); will 6 Nov. 1767, proved 1 Dec. 1767; m. (1) ———; m. (2) 25 June 1754, Mary Angevine; m. (3) Abigail ———.

Child [by second wife]:

Prudence, bapt. 10 Jan. 1723.

Sherwood, Daniel, s. of Isaac.

He settled in Ridgefield, where he d. Aug. 1749 ae. 63 (g. s.); m. Ruth ———, who d. 11 Dec. 1748 ae. 58 (g. s.).*

Will 19 Aug., proved 4 Sept. 1749; four sons, Daniel, Nathan, Isaac, John; daus. Hannah, Abigail; dau. Ruth Lobdell; Capt. Richard Olmsted and Samuel Olmsted, Exec'rs.

Children, recorded at Ridgefield:

Hannah, b. 7 Mar. 1712, d. in 1754; m. 24 Mar. 1750/1, Vivus Dauchy, as his second wife.

Daniel, b. 21 Nov. 1714, d. at Ridgefield, 17 May 1766; m. 29 Apr.

---

* Contributed by Starr S. Sherwood, Esq., of Bethel, Conn.

1736, Jerusha Whitney. His estate was distributed, 27 Nov. 1786, to 3d son Henry, 4th son John, youngest dau. Sarah Sherwood, eldest dau. Jerusha wife of Nehemiah Barlow, youngest son Richard, eldest son Daniel, 4th dau. Mary wife of Nathan Foster, 2d dau. Elizabeth wife of John Lobdell, 3d dau. Ruth Sherwood, 2d son Ebenezer Sherwood.

Abigail, b. 3 Apr. 1716; m. 16 Mar. 1745/6, Henry Elias.

Rebecca, d. 12 Feb. 1719.

Nathan, b. 16 May 1720; m. 4 Jan. 1743/4, Lois Hard, of Newtown.

Ruth, b. 29 Mar. 1722; m. 25 June 1744, John Lobdell.

Isaac, b. 8 Feb. 1723/4; m. 2 Jan. 1746, Naomi ———.

John, b. 15 Mar. 1729; m. Hannah ———.

Sarah, b. 26 May 1731, d. y.

Sherwood, Isaac, s. of Isaac. Lt., Greens Farms company, Fairfield, Oct. 1727.

He d. at Westport, 25 Feb. 1768; m. Rebecca ———, who d. 3 May 1761.

Isaac Sherwood, Jr., conveyed 1729 to son Gabriel, land at Compo on which my father Isaac now liveth; and Gabriel sold 1732 land in homelot where gr. father Isaac Sherwood's house stands at Compo.

Children (incomplete) :

✕Gabriel, b. by 1707; m. by 1728, Martha Seymour. On 22 Mar. 1728, Rachel Seymour of "Sandys Tribe in these Islands, widow of Capt. William Seymour of the same, dec'd." conveyed for love to son and dau. Gabriel Sherwood and Martha his wife, a negro boy Tom and a negro girl Nany, the gift to take effect at her own death.

Elizabeth, b. abt. 1708, d. at Cooperstown, N. Y., 11 Aug. 1792; m. (rec. Norwalk) 24 Feb. 1728/9, Stephen Buckingham.

Jane, d. 12 Apr. 1778; m. 4 Aug. 1741, Thomas Disbrow, 3d.

Sherwood, John, s. of Isaac.

He m. Abigail Frost, dau. of Daniel.

John Sherwood and Abigail his wife, she being dau. of Sergt. Daniel Frost of Fairfield dec'd, conveyed 24 Dec. 1736 to son-in-law Daniel Frost. On 2 Mar. 1748/9, John Sherwood and wife Abigail alias Frost of Stamford conveyed to son and dau. David Cressey and Eunice Cressey alias Sherwood of Fairfield, land from Abigail's father.

Child:

> Eunice, m. (1) Daniel Frost, her first cousin; m. (2) 26 Mar. 1745, David Cressey.

Sherwood, David, s. of Isaac.

He m. at Fairfield, 16 Mar. 1709, Sarah Meeker, dau. of John.

He d. at Westport, 5 Nov. 1759; she d. there 17 Jan. 1748/9.

Will 13 Oct. 1759, proved 20 Nov. 1759; son David; daus. Sarah Carley, Hannah Couch; sons Joseph, Jabez, Andrew, Abel; son-in-law Joseph Couch, Exec'r. Distribution to same, 24 Apr. 1760, Sarah being called wife of John Carely.

Children, recorded at Fairfield:

> Sarah, b. 8 Jan. 1710; m. John Carley, with whom she was living 1760 in the Oblong, Dutchess County, N. Y.
>
> XJoseph, b. 16 May 1712; living 1760 in the Oblong, N. Y.; m. Mary ———.
>
> XJabez, b. 8 Apr. 1714, m. Oct. 1742, Elizabeth Fillio.
>
> XAndrew, b. 10 Oct. 1716, d. at Danbury in 1761; adm'n granted, 12 Oct. 1761; m. Ann ———.
>
> David, b. 15 Mar. 1718, d. 16 Mar. 1722.
>
> XAbel, b. 20 Dec. 1720; rem. to New Fairfield by 1760; d. in Army between 15 Apr. and Nov. 1761; adm'n granted, 1 Dec. 1761; m. 1 Jan. 1749/50, Hannah Fountain, dau. of Aaron, b. 2 Apr. 1729; she m. (2) Elisha Perry.
>
> XDavid, b. 1 Oct. 1723; m. 16 Jan. 1749/50, Eunice Cable.
>
> Mary, b. 10 Aug. 1725, d. y.
>
> Hannah, b. 4 Mar. 1728; m. (1) 7 May 1747, Joseph Couch; m. (2) 21 Nov. 1773, Capt. Gideon Hurlbut.

Sherwood, Thomas, s. of Isaac.

He d. in hospital in Albany, 5 Aug. 1756. He was a private in the company of Capt. Whiting of Stratford. He m. Ellen Churchill, dau. of Robert, bapt. 20 Oct. 1695, d. 1 Oct. 1754.

Nehemiah Sherwood of Fairfield, Benjamin Stuart and Ellen his wife of Norwalk, and Sarah Sherwood of Fairfield, conveyed 1756 to John Sherwood of Fairfield, land with house and shop at Greens Farms. Isaac Sherwood, Jr., of Fairfield, conveyed 1756 to John Sherwood, Jr., of Fairfield, right in the homelot of mother Ellenor Sherwood dec'd.

Children:

> Thomas, b. abt. 1719, d. at Westport, 11 Sept. 1748 in 29 yr. (g. s.). Adm'n on estate of Thomas, Jr., granted to John Andrews, 1 Nov. 1748. Distribution 6 Feb. 1749; Isaac, Jonathan, Nehemiah, John Sherwood; Samuel Bennett and wife; Elinor and Sarah Sherwood.
> Abigail, m. Samuel Bennett, of Ridgefield.
> Isaac.
> Eleanor, m. 7 Feb. 1749/50, Benjamin Stewart, of Norwalk.
> Jonathan.
> ✕Nehemiah.
> ✕John, d. in 1777; m. at Westport, 24 Mar. 1761, Mary Gorham; dau. of Joseph, b. 25 Dec. 1739.
> Sarah, m. 10 Mar. 1757, John Fillio,* of Norwalk.

SHERWOOD FAMILY (STRATFORD)

Sherwood, Thomas.   Deputy (Stratford) to Conn. Leg., Sept. 1645, Sept. 1649, May 1650, Oct. 1653, Oct. 1654; war committee for Stratford, Oct. 1654.

He m. by 1642, Sarah Seabrook, dau. of Robert, b. abt. 1623.

Winthrop in 1657 mentioned the wife of Thomas Sherwood of Stratford, ae. 34, with an unweaned child, and son John ae. 4.

Mentioned 1 Jan. 1657 [1657/8] as "having departed this life" [Stratford rec.].

Will 4 June 1657; wife Sarah; sons John and Thomas (under 18); dau. Mary, a fourth of all my lands; my daus.; overseers, Mr. Blackman, Isaac Nichols, John Birdsey, Henry Wakelee, and John Welles.   Inv. 4 June 1658.

John Wheeler conveyed, 8 Feb. 1672 [1672/3], to Jehiel Preston right in land given to his wife by her Grandfather Seabrook; and Samuel Stiles conveyed in similar terms, 24 May 1673.

Children:

> Sarah, b. [say 1643], d. at Woodbury, 12 Mar. 1703/4; m. (rec. Stratford) beginning of Dec. 1662, John Wheeler.
> Elizabeth, b. [say 1645], d. at Woodbury, 3 June 1719; m. (rec. Stratford) last of Dec. 1664, Samuel Stiles.
> Mary, b. [say 1650]; m. (rec. Milford) 13 July 1670, Josiah Tibbals.
> +John, b. abt. 1653.
> Thomas, b. abt. 1656, for we assume that he was the infant mentioned by Winthrop; d. in 1676. Inv. 6 May 1676, at Stratford, given in by

---

* Or Fillaud; apparently a French name,—now spelled Philo.

John Pickett, Sr., and John Sherwood. An account of debts signed by John Smith, Sr., and Jonathan Law, was dated 28 Feb. 1675 [1675/6], and shows amounts due to Samuel Clark, John Smith the smith, Goodman Merwin, Goodman Smith the tailor, and John Smith, Jr. [These were Milford men, and their names suggest that Thomas had been apprenticed in Milford in his youth.]

Sherwood, John, s. of Thomas.

Born at Stratford about 1653, d. there in 1689; m. at Stratford, 23 Apr. 1685, Sarah Hurd. She was dau. of John, b. 17 Feb. 1665/6; and m. (2) 2 July 1691, Samuel Beecher.

Will 8 Oct. 1689; wife Sarah; son Thomas; dau. Elizabeth; if both children die, then to the Church in Stratford; Mr. Israel Chauncey, Mr. Samuel Sherman, Jr., and brother Samuel Stiles, Exec'rs. Inv. 5 Nov. 1689.

Samuel Beecher and Sarah his wife conveyed to Thomas Sherwood her right as widow of John Sherwood; also in 1714 to dau. Elizabeth Sherwood, "considering her lameness and decrepit condition." [Stratford Deeds.]

Children, recorded at Stratford:

XThomas, b. 22 Nov. 1686, d. at Stratfield, 7 May 1727 in 41 yr. (g. s.); Dr.; will 4 May 1727, proved 6 June 1727; m. (rec. Stratford, date nearly indecipherable), 10 Jan. 1708/9, Abigail Darling of Jamaica, L. I. On 30 May 1753, dower was set to Mrs. Fordice under will of her former husband, Doctor Thomas Sherwood.

Elizabeth, b. Aug. 1688.

Silliman, Daniel.

This surname was originally Sillivant, and traditionally Dutch. The first of the name in Connecticut was a Daniel Sillivant who m. (1) before 1652, Abigail Cole, dau. of James of Hartford. She soon died, and he m. (2) at New Haven, 17 Oct. 1654, Elizabeth Lamberton, dau. of Capt. George. He d. in Virginia leaving a will proved June 1655, giving property to widow. She, in Oct. 1655, conveyed to John Cole the house and land given to her husband and his former wife Abigail by the latter's father in his will. She m. (2) 9 Mar. 1656/7, William Trowbridge of New Haven. It may be queried whether perhaps this Daniel had been married previously in Virginia, where early in the next century a Silliman family was located.*

Daniel of Fairfield, perhaps related to the earlier Daniel, m. (by marriage contract July 1661) Peaceable, widow of John Eggleden.

Record 4 Mar. 1663/4: Daniel Silliman had m. the widow of John Eggleden; her son was apprenticed to Joseph Middlebrook.

Married (2) Hannica (also called Hannah), widow of Henry Hendricks.

Inv. of Daniel, Sr., 2 Jan. 1690 [1690/1]; widow Hannica (marriage contract referred to); adm'n granted to Daniel and Robert. Heirs named: Daniel, Thomas, Robert.

Daniel Silliman was involved in the Benfield case, 1666, and the testimony contains considerable information about him. Gold wrote of him that he had small property, did little labor, and traded with the Indians. George Squire, Jr., testified that, it having been reported that a fleet of Dutch and French was coming to New England, Silliman said he "hoped he should get his foot aboard a man of warre once more." This indicates that he served in the navy in his youth. Prob. he was a man of adventurous spirit, and a shrewd trader; but the ability that soon characterized the Silliman line seems to have derived largely from the excellent intermarriages with families of mental distinction, notably the Hull and Selleck alliances.†

Children [by first wife]:

+Daniel.
    Thomas, d. intestate; Inv. 16 Jan. 1692 [1692/3]; Daniel and Robert
      to administer.
+Robert.

Silliman, Daniel, s. of Daniel.

His wife in 1687 was dau. of Richard Ogden. Abigail, wife of Daniel, bapt. at Fairfield, 30 Dec. 1694. Prob. they were identical. Inv. 4 Feb. 1696/7, sworn to by Abigail Silliman. Robert Silli-

---

* Mary "Sillaven" m. (rec. Fairfield) 28 Dec. 1699, Samuel Gregory. Perhaps she was dau. of an Owen Sillivan who is mentioned as having a house at Stratfield at that period.

† The compiler inclines to the view that he was of Dutch extraction. Not only did he m. a Dutch woman for his second wife, but he lived on "Holland Hill," and his bold remark about a man of war *may* imply that it was the *Dutch* navy in which he served.

man appointed Adm'r, and with their mother was to place out the children Daniel and John, and also the daus. The daus. Mary and Peaceable named; youngest child under four yrs. Partial distribution made to Abigail and Mary Silliman, and they receipted 25 Feb. 1711/2 to their uncle Robert Silliman. Jemima dau. of Daniel Silliman, chose her brother-in-law Samuel Squire for guardian, 2 Feb. 1714/5.

Children, all but youngest bapt. at Fairfield 12 May 1695:

    ✕Daniel, b. abt. 1686, d. in 1717; adm'n granted 1 May 1717; m. 20 Jan. 1714, Thankful Howes, dau. of Joseph, b. Apr. 1692; she m. (2) Capt. John Osborn.

    ✕John, b. 31 Dec. 1687 (age at death), d. 29 Nov. 1752 ae. 64 yrs. 11 mos. wanting 2 days (g. s., Fairfield); Capt.; m. (1) abt. 1716, Anna Burr, dau. of Nathaniel, bapt. 5 Apr. 1696, d. 1 Oct. 1740 in 45 yr. (g. s.); m. (2) by marriage agreement dated 4 Oct. 1741, Ann (Wilson), widow of Daniel Wilson, who d. 14 Aug. 1756 in 70 yr. (g. s.).

    Abigail, m. (1) David Adams; m. (2) 22 Mar. 1737, John Hide.

    Mary, b. abt. 1692/3, d. 26 June 1748 in 56 yr. (g. s., Fairfield); m. abt. 1714, Lt. Samuel Squire.

    Peaceable, m. at Stratfield, 18 Nov. 1713, Jonathan Hubbell; rem. to Newtown.

    Jemima, bapt. 11 Apr. 1697; m. (rec. Stratford) 19 Dec. 1717, Thomas Gilbert, of Stratford.

Silliman, Robert, s. of Daniel   Deputy for Fairfield, May 1722, May and Oct. 1723, May 1724, May and Sept. 1727, May 1728.

His wife Sarah was named as dau. in will 1695 of Cornelius Hull. She was prob. widow of John Knapp, for Silliman entered caveat against Knapp estates, claiming a right in Est. of John Knapp and also in Est. of "his Mother-in-law" Elizabeth Knapp. Robert also purchased a right from Moses Knapp, and in 1718 made a distribution agreement with Daniel Knapp, bro. of Moses.

Will 26 July 1746, proved 10 Aug. 1748; grandson Samuel Sherwood; daus. Sarah wife of Samuel Hall, Martha wife of Nathaniel Burr, and Rebecca wife of Ebenezer Jennings; sons Robert, Nathaniel, Ebenezer; dau. Ann; three sons-in-law Exec'rs.

Children, bapt. at Fairfield:

    ✕Robert, b. (no record; abt. 1692), d. at Fairfield in 1767; will 12 Nov. 1761, proved 1 Dec. 1767; m. (1) 20 Nov. 1715, Ruth Tread-

well, who d. 15 Mar. 1756 ae. 58 yrs. 1 mo. 15 days (g. s., Stratfield) ; m. (2) 14 Dec. 1756, Mary Morehouse; she was widow of
Abijah Morehouse, and m. (3) 11 Oct. 1768, John Bradley; prob.
she was born Mary Summers.

Sarah, bapt. 16 Sept. 1694, d. at Stratfield, 6 Feb. 1770; m. at Stratfield, 29 July 1714, Samuel Hall.

XNathaniel, b. 10 Aug. 1696, bapt. 27 Sept. 1696, d. at Fairfield in
1763; will 21 July 1763, proved 2 Aug. 1763; m. 2 May 1723,
Hannah Booth; dau. of Joseph; d. in 1767. Adm'n on her Est.
granted 14 July 1767.

Ann, bapt. 12 Mar. 1698/9; m. 27 June 1728, Dea. Lemuel Sherwood.

Martha, bapt. 24 Aug. 1701; m. 10 Nov. 1726, Nathaniel Burr.

Rebecca, bapt. 8 Apr. 1705, d. 2 Jan. 1790 in 85 yr. (g. s., Fairfield) ;
m. Ebenezer Jennings; no issue. Adm'n on her Est. was granted,
26 Feb. 1790, to Ebenezer Burr, Jr. Distribution to the heirs of
Ebenezer Silliman dec'd, Robert Silliman dec'd, Nathaniel Silliman
dec'd, Martha Burr dec'd, and Sarah Hall dec'd.

XEbenezer, bapt. 21 Sept. 1707, d. 11 Oct. 1775 in 68 yr. (g. s., Fairfield) ; will 19 Dec. 1774, proved 25 Nov. 1775; Yale Coll. 1727;
m. (1) 8 Oct. 1728, Abigail Selleck, b. [at Stamford, 6 Feb.
1706/7, by age at death making allowance for calendar change], d.
16 Mar. 1772 ae. 65 yrs. 1 mo. wanting 1 day (g. s.) ; m. (2) (by
marriage contract dated 22 July 1773) Abigail, widow of Benjamin
Hall, and dau. of Rev. John Williams of Deerfield; she d. at Deerfield, 3 Dec. 1781 ae. 73.

Skidmore, Thomas.

Blacksmith, of Westerleigh, near Bristol, Eng., sent over cattle
in 1636 for John Winthrop. Came in 1639 and settled in
Cambridge, Mass.

Married (1) Ellen ———.

Married (2) Joanna, widow of Nathaniel Baldwin, previously
widow of Richard Westcott. Winthrop in 1667 referred to her
as aged 55, wife of Thomas Skidmore of Fairfield, and mother of
the wife of John Weed of Stamford; and also stated that she was
sister of the wife of Robert Sanford of Hartford.

Married (3) after 1672, Sarah, widow first of Edward Treadwell, second of Henry Whelpley, and third of Ralph Keeler. She
d. late in 1684.

The will of Joanna Skidmore, wife of Thomas, 1667, named
her Westcott and Baldwin children.

Will of Thomas of Fairfield, 20 Apr. 1684, proved 8 Dec. 1684;
wife Sarah, all Est. for life; at her decease, equally to my grand-

child John Higby that married my wife's dau., and to my grandchild John Skidmore. His widow swore to the Inv. 15 Nov. 1684,
but on 8 Dec. "Sara is alsoe within a fortnight after her husbands
deceas alsoe taken away ₽ death."

Children [by first wife]:

> Thomas, b. abt. 1628; ae. 53 when he testified [in Stratford records]
> at Huntington, 11 Aug. 1681.
> Dorothy, b. [say 1631]; m. (rec. Stratford) 20 July 1652, Hugh
> Griffin.
> Jedidah, m. Edward Higby.
> John, b. at Cambridge, 11 Apr. 1643, d. at Jamaica, L. I., in 1680;
> will 15 Feb. 1678/9, proved 9 July 1680; children John, Samuel,
> Thomas, Joseph, Abigail. He m. Susanna ———, who d. before
> him.
> Grace, m. John Goulding, of Huntington, who received a farm from
> his father-in-law Thomas Skidmore in 1683/4.

Skidmore, John.

Grandson of Thomas, and mentioned in his will; b. abt. 1662,
and d. at Stratford, 22 Jan. 1740/1 ae. 78 (Christ Church rec.);
m. Mary ———, b. abt. 1665, d. at Stratford, 28 Nov. 1748 ae. 83.
[Perhaps she was dau. of Peter Norton of Fairfield, *q. v.*]

Children:

> John, d. at Stratford, 10 Mar. 1724/5.
> Ellen, m. at New Haven, 21 Dec. 1721, Enos Bradley.
> Thomas, b. abt. 1693, d. at Newtown, 21 July 1761 ae. 68 (g. s.); will
> 24 Feb. 1761, proved 10 Aug. 1761; m. Martha ———, who d. 23
> Dec. 1774 ae. 80 (g. s.).
> Mary, b. abt. 1697, d. at Huntington, 18 June 1773 ae. 76 (g. s.); m.
> at Stratford, 19 Apr. 1722, Thomas Lattin.
> Abigail,* d. at Waterbury, 30 Dec. 1771; m. at New Haven (she
> called of Stratford), 19 Dec. 1733, Benjamin Wilmot.

Slawson, George. Magistrate at Stamford, 1657, 1659.
Deputy (Stamford) to New Haven Leg., Oct. 1663.

Of Lynn 1637, rem. soon to Sandwich, and very early to
Stamford.

He m. (2) at Fairfield, 16 Dec. 1680, Mary (Williams) Jennings, widow of Joshua; she d. abt. Dec. 1697.

---

* Her parentage not positive.

Will 19 Dec. 1694, codicil 9 Jan. 1694 [1694/5]; wife, referring to marriage covenant; sons John and Eleazer; dau., John Gold's wife. Inv. states that he d. 17 Feb. 1694/5.

[For his widow's will, see JOSHUA JENNINGS.]

Children:

+John.
+Eleazer, b. abt. 1641.
  Hannah, m. (1) John Gold; m. (2) 20 Sept. 1714, Dea. Samuel Hoyt.

Slawson, John, s. of George.

He m. (1) at New Haven, 22 Nov. 1663, Sarah Tuttle; she was dau. of William, bapt. Apr. 1642; and was killed by her brother Benjamin 17 Nov. 1676, for which he was executed [Conn. Archives].

He m. (2) by 1679, Elizabeth Benedict, dau. of Thomas, who d. before him. He prob. m. (3) after 1690, Hannah, widow of John Gibbs, and dau. of John Punderson, bapt. at New Haven, May 1642, d. there 18 Jan. 1715/6.

He d. at Stamford, 16 Oct. 1706.

Agreement for distribution made 11 Jan. 1706/7 by the children, John, Jonathan, and Thomas Slawson, Sarah wife of Ebenezer Bishop, Elizabeth wife of Nathaniel Pond, and Mary Slawson.

Children [by first wife], recorded at Stamford:

  John, b. 9 Sept. 1664, d. at Stamford in 1745; adm'n granted 7 Oct. 1745; m. Mary Holmes, dau. of Stephen.

  Sarah, b. 20 Jan. 1667 [1667/8], d. at Stamford, 11 Jan. 1743/4; m. 2 Oct. 1700, Ebenezer Bishop.

  Jonathan, b. 25 July 1670, d. at Stamford, 19 Nov. 1727; Ens.; m. (1) 4 Feb. 1699/1700, Mary Waterbury, b. 20 Mar. 1679 [1679/80], d. 12 May 1710; m. (2) 11 July 1711, Rose Stevens, dau. of Obadiah, b. 14 Oct. 1683.

  Elizabeth, b. 30 Jan. 1672 [1672/3], d. at Stamford, 11 May 1711; m. abt. 1697, Nathaniel Pond.

Children [by second wife], recorded at Stamford:

  Mary, b. 21 Apr. 1680, living 1707.

  Thomas, b. 3 Feb. 1681/2, d. at Stamford, 30 Mar. 1710; Inv. 10 Nov. 1710; adm'n granted to John Slawson and Nathaniel Pond. He m. 14 Apr. 1709, Sarah Stevens, dau. of Joseph, b. 27 Jan. 1686 [1686/7]. His widow Sarah made agreement, 26 Aug. 1710, with

John and Jonathan Slawson, Nathaniel Pond, and Sarah Bishop; showing that Thomas had not issue. Sarah m. (2) 13 Feb. 1711/2, Jabez Smith.

Hannah, b. 12 Mar. 1685/6, d. y.

Slawson, Eleazer, s. of George.

Born abt. 1641, d. at Stamford abt. May 1698; m. (1) by 1672, Mary Chapman, dau. of John; m. (2) Susannah ———; and we suppose it was she who m. (2) 24 Oct. 1700, Samuel Hoyt, and d. 26 Mar. 1707.

On 6 June 1692, Eleazer, ae. 51, testified in favor of the accused witch, Elizabeth Clawson, that he had lived her near neighbor for many years, and always observed her to be a woman for peace, and without malice.

Will 29 Apr. 1698, proved 22 Jan. 1699; son Eleazer; dau. Martha; three younger sons; wife; twenty barrels of cider at Huntington; son James to administer, with assistance of his uncle John Slawson and Mr. David Waterbury as overseers. Inv. 27 May 1698.

On 20 Dec. 1717, Ebenezer and Nathaniel Slawson of Stamford receipted to bro. James for portion in Est. of father and mother Eleazer and Susannah Slawson.

Children [by first wife] :*

> Eleazer, b. by 1672; as "Jr." conveyed 1692/3 to Joseph Brown, interest in Est. of John Chapman; m. at Stamford, 9 May 1711, Hannah Webb, who d. 26 June 1723.
>
> Martha.

Children [by second wife] :

> James, d. at Stamford in 1759; Inv. 22 May 1759; m. (1) at Stamford, 3 Dec. 1702, Mehitabel Ambler, who d. 8 Feb. 1736/7; m. (2) Sarah, widow of John Webster, and dau. of Jeremy Jagger, b. abt. 1677, d. 1759-60.
>
> Ebenezer, m. Ann ———.
>
> Nathaniel, b. abt. 1696, d. at Kent, 8 Mar. 1787 ae. 91 (g. s.) ; called of Stamford 1719, of Norwalk 9 Jan. 1719/20 [Stamford Deeds] ; res. Wilton and Kent; m. Margaret Belden, dau. of William, who d. 14 Apr. 1780 in 80 yr. (g. s.).

Smedley, Samuel, s. of Samuel.

Baptist Smedley of Concord (d. 16 Aug. 1675) m. 27 Mar. 1645, Katharine Shorthose; had son Samuel, b. 27 Mar. 1646,

---

* The will of Thomas Lawrence, *q. v.*, proves that his half-sister Mary Chapman was mother of Eleazer, Jr., and Martha.

killed in K. Philip's War, 2 Aug. 1675; he m. 11 July 1667, Hannah Wheeler, and had a son Samuel, b. 28 Feb. 1673 [1673/4]. The last-named, called son of Samuel "sometime of Concord deceased," 4 Apr. 1690 appeared at Fairfield and chose Mr. Simon Davis of Concord as guardian.* We suppose from this that he lived as a boy with Wheeler relatives in Fairfield; and he certainly returned here.

He m. (1) (rec. Stratfield) 30 Nov. 1700, Abigail Dimon, dau. of Moses, b. 20 Aug. 1676.

He m. (2) 14 Feb. 1720/1, Martha, widow of Samuel Treadwell, and dau. of Robert Turney, b. 5 June 1676. Samuel Smedley's wife d. at Stratfield, 3 Jan. 1733/4.

Children [by first wife], recorded and bapt. at Stratfield:

> Abigail, b. 7 Nov. 1701.
>
> Samuel, b. 1 Sept. 1703(?), bapt. 6 Sept. 1702, d. at Litchfield, 16 Feb. 1756 ae. 54; m. 1 Feb. 1729, Esther Kilbourn.
>
> ✕James, b. 28 May 1705, bapt. 3 June 1705, d. at Fairfield, 4 Nov. 1771 in 67 yr. (g. s.); Col.; will 15 Sept. 1766, proved 19 Nov. 1771; m. (1) at Fairfield, 20 Oct. 1731, Jane Sturges, who d. 22 Sept. 1747; m. (2) 4 Jan. 1747/8 Widow Mary Dimon; widow of Ebenezer Dimon, and dau. of Col. John Burr, bapt. 4 July 1708, d. 12 Sept. 1766.
>
> John, b. 29 May 1706(?), bapt. 29 June 1707.
>
> Hannah, b. 18 May 1710(?), bapt. 29 May 1709.
>
> Esther, b. 8 Aug. 1712(?), bapt. 12 Aug. 1711.
>
> Ephraim, b. 27 Oct. 1713, bapt. 1 Nov. 1713, d. at Litchfield, 21 Aug. 1785 ae. 72; m. Concurrence Hurd, of Woodbury, who d. 16 May 1808 ae. 89.
>
> Damaris, b. 27 Dec. 1715, bapt. 19 Feb. 1716.

SMITH FAMILY (FAIRFIELD)

Smith, Giles.

Born abt. 1603, since he was freed from training Apr. 1663, having then attained age of 60. Settled in Hartford by 1639, where he received land "by courtesy of the town"; not a proprietor or freeman.

He wrote letter to John Winthrop, Jr., at New London, 22 Feb.

---

* Case 20544, Middlesex Probate Records; we are indebted to Mr. Clarence A. Torrey, of Dorchester, Mass. for this information. Samuel's mother was dau. of Ephraim Wheeler of Fairfield; see Appendix for further discussion.

1649, saying he was coming to settle there. Here he was one of the earliest settlers, but shortly rem. to Fairfield, where he entered for record 17 Dec. 1651, land purchased from George Stuckey, and by 1658 bought land also from John Fossecar and William Hayden. He d. in 1669.

He m. (1) ———.

He m. (2) Eunice, widow of Jonathan Porter [q. v.] of Huntington, L. I.

Will 10 Sept. 1669, proved 14 Jan. 1669 [1669/70]; to wife, Est. I had with her, mentioning her former husband Jonathan Porter; sons Samuel, Eluzy, John; daus. Elian, Elizabeth Jackson, Johanna Gray; friends Jehu Burr and John Banks, overseers. Inv. 5 Jan. 1669 [1669/70].

Children [by first wife]:

>   Ellen, b. [say 1634]; m. at Fairfield, 21 Feb. 1651 [1651/2], George
>   Godwin [Col. Rec.].
>   +Samuel.
>   Elizabeth, m. John Jackson.
>   +Eluzai.
>   Johanna, bapt. at Hartford, 25 Mar. 1649, d. between 1671 and 1676;
>   m. by 1669, Jacob Gray.
>   +John.

Smith, Samuel, s. of Giles.

He m. in 1665, Sarah Frost, dau. of Daniel, whose will 1684 called her Sarah Smith. The will of Isaac Frost 1684 named his sister the wife of Samuel Smith, and her son John. Engagement of marriage between Samuel Smith of Fairfield, son of Giles, and Sarah Frost, dau. of Daniel of Bankside, 11 Mar. 1664/5. Samuel, Sr., of Fairfield, conveyed 11 Dec. 1695 to son Samuel, land bought from John Godwin and others; signed also by Sarah Smith.

Will 27 Feb. 1698 [1698/9], proved 21 Mar. 1698 [1698/9]; sons John and Samuel had deeds of gift; daus. Elizabeth and Sarah, five shillings each; all land to son Joseph; dau. Hester, £30; to wife, all land and half of house for life. Inv. 12 Mar. 1698 [1698/9].

He renewed his Covenant with Fairfield Church, 17 Feb. 1694/5, and his children Joseph and Hester were bapt. that date.

Children:

+John, b. abt. 1668.
+Samuel.
  Elizabeth.
  Sarah.
  Abigail, b. at Fairfield, 10(?) Feb. 1679 [1679/80].
+Joseph.
  Esther, b. abt. 1685, d. at Redding, 26 Sept. 1769 ae. 84; m. abt. 1702, Thomas Williams.

Smith, Eluzai, s. of Giles.

Called Eluzy in his father's will, and Elusare in Col. Records; he lost his house by fire, and taxes were therefore remitted 1678 on petition of Mr. Hill.

He m. Rebecca Rowland, dau. of Henry, who was his wife in 1690. About 1697 he rem. to Fairfield, Salem County, N. J., and was living there in 1706. Possibly his widow m. (2) ——— Rice, and one of the daus. may have m. Moses Ward.

Children, bapt. at Fairfield, the first four on 18 Apr. 1697:

  Abigail.
  Rebecca.
  Helena.
  Elizabeth.
  Jonathan, bapt. 17 Nov. 1696.

Smith, John, s. of Giles.

He m. Elizabeth Jennings, dau. of Joshua. Her mother Mary (Williams) (Jennings) Slawson gave a legacy to the latter's grandson John Smith by will 1697.

Inv. of John, Sr., 30 Oct. 1690; Samuel Smith, Adm'r, with Joseph Jennings and Samuel Drake to assist. He left one child, a minor. On 7 Nov. 1706, his son John chose cousin Samuel Smith for guardian; and on 2 Sept. 1710 acknowledged receipt of portion from Capt. John Osborn, giving acquittance to Sarah widow of Capt. Osborn.

Child:

+John, b. (rec. Greenfield) 8 Mar. 1689 [1688/9].

Smith, John, s. of Samuel.   Sergt., Fairfield Trainband.

Born abt. 1668, d. at Greenfield, Jan. 1747/8 ae. abt. 80; m. abt. 1691, Martha ———.

He was bapt. at Fairfield Church, together with his wife Martha, 17 Feb. 1694/5. He conveyed to son John, 27 Apr. 1719, right in land from father Samuel.

Children, three recorded at Fairfield, bapt. at Fairfield Church:

  ✕John, b. 17 May 1692, bapt. Oct. 1695, d. at Greenfield, 27 Sept. 1751 ae. near 60; m. Mary Jennings, dau. of Isaac, b. 4 July 1705.

  Martha, b. 16 Mar. 1694, bapt. Oct. 1695.

  Mary, bapt. 10 May 1696; m. 10 Aug. 1722, Obadiah Platt.

  Abigail, bapt. 6 Aug. 1699.

  ✕Eleazer, b. 15 Feb. 1701 [1701/2], bapt. 19 Apr. 1702, d. at Redding, 2 Oct. 1774 ae. 74; m. Eunice Bulkley, dau. of Capt. Gershom, bapt. 4 Jan. 1701/2.

  Sarah, bapt. 9 Apr. 1704.

  Margery, bapt. 26 Jan. 1706/7, d. at Redding, 5 Dec. 1769 ae. 62; m. 22 Aug. 1728, Timothy Platt.

  David, bapt. 20 Mar. 1708/9, d. y.

  ✕Samuel, bapt. 19 Apr. 1713,* d. at Greenfield in 1756; adm'n granted to Mary, 6 July 1756; m. (called son of John) 10 Nov. 1737, Mary Winton, dau. of John, b. 4 Sept. 1717.

Smith, Samuel, s. of Samuel.

He was bapt. at Fairfield Church, as Samuel, Jr., 24 Feb. 1694/5; d. at Fairfield, 19 Dec. 1711. He m. (1) 9 Jan. 1696, Abigail Lyon. She was dau. of Richard, and d. 6 Mar. 1698.

He m. (2) 27 Oct. 1699, Deborah Jackson. She was dau. of Moses, b. 8 Feb. 1678; and m. (2) by 1716, Thomas Bailey.

Adm'n granted, 6 Feb. 1711/2, to widow Deborah and to her brother-in-law John Smith. Distribution ordered to six daus. On 19 July 1716, Deborah and Rebecca Smith chose father-in-law Thomas Bailey guardian, and he was appointed for Sarah, Esther, and Hellinah; he was also granted adm'n in place of Sergt. John Smith and Deborah Bailey. In 1717 Deborah asked to have Bailey removed as her guardian, and chose Robert Jackson. Distribution, 1 Apr. 1729: Abigail wife of William Odell, Deborah wife of Hezekiah Odell, Rebecca wife of Thaddeus Gregory, Sarah

---

  * The Greenfield Church records, in copying the baptisms of John Smith's children, erroneously gives bapt. of Samuel as 8 Feb. 1712/3; this record belongs to the son of John "Jr."

Redfield heir to Sarah dec'd wife of James Redfield, Esther wife of Enoch Gregory, and Elliner wife of Ebenezer French.

Children by first wife:

Abigail, b. 23 Sept. 1696, bapt. 25 Oct. 1696, d. Jan. 1736 in 40 yr. (g. s., Stratfield); m. at Stratfield, 2 Oct. 1718, William Odell.
Sarah, b. 23 Dec. 1697, bapt. 17 Apr. 1698, d. Mar. 1700.

Children by second wife:

Deborah, b. 15 Nov. 1699, bapt. 19 Nov. 1699, d. June 1700.
Deborah, b. 28 Mar. 1702, bapt. 29 Mar. 1702, d. 27 June 1756 in 55 yr. (g. s.); m. Hezekiah Odell.
Rebecca, b. 20 Mar. 1704, bapt. 26 Mar. 1704; m. Thaddeus Gregory.
Sarah, b. 2 Jan. 1706/7, bapt. 5 Jan. 1706/7; m. James Redfield.
Esther, bapt. 22 May 1709, d. 16 July 1790 in 83 yr. (g. s., Stratfield); m. Enoch Gregory.
Eleanor, bapt. 8 Apr. 1711; m. Ebenezer French.

Smith, Joseph, s. of Samuel.

Died at Fairfield abt. 1721; m. Hannah ———. She m. (2) Samuel Davis.

Inv. 6 Feb. 1720/1. Adm'n granted to widow Hannah and Sergt. Samuel Osborn; the widow's mother-in-law Sarah Smith was living. Two of the sons, Benjamin and Samuel, being in their nonage, the Court appointed Thomas Williams, Jr., for their guardian, 19 June 1721.

Benjamin Smith of Fairfield, and Samuel Stuart, Jr., and wife Elizabeth of Norwalk, children of Joseph Smith of Fairfield dec'd, conveyed land 1732, reserving dower right of gr. mother Sarah Smith and mother Hannah Davis. Benjamin Smith also conveyed 1732 land in Greenfield, excepting dower set to mother the wife of Samuel Davis, and to my gr. mother Smith. "Simon" Stuart of Norwalk and wife Abigail of Norwalk conveyed 1742 land distributed to her from her father Joseph Smith dec'd and bro. David Smith dec'd.

Children, bapt. at Fairfield:

Joseph, bapt. 9 June 1706.
✕Benjamin, bapt. 2 May 1708; m. 1 Jan. 1730, Sarah Gray.
Elizabeth, bapt. 26 Nov. 1710; m. abt. 1727, Samuel Stewart of Wilton. They conveyed, 15 Dec. 1727, right in homestead of her father

Joseph Smith, also their right in David's share, reserving dower right of Grandmother Smith and Mother Davis.

Samuel, bapt. 1 Nov. 1713.

David, bapt. 24 June 1716, d. y.

Abigail, bapt. 22 Mar. 1718/9; m. (rec. Wilton) 15 Nov. 1739, Simeon Stewart.

Smith, John, s. of John.

Born 8 Mar. 1688/9; living 1758 in Dutchess County, N. Y. Called "Mill" John Smith, to distinguish him from others of the name, he m. (rec. Greenfield) Aug. 1710, Elizabeth Jessup. She was dau. of Edward, b. 11 Feb. 1693/4, and was bapt. at Fairfield Church as wife of John, Jr., 13 Apr. 1712.

John Smith, son of John, dec'd, with the consent of wife Elizabeth, conveyed his homelot to John Bedient.

Children, recorded at Greenfield:

XSamuel, b. 28 Jan. 1711/2, bapt. 8 Feb. 1711/2, d. at Greenfield in 1755; will 27 Apr. 1755, proved 1 July 1755; called "sailor" in Greenfield records and "2d" in Probate records; m. by 1740, Olive Davis, dau. of Samuel, bapt. 1 June 1718.

Elizabeth, b. 15 Aug. 1715, bapt. 2 Oct. 1715; m. 11 Jan. 1733, Joseph Davis.

XDaniel, b. 19 June 1719, bapt. 19 July 1719.

Jehiel, b. 2 Sept. 1721, bapt. 8 Oct. 1721, d. ae. abt. 21 upon return from Expedition to Cuba.

Deborah, b. 10 Mar. 1724, bapt. 24 May 1724, d. 9 Aug. 1748 ae. 23 (g. s.); m. 24 Feb. 1747, John Squire.

Joseph, b. 24 Apr. 1726, bapt. 22 May 1726; adm'n on Est. of Joseph Smith of Fairfield was granted to John Lyon, 6 Aug. 1754; m. at Westport, 3 Oct. 1752, Esther Lyon, dau. of John, bapt. 2 Feb. 1726/7.

Charity, b. 1 Sept. 1729, bapt. 1 Sept. 1729.

John, b. 24 Oct. 1731, bapt. 25 Oct. 1731, d. y.

Noah, b. 24 Oct. 1731, bapt. 25 Oct. 1731.

Grace, b. 11 Dec. 1733, bapt. 16 Dec. 1733.

XJohn, b. 2 Feb. 1736/7, bapt. in infancy; m. 3 May 1759, Molly Hubbell of Stratford.

Smith [STRATFORD].

This surname, so common in adjacent towns, has few early entries in Stratford. Elizabeth Smith, quite likely a widow, m.

1 June 1698, as his second wife, Samuel Peat, Sr. William and Rebecca Smith of Stratford were perhaps children of Walter of Milford. Rebecca m. 26 Mar. 1706, Benjamin Blackman. William Smith m. 6 Nov. 1701, Abigail Blackman; the will of William, 24 Jan. 1748/9, proved 30 Jan. 1748/9, gave to son Josiah Smith his joiner tools; remembered gr. children William and Samuel, sons of his son William Smith; and daus. Abigail wife of Benjamin Bundey, and Elizabeth wife of John Oatman, Jr. Perhaps it was William, Jr., who was a smith and bought land 1726. Joanna, dau. of William, was bapt. at Stratford (rec. Stratfield) 23 July 1704. Josiah m. at Stratfield, 8 Oct. 1735, Prudence Kimberly.

Mr. John Smith m. 5 Jan. 1715/6, Widow Mary Dunlap [b. 14 July 1683, widow of Mr. Archibald Dunlap, and dau. of John and Hannah (Staples) Beach]. He did not long survive; Widow Mary Smith d. 4 Oct. 1725. Daniel Hubbell of Stratfield [husband of Hester Beach] was appointed guardian, 6 Jan. 1726, to John, son of John and Mary Smith dec'd; and the boy chose Benjamin Cogshall of Stratford for guardian, 14 Feb. 1735/6.

John Smith of Stratfield, will 8 Nov. 1731, proved 6 Dec. 1731, named son Peter and dau. Charity. Peter Smith, late of New York City, but now of Stratfield, appears in Stratford Deeds 1728, then disappears.

Smith [NORWALK].

Two early Smith settlers: Richard, whose dau. Elizabeth m. 17 Mar. 1674/5, John Whitney; and Thomas, perhaps father of Samuel who m. Rachel Marvin, bapt. 30 Dec. 1649.

Will of Samuel, 8 May 1730, proved 18 Nov. 1745; sons Samuel, Nehemiah; dau. Rachel; children of dau. Sarah; daus. Lydia, Hannah, Ruth.

Nehemiah Smith m. by 1715, Elizabeth Clapham, bapt. at Fairfield, 19 Sept. 1697. Will of Nehemiah, 26 Jan. 1757, proved 15 Apr. 1757; wife Elizabeth; son Nehemiah (long gone from me), son Peter, land in New Canaan; son Matthew; son Daniel; daus. Elizabeth Street, Lydia Burr, Rebecca Hanford, Rachel Street.

In 1668 Winthrop mentioned Joseph Smith of Jamaica, L. I., as brother of Goody Higbee, and also called Smith's wife Ruth. He prob. m. Ruth Beardsley, dau. of William of Stratford. He, lately of Long Island, in 1675 bought land in Norwalk. He may have been son of Thomas and bro. of Samuel of Norwalk. In 1729, Samuel Smith of Norwalk, formerly of Jamaica, L. I., son to Ebenezer Smith of Jamaica, dec'd, chose Nehemiah Smith of Norwalk for his guardian.

Smith, Henry.

Of Stamford, will 4 July 1687; son John Smith; gr. son John Knapp; dau. Hannah Laurence. Inv. 5 July 1687. His wife Ann d. second week in June 1685. In 1664 Ann was mentioned as having by a previous marriage, children Rebecca, Ruth, and Abraham, surname not stated.

Children:

> John, d. at Stamford, 3 Nov. 1711; m. (1) Elizabeth ———, who d. 6 Oct. 1703; m. (2) Phebe ———.
> Hannah, m. (1) Caleb Knapp; m. (2) Thomas Lawrence.
> Samuel, d. 16 Oct. 1658.
> Mary, d. 3 Dec. 1658.
> Daughter, d. 9 Aug. 1661.

Sprague, William.

He m. Hannah Hide, dau. of Humphrey.

He had land by gift from his father-in-law Humphrey Hide, recorded 23 Oct. 1680; and purchased from Robert Seeley prior to Feb. 1679/80. Samuel Coley sold his share in the homelot of his gr. father Humphrey Hide to William Sprague, 25 June 1696.

Children, recorded at Fairfield:

> Humphrey, b. 8 June 1680.
> Ann, b. 12 Mar. 1683; m. Joseph Ogden.

Squire, George. Sergt., Fairfield Trainband.

He was of Concord by 1641, and rem. to Fairfield with the Rev. Mr. Jones' contingent.

Born abt. 1618; he, ae. 68, testified 14 Jan. 1686 [1686/7], together with wife Ann.

Ann Squire had a small legacy in the will of Ann Wheeler of Fairfield 1659.

Will 7 Aug. 1691; son Thomas, had rec'd portion; sons John, Jonathan; son-in-law John Seeley, having married my dau. Sarah; son Samuel; gr. son George Squire all right given to my son George,—this gr. son "hath ben specially for sum years formerly very weakly". Witnesses: Nathan Gold, Sr., and John Thompson. Inv. 4 Nov. 1691, calls him Sergt.

Samuel Squire, as Exec'r of will of father George, conveyed 25 Sept. 1694 to cousin [nephew] George Squire, all right my father had in land given to my bro. George dec'd.

Children (one son, not named, was b. at Concord, 11 Mar. 1642/3):

+Thomas.
+George, b. abt. 1647.
+John.
+Samuel, b. 27 Jan. [1651/2]. (Col. Rec.)
+Jonathan.
  Sarah, d. abt. 1690; m. abt. 1685, John Seeley.

Squire, William.

Of Eastchester; his widow Barbara was about to marry John Clark, formerly of Westchester, 11 Aug. 1680,* and bound the realty to the overseers until her children should come of age.

On 7 Oct. 1686, Henry Jackson of Fairfield having died, to whom Mary Squire was apprenticed, her mother Barbara Squire, widow, chose John Jackson for her dau. to serve out her time with.

Squire, Thomas, s. of George.   Sergt., Woodbury Trainband.

Propounded for freeman, Conn., May 1672.

He d. at Woodbury, 9 Apr. 1712; m. Elizabeth ———, who d. as "Aged Widow" Jan. 1743. Elizabeth Squire received a cow by will 1689 of Henry Wakelee.

Inv. of Sergt. Thomas who d. 9 Apr. 1712, taken 12 June 1712; widow Elizabeth made oath.

Prob. m. a first wife and had a child:

  Mary, m. in 1688, Nathan Bailey, of Westchester. Marriage covenant
    made 8 Mar. 1687/8 between Mary Squire, now living at Mr.

---

* This record is in a group of records belonging to 1686-87; and as Barbara was still unmarried Oct. 1686, we suspect that the date was misread and should be 1686.

William Barnes' house in Westchester, dau. of Thomas Squire of Woodbury, and Nathan Bailey of Westchester, by which Bailey agreed to settle £140 upon Mary as her dower at his decease. On 5 Dec. 1688, Nathan Bailey and Mary his wife made agreement, she relinquishing all right of dower on condition that she have liberty to dwell where she please and take employment as she please for an honest livelihood. On 22 Aug. 1689, they annulled their contract of separation, and joined in a deed.

Children, first eight bapt. together at Woodbury, Aug. 1696:

Thomas, b. [by 1680]; Sergt.; m. (rec. Woodbury) 13 Sept. 1704, Hannah Welton; she was dau. of John, b. at Waterbury, 1 Apr. 1683, d. after 1742.

Samuel, b. [say 1682], d. at Woodbury, 26 May 1727; Sergt.; m. by 1714, Elizabeth Mitchell, dau. of John, bapt. May 1693, d. in 1761; she m. (2) 24 Apr. 1735, Jonathan Mitchell.

Hannah, m. 12 Apr. 1699, Henry Castle.

Ebenezer, b. [say 1686]; m.(1) 8 July 1714, Ann Huthwitt; she was dau. of John and d. 3 May 1729; m. (2) Ellen ———, prob. widow of Samuel Hickock.

Martha, b. [say 1688], d. after 1754; m. (rec. Fairfield) 31 Jan. 1712, Jonathan Middlebrook.

Sarah.

Elizabeth, d. at Woodbury, 16 June 1707.

John, b. [say 1695], d. at Woodbury, in 1760; will 29 Apr. 1754, proved 26 Dec. 1760; m. (rec. Woodbury) 23 Sept. 1729, Elizabeth Wakelee. She was widow of Joseph Wakelee and dau. of John Clark, b. 1 Dec. 1702.

Joseph, b. at Woodbury, 25 Dec. 1698, d. there 1746; Inv. 10 June 1746; m. by 1727, Mary ———.

Squire, George, s. of George.

Born abt. 1647; testified in Benfield case, May 1666, ae. 19; propounded for freeman, Conn., May 1672; d. in 1674.

Inv. of George, Jr., taken 25 Dec. 1674 by William Ward and Samuel Morehouse. Sergt. George Squire, his father, made oath.

Probable child:

✕George, settled in Durham abt. 1711; m. at Easthampton, L. I., 29 Jan. 1701/2, Jane Edwards.

Squire, John, s. of George.

He settled in Easthampton, L. I., and is said to have m. Ann Edwards, dau. of William.

Perhaps he was the John who d. at Saybrook, June 1702; and if so, it may have been his widow who m. Capt. Josiah Hobart. Recompence and Thomas Squire, children of Mrs. Hobart by her former husband, were bapt. at Easthampton, 9 Dec. 1705, her eldest having been [previously] bapt. by Mr. James. As Rev. Thomas James d. in 1696, the eldest Squire child was bapt. before then; and may be a John Squire who was b. abt. 1692.*

Squire, Samuel, s. of George. Deputy for Fairfield, May 1700, May 1702, May 1703, Oct. 1704. Ens., east company, Fairfield, May 1705. County Marshal.

In 1696 he was appointed attorney by his "brother" Joseph Seeley. He m. Sarah Seeley, dau. of Capt. Nathaniel.

Capt. Samuel d. at Fairfield, 8 Nov. 1711.

Will 23 Oct. 1711, proved 5 Dec. 1711; wife; sons Joseph, John, Samuel; daus. Sarah and Rebecca Squire; wife and son Joseph, Exec'rs.

All his children were bapt. at Fairfield Church, the first four on 16 Apr. 1704, and the last two as children of "Ens." Samuel.

Children:

   ×Joseph, b. [say 1689], d. at Fairfield, abt. June 1720; cordwainer; will 27 May 1720, proved 5 July 1720; m. (1) 1715, Abigail Hill, dau. of William, b. 8 Jan. 1694/5; m. (2) at Fairfield Church, 19 Nov. [1718 or 1719], Sarah Jennings, dau. of Joseph, bapt. 22 Aug. 1697, d. in 1773; she m. (2) Zechariah Mead.

   ×John, b. [say 1691], d. at Fairfield in 1748; will 5 Apr. 1745, proved 5 Apr. 1748; m. abt. 1717, Sarah Rumsey, dau. of Isaac, bapt. 30 Aug. 1696.

   ×Samuel, b. abt. 1693, d. at Fairfield, 27 Jan. 1773 in 81 yr. (g. s.); Lt.; Inv. 6 Apr. 1773; m. abt. 1714, Mary Silliman, dau. of Daniel, b. abt. 1692/3, d. 26 June 1748 in 56 yr. (g. s.).

   Sarah.

   Rebecca, bapt. 17 June 1705, d. at Redding, 26 Mar. 1779 in 75 yr. (g. s.); m. 12 May 1730, Lemuel Sanford.

   Benjamin, bapt. 15 June 1707, d. y.

Squire, Jonathan, s. of George.

Prob. m. Mary Seeley, dau. of Capt. Nathaniel. [Jonathan named a son Nathaniel, who in turn named a son Seeley.]

* For this plausible theory we are indebted to Mrs. C. W. Nichols, of New Britain, Conn.

Mary wife of Jonathan Squire made a charge against Philip Lewis, July 1703, which appears not to have been prosecuted.

Jonathan, Sr., of Fairfield West Parish [Westport], agreement 26 Aug. 1723 with sons Jonathan and Nathaniel, the latter to pay to his sister Abigail, and if Nathaniel die childless, half to my dau. Ann's children and half to Jonathan's children. [Fairfield Deeds.]

Children, three bapt. at Fairfield:

    Ann, bapt. at Woodbury, Apr. 1685; m. ———.

    Mary, bapt. with Ann, Apr. 1685, d. y.

    ✕Jonathan, b. [say 1687], rem. by 1739 to Cornwall; m. (1) at Stratfield, 1 Feb. 1710/1, Bethia Odell; she was dau. of John, b. 27 Feb. 1692/3; m. (2) after 1730, Hannah, widow of Samuel Hall, and dau. of Luke Guire, b. abt. 1697, living 1752.

    ✕Nathaniel, b. [say 1690]; m. at Fairfield, 20 Jan. 1723, Sarah Higgins.

    Mary, bapt. 9 Sept. 1694.

    Abigail, bapt. 11 Nov. 1694, d. 1 Aug. 1777 in 84 yr. (g. s., Stratfield); m. 10 Jan. 1720, Stephen Hubbell.

    Deborah, bapt. 23 July 1699, d. at Woodbury, 9 Feb. 1724/5. Inv. taken at Fairfield, 18 Feb. 1724/5. Adm'n granted to her father Jonathan.

    ✕?Seeley, of Norwalk; m. Phebe Sears, who m. (2) at Wilton, 24 Nov. 1747, Thaddeus Hubbell.

Stacy, Simon.

Of Fairfield, Inv. 14 Apr. 1691. No land; eleven books were the largest item. Taken by John Thompson and Thomas Jones. Jonathan Fanton appointed Adm'r.

Was he son of Simon of Ipswich, Mass.?

Staples, Thomas. Deputy (Fairfield) to Conn. Leg., Sept. 1649, Sept. 1650, Oct. 1661.

He was an original settler of Fairfield, 1639.

In 1653 when Goody Knapp was tried and executed as a witch, Staples' wife placed herself under suspicion, to which her unusual intelligence had already made her liable, by expressing doubt, saying for example "it was long before she could believe this poor woman was a witch, or that there were any witches, till the word of God convinced her."* Mr. Ludlow reported the suspicions of her to Rev. Mr. Davenport, but Thomas Staples boldly brought the matter to an issue by suing Mr. Ludlow for slander in the New Haven Colony Court, which awarded him damages of £10. In 1692, during the witchcraft epidemic, Mrs. Staples was accused again, together with her dau. Mary Harvey and gr. dau. Hannah Harvey, but no evidence sufficient for indictment was produced.

In 1664 Winthrop treated Staples' wife of Fairfield and the children, specifying their ages thus: Mary 18, Mehitabel 12-13, Hester 8, John ½.

The estate of Thomas was settled, 12 Jan. 1688 [1688/9] by arbitrators between Mary widow of Thomas Staples, Sr., Thomas Staples, Mehitabel Staples, and John Staples, and Mr. Josiah Harvey and John Beach in right of their now wives.

Will of Mary Staples, 12 Sept. 1696; sons Thomas, John; daus. Mary wife of Josiah Harvey and Hannah wife of John Beach; friend Widow Mary Slawson, as a token of my love, for her kindness to me; gr. child Hannah Harvey; gr. child Mehitabel Fanton; to Nathan Gold, a book by Dr. Preston. [Not recorded; from Files.]

Children:

    Mary, b. abt. 1646; m. Josiah Harvey.
    Mehitabel, b. abt. 1651, d. by 1693; m. after 1688, Jonathan Fanton.
  +Thomas, b. [Mar. 1650/1, if g. s. is correctly read].
    Hester, b. abt. 1656, d. y.
    Hannah, b. [say 1659]; m. (rec. Stratford), 18 Dec. 1679, John Beach.
  +John, b. abt. 1663.

Staples, Thomas, s. of Thomas.

He m. (1) Sarah, widow of Richard Ogden, 2d.

He m. (2) Mary, widow of Michael Clugston, and dau. of Rev. Samuel Wakeman.

He d. at Fairfield, 6 Jan. 1737 [1737/8], ae. 86 yrs. 10 mos. (g. s.).

---

* The Bible affords support to the belief in witchcraft. Accused witches in colonial times were usually either weak-minded women, or else of a superior mental endowment which made them seem eccentric in the eyes of their contemporaries.

Child [by first wife] :

> ╳Thomas, bapt. 14 Sept. 1701, d. 31 July 1772 (Perry Diary) ; m.
> Deborah Sturges, dau. of Joseph, bapt. 1 June 1708.

Child [by second wife] :

> Samuel, bapt. 30 May 1708, d. at Easton, 21 Feb. 1787 in 79 yr.
> (g. s.) ; will of Samuel of North Fairfield Parish, 7 Feb. 1787,
> proved 5 Mar. 1787, gave £300 for support of the ministry in that
> parish; £25 for a bell to give notice of Divine Service; and
> residue for schooling of poor children in North Fairfield and
> Norfield parishes, appointing Samuel Wakeman, Ephraim Lyon and
> David Silliman, guardians of the poor [Trustees] ; friend Lloyd
> Wakeman, Exec'r.

Staples, John, s. of Thomas.

Born at Fairfield abt. 1663, d. there 19 Feb. 1747/8 in 88 yr.
(g. s.) ; m. (1) Abigail Canfield, dau. of Thomas, of Milford,
bapt. 3 Dec. 1665. The will of Phebe Canfield, 28 July 1690,
named her dau. Abigail Staples.

He m. (2) (by marriage contract, 10 June 1724) widow Elizabeth Rowland; prob. widow of Israel Rowland, and perhaps dau.
of Robert Turney.

Will 4 May 1744, proved 18 Apr. 1748; wife Elizabeth; son
Thomas; five daus., Abigail wife of Ignatius Nichols, Hannah
Staples, Eunice wife of Zechariah Clark, Damaris Staples, and
Phebe wife of Isaac Jennings, Jr.

Moses Jennings, one of the heirs of John Staples, asked for distribution, 21 Aug. 1770, of part of John's Est. which he gave by
will in common among some of his children.

Abigail Staples renewed her Covenant at Fairfield Church, 28
July 1695, and her first four children were bapt. that date.

Children [by first wife], bapt. at Fairfield:

> Abigail, b. abt. 1689, d. at Greenfield, 12 Dec. 1745 ae. 57 (g. s.) ; m.
> Ignatius Nichols.
> ╳Thomas, b. abt. 1691, d. at Greenfield, 23 Nov. 1773 ae. 84; Inv. 8
> Dec. 1774; m. 24 May 1723, Deborah Rowland, bapt. 3 Oct. 1703,
> d. 12 Aug. 1774 ae. 68.
> Hezekiah, b. abt. 1693, d. y.
> Mehitabel, b. abt. 1695; m. at Fairfield, 1 Apr. 1722 (rec. Stratford,
> 30 May 1723), George Barley of Stratford.
> Hannah, bapt. 14 Feb. 1696/7.

John, bapt. 16 Nov. 1701, d. 27 June 1737 in 36 yr. (g. s., Fairfield).
Adm'n granted, 12 July 1737, to Isaac Jennings, Jr.   Agreement of
heirs, 2 May 1739; Thomas Staples, Ignatius Nichols and Abigail
his wife, George Barlow [signed Barley] and Mehitabel his wife,
Isaac Jennings, Jr., and Phebe his wife, all of Fairfield, Zachariah
Clark and Eunice his wife, and Hannah Staples, of Stratford, and
Damaris Staples of Milford; bros. and sisters of John [Pro. Files].
Damaris, bapt. 21 May 1704.
Eunice, bapt. 21 May 1704;   m. (rec. Stratford) 21 Nov. 1727,
Zechariah Clark.
Phebe, bapt. 16 Mar. 1706/7, d. in 1768; m. at Fairfield, 1 June 1731,
Isaac Jennings, Jr.

Stevens [Killingworth Family].

John, of Guilford 1646, d. 2 Sept. 1670; had four children, of
whom:

Thomas, of Killingworth 1665, d. 18 Nov. 1685; m. Mary
Fletcher, dau. of John of Milford, and had thirteen children, of
whom the youngest son, Jonathan, b. 2 Feb. 1674/5, d. 2 June
1746, m. Deborah Stiles, dau. of Isaac of Stratford; the eldest son
of Thomas was:

James, b. 21 Feb. 1651, went to sea 1695 and was never heard
from; Inv. 21 May 1699; names and ages of the six children
stated.   He m. Mary, perhaps the dau. of Henry Wakelee, who
was called Mary Stevens in the will of her father 1689.   Adm'n
on Mary's Est. was granted, 18 Nov. 1729, to James Stevens.
Distribution was ordered to the son and daus., and was made
1 July 1737, the daus. being named as Mary Chapman, Hannah
Sanford, Sarah Rogers, Patience Baldwin, and Mercy Turney.

On 12 Mar. 1724/5, Widow Mary Stevens conveyed lands to
her son James Stevens of Killingworth, son Robert Chapman ⁀f
East Haddam, son Thomas Sanford of Fairfield, son Daniel
Baldwin of Milford, dau. Mercy Stevens of Killingworth, and
dau. Sarah Rogers of New London.

Children, recorded at Killingworth:

Mary, b. 3 Dec. 1674; m. Robert Chapman.
James, b. 11 Oct. 1676, d. Sept. 1764; m. Hannah Barnes, dau. of
John and Mercy (Betts) Barnes of New Haven, b. 23 Dec. 1670;
with whom he conveyed property in New Haven in 1721 and 1730.
No authority has been found for the usual statement that his wife

was Hannah Hull; but his son James, b. 27 Mar. 1706, m. 5 Nov. 1729, Hannah Hurd.

Hannah, b. 8 Apr. 1679; m. Thomas Sanford.

Sarah, b. 20 Jan. 1680 [1680/1]; m. 27 May 1699, James Rogers.

Patience, b. 24 Apr. 1683, d. at Meriden, 13 Mar. 1771 ae. 89 (g. s.); m. Daniel Baldwin.

Mercy, b. 7 Mar. 1685 [1685/6]; m. between 1725 and 1731, Thomas Turney, who was of Killingworth in 1731 when he appeared with Mercy in connection with Mary Stevens's Est.

Stewart, Robert.

First appeared in Milford, and on 8 Mar. 1659/60 bought the homelot of Samuel Hale in Norwalk, where he d. in 1688.

He m. at Norwalk, 12 June 1661, Bethia Rumble, dau. of Thomas of Stratford.

Inv. 5 Dec. 1688; lands appraised 27 Aug. 1688. Widow Bethia; nine children, ages: James 26, John 21, Samuel 11 next May, Abigail Cosier 25, Deborah Stewart 19, Elizabeth Stewart 17, Phebe 15, Sarah 13, Rachel 3.

Children, first six recorded at Norwalk:

+James, b. 19 Mar. 1662/3.

Abigail, b. middle of Aug. 1664; m. Richard Cosier.

John, b. 18 Mar. 1666/7, d. at Wilton, 17 June 1749 ae. 83; m. Abiah ———, who d. 30 July 1748 ae. abt. 60.

Deborah, b. May 1669; m. (rec. Stratford) Nov. 1708, Joseph Beardsley, Jr.

Elizabeth, b. latter end of Sept. 1671.

Phebe, b. middle of Feb. 1673 [1673/4].

Sarah, b. abt. 1676.

+Samuel, b. May 1678.

Rachel, b. abt. 1685; m. Daniel Raymond.

Stewart, James, s. of Robert. Ens., north company, Norwalk, May 1710.

Born at Norwalk, 19 Mar. 1662/3, d. there in 1751; m. Experience ———.

Will 19 Jan. 1749/50, proved 12 June 1751; wife Experience; two sons James and Robert; daus. Hannah wife of John Taylor, Deborah wife of James Pickett, Mary wife of John Morehouse; children of dec'd dau. Eunice late wife of John Parret; son Robert and son-in-law John Taylor, Exec'rs.

James Stuart of Kent, John Taylor and Hannah his wife, Robert Stuart, Deborah Pickett, Elizabeth, Hannah and Sarah Parrot, all of Norwalk, John Morehouse and Mary his wife, and John Parrot, all of Fairfield, conveyed to John Taylor, 3d, 6 Apr. 1753.

Children:

> James, d. at Kent, 31 Jan. 1776; settled in Kent by 1741; m. (1) Eleanor Guire, dau. of Luke of Fairfield, b. abt. 1691, living 1752; m. (2) Jemima ———, who d. 24 Dec. 1775.
>
> Hannah, b. abt. 1699, d. at Westport, 2 May 1774 ae. 75; m. 19 Jan. 1726/7, John Taylor, Jr.
>
> Eunice, d. at Norwalk, 30 Mar. 1735/6; m. 4 Mar. 1723/4, John Parrot.
>
> Deborah, m. 14 Apr. 1726, James Pickett.
>
> Robert, m. abt. 1738, Sarah Lounsbury, b. at Stamford, 13 June 1708, d. after 1791, who had been previously the wife of ——— Britto, and was mother of Stephen Britto.
>
> Mary, m. John Morehouse, of Fairfield.

Stewart, Samuel, s. of Robert.

Born at Norwalk, May 1678, d. at Wilton, 5 June 1753 ae. 76. He m. Hannah Bennett, dau. of Thomas, b. at Fairfield, 20 Aug. 1680.

Will 5 Sept. 1748, proved 29 June 1753; eldest son Samuel; 2d son James; 3d son Simeon; youngest son Nathan; dau. Dorothy; gr. children Joseph and Elizabeth Araton, and Samuel and Dorothy St. John, referring to their dec'd mothers; gr. children Mary Araton and Sarah St. John.

Stiles, Francis.

Bapt. at Milbrook, co. Bedford, 1 Aug. 1602, d. prob. at Stratford before 1665. Carpenter, came from London in the *Christian,* 1635, and joined the Windsor settlers, where he had four children born. In 1647 he was of Saybrook, and by 1654 of Stratford.

He m. Sarah ———; who m. (2) Robert Clark, and d. in 1683. She was sister of the first wife of William Hayden of Windsor.

Will of Sarah Clark wife of Robert of Stratford, 5 June 1677, proved 2 Feb. 1682 [1682/3]; "aged and infirm"; sons Samuel, Ephraim, Benjamin, Thomas; children of dau. Hannah Hinman, mentioning Titus; gr. children Sarah and Hannah Blackman;

children of dau. Mary Washburn, mentioning Sarah; sister's children, Daniel and Nathaniel Hayden, and Mary Everts at Guilford.

Children:

    Mary, m. Hope Washburn.
    Daughter, m. abt. 1657, James Blackman.
    Hannah, m. Edward Hinman.
    +Thomas.
    +Samuel, b. abt. 1643.
    +Ephraim, b. at Windsor, 3 Aug. 1645.
    +Benjamin, b. abt. 1651.

Stiles, Samuel, s. of Francis. Ens., Woodbury Trainband, Oct. 1690; Lt., May 1705.

Married at Stratford, last of Dec. 1664, Elizabeth Sherwood, dau. of Thomas. Mrs. Elizabeth d. at Woodbury, 3 June 1719. Lt. Samuel d. at Woodbury, 14 Feb. 1726/7 ae. 84.

Ebenezer Bronson and Francis Stiles, both of Woodbury, purchased from Samuel Castle of Danbury, 10 Aug. 1699; and Ebenezer Bronson entered in Woodbury records land purchased "from his father" Ens. Samuel Stiles, 27 Nov. 1704. Bronson had land by gift from his father Lt. Samuel Stiles, 2 May 1710.

Stiles, Thomas, s. of Francis.

He d. at Stratford in 1683.

Isaac Bennett, ae. abt. 28, testified 24 Oct. 1683, that he watched with Stiles about three days before he died, Hope Washburn and Mary his wife being present, and he desired Bennett to write his will. He gave to father-in-law Robert Clark the £20 his mother willed him, Clark having been a good father to him; lands to Francis son of his bro. Benjamin; bros. Samuel and Ephraim Stiles; bro. and sister Hope and Mary Washburn. Robert Clark was appointed Adm'r.

Stiles, Ephraim, s. of Francis. Deputy (Stratford), Oct. 1686, Jan. 1687, Oct. 1690, Oct. 1692, Mar. 1693, May 1695, May 1696, May 1697, Oct. 1699, Oct. 1702, May 1704, May and June

1709, Oct. 1710; Committee of Safety, Fairfield County, May 1704.

Born at Windsor, 3 Aug. 1645; Mr. Ephraim d. at Stratford, 21 June 1714; ae. 69 (g. s., which in Orcutt's *History* gives year as 1745, an obvious misreading).

Married (1) at Stratford, 28 July 1669, Ruth "sometimes ye wife of Obadiah Wheeler dec'd." She was bapt. at Milford, 5 Feb. 1642/3, dau. of John Rogers of Milford, and was widow first of Thomas Goodwin of Milford, and next of Obadiah Wheeler.

Married (2) Bathsheba Tomlinson, dau. of Henry, b. 3 Jan. 1661/2. She m. (2) 1 Dec. 1714, Mr. Benjamin Curtis, and d. 9 Feb. 1735 ae. 74 (g. s.). Adm'n on her Est. was granted to David Judson, 4 Mar. 1734/5.

Mr. Ephraim d. at Stratford, 21 June 1714.

He was called bro. in will of Sergt. Edward Hinman 1681; bro. in will of James Blackman 1689; and son in will of Henry Tomlinson 1681.

Will 23 July 1712, proved 30 June 1714; wife Bathsheba; dau. Elizabeth Curtis and her son Stiles Curtis, "Mr. Curtiss having promised before her marriage to acknowledge his son Ephraim as his Eldest son"; daus. Sarah Welles and Phebe Stiles.

Ephraim Curtis, Thomas Welles, and David Judson agreed to distribute Est. of mother Bathsheba Curtis, 24 Mar. 1734/5.

Children of Ephraim and Bathsheba, recorded at Stratford:

> Elizabeth, b. 18 Feb. 1687 [1687/8], d. at Stratford, 5 Oct. [1778] in 91 yr. (g. s.) ; m. 26 June 1707, Ephraim Curtis.
> Sarah, b. 4 Nov. 1693; m. 31 Aug. 1710, Thomas Welles.
> Phebe, b. 25 Mar. 1696, d. at Stratford, 20 May 1765 ae. 69 yrs. 2 mos. (g. s.) ; m. 29 Oct. 1713, David Judson.

Stiles, Benjamin, s. of Francis.

Born abt. 1651, d. at Stratford, 13 Apr. 1711 ae. abt. 60. He m. Abigail Rogers, dau. of John of Milford, b. 20 June 1654. Widow Abigail d. at Woodbury, 7 Oct. 1723.

Inv. 4 Dec. 1711, of Benjamin Stiles of Stratford who was late of Woodbury and d. in Stratford, 13 Apr. 1711. Children: Francis Stiles, Sarah wife of Thomas Wheeler, Ruth wife of John

Wheeler, Abigail wife of Samuel Munn. Adm'n granted, 21 Nov. 1711, to Thomas Wheeler and Francis Stiles.

On 20 Dec. 1711, the three sons-in-law with their wives conveyed to Francis Stiles of Woodbury, land from father Benjamin Stiles of Stratford dec'd. [Woodbury Deeds.]

Children, bapt. at Woodbury:

> Sarah, bapt. Apr. 1681; m. at Woodbury, 20 Aug. 1701, Thomas Wheeler.
>
> Francis, bapt. May 1682, d. at Woodbury, 9 Sept. 1748; Lt.; m. at Woodbury, 21 Sept. 1709, Mary Johnson.
>
> Ruth, bapt. May 1683; m. at Woodbury, 17 Nov. 1704, John Wheeler.
>
> Thomas, bapt. Nov. 1685, d. y.
>
> Abigail, bapt. Apr. 1689; m. abt. 1708, Samuel Munn.

Stiles, Isaac, s. of John.

His father John (bro. of Francis) was bapt. at Milbrook, co. Bedford, 25 Dec. 1595, and d. at Windsor, 4 June 1662. Isaac was called (by the Episcopal clergyman who bapt. him 27 Jan. 1710/1) the first male child born in Conn., which would place his birth in 1635, though the clergyman (Mr. Sharp) supposed him to be 80 at baptism.

Married Hannah Palmer, dau. of Henry, b. at Wethersfield, 14 Aug. 1645, and received from his father-in-law land in Wethersfield, where he lived until abt. 1673; rem. to Stratford, and d. there 5 Jan. 1714/5.

Children, recorded at Stratford:*

> +Isaac, b. abt. 1664.
>
> Sarah, b. 18 [no month stated] 1677, d. at Stratford in 1738/9; m. William Perry; no issue. Her will, 28 Oct. 1738, proved 24 Jan. 1738/9; bro. Jonathan Stiles, and his children, Joseph, John, Hannah Smith, and Rebecca Stiles; sister Deborah Stephens; nephew Isaac Stiles; Rev. Mr. Mills of Ripton; Joseph Johnson, Sr., of Derby.
>
> Deborah, b. Jan. 1682 [1682/3], d. at Killingworth, Mar. 1748; m. Jonathan Stevens of Killingworth.
>
> Jonathan, b. 10 Mar. 1688 [1688/9], rem. to N. J.; m. (1) Rebecca Canfield, dau. of Thomas, Jr., b. at Milford, 28 Jan. 1682 [1682/3]; is said to have m. (2) Elizabeth (Taylor), widow of his cousin

---

* Prob. between Isaac and the first recorded child (Sarah) there were also sons John and Joseph, who d. early, and perhaps others who d. young.

John Stiles of Windsor. Jonathan and Rebecca had children rec.
at Stratford: Joseph, b. 7 Oct. 1706; John, b. 8 May 1709; Thomas,
b. 13 Dec. 1711; Rebecca, b. 14 Sept. 1719; Ephraim, b. 12 Feb.
1723/4. He was of Hanover, N. J., 1735; of Pequanock, N. J.,
1746.

Stiles, Isaac, s. of Isaac.

Born abt. 1664, d. at Stratford in 1691; m. Hannah Rose, dau.
of Robert, b. [say 1668]. She m. (2) (rec. Derby) 9 May 1693,
Samuel Harger, and (3) 28 Mar. 1700, John Tibbals.

Inv. of Isaac, Jr., 15 Dec. 1691; included a right in homelot of
Robert Rose, value at present unknown. Widow Hannah made
oath, she to administer with Isaac Bennett. Division ordered,
22 Nov. 1710, to the son and dau. Lt. Agur Tomlinson on behalf
of the orphans of Stiles appealed to the Court of Assistants in
Hartford.

Children:

> Dorcas, d. at Killingworth, 7 Nov. 1748; m. (rec. Killingworth) 7
> Jan. 1712/3, John Sheather, Jr., of Killingworth.
> Isaac, b. abt. 1691, d. at Woodbury, in 1787; m. (1) (rec. Stratford)
> 25 Feb. 1718/9, Abigail Adams of Milford; m. (2) before 1724,
> Sarah ———.

Stites.

JOHN of Hempstead, L. I., was father of Richard (1646-1702),
of Hempstead; who was father of William (who follows), and
presumably also of Margaret who m. 8 Dec. 1702, Francis Hall of
Stratfield.

WILLIAM (1676-1727), of Hempstead, m. Mary Hall, dau. of
Isaac, b. at Fairfield, 7 Aug. 1681. They had the following children bapt. at Stratfield:

> John, bapt. 7 Apr. 1706.
> Rebecca, bapt. 23 Nov. 1707.
> Hezekiah, bapt. 25 Dec. 1709.
> Richard, bapt. 17 May 1717.
> Sarah, bapt. 17 May 1717.

Stolion, Mrs.

Mrs. Stolion was in New Haven by Aug. 1641; had an adult
son, inferentially the Abraham who took the oath of allegiance in

1644. She was quite a trader, and involved in several law-suits. On 25 May 1646, she was lying dangerously ill and about to die.

The name being uncommon, we have small scruple in identifying her with the Mrs.* Stolion who had a dwelling house in Fairfield which was sold to Thomas Wheeler, Jr., and by him to Richard Lyon, and by him to Thomas Dunn, who entered it on record 21 Jan. 1653 [1653/4]. Perhaps she was a very early settler in Fairfield, before she appeared in New Haven.

The name also appears early at New London. Fairfield records enter the gift, 7 Apr. 1683, by Edward Stollyon of New London, mariner, to Pascoe Foot of New London, who had married his dau. Margaret, of one-half of the brigantine (30 tons) *Edward & Margaret,* towards her "portion."

Stratton, Cornelius.

Son of John and Sarah of Easthampton, L. I.; d. at Easthampton, 27 Mar. 1704; m. (1) ———.

He m. (2) by 1695, Martha Hull, dau. of Cornelius of Fairfield, and d. at Easthampton, 27 Mar. 1704. She was widow of ——— Smith. Apparently she had a son Samuel by both first and second husbands. She m. (3) ——— Adams, and was called of Huntington, L. I., when adm'n was granted, 28 Aug. 1727, to her sons Joseph and Samuel Stratton. She may have d. before 1710.

There being two of the sons of Cornelius Stratton late of Long Island dec'd providentially cast into this Government, on 6 Dec. 1710 the Fairfield Pro. Court appointed his uncle Samuel Hull of Fairfield guardian for Samuel Stratton.

On 15 Apr. 1718, Samuel Smith and Joseph Stratton of Huntington, L. I., conveyed to Thomas Harvey of Fairfield right from gr. father Cornelius Hull dec'd which he gave to our mother Martha Stratton of Easthampton, L. I., his dau.

Samuel Stratton of Fairfield conveyed 7 Oct. 1723 to Jacob Gray, land laid out to my gr. father Cornelius Hull dec'd and given by will to my mother Martha. On 28 Aug. 1727, Joseph and Samuel Stratton and Samuel Smith, Jr., all of Huntington, L. I., conveyed land given to our mother by Cornelius Hull.

---

* The prefix was written with a capital 'M' followed by a small raised quirk, and may have been intended for 'Mr.' instead of 'Mrs.'; it has been read both ways. So it may have been Mrs. Stolion's husband who early owned the Fairfield lot.

Child [by first wife]:

> Eliphalet, b. prob. by 1695, d. 21 Sept. 1753 ae. 55 (58?); m. 15
> Mar. 1715, Phebe Conkling.*

Children by Martha Hull:

> Joseph, b. by 1697, since he gave a conveyance in 1718; d. at Hunting-
> ton in 1751; m. Elizabeth ———. Among their children were
> John and Cornelius who settled in Fairfield.
> Samuel, b. abt. 1699, d. at New Canaan, 10 Mar. 1791 ae. 92; m. 2
> Apr. 1728, Ruth Platt. He lived in Huntington, L. I., but his will
> was proved in Fairfield.†
> Rebecca, bapt. 8 Aug. 1703, d. 3 Feb. 1721.

Stratton, John.

Of Woodbury, adm'n granted 11 Dec. 1716 to John Hall and
Henry Wakelee. Distribution ordered to widow, son Thomas, and
Henry Wakelee in right of his wife Rachel dec'd, by whom he had
a dau. Rachel.

Mrs. Priscilla Stratton d. at Stratford, 11 Apr. 1738 ae. 86
(g. s.).

Children:

> Rachel, d. at Stratfield, 10 Mar. 1708 [1708/9] ae. [—] (g. s.); m.
> 12 Dec. 1706, Henry Wakelee.
> Thomas, m. at Stratford, 5 Sept. 1717, Mary Johnson; dau. of George,
> b. 10 Oct. 1695.

Strickland, John. Sergt., Wethersfield Trainband, 1636. Deputy to Conn. Leg., Sept. 1641.‡

He was an original settler of Charlestown, Mass., 1630; rem.
to Watertown, and in 1636 to Wethersfield. That same year, as
Sergt. led a band to Saybrook to relieve Mr. Mitchell from depre-

---

* To fit the marriage in 1715, Eliphalet's birth is likely to have occurred earlier
than 1698, the year derived from his alleged age at death. The same conclusion may
be based on Eliphalet's failure to convey any right from Martha Hull in Fairfield,
which leads to the belief that he was son of a former wife. Joseph, a son of Martha,
conveyed in 1718, hence must have been born at least as early as 1697. Eliphalet's
birth must therefore be placed as early as 1695, and probably earlier.

† His will, dated 9 Nov. 1790, refers to himself as old, and now in Huntington;
eldest dau. Ruth, wife of Isaac Mulford Huntting of Great Nine Partners, Dutchess
County; other dau., wife of Samuel Cooke Silliman of Norwalk; son Eliphalet of
Flushing, Queens County, L. I., and Eliphalet's eldest son Samuel.

‡ If he represented Fairfield, as we incline to believe, he was the first Deputy for
Fairfield on record, the next being Henry Gray in 1643.

dations of the Indians.   Probably he took active part in the Pequot War, 1637.

With Edmund, supposedly his brother, he was among the early settlers of Fairfield; for he testified in 1659, being then of Huntington, L. I., and stated that he formerly lived at Uncoway now called Fairfield and was deputed with others to treat with Stratford men about town bounds.   In 1644 he was a Patentee of Hempstead, L. I., where he still lived in 1653.   His son-in-law Jonas Wood drew a lot for him at Southampton in 1650.   He lived a few years at Huntington, then rem. (by 1664) to Jamaica, L. I., where he d. in 1672.

Strickland, Edmund.

Testimony taken in 1672 shows that he was an original lot-owner in Fairfield (1639).   He rem. to Newtown, L. I.

Strong, Benajah.

Born 24 Sept. 1682, son of Thomas of Northampton, Mass.

Married (1) Mehitabel Burr, dau. of Daniel.

Married (2) at Stratfield, 8 Oct. 1713, Sarah Sherman; dau. of Capt. David, b. [say 1691].   She m. (2) Samuel Barlow, and (3) Samuel Rowland.

Adm'n granted, 2 June 1714, to widow Sarah Strong, with Capt. David Sherman and Ephraim Strong.   Adino Strong of Woodbury was appointed guardian of the dau. Mehitabel.

On 21 Apr. 1718, John Andrews of Fairfield, guardian for Mabel dau. of Benajah Strong of Fairfield dec'd, conveyed to Samuel Barlow, Jr., her right excepting dowry of Sarah now wife of said Barlow who was widow of said Strong.   On 19 Dec. 1720, David Sherman of Stratfield, guardian to Bethia, dau. of Benajah Strong dec'd, with Samuel Barlow, Jr., who had purchased share of Mabel Strong, the other dau., and Sarah now wife of said Samuel, conveyed house and lot.

Child by first wife:

> Mehitabel [also called Mabel], bapt. at Fairfield, 15 Nov. 1713.

Child by second wife:

> Bethia, bapt. at Stratfield, 24 Oct. 1714; m. 7 Mar. 1738/9, Nathan Comstock of Wilton.

Stuckey, George.

He was in Windsor by 1640, purchasing land originally granted to John Taylor; built a house and sold to Richard Weller in 1645. That was probably the date of his removal to Fairfield, where he purchased property from Nicholas Knell, and sold it to Giles Smith, who had it recorded in his name 17 Dec. 1651.

We must suppose that he had a wife when he built in Windsor, and that she died; and he appears to have m. (2) the widow [Elizabeth] of a "Goodman" Close who was living in 1645.

He bought land in Stamford, 1650, and his wife Elizabeth d. there 4 Sept. 1656. He m. (3) 29 Oct. 1657, Ann Quinby. She was widow of William Quinby of Stratford. He d. 28 Nov. 1660, and his widow removed with her children to Westchester, N. Y.

Will 23 Aug. 1660; wife Ann; dau. Elizabeth; Mary sister of Thomas Close; Hannah Close; dau.-in-law Mary Close.

Child [by first or second wife] :
    Elizabeth.

Sturges, John.

Born abt. 1624, d. at Fairfield in 1700; m. Deborah Barlow, dau. of John, who called her Deborah Sturges in his will 1674.

He had a legacy in will of Daniel Finch 1667. Testified Nov. 1686, aged 62.

Will 4 Mar. 1697/8; sons Jonathan, Joseph, John; dau. Deborah Redfield, to whom he gave a negro boy; gr. son Christopher Sturges; son-in-law Richard Stratton and his five children by dau. Sarah; dau. Abigail wife of Simon Couch, to whom he gave a negro boy; son Thomas, not known to be living, if he return home. [Not recorded; from Files.]

Children :
    +Jonathan.
    +Joseph, b. abt. 1654.
    Sarah, m. Richard Stratton.
    Deborah, m. (1) Benjamin Seeley; m. (2) James Redfield.
    +John.
    Abigail, b. abt. 1673, d. at Westport, 14 Sept. 1730 ae. abt. 57 (g. s.) ;
        m. (1) Simon Couch; m. (2), Ens. John Andrews.
    Thomas, "absent" 1698.

Sturges, Jonathan, s. of John.   Deputy for Fairfield, May 1707.

He m. (1) Susannah Banks, dau. of John, whose will 1684 named dau. Susannah Sturges and gr. son Jonathan Sturges.

He m. (2) last day of July 1692, Sarah Osborn, dau. of David of Eastchester, b. [say 1673], d. at Milford, 17 June 1727.   She m. (2) Hon. Peter Burr; and (3) 1 June 1726, Gov. Jonathan Law.

He d. at Fairfield, 29 Nov. 1711.

Will 5 Sept. 1711, codicil 20 Oct. 1711; wife Sarah; three daus. Sarah, Abigail, Eunice; three sons, Jonathan, Peter, David; bro. John Sturges.   Inv. 19 Dec. 1711.

Children [by first wife]:

    XJonathan, b. abt. 1679, d. at Fairfield, 8 May 1744 in 65 yr. (g. s.); Lt.; will 13 Oct. 1742, proved 8 May 1744; m. (1) abt. 1704, ———; m. (2) Jerusha Thompson, dau. of John, b. 11 May 1685, d. 16 Feb. 1745 [1745/6] in 62 yr. (g. s.).

    XPeter, b. abt. 1685, d. at Fairfield, 6 May 1757 in 72 yr. (g. s.); adm'n granted 9 May 1757; m. Hannah Jennings, dau. of Joshua, b. abt. 1692, d. 6 Aug. 1771 in 80 yr. (g. s.); her will 30 Nov. 1763, proved 20 Aug. 1771.

Children [by second wife]:

    XDavid, b. 7 Jan. 1695, bapt. (with Sarah) 13 Sept. 1702, d. at Fairfield, 17 Dec. 1721* ae. abt. 27 (g. s.); m. Mary ———, b. abt. 1698, d. 5 Mar. 1721 ae. abt. 23 (g. s.).   Adm'n on David's Est. granted, 22 Jan. 1720/1, to bros. Jonathan Sturges and Andrew Burr.

    Sarah, b. 22 Dec. 1701 [error for 1700], bapt. 13 Sept. 1702, d. at Fairfield, 9 Dec. 1745 ae. 45 yrs. wanting 13 days (g. s.); m. 30 Apr. 1719, Andrew Burr.

    Abigail, b. 8 Sept. 1704, bapt. 10 Sept. 1704, d. at Fairfield, 26 June 1753 in 49 yr. (g. s.); m. 26 Nov. 1725, Thaddeus Burr.

    Eunice, b. 3 June 1709, bapt. 5 June 1709, d. 16 Oct. 1740; m. 13 Apr. 1731, James Dennie.

Sturges, Joseph, s. of John.

Born abt. 1654, d. at Fairfield, 12 May 1728 in 75 yr. (g. s.); m. (1) ———; m. (2) Sarah, widow of David Watkins, and dau. of Jeremiah Judson, b. at Stratford, 7 Apr. 1662.   She renewed her Covenant at Fairfield Church, 24 May 1696.   She

---

* Apparently should be 1720.

must have d. in 1700, and very soon after her death Joseph m.
(3) Mary, widow of Thomas Morehouse, Jr., and dau. of Eliphalet
Hill, b. at Boston, 1 Apr. 1670, d. at Fairfield, 9 July 1746 in 77
yr. (g. s.).

Will 9 Mar. 1727/8, proved 4 June 1728; wife Mary; children
Christopher, David, Jeremiah, Solomon, Benjamin, Esther Lines,
Abigail Osborn, Sarah Sherman, Jane, Deborah; gr. dau. Mary
Dimon.

Will of Mary Sturges, 9 July 1746, proved 22 July 1746; son
Benjamin Sturges, Jr.; gr. dau. Mary Dimon; daus. Esther wife
of William Hill, Abigail wife of Samuel Osborn, Jane wife of
James Smedley, and Deborah wife of Thomas Staples.

Child [by first wife]:

XChristopher, b. [say 1680], d. at Stamford, 4 Apr. 1755; will 13 Feb.
1752, proved 28 Apr. 1755; m. abt. 1701, Mary Godwin, dau. of
Samuel of Eastchester, who d. at Stamford, 17 Feb. 1746.

Children [by second wife], bapt. at Fairfield:

Joseph, bapt. 24 May 1696, d. y.

XDavid, bapt. 24 May 1696; m. Hannah Osborn, bapt. 2 Jan. 1703/4.

XJeremiah, bapt. 24 May 1696; res. Newtown 1769; m. 1 Sept. 1720,
Ann Barlow; dau. of John, 3d, b. 6 Oct. 1699, d. at Westport, Nov.
1764.

XSolomon, bapt. 15 May 1698, d. at Fairfield, 1779; m. 3 Mar. 1725,
Abigail Bradley.

Sarah, bapt. 10 Mar. 1699/1700; m. Benoni Sherman, of Stratford;
rem. to Newtown.

Children [by third wife], bapt. at Fairfield:

Esther, bapt. 2 Mar. 1700/1; m. (1) Benjamin Lines; m. (2)
William Hill.

Abigail, bapt. 14 June 1702; m. abt. 1723, Samuel Osborn.

Jane, bapt. 12 Mar. 1703/4, d. 22 Sept. 1747; m. 20 Oct. 1731, James
Smedley.

Mary, bapt. 30 Sept. 1705; renewed Covenant at Fairfield Church,
25 Aug. 1723; d. at birth of her child as stated in suit brought by
the Executors of the Est. of Joseph Sturges against John Dimon,
reputed father of the child, in 1729; her dau. Mary was bapt. 7
Mar. 1724/5, and was known as Mary Dimon.

Deborah, bapt. 1 June 1708; m. Thomas Staples.

XBenjamin, bapt. 5 Feb. 1709/10, d. in Apr. 1760; will 7 Apr. 1760,
proved 23 Apr. 1760; m. Elizabeth Barlow; dau. of Samuel, bapt.
20 June 1714.

Sturges, John, s. of John.

Will of John, Sr., 12 Mar. 1729/30, proved 5 Jan. 1743/4; wife Abigail; children John, Benjamin, Ebenezer, Eleazer, Elnathan, Margery, Mary, Dorothy, Elizabeth, and Abigail Gregory; mentioned deeds of gift to children.

Will of Abigail, 13 Oct. 1748, proved 17 Sept. 1750; son Elnathan, Exec'r; dau. Margery wife of Christopher Godfrey; dau. Mary wife of Francis Bradley; five daus., Abigail, Margery Mary, Dorothy, and Elizabeth.

Children, bapt. at Fairfield:

Abigail, m. Benjamin Gregory.

Margery, b. abt. 1689, d. at Westport, 4 Nov. 1759 in 71 yr. (g. s.); m. 11 Feb. 1711, Christopher Godfrey.

✕John, b. [say 1692]; m. Sarah ———, who d. at Westport, 16 Dec. 1757.

✕Benjamin, b. 19 Nov. 1694 [Old Style, by age at death], bapt. 30 Dec. 1694, d. at Redding, 20 July 1765 ae. 70 yrs. 7 mos. 20 days (g. s.); m. 9 Feb. 1715, Sarah Adams; dau. of Nathan, b. abt. 1695, d. ("Widow Sturges") 4 Feb. 1775 ae. 80.

Ebenezer, bapt. 23 May 1697, d. y.

Mary, b. (rec. Greenfield) 8 Aug. 1699; m. 29 Apr. 1719, Francis Bradley.

Dorothy, b. (rec. Greenfield) 28 Aug. 1700 [error for 1701], bapt. 28 Sept. 1701; m. at Greenfield, 8 Oct. 1719, David Williams.

Ebenezer, bapt. 30 Oct. 1703; res. 1728, Elizabeth, N. J., and conveyed land bounded on land of his father John Sturges; but Martha, dau. of Ebenezer, was bapt. at Greenfield, 27 Dec. 1731.

✕Eleazer, bapt. 3 Mar. 1705/6, d. after 1774; m. 23 Apr. 1724, Abigail Osborn; dau. of Samuel, bapt. 27 Apr. 1707.

Elizabeth, bapt. 29 Aug. 1708, d. at Westport, 20 July 1787; m. 13 Sept. 1726, Samuel Couch.

✕Elnathan, b. 20 Jan. 1710/1, bapt. 5 Feb. 1710/1; res. 1763 Ridgefield; m. 14 Mar. 1733, Rebecca Turney, b. 4 Aug. 1717.

Summers, Henry.

Bought land in Stratford, 1668; it is not known how, if at all, he was related to Henry Summers of Woburn, Mass.

Married (1) Sarah Gregory, dau. of Judah.

Removed to Milford and m. (2) Mary, widow of Ephraim Wheeler, and dau. of Richard Holbrook, bapt. at Dorchester, 17 Mar. 1650. She conveyed as widow of Henry Summers, mentioning her former name Wheeler, to her son Joseph Summers for his dutiful care, land in Milford, 26 Mar. 1722.

Will 1 Sept. 1713, proved 17 June 1717; wife to be maintained by son Joseph with the provision made for her by her first husband and her own help; one shilling apiece to children, Samuel, Henry, John, children of dau. Sarah, dau. Hannah, Mary Summers, daus. Abigail, Patience, Martha; to son Joseph, all lands in Milford; bro. Joseph Wheeler and son Joseph Summers, Exec'rs. Wheeler refused the trust. The Exec'r reported that he had paid legacies to John Summers, Abigail Hall, Hannah Scovill, Mary Summers, Patience Hubbell, and Martha Morehouse; and tendered legacies to Samuel and Henry Summers, which they refused.

Children [by first wife]:

+Samuel, b. abt. 1669.
+Henry.
  Sarah, m. ————.
  Hannah, m. ———— Scovill.
  Mary, m. (rec. Stratford) 24 Dec. 1718, Jonathan Curtis.
  Abigail, b. [say 1681]; m. John Hall.
  Patience, b. abt. 1683, d. at Trumbull, 29 Sept. 1753 in 71 yr. (g. s.); m. abt. 1705, James Hubbell.
+John, b. [say 1685].
  Martha, b. [say 1688]; m. 6 Oct. 1708, Noah Morehouse.

Child [by second wife]:

  Joseph, bapt. at Milford, 24 Mar. 1695, d. abt. 1769; m. at Milford, 4 Mar. 1729/30, Sarah Gillet, dau. of John and Sarah (Tryon) Gillet, b. at Wethersfield, 23 Feb. 1707/8.

Summers, Samuel, s. of Henry.   Sergt., Stratfield Train Band (called Sergt. at bapt. of child 1717, and in Inv. 1728).

Will of Samuel of Stratfield, 3 May 1728, proved 4 June 1728; wife Abigail; sons Samuel, David, Nathan, Daniel, Jabez; daus. Abigail, Deborah, Sarah, Hannah, Ruth; eldest son Samuel; witnesses, John Wheeler, Joseph Booth, Samuel Cooke.

Samuel Summers had land at Stratford by exchange with his uncle Samuel Gregory.

Abigail, widow of Samuel, d. 24 Jan. 1767 in 89 yr. (g. s., Newtown).

Will of Abigail, 23 Jan. 1767, proved 2 Mar. 1767; sons Samuel,

Jabez; daus. (not named); Ruth's heirs.   Distribution: Solomon Burton, Ruth Osborn, and Abigail Hubbell, children of Abigail's dau. Ruth; Sarah and Jacob Starling, children of Abigail's dau. Sarah; John, Aden, and Lucy Jackson, Mary Osborn, Ann Stevens, and Lois Jackson, children of Abigail's dau. Abigail; David and Benjamin Beardsley, Lois Porter, Abigail Curtis, and Ruth Blackman, children of Abigail's dau. Deborah; John and David Sterling, and Deborah Turner, children of Abigail's dau. Sarah; Samuel, Joseph, Enoch, John, and Zacheriah Lacy, Eunice Sherwood, Sarah, Ruth, and Abigail Lacy, children of Abigail's dau. Hannah.

Children, bapt. at Stratfield Church:

×Samuel, bapt. 30 June 1700; res. Newtown; Ens.; m. Rebecca Turney, dau. of Robert.

Abigail, bapt. 30 June 1700, d. y.

×David, bapt. 8 Feb. 1702, d. 28 Jan. 1761 in 59 yr. (g. s., Trumbull); m. (1) Abiah Treadwell, bapt. 13 Jan. 1706, d. 5 Dec. 1737 ae. 32 (g. s.); m. (2) Lydia, widow of John Harrington and dau. of Josiah Rogers of Branford, who d. 5 Jan. 1796 in 84 yr. (g. s., North Branford).

×Nathan, bapt. 14 Nov. 1703, d. 13 Dec. 1772 in 70 yr. (g. s., Stratfield); m. (1) 10 Nov. 1730, Martha Treadwell, who d. 26 Oct. 1751 in 50 yr. (g. s.); m. (2) 30 Oct. 1754, Comfort (Titherton) Lattin, who d. 4 Oct. 1763 in 63 yr. (g. s.).

Abigail, bapt. 21 Oct. 1705; m. John Jackson.

Deborah, bapt. 13 Mar. 1709; m. Benjamin Beardslee.

Sarah, bapt. 23 Dec. 1711; m. Jacob Stirling.

×Daniel, m. 19 Mar. 1741, Eunice Burroughs.

Hannah, bapt. 2 June 1717, d. at Stratfield, 14 Oct. 1755 ae. abt. 43 (g. s.); m. Edward Lacy.

Ruth, bapt. 27 June 1719; m. Solomon Burton.

Jabez, b. [25 July 1721 by age at death], d. 21 Aug. 1801 ae. 80 yrs. 27 days (g. s., Stratfield); m. Abiah Rowland, who d. 8 Sept. 1807 in 84 yr. (g. s.).

Summers, Henry, s. of Henry.

As a youth, in 1689, he lived with Henry Wakelee [his mother's stepfather].

He m. Sarah Woodruff, bapt. as his wife at Stratfield, 11 May 1707. She was dau. of Matthew Woodruff by his wife Mary, dau. of Mr. Robert Plumb of Milford. Henry Summers in behalf of Sarah his wife consented 1703 to an agreement of Plumb heirs.

Will 27 Feb. 1740/1, proved 3 Dec. 1745; wife Sarah, entire estate.

Children, bapt. at Stratfield:

> Henry, bapt. 29 Aug. 1703; m. Sarah Booth, dau. of Joseph, 2d.
> Sarah, bapt. 2 Mar. 1707.
> Rebecca, bapt. 3 June 1711.
> Abiah, bapt. 8 Feb. 1713, d. at Wilton, 23 June 1795; m. Michael Middlebrook.
> Mary, b. abt. 1718, d. at Greenfield, 18 May 1776 in 58 yr.; m. (1) abt. 1737, Abijah Morehouse; m. (2) 14 Dec. 1756, Robert Silliman; m. (3) 11 Oct. 1768, Lt. John Bradley.

Summers, John, s. of Henry.

Born [say 1685].
He m. at Stratfield, 3 Aug. 1710, Mary ———.

Children, bapt. Stratfield:

> John, bapt. 11 May 1712.
> Joseph, bapt. 19 May 1717, d. at Stratford in 1777; m. at Newtown, 11 Jan. 1743/4, Abiah Booth, dau. of Ebenezer, b. 11 Feb. 1720. His will, 28 Feb. 1777, named: wife Abiah; son Elijah; three daus., Phebe Hinman, Ruth, Eunice.
> Prudence, m. (1) [Thomas?] Curtis; m. (2) 29 Dec. 1761, Daniel Morris.
> Others?

Taintor, Charles. Deputy (Fairfield) to Conn. Leg., May 1647, May 1648.

Settled in Wethersfield 1643 or earlier, sold his lot there to Josiah Churchill, and soon removed to Fairfield, where he d. in 1658.

John Burr bought land in Fairfield from Charles and Michael Taintor, 1656.

Inv. 20 Oct. 1658; presented by John Banks as Estate "his father Tainter hath left in Fairfield." Thomas Staples was desired to care for estate until his heir, Exec'r, or Adm'r demand it. [Fairfield Pro. Rec.]

Adm'n granted to his son Michael, 1 Dec. 1659 [Hartford Pro. Rec.].

Children:

>Daughter, m. John Banks.
>
>Michael, settled in Branford, where he d. in 1673; Inv. 20 Mar. 1672/3; Deputy (Branford), May 1670, May 1672; m. by 1649, Elizabeth Rose, dau. of Robert, who d. 22 July 1659; descendants in Branford and Colchester.
>
>Prob. others.

Taylor, John.

He may be the John Taylor who was at Lynn in 1630; from Haverhill, co. Suffolk, and on passage lost wife and child. He m. (perhaps as his second wife) a widow, Rhoda ———, and came to Windsor 1639. He served on a jury, June 1644, and was appointed an arbiter of a civil action.* He died about 1646, traditionally lost at sea. His will, 24 Nov. 1645 (but not entered for probate until 6 Sept. 1694, after death of his widow), mentioned his wife, two sons, and daus.-in-law. Rhoda, a widow, had prob. two daus. by her first husband. She m. (3) Walter Hoyt, with whom she rem. to Norwalk. The son Thomas went with them, and received land from Walter Hoyt by deed Apr. 1674.

Children:

>+John.
>+Thomas.

Taylor, John, s. of John.   Capt., Hampshire County Troop.

He settled in Northampton, Mass., where he m. 18 Dec. 1662, Thankful Woodward, dau. of Dr. Henry.

As Capt. of the Hampshire Troop, in pursuit of Indians, he was killed 13 May 1704.

Children, recorded at Northampton:

>Thankful, b. 29 Oct. 1663, d. 4 Apr. 1701; m. 22 Mar. 1680, Benjamin Wright.
>
>Joanna, b. 27 Sept. 1665, d. 23 Jan. 1741; m. (1) 22 Mar. 1681, Thomas Alvord; m. (2) abt. 1690, Samuel King; m. (3) 26 Nov. 1702, Deliverance Bridgeman; all of Northampton.
>
>+John, b. 10 Oct. 1667.
>
>Rhoda, b. 26 Sept. 1669, d. 21 Jan. 1759; m. Samuel Parsons; settled in Durham, Conn.

---

* He was not a Deputy, 9 Apr. 1641, as sometimes stated. The name "Mr. Taylcoate" appears as a Deputy at that session, by whom Mr. Talcott of Hartford was meant.

Elizabeth, b. 13 Jan. 1672, d. 30 June 1681.

Mary, b. 13 Oct. 1673, d. 14 Feb. 1709; m. abt. 1704, Joseph Atherton.

Jonathan, b. 19 Sept. 1675, d. before Feb. 1723.

Mindwell, b. 19 Aug. 1677, d. 6 Nov. 1761; m. 2 June 1696, Jonathan Burt.

Lydia, b. 18 Mar. 1678/9, d. 3 Feb. 1722; m. 24 July 1707, Samuel Pomeroy.

Thomas, b. 4 Nov. 1680, d. at Deerfield, Nov. 1717; m. 31 Aug. 1715, Thankful Hawks; she m. (2) 15 Nov. 1718, Daniel Ashley; and (3) 6 Mar. 1729, William Syms.

Elizabeth, b. 17 Sept. 1682, d. at Danbury, abt. Aug. 1766; m. (1) 26 Feb. 1706/7, Joseph Mygatt; m. (2) abt. 1726, Benjamin Stephens.

Experience, b. Oct. 1684, d. y.

Samuel, b. 30 Aug. 1688, d. 5 Mar. 1735; m. (1) 9 Aug. 1715, Sarah Munn; m. (2) 16 July 1718, Mary Hitchcock, b. 20 Mar. 1699/1700, d. at Charlemont, 17 June 1787. She m. (2) 2 Sept. 1737, Daniel Arms, and (3) 20 Aug. 1754, Ebenezer Barnard.

Taylor, Thomas, s. of John. Deputy (Danbury), May 1697, May 1702, May and Oct. 1706, May and Dec. 1707; Ens., Danbury Trainband, Oct. 1696.

He m. at Norwalk, 14 Feb. 1677 [apparently an error—1667/8], Rebecca Ketchum, dau. of Edward of Stratford, dec'd.

Children, four recorded at Norwalk:

Thomas, b. 26 Nov. 1668, d. 1758; m. (1) Phebe Benedict, dau. of James; m. (2) Abigail ———. His will, 5 May 1746, proved 10 July 1758, named wife Abigail; sons Thomas, David; daus. Mary wife of Benjamin Sperry and Elizabeth wife of Jabez Davis.

Deborah, b. June 1671, d. 1750; m. Daniel Betts of Norwalk.

John, b. Dec. 1673, d. 1742 ae. 70; m. Mary Bushnell, dau. of Francis, b. 21 Dec. 1679.

Joseph, b. Dec. [1674], d. 1764 ae. 90; will 21 Jan. 1764, proved 21 Mar. 1764; m. Sarah ———.

Daniel, b. [Oct. 1676], d. at Danbury, 12 Aug. 1770 ae. 94 wanting 2 mos.; m. (1) Elizabeth Benedict, dau. of James; m. (2) Rachel Starr, who d. 3 July 1741; m. (3) 1 June 1742, Elizabeth Bouton.

Timothy, b. abt. 1678, d. 1735 ae. 56; will 22 Sept. 1735, proved 23 [Oct. or Nov.] 1735; m. Mary Davis, dau. of John of Derby.

Nathan, b. abt. 1682, d. 1782 ae. 100; m. Hannah Benedict, dau. of Daniel.

Rebecca, b. abt. 1684, d. ae. 98; m Daniel Benedict.

Theophilus, b. abt. 1687, d. 1777 ae. 90; m. (1) [Rebecca?] Bushnell; m. (2) Sarah Gregory.

Eunice, b. abt. 1689, d. ae. 90; m. Lt. Benjamin Starr.

Taylor, John, s. of John, 2d. Quarter-Master, Fairfield County Troop, May 1717; Lt., Oct. 1718.

Born at Northampton, 10 Oct. 1667, d. at Norwalk, 18 Nov. 1744; m. (1) Wait Clapp, dau. of Preserved and Sarah (Newberry) Clapp, b. at Northampton, 18 Nov. 1670, d. at Norwalk, 29 Jan. 1721/2. He m. (2) Sarah, widow of James Bennett, and dau. of Philip Lewis of Fairfield.

This family lived mostly in Westport, on the Norwalk side.

Will 9 Oct. 1744, proved 4 Dec. 1744; three daus., Wait wife of Jachin Gregory, Sarah wife of Nathaniel Bates, and Mary wife of Asahel Raymond; son Abner, land on east side Saugatuck River, and estate in Northampton, Mass.; five sons, John, Abner, Noah, Josiah, Reuben.

Children, first five born at Northampton, last five at Norwalk:

Wait, b. 27 Mar. 1690, d. Sept. 1692.

John, b. 20 Feb. 1691, d. 19 Mar. 1692.

Wait, b. abt 1693; m. Jachin Gregory.

✕John, b. 10 June 1695, d. at Norwalk, 3 May 1774 ae. near 70 [79?] (g. s.); m. (1) 6 Nov. 1723, Sarah Lockwood, dau. of Daniel, of Norwalk, who d. 24 Jan. 1724/5; m. (2) 19 Jan. 1726/7, Hannah Stewart, dau. of Lt. James, b. abt. 1699, d. at Westport, 2 May 1774 ae. 75.

Abner, b. 19 Sept. 1697; m. Hannah ———.*

✕Noah, b. 5 Oct. 1699, d. at Westport, 15 Feb. 1768; m. (1) Sarah Bennett, dau. of James, of Stratfield, bapt. 12 May 1706, d. at Westport, 9 May 1744 ae. 39; m. (2) at Wilton, 31 Jan. 1745/6, Elizabeth (Clark), widow of Capt. Matthew Marvin, b. 4 May 1710, d. at Westport, 29 Aug. 1766 in 56 yr.

✕Josiah, b. 17 Oct. 1701, d. at Westport, 11 Feb. 1781; m. (rec. Norwalk) 2 Aug. 1729, Thankful French; dau. of Samuel of Stratfield, bapt. 23 Jan. 1707/8.

✕Reuben, b. 21 Nov. 1703, d. at Norwalk in 1752; adm'n granted, 23 June 1752; m. Eunice Couch, dau. of Samuel, bapt. 2 Mar. 1706/7.

Sarah, b. 22 Nov. 1706; m. (at Norwalk, rec. Stamford), 9 Dec. 1728, Nathaniel Bates.

Mary, b. 2 Oct. 1709; m. Asahel Raymond.

Theale, Nicholas.

Of Watertown, Mass., 1638; rem. 1645 to Stamford, where he d. 19 Aug. 1658. He m. Elizabeth ———, who m. (2) abt. 1659, Thomas Ufford, and d. 27 Dec. 1660.

---

* One child, Hannah, perhaps their youngest, was bapt. at Westport, 15 May 1743.

Will presented 1659, witnessed by Nicholas Knapp and Joseph Theale, noted the wife, son and dau.

In 1660 after Ufford's death, his children made an agreement with his widow (formerly the widow Theale) and her children; signed by the widow and her children (Joseph Theale and William Ratliffe), and on behalf of Thomas Ufford's children by Alexander Bryan, John Archer, Thomas Ufford of Stratford, John Ufford, and Roger Terrill. [The interest of Bryan and Archer does not appear.]

Children, recorded at Watertown:

+Joseph, b. 24 Oct. 1640.
  Elizabeth, b. 5 June 1643, m. at Stamford, 29 Oct. 1659, William Ratliffe.

Theale, Joseph, s. of Nicholas. Deputy (Stamford) to Conn. Leg., Oct. 1671, Oct. 1673, Oct. 1674, May and Oct. 1675, Oct. 1676, Oct. 1677, May and Oct. 1678, May and Oct. 1679, May and Oct. 1680, May 1681, May 1682; Deputy for Greenwich, Oct. 1683; Chief Military Officer, Bedford Trainband, May 1682.

Of Stamford, made freeman 1662; rem. 1682 to Bedford, N. Y., with the founders of that town, which was established by Conn. Colony that year, and later fell within the bounds of Westchester County, N. Y.

We suppose that for a second wife he m. after 1695, Rebecca, widow of Cornelius Hull, and dau. of Rev. John Jones, of Fairfield, b. in England abt. 1633; for an execution dated 27 Sept. 1710 and recorded in Fairfield, describes land bounded by the homelot of Rebecca Theel formerly Hull.

Thomas, John.

Perhaps related to the older John Thomas of New Haven, where he settled at marriage. We should guess he was not that John who was paying court in 1665 to the dau.-in-law of Rev. Adam Blackman [see his will], for our John appears not to have m. until a dozen years later.

New Haven Deeds prove that he m. Mary Blakeslee, dau. of Samuel, b. 2 Nov. 1659. They rem. to Woodbury, where his widow Mary was living in 1735, having m. (2) Alexander Alcorn. John d. in 1709.

Will 8 June 1709; called to go in expedition against Canada; wife Mary; five sons, Jeremiah, Jonathan, John, Samuel, Ebenezer; dau. Hannah Taylor; son-in-law Robert Churchill. There are five sons living besides that dau. at Mr. Sackett's Farm; names and ages: Jeremiah, 24, 15 this present Feb. 1709/10; Jonathan, 18, 22 Apr. next; John, 14, the last of last Aug.; Samuel, 11, 12 of last June; Ebenezer, 9, 11 of next Mar.

Children, first four recorded at New Haven, last three at Woodbury:

> Hannah, b. 20 Apr. 1678; m. Jonathan Taylor; divorced 1708.
>
> Rebecca, b. 20 Sept. 1680; prob. was the dau. who m. Robert Churchill of Fairfield, and apparently d. before 1709.
>
> Jeremiah, b. 16 Feb. 1684 [1684/5], or 15 Feb. [Pro. Rec.], d. at Roxbury, 10 Dec. 1752; m. Susannah Lane, dau. of Charles, who d. 18 May 1767.
>
> Mary, b. 9 May 1687, prob. d. y.
>
> Jonathan, b. 22 Apr. 1692.
>
> John, b. 30 Aug. 1695, d. at Woodbury, 27 July 1715. Inv. 27 Aug. 1715. Agreement for distribution made 1 Dec. 1732 by Jeremiah Thomas of Woodbury, Samuel Thomas of Waterbury, John Hurd and David Leavenworth of Woodbury, and Robert Churcher of Fairfield, interested by right or purchase. Leavenworth had purchased from Patience, sister of Robert Churcher, Jr.
>
> Samuel, b. 10 Sept. 1699 (at night), or 12 June [Pro. Rec.], d. at Cape Breton, 2 Jan. 1745/6; m. at Waterbury, 8 Apr. 1725, Rebecca Warner.
>
> Ebenezer, b. 25 Mar. 1701, or 11 Mar. [Pro. Rec.], d. at Roxbury, 23 Nov. 1780; m. (1) 11 Oct. 1721, Sarah Mitchell; dau. of Abraham; she d. 28 Mar. 1760; m. (2) 14 Aug. 1760, Joanna (———) Galpin, prob. widow of Joseph.

THOMPSON FAMILY (FAIRFIELD)

Thompson, John.

He had a grant of 2½ acres in Fairfield, recorded 7 Jan. 1660 [1660/1].

Inv. June 1657. Widow; ages of children: Elizabeth 13, Mary 8, John 6, Hester 3. The widow Elizabeth made marriage covenant, 25 Dec. 1657, with Daniel Finch of Fairfield, and was dead in 1658. Francis Hall and George Godwin were appointed feofees, and at Godwin's death, William Heyden was appointed in his room. Hall and Heyden were appointed Adm'rs of John Thompson's Est. in room of Elizabeth Finch.

On 28 Jan. 1673 [1673/4], Elizabeth wife of Thomas Bennett, Mary wife of John Bennett, and Esther Thompson, entered for record land which was theirs by virtue of execution in William Heyden's estate; and John Bennett purchased from Thomas Bennett a third part, and from Hester Thompson a third part. On 4 Apr. 1672, in a sale from Turney to Wheeler, the bounds mention "land of John Tomsons Children sometimes the land of Willm Hayden."

Children:

> Elizabeth, b. abt. 1644; m. Thomas Bennett.
> Mary, b. abt. 1649; m. John Bennett.
> +John, b. abt. 1651.
> Hester, b. abt. 1654; m. John Grumman.

Thompson, John, s. of John.

Born (presumably at Fairfield) abt. 1651; Dea. John d. 1 Mar. 1734 ae. 83 (g. s., Fairfield). He m. in 1684, Sarah Gold, dau. of Nathan, b. abt. 1661, d. 4 June 1747 in 87 yr. (g. s.).

Will 8 May 1723, proved 23 Mar. 1736; wife Sarah; "my three children"; sons John, David; dau. Jerusha Sturgis. Inv. of Dea. John, 10 Mar. 1741/2.

Will of Sarah, 20 Jan. 1746/7, proved 7 July 1747; called herself widow of Dea. John; all estate to son John.

Children, recorded at Fairfield:

> Jerusha, b. 11 May 1685, d. 16 Feb. 1745 [1745/6] in 62 yr. (g. s., Fairfield); m. Jonathan Sturgis. Her will, 8 Feb. 1745/6, proved 21 Feb. 1746; to Trinity Church; cousins Nathan, Daniel, John, Abigail, Jerusha, Sarah, Ann, and Mary Thompson.
> John, b. 21 Feb. 1686 [1686/7], d. 10 Apr. 1759 in 73 yr. (g. s., Fairfield). Adm'n granted, 23 Apr. 1759, to Jerusha Thompson, who gave bond with Sarah Dennie. Distribution, 12 Feb. 1761, to Sarah, John, Jerusha and Mary, surviving children of David Thompson of Fairfield dec'd.
> Sarah, b. 4 Oct. 1689, d. y.
> ✕David, bapt. 3 May 1696, d. in 1736; adm'n granted to widow Abigail, 21 July 1736; m. abt. 1718, Abigail MacKenzie, b. 4 Aug. 1700, d. after 1761.

Thompson, William.

On 17 Mar. 1688 [1688/9], Richard Blackleach of Stratford conveyed to William Thompson, now resident in Fairfield, for £60, sixty acres in the woods in Stratford bounds [Fairfield Deeds].

Children, recorded at Fairfield:

> Mary, b. 20 Nov. 1685.
> Martha, b. 3 Sept. 1688.

THOMPSON FAMILY (STRATFORD)

Thompson, John.

A very early settler in Stratford, where he d. in 1678/9; m. Mirable ———.

Will 17 July 1678, proved 29 Jan. 1678 [1678/9]; dau. Hurd; son-in-law Jonathan Curtis; Samuel Galpin; dau. Mary; sons John, Ambrose; wife Mirable. Receipt 24 Mar. 1678/9 from John Hurd, Sr., Jonathan Curtis, and Samuel Galpin, of legacies under will of father-in-law John Thompson dec'd.

"Marable" d. at Stratford, 13 Apr. 1690.

Children, recorded at Stratford:

> +John, b. Sept. 1641.
> Sarah, b. in 1642, d. 24 Jan. 1717/8 (Stratford); m. (1) 1 Dec. 1662, John Hurd, Sr.; m. (2) Thomas Barnum.
> Abigail, b. 1 May 1646, d. 2 Mar. 1731; m. (1) abt. 1670, Jonathan Curtis; m. (2) Nicholas Hughes; m. (3) 1 Aug. 1695, Mr. Samuel Sherman.
> Esther, b. Jan. 1649 [1649/50], d. 27 Aug. 1678; m. 22 Mar. 1676/7, Samuel Galpin.
> +Ambrose, b. 1 Jan. 1651 [1651/2].
> Mary, b. 20 July 1655, d. at Woodbury, 18 Jan. 1710/1 in 56 yr.; m. abt. 1677, Matthew Mitchell.

Thompson, John, s. of John.

Born at Stratford, Sept. 1641; d. there in 1681.

Will 8 Oct. 1681; my mother, all est. for life; John son of Ambrose Thompson now at Woodbury; two cousins William and Jonathan Curtis; residue to cousins, viz.: the children of John Hurd, Sr., of Jonathan and Abigail Curtis, the child of Ambrose

Thompson, the child of Matthew Mitchell; my sister Abigail Curtis; my sister Hurd.

Receipt May 1690 to bro. Ambrose Thompson from Sarah widow of John Hurd, Sr. (for his children Mary and Esther Hurd) and from Abigail Huse (mother of William, Jonathan and Sarah Curtis, children of Jonathan and Abigail Curtis); also from Matthew Mitchell of Woodbury to Ambrose Thompson for legacy given to his child by John Thompson, Jr.; also from John Hurd, Isaac Hurd, Sarah Sherwood, and Hannah Hurd, children of John Hurd, Sr., and Abigail Curtis, child of Jonathan Curtis, to uncle Ambrose Thompson for legacies left them by John Thompson, Jr., son of John Thompson, Sr., after decease of our gr. mother Marable Thompson.

Thompson, Ambrose, s. of John. Deputy (Stratford), May 1697, Oct. 1704, May 1705, Oct. 1706, May 1710, May 1712, Oct. 1716, May 1717.

Born at Stratford, 1 Jan. 1651/2; d. there 7 Sept. 1742 in 92 yr. (g. s.); m. by 1679, Sarah Welles, dau. of Mr. John, who d. 23 Mar. 1730 ae. abt. 71 (g. s.).

Will 23 Feb. 1740/1; dau. Elizabeth Thompson; son Thomas Thompson; dau. Hannah Thompson; son John Thompson, Capt. David Judson, and Mr. Daniel Hawley, Exec'rs.

Children, recorded at Stratford:

> John, b. abt. 1680, d. at Stratford, 20 July 1765 in 85 yr. (g. s.); Deacon; will 19 Mar. 1761, proved 1 Aug. 1765; m. (1) 15 Nov. 1705, Ruth Curtis, who d. 23 Apr. 1721; m. (2) 30 Nov. 1721, Mrs. Martha DeForest, widow, who d. 7 Feb. 1740/1; in 63 yr. (g. s.); m. (3) 7 July 1741, Mehitabel Webb; widow of Rev. Joseph Webb of Fairfield, previously of Benjamin Coney, and dau. of John Glover, b. at New Haven, 1 May 1679.
>
> Ambrose, b. 17 Nov. 1682, d. at Stratford, 3 May 1768 in 86 yr. (g. s.); m. 22 May 1707, Ann Booth, who d. 22 Sept. 1774 in 86 yr. (g. s.).
>
> Sarah, b. 26 Aug. 1685; m. 10 June 1708, Joseph Birdsey.
>
> Ebenezer, b. [say 1688], d. 21 May 1757; will 1 Dec. 1755, proved 30 June 1757; m. 7 Aug. 1712, Comfort Pickett, who d. at Huntington, 7 Nov. 1773 ae. 78.
>
> Thomas, b. 24 Dec. 1691; m. 11 Aug. 1720, Ruth Seeley, who d. 12 Feb. 1721/2.
>
> Elizabeth, b. 28 Feb. 1694/5, d. 3 July 1753, unm.
>
> Hannah, b. 25 Sept. 1700.

Thornton, Thomas. Deputy (Stratford) to Conn. Leg., May 1651; war committee for Stratford, May 1653.

From Dorchester to Windsor by 1640; sold his property there to Thomas Ford and Ford's son-in-law John Strong about 1647, and rem. to Stratford. He was prob. a tanner, but of his later history we have learned nothing.

Children:

> Thomas, d. at Hartford, 22 Sept. 1703; a tanner; m. at Milford, 5 Aug. 1674, Hannah Farrand, dau. of Nathaniel, Sr.
> Priscilla.
> Samuel, b. at Windsor, 13 July 1645.
> Ann.
> Theophilus, b. at Stratford, 10 June 1651.

Thorp, John, s. of William.

Bapt. at New Haven, July 1643; lived there 1666 when he was before the Court with Rebecca Potter, who accused him of the paternity of her child; rem. to Fairfield, where he had a grant 3 Sept. 1679.

He m. (1) Hannah Frost, dau. of Daniel.

He m. (2) after 1698, Mary, dau. of Robert Meeker, and widow first of Samuel Adams and second of Moses Lyon.

He conveyed to his son John, 17 Aug. 1700. Samuel Thorp sold land 1721 which he had by gift from father John dec'd, which descended to him and his bro. Daniel; mentioned also land of his bro. John.

Adm'n on Est. of John, Sr., granted to son Samuel Thorp and John Gold both of Fairfield, 17 Oct. 1720.

Children [by first wife]:

> ✕John, b. abt. 1679, d. at Greenfield, 1 Mar. 1742 ae. 63 (g. s.); will 28 Feb. 1741/2, proved 22 Mar. 1741/2; m. (rec. Greenfield) 15 May 1699, Mary Davis, b. abt. 1678, d. 27 Jan. 1758 ae. 80 (g. s.).
> ✕Samuel, b. abt. 1684, bapt. at Greenfield as an adult, 5 June 1726, d. at Greenfield, 26 Apr. 1758 ae. abt. 74; adm'n granted, 8 Nov. 1758; m. abt. 1708, Margaret ———,* b. abt. 1687, bapt. 24 Feb. 1694/5, d. 3 Nov. 1767 ae. abt. 80.

---

* It has been suggested that she was Margaret, dau. of Dr. Peter Bulkley. In favor of this assumption, no other marriage has been proved for Margaret Bulkley; the Thorps named a son Gershom; and a nephew of Samuel Thorp m. a niece of Margaret Bulkley. Against it, Margaret Bulkley was prob. b. a few years earlier than 1687, since she was one of the "two eldest daus." named in 1691 in her father's will, and this consideration outweighs the favorable ones.

Children [prob. by second wife] :

> ╳Peter, bapt. at Fairfield as an adult, 9 Jan. 1725/6; m. abt. 1725, Sarah ———.
> ╳Daniel, b. ———, d. at Westport, 26 Feb. 1749; m. by 1731, Hephzibah Luff, dau. of John of Stratford, who d. 16 Mar. 1752.

Titherton, Daniel. Daniel (Stratford) to Conn. Leg., May 1647, May 1649, May 1652, May 1654.

Will 23 Dec. 1660, proved 6 July 1661; wife Jane; son Timothy (under 18) ; son Daniel (a tub I brought from England) ; son Samuel; dau. Wilcocks; daus. Mary and Elizabeth (not married) ; mentioned estate in England; signed with mark (DT). Witnesses, Jasper Gunn, Moses Wheeler. Inv. 16 July 1661.

Children, youngest recorded at Stratford:

> John, b. abt. 1639 [Winthrop called him ae. 18 in 1657], d. y., perhaps in 1657.
> +Daniel.
> Daughter, m. John Wilcoxson.
> Mary, d. before 1695; m. 19 June 1665, Samuel Sherman.
> +Timothy, b. 25 Mar. 1651.
> Elizabeth, m. Thomas Welles.
> +Samuel.

Titherton, Daniel, s. of Daniel.

Died and buried at Stratford, 30 Nov. 1709.
Adm'n granted, 5 Dec. 1709, to Lt. John Clark and John Porter. They, as husbands of the daus., made agreement to divide Est., 7 June 1710.

Children, recorded at Stratford:

> Sarah, b. 12 Oct. 1673; m. 11 Aug. 1692, John Clark.
> Mary, b. 11 June 1676; m. 8 Oct. 1696, John Porter.

Titherton, Timothy, s. of Daniel.

Born at Stratford, 25 Mar. 1651.
He m. at Stratford, 3 Oct. 1692, Patience Wakelee.
Will 20 May 1737, proved 2 Sept. 1740; wife Patience; daus. Jane wife of Samuel Brown of Stratford, Sarah wife of Ebenezer Hubbell of Stratfield, Mary wife of David Peet of Stratfield, Hannah Titherton, and Susanna Stoddard (Widow) ; son Timothy.

Children, recorded at Stratford:

> Jane, b. 30 Mar. 1694; m. 14 Jan. 1724/5, Samuel Brown, of New Haven.
>
> Timothy, b. 25 Aug. 1695, d. at Stratford, 1757/8; will 22 May 1757, proved 18 Jan. 1758; m. Mary ———; no issue. His will named wife Mary, and his sisters and their heirs (without specifying them).
>
> Sarah, b. 31 Jan. 1696 [1696/7], d. at Easton, 20 May 1788 in 93 yr. (g. s.); m. Ebenezer Hubbell.
>
> Mary, b. 4 Nov. 1698; m. 1 Oct. 1719, David Peat.
>
> Hannah, b. 4 Nov. 1698.
>
> Susannah, b. 2 Oct. 1700; m. ——— Stoddard.*

Titherton, Samuel, s. of Daniel.

He m. at Stratford, 14 July 1693, Hannah Hurd.

Inv. 6 Mar. 1710/1. Widow Hannah. Children: Abigail, abt. 18; Comfort, abt. 12.

Children, recorded at Stratford:

> Abigail, b. 17 May 1696.
>
> Comfort, b. 17 Aug. 1701, d. at Stratfield, 4 Oct. 1763 in 63 yr. (g. s.); m. (1) 8 Nov. 1721, David Lattin; m. (2) at Trumbull, 30 Oct. 1754, Nathan Summers.

Tolles, Henry.

The birth of his son Henry at "Seabrooke" the first week in Nov. 1669 is recorded in Fairfield, where he was living (we must suppose) when the entry was made. The younger Henry settled in West Haven.

Tomlinson, Henry.

George Tomlinson m. Jan. 1600, at St. Peter's, London, Mary Hyde; who have been claimed as parents of Henry, bapt. Nov. 1606, at St. Peter's, Werbury, co. Derby, Eng.

He took the oath at Milford, 1652, and kept the tavern there in 1656; was a weaver, and removed to Stratford by 1659.

He d. at Stratford, 16, bur. 17 Mar. 1680/1. His widow Alice m. (2) Dea. John Birdsey, and d. 25 Jan. 1697/8.

---

* Yet Stratford records state that Jesse Persons (so called), son of Susannah Titherton, was b. 8 Sept. 1727; and that Judah, dau. of Robert and Susannah Persons, was b. 17 May 1733; seeming to imply that Susannah became the wife of Robert Persons. How then was she a Widow Stoddard in 1737?

Will 15 Mar. 1680/1, proved 28 Apr. 1681 (he d. 16 Mar. 1680/1) ; wife Alice ; son Agur ; married children, Jonas, dau. Harger, Mary Pierson, Tabitha Wooster, Phebe Wooster, Bashua Stiles ; dau. Margaret Harger ; gr. son Timothy Wooster ; son Ephraim Stiles.   In 1688 the widow had m. John Birdsey, Sr.

Children, last three recorded at Stratford :

>Abram, d. at Stratford, 30 May 1662.
>
>Margaret, d. at Derby, 17 Mar. 1697/8 ; m. (1) 5 Nov. 1662, Jabez Harger ; m. (2) John Tibbals.
>
>+Jonas.
>
>Tabitha, d. abt. 1691 ; m. (1) Edward Wooster ; m. (2) Dr. John Hull.
>
>Mary, d. at Derby, 25 Sept. 1715 ; m. Stephen Pierson.
>
>Phebe, b. 14 Aug. 1656, d. Mar. 1739/40 ae. abt. 80 (g. s., Derby) ; m. Thomas Wooster.
>
>+Agur, b. 1 Nov. 1658.
>
>Bathsheba, b 3 Jan. 1661/2, d. at Stratford, 9 Feb. 1735 ae. 74 (g. s.) ; m. (1) Ephraim Stiles ; m. (2) 1 Dec. 1714, Benjamin Curtis.

Tomlinson, Jonas, s. of Henry.

Settled in Derby, where he d. in 1693.   Married Hannah ———, who d. in 1723.

Will 27 Nov. 1692, proved June 1693 ; wife Hannah ; children (unnamed) ; sworn to by William Tomlinson, ae. 50, and Mary Washburn, ae. 21.

Adm'n on Est. of Hannah of Derby was granted, 4 Feb. 1723, to eldest son Abraham ; the four children (unnamed) were the heirs.

On 9 May 1720, John Riggs and Elizabeth his wife, and Andrew Smith and Sarah his wife, conveyed to bros. Abraham and Samuel Tomlinson, right from father Jonas Tomlinson dec'd.   [Derby Deeds.]

Children :

>Sarah, m. 21 May 1696, Andrew Smith.
>
>Elizabeth, d. at Derby, 17 Apr. 1747 (g. s.) ; m. 23 Feb. 1699/1700, John Riggs.
>
>Abraham, d. at Derby in 1739 ; will 22 Apr. 1731, proved 24 Apr. 1739 ; m. (1) abt. 1711, Mary Perkins, dau. of John, b. at New Haven, 9 Oct. 1689 ; m. (2) at Stratford, 4 July 1728, Lois Wheeler ; widow of Samuel Wheeler of Stratford, previously widow of

Ebenezer Riggs; also divorced wife of John Obartus, and dau. of Joseph Hawkins, b. at Derby, 6 Nov. 1681, d. there 11 Sept. 1767 ae. 87 (g. s.).

Samuel, bapt. at Woodbury, Dec. 1687; m. abt. 1711, Hannah ———.

Tomlinson, Agur, s. of Henry. Ens., Troop raised to march to Albany, Apr. 1690; and in 1696 the Col. Rec. call him Lt.

Born at Stratford, 1 Nov. 1658; Lt. Agur d. there 5 Mar. 1727/8; in 70 yr. (g. s.).

Will 3 Oct. 1727, proved 21 Mar. 1728; wife Abigail; gr. sons Josiah and Timothy Wilcoxson; kinswoman Abigail Pierce (under 18) that now lives with me; son Zachariah.

Married (1) at Stratford, 13 Dec. 1681, Elizabeth Judson. She was dau. of Jeremiah, b. 24 Feb. 1658 [1658/9].

Lt. Agur m. (2) at Stratford, 19 Oct. 1692, Sarah Hawley, widow. She was widow of Ephraim Hawley, and née Welles of Wethersfield. She d. at Stratford, 29 June 1694.

Lt. Agur m. (3) at Stratford, 14 Apr. 1702, Mis^t Abigail Brown. She had been adm. to Stratford Church, 31 Aug. 1701, by letter from Haverhill.

Children by Elizabeth, recorded at Stratford:

Alice, b. (no record), d. 11 Oct. 1684.
Elizabeth, b. 11 Aug. 1684, d. before 1713; m. June 1707, John Wilcoxson.

Child by Sarah, recorded at Stratford:

Zechariah, b. 31 Oct. 1693, d. at Stratford, 15 Apr. 1768 in 75 yr. (g. s.); m. 25 Mar. 1718/9, Hannah Beach, who d. 5 Oct. 1740 in 37 yr. (g. s.); her will 30 Sept. 1740.

Tomlinson, William.

Perhaps nephew of Henry Tomlinson.

Born abt. 1643; d. at Derby, 9 Dec. 1711.

William, Sr., conveyed 20 Mar. 1711 to sons John and Isaac. On 4 Apr. 1712, William conveyed to bros. John and Isaac, right from father William dec'd; the same date, James Hard and Elizabeth his wife conveyed to bros. John and Isaac Tomlinson, right from father William dec'd. [Derby Deeds.]

Children:

> Elizabeth, m. James Hard.
> William, d. at Derby in 1736; will 10 Mar. 1735/6, proved 6 Dec. 1736; m. [possibly a dau. of Benjamin and Ruth (Williams) Gaylord of Windsor].
> John, b. at Derby, 19 Sept. 1686, d. there 18 Nov. 1756 ae. 71; adm'n granted, Dec. 1756; m. (1) 27 Mar. 1712, Elizabeth Wooster, dau. of Thomas; m. (2) abt. 1744, Hannah (Merwin), widow of John Collins; she m. (3) Andrew Sanford, 4th, of Milford.
> Isaac, b. abt. 1689, d. at Derby, 27 Jan. 1754; in 64 yr. (g. s.); m. (rec. Derby) 25 Mar. 1712, Patience Gaylord; perhaps dau. of Benjamin and Ruth (Williams) Gaylord of Windsor.

Tompkins, John.

Of Concord, Mass.; came with Jones contingent to Fairfield, where he died, and his widow m. William Heyden and rem. to Eastchester, N. Y.

He died so early that his will is not found; but on 7 Mar. 1660/1, John Wheeler and George Squire, as overseers to [the younger] John "Tomkins," sued William Hayden for £30 for neglect in executing the will of John Tompkins. They won the suit, and Hayden was ordered to surrender the lands to [the son] John. Since William Hayden [of Windsor] sat on the jury which tried the case, it is obvious that a different man of the same name was the defendant.

On 27 Dec. 1687, William Hayden of Eastchester put it upon record that he had sold out of his possession land at Eastchester, to his sons-in-law Nathaniel and John Tompkins. [Westchester Deeds.]

Children, two recorded at Concord:

> Ruth, b. 1 June 1640.
> John, b. 25 Sept. 1642; propounded for freeman of Conn., May 1669, then residing at Fairfield; sold Fairfield property to John Wheeler by 1673, and rem. to Eastchester.
> Nathaniel, d. at Eastchester, 6 Sept. 1684; purchased land from Mr. John Pell, 1681; will 2 Sept. 1684, named wife Elizabeth, bro. John Tompkins, and Nathaniel White, Exec'rs; children, Nathaniel, Ann, Elizabeth, Mary, and Rebecca, all under age.

Travis, Garret.

Of Rye, N. Y.

Children:

Philip, had legacy 1680 by will of John Hurd, Sr., of Stratford.
James.
Robert, m. a dau. of Philip Galpin of Stratford and Rye. A Robert, prob. of the next generation, m. by 1723 Mary Ogden, dau. of Richard, bapt. at Fairfield, 19 Apr. 1696.
John; his Inv., taken at Rye, 20 Nov. 1677, calls him son of Garret, and is signed by John Gelpin, Joseph Horton, Joseph Gelpin. He was "slayne in the Late warr." Distribution ordered to eldest bro. Philip Travis (Adm'r); to James Travis; to bro. Robert Travis and sister Hannah Travis.
Hannah.

Treadwell, Samuel, s. of Edward.

His father Edward was of Hempstead, L. I. His mother Sarah m. (2) about 1661, Henry Whelpley of Fairfield; m. (3) about 1663, Ralph Keeler of Norwalk; and (4) after 1672, Thomas Skidmore of Fairfield; and d. abt. Nov. 1684.

Samuel m. Ruth Wheeler, dau. of Ephraim, who d. in 1719.

He d. at Stratfield in 1718.

His sister Rebecca m. 1 May 1679, John Higbee, of Middletown. Perhaps the Elizabeth Treadwell, who m. at Concord, Mass., 23 Mar. 1676/7, Joseph Heyward, was another sister.*

Will of Ruth, 19 Jan. 1718/9, proved 10 Feb. 1718/9; widow of Samuel, Sr.; son Edward, Exec'r; gr. daus., daus. of son Samuel dec'd, of son Edward, of son John dec'd, of son Ephraim dec'd, and of son Timothy.

Children, three recorded at Fairfield:

+Samuel.
+Edward.
+John, b. 11 Feb. 1674 [1674/5].
Ruth, b. 20 Jan. 1679 [1679/80], "R. T." d. 1699 (g. s., Stratfield).
+Ephraim, b. 7 Mar. 1681 [1681/2].
+Timothy, b. abt. 1684.

Treadwell, Samuel, s. of Samuel.

He d. at Stratfield, 28 Feb. 1717 (g. s.); m. Martha Turney, dau. of Robert, b. 5 June 1676. She m. (2) 14 Feb. 1720/1, Samuel Smedley, and d. at Stratfield in 1734.

---

* For the Long Island branch founded by Samuel's brother John, see *New York Gen. and Biog. Record*, Apr. 1911.

Will 2 Feb. 1716/7, proved 25 Mar. 1717; wife Martha; children David, Zachariah, Martha, Abiah, Robert, Stephen, Josiah; land in common with bros. John and Edward Treadwell and Joseph Booth, and land bought from Joseph Bennett; codicil 22 Feb. 1716 [1716/7].

Adm'n on Est. of Martha Smedley was granted, 8 Nov. 1734, to Zachariah Treadwell.

David Summers in right of his child David, issue by his late wife Abiah, with Nathan Summers and Martha his wife, all of Stratford, conveyed 1740 land which belonged to mother Mrs. Martha Smedley of Fairfield dec'd as her dowry in Est. of our father Mr. Samuel Treadwell her former husband, and right in Est. of our bro. Robert Treadwell dec'd.

Children, bapt. at Stratfield:

> ✕David, bapt. 17 July 1698, d. in 1727; adm'n granted, 1 Mar. 1726/7, to Sarah Treadwell; m. Sarah ———.
> ✕Zachariah, bapt. 6 Oct. 1700, d. 16 Sept. 1786; will 11 Sept. 1783, proved 14 Nov. 1786; m. Jerusha [prob. dau. of John Hubbell, Jr., bapt. 14 June 1713], d. in 1793.
> Martha, bapt. 23 Aug. 1702, d. at Stratfield, 26 Oct. 1751 in 50 yr. (g. s.); m. Nathan Summers.
> Rebecca, bapt. 27 Aug. 1704, d. y.
> Abiah, bapt. 13 Jan. 1706, d. at Stratfield, 5 Dec. 1737 ae. 32 (g. s.); m. David Summers.
> Robert, bapt. 30 Nov. 1707, d. in 1739, unm. Adm'n granted, 5 Dec. 1739, to Zechariah Treadwell.
> ✕Stephen, bapt. 22 Oct. 1710, d. at Stratfield, 23 Nov. 1753 in 44 yr. (g. s.); adm'n granted, 1 Jan. 1754, to widow Sarah; m. at Stratfield, 5 Feb. 1750/1, Sarah Wakelee, dau. of Joseph, bapt. 1 Dec. 1717; she m. (2) John Truesdale of Norwalk.
> ✕Josiah, bapt. 8 Nov. 1713; m. (1) Ann Wakelee, dau. of Jonathan, bapt. 7 Dec. 1712; m. (2) Deborah Beardsley, dau. of John, b. 10 Sept. 1719.

Treadwell, Edward, s. of Samuel.

He m. (1) Mary Turney, dau. of Robert, b. 9 Dec. 1673.

He m. (2) at Fairfield Church, 26 May 1743, Sarah Trowbridge; widow of Samuel Trowbridge, and dau. of Edward Lacy.

Will 20 Jan. 1753, proved 6 Mar. 1753; wife Sarah, all personal estate; I have given children their portions.

Children, bapt. at Stratfield:

> Mary, bapt. 25 Dec. 1695, d. y.
>
> Ruth, b. [20 Jan. 1697/8 Old Style, by age at death], bapt. 20 Mar. 1698, d. at Stratfield, 15 Mar. 1756 ae. 58 yrs. 1 mo. 15 days (g. s.) ; m. at Stratfield, 20 Oct. 1715, Robert Silliman.
>
> ✕Benjamin, bapt. 18 Feb. 1700; m. Mary Kimberly, dau. of Nathaniel of New Haven, b. 24 July 1698.
>
> Elizabeth, bapt. 1 Mar. 1702 (a twin dau.), m. after 1741, John Root, of Woodbury.
>
> Daughter (twin), b. and d. 1702.
>
> Elnathan, bapt. 5 Nov. 1704.
>
> Sarah, bapt. 2 June 1706, d. abt. 1785; m. at Stratfield, 13 June 1733, Ezekiel Sanford.
>
> Mary, bapt. 27 Feb. 1709, m. at Fairfield, Nov. 1729, Benjamin Banks.
>
> Mercy, bapt. 1 July 1711.
>
> Tabitha, bapt. 24 Apr. 1715, d. at Woodbury, 29 Feb. 1792 ae. 77; m. at Fairfield Church, 4 Sept. 1751, Thomas Minor.

Treadwell, John, s. of Samuel.

Born at Fairfield, 11 Feb. 1674/5, d. at Stratfield in 1716; m. at Woodbury, 8 Feb. 1699/1700, Abigail Minor; dau. of Capt. John, bapt. at Woodbury, Feb. 1680/1. She m. (2) (rec. New Haven) 22 Nov. 1721, Lt. Richard Miles.

Adm'n granted, 1 Feb. 1715/6, to Dea. Thomas Hawley of Stratfield with the widow Abigail.

Inv. presented 2 May 1716; dates of birth of the surviving children stated. In 1721 the sons John and Hezekiah chose Mr. Joseph Booth of Stratfield for guardian; and the Court appointed Mr. Thomas Hawley guardian for Ephraim and Jabez. Ephraim chose Joseph Booth for guardian, 27 July 1728.

Hezekiah Treadwell of Stratford and Ephraim Treadwell of Farmington conveyed, 20 May 1740, right in Newtown common land which descended to them from father John of Stratfield dec'd. [Newtown Deeds.]

Children, bapt. at Stratfield:

> Adoniram,* b. 14 Jan. 1700 [1700/01], bapt. 19, 1701; rem. to New Milford.
>
> Abigail, b. 7 Oct. 1702, bapt. 11 Oct. 1702, d. at Redding, 6 Sept. 1759 in 56 yr. (g. s.) ; m at Fairfield, 1 Mar. 1722, Stephen Morehouse.
>
> John, b. 7 June 1705, bapt. 10 June 1705.

---

* Name given in probate rec. as "Benja."

XHezekiah, b. 3 Nov. 1707, bapt. 9 Nov. 1707, d. at Stratfield in 1761;
 Lt.; will 3 Feb. 1761, proved 3 Mar. 1761; m. Mehitabel Fairchild,
 dau. of Agur, b. Apr. 1711, d. in 1764; Inv. 23 Mar. 1764.
Ephraim, b. 4 July 1710, bapt. 9 July 1710, d. at Farmington in 1782;
 Ens., 2d Co., Farmington, Oct. 1750; Capt., Oct. 1752; will 18 Dec.
 1781, proved 11 Feb. 1782; m. at Farmington, 30 Apr. 1741, Mary
 Porter.
Joseph, bapt. 23 Nov. 1712, d. y.
Jabez, b. 4 Nov. 1715, bapt. (as son of John dec'd) 4 Mar. 1716.

Treadwell, Ephraim, s. of Samuel.

Born at Fairfield, 7 Mar. 1681/2; "E. T." d. 1708 (g. s., Stratfield). Prob. he d. early in 1708/9. He m. Ruth Wakelee, dau.
of Jacob, b. at Stratford, 27 Aug. 1681. She m. (2) John Lacy.

Adm'n granted, 4 Feb. 1708 [1708/9] to widow Ruth and her
father-in-law Samuel Treadwell. Distribution made Mar. 1726/7
to widow Ruth wife of John Lacy; Samuel Treadwell; Jacob
Treadwell; Ruth Treadwell.

Children, bapt. at Stratfield: ,

XSamuel, bapt. 19 Mar. 1704, d. at Stratfield in 1787; m. ———.
XJacob, bapt. 6 Jan. 1706; m. Hannah Trowbridge.
Ruth, bapt. 23 May 1708; m. (1) Peter Coley, and (2) James Tongue,
 both of Ridgefield. On 15 June 1728, Peter Coley and Ruth his
 wife of "Greenfarms" conveyed to Nathan Hurd of Stratfield part
 of Ruth's portion from her father, and part of homestead where our
 father and mother Lacy now dwell, bounded north on bro. Samuel
 Treadwell.

Treadwell, Timothy, s. of Samuel.

Born abt. 1684, d. at Stratfield abt. 20 Sept. 1720 ae. abt. 37
(g. s.). He m. (1) Sarah Sherwood, dau. of Matthew, Jr.

He m. (2) at Stratfield, 24 Mar. 1713/4, Deborah Burr, dau. of
Maj. John.

His dau. Ruth chose Lt. Richard Hubbell for guardian, 24 Mar.
1726/7. Distribution 2 May 1727; Widow Deborah; son Samuel;
daus. Ruth and Deborah Treadwell.

Children [by first wife], bapt. at Stratfield:

Elizabeth, bapt. 17 Feb. 1706, d. 10 May 1709 in 4 yr. (g. s.).
Sarah, bapt. 15 Feb. 1708, d. 24 Dec. 1709 (g. s.).
Ruth, bapt. 29 Oct. 1710; m. at Fairfield, 1 June 1727, Jabez
 Wakeman.

Children [by second wife], bapt. at Stratfield:

Sarah, bapt. 28 Oct. 1716, d. y.

Samuel, bapt. 8 Mar. 1719, d. in 1740, unm. Adm'n granted, 20 Oct. 1740, to Jabez Wakeman of Fairfield. Will, 21 May 1740, proved 31 July 1740; mother Deborah Treadwell; sister Deborah Treadwell and cousin Tabitha Treadwell, residue after mother's death; Jabez Wakeman in right of his wife, one of the heirs, appealed, and the will was not approved [Pro. Files].

Deborah, m. Hope Chapman.

Trowbridge, Samuel, s. of William. Soldier in the Province galley, May 1695.

Born at New Haven, 7 Oct. 1670; d. at Fairfield in 1741/2; m. at Stratfield, 30 Dec. 1697, Sarah Lacy; dau. of Edward. She m. (2) 26 May 1743, Edward Treadwell.

Will 11 Feb. 1741/2, proved 25 Mar. 1741/2; four Remaining Children, Samuel, Elizabeth, Hannah, Sarah; wife Sarah.

Children, recorded and bapt. at Stratfield:

Sarah, b. 18 Jan. 1698/9, bapt 22 Jan. 1699, d. 25 May 1699.

Samuel, b. 26 Aug. 1700, bapt. 8 Sept. 1700, d. at New Fairfield, 24 Nov. 1782; Dea.; m. (1) 30 Aug. 1722, Sarah Seeley, dau. of Lt. James, b. 29 June 1703, d. 15 Mar. 1752;* m. (2) at Roxbury, 1 Nov. 1753, Comfort, widow of Lt. Joshua Hurlbut; m. (3) at New Milford, 9 Feb. 1774, Mrs. Anne Moger.

John, b. 4 Dec. 1705, bapt. 9 Dec. 1705, d. at Fairfield, 26 Oct. 1741. Will 1 July 1741, proved 8 Dec. 1741; father Samuel Trowbridge, Exec'r; bro. Samuel, Jr.; sisters Elizabeth Nichols, Hannah Treadwell, Sarah Bennett.

Elizabeth, b. 25 June 1710, bapt. 30 July 1710; m. 13 Oct. 1730, Benjamin Nichols.

Hannah, b. 22 Oct. 1712, bapt. 26 Oct. 1712; m. Jacob Treadwell.

Sarah, b. 15 Nov. 1715, bapt. 19 Feb. 1716; m. Daniel Bennett.

Try, Michael. Deputy (Fairfield) to Conn. Leg., Oct. 1657.

Came to Windsor by 1640, where his wife died 1646; soon after sold his property there and rem. to Fairfield, where he d. in 1677. His first name was often spelled Mihil.

Married (1) ——— Phillips, sister of George of Windsor. Presumably she was the wife who d. at Windsor, 19 May 1646. He m. (2) by 1653, Margery, widow of Richard Root of Fairfield.

---

* For children, see *Trowbridge Genealogy,* pp. 131, 132. Four were recorded at Stratfield: Abigail, b. 9 July 1724, m. [Ephraim?] Lacy; Stephen, b. 30 Jan. 1726/7; Seth, b. 24 June 1729; William, b. 13 Mar. 1732/3.

Est. of George Phillips, who d. at Windsor 9 July 1678, was ordered divided, two-thirds to John Saunders alias Phillips, his brother's son, and one-third to John Grumman, husband of his sister's dau. [The wife of George Phillips was mentioned by Winthrop as above 60 yrs. in 1657.]

Will 13 Apr. 1676; to dau. Sarah wife of John Grumman, £10; gr. child John Grumman, housing and lands near Uncaway River; gr. child Samuel Grumman, houselot by Robert Turney's; gr. child Thomas Grumman, land in Concord Field and long lot; gr. child Mihil Grumman, £10 and rest of long lot; to my kinsman John Roots, the bed my deceased wife gave him, also meadow at the Indian Field; to Benoni Galpin, if he serve out his time with my Exec'rs; residue to gr. children Mihil, Elizabeth, and Sarah Grumman equally; lands entailed to male gr. children; dau. Sarah and gr. son John Grumman, Exec'rs; friends Lt. Banks and Sergt. Squire, overseers. Codicil 17 Apr. 1676; legacy of ten shillings to Richard Lyon, Sr. Inv. 26 Apr. 1677.

Child [by first wife]:

Sarah, d. in 1691; m. [prob. by 1655], John Grumman.

Turney, Benjamin.

He settled in Concord, Mass., by 1639, and was made freeman, June 1641; and removed, we suppose in Sept. 1644 with Rev. Mr. Jones, the Wheelers, and others, to Fairfield. Here he d. in 1648; and it may be guessed that he or his wife was closely related to Ann wife of Thomas Wheeler, Sr., for in her will 1659, which was witnessed by Robert Turney, Mrs. Wheeler gave her best hat to Rebecca Turney.

He m. Mary ———, who m. (2) Joseph Middlebrook.

Inv. 6 June 1648, presented by Mary Turney, 10 Nov. 1648. Ages of children: Mary 17, Robert 15, Judith 13, Ann 11, Rebecca 8, Sarah 6, Ruth 4, Benjamin 3. Receipts were given to Joseph Middlebrook in 1661 by Nathaniel Seeley in behalf of his wife and for use of sister Sarah; John Wheeler in behalf of his wife and for use of sister Ruth Turney and bro. Benjamin Turney and sister Rebecca; and Stephen Sherwood who m. the said Rebecca acknowledged receipt of her portion; also Thomas Sherwood receipted to Middlebrook for his wife's portion. John Wheeler by 1673 purchased from Stephen and Matthew Sherwood all their interest in right of their wives, the daus. of Benjamin Turney dec'd.

A Richard Turney settled early in Virginia and is claimed as ancestor by some of the southern Turneys. Joseph of Stamford, whose record we give below, was prob. closely related to Benjamin.

Children, three recorded at Concord:

> Mary, b. abt. 1631, d. before 1674; m. abt. Oct. 1649, Nathaniel Seeley; who had land recorded 2 Feb. 1673/4 by virtue of marriage with his wife Mary, dau. of Benjamin Turney dec'd, bounded on a meadow pertaining to the child of Ruth Bouton dec'd.
> +Robert, b. abt. 1633.
> Judith, b. abt. 1635, d. abt. 1672; m. John Wheeler.
> Ann, b. abt. 1637; m. by 1659, Thomas Sherwood.
> Rebecca, b. 16 Feb. 1639/40; m. Stephen Sherwood.
> Sarah, b. 11 Dec. 1641; m. by 1670, Matthew Sherwood.
> Ruth, b. 28 Jan. 1643/4, d. in 1666; m. Richard Bouton.
> +Benjamin, b. abt. 1645.

Turney, Joseph.

Prob. a nephew of Benjamin Turney, of whose son Robert's estate he was an overseer.

He m. (2) in 1691, Mary, widow of Joshua Hoyt, and dau. of Francis Bell, b. abt. 1646.

Died at Stamford, 24 Dec. 1713; widow Mary, d. 29 Sept. 1724.

Will 30 July 1713, proved 9 June 1715; wife to have negro girl; son and heir Thomas Turney now present here and bound for London, all Est., and to be Exec'r; Capt. Joseph Bishop and Mr. Daniel Smith of Stamford, overseers. Inv. sworn by widow Mary.

Joseph conveyed 22 Dec. 1713 to his gr. son-in-law Nathan Ferris; Mary, widow of Joseph, conveyed 14 Mar. 1717, to son-in-law Joseph Ferris, Sr. Mary, widow of Joseph, receipted to son-in-law Thomas Turney, 21 Feb. 1715/6. [Stamford Deeds.]

Mary Turney, ae. abt. 46, testified Oct. 1692 in Clawson witch-craft trial.

Children [by first wife]:

> Edward, d. at Stamford, 11 Feb. 1705 [1705/6]; Inv. 4 Aug. 1715; brother Thomas, only heir.
> Thomas, may be the Thomas Turney who settled at Killingworth and m. Mercy Stevens, dau. of James, b. 7 Mar. 1685. He was of New Haven, 18 Mar. 1722/3 [Stamford Deeds].

Turney, Robert, s. of Benjamin. Capt., Fairfield Trainband, Oct. 1685.

Born abt. 1633, d. at Fairfield abt. Jan. 1690; m. Elizabeth Holly, dau. of John, whose will 1681 called her Elizabeth Turney.

Will 31 Dec. 1689; sons Benjamin, Robert; wife Elizabeth; Joseph Jennings in right of his wife; Ephraim Wheeler in right of his wife; daus. Elizabeth, Mary, Ruth, Martha, Rebecca; bro.-in-law, Samuel Wilson, Exec'r; brethren Sergt. John Wheeler and Benjamin Turney, overseers; mentioned meadow between Samuel Morehouse's heirs and Ruth Bouton's heirs. Inv. of Capt. Robert, 17 Jan. 1689 [1689/90]. Sergt. John Wheeler being dead, Mr. Joseph Turney was appointed to take his place, 12 June 1690.

Samuel Wilson of Fairfield, Exec'r of Robert Turney's will, conveyed 5 Dec. 1716 to Robert Turney, Jr., in consideration of amounts the latter had paid to his sisters Martha Treadwell, Mary Treadwell, and Ruth Turney, and to Timothy Wheeler.

Children, recorded at Fairfield:

>Abigail, b. 25 Feb. 1661 [1661/2]; m. Joseph Jennings.
>Sarah, b. 27 Sept. 1663; m. Ephraim Wheeler.
>Elizabeth, b. 15 July 1668; prob. m. (1) abt. 1690, Israel Rowland; and (2) (by contract 10 June 1724) John Staples.
>Rebecca, b. 10 July 1671; m. at Stratfield, 11 Apr. 1689, Timothy Wheeler.
>Mary, b. 9 Dec. 1673; m. Edward Treadwell.
>Martha, b. 5 June 1676, d. at Stratfield, 3 Jan. 1733/4; m. (1) Samuel Treadwell; m. (2) 14 Feb. 1720/1, Samuel Smedley.
>Benjamin, b. abt. 1679, d. at Stamford in 1698. Inv. 29 Apr. 1698 of Benjamin son of Capt. Turney who d. at Stamford ae. abt. 19 yrs.; only item was a bed valued at £5 which was ordered to be divided by Samuel Wilson to the surviying children of Capt. Turney.
>+Robert, b. [say 1682].
>Ruth.

Turney, Benjamin, s. of Benjamin.

Born abt. 1645, d. at Fairfield in 1694; m. (rec. Fairfield) 16 Nov. 1671, Rebecca Keeler; dau. of Ralph, bapt. 9 Feb. 1650/1. She m. (2) (rec. Wallingford, m. by Capt. Gould) 21 Sept. 1699, Dr. John Hull.

He bought land from Joseph Patchen, Sr., 20 Apr. 1671.

Inv. of Benjamin dec'd in year 1694; widow Rebecca with her son Benjamin appeared in Court, 28 Nov. 1694. Ages of children; Benjamin 22, Robert 20, Thomas 15, Rebecca 18, Sarah 15, Jemima 8, Jonah 4.

Children, first four recorded at Fairfield:

> Benjamin, b. 3 Sept. 1672, prob. d. unm. In 1700, Robert Turney maintained his blind bro. Benjamin.
> +Robert, b. 6 Mar. 1673 [1673/4].
> Rebecca, b. 16 Oct. 1676.
> +Thomas, b. 5 Jan. 1678 [1678/9].
> Sarah, b. [perhaps 1681]; m. Daniel Adams.
> Jemima, b. abt. 1686.
> +Jonah, b. abt. 1690.

Turney, Robert, s. of Robert.

Born [say 1682], d. at Fairfield in 1764.

He m. Elizabeth Wilson, dau. of Samuel.

He and his wife Elizabeth renewed their Covenant at Fairfield Church, 26 Oct. 1712. At the bapt. of children, he was designated "Jr." and "of Town," to distinguish him from his cousin. Samuel Wilson conveyed 1724 to son-in-law Robert Turney, Jr., land for his wife's portion.

Adm'n granted, 27 Nov. 1764, to Nathaniel Burr of Fairfield. Distribution to eldest son John, son Stephen, and dau. Mary wife of Capt. Nathaniel Burr.

Children, bapt. at Fairfield:

> Mary, bapt. 26 Oct. 1712, d. by 1785 and prob. earlier; m. 23 Nov. 1732, Nathaniel Burr, Jr.
> Elizabeth, bapt. 23 May 1714, d. y.
> ✕John, bapt. 31 Mar. 1716/7; m. 28 Dec. 1742, Esther Gold, dau. of Samuel.
> ✕Stephen, bapt. 28 May 1721, d. at Fairfield in 1786; will 24 Jan. 1786, proved 6 Feb. 1786; m. (1) 5 Nov. 1744, Hester Middlebrook, who d. 9 Mar. 1747; m. (2) 17 Dec. 1747, Sarah Squire; m. (3) 9 Feb. 1773, Widow Abiah Mitchell, dau. of Josiah Treadwell.

Turney, Robert, s. of Benjamin.

Born at Fairfield, 6 Mar. 1673/4, d. at Fairfield, 1741; m. Rebecca, widow of Luke Guire, and dau. of John Odell; she d. by end of 1741.

Will 25 Nov. 1740, proved 7 May 1741; wife Rebecca; sons Robert, John; three daus., Rebecca Summers, Deborah Burr, Jerusha Bradley. Distribution to dau. Jerusha wife of Joseph Bradley, sons Robert and John, dau. Rebecca wife of Samuel Summers, and dau. Deborah wife of James Burr.

Adm'n on Est. of Rebecca granted, 11 Jan. 1741/2, to Mr. Robert Turney.

Children, bapt. at Fairfield:

> XRobert, bapt. 30 Aug. 1702, d. at Trumbull, 1 Jan. 1753 in 50 yr. (g. s.) ; adm'n granted 6 Mar. 1753; m. Rebecca Burr, dau. of Daniel, bapt. 29 Oct. 1710, d. at Trumbull, 7 Sept. 1794 in 84 yr. (g. s.) ; she m. (2) 3 June 1756, Jonadab Bassett.
> Rebecca, m. Samuel Summers, of Newtown.
> Abigail, bapt. 23 Mar. 1706/7, d. y.
> XJohn, bapt. 22 May 1709, d. at Trumbull, 11 Aug. 1786 in 78 yr. (g. s.) ; m. at Stratfield, 23 May 1734, Hannah Porter; dau. of Nathaniel, bapt. 8 July 1705, d. 1 June 1790 in 85 yr. (g. s.).
> Deborah, bapt. June 1711; m. James Burr.
> Jerusha, bapt. 17 May 1713, d. at Greenfield, 16 Jan. 1746 in 34 yr. (g. s.) ; m. 9 Nov. 1732, Joseph Bradley, Jr.

Turney, Thomas, s. of Benjamin.

Born at Fairfield, 5 Jan. 1678/9, d. there in 1761; m. at Stratfield, 24 Nov. 1709, Abigail Welles.

Will 9 Apr. 1756, proved 5 Jan. 1762; wife Abigail; son Thomas; gr. son William Osborn; son Samuel; five gr. children, Elizabeth, Reuben, Benjamin, Abigail, and Eunice, children of dau. Abigail Whitehead dec'd; four daus., Rebecca, Sarah, Jemima, Ann; gr. children Dorothy, Hezekiah, and Isaac Osborn, children of dau. Elizabeth; son Thomas and son-in-law Elnathan Sturgis, Exec'rs.

He conveyed 7 June 1759 to daus. Rebecca Sturgis and Ann Turney, and gr. children Elizabeth, Andrew, Peter, Aaron, Sarah, Gershom, Turney, and Nathan Bulkley, children of dec'd dau. Sarah, and Jemima and Mehitabel Barlow, children of dec'd dau. Jemima.

Children:

> Abigail, m. Nathaniel Whitehead.
> Benjamin, b. abt. 1713, d. at Greenfield, 7 Mar. 1755 in 42 yr. (g. s.) ; m. at Redding, Oct. 1740, Eunice Lyon, who d. 8 Jan. 1744 ae. 22

(g. s.). Inv. 3 Apr. 1755 sworn by Elnathan Sturgis and Thomas Turney, Jr., Adm'rs; his father Thomas mentioned. Distribution to bro. Thomas and 2d bro. Samuel; heirs of Abigail, eldest sister; Sarah, 4th sister; Rebecca, 3d sister; Ann, 6th sister; Jemima, 5th sister; heirs of Elizabeth, 2d sister.

Elizabeth, b. abt. 1715, d. 16 Feb. 1741 in 26 yr. (Bible rec.); m. 7 Nov. 1733 (Bible rec.), William Osborn.

Rebecca, b. 4 Aug. 1717; m. 14 Mar. 1733, Elnathan Sturgis.

✗Thomas, m. 28 Dec. 1746, Martha Lyon, dau. of Samuel.

✗Samuel, d. at Greenfield, 27 Aug. 1777, ae. upwards of 50; m. 5 Nov. 1750, Mary Baker, dau. of Benjamin.

Sarah, d. abt. 1758; m. 1 Jan. 1741, Peter Bulkley.

Jemima, m. 25 Jan. 1751, Nehemiah Barlow.

Ann, m. John Olmstead, Jr., of Ridgefield, whose wife she was in 1762.

Turney, Jonah, s. of Benjamin.

Born abt. 1690. He m. Mary Guire, dau. of Luke, b. abt. 1695.

In 1734 Thomas Turney of Greenfield conveyed Stratford land to bro. Jonas of Stratfield.

On 4 Mar. 1754, Jonah and Mary his wife of Stratford conveyed land distributed to Mary from Edward Adams' right in commonage of Fairfield.

On 12 Mar. 1753, Jonah of Stratford conveyed for love to son Daniel Turney of Stratford, land in Stratford below Jacob's Brook with a new dwelling house.

Samuel Bassett and Eunice his wife, and Daniel Turney and Katee his wife, all of Stratford, for £200 received from mother Hannah Beach, conveyed, 4 Dec. 1749, to bro. David Beach a right to house and land of father David Beach dec'd.

This branch has not been traced further.

Ufford, Thomas.

Came in the *Lion* 1632, settled in Roxbury; rem. with Pynchon to Springfield 1635; and within a few years to Milford. There his wife Isabel joined the church, Jan. 1644/5, and he on 11 Feb. 1644/5. His wife d. before him, and he m. (2) abt. 1659, Elizabeth, widow of Nicholas Theale of Stamford. She d. 27 Dec. 1660; and he earlier that year.

Inv. 6 Dec. 1660; estate in Milford and Stratford; sons Thomas and John mentioned.

Children:

+Thomas.
Abigail, m. Roger Terrill, of Milford.
+John.

Ufford, Thomas, s. of Thomas.

He early owned land in Wethersfield, where he m. Frances Kilbourn, dau. of Thomas. Settled in Stratford, where the record states he and wife d. in 1683.

Will 17 May 1683, proved 2 Jan. 1683 [1683/4]; cousin Samuel, son of bro. John of Milford; wife Frances; children of bro. John Uffoot and children of bro. Roger Terrill.

Inv. of Frances Ufford, 2 Jan. 1683 [1683/4]. Distribution ordered to bro. John Kilbourn of Wethersfield; children of sister Mrs. Margaret Law; sister Lydia wife of Robert Howard; sister Mary wife of John Root, Sr.

Ufford, John, s. of Thomas.

He remained in Milford, where he d. in 1692. He m. (1) Hannah Hawley, sister of Mr. Joseph of Stratford. They agreed to disagree, and she succeeded in divorcing him on the ground that he was unqualified for the marital relation, and m. (2) Capt. John Beard, of Milford. The New Haven Colony Court, which had granted the divorce, felt badly used and made an inquiry when John sought to m. Martha* Nettleton (orphan dau. of Samuel of Branford and Fairfield), then an apprentice in the elder Ufford's household. The marriage was permitted, and apparently took place abt. June 1657.

Will 29 July 1689, proved 4 May 1692; eldest dau. Martha Carrow and her son Samuel Carrow; two youngest daus. Elizabeth and Lydia Uffet; dau. Mary Pickett; son Samuel (his uncle hath given him a large legacy); son John.

Children, recorded at Milford:

Thomas, b. 20 Aug. 1657, d. y.
Martha, b. 12 Aug. 1659, d. at Durham, 14 Feb. 1739 ae. 70(?); m. (1) Peter Carrow, of Milford; m. (2) by 1699, Samuel Camp, son of Nicholas, 2d.
Mary, b. 20 June 1661; m. (rec. Stratford) 13 Sept. 1683, Daniel Pickett.

---

* Her name erroneously reads *Hannah* in the *overwritten* original marriage record.

John, b. 3 Feb. 1665, d. y.

John, b. 21 Jan. 1666 [1666/7], d. at Milford in 1712; m. Abigail ———.

+Samuel, b. 25 June 1670.

Elizabeth, b. 19 Feb. 1672 [1672/3], d. in 1699. Inv. 18 May 1699, sworn by her sister Lydia, ae. abt. 21. Distribution to bros. and sisters: John and Samuel Uffort; Martha Camp (with Samuel Camp); Mary Pickett (with Daniel Pickett); Lydia Uffort.

Lydia, b. 21 Oct. 1677; m. 1 Feb. 1704/5, Samuel Camp, Jr.

Ufford, Samuel, s. of John. Ens., 1st company, Stratford, May 1714; Lt., south co., Stratford, May 1720.

Born at Milford, 25 June 1670; Lt. Samuel d. at Stratford, 30 Dec. 1746 in 77 yr.; m. at Stratford, 5 Dec. 1694, Elizabeth Curtis, dau. of Joseph, b. 17 Jan. 1677/8.

Adm'n granted, 6 Jan. 1746/7, to sons Thomas and Joseph. Distribution named daus. as Martha Hubbell, Elizabeth Beers, Eunice DeForest, Bethia Hawley, heirs of Abigail Beach, Anna Patterson, Mary Hawley.

Children, recorded at Stratford:

Martha, b. 28 Sept. 1695; m. 18 June 1713, Josiah Hubbell.

Elizabeth, b. 3 Apr. 1698; m. 10 May 1717, Josiah Beers.

Abigail, b. May 1700, d. at Cheshire, 2 Dec. 1738; m. 9 May 1720, Elnathan Beach.

Anna, b. 8 Aug. 1702; m. (1) 30 Nov. 1720, Joseph Burton; m. (2) 22 Aug. 1723, William Patterson.

Mary, b. 16 Apr. 1704, bapt. at Stratford ("Elizabeth", says Stratfield rec. in error) 23 July 1704; m. 12 Dec. 1723, Nathaniel Hawley.

Thomas, b. 22 Jan. 1705/6, d. in 1770; Inv. 18 Dec. 1770; m. (1) 30 Dec. 1725, Phebe Judson [error for Phebe Welles, dau. of John and Mary (Judson), b. 17 Feb. 1707]; m. (2) Sarah, widow of James Beach, and dau. of John Curtis.

Bethia, b. 12 May 1708; m. [Oliver?] Hawley.

Sarah, b. 15 Mar. 1710.

Samuel, b. 12 Apr. 1712; m. 21 Dec. 1738, Joanna Moss, dau. of John.

Eunice, b. 2 Nov. 1713; m. 8 June 1733, Edward DeForest.

Joseph, b. 15 Nov. 1715; will 11 Dec. 1753; m. 24 Feb. 1742/3, Ruth Lewis, dau. of Edmund.

John, b. 23 Nov. 1717, d. 15 May 1721.

Ebenezer, m. 17 Nov. 1743, Jane Moss.

Usher, Robert, constable at Stamford (under New Haven Colony), 1662, 1663; Deputy to Conn. Leg., May 1665, May 1667.

Of New Haven, where he took Oath of Fidelity, 1644; rem. to Stamford.

He m. at Stamford, 12 May 1659, Elizabeth Jagger. She was widow of Jeremy.

Will 21 Sept. 1669; two children, Robert and Elizabeth; to Deborah Rose, £5; to Richard Cousins, £1; brother Mr. Hezekiah Usher of Boston to have my two children if he send for them, and if my wife can consent to part with them. Inv. 26 Oct. 1669.

Richard Cousins, mentioned in the will, and prob. a relative, settled in Saybrook; Deborah Rose, possibly a sister of Cousins, was supposedly first wife of the second John Rose of Branford.

Children:

> Elizabeth, b. 25 Feb. 1659/60.
> Robert, perhaps son by a former marriage; settled in Dunstable, Mass.

Vicars, Philip.   [Surname also spelled Vickers.]

Blacksmith, of Fairfield 1692; perhaps related to George Vicars who m. Rebecca Phippen, stepdau. of George Hull. He prob. m. (1) Abigail ———, who was admitted to Fairfield Church 2 June 1695, and (2) Hannah Pardee, dau. of George, b. at New Haven, 7 July 1672.

He sold land in Fairfield to Mr. John Campbell of Boston, 1698, and sold other land 1701, and rem. to Fairfield, Salem County, N. J., where he d. in 1703 leaving widow Hannah.

Vowles, Richard.   Deputy (for Hastings?) to Conn. Leg., Oct. 1665, and for Rye, Oct. 1668, May 1669.

The surname is also spelled Fowles. The family of a Richard Fowle of Frittenden, co. Kent, Eng., whose daughter Joan was wife of Richard Borden of Portsmouth, R. I., may be seen in *New Eng. Hist. and Gen. Register,* vol. 75, p. 232.

He m. Mary Sadler, dau. of John of Wethersfield.

Bought house in Fairfield, 25 Nov. 1661, from Thomas Bassett.

Removed to Greenwich, thence to Hastings 1663, a town which did not long survive under that name, and remained at Rye; died apparently about 1685.

Winthrop in 1669 wrote of Mary wife of Richard Fowle of Hastings an island near Rye,—she is Goodman Sadler's dau. of Wethersfield; her age he stated in 1668 as 40 yrs.

Had son Jonathan living 1713 at Rye. Jonathan conveyed 1707 to his cousin John Odell; and in 1698 with his wife Deborah to kinsman John Church. Aged abt. 57, Jonathan testified 16 May 1704.

Wakelee, James.

He had lands recorded in Hartford, Feb. 1639/40. For several years thereafter, his name frequently appears in law-suits, and he sometimes acted as attorney for others. He m. 5 Oct. 1652, Alice, widow of James Boosey of Wethersfield, and removed there. Constable of Wethersfield, Mar. 1656/7; served on several juries, 1655-62. Before Jan. 1663 he fled from his wife and family to Rhode Island. In May 1663, Henry Wakelee had a power of attorney from James. It seems that James forfeited a bond of £150 which he had given for his appearance, and his housing and land were ordered sold. He had been accused of a capital crime, presumably witchcraft.

Attempts of James and Alice to divorce each other were unsuccessful. She d. at Wethersfield, 30 Aug. 1683. He petitioned in 1681 vainly for the remission of his forfeiture, and is said to have been living in Providence as late as 1690, when he must have been quite old, as he certainly was b. by 1610, and we should guess that he was b. by 1600.

The relationship of James to Henry and Richard Wakelee is not exactly determined, but it is a reasonable guess that they were his sons by an earlier marriage.

Probable children :*

+Henry, b. by 1620.
Richard, b. by 1634; freeman, 1657; taxed in Hartford, 1655-57; settled early in Haddam, where he was a freeman in 1669 and d. by 6 Aug. 1681; left widow, two sons, and a dau.† His widow Rebecca m. (2) Daniel Cone, Sr.

---

* We do not know how many times James was married, and by an intermediate wife he could have been father of Rebecca "Wiekle" whose marriage 25 Apr. 1665 to Ezekiel Sanford is recorded at Fairfield. Supposing her born abt. 1645, it is unlikely that she was dau. of Henry by his only known wife (m. 1649), but she could have been dau. of Henry by an earlier unknown wife, though not mentioned in his will.

† A dau. Rebecca, b. 12 Aug. 1672, and a son Richard (Sergt.), b. 31 Mar. 1678, d. 23 June 1756 in 79 yr., by Haddam records. The dau. Rebecca m. by 1692, John Booge.

Wakelee, Henry [s. of James?]. Colonial grant of 50 acres, May 1669, doubtless for service in Pequot War (1637). Granted 200 acres, May 1681, for service to the Colony in or about Mattebeseck [Waterbury] (not laid out until 1716, and then assigned by James, son of Henry, to Benjamin Fairweather of Stratfield).

Res. Hartford, but removed early to Stratford. His service at Mattebeseck prob. refers to a punitive expedition of 100 men sent out in Aug. 1639, as a sequel to the Pequot War.

Married 4 Sept. 1649, Sarah, widow of Judah Gregory, and dau. of Henry Burt of Springfield. He was granted adm'n, 15 May 1650, on the "Estate of his wive's other husband."

Will 11 July 1689, codicil 5 Apr. 1690, exhibited 8 Nov. 1690; wife Sarah; sons Deliverance, James, Jacob; daus. Patience and Abigail (single); to Thomas Lattin, five sheep; to Elizabeth Squire, a cow; to dau. Mary Stevens, a cow; to "Henry Sumers y^t Lives with me besides what I have Given: A Cow." Witnesses: Zechariah Fairchild, Samuel Preston.

Children:

+Deliverance, b. abt. 1651.
+James.
+Jacob.
Mary, m. ―――― Stevens, prob. James Stevens of Killingworth.
Patience, m. at Stratford, 3 Oct. 1692, Timothy Titherton.
Abigail [b. abt. 1665, d. Aug. 1753 ae. 88; m. abt. 1691, John Beardsley.]
?Mercy, m. (1) by 1687, Thomas Lattin; m. (2) at Stratford, 31 Aug. 1721, Mr. Moses Wheeler; m. (3) at Stratford, 9 May 1726, Mr. John Burritt.

Wakelee, Deliverance, s. of Henry.

Born about 1651, d. at Stratford, 6 Nov. 1707; in 57 yr. (g. s.).

Married (rec. Stratford) 3 Dec. 1678, Hannah Nash. She was dau. of Edward.

Will 15 Oct. 1707, proved 5 Dec. 1707; aged mother Sarah Wakelee; Mary Summers, which long lived with me and hath been very kind to me, to share with my two daus., Sarah and Mary Wakelee; brother-in-law Timothy Titherton, Exec'r, with Ambrose Thompson, Sr.

Children, recorded at Stratford:

Hannah, b. 15 Oct. 1679, d. Aug. 1683.

Ebenezer, b. 23 Oct. 1681, d. 27 Mar. 1683.

Henry, b. 1 Dec. 1683, d. 7 Dec. 1683.

Sarah, b. 1 Dec. 1683; m. (rec. Norwalk) 12 June 1710, Nathaniel Ketchum.

Mary, b. 3 Mar. 1688/9; m. 25 Nov. 1708, Joseph Burritt.

Wakelee, James, s. of Henry.

Married (1) [possibly Hannah Peat, b. 6 Dec. 1667; see JACOB WAKELEE].

Married (2) at Stratford, 26 Feb. 1701/2, Hannah Griffin. She was dau. of Hugh, b. about 1675.

He, of Stratford, conveyed 1725 to son Joseph of Stratford; on 3 Feb. 1728/9, being of Stratford, now resident in Guilford, he conveyed to son-in-law Nehemiah Allen land in Ripton parish.

Children, first two recorded at Stratford:

✕James, b. 28 Dec. 1688, d. at Stratford in 1762; will 23 Apr. 1745, proved 4 May 1762; m. Sarah Shelton.

Henry, b. 15 May 1691.

✕Joseph, d. in 1729; will dated Stratford 10 July 1729, proved at Woodbury; m. 24 Apr. 1723, Elizabeth Clark. She m. (2) at Woodbury, 23 Sept. 1729, John Squire.

Dinah, m. 26 Nov. 1719, David Curtis.

Abigail.

Hannah, m. 30 May 1728, Nehemiah Allen.

Wakelee, Jacob, s. of Henry.

Called "Dr." in 1726.

He m. (1) ———, widow of Richard Wallis of Norwich.

[He m. (2) Hannah Peat, dau. of John, b. 6 Dec. 1667. This statement is made in *Hist. of Stratford*, also in *Hist. of Fairfield*, where Hannah Peat is the only wife attributed to Jacob. It is obvious that she was not old enough to be mother of the older children; she was wife of a Wakelee in 1694, and could have been second wife of Jacob, or first wife of James Wakelee.]

Will 30 Dec. 1726, codicil 7 Jan. 1726/7, proved 24 Feb. 1726/7; sons Jonathan, Henry, Joseph, Israel, Nathaniel; daus. Ruth wife of John Lacy, Ann wife of Timothy Wheeler, Jr.; grandsons Jacob son of Jonathan, and Timothy son of Timothy Wheeler.

Witnesses: John Fairchild, Alexander Fairchild, Jr., and Thomas Sherwood.

Children [by first wife], recorded at Stratford:

Jacob, b. 10 Feb. 1677 [1677/8], d. y.

×Jonathan, b. 9 Feb. 1678/9, d. at Stratfield, in 1743; will 13 Dec. 1742, proved 7 June 1743; m. abt. 1704, Mary Beardsley, dau. of Samuel, b. 1 May 1680, d. after 1742.

Ruth, b. 27 Aug. 1681; m. (1) abt. 1703, Ephraim Treadwell; m. (2) John Lacey.

×Henry, b. 27 Jan. 1683 [1683/4], d. at Stratfield, 9 Jan. 1743 [1743/4] in 60 yr. (g. s.); Corp'l in Canadian Expedition, 1709; adm'n granted, 13 Feb. 1743/4, to Nathan Seeley; m. (1) (rec. Stratford) 12 Dec. 1706, Rachel Stratton, who d. 10 Mar. 1708 [1707/8 by Stratford rec.] ae. [—] (g. s., Stratfield); m. (2) (rec. Stratford) 26 Jan. 1710/1, Sarah Frost.

×Joseph, b. 17 Sept. 1686, d. bef. 16 Apr. 1760 (agreement of heirs); m. ———.

×Israel, b. 4 Feb. 1689 [1689/90], d. 29 Mar. [1786] in 75 yr. (g. s., Trumbull); will 29 Apr. 1768, proved 8 May 1786; m. Abigail ———, b. abt. 1688, d. 12 Nov. 1765 in 78 yr. (g. s.).

×Nathaniel, b. (no record), d. at Stratfield, in 1771; adm'n granted, 19 Feb. 1771, to Ephraim Fairchild; m. Rebecca ———.

Ann, b. abt. 1693, d. at Stratfield, 18 July 1764 in 72 yr. (g. s.); m. at Stratfield, 29 Jan. 1712/3, Timothy Wheeler.

Wakeman, John. Magistrate (New Haven), Oct. 1641, Apr. 1642, Oct. 1642, Apr. 1643, Oct. 1643, Mar. 1644, Oct. 1644, May 1655, May 1656, May 1657, May 1658, May 1659, May 1660; Deputy (New Haven) to New Haven Leg., Apr. 1646, Oct. 1646, Oct. 1647, May 1648, May 1655, May 1656, May 1657, May 1658, May 1660; Treasurer, New Haven Col., May 1655, May 1656, May 1657, May 1658, May 1659, May 1660; Assistant, New Haven Col., May 1661 (declined).

Son of Francis and Anne (Goode) Wakeman, bapt. at Bewdley, co. Worcester, Eng., 29 Mar. 1601, d. at Hartford in 1661; m. 28 Jan. 1628/9, Elizabeth dau. of William and Helen (Vickaris) Hopkins, bapt. at Ribbesford Church, co. Worcester, 7 Oct. 1610, d. at New Haven in 1658.

An early but not original signer of the New Haven compact; sold his house and homelot to John Punderson, June 1659, and in May 1660 it was doubtful whether he should remain in New Haven; was on the eve of moving, May 1661; so d. soon after settling in Hartford.

The religious preamble to his will indicates that he was thoughtful and tolerant to a degree unusual in his generation.

Will of John of New Haven, 18 June 1660; dau. Helena wife of John Talcott of Hartford, and their children John, Elizabeth and Samuel; son Samuel and his sons Samuel and John; dau. Elizabeth wife of Samuel Kitchell and her dau. Elizabeth; bro.-in-law Adam Nichols of Hartford, his wife Anna Nichols my sister, and their children John, Hannah, Sarah, Ebenezer; Hannah Cheever (under 18), £5; servant Thomas Huxley; mentioned cousin John Walker; friends and brethren Henry Glover and James Bishop, overseers; sisters Davis and Glover to assist with counsel. Witnesses: Martha Davis, Ellen Glover. Inv. taken at Hartford, 14 Sept. 1661.

Children:

> John, bapt. 25 July 1630, d. 19 Jan. 1636.
> Helena, bapt. 23 Dec. 1632, d. at Hartford, 2 June 1674; m. 29 Oct. 1650, Lt.-Col. John Talcott. One of their children was Hannah, b. 8 Dec. 1663, m. Nathan Gold, 2d, of Fairfield. By his second wife, Talcott was father of Ruth, b. 12 Sept. 1677, m. John Reed of Fairfield; and of Rachel, b. 23 Feb. 1681/2, m. Gershom Bulkley of Fairfield.
> +Samuel, bapt. 7 June 1635.
> Elizabeth, bapt. 16 Sept. 1638; m. at New Haven, 11 Mar. 1656/7, Samuel Kitchell; rem. to Newark, N. J.

Wakeman, Samuel. Deputy (Cambridge) to Mass. Leg., May 1635; Constable, Hartford, Apr. 1636.

Son of Francis, and younger bro. of John, bapt. at Bewdley, co. Worcester, 25 Sept. 1603, killed at Providence in the Bahamas, summer of 1641; m. Elizabeth ———, who m. (2) before 1645, Nathaniel Willett of Hartford.

He came in the *Lion,* arriving Nov. 1631, and settled in Roxbury. Rev. John Eliot of Roxbury tells when Wakeman came; "he buryed his only child at sea . . . . Elizabeth his first borne here."

Samuel's Est. was settled, 4 Dec. 1645, on Nathaniel Willett, he to pay £40 to the eldest son at 21, and £20 apiece to the three daus. at 18. Ezbon Wakeman receipted 1657 to father-in-law Nathaniel Willett. Hannah Hacleton, dau. of Samuel Wakeman, gave receipt, 6 Sept. 1662, as did also Joseph Arnold and Elizabeth his wife; and John Kelly receipted for his wife's portion, 10 June 1663.

Children:

Child, d. at sea 1631.
Elizabeth, b. [say 1633]; m. Joseph Arnold.
+Ezbon, b. [say 1635].
Joanna, b. [say 1637]; m. Francis Hackleton, of Northampton.
Daughter, b. [say 1640]; m. John Kelly, of Hartford.

Wakeman, (Rev.) Samuel, s. of John. Colonial grant of 200 acres, May 1673. Preached Election Sermon, 1685, and again (perhaps 1690).

Bapt. at Bewdley, co. Worcester, Eng., 7 June 1635, d. at Fairfield, 8 Mar. 1691/2; m. at New Haven, 29 Oct. 1656, Hannah Goodyear, dau. of Dep.-Gov. Stephen; she m. (2) Nathaniel Burr, and d. in 1721.

Ann Wakeman testified in the witchcraft trials, Sept. 1692. It is odd that in this and the probate record (1721) her name appears as "Ann"; but this name was sometimes used interchangeably with "Hannah", and no evidence has been found to suggest that Mr. Wakeman had more than one wife.

Will 8 Mar. 1692; £3 to Church for silver bowl; £3 to a grammar school in Fairfield; £2 to the poor, ten shillings of it to Thomas Jones; Indian servant Jane to have liberty at 26 (in 1698) and £5; son Samuel dec'd had portion (and the loan of silver money at his last marriage); sons Joseph and Jabesh (latter to be brought up to learning) and dau. Mary; wife; son John, Exec'r. Inv. 8 Apr. 1692.

Adm'n on Est. of Mrs. Ann Burr of Fairfield granted, 9 Nov. 1721, to Capt. Joseph Wakeman, who presented Inv. "of his mother."

Children, first recorded at New Haven:

+Samuel, b. 12 Oct. 1657.
+John, b. abt. 1660.
Ann, m. (1) Nathaniel James; m. (2) 2 Oct. 1690, Capt. Abraham Howell, of Southampton, L. I.
Ebenezer, d. at Fairfield in 1690/1. Inv. 26 Feb. 1690 [1690/1]; adm'n granted to his father, 2 Dec. 1691. Distribution ordered to three bros., and sisters. The Adm'r being dead, 16 Jan. 1692 [1692/3], Sergt. John Wakeman was appointed. On 6 Sept. 1694, John Wakeman, Albert Dennie, Abraham Howell, Michael Clugston, and Joseph Wakeman, conveyed to bro. "Jabish" all interest in estate of bro. Ebenezer.

Elizabeth, m. by 1693, Albert Dennie.

+Joseph, b. abt. 1670.

Mary, m. (1) by 1694, Michael Clugston; m. (2) abt. 1706, Thomas Staples.

+Jabez, b. abt. 1679.

Wakeman, Ezbon, s. of Samuel.

Settled in Stratford, rem. to Fairfield, and d. in 1683.

Married at Stratford, 28 June 1666, Hannah Jordan of Guilford. She was dau. of John Jordan, and m. (2) abt. Sept. 1684, Mr. Joseph Bastard.

Inv. dated 1683; widow made oath 16 Nov. 1683. Lt. Ezbon left wife Hannah and dau. Abigail.

Child:

Abigail, b. [say 1668]; m. (soon after 9 Nov. 1685), Capt. Thomas Hill.

Wakeman, Samuel, s. of Samuel.

Born at New Haven, 12 Oct. 1657, d. at Fairfield in 1691; m. (1) Mary Burr, dau. of Jehu 2d; m. (2) Sarah Knowles, dau. of John. She m. (2) at Fairfield, 18 Nov. 1696, Dugal MacKenzie.

Will 23 Feb. 1690 [1690/1]; dau. Mary had portion by deed of gift; wife Sarah, and child she now goes with; if the child does not live, then the Est. wife brought to be to her heirs, and my own Est. to bro. Joseph Wakeman; bro. John Wakeman and wife, Exec'rs.

Inv. 4 June 1691; adm'n granted to widow Sarah. On 1 Nov. 1691, Capt. John Burr and Sergt. John Wakeman were appointed overseers of the dau. Mary.

On 2 Mar. 1693/4, Samuel Hubbell of Fairfield, having received £50 from Sarah Wakeman, Exec'x to her husband Samuel Wakeman, Jr., of Fairfield dec'd for use of his dau. Mary Wakeman, it being given her by her father by deed of gift, conveyed etc.

Child [by first wife]:

Mary, b. [say 1688]; named in will of her gr. father Burr 1690; was living in Milford 1711. On 28 June 1714, Joseph Wakeman of Fairfield, and Mary Wakeman resident in Milford, single woman, discharged Mr. Dugall MacKenzie of all claim to property which Samuel Wakeman of Fairfield died possessed of, excepting only his dwelling house; witnessed by Jonathan Law and Sylvanus Baldwin.

Child [by second wife] :

Sarah, b. 13 May 1691, d. 28 Dec. 1710.

Wakeman, John, s. of Samuel. Deputy for Fairfield, Apr., May and Oct. 1690, Oct. 1692, Sept. and Oct. 1693, May* and Oct. 1694, May and Oct. 1696, May and Oct. 1697, Jan. and Oct. 1698, Oct. 1699, Oct. 1700, Oct. 1701, May and Oct. 1703, Oct. 1705, May 1706, Oct. and Dec. 1707, Oct. 1708. Lt., Fairfield Trainband, May 1697; Capt., May 1704; Capt., east company, Fairfield, May 1705. Commissioner for Fairfield, 1694-98; Justice, 1698-1709; Committee of Safety, Fairfield County, May 1704.

Born abt. 1660; testified in Disbrow witch trial, 1692 ae. 32; d. at Fairfield, 15 Feb. 1708/9; m. at Fairfield, 24 Apr. 1687,† Martha Hubbell; dau. of Richard, d. 5 June 1710.

Inv. 6 Dec. 1709; widow Martha made oath. Adm'n granted to her, 9 Nov. 1709, "he having been deced sometime since." Distribution of Est. of Capt. John, 7 Mar. 1710/1; Samuel, Stephen, John, Elizabeth, Ann, and Martha Wakeman.

Will of Martha, 23 Mar. 1709/10, proved 6 Sept. 1710; son Samuel; daus. Helena, Elizabeth, Ann, Martha; sons Stephen and John (under 21) ; bro. Richard Hubbell, Exec'r.

On 12 Sept. 1710, Elizabeth chose Sergt. Samuel French for guardian, and Samuel chose Maj. Peter Burr; the Court appointed Capt. Joseph Wakeman for Stephen and Joseph, and Maj. Peter Burr for John. Lt. Samuel Hubbell, guardian of Ann and Martha, being dec'd (7 Oct. 1713), they chose their uncle Ens. Richard Hubbell.

Children, recorded at Fairfield :†

Eleanor, b. 24 Aug. 1689, d. 21 Feb. 1710/1.

×Samuel, b. 24 Feb. 1692/3, d. at Greenfield, 19 Oct. 1771 ae. 78 yrs. 7 mos. 23 days (g. s.) ; Lt. and Deacon; will 14 June 1764, proved 5 Nov. 1771; m. Elizabeth ———, b. abt. 1695, d. 14 Mar. 1759 in 64 yr. (g. s.).

Elizabeth, b. 1 June 1695, bapt. 2 June 1695; m. James Bennett.

Ann, b. 24 Mar. 1698, bapt. 17 Apr. 1698; m. by 1717, Benjamin Hill.

---

* Called Mr. Samuel, but no Samuel was living on that date, and John must be meant; the same applies to record of Commissioner for 1694.

† Dates of marriage and births of children are entered in the probate records.

Martha, b. 24 Sept. 1700, bapt. 22 Oct. 1700; m. 2 Feb. 1720/1, Israel Chauncey.

✗Stephen, b. 15 Oct. 1702, bapt. 1 Nov. 1702, d. at Fairfield, in 1761; adm'n granted, 1 Sept. 1761; m. 28 Apr. 1727, Rebecca Morehouse, dau. of Daniel, bapt. 24 Feb. 1711/2, d. in 1761; adm'n granted on her Est., 1 Dec. 1761.

✗John, b. 29 Aug. 1705, bapt. 16 Sept. 1705; m. 8 Apr. 1730, Catherine Gilbert, dau. of Moses, bapt. 3 July 1709, d. at Greenfield, 9 Apr. 1777 ae. 68.

Wakeman, Joseph, s. of Samuel. Lt. for war service, Dec. 1704; Lt., east company, Fairfield, May 1705; Capt. (in place of bro. John, resigned) May 1708; Deputy for Fairfield, May 1705, Oct. 1706, May, Oct., and Dec. 1707, May and Aug. 1710, May and June 1711, May 1712, May and Oct. 1713, May and Oct. 1714, May and Oct. 1715, May and Oct. 1716, May and Oct. 1717, May and Oct. 1718, May and Oct. 1719, Oct. 1720, May and Oct. 1721, Oct. 1722; Assistant, 1724, 1725, 1726; Commissioner, N. Y. Boundary, Oct. 1713, May 1718, Mar. 1719, Mar. 1725; Justice, 1709, 1710, 1721; Judge of Probate, Fairfield, Jan. 1725 to death; Judge, Fairfield County Court, May 1725, but declined.

Born at Fairfield abt. 1670, d. there 5 Dec. 1726 ae. 56 (g. s.); m. by 1698, Elizabeth Hawley, dau. of Ebenezer, b. 6 May 1679, d. 18 Aug. 1753 in 74 yr. (g. s.); she m. (2) Col. John Burr.

He renewed his Covenant at Fairfield Church, 19 Mar. 1699. In 1706 he conveyed right in land which my mother-in-law Esther Lord of Fairfield sold to Robert Silliman, which formerly belonged to her former husband Ebenezer Hawley.

Will 3 Dec. 1726, proved 4 Jan. 1726/7; wife Elizabeth; son Joseph; daus. Katherine Burr, Elisabeth Burr; son Jabez; dau. Mary Wakeman; son Samuel, to be educated at College; son Stephen; gr. child Ebenezer Wakeman (his father Ebenezer had full portion); £3 for silver tumblers to Fairfield Church; £3 to Rev. Joseph Webb of Fairfield; £3 to Rev. Samuel Cooke of Stratfield.

Will of Elizabeth Burr, widow, 28 June 1753, proved 27 Aug. 1753; three sons, Joseph, Jabez, and Stephen Wakeman; dau. Catherine Burr; Seth, Samuel, Daniel, Ebenezer, Nehemiah, and Charles Burr, children of dec'd dau. Elizabeth; Ellen and Elizabeth Burr, children of said dau. Elizabeth; gr. child Catherine Wakeman, dau. of dec'd son Samuel, and his daus. Hannah, Mary, and Elizabeth, and his son Andrew; gr. son Ebenezer Wakeman, son of dec'd son Ebenezer; gr. son William Burr, son of dec'd dau. Mary; £5 each to Widow Sarah Hill and Widow Squire, both of Fairfield, and Widow French of Stratfield.

Children, bapt. at Fairfield:

XEbenezer, b. 10 Feb. 1698/9 [by age at death], bapt. 19 Mar. 1698/9, d. at Fairfield, 25 Sept. 1726 ae. 27 yrs. 7 mos. 15 days; grad. Yale Coll. 1720; m. 24 June 1724, Sarah Sturgis; dau. of Jonathan, bapt. 27 July 1707, d. 15 May 1756 in 52 yr. (g. s.); she m. (2) 26 July 1727, Lothrop Lewis.

Catherine, bapt. 21 Apr. 1700, d. at Stratfield, 25 Sept. 1753 in 53 yr.; m. 18 Oct. 1722, John Burr, Jr.

Elizabeth, bapt. 19 Apr. 1702, d. at Fairfield, 16 June 1753 in 51 yr. (g. s.); m. June 1722, Seth Samuel Burr.

XJoseph, bapt. 14 May 1704, d. at Westport, 23 Sept. 1762 in 59 yr. (g. s.); will 8 Feb. 1753, proved 5 Oct. 1762; m. 31 Oct. 1727, Abigail Allen; dau. of Gideon, bapt. 24 June 1705, d. 1 Jan. 1804 in 100 yr. (g. s.).

XJabez, bapt. 10 Mar. 1705/6, d. at Greenfield, 10 Oct. 1774 ae. 68; will 17 Mar. 1774, proved 1 Nov. 1774; m. 1 June 1727, Ruth Tread-well; dau. of Timothy, bapt. 29 Oct. 1710.

Samuel, bapt. 30 Jan. 1708/9, d. soon.

Mary, bapt. 23 July 1710, d. at Stratfield, 19 Mar. 1742/3 in 33 yr. (g. s.); m. 4 Aug. 1736, William Burr.

XSamuel, bapt. 1 Nov. 1713, d. at Fairfield, 15 Aug. 1752 in 39 yr. (g. s.); adm'n granted, 5 Dec. 1752; m. Ruth ———.

XStephen, bapt. 10 Mar. 1716/7, d. at Westport, 25* Mar. 1760 in 44 yr. (g. s.); grad. Yale Coll. 1738; will 8 Feb. 1760, proved 1 Apr. 1760; m. (1) Mary Booth, dau. of Joseph, bapt. 22 June 1718, d. 16 Aug. 1741 in 24 yr. (g. s.); m. (2) 11 Jan. 1743/4, Sarah Jessup, dau. of Edward, b. 14 July 1726; she m. (2) 2 June 1768, Capt. David Banks of Greenfield, and d. in 1805 in 78 yr.

Wakeman, (Rev.) Jabez, s. of Samuel.

Born abt. 1679, d. at Newark, N. J., 8 Oct. 1704; m. 29 Sept. 1702, Eunice Howell, dau. of Col. Matthew and Mary (Halsey) Howell, of Southampton, L. I., b. 18 Aug. 1678, d. at Hartford, 25 May 1738; she m. (2) 26 June 1706, Gov. Joseph Talcott.

He was grad. from Harvard 1697; pastor of First Church, Newark.

---

* Perhaps a misreading; 23 by church record.

Child:

> Samuel, b. in 1703, d. 29 Sept. 1704 in 2 yr.

Walker, Robert.

Linen webster, from Manchester, co. Lancaster, he was b. abt. 1607, and testified 10 Apr. 1679, aged 72. Joined the Boston Church in 1632; freeman, 14 May 1634; a founder of Old South Church, 1669; and d. at Boston, 29 May 1687.

He m. Sarah ———, who d. 21 Dec. 1695.

Sewall's Diary notes their deaths, and calls Robert "a very good man."

Children, recorded at Boston:

> Elishua, b. 14 Feb. 1635/6; m. at Boston, 12 Dec. 1660, Benjamin Thurston.
> +Zechariah, b. 15 Sept. 1637.
> John, b. 22 Sept. 1639, d. 22 July 1652.
> Sarah, b. 15 Nov. 1641.
> +Jacob, b. 21 Mar. 1643/4.
> +Joseph, b. July 1646.
> Thomas, b. [12 Apr. 1649], bapt. 22 Apr. 1649 (ae. abt. 10 days).
> Mary, b. [12 Apr. 1649], bapt. 22 Apr. 1649 (ae. abt. 10 days).
> Timothy, bapt. 1 Sept. 1650.
> Eliakim, b. 3 July 1652, d. 30 Sept. 1654.
> Mary, b. 1 Nov. 1654.
> John, b. 14 July 1656, d. 20 July 1657.

Walker, (Rev.) Zechariah, s. of Robert.

Born at Boston, 15 Sept. 1637, d. at Woodbury, 20 Jan. 1699/1700.

He m. (1) Mary Prudden, dau. of Rev. Peter, bapt. at Milford, 4 Dec. 1641; and she was dead by 1681, when her mother made her will, leaving two children then surviving.

He m. (2) Susanna Rossiter, dau. of Bryan, b. at Guilford, 18 Nov. 1652, d. at Woodbury, 26 Apr. 1710.

Educated at Harvard, but did not graduate; minister at Jamaica, L. I., 1663 to 1668. Then he rem. to Stratford as pastor of portion of the Society there, and went with the first settlers to Woodbury, where he was the first minister.

Children [by first wife], recorded at Stratford:

+Zechariah, bapt. 22 May 1670.
Abigail, bapt. 22 May 1670, d. y.
Elizabeth, b. 1 Mar. 1673/4, d. at Woodbury, 22 Sept. 1741 ae. 67;
m. Samuel Bull; no issue.

Walker, Jacob, s. of Robert.

Born at Boston, 21 Mar. 1643/4.
Married at Stratford, 6 Dec. 1670, Elizabeth, late wife of
Samuel Blackman. She was dau. of Moses Wheeler.

Children, recorded at Stratford, bapt. at Woodbury:

+Samuel, b. 6 or 7 Nov. 1671, bapt. Dec. 1671.
Moses, bapt. Dec. 1673, d. y.
+John, b. 29 Oct. 1674.
Elizabeth, bapt. Mar. 1675/6; m. Luke Hitchcock, of Springfield,
Mass., with whom she conveyed 1735 right in Stratford land laid
out to "our father" Jacob Walker dec'd.
Mary, b. 6 Jan. 1678 [1678/9]; m. 22 Nov. 1699, Abraham Wooster.
Mercy, b. 11 Mar. 1681 [1681/2].
Jacob, d. in 1716. Adm'n granted to father Jacob, 4 Apr. 1716, and
bro. Samuel later added.

Walker, Joseph, s. of Robert.

Born at Boston, July 1646, d. at Stratford, in 1687.
He m. at Milford, 14 Nov. 1667, Abigail Prudden, dau. of Mr.
Peter. She was bapt. at Milford, 13 Feb. 1647/8, and d. at
Stratfield abt. Jan. 1717/8, having m. (2) (by marriage contract,
16 Apr. 1688), Sergt. Richard Hubbell.
Inv. 19 Nov. 1687; widow Abigail.

Children, three recorded at Stratford:

+Robert, b. at Milford, 5 Aug. 1668, bapt. at Woodbury, 22 May 1670.
Sarah, b. 23 Jan. 1669 [1669/70], bapt. at Woodbury, 22 May 1670,
d. y.
Abigail, b. 18 Feb. 1671 [1671/2], bapt. at Woodbury, Feb. 1671/2;
m. John Bostwick.
Joseph, b. at Boston, 8 Dec. 1674, d. y.
Joanna, b. at Boston, 5 May 1677; m. Samuel Odell.
Mary, b. 18 Dec. 1680, "10 in the night," d. y.

Walker, Zechariah, s. of Zechariah. Deputy (Woodbury), May 1720.

Bapt. at Stratford, 22 May 1670, d. at Woodbury, 21 Dec. 1753; m. Elizabeth ———, who d. 19 Dec. 1749. He was Deacon of the Church.

Will 11 May 1739, codicil 26 May 1743, proved 14 Feb. 1754; wife Elizabeth; sons Timothy, Josiah, Zechariah; three daus., Mary Judson, Abigail Prentice, Elizabeth Martin; sons Peter, Gideon; mentioned land that brother Bull improves.

On 9 Dec. 1706, he conveyed to Gideon Allen of Fairfield, a legacy of twenty shillings per year in England, granted by my gr. mother Joanna Prudden of Milford dec'd to my dec'd mother Mary and to her heirs; witnessed by Peter and Abigail Burr.

Children, recorded at Woodbury:

> Mary, bapt. Jan. 1689/90; m. 13 Feb. 1706/7, Joseph Judson.
> Abigail, bapt. Sept. 1691; m. Valentine Prentice.
> Timothy, bapt. June 1693, d. at Woodbury, 15 June 1786; Capt.; m. Sarah ———.
> Josiah, bapt. Sept. 1694; m. 24 Dec. 1719, Phebe Hurlbut.
> Joseph, b. 26 Dec. 1699, d. 1 June 1727.
> Zechariah, b. 14 May 1702, about 2 P. M., bapt. June 1702.
> Peter, b. 24 Oct. 1706, bapt. Feb. 1706/7, d. at Woodbury, 16 Apr. 1788; m. (1) at Stratfield, 28 Feb. 1732/3, Mary Hawley; m. (2) at Woodbury, 13 Nov. 1740, Rhoda Sherman.
> Elizabeth, b. 16 Dec. 1708, bapt. Dec. 1708; m. 26 June 1729, Caleb Martin.
> Gideon, b. 16 Dec. 1711, bapt. Dec. 1711, d. at Woodbury, 30 Apr. 1781 ae. 70; m. 6 Nov. 1735, Mary Munn.

Walker, Samuel, s. of Jacob.

Born at Stratford, 6 or 7 Nov. 1671, d. there in 1721. He settled in Wethersfield, where he m. 23 Feb. 1696/7, Abigail widow of John Crane, and dau. of Nathaniel Butler. She m. (3) Samuel Wright, of Wethersfield, and d. there 1 Jan. 1740.

He returned to Stratford, and Inv. was filed 22 Nov. 1721. Adm'n granted to widow Abigail.

Inv. of Est. of widow Abigail Wright, "late of Wethersfield or Stratford", was taken 25 Apr. 1740 and exhibited by Enos Sherman, Adm'r.

Children, four recorded at Wethersfield, one at Stratford:

> Abigail, b. 11 Apr. 1698; m. at Stratford, 28 Jan. 1724/5, Enos Sherman.
>
> Ann, b. 14 Dec. 1701; m. Daniel Sherwood, with whom she conveyed 1729 right from father.
>
> Elizabeth, b. 23 July 1704, m. at Stratford, 15 Feb. 1727/8, Thomas Lake.
>
> Sarah, b. 1 Nov. 1706, d. at Wethersfield, 12 May 1764 in 58 yr. (g. s.); m. at Wethersfield, 22 Apr. 1725, Timothy Wright, with whom she conveyed 1735 an interest in Stratford realty inherited from Jacob Walker, excepting the dower right of Widow Abigail Wright, formerly widow of Samuel Walker.
>
> Mary, b. 26 Dec. 1711, d. at Wethersfield, 10 Nov. 1796 ae. 84; m. at Wethersfield, 10 Apr. 1740, William Woodhouse.

Walker, John, s. of Jacob.

Born at Stratford, 29 Oct. 1674.

He m. (rec. Stratford) 15 Oct. 1705, Tabitha Wooster; dau. of Edward.

Mis^t. Tabitha Walker m. 11 Oct. 1726, Joseph Birdsey.

John gave a conveyance 23 Aug. 1707, in which he states that gr. father Moses Wheeler by deed gave to his sons Samuel and Moses Wheeler and son-in-law Jacob Walker (22 Apr. 1686), said land being undivided and uncle Samuel Wheeler having given his part by will to his wife, now Mrs. Elizabeth Nisbett, and father Jacob Walker and aunt Elizabeth Nisbett have conveyed their share to John, etc.

Children, first recorded at Stratford:

> Sarah, b. 12 Oct. 1708; no further record found.
>
> Hannah, b. abt. 1710, d. at Redding, 16 July 1769 ae. 59; m. at Stratford, 25 Jan. 1727/8, Joseph Hawley. They, of Redding, conveyed 8 May 1749 to their father Joseph Birdsey and mother Tabitha Birdsey of Stratford, land in Derby laid out to John Walker in 1727.

Walker, Robert, s. of Joseph.

Born at Milford, 5 Aug. 1668, d. at Stratford, 1 Apr. 1743 in 75 yr. (g. s.); m. at Stratford, 1 Aug. 1695, Ruth Wilcoxson. She was dau. of Timothy, b. 31 Aug. 1677.

Deacon in the Cong. Church.

Will 18 Jan. 1742/3, proved 18 Apr. 1743; wife Ruth; sons Robert, James; daus. Sarah Hawley, Abigail Nichols, Joanna Beard, Ruth Youngs, Mary Sherwood, Phebe Bliss, Eunice Walker, Martha Walker; son James and sons-in-law James Beard and John Sherwood, Exec'rs.

On 20 Dec. 1743, Ruth Walker, Sarah Hawley, Abraham Nichols and Abigail his wife, James Beard and Joanna his wife, and James, Eunice, and Martha Walker, all of Stratford, and John Sherwood and Mary his wife of Fairfield, conveyed to Robert Walker a right from Robert Walker dec'd.

Children, recorded at Stratford:

Sarah, b. 23 July 1697; m. 20 Dec. 1716, John Hawley.

Abigail, b. 26 Oct. 1699; m. 25 Dec. 1718, Abraham Nichols.

Johanna, b. 3 Oct. 1702; m. James Beard.

Robert, b. 1 Apr. 1705, bapt. 14 Oct. 1705, d. at Stratford, 13 July 1772 ae. 68 (g. s.); grad. Yale Coll. 1730; Assistant, Judge, Col.; will 6 May 1771, proved 3 Aug. 1772; m. 3 Jan. 1738/9, Rebecca Lewis, b. 22 July 1716, d. 28 Feb. 1805 in 89 yr. (g. s.).

Ruth, b. 19 Sept. 1707, d. at Stratford in 1750; m. ——— Youngs; on 4 July 1744, being "late of Goshen, N. Y., now of Stratford", she conveyed to bro. Robert Walker. Her will, 20 Mar. 1750, proved last Monday in Apr. 1750, gave all to dau. Ruth Youngs, but if she die under age or unmarried, then to my six sisters, Abigail wife of Abraham Nichols, Joannah wife of James Beard, Mary wife of John Sherwood, Phebe wife of Rev. Mr. Daniel Bliss, Eunice wife of Gideon Wells, and Martha Walker, my brothers and other sister being otherwise provided for.

Mary, b. 28 May 1710, d. at Stratfield, 12 June 1767 in 58 yr. (g. s.); m. at Stratfield, 14 June 1733, Sergt. John Sherwood.

Phebe, b. 1 Feb. 1712/3; m. Daniel Bliss, of Concord, Mass., with whom she conveyed, 30 Sept. 1744, land from father Robert Walker.

James, b. abt. 1715, d. at Stratford, 9 June 1796 in 81 yr. (g. s.); Justice; m. 4 Jan. 1738/9, Jerusha Nichols, b. 27 Mar. 1717, d. 8 July 1803 in 87 yr. (g. s.).

Eunice, m. Gideon Welles.

Martha.

Waller, Joseph.

Of Boston 1670, soon removed to Fairfield, and d. in 1672; m. Lydia ———.

Inv. 25 Dec. 1672, sworn by widow Lydia; minor children Joseph and Lydia. The widow was about to m. John Davis.

Children, first recorded at Boston:

+Joseph, b. 3 Feb. 1669 [1669/70].
　Lydia, b. [say 1672].

Waller, Joseph, s. of Joseph.

Born at Boston, 3 Feb. 1669/70; lived in childhood in Fairfield; settled early in Woodbury; m. Abigail ———.

Joseph, Sr., of Woodbury, d. at Chestnut Ridge or Lonetown [Redding], 13 Apr. 1727.

Children, recorded at Woodbury:

Sarah, b. [say 1695], bapt. 30 Aug. 1702.

Lydia, b. [say 1696], bapt. 30 Aug. 1702; m. (rec. New Milford), 12 Dec. 1723, John Weller.

Abigail, b. 25 Sept. 1698 (called 3d dau.), bapt. 30 Aug. 1702.

Joseph, b. 3 Apr. 1701, bapt. 30 Aug. 1702, d. at New Milford, 8 July 1788 in 88 yr. (g. s.); blacksmith; m. (1) at Litchfield, 8 Dec. 1726, Hannah Buel, who d. at New Milford, 4 Feb. 1746/7; in 44 yr. (g. s.); m. (2) at New Milford, 22 Sept. 1748, Mrs. Abigail Starr, who d. at Danbury, 24 July 1791 in 88 yr.

Samuel, b. 18 Mar. 1702/3, bapt. Mar. 1702/3, living at Kent in 1753; m. Esther Hurd, dau. of Joseph, b. 9 Apr. 1709, d. at Woodbury, 6 Oct. 1749.

Martha, b. 4 Sept. 1705, bapt. Sept. 1705.

Mary, bapt. May 1708; m. 30 Oct. 1729, Benjamin Wheeler.

Bathsheba, b. 19 May 1710, bapt. May 1710.

Daniel, b. 19 May 1713, bapt. May 1713, d. latter end of May 1713.

Daniel, b. 23 May 1714.

Phineas, b. 31 Oct. 1717, bapt. 3 Nov. 1717, d. at Cornwall, 25 June 1787; m. Apr. 1749, Rhoda Taylor of Danbury, who d. at Windsor, N. Y., at home of son Nathan.*

Wallis, Richard.

Of Lyme and Norwich.

His widow m. [prob. by 1677] Jacob Wakelee, of Stratford.

Inv. 4 June 1675; adm'n granted to widow. Distribution order; to eldest dau. Abigail, lands at Norwich; to younger dau. Johanna, lands at Lyme; to the widow, residue, and use of lands until daus. attain 18 yrs. or marry. Overseers, Simon Huntington and John Birchard.

---

* Nathan Waller, b. at Cornwall, 17 Mar. 1753, d. at Wilkes-Barre, Pa., 11 July 1831; m. at Wilkes-Barre, 4 May 1773, Elizabeth Weeks, b. "at Fairfield, Conn.", 6 Mar. 1754, d. at Windsor, N. Y., 22 Sept. 1822. Their son, Phineas, b. at Wilkes-Barre, 31 July 1774, d. at Bloomsburg, Pa., 3 June 1859; m. (1) Hannah Bradley, of Washington, D. C., and (2) Elizabeth Jewett, of New London, Conn.; whence a distinguished Waller line.

Children:

> Abigail, b. abt. 1670; on 8 Feb. 1685 [1685/6], being ae. abt. 15, she chose her father-in-law Jacob Wakelee* for guardian; m. at Stratford, 5 Jan. 1692 [1692/3], John Hurd.
>
> Johanna.

Ward, Andrew. Commissioner appointed by Mass. to govern Conn., Mar. 1636; Assistant, Conn. Col., Apr. 1636, Sept. 1636, Mar. 1637, May 1637; Deputy (Wethersfield) to Conn. Leg., Nov. 1637, Mar. 1638, Apr. 1638, Aug. 1639, Sept. 1639, Jan. 1640; Magistrate (Stamford town), Oct. 1642; Dep. Magistrate, Apr. 1643; Deputy (Stamford) to New Haven Leg., Apr. 1644; Assistant, New Haven Col., Oct. 1646; Deputy (Fairfield) to Conn. Leg., May 1648, May 1649, Sept. 1649, May 1650, Sept. 1650, May 1651, May 1652, May 1653, Sept. 1653, May 1654, Oct. 1654, May 1655, May 1656, Oct. 1656, Oct. 1658; war committee for Fairfield, May 1653, Oct. 1654.

The statements in the preface to the *Andrew Ward Genealogy* with regard to Andrew's being of the family of Richard Ward of Gorleston or Homersfield have been investigated.† No such person as Richard Ward was found; no Gunville family existed in that vicinity as lords of the manor; and every reference given has proved to be fictitious. It is likely that these statements were the invention of a fraudulent genealogist, innocently accepted by members of the Ward family, through whom they found their way into the book.

It is certain that he m. in England, Hester Sherman, who was bapt. 1 Apr. 1606 at Dedham, co. Essex, and we should look for his antecedents in that quarter. The will of Robert Lockwood‡ of Eye, near Yaxley, co. Essex (who m. Margery Sherman), in 1558 named his daus. Mary wife of John Ward and Ann wife of Anthony Barker. David Rawson of St. Gregory's, London, father of Edward (Sec. of Mass. Col.), and son of Edward and Bridget (Ward) Rawson, in his will 1616 named his uncle John Ward, and Andrew Ward (a minor), son of his uncle Ralph. Now Dr. John Ward of Ipswich, Mass., besides mentioning various

---

* Correct page 314, where by a clerical blunder Abigail was called stepdau. of Henry instead of Jacob Wakelee.

† By Col. Charles E. Banks for Mrs. Finley J. Shepard.

‡ The Lockwoods of Fairfield were prob. of this tribe.

Sherman cousins in his will 1652, gave £20 each to the two youngest sons of his "Cousin Ward of Wethersfield." Dr. John Ward was son of John Ward (will 1631) of Stratford St. Mary, co. Suffolk, just across the River Stour from Dedham, co. Essex. The mother of Dr. John Ward was Anne, whose will 1635 made Dr. John Clarke of Colchester Executor. This was the Dr. John Clarke who settled later in Newbury, Mass., the same town to which the younger Edward Rawson had come in 1637.

Andrew may have been the son of Ralph, nephew of John of Stratford, and cousin of Dr. John Ward and of Sec. Rawson; but positive proof has not been found.*

He first settled in Watertown, Mass.; was a founder of Conn. Colony and an original settler at Wethersfield; he was also a founder of Stamford in 1641, having with Robert Coe on behalf of the Wethersfield men arranged with New Haven Colony for the settlement there; and rem. 1647 to Fairfield, where he died in 1659. He m. Hester Sherman, dau. of Edmund, bapt. 1 Apr. 1606, d. in 1666.

Will 8 June 1659; wife Ester; son John, £50, when 21; dau. Sarah, £40; dau. Abigail, £40, when 18; housing and lands to sons Andrew and Samuel, to be divided when the eldest (Andrew) is 21; the rest of his children have had full portions except Edmund, who is to have £20 "if he come to this place." Inv. 18 Oct. 1659; Esther and son William granted adm'n.

Will of Hester, 27 Dec. 1665; son William, £5; dau. Mary Burr, £2; sons Andrew and Samuel, £8 each; dau. Abigail, £10; children of dau. Anna Nichols, £9; gr. child Hester Ward, £9; son John's child, £9; gr. children Sarah and Nathaniel Burr, children of dau. Sarah, £9; clothing to daus. Ann, Mary, Sarah, Abigail; sons William and Andrew, Exec'rs; to Daniel Burr and Hester Burr, 10 shillings each. Inv. 30 Jan. 1665 [1665/6].

It is reasonable to suppose that Edmund was eldest son, named for Hester's father Edmund Sherman, but dead before Hester made her will; yet Elizabeth Barker of Nayland, co. Suffolk (five miles from Stratford, where the Dr. John Ward family lived), in

---

* Stephen and Joyce (Traford) Ward had a son Richard of Faxton, co. Northampton, whose will in 1640 named various relatives, including a brother Andrew; but as this Andrew was in England in 1640, he was not the emigrant. However, Richard gave a legacy to Gov. Thomas Dudley in New England, and a clue may be found here.

her will 1627 named her gr. child Edmund Ward. It should be considered as a possibility that Andrew Ward m. (1) a Barker, mother of Edmund; and that Edmund returned to England, not being of "this place" when Andrew made his will; and this theory would explain Hester's will not naming him, even if he was then living.

Children:

Edmund.

Ann, b. abt. 1629 [she had children from 1650 to 1676], d. at Woodbury, 23 July 1718 in 98 yr. "as is supposed on good grounds", the record states, but she could not have been nearly so old; m. abt. 1649, Caleb Nichols.

+William, b. [say 1631].

?Hester, b. [say 1633], d. abt. 1663/4; m. (1) Joseph Boosey; m. (2) abt. 1658, Jehu Burr, Jr.

Mary, b. [say 1635], d. [between 1665 and 1672]; m. [prob. John] Burr.

+John, b. [say 1637].

Sarah, b. [say 1640]; m. abt. 1660, Nathaniel Burr.

+Andrew, b. [say 1642].

+Samuel, b. [say 1644].

Abigail, b. [say 1647]; m. (1) [2 May 1670 by *Ward Gen.*] Moses Dimon; m. (2) in 1685, Edward Howard.

Ward, (Dr.) William.   Surgeon, K. Philip's War, Jan. 1675/6.

He m. Deborah Lockwood, dau. of Sergt. Robert, b. at Watertown, Mass., 12 Oct. 1636. She m. (2) John Topping, of Southampton, L. I.

Inv. 4 Mar. 1675/6; calls him Ens.; Widow made oath.

Marriage agreement between Ebenezer Hawley and Hester Ward, dau. of Mrs. Deborah Topping of Southampton, 19 Apr. 1678.

Child:

Esther [or Hester], b. abt. 1664, d. at Fairfield, [date gone, 1732] ae. 67 (g. s.); m. (1) (by contract 19 Apr. 1678) Ebenezer Hawley; m. (2) at Fairfield, 17 Oct. 1682, Ephraim Nichols; m. (3) at Fairfield, Nov. 1691, Eliphalet Hill; m. (4) abt. 1697, Robert Lord.

Ward, John, s. of Andrew.

He m. at Middletown, 18 Apr. 1664, Mary Harris; dau. of William, b. at Rowley, Mass., 1 Mar. 1645/6. He d. in 1683/4, and she m. (2) Jan. 1687/8, Josiah Gilbert, of Wethersfield, and d. in 1721.

Inv. 22 Feb. 1683/4. Ages of children: John 18, Andrew 16, Esther 14, Mary 11, William 9, Samuel 4, and one unborn. Adm'n granted to the widow. The order of distribution mentions that the eldest son had £10 by will of gr. mother [Hester Ward's £9 must have accumulated interest before her gr. son rec'd it]. William Harris, father of the widow, with Mr. Hamlin, appointed to assist the widow.

Adm'n on Est. of Mary Gilbert of Middletown granted, 4 Mar. 1728/9, to son William Ward. Her daus. Esther Cornwell of Middletown and Mary Percival of Haddam testified.

Children, recorded at Middletown:

> John, b. 15 Nov. 1665, d. in 1709.
>
> Andrew, b. 1 Dec. 1667, d. at Middletown, in 1728/9; adm'n granted, 4 Mar. 1728/9, to bro. William; Andrew returned 1698 from Boston to Middletown, insane, and was cared for by bros. William and Samuel at great cost and trouble; on 21 Jan. 1730/1, Mrs. Elizabeth Ward, widow of Samuel, appeared with William at Court in connection with Andrew's Est.
>
> Esther, b. 15 Dec. 1669, d. at Middletown, 13 July 1734; m. 22 Jan. 1692, William Cornwell.
>
> Mary, b. Aug. 1672; m. (1) ——;* m. (2) James Percival, Sr., of Haddam.
>
> William, b. 30 June 1674, d. at Middletown, 6 Apr. 1745; Sergt.; m. 9 July 1702, Abigail Collins.
>
> Samuel, bapt. 12 Oct. 1679, d. at Middletown, 25 June 1715; Inv. 26 July 1715; m. 10 Aug. 1710, Elizabeth Adkins, dau. of Josiah, b. 11 Aug. 1687.

Ward, Andrew, s. of Andrew.

He m. Tryal Meigs, dau. of John.

On 20 Dec. 1668, Samuel Ward sold to Andrew Ward land at Fairfield bounded on Nathaniel Burr's land; witnesses, William Ward and John Burr.

Children, recorded at Killingworth:

> Andrew, b. [no record, abt. 1669], d. at Guilford, 7 Aug. 1756; Capt.; m. 19 Nov. 1691, Deborah Joy; dau. of Jacob, b. 23 Feb. 1673, d. 22 Feb. 1752.

---

* She did not, as claimed by the *Andrew Ward Genealogy,* m. Benjamin Cornwell and bear children when over sixty years old.

John, b. 16 Mar. 1671, d. 1700.

Abigail, b. 15 Sept. 1672, d. 10 Aug. 1733; m. 25 Jan. 1693, Samuel Norton.

Sarah, b. 15 Nov. 1674, d. 8 Dec. 1763; m. 15 Nov. 1693, Stephen Bradley.

Peter, b. 14 Oct. 1676, d. 18 Dec. 1763; Capt.; m. 30 Mar. 1699, Mary Joy; dau. of Jacob, b. 17 Sept. 1680.

William, b. 18 Oct. 1678, d. at Wallingford, 19 Dec. 1768 ae. 90 (g. s.); Capt.; m. (1) 14 Dec. 1701, Lettice Beach, dau. of John and Mary (Royce) Beach, b. 24 Dec. 1679; m. (2) in 1755, Ruth ———.

Samuel, b. 24 Sept. 1680, d. 30 Apr. 1681.

Hester, b. 2 May 1684, d. 17 June 1684.

Mary.

Anna, b. abt. 1689, d. 1 June 1746; m. (1) 10 Nov. 1709, Samuel Rossiter, of Guilford; m. (2) 26 Apr. 1716, Daniel Parmelee.

Ward, Samuel, s. of Andrew. Sergt., Fairfield Trainband; Deputy (Fairfield), May and July 1691.

He m. (1) ——— Ogden, dau. of Richard. Statements that her name was Alice are based on a misreading of a probate entry [see RICHARD OGDEN].

He m. (2) Hannah, widow of Jonathan Nichols of Stratford, dau. of Mr. Anthony Howkins and granddau. of Gov. Welles, b. at Farmington abt. 1661. She m. (3) John Judson of Woodbury, where she d. 23 July 1698. Her will, made the day before her death, named her three Nichols children and her dau. Hannah Ward.

Inv. 8 Jan. 1692 [1692/3]. Adm'n granted to widow Hannah and son Edmund Ward, 16 Jan. 1692 [1692/3]. Allowance made to widow, 29 Mar. 1692/3 for bringing up Sergt. Ward's youngest child and the other three children of her former husband Jonathan Nichols; mention made of the eldest son, the other five sons, and one dau. On 12 Apr. 1694, the Adm'r Edmund having rem. out of Colony, Nathaniel Burr and Eliphalet Hill were instructed (as overseers) to proceed with the adm'n.

Children [by first wife]:

Edmund, b. abt. 1671, d. in 1712; res. 1693 Fordham, N. Y., 1700 East-chester; ae. 39 in 1710 Census of Eastchester; m. abt. 1693, Mary Hoyt, dau. of Moses. Children rec. Eastchester: Mary, b. 23 May 1694; Eleanor, b. 2 May 1696; Sarah, b. 1 Nov. 1698; Abigail, b. 26 Jan. 1700; Miriam, b. 21 Jan. 1703; Edmund, b. 9 Dec. 1705; and Samuel, b. 14 Mar. 1708.

Sarah.

Samuel, d. in 1706; in Eastchester Census 1698, with Hannah [prob. wife] and Abigail [prob. dau.].

William, b. abt. 1678; res. Pelham, N. Y.; m. Hannah Pell, dau. of John of Pelham Manor.

John, b. abt. 1685, d. at Peekskill, N. Y., 6 Dec. 1767; ae. 25 in 1710 Census of Eastchester; m. (1) Rebecca Fowler, dau. of Henry and Abigail (Hoyt) Fowler; m. (2) Elizabeth ———.

×Moses, d. at Fishkill, N. Y., in 1746; m. [possibly ——— Smith, dau. of Eluzai].

Child [by second wife] :

Hannah, b. abt. 1692, d. abt. 1772; m. [at Stratfield, 25 Oct. 1709] Peter Bulkley.

Washburn, William.

Settled at Stratford and rem. to Hempstead, L. I.

Children :

+John.
+Hope.
William.
Mary, m. Richard Willets.
Daughter, m. Robert Williams.
Martha, m. Edmund Titus, of Hempstead.
Two other daus.

Washburn, John, s. of William.

Called son of William, he m. at Stratford, 17 June 1655, Mary Butler, dau. of Richard.

He removed to Hempstead, L. I.

Child, recorded at Stratford :

John, b. 20 Nov. 1657; said to have m. Sarah Cornell, dau. of Richard, and to have had children John, Susanna, and Mary.

Washburn, Hope, s. of William.

He m. Mary Stiles, dau. of Francis. Rem. from Stratford to Derby, where he d. in 1696; she d. 11 Jan. 1712.

Agreement 16 Nov. 1696 of widow Mary and children William, Samuel, Sarah, and Jane Washburn, and John Johnson on behalf of wife Mary Washburn.

Children, first five recorded at Stratford:

Sarah, b. Dec. 1661; m. at Derby, 6 May 1713, Samuel Riggs; no issue.

John, b. May 1666, d. y.

William, b. 16 Mar. 1668/9, d. at Derby, 18 Jan. 1741 [1741/2] ae. 72 yrs. 10 mos. 16 days (g. s.); will 14 Jan. 1742, proved 9 Feb. 1741/2; m. 20 Aug. 1696, Hannah Wooster, bapt. 31 Oct. 1675, d. in 1743; her will 1 Dec. 1742, proved 21 Nov. 1743.

Samuel, b. 5 Mar. 1670/1, d. at Derby in 1724; adm'n granted, 22 Apr. 1724; m. 30 Nov. 1713, Susannah, widow of Sylvester Wooster; she m. (3) ——— Northrup.

Ephraim, b. 31 Aug. 1673, d. y.

Mary, b. July 1675; m. 24 Sept. 1694, John Johnson, of Derby.

Jane, b. 6 Aug. 1678.

Watkins, David.

He m. Sarah Judson, dau. of Jeremiah, b. at Stratford, 7 Apr. 1662. He d. in 1688, and she m. (2) Joseph Sturges of Fairfield.

Inv. 28 July 1688; widow Sarah appointed Adm'x, Dec. 1688; her dau. mentioned.

Child:

Mary, prob. m. Samuel Welles, Jr.

Watkins, Joseph.

He m. at Stratford, 4 Dec. 1688, Johanna Blackman; dau. of Samuel, b. 4 Dec. 1667. She m. (2) abt. 1714, Jesse Lambert; and (3) 24 Nov. 1725(?), Mr. Samuel Camp, of Newark, N. J.

Mr. Joseph d. at Stratford, 23 Dec. 1711.

Adm'n granted to widow Johanna, 3 Jan. 1711/2. Joseph and Elizabeth, children of Joseph, chose Richard Hubbell for guardian, 5 Jan. 1714 [1714/5], and he was appointed for Hezekiah. On the same date, the Court appointed David Watkins guardian of Benjamin and Ephraim; and Johanna chose her father-in-law Jesse Lambert.

The estate of Joanna Camp, late of Newark, was distributed, 5 Dec. 1729, to David, Elizabeth, heirs of Samuel Watkins, Joanna, Benjamin, Joseph, Ephraim, Hezekiah.

Children, recorded at Stratford:

David, b. 6 Nov. 1691; settled in N. J. On 24 May 1755, David Watkin of Elizabeth Town, Essex County, N. J., son and heir at law of David Watkin late dec'd, conveyed land in Stratford to Hezekiah Watkin of New Windsor Parish, N. Y., Minister of the Gospel.

Samuel, b. 17 July 1693, d. in 1725; adm'n granted, 6 July 1725, to widow Deborah; m. 17 Jan. 1716/7, Deborah Janes; she m. (2) 29 Oct. 1727, Mr. Nehemiah Loring.

Jonathan, b. last day of June 1695, d. 17 Aug. 1696.

Joseph, b. 28 Sept. 1697, d. 9 May 1698.

Joseph, b. 28 Aug. 1699, d. in 1736; adm'n granted, 15 Mar. 1736, to Benjamin Watkins; he was of Elizabeth, N. J., 1724; m. ———.

Johanna, b. 25 Sept. 1700.

Elizabeth, b. 10 Aug. 1702, d. at Greenfield, 2 Mar. 1737/8; m. (1) 7 Feb. 1723/4, Edward Wooster; m. (2) Thomas Harvey.

Benjamin, b. 28 Sept. 1704, bapt. at Stratfield, 5 Nov. 1704.

Ephraim, bapt. (at Stratford, rec. Stratfield) 20 Oct. 1706; res. 1747, Ulster County, N. Y.; m. 21 Nov. 1727, Joanna Birdsey.

Hezekiah, bapt. (at Stratford, rec. Stratfield) 3 Apr. 1709, d. at New Windsor, Ulster County, N. Y., 10 Apr. 1765; grad. Yale Coll. 1737; Episcopal missionary in Ulster County; will 22 Mar. 1765, proved 1 June 1765; named cousins Tabitha Tuthill, Eunice Reeve, Bridget Goldsmith; nephews Edward Wooster, and Joseph, Samuel, Ephraim, and Hezekiah Watkins.

Webb, (Rev.) Joseph. Minister at Fairfield, had colonial grant of 200 acres, May 1699; preached Election Sermon, 1701.

Grad. Harvard Coll. 1684.

He m. (1) (rec. at Derby and Fairfield) 8 July 1691, Mrs. Elizabeth Nichols. She was dau. of Isaac Nichols, b. at Stratford, 2 Apr. 1668, d. at Fairfield, 15 Feb. 1718 ae. 50 yrs. 10 mos. 15 days (g. s.).

He m. (2) (rec. Stratford) 21 Sept. 1721, Mrs. Mehitabel Coney; widow of Benjamin Coney, and dau. of John Glover, b. at New Haven, 1 May 1679. She m. (3) at Fairfield (rec. also at Stratford) 7 July 1741, John Thompson.

He d. at Fairfield, 12 Sept. 1732 ae. 66 (g. s.).

Adm'n granted, 30 Oct. 1732, to Mr. Samuel Pumroy of Newtown, L. I., and Mr. Joseph Webb of Newark, N. J. Prenuptial agreement with Mrs. Mehitabel Coney dated 21 Sept. 1721. Agreement 14 Nov. 1732 regarding Est. of Rev. Joseph, lands in Reddings, etc., some of which belonged to his former wife Elizabeth;

made by Joseph Webb of Newark, N. J., Samuel Pumroy and
Elizabeth his wife of Newtown, Queens County, Island of Nassau,
and John Dennie and Sarah his wife, Abigail Webb, and Josiah
Webb, all of Fairfield.

Children, recorded at Fairfield:

> Joseph, b. 21 Sept. 1693; grad. Yale Coll. 1715; pastor at Newark,
> N. J., 1718-36; drowned on Conn. River, 20 Oct. 1741, with only
> son; m. at Stratfield, 3 Feb. 1736, Elizabeth Starr. Adm'n granted
> at New Haven, 27 Oct. 1741, to bro. Josiah of Fairfield. Receipts
> exhibited 1745 by the Adm'r from Mr. Thomas Hill as attorney for
> John Dennie and Sarah his wife, and from Capt. John Phillips and
> Abigail his wife.
>
> Nehemiah, b. 26 Feb. 1694 [1694/5], bapt. 3 Mar. 1694/5, d. in 1722.
> Adm'n granted, 7 May 1722, to Rev. Joseph Webb.
>
> Elizabeth, b. 14 Feb. 1696/7, bapt. 21 Feb. 1696/7; m. Rev. Samuel
> Pomeroy, of Newtown, L. I.
>
> Mary, b. 10 Mar. 1698/9, bapt. 12 Mar. 1698/9, d. y.
>
> Grace, b. 3 Dec. 1700, bapt. 8 Dec. 1700, d. 17 May 1722 ae. 21 yrs.
> 6 mos. 4 days (g. s.).
>
> Sarah, b. 30 Jan. 1702/3, bapt. 31 Jan. 1702/3; m. John Dennie.
>
> Abigail, b. 1 Mar. 1704/5, bapt 4 Mar. 1704/5; m. Capt. John
> Phillips.
>
> ✕Josiah, b. 15 Mar. 1706/7, bapt. 16 Mar. 1706/7, d. at Westport, 8
> Apr. 1776; m. (1) Nov. 1729, Susannah Disbrow, dau. of Thomas;
> b. May 1717, d. at Westport, 25 Dec. 1748(?); m. (2) Oct. 1750,
> Hannah Sherwood, who d. at Westport, 14 Mar. 1764.

Webster, Nicholas.

Settled in Stamford and m. Sarah, dau. of John Waterbury,
formerly wife of Zachariah Dibble, whom she had divorced in
1672. He d. in 1687, and she m. (3) Edward Trehern. She d.
2 Sept. 1712, and Edward d. 14 May 1714.

Sarah m. (1) 10 May 1666, Zachariah Dibble, by whom she had
one child: Zachariah, b. 19 Dec. 1667, d. 22 Jan. 1711/2; m. 13
Aug. 1698, Sarah Clements, and was ancestor of the Dibbles of
Stamford; his son, the third Zachariah, b. 16 July 1699, m. 15
June 1725, Sarah Sturges, who d. 2 Jan. 1735/6.

Will of Nicholas Webster, 4 May 1687; wife Sarah; sons
John, David; dau. Rachel; bro. Jonathan Waterbury; Zachariah
Dibble "if he settles in Stamford." Inv. Aug. 1687.

Will of Edward Trehern, 11 May 1714, proved 6 Apr. 1715;

Nathaniel Wiat, son of my dau.-in-law Rachel Atwood; my dec'd wife's three children, John and David Webster and Rachel Atwood; son John Webster and son Henry Atwood, Exec'rs.

Children:

> John, d. 8 Mar. 1717; Inv. 29 Nov. 1717; m. 9 Apr. 1702, Sarah Jagger.
>
> David, d. 11 Dec. 1732; m. (1) 13 June 1706, Abigail Holly, who d. 16 Apr. 1707; m. (2) 1 Dec. 1709, Mercy Morehouse.
>
> Rachel, m. 18 Aug. 1708, Henry Atwood. Her son Nathaniel Wyatt was b. 18 July 1697.

Weed, Jonas.

Came on the *Arbella,* 1630, settled at Watertown, Mass., and was made freeman, 18 May 1631. In 1635 was a first settler in Wethersfield, Conn., and a founder of Stamford in 1641. He d. in Stamford in 1676, and his widow Mary early in 1690.

Will 26 Nov. 1672; Inv. 7 Nov. 1676; wife Mary; eldest son John; son Daniel; son Jonas; dau. Mary wife of George Abbot; dau. Dorcas wife of James Wright; son Samuel; to John Rockwell, five shillings, and £5 in Daniel's hands for Elizabeth; dau. Sarah, "if she return to the truth"; dau. Hannah wife of Benjamin Hoit; wife Mary and son John, Exec'rs.

Inv. of Mary Weed, 10 Mar. 1689/90.

Children:

> +John.
>
> Mary, m. George Abbott.
>
> +Daniel.
>
> +Jonas.
>
> Dorcas, b. [say 1640], d. at Wethersfield, 24 Dec. 1692; m. (rec. Wethersfield) 20 Nov. 1660, James Wright.
>
> Samuel, d. at Danbury in 1708; Inv. 9 Sept. 1708; m. Mary ———; Pro. Rec. mentions adult son Jacob, and minor children Samuel, Jonas, Elizabeth Prob. there were other adult children.
>
> Elizabeth, m. John Rockwell, of Rye, who d. by 1677.
>
> Sarah.
>
> Hannah, b. [say 1650], d. at Stamford, 9 Nov. 1711; m. 5 Jan. 1670, Benjamin Hoyt.
>
> Child, d. 15 July 1656.

Weed, John, s. of Jonas.

He m. (1) Joanna Westcott, dau. of Richard, who d. by 1678.
He m. (2) Mary, who m. (2) Josiah Forman, of Newtown,
L. I., and d. 31 Mar. 1714.

Inv. exhibited 12 Mar. 1689/90 by the Widow; eight children
named.

Will of Marah Firman of Stamford, widow of Josiah of Newtown, L. I., 27 Mar. 1714; son Isaac Weed; dau. Mary Lockwood; dau. Hannah Scofield; dau. Rebecca Firman; son-in-law
Samuel Weed; gr. children, the immediate children of son Joseph
Weed dec'd; Rebecca Weed, widow of son Joseph; son-in-law
Samuel Scofield, Exec'r. She d. 31 Mar. 1714; Inv. 29 Apr.
1714.

Children [by first wife], recorded at Stamford:
+Jonas, b. 5 Feb. 1667 [1667/8].
+Daniel, b. 11 Feb. 1669 [1669/70].
  John.
  Samuel, Deputy for Stamford, May 1718, and May 1721; Lt., 1st Co.,
    Stamford, Oct. 1722; m. 17 Apr. 1701, Abigail Scofield, who d.
    5 May 1734.

Children [by second wife], recorded at Stamford:
  Joseph, b. 7 Jan. 1678/9, d. 16 Dec. 1711 [Pro. Rec., which calls him
    son of John]; m. 10 Dec. 1701, Rebecca Higginbotham. Widow
    Rebecca swore to Inv. 3 Mar. 1711/2, and was appointed to admin-
    ister with his bro. Samuel. Three daus., of whom Rebecca was
    appointed guardian.
  Isaac, b. 20 Apr. 1682.
  Mary, b. 21 Apr. 1684; m. [prob. Gershom] Lockwood, [Jr., of
    Greenwich].
  Hannah, b. 22 Mar. 1687; m. Samuel Scofield.

Weed, Daniel, s. of Jonas. Deputy (Stamford) to Conn. Leg.,
Oct. 1694, Oct. 1695, May 1696.

He died at Stamford, 29 Nov. 1697; adm'n granted to widow
and Jonas Weed of Stamford; the children are four sons and one
dau. On 24 Jan. 1699, adm'n was granted to the widow with her
son Abraham.

He m. Mary ———, who d. 1 Apr. 1714.

Children, recorded at Stamford:

Sarah, b. 18 Nov. 1675; m. 11 Aug. 1698, Lt. David Waterbury.
Abraham, b. 18 Aug. 1680, d. 26 Dec. 1711; Widow Susanna with
Mr. John Bell appointed to administer, 6 Feb. 1711/2; m. 11 Apr.
1706, Susanna Bell, b. 25 Dec. 1686; she m. (2) 26 May 1715,
Thomas Talmadge, and d. at New Canaan, 23 Nov. 1756 ae. 70
(g. s.).
Daniel, b. 19 Mar. 1685; m. Elizabeth Scofield.
Ebenezer, b. 22 Oct. 1692, d. in 1765; will 14 Mar. 1765; m. 28
May 1713, Mary Bell.
Nathaniel, b. 22 Oct. 1696; m. Mary [Reed?].

Weed, Jonas, s. of Jonas.

He d. at Stamford, 19 Nov. 1704; m. 16 Nov. 1676, Bethia
Holly, who d. 24 Dec. 1713.

Inv. 10 Jan. 1704/5; widow Bethiah made oath; she with sons
Jonas and Benjamin to administer.

Children, recorded at Stamford:

Jonas, b. 26 July 1678; Deputy for Stamford, May and Oct. 1718;
m. 20 Jan. 1703/4, Sarah Waterbury, b. 10 Jan. 1684/5, d. 5 Feb.
1726/7.
Benjamin, b. 5 Apr. 1681; m. 27 Feb. 1706/7, Mary Penoyer, b. 22
Nov. 1688, d. 27 Sept. 1732.
Jonathan, b. 15 Apr. 1684, d. 19 Dec. 1728; m. Mary ———.

Weed, Jonas, s. of John.

Born 5 Feb. 1667/8, d. at Stamford, 18 Nov. 1706; m. Mary
Scofield, dau. of Daniel. She m. (2) 31 Dec. 1707, Samuel Hoyt.

Inv. 8 Jan. 1706/7; states that he d. 20 Nov. 1706. Widow
Mary and Samuel Weed to administer. Sons and daus.; Samuel
Weed to be guardian of John and Nathan; Widow Mary appointed
for Miles and Sarah.

Children, recorded at Stamford:

Abigail, b. 5 Apr. 1695; m. 20 Jan. 1714, Jeremiah Scofield.
John, b. 19 Nov. 1698.
Miles, b. 24 Feb. 1700/1; m. 19 Dec. 1723, Joanna Weed.
Sarah, b. 10 Mar. 1702/3; ?m. 29 Dec. 1726, Nathan Scofield.
Nathan, b. 20 May 1705; m. 28 May 1730, Isabel Youngs.

Weed, Daniel, s. of John.

Born 11 Feb. 1669/70.
He m. 23 Sept. 1697, Mary Webb.

Children, recorded at Stamford:
>Joseph, b. 18 Aug. 1698.
>David, b. 19 Aug. 1700; m. 31 May 1723, Sarah Pettit.
>Joanna, b. 8 Nov. 1702; m. 19 Dec. 1723, Miles Weed.
>Daniel, b. 14 May 1705; m. 16 Nov. 1732, Susanna Guernsey.
>Ebenezer, b. 19 Mar. [1709/10?].
>Sarah, b. 6 Jan. 1709/10; ?m. 23 June 1726, Nathaniel Webb.
>Samuel, b. 27 July 1712.

Welles, Thomas. Assistant, Conn. Col., 1637-54; Moderator, Mar. 1654; Dep. Governor, 1654, 1656, 1657, 1659; Governor, 1655, 1658; Treasurer, 1639, 1648, 1649, 1650; Secretary, 1641, 1643, 1644, 1645, 1647; Commissioner to United Colonies, 1649, 1654, 1659; war committee for Wethersfield, May 1653, Oct. 1654.

Son of Robert and Alice of Stourton in Whichford, co. Warwick, Eng., he m. (1) soon after 5 July 1615, Alice Tomes, dau. of John. They came to New England with their six children in 1635/6, and after a sojourn in Cambridge rem. to Hartford, where from the first he was prominent in the colonial government. He m. (2) abt. 1646, Elizabeth (Deming), widow of Nathaniel Foote, and the same year rem. to Wethersfield, where he d. 14 Jan. 1659/60.

Children [by first wife], born in England:
>+John.
>>Thomas, d. at Hartford in 1668; Quartermaster, Conn. Col. Troop, Mar. 1658; Patentee, Royal Charter, 1662; Deputy for Hartford, May 1662; Assistant, 1668; m. 23 June 1654, Hannah (Tuttle), widow of John Pantry, who d. 6 Aug. 1683. Of their children: Rebecca, b. May 1655, d. at Stratford, 5 Nov. 1717 ae. 62 (g. s.), m. (rec. Stratford) 18 Aug. 1680, Capt. James Judson; and Samuel, b. Oct. 1662, m. Ruth Judson, dau. of Joseph, b. 27 Oct. 1664.
>>Samuel, d. at (Wethersfield?), 15 July 1675; Deputy for Wethersfield, Oct. 1657, May and Oct. 1658, May and Oct. 1659, May 1660, May and Oct. 1661, May 1675; Ens., Wethersfield Trainband, Mar. 1658; Lt., May 1665; Capt., May 1670; Commissioner for Wethersfield, 1665-75; member of Council, K. Philip's War, 1675;

m. (1) abt. 1659, Elizabeth Hollister, dau. of John; m. (2) Hannah
Lamberton, who m. (2) Lt.-Col. John Allyn. Among the children
(by first wife) were: Sarah, b. 29 Sept. 1664, d. at Stratford, 29
June 1694, m. (1) (rec. Stratford) 4 Dec. 1683, Ephraim Hawley,
and (2) 19 Oct. 1692, Lt. Agur Tomlinson; Ann, b. in 1668, d.
at Wethersfield in 1739, m. (1) 19 July 1687, Capt. James Steele
of Wethersfield, and (2) (rec. Stratford) 20 Nov. 1718, Capt.
James Judson; and Elizabeth, b. in 1670, d. 1 Apr. 1747 ae. 76
(g. s., Shelton); m. 4 Apr. 1692, Daniel Shelton of Stratford.
Mary, m. ————.
Ann, d. in 1680; m. (1) 14 Apr. 1646, Thomas Thomson, of Farming-
ton; m. (2) early in 1656, Anthony Howkins.* One of her children by first husband, Mary, bapt. 7 June 1653, m. 20 May 1673,
Samuel Hawley.
Sarah, b. abt. 1631, d. at Wethersfield, 12 Dec. 1698 ae. 67 (g. s.); m.
Feb. 1653/4, Capt. John Chester.

Welles, John, s. of Thomas. Deputy (Stratford) to Conn.
Leg., May and Oct. 1656, May and Oct. 1657; Assistant, 1658,
1659.

He m. by 1647, Elizabeth Bourn; she m. (2) at Stratford, 19
Mar. 1662/3, John Wilcoxson.

Will 19 Oct. 1659; wife Elizabeth, mentioning what is due her
in England; dau. Temperance; sons John, Thomas, Samuel;
father, brother Samuel, "brothers." Inv. Oct. 1659. Ages of
children: John 11, Thomas 8, Robert 8, Temperance 5, Samuel 3,
Sarah 1.

Children:

+John, b. abt. 1648.
+Thomas, b. abt. 1651.
    Robert, b. abt. 1651, d. at Wethersfield, 22 June 1714; Capt.; m. (1)

---

* Anthony Howkins, of Windsor, rem. to Farmington 1656; Deputy for Farmington, Oct. 1657, May 1658, May and Oct. 1660, May and Oct. 1661, May and Oct.
1662, May and Oct. 1663, May and Oct. 1664, May and Oct. 1665, Oct. 1666, May
and Oct. 1667; Patentee, Royal Charter, 1662; Assistant, 1668-74; Commissioner for
Farmington, 1663, '64, '66, '67; member of War Council, Nov. 1673. He d. 28 Feb.
1673/4; by his first wife (name unknown), who d. at Windsor 12 July 1655, he had
children: 1. Mary, b. 16 July 1644; m. John Judd. 2. Child, d. 1647. 3. Ruth, b.
24 Oct. 1649; m. abt. 1676/7, Capt. Thomas Hart (as his second wife). 4. John, b.
18 Feb. 1651/2, Sergt. at Farmington, d. in K. Philip's War, 1676. By his second
wife (Ann Welles), Anthony had children: 5. Sarah, bapt. June 1657, d. in 1678,
unm. 6. Elizabeth, b. abt. 1659; m. (rec. Stratford) 30 Oct. 1678, Paul Brinsmade.
7. Hannah, b. abt. 1661, d. at Woodbury, 23 July 1698; m. (1) (rec. Stratford) 21
Dec. 1681, Jonathan Nichols; m. (2) Sergt. Samuel Ward, of Fairfield; m. (3) John
Judson, of Woodbury.

at Wethersfield, 9 June 1675, Elizabeth Goodrich, dau. of Ens. William, who d. 17 Feb. 1697/8 ae. abt. 40; m. (2) at Boston, 13 Oct. 1698, Mary Stoddard. His dau. Prudence m. 20 Oct. 1700, Rev. Anthony Stoddard, of Woodbury.

Temperance, b. abt. 1654, d. after 1728; m. 29 Nov. 1681, Mr. Jonathan Pitman.

+Samuel, b. abt. 1656.

Sarah, b. abt. 1658, d. at Stratford, 23 Mar. 1730 ae. abt. 71 (g. s.); m. Ambrose Thompson.

Welles, John, s. of John. Deputy (Stratford), Aug. 1689, Oct. 1693.

Born abt. 1648, d. at Stratford, 24 Mar. 1713.

Will 21 Mar. 1713, proved 22 Apr. 1713; wife Mary; sons Thomas, John, Joseph, Robert; daus. Mary, Sarah, Comfort, Elizabeth, Hannah.

Wife was called Mary at birth of child 1673.

Children, recorded at Stratford:

Mary, b. 29 Nov. 1670; m. 24 Apr. 1695, Jeremiah Judson.

Sarah, b. 2 Jan. 1673 [1673/4]; m. ——— Everts, of Jamaica, L. I.

John, b. abt. 1676, d. at Stratford, 19 Feb. 1734/5; or 17 Feb. 1735 ae. 59 (g. s.); Capt.; will 13 Feb. 1734/5, proved 4 Mar. 1734/5; m. 15 Dec. 1698, Mary Judson; dau. of Isaac, b. 10 Oct. 1679, d. 6 Jan. 1743 ae. 64 (g. s.).

Joseph, b. 21 June 1679, d. at Stratford, abt. 1765; Est. distributed 3 Mar. 1766; m. 3 Feb. 1714/5, Sarah Preston; dau. of Hachaliah, bapt. at Woodbury, Nov. 1683.

Comfort, b. [say 1681], d. 1 June 1717; m. 8 June 1704, Abel Birdsey.

Thomas, b. ———, d. at Stratford, in 1755; will 28 June 1753, proved 6 May 1755; m. 31 Aug. 1710, Sarah Stiles.

Elizabeth, m. 5 July 1711, Joseph Curtis.

Robert, b. Sept. 1688, d. at Stratford, in 1758; will 17 Nov. 1758, proved 5 Dec. 1758; m. 24 Oct. 1720, Eunice Curtis; dau. of Josiah, b. 1 Aug. 1699.

Hannah, m. 27 Nov. 1712, Nathaniel Curtis.

Welles, Thomas, s. of John.

Born abt. 1651; Dea. Thomas d. at Stratford, 7 Jan. 1719/20 ae. abt. 70; m. Elizabeth Titherton, dau. of Daniel, who d. abt. 1729. No issue.

Will of Thomas, Sr., 8 Dec. 1717, proved 26 Jan. 1719/20; wife

Elizabeth; cousins John Thompson, John Welles, Ambrose Thompson, Joseph Welles, Robert Welles, Ebenezer Thompson, Thomas Thompson; sister Temperance Pitman; cousins Thomas, Joseph, Robert, and Gideon Welles of Wethersfield, Josiah Beers, Samuel and Thomas Welles of Stratford; movable estate to cousins John Welles, John Thompson, Joseph Welles, Sarah Evert of Jamaica, L. I., and Elizabeth wife of Joseph Curtis. There being realty not disposed of by will, distribution was ordered to the next of kin, viz.: children of dec'd brothers John and Robert, bro. Samuel Welles of Wethersfield, and sisters Temperance wife of Mr. Jonathan Pitman and Sarah wife of Mr. Ambrose Thompson, both of Stratford.

John Porter was appointed Adm'r of the Est. of Elizabeth Welles of Stratford, 11 Aug. 1729. Timothy Titherton, Richard Nichols, and John Wilcoxson, heirs to Elizabeth, appealed to the Superior Court.

Welles, Samuel, s. of John.   Sergt., Stratfield Trainband.

Born abt. 1656, d. at Stratfield in 1729.

He m. (1) Abigail Wheeler, who joined Stratfield Church, 10 July 1695, by letter from Fairfield. That she was dau. of Sergt. Ephraim Wheeler is indicated by a deed given in 1723 by Timothy Wheeler, Sr. [son of Ephraim], of Stratfield, in which he mentions adjacent land of " my brother Wells."

He m. (2) after 1700, Elizabeth, widow of Daniel Comstock, and dau. of John Wheeler, b. abt. 1667, d. abt. 1706.

He m. (3) at Stratfield, 25 Oct. 1711, Abigail Jones.

Agreement of children and heirs, 11 Mar. 1728/9; Samuel Welles, Thomas Turney and Abigail his wife, John Hubbell and Ann his wife, and John Clugstone and Elizabeth his wife, allowing one-third to their mother-in-law Abigail Welles.

Children [by first wife] :

+Samuel, b. at Stratford, 15 Oct. 1686.
Abigail, m. at Stratfield, 24 Nov. 1709, Thomas Turney.
Ann, m. at Stratfield, 6 Nov. 1711, John Hubbell.
Elizabeth, bapt. at Stratfield, 31 Jan. 1697, d. at Stamford, 31 Aug. 1730; m. at Stratfield, 11 June 1718, John Clugstone.

Welles, Samuel, s. of Samuel.

Born at Stratford, 15 Oct. 1686; d. at Stratfield, 16 Apr. 1751.
He m. Mary, prob. dau. of David Watkins.*

Will 13 Nov. 1744, proved 23 Apr. 1751; wife Mary; daus.
Sarah Blackman, Abigail Prince, Mary Hubbell, Prudence and
Hester Welles; eldest son David; youngest son Jedediah; son
Samuel.

Children, bapt. at Stratfield:

Sarah, bapt. 21 Dec. 1712; m. 20 Dec. 1732, Nathan Blackman.
Abigail, bapt. 21 Dec. 1712; m. 9 Aug. 1733, Samuel Prince.
Mary, bapt. 25 Apr. 1714; m. 2 Dec. 1736, Andrew Hubbell.
Prudence, bapt. 15 July 1716.
David, bapt. 20 July 1718; m. 6 Sept. 1750, Ruth Burroughs, dau. of
    Stephen, b. 25 Apr. 1731, d. at Stratfield, 3 July 1766 in 35 yr.
    (g. s.).
Samuel.
Jedediah, m. 29 Nov. 1750, Lucy French, b. abt. 1729, d. at Stratfield,
    28 Oct. 1751 in 23 yr. (g. s.).
Hester.

Welles, John, s. of Hugh.

Rem. from Wethersfield to Stratford, and thence to Hatfield,
Mass., where he d. 18 Oct. 1692.

Married Sarah Curtis, dau. of William, b. at Stratford, 10 Oct.
1642.

---

* By Stratfield Church records, Samuel and *Sarah* his wife joined 21 Dec. 1712.
On 22 Mar. 1734/5, Samuel Prince and Abigail his wife conveyed land formerly given
us by our father and mother Samuel and *Sarah* Welles of Stratfield, part of 18
acres formerly Mr. Jeremiah Judson's dec'd. Yet on 1 Apr. 1734, Samuel Welles and
Mary his wife of Stratfield conveyed to our dau. Sarah Blackman; and on 8 Aug.
1741, Nathan Blackman and Sarah his wife conveyed the right received by deed from
father and mother Mr. Samuel Welles and *Mary* his wife. In several deeds, in
1738 and earlier, Samuel Welles and wife *Mary* joined other heirs of Jeremiah Judson,
Sr., and she must obviously have been a gr. dau. of Judson; but the *Hist. of Stratford* errs in calling her dau. of Jeremiah Judson, Jr. Almost certainly, she was
the dau. of David and Sarah (Judson) Watkins, and named a child for each parent.
If there was a first wife Sarah, she would have been mother of most of the children, and it is difficult to assign her a reasonable date of death in view of the terms
in which some of the deeds are couched. We conclude that *Sarah* is a recorded
error, the name perhaps having been written Marah (variant of Mary) in original
documents.

Children, first two recorded at Stratford [last six from *Hist. of Hadley*] :

> Sarah, b. 28 Sept. 1659, m. at Stratford, 1 Feb. 1677/8, Benjamin Beach.
> Mary, b. 29 Aug. 1661.
> Abigail, b. [say 1663] ; m. (rec. Stratford) 3 Nov. 1684, John Charles.
> Hannah, b. 12 Nov. 1665, d. 24 Nov. 1676.
> Hester, b. 26 Apr. 1668.
> John, b. 15 Sept. 1670, d. at Hatfield, 21 Apr. 1720 ; m. Rachel Marsh, dau. of Samuel.
> Elizabeth, b. 21 June 1675, slain 20 Sept. 1677.
> Jonathan, b. 14 Dec. 1682.
> Elizabeth, b. 10 Jan. 1686.

Westcott, Richard.   Served in Pequot War, 1637.

He settled in Wethersfield by 1636 and bought Samuel Clark's homestead ; sold it to John Stoddard, 1645, and removed to Fairfield, where he d. before 11 Mar. 1649/50.

He m. Joanna, sister of the wife of Robert Sanford of Hartford. She m. (2) Nathaniel Baldwin of Fairfield, and (3) Thomas Skidmore of Fairfield.

On 14 Feb. 1664 [1664/5], John Weed of Stamford, husband of Joanna dau. of Richard Westcott, receipted to his father-in-law Thomas Skidmore. Daniel Westcott receipted same date ; and on 4 Jan. 1669 [1669/70] Moses Knapp, husband of Abigail Westcott receipted, and on 9 Nov. 1666 John Westcott receipted.

Children :

> +John, b. [say 1641].
> +Daniel, b. abt. 1643.
> Joanna, b. [say 1645] ; m. by 1665, John Weed, of Stamford.
> Abigail, b. [say 1647] ; m. by 1669, Moses Knapp, of Stamford.

Westcott, John, s. of Richard.

With his bro. Daniel he settled in Stamford, where he m. Ruth Hyatt, dau. of Thomas, b. abt. 1650. He rem. to Mamaroneck, Westchester County, where he was living in 1676 and 1698. On 26 June 1675, he purchased land in Westchester County from John and Mary (Richbell) Mott. Ruth, ae. 60, was living at Bedford with her son Thomas in 1710.

Children (record incomplete) :*

> Richard, b. abt. 1668; m. Rachel Holmes, dau. of John, b. abt. 1670.
> The children in the Bedford Census 1710 were: Rachel, b. abt.
> 1695; Ruth, b. abt. 1697; Rose, b. abt. 1701; Richard, b. abt. 1704;
> Daniel, b. abt. 1707; and Millicent, b. in 1710.
>
> John, b. abt. 1679, d. at Wilton in 1743; will 23 Mar. 1743, proved
> 4 June 1743; m. at Stamford, 9 Apr. 1702, Rose Holmes, b. abt.
> 1678. His will named wife Rose and children John, Nathaniel,
> Samuel, Joanna, Abigail, Eleanor. The children in the Bedford
> Census, 1710, were: Martha, b. abt. 1703; John, b. abt. 1704;
> Samuel, b. abt. 1706; and Johanna, b. abt. 1709.
>
> Thomas, b. abt. 1686; m. Elizabeth ———, b. abt. 1691.

Westcott, Daniel, s. of Richard.   Deputy (Stamford) to Conn.
Leg., Oct. 1691, May and Oct. 1692, May and Oct. 1694.

Born abt. 1643; ae. 49 in 1692; settled in Stamford, where he
bought land in 1669.   On 3 Jan. 1680 [1680/1] he sold to Mr.
William Read land in Fairfield, not to be entered until the death
of Thomas Skidmore.   He served in K. Philip's War, 1675, and
was called Sergt.   Selectman at Stamford, 1676-81.

He m. Abigail Gaylord,† dau. of Samuel of Windsor, b. 29 Sept.
1653.

He joined the contingent which went from Fairfield County to
Cohansey, N. J., and d. in 1704.   Will of Daniel of Caesaria River,
Salem County, N. J., yeoman, 30 Nov. 1702, proved 14 Feb.
1703/4; wife Abigail; children Samuel, Daniel, Ebenezer, Mary,
Joanna Foster, Abigail Lummus; children Daniel, Ebenezer, and
Mary, to be sent to cousin Jonas Weed in Stamford, shoemaker,
if his widow cannot maintain them.

In 1692, his French girl, Katharine Branch,‡ ae. 17, showed
symptoms of being bewitched, threw fits, and reveled in the attention she attracted.   Sergt. Westcott took the matter seriously and
in May 1692 made the formal complaint which resulted in the trial
of Elizabeth (wife of Stephen) Clawson and of Mercy (wife of

---

* Ruth "Wascot" who m. (rec. at Killingworth), 1 Jan. 1696, Samuel Wilcoxson, is
usually placed as dau. of John, but more likely dau. of Robert of the R. I. family,
perhaps b. 1676, the year Robert was killed in K. Philip's War.

† Probate records, estates of her father and brother, according to Manwaring's *Digest*
call her wife of *Joseph* Westcott of Stamford. There was no Joseph of Stamford at
that time. We are indebted to William M. Clevenger, Esq., of Atlantic City, N. J.,
who informs us that in the original files Abigail's husband signed as *Daniel*. Mrs.
H. B. Houghton of Bridgeport, Conn., has also been generous with Westcott data.

‡ She had a brother at St. Christopher's.

Thomas) Disbrow. The testimony mentions Westcott's wife Abigail and eldest dau. "Johannah", and states his age. Lydia Penoyer* testified that her aunt Abigail Westcott said "her servant girl Caten branch was such a Lying gairl that not anyboddy Could beleiue one word what shee said"; and Abigail further showed good sense by asserting her disbelief that any of the accused women were witches.

Children:

> Joanna, m. —— Foster.
> Abigail, m. —— Lummus.
> Samuel, of Cohansey, N. J.; m. Elizabeth Coley, dau. of Peter, b, at Fairfield, 1 Dec. 1680.
> Daniel, of Cohansey, N. J., d. in 1742; will 14 Oct. 1742, proved 3 Dec. 1742; m. Elizabeth [?Foster].
> Ebenezer, of Fairfield, N. J., d. in 1749; will 7 Jan. 1748/9, proved 25 Feb. 1748/9; m. Barbara ——.
> Mary.

WHEELER FAMILY (FAIRFIELD)

Wheeler, Thomas, "Sr."

Known as Thomas, Sr., came to Concord, whence he came (with the Jones contingent in Sept. 1644 as we suppose) to Fairfield. Here land was recorded to him, and adjacent land to Thomas, Jr., in Jan. 1649 [1649/50]. This Thomas, Jr., we take to be the brother named 1654 in his will, but whether actual brother or brother-in-law the evidence is inadequate to establish. Though rare, brothers sometimes were given identical names, but usually they were half-brothers, with different mothers. Ephraim Wheeler was certainly brother of Thomas, Sr.

Will 5 May 1654, proved 23 Aug. 1654; wife Ann; elder son Thomas, property in Concord; dau. Sarah wife of Thomas Sherwood and their son Thomas; dau. (not named) and four gr. children, Mary, James, Thomas, and John Bennett; son John, lands in Fairfield; brother Thomas Wheeler Lieutenant, Robert Lockwood, and Andrew Ward, all of Fairfield, overseers. Ephraim Wheeler was an appraiser.

---

* Wife of Thomas Penoyer, and presumably dau. of Moses and Abigail (Westcott) Knapp.

Will of Ann Wheeler, 21 Aug. 1659; elder son Thomas, his wife and children; children of dau. Hannah, mentioning Sarah and Hannah Bennett; gr. child Sarah Sherwood; Annis Sherwood, wife of my son-in-law; to Rebecca Turney, my best hat; to Ann Squire, a petticoat. Inv. 20 Oct. 1659. The illegible conclusion of the will may have named her son John.

The *Wheeler Family in America,* which we cannot follow implicitly with regard to this Wheeler family, states that Thomas m. at Cranefield, co. Bedford, Eng., 5 May 1613, Ann Halsey; and the baptisms of their children at Cranefield, given below, are from the same source.

Children:

    Mary, bapt. 20 Oct. 1615, no further record.

    Anna, bapt. 20 Feb. 1617; she was, we suppose, the dau. always called Hannah in Fairfield records, who m. (1) James Bennett, and (2) Joseph Middlebrook.

    William, bapt. 16 Mar. 1618, no further record, and d. y.; for his brother Thomas was called "elder son" in will of both parents.

    Thomas, bapt. 8 Apr. 1620; of Concord. [See the following article.]

+John, bapt. 27 Feb. 1624.

    Sarah, bapt. 10 Aug. 1628; m. Thomas Sherwood, Jr.

Wheeler, Thomas. Ens., Conn. Col. Troop, May 1653, having previously held title of Lt.

For all his activity and prominence, the identity of this man has been an enigma. Savage identifies him with Thomas, Sr., of Fairfield, which is certainly wrong, as the Lieutenant was living after the death of Thomas, Sr. Orcutt makes him son of Thomas, Sr., and then proceeds to identify him further with Thomas of Milford; and the *Wheeler Family in America* follows this solution.

Now the Thomas who was appointed Ensign in 1653 by Conn. Colony was distinctly called "Lt. Thomas of Fairfield." But the Milford Thomas was living *there* by 1640, and until 1657 continued to have his children bapt. there with great regularity at two-year intervals. As Milford was in New Haven Colony in 1653, it should be obvious that he could not be the man on whom Conn. Colony conferred this commission in its colonial troop which was raised for possible war service during the trouble with the Dutch.

The Milford Thomas located there before there were any Wheelers in Fairfield; never lived in Fairfield, nor, so far as we

have ascertained, in Stratford, though he purchased land in the
latter place which he conveyed to two of his sons, still being called
"of Milford"; and New Haven Col. Rec. mention him in 1659 as
marshal at Milford, and his house at Milford (though he not
living in it) in 1660, together with other references showing him
active at Milford, and not one mention which gives him any military title; while Lt. Thomas Wheeler, mentioned both times by
that title, was in 1658 and 1663 requesting New Haven Colony to
accept within its jurisdiction his purchases from the Indians near
Derby.

There are but two men of the name Thomas Wheeler with whom
it is possible to identify the lieutenant. One was the son of
Thomas, Sr., of Fairfield; he in his father's will received the Concord estate, and we follow Savage and Mrs. Schenck rather than
the *Wheeler Family in America* in believing that he settled in
Concord, whether or not he ever resided in Fairfield. If the children who were recorded to Thomas in Concord from 1649 to
1662 belonged to this man and were actually born in Concord, that
would preclude his being the lieutenant who was active in Conn.
during that period.

Without research in Concord, the evidence at hand is insufficient
and too confusing to permit a definite conclusion. We are inclined
to believe that Thomas, son of Thomas, Sr., remained in Concord,
had wife Sarah, and children born at Concord: Sarah, b. 10 July
1649; Joseph, b. 18 Aug. 1651; Ann, b. 20 Dec. 1653; John, b.
18 Feb. 1655/6; Mary, b. 20 Dec. 1658; and Thomas, b. 29 Mar.
1662.

The Thomas, Jr., who had a homelot in Fairfield by 1650, was
prob. the brother named in the will of Thomas, Sr., in 1654. Perhaps he was a younger half-brother, born as late as 1610. Doubtless he came to Fairfield in 1644, and on 16 June 1650 he sold to
Henry Jackson land which had been purchased from Robert
Hawkins and Richard Vowles. In 1653/4 he sold his homelot and
several other pieces of land, being called "Jr." and in one instance
"the younger"; and not long after rem. to Stratford, being called
of that town when he bought land in Derby from the Indians in
1657. At Derby he remained as a trader until 1664, when he sold
the property there to Mr. Alexander Bryan of Milford, and
returned, as we suppose, to Mass.

Since Lt. Thomas Wheeler in 1658 and 1663 had dealings with

New Haven Colony, there being an uncertainty whether his Derby holdings fell within its jurisdiction or in that of Conn. Colony, and was definitely called lieutenant in these transactions, we need not hesitate to identify him with the Lt. Thomas of Fairfield who received a commission from Conn. Colony in 1653, at which time he lived within the bounds of that colony.* His history is therefore traced from his advent in Fairfield in 1644 until he left Derby in 1664. His appointment as Lt. is not found in Conn. records, and may have been by Mass. before he came to Fairfield. It is reasonable, as he disappears from Conn., to assume his return to Concord and to believe that he was the Capt. who was wounded in K. Philip's War, 1675; for inexperienced men were not appointed to serve in high military positions in the Indian wars, and our Lt. Thomas had had sundry dealings with the Indians, as Conn. records attest.

It is further likely, though Savage makes the same Thomas marry both Ruth and Sarah (in that order), that it was Lt. Thomas who m. Ruth Wood, dau. of William of Concord; whose will in 1670 named both Ruth and her husband, thereby invalidating the supposition that he already had a second wife Sarah.† It should be noted that when he bought his Derby land in 1657, the deed was witnessed by Ruth and Timothy Wheeler. Ruth was doubtless his wife, and Timothy a youthful son. This may have been the Timothy who m. at Concord, 29 June 1670, Ruth Fuller, and d. 7 June 1678. A dau. Alice d. at Concord, 17 Mar. 1640/1, before Thomas came to Fairfield; and a dau. Ruth m. 7 May 1673, Ephraim Jones of Concord. Capt. Thomas d. 16 Dec. 1686; and it appears he had a second wife Hannah who, with his son Thomas, administered his estate.

Wheeler, Ephraim. Sergt., Fairfield Trainband.

Brother of Thomas, Sr., settled in Fairfield; d. in 1670; m. Ann ———, who d. before 1708.

Will 22 Sept. 1669, proved 1 Nov. 1670; wife Ann; son Isaac; daus. Mary, Ruth, Hannah (she not living in Fairfield); sons

---

* Lt. Thomas testified concerning Indian claims [not dated, but apparently 1659] and spoke of having been formerly an inhabitant of Fairfield.

† Sarah, if our conclusions are correct, was the only known wife of Thomas of Concord, son of Thomas, Sr., of Fairfield.

Samuel, Timothy, Ephraim; daus. Rebecca, Judith, Abigail; cousin John Wheeler.

Ann Wheeler, Exec'x of her husband Ephraim's will, and with consent of her son Isaac, conveyed to two sons Timothy and Ephraim.

Children:

+Isaac, b. at Concord, 13 Dec. 1642.
Mary, m. by 1669, ———.
Ruth, d. at Stratfield in 1719; m. Samuel Treadwell; entered Feb. 1673/4 land from Sergt. Ephraim Wheeler as his wife's portion.
Hannah, m. (rec. Concord), 11 July 1667, Samuel Smedley, of Concord, by whom she was mother of Samuel Smedley of Stratfield.
Rebecca, m. Samuel Gregory; entered Apr. 1682 land of wife Rebecca from her father Sergt. Ephraim Wheeler.
Judith.
Samuel.
+Timothy.
Abigail, m. abt. 1685, Sergt. Samuel Welles.
+Ephraim.

Wheeler, John, s. of Thomas.   Deputy (Fairfield) to Conn. Leg., Oct. 1657, May 1658, May 1659, May 1660, Oct. 1671, May and Oct. 1672, Oct. 1674, May 1677, Oct. 1678, May and Oct. 1681, Oct. 1682, July and Oct. 1684,* Oct. 1685, Oct. 1687, May and June 1689.   Sergt., Fairfield Trainband.

Bapt. at Cranefield, co. Bedford, 27 Feb. 1624, d. at Fairfield in 1690.

Inv. 5 Apr. 1690. Widow; children, John 26, Thomas 21, Joseph 16, Obadiah 8, Jonathan 3, David 1, Judan 29, Elizabeth 23, Mary 19, Rebecca 18, Hannah 14, Abigail 10, Ann 6.   In 1698, twelve children were living; one son d. last winter.

On 8 Jan. 1673 [1673/4], he entered land by virtue of marriage with dec'd wife Judith, as part of her portion, on the upland lot of Benjamin Turney dec'd.   On 5 Jan. 1673 [1673/4], Henry Rowland entered 24 acres formerly bought of Mr. John Jones dec'd, and put the greater part of it in hands of John Wheeler "my son in law."

---

* The name John Fyler appears in Colonial Records as Deputy for Fairfield, May 1684. This name has not been found at Fairfield and is prob. error for John **Wheeler,** who was Deputy at the other sessions that year.

He m. (1) Judith Turney, dau. of Benjamin, b. abt. 1635. He gave rec't for his wife's portion 1661; and was called bro. by Robert Turney, 1689.

He m. (2) by 1673, Elizabeth Rowland, dau. of Henry, who d. abt. Mar. 1702/3.

Agreement was made, 3 Apr. 1700, between Elizabeth widow of John Wheeler, guardian of her children Jonathan, David and Ann, with John, Mary, and Abigail Wheeler, Nathaniel Porter, Samuel Wheeler and Joseph Wheeler; witnesses, Philip Lewis, Elizabeth Comstock, and Robert Turney. The above were the signers, but the body of the document mentioned John, Joseph, Thomas, Jonathan, David, Rebecca, Mary, Abigail, Ann, and Hannah Wheeler.

Will of Elizabeth, widow of John, 21 Feb. 1702/3; daus. Abigail and Ann; son Joseph; two youngest sons, Jonathan and David. Inv. 23 Mar. 1703. Adm'n granted to son Joseph, who was chosen guardian by Jonathan and David.

Children [by first wife] :

> Jude-Ann (or Judith), b. abt. 1661, d. before 1706 without issue; m. Joshua Knowles, who had land recorded 23 Mar. 1690 by gift of his father-in-law Sergt. John Wheeler.
>
> +John, b. abt. 1664.
>
> Elizabeth, b. abt. 1667; m. (1) (rec. Norwalk) 13 June 1692, Daniel Comstock; m. (2) Samuel Welles.
>
> Thomas, b. abt. 1669, d. unm.; a letter written by him from Barbados, 19 July 1696, to his bro. John, describes himself as aboard a man of war, the *Play,* bound to London, mentions his mother and gives lands to five brothers if he return not. On 12 Mar. 1704/5, his relatives being informed he was dec'd, the Court accepted the letter as a will, and distribution was made to the four brothers.
>
> Mary, b. abt. 1671, d. at Stratfield, 7 Jan. 1710/1; m. abt. 1701, John Beardsley, of Stratfield. On 16 Dec. 1703, he gave a discharge to Joseph Wheeler for all legacies from the beginning of the world until that date.
>
> Rebecca, b. abt. 1672, d. between 1708 and 1713; m. (1) abt. 1693, Isaac Wheeler, Jr.; m. (2) abt. 1699, Nathaniel Porter.

Children [by second wife] :

> +Joseph, b. abt. 1674.
>
> Hannah, b. abt. 1676; m. (1) Sergt. Samuel Wheeler; m. (2) 24 Aug. 1708, Dr. John Wheeler.
>
> Abigail, b. abt. 1680, d. in 1706, unm. Inv. 31 Dec. 1706. Next of kin: John, Joseph, Jonathan, and David Wheeler; and those who m. the sisters,—Nathaniel Porter, Samuel Beardsley [*sic*], John

Beardsley, Ann Wheeler, and Daniel Comstock who represents his dec'd mother. Distribution 14 Apr. 1707, to John, Joseph, Jonathan and David Wheeler, Sergt. Samuel Wheeler, John Barley [*sic*], Ann Wheeler, and Daniel Comstock in right of his mother Elizabeth Welles.

Obadiah, b. abt. 1682, d. between 1696 and 1698.

Ann, b. abt. 1684; m. Lemuel Sherwood.

+Jonathan, b. abt. 1687.

+David, b. abt. 1689.

Wheeler, Isaac, s. of Ephraim. Deputy (Fairfield), May and Sept. 1693; Ens., Stratfield Trainband, May 1697.

Born at Concord, Mass., 13 Dec. 1642, d. at Stratfield 1 Apr. 1712 ae. 70 (g. s.); Deacon of Stratfield Church. He m. (1) ————,* and (2) Susannah, widow of Samuel Hall. She d. by 1751.

Nuncupative will, 11 Apr. 1712 (four days before he died, so the g. s. is prob. misread and should be read 15 instead of 1 Apr.); he was "much troubled about John Patchin", his faithful servant for thirty yrs.; "I would not have him wronged he is grown A poor old Creature", so provision is made to maintain him; wife; testified by Mr. James Bennett and Mrs. Mary Bennett, 29 Apr. 1712. Also, Sergt. John Odell, David Hall, and John Wheeler testified to his will regarding his dec'd son Samuel's heirs, mentioning gr. son Samuel; gr. sons Isaac and Ebenezer; his son-in-law Samuel Hall; son-in-law David Hall, upon consideration of his being kind to his mother. Adm'n was granted to widow Susannah. Distribution order to Widow, and five daus. and three gr. sons, viz.: Sarah wife of John Odell, Rebecca wife of Capt. David (*sic*) Sherman, Mary wife of Henry Jackson, Experience wife of Lemuel Sherwood, and Mercy Sherman, and the gr. sons, Isaac, Ebenezer, and Samuel Wheeler.

On 21 Mar. 1751, the realty of Dea. Isaac formerly distributed to his widow as dower was set to the heirs; heirs of Mercy wife of Capt. David Sherman; heirs of Sarah Odell of Stratfield; Rebecca Sherman of Newtown; Samuel Wheeler of Fairfield; heirs of Experience wife of Lemuel Sherwood; heirs of Ebenezer Wheeler; heirs of Isaac Wheeler.

---

* He was *not* the Isaac Wheeler of Lancaster, Mass., who by wife Experience had twin children, Isaac and Experience, b. 22 Nov. 1684, and a son John, b. 24 July 1686.

Children [by first wife] :

> Sarah, b. abt. 1665, d. at Stratfield, 25 Oct. 1743 in 79 yr. (g. s.) ; m. John Odell.

+Isaac.

> Mercy, b. abt. 1670, d. at Stratfield, 19 Aug. 1745 in 75 yr. (g. s.) ; m. abt. 1690, Capt. David Sherman; they conveyed 1732 land set to her in distribution of Dea. Isaac Wheeler's Est.

> Rebecca, b. abt. 1672, d. at Newtown, 2 Sept. 1751; m. at Stratford, 19 Dec. 1694, Daniel Sherman.

+Samuel.

> Mary, b. abt. 1683, d. at Stratfield, 18 Sept. 1743 in 61 yr. (g. s.) ; m. (1) 16 Jan. 1703/4, Henry Jackson; m. (2) Samuel Sherwood. Mary Sherwood, widow of Capt. Samuel, conveyed 1733 right from father Wheeler dec'd.

> Experience, b. abt. 1686, d. at Stratfield, 27 Aug. 1721 ae. 35; m. at Stratfield, 17 May 1711, Lemuel Sherwood.

Wheeler, Timothy, s. of Ephraim.

He m. (1) at Stratfield, 11 Apr. 1689, Rebecca Turney; dau. of Robert, b. 10 July 1671.

He m. (2) Margery ———.

He conveyed land to his son Timothy, 28 Aug. 1713. In 1708 he sold to Mr. Richard Sackett of the Province of New York, brewer, land formerly the dower of my mother Mrs. Ann Wheeler dec'd, mentioning his bro. Ephraim Wheeler. He conveyed 4 Mar. 1722/3 to son Timothy, land bounded on "my brother Wells his Land."

Will 13 Apr. 1730, proved 20 June 1730; wife Margery; daus. Rebecca Bostwick and Abigail Wheeler; son Timothy, Exec'r.

Children [by first wife], recorded Stratfield:

+Timothy, b. 24 Apr. 1691.

> Samuel, b. 28 May 1692, d. y.

> Benjamin, b. 22 Mar. 1695, bapt. 14 July 1695, d. y.

> Rebecca, b. 30(?) Oct. 1697, bapt. 21 Oct. 1697; m. (rec. New Milford) 23 July 1724, Joseph Bostwick. They receipted 1732 to her bro. Timothy Wheeler, only son and Exec'r, for her right in Est. of father Mr. Timothy Wheeler, Sr.

> Abigail, b. 30 Dec. 1703, bapt. 7 May 1704; m. Jonathan Wheeler. They receipted 1733 to bro. Timothy Wheeler for her right in Est. of father Timothy Wheeler, Sr.

Wheeler, Ephraim, s. of Ephraim.

He m. (1) Sarah Turney, dau. of Robert, b. 27 Sept. 1663.

He m. (2) Sarah Sherwood, dau. of Matthew, b. abt. 1676, d. at Stratfield, 25 May 1743 in 67 yr. (g. s.) ; she m. (2) Benjamin Fairweather, and (3) Anthony Nouguier.

Inv. 27 Nov. 1705, taken by James Bennett, Sr., and Richard Hubbell at request of Thomas Merwin of Fairfield, Adm'r. The son Andrew chose Samuel Treadwell, Sr., for guardian, and Jedediah chose Ens. Samuel Sherwood, 4 Apr. 1716.

Children [by second wife], bapt. at Stratfield:

> Katharine, b. 20 Mar. 1693/4, d. at Newtown, 16 Mar. 1742 in 49 yr.; m. at Stratfield, 19 Jan. 1709/10, Peter Hubbell.
> Abiah, b. 28 Dec. 1696, bapt. 31 Jan. 1697; m. John Cornwell.
> Andrew, b. 15 Feb. 1698/9, bapt. 19 Feb. 1699, d. at Newtown, by 1782 [mutual agreement of heirs] ; m. ———.*
> Jedediah, b. 28 Dec. 1700, bapt. 29 Dec. 1700, d. in 1724; Inv. 19 Aug. 1724; adm'n granted to mother Sarah, widow of Mr. Benjamin Fayerweather.

Wheeler, John, s. of John.   Ens., east company, Fairfield, May 1709; Lt., May 1712.

Born abt. 1664, d. at Fairfield, 19 Mar. 1754 ae. 92 (g. s.) ; m. (1) at Fairfield, 22 Mar. 1692, Abigail Burr. She was dau. of Nathaniel, b. abt. 1668, d. 7 Feb. 1711/2. He m. (2) 17 Oct. 1712, Lydia Porter of Windsor. She was, possibly, Lydia, twin dau. of the third John and Joanna (Gaylord) Porter, b. 28 Nov. 1689, though the *History of Windsor* kills her off in infancy. She d. 12 Nov. 1747 in 57 yr. (g. s.), so may have been a second Lydia, b. abt. 1691, and not recorded.

He renewed his Covenant at Fairfield Church, 16 Sept. 1694.

Children by first wife, recorded at Fairfield:

> ╳John, b. 20 July 1694, bapt. 16 Sept. 1694, d. at Fairfield, 19 Feb. 1725/6 in 32 yr. (g. s.) ; m. by 1722, Elizabeth Burr, dau. of John, bapt. 2 Feb. 1701/2, d. at Woodbridge, 3 Aug. 1769 in 69 yr. (g. s.) ; she m. (2) at Stratfield, 3 Apr. 1733, Ezra Dibble; and (3) Capt. Ebenezer Beecher.
> Sarah, b. 11 Feb. 1696 [1696/7], bapt. 21 Mar. 1696/7.
> Abigail, b. 16 Aug. 1698 [1699?], bapt. 13 Aug. 1699; m. 5 July 1722, Samuel Merwin.

---

* One son, Jedediah, bapt. at Stratfield, 12 Dec. 1731.

Mary, b. 4 Nov. 1701, bapt. 28 Dec. 1701, d. 11 Dec. 1713/4.

Elizabeth, b. 2 Apr. 1703 [should be 1704], bapt. 16 Apr. 1704, d. 8 Feb. 1786 in 84 yr. (g. s.) ; m. 10 May 1727, John Dimon.

Ann, b. 16 Jan. 1706, bapt. as Judith-Ann, 10 Mar. 1705/6; m. (as Judith-Ann) at Stratfield, 25 Jan. 1733, Samuel Odell.

Children by second wife, recorded at Fairfield :

Mary, b. 11 Oct. 1713, bapt. 27 Dec. 1713, d. 28 Feb. 1720/1.

✕Obadiah, b. 15 Mar. 1716, bapt. 15 Apr. 1716, d. at Fairfield, 6 Nov. 1753; Inv. 11 Jan. 1754; m. Mary ———.

Daniel, b. 15 July 1718, bapt. 10 Aug. 1718, d. before 1788; m. Esther Nichols, dau. of Ignatius, who d. abt. 1788; no issue. Adm'n on Ests. of Esther Wheeler and Daniel Wheeler was granted, 2 Sept. 1788, to Ebenezer Nichols of Weston; her estate was distributed to her relatives.

✕Jabez, b. 25 Feb. 1722, bapt. 15 Apr. 1722, d. at Easton by 1810; Dea.; Capt.; m. (1) 9 Dec. 1742, Charity Beach, bapt. Mar. 1724, d. at Greenfield, 4 Sept. 1761 in 38 yr.; m. (2) Mary Wheeler, dau. of Isaac, bapt. 27 Jan. 1733/4, d. in 1810.

✕Ichabod, b. 11 Jan. 1725 [1725/6], bapt. 6 Mar. 1725/6, d. 14 Sept. 1806 in 81 yr. (g. s., Fairfield) ; Capt.; m. 1 Jan. 1752, Deborah Burr, dau. of Capt. John, who d. 5 May 1799 in 69 yr. (g. s.).

✕John, b. 3 June 1729, bapt. 8 June 1729, d. at Easton, 3 Feb. 1819 in 90 yr. (g. s.) ; m. (1) Ann ———, who d. at Easton, 17 Mar. 1767 in 38 yr. (g s.) ; m. (2) 12 July 1767, Ruth Seeley; widow of Stephen Seeley and dau. of Zechariah Sanford, b. 19 June 1737; m. (3) Abiah ———, who d. 4 July 1828 ae. 89 (g. s.).

Wheeler, Joseph, s. of John.

Born abt. 1674, d. at Greenfield, 13 July 1759 ae. 84. He renewed his Covenant at Fairfield Church.

He m. at Fairfield, 7 Dec. 1705, Deborah Nichols; dau. of Ephraim, b. 1 Jan. 1685/6. She d. at Greenfield, 14 Sept. 1748 in 63 yr. (g. s.).

Will 9 Mar. 1758, proved 20 July 1759; sons Joseph, Ephraim, Thomas (for care of his mother) ; dau. Catherine Osborn; two gr. children Lazarus and Hannah Wheeler.

Children, recorded at Greenfield :*

✕Joseph, b. 16 Nov. 1706, bapt. 26 Jan. 1706/7; m. 10 Sept. 1729, Abigail Perry; dau. of Joseph, bapt. 8 Feb. 1710/1.

---

* This family is also entered in the Fairfield town records, five dates out of six being at variance with the Greenfield records. Experience with such discrepancies leads us to credit the Greenfield rather than the town record, with the exception that we have followed the latter in making Joseph b. 1706 instead of 1705. The baptisms are from Fairfield Church records, which the Greenfield records repeat with but one error.

XThomas, b. 16 July 1708, bapt. 15 Aug. 1708, d. at Greenfield, 22 Feb.
1796 in 88 yr. (g. s.); m. (1) Mary Sanford, dau. of Thomas,
bapt. 2 May 1714, d. 24 Feb. 1753 in 39 yr. (g. s.); m. (2) 17 Apr.
1760, Sarah, widow of Joseph Perry, Jr., and dau. of Peter Bulkley,
bapt. 29 Nov. 1713, d. 22 Apr. 1789 in 76 yr. (g. s.).

Esther, b. 31 Aug. 1710, bapt. 29 Oct. 1710, d. Apr. 1732.

Catherine, b. 16 Nov. 1712, bapt. 8 Feb. 1712/3; m. Sept. 1733,
Jonathan Osborn.

XEphraim, b. 25 Mar. 1716, bapt. 15 Apr. 1716, d. at Redding abt. 1806;
m. Martha Bulkley, dau. of Daniel, bapt. 2 July 1721.

XSeth, b. 26 Mar. 1721, bapt. 28 May 1721, d. at Redding, 11 Aug. 1751
in 30 yr.; adm'n granted, 1 Oct. 1751; m. at Redding, 27 Oct. 1746,
Ruth Knapp.

Wheeler, Jonathan, s. of John.

Born abt. 1687, d. at Fairfield, 20 Feb. 1772 ae. 86 (g. s.); m.
Abigail Wheeler, dau. of Timothy, b. 30 Dec. 1703.

On 31 Mar. 1733, he gave a receipt to his (former) guardian,
Joseph Wheeler, for his share in the estates of mother Elizabeth,
bro. Thomas, and sister Abigail.

Adm'n granted, 3 Mar. 1772, to Jonathan Wheeler. Distribution 28 Jan. 1775; widow Abigail; eldest son Jonathan; heirs
of Sarah Cope; heirs of Abel Wheeler.

Children:

Jonathan, d. at Fairfield in 1777; Inv. 2 June 1777.

Sarah, bapt. at Stratfield, 15 Oct. 1732; m. ——— Cope.

XAbel, b. abt. 1737, d. at Fairfield, 27* Mar. 1772 in 36 yr. (g. s.);
will 26 Feb. 1772, proved 13 Apr. 1772; m. 27 Mar. 1758, Rebecca
Whittier, dau. of John; she was bur. 22 Nov. 1806 ae. 67 (Trinity
Church rec.).

Wheeler, David, s. of John.

Born abt. 1689, d. at Fairfield in 1775.

He m. (1) 28 Mar. 1716/7, Esther Nichols; dau. of Ephraim,
b. 18 Dec. 1689.

He m. (2) Martha ———.

Will 18 Apr. 1774, proved 4 Dec. 1775; wife Martha; dau.
Eunice wife of John Nichols; son David; negro slave Tom to
have freedom at death of myself and wife.

---

*26 by town record.

Children [by first wife], recorded at Fairfield:

Eunice, b. 24 Dec. 1717, bapt. 1 Nov. 1719, d. at Stratfield, 9 Apr.
1785; m. (1) Ephraim Morehouse; m. (2) John Nichols.

Temperance, b. 6 Nov. 1721, bapt. 18 Feb. 1721/2, d. y.

Patience, b. 1 Oct. 1723, bapt. 6 Oct. 1723, d. y.

XDavid, b. 6 Apr. 1726, bapt. 2 July 1727, d. 10 May 1806 ae. 79
(Wheeler Journal); m. at Stratfield, 6 Oct. 1749, Lois Chauncey,
b. 28 Oct. 1727, d. 2 Feb. 1793 (Wheeler Journal).

Wheeler, Isaac, s. of Isaac.

He m. abt. 1693, Rebecca Wheeler, dau. of Sergt. John, b. abt.
1672; she m. (2) abt. 1699, Nathaniel Porter.

Inv. of Isaac of Fairfield Village [Stratfield], 18 Apr. 1698.
Widow to administer, with his father Isaac. On 18 July 1699, the
ages of the children (two sons and a dau.) are stated as 6, 4, and
2. Isaac and Ebenezer, sons of Isaac, Jr., chose their father-in-
law Nathaniel Porter as guardian. Distribution made to the three
children, 4 Apr. 1716.

Children:

XIsaac, bapt. at Fairfield, 11 Nov. 1694, d. 17 Nov. 1733; will 16 Nov.
1733, proved 6 Dec. 1733; m. Mary Wakelee, dau. of Jonathan, b.
10 June 1708, d. 5 July 1768 ae. 60 (g. s., Easton); she m. (2)
Isaac Bennett, Jr.

XEbenezer, bapt. at Stratfield, 8 Feb. 1696, d. in 1744; will 24 Jan.
1743/4, proved 6 Mar. 1743/4; m. Abigail Edwards, dau. of John,
bapt. 25 Apr. 1703.

Elizabeth, bapt. at Stratfield, 26 Dec. 1697; m. Henry Stevens, of
Fairfield, with whom in 1726 she conveyed right to land in Stratford from estate of her father, Isaac Wheeler, Jr.

Wheeler, Samuel, s. of Isaac. Sergt., Stratfield Trainband.

He m. Hannah Wheeler, dau. of Sergt. John, b. abt. 1676.

She m. (2) 24 Aug. 1708, Mr. John Wheeler, Physician.

Inv. 8 Mar. 1707/8; Widow Hannah; son ae. 7 and dau. ae.
5. Adm'n granted to Widow and Ens. David Sherman. Distribution 25 July 1727; Hannah wife of Dr. John Wheeler who was
relict to the dec'd; Samuel Wheeler, eldest son; Hannah Wheeler,
eldest dau.; Mara Wheeler, 2d dau. Agreement, 7 June 1734,
between Samuel Wheeler, and Hannah wife of Robert Chauncey,
both of Stratfield, and Mara wife of John Fairchild of New Fair-

field; mentioning father Samuel Wheeler dec'd and dower of mother Hannah wife of Dr. John Wheeler.

Hannah Thompson sued and obtained judgment, May 1710, against John Wheeler and Hannah his wife, and David Sherman, of Stratfield, as Adm'rs of the Est. of Samuel Wheeler; and by Aug. 1710 she m. Thomas Fell of New York City and they sold to John Odell the land taken by the judgment.

Children, bapt. at Stratfield:

> Samuel, bapt. 20 Apr. 1701; chose his father-in-law Dr. John Wheeler for guardian, 5 June 1712; d. at New Fairfield, in 1773; will 26 Mar. 1773; m. Abigail Lacy, dau. of Edward, bapt. 3 June 1705.*
>
> Hannah, bapt. 31 Jan. 1703; m. 6 June 1722, Robert Chauncey; they conveyed 1738 to John Wheeler, Jr., mentioning mother, wife of Dr. John Wheeler.
>
> Mary, b. (rec. at Fairfield as dau. of Sergt. Samuel of Stratfield dec'd) 22 July 1708, bapt. (as dau. of Widow Hannah) 24 July 1708; m. John Fairchild; of New Fairfield 1735, when they conveyed to John Wheeler, Jr., of Stratfield, right in dower of mother, wife of Dr. John Wheeler. In 1728, while still of Stratfield, they sold part of the long lot of Dea. Isaac Wheeler dec'd.

Wheeler, Timothy, s. of Timothy.

Born 24 Apr. 1691; d. at Stratfield, 5 Mar. 1752 in 62 yr. (g. s.); m. at Stratfield, 29 Jan. 1712/3, Ann Wakelee, b. abt. 1693, d. 18 July 1764 in 72 yr. (g. s.).

Adm'n granted, 24 Mar. 1752, to Timothy and Benjamin Wheeler, both of Fairfield. Distribution, 20 Mar. 1753: widow; Samuel Cable, son of Ann Cable; Eaidin Allen; Abigail Wheeler; Rebecca Cable; Timothy Wheeler; Benjamin Wheeler; Hezekiah Wheeler.

---

* His will named his wife Abigail, eldest son Jedediah, youngest son Samuel, son Enoch, and dau. Anne wife of James Pardee. Of these, Samuel m. Chloe Kidder and had issue. Enoch m. Eunice Newcomb of Amenia, and d. 1810; his will, 14 Apr. 1809, proved 9 June 1810, named wife; dau. Charity widow of Dimon Bradley; gr. children (Elizabeth, Polly, Enoch, Dimon, and another), the five children of dec'd dau. Huldah late wife of Daniel Stevens; and four children, James, Nehemiah, Charity, and Elizabeth wife of James Hendrick. Jedediah Wheeler, b. 1729, m. Elizabeth Rundle, and had children: Abigail, b. 1767, m. Paul Wellman; Luther, b. 1768, m. Lucy Rundle; Eli, b. 1770, m. Grizzel Osborn; Rhoda, b. 1771, m. Eleazer Osborn, Jr. The compiler is indebted to Mrs. Thomas D. Watkins, of Utica, N. Y., for part of this information.

Children:

Ann, b. 2 Dec. 1713, bapt. at Stratfield, 6 Dec. 1713; m. 27 July 1731, Samuel Cable.

Rebecca, b. 14 Feb. 1719/20, d. at Stratfield, 23 Feb. 1799 ae. 80 yrs. 9 days (g. s.); m. Andrew Cable.

✕Timothy, b. 6 Nov. 1722, d. at Stratfield, 11 Oct. 1776; will 5 Oct. 1776, proved 31 Mar. 1777; m. 9 Aug. 1744, Abigail Burritt.

✕Benjamin, b. 18 July 1725, d. at Stratfield, 26 Dec. 1798 in 74 yr. (g. s.); m. at Trumbull, 20 Apr. 1749, Mary Middlebrook, dau. of John, b. abt. 1727, d. 13 Aug. 1798 in 71 yr. (g. s.).

Abigail, b. 18 Feb. 1727/8.

✕Hezekiah, bapt. 30 Apr. 1732, bur. 25 Dec. 1809 ae. 78 (Trinity Church rec.); m. 19 Dec. 1754, Abigail French, bapt. 10 Feb. 1733/4, bur. 22 Sept. 1795 ae. 61 (Trinity Church rec.); will of Abigail, 17 Aug. 1795, proved 9 Oct. 1795.

Edra, bapt. 13 July 1735, d. at Stratfield, 20 Feb. 1809 in 74 yr. (g. s.); m. 8 Sept. 1752, Nehemiah Allen.

WHEELER FAMILY (DR. JOHN OF STRATFIELD)

Wheeler, (Dr.) John. Chirurgeon and physician, Expedition against Canada, May 1709.

He m. (rec. Fairfield) 24 Aug. 1708, Mrs. Hannah Wheeler. She was widow of Sergt. Samuel Wheeler, and dau. of Sergt. John Wheeler, b. abt. 1676.

He d. at Stratfield, 12 Sept. 1747 in 64 yr. (g. s.).

Inv. 3 Nov. 1747. Agreement, 10 May 1748, of Widow Hannah, and sons John and David.

Children, first recorded at Fairfield; bapt. at Stratfield:

John, b. 12 Nov. 1709, bapt. 5 Mar. 1710, d. at Stratfield, 12 Sept. 1790 ae. 80 yrs. 10 mos. 3 days (g. s.); m. Dorothy Sherman, dau. of Capt. David, bapt. 29 Aug. 1714, d. 9 Oct. 1800 in 87 yr. (g. s.).

Ann, bapt. 12 Oct. 1712, prob. d. y.

✕David, bapt. 20 Sept. 1713, d. in 1767; m. Betty ———.

Nehemiah, b. abt. 1720, d. 28 Nov. 1726 in 7 yr. (g. s., Stratfield).

WHEELER FAMILY (JOSEPH OF STRATFIELD)

Wheeler, Joseph.

He m. Mary ———, who d. at Middletown in 1740/1.

Joseph and his wife were admitted to Stratfield Church, 1695, by letter from Concord.

Inv. 29 May 1698 of Joseph Wheeler of Fairfield Village [Stratfield]. Ephraim, son of Joseph and Mary, b. latter end of July 1698. Widow Marah made oath. Ephraim chose his bro.-in-law Edward Higby for guardian, July 1715/6. Joseph's widow was empowered, Sept. 1699, to place out their children, with the advice of Ens. Wheeler.

Josiah Adkins and Mary his wife, and Edward Higby and Rebecca his wife, all of Middletown, conveyed 1715 to mother Mary Wheeler of Stratford. Elizabeth and Jane Wheeler of Middletown conveyed 1714 to Edward Higby, right from father Joseph Wheeler. Joseph Wheeler, son of Joseph of Stratford dec'd, conveyed 1716 to mother Mary Wheeler. [Stratford Deeds.]

Adm'n on Est. of Mary Wheeler of Middletown was granted, 27 Jan. 1740/1, to Edward Higby, with Benjamin Butler surety.

Children, first two recorded at Concord, last rec. Stratfield:

> Rebecca, b. 2 Apr. 1679, d. at Middletown, 22 Oct. 1771; m. 29 Nov. 1706, Edward Higby, of Middletown.
>
> Joseph, b. 7 Oct. 1682.
>
> Mary, m. 16 Dec. 1708, Josiah Adkins, of Middletown.
>
> Elizabeth.
>
> Jane, m. (by Capt. Ward,* rec. Wallingford) 1 June 1714, Samuel Doolittle.
>
> Ephraim, b. 28 July 1697, bapt. 1 Aug. 1697.

WHEELER FAMILY (MOSES OF STRATFORD)

Wheeler, Moses.

He d. 15 Jan. 1698 ae. 100 (g. s., Stratford).

Gift of Moses, Sr., shipwright, to his sons Samuel and Moses and son-in-law Jacob Walker, 22 Apr. 1686.

Will 19 Feb. 1689/90; mentions gifts to children, has only house and movables to bequeath; son Samuel; dau. Miriam; son Moses; dau. Mary; Elizabeth wife of son Samuel; Mr. Israel Chauncey and Mr. Joseph Hawley, overseers. Inv. 1 Mar. 1697/8.

Jacob Walker conveyed to son John, 1707, mentioning deed 1686 from father-in-law Moses Wheeler to himself and bros.-in-law

---

* Of Middletown.

Samuel and Moses Wheeler. Elizabeth Nisbett conveyed 1707 to kinsman John Walker, referring to her husband Samuel Wheeler and father-in-law Moses Wheeler. A deed 1716 mentions land Moses Wheeler dec'd left to four gr. children, viz.: James and Robert (sons of Moses Wheeler) and Robert (now dec'd) and Samuel Fairchild (sons of his dau. Mary Fairchild now Beach). Elizabeth Wheeler alias Delaport Poisson conveyed 1715 to bro. Moses Wheeler, Edward Delaport signing with her. [Stratford Deeds.]

Children, recorded at Stratford:

> Elizabeth, b. 6 Aug. 1642; m. (1) latter end of Nov. 1660, Samuel Blackman; m. (2) 6 Dec. 1670, Jacob Walker.
> Miriam, b. 28 Mar. 1647; m. (1) abt. 1667, James Blackman; m. (2) Edward Groom.
> +Samuel, b. 28 Apr. 1649.
> +Moses, b. 5 July 1651.
> Mary, b. 13 Sept. 1655; m. (1) Samuel Fairchild; m. (2) 5 Apr. 1705, Benjamin Beach; m. (3) (rec. Wallingford) 31 July 1716, Thomas Yale.
> Joanna, b. 5 Mar. 1658/9, d. y.

Wheeler, Samuel, s. of Moses.

Born at Stratford, 28 Apr. 1649, d. early in 1699.

Married at Stratford, 29 May 1678, Elizabeth Harris; not a native of New England. No issue.

She m. (2) at Stratford, as Mis^t Elizabeth Wheeler, 16 Sept. 1703, Mr. Hugh Nesbitt; m. (3) at Stratford, 20 Nov. 1712, Mr. Edward Poisson; m. (4) at Stratford, 27 Aug. 1717, Mr. Richard Blackleach.

Will 30 Nov. 1698; he had given dwelling house to wife Elizabeth by deed of gift; gives her now his whole Est., with right to dispose and bequeath it; "If she see good to remove her selfe out of this Country towards her Native Land" and desires to sell realty, my bro. Moses Wheeler to have the first refusal.

Wheeler, Moses, s. of Moses.

Born at Stratford, 5 July 1651, d. there 30 Jan. 1724/5; in 74 yr. (g. s.).

Will 1 Jan. 1724/5, proved 15 Feb. 1724/5; wife, mentioning marriage agreement; son James, £40; sons Nathan and Robert and dau. wife of Samuel Perry, £5 each; son Samuel's children and gr. dau. Sarah Jessup, £2 each; residue to son Elnathan, Exec'r. Robert and Nathan Wheeler appealed. Inv. 3 Feb. 1724/5.

Called Jr., he m. (1) (Stratford rec.) 20 Oct. 1674, Sarah Nichols, dau. of Caleb.

Married (2) in Dec. 1698, Ruth Bouton. She was dau. of Richard, b. abt. 1665.

Married (3) 31 Aug. 1721, Mercy Lattin. She was widow of Thomas Lattin, and prob. dau. of Henry Wakelee. She seems to have m. (3) 9 May 1726, Mr. John Burritt.

Children [by first wife], recorded at Stratford, two bapt. at Woodbury:

> Moses, b. 8 July 1675, bapt. July 1675, d. y.
>
> Caleb, b. 29 Jan. 1676 [1676/7], d. y.
>
> Sarah, b. 21 June 1678, bapt. Jan.(?) 1678; m. Richard Blackleach.
>
> Nathan, b. 31 Jan. 1680 [1680/1], d. at Stratford, 7 Nov. 1765 in 86 yr. (g. s.); m. (1) Mary ———, who d. 2 Feb. 1712/3; m. (2) 16 Dec. 1716, Mary Stebbins of Springfield; m. (3) Elizabeth Beach, dau. of Nathaniel, b. 11 or 12 Nov. 1689, d. 22 Jan. 1739/40 in 51 yr. (g. s.); m. (4) Elizabeth ———.
>
> Samuel, b. 27 Feb. 1681 [1681/2], d. at Stratford, 26 Mar. 1721; will 22 Mar. 1721, proved 27 Apr. 1721; m. (1) 3 May 1708, Mary Brinsmade, b. abt. 1684, d. 26 July 1712; m. (2) Lois, widow of Ebenezer Riggs, and dau. of Joseph Hawkins; she m. (3) 13 Mar. 1721/2, John Obartus, from whom she obtained a divorce, and m. (4) 4 July 1728, Abraham Tomlinson of Derby.
>
> James, b. 23 Oct. 1683.
>
> Robert, b. 18 May 1686, d. 23 Feb. 1753 in 68 yr. (g. s., Shelton); adm'n granted, 24 Mar. 1753; m. June 1708, Sarah Bennett, who d. abt. 1773; her will, 11 Mar. 1757, proved 8 Jan. 1774.
>
> Elizabeth, b. 8 Aug. 1687; m. Samuel Perry.

Children [by second wife], recorded at Stratford:

> Elnathan, b. 31 Jan. 1703, d. at Stratford, 14 Mar. 1761 ae. 58 (g. s.); Dea.; will 25 July 1759, proved 7 Apr. 1761; m. 8 Dec. 1726, Martha Deforest; dau. of David, b. 13 Apr. 1700, d. 5 Aug. 1764 ae. 64 (g. s.).
>
> Nathaniel, b. 16 Dec. 1705, bapt. at Stratford, 10 Feb. 1706 (Stratfield rec.), d. 31 Jan. 1723/4 in 19 yr. (g. s)

Wheeler, Thomas. Deputy (Milford) to Conn. Leg., May and Oct. 1670, May 1671.

He was adm. to Milford Church, 9 Aug. 1640, and d. at Milford, 26 Nov. 1672. His wife Jane was adm. 27 Sept. 1640, and buried 11 June 1673. She is called Joan in probate records; no evidence has been seen for the oft-repeated assertion that she was a Bryan.

Nor can we accept Orcutt's statement that the Milford Thomas was son of Thomas, Sr., of Fairfield, despite its acceptance by the compiler of the bulky *Wheeler Family in America,* for the Milford Thomas was certainly too old a man to permit of such identification. The wills of Thomas and of William of Stratford prove that they were brothers, but of their parentage we permit ourselves no guess.

Will 18 Nov. 1672, proved 11 June 1673; eldest son John and John's three eldest daus., Sarah, Mary, Elizabeth; 2d son Nathaniel and his dau. Esther; sons Ephraim and Joseph; son Thomas; my bro.'s children here, viz., William, Thomas, Sarah; wife Joan.

Inv. of his widow Joan, 23 June 1673.

John and Obadiah Wheeler had land in Stratford 1667, by gift from father, Thomas of Milford.

Children, recorded at Milford:

+John, b. abt. 1636, bapt. 16 Aug. 1640.

Samuel, b. [say 1639], bapt. 16 Aug. 1640, d. in 1668; Inv. 24 June 1668.

Nathaniel, bapt. 20 Feb. 1641/2; rem. to Newark, N. J.; m. at Milford, 27 June 1665, Esther Botsford, dau. of Henry; had issue.

Obadiah, bapt. 10 Mar. 1643/4, d. at Stratford in 1668; m. Ruth, widow of Thomas Goodwin, dau. of John Rogers, bapt. 5 Feb. 1642/3; she m. (3) 28 July 1669, Ephraim Stiles. Obadiah's will named only wife Ruth and father Wheeler; no issue; the dau. Ruth sometimes attributed to him belonged to his predecessor Goodwin.

+Ephraim, bapt. Apr. 1646.

Eleazer, bapt. 30 Apr. 1648, d. 10 Aug. 1649.

+Thomas, bapt. 28 July 1650.

Josiah, bapt. 5 June 1653, d. y.

Joseph, b. 23 Nov. 1655, bapt. 2 Dec. 1655, d. y.

Joseph, b. 13 Mar. 1656/7, rem. to Newark, N. J.; m. at Milford, June 1678, Patience Holbrook; she was dau. of Richard. They had children rec. at Milford: Patience, b. 7 June 1679; Anna, b. 20 Feb. 1680 [1680/1]; Joseph, b. 1 Dec. 1683. Joseph, Jr., m. at Milford, 27 Mar. 1707, Sarah Crane.

Wheeler, William.

Of Stratford, brother of Thomas of Milford, d. at Delaware in 1666. He m. Sarah ———, who m. (2) in 1666, William Brooks of Milford, and took her children there to live. She d. at Milford, 5 June 1709 in 88 yr.

Will 17 Jan. 1666, proved 8 Nov. 1666; wife Sarah; bro. Thomas Wheeler; two sons and dau.; Nathaniel Wheeler was a witness. Sarah Brooks presented the Inv.

His children are named in will of his bro. Thomas as living at Milford. The will of William Brooks, 1 Dec. 1684, named wife Sarah; two shillings to the wife of Thomas Wildman, she having rec'd her portion, "and I doe further declare y^t I know not that shee is any wayes related to mee"; William and Thomas Wheeler, sons of my wife; Sarah wife of James Biscoe; Hannah dau. of Elder Buckingham; Richard Bryan and Jobamah Gunn.

Children:

   Sarah, m. at Milford, 6 Dec. 1676, James Briscoe.
+William.
+Thomas, bapt. at Milford, 16 Feb. 1672/3 as son of "sister Brooks."

Wheeler, John, s. of Thomas.

Bapt. at Milford, 16 Aug. 1640, d. at Woodbury, 3 Dec. 1716 in 81 yr.

Married (1) at Stratford, beginning of Dec. 1662, Sarah Sherwood, dau. of Thomas, who d. 12 Mar. 1703/4.

He m. (2) at Milford, 3 July 1706, Mrs. Ruth Plumb. She was bapt. at Milford, 20 Feb. 1642, the dau. of George Clark, "Farmer", and was widow first of Thomas Fitch, Jr., of Norwalk, and afterwards of Robert Plumb of Milford.

Will 23 July 1712, proved 2 Dec. 1716; wife Ruth; eldest son Thomas; son John; dau. Elizabeth Burch; gr. son Nathan Mitchell; gr. daus. Hannah and Sarah Mitchell; gr. children, children of Elizabeth Burch; gr. child Ruth Richardson; gr. child Joseph Tuttle.

Children [by first wife], recorded at Stratford, bapt. at Woodbury:

> Sarah, b. 24 Feb. 1663 [1663/4], bapt. 19 Jan. 1670/1; m. by 1687, Abraham Mitchell.
>
> Mary, b. 26 Aug. 1666, bapt. 19 Jan. 1670/1, d. at Woodbury, 20 June 1701, unm.
>
> Elizabeth, b. middle of Feb. 1669 [1669/70], bapt. 19 Jan. 1670/1; m. (rec. Stratford) June 1696, Jeremiah Burch.
>
> Thomas, b. 2 Apr. 1673, bapt. 25 May 1673, d. at Woodbury, by fall of a tree, 21 Mar. 1727/8; m. at Woodbury, 20 Aug. 1701, Sarah Stiles.
>
> Ruth, b. [30 June 1679],* bapt. June 1678, d. at Waterbury, 10 Feb. 1701 [1701/2]; m. (rec. Waterbury) 22 Apr. 1701, John Richardson [rec. also Woodbury, 23 Apr. 1701].
>
> Dinah, bapt. Feb. 1680/1; m. at Woodbury, 13 Feb. 1706/7, Ephraim Tuttle.
>
> John, bapt. May 1685, d. at Woodbury, 19 May 1727; m. at Woodbury, 17 Nov. 1704, Ruth Stiles.

Wheeler, Ephraim, s. of Thomas.

Bapt. at Milford, Apr. 1646, d. there in 1684/5; m. at Milford, 8 Sept. 1675, Mary Holbrook, dau. of Richard. She m. (2) Henry Summers.

Inv. 27 Feb. 1684 [1684/5]. Adm'n granted, 25 Mar. 1685, to widow Mary. Eldest son Obadiah and three other children. In Nov. 1696 it was reported to the Court by Mr. Silvanus Baldwin that the two sons were dead, and only two daus. now living. Silvanus Baldwin was appointed guardian, June 1697, to Abigail, ae. 12.

Children, recorded at Milford:

> Obadiah, b. 15, bapt. 18 June 1676, d. y.
>
> Mary, b. Feb., bapt. 3 Feb. 1677 [1677/8], d. at Milford, 31 Jan. 1730 [1730/1] ae. 53 (g. s.); m. Eliphal Gillet.
>
> Thomas, b. 25 June, bapt. 25 July 1680, d. y.
>
> Ephraim, b. 5 Jan. 1681 [1681/2], d. y.
>
> Abigail, b. 8 Feb. 1683 [1683/4]; m. (rec. Derby) 28 July 1703, John Brinsmade.

---

* Cothren gives this birth as recorded at Woodbury, but the present compiler failed to find this entry.

Wheeler, Thomas, s. of Thomas.

Bapt. at Milford, 28 July 1650, d. there Apr. [1727, g. s., mostly illegible] ; m. (rec. Milford) 1 June 1685, Anna French, dau. of Francis of Derby.

Will 1 Jan. 1724/5, proved 28 Apr. 1727; dau. Anna Munn; gr. dau. Mary Hine; dau. Thankful Ashburn; dau. Joanna, one shilling in addition to what I have already given; right in common lands to daus. Thankful and Joanna; son-in-law Daniel Munn; son-in-law Stephen Hine; son Obadiah Wheeler and Joanna Wheeler, Exec'rs.

Children:

> Anna, m. Daniel Munn.
> Mercy, m. Stephen Hine, of Woodbridge.
> Obadiah, b. abt. 1694, d. at Newtown, 24 Feb. 1770 in 76 yr. (g. s.) ;
>   Capt.; m. (1) Joanna ———, b. abt. 1695, d. 15 Jan. 1758 in 60 yr.
>   (g. s.) ; m. (2) Miriam ———.
> Thankful, m. Joseph Ashburn.
> Joanna.

Wheeler, William, s. of William.

Blacksmith, d. at Milford, 12 Nov. 1705; m. at Milford, 10 Apr. 1682, Ruth Smith, who d. 27 Sept. 1705 in 42 yr. (g. s.).

Children, recorded at Milford:

> Ruth, b. 14 Jan. 1682/3, bapt. 30 June 1695; m. abt. 1701 Josiah
>   Rogers, of Branford.
> Sarah, bapt. 30 June 1695; m. (rec. Branford) 8 Apr. 1713, Samuel
>   Beers.
> Samuel, bapt. 30 June 1695, d. 22 Oct. 1705.
> Rebecca, b. abt. 1691 (aged 14 in Dec. 1705), bapt. 30 June 1695, d. y.
> Elizabeth, b. 12 Jan. 1696 [1696/7], bapt. 17 Jan. 1696/7, d. at Bran-
>   ford, 25 Aug. 1755 in 59 yr. (g. s.) ; m. (rec. Branford) 28 Nov.
>   1722, Noah Rogers.
> William, bapt. 7 July 1700, prob. d. y.
> Rhoda, b. 9 Dec. 1701, bapt. 28 Dec. 1701; m. Nathaniel Wheadon, of
>   Branford.

Wheeler, Thomas, s. of William.

Called "Jr." in Milford to distinguish him from his cousin; rem. to Durham.

Married Mary ——, who was adm. to Milford Church, 3 Oct. 1697, the four eldest children being bapt. that date.

On 10 Nov. 1729, Thomas Wheeler formerly of Milford, now of Durham, conveyed to son Job of Durham. In 1713, then of Milford, he conveyed land which the town of Milford granted him in 1688.

Children, recorded at Milford:

Mary, m. (rec. Durham) 15 Dec. 1711, Samuel Parsons.
Eleanor, m. (rec. Durham) 14 Jan. 1713/4, Joseph Seward.
Abigail, m. (rec. Milford) 27 Oct. 1714, Joseph Merchant.
Joseph.
William, bapt. 5 Dec. 1697.*
Job, bapt. 25 Dec. 1698, m. (rec. Durham) 29 Apr. 1731, Jane Squire.
Jemima, bapt. 3 Aug. 1701.
John, bapt. 26 Sept. 1703, d. 4 Oct. 1703.
Elizabeth, b. 9 June 1705.

WHEELER FAMILY (NEW HAVEN)

Wheeler, Thomas.

Called "Old Thomas", he d. at New Haven, 22 Jan. 1672 [1672/3]. His connection with other Wheeler families has not been ascertained. He had at least one child, Thomas, Jr., who d. in 1656 leaving wife Alice who m. (2) in 1657, Josiah Stanborough of Southampton, L. I.

The will of Josiah Stanborough, 6 July 1661, named wife "Alce", sons Peregrine and Josiah; daus. Sarah and Mary. Alce Stanborough, 3 Sept. 1661, released the Exec'r of liability for estate belonging to her three children by her former husband.

Thomas Wheeler, Jr., had a son Thomas, b. at New Haven, 21 Apr. 1652; an older son was prob. John Wheeler who m. at Southampton, 9 Dec. 1669.

---

* It is not certain this was the William who m. Jemima Plumb. William Wheeler of Boston (s. of Henry) d. in 1704; m. at Boston, 16 May 1686, Ann Phippen, dau. of Gamaliel, b. 28 Apr. 1666. They had three children rec. at Boston: Ann, b. 19 July 1692; Hannah, b. 18 Mar. 1695; and William, b. 27 Apr. 1697; also, Mehitabel dau. of Mrs. Wheeler of Boston, bapt. at Milford 17 Apr. 1701. William Wheeler, a minor child whose mother hath been residing in Milford near the space of four years, chose James Prime, Jr., guardian, 7 June 1714. This William was then ae. 17 and living in Milford, while the family of Thomas had by then rem. to Durham; so it was prob. this William (s. of William of Boston) who m. Jemima Plumb.

Wheeler [Unplaced].

Hester m. at Stratford, 29 Jan. 1704/5, Joseph Blackman.
Kezia m. at Stratford, 29 Dec. 1725, John Beardsley.

Whelpley, Henry.

He settled early in Stratford, and soon removed to Fairfield, where he d. in 1662. Inv. £280. On 6 June 1662, the Court ordered £300 to be paid to his widow "of ye estate of her former husband Treadwell," any deficit to be made up out of Whelpley's estate, and £20 as dower; the balance to be divided between Whelpley's children.

He m. (2) not long after 1659, ———, widow of John Whitlock. On 30 Nov. 1684, David Whitlock for himself and brothers and sisters receipted to Rebecca widow of Joseph Whelpley for portions, Henry Whelpley dec'd having become responsible for their payment by marrying David's mother.

She did not long survive, and he m. (3) about 1661, Sarah, widow of Edward Treadwell, of Hempstead, L. I. She m. (3) about 1663, Ralph Keeler of Norwalk, and (4) Thomas Skidmore of Fairfield. The deeds show that Alexander Knowles, Michael Try, Cornelius Hull, and William Hill, Adm'rs of Henry Whelpley's estate, sold land to Ralph Keeler, who had married Whelpley's widow, and that Ralph Keeler sold it 1664 to Isaac Wheeler.

Children:

> Daughter, m. George Kniffen.
> +Nathan.
> +Joseph.
(prob.) Jonathan, of Greenwich, whose will, 21 Jan. 1712/3, proved 6 Mar. 1712/3, mentioned his wife Sarah, and children (not all named) Hannah, Mary Marshall, eldest son Jonathan (his gristmill), youngest child Sarah Whelpley.

Whelpley, Nathan, s. of Henry.

On 10 Aug. 1687, the will of Nathan Whelpley, mariner, was exhibited by Mr. Richard Blackleach, ae. abt. 33, who testified that abt. 18 Oct. last he was at Barbados with Whelpley, Master of the bark *Laurel* belonging to Stratford; he gave to Samuel Kniffen, his sister's son, his house at New Haven; residue to his relatives in New England. John Prior, ae. abt. 28, also testified. Adm'n was granted, 5 Oct. 1687; George Kniffen and Rebecca Whelpley were appointed Adm'rs; they not accepting, Mr. Joseph Hawley, Mr. Richard Blackleach, and Daniel Burr were appointed. [Fairfield Pro.]

Inv. presented at New Haven, 8 June 1687.

Whelpley, Joseph, s. of Henry.

He m. Rebecca Bulkley, dau. of Thomas, who d. in 1690; he d. in 1682.

Inv. 7 Nov. 1682. Widow and three children,—Sarah, Rebecca, Joseph.

Inv. of Rebecca, widow of Joseph, 19 Nov. 1690. Adm'n granted to John Bulkley and William Hill. Sarah Whelpley gave receipt, 29 Nov. 1694, to uncle John Bulkley and cousin William Hill [the former was her mother's bro., the latter was son of her mother's sister]. Sarah Whelpley witnessed a Bulkley deed, 20 Sept. 1698.

Children, recorded at Fairfield:

Sarah, b. 30 June 1676, living 1698; see THOMAS NASH.
Rebecca, b. 2 Apr. 1679, d. 19 Apr. 1709.
+Joseph, b. 7 Oct. 1682.

Whelpley, Joseph, s. of Joseph.

Born at Fairfield, 7 Oct. 1682, d. there in 1708; m. by 1707, Deborah Burr, dau. of Daniel; she m. (2) Joseph Perry.

Inv. 6 Mar. 1707/8. Adm'n granted to Rebecca Whelpley and John Andrews. On 3 Mar. 1708, Deborah *Burr* widow of Joseph Whelpley was appointed with John Andrews to make Inv.; her maiden name apparently was used by inadvertence in this record, which also calls her Deborah Whelpley.

Child, recorded at Fairfield:

Sarah, b. 17 Jan. 1707, d. at Greenfield, 12 Sept. 1777; m. Nov. 1724, Samuel Bradley.

Whidden, Richard.

He m. at Fairfield, 15 Apr. 1686, Sarah Hill. She was dau. of William; and d. 28 Mar. 1697. He d. 24 Oct. 1690.

Inv. 3 Nov. 1690 of Richard, mariner, of Fairfield. Widow Sarah; daus. Elizabeth and Sarah. Nuncupative will expressed to John Thompson and Nathan Gold.

The widow being dec'd, and the estate not settled, and Elizabeth having come of age, William and John Hill were appointed to administer, 3 Jan. 1705/6.

Children, recorded at Fairfield:

> Elizabeth, b. 19 Sept. 1688; m. 22 Jan. 1705/6, Joseph Bennett.
> Sarah, b. 29 Dec. 1689, d. abt. 1739, unm. Adm'n granted, 19 Dec. 1739, to Samuel Gold.

Whitacus, Jonathan. [Surname also spelled Whitaker.]

Supposedly son of John of Watertown, Mass., he settled in Concord, whence he rem. to Fairfield, where his wife may have had relatives. He m. Sarah ————.

Sarah Whitacus was adm. to Stratfield Church by letter from Concord, 17 June 1705.

Children, first recorded at Concord, second recorded and bapt. at Fairfield, third recorded and bapt. at Stratfield:

> Sarah, b. 28 Nov. 1695.
> Jonathan, b. 28 May 1698, bapt. 10 July 1698.
> Mary, b. 22 May 1700, bapt. 26 May 1700.

Whitlock, John.

Inv. 14 Oct. 1659. Widow Whitlock made oath. No will; children under age.

His widow m. Henry Whelpley, and d. prob. by 1661. On 30 Nov. 1684, David Whitlock for himself and bros. and sisters gave receipt to Rebecca widow of Joseph Whelpley for portions due from Henry Whelpley dec'd who married David Whitlock's mother.

Children:

> +David.
> +John.
> Daughters, one of whom was doubtless the Sarah Whitlock, 12 yrs. old, mentioned by Winthrop 1667 as at Thomas Sanford's in Milford, fatherless and motherless.

Whitlock, David, s. of John.

He m. Mary Sherwood, dau. of Thomas, 2d.

Thomas Sherwood, Sr., conveyed 1 Jan. 1697/8, to dau. Mary wife of David Whitlock.

Will 11 Feb. 1713/4, proved 4 May 1722; wife Mary; to son David, lot that was my father-in-law Thomas Sherwood's; son Samuel; dau. Abigail Rowland; dau. Mary.

Children, last two bapt. at Fairfield:

 ✕David, b. abt. 1681, d. at Greenfield, 30 May 1761 ae. abt. 80; m. (1) before 1720, Margaret ———; m. (2) by 1737, Ruth Williams, dau. of Thomas, b. abt. 1688, d. at Greenfield, 17 June 1773 ae. 85. In 1726, being then of Ridgefield, he conveyed land which his mother Mary Whitlock had from her father Thomas Sherwood.
 ✕Samuel, b. ———, d. at Danbury by 1751; Est. distributed 17 Sept. 1751; m. Sarah ———.
 Abigail, m. Joseph Rowland, 2d.
 Sarah, bapt. 6 Jan. 1694/5.
 Mary, bapt. 4 July 1697.

Whitlock, John, s. of John.

As a youth, he was appointed to beat the drum, 15 Feb. 1671 [1671/2].

He m. Sarah Sherwood, dau. of Thomas, 2d. He renewed his Covenant with Fairfield Church, 6 Jan. 1694/5; and d. in 1698.

John Whitlock [Jr.] conveyed 19 Nov. 1722 to bro. Thomas, land laid out to gr. father Thomas Sherwood.

Inv. 7 Apr. 1698. Adm'n granted to widow with Ens. John Osborn. Agreement, 6 May 1713, between John and Thomas, sons of John dec'd.

Children, first three bapt. at Fairfield, 6 Jan. 1694/5:

 ✕John, d. at Fairfield in 1733; will 15 Mar. 1732/3, proved 1 May 1733; m. Abigail Adams, dau. of Lt. Abraham.
 Hannah, prob. b. abt. 1685, for "Old Joseph Beers wife" d. 10 Mar. 1771 in 86 yr. (Perry Diary); m. 1 Mar. 1711, Joseph Beers.
 ✕Thomas, m. 24 Jan. 1716, Damaris Hide.
 Sarah, bapt. 30 June 1695; receipted for portion to bro. John, 6 May 1713.

Whitney, Henry.

His English origin is unknown, the ancestry assigned to him in the splendid genealogy by Phoenix having proved false.

A miller; bought at Southold, L. I., 8 Oct. 1649, with Edward Treadwell and Thomas Benedict. He rem. by 1658 to Huntington, L. I.

He m. (1) ———; m. (2) Sarah, widow of Edward Ketchum of Stratford. In 1660 he objected to Joseph Whitman as suitor to his dau. [stepdau.] Sarah Ketchum. He rem. abt. 1662 to Jamaica, L. I., and by 1665 to Norwalk, where he d. in 1673.

Will 5 June 1672; wife; son John; Thomas Benedict, Sr., Walter Hoyt, and Thomas Fitch, Sr., my beloved brethren and friends, overseers. Inv. 8 Nov. 1673.

Child [by first wife] :
+John.

Whitney, John, s. of Henry.

A miller; had a grant of land in Southold, L. I., 1666; rem. to Norwalk with his father. He m. (rec. Norwalk) 17 Mar. 1674/5, Elizabeth Smith, dau. of Richard; she d. after 3 Apr. 1741.

Adm'n granted, 11 Oct. 1720, to son-in-law Joseph Keeler.

Children, recorded at Norwalk:

John, b. 1 Mar. 1676/7, d. at Norwalk, 3 Feb. 1712/3; miller; m. 4 Mar. 1709/10, Elizabeth Finch, dau. of Joseph of Greenwich.

Joseph, b. 1 Mar. 1678 [1678/9], d. at Norwalk in 1741; mill-wright; will 21 Mar. 1740/1; m. 6 July 1704, Hannah Hoyt, dau. of Zerubbabel.

Henry, b. 21 Feb. 1680 [1680/1], d. at Ridgefield, 26 Apr. 1728; weaver; m. 14 June 1710, Elizabeth Olmstead, dau. of Lt. John.

Elizabeth, b. abt. 1684, d. at Ridgebury, 17 Mar. 1763 ae. 79 (g. s.); m. Joseph Keeler.

XRichard, b. 18 Apr. 1687.

Samuel, b. abt. 1688, d. at Stratford, 6 Dec. 1753 in 66 yr. (g. s.); m. at Stratford, 18 Jan. 1721/2, Ann Laborie, who m. (2) 23 July 1759, Benjamin Banks of Greenfield.

Ann, b. abt. 1691, d. at Sharon, 9 May 1773 ae. 82 (g. s.); m. 13 Oct. 1709, Matthew St. John.

Eleanor, b. [27 Jan. 1693/4], d. at Norwalk, 25 Jan. 1777 ae. 81 yrs. 11 mos. 19 days (g. s.); m. 13 June 1717, Jonathan Fairchild.

Nathan, res. Ridgefield; m. Sarah Platt, dau. of John, b. 30 May 1697.

Sarah, d. at Ridgefield, 22 Oct. 1720; m. 13 June 1717, Samuel Smith.
Josiah, d. at Norwalk by 1750; m. 30 Oct. 1729, Eunice Hanford,
dau. of Eleazer.

Wilcoxson, William. Deputy (Stratford) to Conn. Leg., May 1647.

Born abt. 1601; came in *Planter,* Apr. 1635, ae. 34, with wife Margaret, ae. 24, and John (their son) ae. 2. Was first located at Concord. He early settled in Stratford, where he d. in 1652; his widow m. William Hayden of Windsor.

Will 29 May 1651; wife Margaret; eldest son; the rest of my sons; daus.; £40 to be sent to Concord to be ordered as in a letter to Bulkley already sent; overseers, Adam Blackman, Thomas Thornton, Philip Grove, and William Beardsley. Inv. 16 June 1652.

Agreement 22 Oct. 1668, of children and heirs, referring to their mother's marriage; the heirs named in document and signatures were Widow Margaret (now) Hayden, Henry and Elizabeth Stiles, Daniel and Hannah Hayden, John and Sarah Meigs, and John, Joseph, Phebe, Timothy, Johanna, Samuel and Obadias Wilcoxson.

Children:

+John, b. abt. 1633.

+Joseph, b. [say 1635].

+Timothy, b. abt 1637; Winthrop in 1660 called him of Stratford, ae. 23, and mentioned that his mother was William Hayden's wife of Windsor; in 1658 he called him ae. 20.

+Samuel, b. abt. 1640; Winthrop in 1658 called him 17 or 18 yrs. old, son of "Goody Hayden."

Elizabeth, b. [say 1642]; m. (rec. Windsor) 16 Apr. 1663, Henry Stiles.

Hannah, b. [say 1644]; m. (rec. Windsor) 17 Mar. 1664/5, Daniel Hayden.

Sarah, b. [say 1646]; m. (rec. Killingworth) 7 Mar. 1665 [1665/6], John Meigs.

+Obadiah, b. [say 1648].

Phebe, b. abt. 1651, d. 20 Sept. 1743 ae. 93; m. (1) (rec. Stratford) 11 Dec. 1669, John Birdsey; m. (2) John Beach.

Johanna, b. [say 1653].

Wilcoxson, John, s. of William.

Born abt. 1633; Deacon of Stratford Church; d. in Nov. 1690.

Nuncupative will of John, Sr., 8 Nov. 1690, expressed to Samuel Sherman and John Birdsey; to Barnabas Beers, half an acre of his home lot; to son John, his dwelling house and rest of his home lot; confirmed to children land formerly given; gr. children Dorothy Blackman and Susannah Wilcoxson; daus. Patience and Hannah had rec'd sufficient. Inv. 17 Nov. 1690.

Married (1) ——— Titherton, dau. of Daniel, whose will 1660 named dau. Wilcocks.

Married (2) at Stratford, 19 Mar. 1662/3, widow Elizabeth Welles. She was Elizabeth Bourn, widow of Mr. John Welles.

Child by first wife, born at Stratford:

+John, b. Mar. 1657.

Children by second wife, born at Stratford:

    Patience, b. 1 Feb. 1663 [1663/4]; m. 24 Oct. 1681, Ebenezer Blackman.

    Hannah, b. 14 Feb. 1664 [1664/5], d. 10 July 1701 ae. 38 (g. s.); m. Joseph Booth.

    Elizabeth, b. July 1666, d. 11 Oct. 1694; m. 4 Apr. 1688, Barnabas Beers.

    Mary, b. Apr. 1668.

Wilcoxson, Joseph, s. of William.

He m. Ann ———, rem. to Killingworth, and d. by 1684.

Children, first two recorded at Stratford, three at Killingworth:

    Joseph, b. 29 Oct. 1659, d. at Killingworth, 29 Sept. 1747; Lt.; will 9 May 1747, proved 6 Oct. 1747; m. at Killingworth, 14 Feb. 1693 [1693/4], Hannah Kelsey, dau. of John, b. 13 Sept. 1668, d. 2 Feb. 1729/30.

    Thomas, b. 13 Nov. 1661.

    Samuel, b. abt. 1663; m. 1 Jan. 1696, Ruth Westcott.

    Hannah, b. 19 Jan. 1665 [1665/6], d. at Wallingford, 6 Feb. 1707/8; m. (1) 8 Dec. 1686, Peter Farnum; m. (2) (rec. Wallingford) 24 Aug. 1707, Nathaniel Royce.

    Nathaniel, b. 29 Aug. 1668, d. at Killingworth, 13 June 1712; m. 21 Nov. 1695, Hannah Lane.

    William, b. 9 Jan. 1671.

    Margaret, b. abt. 1673, d. 9 Feb. 1763 ae. 90; m. Joseph Graves, of Guilford.

    John, b. abt. 1675.

Wilcoxson, Timothy, s. of William.

Born abt. 1637; Deacon Timothy d. at Stratford, 13 Jan. 1713 [1713/4]. Apparently the date should be 1710/1.

Inv. 9 Feb. 1710/1; widow Johanna. On 7 Oct. 1713, it was reported that Joanna had died without completing adm'n of husband Timothy's Est.; and Robert Walker and Joseph Hawley were appointed.

Will of Johanna, widow of Timothy, 4 Aug. 1713; gr. child Phebe Fairchild, dau. of son-in-law Joseph Fairchild, late of Stratford dec'd; gr. dau. Sarah Fairchild; daus. (not named); residue to children of son Joseph Fairchild and Johanna his wife, now both dec'd.

Thomas Beach and Eliasaph Preston of Wallingford, and Joseph Hawley and Thomas Gridley of Farmington, and Robert McEwen and Robert Walker of Stratford, interested in a house and land with Joseph Fairchild which were given us by father Timothy Wilcoxson, conveyed 3 Dec. 1706 to Fairchild.

Married at Stratford, 28 Dec. 1664, Johanna Birdsey. She was dau. of John. Wife was called Johanna at birth of child 1677. She d. at Stratford (as widow) Aug. 1713.

Children, recorded at Stratford:

> Johanna, b. 8 July 1667, d. at Stratford, 15 Aug. 1713; m. Joseph Fairchild.
> Phebe, b. 2 [or 3] Aug. 1669, d. at Wallingford, 30 Apr. 1758; m. abt. 1688, Thomas Beach.
> Sarah, b. 26 Dec. 1671; m. 20 June 1695, Robert McEwen.
> Elizabeth, b. 6 Nov. 1673, d. at Farmington, 10 Sept. 1762 in 89 yr. (g. s.); m. 7 June 1697, Joseph Hawley.
> Ruth, b. 31 Aug. 1677, d. after 1743; m. 1 Aug. 1695, Robert Walker.
> Rebecca, b. 13 July 1680, d. at Wallingford, 2 Sept. 1716; m. (1) (rec. Wallingford) 26 May 1701, Benjamin Royce; m. (2) (rec. Wallingford) 31 Jan. 1704, Eliasaph Preston.
> Hannah, b. 18 Sept. 1685, d. at Farmington, 19 Nov. 1733; m. (rec. Farmington) 31 Oct. 1704, Thomas Gridley.

Wilcoxson, Samuel, s. of William. Sergt., Simsbury Trainband; Deputy (Simsbury), May and June 1689, May and Oct. 1694, Oct. 1695, Oct. 1696, May and Oct. 1697, Jan. and May 1698, May 1699, May 1700, May and Oct. 1701, May and Aug. 1710, May 1711, May 1712.

Born abt. 1640; d. at Simsbury, 12 Mar. 1712/3. This branch often dropped the final syllable from the surname.

Agreement of heirs, 12 Mar. 1712/3; made by the children, Samuel, William, Joseph, and Margaret Wilcoxson.

Children:

> Samuel, b. at Windsor, 15 Apr. 1666, d. at Simsbury, 13 Sept. 1713; Inv. 30 Oct. 1713; m. abt. 1691, Mindwell Griffin.
>
> William, d. at Simsbury, 22 Mar. 1733; Sergt.; will 19 Mar. 1732/3, proved 1 May 1733; m. abt. 1699 Elizabeth ———.
>
> Joseph, m. at Simsbury, 29 Apr. 1703, Abigail Thrall, dau. of Timothy, who d. 10 July 1725.
>
> Margaret, d. at Simsbury in 1714; Inv. 21 Dec. 1714; had a son Benoni, b. 7 Dec. 1714/5 (*sic*), bapt. 6 Nov. 1715, who received her Est. by order of Court; her bro. Joseph appealed.

Wilcoxson, Obadiah, s. of William.

Settled in Killingworth; rem. before 1676 to East Guilford, where he d. in 1714. This branch spelled the name Wilcox.

He m. (1) Mary Griswold, dau. of Michael, b. at Wethersfield, 28 Jan. 1650 [1650/1], d. at Killingworth, 8 Aug. 1670. Her father's will 10 Sept. 1678 gave one shilling to his son-in-law Obadiah Willcox.

He m. (2) by 1676, Lydia Alling, dau. of Corp. John, b. at New Haven, 26 Dec. 1656. The will of John Alling, 6 May 1689, named his gr. children Ebenezer and Mary "Wilcocks."

He m. (3) Silence Mansfield, dau. of Joseph, b. at New Haven, 24 Oct. 1664. She m. (2) 30 Oct. 1719, George Chatfield, of Killingworth, as his second wife.

He was released from training, Nov. 1694, because of lameness.

Will 18 Dec. 1710, proved 1 Nov. 1714; wife Silence; son Ebenezer, land in Durham; son John, land at "Hassaka Gusell"; son Joseph, land in Guilford; dau. Mary (had rec'd most of portion); daus. Mindwell, Jemima, Thankful; mentioned sons Obadiah and Timothy dec'd. Inv. 28 Oct. 1714. Thomas Munson in right of wife Mary appealed from probate of will. On 12 Sept. 1723, Silence Wilcockson exhibited receipts from five of the legatees, and declared the others had received their portions. [Her name at that date was Chatfield, despite the retention of her former name by the probate record.]

Statements that Obadiah had a son Janna, or children by his first wife, are false; Janna derived from the Wilcox family of Middletown.

Children [by second wife]:

Mary, b. 11 Dec. 1676; m. (rec. New Haven) 15 Sept. 1694, Thomas Munson.

Lydia, b. 14 Oct. 1678, d. 4 Nov. 1678.

Obadiah, b. 14 Dec. 1679, d. y.

Ebenezer, b. 20 Sept. 1682; res. 1715 Hebron.

Children [by third wife]:

Timothy, b. 15 Nov. 1690, d. before 1710, unm.

John, b. 9 Nov. 1692, d. at East Guilford, 1 May 1753; will 26 Apr. 1753, proved 5 June 1753; m. 11 Jan. 1718/9, Deborah Parmelee.

Joseph, b. abt. 1694, d. at East Guilford, 15 July 1770; m. in 1722, Hannah Goodale.

Mindwell, b. [say 1696], d. 3 Feb. 1770; m. 20 Apr. 1714, Daniel Hill, of Guilford.

Jemima, b. 30 Oct. 1699, d. at Southington, 11 Oct. 1764; m. (rec. Wallingford) 24 Feb. 1726, John Merriman.

Thankful, b. 4 Apr. 1702; m. 6 Sept. 1722, Samuel Norton, of Guilford.

Wilcoxson, John, s. of John.

Born at Stratford, Mar. 1657; was living there in 1735 when his son John was still called "Jr." No record of death or probate found.

He conveyed lands to his sons John and William, 1 Mar. 1726/7; William conveyed to bro. John, Jr., 15 Nov. 1728; William and John [Jr.] mentioned their dec'd gr. father John Wilcoxson in a deed in 1725.

His wife has not been ascertained.

Children:

John, b. abt. 1684, d. at Stratford, 12 Sept. 1748 in 65 yr. (g. s.); Lt.; will 13 May 1748, proved 4 Oct. 1748; m. (1) June 1707, Elizabeth Tomlinson, b. 11 Aug. 1684, by whom he had two sons; m. (2) 19 Mar. 1713, Sarah Curtis, who d. soon without surviving issue; m. (3) 13 Jan. 1714/5, Deborah Brinsmade, b. abt. 1692, d. abt. 1758; her will 12 Nov. 1757, proved 17 Feb. 1758.

William, b. (no record), d. at Stratford abt. 1754; will 11 Jan. 1754; m. 11 Dec. 1712, Esther Brinsmade, b. abt. 1689, d. abt. 1785; her will 4 Dec. 1777, proved 22 Apr. 1785.

Susannah, named in her gr. father's will.

Perhaps other daus.

Wildman, Thomas.

Of Bedford, died in Sept. 1689 leaving a widow, four sons and two daus.; and the first son and one of the daus. being of age to receive their portion, and the children of age to choose their guardian have chosen Abraham Ambler of Stamford; the heirs made agreement, signed at Stamford 30 Oct. 1697 by Sarah Seymour, Abraham Wildman, Abraham Ambler, and Martha Ambler. The Inv. was attested by Sarah Seymour, relict of Thomas Wildman, now wife of Thomas Seymour, at Norwalk.

His wife in 1684 was named in will of William Brooks of Milford, apparently being his reputed dau. [see WILLIAM WHEELER]. Prob. she was the same wife Sarah who survived him and m. (2) Thomas Seymour of Norwalk.

Children:

    Abraham, d. at Danbury in 1750; will 22 Mar. 1745/6, proved 10 Oct. 1750; m. (1) ———; m. (2) Abigail, a widow.

    Martha, m. [John] Ambler, of Stamford.

    Thomas, d. at Danbury in 1752; adm'n granted, 4 Dec. 1752; m. abt. 1705, Lydia, widow of Joseph Forward, and dau. of Judah Gregory, b. 9 Jan. 1676/7.

    John, of Norwalk, d. by 1732; Capt.; adm'n granted, 5 July 1732; m. (rec. Stratford) 19 Apr. 1716, Sarah Fairchild.

    Son.

    Daughter.

Williams, Richard.

One of the first settlers of Branford, 1645.

He purchased land at Fairfield, before 11 Aug. 1656, from Humphrey Hide; and leased land at Fairfield from heirs of Samuel Nettleton, 26 Oct. 1658; removed there, but soon disappears from Fairfield records. In 1677 he was living in New London County, and was then prosecuted (and thought himself persecuted) by Isaac Hall of Fairfield.

Children, two recorded at Branford:

    Samuel, b. 3 Sept. 1655.

    Daniel, b. 15 Apr. 1657.

    Others.

Williams, Robert.

Accused of stealing at Fairfield, Nov. 1685.

Williams, Thomas.

Of Fairfield 1678, when with Thomas Jones he was fined for selling liquor to Indians.

He m. Ruth Bradley, dau. of Francis, whose will 1688/9 called her the wife of Thomas Williams.

In Feb. 1736/7, his children, Thomas Williams, Jr., John Williams, Daniel Williams, David Williams, Benjamin Williams, and Ruth wife of David Whitlock, were ordered to pay equally for his maintenance. [Fairfield County Court Rec.]

[Adm'n on the Est. of Thomas Williams, a transient person of Stratfield, was granted to James Seeley of Fairfield, 17 Apr. 1727. This man's identity is unknown.]

Children:

XThomas, m. abt. 1702, Esther Smith, dau. of Samuel, b. abt. 1685, d. at Redding, 29 Sept. 1769 ae. 84.

XJohn,* m. Martha ———.

Ruth, b. abt. 1688, d. at Greenfield, 17 June 1773 ae. 85; m. David Whitlock.

XDaniel, d. at Norwalk; adm'n granted, 5 Sept. 1769; m. by 1724, Deborah ———.

XDavid, b. (rec. Greenfield) May 1696, bapt. at Fairfield, 10 July 1720; d. at Greenfield, Apr. 1752 ae. just 56; Sergt.; will 9 Apr. 1752, proved 7 May 1752; m. 8 Oct. 1719, Dorothy Sturges, b. 28 Aug. 1700.

XBenjamin, b. [by 1700], bapt. at Greenfield in 1733, d. at Redding abt. Jan. 1749; will 13 Jan. 1748/9, proved 7 Feb. 1748/9; m. by 1723, Rebecca Mallory, dau. of William; she renewed Covenant at Fairfield, 2 June 1723, and was living 1750.

Wilson, Anthony. Deputy (Fairfield) to Conn. Leg., Apr. 1646.

He m. (1) (apparently by agreement dated 5 Aug. 1642) Rachel, widow of John Brundage of Wethersfield. She did not long survive, and he m. (2) Elizabeth Hill, dau. of William. He m. (3) abt. 1659, Sarah, widow of Thomas Bulkley, and dau. of Rev. John Jones, b. abt. 1620, d. in 1683.

---

* See JOHN APPLEGATE.

Will (date gone) ; wife Sarah and the legacies of her children; only dau. Sarah Wilson; cousins Thomas Wilson, Peter Clapham, Edward Wilson, and Samuel Wilson who lives with me; brother William Hill and my mother Hill; brother Samuel Wilson; bro. Thomas Wilson's children; sister Ann's children; bro. John Wilson's children; bros. William, Ignatius, and James Hill; three horses to be sent to Barbadoes to be turned to England to pay an engagement to bro. Samuel. Inv. 8 Apr. 1662.

His sister Ann may have been mother of his nephew Peter Clapham.

Child [by second wife] :

Sarah, b. [say 1650] ; m. Joseph Rowland.

Wilson, Samuel.

Brother of Anthony, with whom he may have been at Fairfield for a time; Mary dau. of Samuel and Jane of Fairfield d. at Boston in 1654. But if so, he rem. to New York, and had a second wife Elizabeth.

He may have been the same Samuel who took the oath of allegiance at New Haven, 1644, bought the house and homelot of Edward Wigglesworth, Sept. 1646, which he sold to Thomas Powell, Feb. 1648/9, and was noted as about to leave New Haven that year.

Will of Samuel of New York City, 14 Dec. 1688, proved 8 Jan. 1688/9; wife Elizabeth; two sons Joseph and Ebenezer; Samuel, son of son Joseph; £30 to Samuel Wilson of Fairfield, son of my bro. John dec'd.

Wilson, John.

Brother of Anthony.

Children :

+Thomas.
+Samuel.
Others ?

Wilson, Thomas, s. of John.

He owned land in Fairfield in 1670. In 1686 he took legal action on behalf of Hannah Abbott [dau. of Peter], but his interest does not appear. He d. at Fairfield in 1691; m. Hannah ————, who d. in 1694.

Inv. 2 Nov. 1691. Widow Hannah; one dau. (under 18).

Inv. of Hannah presented 5 Nov. 1694 by her only child Sarah wife of Elnathan Hanford.

Child:

> Sarah, m. abt. 1695, Elnathan Hanford, whose will 1701 named uncle Samuel Wilson.

Wilson, Samuel, s. of John.

Brought up at Fairfield by his uncle Anthony, he was generously remembered in his uncle Samuel's will. He d. early in 1729; was one of the twelve original proprietors of New Fairfield.

He m. in 1679, Phebe Middlebrook, dau. of Joseph, who joined him in agreement 1687. She renewed her Covenant at Fairfield Church, 7 Mar. 1696/7 and their six children were bapt. that date. She received land from her father 12 June 1679, when intending marriage.

Samuel conveyed to son John, 1727; to son-in-law Robert Turney, 1727; and to son Daniel, all right at New Fairfield, 1727. Daniel Wilson conveyed, also 1727, to bro. Joseph. Robert Turney and Elizabeth his wife conveyed 1728 to bro. Daniel Wilson. Daniel conveyed, Dec. 1728, to Henry Stevens of Stratford, one quarter of father Samuel's right in New Fairfield. Daniel conveyed, Mar. 1728/9, to Richard Smith of Groton, another quarter of the right in New Fairfield of his father Samuel dec'd. No probate of Samuel's estate has been found, and it was presumably settled by these and other conveyances.

Children:

> John, b. [say 1680].
> Isaac, b. [say 1682].
> ✕Daniel, b. abt. 1684, d. at Fairfield, 16 Aug. 1739 in 55 yr. (g. s.);
> will 21 Apr. 1733, proved 14 Sept. 1739; no children, gave all to
> wife; m. Ann Wilson, dau. of Nathaniel, b. abt. 1687, d. 14 Aug.
> 1756 in 70 yr. (g. s.); she m. (2) by agreement dated 4 Oct. 1741,
> Capt. John Silliman.

✕Joseph, d. at Fairfield abt. 1736; adm'n granted 3 Feb. 1735/6; m. Abigail ———, who d. abt. 1759; her Inv. 8 Jan. 1760.
Stephen.
Elizabeth, m. by 1711, Robert Turney.

Wilson, Edward.

He settled in Fairfield, and was prob. related to the Anthony Wilson family; but how, does not appear.

Inv. 12 Nov. 1684. Son Nathaniel; dau. Mary wife of Jonathan Morehouse.

Children:

+Nathaniel.
Mary, m. Jonathan Morehouse.

Wilson, Nathaniel, s. of Edward.

He m. Elizabeth Hendrick, dau. of Henry. She was bapt. at Fairfield, 27 Jan. 1694/5; and the two children, the following 7 Apr.

Will 15 Nov. 1726, proved Nov. 1733; wife Elizabeth; son Nathaniel; dau. Ann wife of Daniel Wilson; Mary Morehouse who lives with me.

Children:

Ann, b. abt. 1687, d. 14 Aug. 1756 in 70 yr. (g. s., Fairfield); m. (1) Daniel Wilson; m. (2) in 1741, Capt. John Silliman.
✕Nathaniel, b. abt. 1689, d. 8 May 1769 in 80 yr. (g. s., Fairfield); will 8 Nov. 1768, proved 4 July 1769; m. Ruth Adams, dau. of Nathan, bapt. 11 Oct. 1696, d. 13 June 1775 in 78 yr. (g. s.).

Wilson, Benjamin.

Perhaps related to the Anthony Wilson family.
He m. Jane Olmstead, dau. of Lt. John, b. abt. 1677.
Rem. from Norwalk to Ridgefield.

Children, three recorded at Norwalk, four at Ridgefield:

Sarah, b. 24 Sept. 1698.
Nathan, b. 30 Sept. 1701; m. 5 June 1727, Phebe Hobart.
Thomas, b. 9 Oct. 1703; m. 30 Jan. 1729, Elizabeth Brooks.
Rebecca, b. [say 1706], d. 27 Oct. 1789; m. 15 Apr. 1731, Benjamin Rockwell.

Benjamin, b. 17 June 1709, d. at Ridgefield, June 1757; m. 2 June 1737, Deborah Bennett.

Mary, b. 3 July 1712.

Jane, b. 28 Dec. 1714; m. 22 Sept. 1735/6, Joseph Keeler.

Abigail, b. 28 Mar. 1721.

Winter, John.

Of Westchester, N. Y., m. Posthume, doubtless dau. of John Brundish of Fairfield. His name appears often in Westchester County Deeds, and he had a son John.

On 22 May 1674, John "Wintar" of Westchester sold to Joseph James of Fairfield, land in that town which Francis Frenchard and Ebenezer Jones bought of Elias Douty. The surname in this deed has been read erroneously as "Winton".

Winton, Andrew.

He lived in Fairfield in 1684, when two indentured Scotch servants were assigned to him [prob. to "work out" their passage] by Andrew Alexander of East Jersey; assignment witnessed by Josiah Harvey and Thomas Merwin. They were Duncan Garnoch and Margaret his wife; and he released them, 2 July 1685.

On 29 May 1698 was bapt. at Fairfield, John Winton, son of Hannah Fountain. The rarity of the surname, in connection with the fact that John conferred the name Andrew on a son, warrants the assumption that Hannah, second wife of Aaron Fountain, was widow of Andrew Winton. As Hannah Fountain had four children by her second husband in 1698, her marriage to him should be placed as early as 1690, and Andrew's death [unless there was a divorce] falls between 1685 and 1690.

Probable child:

XJohn, b. [say 1685], bapt. 29 May 1698; m. abt. 1711, Susanna Adams, dau. of Lt. Abraham, b. abt. 1688, d. at Greenfield, 7 Feb. 1749/50 ae. abt. 61.

Woolly, Robert.

He bought the homelot in Fairfield originally belonging to Daniel Bulkley, and sold it prior to 5 Mar. 1649 [1649/50] to Thomas Dunn. We assume that he was the man of this name who later lived in Southampton, L. I.

Wooster, Edward. Constable of Derby, 1669.

In 1651 he obtained permission from Milford to settle in Paugasset (later Derby), and with his brother-in-law Thomas Langdon became the first settler there.

He m. (1) Dorothy, prob. sister of Thomas Langdon. She was treated in 1663 by Winthrop, who stated her name as Dorothy; and she d. prob. that year or soon after. He m. (2) by 1665, Tabitha Tomlinson, dau. of Henry of Stratford. She m. (2) abt. 1690 Dr. John Hull, and d. in 1691. Edward d. 8 July 1689.

Children [by first wife] :

> Elizabeth, b. [say 1652], d. before 1676; m. (rec. Stratford) 16 Nov. 1671, Ebenezer Johnson.
> Mary, b. 2 Nov. 1654 (rec. Milford), d. y.
> Thomas, b. abt. 1656, d. at Derby, 9 Jan. 1712/3; Lt.; m. abt. 1678, Phebe Tomlinson, dau. of Henry, b. 14 Aug. 1656, d. Mar. 1739/40.
> Edward, b. [say 1658], bapt. at Milford, 12 June 1670, d. y.
> David, b. [say 1660], bapt. 12 June 1670, d. at Derby, 29 Mar. 1711; m. Mary Lobdell, dau. of Simon, who d. before 1723.

Children [by second wife] :

> Henry, b. 18 Aug. 1666 (rec. Milford), bapt. 4 July 1669, d. in the Canadian Expedition, 1709, unm.
> Ruth, b. 8 Apr. 1668 (rec. Milford), bapt. 4 July 1669, d. before 1691; m. in 1687, Samuel Bowers.
> Timothy, b. 12 Nov. 1670 (rec. Milford), bapt. 18 Dec. 1670; m. 23 May 1699, Anna Perry, dau. of Arthur, b. 22 Jan. 1679/80.
> +Abraham, bapt. at Milford, 16 Mar. 1672/3.
> Hannah, bapt. 31 Oct. 1675, d. in 1743; m. 20 Aug. 1696, William Washburn, of Derby.
> Sylvester, b. [say 1678], d. at Derby, 16 Nov. 1712; m. abt. 1700, Susanna ———; she m. (2) 30 Nov. 1713, Samuel Washburn, and (3) in 1724, ——— Northrop.
> Tabitha, b. [say 1680]; m. (1) (rec. Stratford) 15 Oct. 1705, John Walker; m. (2) 11 Oct. 1726, Joseph Birdsey.
> Jonas, b. [say 1682], lived in Huntington; Lt.; m. Jane Nichols, dau. of Benjamin.
> Ebenezer, bapt. at Milford, 5 Aug. 1688; res. Stamford; m. Margaret Sawtell, dau. of Zechariah.

Wooster, Abraham, s. of Edward. Ens., Ripton Trainband, May 1717; Capt., May 1728.

Bapt. at Milford, 16 Mar. 1672/3, d. at Stratford, 1 Sept. 1743 ae. 70 (g. s.) ; m. at Stratford, 22 Nov. 1699, Mary Walker.

He lived in Ripton parish, Stratford [later Huntington], from marriage until death, and not in Derby as claimed by Orcutt.

Will 31 Aug. 1739, proved 29 Sept. 1743; wife Mary; sons Joseph, David; daus. Sarah Hemingway, Mary Harrison, Hannah and Ann Wooster.

Children, recorded at Stratford :*

> Ruth, b. 26 Sept. 1700, d. y.
>
> Joseph, b. 16 Jan. 1702/3, d. at Stratford, 30 Dec. 1791 ae. 89 (g. s.); Col.; m. Dec. 1751, Lucy Nichols, dau. of Theophilus, who d. 18 Oct. 1760 ae. 32 (g. s.).
>
> Sarah, b. 2 Apr. 1705, bapt. at Stratford (rec. Stratfield) 10 Feb. 1705/6; m. (1) 16 Aug. 1726, Charles Johnson, of Derby; m. (2) abt. 1740, Rev. Jacob Hemingway, of East Haven.
>
> Mary, b. 3 Apr. 1707, bapt. at Stratford (rec. Stratfield) 27 Apr. 1707, d. 4 Feb. 1791; m. 1 Jan. 1728/9, David Harrison, of Northford.
>
> Hannah, b. 23 Feb. 1709.†
>
> David, b. 2 Mar. 1710/1, d. at Danbury, 2 May 1777 ae. 66 (g. s.); grad. Yale Coll. 1738; Capt. in Cape Breton Expedition, 1745; Col. in Crown Point Expedition, 1757; Brig.-Gen., Revolutionary War; res. New Haven, where he m. 6 Mar. 1745/6, Mary Clap, dau. of Thomas, b. at Windham, 25 Apr. 1729, d. 6 June 1807 ae. 78 (g. s.).
>
> Ann, m. by 1750, Thomas Robinson, of East Haven.

Yeo, Thomas.

He m. abt. 1650, Sarah Phippen, dau. of David, of Boston; and rem. to Fairfield with the family of his wife's mother when she m. George Hull.

Inv. 10 Sept. 1658; widow.

Children, recorded at Boston:

> Elizabeth, b. 1 Oct. 1652; on 16 Apr. 1670, she witnessed an exchange of land between Nathan Gold and Thomas Morehouse.
>
> Thomas, b. 24 Apr. 1654.

* The claim has long been made that he had also a son Abraham, who m. Martha Hull and lived in Oxford and Waterbury. In the *New Eng. Hist. and Gen. Reg.*, vol. 75, p. 181, the present writer gave evidence tending to place this Abraham hypothetically as a son of Sylvester. Later discoveries negative that supposition. Abraham, son of Mary Hinman, was bapt. July 1697; her bro. Samuel Hinman gave by will to Abraham Wooster, son of his sister Mary. Abraham and Martha (Hull) Wooster named a son Hinman. Their grandson, Rev. Benjamin Wooster, who served under Gen. David Wooster as a boy in the Revolution, and undoubtedly knew the family history, left an autobiography in which he wrote that his grandfather "was the son of Abraham Wooster (the father of Gen. David Wooster) but by a different Mother."

† Family records, which the compiler has not verified but is inclined to credit, state that she m. (1) [abt. 1739] Capt. Elnathan Beach of Cheshire, as his second wife; and that she m. (2) Dr. Jonathan Bull of Hartford.

Young, John.

Died at Stratford, 7, bur. 8 Apr. 1661. His estate was administered in 1662 by Isaac Nichols and Henry Tomlinson, with the advice of Mr. Gold and Mr. Sherman.

Possibly he was the John Young who purchased land in Windsor 1641, and sold it 1649, having lost his wife Alse [Alice] by hanging, 26 May 1647, the first victim of the witchcraft delusion in Conn. Her name has also been stated as Achsah, but the authority is not so good; and the present writer has not seen the original entry in Matthew Grant's Diary.

ADDENDA

Since the publication of the earlier parts of the present volume, further research has brought new facts to light; in particular, a page by page inspection of certain unindexed volumes of the Stratford Land Records, made by the compiler on behalf of Mrs. Turney Sharps; and items have also been picked up when searching in Danbury, Stamford, Newtown, and elsewhere. Col. Charles E. Banks, of Boston, Mass., has contributed valuable suggestions, and two or three corrections; and several have furnished additions and corrections which are acknowledged individually under the specific families below.

Abbott, George. (Page 5.) Mrs. C. F. Heine of Bridgeport, Conn., kindly called our attention to the will (1676) of the first Jonas Weed of Stamford which names his dau. Mary wife of George Abbott. Since some of the Abbott children had Weed names, it is likely that Mary Weed was their mother, but it is not certain that she was his first wife or mother of all the children.

Adams, Nathan, s. of Edward. (Page 10.) Stratford Deeds prove that in 1734 and 1736 he was the (fourth) husband of Jane (Blackman) (Russell) (Griffin) Clark. In 1734 they conveyed to Zachariah Clark right that accrued to Jane Adams by gift from Thomas Griffin "one of her former Husbands"; in 1736 they conveyed to Zachariah Blackman land distributed to Miriam (or her representatives) "yᵉ Daughter of Mʳ Moses Wheeler Senʳ." Jane was Nathan's second wife, and Anna ———— his third.

Adams, Freegrace. (Page 12.) Danbury Probate Records add to our knowledge of his family.

John d. in 1786 (will 16 Mar. 1782, proved 4 Apr. 1786); m. (1) Sarah Curtis, dau. of Jonathan; m. (2) Mary Patterson, dau. of Andrew, b. 27 Mar. 1706. By first wife he had: Sarah-Curtis, who m. Asa Chambers. By second wife he had: Reuben, d. in 1787 (will 30 Mar. 1786, proved 9 Apr. 1787), who m. Naomi ———— (d. 29 Apr. 1777 in 25 yr., g. s.), and had children, Mary-Patterson and Joseph-Stevens.

Samuel d. in 1787 (will 12 Jan. 1786, proved 13 Aug. 1787); no issue.

Ephraim d. 24 Nov. 1786 in 76 yr. (g. s., Newtown) ; will 21 June 1784; no issue.

Sarah m. 5 Oct. 1743, Daniel Stevens, of New Fairfield.

Mehitabel apparently d. unmarried.

Abiah m. 19 Dec. 1750, Nathan Sherman.

Barlow. (Page 30.) Francis, b. 1702, m. Elizabeth Mitchell, dau. of Daniel.

Beach, Isaac. (Page 43.) His dau. Hannah m. Joseph Prince of Stratford, whose will 2, proved 31 Dec. 1747 named sons Joseph and William, daus. Mary and Martha, crazy sister Mary Prince of Middlebury, Plymouth County, Mass., and made wife Hannah and bro. Mr. William Beach Exec'rs. Prince was a mariner, and owned half of the sloop *Mary,* and in partnership with "Capt. Bennett" a half of the sloop *Darbe.*

Beardsley, William. (Page 46.) The daus. Ruth and Rebecca were correctly assigned to William on the strength of the distribution of the estate of their bro. John. Confirmation has been found. On 31 Oct. 1719, Joseph Smith of Jamaica, L. I., conveyed to Nathan Beardsley of Stratford land set to my mother Mrs. Ruth Smith in the distribution of the estate of Capt. John Beardsley. Rebecca, dau. of William, m. (1) Israel Curtis of Woodbury, and (2) a Beebe of Danbury, whom we must identify with James Beebe (page 54), whose third wife she doubtless was. On 31 Mar. 1719, Israel Curtis of Danbury conveyed to William, Daniel and John Beardsley, Jonathan Wakelee, John Parruck, and Nathan Beardsley (later referred to as children of Samuel Beardsley dec'd), land in Stratfield set out to my mother Rebecca Beebe from the estate of Capt. John Beardsley. Joseph Beardsley (son of William) was of Brookhaven, L. I., in 1684. Mrs. Rebecca Beebee, "the aged widow," d. at Woodbury, 17 Feb. 1739.

The Stratfield Plantation Book gives somewhat different dates for some of the children of John Beardsley (pages 51, 52). His first wife died 7 Jan. 1710/1. The son John was b. 6 Sept. 1704; Obadiah, 17 June 1706; Samuel, 9 Oct. 1712; and Martha, 16 Mar. 1728. The youngest child was called Johanna at birth and marriage, but Hannah in the recorded will of her father.

Bedient. (Page 53.) In making Mordecai the progenitor of the Fairfield Bedients, we followed the abstracts in the very useful "Westchester Miscellanea" published in the *New York Gen. and Biog. Record.* For a different account, see Savage's *Gen. Dict.,* vol. 1, p. 152; there is no question of the existence of the bros. Morgan and Thomas mentioned therein, or of their mother Mary. Morgan died early; if this Thomas was the man later of Fairfield, it is necessary to assume that younger bros. John and Mordecai came over later, and that the abstracter of "Westchester Miscellanea" erred in giving the father's name as Mordecai. The problem is involved, and for a positive solution research and study of all the original records involved would be required.

Beebe, James. (Page 54.) He apparently m. (3) after 1704, Rebecca, widow of Israel Curtis of Woodbury, and dau. of William Beardsley of Stratford. See BEARDSLEY above.

Beers. Family of Ephraim, son of Anthony (page 56). John may be the man on whose estate adm'n was granted, 3 Mar. 1761, to Nathaniel Squire. He and Anthony prob. lived in the Westport section of Norwalk. Their daus. were named in the will of their sister Mary; the Norwalk Land Records would likely yield information concerning their sons. These branches are difficult, the probate records yielding meagre data; and as they lived chiefly across the Fairfield boundary line, are omitted from consideration herein.

Bell, Jonathan. (Page 60.) His dau. Susannah, b. 25 Dec. 1686, m. (1) 11 Apr. 1706, Abraham Weed, and (2) 26 May 1715, Thomas Talmadge, and d. at New Canaan, 23 Nov. 1756 ae. 70 (g. s.).

Bennett. (Page 75, line 1.) Hannah, dau. of ISAAC, m. at Stratford, 29 Jan. 1721/2, Caleb Perry.

(Page 72.) The surviving children of JOSEPH made a distribution of his realty, 15 June 1744, recorded in Fairfield Deeds. Richard was then of New Hanover, Burlington County, N. J.; Abiah and her husband Samuel Bennett, of Ridgefield; Mary, of Stratford; and Joseph, "non compos mentis", of Fairfield.

(Page 74.)   The wife of Hezekiah was Hannah Hendrick. His father Jeremiah d. at Stratfield, 27 Aug. 1773; and Jeremiah's wife d. June 1772.

Birdsey, John.   (Page 76.)   His wife Philippa was prob. dau. of Rev. Henry Smith of Wethersfield. See will of John Blackman, page 82.

Bishop, (Rev.) John.   (Page 77.)   It was his dau. Rebecca who m. Rev. Joseph Whiting; he gave a receipt in 1695 for portion due to my wife Rebecca according to the will of her father Mr. John Bishop dec'd.   In 1718, Joseph Whiting of Southampton, Clerk, conveyed to son Joseph Whiting of Stamford, two pieces of land bounded on Bishop land.   Rebecca (Bishop) Whiting d. at Southampton, 26 Apr. 1726 ae. 63 yrs. 2 mos. (g. s.).

(Page 79.)   Alexander Bishop m. Susanna Holly, b. 8 Apr. 1711.

Blackman.   (Pages 84 and 85.)   On 6 Dec. 1710, Abigail wife of Ebenezer Blackman and Prudence wife of John Osborn, Jr., testified concerning the nuncupative will of Adam Blackman, made on 18 Aug. last, when he was about to go to Port Royal; he named Ebenezer Blackman and the latter's son John, dau. Dorothy Foot, and maiden dau. Elizabeth; also, Jane wife of James Clark.   Was this Adam the son of Deliverance?   There was also an Adam, son of Joseph (page 86), who in 1735 conveyed to his bro. Joseph, mentioning his dec'd father Joseph. Perhaps this was the Adam who m. Ruth Beecher.

Jane (page 84) m. (4) Nathan Adams of Fairfield.

Mary (page 87) m. at Ridgefield, 8 May 1740, James Benedict, Jr.   In 1761 they conveyed to Nathaniel Whitehead, their right in houselot of father John Blackman dec'd.

Dorothy (page 87) perhaps m. (1) John Butler, Jr.

Abigail (page 87) was living unmarried 1767, when she conveyed to John Whitehead, her right in house of father John Blackman in Greens Farms; hence doubtless was the Abigail who d. 26 Aug. 1772.

Booth.   (Page 91.)   Zechariah m. (2) Sarah (Gilbert) Merchant; see Gilbert below.   The reference on page 89 to "Private

Controversies" should be to "Towns and Lands", Conn. Archives. JOSEPH (page 90) m. (2) Elizabeth, perhaps Bostwick, b. 1 Oct. 1677; she m. (2) 12 Nov. 1712, John Mix of New Haven, where she d. May 1716.

John, s. of Richard.   (Page 89.)   With regard to his children, Mrs. Katharine H. Fogarty of Bridgeport has found a deed in Stratford in 1736 from John Booth, Ambrose Thompson and Ann his wife, Benjamin Brooks and Mary his wife, Richard Chapman and Sarah his wife, and Jonathan Booth of Newtown, to Thomas Booth; which proves us right in placing Mary and Sarah as daus. of John Booth, but suggests that we may have erred in following Orcutt as to the marriage of Sarah unless she, like Mary, was twice married.

It was not DEA. JOSEPH (page 90) who m. Sarah Blackman. He m. (3) Sarah (Thompson) Sherman, bapt. 20 Mar. 1709.

Bostwick. ELIZABETH (page 92), b. 1 Oct. 1677, perhaps m. (1) Joseph Booth, and (2) John Mix. EPHRAIM (page 94) was of Greenwich, 1736.

Bulkeley, (Rev.) Peter. (Page 109.)   Col. Charles E. Banks, the eminent authority on English research, kindly sends an excerpt from a letter written to William Morton by John Blackiston, 22 May 1635, referring to departure for New England: "m[r] Buckley is gone wth his wife m[rs] Grace Cheetwood whom he married a month agoe." This fixes the date of marriage as early April, 1635, instead of late in 1634.

Burr. (Page 131.)   The will of Samuel Burr, 6 Mar. 1772, proved 6 Apr. 1773, mentioned marriage covenant with wife Ruth, children Samuel, Daniel, Nehemiah, Charles, Elizabeth, Ellen, and children of dec'd son Ebenezer and of dec'd dau. Mehitabel. The distribution calls Ellen, wife of Abel Gold, and Elizabeth, wife of Samuel Silliman, and refers to heirs of Mehitabel Squire.

(Page 121.)   A conveyance of land in Newtown, 1 June 1757, throws light on the family of Samuel Burr of Charlestown. William Downs Cheever and Elizabeth his wife, and Zachariah Brigden and Sarah his wife, all of Boston, called themselves the only heirs of Samuel Burr late of Charlestown, dec'd.

(Page 124.)   Daniel Burr's will, 5 Feb. 1719/20, not approved

[Pro. Files], named wife Elizabeth; two sons Stephen and Peter, Exec'rs; two youngest sons, Moses and Aaron; gr. son Daniel (under 21), apparently the son of Jehu; son David; five daus. Hannah Burr, Mary Meeker, Elizabeth Hull, Jean Burr, Esther Burr; eldest son Jehu, to whom he had already given land at Newtown; witnesses, Peter Burr, Samuel Hubbell, Abigail Burr.

Burroughs, John. (Page 133.) His son Edward, b. 14 Mar. 1696, was of "Fairfield in Cohansey", West Jersey, 1722, when he conveyed land set to him in distribution of his father John's estate. This Edward has sometimes been identified erroneously with an older man, Mr. Edward Burrough, whose name was usually spelled without the final 's'.

Bushnell. (Page 134.) In calling Francis of Norwalk and Danbury, son of Richard, the compiler unwisely followed the account given in vol. 53 of the *New Eng. Hist. and Gen. Register,* and in vol. 72, p. 210 of the same. Subsequent research on the Bushnell family makes it clear that Francis was the son of Lt. William Bushnell, of Saybrook, b. Jan. 1649/50.

Butler, John.

We suppose that the Dr. John of Stratford who d. 1696 leaving a widow Mary and a farm at Saugatuck (see vol. 1, pp. 135, 136) is identical with the man to whom the following records pertain.

Adm'n on Est. of John Butler, *formerly* of Norwalk, was granted 1 Feb. 1722/3, to Samuel Richards of Norwalk and to Mary Lockwood, widow of Robert Lockwood of Fairfield, formerly widow of said Butler. Mary Lockwood was referred to as mother-in-law of Samuel Richards. Distribution was ordered to the only son John, and to the two daus., Wait wife of Robert Lockwood, and Hellinah Butler.

Children:

> John, called of Fairfield, d. by 1735; m. Dorothy ———. On 5 June 1735, Dorothy Butler was appointed guardian to her dau. Mary, child of John Butler. Stephen, son of John, chose Ephraim Jackson of Fairfield for guardian, 8 Mar. 1742/3. It is believed that Dorothy was the dau. of John Blackman (see p. 87) who in 1744

was wife of William Williams of Cortlandt, N. Y.; this Dorothy
was sister of Martha Blackman, the wife of Ephraim Jackson.*
Wait, m. Robert Lockwood, Jr.
Hellinah or Ellen, called of Fairfield, d. by 1732; adm'n on her
estate was granted, 4 Apr. 1732, to Samuel Richards of Norwalk,
and he was appointed guardian to her dau. Prudence.

Castle, Henry, s. of Henry. (Page 139.) His second wife was
Ruth Richardson, dau. of Thomas, b. at Waterbury, 10 May 1681.
The second wife of Isaac, on same page, was her sister, Joanna
(Richardson) Warner.

Clugston, Michael. (Page 150.) His son Samuel was Lt., 2d
Co., Norwalk, May 1737, and Capt., Oct. 1740; and Deputy for
Norwalk, Oct. 1739, and May and July 1740. The other son,
John, had *three* wives, all named Elizabeth. He m. (1) 11 June
1718, Elizabeth Welles, who d. at Stamford, 31 Aug. 1730. He m.
(2) at Greenwich, 27 Feb. 1734/5, Elizabeth Peck, and it was she
and not the first Elizabeth who d. at Redding, 1 Sept. 1745. He
m. (3) at Fairfield, 24 Mar. 1747/8, Elizabeth Rowlinson.

Cobbitt. (Page 151.) Mr. Samuel and Mrs. Sarah his wife
were admitted to Fairfield Church by letter from church in New
Bristol. The printed records of Bristol, R. I., contain births of
the following children of Samuel and Sarah: Sarah, b. 3 Jan.
1689; Samuel, b. 16 Aug. 1693; Thomas, b. 18 Oct. 1695, d.
2 Dec. 1695; John, b. 9 Oct. 1696.

Coley. (Page 156.) Ebenezer, bapt. 4 May 1712, left a will
dated 19 Jan. 1734/5, proved by the witnesses 27 Jan. 1734/5;
named mother Hannah Coley and aunt Sarah Rowlerson, with
residue equally to bros. and sisters; Peter Coley appealed and the
will was not approved. [Pro. Files.]

Crofut, James. (Page 166.) His son Josiah m. Sarah dau. of
James and Rachel (Starr) Benedict; another son, Matthew, m.
her sister Rebecca Benedict. [Information contributed by Mr.
Henry M. Bradley, Jr., of Derby, Conn.]

---

* Stephen and James, children of Dorothy Williams, were bapt. at Greens Farms,
3 Oct. 1742. These were prob. Butler children.

Curtis, Israel, s. of John. (Page 171.)   He m. Rebecca, dau. of William Beardsley; she m. (2) James Beebe of Danbury.   See BEARDSLEY in the Addenda above.

Benjamin, s. of John. (Page 172.)   Stratford Deeds bear out the belief expressed in the footnote on p. 173 that Benjamin had more daus. On 19 Sept. 1733, John and David Curtiss, John Thompson, Zachariah Booth, Nathan Beardslee and Dinah his wife, and Daniel Beach and Esther his wife, all of Stratford, and James Curtiss of Durham, and Ephraim Hawley and Phebe his wife of New Milford, made mutual distribution of the estate of their father Mr. Benjamin Curtiss, and stated "we are the only heirs." Thus Phebe and Dinah, as suggested, were daus. of Benjamin, but Martha was not, and remains still unplaced.

Dickerson, Thomas, s. of Thomas. (Page 183.)   Of the children, Elizabeth, b. 9 June 1693, m. William Lyon of Newtown; Daniel was of Newtown, 1716; Nathaniel was of Stratford, 1718; and Sybil was of Newtown, 1720.   [Stratford Deeds.]

Dunbar, John. (Page 189.)   Anne Dunbar was admitted to full communion at Fairfield by letter from Salem, 21 Oct. 1694, the same day that John's son John was baptized. She must have been John's wife, and mother of Sarah and John, Jr. Anne d. soon, and John thereafter made the two marriages ascribed to him. Since the publication of the *Salisbury Family-Histories,* John of Fairfield and New Haven has always been identified with John of Hingham who m. in 1679 Mattithiah Aldridge. Perhaps his earlier career should be reviewed and his identity verified.

Dunning (Page 190).   The second marriage of the younger Benjamin (Sergt.), was taken from a supposedly reliable printed source. He certainly had a second wife Elizabeth, named in his will, and she may have been Elizabeth Minor as stated; but the date 1710 is certainly a few years too early. The bros. Benjamin and John were bapt. at Stratfield, 30 May 1703. By wife Mary, Benjamin had children (rec. Newtown, bapt. Stratfield): Mary, b. 6, bapt. 20 July 1707; m. Joseph Stilson. Benjamin (Capt.), b. 9, bapt. 14 Aug. 1709; m. Sarah Burritt. David, b. 6 Sept. 1711, bapt. 11 May 1712; m. Hannah ———. Sarah, b. 14 Aug., bapt. 25 Oct. 1713; m. Jehiel Hawley. Other children (named in will): Abiel. John, b. by 1725, d. at Stratford, 1764; m. Anna Kimberly. Michael, b. 20 July 1732. Amos, b. 20 Jan. 1733/4. The last two, and possibly the last four, were by Elizabeth.

Fanton, Jonathan. (Page 199.) A partition deed, dated 30 Apr. 1765, of the heirs of Sarah Fanton of Fairfield, who died interstate, is found in the Land Records, signed by John Fanton and Sarah Jennings of Fairfield and Richard Welton and Gershom Scott of Waterbury. The dau. Sarah, bapt. 18 Nov. 1694, m. John Jennings.

Fairchild, Samuel, s. of Thomas. (Page 195.) His son Robert (named in gr. father Wheeler's will) apparently d. young before him. The three sons mentioned, but not named, in the probate entry in 1705, were apparently Samuel, Edward, and *Jonathan,* for in 1721 Jonathan Fairchild of Norwalk sold land in Stratford inherited from his father Samuel dec'd. Jonathan was ancestor of the Norwalk branch; his will, 2 June 1769, proved 15 Dec. 1772, named wife, sons Thomas and Abraham, heirs of son Daniel dec'd, son Samuel, and daus. Sarah and Ellen.

Ferris, Zechariah. (Page 200.) Stratford Deeds prove that he left four surviving children: Zechariah of New Milford, Sarah wife of Joseph Halsted of Hempstead, L. I., and Samuel of Newtown; and also Mary who in 1722 was widow of John Sturdevant of Ridgefield. Presumably he was the John (son of William) Sturdevant who was b. at Norwalk, 20 July 1676. The marriage is found of John Sturdevant to Mary Jackson at Stratfield, 28 Apr. 1709. Presumably this was Mary Ferris, so she must have been the young widow of one of the Jacksons, not identified.

Finch, Isaac, s. of John. (Page 203.) His eldest son John, b. 20 Sept. 1659, left a will dated 15 Mar. 1702/3, not proved [Pro. Files], in which he mentioned son-in-law Joseph Webb, "my father's bed", bro. Isaac Finch, dau.-in-law Sarah Webb, sister Elizabeth Pettit, mother Ann Finch, and bro. Benjamin Finch. The Inv. states that he d. 17 Mar. 1702/3; adm'n granted to

Abraham Finch. He perhaps m. (1) Sarah Pettit, gr. dau. of Sarah (———) (Scofield) Merwin [see will of latter under Scofield; she called John Finch her gr. son]; and if so, had children by her who evidently d. before him. He certainly m. (2) Hannah, widow of Joseph Webb, mother of the Joseph and Sarah Webb named in Finch's will as his stepchildren. She (who m. Webb in 1672 as Hannah Scofield) was seemingly not dau. of Sarah (———) (Scofield) Merwin.

French, Samuel. (Page 209.) Stratford Deeds prove that it was not Sergt. Samuel, the carpenter of Stratfield, but Samuel the joiner of Stratford (page 210), who was nephew of Mr. Jonathan Pitman. For calling attention to this, we are indebted to Mr. Mansfield J. French, of Syracuse, N. Y., who also suggests that the Deborah French bapt. 2 Aug. 1696 may have been the mother and not a child of Sergt. Samuel.

The dau. Elizabeth prob. m. Michael Slater or Slaughter, b. at Eastchester, N. Y., 18 Nov. 1689. The will of Michael of Eden, Chewan County, N. C., about 1740, named wife Elizabeth and seven daus., Anna, Abigail, Elizabeth, Rebecca, Deborah, Nancy, and the youngest not named.

The reading of Sergt. Samuel's gravestone is incorrect; he d. 23, not 20 Dec. 1732.

Gilbert. (Page 223, line 2.) Sarah, b. 10 Nov. 1705, d. at Stratford in Apr. 1788 (will 5 Apr., proved 28 Apr.); m. (1) 24 Aug. 1724, John Marchant; m. (2) Zechariah Booth. Proved by her will, of which an abstract was kindly furnished by Mrs. Katharine H. Fogarty of Bridgeport, Conn.

Glover, John (1674-1752), page 225. A record of his family was made after his settlement in Newtown [Land Records, vol. 2, p. 83]. It states his first marriage, 27 Nov. 1700, to Margery *Hubbell,* thus confirming our conclusions stated on pages 225 and 302; the births of the son John at New Haven, Dec. 1701, and of the son Henry at Stratford, Oct. 1703; the death of Margery on 14 Mar. 1703/4; the second marriage of John, 14 July 1707, to Bethiah Bickley, and the births of their children: Benjamin, b. at Stratford, 26 May 1708; Bethiah, b. at Newtown, 6 Dec. 1710;

Mary, b. at Newtown, 5 May 1713; and Daniel, b. at Newtown, 13 Mar. 1717. John's first purchase in Newtown was made 1710 from Richard and Josiah Hubbell [his wife's brothers].

Gregory, Benjamin, s. of Samuel. (Page 241.) On 8 Apr. 1712, his wife and children absenting themselves from him, he published his refusal to pay any debt contracted by his wife [Stratfield Plantation Book].

EBENEZER, s. of Samuel (page 241) had three children recorded at Stratfield: Eunice, bapt. 7 Nov. 1731; Naomi, bapt. 12 Aug. 1733; Naomi, bapt. 16 Mar. 1735. Ebenezer d. at Stratfield, suddenly, 8 Mar. 1749/50.

Griffin, Thomas. (Page 243.) The compiler is indebted to Mr. Clarence A. Torrey, of Dorchester, Mass., for calling attention to the stupid oversight in entering 1703, the date of probate action, as the date of Thomas's death, when his widow had remarried in 1698. Inspection of the files shows that the will and inventory were accepted and ordered recorded, 7 Nov. 1693, so the death of Thomas should be placed in 1693. However, the will was *not* recorded and is not in the files, and the inventory was not entered until 1703; and the dates in the record volume are correctly stated on page 243. It appears that the will, instead of being nuncupative as the mention of it in the record volume led us to infer, actually was *lost*.

Hall, Samuel, s. of Samuel. (Page 255.) It was his widow Sarah who d. at Stratfield, 6 Feb. 1770.

RICHARD, b. 1713 (page 254); his wife Hannah Booth did not die in 1768, in which year action was taken on her estate, but some years previously; and Richard had a second wife Hannah who was named in his will.

JABEZ (page 254) settled in New Fairfield by 1753 [Fairfield Deeds].

Hanford, (Rev.) Thomas. (Page 256.) He was son of Theophilus and Eglin (Mortimer) Hanford, according to some accounts which have appeared in print. These statements have not been verified by the compiler, who sees no good reason to doubt that Eglin was a Hatherly. Col. Banks suggests the possibility that the name Eglin may be a misreading for Eylin, i.e., Ellen, and we pass the suggestion along to those who may have the opportunity of consulting original records in which her name appears.

Thomas, 3d (page 258), prob. d. in 1747, soon after will was made; for the marriage record of his dau. Mary, 27 Oct. 1747, calls him deceased [Darien Church rec.].

Higbee. See the published genealogy of the family for further data. It seems that the Betts wife belonged to Edward, Jr.

Hubbell, James, s. of Richard. (Page 306.) His dau. Patience, b. 8 Apr. 1722, m. at Trumbull, 4 Dec. 1740, Nathan Nichols.

John, s. of Richard (page 306), had a second wife, a widow Abigail [Brinsmade?], who on 20 June 1774 gave a receipt to her son-in-law Benjamin Hubbell [her stepson], referring to her son Brinsmade. The dau. Jerusha, bapt. 14 June 1713, m. Zachariah Treadwell.

Hurd, John. (Page 314.) His wife Abigail Wallis was stepdau. of *Jacob,* not of *Henry* Wakelee. His son John, b. 1701, prob. m. at Windham, 16 Sept. 1725, Sarah Hendee, dau. of Richard. Enos, b. 1713, m. Elizabeth Oatman.

Jennings, Sarah, dau. of Joseph (page 334), bapt. 22 Aug. 1697; m. (1) 19 Nov. [1718 or 1719], Joseph Squire; m. (2) Zachariah Mead. She d. without issue in 1773. Her will, 4 Jan. 1771, proved 6 July 1773, named: sister Martha Jennings of Fairfield; ⅓ of residue to Elizabeth wife of Thaddeus Bennett, and ⅔ to Ruth Hollingsworth.

John, s. of Joseph (bottom of page 333), m. Sarah Fanton, bapt. 18 Nov. 1694.

Johnson, Nicholas. (Page 343.) He was admitted to full communion at Fairfield, 19 Apr. 1696; removed to Cohansey, N. J., where he d. in 1733; will 1 Sept. 1732, proved 27 Feb. 1732/3, named wife Mary, sons Nicholas, Othniel, and Nathaniel, daughters Sarah Haries, Hannah Peterson, Ann Smith, Temperance and Sarah Johnson.

Jones, Thomas, s. of Thomas. (Pages 344, 345.) His will named also his son Eliphalet, who had been abroad for several years, providing for him if he should come in person to Fairfield. The inventory was made 13 Jan. 1723/4, over a month before the probation of the will.

Judson. ELIPHALET (page 352) called himself in 1736, late of Stratford, now of Eggs Harbor. Mary (Mitchell), widow of JONATHAN, m. (2) 9 Dec. 1729, Stephen Terrell of Woodbury.

Lewis, Philip. (Page 379.) It was difficult to obtain a full record of his family, as the probate record of his estate is defective. He had two wives and two sets of children. His [second] wife Elizabeth was admitted to Fairfield Church by letter from Hartford, 1694, and we must believe that she was mother of the younger children. The Elizabeth Lewis, Jr., who witnessed a deed in 1709 (see page 380) was, without doubt, a dau. of Philip.

Lockwood. (Page 387, sixth child of John.) ELIZABETH m. Robert Matthews. She was of New York City and d. before 1757; her dau. Susanna m. Francis Thurman of New York (he d. 1757-8), and conveyed right in land of John Lockwood, bounded north on land of the heirs of the late wife of David Adams, and south on land set to the wife of Josiah Bagley.

The first ROBERT (page 380) was son of Edmond of Combs, co. Suffolk, and bapt. 18 Jan. 1600; his bro. Edmond was bapt. 9 Feb. 1594. They came in the Winthrop fleet, 1630. [Charles E. Banks: *The Winthrop Fleet* (1930), pp. 79, 80.]

Robert, s. of Joseph. (Page 385.) He m. (2) after 1696, Mary, widow of John Butler, and she was mother of his younger children, almost certainly of Daniel, Abigail, Joseph, Gershom, and Jehiel, and possibly of others. Robert had a first unknown wife, who was certainly mother of the eldest son, Robert, Jr., who m. his stepsister Wait Butler. The maternity of the daus. is in doubt. The son Joseph was "late of Fairfield, now of Norwalk", Mar. 1767, when he sold land in the Beacham long lot; in Sept. 1767 he was of Sharon, and sold land in the Beacham long lot, bounded on land of the heirs of Gershom and Jehiel Lockwood. On 7 Jan. 1768, Joseph of Sharon conveyed a right in Fairfield to his son Joseph of Sharon; the latter conveyed the same, 1 Feb. 1768, to James Lockwood, Jr., of Norwalk; and the last-named, on 25 Nov. 1768, conveyed it back to Joseph Lockwood, "late of Norwalk, now of Sharon."

Mitchell, Daniel. (Page 417.)   His dau. Elizabeth, b. 1703, m. Francis Barlow.

Morehouse.   Children of Lemuel (page 427).   Mary m. abt. 1738, Isaac Keeler.   Rebecca m. (2) John Videto of Danbury, and d. in 1789; her will, 29 May, proved 19 June 1789, named her husband John Videto; Rebecca Morehouse, dau. of bro. John of Brookfield; sister Hannah Osborn of Ridgefield; Rachel wife of Samuel Wallace, Ruth wife of Ezra Abbot, and Sarah wife of Peter Crane, the three heirs of bro. Lemuel Morehouse dec'd; Isaac, Jacob, and Elijah Keeler, and Mary wife of John Lee, heirs of sister Mary Keeler, late of Salem, N. Y., dec'd; and Thomas and Martha Northrup, heirs of sister Rachel Northrup, late of Ridgefield, dec'd.

Samuel, s. of Samuel (top of page 422), d. 25 Nov. 1732.

Nichols, Caleb. (Pages 435, 436.)   The brief abstract of his will omits the mention he made of his three sons-in-law, Moses Wheeler, John Prentis, and William Martin.

Ogden, Richard.   Referring to his nameless dau. (page 448) who m. John Pine, the census of Hempstead, L. I., 1698, lists a John Pine, with Abigail (prob. his second wife), Mary (perhaps the child he had by the Ogden wife), and Daniel, Abigail, Ruth, and Phebe (presumably children by the second wife).   With regard to the daus. of Richard Ogden, who m. Samuel Ward and Daniel Silliman, their names have been stated in printed sources, but we lack confidence in these statements.   The name *Hannah* for wife of Samuel Ward is obviously a confusion with Ward's second wife, whose name was Hannah. The name Thankful for Silliman's wife seems to confuse him with a later Daniel whose wife's name was Thankful; and the evidence is good for calling this Ogden girl *Abigail*.

SARAH (dau. of Richard, 2d, page 449, last line), m. Monmouth Hart, Sr., of Rye, N. Y. [Contributed by Mrs. May Hart Smith, of Ontario, Calif.]

JONATHAN (s. of Richard, 2d, page 450, top line), settled in Fairfield, N. J., prob. with his bro. Richard, 3d.

Osborn, John, s. of John. (Page 459.) His second wife (Thankful Silliman) d. 25 July 1777 by the Perry Diary; the entry reads "Widow Osborn, Stephen Osborn's mother."

Richard, s. of David. (Page 457.) His second wife, whom he m. abt. 1722, was Sarah, widow of Thomas Rockwell of Norwalk, and dau. of John Ruscoe.

ERRATA

Page 101, line 4 from bottom. For *Walderswich,* read *Walberswich.*

Page 279, lines 5, 7, and footnote. For St. Mary *Archer,* read *Arches.*

Page 307, line 15. For *Crew Kerne,* read *Crewkerne.*

Page 456, top line. For *28,* read *25.*

Page 462, 7th line from bottom. For *Zephaniah* Clark, read *Zechariah.* In 1758, he and wife Olive lived in Farmington.

Page 537, line 6. The second wife of Thomas Seymour was *Sarah,* not *Elizabeth,* widow of Thomas Wildman. Elizabeth ———— was a third wife.

APPENDIX

Several families in this volume presented serious problems to the genealogist, and we have not always arrived at conclusions in agreement with what has heretofore found general acceptance. To meet the request for a statement of reasons for reaching some of these conclusions, the following notes are appended.

FAIRCHILD

Mary Fairchild m. 12 Mar. 1712/3, Benjamin Brooks.
Mary Fairchild m. 14 Feb. 1721/2, Ephraim Burritt.
Mary Fairchild m. 7 Mar. 1728/9, Samuel Adams.

To answer the requirements of these three marriages, just three Mary Fairchilds were found in record sources. One was Mary, dau. of Zechariah, b. 1698. The second was Mary (Booth), left a widow by Zechariah's son Agur in 1712. The third was Mary, b. 1708, dau. of Samuel, a cousin of the above Mary and Agur.

If Orcutt can be believed, both Mary (b. 1698) and Mary (b. 1708) married Samuel Adams in 1729. Most accounts make her dau. of Zechariah, b. 1698; but this would make her 31 at marriage, 53 when her youngest child was born, and 105 at death. Actually, the *Conn. Herald* at the time of her death in 1803 stated her age as 105. Despite this, Samuel Fairchild's dau. was called Mary Adams in the probate records, and wife of Samuel Adams in Fairfield Land Records when she conveyed inherited property with other children of Samuel Fairchild. We are therefore correct in calling this Mary, dau. of Samuel, b. 1708.

The deed recently discovered in Stratford by Mrs. Katharine H. Fogarty, in which Benjamin Brooks and Mary his wife joined with other heirs of John Booth, identifies this Mary with the widow Mary (Booth) Fairchild. This leaves Mary dau. of Zechariah (b. 1698) free for the marriage to Ephraim Burritt in 1722, when she was nearly 24 years old. Thus all three Marys are accounted for, with record evidence for the history of two of them. Orcutt's account of them was inherently improbable, and is proved incorrect.

FINCH

The *Hist. of Wethersfield* and other authorities state that there was an antique Abraham Finch early at Wethersfield, where he

was known as "Old Finch," and that he was father of the
Abraham who was killed by the Indians, and father also of Daniel
of Fairfield. This account seems incredible to the present writer,
and necessitates a pedigree as follows:

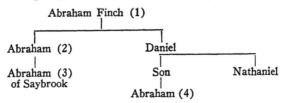

It is the writer's belief that Abraham (1) is fictitious; that
Abraham (2) who was killed by the Indians was son of Daniel;
and that Abraham (3) and Abraham (4) are identical. The con-
ventional pedigree above is built on a single record; for in 1640,
in records of the estate of Abraham (2), who left an only son
Abraham (3), the child's grandfather, erroneously called Abraham,
offered to educate it. The child's grandfather should have been
called Daniel.

Except for this probate entry, no mention has been found of the
alleged Abraham (1). He had no probate of his own, and is not
mentioned in the Colonial Records. It was Daniel who was Constable of Wethersfield in 1636, and all references to "Old Finch"
can apply to Daniel, since he had an adult son at that date. The
estate of Daniel at Fairfield was committed by the Court to the
management of his grandson Abraham Finch in 1657. Hence
Daniel did have a grandson Abraham (mentioned also in his will
at Fairfield), and this grandson was of age in 1657, so was presumably born about 1635. Daniel's son, the father of Abraham
(4), was therefore born not long after 1610, and Daniel's own
birth may be placed in the neighborhood of 1585. This makes him
old enough to be called "Old Finch" in the Wethersfield records of
the 1640's. If Daniel's father, the fictitious Abraham (1), was
in Wethersfield in 1640, he was old indeed, excessively old to have
been a Pilgrim to these shores.

The explanation is simple. Correct the one record in which
Daniel was erroneously referred to as Abraham because of a
clerical error, and everything is plain. Daniel was father of the
Abraham (2) who was killed by the Indians. This Abraham's
widow married a Saybrook man, and the only child (Abraham)

eventually settled in Saybrook. Daniel's grandson Abraham was in Fairfield with him for a time, but after Daniel's death completely disappears from Fairfield records. Why? Because he had gone to his mother's people in Saybrook. When Abraham (3) died in Saybrook (will presented 5 June 1667), the probate records refer to property he had at Wethersfield, and also to livestock he had at Fairfield. The last fact identifies him as Daniel's grandson. The correct pedigree is:

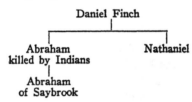

Daniel Finch

Abraham
killed by Indians

Nathaniel

Abraham
of Saybrook

BRADLEY—DAVIS

Samuel Bradley of Fairfield conveyed to his kinsman, James Davis; in selling the land, James referred to Samuel Bradley as his uncle.

The identity of Samuel Bradley is a complete mystery, and no place for him has been found in either the Fairfield or in the New Haven Bradley family.

James and Joseph Davis were bapt. as adults at Greenfield, 26 June 1726. They were of age to be brothers or cousins, as was also Benjamin Davis of Greenfield. They may have been sons of John Davis, Jr., of Fairfield (see page 180).

The same names occur in the Concord and East Cambridge branches of the descendants of Dolor Davis; for James Davis (1668-1727) by his wife Ann Smedley (1676-1760) had sons James (b. 1701), Joseph (b. 1708), and Benjamin (b. 1712). Because of the connection of the Smedley family with Fairfield, the compiler believed that we might find here the origin of the Fairfield Davis trio. Mr. Clarence A. Torrey, of Dorchester, Mass., very kindly searched records in Massachusetts, and found that the James born in 1701 died in 1728; and that the Benjamin born in 1712 had wife Sarah and lived in Concord and Groton. Hence this promising clue evaporated into a remarkable coincidence, and unless the Fairfield Davises were sons of John, Jr., of that place, we have no suggestion to offer.

HOLDSWORTH—HOLLINGSWORTH—JONES

The problem of the identity of Susanna, second wife of Rev. John Jones, and mother of the noted "witch" Mercy (Holsworth) (Nichols) Disbrow, has been accorded further consideration (see pages 289 and 343).

The enticing theory, which was offered merely as a theory, that the name Holsworth was an abbreviated form of Hollingsworth, must probably be abandoned; for the evidence seems to be strong that Susanna, widow of the first Richard Hollingsworth, continued her residence at Salem and hence did not marry Mr. Jones.

Milford Church Records contain the baptism, 2 Sept. 1677, of "Joshua Hollinsw   of Salem Church", the surname being left thus incomplete. This was probably another child of the second Richard Hollingsworth, who came about that time from Salem to Milford; though the entry is made without statement of parentage, which was customarily entered in the Milford Church Records.

Attention is again called to the brothers Joseph and Joshua Holdsworth, mariners of Boston, of whom the former died unmarried, and the latter married, 10 May 1669, Sarah Rawlins. Further record of them has not been found.

Jonas Holdsworth was listed without a family in the 1698 Census of Southold, L. I. He was a school-teacher, and clerk of the Court of Sessions in 1665 and later; hence a man of education and standing, as we would expect of a stepson of Mr. Jones. Apparently the dates would permit of his being a son of Mrs. Susanna Jones, since she had a daughter born about 1637. This may bring a solution of the problem nearer.

SAMUEL SMITH

Three men named Samuel Smith were born at Fairfield in the years 1712 and 1713. Their histories were difficult to untangle, but a recent search of the later land records seems to indicate that we have reversed the marriage and death records of Samuel, son of John (bapt. 19 Apr. 1713, page 571) and of the other Samuel, son of John (b. 28 Jan. 1711/2, page 573). The third Samuel, son of Joseph (bapt. 1 Nov. 1713, page 573), settled in Redding, and m. 25 Aug. 1736, Lydia Hull. The second volume will set forth their histories in greater detail.

LUDLOW

Roger Ludlow was bapt. at Dinton, co. Wilts, Eng., 7 Mar. 1590, and his ancestry was as stated on pages 388 to 390. See the *New Eng. Hist. and Gen. Register,* vol. 42, pp. 181-184, for a more complete account than that of Col. Chester.

MONROE

The first wife of David Monroe (mother probably of most if not all of his children) was Elizabeth Ted, to whom he was married 27 May 1690 at Huntington, L. I., where the record calls him David Roe alias MunRoe.

INDEX

The following index, containing over 11,000 references, does *not* include names occurring in their natural order under their proper family histories. It indexes all names occurring incidentally or outside of their family position, such as the names of wives and husbands. Since only a few pages are devoted to each surname in the book, and the surnames are arranged alphabetically, it is believed that those who use the book can readily find what they seek by glancing through the pages that deal with the family in which they are interested. The index capitalizes the surnames of families that received special treatment in their proper order, and the first reference in such case is to the page on which the account of that family begins.

Martha, 327, 709.
Mary, 153, 159, 523, 706.
Nathan, 659.
Phebe, 146.
Rebecca, 174.
Ruth (Beardsley), 597.
Samuel, 359, 638, 649, 677.
Sarah, 90, 159, 250, 584, 707.
Zechariah, 145, 153, 182, 221, 222, 244, 703.
Blagge, Elisha, 175.
Mary, 146.
Prudence, 463.
Blakeslee, ———, 16.
Abigail, 429.
Ebenezer, 429.
Mary, 602.
Miriam, 401, 480, 481.
Samuel, 361, 481, 602.
Blatchley, Joseph, 299, 356.
Samuel, 17.
Bliss, Daniel, 641.
Nathaniel, 220.
BLOOMER, family, 87.
Blouds, Sarah, 200.
Blount, Elizabeth, 389.
William, 389.
Blux, Katharine, 328.
Boardman, Daniel, 440, 531, 546.
Isaac, 360.
Mabel, 440.
Bodlie, John, 279.
Katherine, 279.
Boltwood, Mary, 54.
Robert, 54.
Booge, John, 627.
Boosey, Alice (———), 627.
Esther (Ward?), 117, 118, 119, 120.
James, 118, 627.
Joseph, 117, 118, 645.
BOOTH, family, 87, 706.
Abiah, 43, 547, 598.
Abiel, 72.
Abigail, 372.
Ann, 606, 707.
Bethia, 172, 265.
Daniel, 72.
Ebenezer, 43, 90, 144, 400, 598.
Elizabeth, 49, 412.
Elizabeth (———), 90.
Ephraim, 67, 71, 264, 265, 441, 555.
Hannah, 254, 564, 713.
Hannah (———), 89.
James, 89, 148, 547.
Johanna, 265, 555.
John, 144, 242, 264, 707, 718.
Jonathan, 214, 707.
Joseph, 41, 42, 86, 255, 256, 423, 564, 596, 598, 614, 615, 636, 690, 707.

Martha, 90.
Mary, 71, 104, 196, 400, 636, 707, 718.
Mary (French), 210.
[Richard], 82.
Richard, 172, 264, 367, 412.
Sarah, 598, 707.
Sarah (———), 90, 91.
Simon, 211, 212.
Thomas, 159, 354, 707.
Zechariah, 172, 173, 706, 710, 712.
Boradel, Margaret, 415.
Borden, Richard, 626.
BOSTWICK, family, 91, 707.
Abigail, 314.
Abigail (Walker), 301.
Benjamin, 340.
David, 285, 398.
Elizabeth, 176, 707.
Elizabeth (———), 93.
Ellen (———), 91, 488.
Ephraim, 707.
Jane, 441.
John, 103, 135, 384, 498, 638.
Joseph, 669.
Lemuel, 325.
Martha, 146, 546.
Meredith [or Merriday], 47.
Rebecca, 478.
Samuel, 336.
Susanna, 314.
Zechariah, 146, 314, 513.
Botsford, Amos, 72.
Christian, 72.
Elizabeth, 23.
Esther, 679.
Gideon, 72.
Hannah, 24, 311.
Henry, 23, 24, 518, 532, 679.
Jabez, 378.
John, 72.
Joseph, 72.
Mary, 518.
Miriam, 532.
Moses, 378.
Bourn, Elizabeth, 656, 690.
BOUTON, family, 94.
Alice (———), 94, 402.
Bridget, 357.
Eleazer, 268, 408, 538.
Elizabeth, 600.
John, 268, 269, 273, 292, 293, 355, 357, 402, 403, 408, 427, 515, 538.
Joseph, 238.
Mary, 427.
Mary (Pettit), 96.
Nathaniel, 268, 408.
Rachel, 403, 514.
Richard, 292, 486, 619, 678.

INDEX

Orton, John, 352.
  Mary (Tudor), 352.
  Samuel, 352.
Orvis, Samuel, 20.
OSBORN, family, 455, 717.
  Aaron, 427.
  Abigail, 281, 357, 450, 595.
  Daniel, 462.
  David, 112, 281, 375, 482, 593.
  Dorothy, 622.
  Eleazer, 461, 674.
  Elizabeth, 53, 99, 207.
  Elizabeth (———), 329.
  Grizzel, 461, 674.
  Hannah, 23, 512, 594.
  Hannah (———), 130.
  Hannah (Morehouse), 716.
  Hezekiah, 622.
  Isaac, 622.
  Jeremiah, 67, 88, 152.
  John, 34, 57, 65, 66, 78, 122, 222, 344, 380, 448, 468, 474, 512, 563, 570, 687.
  Jonathan, 519, 672.
  Joseph, 68, 130, 305, 329.
  Lois (———), 462.
  Mary, 54, 67, 88, 362, 474.
  Mary (Jackson), 597.
  Mehitabel, 47.
  Priscilla, 526.
  Prudence (Blagge), 706.
  Rachel, 427.
  Rebecca (———), 458.
  Richard, 18, 19, 23, 53, 54, 104, 357, 463, 468, 526, 717.
  Ruth (Burton), 597.
  Samuel, 163, 447, 511, 572, 594, 595.
  Sarah, 78, 104, 125, 131, 375, 380, 447, 458, 467, 468, 470, 553, 593.
  Sarah (———), 462.
  William, 622, 623.
Outman, John, 330.
Oviatt, Abigail, 11.
  Dorothy, 11.
  Samuel, 11.
  Thomas, 11, 358.
Oysterbank, Jacob, 142.
Paget, Henry, 500, 501.
Painter, Shubael, 189.
PALMER, family, 463.
  Bridget, 455.
  Bridget (———) (Baxter), 39.
  Grace, 412.
  Hannah, 587.
  Henry, 587.
  John, 39, 455.
  Joshua, 519.
  Moses, 220.

Rebecca (———), 40.
  Samuel, 167.
Pantry, John, 655.
Pardee, Elizabeth, 238, 454.
  George, 238, 454, 626.
  Hannah, 626.
  James, 674.
Parker, Edward, 101.
Parks, Hannah, 373.
Parmelee, Barbara, 152.
  Daniel, 647.
  Deborah, 693.
  Hannah (———), 312.
  John, 152, 193, 268.
  Joseph, 362, 363.
  Noah, 539.
  Samuel, 438.
  Sarah, 268.
  Stephen, 24.
Parrott, Parrot, Elizabeth, 584.
  Hannah, 584.
  James, 94.
  John, 94, 583, 584.
  Sarah, 584.
  Sarah (———), 441.
PARRUCK, family, 464.
  Abigail, 406.
  John, 48, 306, 371, 704.
  Sarah, 306.
Parsons, Hannah, 153.
  Jesse, 609.
  Judah, 609.
  Robert, 609.
  Samuel, 153, 599, 683.
PATCHEN, family, 464.
  Jacob, 137, 247, 300.
  John, 668.
  Joseph, 8, 69, 137, 192, 193, 234, 419, 421, 472, 620.
  Mary (———), 465.
PATTERSON, family, 466.
  Andrew, 52, 468, 547, 703.
  Charles, 441.
  Elizabeth, 424.
  Eunice (Nichols), 545.
  John, 176, 177.
  Mary, 703.
  Sarah, 42.
  William, 134, 625.
Payne, Elizabeth, 516.
Peacke, Ann, 467.
PEACOCK, family, 466.
  Deborah, 144.
  John, 44, 116, 144.
  Mary, 44.
  Phebe, 116.
Pearsall, Daniel, 36.
PEAT, Peet, family, 467.
  Benjamin, 135, 195, 354, 420, 469.

CPSIA information can be obtained
at www.ICGtesting.com
Printed in the USA
JSHW050709070323
38453JS00023B/53